D0087046

7th EDITION

The Management of Business Logistics

A Supply Chain Perspective

John J. Coyle
The Pennsylvania State University

Edward J. Bardi
University of Toledo

C. John Langley Jr.
Georgia Institute of Technology

The Management of Business Logistics: A Supply Chain Perspective, 7e
John J. Coyle, Edward J. Bardi, C. John Langley Jr.

Team Leader:
Melissa Acuña

Senior Acquisitions Editor:
Charles McCormick, Jr.

Developmental Editor:
Mardell Toomey

Marketing Manager:
Larry Qualls

Media Development Editor:
Christine Wittmer

Media Production Editor:
Robin Browning

Production Editor:
Chris Hudson

Manufacturing Coordinator:
Diane Lohman

Compositor:
Shepherd, Inc.

Printer:
Transcontinental
Louiseville, Quebec

Design Project Manager:
Michelle Kunkler

Cover and Internal Designer:
Joseph R. Pagliaro Graphic Design

Cover Images:
©PhotoDisc, ©CORBIS,
©DigitalVision

Printed in Canada

9 09 08 07

For more information contact South-Western, 5191 Natorp Boulevard, Mason, Ohio 45040.
Or you can visit our Internet site at: http://www.swcollege.com

Library of Congress Cataloging-in-Publication Data

Coyle, John Joseph, 1935–
The management of business logistics/John J. Coyle, Edward J. Bardi, C. John Langley, Jr.—7th ed.
p. cm.
Includes bibliographical references and index.
ISBN: 978-0324-00751-0
ISBN: 0-324-00751-5
1. Business logistics. I. Bardi, Edward J., 1943– II. Langley, C. John, 1946– III. Title.
HD38.5 .C69 2002
658.7—dc21 2001055131

To our respective wives, Barbara, Carol, and Anne,
and our children, John and Susan, Susan and Pamela,
and Sarah and Mercer

Brief Contents

Contents

PREFACE

Logistics and the closely related concept of supply chain management are necessary cornerstones of competitive strategy, increased market share, and shareholder value for most organizations. Now more than ever, students who are currently planning to pursue a career in business will benefit from a clear understanding of this field. With this edition we have tried to cover, as comprehensively as possible, the changes in the way business is being done, with a particular emphasis on technology and from a supply chain perspective. We have tried to capture some of the excitement of the escalating rate of change that is continuing into the 21st century and demonstrate that there is a growing recognition of the importance of logistics and its related activities.

The topics of Change and Change Management have been popular with authors and speakers for several decades; these topics are no longer new but are still extremely relevant. Our last edition, for example, featured the recurring themes of challenge and change. The current edition builds upon those themes. What is different now is the *rate* of change. The rapidity of change in the economic and technological landscapes, in particular, increases the significance of analyzing and adapting to change in an appropriate manner. For most managers, the rapid buildup and subsequent fallout from the so-called dot-com revolution is still fresh. Change is what is currently central to the significance and importance of logistics and supply chain management. The changes that we have seen since the first edition was published in 1976 led to an even more fundamental revision than just adding several new chapters and rewriting existing chapters. We felt a strong need to integrate the supply chain concept more completely into the text. It should be noted that the fifth edition, which was published in 1992, did discuss supply chain management as being an important new concept. In the sixth edition (1996), the first chapter, which was new, was devoted entirely to supply chain management, and some of the subsequent chapters incorporated the supply chain perspective into the discussion. The importance and recognition of supply chain management has become so prevalent since the publication of the sixth edition that we debated changing the title of the text to *Supply Chain Management.* After careful (and sometimes lively) discussion, we decided to use "A Supply Chain Perspective" as the subtitle. Logistics is still very important and a critical part of supply chain management. The relationship between the two concepts is explored in Chapter 2.

The seventh edition is reflective of the growth in strategic value and the increasing importance of its relationship to other functional areas. Examples include the focus on demand management in Chapter 3, and the addition of new chapters on performance measurement (Chapter 13) and financial analysis (Chapter 15).

The seventh edition is again divided into three major sections and a total of sixteen chapters. Part One provides an overview of supply chain management and some of its important related components. Chapter 1 is devoted to a comprehensive discussion of supply chain management. Chapter 2 presents an overview of all of the important dimensions of logistics and discusses its relationship to supply chain management. Chapter 3 discusses demand management and customer service, or the outbound side of logistics systems, by addressing the current issues of demand forecasting and collaborative planning, forecasting, and replenishment (CPFR). Chapter 4 focuses on procurement, or the inbound side of logistics systems, and includes discussion of two new topics: electronic procurement and material and service strategic importance. Chapter 5 provides a comprehensive overview of global logistics with particular emphasis on global supply chains.

Part Two of the text examines the various processes associated with logistics and supply chain management. Managing inventory is a critical ingredient to successfully managing supply chains. It is frequently the largest asset on the balance sheet for many companies and has an important influence on the cost of goods sold as well as customer service. The first two chapters of Part Two are devoted to inventory management. Chapter 6 explores the rationale for carrying inventory as well as the basic types of inventory costs and inventory classification. Chapter 7 focuses on techniques of inventory control, both old and new. The relationship between this chapter and Chapters 3 ("Demand Management and Customer Service") and 4 ("Procurement and Supply Management") is very important.

Transportation management, like inventory management, is critical to successful supply chain management. Transportation can be viewed as the glue that holds supply chains together, and in today's "just-in-time environment" has become more important than ever. Chapters 9 and 10 are devoted to transportation. Chapter 9 provides an overview of our domestic transportation system and includes three new sections: impact of the ICC Termination Act; electronic auctions; and the role of consolidators to support small dot-com shipments. Chapter 10 explores the management of transportation from a user perspective, and it also includes several new sections such as EDI and Internet applications and the impact of the ICC Termination Act.

The remaining chapter in Part Two (Chapter 8) examines the role of warehousing in logistics and supply chain systems. This chapter contains several new additions, including: flowcharts describing basic warehousing decisions and operations; warehousing metrics; and an appendix describing materials handling equipment.

Part Three focuses on key strategic issues for logistics and supply chains. Chapter 11 explores the area of supply chain relationships and the use of third party logistics services. The focus is on how to create value through collaboration in supply chains. This chapter essentially is a new chapter for the seventh edition, reflecting the contemporary interest in these topics.

Chapter 12 examines the role and importance of information systems in the effective management of supply chains. It provides a comprehensive overview of the topic and relates to the discussion of E-commerce applications presented in previous chapters.

Chapter 13 is a new chapter devoted to performance measurement. While this topic has been addressed in previous editions, the discussion was part of several chapters. The supply chain concept, with its boundary-spanning approach that incorporates a group of companies, has intensified the need for metrics to gauge performance efficiency and effectiveness. Network design and facility location has been a continuing topic of interest in all the previous editions of this text. The seventh edition also includes a chapter (14) on this timely and important topic.

Chapter 15 is a new chapter that examines how finance and financial techniques can be used to more effectively manage the internal and external dimensions of the supply chain. It could be considered an extension of Chapter 13 because it discusses financial metrics.

The final chapter discusses cutting edge strategies that the leading companies have used to gain competitive advantage. The chapter also examines major macro trends that will impact the future of logistics and supply chain management.

Features

- Learning Objectives at the beginning of each chapter provide students with an overall perspective of chapter material and also serve to establish a baseline for a working knowledge of the topics that follow.
- *Logistics Profiles* are the opening vignettes at the beginning of each chapter that introduce students to the chapter's topics through familiar, real-world companies, people, and events.
- *On the Line* features are applied, concrete examples that provide students with hands-on managerial experience of the chapter topics.
- *Supply Chain Technology* boxes (a new feature!), also found in each chapter, help students relate technological developments to supply chain management concepts and logistics practices.
- Key Terms in the margins help students to become more familiar with logistics terminology and aid in independent study of the chapter material.
- End-of-chapter Summaries and Study Questions reinforce material presented in each chapter.
- Short Cases at the end of each chapter build upon what students have learned in each chapter. Questions that follow the cases sharpen critical thinking skills.

Ancillaries

Instructor's Manual with Test Bank (ISBN 0-324-17973-1), prepared by Andrew Melendrez Stapleton of The University of Wisconsin, LaCrosse, includes chapter outlines, answers to end-of-chapter study questions, commentary on end-of-chapter short cases and end-of-text comprehensive cases, teaching tips, and transparency masters. Also includes test bank with 10 T/F questions, 25 multiple choice, and two essay questions per chapter.

PowerPoint (0-324-007-523), prepared by John Cancro of The Pennsylvania State University, includes more than 300 slides that cover main chapter topics and contain graphics from the main text. The PowerPoint presentation, available on CD-ROM, is packaged in the back of the instructor's manual with test bank.

Web site provides additional resources for students including Web site exercises and e-lectures. The instructor's manual is available as downloadable files so that instructors can easily customize teaching plans and notes.

Acknowledgments

The authors are indebted to many individuals at our respective academic institutions as well as other individuals with whom we have had contact in a variety of venues. Our university students and our executive program students have provided an important sounding board for the many concepts, techniques, metrics, and strategies presented in the book. Our faculty and corporate colleagues have provided invaluable insights and appropriate criticism of our ideas. Some individuals deserve special consideration: Dr. David A. Lindsley (University of Toledo); Mark J. Basile (DuPont Corporation); Dr. Robert Novack (Penn State University); Dr. Alan J. Stenger (Penn State University); Ms. Tracie Shannon (Penn State University); and especially Ms. Jean Beierlein (Penn State University).

A very special note of thanks and appreciation is due to our wives, Barbara, Carol, and Anne, who have provided support and encouragement and have given up time from our personal schedules to allow us to complete this task. Our children, John and Susan, Susan and Pamela, and Sarah and Mercer, who have made our lives meaningful, also deserve mention. A new special dimension has been added by our grandchildren, Lauren, Matt, Elizabeth Kate, Emily, Ben, Cathryn, Maggie, Kate, and Lauren.

We extend our appreciation to the members of our South-Western team, who are very professional: Charles McCormick, Jr., Senior Acquisitions Editor; Mardell Toomey, Developmental Editor; Chris Hudson, Production Editor; and Larry Qualls, Marketing Manager.

Special thanks should be given to the following reviewers who provided meaningful input for our seventh edition:

Steve Clinton, Ph.D.
Arizona State University

Guy Cyr
York College

Thomas J. Goldsby
Iowa State University

Kent N. Gourdin
University of North Carolina

Joe B. Hanna
Western Illinois University

Tenpao Lee
Niagra University

Amanda Luthy
University of Tennessee

Gary Merlo
Westfield State College

John Ozment
University of Arkansas

Richard D. Stone
Shippensburg University

Joel D. Wisner
University of Nevada

Gary Wilson
Elmhurst College

About the Authors

John J. Coyle is Professor Emeritus of Business Administration and Director of Corporate Relations for the Center for Supply Chain Research at Penn State University. He served for 30 years as the Faculty Representative to the NCAA and the Big Ten for Penn State. He holds a bachelor's degree and master's degree from Penn State, and he earned his doctorate at Indiana University, Bloomington, where he was a U.S. Steel Fellow. Dr. Coyle is the co-author of two best-selling textbooks, *The Management of Business Logistics* and *Transportation*. He was editor of the *Journal of Business Logistics* from 1990 to 1996. He currently serves on the editorial review board of *Journal of Business Logistics, Supply Chain Review,* and *International Journal of Physical Distribution and Logistics*. In 1991 Dr. Coyle received the Council of Logistics Management's top honor—the Distinguished Service Award.

Edward J. Bardi is Visiting Professor of Business Logistics at Penn State University, Principal of Bardi Consulting, and Professor Emeritus of Logistics and Transportation at the University of Toledo. Prior to joining the Penn State faculty, Dr. Bardi held faculty positions at the University of Toledo and Iowa State University. Dr. Bardi has served as a consultant to numerous businesses and public agencies in the areas of transportation, distribution, reverse logistics, private trucking, warehouse location and operation, marketing, business organization, and economic development. He is a popular seminar leader of transportation and logistics/supply chain management development programs. Dr. Bardi is a co-author of two textbooks, *The Management of Business Logistics* and *Transportation*. He has published numerous articles dealing with business logistics, transportation management, carrier selection, economic development, and employee household goods movement in various academic and professional journals.

C. John Langley, Jr., is Professor of Supply Chain Management and Director of Supply Chain Executive Programs in the School of Industrial and Systems Engineering and The Logistics Institute at the Georgia Institute of Technology. Previously, he served for 28 years at the University of Tennessee where he was the John H. "Red" Dove Distinguished Professor in Logistics and Transportation. Dr. Langley is a former President of the Council of Logistics Management, and was a recipient of the Council's Distinguished Service Award. Dr. Langley has co-authored several books, and his research publications have appeared in leading professional journals. In addition to his university duties, Dr. Langley actively consults with firms in the logistics profession. He also serves on the boards of directors of Averitt Express, Inc., and Landair Transportation, Inc., and on corporate advisory boards for several firms in the E-commerce business.

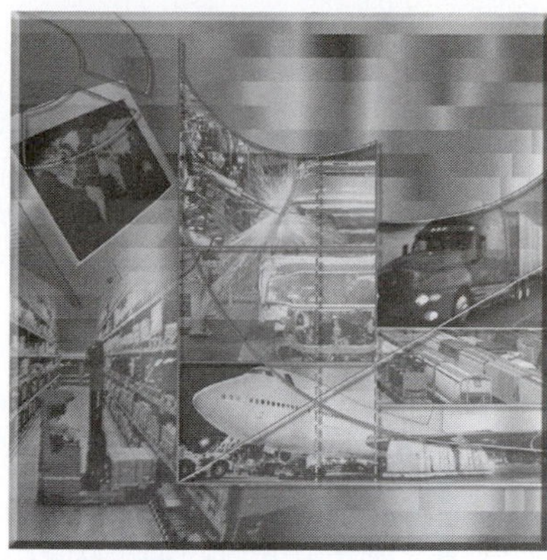

PART I

Supply chain management is a fundamental concept that has evolved to enable organizations to improve their efficiency and effectiveness in the global and highly competitive environment of the twenty-first century. It is the goal of this book to assist in helping to make those changes that are critical to successful supply chain implementation.

Chapter 1 provides the foundation and base case for supply chain management. An overview is presented of the rationale and development of the concept. The important characteristics and dimensions of supply chain management are explored.

Chapter 2 focuses on business logistics and its relationship to supply chain management. The logistics concept is examined in detail as well as the relationship with other functional areas in a business organization.

Chapter 3 examines the customer interface in logistics and supply chain systems. Customer satisfaction and service have become major focal points of the business community. Customers are no longer taken for granted by successful companies. Logistics and supply chain management play a very important role in assisting companies in keeping their customers "happy."

Chapter 4 provides the supply side perspective on logistics and supply chain systems, as opposed to the demand side provided in Chapter 3. Procurement has become much more complex and challenging. Chapter 4 examines the important aspects of procurement in this complex, global environment and provides meaningful managerial insights for its successful management.

Chapter 5 focuses on global logistics. Global sourcing, marketing, manufacturing, and distribution require companies to evaluate their businesses using global network analysis. Supply chain managers must appreciate and understand not only the general issues but also the important specific requirements of global material flows.

CHAPTER 1

SUPPLY CHAIN MANAGEMENT

LEARNING OBJECTIVES

After reading this chapter, you should be able to do the following:

- Understand the development of supply chain management in leading corporations.
- Appreciate the importance and role of supply chain management among private and public organizations.
- Understand the contributions of a supply chain approach to organizational efficiency and effectiveness.
- Analyze the benefits that can accrue from implementing effective supply chain practices.
- Understand the major challenges and issues facing organizations developing and implementing supply chain strategies.
- Discuss the major change drivers in our economy and in the global marketplace.

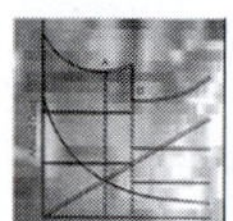

LOGISTICS PROFILE

SAB Distribution

"It is unbelievable how the old adage of eliminating the middleman has taken on a new meaning in today's economy. My predecessor, Pete Swan (CEO, SAB Distribution), used to complain about the rate of change during the 1980s and how the manufacturers and the large retailers were squeezing the distributors and wholesalers," stated Sue Purdum, the current CEO of SAB. "Pete decided to retire at 60 because of the pressure that he felt to somehow remain profitable under the competitive circumstances of the 1980s. If Pete were still here today, I swear that he would have bleeding ulcers."

SAB Distribution was established in 1949 in Harrisburg, Pennsylvania, by three World War II veterans who had served in the U.S. Navy as supply officers. They completed their interrupted college programs after the war. All three worked for several years after graduation for local companies. Then, they decided to go into business for themselves. Harrisburg was in the center of the state and also the state capital. The Pennsylvania Railroad provided transportation service, and the developing highway network boded well for improvements in the transportation access to the many communities within a hundred-mile radius of Harrisburg.

Skip, Al, and Bob felt that their naval experience as supply officers along with their business administration degrees from Penn State put them at a strategic advantage in developing a food-wholesaling company to serve small- to medium-size retail food stores. They focused initially on nonperishable food items but expanded during the 1960s and 1970s into perishables and nonfood items to meet the competition of other wholesalers and larger retailers.

The company was incorporated in 1978 because none of the founders' children wanted to be involved in the family business. Peter Swan joined the company in 1960 and had held several management positions in the company. When the founders were ready to retire in 1983, Pete was named CEO at SAB Distribution, which had grown to be a $180 million company with its own large warehouse in Camp Hill, Pennsylvania, and a market area that stretched across Pennsylvania into parts of Delaware, New Jersey, Ohio, and New York.

The gross sales of SAB had leveled off during the last half of the 1980s, and costs had risen, which had a negative impact on profit margins. A majority of the stock was held by family members of the three founders, and they were not happy with their dividends. Feeling the pressure, Pete Swan retired in 1995, and Sue Purdum took over. Sue had had a successful career in retailing after finishing her MBA at Slippery Rock University in Western Pennsylvania.

Ms. Purdum had managed to improve the profitability of SAB during her first five years by focusing upon efficiency in the warehouse, improved order fulfillment to customers, and establishing partnerships with a select number of motor carriers with major hub terminals in the Harrisburg area. Also, she was aggressive in investing in technology such as EDI to interface with major vendors.

Sue Purdum had recently met with her executive committee and made the following observations: "SAB is at another crossroad in our development. We cannot cut costs much more without causing ourselves to "bleed" in other areas. Our sales have been flat for two years, and our margins are not what they need to be. We need to get better or recommend a merger to the Board. Milroy Distribution wants to buy SAB, and some of our family stockholders want to take advantage of this opportunity. I need your help, guidance, and wisdom. Where do we fit in the supply chain? What should be our role? How can we be more profitable?"

INTRODUCTION

supply chain strategies

During the 1990s, supply chain management became a part of the CEO, CFO, COO, and CIO vocabularies. The dynamics of the global marketplace had changed dramatically. The lexicon of many private and public organizations expanded to include supply chain management and related concepts and strategies such as continuous replenishment, pull distribution systems, reduced cycle times, and so on. The *Wall Street Journal, Business Week, Forbes, Fortune,* and other major business periodicals and publications featured articles related to supply chain management and logistics.

1990s

The 1990s were obviously a decade of great change from a global perspective as well as for the U.S. economy. The dim, dire outlook that was envisioned for the U.S. economy in the late 1970s and early 1980s changed as the 1990s turned out to be a decade of great growth and overall economic well-being. Employment reached levels never envisioned by macro economists in the 1960s and 1970s as unemployment was reduced below 5 percent in many areas of the U.S. economy. The doom and gloom of the early 1980s were replaced to a large extent by perpetual optimism and boundless expectations.

rapid change

The economic prosperity also included much turbulence, and many individuals have taken note of the rapid rate of change:

> More change has occurred in the 1990s than the previous nine decades of the twentieth century.[1]
>
> We live in an era of almost continuous change, there is no steady state any more, it is like constant whitewater.[2]

But perhaps more profound are the following:

> Change is inevitable, growth and improvement are optional.[3]
>
> You either change and get better or you slip and get worse, you cannot stay the same.[4]

The scenario described in the SAB case at the beginning of this chapter is not unique. Many companies have experienced challenging changes in the marketplace that have eliminated their "comfort zone" and forced them to respond. Some organizations have responded well and have improved their competitive position, while others have failed the "test" and have been subjected to a less-positive outcome.

SAB has to understand the forces of change at a macro level and reposition themselves. They appear to have some perception of supply chain management, which has evolved as a response to the macro-level change drivers in the economy, but they need a better understanding to move ahead and improve their financial viability.

Given the preceding commentary, the next step should be to examine in detail the major forces of change in our economy that produced a variety of outcomes in the 1990s and continue to shape the business landscape in the twenty-first century.

THE CHANGING BUSINESS LANDSCAPE: DRIVING FORCES

As indicated previously, the rate of change has accelerated both in the U.S. economy and globally. Businesses and public organizations have had to respond to the changes and the inherent dynamics of their environment. A key to understanding how to respond is to have some perspective and understanding of the forces of change.

The Empowered Consumer

impact on logistics

Understanding consumer behavior has been a focus of marketing analysis and strategy development for many years. Typically, such analyses examine consumers in total and/or major groupings or segments to understand their needs and to respond to them with products and services. Such analyses have some implications for logistics and supply chain management, but they have been viewed at times in the past as being somewhat indirect impacts. Today, the impact of the consumer is much more direct for supply chain and logistics managers.

informed consumers

The consumers in today's marketplace are enlightened and empowered by the information that they have at their disposal from the Internet and from many other sources. Their access to supply sources has expanded dramatically beyond their immediate locale by virtue of catalogs, the Internet, and other media. Consumers have the opportunity to compare prices, quality, and service. In turn, they demand competitive prices, high quality, tailored/customized products, convenience, flexibility, and responsiveness. They tend to have a low tolerance level for poor quality in products and/or services.

changing demographics

The demographics of our society, with the increase in two-career families and single-parent households, have made "time" a critical dimension for many consumers. They want and demand quicker response times and more convenient offerings according to their schedules. The five-day week with 9 A.M. to 6 P.M. service for customers is no longer acceptable or tolerated. Twenty-four hours/seven days is frequently the expectation with a minimum of wait time. The age-old axiom of "let the buyer beware" should probably be changed to "let the seller beware." Today's consumers do not have the loyalty of previous periods or much patience with inferior quality in any area.

increased importance of logistics and supply chains

Why is this consumer revolution so important in a supply chain/logistics content? The reason is that the supply chain/logistics requirements have dramatically increased to serve the consumers of today. If retail establishments have to be open twenty-four hours/seven days per week, this places greater demands upon the supply chains that serve them. Also, the pressure from consumers related to price put pressure in turn upon the supply chain to operate as efficiently as possible. SAB Distribution should evaluate its role in helping its customers respond to the new consumer. How can it add value for its customers who have to compete with the larger retail chains and other types of suppliers?

Power Shift in the Supply Chain

Traditionally, manufacturers were the dominant force in supply chains or distribution channels. This was particularly true for consumer products. The manufacturers designed, produced, promoted, and distributed their products. Vendors/suppliers and wholesalers, distributors, and retailers were usually smaller in size and depended upon the leadership of the large manufacturers. During the post–World War II era with the introduction of television advertising, manufacturers' brands took on increased significance. Distribution and logistics systems were not accorded as much attention as product development, promotion, and/or brand management.

large retailers

During the 1980s and 1990s, a significant change occurred in the relative economic power in a number of supply chains with the trend toward retail consolidation and the emergence of giant retailers such as Wal-Mart, Kmart, Toys R Us, Home Depot, and so on. For example, in 1999, Wal-Mart was the third largest company on the *Fortune* 500 list in terms of sales with annual sales of $146 billion. It has been predicted that Wal-Mart soon will surpass General Motors as the largest company in terms of sales. A comparison of the *Fortune* 500 list during the 1990s shows that many retailers of products and/or services have moved up on the list.

focus upon distribution costs

What is the significance of this shift in power to the supply chain? The consolidation of economic power at the retail end of the supply chain led to very large retailers whose basic competitive strategy was usually based upon lower prices. This strategy focused attention upon the distribution systems of manufacturers that tended to treat their customers similarly and not pay attention to how their order-fulfillment strategies affected the efficiency of the retailers. Such an approach tended to increase operating costs for retailers.

changing strategies

The large retailers were able to exert pressure back in the supply chain to force manufacturers to change their logistics and supply chain strategies to include tailored pallet packs, scheduled deliveries, continuous replenishment systems, and so on. Manufacturers found that a small number (15 percent to 20 percent) of their customers accounted for a substantial share (75 percent to 85 percent) of their sales. Such important customers had to be accorded special treatment, and that treatment frequently translated into improved logistics systems, which had an important positive impact upon the retailers' efficiency. In other words, the consolidation of economic power at the retail level probably caused more change and focus upon improved logistics systems during the 1990s than manufacturers had implemented during the previous three decades.

How has SAB been affected by the retail consolidation? It is safe to observe that SAB has been impacted profoundly by this change also. Independent distributors serving small- to medium-size retailers often do not have the economic leverage to demand the price/service treatment accorded large retailers. Their customers have problems competing in the marketplace on a price basis against the large retailers. SAB and its retail customers have to respond to the price competition of the large retailers in proactive ways that add value for consumers to maintain their market share. What do you think SAB can do?

Deregulation

changing economic controls

The infrastructure of many businesses is based upon transportation, communications, energy, and financial systems. These four "legs" of business operations have undergone fundamental change during the 1980s and 1990s because of government deregulation. All four had for many years been subjected to comprehensive regulation that developed in an era when it was felt that businesses needed to be protected from the supposed monopoly power that these industries possessed. The regulations were probably philosophically sound in an earlier era in U.S. industry, but much had changed during the 1960s and 1970s, not only among domestic organizations but also globally. The net effect of the comprehensive and complex regulations affecting these four industries was a bureaucratic system that tended to stymie innovation and resulted in relatively high prices being charged in these four important sectors of our economy.

changes in transportation

Beginning in the late 1970s and into the 1980s, transportation was deregulated in terms of economic controls such as rates and areas of service. The net effect was that it became possible for transportation services to be purchased and sold in a much more competitive environment. The results were, frequently, lower prices to users and better service. It became possible for carriers and shippers to negotiate and to make changes in their respective operations to allow carriers to operate more efficiently and lower their prices. New carriers entered the marketplace, particularly in the motor carrier industry, and some established carriers were forced out of business in the new, more competitive environment of the 1980s. Certain sectors of transportation underwent consolidation through mergers and acquisitions, most notably railroads and airlines. Transportation companies have also been liberated to the extent that they can now offer more than just pure transportation services. Many motor carriers, for example, have declared themselves as logistics services companies and offer an array of related services that can include order fulfillment, inventory management, and warehousing. They have moved aggressively ahead in the new business environment where companies view outsourcing and partnerships as a potential strategic advantage.

change in financial institutions

The financial industry was also deregulated. The distinction between commercial banks, savings and loan associations, and credit unions, for example, has blurred as these institutions have been allowed to broaden their array of services and make the financial market more competitive and, like the transportation industry, more responsive to customer needs in the new environment for the consumers and retailers described in the previous two sections. Brokerage and insurance companies have also been impacted by the deregulation of this broad financial industry.

The changes have fostered many changes in the ways that businesses can operate. For example, the opportunity to invest cash at the end of the day in the global overnight money market in periods of six to ten hours made many companies more cognizant of the value of asset liquidity and asset reduction, especially inventory. Payment transactions for buyers and sellers have also changed dramatically with the alternatives in financial practices made possible and fostered by deregulation. The purchase cards used by many procurement departments for maintenance, repair, and operating (MRO) items are just one example of the efficiencies that were made possible by the deregulation.

change in communications industry

The communication industry was also made more competitive; but the scenario was different since the major cause of change was a Supreme Court decision that split up the AT&T/Bell telephone system into regional companies and separated the "long-lines system" of AT&T and made it accessible to other companies, such as MCI, who wanted to sell telephone services. Like the other two industries discussed, the communication industry has undergone much change and more is coming with the possible integration of related services such as cable, telephone, computers, and wireless access. Businesses and the general consumer population are all being impacted by the many changes in this industry from cell phones and pagers to E-mail, electronic data interchange (EDI), and the Internet. Communication efficiency and effectiveness have led to dramatic improvements and opportunities in logistics and supply chains, for example, inventory visibility, quick response replenishment, improved transportation scheduling, order entry, and so on. Supply chain practices have been improved dramatically, leading to lower cost and better customer service. Some people argue that the best is yet to come.

utility industry

The final industry segment is the energy industry, specifically, electric power, which is being deregulated on a state-by-state basis. In the states in which deregulation has occurred, businesses and households are able to choose their electricity provider. In other words, there are competitive alternatives, which have resulted in lower prices to users. It is likely that as deregulation becomes more widespread there will be more profound effects upon the industry similar to what has occurred in transportation, finance/banking, and communication. However, initially, some of the changes will appear chaotic or negative as the industry adjusts to deregulation. Such adjustments occurred among transportation companies, financial institutions, and in communications, for example, bankruptcy, scandals, and so on. The long-run impact will be more positive with lower prices and new services for users. It is also likely that the structure of the energy industry will change.

Sue Purdum, CEO of SAB, has attempted to take advantage of the changes brought about by deregulation. Her predecessor, Pete Swan, had initiated changes with the help of SAB's traffic manager, Doug Thomas. They began a strategy of reducing the number of carriers that they purchased transportation service from in order to improve their leverage with the carriers to lower rates and improve service reliability for customer deliveries. Ms. Purdum has improved the transportation purchasing even more through strategic alliances based upon information exchange and EDI. She wants to take advantage of other opportunities made possible by deregulation in the other three sectors just discussed.

Globalization

global marketplace

It is difficult to single out one of the five change drivers and point to it as having the biggest impact. However, if one were to be selected as being the most important, many individuals would argue that it is probably globalization. In the eyes of some individuals, globalization has replaced the so-called "cold war" of the post–World War II era as the dominant driving force for world economics.[5] The concept of the "global marketplace" has taken on new meaning for all enterprises (small, medium, and large) and for individual consumers. Changes in government policy and the "new" technologies have made the global economy concept a fact of life.

global network

In the United States, globalization has evolved from the 1970s, when U.S. companies began to practice more aggressive global sourcing or procurement of materials, parts, and supplies, to the 1980s, when aggressive marketing in international markets became more commomplace among larger companies, to the 1990s, when a true global perspective began to be taken and companies sought to rationalize global networks by asking:

- Where in the world should they source?
- Where in the world should they manufacture?
- Where in the world should they market their products?
- Where in the world should they warehouse and distribute from?
- What global transportation strategies should they utilize?

global alternatives

The liberalization of international trade has been aggressively pursued by a number of countries, which has opened up new markets and sources of supplies for most companies. Not only large businesses but also small- and medium-size companies have been able to participate in the globalization. The opportunities have been enhanced by the technology revolution, which is discussed in the next section. The consumer has benefited from the many alternative sources of supply for wholesalers and retailers, which has lowered prices, raised product quality, and dramatically increased choice alternatives to the consumer.

no geography

With the changes occurring from Internet and other related technologies, some individuals are arguing that there is "no geography" any more. Products and services can be bought and sold anywhere in the world no matter how large or small the enterprise. Product and service information is available on a real-time basis, and comparisons can quickly be made. Such openness of markets and sources is both a threat and an opportunity and has profoundly impacted how businesses operate and how consumers view their purchase opportunities.

The significance of the global environment can easily be demonstrated. Consider, for example:

- About 25 percent of the output of U.S. firms is produced overseas.
- About 25 percent of U.S. imports are between foreign affiliates and U.S. parent companies.
- Since the 1980s, well over 50 percent of U.S. companies have increased the number of countries in which they operate.
- International sales account for about 50 percent of sales of most of the 100 largest companies in the United States.

supply chain challenges

Supply chain management, therefore, usually has to be labeled *global supply chain management* in today's environment. Globalization presents some special challenges and issues for business organizations. The distance factor alone becomes significant with shipments moving thousands of miles from vendors and/or to customers. In an environment of reduced cycle times, expected higher levels of reliability, and emphasis upon efficiency, the distance factor presents some special challenges to logistics and supply chain managers.

Wal-Mart's challenges

Even companies as successful as Wal-Mart have slipped and occasionally stumbled with global ventures. When Wal-Mart entered the Brazilian markets, they found the competition brutal. They needed to adapt to local tastes in stocking their stores. Footballs were replaced with soccer balls; American-style jeans were replaced with "knock-offs"; and new items for the deli counter included sushi and "feiyoada fixings." Product line adjustment, however, may have been the easy part. Doing things the "Wal-Mart way" caused friction with local vendors and employees. Large stores in Brazil encountered problems achieving the economy of scale of their U.S. counterparts. "Disappointed but not discouraged" probably best describes Wal-Mart's situation in South America. Wal-Mart feels that there is tremendous potential for growth and expansion, and it is confident that it can adjust and be successful.[6]

The logistical aspects of operating in the South American markets have been especially challenging to Wal-Mart. Order placement to on-shelf availability (order-fulfillment time) is accomplished with relative ease in the United States by Wal-Mart working with its vendors and associated transportation companies. In São Paulo, bumper-to-bumper traffic impedes timely delivery and smooth replenishment for the Wal-Mart systems. Mysterious disappearance of shipments also exacerbates the situation. While globalization presents Wal-Mart and other companies with new and expanded opportunities, there are many logistical and supply chain challenges that they have to overcome.

new supply sources

SAB also has been impacted by globalization in many ways. The population bases of central and southern Pennsylvania, as well as other areas of SAB's market, have become much more diverse. Its product lines have had to change to respond to this change in tastes; its recruiting practices have had to change; new sources of supply have opened up, especially for fresh fruits and vegetables, for example, Central and South America. Sue Purdum is cognizant of these significant changes and wants to capitalize on the opportunities. She is, however, also aware that she could encounter some problems. Some of SAB's customers are smaller retail stores and are reluctant to change. Also, importing from global vendors is a special challenge to mid-size companies like SAB.

The discussion of globalization provides a convenient segue for the discussion of the fifth change driver, namely, technology.

Technology

Technology can be viewed legitimately as a facilitator of change on a micro basis since it enables companies to implement many of the strategies to be discussed in later section of the book. However, technology can also be classified as a change driver on a macro or external basis. The revolution that has occurred in technology—hardware and software—has forced many companies to change the way they "do business."

Information Age

We live in an era that has been described by some individuals as the "Information Age," but this description does not do our present environment justice. There is no question that businesses and consumers have much more information available today, which influences how they buy and sell goods and services; but technology has also changed the modus operandi in the marketplace. It was traditional for consumers/customers to buy at the business "place" in accordance with the business time schedule. The time aspect has changed, as previously noted, since it has become more customary for many businesses to be accessible twenty-four hours a day, seven days a week. Now, the Internet and related technology are changing the place aspect.

my time, my place

Buyers no longer have to go to the seller's place or a "space" to view and buy products. It can be argued that this is not new but rather an extension of catalog sales, but the Internet is so much more dynamic and accessible. It would be analogous to comparing the Model T Ford with a brand new Lincoln or Cadillac. Technology has sparked and enhanced the so-called consumer revolution, but it is much more impactful than consumer purchasing practices.

There is a separate chapter devoted to technology in the supply chain, which explores in more detail the role and impact of technology in the supply chain. In this section, technology needs to be addressed on a more general basis as a change agent. Suffice it to say that technology changed how buyers and sellers interact in the marketplace, both business-to-business (B2B) and business-to-consumer (B2C), and how business operates. Asset visibility, precision logistics, tailored/customized services, and so on are concepts based upon the technology currently available. While not a panacea for success, technology certainly provides the opportunity to improve efficiency and customer service.

warehouse technology

SAB Distribution's CEO, Sue Purdum, has recognized the importance of technology. The SAB warehouse was the initial target of her efforts. Bar codes and optical scanning equipment were introduced to improve order picking and fulfillment time; conveyers were added in selected sections of the warehouse to improve productivity; and new forklift trucks that could handle slip sheets were purchased. Subsequently, EDI technology was purchased to interact with major vendors and their transportation partners in an effort to reduce order cycle time and improve vendor order fill accuracy. Ms. Purdum knew that "more was better," but she needed to carefully analyze what technology would serve SAB's needs the best. How could SAB use technology to offset the cost advantage of the large retailers and make SAB and/or its retail customers more competitive? How could she utilize the Internet to improve SAB's effectiveness and perhaps tap new markets? New technology requires investment of capital, which has serious implications for SAB's already strained financial resources and profit margin.

SAB Distribution is being buffeted by all of these change drivers. The marketplace is much more competitive; consumers are much more demanding and knowledgeable. Globalization and deregulation have made SAB much more vulnerable in its regional marketplace and much less insulated against larger competitors. These change drivers represent both opportunities and threats for SAB, as well as for other businesses both large and small.

The rate of change has accelerated, as previously noted, with consequent negative impacts if organizations do not change also. But such change can also have positive impacts if appropriate actions are taken. For example, deregulation of transportation led to the demise of some very large, financially successful transportation companies who prospered in an era of regulation but could not cope in the deregulated, competitive marketplace of the 1980s. On the other hand, some other companies emerged in this more competitive environment—for example, Federal Express, Schneider National, and J. B. Hunt—as large and economically viable organizations. They changed in response to the new environment. What does SAB Distribution have to do to function in the twenty-first century? One aspect of change that SAB has to be cognizant of is the supply chain management approach that has emerged during the 1990s in response to the change drivers discussed and some related developments. What should SAB's role be in the new supply chain era?

On The Line

Extreme Enterprise

Integrating new enterprise and supply chain management solutions allowed Columbia Sportswear to keep up with its raging sales numbers. The company has increased accuracy and set new productivity marks since implementing the enterprise-wise solution.

Earl Scheib promised to paint any car for $99.99. Victor Kiam liked Remington razors so much that he bought the company. However, no company owner/pitchman can match Mother Boyle when it comes to ensuring product quality. Whether it is dangling from a cliff or racing a four-wheel drive vehicle with her son Tim strapped to the roof, Columbia Sportswear's ads proclaim that before the company's products pass Mother Nature, they must pass Mother Boyle. One ad had Gert Boyle donning a tattoo on her bicep that read "Born to Nag"—proving to any doubters that she was, in fact, one tough mother.

There is no denying that the ad campaign was more successful than anyone could have predicted. Since launching the television and print spots in 1984, Columbia has seen its annual revenue increase from $3 million to $470 million in 1999. But, the company had to meet the logistical challenge of satisfying customer demand. That daunting task was left to Columbia's domestic distribution center (DC) located just outside of Portland, Oregon. As far as company growth was concerned, it was a slight case of being careful what you wished for.

The company's growth reached a point in 1997 where all cylinders in the DC had to be hitting just right in order to keep up with demand. The DC, which was built in 1994 and expanded once, was scheduled to receive another addition. Once completed, the facility would have more than one million square feet of floor space. Also, Columbia had secured new customer accounts that altered the way the company did business. "We took on some key accounts that added significant volume to our distribution. In addition to the volume, it was also the amount of shipping we had to do," recalled Dan Dougherty, technical services manager at Columbia. "One particular account had well over 1,000 stores with several subdivisions in each store. Each subdivision received individual shipments one to three times each month. With this one account, we essentially added 15,000 to 20,000 new customers overnight."

Because Columbia only operates a handful of outlet stores and one flagship store (Portland, Oregon), distribution to its thousands of accounts is really where the rubber meets the road for the outdoor clothing manufacturer. This point was not lost on Tim Boyle, president and CEO at Columbia. "Tim handed down a mandate that stated distribution would not constrain the growth of the company. You can simply say those words, or you can back them up with your pocketbook. Tim did the latter," says Dougherty. "As a result, distribution is not a constraint. We are able to keep up with a raging sales force that is selling a very hot product."

At this point, Columbia continues to set new shipping records. On the inbound side of operations, the company recently established a new mark by receiving more than 2 million units in a month. On the outbound side, the company set a record by shipping 172,000 units in one day and more than 2 million units in one month.

Source: Ed Hess, *Integrated Solutions Magazine* (May 2000): 30–34.

The Supply Chain Concept

While reference to supply chain management can be traced to the 1980s, it is safe to say that it was not until the 1990s that the term *supply chain management* captured the attention of senior level management in numerous organizations. They recognized the power and potential impact of a supply chain approach to making organizations more globally competitive and helping to increase their market share with consequent improvements in shareholder value.

Development of the Concept

total systems cost

Note that supply chain management is not a brand new concept. Rather, supply chain management represents the third phase of an evolution that started in the 1960s with the development of the physical distribution concept and focused upon the outbound side of the firm's logistics system. A number of studies[7] during the 1950s and 1960s indicated the potential of the systems concept. The focus was upon total systems cost and analyzing trade-off scenarios to arrive at the best or lowest physical distribution system cost. As is explained in more detail in the next chapter, the system relationship among transportation, inventory requirements, warehousing, exterior packaging, materials handling, and some other activities or cost centers was recognized. For example, the selection and use of a mode of transportation, such as rail, impact inventory, warehousing, packaging, customer service, and materials handling costs; whereas motor carrier service would have a different impact on the same cost centers.

Evaluating alternate combinations of transport carriers, number and size of warehouses, location of plants and warehouses, inventory levels, and so on was an effective way to lower the total cost of the physical distribution system. Attempting to select the lowest-cost transportation alternative could, for example, lead to higher inventory, packaging, warehousing, and handling costs, which could more than offset the low transportation cost and lead to higher physical distribution system costs. Conversely, a higher-cost transportation alternative with better service could lower those same costs and, perhaps, result in lower total cost.

outbound logistics

The initial focus upon physical distribution or outbound logistics was logical since finished goods were usually higher in value, which meant that their inventory, warehousing, materials handling, and packaging costs were relatively higher than their raw material counterparts. The impact of transportation selection was, therefore, more significant. Managers in certain industries such as consumer package/grocery products, high-tech companies, and other consumer product companies—as well as some academicians—became very interested in physical distribution management. A national organization, the National Council of Physical Distribution Management (NCPDM), was organized to foster leadership, education, research, and interest in this area.

inbound logistics

The 1980s, as was noted, were a decade of change with the deregulation of transportation and financial institutions. The technology revolution was also well under way. During the 1980s, the logistics or integrated logistics management concept began to be used in a growing number of organizations. Logistics, in its simplest form, added inbound logistics to the outbound logistics of physical distribution (see Figure 1–1 and Figure 1–2). This was a very logical addition since deregulation of

FIGURE 1–1 A View of Business Logistics in a Company

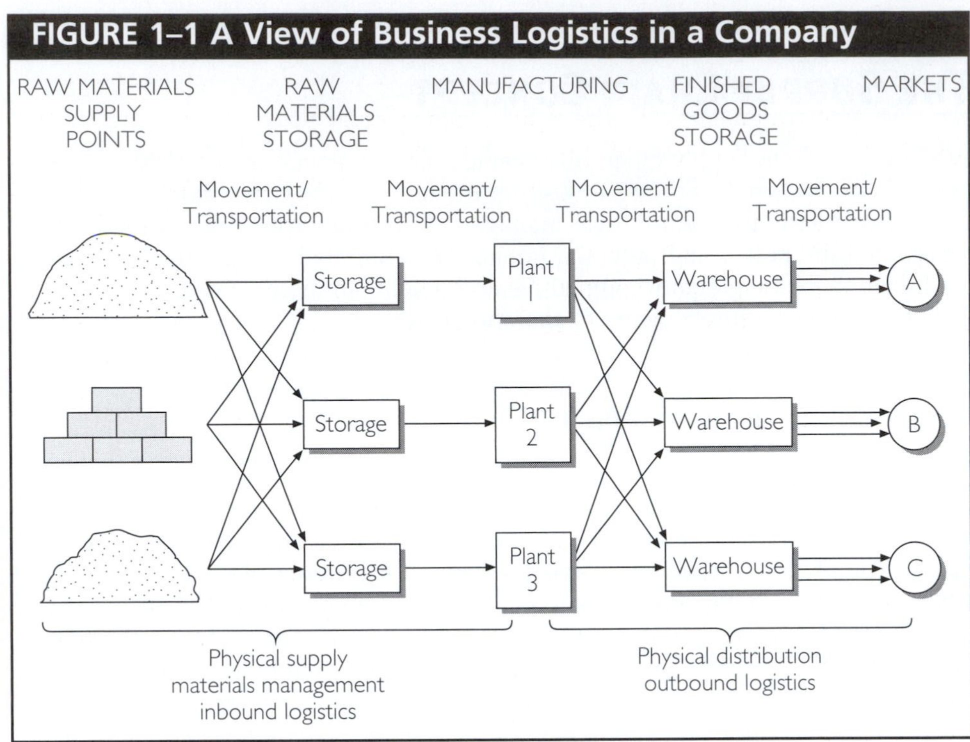

Source: Center for Supply Chain Research, Penn State University.

FIGURE 1–2 Integrated Logistics Management

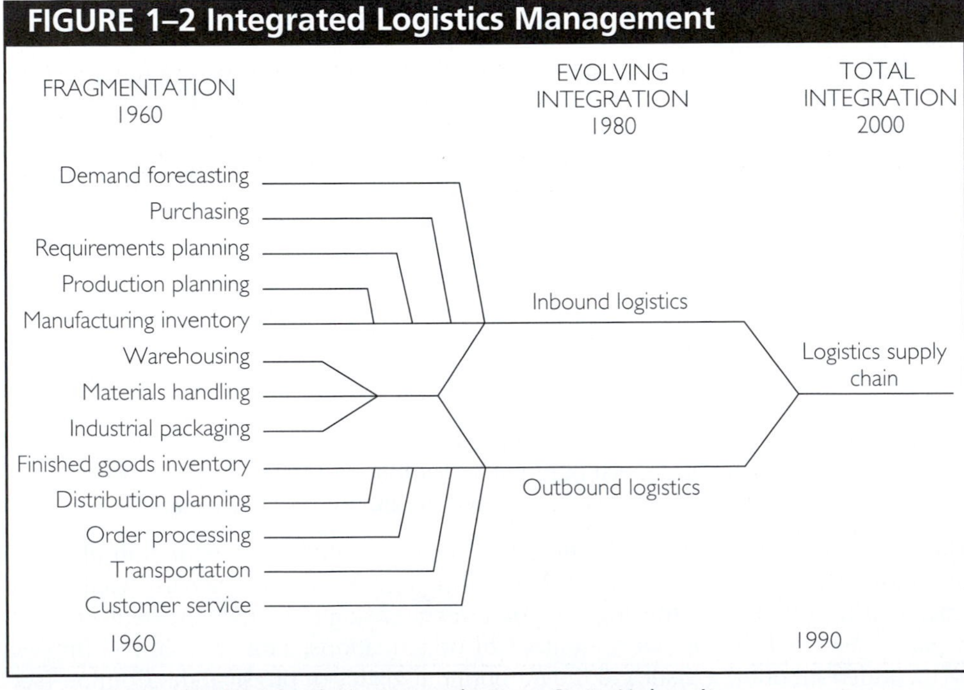

Source: Center for Supply Chain Research, Penn State University.

transportation provided an opportunity to coordinate inbound and outbound transportation movements of large shippers, which could positively impact a carrier's operating cost by minimizing empty backhauls, leading to lower rates for the shipper. Also, international or global sourcing of materials and supplies for inbound systems was growing in importance. As previously noted, global transportation presents some special challenges for production scheduling. Therefore, it became increasingly apparent that coordination with the outbound logistics system was critical for success.

value chain

The underlying logic and rationale of the systems or total cost concept were still the basis for the logistics concept. However, the value chain concept had also been developed as a tool for competitive analysis and strategy. As can be seen in the value chain illustration (Figure 1–3), inbound and outbound logistics are important, primary components of the value chain, that is, contributing "value" to the firm's customers and making the company financially viable. The more integrated nature of marketing, sales, and manufacturing with logistics is also an important dimension of the value chain.

As already stated, supply chain management came into vogue during the 1990s and continues to be a focal point for making organizations more competitive in the global marketplace. Supply chain management can be viewed as a pipeline or conduit for the efficient and effective flow of products/materials, services, information, and financials from the supplier's suppliers through the various intermediate organizations/companies out to the customer's customers (see Figure 1–4) or the system of connected logistics networks between the original vendors and the ultimate final consumer. The extended enterprise perspective of supply chain management represents a logical extension of the logistics concept.

terminology

Before discussing and analyzing the supply chain concept in more detail, it is worth noting that a growing number of terms are being utilized by individuals and organizations that are presented as being more appropriate, comprehensive, and/or advanced than *supply chain management.* Such terms include *demand chain management, demand flow management, value chain management, value networks,*

FIGURE 1–3 Generic Value Chain

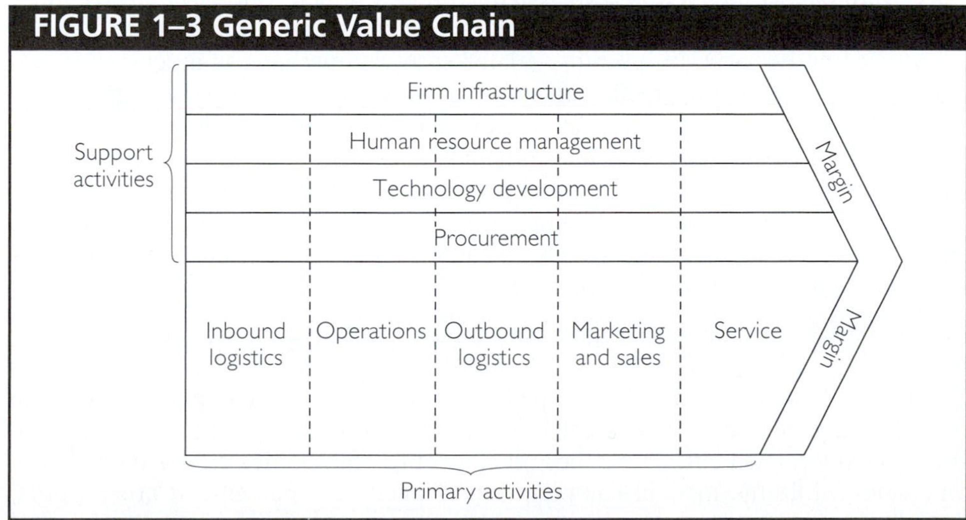

Source: Michael Porfun, *Competitive Advantage* (New York: The Free Press, 1985), 37.

FIGURE 1–4 Logistics Supply Chain

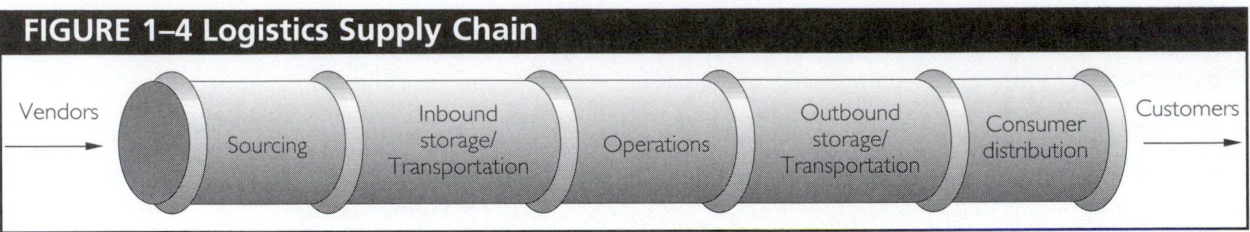

and *synchronization management. Supply chain management* is viewed by some individuals to be too narrowly focused and/or focused upon supplies and materials, not demand for finished products. The definition of supply chain management proposed in this book is broad and comprehensive; therefore, demand and value are very relevant as well as synchronization of flows through the pipeline or supply chain. Therefore, it can be argued that *supply chain, demand chain, value network, value chain,* and so on can be used as synonyms. Also, there appears to be a much more widespread use and acceptance of the term *supply chain management* and the broader and more comprehensive viewpoint of supply chain management espoused in this chapter and throughout the book.

Business Case for Supply Chain Management

A logical question to be asked is, why has supply chain management attracted so much attention among CEOs, CFOs, COOs, CIOs, and other senior executives? There are a myriad of reasons, but the business case for supply chain management can be demonstrated with two well-known studies.

ECR In the early 1990s, the Grocery Manufacturer's Association (GMA) commissioned a study by one of the large consulting organizations, which specializes in logistics and supply chain management to research and analyze its supply chain. Figure 1–5 illustrates one of the major findings of the study: on average, this industry had 104 days of inventory in its outbound supply chains. The consulting company recommended a set of initiatives that would lead to reducing that to *sixty-one* days of inventory. There are two important points here. First, it was estimated that at least $30 billion per year could be saved in inventory-related *costs* and perhaps as much as $50 billion per year by reducing pipeline inventory to sixty-one days. Such savings had the potential of having a significant impact upon consumer prices or what might be called "landed prices." Second, this study only considered part of the supply chain, which, therefore, understated the total potential. The potential savings of $30 billion demonstrated the power of looking at the supply chain as opposed to just looking at one individual company or one segment of the supply chain. The latter perspective often results in suboptimization.

best-in-class Another demonstration of the significance of focusing upon the supply chain came from the Supply Chain Council, which published a comparison for 1996 and 1997 of "best-in-class" companies (top 10 percent) and the median companies who were reporting their metrics to the Council. As can be seen from Figure 1–6, in 1996, the supply chain–related costs of the best-in-class (BIC) companies were 7.0 percent of total sales while the median company experienced 13.1 percent. In other words, the best-in-class companies spent 7.0 cents of every sales/revenue dollar for supply chain–related costs while the median company spent 13.1 cents of every sales

FIGURE 1–5 Comparison of Average Throughput Time of Dry Grocery Chain before and after ECR Implementation

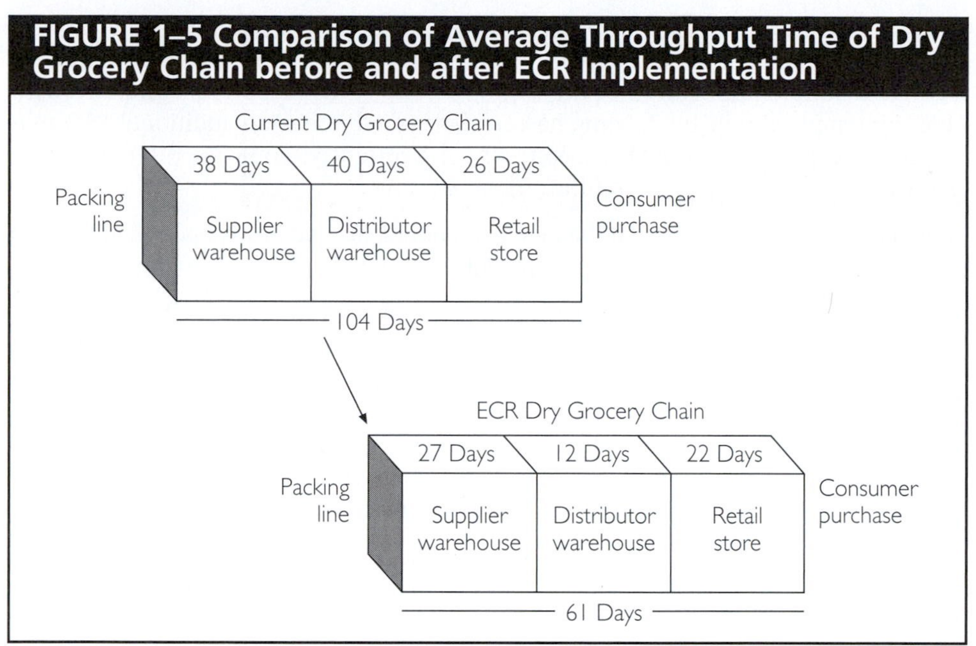

Source: Kurt Salmon Associates, Inc., *Efficient Consumer Response Enhancing Consumer Value in the Grocery Industry* (January 1993).

FIGURE 1–6 Total Supply Chain Management Cost—All Sectors

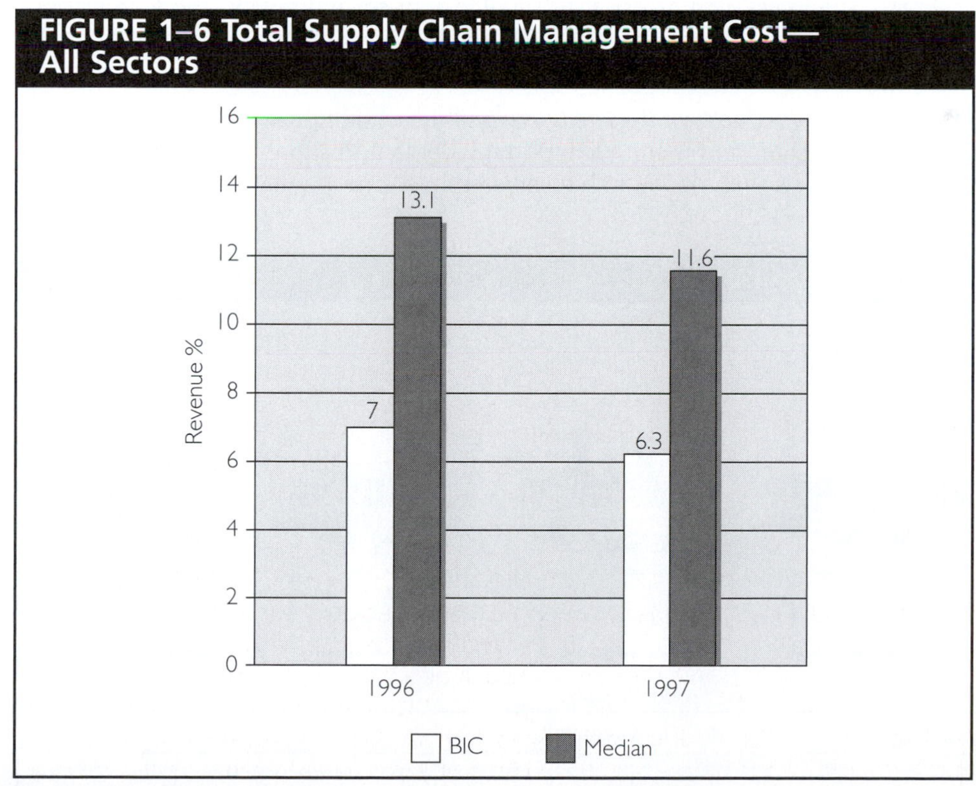

Source: Supply Chain Council.

dollar on supply chain–related costs. In 1997, the respective numbers were 6.3 percent and 11.6 percent for best-in-class companies versus the median company. If we take a simple application of these numbers for a hypothetical company with $100 million in sales in 1997, being best in class would mean an additional $5.3 million of gross profit to an organization, which frequently would be the equivalent profit from another $80–100 million of sales.

There have been other reports in the business periodicals and newspapers, but the two cases cited offer ample evidence of the potential savings of a supply chain perspective.

complexity of supply chain

At this point, a more detailed analysis and discussion of the supply chain is appropriate. Figure 1–7 presents a simplified, linear example of a hypothetical supply chain. Real-world supply chains are usually more complex than this example because they may be nonlinear and/or have more supply chain participants. Also, this supply chain does not adequately represent the importance of transportation in the supply chain. In addition, some companies may be part of several supply chains. For example, IBM considers its PC business as part of a different supply chain than its mainframe computers.

extended enterprise

Figure 1–7, however, does provide sufficient perspective at this juncture to understand the basics of a supply chain. The definition that is a part of the illustration indicates several very important points. A *supply chain* is an extended enterprise that crosses over the boundaries of individual firms to span the logistical related activities of all the companies involved in the supply chain. This extended enterprise attempts to execute or implement a coordinated, two-way flow of goods/services, information, and financials (especially cash). The three flows enumerated at the bottom of the illustration are very important to the understanding of supply chain management. The integration across the boundaries of several organizations in essence means that the supply chain needs to function like one organization in satisfying the ultimate customer.

two-way flow of products

The top flow—*products and related services*—has traditionally been an important focus of logisticians and is still an important element in supply chain management. Customers expect their orders to be delivered in a timely, reliable, and damage-free

FIGURE 1–7 Integrated Supply Chain

The supply chain can be viewed as a series of integrated enterprises that must share information and coordinate physical execution to ensure a smooth, integrated flow of goods, services, information, and cash through the pipeline.

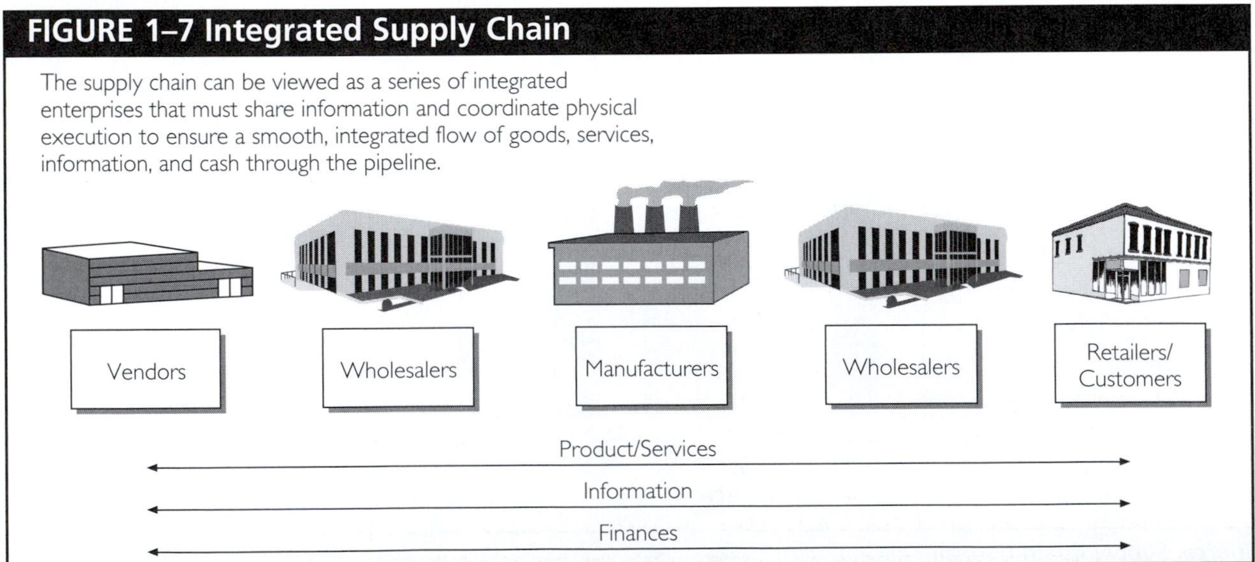

manner; and transportation is critical to this outcome. Figure 1–7 also indicates that product flow is a two-way flow in today's environment because of the growing importance of reverse logistics systems for returning products that are unacceptable to the buyer, damaged, obsolete, or worn out. There are numerous reasons for this growth in reverse systems, which are explored in a later chapter, but there is no question that it is a growing phenomenon of supply chains. Note also that networks for reverse systems usually have to be designed differently than forward systems. The location, size, and layout of facilities are frequently different; and the transportation carriers need to be utilized differently.

information flows

The second flow indicated is the *information flow,* which has become an extremely important factor for success in supply chain management. Traditionally, we have viewed information as flowing in the opposite direction of products, that is, from the market/customer back to the wholesalers, manufacturers, and vendors. The information was primarily demand or sales data, which were the trigger for replenishment and the basis for forecasting. Note that, other than the retailer or final seller, the other members of the supply chain reacted to replenishment orders. If there were long time intervals between orders, the members of the supply chain were faced with much uncertainty about the level and pattern of the demand.

information sharing

One of the realizable outcomes of supply chain management is the sharing of sales information on a more "real-time" basis, which leads to less uncertainty and, therefore, less safety stock. In a sense, the supply chain is being compressed or shortened in the form of time/information flow back from the marketplace, which leads to a type of supply chain compression—inventory compression. In other words, inventory can be eliminated from the supply chain by timely, accurate information about demand. If point-of-sale (POS) data were available from the retail level on a real-time basis, it would help eliminate the bullwhip effect associated with supply chain inventories and would significantly reduce cost.

inventory visibility

Note that the illustration also indicates a two-way flow for information. In a supply chain environment, information flowing forward in the supply chain has taken on increased significance and importance. Forward information flow can take many forms such as advance shipment notices (ASNs), order status information, inventory availability information, and so on. The overall impact has been to reduce uncertainty with respect to order replenishment, which also contributes to lowering inventory and improving replenishment time. A related aspect of forward information flow has been the increased utilization of bar codes and radio frequency (RF) tags, which dramatically increase inventory visibility, which again helps reduce uncertainty and safety stock; but also, the vastly improved visibility of pipeline inventory makes possible many opportunities for improved efficiency such as transportation consolidation and merge-in-transit strategies.

The combined two-way flow of timely, accurate information has lowered supply chain–related costs while also improving effectiveness/customer service; but there is much more improvement that can be made.

cash flow

The third and final flow is *financials* or, more specifically, cash. Traditionally, financial flow has been viewed as one-directional—backward—in the supply chain or, in other words, payment for goods, services, and orders received. A major impact of supply chain compression and faster order cycle times has been faster cash flow. Customers receive orders faster; they are billed sooner; and companies collect sooner. The faster cash-to-cash cycle or order-to-cash cycle has been a financial bonanza for many companies because of the impact on profitability. Dell

Computer, which has been the focus of much attention compared to other computer companies, especially Compaq, has been a major beneficiary of a compressed supply chain and the related faster cash flows. As Figure 1–8 illustrates (see fourth quarter of 1997), Dell is turning its inventory fifty turns per year (about one per week) compared to ten turns (five weeks) for Compaq computer. More importantly for this discussion, since they fulfill their orders in seven to ten days, they often receive payment (in ten to twelve days) before they pay their vendors. In essence, they have a negative cash flow.

The supply chain perspective is very dynamic and provides an opportunity to reduce the cost of doing business and improve customer service for many companies. At the same time, it is not easy to implement. To gain an understanding of these challenges, we will examine the major characteristics of supply chain management.

SAB Distribution is obviously a part of a supply chain with an intermediate position between manufacturers and retailers. Wholesalers had a traditional role, which was buying products in volume quantities at volume prices and selling a mix of products in smaller quantities at higher prices to retailers. They frequently played a role in promoting and financing product sales in addition to distributing the item. Manufacturers and retailers depended upon them for efficiency in their operations. Large-scale retailers and manufacturers willing and able to provide more tailored, customized services have put wholesalers in jeopardy. SAB has felt this changing environment. It needs to reevaluate its role in relation to its retailers. What changes can SAB make to allow its customers (retailers) to be more competitive?

FIGURE 1–8 Running Lean

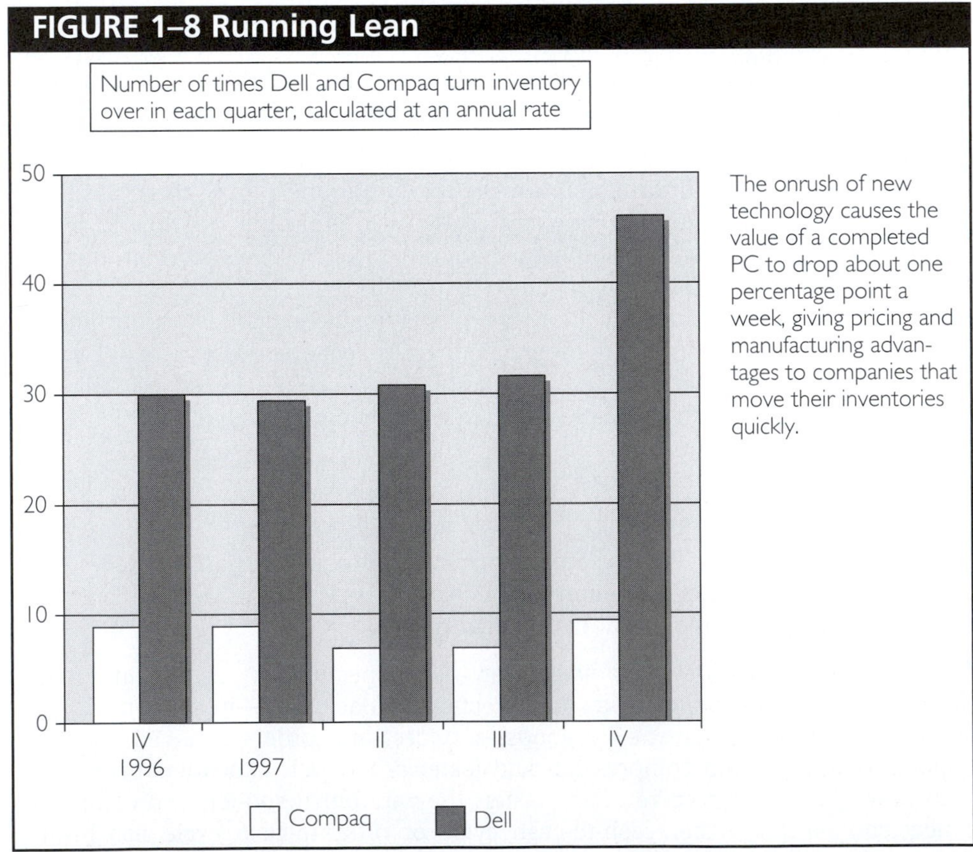

Source: Paine Webber.

SUPPLY CHAIN TECHNOLOGY

ENABLING RETAILERS TO CONQUER THE WORLD

Federated Department Stores is a retail leader in using technology to improve and streamline logistics. The company created Federated Logistics & Operations (FLO) in 1994 to coordinate merchandise distribution, logistics, and vendor technology across the company. FLO serves Federated's bricks-and-mortar and on-line retail operations—which include Burdines, Macy's, Rich's/Lazurus, Bloomingdale's, Goldsmith's, Stern's, and The Bon Marche. Leveraging state-of-the-art technology is part of FLO's mission; and it has been highly successful, saving Federated more than $150 million over the last five years.

Federated was one of the first department stores to partner with vendors to provide floor-ready merchandise. It also created the FASST (Federated Accelerated Sales & Stock Turn) stock replenishment plan. Using an advanced group to retail merchandise technologies, FASST enables a buyer to write a merchandise order that is processed electronically for access by both Federated and the supplier. Shipping labels and merchandise tickets are derived directly from that order.

FLO continues to seek improvement in its seven distribution centers that serve Federated's 400-plus stores. Two DCs each in New Jersey and California and one in Florida handle small-ticket products. Big-ticket items are handled out of separate facilities in California, New Jersey, and Florida. DCs in California, Georgia, and Washington handle both small- and big-ticket items, but "we treat them as separate operations—they're very different in scope," says FLO president Peter Longo.

"We spent the first five years of our life at Federated Logistics bringing supply chain technology, material handling, and DC management to world-class status in small-ticket operations," Longo says. "Our initiative this year is to replicate that success for big-ticket operations, applying the systems, technology, and profit improvement to furniture and bedding delivery and to order fulfillment."

The time frame? "Yesterday!" he says. FLO is already replatforming the operating support system, which will be ready mid-2001.

BUILDING A B2B BUSINESS

"An involving issue for all retailers, including Federated, is the B2B application for the Internet," Longo says. As information becomes more readily available and usable in a proprietary Web-based application, Federated is determining how to use logistics data to better serve merchants at the front end of the process and the stores that receive orders.

The retailer is building a proprietary Web-based application that "graphically and in text connects everything you want to know about a purchase order—from ship date to transportation to the DC and shuttle to the store," Longo says. This will enable a merchant to track an order from beginning to end simply by pointing and clicking. And the stores will get an advanced view of the orders. Accurately knowing when a shipment will arrive—and what products will be received—lets stores improve staff planning and workload management.

Federated wanted to leverage further the power of logistics data and make it available to both front- and back-end users, Longo says. This led to FLO's second major B2B initiative, a collaborative effort involving Manhattan Associates' *InfoLink.* Manhattan Associates is an Atlanta-based provider of warehouse and transportation management systems. The companies are working to build a collaborative Business Community Integration solution that will allow real-time communication between retailers and suppliers. *InfoLink* uses Extensible Markup Language (XML) technologies to facilitate supplier and retailer B2B capabilities.

Federated and Manhattan Associates have recently completed a pilot program using *InfoLink* to communicate with three of the retailers' vendors. "We believe the program will evolve into an exception-based, Web-based information link that will look at such factors as ship dates, allocations, sizes, ranges,

(continued on next page)

Supply Chain Technology *continued*

and colors," Longo says. "In addition to providing end-to-end inventory visibility, the system will deliver a series of exception alerts that give information to the people that need it at the earliest point in the cycle."

FLO's supply chain improvement efforts are paying off handsomely. Nearly 90 percent of merchandise is received floor-ready, compared to just 41 percent in 1995. Almost 98 percent of orders from domestic vendors are received with an EDI vendor ship notice. On average, 75 to 80 percent of each day's receipts are processed and shipped to the stores on the date of receipt—nearly twice the quantity as in 1995. On the expense side, processing cost has been reduced by more than 50 percent in that same time frame.

"No matter what our specific goals are," Longo says, "FLO will continue to be driven by a passion for creating large changes in supply chain management, which will benefit Federated and our resources."

Source: Leslie Hanson Harps, *Inbound Logistics* (August 2000): 33–43.

Characteristics of Supply Chain Management

The definition of supply chain management presented previously suggested a number of important factors and related characteristics that are key to successful implementation. The key factors are inventory, cost, information, customer service, and collaborative relationships. Each of these deserves some special consideration.

inventory visibility

Inventory. Managing the flow and level of inventory is a central focus of supply chain management and a major performance metric to gauge success. In simplistic terms, the level of inventory must be sufficient to provide acceptable customer service but low enough to minimize supply chain costs. To maintain the balance between supply of and demand for inventory stock, the supply chain requires integrated management to avoid duplication among members of the supply chain. Visibility of inventory as it moves through the supply chain is necessary to reduce or eliminate uncertainty, which eliminates safety stock. This includes visibility of inventory being held in warehouses and other storage facilities as well as inventory in transit. The use of bar coding, RF tags, and other related technology provides the opportunity to reduce safety stock or buffer stock, which usually is accumulated at the interface between organizations in the supply chain and frequently duplicated by both organizations. This is illustrated in Figure 1–9 by the bulges in the pipeline.

pull systems

Another important characteristic of effective inventory management is to attempt to pull it through the supply chain in response to demand as opposed to pushing out inventory in advance of demand, which tends to inflate inventory levels and lead to obsolete inventory and lower inventory turnover. A number of companies, such as Dell Computer Company, have been successful in implementing pull systems, which has had a dramatic impact upon their inventory turnover. Essentially, personal computers that are ordered via telephone, fax, or the Internet are assembled/produced after the order is received. Dell can frequently produce the customized computer in forty-eight hours or less and ship it to its customers. Such a strategy has a dramatic impact on finished goods inventory. In

FIGURE 1–9 Traditional Supply Chain/Pipeline Inventory Flow: 1970s and 1980s

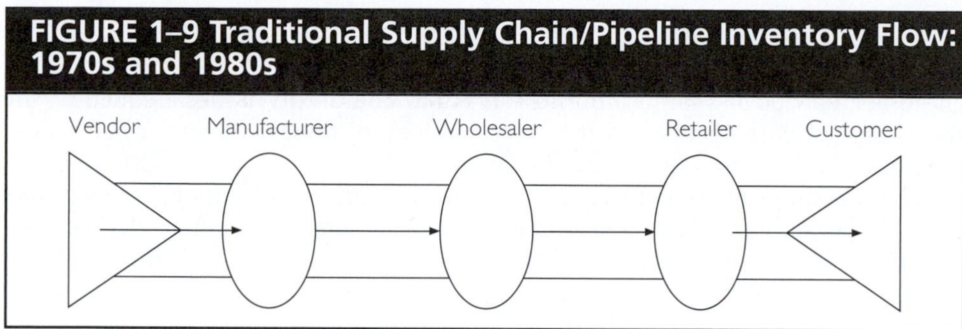

Source: Center for Supply Chain Research, Penn State University.

conjunction with the outbound strategy, there is a complementary JIT arrangement with vendors on the inbound side.

While it is not possible for all companies to produce products after they are ordered (build to order), for example, consumer food product companies, there are related strategies—such as postponement, which is discussed in later chapters—that contribute to the same objective, that is, lower pipeline/supply chain inventories.

landed cost

Cost. As indicated previously, efficiency or lowering cost is an important objective of supply chain management. However, note that the focus has to be upon the cost at the end of the supply chain, which is, in essence, the total cost or what is sometimes called the *landed cost* at the end of the pipeline. This means that the companies that are part of a supply chain need to be cognizant of what impact their approach and activities have upon their vendors and/or customers. Far too often, companies attempt to optimize their own costs, which may have a negative impact on their venders or customers. In some instances, companies are just not aware of the impact of their strategies and/or tactics. In today's environment, as indicated previously, global supply chains are competing against global supply chains. Companies have to coordinate their supply chain activities by sharing information and using joint planning to accomplish the cost objective. In essence, this builds upon systems theory and total cost analysis that was discussed earlier in this chapter. Such an outcome is far more difficult to achieve when you are dealing with several companies rather than one.

Information. Managing the flow of information is a key factor for both efficiency and effectiveness in the supply chain. As previously indicated, it must be a two-directional flow to really maximize the potential of supply chain management. A key characteristic is sharing information up and down the supply chain related to the flow and demand requirements. If information is shared, it can potentially be available on a real-time basis. If the information also has a high level of integrity and accuracy, then it significantly reduces uncertainty, which, in turn, reduces safety stock and obviously lowers inventory.

real-time information

As important as sharing real-time information is to the successful management of supply chains, there is some reluctance in companies to share. This reluctance is usually based upon a fear that companies will lose competitive advantage if, for example, demand information or production information will inform competitors of what to expect and perhaps lead to lost sales. Often, such fears are not founded upon logistical analysis. Even if there is some disadvantage to sharing information, the advantages may far outweigh the disadvantages.

The other barrier to sharing information is the complexity issue. Frequently, an abundance of data is collected by the technology of optical scanners, bar codes, computers, and so on; but turning this plethora of data into useful information for decision making can be a challenge. Consider the amount of data being collected every day at all of the scanners at retail outlets. The amount of data collected is so overwhelming that it is very difficult to summarize, synthesize, and manipulate it into useful form in a timely manner.

Nevertheless, much progress has been made with information sharing; more is likely to come in the future as we demonstrate the positive outcomes of such an approach. Shared information of high integrity on a real-time basis is the key to supply chain success.

Customer Service. As indicated previously, the decade of the 1990s has been described in some quarters as the information decade because of the impact that information technology has had on how businesses can operate in terms of efficiency and effectiveness. Some individuals argue that the 1990s was the decade of customer service. Actually, a good argument can be made for either descriptor for the 1990s, but we should recognize that there is a synergy between the information and customer service. Timely information of high quality makes possible improved customer service and also lower cost, which can mean lower prices to customers.

In the context of our discussion of supply chain characteristics, customer service is a very important attribute of successful supply chains. In the final analysis, the success of today's global supply chains is the value that they add for their ultimate customers in terms of the supply chain's landed cost/price and the related services that are provided. Information technology can play a significant role in facilitating customer service that provides the opportunity for a global supply chain to remain competitive and, hopefully, gain market share.

levels of customer service

Customer service has three recognized levels from a supply chain and logistics perspective. The minimum level is reliable, on-time delivery and accurately filled orders. In today's environment, this basic level of service is necessary to retain customers. To increase sales with customers (especially large customers), it is necessary to be responsive to their special needs and requests. This second level may entail, for example, scheduled deliveries, advanced shipment notices, tailored pallet packs, and so on.

To sustain and grow market share, the third and highest level of customer service is required, namely, adding value for important customers. Examples of value-adding services may include vendor-managed inventory, collaborative planning and forecasting, supply chain visibility of inventory, and so on.

The importance of existing and potential customers has to be evaluated to develop priorities for extending the highest two levels of customer service. Many companies find that a relatively small percentage of their customers generates a significant share of their sales. These "A" customers require priority-type service, which an effective supply chain partner should be able to provide.

supply chain collaboration

Relationships. Collaboration among supply chain "partners" is another important ingredient to supply chain success and to the ultimate goal of integration, that is, operating the whole supply chain as if it were a single organization. Concepts such as partnerships and alliances have become a part of the vocabulary of logistics and supply chain managers and indicate that the more traditional adversarial basis to business interactions has been changing. The cooperative, collaborative approach is a recognition to some extent of the characteristics already discussed. However, supply chain relationships need to incorporate more than shared information and a focus upon total supply chain cost. Collaboration in planning strategy and tactics among supply chain partners is also needed. The collaborative planning utilized, for example, by Chrysler in working with its vendors has led to significant cost reduction in producing its cars.[8] The cooperative planning for a supply chain approach needs to include an internal, cross-function team and external efforts with vendors, carriers, distributors, and so on. The reported successes of Collaborative Planning and Forecasting Requirements (CPFR) among supply chain members provide another example of the power of collaborative planning and information sharing among supply chain members.[9] This topic is so important that a separate chapter is devoted to supply chain partnerships or relationships.

In addition to the collaborative planning, there is a need to share risks and rewards. Most organizations function in an environment where they attempt to minimize their own risk and maximize their own rewards, which may mean that outcomes are achieved at the expense of other companies. The more cooperative, collaborative approach defined by a supply chain approach, or the "win-win" outcome, is the objective of collaboration strategies.

An underlying dimension of collaboration and partnering is a recognition that in the cast-changing environment of today's global marketplace, successful organizations need to focus upon their core competencies and outsource other activities to supply chain partners. Such an approach allows more flexible, responsive, and agile responses to the changing business environment.

SAB Distribution needs to understand its supply chain mission in terms of the characteristics discussed here—namely, inventory, landed cost, information, and collaboration. Intermediaries, such as wholesalers, will continue to be important to some supply chains. They will probably have to change and adapt to a differing role than they played in the past. The same may also be true of their "partners."

SUMMARY

- The 1990s was a decade of great change and also a period during which the importance of logistics and supply chain management reached the board rooms of major corporations worldwide.
- The accelerated rate of change in our economy was driven by a number of macro level forces, namely: An empowered consumer; a shift in economic power toward the end of the supply chain; deregulation of key industries; globalization; and technology. All of these forces of change elevated the importance of supply chain management as a strategic weapon for competitive advantage.
- The conceptual basis of the supply chain is not new. In actuality, we have gone through several evolutionary stages starting with physical distribution

management in the 1970s, which evolved into logistics management in the 1980s and then supply chain management in the 1990s.

- There are a number of terms being used that may be considered synonymous with how supply chain management is defined in this text, namely, *demand chain, demand flow, value networks,* and so on.
- Supply chain management is involved with integrating three key flows across the boundaries of the companies in a supply chain—product/materials, information, and financials/cash. Successful integration or coordination of these three flows has produced improved efficiency and effectiveness for companies.
- The key factors of successful supply chain management include inventory, cost, information, customer service, and collaboration relationships. Focusing on the management of these factors is critical to the implementation of a supply chain strategy.

Study Questions

1. Consumers have been described as one of the driving forces of change during the 1990s. In fact, reference is made to the "empowered consumer." How has the role of the consumer changed? What has been the impact upon supply chains?
2. Consolidation at the retail level has been an important economic development during the 1980s and the 1990s. What impact has retail consolidation had upon supply chains?
3. "Deregulation of transportation, communications, and financial organizations has resulted in lower prices and better service and has been a cornerstone of the development of supply chain management." Do you agree or disagree? Why?
4. Some individuals argue that globalization has impacted all businesses whether they are large or small. It is relatively easy to understand why and how large companies are impacted by globalization, but why and how would a relatively small company, such as SAB, and its supply chain be impacted by globalization?
5. Technology has been labeled as both an external change driver for supply chains and also as an internal factor for change. Why?
6. Supply chain experts point out that supply chain management encompasses three important flows. What are these three flows? Why are they important to effective supply chain management? Discuss the direction of these flows.
7. Supply chains have been described as "extended enterprises." What does this description mean? What special challenges are presented by this concept?
8. Successful supply chains manage inventory and information flows. What is the nature of the relationship between these two flows?
9. What is meant by the term "landed cost"? Why is it important in supply chain management?
10. "Collaboration is one of the key factors for successful supply chain management." Do you agree or disagree? Why?

NOTES

1. Charles Durney (presented at Council of Logistics meeting, Philadelphia, Pa., June 2000).

2. James Tompkins (presented at Warehouse of the Future Conference, Atlanta, Ga., May 2000).

3. Anonymous, *Logistics* (July–August 2000): 43.

4. Joe Paterno, football coach, speech (September 1998) presented at Penn State University.

5. Thomas L. Friedman, *The Lexus and the Olive Tree* (New York: Farrar, Straus and Giroux, 1999), 1–25.

6. Ibid., 30–35.

7. George Smerk, George Wilson, and John Spychalski, *Physical Distribution Management,* vol. 1 (Bloomington, Ind.: Indiana University Press, 1964), 15–21.

8. Thomas T. Stallkamp, "Chrysler's Leap of Faith," *Supply Chain Management Review* (Summer 1998): 18–21.

9. Ibid.

CASE 1–1 ■ Central Transport, Inc.

Doug Thomas, president and CEO of Central Transport, had just returned from a meeting called by Sue Purdum, president and CEO of SAB Distribution. He immediately sat down and wrote the following E-mail message to all of his senior staff:

> *I need your collective wisdom and input to help me respond to a challenge given to me by Sue Purdum of SAB Distribution. SAB, as you know, has been one of our best customers for many years. Our growth has been tied to its growth since we are one of its core carriers. As it expanded its customer base throughout Pennsylvania and neighboring states, we have expanded our route network to meet its requirements. Our founder, John Spychalski, was a personal friend of the three founders of SAB Distribution. While that personal relationship has changed with changes in both of our organizations, Central has maintained a partnership approach with SAB. My belief is that if it wins, we win.*
>
> *SAB, according to Ms. Purdum, has been faced with a growing level competition both directly and indirectly in the two small medium-size communities where its retail store customers are located. Its profit margins have narrowed, and Ms. Purdum is under pressure from her board (most of whom are descendants of the three founders) to improve SAB's profitability. To her credit, she initiated a number of changes after she became president and CEO five years ago.*

According to Ms. Purdum, she has to reduce her cost-of-sales and/or improve her level of customer service to add more value to her customers. Transportation from SAB's warehouse to its customer stores is a major part of its cost-of-sales. Also, our ability to deliver her customer's orders in a timely and reliable manner impacts significantly SAB's customer service.

Ms. Purdum would like our senior management team to consider what we could do to help SAB remain competitive and improve its profitability. Obviously, we could reduce our rates by 10 percent, but that only shifts the problem to us unless we can reduce our operating costs by 10 percent to offset the rate reduction. We need to be creative and think of ourselves as a supply chain partner with SAB and its suppliers and customers.

Help Mr. Thomas develop a "white paper" to respond to Ms. Purdum by addressing the following:

Case Questions

1. Why and how has the competitive marketplace changed for SAB?
2. Provide additional rationale for the collaborative perspective suggested by Mr. Thomas.
3. Using the success factors for supply chain management as a framework, recommend what Central Transport can do to help SAB improve its efficiency and effectiveness.

CHAPTER 2

DIMENSIONS OF LOGISTICS

LEARNING OBJECTIVES

After reading this chapter, you should be able to do the following:

- Understand the role and importance of logistics in private and public organizations.
- Discuss the impact of logistics on the economy and how effective logistics management contributes to the vitality of the economy.
- Understand the value-added roles of logistics on both a macro and micro level.
- Explain logistics systems from several perspectives.
- Understand the relationship between logistics and other important functional areas in a company, including manufacturing, marketing, and finance.
- Discuss the important management activities in the logistics function.
- Analyze logistics systems from several different perspectives to meet different objectives.
- Determine the total costs and understand the cost trade-offs in a logistics system from a static and dynamic perspective.

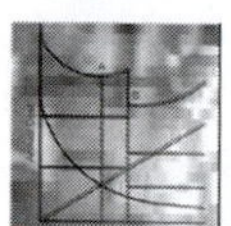

LOGISTICS PROFILE

Jordano Foods Case

Susan Weber, vice president of logistics for Jordano Foods, had just completed the following E-mail message to the other members of the executive committee of the company.

E-MAIL MESSAGE

I just returned from a lengthy meeting with Sue Purdum, CEO, of SAB Distribution. Sue is under great pressure from her board of directors to improve SAB's profitability. SAB has received an offer from another distributor to purchase the company, and several members of the SAB board have recommended that the offer be accepted. Sue Purdum feels strongly that SAB can be "turned around," that is, profitability and growth can be improved. She is meeting with all of SAB's major vendors and customers to request a more collaborative supply chain approach in their supply chain.

I am not certain that I understand all of the dimensions of supply chain management, but Sue Purdum's ideas make sense to me. She feels that if she can work more closely with SAB's major vendors (we are their sixth largest vendor) and major customers (top fifteen to twenty), a significant cost reduction can be realized. She also is convinced that these cost savings would not be at the expense of service. In fact, she gave examples of where companies in a supply chain have reduced cost and improved service. I was concerned about how the cost savings would be shared. Sue Purdum assured me that it would be a win-win approach. She feels strongly that most of the savings should go toward lowering prices to make our supply chain more competitive. The improved competitiveness would result in increased sales for all members of the supply chain, which would improve our profits.

One way to look at Sue Purdum's message is that the major supply chain members have to not only improve their internal logistics systems but also to try to coordinate their logistical activities by collaborating and sharing appropriate information.

I am going to ask Paul Durkin, warehouse manager, Tracie Shannon, inventory manager, Sue Kolbe, transportation manager, and Jean Beierlein, customer service manager, to serve as a facilitating group. We will be holding weekly meetings and will update all directors and managers on a monthly basis. Your input will be an important part of this program.

BACKGROUND ON JORDANO FOODS

Jordano Foods was founded in 1950 in Lewistown, Pennsylvania, by two brothers, Luigi and Mario Jordano. The parents of the two brothers operated a restaurant in Burnham, Pennsylvania, featuring Italian cuisine. Marie Jordano was famous for her culinary skills. She developed her own recipes for pasta sauce, meatballs, fresh and dry pasta, and so on. Luigi and Mario worked in the restaurant prior to establishing Jordano Foods. The brothers felt that they could capitalize on the family recipes by selling pasta, sauces, and some related Italian food products to other restaurants in nearby communities in central Pennsylvania.

Their initial venture was so successful that they expanded their product line and began to sell their products to small- to medium-sized wholesalers and distributors throughout Pennsylvania. They built a plant in Lewistown, Pennsylvania, to produce their food products and subsequently built another plant in Elizabethtown, Pennsylvania, and a warehouse in Mechanicsburg, Pennsylvania.

CURRENT SITUATION

The 1980s and 1990s were decades of significant growth for Jordano Foods. Mario and Luigi were still active in the company as president/CEO and chairman of the board, respectively. Sales now exceeded $300 million per year, and a third plant had been built in the western part of Pennsylvania near Uniontown. A group of professional managers has been developed in the company to head up the major functional areas. Susan Weber was hired in 1995 to head up the logistics area, which had not received much attention prior to Susan's being hired. Her career at P&G had provided her with

(continued on next page)

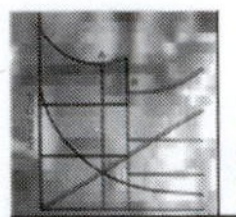

LOGISTICS PROFILE

Jordano Foods Case *continued*

much experience in all phases of logistics. It was her experience with systems planning that was particularly attractive to Mario Jordano when she was interviewed.

The change to a relatively small company was initially a challenge for Susan, but, at this point in time, she was very comfortable in her role. Under her leadership, a number of initiatives in inbound transportation and inventory control had been implemented. She was very supportive of Sue Purdum's collaborative approach. She had been involved in some of P&G's initial collaborative efforts with vendors. She wanted her working group to analyze how they could improve their inbound and outbound logistics systems not only to operate more efficiently but also to provide better service to their plants (inbound) and to their customers, such as SAB Distributors (outbound).

Ms. Weber realized the functional team she had appointed would need to operate with a systems perspective but also that the whole team would have to coordinate with manufacturing/processing and with marketing. She was concerned about the coordination with manufacturing and marketing because, traditionally, they had operated very independently and seemed reluctant to consider proposals she had made in the past for closer ties and discussions about trade-offs between the areas.

Ms. Weber was trying to keep an open mind. She realized that the Jordano Brothers had managed and developed the manufacturing and marketing functions during the formative years and these two areas were regarded as cornerstones of the company's success. Logistics was a new functional area for Jordano Foods. There were skeptics in the company who questioned logistics' value-add to the profitability and competitive position of Jordano Foods.

Susan Weber's "plate" was indeed "full" with both internal and external challenges and pressure to prove the importance of the logistics function. As you proceed through this chapter, identify areas for Jordano Foods to improve its logistics processes and its supply chain relationships with SAB distributors.

INTRODUCTION

As indicated in the previous chapter, supply chain management has captured the attention and interest of many high-level executives. Logistics is misunderstood and often overlooked with the excitement surrounding supply chain management and all of the related technology that has been developed to support the supply chain. The "glitter and glitz" associated with the E-supply chain, E-tailing, E-business, and so on seem to overshadow the importance of logistics in a company and the need for efficient and effective logistical support in a supply chain. Logistics may be regarded by some individuals as mundane and staid when compared to supply chain initiatives such as compression and postponement.

order fulfillment

Logistics professionals and other knowledgeable managers realize, however, that, in spite of all the hype about the Internet, successful companies must manage order fulfillment to their customers effectively and efficiently to build and sustain competitive advantage and profitability. The much noted E-tailing debacles of the 1999

Christmas season provide ample proof of the need for good, basic logistics systems. Sophisticated and "sexy" front-end systems cannot stand alone in the competitive global marketplace of today—back office execution is critical for customer satisfaction. In fact, the speed of ordering via the Internet and other technologies exacerbates the need for an efficient and effective logistics system that can deploy appropriate levels of inventory, speed completed orders to customers, and manage any returns. The often-quoted adage of "Good logistics is business power" is very appropriate because it helps build competitive advantage. At the end of the day, if you cannot get your products to your customers, you will not stay in business very long. This is not to say that you do not need quality products and effective marketing. Both are obviously very important, but they must be combined with effective and efficient logistics systems for long-run success and financial viability.

The big challenge is to manage the whole logistics system in such a way that order fulfillment meets and, perhaps, exceeds customer expectations. At the same time, the competitive marketplace demands efficiency—controlling transportation inventory and other logistics-related cost centers. As is discussed subsequently, cost and service trade-offs may have to be considered when evaluating customer service levels and the associated total cost of logistics; but both goals, efficiency and effectiveness, are important in today's competitive environment.

It is important at the outset to distinguish between logistics management and supply chain management or, more appropriately, relate the two concepts to each other. In the proceeding chapter, supply chain management was defined using a pipeline analogy with the start of the pipeline representing the initial vendor/supplier and the end of the pipeline representing the ultimate customer (see Figure 2–1). In other words, it was an extended set of enterprises from the vendor's vendor to the ultimate customer.

Another perspective on supply chain management is that it is a network of the logistics systems and related activities of all of the individual companies/organizations that are a part of a particular supply chain. The individual logistics systems obviously play a role in the success of the overall supply chain. The coordination or integration of the logistics systems in a supply chain is a challenge. In order to fully appreciate the dynamics of this challenge, it is necessary to examine and dissect an individual logistics system. In the Jordano Foods case, Ms. Sue Purdum needs to understand the intrafirm logistical relationships before she can synchronize with the whole SAB supply chain. The focus in this chapter is upon the dimensions of the individual logistics system but always recognizing that no logistical organization operates in a vacuum. For example, the inbound part of a manufacturer's logistics system interfaces with the outbound side of its vendor's logistics

FIGURE 2–1 Contemporary Supply Chain Pipeline

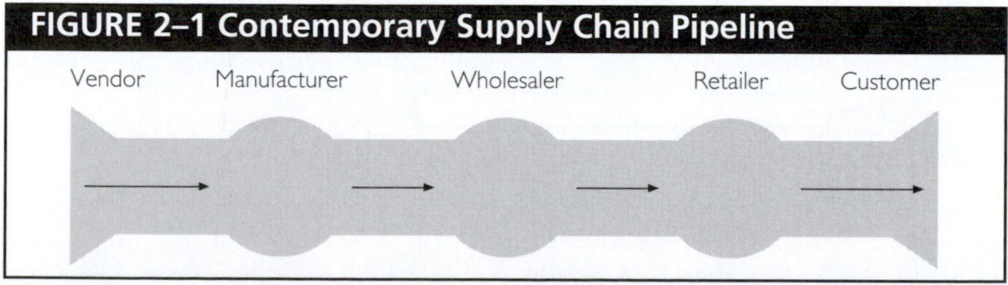

Source: Center for Supply Chain Research, Penn State University.

system. The outbound portion of the manufacturer's logistics system interfaces with the inbound side of its customer's logistics system.

As indicated in previous editions of this text, logistics has come a long way since the 1960s. The growing appreciation of the value associated with good logistics and the improved management of logistics systems have resulted in significant change and improved efficiency. To gain some appreciation of the strides that have been made, it is useful to examine logistics-related cost in the economy.

LOGISTICS IN THE ECONOMY: A MACRO PERSPECTIVE

The overall, absolute cost of logistics on a macro basis will increase with growth in the economy. In other words, if we produce and consume more goods and services, there will be increased total costs associated with all of the logistical activities of each and every organization. To determine the efficiency of the logistics system, we need to measure total logistics cost in terms of gross domestic product, which is a widely accepted barometer or metric used to gauge the rate of growth in the economy.

As indicated in Figure 2–2, logistics costs as a percentage of gross domestic product (GDP) have declined since 1980 from about 16 percent down to under 10 percent. In fact, logistics costs were closer to 20 percent of GDP in the early to mid-1970s. Robert Delaney, vice president of Cass Logistics in St. Louis, has developed and published this macro-level metric for logistics for over ten years. His annual reports are a widely recognized barometer for logistics costs.

FIGURE 2–2 Logistics Costs as a Percentage of GDP

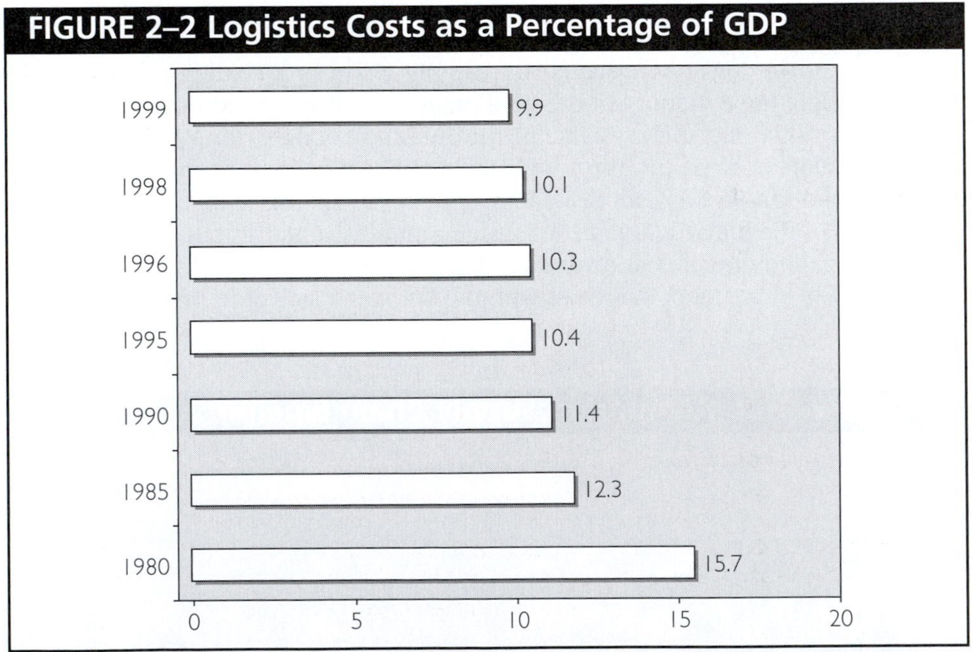

Source: Robert Delaney, Cass Information Systems.

declining costs

As can be readily seen from Figure 2–2, logistics costs on a relative basis (relative to GDP) have declined over the course of the last twenty-plus years. That is, there has been a significant improvement in the efficiency of the overall logistics systems of the various companies operating in the economy. This reduction in relative cost allows companies to be more competitive since it directly impacts the cost of producing goods (COGS). It can be argued that the turnaround that has occurred in the United States' global, economic viability is due in part to the improvement in the logistics cost. The 1990s are in stark contrast to the 1970s and early 1980s when our national economic competitiveness was seriously questioned in relation to the countries in Western Europe and on the Pacific Rim.

Some additional understanding of logistics can be gained by examining the three major cost categories that Delaney includes in his measure of annual logistics costs—carrying cost, transportation cost, and administrative costs. Simply stated, carrying costs are all the expenses associated with holding goods in storage. Carrying costs include interest expenses (or the opportunity cost associated with the investment in inventory), warehousing, risk-related costs (obsolescence, deterioration, damage), and service-related costs (insurance, taxes). Transportation costs are the total national expenditures for the movement of freight in the United States. The third category of logistics costs is the administrative cost associated with managing the logistical activities. Figure 2–3 depicts the breakdown of these cost categories for 1999.

It is very likely that the total cost of logistics presented in Figure 2–3 for 1999 of $921 billion understates the true cost of logistics in the economy because it does not appear to include some of the logistical activities that are discussed in this chapter. Nevertheless, the cost estimate provided by Delaney captures the major

FIGURE 2–3 Total Logistics Costs—1999

		$ Billions
Carrying Costs—$1,376 Trillion All Business Inventory		
Interest		70
Taxes, obsolescence, depreciation, insurance		187
Warehousing		75
	Subtotal	332
Transportation Costs		
Motor Carriers		
Truck—Intercity		300
Truck—Local		150
	Subtotal	450
Other Carriers		
Railroads		36
Water (International 16, Domestic 6)		22
Oil pipelines		9
Air (International 7, Domestic 19)		26
Forwarders		6
	Subtotal	99
Shipper Related Costs		5
Logistics Administration		35
	Total logistics cost	921

Source: Robert Delaney, Cass Information Systems.

cost categories; but, more importantly, the ten-year trend of logistical costs in the economy is represented in Figure 2–2.

The declining trend for logistics cost relative to gross domestic product indicated in Figure 2–2 is very important to note. The decline started in the early 1980s and was closely related to the deregulation of transportation, which permitted much more flexibility for carriers to adjust their rates and service in response to competition. Overall, transportation rates/prices declined in response to the then new, less regulated environment (Chapter 9 discusses the overall deregulation outcomes in much more detail). A second factor contributing to the trend has been the improved management of inventory levels. This has been the result of more attention being focused upon the investment in inventory and the associated better management tools and techniques for more effective decisions (Chapter 7 and Chapter 8 discuss these tools in more detail).

On a macro basis, the Federal Reserve publishes data on the ratio of inventory to sales (see Figure 2–4). In other words, how much inventory do companies carry to support sales? Typically, one might expect inventory to increase with increased sales. Figure 2–4 indicates a very interesting trend of inventory levels declining relative to sales. This is a measure of efficiency and clearly indicates that companies are improving in managing their inventory. Overall, companies have been supporting growing sales levels with a much lower level of inventory on a relative basis.

In addition to the managerial focus upon managing inventory and transportation more effectively, the total logistics system has received increased attention. It certainly appears that U.S. managers have realized the power of the message delivered by Peter Drucker in an article written for *Fortune* in 1962:[1]

> Distribution is one of the most sadly neglected but most promising areas of American business. . . . We know little more about distribution today than Napoleon's contemporaries knew about the interior of Africa. We know it's there, and we know it's big; and that's about all. . . . Most of our present concepts focus on production or on the stream of money and credit, rather than on the flow of physical goods and its economic characteristics. . . . To get control of distribution, therefore, requires seeing—

FIGURE 2–4 Inventory-Sales Ratio

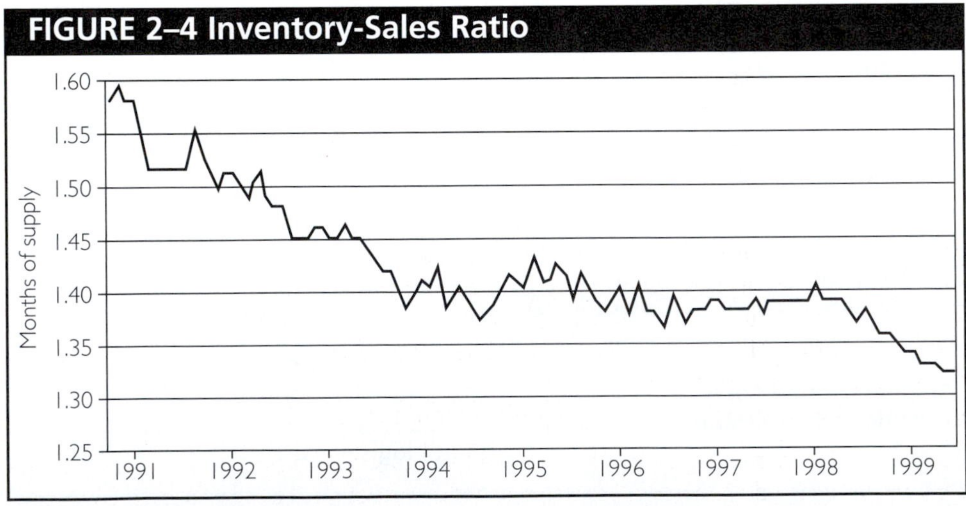

Source: Federal Reserve Bank of St. Louis.

and managing—it as a distinct dimension of business and as a property of product and process rather than as a collection of technical jobs.

The industrial purchaser has to know his own business. . . . [H]e has to know what the product or supply he buys is supposed to contribute to his company's end results. . . . My purpose is to point to distribution as an area where intelligence and hard work can produce substantial results for American business. Above all, there is a need for a new orientation—one that gives distribution the importance in business design, business planning, and business policy its costs warrant.

The two largest cost categories in any company's logistics system are transportation and inventory cost. As indicated, transportation is usually the single largest cost in any logistics system.

importance of motor carriers

Note the magnitude of the motor carrier share of the total freight expenditures—$450 billion versus $99 billion for all other carriers. This level of expenditure is not based necessarily upon the lowest transportation rates/prices but reflects the value to shippers/users of the service provided by the motor carriers. This point is discussed in the chapter on Transportation, but it is worth noting here because logistics management requires looking at the total cost of all the logistics activities, not just one cost such as transportation.

Also worth noting is that one of the most frequent trade-offs in logistics systems in a company is between transportation and inventory cost. For example, a company may be willing to pay the much higher rates/prices for air freight service because of the savings it will experience in inventory-related costs. In making this trade-off evaluation, companies are using a systems approach (which is discussed in more detail subsequently) to arrive at the best/lowest total cost.

WHAT IS LOGISTICS?

increased recognition

The term *logistics* has become much more widely recognized by the general public in the last twenty years. Television advertisements, for example, laud the importance of logistics. Transportation companies, especially trucking companies, frequently refer to their organizations as logistics companies and paint it on the side of their trailers. The Persian Gulf War probably contributed to increased recognition because of the frequent mention by news commentators of the logistical challenges associated with the so-called 7,000-mile "supply pipeline" to support the war effort in the Persian Gulf countries.

service quality

Another factor contributing to the recognition of logistics has been our increased sensitivity to not only product quality but also the associated service quality. For example, the previously mentioned failures during the Christmas season of 1999 associated with Internet retailers were widely publicized and often referred to as logistics system failures. But even prior to that time, when stores were out of stock of some item that we wanted to purchase or we did not receive a delivery of a package when we expected it, we would blame the logistics system.

Even with the increased recognition of the term *logistics,* however, there is still confusion about the definition of logistics or what it really means. Some of the confusion can be traced to the fact that there are a number of terms that are used by individuals when they refer to what has been described in this chapter. For example, consider the following list:

Logistics management
Business logistics management
Integrated logistics management
Materials management
Physical distribution management
Marketing logistics
Industrial logistics
Distribution

Logistics management is the most widely accepted term and encompasses logistics not only in the private business sector but also in the public/government and nonprofit sectors. In addition, service companies including banks, hospitals, restaurants, hotels, and so on have logistics challenges and issues, and logistics management is an appropriate form for the service industry.

Part of the definition problem is also traceable to the fact that logistics has been described by a variety of sources that have somewhat different perspectives. Table 2–1 illustrates a number of these definitions along with the perspective or connection.

For the purposes of this text, the definition of the Council of Logistics Management is utilized. However, it is important to recognize that logistics owes its origins to the military who have long recognized the importance of logistical activities for national defense.

The military definition of logistics encompasses supply items as well as personnel. It is reported that the term *logistics* became a part of the military lexicon in the eighteenth century in Europe. The logistics officer was responsible for encamping and quartering the troops as well as stocking supply depots.[2]

The logistics concept began to appear in the business-related literature in the 1960s under the label of *physical distribution,* which had a focus on the outbound side of the logistics system (see Figure 2–7). During the 1960s, military logistics began to focus upon engineering dimensions of logistics—reliability, maintainability, configuration management, life-cycle management, continuing supply support, and so on—with increased emphasis upon modeling and quantitative analysis.[3] In contrast, the business or commercial applications were usually more focused upon consumer nondurable goods related to marketing and physical distribution of finished products. The engineering-related logistics, as practiced by the military, attracted attention among businesses that produced industrial products that had to be maintained with repair parts over the life cycle of the product, for example, generators, airplanes, manufacturing equipment, and so on. In fact, engineers developed a separate professional organization called the Society of Logistics Engineers (SOLE), which has had active participation from both the military and commercial enterprises.

As indicated in the previous chapter, the business or commercial sector approach to logistics developed into inbound logistics (materials management to support manufacturing or operations) and outbound logistics (physical distribution of finished goods to support marketing) during the 1970s and 1980s. Then, in the 1990s, the business or commercial sector began to view logistics in the context of a supply or

TABLE 2–1 Logistics Definitions

Perspective	Definition
Inventory	Management of materials in motion and at rest
Customer	Getting the right product, to the right customer, in the right quantity, in the right condition, at the right place, at the right time, and at the right cost (called the "seven Rs of logistics")
Dictionary	The branch of military science having to do with procuring, maintaining, and transporting material, personnel, and facilities
International Society of Logistics	The art and science of management, engineering, and technical activities concerned with requirements, design, and supplying and maintaining resources to support objectives, plans, and operations
Utility/Value	Providing time and place utility/value of materials and products in support of organization objectives
Council of Logistics Management	That part of the supply chain process that plans, implements, and controls the efficient, effective flow and storage of goods, services, and related information from point of origin to point of consumption in order to meet customer requirements
Component support	Supply management for the plant (inbound logistics) and distribution management for the firm's customers (outbound logistics)
Functional management	Materials requirements determination, purchasing, transportation, inventory management, warehousing, materials handling, industrial packaging, facility location analysis, distribution, return goods handling, information management, customer service, and all other activities concerned with supporting the internal customer (manufacturing) with materials and the external customer (retail stores) with product
Common culture	Handling the details of an activity

Source: Adapted from Stephen H. Russell, "A General Theory of Logistics Practices," *Air Force Journal of Logistics* 24, no. 4 (2000): 15.

demand chain that linked all of the organizations from the vendor's vendor to the customer's customer. As discussed in the previous chapter, supply chain management requires a collaborative, coordinated flow of materials and goods through the logistics systems of all the organizations in the network.

In the twenty-first century, logistics should be viewed as a part of management and has four subdivisions:[4]

- *Business logistics:* That part of the supply chain process that plans, implements, and controls the efficient, effective flow and storage of goods, services, and related information from point of origin to point of use or consumption in order to meet customer requirements
- *Military logistics:* The design and integration of all aspects of support for the operational capability of the military forces (deployed or in garrison) and their equipment to ensure readiness, reliability, and efficiency

- *Event logistics:* The network of activities, facilities, and personnel required to organize, schedule, and deploy the resources for an event to take place and to efficiently withdraw after the event
- *Service logistics:* The acquisition, scheduling, and management of the facilities/assets, personnel, and materials to support and sustain a service operation or business

All four subdivisions have some common characteristics and requirements such as forecasting, scheduling, and transportation, but they also have some differences in terms of their primary purpose. All four, however, can be viewed in a supply chain context, that is, upstream and downstream there are other organizations that play a role in their overall success and long-run viability. (Our focus in this text is upon logistics management in the business sector.)

A general definition of logistics that could be used that appears to encompass all four subdisciplines is:

> Logistics is the process of anticipating customer needs and wants; acquiring the capital, materials, people, technologies, and information necessary to meet those needs and wants; optimizing the goods- or service-producing network to fulfill customer requests; and utilizing the network to fulfill customer requests in a timely way.

From the perspective of Jordano Foods, its focus should be upon its inbound logistics system (its vendors who provide the raw materials and supplies for its finished products) and its outbound logistics system (meeting the requirements of its customers). However, Ms. Weber has the additional challenge of the overall supply chain's requirements.

Value-Added Role of Logistics

types of utility

As Figure 2–5 illustrates, four principal types of economic utility add value to a product or service. Included are form, time, place, and possession. Generally, we credit manufacturing activities with providing form utility, logistics activities with time and place utility, and marketing activities with possession utility. We discuss each briefly.

what

Form Utility. *Form utility* refers to the value added to goods through a manufacturing, production, or assembly process. For example, form utility results when raw materials are combined in some predetermined manner to make a finished product. This is the case, for example, when a bottling firm adds together syrup, water, and carbonation to make a soft drink. The simple process of adding the raw materials together to produce the soft drink represents a change in product *form* that adds value to the product.

In today's economic environment, certain logistics activities can also provide form utility. For example, breaking bulk and product mixing, which typically take place at distribution centers, change a product's form by changing its shipment size and packaging characteristics. Thus, unpacking a pallet of breakfast cereal into individual consumer-size boxes adds form utility to the product. However, the two principal ways in which logistics adds value are in place and time utility.

where

Place Utility. Logistics provides *place utility* by moving goods from production surplus points to points where demand exists. Logistics extends the physical

FIGURE 2–5 Fundamental Utility Creation in the Economy

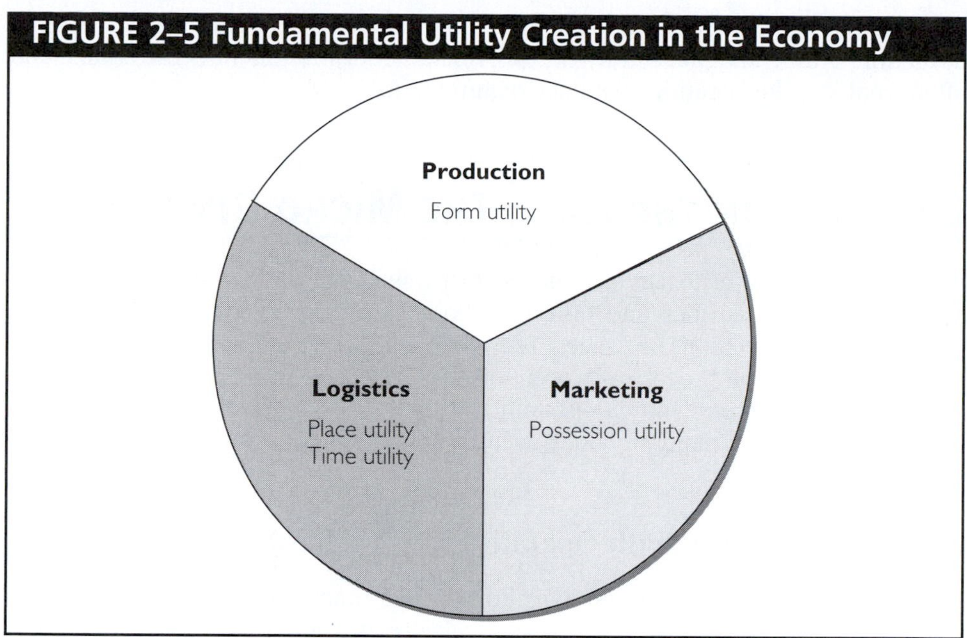

Source: Center for Supply Chain Research, Penn State University.

boundaries of the market area, thus adding economic value to the goods. This addition to the economic value of goods or services is known as *place utility.* Logistics creates place utility primarily through transportation. For example, moving farm produce by rail or truck from farm areas to markets where consumers need this produce creates place utility. The same is also true when steel is moved to a plant where the steel is used to make another product. The market boundary extension added by place utility increases competition, which usually leads to lower prices and increased product availability.

when

Time Utility. Not only must goods and services be available *where* consumers need them, but they must also be at that point *when* customers demand them. This is called *time utility,* or the economic value added to a good or service by having it at a demand point at a specific time. Logistics creates time utility through proper inventory maintenance and the strategic location of goods and services. For example, logistics creates time utility by having heavily advertised products and sale merchandise available in retail stores at precisely the time promised in the advertising copy.

To some extent, transportation may create time utility by moving something more quickly to a point of demand. For example, substituting air transportation for warehousing adds time utility. Time utility is much more important today because of the emphasis upon reducing lead time and minimizing inventory levels through logistics-related strategies such as JIT inventory control.

why

Possession Utility. *Possession utility* is primarily created through the basic marketing activities related to the promotion of products or services. We may define *promotion* as the effort, through direct and indirect contact with the customer, to increase the desire to possess a good or to benefit from a service. The role of logistics in the economy depends upon the existence of possession utility, for time or place utility make sense only if demand for the product or service exists. It is also true that marketing depends upon logistics, since possession utility cannot be acted upon unless time and place utility are provided. Order fulfillment is the critical and often final step for meeting customer requirements.

LOGISTICS IN THE FIRM: THE MICRO DIMENSION

Another dimension of logistics is the micro perspective, which examines the relationship between logistics and other functional areas in a company—marketing, manufacturing/operations, finances and accounting, and others. Logistics, by its nature, focuses upon processes that cut across traditional functional areas, particularly in today's environment with its emphasis upon the supply chain. Consequently, logistics interfaces in many important ways with all the other functional areas.

Logistics Interfaces with Operations/Manufacturing

length of production runs

A classic interface area between logistics and manufacturing management relates to the length of the production run. We typically associate production economies with long production runs with infrequent production line setups or changeovers. These can, however, easily result in excessive inventories of certain finished products and in limited supplies of others. Thus, the ultimate production decision requires management to carefully weigh the advantages and disadvantages of long versus short production runs. Many industries today tend toward shorter production runs and toward doing whatever it takes to reduce the time and expense normally associated with changing production lines from one product to another. This is particularly true for firms employing the just-in-time (JIT) approach to inventory and scheduling. The trend is toward "pull" systems, manufacturing/logistics systems where the product is "pulled" in response to demand as opposed to being "pushed" in advance of demand. The lower inventory levels decrease logistics costs.

seasonal demand

The production manager is interested in minimizing the effects of seasonal demand for products. Fully anticipating such demand is not always possible, however; thus, having desired product quantities available when and where needed is not always possible. For example, cold weather and snow accumulation in various parts of the country easily influence sales of snow skis or snowmobiles. To keep costs low, to avoid overtime and rush situations, and to prepare for the sales schedule, production managers usually like to produce well ahead of the season and to produce a maximum amount. Such advance production may not be economically feasible because of inventory storage costs. However, production managers have to consider this problem in an attempt to keep production costs down. Therefore, the logistics department, in conjunction with production or manufacturing, must be prepared to accept seasonal inventory, which can start to accumulate three to six months before sales occur. For example, Hallmark Cards begins to accumulate Christmas items at its Kansas City warehouse during the summer months, so that the company will be prepared to ship to retailers and other customers during the fall.

supply-side interfaces

Since the logistics manager is responsible for the inbound movement and storage of raw materials that will feed the production line, logistics and production also interface on the supply side. A shortage or stockout situation could result in the shutdown of a production facility or an increase in production costs. The logistics manager should ensure that available quantities of raw materials and other production inputs are sufficient to meet production schedules yet are conservative in terms of inventory carrying costs. Because of the need for this type of coordination, many firms today have shifted the responsibility for production scheduling from manufacturing to logistics management. The end result is a broadening of overall logistics responsibility.

protective packaging

Another activity at the interface of logistics and operations is packaging, which many firms treat as a logistics activity. In the context of either operations or logistics management, the principal purpose that packaging serves is to protect the product from damage. This is distinct from whatever value the product package may have for marketing or promotional reasons.

foreign and third-party alternatives

The interface between logistics and operations is becoming more critical, given recent interest in the procurement of raw materials and other production inputs from foreign sources. Also, many firms today are making arrangements with third-party manufacturers, or "co-packers," to produce or assemble some or all of the firms' finished products. These arrangements are especially prevalent in the food industry, where many firms manufacture only food items to be sold under someone else's label.

The interface with manufacturing is very important for Jordano Foods' logistics group. The seasonal supply of some raw materials—for example, tomatoes—and the need to import some items require close coordination for the inbound side of the logistics system.

Logistics Interfaces with Marketing

Logistics is sometimes referred to as the other half of marketing. The rationale for this definition is that the physical distribution or outbound side of a firm's logistics system is responsible for the physical movement and storage of goods for customers and thus plays an important role in selling a product. In some instances, physical distribution and order fulfillment may be the key variables in selling a product; that is, your ability to provide the product at the right time in the right quantities may be the critical element in making a sale.

marketing mix

This section briefly discusses the interfaces between logistics and marketing, activities in each principal area of the marketing mix. The material is organized according to the four Ps of marketing—price, product, promotion, and place.[5] In addition, recent trends in the interface area between logistics and marketing will be discussed.

carrier pricing

Price. From a logistics perspective, adjusting quantity prices to conform with shipment sizes appropriate for transportation companies may be quite important. Railroads, for example, publish minimum weight requirements for carload lots—for instance, 30,000 pounds. Motor carriers typically publish four or five rates that will apply to the same commodity shipped between two points depending upon the size (weight) of the shipment. The larger the size, the lower the unit rate charged. In other words, a price discount schedule for shipping larger volumes at one time applies because the transportation company experiences economy if the customer sends larger shipments.

matching schedules

Companies selling products also typically provide a discount schedule for larger purchase quantities. If such discount schedules relate to transportation rate discount schedules in terms of weight, then the company may be able to save itself some money or save money for customers, depending on the sale terms. For example, if a company sells on a delivered-price basis (price includes transportation charges) and if its price schedule matches the transportation shipping requirements on a weight basis, the company should be able to get lower rates with larger purchases and thus save money. So when the company calculates the number of units that it wants to sell to a customer for a particular price, it should see how the weight of that number of units compares with the weight requirement for a transportation rate. In many instances, increasing the quantity purchased in order to produce a total shipment weight that will qualify for a lower per unit transportation weight becomes advantageous. Even if the firm were selling goods on a free on board (FOB) point-of-origin basis (transportation charges paid by the buyer), this approach would enable the firm's customers to qualify for the lower rate and thus save money.

Although it is not always possible to adjust prices to meet rate breaks and to have a quantity convenient to deal with, organizations should investigate such alternatives. In some organizations, entire pricing schedules conform to various quantities the company can ship by motor and railroad or by other modes of transportation. Under the Robinson-Patman Act and related legislation, transportation cost savings are a valid reason for offering a price discount.

volume relationships

In addition, the logistics manager may be interested in the volume sold under different price schedules, because this will affect inventory requirements, replacement times, and other aspects of customer service. Although this is somewhat difficult to analyze, a firm may consider the logistics manager's ability to provide sufficient volumes within an attractive price schedule. Such a situation may be particularly true when price specials generate extra sales at particular times of the year. The logistics manager must be apprised of such specials so that he or she can adjust inventory requirements to meet projected demand.

Product. Another decision frequently made in the marketing area concerns products, particularly their physical attributes. Much has been written about the number of new products that come on the market each year in the United States. Their size, shape, weight, packaging, and other physical dimensions affect the ability of the logistics system to move and store products. Therefore, the logistics manager should offer input when marketing is deciding upon the physical dimensions of new products. The logistics manager can supply appropriate information about the movement and storage of the new products. In addition to new products, firms frequently refurbish old products in one way or another to improve and maintain sales. Very often such changes may take the form of a new package design and, perhaps, different package sizes. The physical dimensions of products affect the use of storage and movement systems. They affect the carriers that a firm can use, equipment needed, damage rates, storage ability, use of materials-handling equipment such as conveyors and pallets, exterior packaging, and many other logistics aspects.

It is very difficult to convey the frustration that some logistics managers experience when discovering a change in a product package that makes the use of standard-size pallets uneconomical, or that uses trailer or boxcar space inefficiently or in a way that could damage products. For example, when Gillete first introduced the Daisy razor, the logistics group did not learn until late in the game that they had to deal with light and bulky floor stand displays, with consequent low weight density. Not only would the floor stand displays not fit on the warehouse conveyors, but they had to be shipped at a rate that was 150 percent higher than the existing rate for the product itself. Gillette eventually corrected the situation, but it was an expensive lesson. These things often seem mundane and somewhat trivial to people concerned about making sales to customers, but they greatly affect an organization's overall success and profitability in the long run.

No magic formulas can spell out what firms should do in these cases, but we can keep in mind that interaction can allow the logistics manager to provide input about the possibly negative aspects of decisions. It may well be that logistics can do nothing and that the sale is most important; but often the logistics manager can recommend small changes that make the product much more amenable to a logistics system's movement and storage aspects while having no real effect upon the sales of the product itself.

consumer packaging

Another marketing area that affects logistics is consumer packaging. The marketing manager often regards consumer packaging as a "silent" salesperson. At the retail level, the package may be a determining factor in influencing sales. The marketing manager will be concerned about package appearance, information provided, and other related aspects; for a customer comparing several products on the retailer's shelf, the consumer package may make the sale. The consumer package is important to the logistics manager for several reasons. The consumer package usually has to fit into what is called the *industrial package,* or the external package. The size, shape, and other dimensions of the consumer package will affect the use of the industrial packages. The protection the consumer package offers also concerns the logistics manager. The physical dimensions and the protection aspects of consumer packages affect the logistics system in the areas of transportation, materials handling, and warehousing.

Promotion. Promotion is a marketing area that receives much attention in an organization. Firms often spend hundreds of thousands or even millions of dollars on national advertising campaigns and other promotional practices to improve a sales position. An organization making a promotional effort to stimulate sales should inform its logistics manager so that sufficient inventory quantities will be available for distribution to the customer. But even when logistics is informed, problems can occur. For example, when Gillette introduced the disposable twin-blade Good News razor, the company's original plan called for three consecutive promotions. The national launch promotion was to achieve sales of twenty million units. A following trade deal promotion was to net ten million in sales, and Gillette expected a third promotional campaign to net an additional twenty million—for a total of fifty million in sales. As it turned out, the first promotion sold thirty-five million—seventy-five percent over the plan. Needless to say, this placed quite a burden on the logistics group to try to meet the demand.

push versus pull

We should look beyond the simple relationship between increasing sales and analyzing basic promotion strategies to see how they affect the logistics department. Marketing managers often classify their promotion strategies into two basic categories: push or pull. What they are implying is that they can try to either "push" the product through the distribution channel to the customer or "pull" it through.[6] We discuss distribution channels subsequently in more detail. Briefly, they are the institutions that handle products after manufacture but before sale to the ultimate consumer. They include organizations such as wholesalers and retailers.

channel competition

Producers frequently compete to get distribution channels to give their products the sales effort they feel their products deserve. For example, a cereal producer may want to ensure sufficient space for its product on the retailer's shelf or ensure that wholesalers hold product quantities sufficient to satisfy retailers, believing that ultimately the final consumer demand for the product will influence the retailer and the wholesaler. By selling popular products, they improve their profitability. The higher the product turnover, the more likely they are to make a profit; the happier they are with a particular product, the more willing they are to give it space and a better position in the store.

pull strategy

Companies can attempt to improve their sales by *pulling* their product through the distribution channel with national advertising. Promotional advertising attempts to create or stimulate sales to customers and to get customers into the retail store asking for a product they have seen advertised in a magazine, have heard advertised on the radio, or, more likely, have seen advertised on television. The purchases will likely influence the retailer, and the retailer will influence the wholesaler, if any, from whom the retailer purchases. Some companies feel that the best approach in promoting a product is to pull it through distribution channels by directly stimulating demand at the consumer level.

push strategy

The other basic approach is the *push* method. Implied in the push approach is cooperation with the channels of distribution to stimulate customer sales—in other words, producers may pay part of local advertising costs or provide special store displays to stimulate sales. In cooperating with the wholesaler, a manufacturer may be able to offer retailers a special price at a particular time to stimulate product demand. The emphasis is upon having the distribution channel work with the company. This contrasts with the pull approach, wherein the company stimulates sales somewhat independently of the retailer by national advertising or by advertising a product on a broad regional scale.

logistics impact

We can offer arguments both for and against these two approaches. In fact, some companies combine the two in their promotion efforts. From the logistics manager's point of view, however, push and pull are often different as far as logistics system requirements are concerned. The pull approach is more likely to generate erratic demand that is difficult to predict and that may place emergency demands upon the logistics system. Broad-scale national advertising has the potential to be extremely successful, but predicting consumer response to new products is often difficult. Such advertising may also strain the logistics system, requiring emergency shipments and higher transportation rates. Frequent stockouts may also result, requiring additional inventory. The Gillette situation is an example of such a case. On the other hand, a push approach may have a more orderly demand pattern. Cooperation with the retailer allows manufacturers to fill the "pipeline" somewhat in advance of the stimulated sales rather than quickly, on an almost emergency basis, as retailers and consumers clamor for some successfully promoted new product.

wholesalers versus retailers

Place. The place decision refers to the distribution channels decision and thus involves both transactional and physical distribution channel decisions. Marketers typically become more involved in making decisions about marketing transactions and in deciding such things as whether to sell a product to wholesalers or to deal directly with retailers. From the logistics manager's point of view, such decisions may significantly affect logistics system requirements. For example, companies dealing only with wholesalers will probably have fewer logistics problems than will companies dealing directly with retailers. Wholesalers, on the average, tend to purchase in larger quantities than do retailers and to place their orders and manage their inventories more predictably and consistently, thereby making the logistics manager's job easier. Retailing establishments, particularly small retailers, often order in small quantities and do not always allow sufficient lead time for replenishment before stockouts. Consequently, manufacturers may need to purchase time-sensitive transportation service at a premium price to meet delivery needs.

SUPPLY CHAIN TECHNOLOGY

E-LOGISTICS: WEAPONS FOR A NEW WORLD

The logistics of electronic commerce are not easy. Selecting the right tools and making systems integration a high priority are crucial steps in making it work.

Bewitched by the entrancing vision of a virtual world, few Internet business start-ups realized how vital sophisticated logistics would prove in the virtual economy. A floor of dot-com commercials and over-hyped coverage created expectations of a world where product would leap invisibly from factory floors to consumer mailboxes.

Things have not quite worked out that way. Indeed, E-commerce is presenting one of the greatest logistics challenges in history, with consumers demanding service levels that are frequently equal to or better than those found in the most stringent JIT agreements—and they want it all for free.

E-logistics has also brought back a burden many companies have worked hard to reduce in recent years: inventory. In an amazingly short time, E-logistics has begun to reverse the trend toward tighter, smaller inventories that has helped drive costs down for American businesses in recent years.

Consumer demands for next-day or even same-day delivery mean that E-commerce providers, small and large, need to keep enormous amounts of product not only on hand but in distribution centers across the country. It is possible to get around this by using service providers, but, in the end, someone has to have product ready to move, and someone has to pay for that capability.

Businesses that neglect E-logistics' realities face some real dangers. Some companies put on a pretty face last year and were so busy trying to initiate sales that they did not do what it takes to get goods to the consumers.

Though the tests posed by E-logistics are becoming increasingly clear, the solutions for the situation are not. Part of that problem simply springs from the realities of "Internet time." E-logistics user providers must deal with a technological and economic environment that is changing so rapidly that the rules rarely seem to hold from one month to the next. All too often, companies find themselves confronting a crazy quilt of potential solutions. Basic development work is still underway in many areas.

Source: Tony Seideman, *Logistics Management & Distribution Report* (Cahners Publishing, April 2000): e33–e35.

customer service

Recent Trends. Perhaps the most significant trend is that marketers have begun to recognize the strategic value of place in the marketing mix and the increased revenues and customer satisfaction that may result from high-quality logistical services. As a result, many firms have recognized *customer service* as the interface activity between marketing and logistics and have aggressively and effectively promoted customer service as a key element of the marketing mix. Firms in industries such as food, chemicals, and pharmaceuticals have reported considerable success along these lines.

LOGISTICS INTERFACES WITH OTHER AREAS

While manufacturing and marketing are probably the two most important internal, functional interfaces for logistics in a product company, there are other important interfaces. The finance area has become increasingly important during the last decade. The impact that logistics can have upon return on assets (ROA) or return on investment (ROI) is very significant. We define ROA as follows:

ROA = revenue − expenses/assets

or

ROA = gross profit/assets

Logistics can impact ROA positively in several ways. The reduction in inventory during the 1990s has already been mentioned. Inventory is an asset on the balance sheet; lowering inventory (assets) in the preceding equation increases ROA. In addition to inventory, there has been improvement to the utilization of other logistics-related assets, namely, warehouse and transportation equipment investment.

It was also pointed out in this chapter that logistics costs have been reduced in some companies, which improves gross margin or gross profit and increases ROA. Finally, the focus upon customer service (which is discussed in more detail in a subsequent chapter) can increase revenue or sales. As long as the increase in sales is not offset by higher cost for customer service, then ROA will also be increased.

Increasingly, CFOs in companies have become very knowledgeable about logistics because of the impact that it can have upon key functional metrics such as ROA or ROI. These metrics are important barometers for the external financial community to gauge the financial viability of a given company.

On the "other side of the coin," logistics managers have to justify increased investment in logistics-related assets using acceptable financial parameters related to "payback" periods. Consequently, logistics managers must be knowledgeable about financial metrics and standards of performance. This topic is the focus of a later chapter in the text.

Accounting is also an important interface for logistics. Accounting systems are critical for providing appropriate cost information for analysis of alternative logistics systems. Far too often in the past, logistics-related costs were not measured specifically and were often lumped into overhead, which made it extremely difficult to systematically monitor logistics costs.

The recent interest in direct product profitability and the related cost accounting systems such as activity-based costing (ABC) has been beneficial to improving the quality of logistics analyses. Accounting systems are also critical for measuring supply chain trade-offs and performance.

The next section focuses upon activities that are typically a part of the logistics function.

Logistical Activities

The logistics definitions discussed earlier indicate activities for which the logistics manager may be responsible:

- Traffic and transportation
- Warehousing and storage
- Industrial packaging
- Materials handling
- Inventory control
- Order fulfillment

- Demand forecasting
- Production planning
- Purchasing
- Customer service levels
- Plant and warehouse site location
- Return goods handling
- Parts and service support
- Salvage and scrap disposal

This list is quite comprehensive; some companies with well-organized logistics areas may not place responsibility for all of these activities within the logistics area. For example, companies having a physical distribution focus may not include procurement in their logistics organization.

Scope of Activities

The development of interest in logistics after World War II contributed to the growth in activities associated with logistics. Given the scope of this growth, it is worthwhile to discuss these activities and their relationship to logistics.

Transportation. Transportation is a very important part of the logistics system. A major focus in logistics is upon the physical movement or flow of goods or upon the network that moves the product. This network is composed of transportation agencies that provide the service for the firm. The logistics manager is responsible for selecting the mode or modes of transportation used in moving the raw materials and finished goods or for developing private transportation as an alternative.

transportation trade-off

Storage. A second area, which has a trade-off relationship with transportation, is storage. It involves two separate but closely related activities: inventory management and warehousing. A direct relationship exists between transportation and the level of inventory and number of warehouses required. For example, if firms use a relatively slow means of transport, they usually have to keep higher inventory levels and usually have more warehousing space for this inventory. They may examine the possibility of using faster transport to eliminate some of these warehouses and the inventory stored therein.

A number of important decisions are related to storage activities (inventory and warehousing), including how many warehouses, how much inventory, where to locate the warehouses, what size the warehouse should be, and so on. Because decisions related to transportation affect storage-related decisions, a decision framework to examine the trade-offs related to the various alternatives is essential to optimize the overall logistics system (discussed in detail in Chapter 8).

modal impact

Packaging. A third area of interest to logistics is industrial (exterior) packaging. The type of transportation selected affects packaging requirements both for moving the finished product to the market and for the inbound materials. For example, rail or water transportation usually requires additional packaging expenditures because of the greater possibility of damage. In analyzing trade-offs for proposed changes in transportation agencies, logistics personnel generally examine how the change will influence packaging costs. In many instances, changing to a premium transport means, such as air, will reduce packaging costs because there is less risk of damage. In fact, some items may not be packaged when shipped via air freight; for example, clothing is frequently shipped on hangers.

efficiency

Materials Handling. A fourth area to be considered is materials handling, which is also of interest to other areas in the typical manufacturing organization. Materials handling is important to efficient warehouse operation. Logistics managers are concerned with the movement of goods into a warehouse, the placement of goods in a warehouse, and the movement of goods from storage to order-picking areas and eventually to dock areas for transportation out of the warehouse.

Materials handling is usually concerned with mechanical equipment for short-distance movement; such equipment includes conveyors, forklift trucks, overhead cranes, and containers. Production managers may want a particular pallet or container type that is not compatible with logistics warehousing activities. Therefore, the materials-handling designs must be coordinated in order to ensure congruity between the types of equipment used. In addition, the company may find it economical to use the same type of forklift trucks in the plants and in the warehouses.

Order Fulfillment. Another activity area that logistics may control is order fulfillment, which generally consists of activities involved with completing customer orders. Initially, one might question why the logistics area would concern itself directly with order fulfillment. However, one important physical distribution factor is the time elapsing from the time when a customer decides to place an order for a product until the time that those goods are actually delivered in a satisfactory condition, that is, the lead time.

For example, assume that the present system takes a total lead time of eight days for transmittal, processing, order preparation, and shipping. Order processing may take four days, and order preparation may take an additional two days, which means that the goods have to be transported to the customer in two days. The short delivery time may require a premium means of transportation. If order processing is considered part of the logistics system, then the company might examine improvements, such as using telephone calls and more computer equipment for processing, to reduce order processing time to two days or less. This would allow the firm to use much cheaper transportation and still get the goods to the customer within eight days. Looking from a time perspective or in terms of total lead time, we can see that order fulfillment is quite important to the logistics function.

inventory accuracy

Forecasting. Another activity important to the logistics area is inventory forecasting. Accurate forecasting of inventory requirements and materials and parts is essential to effective inventory control. This is particularly true in companies using a just-in-time (JIT) or materials requirement planning (MRP) approach to control inventory. Logistics personnel should develop forecasts in those situations to ensure accuracy and effective control. Too frequently, forecasts developed by marketing staff reflect sales objectives rather than inventory requirements.

time perspective

Production Planning. Another area of growing interest for logistics managers is production planning, which is closely related to forecasting in terms of effective inventory control. Once a forecast is developed and the current inventory on hand and usage rate are assessed, production managers can determine the number of units necessary to ensure adequate market coverage. However, in multiple-product firms, production process timing and certain product line relationships require close coordination with logistics or actual control of production planning by logistics. The integration of production planning into logistics is becoming increasingly common in large corporations.

Purchasing. Purchasing, or procurement, is another activity that we can include in logistics. The basic rationale for including purchasing in logistics is that transportation cost relates directly to the geographic location (distance) of raw materials and component parts purchased for a company's production needs. In terms of

ON THE LINE

TOYOTA TUNES UP ITS DISTRIBUTION NETWORK

Two years ago, Toyota Motor Sales USA, Inc., decided that its U.S. distribution network was due for a tune-up. The three-decade-old system of warehouses had been established at a time when the Japanese automaker sourced most of its parts from overseas to serve a small network of U.S. dealerships; but that scenario changed in the '90s when Toyota shifted more of its business to North American parts suppliers and its dealership network exploded.

Under the existing system, the Torrance, California-based company has been providing U.S. after-sales support to 1,200 car dealerships, 200 Lexus luxury car dealers, and 100 forklift dealers via a two-tiered system. The first tier consists of two large distribution centers (DCs)—one in Ontario, California; the other in Hebron, Kentucky. Those two sites, in turn, feed parts to nine smaller sites located around the country—in Los Angeles; San Francisco; Portland, Oregon; Kansas City, Missouri; New York; Cincinnati; Baltimore; Chicago; and Boston. The company also operates a facility strictly for Lexus parts in Jacksonville, Florida.

Toyota had not undertaken a strategic network analysis since 1978; but its operation has changed significantly since that time. For starters, its customer base has grown. It also sources differently today, bringing in 55 percent of its parts from North American suppliers rather than from Japan. Finally, in addition to supporting its Toyota models, the company has added parts distribution for its Lexus line of luxury automobiles, which were first introduced in 1989. "The decision to go through with a network analysis/simulation was strategic," says Susan Dexter, a business process change manager at Toyota who oversaw the project. "We wanted to be proactive and make sure that we could continue our high levels of customer service in light of our projected growth over the next three to five years."

But what would be the optimal network for an organization that moves more than 8 million parts and accessories around the country each month? To answer that question, Toyota turned to computer modeling. Using network simulation software, the automaker decided it would first examine the distribution network used for its Lexus division and then look at the entire network. "We wanted to do a comprehensive study of our DCs to see if they were in the right place to meet the dealers' needs," says Dexter. "Our objective was to develop a parts logistics network to support business growth and maximize customer satisfaction," she adds. "If we could save a few dollars, that would be great, too."

The results of the software modeling revealed that Toyota could improve customer service to dealers while cutting costs by opening a new distribution center. Despite the start-up costs, the study showed, a new DC that would strictly handle Lexus parts would quickly pay for itself by eliminating the need for premium-priced expedited transportation and also alleviate overcrowding at an existing distribution center. On top of that, the model indicated that customer service could be improved with faster delivery.

Source: James A. Cooke, *Logistics* (March 2001): 40.

transportation and inventory costs, the quantities purchased would also affect logistics cost. Including purchasing within the logistics area is primarily a matter of whether this more effectively coordinates and lowers costs for the firm. As was noted previously, a growing number of companies added purchasing to the logistics function during the 1970s and 1980s.

Customer Service. Another area of importance is customer service. Customer service is a complex topic and one that concerns other functional company areas. Customer service levels in many ways glue together other logistics areas. Decisions about inventory, transportation, and warehousing relate to customer service requirements. While customarily the logistics area does not completely control customer service decisions, logistics plays an extremely important role in ensuring that the customer gets the right product at the right place and time. Logistics decisions about product availability and inventory lead time are critical to customer service.

Site Location. Another area that is important to logistics is plant and warehouse site location. We discuss this activity at some length in a later chapter. A location change could alter time and place relationships between plants and markets or between supply points and plants. Such changes will affect transportation rates and service, customer service, inventory requirements, and possibly other areas. Therefore, the logistics manager is quite concerned about location decisions. In fact, plant location, as discussed in a subsequent chapter, is frequently as important as warehouse location. Transportation cost is frequently a very important factor in deciding on a location.

Other Activities. Other areas may be considered a part of logistics. Areas such as parts and service support, return goods handling, and salvage and scrap disposal indicate the reality of logistical activities managed in companies producing consumer durables or industrial products. Here, a very integrative approach is necessary. Logistics offers input into product design as well as into maintenance and supply services, since transportation and storage decisions affect these areas. (The definitions of logistics and materials management imply the importance of such activities to systematic logistics management in such companies.)

APPROACHES TO ANALYZING LOGISTICS SYSTEMS

The analysis of logistics systems frequently requires different views or perspectives of logistical activities. The best perspective to take depends upon the type of analysis that is needed. For example, if a company wants to analyze the long-run system design of its logistics system, a view of logistics that focuses upon the company's network of node and link relationships would probably be most beneficial. On the other hand, if a company is evaluating a change in a carrier or mode of transportation, it should probably analyze the logistics system in terms of cost centers. In this section, we discuss four approaches for analyzing logistics systems: materials management versus physical distribution, cost centers, nodes versus links, and logistics channels.

Materials Management versus Physical Distribution

The classification of logistics into materials management and physical distribution (inbound and outbound logistics) is very useful to logistics management or control in an organization. Frequently, the movement and storage of raw materials in a firm is different from the movement and storage of finished products. For example, a steel company may move required raw materials of iron ore and coal by barge and large rail carload. Storage may require nothing more elaborate than land where these items can be dumped and piled for future use. On the other hand, the finished steel will very often be moved by motor carrier, and the storage will require an enclosed facility for protection against the elements and, perhaps, elaborate materials-handling equipment.

cost differences

The different logistics requirements that may exist between materials management and physical distribution may have important implications for the design of an organization's logistics system. Great differences may result in different logistics system designs for materials management and physical distribution. Companies may find it convenient to view their logistics system from these two perspectives, and somewhat different management approaches for each may result. Note that, in spite of such differences, close coordination between materials management and physical distribution is still necessary.

Additional perspectives related to viewing logistics in terms of materials management/ inbound logistics and physical distribution/outbound logistics deserve consideration. In fact, from the inbound and outbound requirements perspective, we may classify companies into four different types of logistics systems.

Balanced System. Some companies have a reasonably balanced flow on the inbound and outbound sides of their logistics systems. In other words, they receive supplies from various vendors in different locations and ship to various customers in different locations. Consumer product companies such as General Foods, Pillsbury, and General Mills typically fit this description. While these companies may emphasize the physical distribution or outbound side because of the importance of customer service, both inbound and outbound logistics are important.

Heavy Inbound. Some companies have a very heavy inbound flow and a very simple outbound flow. An aircraft company such as Boeing is a good example. It uses thousands of parts manufactured by hundreds of vendors to assemble and produce a finished airplane. Once the airplane is finished and tested, the company simply flies it to the customer (Delta Airlines, for example), who ordered it two or three years before delivery. The process requires no warehousing, special transportation arrangements, or packaging. In contrast, the inbound side requires detailed scheduling, coordination, and planning to ensure that parts arrive in time. Varying lead times for parts from vendors present a complex logistics challenge. Auto manufacturers, using twelve thousand to thirteen thousand parts per car, also fit this model. Their outbound systems, while more complex than an aircraft company's, are not nearly as complex as their inbound systems.

Heavy Outbound. A chemical company like Dow offers a good example of a logistics system with heavy outbound flow. Inbound crude oil by-products, salt water, and other raw materials flow from a limited number of sources and frequently move in volume over relatively short distances. On the outbound side, a wide variety of industrial and consumer products are produced that need storage, packaging, and transportation to the final customer. Therefore, in a company with heavy outbound, the physical distribution side of logistics system is more complex.

Reverse Systems. Some companies have reverse flows on the outbound side of their logistics systems. This is true of companies producing durable products that the customer may return for trade-in, for repairs, or for salvage and disposal. Companies that produce computers, telephone equipment, and copy machines have these characteristics. Companies that deal with returnable containers also fit this model. Increased concern with the environment will require more companies to develop reverse logistics systems to dispose of packaging materials on used products.

Cost Centers

We previously mentioned the management activities that many firms include in the logistics area, namely, transportation, warehousing, inventory, materials handling, and industrial packaging. We also emphasized the need to consider these activities as being highly interrelated. By looking at these activities as cost centers, one can analyze possible trade-offs between and among them that could result in lower overall cost and/or better service.

trade-offs

The breakdown of logistics into various cost centers or activity centers represents a second approach to logistics system analysis. Firms frequently analyze logistics systems by dividing them into cost or activity centers, since reducing total logistics costs and/or improving service most frequently occurs by trading off one activity center against another. For example, shifting from rail to motor carrier may result, because of faster and more reliable service, in lower inventory costs, which offsets the higher motor carrier rate (see Table 2–2). Another possibility might be increasing the number of warehouses, thereby raising warehousing and inventory costs but possibly reducing the cost of transportation and lost sales enough to lower total costs (see Table 2–3).

TABLE 2–2 Analysis of Total Logistics Cost with a Change to a Higher Cost Mode of Transport

Cost Centers	Rail	Motor
Transportation	$ 3.00	$ 4.20
Inventory	5.00	3.75
Packaging	4.50	3.20
Warehousing	1.50	.75
Cost of lost sales	2.00	1.00
Total cost	$15.00*	$13.00*

*Costs per unit.

TABLE 2–3 Analysis of Total Logistics Cost with a Change to More Warehouses

Cost Centers	System 1 Three Warehouses	System 2 Five Warehouses
Transportation	$ 850,000	$ 500,000
Inventory	1,500,000	2,000,000
Warehousing	600,000	1,000,000
Cost of lost sales*	350,000	100,000
Total cost	$3,300,000	$3,600,000

*Expected cost based upon probabilities, of not having stock/inventory available when customers want it.

The activity or cost center perspective is very useful in reviewing various trade-offs for lower cost and/or improved service to the customer or plants. However, as Table 2–3 indicates, not every change results in lower total costs.

Nodes versus Links

A third approach to analyzing the logistics system in an organization is in terms of nodes and links (see Figure 2–6). The *nodes* are established spatial points where goods stop for storage or processing. In other words, the nodes are plants and warehouses where the organization stores materials for conversion into finished products or goods in finished form for sale to customers (equalization of supply and demand).

The other part of the system is the *links,* which represent the transportation network connecting the nodes in the logistics system. The network can be composed of individual modes of transportation (rail, motor, air, water, or pipelines) and of combinations and variations that we discuss later.

From a node-link perspective, the complexity of logistics systems can vary enormously. One-node systems may use a simple link from suppliers to a combined plant and warehouse and then to customers in a relatively small market area. At the other end of the spectrum are large, multiple-product firms with multiple plant and warehouse locations. The complex transportation networks of the latter may include three or four different modes and perhaps private as well as for-hire transportation.

The node-and-link perspective, in allowing analysis of a logistics system's two basic elements, represents a convenient basis for seeking possible system improvements. As we have noted, the complexity of a logistics system often relates directly to the various time and distance relationships between the nodes and the links and to the regularity, predictability, and volume of flow of goods entering, leaving, and moving within the system.

FIGURE 2–6 Nodes and Links in a Logistics System

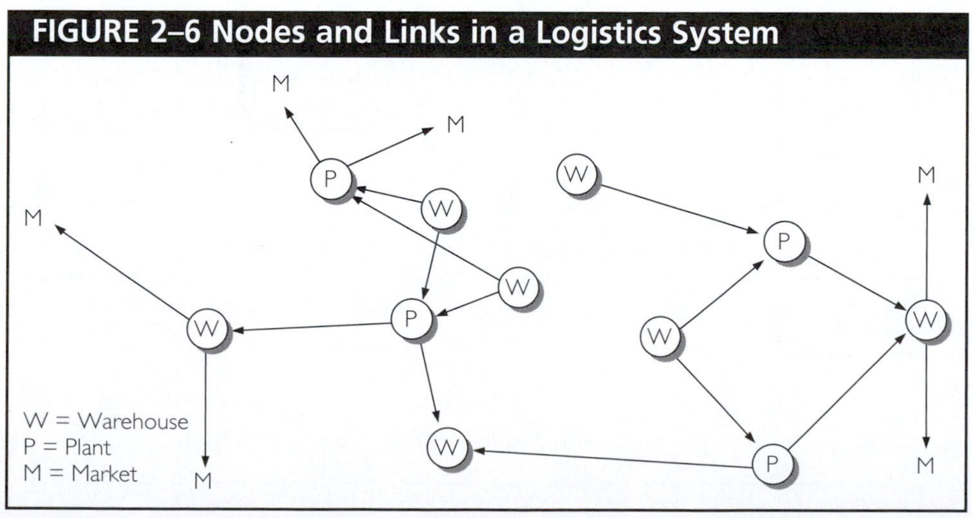

Logistics Channel

A fourth approach to logistics system analysis is to study the *logistics channel,* the network of intermediaries engaged in transfer, storage, handling, communication, and other functions that contribute to the efficient flow of goods. We can view the logistics channel as part of the total distribution channel, which includes, in addition to the logistical flow, a transaction flow of specific interest to the marketing specialist.[7]

The logistics channel can be simple or complex. Figure 2–7 shows a simple channel in which an individual producer deals directly with a final customer. The control in this channel is relatively simple. The individual manufacturer controls the logistical flows since it deals directly with the customer.

Figure 2–8 presents a more complex, multi-echelon channel, with a market warehouse and retailers. The market warehouse could be a public warehouse. In this instance, the control is more difficult because of the additional storage and transportation.

FIGURE 2–7 A Simple Logistics Channel

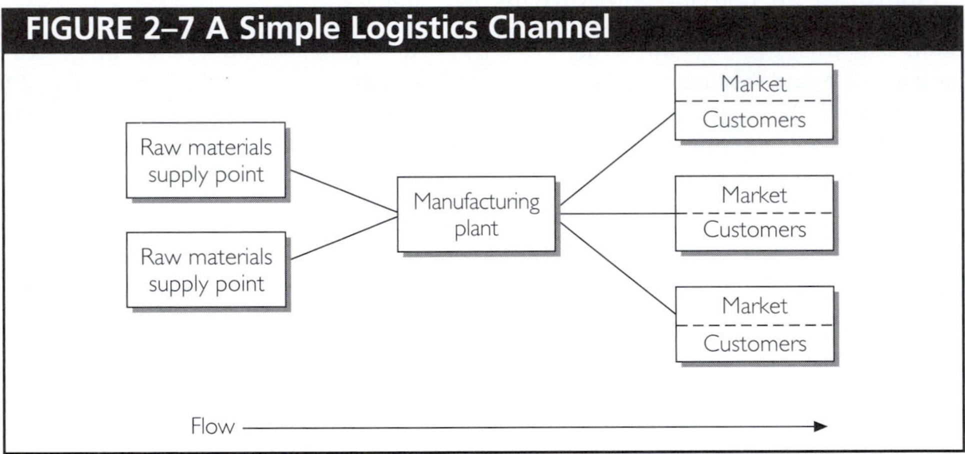

FIGURE 2–8 A Multi-Echelon Logistics Channel

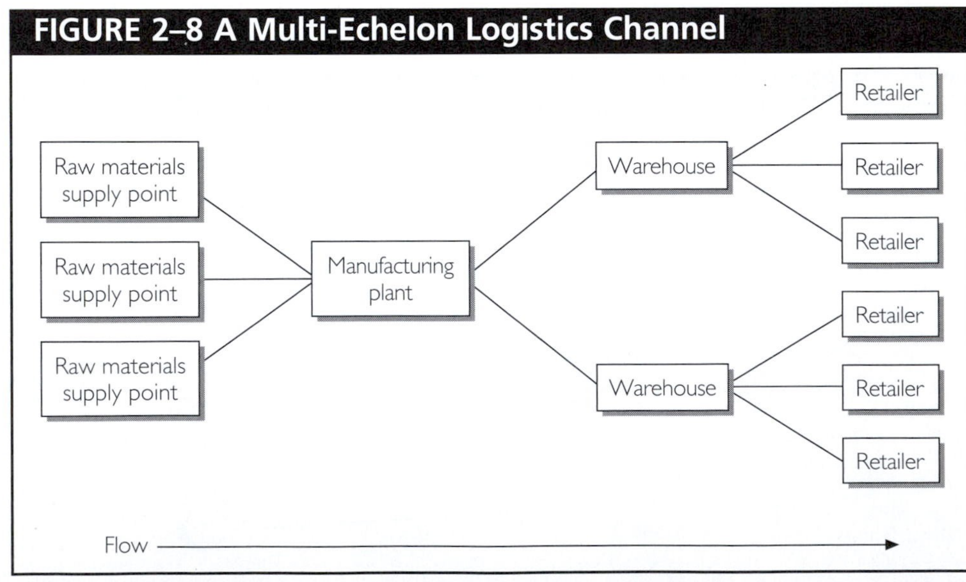

Figure 2–9 illustrates a complex, comprehensive channel. In this instance, the task of achieving an effective logistical flow in the channel is far more formidable. This figure very realistically portrays the situation confronting many large organizations operating in the United States.

Some instances involving production of a basic good like steel, aluminum, or chemicals may further complicate the situation because companies may be a part of more than one channel. For example, the steel may be sold to auto manufacturers, container manufacturers, or file cabinet producers. Duplication of storage facilities, small-shipment transportation, conflict over mode choices, and other problems may contribute to inefficiency in the channel. Communications problems may also exist.

FIGURE 2–9 A Complex Logistics Channel

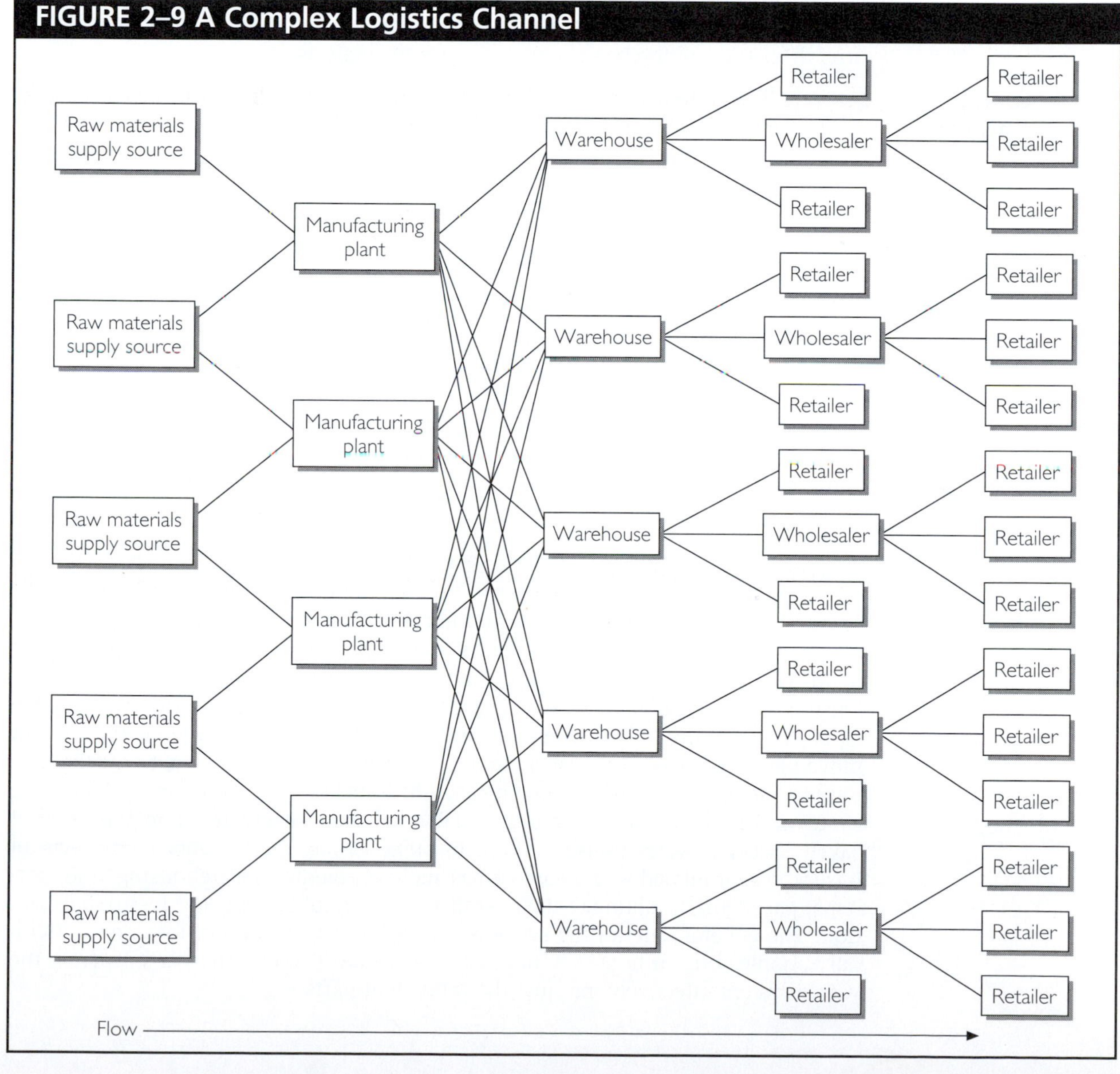

In attempting to overcome these problems, companies employ different strategies. For example, some organizations integrate vertically in order to control the product over several stages in the logistics channel. Some strong companies dominate the channel to achieve efficiency. In any case, we can appreciate the complicating factors of the complex channel. The various approaches to logistics should provide additional insights into relevant logistics activities. A discussion of systems analysis in logistics may further aid your understanding of logistics.

LOGISTICS AND SYSTEMS ANALYSIS

An earlier section pointed out that improvements in analysis and methodologies have facilitated the development of logistics. One such improvement was systems analysis, or the systems concept. A convenient starting point for this section is a brief discussion of the basic nature of systems analysis.

concept of a system

Essentially, a system is a set of interacting elements, variables, parts, or objects that are functionally related to one another and that form a coherent group. The systems concept is something to which most people have been exposed at an early educational stage; for example, in science, your instructor probably taught you about the solar system and how relationships among the planets, the sun, and the moon resulted in day and night, weather, and so forth. Later, in learning about the human body in biology, you viewed the parts of the body, such as the heart and the blood vessels, and their relationships as another system.

Perhaps in a power mechanics class, you learned about the internal combustion engine as a system. You probably learned that engine parts, such as the pistons, could have been larger in size and more efficient but that their very efficiency may have overloaded other parts of the engine, causing it to break down. So the pistons had to be designed in harmony with other parts of the engine. In other words, the overall performance of the engine was more important than the performance of one part.

Cost Perspective

optimization

The preceding engine analogy provides insight into business system characteristics. If we measure efficiency by cost, an individual part of the system not operating at its lowest cost may contribute to the system's overall efficiency. For example, in a logistics context, perhaps water transportation is the cheapest alternative available to some company. If the company optimizes transportation alone, then water movement would be the best approach. However, moving freight by water may require increased inventory holdings, with associated increases in warehousing space and other costs. These additional costs may be greater than the amount saved by using water transportation. In other words, the transportation decision has to be coordinated with related areas such as inventory, warehousing, and, perhaps, packaging to optimize the overall system or subsystem, not just transportation. The general tenet of the systems concept is that we do not focus on individual variables but on how they interact as a whole. The objective is to operate the whole system effectively, not just the individual parts.

Level of Optimality

functional relationships

Another aspect of the systems concept is that *levels of optimality* exist in the firm. We just stated that a firm should not optimize transportation at the expense of related logistics areas such as warehousing and packaging. At the same time, logistics is only one subsystem in the firm, and therefore the firm should not optimize it at another area's expense. For example, the logistics manager may want to give five-day delivery service to certain customers in order to eliminate some warehouses and inventory; but this may conflict with marketing, since the firm's competitors give three-day delivery service in the same sales area. Clearly, the firm must work out some compromise after analyzing the situation. Logistics may have to accept the three-day service as a working constraint imposed because of competition and may have to design the best system within this constraint. Some individual or group at the organization's senior executive level has to examine the trade-offs between marketing and logistics in terms of the total organization's efficiency or profit.

constraints

In addition to marketing, the firm has to consider production, finance, and other areas (see Figure 2–10). In other words, the overall firm is a system that should be optimized. The firm may have to suboptimize internal subsystems to achieve the best overall position. Generally, this means that logistics may work within constraints such as set delivery times, minimum production run orders, and financial limits on warehouse improvements and construction. Such constraints, occasionally somewhat arbitrary, should be flexible within reason. Ideally, logistics managers should make decisions such as delivery times on a more individual or short-run basis, but organizations are sometimes too complex to make this possible from an operational standpoint. A dynamic simulation model would help to solve some of these problems and to allow

FIGURE 2–10 Levels of Optimality in Economic Environments

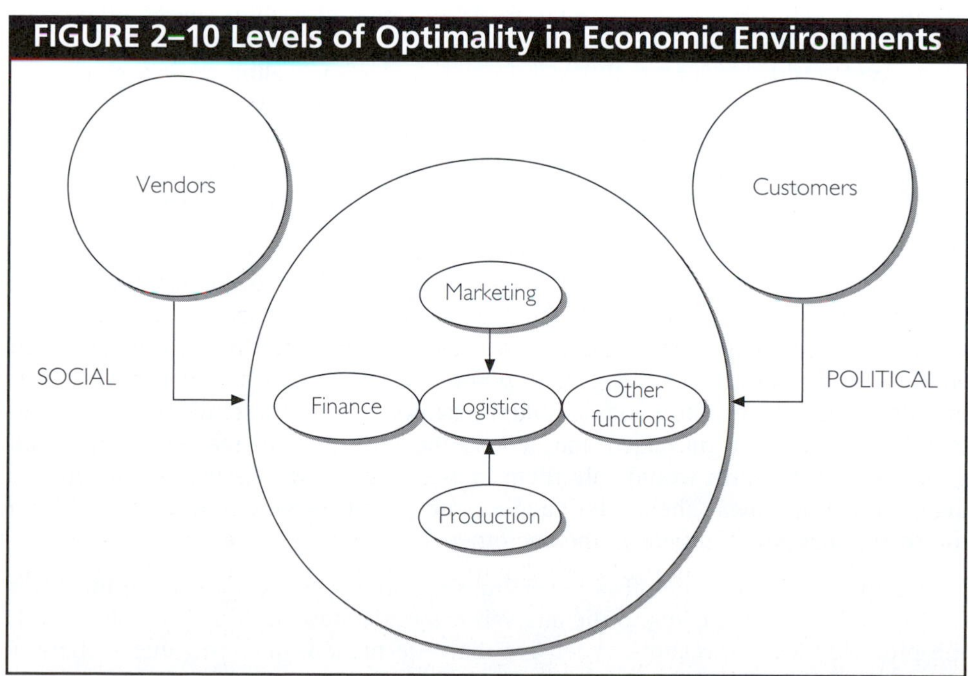

more flexibility. We say more about this point in the chapters covering management of logistics systems.

One other point about optimality levels is that firms producing intermediate goods such as steel or having a multiple-product line very often operate in several supply chains.[8] Therefore, one might consider supply chain optimization or the external effects of a firm's decisions as a higher optimality level. For example, a container or pallet designed for shipping a firm's product in a manner consistent with the firm's overall needs may not be compatible with the ordering and receiving needs of customers. Therefore, in the final analysis, such an improvement may harm the supply chain's overall efficiency. The increased focus upon supply chains discussed in Chapter 1 necessitates optimization at this higher level. It will be challenging, but the payoff potential is high.

Techniques of Logistics System Analysis

In this section, we consider total cost analysis techniques for logistics systems. We examine only the more basic methods; more sophisticated techniques of total cost analysis are discussed in a later section. The basic approaches examined here unite some of the concepts discussed thus far and provide a background for the material discussed in the book's next section.

Short-Run/Static Analysis

One general approach to total cost analysis for business logistics is known as *short-run analysis.* In a short-run analysis, we would look at a short-run situation and develop costs associated with the various logistics cost centers described previously. We would develop such cost information for each alternative system considered. We would then select the system with the lowest overall cost, as long as it was consistent with constraints the firm imposed on the logistics area. Some authors refer to this short-run analysis as *static analysis.*[9] Essentially, they are saying that this method analyzes costs associated with a logistics system's various components at one point in time or at one output level.

Example. For an example of static analysis, see Table 2–4. In this instance, a firm is presently using an all-rail route from the plant and the associated plant warehouse to the customers. At the plant warehouse, the chemicals are bagged and then shipped by rail to the customer. A proposed second system would use a market-oriented warehouse. The goods would be shipped from the plant to the market warehouse and then packaged and sent to the customer. Instead of shipping all goods by rail, the firm would ship them by barge to the warehouse, taking advantage of low bulk rates. Then, after bagging, the chemicals would move by rail from the warehouse for shipment to the customer.

In this example, the trade-off is lower transportation costs versus some increases in storage and warehousing. If the analysis is strictly static (at this level of output), the proposed system is more expensive than the present one. So, unless analysis provided additional information more favorable to the proposed system, the firm would continue with its present system.

TABLE 2–4 Static Analysis of C & B Chemical Company (50,000 Pounds of Output)

Plant Logistics Costs*	System 1	System 2
Packaging	$ 500	$ 0
Storage and handling	150	50
Inventory carrying	50	25
Administrative	75	25
Fixed cost	4,200	2,400
Transportation Costs*		
To market warehouse	0	150
To customer	800	100
Warehouse Costs*		
Packaging	0	500
Storage and handling	0	150
Inventory carrying	0	75
Administrative	0	75
Fixed cost	0	2,400
Total cost*	$5,775	$5,950

*In thousands of dollars.

However, we have two reasons to select the proposed system. First, we have no information about customer service requirements. The new market-oriented warehouse might provide better customer service, therefore increasing sales and profit and offsetting some of the higher cost of System 2.

Second, if we use a longer-run perspective—*dynamic analysis*—to look at the example (Figure 2–11), we find that although System 1 gives a lower cost at an output of 50,000 pounds, at approximately 70,500 pounds, System 2 becomes less expensive than System 1. Therefore, a company experiencing rapid sales growth may want to plan the shift to System 2 now. The start-up time for the new warehouse may necessitate the immediate planning.

Another reason why a firm might switch to System 2, even though it is presently experiencing lower costs with another system, is that the firm expects the second system to result in lower costs in the future. Since setting up a new system usually takes time, the firm may initiate the change in the near future. If this firm is growing relatively rapidly, it may achieve an output of 70,500 pounds in a fairly short time.

Long-Run/Dynamic Analysis

The second way to project the optimum system is to mathematically calculate the point of equality between the systems. In the example used here, System 1 and System 2 are equal at about 70,500 pounds of output. If we use a graph to determine

FIGURE 2–11 Dynamic Analysis

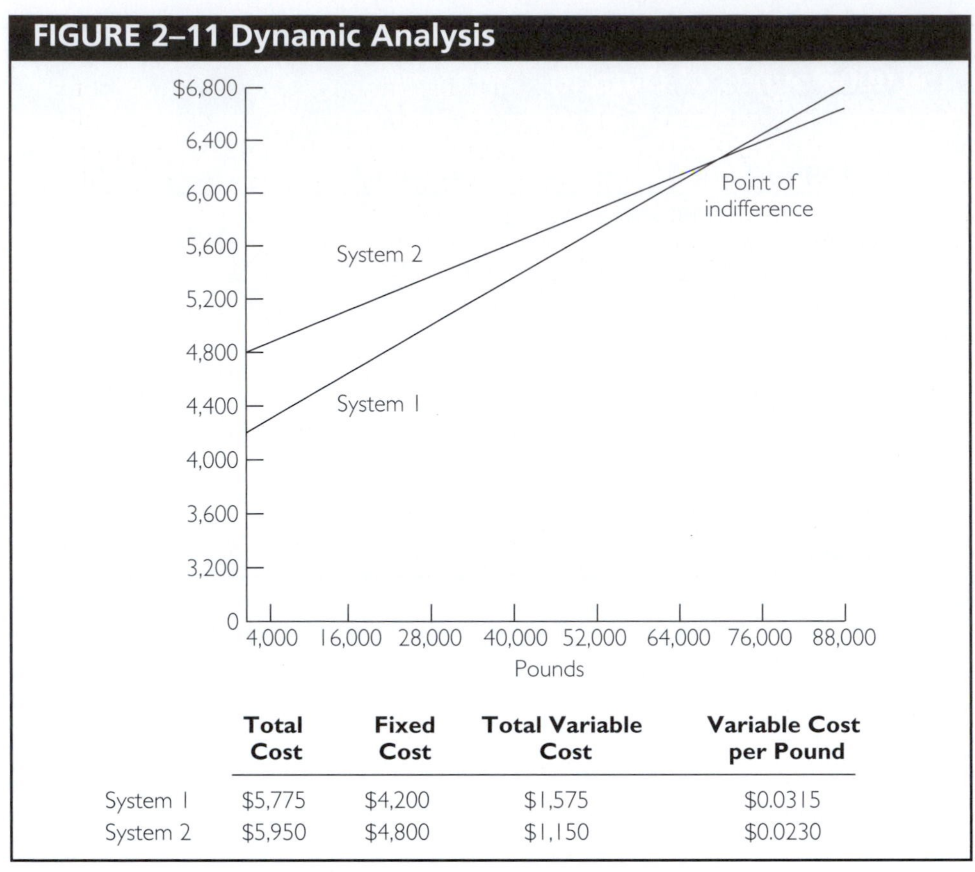

	Total Cost	Fixed Cost	Total Variable Cost	Variable Cost per Pound
System 1	$5,775	$4,200	$1,575	$0.0315
System 2	$5,950	$4,800	$1,150	$0.0230

the equality point, complete accuracy is difficult. For a mathematical solution, we simply need to start with the equation for a straight line ($y = a + bx$). In this particular case, a would be the fixed costs and b would be the variable cost per unit. The x would be the output level. If we want to solve for the point at which the two systems are equal, we can set the two equations up as equal and plug in the cost information appropriate to solve these equations. As is demonstrated here, at approximately 70,500 pounds the two systems are equal, and we see a point of indifference between the two systems:

System 1

Total cost = fixed cost + variable cost/unit × number of units

$$y = 4{,}200_1 + 0.0315x$$

System 2

$$y = 4{,}800 + 0.0230x$$

Trade-off point

$$4{,}800_1 + 0.0230x = 4{,}200_1 + 0.0315x$$
$$600_1 = 0.0085x$$
$$x = 70{,}588 \text{ pounds}$$

A particular firm may consider more than two logistics systems at one time. Many examples show a firm considering three or sometimes four systems. We can use the same basic methodology for plotting and mathematically solving for the points of indifference regardless of how many systems we analyze. Further, in a particular situation involving two systems, the cost functions may not necessarily intersect. Hence, one function will be lower than the other over the entire output range. When a firm considers three or more systems, two of them may intersect while the other occurs at a higher level in the quadrant. If we have three intersecting systems, two relevant intersection points or two relevant points of indifference usually occur. A third intersection would occur at a point above some other cost function and would not be relevant.

LOGISTICS IN THE FIRM: FACTORS AFFECTING THE COST AND IMPORTANCE OF LOGISTICS

This section deals with specific factors relating to the cost and importance of logistics. Emphasizing some of the competitive, product, and spatial relationships of logistics can help to explain the strategic role of a firm's logistics functions.

Competitive Relationships

Frequently, competition is narrowly interpreted only in forms of price competition. While the price issue is certainly important, in many markets, customer service can be a very important form of competition. For example, if a company can reliably provide customers with its products in a relatively short time period, then its customers can often minimize inventory cost. A company should consider minimizing buyer inventory costs to be just as important as keeping product prices low, since minimizing such costs will contribute to more profit or in turn enable the seller to be more competitive. Therefore, customer service is of great importance to the logistics area.

length of order cycle

Order Cycle. That order cycle length directly affects inventory requirement is a well-accepted principle of logistics management; stated another way, the shorter the cycle, the less inventory is required. Figure 2–12 shows this relationship. We discuss order cycles in greater detail in the chapter dealing with order processing and information systems. For now, we can define *order cycle* as the time it takes for a customer to receive an order once he or she has decided to place it. It includes elements such as order transmittal time, order preparation time, and transportation time.

Figure 2–12 shows that longer order cycles usually require higher inventories. Therefore, if a firm can improve customer service by shortening customer order cycles, its customers should be able to operate with less inventory. It follows, then, that such a cost reduction could be as important as a price reduction.

nature of product

Substitutability. Substitutability very often affects the importance of customer service. In other words, if a product is similar to other products, consumers may be willing to substitute a competitive product if a stockout occurs. Therefore, customer service is more important for highly substitutable products than for products that customers may be willing to wait for or back order. This is one reason firms spend so much advertising money making customers conscious of their brands. They want consumers to ask for their brands, and, if their brands are temporarily not available, they would like consumers to wait until they are.

FIGURE 2–12 The Relationship between Required Inventory and Order Cycle Length from a Customer Perspective

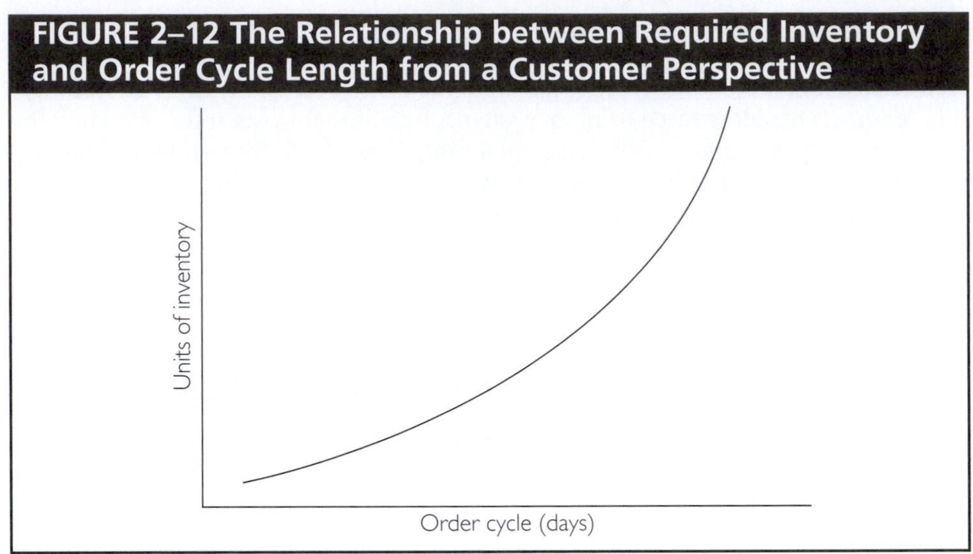

Product substitutability varies greatly. Usually, the more substitutable a product, the higher the customer service level required. As far as a logistics manager is concerned, a firm wishing to reduce its lost sales cost, which is a measure of customer service and substitutability, can either spend more on inventory or spend more on transportation.

relationship to lost sales

Inventory Effect. Figure 2–13 shows that, by increasing inventory costs (either by increasing the inventory level or by increasing reorder points), firms can usually reduce the cost of lost sales. In other words, an inverse relationship exists between the cost of lost sales and inventory cost. However, firms are generally willing to increase the inventory cost only until total costs start to go up. They are typically willing to spend increasing amounts on inventory to decrease lost sales cost by larger amounts—in other words, up to the point at which the marginal savings from reducing lost sales cost equal the marginal cost of carrying added inventory. A related trade-off is information for inventory.

relationship to transportation

Transportation Effect. A similar relationship exists with transportation, as we can see in Figure 2–14. Companies can usually trade off increased transportation costs against decreased lost sales costs. For transportation, this additional expenditure involves buying a better service—for example, switching from water to rail, or rail to motor, or motor to air. The higher transportation cost also could result from shipping more frequently in smaller quantities at higher rates. So, as indicated in Figure 2–14, firms can reduce the cost of lost sales by spending more on transportation service to improve customer service. Once again, most firms willingly do this only up to the point where the marginal savings in lost sales cost equal the marginal increment associated with the increased transportation cost.

Although showing inventory cost and transportation cost separately is convenient here, companies often spend more for inventory and for transportation almost simultaneously to reduce the cost of lost sales. In fact, improved transportation will usually result in lower inventory cost. (The lower inventory cost stems from smaller carrying capacity and faster transit times.) In other words, the situation is much more interactive and coordinated than is indicated here.

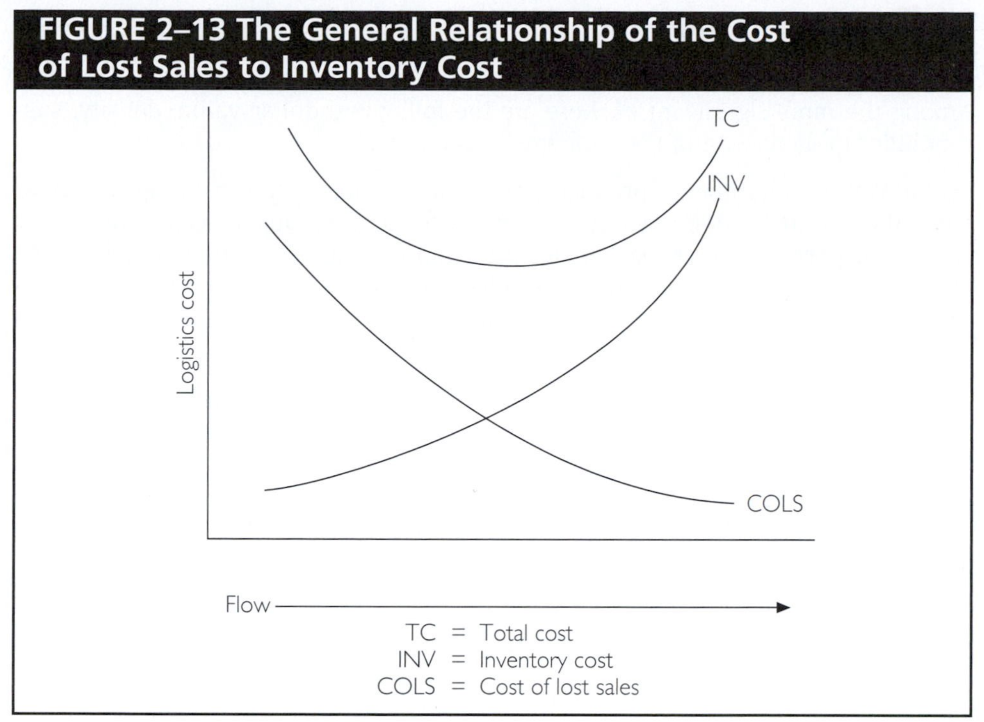

FIGURE 2–13 The General Relationship of the Cost of Lost Sales to Inventory Cost

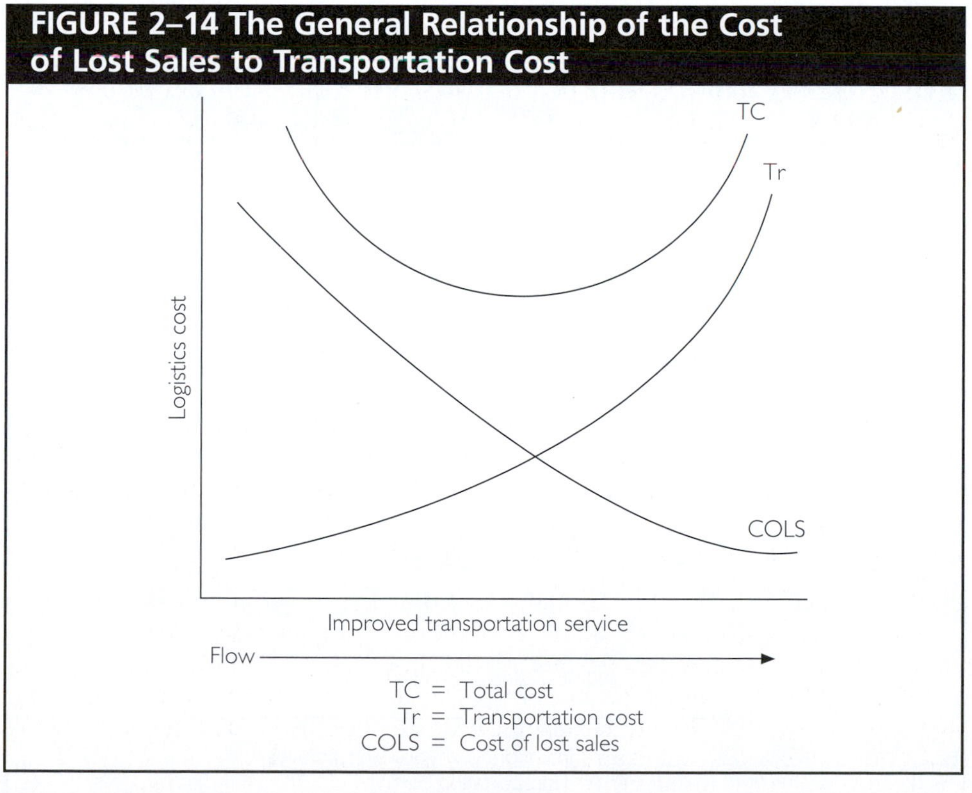

FIGURE 2–14 The General Relationship of the Cost of Lost Sales to Transportation Cost

Product Relationships

A number of product-related factors affect the cost and importance of logistics. Among the more significant of these are the following: dollar value, density, susceptibility to damage, and need for special handling.

Dollar Value. A number of product aspects have a direct bearing on logistics cost. First, the product's dollar value typically affects warehousing costs, inventory costs, transportation costs, packaging costs, and even materials-handling costs. As Figure 2–15 indicates, as the product's dollar value increases, the cost in each indicated area also rises. The actual slope and level of the cost functions vary from product to product.

impact on rates

Transportation rates reflect the risk associated with the movement of goods. There is often more chance for damage with higher-value goods; damage to such goods will cost the transportation company more to reimburse. Transportation companies also tend to charge higher rates for higher-value products because their customers can typically afford to pay a higher rate for such products. A relationship exists between the product value and the rate amount in transportation rate structures.

impact on warehousing

Warehousing and inventory costs also go up as the dollar value of products increases. Higher value means more capital in inventory, with higher total capital costs. In addition, the risk factor for storing higher-value products increases the possible cost of obsolescence and depreciation. Also, since the physical facilities required to store higher-value products are more sophisticated, warehousing costs increase with increased dollar value.

FIGURE 2–15 The General Relationship of Product Dollar Value to Various Logistics Costs

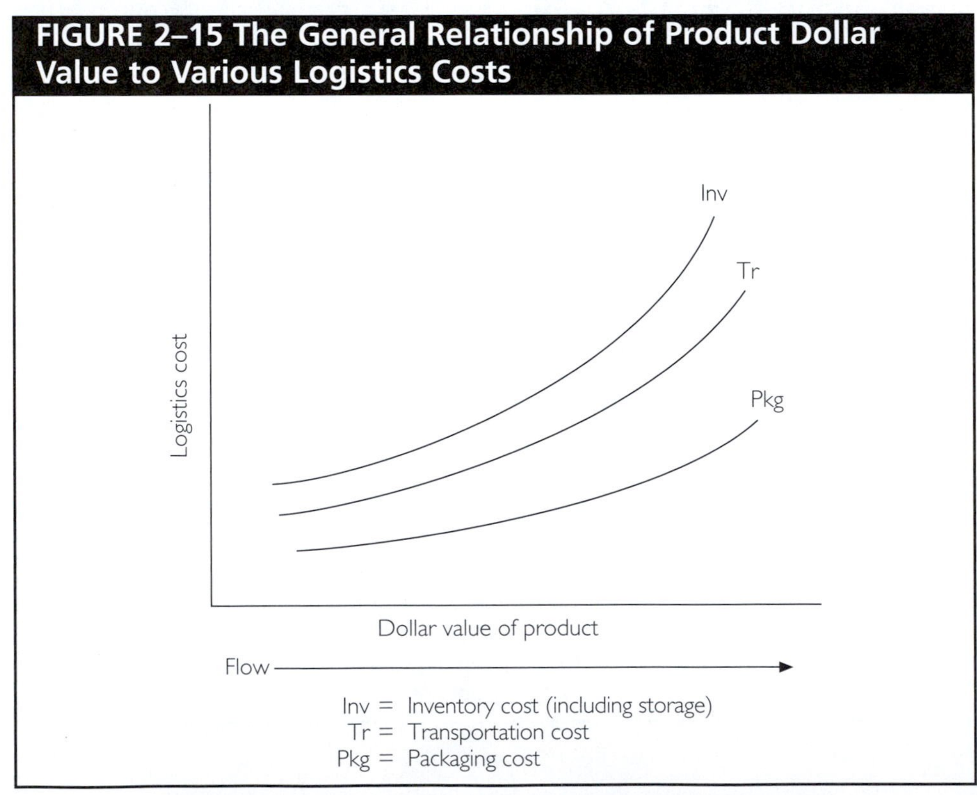

impact on packaging

Packaging cost also usually increases, because the firm uses protective packaging to minimize damage. A company spends more effort in packaging a product to protect it against damage or loss if it has higher value. Finally, materials-handling equipment used to meet the needs of higher-value products is very often more sophisticated. Firms are usually willing to use more capital-intensive and expensive equipment to speed higher-value goods through the warehouse and to minimize the chance of damage.

weight/space ratio

Density. Another factor that affects logistics cost is density, which refers to the weight/space ratio. An item that is lightweight compared to the space it occupies—for example, household furniture—has low density. The Gillette packaging situation described previously is another good example. Density affects transportation and warehousing costs, as Figure 2–16 shows. As we move from low density to high density, warehousing costs and transportation costs tend to fall.

In establishing their rates, transportation companies consider how much weight they can fit into their vehicles, since they quote their rates in terms of dollars and cents per hundred pounds. Therefore, on high-density items, they can afford to give a lower rate per hundred pounds because they can fit more weight into a car. Density also affects warehousing costs. The higher the density, the more weight can fit in an area of warehouse space—hence, the more efficient the use of warehousing space. So both warehousing cost and transportation cost tend to be influenced in the same way by density.

Susceptibility to Damage. The third product factor affecting logistics cost is susceptibility to damage (see Figure 2–17). The greater the risk of damage, the higher the

FIGURE 2–16 The General Relationship of Product Weight Density to Logistics Costs

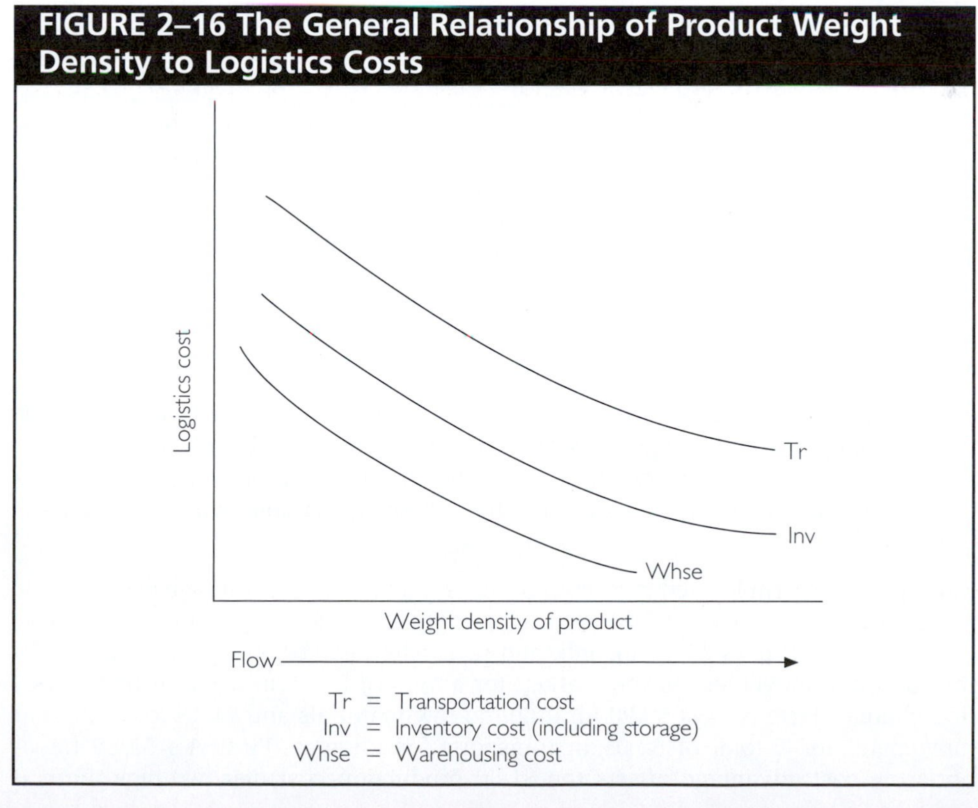

FIGURE 2–17 The General Relationship of Product Susceptibility to Loss and Damage to Logistics Costs

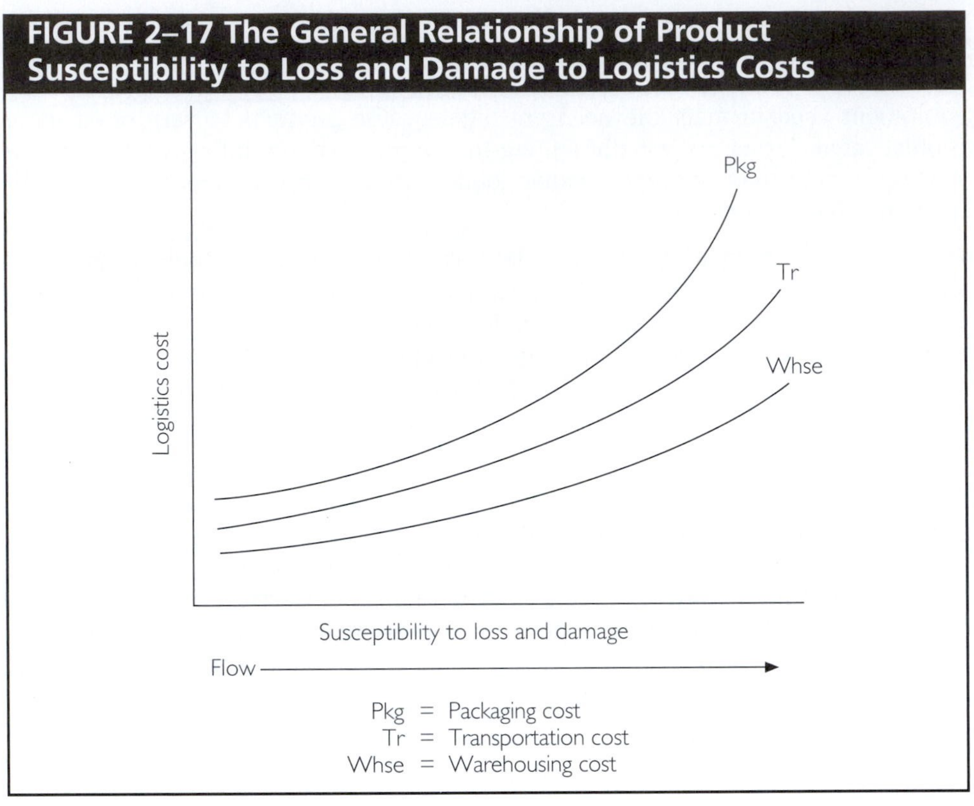

transportation and warehousing costs. Transportation companies, expecting greater product damage will charge higher rates, and warehousing costs will go up either because of damage or because of measures taken to reduce the risk of damage.

Special Handling Requirements. A fourth factor, related to damage susceptibility but somewhat distinct, is special handling requirements for products. Some products may require specially sized transportation units, refrigeration, heating, or stopping in transit. Special handling requirements, whether for transportation or for warehousing, will generally increase logistics cost.

Spatial Relationships

A final topic that is extremely significant to logistics is *spatial relationships,* the location of fixed points in the logistics system with respect to market and supply points. Spatial relationships are very important to transportation costs, since these costs tend to increase with distance. Consider the following example, which Figure 2–18 illustrates.

Example. The firm located at B has a $1.50 production cost advantage over Firm *A*, since Firm *B* produces at $7.00 per unit as opposed to $8.50 per unit for Firm *A*. However, Firm *B* pays $1.35 for inbound raw materials ($0.60 + $0.75) and $3.50 for outbound movement to the market, for a total of $4.85 in per unit transportation charges. Firm *A* pays $0.90 for inbound raw materials and $1.15 for outbound movement, for a total of $2.05 in transportation charges. Firm *A*'s $2.80 transportation cost advantage offsets the $1.50 production cost disadvantage. Firm *B*

FIGURE 2–18 Logistics and Spatial Relations

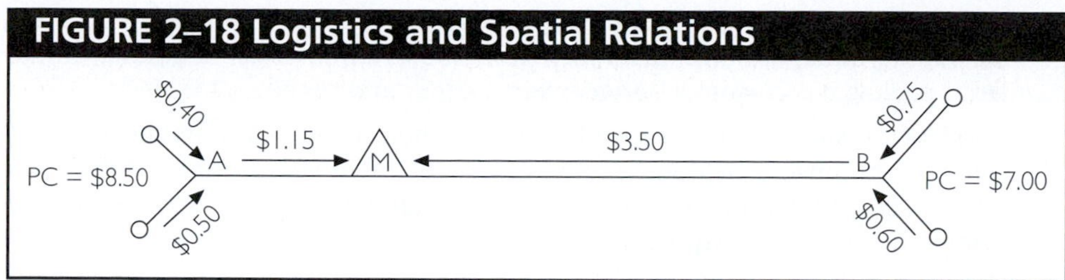

may wish to look at alternative strategies for its logistics system in order to compete more effectively at *M*. For example, firm *B* may base its $3.50/unit transportation cost for shipping to the market on less-than-truckload rates (low-volume movements). The firm may consider using a warehouse at *M* and shipping in higher-volume rail carload lots at lower transportation costs.

distance factor

The distance factor or spatial relationships may affect logistics costs in ways other than transportation costs. For example, a firm located far from one or more of its markets may need to use a market-oriented warehouse to make customer deliveries in a satisfactory time period. Therefore, distance can add to warehousing and inventory carrying costs. It may also increase order processing costs.

Distance or spatial relationships are of such importance to logistics cost that logistics responsibilities include site location. We consider location, or site analysis, in some detail at a later point in the text.

SUMMARY

- Logistics has developed as an important area or function of business since World War II. It has gone through several phases of development in achieving its present status.
- Logistics is a critical part of supply chain management. The coordination and, perhaps, integration of the logistics systems of all the organizations in a supply chain are necessary requirements for successful management of the supply chain.
- Logistics has a number of different definitions because of the broad-based interest in its activities and the recognition of its importance. The definition developed by the Council of Logistics Management is the primary definition used in the text.
- Logistics is an area of management that has four subdisciplines—business, military, service, and event.
- On a macro basis, logistics-related costs have been decreasing on a relative basis, which has helped the U.S. economy regain its competitive position on a global basis.
- Logistics adds place and time value to products and enhances the form and possession value added by manufacturing and marketing.
- Logistics has an important relationship to manufacturing, marketing, finance, and other areas of companies.

- Logistics managers are responsible for a number of important activities, including transportation, inventory, warehousing, materials handling, industrial packaging, customer service, forecasting, and others.
- Logistics systems can be viewed or approached in several different ways for analysis purposes, including materials management versus physical distribution, cost centers, nodes versus links, and channels. All four approaches are viable for different purposes.
- Logistics systems are frequently analyzed from a systems approach, which emphasizes total cost and trade-offs when changes are proposed. Either a short-run or a long-run perspective can be used.
- The cost of logistics systems can be affected by a number of major factors, including competition in the market, the spatial relationship of nodes, and product characteristics.

STUDY QUESTIONS

1. Compare and contrast the four subdivisions of logistics management.
2. Compare and contrast logistics management with supply chain management.
3. On a macro-economic basis, the ratio of inventory to sales has declined over the last fifteen years. Is this good or bad? Why? What factors have contributed to this trend? Is this trend likely to continue in the future? Why or why not?
4. Logistics costs as a percentage of GDP have been decreasing in recent years. What factors have contributed to this relative decline? What does the future hold for logistics costs?
5. Discuss the ways in which logistics contributes to economic value in the economy and in a firm.
6. Manufacturing companies have traditionally used long production runs as a means to gain a cost advantage in the marketplace. What is the impact of these long production runs upon logistics? The current approach to manufacturing is to have shorter production runs and more flexible setups. What impact does this approach have upon logistics costs? Manufacturing costs? What are the trade-offs?
7. Physical distribution has a special relationship to marketing. Why is this relationship so special? What is the nature of the overall relationship between logistics and marketing? Is the relationship becoming more or less important?
8. Logistics comprises a relatively large number of managerial activities. Discuss five of these activities and why they are important to logistics systems.
9. Compare and contrast the static analysis of logistics systems with dynamic analysis.
10. What product characteristics affect logistics costs? Discuss the effect of these characteristics upon logistics costs.

NOTES

1. Peter F. Drucker, "The Economy's Dark Continent," *Fortune* (April 1962): 103.
2. Stephen H. Russell, "Growing World of Logistics," *Air Force Journal of Logistics* 24, no. 4 (2000): 13–15.
3. Ibid.
4. Ibid.
5. E. Jerome McCarthy and William E. Perrault Jr., *Basic Marketing: A Managerial Approach,* 9th ed. (Homewood, Ill.: Richard D. Irwin, 1987), 46–52.
6. Philip Kotler, *Marketing Management: Analysis, Planning, and Control,* 5th ed. (Englewood Cliffs, N.J.: Prentice-Hall, 1984), 463–64.
7. Roy Dale Voorhees and Merrill Kim Sharp, "Principles of Logistics Revisited," *Transportation Journal* (Fall 1978): 69–84.
8. J. L. Heskett, Robert M. Ivie, and Nicholas A. Glaskowsky Jr., *Business Logistics: Management of Physical Supply and Distribution* (New York: Ronald Press, 1973), 26.
9. Op. cit., 454–69.

CASE 2–1 ■ Lycoming Electric Company

The Lycoming Electric Company is contemplating opening a new generating plant along the Susquehanna River because of increased electric power demand in that region. According to the president and manager of Lycoming Electric, Traci Shannon, "We've had very little problem finding the appropriate location for the plan along the river. However, since we rely on the burning of coal to produce the electricity, and since there is no possibility of using the river flow to generate electricity because of its current and speed, our biggest problem lies in determining which mode of transportation to use in acquiring the needed coal."

According to its planning department, Lycoming Electric will need 30 cwt. (3,000,000 lbs.) of coal per year in its plant. Skip Grenoble, logistics manager, presented to Ms. Shannon the only feasible systems available to transport such a large amount of coal to the new plant (see exhibit). According to Mr. Grenoble, "The rail system will result in a lower total cost, but the actual transportation costs will be higher than in the barge system because the nature and size of the barge equipment will necessitate our ordering in larger amounts. This, however, will also result in a lower annual ordering cost for the barge system because ordering in larger lots will reduce the amount of necessary orders. Administrative costs for the rail system will be higher due to the addition of an extra manager to handle necessary paperwork and other duties. The fixed cost for the rail system will include a rail siding, unloading equipment, and a conveyor system to get the coal inside the plant. When comparing these two systems to determine which is the most suited to our plant facility and overall efficiency, we must make our decision not on total cost alone but on how each system will contribute to our overall profitability." The relevant cost information is summarized in the following exhibit:

	Rail	**Barge**
Transportation costs	$ 23,000	$ 14,500
Inventory costs		
Carrying	1,346	2,266
Handling	1,760	2,000
Ordering	1,900	1,350
Fixed costs	99,444	116,391
Total costs	$127,450	$136,607

Case Questions

1. If you were the logistics manager of Lycoming Electric, which system would you advise Ms. Shannon to initiate? What criteria did you use to arrive at your decision?
2. At what level of demand in pounds of coal per year would these two systems be equal?
3. Graphically represent these two systems and their trade-off point.
4. What other factors might Ms. Shannon and Mr. Grenoble want to consider before making a final decision?

CASE 2–2 ■ Best Foods, Inc.

Best Foods, Inc., a major U.S. food products company located in Philadelphia, developed a new type of coffee and planned to test market the coffee nationwide. In addition to the test marketing, Best wanted to saturate the coffee market with its new product by selling the coffee at a $2.50-per-pound introductory price for one week. The second week of the introductory campaign, Best planned to increase the price per pound to $2.75, but all one-pound cans were three inches higher to accommodate enclosing a free stainless steel measuring scoop.

Two weeks before the product introduction, the marketing department, using all forms of media, advertised heavily throughout the United States. Posters, billboards, newspapers, radio, and television all carried advertisements for the new coffee. Raffle drawings were established in all the major grocery store chains nationwide, with Best Foods providing the prizes.

In conjunction with the marketing department, production runs for the new coffee started one month before the introduction. Estimated demand for the new product started one month before the introduction. Estimated demand for the new product was 1 million units for the first week and 1.25 million units for the second week.

Production runs had to be started early to meet the estimated product demand and to allow for a break in the production for the second week to set up for the new size cans.

Case Questions

1. Describe what interactions needed to take place among the marketing, production, and logistics departments. Explain the logistics department's role in the introduction of the new product.
2. Why was it necessary for the logistics department to be cognizant of all the planned changes in the promotion and production schedules for the new product introduction? Discuss various problems that may have arisen (for example, the second-week change in can size and weight) and what the logistics department's responsibilities were with respect to changes.

CHAPTER 3

DEMAND MANAGEMENT AND CUSTOMER SERVICE

LEARNING OBJECTIVES

After reading this chapter, you should be able to do the following:

- Understand the critical importance of outbound-to-customer logistics systems.
- Appreciate the growing need for effective demand management as part of a firm's overall logistics and supply chain expertise.
- Know the types of forecasts that may be needed, and understand how collaboration among trading partners will help the overall forecasting and demand management process.
- Identify the key steps in the order-fulfillment process, and understand how effective order management can create value for a firm and its customers.
- Realize the meaning of customer service, and understand its importance to logistics and supply chain management.
- Understand the difference between logistics and marketing channels, and understand that goods may reach their intended customer via a number of alternative channels of distribution.

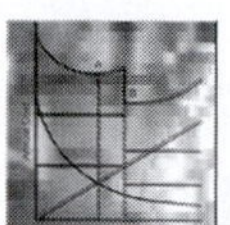

LOGISTICS PROFILE

How Scan-Based Trading Changed Distribution at Dreyer's

Not only has scan-based trading changed the payment process at Dreyer's Grand Ice Cream, but it has altered distribution operations as well. Six years ago, the ice-cream maker began instituting scan-based trading, a practice whereby the merchant pays the manufacturer for products based on what is actually scanned at the checkout counter. According to the director of distribution for Dreyer's, an Oakland, California-based company, the retailers send them daily scanned data, and they pay Dreyer's directly from the scanned data.

For starters, the implementation of scan-based trading has changed the way inventory is managed because there is no longer a transfer of product ownership at the store. "In essence, the inventory remains Dreyer's inventory until it's scanned," says the director of distribution. "The handoff at the back door doesn't happen."

Because consumer takeaway drives what Dreyer's stocks, the ice-cream manufacturer has shifted to a closed-loop distribution system. As a result, they reported having more detailed knowledge of what is selling at each location, and the traditional invoice discrepancies are being eliminated.

In-store vendor control of inventory also has eliminated the time-consuming validation of product delivery at each store. Previously, it took drivers up to one half hour to count inventory and validate items against the store's pricing files. This has had other benefits as well. Notably, deliveries are no longer restricted to the normal receiving hours of the retail stores. Also, from the perspective of fleet operations, Dreyer's is able to promote 24/7 availability of product to its customers. The removal of delivery-window constraints has allowed Dreyer's to optimize its 800-vehicle fleet for direct store delivery. Although the company has experienced sales increases of 10 percent to 15 percent per year, it has not had to add vehicles to its fleet since it adopted scan-based trading.

Improved fleet utilization has freed up resources that Dreyer's can reassign to in-store stocking tasks. (Unlike other companies, the drivers strictly operate the trucks; a separate workforce does the stocking.) In short, the money saved on distribution has been reinvested in stocking and merchandising. The feeling is that Dreyer's can take the money saved on distribution and reinvest it in stocking and merchandising. If available funds can be spent on people in stores, instead of trucks, then more value is offered to the customer. With the increases in efficiency of truck delivery, the focus at Dreyer's has shifted from delivery of the product to a partnership of selling products at the store level. If the product does not sell, the manufacturer does not get paid.

Source: Adapted from James Aaron Cooke, "Scan and Supply," *Logistics Management and Distribution Report* (June 2000): 67.

Outbound-to-Customer Logistics Systems

outbound logistics

In an effort to better serve their customers, many firms have placed significant emphasis on what may be termed their *outbound-to-customer logistics systems.* Also referred to as *physical distribution,* this essentially refers to the set of processes, systems, and capabilities that enhance a firm's ability to serve its customers. For example, the ways in which retailers such as L. L. Bean, Lands' End, and Eddie Bauer fulfill their customers' orders are examples of outbound logistics. This topic has been of significant historical interest in the study of logistics and supply chain management, and this chapter highlights key areas of concern relating to this general topic.

materials management

Correspondingly, the topic of *inbound-to-operations logistics systems* refers to the activities and processes that precede and facilitate value-adding activities such as manufacturing, assembly, and so on. Other terms that focus on these elements of the supply chain include *materials management* and *physical supply.* A typical example would be the movements of automotive parts and accessories that need to move from vendor locations to automotive assembly plants. Although many of the principles of inbound logistics are conceptually similar to those of outbound logistics, there are important differences that must be recognized. Thus, the topic of inbound logistics systems is the focus of the next chapter, which is titled "Procurement and Supply Management."

Examples of Successes

As a practical matter, in many firms the outbound-to-customer logistics system receives far more attention than the inbound-to-operations system. While this is changing quickly, it is largely due to the historical priority firms have had on improving service to their customers. This has led to an emphasis on attributes such as product availability, on-time and order delivery, timely and accurate logistics information, overall responsiveness, and post-sale customer support. Very simply, providing the customer with an acceptable level of service has been of greater concern, historically, than assuring the efficient and effective flow of materials to value-adding operations. In today's business environment, successful firms find it necessary to place an equal emphasis on being proficient in both of these areas.

"customer insight day"

The automotive industry provides an interesting example of the kinds of progress being made. In order to make sure buyers get the vehicle they want, top executives of one U.S.-based auto manufacturer recently held a "customer insight day," in which they sat at a table and talked with real customers about their cars and how their cars fit into their lives. In addition, these same executives visit at least two of the company's dealerships each year. In essence, they are working to change the basic dealer strategy, which currently is to sell from stock. Since studies have shown that only 60 percent of auto customers typically get what they want, their goal is to make it 100 percent. To achieve this, emphasis has been placed on developing a process whereby a dealer can change an order shortly before the car is built, and on identifying better means to transport finished vehicles to consumer buyers in a more timely and consistent manner.

Another goal is to make order entry and vehicle configuration more accurate and efficient. They want to be able to tell a buyer when his/her vehicle will be ready, and stand by it. Not long ago, this particular manufacturer was making only 60 percent of the vehicles in the week that were planned; this percentage has increased to 90 percent in recent years. Last, the company has created a special team to work with its suppliers to align its production strategy with its forecast. The desired end result is to shorten the time needed to get a car to the customer.[1]

supply chain consolidation

Another example is that of a major computer disk drive manufacturer that experienced rapid consolidation in its supply chain. In response to a series of acquisitions that brought together eight different companies operating in eight different ways, the company initiated a supply chain project that focused everyone's attention on the needs of the customer. This action enabled them to begin breaking down all of the silos that existed between the companies and, in the process, drove out inefficiencies. In addition to being able to lower prices for its customers, this firm was able to reduce production time for its disk drives by 50 percent. Shortening the forecast was another benefit of this effort. Previously, monthly sales forecasting cycles—a long time in the high-tech/electronics industry—were used on a regular basis. More recently, the focus has shifted to weekly forecasts and, ultimately, to having forecasts on a daily basis. As a result, costs are expected to continue to decline, with service to the customer expected to improve.[2]

Organization of This Chapter

Considering the complexity of the topic at hand, this chapter has a relatively aggressive agenda of topics to be discussed. First, a discussion of demand management provides an overview of the importance of effectively managing outbound-to-customer activities and processes. Second, the topic of forecasting is addressed in a general sense. Third, the more recent emphasis on collaborative forecasting approaches is covered. Fourth, attention is directed to the customer order cycle and how orders are placed, received, processed and shipped to the customer. Fifth, the role and importance of customer service are examined. A sixth topic is how to understand and quantify the costs that may be incurred when needed merchandise is not available for the customer. Last, a few comments regarding channels of distribution are necessary to put the overall topic of outbound logistics in its broader, more meaningful context.

DEMAND MANAGEMENT

According to Blackwell and Blackwell,[3] *demand management* may be thought of as "focused efforts to estimate and manage customers' demand, with the intention of using this information to shape operating decisions." Traditional supply chains typically begin at the point of manufacture or assembly and end with the sale of product to consumers or business buyers. Much of the focus and attention has been related to the topic of product flow, with significant concern for matters such as technology, information exchange, inventory turnover, delivery speed and consistency, and transportation. This notwithstanding, it is the manufacturers—who are many times far removed from the end user or consumer market—who determine what will be available for sale, where, when, and how many. If this seems to reflect a disconnect between manufacturing and demand at the point of consumption,

On The Line

Ingram Micro—A Demand Chain Leader

Demand chain creation usually begins with the vision of a company leader who is determined to make operations fully complement a consumer-centered strategy. In many cases, the company will take the lead role, inculcating its supply chain partners with that same vision. In other cases, it may turn to outside resources, such as a consulting firm or service provider, for help in this effort.

Ingram Micro took the leadership approach in creating a demand chain among its supply chain partners. The Seattle-based company is the world's leading wholesale distributor of technology products and services. This $22 billion giant distributes more than 200,000 products from 1,500 manufacturers to over 140,000 resellers in 130 countries.

The company's COO explains that Ingram Micro is committed to reinventing technology distribution by putting the customer first . . . but the company's initiative does not stop there. The focus goes beyond Ingram's customers to address the needs of its customers' customers—or end-use customers. The role of distribution in any industry is to extract products from a multitude of manufacturers and distribute them to a broad set of businesses, markets, and consumers. This is true in the technology market in which Ingram competes as well. Consumers look for solutions to their computing needs, which can involve putting together a complex system of products and features—not just a single product from a single vendor.

The accompanying diagram depicts Ingram Micro's model for technology distribution. The intent is that the model begins and ends with the end user—the consumer. After listening to the needs of the end consumer, Ingram communicates this information to its customers (resellers), who design, sell, and support the products and services consumers want. In conjunction with manufacturers, the company then puts the products together and delivers them directly to the end user on the reseller's behalf. The company has chosen the terminology *demand chain,* rather than *supply chain,* because its central focus is to meet consumer demand.

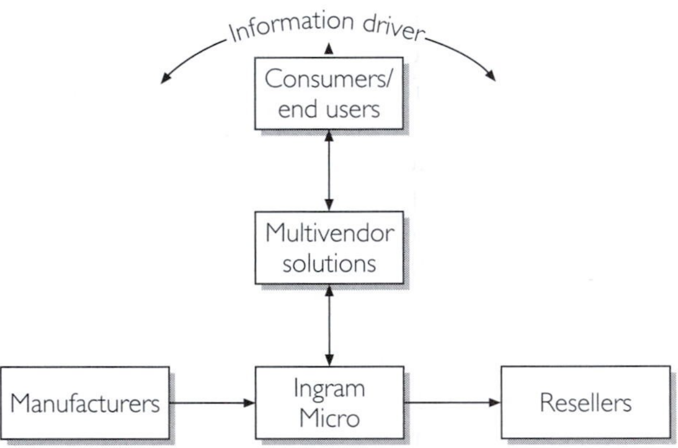

Source: Figure and text adapted from Roger D. Blackwell and Kristina Blackwell, "The Century of the Consumer: Converting Supply Chains into Demand Chains," *Supply Chain Management Review* 3, no. 3 (Fall 1999): 24–25. Reprinted with permission of *Supply Chain Management Review,* a Cahners publication

that is exactly what it is. Thus, any attention paid to demand management will produce benefits throughout the supply chain.

demand management objectives

The essence of demand management is to further the ability of firms throughout the supply chain—particularly manufacturing through the customer—to collaborate on activities related to the flows of product, services, information, and capital. The desired end result should be to create greater value for the end user or consumer, for whom all supply chain activity should be undertaken. The following list suggests a number of ways in which effective demand management will help to unify channel members with the common goal of satisfying customers and solving customer problems:[4]

- Gathering and analyzing knowledge about consumers, their problems, and their unmet needs
- Identifying partners to perform the functions needed in the demand chain
- Moving the functions that need to be done to the channel member that can perform them most effectively and efficiently
- Sharing with other supply chain members knowledge about consumers and customers, available technology, and logistics challenges and opportunities
- Developing products and services that solve customers' problems
- Developing and executing the best logistics, transportation, and distribution methods to deliver products and services to consumers in the desired format

forecasts

As firms identify the need for improved demand management, a number of problems occur. First is that lack of coordination between departments (i.e., the existence of "functional silos") results in little or no coordinated response to demand information. Second is that too much emphasis is placed on forecasts of demand, with less attention on the collaborative efforts and the strategic and operational plans that need to be developed from the forecasts. Third is that demand information is used moreso for tactical and operational than for strategic purposes. In essence, and since in many cases historical performance is not a very good predictor of the future, demand information should be used to create collective and realistic scenarios of the future. Primary emphasis should be on understanding likely demand scenarios and mapping their relationships to product supply alternatives. The end result will be to better match demand as it occurs with appropriate availability of needed product in the marketplace.

supply-demand misalignment

Figure 3–1 provides a view of how supply-demand misalignment may impact overall supply chain effectiveness. Using the PC industry as an example, this figure charts production, channel orders, and true end-user demand over the life cycle of a product. Ignoring the early adopters, end-user demand for PCs typically is at its highest level at the time new products are launched—which is also the time that availability is most precarious. As new, competing products become available, end-user demand begins to taper off, eventually reaching a modest level, at which time the product, now much more available, is generally phased out.

Looking more closely at Figure 3–1, in the first phase of a new product launch, when end-user demand is at its peak and opportunities for profit margins are greatest, PC assemblers are not able to supply product in quantities sufficient to meet demand—thus creating true product shortages. Also during this time frame,

FIGURE 3–1 Supply-Demand Misalignment

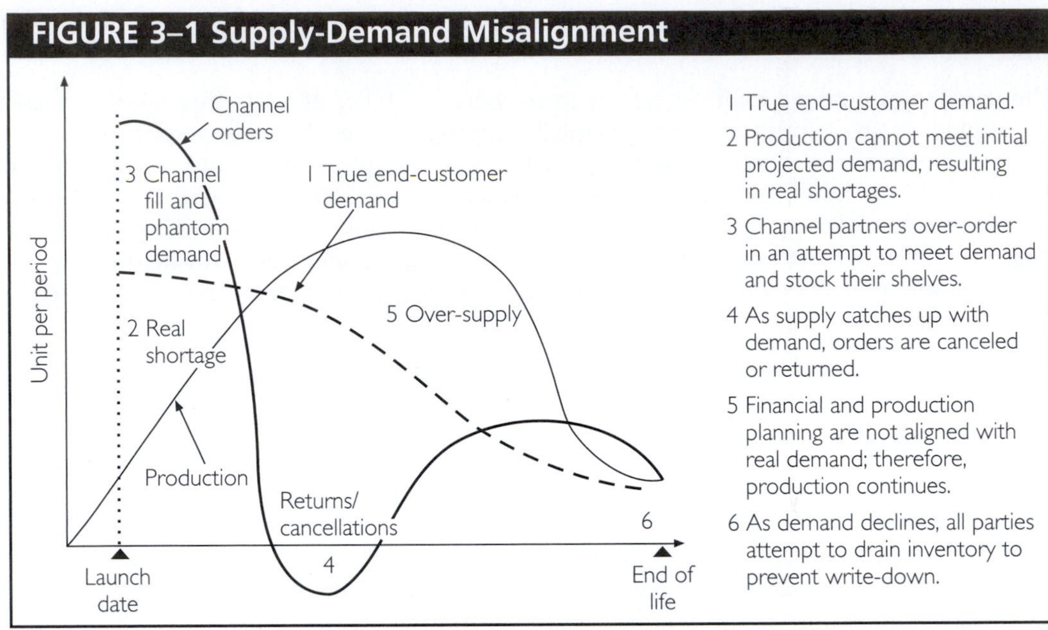

Source: Accenture, Stanford University, and Northwestern University, *Customer-Driven Demand Networks: Unlocking Hidden Value in the Personal Computer Supply Chain* (Accenture, 1997), 15.

distributors and resellers tend to "over-order," often creating substantial "phantom" demand. In the next phase, as production begins to ramp up, assemblers ship product against this inflated order situation and book sales at the premium, high-level launch price. As channel inventories begin to fill, price competition begins to set in, as do product overages and returns. This further depresses demand for the PC product, and the PC assemblers are the hardest hit.

In the final phase noted in Figure 3–1, as end-user demand begins to decline, the situation clearly has shifted to one of over-supply. This is largely due to the industry's planning processes and systems, which are primarily designed to use previous period demand as a gauge. Since much of the previous period's demand was represented by the previously mentioned "phantom" demand, forecasts are distorted. The net result of these behaviors in aligning supply and demand is that a large majority of product is sold during the declining period of profit opportunity, thereby diminishing substantial value creation opportunities for industry participants. Adding insult to injury, substantial amounts of inventory are held throughout the supply chain as a hedge against supply uncertainty. Overall, this situation is one that needs considerable attention.

According to Langabeer,[5] there is growing and persuasive evidence that understanding and managing market demand are central determinants of business success. Aside from this observation, relatively few companies have successfully linked demand management with corporate strategy. Table 3–1 provides a view of how demand data may be used strategically to enhance a company's growth, portfolio, positioning, and investment strategies. As suggested, effective use of demand data can help companies to guide strategic resources in a number of important ways.

TABLE 3–1 How Demand Management Supports Business Strategy

Strategy	Examples of How to Use Demand Management
Growth strategy	• Perform "what if" analyses on total industry volume to gauge how specific mergers and acquisitions might leverage market share. • Analyze industry supply/demand to predict changes in product pricing structure and market economics based on mergers and acquisitions. • Build staffing models for merged company using demand data.
Portfolio strategy	• Manage maturity of products in current portfolio to optimally time overlapping life cycles. • Create new-product development/introduction plans based on life cycle. • Balance combination of demand and risk for consistent "cash cows" with demand for new products. • Ensure diversification of product portfolio through demand forecasts.
Positioning strategy	• Manage product sales through each channel based on demand and product economics. • Manage positioning of finished goods at appropriate distribution centers, to reduce working capital, based on demand. • Define capability to supply for each channel.
Investment strategy	• Manage capital investments, marketing expenditures, and research and development budgets based on demand forecasts of potential products and maturity of current products. • Determine whether to add manufacturing capacity.

Source: Jim R. Langabeer II, "Aligning Demand Management with Human Strategy," *Supply Chain Management Review* (May/June 2000): 68. Reprinted with permission of *Supply Chain Management Review,* a Cahners publication.

TRADITIONAL FORECASTING

demand forecasting

A major component of demand management is *forecasting* the amount of product that will be purchased by consumers or end users. Although forecasts are made throughout the supply chain, the single, most important forecast is that of primary demand. In a truly integrated supply chain scenario, all other demand will emanate directly from—or at least be influenced by—primary demand. One of the key objectives of integrated supply chain management is to further the extent to which all supply chain decisions anticipate, as well as respond to, primary demand as it occurs in the marketplace.

integrating forecasting and production

Figure 3–2 outlines one firm's approach to sales forecasting and its integration with production scheduling activities. The first step is to develop a twelve-month forecast of demand by month by applying traditional demand forecasting approaches (e.g., moving average, exponential smoothing, Box-Jenkins, regression analysis, etc.) to a three-year history file of data on factors such as demand, price, seasonality, availability, deals, and promotions. In the second step, brand and product managers review this forecast and recommend relevant changes. The result is an agreed-upon statement of gross market requirements for the succeeding one- to three-year periods. The third step involves developing aggregate production schedules for the next twelve-month period and allocating specific production requirements to

FIGURE 3–2 Integration of Sales Forecasting and Production

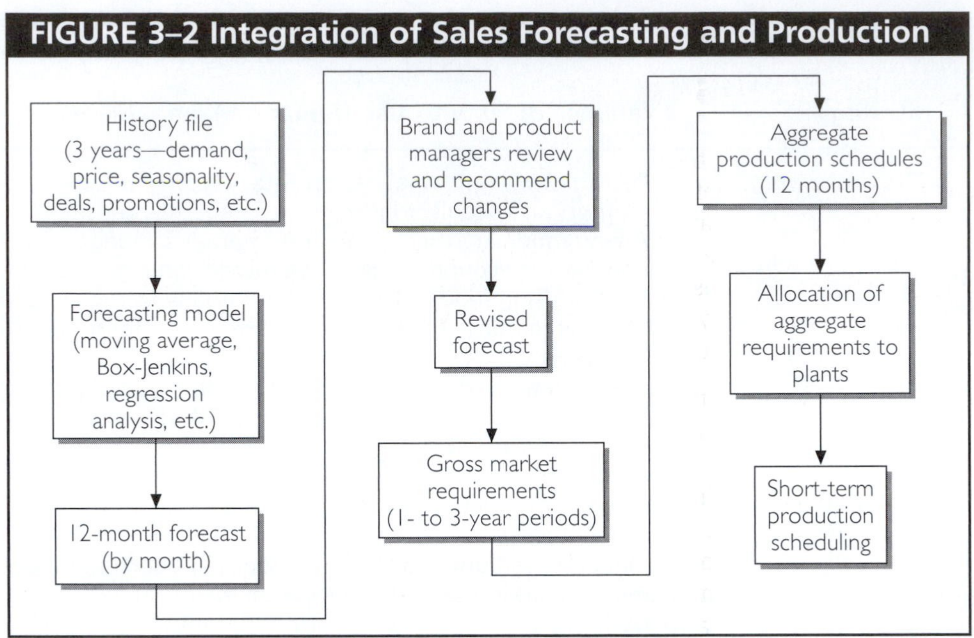

various manufacturing facilities. Finally, the logistics function commonly assumes responsibility for scheduling production on a short-term basis, in order to coordinate demand for finished product with the timing and availability of needed production inputs.

purposes of forecasting

Actually, different approaches to forecasting serve different purposes:

- *Long-term forecasts* usually cover more than three years and are used for long-range planning and strategic issues. These naturally will be done in broad terms—sales by product line or division, throughput capacity by ton per period or dollars per period, and so on. These forecasts might easily go beyond customer demand to other key corporate resources such as production capacity and desired inventory asset levels.
- *Midrange forecasts*—in the one- to three-year range—address budgeting issues and sales plans. Again, these might predict more than demand. The demand forecasts will very likely still be in dollars and now, perhaps, at the level of product family or product line. The first year in a multiyear forecast might be by month, while the following years may be by quarter.
- *Short-term forecasts* are most important for the operational logistics planning process. They project demand into the several months ahead and are focusing increasingly on shorter time intervals. These forecasts are needed in units, by actual items to be shipped, and for finite periods of time.

An important distinction involves the tactical use of demand information by the supply chain, in contrast to the strategic use by an executive-controlled supply chain.[6] On the one hand, "tactical" use of demand data will probably help a company to develop a forecast of projected sales. Alternatively, "strategic" use of the same data can help a company to analyze its product portfolio and its new product development strategies. This strategic use of demand data can help to improve the overall profitability and market positioning of a company.

Collaborative Planning, Forecasting, and Replenishment

Over time, there have been numerous industry initiatives that have attempted to create efficiency and effectiveness through integration of supply chain activities and processes. They have been identified by names such as quick response, electronic data interchange (EDI), short cycle manufacturing, vendor-managed inventory (VMI), continuous-replenishment planning (CRP), and efficient consumer response (ECR). One by one, each fell short of expectations, particularly in its ability to integrate supply chain activities among the many participants.

CPFR

One of the most recent initiatives, aimed at achieving true supply chain integration, is *collaborative planning, forecasting, and replenishment (CPFR®)*.[7] CPFR has become recognized as a breakthrough business model for planning, forecasting, and replenishment. Using this approach, retailers, transport providers, distributors, and manufacturers can utilize available Internet-based technologies to collaborate from operational planning through execution. Whereas historically, for a single product, retailers and manufacturers may have had twenty or more types of forecasts between them—each developed for a special purpose, each more or less accurate, and all trying to predict behavior of buyers in the marketplace—CPFR simplifies and streamlines overall demand planning.

The impetus for the development of CPFR came from an effort in 1995 by Wal-Mart and one of its suppliers, Warner-Lambert Company, particularly with regard to its Listerine™-brand product. In addition to rationalizing inventories of specific line items and addressing out-of-stock occurrences, these two companies collaborated to increase their forecasting accuracy, so as to have just the right amount of inventory where it was needed, when it was needed. The three-month pilot produced significant results and improvements for both parties, sufficient to be responsible for further utilization by Wal-Mart of this approach that used the Internet to facilitate the collaboration.

As suggested in Figure 3–3, CPFR emphasizes a sharing of consumer purchasing data among and between trading partners for the purpose of helping to govern supply chain activities. In this manner, CPFR creates a significant, direct link between the consumer and the supply chain. The effective implementation of CPFR is based on systematic collaboration between trading partners, whereas predecessor approaches are not. In addition, the CPFR movement is responsible for the creation of new technology tools to facilitate the sharing, analysis, and ultimate application of the information by trading partners. Use of the Internet as a low-cost, neutral systems platform and the development of "between-ware" applications are showing great promise.

The CPFR initiative begins with the sharing of marketing plans between trading partners. Once an agreement is reached on the timing and planned sales of specific products, and a commitment is made to follow that plan closely, the plan is then used to create a forecast, by stock-keeping unit (SKU), by week, and by quantity. The planning can be for thirteen, twenty-six, or fifty-two weeks. A typical forecast is for seasonal or promotional items that represent approximately 15 percent of sales in each category. The regular turn items, or the remainder of products in the category, are forecast statistically. Then, the forecast is entered into a system that

FIGURE 3–3 CPFR Business Model

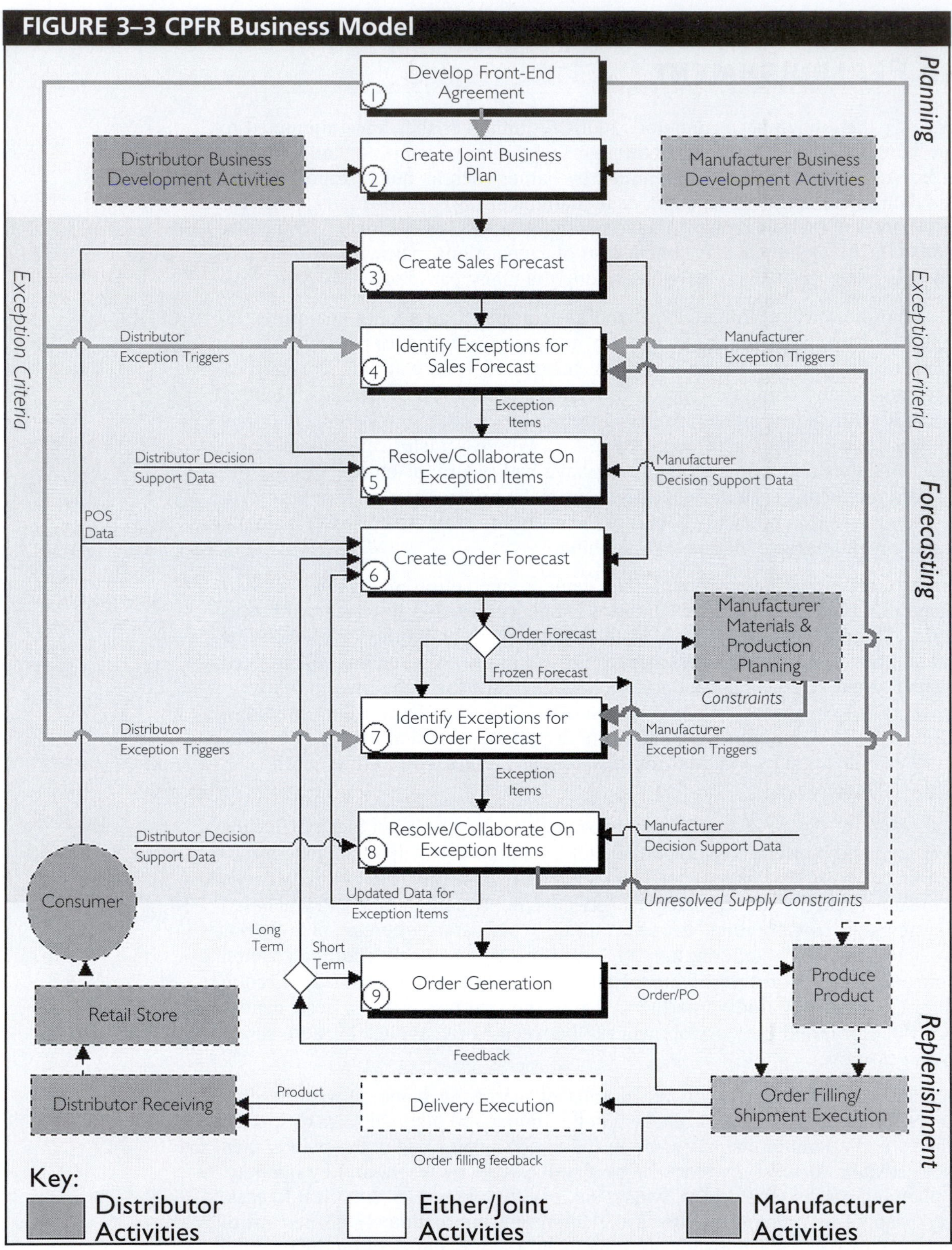

Source: Used with permission of the Voluntary Interindustry Commerce Standards (VICS) Association. CPFR® is a registered trademark of the Voluntary Interindustry Commerce Standards (VICS) Association.

SUPPLY CHAIN TECHNOLOGY

MIDWEST PHARMACEUTICALS

A large Midwest pharmaceutical company manufactures approximately 15,000 different products in its four locations in the domestic United States. These products are grouped into five families, each with approximately 3,000 products. History is collected at the product level. Using the company's statistically advanced demand-management system, a state-of-the-art technology, the company can analyze changes in rates of demand and determine whether the product is in an introduction, growth, maturity, or decline phase of its life cycle. With relatively few inputs, such as expected product life and the data the product was introduced, the system can isolate the seasonal and trend components and determine each product's position in the life cycle.

As the company rolled this information up to the higher or "family" level, demand-chain managers could see that in one family, 72 percent of the products were in the mature stage, while 14 percent were in decline. This finding troubled management because success for companies in the pharmaceutical business depended on continually adding new and innovative products to their portfolios to replace old and declining ones. Accordingly, the company decided to alter its portfolio strategy by immediately investing more heavily into products that could offset those in decline.

Tactical use of demand data would have given this company only a forecast of projected sales. Strategic use of the same data, on the other hand, led management to modify and improve the portfolio and its product investment strategy. In essence, demand management helped make this company more profitable and effective.

Source: Edited from Jim R. Langabeer II, "Aligning Demand Management With Business Strategy," *Supply Chain Management Review* (May/June 2000): 69. Reprinted with permission of *Supply Chain Management Review*, a Cahners publication.

is accessible through the Internet by both supplier and buyer. Either party is empowered to change the forecast, within established parameters.

CPFR results

Only a few CPFR initiatives have published the results of their collaborative efforts, but those that are available are impressive.[8] Nabisco and Wegmans, for example, noted an increase in category sales of more than 50 percent. Wal-Mart and Sara Lee reported a reduction of 14 percent in store-level inventory, with a 32 percent increase in sales. Kimberly-Clark and Kmart have achieved steady increases in category sales growth that exceeded margin growth.

ORDER FULFILLMENT AND ORDER MANAGEMENT

As suggested by Figure 3–4, three critical elements of collaborative planning are collaborative demand planning, joint capacity planning, and synchronized order fulfillment. This type of planning improves quality of the demand signal for the entire supply chain through a constant exchange of information from one end to the other that goes well beyond traditional practices. As a result, the downstream supply chain firms share relevant and useful order information and demand forecasts with those farther upstream. At the same time, upstream firms share updated information relating to product availability and expected inventory levels.

FIGURE 3–4 Collaborative Planning

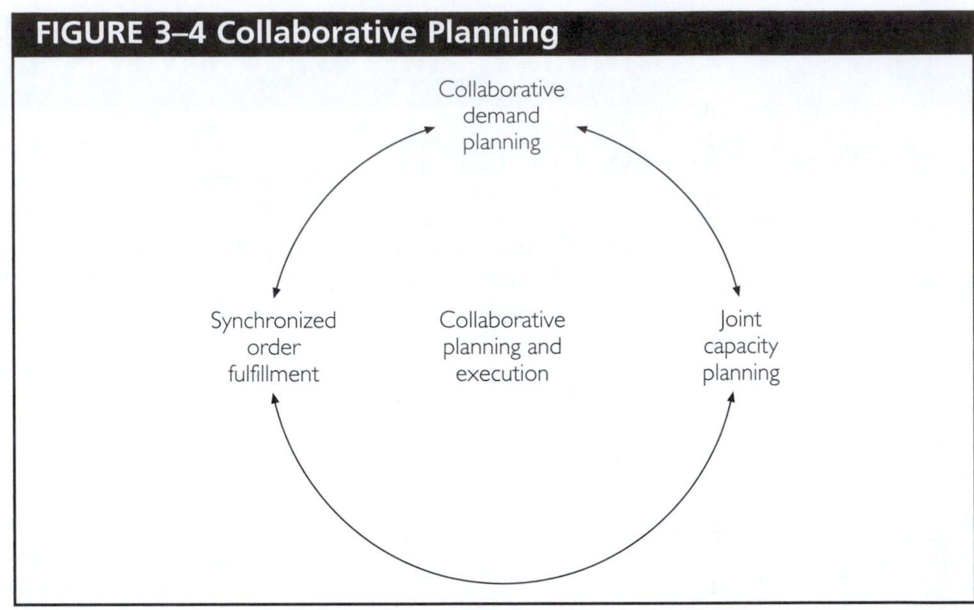

Source: Accenture, Stanford University, and Northwestern University, *Customer-Driven Demand Networks: Unlocking Hidden Value in the Personal Computer Supply Chain* (Accenture, 1997), 29.

FIGURE 3–5 Stages of Order Fulfillment

	Transactional	*Interactive*	*Interdependent*
Information sharing	Limited to basic order information	Some sharing of inventory availability and shipment information	Extensive sharing of inventory, shipment, and sell-through information
Decision making	Independent order decisions—"phantom demand"	Some negotiation of order decisions among partners	Synchronized ordering decisions driven by shared replenishment policies, channel inventory data, and POS information (VMI)
Performance measures	Limited performance measures	Some shared performance measures like lead times, on-time delivery, and inventory availability	Extensive use of performance measures tied to shared risks and rewards
Technology	Limited use of technology	Some use of technology to track orders and material flow	Extensive use of technology to allow real-time tracking of orders and material and an automatic replenishment

Source: Accenture, Stanford University, and Northwestern University, *Customer-Driven Demand Networks: Unlocking Hidden Value in the Personal Computer Supply Chain* (Accenture, 1997), 32.

Figure 3–5 identifies four key stages of order fulfillment (i.e., information sharing, decision-making, performance measures, and technology) and suggests how these stages differ as supply chain activity matures from transactional to interactive to interdependent. This figure clarifies the significant enhancements to the order-fulfillment process that may be expected as supply chain activities become increasingly collaborative.

FIGURE 3–6 Order-Management Functions

- Receive order
- Enter order - manual/electronic
- Verify and check order for accuracy
- Check credit
- Check inventory availability
- Process back order
- Acknowledge order
- Modify order
- Suspend order
- Check pricing and promotion
- Identify shipping point
- Generate picking documents
- Originate shipment
- Inquire order status
- Deliver order
- Measure service level
- Measure quality of service
- Assure continuous improvement
- Handle product returns

The Order-Management System

The order-management system represents the principal means by which buyers and sellers communicate information relating to individual orders of product. The order-processing system, extremely important to the firm's logistics area, is also one of the most important components of the firm's overall management information system.

order management functions

Effective order management is a key to operational efficiency and customer satisfaction. Figure 3–6 provides a list of typical order-management functions. To the extent that a firm conducts all activities relating to order management in a timely, accurate, and thorough manner, it follows that other areas of company activity can be similarly well coordinated. In addition, both present and potential customers will take a positive view of consistent and predictable order cycle length and acceptable response times. By starting the process with an understanding of customer needs, firms can design order-management systems that will be viewed as superior to those of competitor firms. A company's order-management capabilities will contribute toward producing a competitive advantage.

The logistics area needs timely and accurate information relating to individual customer orders; thus, more and more firms are placing the corporate order-management function within the logistics area. The move is good not only from the perspective of the logistics process but also from that of the overall organization. The area of order management has been a primary beneficiary of the enhanced and more responsive computer and information systems available today. In many firms, the area of order management has become an innovator in exploiting new technological advances.

Order and Replenishment Cycles

order cycle

When referring to outbound-to-customer shipments, we typically use the term *order cycle.* The term *replenishment cycle* is used more frequently when referring to the acquisition of additional inventory, as in materials management. Basically, one firm's order cycle is another's replenishment cycle. For simplicity, we shall use the term *order cycle* throughout the remainder of this discussion.

lead time Four principal activities, or elements, constitute lead time, or the order cycle: order placement, order processing, order preparation, and order shipment. These activities are shown in Figure 3–7, along with arrows indicating the principal directions in which product and information flow. Traditionally, the order cycle includes only those activities that occur from the time an order is placed to the time that it is received by the customer. Special activities such as backordering and expediting will affect the overall length of the order cycle. Subsequent customer activities, such as product returns, claims processing, and freight bill handling, are not technically part of the order cycle.

Order Placement. Order-placement time can vary significantly, from taking days or weeks to being instantaneous. Company experiences indicate that improvements in order-placement systems and processes offer some of the greatest opportunities for significantly reducing the length and variability of the overall order cycle. Figure 3–8 shows results of a study by Forrester Research, Inc., showing the means by which companies purchased direct materials in 2000, and their advance plans for 2002.

FIGURE 3–7 Major Components of the Order Cycle

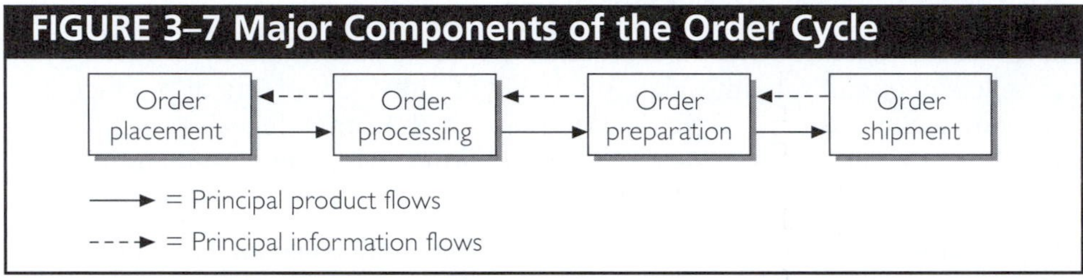

FIGURE 3–8 Order-Placement Trends

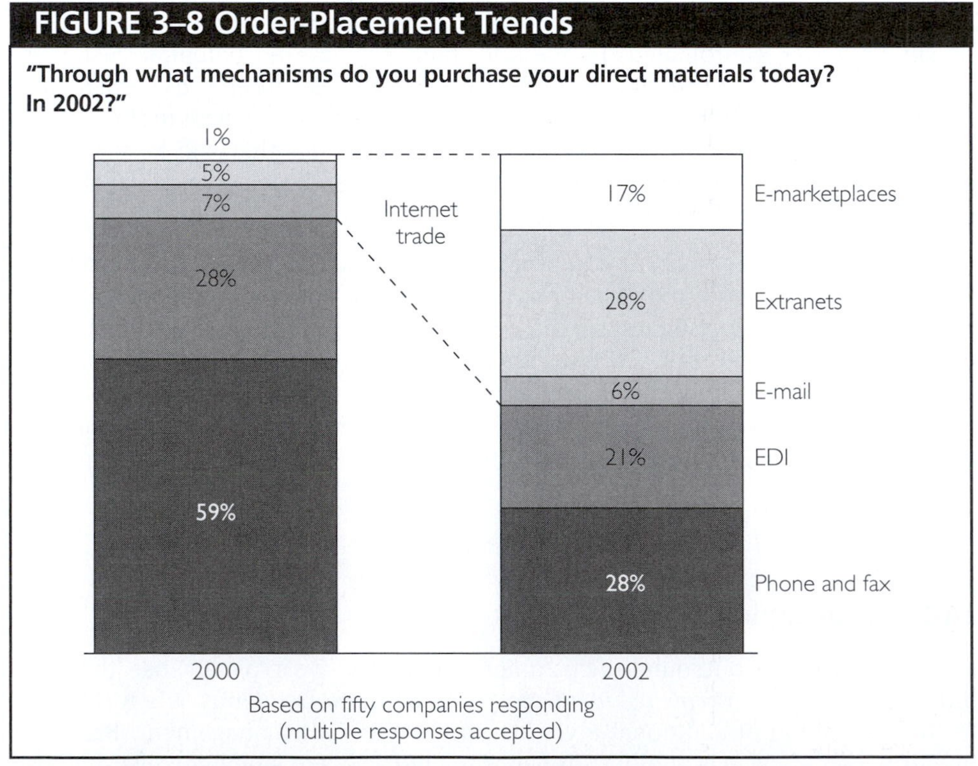

Source: Forrester Research, Inc., *The Forrester Report: On-Line Supply Chain Realities* (Cambridge, Mass.: Forrester Research, Inc., 2000), 3.

Clearly, significant increases were projected for Internet-facilitated resources such as E-marketplaces, Extranets, and E-mail. Those that were expected to show declines in relative use were electronic data interchange (EDI) and phone/fax.

Order Processing. The order-processing function usually involves checking customer credit, transferring information to sales records, sending the order to the inventory and shipping areas, and preparing shipping documents. Many of these functions can occur simultaneously through the effective use of available information technologies. Recent improvements in computer and information systems have led to considerable reductions in the times needed to accomplish these activities.

Order Preparation. Depending on the commodity being handled and other factors, the order-preparation process sometimes may be very simple and performed manually or, perhaps, may be relatively complex and highly automated. Since the time needed to prepare orders for shipment frequently represents a significant bottleneck in the overall order cycle, advance information concerning the composition of individual shipments has become highly desirable. The availability of real-time information systems has helped significantly to see that this information is available in a timely and functional manner.

Order Shipment. Shipment time extends from the moment an order is placed upon the transport vehicle for movement, until the moment it is received and unloaded at the buyer's location. Measuring and controlling order-shipment time sometimes can be difficult when using for-hire transportation services; however, most carriers today have developed the ability to provide their customers with this type of information.

advance shipment notification

One way for receivers of product to increase the likelihood of timely delivery is to ask for advance shipment notification (ASN) from supplier firms. Alternatively, shippers may prefer to receive proof-of-delivery (POD) documentation, preferably electronically, from carriers. This helps to pinpoint the exact time and location of delivery. To improve service to customers, transport firms have moved to the use of Internet-enabled capabilities to provide services such as these to their customers. In addition, carriers have made it easier for customers to track and trace shipments when needed and have provided these same customers with summary reports of shipment times, service levels, and so on.

proof of delivery

One of the major U.S. automobile companies has established an integrated private/contract carriage system and a computerized parts locating and ordering system to produce prompt and dependable delivery service for small, less-than-truckload shipments. The system provides next-day delivery to most of its dealers from the company's eighteen distribution centers located throughout the United States. Approximately 80 percent of the parts deliveries are made at night through a passkey operation. Company drivers are given keys to the dealers' facilities and make deliveries to secured areas. The night deliveries reduce delays normally caused by daytime highway traffic and congestion at dealer facilities. This example shows how a precisely planned and well-executed transportation capability can help to reduce needed time to fulfill customer orders.

Because of the positive changes that have occurred in the transportation environment over a number of years, capable, time-sensitive logistics services are increasingly becoming available. While each of the modes of transport has evidenced considerable improvement in this area, there are significant opportunities to further enhance value-added services for customers. Also, the availability of accurate information on a real-time basis has been identified as a key priority for a growing number of transportation and logistics service providers.

Length and Variability of the Order Cycle. While interest has traditionally centered more on the overall length of the order/replenishment cycle, recent attention has been focused on the variability or consistency of this process. Consistent with the contemporary interest in meeting customer requirements, there also is a concern for making sure that the first priority is to deliver shipments at the time and location specified by the customer.

One landmark customer service study incorporated a series of questions pertaining to the time needed to complete the total order cycle as well as the relative time needed to complete the individual elements of the order cycle.[9] A significant finding was that the greatest portion of the total order cycle time occurred either before the manufacturer received the order from the customer or after the order was shipped. In other words, activities that were at least somewhat external to the manufacturer and over which the manufacturer traditionally had little control consumed more than one-half of the total order cycle time.

order cycle length

This phenomenon is supported by more recent data developed by Accenture (formerly Andersen Consulting), which is shown in Figure 3–9. In this example, the average total time for order transmission and transit to customer (7.0 days) exceeded the average time spent on more internally focused activities such as order edit/entry, pick-ticket generation, and order picking (5.1 days). Also, there were significant differences between the average times for completing the various steps and the 95th percentile times. Results such as this have caused manufacturers to be more aggressive in facilitating the order-placement activity experienced by their customers, particularly through the use of information-based and Internet-enabled capabilities. Similarly, manufacturers have become more interested in seeing that shipments arrive at their customers' locations in a timely manner. This has resulted in the development of strategies to assure greater control over the speed, consistency, and overall quality of transportation services.

FIGURE 3–9 Example of Order Cycle Time Analysis

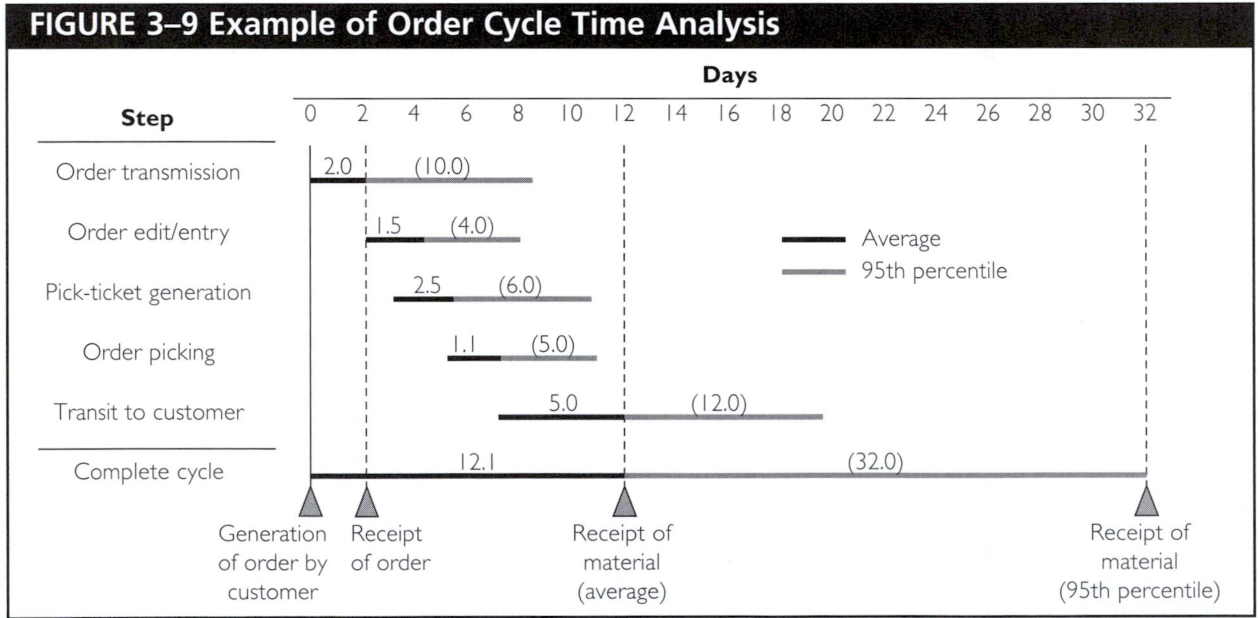

Source: William C. Copacino, "Time to Review Order Management," *Traffic Management* (June 1993): 32. Used with permission.

Any reduction in the length of one or more order cycle components will provide either additional planning time for the manufacturer or a shortened order cycle for the buyer. If a manufacturing firm identifies an opportunity to reduce the length of one or more components of the order cycle, it then can choose to either absorb the extra time into its own system (perhaps as additional planning time) or share it with the customer by shortening the order cycle in a material fashion. In competitive markets, passing such time savings along to the customer whenever possible may be of great value in the marketplace for the manufacturer.

order cycle variability

Variability in the order cycle length also can affect the levels of safety stock carried by purchasers of the firm's products. Specifically, as order cycle variability increases, needed safety stock levels also increase. Conversely, as firms reduce order cycle variability, customers may choose to carry less safety stock. In either instance, order cycle variability links directly to the levels of safety stock a customer must carry.

Ideally, improvement will take the form of shorter order cycle lengths, coupled with improved consistency and reliability. Figure 3–10 illustrates a before-and-after situation in which a firm successfully reduced the length and variability of most of the activities comprising the order cycle. Aside from the improvement in each individual activity, the total order cycle time and variability have decreased noticeably.

E-Commerce Order-Fulfillment Strategies

As firms become more and more involved in E-commerce, it has become apparent that order fulfillment and product distribution are among the most overlooked and, perhaps, the most underestimated in terms of importance. Success in the E-commerce arena is just as much about designing and implementing the basic principles of logistics and supply chain management as it is about marketing the latest technologies.

consumer-direct business needs

According to Ricker and Kalakota,[10] three forces are converging to create an explosion in consumer direct business models: technology forces are making it possible, market forces are making it viable, and social forces are making it inevitable. According to these authors, some of the critical decisions to be made by companies are related to the evaluation of multiple fulfillment planning strategies. Among those that are cited are:

- *Profitable to promise:* Should I take the customer order at this time?
- *Available to promise:* Is inventory available to fulfill the order?
- *Capable to promise:* Does manufacturing capacity allow order commitment?

Thus, five alternative fulfillment strategies are suggested for consideration by firms in the E-commerce business: (1) distributed delivery centers; (2) partner fulfillment operations; (3) dedicated fulfillment centers; (4) third-party fulfillment centers; and (5) build to order (which involves no stock inventory).[11] Regardless of the strategy that is selected, a fundamental requirement of fulfillment logistics is the dedicated collaboration of all supply chain trading partners to eliminate the costs associated with inefficient movement of goods, redundant practices and processes, and excess inventory. Effective collaboration tends to foster not only supply chain efficiency and effectiveness but also the ability to change when needed and to see that strategic processes are continuously improved.

FIGURE 3–10 Order Cycle Length and Variability

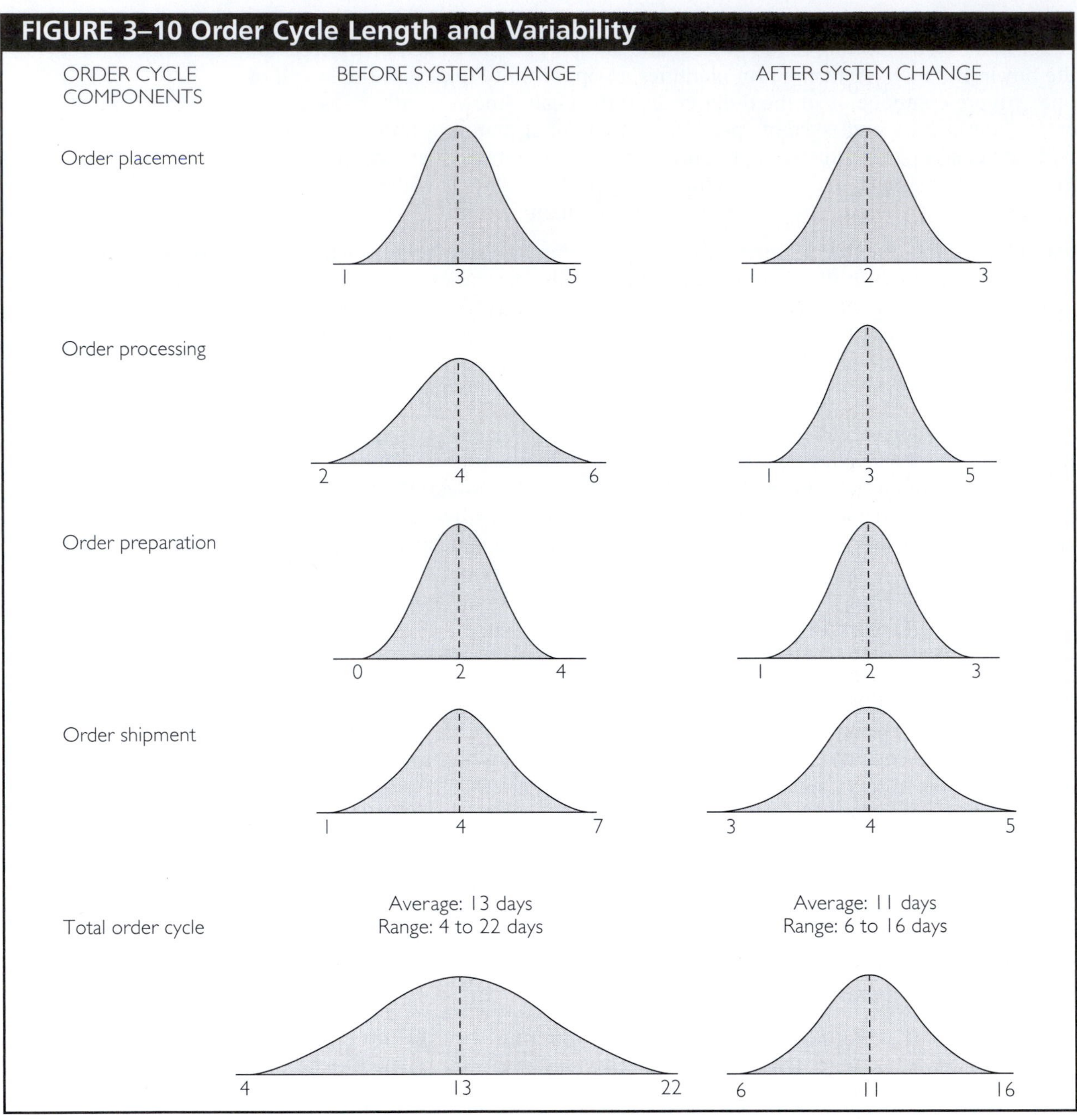

Source: Adapted from Douglas M. Lambert and James R. Stock, "Using Advanced Order-Processing Systems to Improve Profitability," *Business* (April–June 1982): 26.

Customer Service

No discussion of outbound logistics systems would be considered complete without the inclusion of customer service, since customer service is really the fuel that drives the logistics supply chain engine. Having the right product, at the right time, in the right quantity, without damage or loss, to the right customer is an underlying principle of logistics systems that recognizes the importance of customer service.

consumer awareness

Another aspect of customer service that deserves mention is the growing consumer awareness of the price/quality ratio and the special needs of today's consumers, who are time conscious and who demand flexibility. The 1980s and the 1990s evidenced a growing awareness of the special needs of consumers and the distribution network that serves them. Today's consumers are a different breed. They have high standards for quality, and brand loyalty is not necessarily something that they always support. Essentially, they want products at the best price, with the best level of service, and at times convenient to their schedules. Successful companies have adopted customer service approaches that recognize the importance of speed, flexibility, customization, and reliability.

The Logistics/Marketing Interface

Customer service is often the key link between logistics and marketing. If the logistics system, particularly outbound logistics, is not functioning properly and a customer does not receive a delivery as promised, the company could lose future sales. Remember that manufacturing can produce a good product at the right cost, and marketing can sell it; but if logistics does not deliver it when and where promised, the customer will be dissatisfied.

traditional view

We could consider this description of the relationship between logistics and marketing a traditional view. Figure 3–11 depicts this traditional role of customer service at the interface between marketing and logistics. The relationship manifests itself in this perspective through the "place" dimension of the marketing mix, which is often used synonymously with channel-of-distribution decisions and the associated customer service levels provided. In this context, logistics plays a static role that is based upon minimizing the total cost of the various logistics activities within a given set of service levels, most likely as dictated by marketing.

It is safe to say that this particular vision of logistics and its relationship to marketing is one that dominated the logistics literature in the years preceding what might be termed the "supply chain revolution." From this traditional point of view, the usual trade-off was seen as, "if we increase the level of customer service, then logistics costs will automatically increase."

new vision

An interesting example, however, is that of National Semiconductor, a company that reengineered its supply chain to reduce the overall cost of logistics. In so doing, this company also improved in-stock inventory levels, experienced shortened and more consistent order cycles, and significantly improved overall service to its global customers. This situation required a more dynamic, proactive approach that recognized the value-added role of logistics supply chains in creating and sustaining competitive advantage and providing win-win outcomes.

In an effort to promote the true competitive advantages that can arise from a well-run logistics operation, the chief financial officer of Compaq Computer suggested:

> We've done most of what we have to do to be more competitive. We've changed the way we develop products, manufacture, market, and advertise. The one piece of the puzzle that we haven't addressed is logistics. It's the next source of competitive advantage, and the possibilities are astounding.[12]

FIGURE 3–11 The Traditional Logistics/Marketing Interface

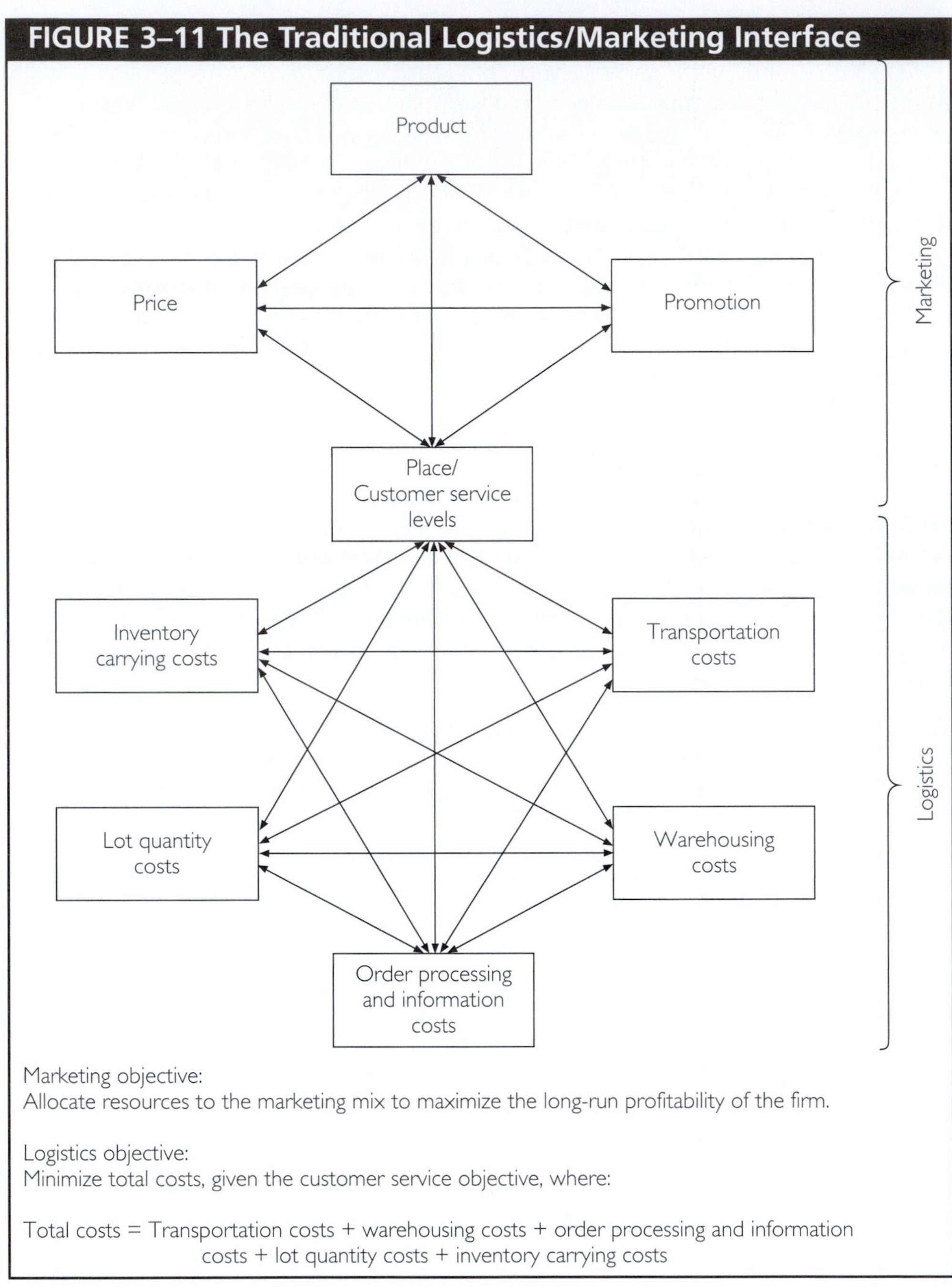

Marketing objective:
Allocate resources to the marketing mix to maximize the long-run profitability of the firm.

Logistics objective:
Minimize total costs, given the customer service objective, where:

Total costs = Transportation costs + warehousing costs + order processing and information costs + lot quantity costs + inventory carrying costs

Source: Adapted from Douglas M. Lambert, *The Development of an Inventory Costing Methodology: A Study of the Costs Associated with Holding Inventory* (Chicago: National Council of Physical Distribution Management, 1976), 7.

service adds value

This new perspective emphasizing value added is providing the basis for National Semiconductor and other companies—such as Sears, Procter & Gamble, Nabisco, Hershey, and Dell Computer—to improve both efficiency and effectiveness. Becton Dickinson (BD) is a good example of a company that has recognized the proactive, value-adding role of customer service in the logistics supply chain. BD has focused on managing the supply chain on an integrated basis, with the intent of providing high levels of customer service and high-quality goods to satisfy customers throughout its supply chain. Essentially, the company envisions delivering the best product and services at the lowest total system cost. Becton Dickinson's commitment to effective supply chain management resulted several years ago in the creation of a Supply Chain Services operating division of the company.[13]

Defining Customer Service

Anyone who has ever struggled to define *customer service* soon realized the difficulty of explaining this nebulous term. Thus, different people will understandably have different interpretations of just what customer service means.

levels of product

We can think of customer service as something a firm provides to those who purchase its products or services. According to marketers, there are three levels of product: (1) the core benefit or service, which constitutes what the buyer is really buying; (2) the tangible product, or the physical product or service itself; and (3) the augmented product, which includes benefits that are secondary to, but an integral enhancement to, the tangible product the customer is purchasing. In this context, we can think of logistical customer service as a feature of the augmented product that adds value for the buyer.[14] Other examples of augmented product features include installation, warranties, and after-sale service.

Extending our thinking along these lines, a firm could achieve a competitive advantage by providing superior levels of logistical customer service. Thus, a potential benefit exists in viewing customer service as a "product" that may add significant value for a buyer.

This view of logistics as it relates to the augmented product is quite consistent with the Becton Dickinson perspective and is one that in today's environment plays a major role in augmenting value along the supply chain. It may not be as exciting to some individuals, but the role is critical for success in the marketplace.

types of customer support/service

A fundamental point to recognize is that customer service is a concept whose importance reaches far beyond the logistics area. Customer service frequently affects every area of the firm by attempting to ensure customer satisfaction through the provision of aid or service to the customer.

Examples of the various forms that customer service may take include the following:

- Revamping a billing procedure to accommodate a customer's request
- Providing financial and credit terms
- Guaranteeing delivery within specified time periods
- Providing prompt and congenial sales representatives
- Extending the option to sell on consignment
- Providing material to aid in a customer's sales presentation
- Installing the product
- Maintaining satisfactory repair parts inventories

This section examines customer service within a logistics supply chain. However, customer service can, as the preceding list indicates, have many interpretations throughout the firm. The numerous nonlogistical aspects of customer service may add value for the customer, and a firm should include these aspects within its overall marketing effort.

levels of involvement

While customer service has no single widely used definition, customer service is often viewed in three principal ways. We can think of them as three levels of customer service involvement or awareness:[15]

definition

- *Customer service as an activity.* This level treats customer service as a particular task that a firm must accomplish to satisfy the customer's needs. Order processing, billing and invoicing, product returns, and claims handling are all typical examples of this level of customer service. Customer service departments, which basically handle customer problems and complaints, also represent this level of customer service.
- *Customer service as performance measures.* This level emphasizes customer service in terms of specific performance measures, such as the percentage of orders delivered on time and complete and the number of orders processed within acceptable time limits. Although this level enhances the first one, a firm must look beyond the performance measures themselves to ensure that its service efforts achieve actual customer satisfaction.
- *Customer service as a philosophy.* This level elevates customer service to a firm-wide commitment to providing customer satisfaction through superior customer service. This view of customer service is entirely consistent with many firms' contemporary emphasis on quality and quality management. Rather than narrowly viewing customer service as an activity or as a set of performance measures, this interpretation involves a dedication to customer service that pervades the entire firm and all of its activities.

The least important level of involvement for most companies would be viewing customer service simply as an activity. From this perspective, customer service activities in logistics are at the transactional level. For example, accepting product returns from customers in a retail store adds no value to product: it is merely a transaction to appease the customers. With the possible exception of making it extremely convenient for customers to return products, this level of customer service typically offers limited opportunities to add value for the customers.

The focus upon performance measures for customer service is very important because it provides a method of evaluating how well the logistics system is functioning. Over time, such measures provide benchmarks to gauge improvement, which is especially important when a firm is trying to implement a continuous improvement program. But this level of involvement is not sufficient.

The final level, customer service as a philosophy, broadens the role of customer service in the firm. However, this still may not be sufficient unless the value-added dimension is included as the goal of the corporate customer service philosophy.

The definition of customer service that is used in this text is as follows:

> Customer service is a process for providing competitive advantage and adding benefits to the supply chain in order to maximize the total value to the ultimate customer.

complexity of customer service

The customer service issue has many dimensions and is truly complex. A firm must fully control numerous customer service elements through effective business logistics management. Successfully implemented, high levels of logistics customer service can easily become a strategic way for a company to differentiate itself from its competitors.

Elements of Customer Service

Customer service is an important basis for incurring logistics costs. Economic advantages generally accrue to the customer through better supplier service. As an example, a supplier can lower customer inventories by utilizing air rather than truck transportation. Lower inventory costs result from air transport's lower transit time, which will lower order cycle time, but the transportation costs will be higher than those for truck transportation. The supplier's logistics manager must balance the high service level the customer desires and the benefits the supplier may gain from possible increased sales against the cost of providing that service. The logistics manager must strike a balance among customer service levels, total logistics costs, and total benefits to the firm. However, as the National Semiconductor example illustrated, there are situations where cost can be lowered and service improved.

food industry example

The food industry illustrates the importance of customer service factors and how they will probably change over time. Table 3–2 lists customer service factors that are important in the food industry. The first column is for 1995; the second column projected customer expectations for 2000. If the table provided data from another industry, the percentages would probably be different, but the upward direction of customer service standards would be the same. Companies both within and outside of the food industry implement such improvements in response to market pressures, and lower costs frequently accompany these improvements.

four main dimensions

Customer service has multifunctional interest for a company; but, from the point of view of the logistics function, we can view customer service as having four traditional dimensions: time, dependability, communications, and convenience. This section explores the ways in which these elements affect the cost centers of both buyer and seller firms.

Time. The *time* factor is usually order cycle time, particularly from the perspective of the seller looking at customer service. On the other hand, the buyer usually refers to the time dimension as the lead time, or replenishment time. Regardless of the perspective or the terminology, several basic components or variables affect the time factor.

control over lead time

Successful logistics operations today have a high degree of control over most, if not all, of the basic elements of lead time, including order processing, order preparation, and order shipment. By effectively managing activities such as these, thus

TABLE 3–2 Customer Service Elements for the Food Industry

Element	1995	2000
Product availability	98%	99%
Order cycle time	9 days	7 days
Complete orders shipped	90%	94%
Accurate invoices provided	90% of invoices	93%
Damaged products	1%	0.5%

Sources: Grocery Manufacturers of America and A. T. Kearney, *Customer Service Data for Food Industry* (1995), 5. Used with permission.

ensuring that order cycles will be of reasonable length and consistent duration, seller firms have improved the customer service levels that they provide to buyers. National Semiconductor Company, discussed previously, is a good example of a firm achieving a significant reduction in order cycle time.

Modifying all of the elements that contribute to lead time may be too costly. The firm may therefore make modifications in one area and permit the others to operate at existing levels. For example, investing in automated materials-handling equipment may be financially unwise for the firm. To compensate for its higher manual order-processing time, the firm could switch from fax to Internet-enabled order transmittal and use motor transportation instead of rail. This would permit the firm to reduce lead time without increasing its capital investment in automated materials-handling equipment.

Guaranteeing a given level of lead time is an important advancement in logistics management. We may see its impact in the efficiencies that accrue both to the customer (inventory costs) and to the seller's logistics system and market position. But the concept of time, by itself, means little without dependability.

Dependability. To some customers, *dependability* can be more important than lead time. The customer can minimize its inventory level if lead time is fixed. That is, a customer that knows with 100 percent assurance that lead time is ten days could adjust its inventory levels to correspond to the average demand (usage) during the ten days and would have no need for safety stock to guard against stockouts resulting from fluctuating lead times.

inventory level and stockout costs

Cycle time. Lead time dependability, then, directly affects the customer's inventory level and stockout costs. Providing a dependable lead time reduces some of the uncertainty a customer faces. A seller who can assure the customer of a given level of lead time, plus some tolerance, distinctly differentiates its product from that of its competitor. The seller that provides a dependable lead time permits the buyer to minimize the total cost of inventory, stockouts, order processing, and production scheduling.

Figure 3–12 graphs a frequency distribution pertaining to overall lead time, measured in days. The graph is bimodal. It indicates that lead time tends to be in the vicinity of either four days or twelve days. The customer typically receives within four days orders that the seller can fill from stock. Orders that the seller cannot fill from available stock, and for which the customer must place a back order, typically result in a total order cycle time of approximately twelve days.

Dependability encompasses more than just lead time variability. More generally, dependability refers to delivering a customer's order with a regular, consistent lead time; in safe condition; and in harmony with the type and quality of items the customer ordered.

Safe delivery. An order's safe delivery is the ultimate goal of any logistics system. As was noted earlier, the logistics function is the culmination of the selling function. If goods arrive damaged or are lost, the customer cannot use the goods as intended. A shipment containing damaged goods aggravates several customer cost centers—inventory, production, and marketing.

lost profits

Receiving a damaged shipment deprives the customer of items for sale or production. This may increase stockout costs in the form of foregone profits or production. To guard against these costs, the customer must increase inventory levels.

FIGURE 3–12 Example of the Frequency Distribution of Lead Time

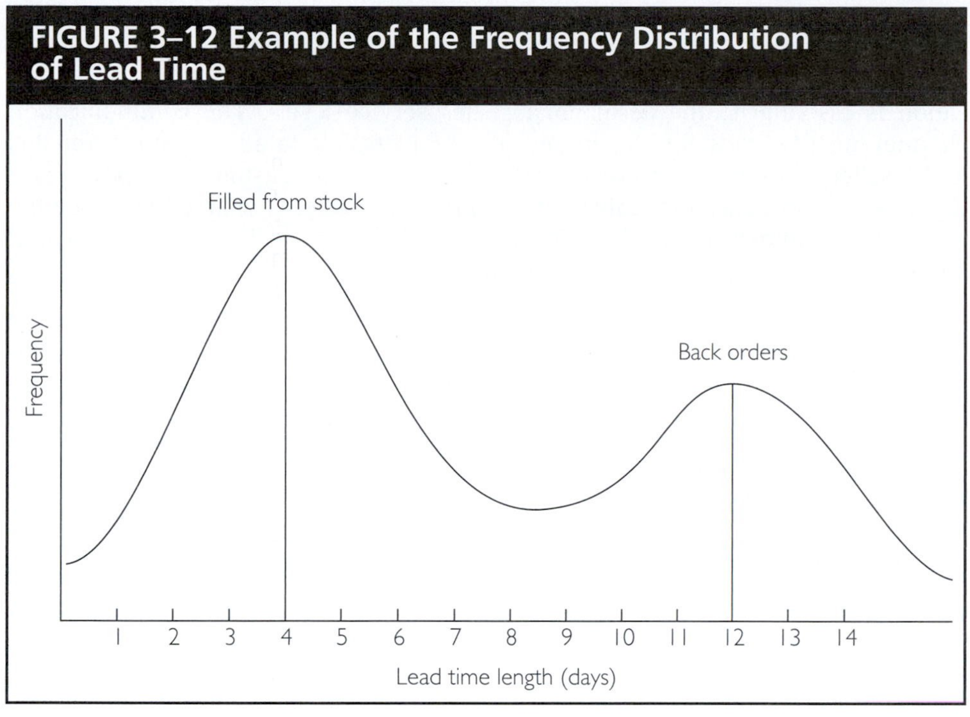

Thus, unsafe delivery causes the buyer to incur higher inventory carrying costs or to forego profits or production. This situation would be unacceptable for a company interested in minimizing or eliminating inventories through some form of just-in-time program.

claims

In addition to the preceding costs, an unsafe delivery may cause the customer to incur the cost of filing a claim with the carrier or returning the damaged item to the seller for repair or credit. (Depending upon the FOB terms of sale and other sales agreement stipulations, the seller, not the buyer, may be responsible for these costs.) The seller will probably be aware of these two costs, since the seller will be more or less directly involved in any corrective actions that may be necessary.

lost sales or lost production

Correct orders. Finally, dependability embraces the correct filling of orders. A customer who has been anxiously awaiting the arrival of an urgently needed shipment may discover upon receiving the shipment that the seller made an error in filling the order. The customer who has not received what was requested may face potential lost sales or production. An improperly filled order forces the customer to reorder, if the customer is not angry enough to buy from another supplier. If a customer who is an intermediary in the marketing channel experiences a stockout, the stockout cost (lost sales) also directly affects the seller.

order information

Communications. The two logistics activities vital to order filling are the communication of customer order information to the order-filling area and the actual process of picking out of inventory the items ordered. In the order information stage, the use of EDI or Internet-enabled communications can reduce errors in transferring order information from the order to the warehouse receipt. The seller should simplify product identification such as product codes in order to reduce order picker errors.

seller-customer channel

However, customer contact can be as important as accurate, electronic flow of information between buyers and sellers. Communication with customers is vital to monitoring customer service levels relating to dependability. Customer communication is essential to the design of logistics service levels. The communication channel must be constantly open and readily accessible to all customers, for this is the seller's link to the major external constraints that customers impose upon logistics. Without customer contact, the logistics manager is unable to provide the most efficient and economical service; in other words, the logistics manager would be playing the ball game without fully knowing the rules.

two-way street

However, communication must be a two-way street. The seller must be able to transmit vital logistics service information to the customer. For example, the supplier would be well advised to inform the buyer of potential service level reductions so that the buyer can make necessary operational adjustments.

In addition, many customers request information on the logistics status of shipments. Questions concerning shipment date, the carrier, or the route, for example, are not uncommon. The customer, who needs this information to plan operations, expects the logistics manager to provide answers on a timely basis.

flexibility

Convenience. *Convenience* is another way of saying that the logistics service level must be flexible. From the logistics operations standpoint, having one or a few standard service levels that applies to all customers would be ideal; but this assumes that all customers' logistics requirements are homogeneous. In reality, this is not the situation. For example, one customer may require the seller to palletize and ship all shipments by rail; another may require truck delivery only, with no palletization; still others may request special delivery times. Basically, logistics requirements differ with regard to packaging, the mode and carrier the customer requires, routing, and delivery times.

different customer requirements

Convenience recognizes customers' different requirements. A seller can usually group customer requirements by such factors as customer size, market area, and the product line the customer is purchasing. This grouping, or market segmentation, enables the logistics manager to recognize customer service requirements and to attempt to fulfill those demands as economically as possible.

customer profitability

We can attribute the need for convenience in logistics service levels to the differing consequences the service levels have for different customers. More specifically, the cost of lost sales will differ among the customer groups. For example, a customer purchasing 30 percent of a firm's output loses more sales for the firm than a customer buying less than 0.01 percent of the firm's output does. Also, the degree of competitiveness in market areas will differ; highly competitive market areas will require a higher service level than less-competitive market areas will. The profitability of different product lines in a firm's market basket will limit the service level the firm can offer; that is, a firm may provide a lower service level for low-profit product lines.

However, the logistics manager must place the convenience factor in proper operational perspective. At the extreme, meeting the convenience needs of customers would mean providing a specific service level policy for each customer. Such a situation would set the stage for operational chaos; the plethora of service level policies would prevent the logistics manager from optimizing the logistics function. The need for flexibility in service level policies is warranted, but the logistics manager should restrict this flexibility to easily identifiable customer groups and must examine the trade-off between the benefits (improved sales and profits or elimination of lost profits) and the costs associated with unique service levels in each specific situation.

Performance Measures for Customer Service

The four traditional dimensions of customer service from a logistics perspective—time, dependability, convenience, and communication—are essential considerations in developing a sound and effective customer service program. These dimensions of customer service also provide the underlying basis for establishing standards of performance for customer service in the logistics area.

Table 3–3 expands these four elements into a format that has been used by companies in developing customer service policy and performance measurement standards. The traditional performance measures that have been used are stated in the right-hand column. Typically, such measures were stated from the perspective of the seller, for example, orders shipped on time, orders shipped complete, product availability when an order was received, order preparation time, and so on.

TABLE 3–3 Elements and Measurement of Customer Service

Element	Brief Description	Typical Measurement Unit(s)
Product availability	The most common measure of customer service. Usually defined as percent in stock (target performance level) in some base unit (i.e., order, product, dollars).	% availability in base units
Order cycle time	Elapsed time from order placement to order receipt. Usually measured in time units and variation from standard or target order cycle. Note: Frequently, product availability and order cycle time are combined into one standard. For example, "95 percent of orders delivered within 10 days."	Speed and consistency
Distribution system flexibility	Ability of system to respond to special and/or unexpected needs of customer. Includes expedite and substitute capability.	Response time to special requests
Distribution system information	Ability of firm's information system to respond in timely and accurate manner to customers' requests for information.	Speed, accuracy, and message detail of response
Distribution system malfunction	Efficiency of procedures and time required to recover from distribution system malfunction (i.e., errors in billing, shipping, damage, claims).	Response and recovery time requirements
Postsale product support	Efficiency in providing product support after delivery, including technical information, spare parts, or equipment modification, as appropriate.	Response time, quality of response

Source: Reprinted with the permission of The Free Press, a division of Simon & Schuster, Inc., from *The Distribution Handbook,* James F. Robeson and Robert G. House, editors. Copyright © 1985 by The Free Press.

The new supply chain environment for customer service has resulted in much more rigorous standards of performance. The performance measures are now stated from the point of view of the customer:

- Orders received on time
- Orders received complete
- Orders received damage free
- Orders filled accurately
- Orders billed accurately

If the seller is concerned only with customer service prior to shipping, as per traditional measures, the buyer may not be satisfied and the seller may not know it, because of problems occurring during the delivery process. Furthermore, the seller using traditional measures would have no basis upon which to evaluate the extent and magnitude of the problem. The current approach, focusing the measurement at the delivery level, not only provides the database to make an evaluation but also, and perhaps more importantly, provides an early warning of problems as they are developing. For example, if the standard for on-time delivery is 98 percent and it slips during a given month to 95 percent, an investigation may show that a carrier is not following instructions or even that the buyer is at fault by not being ready to accept shipments.

delivery time windows

The on-time delivery measure is even more demanding today because buyers often give appointment times for warehouse and/or store deliveries on the outbound side of logistics. For example, the move to just-in-time manufacturing has necessitated the establishment of sometimes very narrow delivery time "windows" for vendors. Overall, making deliveries on time is much more difficult currently and will be even tougher in the future.

Another aspect of the supply chain environment is that the excellent companies are using multiple measures of customer service simultaneously. Using multiple measures makes it much more difficult to achieve high levels of customer service. For example, assume that a company was using only one of the following:

95 percent of orders delivered on time

93 percent of orders filled completely

97 percent of orders delivered damage free

Achieving one of these performance levels—for example, 95 percent of orders delivered on time—would be challenging but very possible by focusing upon the activities necessary to attain the required performance. But trying to achieve all three performance levels simultaneously for every order and to attain a "perfect order" level like 95 percent would be difficult. For example, even if a company hit each of the preceding standards individually, it might find its perfect order measure to be 72 percent or less because the misses would not occur at the same time for a single order. That is, an order might be on time and damage free, but it might not be complete because of a stockout. Consequently, it would not be a perfect order. Achieving a perfect order performance level of 95 percent with three or more measures being utilized simultaneously is indicative of the requirements of today's supply chain environment.

Implementing Customer Service Standards

setting standards

This section highlights the keys for successfully developing and implementing customer service standards.

The first point is to be wary of adopting easily achievable performance standards; such standards may be too low to be of practical value. While setting and adhering to a meaningful standard should help to differentiate your firm from the competition, setting standards at unrealistically low levels will not help to establish a competitive advantage.

levels of quality

Second, some current management philosophies—such as an emphasis on total quality or on creation of the "perfect order"—are very critical of any acceptable quality level set below 100 percent. This does not mean that a firm can achieve 100 percent performance at all times, for the use of 100 percent represents an attitude more than a measurement. From a practical viewpoint, however, establishing a desired quality level that is less than 100 percent will generally limit, rather than encourage, superior performance.

communication with customers

Third, the firm should develop customer service policies and standards through customer consultation. After adopting these standards, the firm should formally communicate them to customers. Certain firms prefer to keep silent about their customer service standards and avoid letting their customers know their exact policies and performance targets. The best approach, however, is to communicate these policies and standards to customers very openly.

control of customer service

Fourth, the firm should develop procedures to measure, monitor, and control the customer service quality called for by the firm's performance measures and standards. Using techniques such as statistical process control (SPC), obtaining feedback, and taking corrective action are essential to success. When customer service standards are ineffective, the firm should not hesitate to amend or discontinue them as appropriate.

Summary of Customer Service

It would be difficult to summarize all the discussion and analysis related to customer service that have been presented here. In an attempt to capture some important overall points about customer service, we offer the following observations:

- If the basics of customer service are not in place, nothing else matters.
- Customers may define service differently.
- All customer accounts are not the same.
- Relationships are not one-dimensional.
- Partnerships and added value can "lock up" customers.

Figure 3–13 offers a more comprehensive view of the issues related to customer service. This list of questions can be used as a guide in developing a sound customer service policy and statement of appropriate standards of performance. The questions posed in Figure 3–13 can also be answered by a cross-functional team to develop a consensus in the area of customer service.

FIGURE 3–13 Customer Service Issues

- What do our customers feel about present levels of service?
- Do their perceptions match up with ours?
- How do our services compare to those of our competitors?
- Are we using appropriate standards and measurements to monitor our service performance?
- Is it possible to segment our customers according to the varying degrees of service they require?
- Can we produce the same levels of service we are presently providing in a more cost-effective manner?
- Can improved customer service be used as a strategic weapon to provide an important competitive advantage?
- In the minds of our customers, how important is service compared to other elements of the marketing mix, such as price, promotion, and products?

Expected Cost of Stockouts

A principal benefit of inventory availability and, hence, of customer service is to reduce the incidence of stockouts. Once we develop a convenient way to calculate the cost of a stockout, we can use stockout probability information to determine the expected stockout cost. Last, we can analyze alternative customer service levels directly by comparing the expected cost of stockouts with the revenue-enhancing benefits of customer service.

This section examines stockout issues that relate more to finished goods inventories than to inventories of raw materials or component parts. Calculating stockout costs for finished goods is generally more formidable than calculating these costs for raw materials. We must, however, address issues relating to both of these inventory types. An earlier section of this chapter dealt specifically with inbound logistics supplies and stockout costs.

effects of stockouts

A *stockout* occurs when desired quantities of finished goods are not available when and where a customer needs them. When a seller is unable to satisfy demand with available inventory, one of four possible events may occur: (1) the customer waits until the product is available; (2) the customer back orders the product; (3) the seller loses a sale; or (4) the seller loses a customer. From the viewpoint of most companies, these four outcomes are listed from best to worst in terms of desirability and cost impact. Theoretically, scenario 1 (customer waits) should cost nothing; this situation is more likely to occur where product substitutability is very low.

Back Order

nature of cost

A company having to back order an item that is out of stock will incur expenses for special order processing and transportation. The extra order processing traces the back order's movement, in addition to the normal processing for regular replenishments. The customer usually incurs extra transportation charges because a back order is typically a smaller shipment and often incurs higher rates. Also, the seller may need to ship the back-ordered item a longer distance—for example, from a plant or warehouse in another region of the country. In addition, the seller may need to ship the back order by a faster and more expensive means of transportation. Therefore, we could estimate the back-order cost by analyzing the additional order processing and additional transportation expense. If customers always back ordered out-of-stock items, the seller could use this analysis to estimate the cost of stockouts. The seller could then compare this cost with the cost of carrying excess inventory.

Lost Sales

direct loss

Most firms find that although some customers may prefer a back order, others will turn to alternative supply sources. In other words, most companies have competitors who produce substitute products; and, when one source does not have an item available, the customer will order that item from another source. In such cases, the stockout has caused a lost sale. The seller's direct loss is the loss of profit on the item that was unavailable when the customer wanted it. Thus, a seller can determine direct loss by calculating profit on one item and multiplying it by the number the customer ordered. For example, if the order was for 100 units and the profit is $10 per unit, the loss is $1,000.

special explanation

Three additional points about lost sales follow. First, in addition to the lost profit, we might include an amount for the cost of the salesperson who made the initial sale. The sales effort was wasted and in that sense was an opportunity loss. Whether including such a cost is valid would depend upon whether the company uses salespeople in its marketing effort. Second, determining the amount of a lost sale may be difficult in some circumstances. For example, numerous companies customarily take orders by telephone. A customer may initially just inquire about an item's availability without specifying how much is desired. If an item is out of stock, the customer may never indicate a quantity and the seller will not know the amount of the loss. Other problems may cause difficulties but are not insurmountable. For example, although developing a system for recording lost sales in telephone-order situations is often difficult, a seller can overcome this problem through sampling techniques. Third, estimating how a particular stockout will affect future sales within other product lines is difficult.

calculation

In the likely event that a firm will sustain lost sales with inventory stockouts, the firm will have to assign a cost along the lines we suggested earlier. Then the firm should analyze the number of stockouts it could expect with different inventory levels. An example of this technique is given later. The seller should then multiply the expected number of lost sales by the profit loss plus additional assigned cost, if any, and compare the cost with the cost of carrying safety stock.

Lost Customer

cost of lost customer

The third possible event that can occur because of a stockout is the loss of a customer; that is, the customer permanently switches to another supplier. A supplier who loses a customer loses a future stream of income. Estimating the customer loss that stockouts can cause is difficult. Marketing researchers have attempted to analyze brand switching for some time. Such analysis often uses management science techniques along with more qualitative marketing research methods. This is usually the most difficult loss to estimate because of the need to estimate how many units the customer may have purchased in the future.

Determining the Expected Cost of Stockouts

procedure

To make an informed decision as to how much inventory to carry, a firm must determine the expected cost it will incur if a stockout occurs. That is, how much money will the firm lose if a stockout occurs?

The first step is to identify a stockout's potential consequences. These include a back order, a lost sale, and a lost customer. The second step is to calculate each result's expense or loss of profit and then to estimate the cost of a single stockout. For the purposes of this discussion, assume the following: 70 percent of all stockouts result in a back order, and a back order requires extra handling costs of $6.00; 20 percent result in a lost sale for the item, and this loss equals $20.00 in lost profit margin; and 10 percent result in a lost customer, or a loss of $200.00.

Calculate the overall impact as follows:

	70% of $ 6.00 =	$ 4.20
	20% of $ 20.00 =	4.00
	10% of $200.00 =	20.00
Total =	estimated cost per stockout =	$28.20

Since $28.20 is the average dollar amount the firm can save by averting a stockout, the firm should carry additional inventory to protect against stockouts only as long as carrying the additional inventory costs less than $28.20.

A firm can easily use this information when formally evaluating two or more logistics system alternatives. For each alternative, the firm would need to estimate the potential number of stockouts and to multiply those numbers by the estimated cost of a single stockout. This would represent a way to include stockout costs in the overall decision-making process.

CHANNELS OF DISTRIBUTION

A *channel of distribution* consists of one or more companies or individuals who participate in the flow of goods, services, information, and finances from the producer to the final user or consumer. This encompasses a variety of intermediary firms, including those that we classify as wholesalers or retailers. Since most companies find that distribution channel decisions are critical to their overall success, this topic should be an educational priority for all corporate managers. In the logistics area, understanding and appreciating the area of channels is a prerequisite to effective strategy formulation, operations, and control.

types of channels

Managing distribution channels requires firms to coordinate and integrate logistics and marketing activities in a manner consistent with overall corporate strategy. Two channels, the logistical channel and the marketing channel, are highly related. The *logistical channel* refers to the means by which products flow physically from where they are available to where they are needed. The *marketing channel* refers to the means by which necessary transactional elements are managed (e.g., customer orders, billing, accounts receivable, etc.). These two channels are illustrated in Figure 3–14.

Effective channel management necessitates a good grasp of the management alternatives and guiding principles applicable to each of these. We should also note the four basic functions of logistical channel members: sorting out, accumulating, allocating, and assorting. We can classify channel systems as either direct or indirect, and we can further subdivide indirect channels into traditional and vertical marketing systems (VMS). With the VMS, some degree of implicit or explicit relationship exists among the firms in the channel and firms in the channel have considerable opportunity to coordinate their activities. As channel members begin to collaborate effectively on matters relating to logistics, the VMS evidences growth in the duration of true supply chain management.

Using the grocery industry as an example, Figures 3–15 shows the numerous channels of distribution that are responsible for delivering these products to consumers. While it is true that several of these channels may compete with one another, collectively

FIGURE 3–14 Logistical and Marketing Channels

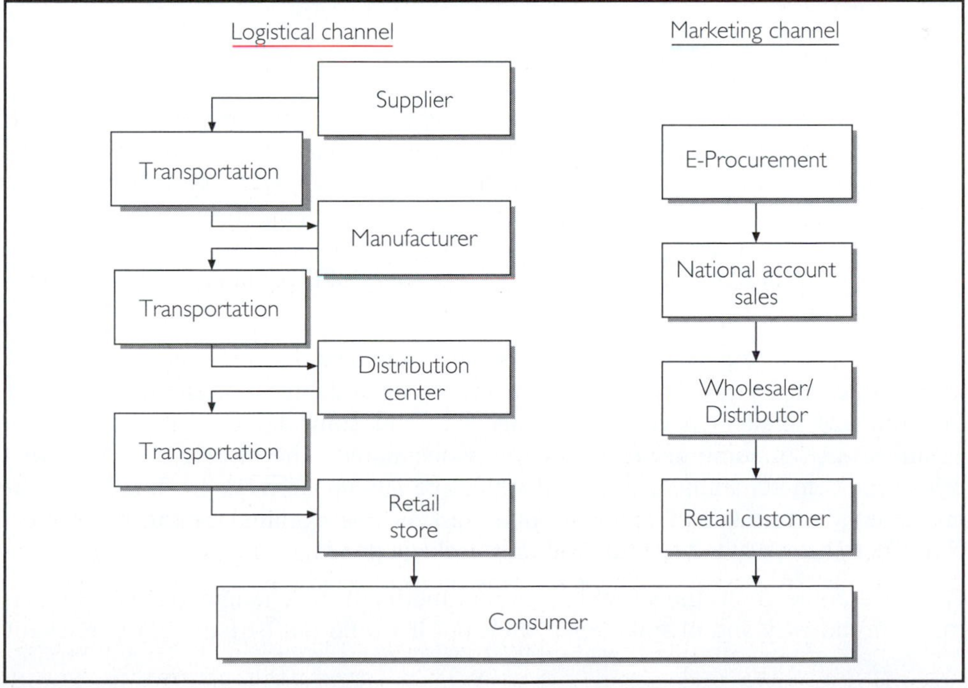

FIGURE 3–15 Examples of Channels of Distribution for the Food Products Manufacturing Industry

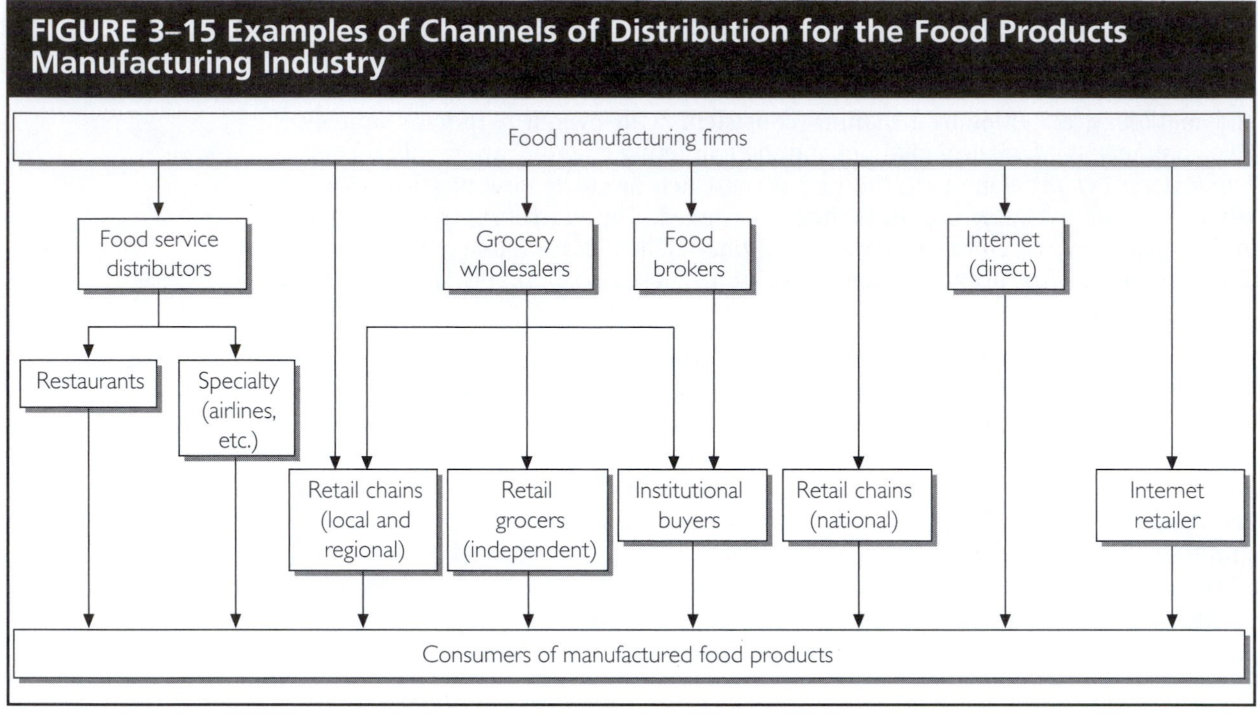

they provide the consumer with a significant members of choice as to where and how to purchase grocery products. Each individual channel represents a unique path from grocery manufacturer to consumer, and a set of effective logistics strategies must be developed for each channel.

The Growth and Importance of Channels of Distribution

A virtual revolution has been occurring in the ranks of the companies that make up the distribution industry, which we have referred to as channels of distribution. Nowhere has this been more apparent than at the retail level, with the dramatic growth in companies that are usually called mass merchandisers, such as Wal-Mart, Kmart, Sears, and Target; the category retailers, for example, Toys R Us, Home Depot, and Staples; and an emerging number of E-commerce retailers, such as Amazon.com.

Much has been written about the mass merchandisers and club stores and their impact upon many small- and medium-size towns and cities where the small- and medium-size retailers have been "squeezed" and some forced out of business. "Main Street" in some instances has been decimated. The more efficient, lower-priced mass merchandisers have a competitive advantage over the smaller retailers. Even the number of regional supermarkets has declined as the mass merchandisers have expanded into food and package goods.

We could argue about the social impact and merits of the changing face of the distribution industry and of small-town USA, but it would not be particularly relevant to our focus on outbound logistics systems. However, this trend toward larger, more efficient retailers has also had a major economic impact on logistics supply chains.

The mass merchandisers and other large retailers have changed the nature of logistics, leading to what some have called the Wal-Mart effect, by demanding customized or tailored logistics systems to meet their particular needs. Historically, the large manufacturers with successful brands, such as Procter & Gamble, General Foods, Nabisco, Hershey, and so on, exercised the most influence and power in the flow of goods to the ultimate consumers. They tended to emphasize product development and brand management with homogeneous (vanilla) logistics systems to all customers.

unique customer requirements

The "new retailers" revolted against this convention. They were not willing to accept the same treatment as JoPa's Deli and Grocery in Brooklyn. They demanded special service, such as scheduled deliveries, special pallet packs, advance shipment notice, cross-docking capability, and so on. They wanted high-quality, specialized logistics services with the lowest possible prices for the products they were purchasing. This revolution was similar to the consumer revolution that we discussed earlier, with its demand for high quality, lowest price, and maximum flexibility.

The 1980s and particularly the 1990s were characterized by a rash of logistics-related strategies and tactics that were developed largely in response to the customer and consumer revolution. Efficient consumer response (ECR), vendor-managed inventories (VMI), continuous replenishment (CR), direct store delivery (DSD), everyday low pricing (EDLP), supply chain management (SCM), quick response (QR), and others are illustrative of the developments and changes that occurred.

The successful retailers have based much of their efficiency upon good logistics systems. Wal-Mart is frequently lauded in logistics circles for its efficiencies in warehousing (cross-docking), transportation, materials handling, and other logistics processes. The new retailers understand the importance of good logistics and know that it gives them business power. Sears Merchandise Group hired Gus Pagonis, the retired three-star general and logistics hero of the Gulf War, who managed that 7,000-mile supply chain. He was brought in to reengineer the logistics system at Sears and has made major strides in this direction.

IKEA, the Swedish furnishings company, is another example of a super retailer who has expanded into a giant enterprise with efficient logistics and good business acumen. IKEA has grown from a small Swedish mail-order operation to the largest retailer of home furnishings in the world, with over 100 stores and revenues near $5 billion. Its logistics operation is the featured centerpiece of its global business system, with a network of fourteen warehouses that link to point-of-sales data in all the stores. The warehouses operate as logistical control points, consolidation centers, and transit hubs. They play a proactive part in the integration of supply and demand, decreasing the need to provide storage for production runs, anticipate retail demand, and eliminate storage.

It is fair to say that the large retailers, wholesalers, and other channel members are reshaping the logistics of supply chains in conjunction with manufacturers and third-party providers. Distributors are key members of many supply chains. Overall, the traditional role of channels of distribution is not an accurate reflection of their importance and scope of influence. They not only help with change, they create change.

SUMMARY

- Outbound-to-customer logistics systems have received the most attention in many companies; but, even in today's customer service environment, outbound and inbound logistics systems must be coordinated.
- Demand management may be thought of as "focused efforts to estimate and manage customers' demand, with the intention of using this information to shape operating decisions."
- Supply-demand misalignment may cause severe problems in the outbound-to-customer logistics channel. Causes of these problems should be identified and removed.
- There is growing and persuasive evidence that understanding and managing market demand is a central determinant of business success.
- Although many forecasts are made throughout the supply chain, the forecast of primary demand from the end user or consumer will be the most important. It is essential that this demand information be shared with trading partners throughout the supply chain and be the basis for collaborative decision making.
- There are various approaches to forecasting, each serving different purposes.
- The recent popularity of CPFR has led companies to more meaningful and productive sharing of forecast information on an inter-firm basis.
- The three critical elements of collaborative planning are collaborative demand planning, joint capacity planning, and synchronized order fulfillment.
- Significant attention needs to be directed to individual elements of the order cycle, the length and variability of each, and the overall performance of the order cycle.
- E-commerce fulfillment creates a number of unique challenges for logistics management.
- Customer service is an area of key interest to both marketing and logistics. Effective customer service represents a key way to create value for the customer.
- Customer service may be viewed in three ways—as an activity, as a performance measure, and as a philosophy.
- To be efficient and effective in providing and managing customer service, we have to provide performance standards and measure performance against these standards. Many standards have been used historically, and current priorities are on making sure they focus on the needs of the buyer as well as the seller.
- Having inventory available reduces the likelihood of stockouts. In the event of an out-of-stock situation, there are a number of costs that may be incurred by the manufacturer. These cost types should be identified, and the expected cost of stockouts should be estimated in advance.
- There are a number of distribution channel alternatives that may be considered by companies today. Effective management of the various choices requires coordination and integration of marketing and logistics activities within the firm, as well as coordination of overall channel-wide activities across the firms in the channel.

STUDY QUESTIONS

1. Why may it be that outbound logistics systems are viewed in some firms as being of greater importance than inbound logistics systems?
2. How do outbound logistics systems relate directly to needs of the customer?
3. How can demand management help to unify channel members, help to satisfy customers, and solve customer problems?
4. What are some of the logistical problems that may arise when supply and demand for a product are not aligned properly?
5. What are the basic types of traditional forecasts? How does collaborative planning, forecasting, and replenishment (CPFR) differ from these traditional approaches?
6. What are the critical elements of collaborative planning? What benefits do they provide for the supply chain?
7. What are the four elements of the order cycle? Why is it important to understand and measure the length and variability of each?
8. In what ways do the challenges of E-commerce order fulfillment impact traditional logistics responsibilities?
9. Customer service is frequently viewed as the primary interface between logistics and marketing. Discuss the nature of this interface and how it may be changing.
10. What is meant by the term "augmented" product? How does this concept relate to customer service and logistics?
11. Companies can have three levels of involvement with respect to customer service. What are these, and what is the importance of each?
12. Discuss the nature and importance of the four logistics-related elements of customer service.
13. Effective management of customer service requires measurement. Discuss the nature of performance measures used in the customer service area.
14. What events may occur when a company is out of stock of a needed product? How may the cost of a stockout be estimated?
15. What is the role of channels of distribution in the outbound logistics system? How has this role been changing in recent years?

NOTES

1. Ernst & Young, *Supply Chain Management in the Connected Economy* (Proceedings of Advantage '99: Accelerating Supply Chain Innovations, 1999), 19.
2. Ibid., 21.

3. Roger D. Blackwell and Kristina Blackwell, "The Century of the Consumer: Converting Supply Chains into Demand Chains," *Supply Chain Management Review* 3, no. 3 (Fall 1999): 22–32.

4. Ibid., 32.

5. Jim R. Langabeer II, "Aligning Demand Management with Business Strategy," *Supply Chain Management Review* (May/June 2000): 66–72.

6. This example provides an excellent contrast between the value of demand information for tactical versus strategic purposes and was adapted from Jim R. Langabeer II, ibid., 69.

7. CPFR® is a registered trademark of the Voluntary Interindustry Commerce Standards (VICS) Association. Much of this information on CPFR has been adapted from Kevin P. Francella, "Will CPFR Supplant ECR?" *Food Logistics* (September 1998): 10.

8. CPFR results information was available at http://www.syncra.com

9. Bernard J. LaLonde and Paul H. Zinszer, *Customer Service: Meaning and Measurement* (Oak Brook, Ill.: Council of Logistics Management, 1976), 119.

10. Fred R. Ricker and Ravi Kalakota, "Order Fulfillment: The Hidden Key to E-Commerce Success," *Supply Chain Management Review* (Fall 1999): 60–70.

11. Ibid.

12. Ronald Henkoff, "Delivering the Goods," *Fortune* (28 November 1994): 64–78.

13. Becton Dickinson and Company, Annual Report, 1994.

14. Philip Kotler, *Marketing Management*, 5th ed. (Englewood Cliffs, N.J.: Prentice-Hall, 1990), 225–26.

15. Bernard J. LaLonde, "Customer Service," Chapter 11 in *The Distribution Handbook* (New York: The Free Press, 1985), 243.

Case 3–1 ■ Walton Seed Company

"We have to do something about our customer service levels and our inventory turns," complained Lisa Williams, CEO for Walton Seed Company, to Jason Greaser, the new director of logistics. Jason immediately wanted to know the details of the problem, since he had just joined Walton Seed and had not had an opportunity to really delve into any of its problems. Lisa responded, "Let me give you some of the background and you can put that education to use that you received at Penn State."

Jason smiled and said, "I am really interested in addressing some of the major problems and issues that Walton Seed has in the logistics area, so I can put my education and experience to good use. We had a similar problem at CBL Electronics, where I did my internship. While I realize that the products are different, there may be some common threads."

Background

Walton Seed Company was founded by Eric Walton in Toledo, Ohio, and subsequently moved to York, Pennsylvania. Traditionally, Walton's niche was as a high-quality seed company selling grass, flower, and vegetable seeds through a mail-order catalog. But it subsequently started to distribute through small, family-owned hardware and variety stores. As the business grew, the company expanded its distribution to several smaller wholesalers, who gave Walton additional market coverage in Ohio, Indiana, Illinois, and New York. Walton still continued its catalog business in the Middle Atlantic states and served retailers directly in Pennsylvania, Maryland, and New Jersey.

The seed business is such that sales are traditionally very heavy in the spring and early summer and drop off dramatically for the rest of the year. Catalog sales help to spread out demand a little by making sales promotions in the January/February mailing, when people start thinking "spring" to help get through the winter; but, overall, sales are still very concentrated. Therefore, Walton pushes inventory out into its warehouse during the fall and winter to be ready for the big spring and summer sales spurt.

During the season, the company runs out of certain types of seeds and has an abundance of others. The wholesalers and retailers complain about the stockouts. Sometimes they will accept substitutions but not often enough. The wholesalers and retailers do not provide in-season sales information and tend to buy large quantities prior to the start of the season.

Another matter worrying Lisa Williams is the decline in the number of independent hardware and variety stores, with the growth of Wal-Mart, Home Depot, Lowe's, and others of similar size. Walton does not sell to those stores, directly or indirectly, because Walton has positioned itself at the higher end of the market with high-quality seeds.

Walton really wants to increase its late summer and fall sales of grass seeds and perennial flower seeds, to spread out demand and also to avoid stockouts, which result in lost sales and customers.

The Problem

"Well, Jason, there you have it in a nutshell," said Lisa. "It is an exasperating situation, and we need your help in solving these problems."

"Wow, you are right!" replied Jason, "There are really challenging issues; I won't be able to claim that you didn't give me anything significant to sink my teeth into. Do you have anything specific that you want me to start with, since this is such a comprehensive set of problems?"

Case Questions

Here are the questions Lisa wants Jason to answer:

1. How can we improve in-season sales forecasting and develop a logistics system that is more responsive to demand and sales?
2. What are some of the special logistical issues that we will need to consider if we attempt to sell to the mass merchandisers?
3. What standard(s) of performance should we use for measuring customer service?
4. What E-commerce alternatives do you feel should be considered?

CHAPTER 4

PROCUREMENT AND SUPPLY MANAGEMENT

LEARNING OBJECTIVES

After reading this chapter, you should be able to do the following:

- Understand the role and nature of procurement and supply management in a supply chain context.
- Explain the different types of inbound systems.
- Discuss the major materials-management activities.
- Understand the procurement process.
- Explain the risk/value technique for determining purchased item importance.
- Identify the four steps necessary for effective procurement.
- Explain the criteria for evaluating vendors.
- Examine the role of E-commerce in the procurement process.

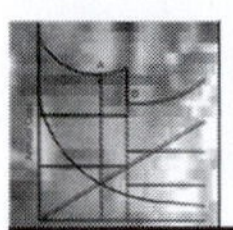

LOGISTICS PROFILE

CBL Plastic Company

"Wow! That sure was a close call. We have to do everything possible to prevent such a situation from occurring in the future," said Bill Marley, president of CBL, to the operations team. Bill was referring to the critical shortage, two hours worth of material in the warehouse, of plastic pellets. Plastic pellets are the primary raw material used in the manufacture of CBL plastic injection molded parts.

Because of the near stockout of plastic pellets, CBL faced a potential operations stoppage. The plastic pellet supplier did not have a sufficient supply of recycled plastic, the base stock from which the pellets are made. After the pellet vendor located a new recycled plastic supplier and began production, a snowstorm hit the area and prevented the trucking companies from delivering the product to CBL.

When the inventory level dropped to a two-hour level, the truck arrived and saved CBL from shutting down the plant. If production had stopped, CBL would have incurred the overhead costs of the plant without any output as well as lost sales because it did not have sufficient inventories of finished product to meet customer orders. Bill did not have a good estimate of the cost of shutting down the plant and lost sales.

Now that the emergency was over, Bill convened his operations team to develop action plans to prevent a stockout of critical raw materials that could force a plant shutdown. To focus the operations team's efforts, Bill developed a number of strategic issues regarding the supply management process. The issues to be explored included:

1. The cost of a raw material stockout
2. The cause of the tier-one plastic pellet vendor's raw material supply problem
3. The availability of raw materials for the tier-two vendors
4. Potential of CBL switching to a backup plastic pellet vendor(s)
5. An analysis of the plastic pellet market, including suppliers, future supply capacity and demand, and raw material availability
6. Definition and identification of CBL's "critical" raw materials
7. The optimum number of vendors for critical raw materials
8. The optimum inventory level for critical and noncritical raw materials
9. Changes needed in policies and operating procedure to prevent supply disruptions

After presenting these issues to the operations team, Bill was certain the team would dig into the problem and come back next week with a list of additional issues and questions. After a few meetings, the team would be able to recommend strategies and tactics that would prevent the almost disastrous stockout condition from occurring again.

INTRODUCTION

Chapter 1 provided an overview of the logistics supply chain and indicated that today's environment requires management of the flow and storage of materials (raw materials, semifinished goods, and finished products) from vendor sources through to the ultimate customer. One convenient way to view the supply chain for a single company is to divide its logistics system into *inbound logistics* (materials management and procurement) and *outbound logistics* (customer service and channels of distribution).

common activities

The focus of this chapter is upon the inbound side of logistics systems, including procurement or purchasing and the related materials-management activities. It is important to note that the inbound and outbound logistics systems share common activities or processes, since both involve decisions related to transportation, warehousing, materials handling, inventory management and control, and packaging, as well as some other activities. Each of these common areas is covered in some detail in subsequent chapters of this book. The purpose of this chapter is to provide an overview of the materials-management and procurement activities of an inbound logistics system.

INBOUND LOGISTICS ALONG THE SUPPLY CHAIN

A dimension of the inbound system that deserves consideration at the outset is the differences that exist among the inbound systems of different companies. These differences have important implications for the design and management of logistics supply chains.

mining firm

As you move along a supply chain made up of a series of individual companies (see Figure 4–1), you will see important differences in the inbound systems of the companies. The start of a supply chain could very well be a mining operation involving the extraction of coal or some ore commodity. In this instance, the inbound logistics system is essentially a part of the extractive or production process. Therefore, inbound logistics would be very difficult to separate out for analysis from the mining operation except to the extent that the extractive company purchases supplies for use in the mining process that must be stored and transported prior to the extractive process. An important point here is that extractive companies would be most concerned about their outbound system, which

FIGURE 4–1 A Food System Supply Chain

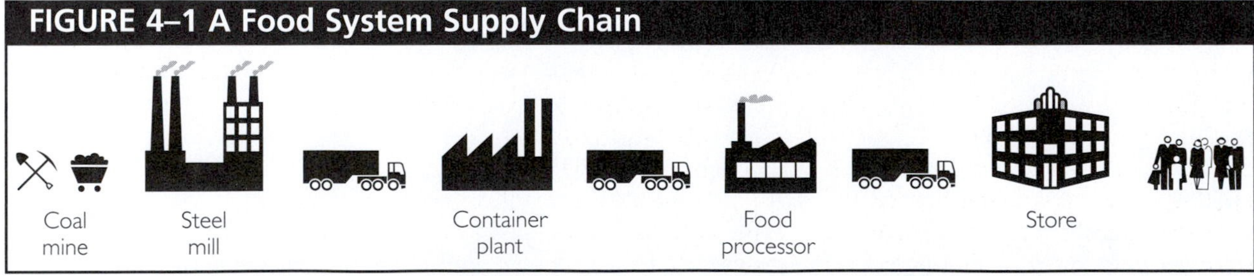

would be involved in delivering appropriate quantities of their commodity at the right time and place to the next firm in the supply chain. The inbound system of the extractive company would probably not receive as much separate attention as would the inbound system at the next firm in the supply chain.

steel firm

As we move along this hypothetical supply chain, the next company could be a steel manufacturer. The coal would be an important raw material for this firm, and it would probably transform the coal to coking coal in its coke plant. However, it could also buy coking coal from an intermediary company that buys coal and specializes in producing coking coal. (Obviously, if the latter were true, we would have another company in our supply chain.)

In addition to the coking coal, the steel company would utilize several raw materials from a variety of vendor sources to produce the steel. These materials would have to be procured in appropriate quantities, transported, stored, and their arrivals coordinated via the production planning process in advance of the manufacturing process for producing the steel. Therefore, the steel company would be very much aware of its inbound logistics system and the need to coordinate inbound logistics activities.

The steel company would have some interesting contrasts between its inbound and outbound systems. On the inbound side, the nature of the raw materials, coking coal, iron ore, and so on are such that they can be shipped in bulk in railcars and barges and stored outside in piles. On the other hand, the finished steel would need more sophisticated transportation, warehouses, inventory control, materials handling, and so on. Therefore, the inbound and outbound logistics systems could have some unique network design requirements.

container firm

Once the steel is produced, it would be ready to move along the supply chain to the next firm, which could be another manufacturer such as an auto or a container manufacturer. Assuming that the supply chain we are concerned about will ultimately result in food products in a store, the next point would be the container company that produces cans of various sizes for the food processors. It is important to note that the steel company would usually be a part of several supply chains. That is, the steel company may also be selling to auto manufacturers, office supply producers, and other types of manufacturers.

food firm

After the can manufacturer, the next step in our supply chain would be the food manufacturing plant, where processed food would be added to the cans of various sizes. Food processing companies frequently add labels later, since the same can of peas, for example, could be sold under as many as eight to ten different company labels. By storing the cans as "brights" and adding the labels when orders are received, the level of inventory can be reduced because of the reduction of uncertainty. That is, it is much easier to forecast the total demand for a certain size of canned peas than it is to forecast the demand for each company's labeled cans of peas, since individual market shares change.

retail store

Once an order for the peas has been received from a retailer, the labels can be added and the peas shipped to the retailer's warehouse or store. When the peas finally end up in the store for sale, we have reached the last point in our supply chain, although you could argue that the cycle is not complete until the can of peas ends up in a consumer's home. In fact, in today's environment, that can may be recycled after the peas are consumed and the materials may start back through part of the supply chain again—a reverse logistics system.

TABLE 4–1 Industry Supply Chain Logistics Emphasis

Industry	Supply Chain Logistics Emphasis
Extractive	One-way; outbound
Manufacturing	Two-way; inbound and outbound
Channel intermediary	Two-way; inbound and outbound
Retailer	Two-way; inbound and outbound
E-tailer	Two-way; inbound and outbound
End User	One-way; inbound

This rather lengthy discussion of the supply chain illustrates a number of interesting aspects of supply chain logistics. It shows that what is inbound for one company is frequently outbound for another company. Also, as we move along the supply chain, we are continually adding value, and the logistics costs will usually also increase because of the higher-value products. In addition, companies may be part of several supply chains.

The preceding discussion also indicates that the location in the supply chain channel determines the emphasis given to logistics. As shown in Table 4–1, an extractive industry has a one-way supply chain channel, outbound logistics. Conversely, an end user has a one-way supply channel that emphasizes inbound logistics. Manufacturers, channel intermediaries, retailers, and E-tailers have two-way supply chain channels, that is, these industries are concerned with both inbound and outbound logistics.

complexity

Another important dimension of our discussion of inbound logistics systems is the difference in complexity that exists among companies. For example, an automobile manufacturer typically has about 13,000 individual parts in the inbound system in order to assemble or manufacture an automobile. The inbound system for the steel plant mentioned previously is relatively simple compared to that of the auto manufacturer. The steel company has a limited number of raw materials that are shipped in bulk and are stored outside. Some aspects of inbound logistics systems for steel production are challenging but not nearly as challenging as the inbound system for automobile production.

As was indicated previously, the focus of this chapter is the inbound systems for logistics. We examine each of the major activities that are a part of inbound systems. The discussion is limited on some of these activities, such as transportation and warehousing, since these topics receive extensive discussion in later chapters.

MATERIALS MANAGEMENT

integration

Effective supply chain management requires careful coordination of the inbound system of logistics, which is frequently referred to as *materials management,* and the outbound system, which is usually called *physical distribution.* While the focus in this chapter is upon the inbound system, the integration of the inbound and outbound systems is extremely important to the efficient and effective management of the logistics supply chain. Information flow is often the key ingredient to the coordination of inbound and outbound logistics systems. Since information regarding product demand flows down the supply chain from the marketplace or customer and materials flow up the supply chain, the possibility exists that decisions related to the flow of materials will not be coordinated with the customer information flowing down. When there is a lack of integration, inefficiencies occur, especially with respect to inventory accumulation and/or lack of appropriate customer service levels. In today's complex environment, information needs to flow quickly in both directions for effective coordination.

Materials management can be described as the planning and control of the flow of materials that are a part of the inbound logistics system. Materials management usually includes the following activities: procurement, warehousing, production planning, inbound transportation, receiving, materials quality control, inventory management and control, and salvage and scrap disposal.

Procurement[1]

importance

Effective procurement of goods and services contributes to the competitive advantage of an organization. The procurement process links members in the supply chain and assures the quality of suppliers in that chain. The quality of the materials and services that are input affects finished product quality and hence customer satisfaction and revenue. Input costs are a large part of total costs in many industries. With the importance of procurement as a determinant of revenues, costs, and supply chain relationships, it is easy to understand why it has recently been receiving more attention from both practitioners and academics.

definition

Procurement can be a complex process that is difficult at times to define, understand, and manage. However, to manage the process, it must be understood; to understand the process, it must be defined. Depending on the circumstances, procurement can be defined, in a narrow sense, as the act of buying goods and services for a firm or, in a broader perspective, as the process of obtaining goods and services for the firm. The procurement process is, however, more than just the culmination of an activity; it is the successful completion of a series of activities that often cut across organizational boundaries. To formalize the definition, then, procurement consists of all those activities necessary to acquire goods and services consistent with user requirements.

Porter, in his value chain, identified the strategic importance of procurement, since it includes such activities as qualifying new suppliers, procuring different types of inputs, and monitoring supplier performance.[2] As such, procurement serves as a critical link between members of the supply chain.

The activities that follow for the procurement process apply to the purchase of both goods and services in industrial markets. (See Figure 4–2 for an overview of the procurement process.) These activities often cut across both functional boundaries (intrafirm) and organizational boundaries (interfirm) and cannot be effectively completed without input from all parties involved in the transaction. The successful completion of these activities maximizes value for both the buying and selling organizations, thereby maximizing value for the supply chain:

1. *Identify or reevaluate needs.* A procurement transaction is usually initiated in response to either a new or an existing need of a user (by an individual or

FIGURE 4–2 Procurement Process

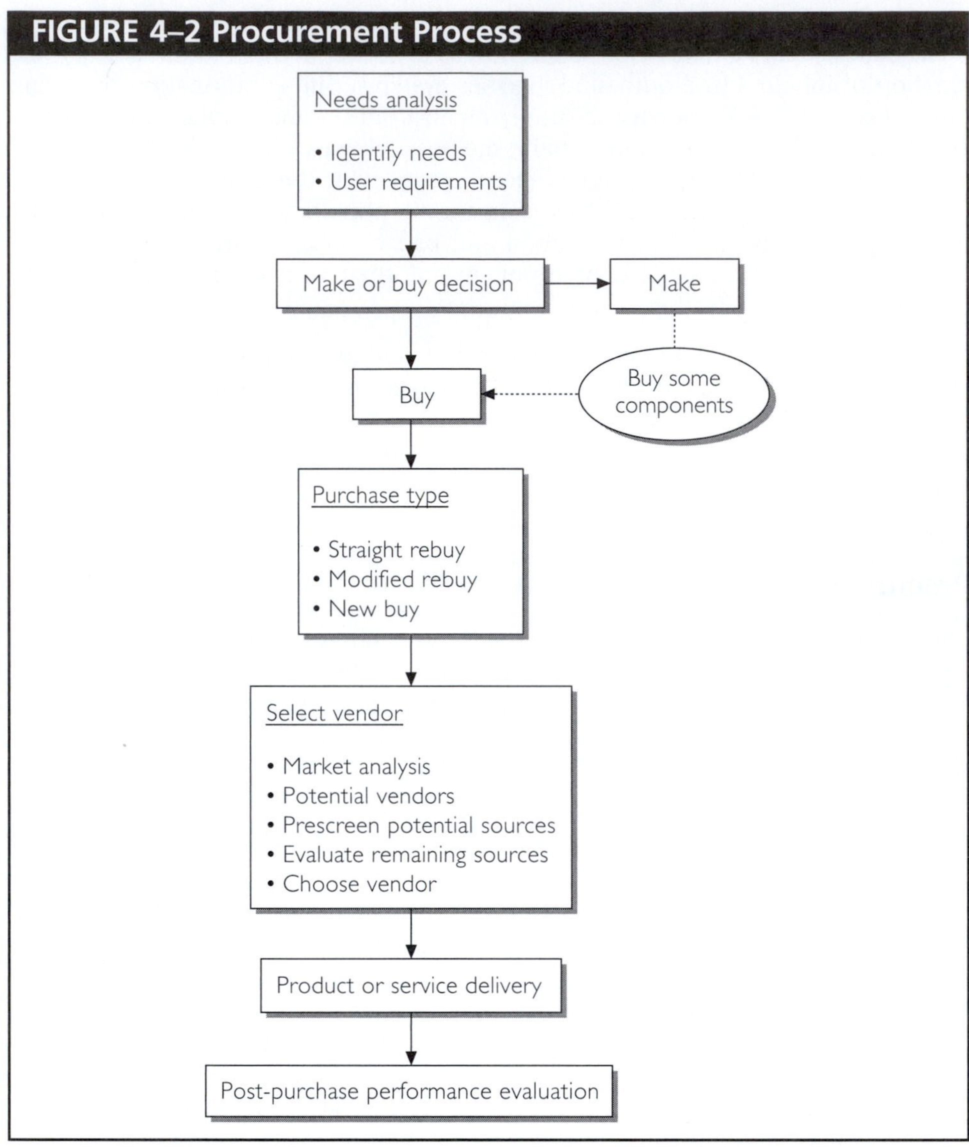

department within the buyer's firm). In some instances, existing needs must be reevaluated because they change. In either case, once the need is identified, the procurement process can begin. The need can be identified by any of a variety of functional areas in the firm or even by someone outside the firm, for example, by customers.

2. *Define and evaluate user requirements.* Once the need has been determined, its requirement must be represented by some type of measurable criteria. The criteria may be relatively simple—for example, criteria for copy machine paper could be 8 ½ by 11-inch white paper of a certain bond weight—or they may be very complex if the company is buying a highly technical product. Using these criteria, the procurement professional can communicate the user's needs to potential suppliers.
3. *Decide whether to make or buy.* Before outside suppliers are solicited, the buying firm must decide whether it will make or buy the product or service to

satisfy the user's needs. Even with a "make" decision, however, the buying firm will usually have to purchase some types of inputs from outside suppliers. This step has become much more important today, when more companies are outsourcing in order to focus upon their "core" activities.

4. *Identify the type of purchase.* The type of purchase necessary to satisfy the user's needs will determine the amount of time needed for the procurement process and the complexity of the process. The three types of purchases, from least amount of time and complexity to most amount of time and complexity, are (1) a straight rebuy or routine purchase; (2) a modified rebuy, which requires a change to an existing supplier or input; and (3) a new buy, which results from a new user need. In a straight rebuy or modified rebuy, several of the activities discussed in the remainder of this section can be eliminated; for example, there is no need to identify all possible suppliers.
5. *Conduct a market analysis.* A source of supply can operate in a purely competitive market (many suppliers), an oligopolistic market (a few large suppliers), or a monopolistic market (one supplier). Knowing the type of market will help the procurement professional determine the number of suppliers in the market, where the power/dependence balance lies, and which method of buying might be most effective—negotiations, competitive bidding, and so on. The information about market type is not always apparent, and some research may be necessary using standard library sources such as *Moody's* or information from a trade association.
6. *Identify all possible suppliers.* This activity involves the identification of all possible suppliers that might be able to satisfy the user's needs. It is important at this stage to include possible suppliers that the buying firm has not used previously. Again, identifying all possible suppliers, especially with today's global environment, can be a challenge and may require some research. If the company is small, it may rely upon more common sources of such information, such as the telephone company's yellow pages directory.
7. *Prescreen all possible sources.* When defining and evaluating user requirements (as described in the second activity), it is important to differentiate between demands and desires. *Demands* for a product or service are those characteristics that are critical to the user; *desires* are those that are not as critical and are therefore negotiable. Prescreening reduces the pool of possible suppliers to those that can satisfy the user's demands. In some instances, prescreening can be a relatively simple task. For example, in the case of the copy paper, the supplier will have it on hand regularly or will not have it available dependably. With parts for a computer, the situation may require a series of tests by internal engineering staff.
8. *Evaluate the remaining supplier base.* With the possible pool of suppliers reduced to those that can meet the user's demands, it is now possible to determine which supplier or suppliers can best meet the user's negotiable requirements, or desires. This activity may be accomplished through the use of competitive bidding if the procurement item or items are fairly simple or standard and there is a sufficient number of potential vendors. If these conditions do not exist, more elaborate evaluation may be necessary, using engineering tests or simulated end-use situations, for example, to test seat belts for cars.
9. *Choose a supplier.* The choice of supplier also determines the relationship that will exist between the buying and supplying firms and how the "mechanics" of this relationship will be structured and implemented. This activity also

determines how the relationships with the nonselected suppliers will be maintained. The actual choice will be based upon criteria to be discussed subsequently, such as quality, reliability, total required price, and so on.

10. *Receive delivery of the product or service.* This activity occurs with the first attempt by the supplier or suppliers to satisfy the user's needs. The completion of this activity also begins the generation of performance data to be used for the next activity.
11. *Make a postpurchase performance evaluation.* Once the service has been performed or the product delivered, the supplier's performance must be evaluated to determine whether it has truly satisfied the user's needs. This also is the "control" activity. If supplier performance did not satisfy the user's needs, the causes for this variance must be determined and the proper corrective actions implemented.

external influences

All of the activities identified in this section are subject to influences beyond the control of the procurement professional. These influences can determine how effectively each activity is performed. They include intraorganizational and interorganizational factors and external factors such as governmental influences. For example, a change in marketing needs or manufacturing process may require repeating all or some of the activities identified before the first iteration is completed. Financial failure of a potential vendor will also cause problems and necessitate repeated activities.

Importance of Item and Service Purchased[3]

The products and services purchased by a company are not all the same. Some products are more important and require greater procurement attention. Applying the same procurement strategies, tactics, and resources to supplying a computer manufacturer with paper clips and computer chips overlooks the differences in criticalness of each item to the firm's survival and profitability. That is, the computer company can survive without paper clips but not without computer chips.

The quadrant technique enables the supply chain manager to assess the importance of each product or service being purchased. The quadrant technique utilizes a two-by-two matrix to determine a procured item's relative importance on the basis of value and risk. The criteria used to delineate importance are *value* or profit potential and *risk* or uniqueness.

value

The value criterion examines product or service features that enhance profits for the final product and the firm's ability to maintain a competitive advantage in the marketplace. For example, a computer chip that is faster or an operating system that is more user friendly will make the computer more desirable, thereby increasing demand for the product and, consequently, increasing profits. Alternatively, the addition of a gold-plated paper clip to the computer instruction manual probably will not increase computer sales or solidify a competitive advantage in the marketplace.

risk

Risk reflects the chance of failure, nonacceptance in the marketplace, delivery failures, and source nonavailability. The risk of a paper clip failure is really not a significant risk for a computer manufacturer. That is, if a paper clip fails to hold a number of pieces of paper together, the operation of the company's computer should not be affected. However, if a computer chip fails, the computer will not operate and the marketplace will respond in a negative way. Thus, the computer chip poses a greater risk than the paper clip to a computer manufacturer.

FIGURE 4–3 Item Procurement Importance Matrix

RISK		
	Distinctives High risk, low value Engineered items	Criticals High risk, high value Unique items Items critical to final product
	Generics Low risk, low value Office supplies MRO items	Commodities Low risk, high value Basic production items Basic packaging Logistics services
	Value or Profit Potential	

importance categories

Figure 4–3 depicts the value risk quadrant and categorizes item importance. Items of low risk, low value are identified as *generics;* and those of low risk, high value are *commodities.* Products or services that are high risk, low value are *distinctives;* while those of high risk, high value are *criticals.*

generics

Generics are low-risk, low-value items and services that typically do not enter the final product. Items such as office supplies and maintenance, repair, and operating items (MRO) are examples of generics. The administrative and acquisition processing costs are more significant than the purchase price of generics, and, for some generics, the administration and processing costs may exceed the price paid for the item or service. The strategic procurement thrust for generics is to streamline the procurement process to reduce the cost associated with purchasing generics. For example, the use of purchasing cards (corporate credit cards) reduces the number of checks written and the administrative costs associated with check payment, bank verification, and so on.

commodities

Commodities are items or services that are low in risk but high in value. Basic production materials (bolts), basic packaging (exterior box), and transportation services are examples of commodities that enhance the profitability of the company but pose a low risk. These items and services are fundamental to the company's finished product, thus making their value high. Risk is low because commodities are not unique items and there are many sources of supply. Because commodities are not unique, there is little brand distinction and price is a significant distinguishing factor. Freight and inventory are major procurement cost considerations for commodities. The procurement strategies used for commodities include volume purchasing to reduce price and just-in-time systems to lower inventory costs.

distinctives

Distinctives are high-risk, low-value items and services such as engineered items, parts that are available from only a limited number of suppliers, or items that have a long lead time. The company's customers are unaware of or do not care about the uniqueness of distinctives, but these products pose a threat to continued operation and/or high procurement cost. A stockout of distinctives results in stopping the production line or changing the production schedule to work around a stocked-out item, and both tactics increase production costs. Alternatively, using premium supply sources or premium transportation will eliminate the stockout but procurement costs will increase. The strategic focus for distinctives is developing a standardization program to eliminate or reduce the uniqueness of the distinctives, thereby changing these items to generics.

criticals

Finally, *criticals* are high-risk, high-value items that give the final product a competitive advantage in the marketplace. As noted earlier, the computer chip used may give the computer a unique speed that differentiates it from all competitors. This unique computer chip increases the computer's value to the customer, and the risk of nonavailability is customer dissatisfaction and reduced sales. Criticals, in part, determine the customer's ultimate cost of using the finished product—in our example, the computer. The procurement strategy for criticals is to strengthen their value through use of new technologies, simplification, close supplier relations, and/or value-added alterations. The focus of critical procurement is on innovation to make the critical item provide greater market value to the finished product.

The preceding discussion of the quadrant technique emphasizes that not all items and services purchased are of equal importance. It also suggests that the supply chain manager must utilize varying procurement strategies based on the value and risk of the item. Greater resources and attention should be directed toward procuring criticals than toward generics. For example, one full-time procurement specialist may be assigned to purchasing one critical item—say, a computer chip—whereas one full-time person may be assigned to the purchase of hundreds of generics—office supplies.

In the next section, our attention is directed toward managing the procurement process.

Managing the Procurement Process. Managing the procurement process can be difficult for a multitude of reasons, ranging from inflexible organizational structures to inflexible organizational cultures. However, most firms should find the process relatively easy. What must be remembered when dealing with these activities is that all firms are different and will have different requirements for the procurement process. A four-step approach can be used and adapted to a firm's particular needs. Based on the previous discussion of the procurement process activities, the following steps can be used to maximize effectiveness:

1. *Determine the type of purchase.* In the procurement process, identifying the type of purchase (the fourth purchase activity) will many times dictate the complexity of the entire process. For example, a straight rebuy situation will mean that all of the procurement activities were completed previously (when the purchase was a new buy or modified rebuy), and the only activities necessary would probably be the fourth, ninth, tenth, and eleventh. A modified rebuy may also not require all of the activities, but a new buy would normally require performing all of the activities discussed earlier.
2. *Determine the necessary levels of investment.* The procurement process requires two major types of investments by the firm: time and information. Time is expended by the individuals involved in making the purchase; the more complex and important the purchase, the more time must be spent on it, especially if it is a new buy. Information can be both internal and external to the firm. Internal information is gathered concerning user requirements

On The Line

How Dell Defines Direct

Before the first E-tailer ever set up shop, Dell Computer turned the personal computer industry on its ear by pioneering the idea of selling custom-built PCs directly to consumers. By developing and then staying focused on what he termed the *direct model,* Michael Dell built a $21 billion company that is both known for supply chain excellence and widely considered to have the right business model for the Internet age.

Michael Dell attributes his company's success to an unrelenting focus on the customer. "From the start, our entire business—from design to manufacturing to sales—was oriented around listening to the customer, and delivering what the customer wanted" has allowed Dell to eliminate all aspects of the business process that do not contribute directly to meeting customer needs.

Dell's success did not come without some growing pains. In the first few years, Dell learned tough but crucial lessons about the importance of parts inventory management and building to what the customers said they needed. And time and again it learned that continued success was tightly tethered to maintaining focus on the direct model.

Forming strong alliances with the suppliers who would make the direct model work was an important task. First Dell chose to source components from expert outside suppliers rather than build them itself. Dell found that this approach gave it the flexibility to rapidly scale operations as customer needs dictated and to gain access to the best components in the world. Further, it believed in supplier partnerships where goals and strategies are shared freely—a dramatic departure from the traditional buy-bid cycle. When this approach to procurement worked so well, Dell was among the first companies to outsource significant portions of its logistics operations to third-party logistics providers.

To avoid the error, cost, confusion, and complexity that come from managing multiple suppliers, Dell partnered with only a few key suppliers and then brought these suppliers close to Dell's own business, both geographically and electronically. Dell required suppliers to site their facilities close to Dell's own manufacturing facilities to allow for better communication and service and faster time to market—all critical for a company that does not begin building a computer until it receives an order.

Today, Dell uses the Internet as a key part of its IT strategy: the company is now creating Web-based links for each of its suppliers to facilitate the rapid exchange of information such as component quality metrics, cost structures, and current and future demand forecasts. Providing suppliers with closer electronic links helps Dell continue to push for improved inventory velocity and better quality data and ultimately reduce the total cycle time from when Dell customers place an order to when they receive it.

Source: "How Dell Defines Direct," *Channels* 5, no. 1 (2000): 7. Reprinted with permission of *Channels,* a UPS Logistics Group publication.

and the implications that the purchase will have for the firm. External information concerning the input to be purchased may be gathered from supply chain members, from potential suppliers, and others. The more complex and important the purchase, the more information is needed for the procurement process to be effective. By determining the type of purchase (which is also a function of the user's needs), the procurement professional can determine the levels of investment necessary in the procurement process. Problems can occur when not enough or too much investment is made to satisfy a particular user's needs.

Determining the level of investment needed in time and information to adequately meet a user's requirements is a firm-specific process. Once the level of investment is decided, the procurement process can take place.

3. *Perform the procurement process.* This is a relatively easy step to describe but can be a complex step to perform, depending on the situation. It includes performing those activities necessary to effectively make a purchase and satisfy the user's requirements. This step also allows the procurement professional to collect data on the time and information actually used in making a specific purchase. The ability to measure the actual investment and how well a user's needs were satisfied is important to the final step in managing the procurement process.
4. *Evaluate the effectiveness of the procurement process.* This is a control step that asks two questions: (1) Were the user's needs satisfied? and (2) Was the investment necessary? Remember, the goal is to invest only enough time and information to exactly satisfy the user's needs. If the procurement process was not effective, the cause could be traced to not enough investment, not performing the proper activities, or mistakes made in performing one or more of the activities. In any case, when the procurement process is not effective, the manager must determine why and take corrective actions to make sure that future purchases will be effective. If the purchase satisfied the user's needs at the proper level of investment, the procurement process was effective and can serve as a reference for future purchases.

supplier relationship

Thus, although the procurement process is complex, it can be managed effectively as long as the manager develops some systematic approach for implementing it. A key factor in achieving efficiency and effectiveness in this area is the development of successful supplier (vendor) relationships. In fact, many professional procurement/materials managers agree that today's global marketplace requires developing strong supplier relationships in order to create and sustain a competitive advantage. Companies such as NCR and Motorola go so far as to refer to suppliers (vendors) as partners and/or stakeholders in their company. When vendors are "partners," companies tend to rely more upon them to provide input into product design, engineering assistance, quality control, and so on.

The buyer-supplier relationship is so important that it deserves special discussion. (Note that in our previous discussion of procurement activities, supplier relations were involved in at least five of the activities.) The next section provides additional discussion of supplier relationships.

vendor partners

Supplier/Vendor Evaluation and Relationships. Many successful companies have recognized the key role that procurement plays in supply chain management and that supplier/vendor relationships are a vital part of successful procurement strategies "Good vendors do not grow on trees" is an adage that is often quoted by procurement professionals. This is especially true when companies reduce the total number of their suppliers, frequently in conjunction with total quality management (TQM) programs or just-in-time (JIT) production and inventory systems.

The strategy to utilize a smaller number of suppliers/vendors frequently means an alliance or partnership with suppliers/vendors because of the need to assure an adequate supply of quality materials over time at an optimum total acquired cost. The partnership/alliance concept encompasses more than just the procurement process, since partnerships are being developed today throughout the supply chain by companies. For example, partnerships are also evolving with transportation companies, contract logistics companies (third-party providers), and channel members.

At this stage, suffice it to say that procurement professionals today recognize that quality management necessitates quality materials and parts. That is, the final product is only as good as the parts that are used in the process. Also, we need to recognize that the customer satisfaction process begins with procurement.

Another dimension of the supplier relationship is that procurement contributes to the competitive advantage of the company, whether the advantage be one of low cost, differentiation, or a niche orientation (using Porter's generic strategies).[4] Therefore, the procurement management program has to be consistent with the overall competitive advantage that a company is seeking to attain in the marketplace. For example, we would expect that Honda or Toyota would approach procurement differently than would Mercedes Benz or Lexus.

Even with a partnership or strategic alliance with a vendor, certain key criteria need to be considered in any procurement situation. The typical but key vendor/supplier selection criteria are discussed in the section that follows.

quality

Vendor Selection Criteria. Figure 4–4 provides an overview of the vendor selection criteria. The most important factor in vendor selection is usually quality. As was indicated earlier, quality often refers to the specifications that a user desires in an item (technical specifications, chemical or physical properties, or design, for example). The procurement professional compares the actual quality of a vendor's product with the specifications the user desires. In actuality, quality includes additional factors such as life of the product, ease of repair, maintenance requirements, ease of use, and

FIGURE 4–4 Overview of Vendor Selection Criteria

Quality

- Technical specifications
- Chemical and physical properties
- Design
- Product life
- Ease of repair
- Maintenance
- Dependability

Reliability

- On-time delivery
- Performance history
- Warranty

Capability

- Production capability
- Technical capability
- Management
- Operating controls
- Labor relations

Financial

- Price
- Financial stability

Desirable Qualities

- Vendor attitude
- Training aids
- Packaging
- Vendor location
- Repair service

dependability. In today's TQM environment, not only are quality standards higher, but the supplier may also have to assume the major responsibility for quality.

reliability

Reliability comprises delivery and performance history, the second- and third-ranked factors for most procurement professionals. To prevent production line shutdowns resulting from longer-than-expected lead times, the buyer requires consistent, on-time deliveries. Also, the performance life of the procured product directly affects the quality of the final product, the manufacturer's warranty claims, and repeat sales. Finally, in cases of material malfunction, the buying firm considers the vendor's warranty and claim procedure a reliability measure. Reliability is often considered a part of a total quality management program. It should also be noted that the growing reliance upon foreign vendors presents some special challenges to the achievement of reliability because of the distances involved.

capability

The third major vendor selection criterion, capability, considers the potential vendor's production facilities and capacity, technical capability, management and organizational capabilities, and operating controls. These factors indicate the vendor's ability to provide a needed quality and quantity of material in a timely manner. The evaluation includes not only the vendor's physical capability to provide the material the user needs, but also the vendor's capability to do so consistently over an extended time period. The buying firm may answer this long-run supply concern by considering the vendor's labor relations record. A record of vendor-labor unrest resulting in strikes may indicate that the vendor is unable to provide the material quantity the user desires over a long time period. A firm that buys from this vendor will incur increased inventory costs for storing material in preparation for likely disruptions in the vendor's business due to labor strife. Again, sourcing from global suppliers makes this assessment more challenging.

financial

Financial considerations constitute the fourth major vendor selection criterion. In addition to price, the buying firm considers the vendor's financial position. Financially unstable vendors pose possible disruptions in a long-run continued supply of material. By declaring bankruptcy, a vendor that supplies materials critical to a final product could stop a buyer's production. This criterion has become especially important in purchasing transportation service from truckload motor carriers. With the trend toward companies utilizing a smaller number of carriers, the financial failure of such a supplier is a major problem and source of disruption in a supply chain.

desirable qualities

The remaining vendor selection factors may be grouped into a miscellaneous category of desirable, but not always necessary, criteria. Although the buyer might find the vendor's attitude difficult to quantify, attitude does affect the vendor selection decision. A negative attitude, for example, may eliminate a vendor for a buyer's consideration. The impression or image that the vendor projects has a similar effect on vendor selection. The importance of training aids and packaging will depend on the material the buyer is purchasing. For example, packaging is important to buyers of easily damaged material, such as glass, but not important to buyers purchasing a commodity that is not easily damaged, such as coal. Training aids would be significant to a firm selecting vendors to supply technical machinery such as computers and robots but not to a firm seeking office supplies. Likewise, a buyer would consider the availability of repair service more important when buying technical machinery.

vendor location

Another vendor selection factor is geographical location. This factor addresses the issue of whether to buy from local or distant vendors. Transportation cost is one obvious aspect of this issue. Other factors, such as the ability to fill rush orders, meet delivery dates, provide shorter delivery times, and utilize greater vendor-buyer cooperation, favor the use of local suppliers. However, distant vendors may provide lower prices, greater technical ability, greater supply reliability, and higher quality. This is again a choice faced more frequently in today's global environment

factor importance

The relative importance of the vendor selection factors will depend upon the material the buyer is purchasing. When a buyer purchases a computer, for example, technical capability and training aids may be more important than price, delivery, and warranties. Conversely, a buyer of office supplies would probably emphasize price and delivery more than the other factors.

All of the criteria just discussed are important or can be important in certain procurement situations. However, the one criterion that generates the most discussion and/or frustration for procurement specialists is price or cost. Therefore, some extended discussion of this criterion is necessary.

The Special Case of Procurement Price[5]

We begin by identifying the four generic sources of prices in procurement situations. This is somewhat basic but important to understand. The discussion of price becomes more complex when one adds an analysis of total acquired cost or value in the procurement process from a supply chain perspective. Total acquired cost and value are discussed after our description of price sources.

commodity markets

Sources of Price. Purchasing managers utilize four basic procedures to determine potential vendors' prices: commodity markets, price lists, price quotations, and negotiations. Commodity markets exist for basic raw materials such as grain, oil, sugar, and natural resources including coal and lumber. In these markets, the forces of supply and demand determine the price that all potential vendors will charge. Reductions in the supply of these materials or increases in demand usually result in increased prices; the converse is true for increases in supply or decreases in demand.

price list

Price lists are published prices that are generally used with standardized products such as gasoline or office supplies. The vendor's catalog, electronic or hard copy, describes the items available and lists their prices. Depending on the status, buyers may receive a purchaser discount from the list price. For example, a vendor may give a 10 percent discount to small-volume buyers (less than $1,000 per month) and a 35 percent discount to large-volume buyers (more than $10,000 per month).

price quotations

Purchasers use the price quotation method for both standard and specialty items. It is particularly useful in promoting competition among suppliers. The process begins with the buyer sending potential vendors requests for quotes (RFQ). An RFQ contains all the necessary information regarding the specifications the purchaser requires and the manner in which potential suppliers are to present their offers. In turn, the vendors examine the cost they will incur in producing the material, considering the quantity the purchaser will order, the purchase's duration, and other factors that will affect the vendor's profitability. Finally, the purchaser compares the vendor's quoted price and offer specifications with those of other vendors.

negotiation

The fourth procedure, negotiation, is useful when the other methods do not apply or have failed. Negotiation is particularly effective when the buyer is interested in a strategic alliance or long-term relationship. The negotiation process can be time-consuming, but the potential benefits can be significant in terms of price and quality. Negotiation is becoming more widely used by logistics managers buying goods and transport services.

FIGURE 4–5 Hierarchy of Price Measurement Approaches

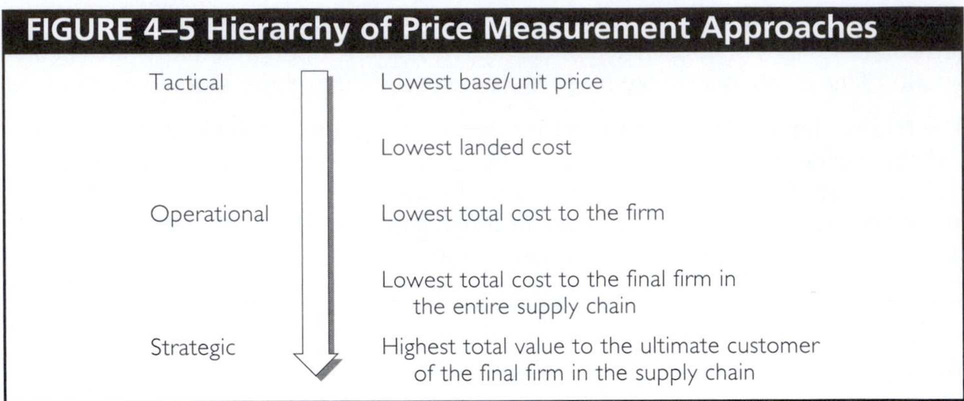

The objective of the procurement process is to purchase goods and services at the "best" price, which may not be the lowest price per unit at the vendor source. This is particularly true from a global supply chain perspective. In all four settings, the base price needs to be evaluated in a total acquired cost context.

A generalized spectrum of expanding procurement approaches to the supply chain concept is presented in Figure 4–5. At the first level, the firm evaluates procurement and logistics functions simply on the basis of lowest price or lowest cost, without strong regard to the total costs to the firm. In this context, it is difficult to attain a total cost savings unless a manager or group becomes directly responsible for the two or more interfacing functions that might offer a total cost savings. As a company attempts to move from the lowest base or unit price to taking a supply chain perspective to create highest value, the procurement function becomes more strategic in nature.

For customer satisfaction, all costs and factors that affect costs and create value should be captured in the total acquired cost. As Figure 4–5 indicates, a hierarchy of costs and other factors build upward from raw materials through manufacturing, to distribution, to final marketing and selection and use by the ultimate customer in order to determine total procurement cost and the highest total value.

For the buyer, the total procurement price is more than just the basic purchase price, as indicated in Figure 4–6. The following discussion starts with the base cost and delineates the additional direct and indirect costs that need to be considered:

Traditional basic input costs. This is the primary price of the product or materials as paid by the firm. It is the traditional price buyers seek through bidding, negotiating, or in requests for quotes. It is easily measured, and it has long been the hallmark against which buyer performance is measured; but, in a supply chain setting, it is only one factor for the firm to evaluate and consider in the acquisition process.

Direct transaction costs. These are the costs of detecting, transmitting the need for, and processing the material flow in order to acquire the goods. It includes the process of detecting inventory need, requisitioning, preparing and transmitting the order documentation to the supplier, receiving the acknowledgment, handling shipping documents, and receiving information about input to inventory. This area was made more efficient during the 1990s with the advent of internal electronic mail systems that automated the purchasing-requisition and order-transmission process.

FIGURE 4–6 Total Procurement Price

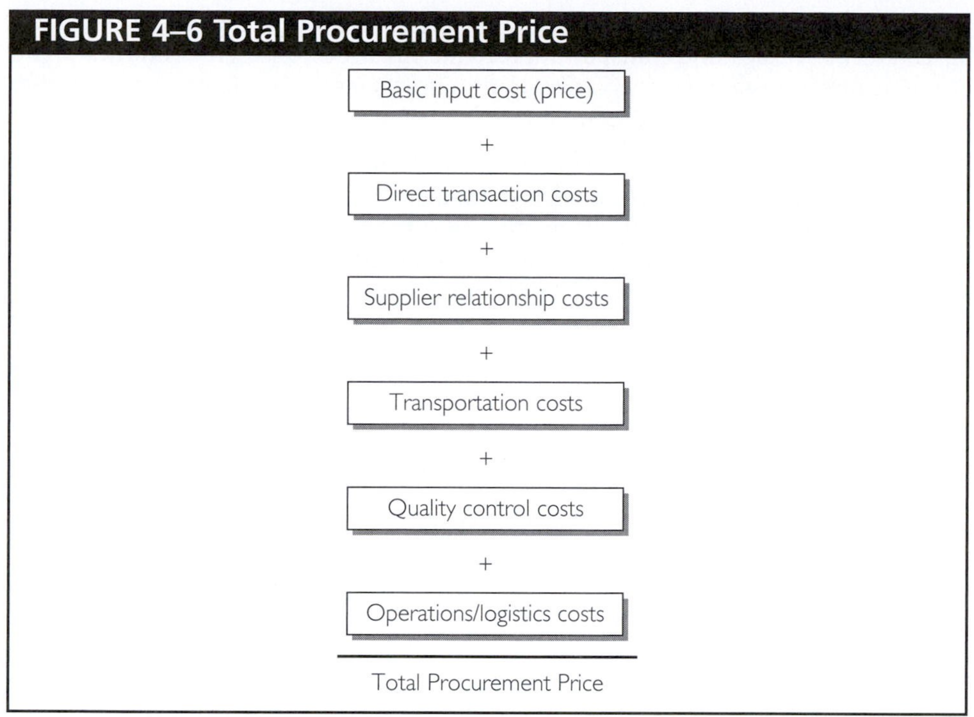

Users inside the firm use electronic means to transmit their needs to purchasing. EDI and the Internet are extensions of this process outbound to the supplier.

The use of blanket or systems contracting can also reduce transaction costs. These include direct ordering by users to suppliers, single consolidated billing, and user inspection and checking. Direct transaction costs are overhead types of costs that are not easily visible, but they represent time and effort that are not available for more productive value-added activities. Suppliers and interfacing carriers that reduce the need for these activities represent value to the buying firm.

Supply relational costs. These are the costs of creating and maintaining a relationship with a supplier. They include travel, supplier education, and the establishment of planning and operational links between purchasing and the supplier's order-entry operation, as well as other links, including ones to traffic, engineering, research, and product development in both firms. In traditional purchasing settings, this includes the process of evaluating and certifying a supplier for quality and preferred supplier programs.

Landed costs. The inbound transportation flow includes two key cost elements: the actual transportation cost and the sales/FOB terms. There are four different transportation options with inbound movements—supplier-selected for-hire carrier or private carrier and buyer-selected for-hire carrier or private carrier.

The sales terms define which firm owns the goods during transportation as well as invoice payment requirements. Transportation terms pertain to the carrier in the move between the supplier and buyer firm. There are nearly a dozen possible transportation terms that include different carrier payment and loss and damage claim options. Each one presents different relative costs to each party in the linkage; and, for supply chain purposes, the one that can perform the task or own the goods at the lowest overall cost has an advantage that can contribute to the overall chain. Both sales and transportation terms must be considered, and there are different direct costs, responsibilities, and indirect implicit costs of cash flow that are affected by each one of them.

Quality costs/factors. Quality pertains to the conformance of goods to a desired specification. It includes the cost of conformance, nonconformance, appraisal, and ultimate use costs. The required quality specification is often balanced against what the supplier can easily provide nearly 100 percent of the time. Often a product specification that is extremely tight requires extra costs but results in higher quality, which may reduce total cost.

Operations/logistics costs. This group includes four key areas:

- Receiving and make-ready costs are the costs of those flow activities occurring between the inbound transportation delivery of a good and its availability for use by production or other processes. These include the cost of unpacking, inspect, counting, sorting, grading, removing and disposing of packaging materials (strapping, banding, stretch-shrink wrapping, pallets, etc.), and moving the good to the use point. A streamlined system such as direct forklift delivery to a production line is an example of an efficient receiving/make-ready process. Some leading edge carriers provide information links to the firm that include inspection checks, sequencing of the loads, and final count checks so that receiving processes can be reduced or eliminated.
- Lot-size costs directly affect space requirements, handling flow, unit price, and related cash flows. These are a major cost of inventories.
- Production costs can be affected by suppliers of even seemingly similar goods. Extruded plastic for high-quality towel rods is an example. The plastic is an extruded tube that must be inflated with air and slipped over a metal or wooden rod. Original raw material quality, differing production processes, and in-transit humidity can cause two suppliers' goods to affect the production line significantly. One might allow assembly of 200 units per hour, while another might split or not form properly, wasting 10 percent of the sleeves and requiring the production line to operate at a slower speed. Thus, each one has a different cost of production operation.
- Logistics costs are also important in both upstream and downstream settings. These are cost factors that are affected by product size, weight, cube, and shape and their resulting impact upon transportation, handling, storage, and damage costs. Purchased goods and packaging materials have a direct bearing upon these subsequent process costs.

All firms in the supply chain add cost and, hopefully, value to a product as it moves through the supply chain. Value is added by reducing total acquired cost or by enhancing the function of the product. Each firm in the supply chain can contribute to or detract from these factors. The key is to focus downstream in the supply chain, but it is also important to note the key role that the procurement process can play at each point along the supply chain by being aware of a product's total acquired cost. Ideally, the focus should be upon the total value at the end of the supply chain. Therefore, the analysis should also include indirect financial costs (payment terms), tactical input costs (vendor capabilities), and strategic business factors (factors that cause customers to buy the product).

Other Materials-Management Activities

As was indicated at the outset of this discussion, price can be a complex factor, since other aspects have to be considered as they relate to the base price. Thus far, the discussion of materials-management functions has focused solely upon procurement. We now turn to the additional materials-management activities.

Warehousing. The *warehousing* function concerns the physical holding of raw materials until a firm uses them. Chapter 8 discusses general warehousing functions and decision areas. Although storing the raw materials a manufacturer will use in the production process is basically the same as storing finished products, raw-materials storage and finished-goods storage differ notably in terms of the type of facility each requires, the value of the stored items, and product perishability.

facilities required

Basic raw materials such as coal, sand, or limestone normally require an open-air warehouse facility; that is, a firm would merely dump the basic raw materials on the ground. Thus, the facility cost for storing basic raw materials is lower than the facility cost for storing other materials—finished goods, components, and other semifinished products, for example—that require an elaborate enclosed structure.

The value of raw materials is usually lower than that of finished goods, since the manufacturer enhances the value of the finished material, or processed raw material, during the manufacturing process. Last, basic raw materials usually suffer less damage and loss than finished goods because raw materials have lower value and need no protection from the elements.

Chapter 8 discusses the warehousing function and the ways in which its activities and decisions affect logistics systems.

Production Planning and Control. In a manufacturing environment, *production planning and control* involve coordinating product supply with product demand. As Figure 4–7 shows, the starting point of the production planning and control process is the demand for the finished product the company produces and sells. This demand is the process's independent variable, since the seller cannot control customer demand.

forecasting

The manufacturer must forecast, or estimate, customer demand. This sales forecast should indicate the sales amount the manufacturer expects for each item and the time period the sales projection covers. After establishing this independent customer demand, the manufacturer can provide the finished product supply either from available inventory or by producing the product. Thus, external demand establishes an internal demand for a finished product; and the manufacturer fills this demand from the existing stocks or from new production.

When demand requires production, the production scheduling manager uses the sales forecast to develop a production schedule. A production planner's main concerns include the following:

- Number of units of a specified product to be produced
- Time intervals over which production will occur
- Availability of materials and machines to produce the number of units required within the specified time frame

Production control results as the production manager specifies time intervals and develops order schedules for raw materials to supply the production schedule. For

FIGURE 4–7 Overview of Production Planning and Control

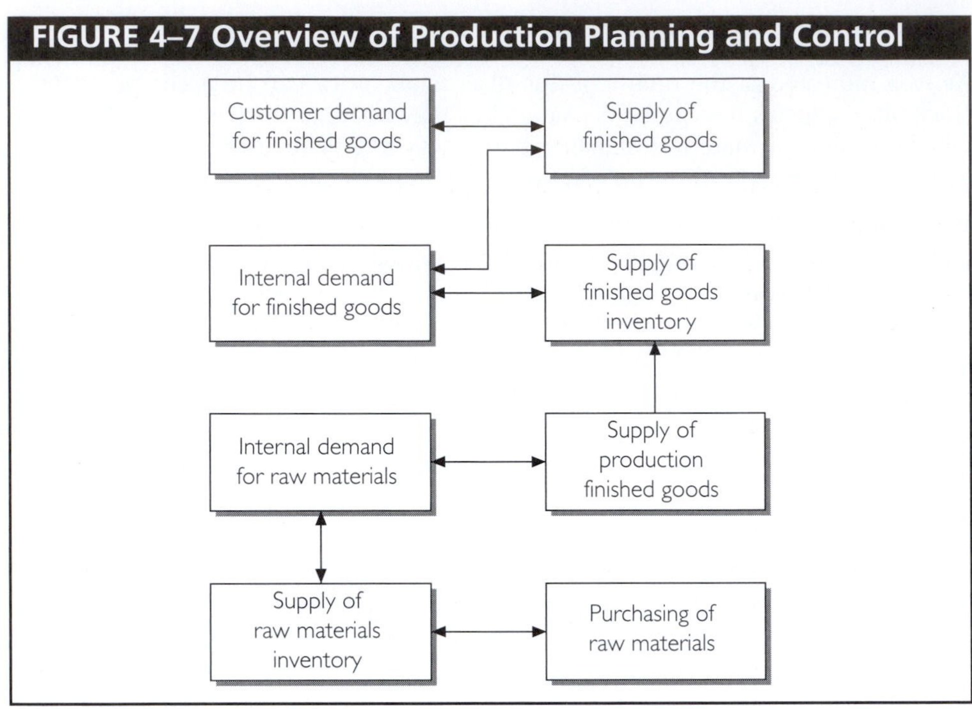

example, suppose that sales forecasts estimate that a firm will sell 10,000 units of product A and 30,000 units of product B in March. The firm makes both products on the same machine, which produces 10,000 units per week. The production planner first determines how much, if any, production the firm requires to satisfy customer demand and to maintain target inventory levels. In this example, low inventory levels require the firm to produce all 40,000 units. Additionally, a special promotion has depleted product A's inventory quickly, giving product A scheduling priority. However, vendor labor strikes have made the material for product A unavailable until week 2. As a result, the production planner first schedules one week of product B, followed by one week of product A and then two weeks of product B. Obviously, this is a simple example.

Transportation. The *transportation* function manages the inbound transportation of materials. Transportation originates with the materials vendor, and the movement's destination is the buyer's plant. The inbound transportation activity supports the firm's supply effort in that the inbound transportation bridges the spatial and temporal gap existing between the buyer and the vendor, or seller.

The management of inbound transportation requires transportation knowledge and expertise similar to that necessary to handle the movement of finished goods outbound from the plant. The transportation manager must decide about the transportation mode, the routes, the rates, claims handling, carrier services, cost analysis, and regulations. Chapter 9 and Chapter 10 discuss these factors in detail.

vendor control

In some situations, the vendor controls inbound transportation. FOB-delivered terms of sale characterize such cases. When the buyer relinquishes the transportation function to the vendor, the buyer assumes that the vendor will ship the materials as cost-efficiently as possible. However, such an assumption is not always true. The buyer should periodically analyze the cost-effectiveness of the vendor's transportation decision.

modal choice

For basic raw materials, the transportation activity may involve rail or water transportation, the modes companies most commonly utilize to ship large volumes of low-value, high-density products, such as coal or sand. With the advent of rail deregulation, many of these shipments are moving into plants under contract rates with the railroads. The contracts usually specify providing a specific rate and service in return for a guarantee that the shipper will tender the carrier a guaranteed amount of freight.

rush shipments

Finally, inbound transportation is normally under less pressure to provide "rush" shipments than is outbound transportation. The demand for raw materials is much more stable and predictable than the demand for finished goods, since economies of production dictate long production runs, which give way to fixed production schedules. However, inbound transportation must occasionally handle a rush shipment—if a plant receives damaged raw materials, for example. Also, with increased use of JIT, inbound transportation requires much stricter schedules. Occasionally, when a problem develops, inbound transportation must expedite (rush) a shipment.

inspection

Receiving. The *receiving* process involves the actual physical receipt of the purchased material from the carrier. The receiving clerk, who must ensure that the goods a firm receives were those ordered and shipped, compares the materials indicated on the buyer's purchase order and the vendor's packing slip with the material the buyer has actually received. If discrepancies exist, the receiving department notifies the purchasing department, the material's users, and the accounts payable department.

damage claims

Another critical inspection during the receiving process involves examining the received material for any physical damage. As is discussed in Chapter 10, claims against the carrier for damage are easier to make if the receiving clerk notes on the bill of lading that the buyer received the shipment in damaged condition. When such a notation appears on the bill of lading, the carrier is presumed guilty of damaging the material. Any legal action places the burden on the carrier to prove that the carrier was not guilty of damaging the freight. Not noting damage on the bill of lading does not preclude the payment of a damage claim, but it puts an additional burden on the receiver (or owner) of the material to prove that the shipment was damaged when the carrier delivered it. Inbound traffic departments and receiving departments usually coordinate freight claims handling activities.

quality standards

Quality Control. The *quality control* function, like the receiving function, attempts to ensure that the items a firm receives are those the firm ordered. However, the quality control function is directly concerned with defining the product's quality in terms of dimensions, design specifications, chemical or physical properties, reliability, ease of maintenance, ease of use, brand, market grade, and industry standard. The quality control area's specific concern is whether or not the product received meets the quality standards the buyer and seller set forth in the purchase agreement.

quality implications

The quality of the materials a manufacturer procures directly affects the quality of the finished product and, consequently, affects the sale of the finished product. If a firm sells a defective product, the product's buyer will become dissatisfied and may refuse to purchase the firm's product in the future. In addition, a manufacturer who uses inferior materials in production may be legally liable for a hazardous or unreliable product. Thus, quality control function responsibilities cover the spectrum from market to legal concerns.

Supply Chain Technology

BibNet Links Michelin's Tire Dealers

Michelin North America's dealers have a better spin on their tire needs than ever before, thanks to the creation of Michelin's on-line supply chain community. Just ask Belle Tire, Inc., Fallen Park, Michigan. The tire dealer, which has about fifty stores in the Detroit area, has been connected for the past three years to BibNet, Michelin's on-line community and, in that time, has reduced inventories, decreased the amount of handling required, and improved order accuracy.

Belle Tire is one of more than 300 Michelin dealers in North America connected to BibNet, which is named after the tire maker's mascot, Bib. These dealers use BibNet to order tires and determine inventory availability at Michelin's eight warehouses.

Michelin began putting BibNet together in 1966, using software from Entigo, a Pittsburgh-based electronic-commerce vendor. BibNet is technically an *Extranet*, which means the dealers dial into a private phone network to gain access to the tire manufacturer's systems and use a standard Web browser to view inventory status and place orders for tires and parts electronically. "It allows for the sales channels to completely automate all of their ordering processes via the Web," says James Graham, Entigo's president.

But, the community offers more to its dealers than just Web-based procurement. Leo Zannetti, Belle Tire's director of purchasing, says that his company also can obtain access to Michelin's tire inventory system (TIMS). TIMS keeps track of the dealer's sales, the stock of tires on hand, and its orders. The system then consolidates the dealer's orders and suggests a shipment replenishment order twice a week.

From all accounts, participation in BibNet has had a positive effect on Belle Tire's operations. Zannetti reports that the software optimization of the procurement process has reduced inventory, resulting in the need for less warehouse space. On top of that, Belle Tire has initiated direct store replenishment for fifteen of its larger stores, which can accommodate tractor-trailer deliveries from Michelin. The other stores are resupplied daily from Belle Tire's main warehouse. "The product that's directly shipped cuts down on handling," says Zannetti. He has identified one other benefit as well: "Because the purchase orders are sent electronically, there are fewer mistakes."

Michelin believes that its on-line community will ultimately eliminate unneeded inventory for both the manufacturer and its dealers. "Because of the visibility of orders from the time the dealer places them to the time they leave the warehouse," says Tom Hall, Michelin's manager of electronic commerce, "there will be fewer mistakes in the order-fulfillment process."

Source: "BibNet Links Michelin's Tire Dealers," *Logistics* (February 2000): 47. Copyright Cahners Business Information. Reprinted by permission.

sample

Normally, inspecting each item that a buyer purchases is neither possible nor desirable. Quality inspectors usually examine a limited sample of the items purchased. For example, a quality inspector wanting to determine whether the life of a given vendor's light bulbs met longevity specifications would test a sample of the vendor's light bulbs. The quality control department would statistically examine the results and, on the basis of the tested sample, would decide to accept or reject the order received. The increased emphasis on quality in recent years has required vendors to develop their own statistical quality control programs. Today, many buyers insist upon total or 100 percent quality.

value of scrap

Salvage and Scrap Disposal. The final activity in the materials-management function involves *disposing of salvage, scrap,* excess, and obsolete materials. Although primarily concerned with buying, the materials management department has assumed this selling responsibility, since most marketing or sales departments must concentrate on selling the firm's finished products.

Scrap and salvage material that is useful to others has a certain value, and the disposal of these items provides income for the firm. The recent recycling trend has provided a ready market for many scrap and salvage items. For example, companies are using used oils and other scrap items such as olive pits and corncobs as fuel sources; and, as recent years of double-digit inflation have sent new equipment prices beyond the ability of many potential buyers to pay, more companies are buying or salvaging used equipment.

disposal

Certain scrap materials cannot be sold but must be disposed of in a safe and prescribed manner. One such commodity group is hazardous wastes—materials that are ignitable, corrosive, reactive (volatile), or toxic. Disposing of these hazardous materials is quite costly, and the generator of such materials is under specific legal liability to dispose of them properly.

The materials-management function, as we indicated, occurs on the inbound side of the logistics pipeline. Customer service and distribution activity channels are on the pipeline's outbound side; but a firm must tightly coordinate both inbound and outbound logistics in today's highly competitive marketplace.

Electronic Procurement

The computer and the World Wide Web have created some dramatic changes in the business world. It is becoming quite common for consumers to research products and services; locate retail outlets; and, with the click of a mouse, purchase goods and services—all in the convenience of one's home. There is much attention to business-to-consumer (B2C) E-commerce, but the majority of the E-commerce transactions are business to business (B2B). B2B purchases are estimated to be $1.3 to $2.0 trillion by 2003.[6]

Procurement was the business process that made early application of E-commerce. Initially, companies utilized electronic data interchange (EDI) technology to connect with their major customers to process purchase orders, send notifications of shipment, and transfer funds. However, EDI technology is costly and requires special technology to implement. The advent of the publicly available Internet has eliminated the investment and technology problems associated with EDI and opened the door to increased application of E-commerce techniques to procurement.

The most common use of E-commerce today is to research vendor and product information. This is a primary reason that some vendors have only a Web site on the Internet to merely advertise their products. However, other companies have advanced on-line procurement systems that permit a buyer to electronically check available stock, negotiate price, issue an order, check on the status of the order, issue an invoice, and receive payment. The ultimate E-commerce procurement system is still in the development stage and will evolve over time.

Advantages

The advantages of E-commerce procurement are shown in Figure 4–8. An obvious advantage is the lowering of procurement operating costs. The reduction of paperwork and the associated cost of paper processing, filing, and storing is a major cost-saving area of E-commerce. Many companies have a goal of being paperless, but few have obtained that goal at this time.

Another paper reduction possible with E-commerce is electronic funds transfer. Paying vendor invoices electronically eliminates the cost of preparing, mailing, filing, and storage of the checks. Estimates of the cost of writing a check vary from a low of $10 to a high of $85, the majority of this cost being the cost of accounts payable personnel.

Reduced sourcing time means increased productivity because a procurement specialist spends less time per order and can place more orders in a given time period. Likewise, the seller utilizing E-commerce can increase the productivity of customer service representatives. Many of the questions asked by the buyer can be answered on-line, thereby saving time for both the buyer and seller personnel.

Given the real-time nature of E-Commerce information, sellers have up-to-date information on demand and can adjust production/purchases to meet the current demand level. This same real-time information enables the buyer to establish controls that will coordinate purchase quantities with requirement quantities and monitor spending levels. That is, the buyer is now in the position of monitoring the quantity of an item ordered, received, and on-hand and comparing it to the amount needed, and doing this in a real-time mode. The same is true for monitoring spending activities against budgeted amounts.

Electronic procurement affords efficiency in the process by utilizing fewer resources to produce a given level of purchases. With a click of the mouse, a purchasing manager can search the world for alternative supply sources of a product or service. With another click of the mouse, the manager can then ascertain information about the sources identified through the electronic search. All of this research is done in the office without phone calls, additional personnel, or outside sources.

FIGURE 4–8 Advantages of Electronic Procurement

Lower operating costs
- Reduce paperwork
- Reduce sourcing time
- Improve control over inventory and spending

Improve procurement efficiency
- Find new supply sources
- Improve communications
- Improve personnel use
- Lower cycle times

Reduce procurement prices
- Improve comparison shopping
- Reduce overall prices paid

A significant efficiency factor of E-commerce is improved communication. The buyer can secure information from the vendor's company—product line, prices, and product availability. The seller can obtain information regarding requests for proposals, blueprints, technical specifications, and purchase requirements from the buyer. Also, the seller can improve customer service by communicating the status of the order, giving the buyer advance notice of any delays in the order fulfillment due to stockout conditions or transportation. As noted earlier, E-commerce permits the seller to gain real-time information to more accurately predict demand.

This improved communication via E-commerce aids in reducing order cycle time. All the time elements incorporated in order cycle time are reduced. The time to place the order is reduced to seconds. The buyer knows prior to placing an order whether the vendor has product available. The seller monitors demand instantaneously and is in a better position to adjust supply with current demand and to reduce or eliminate a stockout condition.

Better use of procurement personnel is made possible by relieving them of the clerical tasks associated with processing the order, such as typing purchase orders, mailing them to the vendor, and checking the status of the order via phone. The procurement manager is now free to focus attention on the long-term strategic procurement issues such as long-term item availability, opportunities for supply chain efficiencies, innovative products, and so on.

Reduced procurement prices have resulted from the ability of a buyer to gain access to pricing information from more potential vendors. With more vendors bidding for the business, the buyers are finding lower prices forthcoming. In addition, the procurement manager has the ability to view on-line the qualities of different vendor products and services, making comparison much easier. The overall effect of increased comparison shopping and increased number of potential vendors is lower prices.

Disadvantages

Like most things in life, E-commerce does have some drawbacks. The most frequently voiced concern about using the Internet for procurement is security. Recent examples of attacks on B2C E-commerce companies such as Amazon.com and eBay where the computers were overloaded with orders and operations were stopped give many executives much concern about E-commerce security. Also, there is concern regarding the vulnerability of credit card numbers transmitted over the Internet or stored on a vendor's system to theft by a computer hacker.

Another problem is the lack of face-to-face contact between the buyer and seller. Buying and selling via E-commerce reduces the ability to build close supplier relationships. This can be overcome by making a concerted effort to develop and enhance personal communications with the vendor.

Other concerns deal with technology. More specifically, there are concerns with the lack of standard protocols, system reliability, and technology problems. Lastly, there is reluctance on the part of some to invest the time and money to learn the new technology. For the most part, these concerns are diminishing daily as new and improved technology is developed and the business community demands the use of E-commerce.

Common Applications

E-commerce is most often used to purchase high-volume, low-value, low-risk items, or generics. The most frequently E-purchased items include office supplies, office equipment, computer hardware/software, and travel. Items within these categories are quite standard, and there are many sellers available. Also, the sellers of these products have been leaders in the development of B2B systems.

This does not mean that other products are not electronically purchased. There is a growing trend toward B2B transactions in such basic products as chemicals, plastics, and metals. Virtually any item purchased by today's businesses will eventually be available through E-commerce within the next few years.

Types of E-commerce Models[7]

There are four basic types of E-commerce business models used in procurement: sell-side system, electronic marketplace, buy-side system, and on-line trading community.

The *sell-side system* is a Web site administered by a seller. The site is usually free to the buyer and offers B2B service with the seller who establishes the site. Examples include OfficeMax (http://www.officemax.com), Staples (http://www.staples.com), McMaster-Carr (http://www.mcmaster.com), Global Computer Supplies (http://www.globalcomputer.com), and Newark Electronics (http://www.newark.com). A buyer can log on to the sell-side Web site and review products, prices, and services and place an order. The buyer cannot track or control spending with the sell-side system, and the Web sites are somewhat difficult to locate.

Another seller-operated B2B service is the *electronic marketplace.* The electronic marketplace is an amalgam of electronic catalogs from vendors within a market. The marketplace is administered by a third party, not one of the vendors. The electronic marketplace provides a one-stop sourcing site for buyers who can examine the offerings of many different vendors at one Web location. Like the sell-side system, the electronic marketplace does not permit the buyer to track or control spending. Examples of electronic marketplaces include the Plastics Network (http://www.plasticsnet.com), E-Chemicals (http://www.e-chemicals.com) and MetalSite (http://www.metalsite.com).

The buyer-controlled B2B service is known as the *buy-side system.* This B2B system is housed on the buyer's system and administered by the buyer. The buyer preapproves the vendors that have access to the system, and the prices of the vendors' products and services have been prenegotiated. These systems permit tracking and controlling procurement spending and reduce unauthorized purchases. However, the cost of the buy-side system is very high due to the cost of developing and administering the system with a large list of vendors. The buy-side system is usually the domain of large companies.

Recently, Ford announced the establishment of buy-side procurement systems. The companies expect to save millions of dollars as a result of processing purchase orders electronically. The Ford system is known as Auto Exchange and will permit its thousands of suppliers to receive and process purchase orders electronically. After focusing on procurement, the system will be used for supply chain planning;

consolidating demand; and, finally, collaborative design and shortening of the product release cycle. Although Ford will benefit from the procurement aspects of its buy-side system, there will be many value-added services, efficiencies, and economies realized from its application to the total supply chain.

The final basic electronic business model is the *on-line trading community.* The on-line trading community is maintained by a third-party technology vendor where multiple buyers and multiple sellers in a given market can conduct business. The difference between the on-line trading community and the electronic marketplace is that the electronic marketplace is focused on providing information about sellers, whereas the on-line community permits the buyers and sellers to conduct business transactions.

The on-line trading company may be viewed as an electronic auction. The buyer indicates the type of product, quantity, and so on desired; and the sellers respond. In a downward auction, the buyer states a maximum time period to receive the best bid from potential vendors. At the end of the time period, the buyer selects the vendor(s) with the lowest price and will conduct negotiations, if necessary, to finalize the transaction. Examples of on-line trading companies include Travelocity (http://www.travelocity.com), eBay (http://www.ebay.com), and the National Transportation Exchange (http://www.nte.net).

Electronic procurement is here and will continue to grow. It will not replace all procurement activities, but it could reach 80 percent or more of a company's total purchase order activity. Electronic procurement focuses on the processing of orders and maintaining a source of real-time information for better decision making. Procurement specialists focus on selecting vendors, negotiating prices, monitoring quality, and developing supplier relations.

Summary

- The supply chain can be viewed as inbound logistics and outbound logistics; the focus of this chapter is on the inbound system. Effective supply chain management requires the careful coordination of inbound and outbound systems.
- Inbound logistics systems can vary in terms of importance, scope, cost, and complexity, depending on where the company is located in the supply chain, the nature of the product, and the market situation in which the product is sold.
- The procurement area plays a major role in materials management, and procurement is an important link in the supply chain.
- The procurement process can be broken down into a set of activities that include identifying a need, defining and evaluating user requirements, deciding whether to make or buy, identifying the type of purchase, performing a market analysis, identifying potential suppliers, prescreening possible vendors, evaluating remaining suppliers, choosing a vendor, receiving delivery of the product or service, and making a postpurchase evaluation.
- Not all purchased items are of equal importance. Using the criteria of risk and value, the quadrant technique classifies items into four importance categories: generics, commodities, distinctives, and criticals. Generics have low risk, low value; commodities have low risk, high value; distinctives have high risk, low value; and criticals have high risk, high value.

- The procurement process activities can be more effectively managed by following a four-step process: (1) determine type of purchase; (2) determine necessary level of investment; (3) perform the procurement process; (4) evaluate the effectiveness of the procurement process.
- In selecting vendors, a number of criteria should be utilized, including quality, reliability, capability, financial viability, and other factors, such as location.
- There are four basic sources of price: commodity markets, price lists, price quotation, and price negotiation.
- The purchase price is a matter of great importance, but it is much more complex than just the base unit price, since it requires the analysis of added value along the supply chain to deliver the highest total value to the ultimate customer.
- In addition to procurement costs, materials management includes warehousing, production planning and control, traffic, receiving, quality control, and salvage and scrap disposal.
- Electronic procurement has become widely used in business because of the publicly available Internet. The advantages include lower operating costs, improved efficiency, and reduced prices, with the primary disadvantage being security. There are four basic types of electronic procurement models: sell-side, electronic marketplace, buy-side, and on-line trading community systems.

Study Questions

1. Inbound logistics systems can vary in scope and complexity among different companies. Explain the differences that can exist between inbound logistics systems. What is the source of the differences?
2. The procurement process can be described in terms of a set of activities that should be used in the purchase of goods and services. Briefly discuss these activities.
3. Maximizing the effectiveness of the procurement process is a major goal of an organization. What steps can be taken to help ensure that the process is maximized?
4. A key part of the procurement process is the selection of vendors. What criteria are commonly used in this selection process? Which criteria should be given the highest priority? Why?
5. What are the major sources of prices in the purchase of goods? Under what circumstances would these sources be utilized?
6. What are the components of total acquired cost? Is it realistic to expect companies to consider all of these components?
7. Using the risk/value technique, categorize the importance of the following items for an automobile manufacturer: engine, tires, gasoline, paper for the employee newsletter, a uniquely designed and engineered muffler, and rail car service to dealers. Describe the rationale you used to ascertain each categorization.

8. What role does warehousing play in materials-management systems? Can the importance of warehousing vary among companies? Explain.
9. Discuss the advantages and disadvantages of using E-commerce in the procurement process.
10. Describe the different types of E-commerce business models available for procurement, and point out their respective benefits and disadvantages.

Notes

1. This section is adapted from R. A. Novack and Stephen W. Simco, "The Industrial Procurement Process," *Journal of Business Logistics* 12, no. 1 (1991): 145–65.
2. Michael E. Porter, *Competitive Advantage* (New York: The Free Press, 1985), 11–16.
3. This section is adapted from Joseph L. Cavinato, "Quadrant Technique: Key to Effective Acquisition and Access," *ARDC Spectrum, Report #11,* Acquisition Research & Development Center, State College, Pa.
4. Porter, 33–34.
5. This section is adapted from J. L. Cavinato, "A Total Cost/Value Model for Supply Chain Competitiveness," *Journal of Business Logistics* 13, no.2 (1992): 285–99.
6. Cherish Karoway Whyte, "E-Procurement the New Competitive Weapon," *Purchasing Today* (April 2000): 25.
7. The material in this section is adapted from Mark Vigoroso, "Buyers Prepare for Brave New World of E-Commerce," *Purchasing* (22 April 1999).

Case 4–1 ■ Durable Vinyl Siding Corp.

The Durable Vinyl Siding Corporation (DVS) is a leading U.S. manufacturer of vinyl siding products for home and commercial buildings. In 2000, the company had record sales of $250 million—a 15 percent increase over 1999 and the tenth year of double-digit growth. Mr. Mark Talbott, president, was very pleased with the positive sales figures for 2000 but was growing increasingly concerned about the trend of the bottom-line numbers. During the past five years, the net profit margin had slipped from 7.2 percent in 1996 to 4.5 percent in 2000.

At the monthly executive team meeting, Mark pointed out the downward trend of net profits and challenged the team to increase the bottom line by 1.0 to 2.0 percentage points for the next year. Mark pointed out to the team members that price pressure from competing siding companies and increasing costs were the primary reasons for the declining profit margins. He asked each team member to develop a strategic plan to accomplish the profit goals.

Margaret Klisure, director of purchasing, was reviewing the purchasing data the procurement team had gathered in preparation for developing a purchasing strategic plan. First, procurement costs had increased from 57 percent of sales in 1996 to 65 percent of sales in 2000. The procurement staff increased by five people during this same time period. DVS now manufactures 1,500 SKUs and purchases over 5,000 SKUs of materials to support the manufacture, sale, and delivery of its finished goods line.

The items purchased include vinyl base products, paints, office supplies, packaging, lumber for pallets, warehouse equipment, maintenance and operating items, and transportation services. In total, DVM spent $162.5 million in 2000 for these items and the operation of the procurement department. For each 1.0 percent reduction in procurement expenditures, Margaret calculated an increase of 0.65 percent in net profits (assuming $250 million in sales).

The purchasing department operation was basically the same as it was in 1996. Margaret was recently appointed director of purchasing following the retirement of the previous director who was the head of purchasing since the founding of the company over twenty years before. Most of the purchasing tasks are completed manually. A computer is used for internal control of inventory levels and for printing invoices. There is no procurement computer system in place, and there is no use of E-commerce for purchasing. The purchasing staff consists primarily of buyers who are assigned to particular product groups; for example, a person is responsible for purchasing all the vinyl raw materials, one person purchases transportation, and so on.

Over the years, the buyers have become very adept at gaining price concessions from vendors. However, this has created some very serious warehousing problems for DVM. For example, last week Mark Talbott called an emergency meeting with the directors of manufacturing, warehousing, sales, and purchasing to seek a solution to the overcrowding in the warehouse. The warehouse was completely full, forcing DVS to go off-site to store finished goods. A review of the items stored in the warehouse indicated that there was a six-month supply of corrugated packaging material, a ten-month supply of paints, and a four-month supply of lumber. Also, the inventory levels of over 50 percent of the finished good SKUs exceeded a two-year supply at current sales levels.

With only one warehouse in the system, DVM had to optimize the utilization of this facility. If DVM had to use an outside warehouse for short-term storage, it incurred a 15 percent penalty in the form of higher storage, order picking, and transportation costs. In addition, the cost of capital rose last year because of the actions of the Federal Reserve; and the total purchasing expenditure included the cost of money tied up in inventory.

Margaret also knew that the buyers' productivity was declining because the annual number of orders was declining in light of the addition of staff last year. The buyers noted the need for more time to research potential vendors and to maintain good vendor relations as the prime reason for the lower productivity.

Margaret's primary objective was to reduce procurement costs while maintaining the product quality and efficiency of procurement. Price concessions from vendors did not appear to be a major source of cost savings, particularly for the basic vinyl raw materials. She concluded that the primary areas for efficiency enhancements were in computerization and E-commerce.

Case Questions

1. What organizational changes would you suggest for DVM procurement?
2. What types of computerization changes would you recommend?
3. How would E-commerce benefit DVS procurement?
4. Would you recommend the same computer and E-commerce strategies for all 5,000 SKUs purchased? If not, how would these strategies differ?
5. What strategies do you suggest for maintaining procurement service levels?

CHAPTER 5

GLOBAL LOGISTICS

LEARNING OBJECTIVES

After reading this chapter, you should be able to do the following:

- Describe the major similarities and differences between domestic and global logistics.
- Discuss the reasons for the increase in global business activity.
- Define a global company.
- Explain Porter's dynamic diamond theory of global competitive advantage.
- Describe the critical changes affecting global logistics.
- Explain the effect of the changing legal and political environment in Europe, Asia, North America, and South America.
- Discuss the North American Free Trade Agreement and its effect on logistics.
- Define the nature and benefit of a Maquiladora.
- Explain the major transportation systems available for global logistics.
- Distinguish among the global logistics intermediaries: freight forwarders, customs house brokers, nonvessel-operating common carriers, and export management companies.
- Explain the criteria used to select a port for global shipments.
- Discuss warehousing and packaging requirements for global shipments.
- Define the role of customs duties and free trade zones.

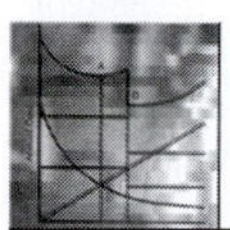

Logistics Profile

The Same but Very Different

Mr. John Rounder, vice president of Worldwide Logistics for Novelty Clothing, Inc., finally had some time to review his notes for the keynote address he was making to the Council of Logistics Management (CLM), a leading supply chain professional organization. After working more than twenty-five years in all phases of logistics and supply chain management (SCM), he was certain that he had something to offer to the CLM membership.

He chose the topic, "The Same but Very Different," because the global supply chain has many of the same fundamental functions and concepts as domestic SCM; but, the differences were quite substantial and required a much different managerial approach. Thus, his presentation would be directed toward global operations but it would build on the domestic supply chain management strategies and techniques familiar to the majority of the members.

First, he enumerated the similarities between domestic and global SCM:

- The conceptual logistics framework of linking supply sources, plants, warehouses, and customers is the same.
- Both systems involve managing the movement and storage of products.
- Information is critical to effective provision of customer service, management of inventory, vendor product and service quality monitoring, and costs control.
- The functional processes of inventory management, warehousing, order processing, carrier selection, procurement, and vendor payment are required for both.
- Economic and safety regulations exist for transportation.

Once John made the audience aware that global SCM is basically the same as domestic, he turned his attention to the major differences:

- Distance is an obvious difference, with the global supply chain typically being greater than the domestic supply chain. For example, the supply chain for sourcing clothing from Pacific Rim manufacturers is approximately eight to ten times greater than that for a domestic supplier.
- Another obvious difference is language. In a domestic supply chain, usually only one language is spoken; whereas, in a global supply chain, two, three, or more languages are utilized. Being able to communicate with a German supplier, a Greek ship owner, a French warehouse operator, and an Italian trucking company requires command of multiple languages.
- The meaning of words must also be examined. For example, the word *ton* has at least three different meanings: a short ton equals 2,000 pounds; a metric ton equals 2,205 pounds; and a long ton equals 2,240 pounds. You can never take for granted that you or your supply chain partner have the same meaning for a ton, so verify the number of pounds in a ton and the meanings of commonly used logistics terms.
- Numerous cultural differences among the people are encountered in a global supply chain. For example, in some countries, conducting business over a lengthy meal is a prerequisite. The national and religious holidays differ from country to country, making it necessary to plan around these downtimes in the system. Finally, the work ethic varies among countries, suggesting that SCM productivity will vary among countries.
- Currency exchange fluctuations are common in the global chain. A devaluation of a country's currency means a price increase for products sourced from that country.
- Political stability is the norm for the U.S. domestic supply chain. However, political instability is the norm in other parts of the world and causes major disruptions in the global supply chain.
- The infrastructure around the world is very different. The size of roadways, trucks, railcars, warehouses, and so on is not the same in all countries.

(continued on next page)

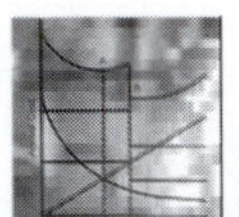

Logistics Profile

The Same but Very Different *continued*

Some developing nations do not have many paved roadways, while in other countries the roads are very narrow precluding the use of the 102-inch-wide trailer, a U.S. standard. For a similar mode, the freight carrying will typically be less than that of the United States.

- Environmental regulations vary considerably in the global supply chain. Some countries—France, for example—require the manufacturer of a product produced outside the country to remove all packaging materials or pay to have it recycled (green stamp in France). Compliance increases global supply chain costs, whereas noncompliance stops the global system in that country.
- Labeling laws differ among countries, with the most common variance being the label printed in the language of the country. Thus, the product label must be printed in the appropriate language or it cannot enter the country.
- Customs regulations are very numerous and different around the world. Each country has regulations controlling the exporting and importing of goods and services. These regulations can change overnight and cause major upheavals in the supply chain.
- Transport regulations around the globe are not the same as those in the United States. For example, ocean carriers registered in countries such as Panama, Liberia, the Cayman Islands, and Bermuda have different safety regulations than those imposed on U.S.-registered vessels. International standards have been developed for such issues as carrier liability, but the standards apply only if the country in which the ship is registered has adopted these rules.
- Probably one of the most time-consuming differences is paperwork. A typical global shipment can require twenty to thirty or more documents, and each one is essential to the movement of the product into or out of a country. It is often said that paperwork moves global shipments; because, without the proper paperwork, the shipment stops!

In conclusion, the global supply chain is much more complex. The same managerial attention to details given the domestic supply chains is required for a global system with serious attention being given to the effects of different cultures, languages, currencies, infrastructures, and regulations of the countries included in the global supply chain.

Global Business Logistics

global sourcing

In recent years, increasing numbers of companies have become aware that the marketplace encompasses the world, not just the United States. For example, many U.S. firms have found that evaluating offshore sourcing alternatives is essential to a well-run logistics and materials-management organization. Alternatively, by developing export markets, U.S. firms have highlighted the need for effective logistics systems and networks throughout the world. Conversely, companies located in other countries have also broadened their sourcing and marketing considerations geographically; like U.S. firms, they look toward global logistics strategies and operations to provide *competitive advantage* through efficiency, effectiveness, and differentiation.

global distribution

key issues

As a practical matter, logistics managers are finding that they need to do much work in terms of conceptualizing, designing, and implementing logistics initiatives that may be effective globally. For this reason, this chapter addresses key issues and topics that are essential to the global aspects of business logistics. Logically, the development of global logistics approaches requires a high degree of coordination between logistics groups, marketing, and purchasing groups in individual companies.

This chapter deals first with the nature of global business and global logistics. Then, two successive sections deal with key global logistics trends and with changing political and legal environments. Finally, the chapter discusses transportation, channel strategies, storage and packaging, and governmental influences.

The Magnitude of Global Business

The growth of world trade is made possible by the planning of logistics companies all over the world. Countries are becoming closer and closer because of the success in logistics. Foreign trade has grown in tonnage and in value for the United States and for most of the other nations of the world. The world is becoming more and more competitive due to the growth in logistics activity. A firm will produce anywhere in the world where it is feasible and leave the transportation from country A to country B to the logistics professionals.

The top ten U.S. trading partners for 1998 and 1999 are presented in Table 5–1. Total trade with these ten countries represents approximately 70 percent of total U.S. imports and 64 percent of total exports. From 1998 to 1999, total trade with these ten countries increased 9.5 percent with the amount of trade increasing for each country except for Singapore, which had the same level of trade in both years. The largest percentage increase in trade was with Korea, which had a 34 percent increase.

TABLE 5–1 Top U.S. Trading Partners

	Value of Trade ($ Billion)	
Country	**1999**	**1998**
Canada	362	329
Mexico	196	173
Japan	188	179
China	94	85
Germany	81	76
United Kingdom	77	73
Korea	54	40
Taiwan	54	51
France	44	41
Singapore	34	34
Total	1,184	1,081

Source: U.S. Bureau of the Census, Foreign Trade Statistics, "Top Ten Countries with which the U.S. Trades," 2000.

foreign sourcing

Outsourcing of materials from foreign suppliers is a critical component of the logistics supply chain of many companies. The major reason for outsourcing is lower costs. For example, many appliance manufacturers will ship all supplies required to make a wiring harness to Mexico where labor rates are less than 20 percent of those in the United States. Lower labor costs in developing nations mean lower prices for materials and higher profits.

focused manufacturing

The trend today is to outsource from any part of the world that offers a cost advantage and to move it to any destination through the global logistics supply chain. For example, some companies are applying this outsourcing concept to production via a managerial concept known as *focused manufacturing*. Focused manufacturing is a strategy in which one or a few plants are designated as the worldwide supplier(s) of a given product or product line. It is the responsibility of global logistics to make certain the finished products are at the right place, in the right quantity, at the right time anywhere in the global marketplace.

Global Markets and Global Corporations

Generally, the global business environment has seen many trade barriers fall over the past decade. Whether the case involves trade between the United States and other countries or between two or more foreign countries, the trend toward facilitating, rather than constraining, global business activity is definitely accelerating. Thanks greatly to the growth and maturation of the ocean and air container shipping industries, distinct national and specific country-to-country international markets have been transformed into truly global businesses.

communications

Global markets have developed because of similar global needs and wants. Through new and extensive communications technologies, people throughout the world learn of and express the desire to have many of the same products. As a result, people have sacrificed traditional product preferences for higher-quality, lower-priced products that are more highly standardized. This preference for nontraditional products is due to economic and cultural factors. The availability of high-quality merchandise at locally reasonable price levels is an attractor to people throughout the world. In addition, the opportunity to own or use products that are used in other countries helps people to feel that they enjoy standards of living that may be comparable to those of more prosperous nations.

global product strategy

We commonly see differences in promotion and in products themselves when manufacturers market their products to potential buyers in various parts of the world.[1] Canon's marketing of a new 35mm automatic camera served as a good example. As a result of extensive customer research conducted in markets worldwide, Canon decided to create a single "world camera" that would respond to the collective preferences of a wide variety of potential purchasers. To customize its appeal to buyers in individual countries, however, Canon positioned the camera differently in various market areas. In the United States, Canon described the camera as easy to use and slanted its appeal toward the growing market of nonprofessional photographers who nevertheless wanted a product of reasonable quality. Alternatively, in Japan, Canon designed the camera to appeal to the consumer as a state-of-the-art example of technological advancement in the photography field. This positioning was very effective, considering many Japanese buyers' strong desire for the latest, most advanced electronic equipment.

Global Competitive Strategy

definition

An interesting distinction is that of a global company versus one whose operations are simply multidomestic. Essentially, global companies formulate strategy on a worldwide basis to exploit new market opportunities.[2] Such companies, which seek to influence their industries' competitive balance, implement global strategy effectively and efficiently. In comparison, multidomestic companies tend to operate within individual markets throughout the world but do not emphasize coordinating individual strategies into a cohesive global strategy.

Global companies tend to be more successful at developing strategies that help them to achieve their business objectives simultaneously at locations throughout the world. These companies are likely to strategically source materials and components worldwide, select global locations for key supply depots and distribution centers, use existing logistics networks when sourcing and distributing new products, and transfer existing logistics technologies to new markets. Examples of U.S.-based global companies include Xerox, IBM, DuPont, Kodak, Philips Consumer Electronics, Merck, Coca-Cola, and McDonald's.

One key to achieving global success is to achieve global business volumes. This not only justifies entering markets and introducing new products in many areas of the world, but also provides business activity sufficient to absorb the significant cost outlays essential to this level of activity.

global operating strategies

Global corporations typically design their operating strategy objectives around four components: technology, marketing, manufacturing, and logistics.[3] While initiatives in all four areas should function synchronously, the logistics system serves as the global infrastructure upon which the other systems operate. Also, firms have recognized that the global logistics system itself may provide a source of competitive advantage.

For example, Toyota has developed the JIT concept for global operations. By refining its information and planning systems, it is capable of outsourcing parts and components from many different nations for its plants in twenty-five countries. Instead of producing automobiles solely in Japan for export throughout the world, Toyota's strategy is to produce more automobiles within the national market and to outsource parts and components from Japan and other nations. The logistics system enables this strategy to operate effectively.

Customer Service Strategies for Global Markets

global competition

Global competition has four prominent characteristics. First, companies competing globally seek to create standardized, yet customized, marketing. Second, product life cycles are shortening, sometimes lasting less than one year. This is true for certain high-tech products such as computers and peripherals, photography items, and audiovisual equipment. Third, more companies are utilizing outsourcing and offshore manufacturing. Fourth, marketing and manufacturing activities and strategies tend to converge and be better coordinated in firms operating globally.[4]

As companies service global markets, logistics networks tend to become more expansive and complex. As a result, it is not unusual to see lead times increase and inventory levels rise. To successfully operate in a time-based competitive environment, firms emphasize managing logistics as a system, shortening lead times when possible, and moving toward the use of "focused" factories that produce limited product lines for geographically specific areas.

customer needs

Perhaps the most important step in designing and implementing global logistics strategies is to understand the service needs of customers in locations dispersed throughout the world. This is a prerequisite to developing effective manufacturing, marketing, and logistics strategies to satisfy the needs of the global marketplace. The whole of the logistics operation should be based around the customers' needs.

Critical Factors and Key Trends

This section first identifies significant factors that have affected the competitive positioning of companies in business environments throughout the world. It then briefly discusses several key logistics and transportation trends that have significantly affected the global business activity of U.S.-based firms and the activity of offshore firms doing business in the United States.

Importance of Competitive Environment

Based on a four-year study of ten countries, Michael Porter has concluded that "a nation's ability to upgrade its existing advantages to the next level of technology and productivity is the key to international (global) success."[5] He feels that a loss of global market share in advanced fields such as transportation and technology shows the United States slipping recently in international trade.

Porter's *dynamic diamond*

To explain his theories of what produces competitive advantage in a global business environment, Porter suggests a *dynamic diamond* containing four elements of competitive advantage that reinforce one another. These elements include

- *Factor conditions:* A nation's ability to transform its basic factors (e.g., resources, education, or infrastructure) into competitive advantage
- *Demand conditions:* Market size, buyer sophistication, and media exposure of available products
- *Related and supporting industries:* May include partners in the supply chain, co-packers and/or co-manufacturers, or marketing and distribution intermediaries
- *Company strategy, structure, and rivalry:* Market structures and the nature of domestic competition

Each element is necessary for success in domestic and global markets, and the presence of competition in domestic markets motivates individual firms to identify productive marketing, manufacturing, and logistics strategies. Creating more competitive business environments, stimulating demand for innovative new products (through the provision of tax credits, for example), placing greater emphasis on research and development, and refocusing trade policies on truly unfair subsidies and trade barriers are strategies for success in global markets.

Critical Changes in Logistics and Transportation

In this section, we discuss briefly five major areas of change: deregulation of the U.S. ocean liner industry, intermodalism, shipment control, trade policies, and currency fluctuations.

Deregulation of the U.S. Ocean Liner Industry. Perhaps the most striking result of the Shipping Act of 1984 and the Ocean Shipping Reform Act of 1998 is the greater reliance on the marketplace to control rates. The elimination of tariff filing and the publishing of rates on the Internet make marketplace controls much more effective. Shippers may negotiate confidential contracts with ocean carriers, and the carriers are not required to match the service contract terms of similarly situated shippers.

marketplace controls

Direct consequences of this shift to marketplace regulation include the use of negotiated rates and service under contracts of carriage, the right of conference carriers to take independent action on rates and service agreements, and the lessening of the role of linear conferences in determining rates and capacity on shipping lanes. Carriers are moving away from conference participation, because the cartel-like arrangements of the conference no longer hold the promise of guaranteed profits for the carriers. The ocean rates are now more flexible to move in response to the laws of supply and demand.

Intermodalism. *Intermodalism* refers to the joint use of two or more transportation modes; moving highway trailers or containers on rail flatcars or in container ships is an example. Figure 5–1 shows intermodal options available to international shippers. Those options include all-water service, mini land bridge, land bridge, and microbridge operations.

intermodal transportation

Toyota uses a microbridge for the movement of parts and components from Japan to its two plants in the United States. The microbridge to Georgetown, Kentucky,

FIGURE 5–1 Types of International Intermodalism

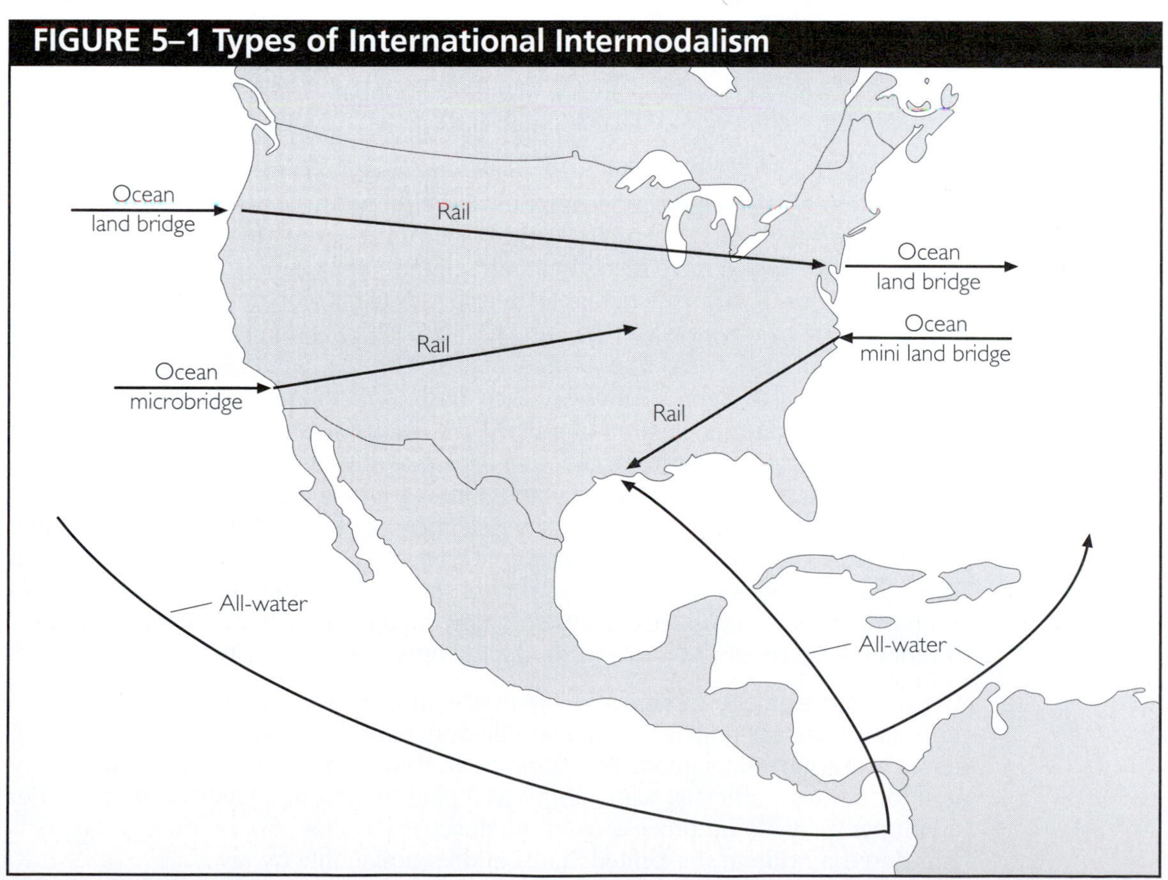

has a lower cost than an all-water movement to an East or Gulf Coast port and then a land shipment by truck or rail to Georgetown. But more important, the cycle time is much lower by the microbridge.

Intermodal operations represent one of the fastest-growing areas in the global logistics arena. By combining the resources of two or more transportation modes, logistics services suppliers can provide a service to the shipper-customer that appears to be seamless, despite the sometimes numerous and complex operations involved in moving the shipper's product.

In international shipping, we have to understand three very fundamental concepts: port to port, port to point, and point to point. *Port to port* refers to moving cargo between two ports, for example, New York and Rotterdam, the Netherlands. *Port to point* refers to moving cargo between a port and final inland destination, for example, Kobe, Japan, and Chicago. Finally, *point to point* implies transportation between the shipper's door and the customer's door. The point-to-point movement is characteristic of intermodalism.

communications and control

Shipment Control. Effective communication and control systems are essential to a competitive global logistics capability. Issues concerning documentation, export-import management, and individual shipments' movements are critical to today's customers; and preferred suppliers are those who can meet these customer requirements.

Most major international transportation companies, particularly the air carriers, have high-tech communication systems that permit the tracking of the progress of the shipment. Federal Express's tracking systems can locate an international shipment within seconds, indicate the time it is expected to be delivered, and identify the person who signed for delivery. Tracking a global shipment poses a problem because of the number of intermediaries and carriers involved, each having different information systems.

free trade agreements

Trade Policies. Although a movement toward eliminating trade barriers worldwide characterized the years following World War II until about 1975, certain countries throughout the world have recently made selective changes in their trade policies. Many countries that are geographically close have negotiated free trade agreements. Europe has established the European Union, an economic community of fifteen European countries. The United States, Canada, and Mexico have joined together to form the North American Free Trade Agreement (NAFTA), a free trade zone. (Both the European Union and NAFTA are discussed in more detail later in this chapter.) Even countries of the Asia-Pacific region that have historically set up protective barriers to restrict imports of goods into their home markets are starting to let down their guard. Australia, New Zealand, Japan, South Korea, Canada, and the United States have joined to found Asian Pacific Economic Cooperation (APEC). However, we should keep in mind that official trade barriers and unofficial barriers such as customs delays still may impair the ability of logistics systems to function effectively in terms of product supply and/or distribution.

Another key element to remember is that countries have different cultures, customs, and business practices. Shipment delays are possible when these cultural differences are not understood. For example, in developing nations, it is quite common for customs officials, who are not well paid, to accept a favor from the carrier or shipper to speed up processing of the documents. The offering of such favors is considered a bribe in the United States and is punishable by law.

The North American Free Trade Agreement has reduced trade barriers such as import duties on a wide number of products moving among the United States, Canada, and Mexico; but physical barriers still remain, especially into Mexico. One such physical barrier takes the form of restricting U.S. trucks and drivers from operating in Mexico, thus requiring all cargo to be handed off to a Mexican trucking company and driver. The United States also restricts Mexican truck operations in the United States.

Currency Fluctuations. Both short- and long-term trends in the value of the U.S. dollar in comparison with the currencies of other nations may easily affect logistics decisions. When the dollar is strong, as it was during most of the 1980s, the United States tends to become a net importer of goods. This is logical, considering that when the dollar is rising in value it is less expensive for U.S. firms to buy other countries' products than it is for other countries to buy U.S. products. Conversely, when the dollar's value declines, as it did during the late 1980s and early 1990s, U.S. exports tend to rise and imports tend to fall.

exchange rates

As Table 5–2 indicates, a stronger U.S. dollar lowers the cost of purchasing an item from Japan. At 100 yen per U.S. dollar, a 5,000-yen item will cost $50.00 (Scenario *A*). However, as the U.S. dollar gains in value (Scenarios *B* and *C*), the cost of the same item drops to $41.67 and $38.46, respectively, thereby making it more economical to import the item from Japan. Conversely, a weaker U.S. dollar lowers the cost of purchasing a U.S. item for Japan. Scenarios *C* to *A* in Table 5–2 indicate that the cost of a $1,000 U.S. item in Japan decreases (130,000 to 100,000 yen) as the U.S. dollar weakens from 130 yen to 100 yen, encouraging the exporting of the item from the U.S. to Japan.

A rise in exports and a decline in imports have a direct link to ocean traffic. When exports are rising, outbound traffic from the United States increases. This, in turn, increases the price for outbound freight as the factors of demand and supply determine prices. At the same time, inbound traffic to the United States is declining and ships traveling to the United States are carrying less freight; hence, shipping rates are lower for inbound traffic due to lower demand. This gives the shipper more power to negotiate rates on inbound shipments.

Fluctuations in world currency values can significantly affect logistics decisions such as inventory positioning, plant and distribution center location, and choice of transportation mode and carrier. Buyers and sellers of logistics services sometimes agree to currency adjustment factors, which help to equalize the effect of short-term changes in relative currency values. Currency adjustment is usually a percent of the basic price.

TABLE 5–2 Effect of Currency Fluctuations on Exports and Imports

Scenario	U.S. $ Value in Japanese Yen	U.S. $ Cost of 5,000-Yen Item	Yen Cost of U.S. $ 1,000 Item
A	100	$50.00	100,000 yen
B	120	$41.67	120,000 yen
C	130	$38.46	130,000 yen

Changing Political and Legal Environments

trading partners

As we indicated earlier, fluctuating trade policies throughout the world can significantly affect global logistics activity. This section describes several instances wherein changing political and legal environments have enhanced opportunities for trade and logistics activity.

Before discussing examples of global logistics issues, we should note that the United States' top five trading partners are Canada, Japan, Mexico, China, and Germany. Table 5–1, earlier in the chapter, shows the value of these countries' trade with the United States in billions of U.S. dollars.

A Single European Market

In one of the most far-reaching commercial efforts the world has ever seen, the fifteen member nations of the European Economic Community (the EEC), formerly the Common Market, have agreed to a single, unified European market. The EEC is popularly called the European Union (EU). Instead of fifteen fragmented markets in Austria, Belgium, Denmark, Finland, France, Germany, Greece, Ireland, Italy, Luxembourg, the Netherlands, Portugal, Spain, Sweden, and the United Kingdom, the plan would create one integrated market of more than 320 million consumers and workers. The map in Figure 5–2 shows the locations of the EU member nations.

The Single European Act of 1987 eliminated trade barriers between EU member nations and facilitated the free movement of goods, services, capital, and people among them. To achieve these goals, the act identified three general barriers for elimination:

- *Physical barriers,* such as customs control and border formalities
- *Technical barriers,* for example, different health and safety standards
- *Fiscal barriers,* such as differences in value-added tax rates and excise duties

At first, these laws most benefited medium-sized companies who competed only with neighboring European Union countries. As the inspection of goods was eliminated between inland borders and free movement of goods was allowed, shorter transportation times resulted.

Other considerable changes have occurred in areas such as documentation and customs procedures, internal trade barriers, national brands and markets, and external trade barriers under the European Union. The area of patent protection has also been incorporated into the EU. At present, when a European company wants patent protection, it has to register in each country individually. The Community Trade Mark (CTM) was established under the EU to simplify the process of protecting intellectual rights. Under the CTM, a trademark can be filed through one application to the CTM office to offer trademark protection in all of the EU.

logistics effects

Of all the changes that the single European market concept encompasses, three affect logistics most directly.[6] The first is the facilitation of intercountry shipment procedures, most notably through the use of a single administrative document (SAD) to reduce border-crossing time. Second is the simplification of customs formalities for shipments simply "passing through" countries en route to others. This

FIGURE 5–2 The Member States of the European Union (EU)

would reduce, for example, the time a container destined for Belgium would spend in customs activities at the entry port of Rotterdam, the Netherlands. Third is the introduction of common border posts, or *banalization*. Essentially, this concept makes a border crossing from Spain to France, for example, a European customs entry, not a French one. Generally, the facilitation of intercountry movements will concentrate European logistics networks of production and distribution into a more concise network of fewer facilities.

competitiveness

Overall, these initiatives will facilitate trade and the emergence of a more competitive business environment among EU member nations. This marketplace will likely attract new competitors, both from Europe and abroad. For example, many U.S. firms have been implementing European market strategies even as this significant change has been occurring. Likewise, as the single European market concept grows and matures, EU member countries will find that they can be more competitive in other parts of the world.

In general, open-market relationships such as these will certainly facilitate trade and help to reduce the cost of doing business. Once again, this reduced cost of doing business would be due to improved efficiency of logistics operations focusing on ocean, rail, and trucking.

Eastern Europe

The countries of Eastern Europe and the Baltic states have broken away from their history of communist government and are fighting the uphill battle of restructuring their economies based on a capitalistic system. Presently the demand in these countries outweighs their capacity to produce. Most of these countries have old infrastructures, especially in the areas of roads and telecommunications, that need to be redesigned.

The Baltic states are working hard to restructure. Their level of reliability in service has recently risen to 80 percent, but it is still not up to par with American standards. Russia seems to be one of the more problematic countries in the Baltic region. Since 1992, $1.6 billion of foreign capital has been invested there, yet there are still no rules governing commercial property or property guarantees. Other Eastern European governments have been selling off their assets in efforts to privatize their economies.

The emergence of a capitalistic Eastern Europe means the probable expansion of the EU. Already certain Eastern European countries have asked for membership but have been denied due to their poor economies. When and if the countries of Eastern Europe join the EU, the largest free trade zone in the world will be created.

The North American Free Trade Agreement

The North American Free Trade Agreement (NAFTA), which became law on January 1, 1994, creates the world's richest trading block with the joining of the United States, Canada, and Mexico (and possibly Central and South American countries in the future). NAFTA encompasses 360 million people and a total market of $6.6 trillion. It will phase out tariffs on more than 10,000 commodities during the next ten to fifteen years. Almost half the tariffs on U.S. and Canadian exports to Mexico were eliminated.

One principal benefit of the removal of these trade barriers is that companies in the three countries should become more involved in cross-border business. As Table 5–1 indicates, Canada is the largest U.S. trading partner, and Mexico is the second largest. The eventual phaseout of tariffs on trade among the three countries will directly reduce the supplier and product discrimination that typically accompanies more insular, protected national business environments.

Since 1989, the United States and Canada have had in effect a Free Trade Agreement designed to open the border between these two countries by eliminating protective measures and tariffs. The result has been an increase in the flow of raw materials and components to manufacturing or processing facilities. Thus, the logistics for U.S./Canada trade is well developed.

Even though the U.S./Canada Free Trade Agreement has been in effect for some time, certain trade barriers still remain. For example, many U.S. companies have yet to recognize certain French/English requirements for packaging and ingredient labeling. Another sensitive issue is that of plant closings, particularly in Canada, as a result of the liberalized trade between the countries. Even though economic efficiency may justify this type of change, it does affect labor issues significant to the well-being of both countries.

Trade with Mexico poses many trade barriers that NAFTA did not eliminate. The logistics barriers include a poor transportation infrastructure, restrictive foreign capital rules, and customs rules. The Mexican highway system is poor when compared to that existing in the United States and Canada. There is only one railroad, which is owned and operated by the Mexican government. There are no national less-than-truckload (LTL) trucking companies, and air transportation is limited to the few airports.

cabotage

Mexican law protects Mexican trucking companies. At present, U.S. and Canadian trucking companies are prohibited from operating in Mexico. Within ten years of the signing of NAFTA, U.S. and Canadian companies can have 100 percent ownership in Mexican trucking companies involved in international commerce (cross-border) only. Foreign trucking companies are restricted from hauling intracountry shipments in all three countries; these are known as *cabotage restrictions.*

Figure 5–3 shows the procedure required to move a truck shipment from the United States into Mexico. The U.S. trucking company moves the shipment to the border, where a Mexican cartage carrier hauls the shipment across the border to Mexican customs and to the Mexican carrier after shipment clearance. The U.S. domestic freight forwarder submits shipment documents to the Mexican customs broker, who submits them to Mexican customs. Mexican customs inspects the documents, collects duties, inspects the goods, and clears the shipment. The Mexican cartage carrier delivers the shipment to a Mexican trucking company, who delivers it to the consignee.

labeling

Another logistics problem is Mexican labeling laws. Changes in labeling requirements are implemented with little notice given to shippers. For example, in early 1995, all imported retail goods were required to be individually labeled with the shipper's and buyer's tax identification numbers. This means that for a truckload shipment containing 30,000 bottles of wine, a label must be affixed to each of the 30,000 bottles before the shipment can clear customs.

Such logistics barriers will eventually be eliminated as NAFTA experience grows. Computerized customs information systems are currently operating in the United States and Canada, with Mexico a few years behind. The electronic transfer of information for NAFTA shipments into Mexico will speed the border crossing and improve logistics service.

In the long run, the goal of NAFTA is to create a better trading environment; but, in the short run, it has created much confusion due to the record keeping required to prove the origin of the product to obtain favorable tariff treatment. NAFTA's impact on logistics involves making the structural changes needed to operate a borderless logistics network in North America. Information systems, procedures, language, labels, and documentation are being redesigned. As new markets and supply sources develop, new transportation and storage facilities as well as intermediaries will be needed.

FIGURE 5–3 A Typical Truck Shipment Crossing into Mexico

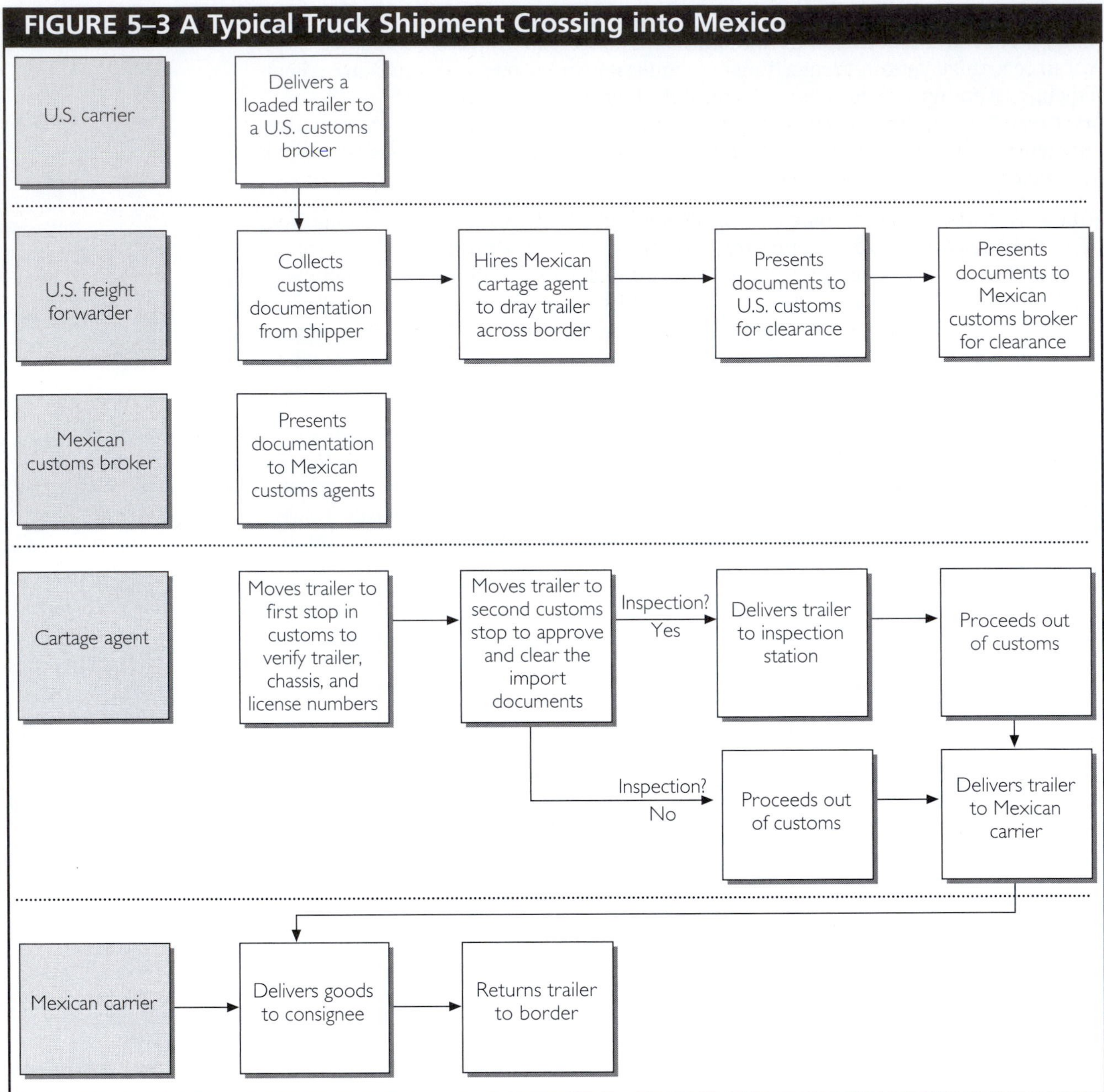

Maquiladora Operations

A concept that has become popular among U.S.-based firms is to use Mexican manufacturing/production facilities for subassembly or component manufacturing, or for final assembly of products such as electronic devices or television sets. While this has been occurring for some time, U.S. firms have only recently begun to include such *Maquiladora operations* (named for the region of Mexico in which many of these plant operations are located) as formal components of their manufacturing and logistics strategies.

Essentially, in a Maquiladora operation, a U.S. manufacturer either operates or subcontracts for a manufacturing, processing, or assembly activity to be performed in Mexico. Mexican production and labor costs are lower than those in the United States, and the operations involve no local content issues. U.S. firms often send semifinished product to Mexico for final assembly, for example, and then have the finished product shipped to the United States. This concept appeals to many companies: U.S. manufacturers operate more than 2,000 Maquiladora facilities in Mexico.

definition

One feature that adds to the feasibility of such an approach is the concept of duty, which involves the importing, storing, manufacturing, and subsequent export of goods with virtually no net payment of customs duties or import charges. The duties are limited to the value-added portion of the goods, primarily labor, returning from Mexico. Effectively, this contributes to the economic efficiency of logistics alternatives such as Maquiladora operations.

Generally, successful Mexican Maquiladora operations have served as role models for this concept's further exploitation in Central and South American countries. Coupled with the prospect of closer trade relations between the United States and Mexico, these alternatives offer considerable advantages to the firms utilizing them.

Central America and South America

Asian Emergence

In perhaps the most significant trend of the past twenty-five years, Pacific Rim countries have emerged as key players in the global business environment. While Japan has achieved a dominant position in global financial markets, other Asian countries in general account for significant portions of global trade growth. Hong Kong, South Korea, Singapore, and Taiwan have all assumed leadership positions in certain markets and product types. This trend is likely to accelerate in the future.

For the first three months of 2000, U.S. imports from Pacific Rim countries accounted for 32.9 percent of total U.S. imports. Japan is the leading supplier of goods from this region, followed by China, Taiwan, and Korea. Also, the Pacific Rim countries purchased 24.7 percent of total U.S. exports during this period, with Japan being the largest consumer, followed by Korea, Taiwan, and Singapore.

Many Asian countries have become preferred sources for many raw materials and components. These countries have become trusted suppliers of finished goods such as apparel, furniture, consumer electronics, and automobiles. The advantage many of these countries offer is low labor cost and high quality.

New Directions

Aside from establishing product sources in other countries, offshore companies are beginning to locate plants and key logistics facilities in countries that use or consume their output. For example, Japanese-based firms such as Toyota have located transplants in the United States. Similarly, U.S. automobile manufacturers such as Ford and General Motors have located transplants in other countries.

Many global manufacturers are using a strategy known as *focus production* in which a given plant produces one or two items of the company's total product line. The plants are typically located in different countries, requiring a global logistics system to tie the focused plant to the customer, who may be located within the producing country or a different country.

focus production

U.S. and global corporations are well advised to examine sourcing and distribution strategies involving countries other than the ones with which they have traditionally been involved. New business opportunities are available in Puerto Rico and Caribbean basin countries and in areas such as Australia and Africa. Trade with Russia and Eastern Europe represents opportunities for sourcing raw materials and components as well as fertile new market areas.

On The Line

Holidays May Be Hazardous to International Logistics Systems

Holidays are normally thought of as a time to retreat from the duties and responsibilities of the job and to spend time with family and friends or travel to a special vacation spot. Holidays provide an opportunity for workers to relax and refresh themselves. In industrialized nations, workers give much time and attention to developing plans that afford maximum opportunity for relaxation during the holiday period. These plans may include visiting a favorite beach, retreating to a mountain hideaway, attending a cultural event, or staying at home. No matter what holiday activity is chosen, the purpose is to have the worker return to the job refreshed and ready to take on the future challenges.

However, holidays may be hazardous to the well-being of international logistics systems. First, the holiday means the workers are not on the job and the logistics activities are not being performed. Orders cannot be filled, shipments cannot be received, and deliveries cannot be made. In essence, the logistics system comes to a halt whenever there is a country holiday.

Like the worker who plans for the holiday respite, the international logistics manager must plan for the logistics disruption holidays create. For example, international sourcing from China during the last week of January poses a problem because this is a holiday period. The international sourcing manager will have to make arrangements for shipments from China to be picked, packed, and shipped prior to this holiday week. In addition, additional time may be required for the transportation function; that is, if the shipment is presented to a China carrier the day before the holiday week, the shipment may get to the terminal and remain there until the holiday period ends.

Holidays vary by country, and the international logistics manager must be acquainted with the country holidays in the company's logistics system. Most countries declare New Years Day as a holiday, but Christmas is not a holiday for all countries, for example, Japan and China. One cannot take for granted that a holiday in one country is being celebrated in another country.

The following table, which was developed using FedEx's holiday schedule, contains the number of holidays for the United States and its top six trading partners. As the table indicates, Japan has the most holidays, sixteen, followed by China with fourteen. The United Kingdom, Canada, and the United States have the least holidays throughout the year. Countries within a region of the world have varying numbers of holidays as evidenced by Italy having eleven; Belgium, ten; Germany, nine; France, eight; and the United Kingdom, four.

Knowledge of international holidays is a key step in keeping the international supply chain functioning properly. By scheduling pickup and deliveries around a country's holidays, the logistics manager can prevent disruptions in the international supply chain and assure that the desired level of logistics service is provided to/from the country.

Also, through proper planning for international holidays, the logistics manager minimizes the international logistics system hazards. In addition, it enables the logistics manager to go off on holiday and return relaxed and refreshed to meet the future challenges of the international logistics system.

(continued on next page)

ON THE LINE *continued*

2001 Holidays for the United States and Its Top Six Trading Partners

United States	Canada	Mexico	Japan	China	Germany	United Kingdom
1/1 5/28 7/4 9/3 11/22 12/25	1/1 4/13 5/21 12/25 12/26	1/1 2/5 3/21 4/12 4/13 5/1 9/16 10/12 11/2 11/20 12/25	1/1 1/2 1/3 1/8 2/12 3/20 4/30 5/3 5/4 5/5 7/20 9/24 10/8 11/3 11/23 12/24	1/1 1/24 1/25 1/26 1/27 1/28 1/29 1/30 5/1 5/2 5/3 11/1 11/2 11/3	1/1 4/13 4/16 5/1 5/24 6/4 10/3 12/25 12/26	1/1 4/13 12/25 12/26
6	5	11	16	14	9	4

Source: Data obtained from FedEx Holiday Schedule. Available from http://www.fedex.com/us/customer/shipsmart/holiday.html

GLOBAL TRANSPORTATION OPTIONS

Global transportation is much more complex than domestic U.S. transportation. The distances involved are greater, and the number of parties involved is typically more extensive. Because of the large expanses of water separating most regions of the world, the major modes of global transport are ocean and air. Land modes also carry significant amounts of freight between contiguous countries, particularly in Europe, where land routes are short. Each of these modes fills a specific niche in the worldwide distribution network. (For an in-depth discussion of global transportation, see Chapter 9 and Chapter 10.)

Ocean

Transport by ship is by far the most pervasive and important global shipment method, accounting for two-thirds of all international movements. Ocean transportation's major advantages are low rates and the ability to transport a wide variety of products and shipment sizes. The primary disadvantages include long transit times (slow speed), low accesibility, and higher potential for shipment damage. The pervasive use of containers has reduced the damage potential and increased accessibility via connections with other modes (rail and truck) for inland origins and destinations.

Ocean shipping comprises three major categories. One is *liner service,* which offers scheduled service on regular routes. Another is *charter vessels,* which firms usually hire on a contract basis and which travel no set routes. Finally are *private carriers,* which are part of a firm's own logistics system. Table 5–3 contains: the top ten ocean carriers for 1999.

liner services

Liner carriers offer common carrier service, sailing on set schedules over specific sea routes. They also offer set tariffs and accept certain standards of liability. Liners usually carry break-bulk shipments of less-than-shipload size. Most container and RO-RO (roll-on, roll-off) ships are liners.

Liners are the property of large steamship companies, many of which belong to shipping conferences. These conferences are voluntary associations of ocean carriers that operate over a common trade route and use a common tariff for setting rates on the commodities they handle. Conferences also work together to attract customers and to utilize member ships as effectively as possible.

In general, conferences provide excellent service with frequent and reliable schedules, published daily in the *Journal of Commerce.* Additionally, conferences help to standardize shipping on many routes by stabilizing prices and offering uniform contract rates.

charters

Firms contract *charter ships* for specific voyages or for specified time periods. *Voyage charters* are contracts covering one voyage. The carrier agrees to carry a certain cargo from an origin port to a destination. The price the carrier quotes includes all of the expenses of the sea voyage. *Time charters* allow the use of a ship for an agreed-upon time period. The carrier usually supplies a crew as part of the contract. The charterer has exclusive use of the vessel to carry any cargo that the contract does not prohibit and assumes all expenses for the ship's operation during the charter period. *Bareboat* or *demise charter* transfers full control of the vessel to the

TABLE 5–3 Top Ten Ocean Carriers

Ocean Carrier	1999 Revenue (U.S. $ Million)
NYK	$10,386
Mitsui OSK Lines	8,307
A. P. Moller	5,886
"K" Line	4,576
NOL/APL	4,277
Hyundai Merchant Marine	4,250
Hanjin Shipping	4,181
Sea-Land	3,809
P&O Nedlloyd Container Line	3,661
OOIL (parent of OOCL)	2,139

Source: Philip Damas, "Who's Making Money?" *American Shipper* (July 2000): 51.

charterer. The charterer is then responsible for the ship and all expenses necessary for the vessel's operation, including hiring the crew.

Chartering usually takes place through *ship brokers,* who track the location and status of ships that are open for hire. When a shipper needs to contract for a ship, the shipper contacts a broker, who then negotiates the price with the ship owner. The ship owner pays the broker a commission on the charter's cost.

private

In a logistics system, *private ocean carriers* play the same role as private carriage in general. In other words, companies utilize private ocean vessels to lower their overall costs and/or to improve their control over transportation service. The major differences between domestic and international private ocean transportation are the scale of investment, the complexity of regulations, and the greater risk international transport entails. In international operations, chartering often provides a very viable substitute for private carriage.

Air

low transit times

The low transit times that air transport provides have had a dramatic effect on international distribution. The tremendous speed of airplanes combined with a high frequency of scheduled flights has reduced some international transit times from as many as thirty days down to one or two days. Recently, these low transit times have spurred the development of international courier services. These couriers offer door-to-door, next-day services for documents and small packages between most large American cities and a growing number of overseas points.

Mostly, however, the world's air carriers have concentrated on passenger service. Air cargo presently accounts for a small percentage of international freight by weight. However, the nature of the cargo, mostly high-value, low-density items, causes the total value of airfreight cargo to be a greater portion of the world total. Air cargoes include high-valued items such as computers and electronic equipment; perishables such as cut flowers and live seafood; time-sensitive documents and spare parts; and even whole planeloads of cattle for breeding stock. Table 5-4 provides a list of major international cargo air carriers.

TABLE 5–4 Major International Cargo Air Carriers

Major International Cargo Air Carriers
Airborne Express
British Airways
Emery Worldwide
Federal Express
Japan Airlines
KLM Royal Dutch Airlines
Lufthansa
Singapore Airlines
DHL Worldwide Express
BAX Global
United Airlines
United Parcel Service

packaging

Because airlines have traditionally concentrated on passenger carriage, airfreight has taken a secondary role. Most airfreight travels as *belly cargo* in the baggage holds of scheduled passenger flights. Only a few major airlines have all-freight aircraft.

In addition to short transit time, air transportation offers an advantage in packaging. This mode requires less stringent packaging than ocean transport, since air transport will not expose the shipment to rough handling at a port, to a rough ride on the oceans, or to the weather. A firm using air transportation may also be able to use the same packaging for international shipping as for domestic shipping. In addition, shippers have developed special containers for air transport. These containers reduce handling costs and provide protection, but they also make intermodal shipments difficult. Their odd shapes usually require shippers to repack the shipment before transporting it by another mode. Recent container-handling innovations have made it possible to load standard twenty-foot containers onto freight aircraft. For example, a carrier can now load a Boeing 747 with up to thirteen TEU containers in addition to any cargo in the belly holds.

high rates

A disadvantage of air carriage is high freight rates, which have prevented many shippers from transporting international shipments by air. Generally, only highly valuable, highly perishable, or urgently needed commodities can bear the higher cost of airfreight.

Motor

Companies most often use motor transport when shipping goods to an adjacent country—between the United States and Mexico or Canada, for example. It is also very common in Europe, where transport distances are relatively short. Motor also plays a large part in intermodal shipments.

advantages

The advantages of international motor transport are basically the same as those for domestic shipments: speed, safety, reliability, and accessibility to the delivery site. However, motor shipment across multiple national boundaries involves a number of different import regulations. To minimize paperwork, these shipments are often made *in bond*—the carrier seals the trailer at its origin and does not open it again until it reaches its destination country.

Rail

International railroad use is also highly similar to domestic rail use. Rail's accessibility is much more limited internationally, however, because border crossing points are scarce. Differing track gauges in various countries also prevent long-distance shipments.

land bridge

Intermodal container shipments are where rail is proving its value. Various *maritime bridge* concepts involve railroads both for transcontinental shipments and to and from inland points. For example, a shipper using a *land bridge* substitutes land transportation for part of a container's ocean voyage, taking several days off the transit time and saving in-transit inventory costs. A prime example of a land bridge occurs on the trade route between Japan and Europe. The all-water route takes anywhere from twenty-eight to thirty-one days. If the shipment travels by water from Japan to Seattle (ten days), then by rail to New York (five days), and by water from New York to Europe (seven days), we have a total shipping time of approximately twenty-two days.

STRATEGIC CHANNEL INTERMEDIARIES

As we indicated earlier, intermediaries play a much larger role in global logistics operations than in the domestic United States. To someone first exposed to global logistics, the scope of services that intermediaries offer is almost overwhelming. However, as the following sections explain, intermediaries play a truly strategic role in helping new and established companies venture into the global arena. Companies are all too grateful for assistance in unraveling operations involving sources and destinations in other countries.

Foreign Freight Forwarders

For a company with little international shipping expertise, the *foreign freight forwarder* is the answer. The foreign freight forwarder, which employs individuals who are knowledgeable in all aspects of international shipping, supplies its experts to small international shippers who find employing such individuals in their shipping departments uneconomical. Foreign freight forwarders are regulated by the Federal Maritime Commission.

forwarder functions

Foreign freight forwarders, like their domestic counterparts, consolidate small shipments into more economical sizes. In the international arena, these larger sizes range from containers up to entire ships. Foreign freight forwarders also perform the routine actions that shipments require. The functions they perform include the following:

- Quoting water and foreign carrier rates
- Chartering vessels or booking vessel space
- Obtaining, preparing, and presenting all documents
- Obtaining cargo insurance
- Paying freight charges
- Collecting and submitting money for shipments
- Tracing and expediting shipments
- Providing language translation
- Arranging inland transportation service

Since no two international sales are exactly alike and since shippers have varying international traffic capabilities, the forwarder usually performs the export work that the shipper cannot handle. The logistics manager must weigh the forwarder's cost against the cost of hiring personnel to perform the same tasks.

income sources

The forwarder derives income from different sources. One source is the fees charged for preparing export documentation. Another source is the commissions the forwarder receives from carriers. These commissions are based on the amount of revenue the forwarder generates for the carrier. The third type of income comes from the price difference between the rate the forwarder charges a shipper and the lower rate per pound it pays for the consolidated shipments. The final two sources are from the provision of inland transportation and warehousing functions.

Airfreight Forwarders. Airfreight forwarders perform the same functions as foreign freight forwarders, but for air shipments only. They do not require a license from the federal government as foreign freight forwarders do. Airfreight forwarders primarily consolidate small shipments, which they present to the air carrier for movement to the destination. In addition, they perform the following functions:

- Obtain, prepare, and present documentation
- Coordinate ground transportation and warehousing
- Trace and expedite shipments
- Publish tariffs and issue air waybills
- Assume liability for damage to the shipment

types

There are two types of airfreight forwarders: consolidators and agents. The consolidator type is not aligned with a particular air carrier and will use the air carrier with the lowest rate. The agent type is aligned with a specific air carrier or carriers and markets cargo space for the carrier(s).

Like the foreign freight forwarder, the airfreight forwarder generates income from fees charged for services provided and the difference between the rate charged the shipper and that paid to the air carrier. The major competitors of airfreight forwarders are the air carriers, who can go directly to the shipper and eliminate the forwarder. For small shipments, the air express carriers, such as Federal Express, Emery, UPS Air, and DHL, compete directly with the forwarders.

Non-Vessel-Operating Common Carriers

consolidator

The *non-vessel-operating common carrier* (NVOCC) consolidates and dispenses containers that originate at or are bound to inland points. The need for these firms arose from the inability of shippers to find outbound turnaround traffic after unloading inbound containers at inland points. Rail and truck carriers often charge the same rate to move containers, whether they are loaded or empty. NVOCCs are regulated by the Federal Maritime Commission.

To reduce these costs, the NVOCC disperses inbound containers and then seeks outbound shipments in the same containers. It will consolidate many containers for multiple-piggyback-car or whole-train movement back to the port for export. They also provide scheduled container service to foreign destinations.

The shippers and receivers of international shipments gain from the shipping expertise NVOCCs possess and from the expanded and simplified import and export opportunities. The ocean carrier gains from the increased market area made possible by NVOCCs' solicitation services.

Export Management Companies

Often a firm wishes to sell its products in a foreign market but lacks the resources to conduct the foreign business itself. An *export management company* (EMC) can supply the expertise such firms need to operate in foreign environments.

obtain orders

EMCs act as agents for domestic firms in the international arena. Their primary function is to obtain orders for their clients' products by selecting appropriate markets, distribution channels, and promotional campaigns. The EMC collects and analyzes credit data for foreign customers and advises exporters on payment terms. It also usually collects payments from foreign customers. EMCs may also supply documentation, arrange transportation, provide warehouse facilities, maintain a foreign inventory, and handle break-bulk operations.

exclusive agent

A firm usually contracts an export management company to provide its exclusive representation in a defined territory. The EMC may either purchase the goods or sell them on commission. In order to present a complete product line to importers, an EMC will usually specialize in a particular product type or in complementary products.[7]

Using an export management company has several advantages. First, EMCs usually specialize in specific markets, so they understand in detail what an area requires. They will have up-to-date information on consumer preferences and will help the exporter to target its products most effectively. Second, EMCs will usually strive to maintain good relations with the governments of the importing countries. This enables them to receive favorable customs treatment when introducing new products. EMCs also remain current on documentation requirements. This helps the goods they are importing to enter with few holdups.

Export Trading Companies

An *export trading company* (ETC) exports goods and services. The ETC locates overseas buyers and handles most of the export arrangements, including documentation, inland and overseas transportation, and the meeting of foreign government requirements. The ETC may or may not take title to the goods.[8]

A trading company may also engage in other aspects of foreign trade, in which case it becomes a *general trading company.* One reason Japan has been successful in international trade is because of its large general trading companies, the *sogo shosha.* These firms, which consolidate all aspects of overseas trade into one entity, may include banks, steamship lines, warehouse facilities, insurance companies, sales forces, and communications networks.

advantages

A trading company allows small- to medium-size firms, which do not in themselves possess the resources, to engage in foreign trade. The trading company purchases their goods and sells them on the international market, taking care of all the intermediate steps. Having all the functional areas under one control makes coordination easy and speeds response time when markets fluctuate.

Customs House Brokers

Customs house brokers oversee the movement of goods through customs and ensure that the documentation accompanying a shipment is complete and accurate for entry into the country. U.S. customs house brokers are licensed by the Department of the Treasury.

Customs house brokers operate under power of attorney from the shipper to pay all import duties due on the shipment. The importer is ultimately liable for any unpaid duties. The brokers keep abreast of the latest import regulations and of the specific requirements of individual products.

Today, customs house brokers use computers to transfer the information required to clear shipments for import. In the United States, the Automated Broker Interface system is used; in Canada, the system used is PARS (Pre-Arrival Review System). The use of computers has greatly reduced the time required for customs clearance and has reduced overall transit time for international shipments.

Ship Brokers

A *ship broker* acts as an intermediary for shippers desiring to charter a ship. The ship broker is a sales and marketing representative for ship owners and a purchasing representative for the shipper. The ship broker knows when ships will be or could be in port and coordinates this with the needs of the shipper.

Ship Agents

The *ship agent* is the local representative of the ship operator when the ship is in dock. The ship agent arranges for the ship's arrival, berthing, clearance, loading and unloading, and for the payment of all fees while the ship is in port. Shippers can contact the ship agent for information regarding the arrival of the ship, the dock location, and arrangements for picking up or delivering the shipment.

Export Packers

rationale

Export packers supply export packaging services for shipments when the exporter lacks either the expertise or facilities. Having a specialist package the export has two distinct advantages. First, it helps the goods move through customs more easily. Many countries assess duties on the weight of the entire package, not just the contents. Export packagers, who know various countries' requirements, know what materials and methods to use in constructing the most economical crate or container.

A second reason to use an export packager is to ensure adequate protection for the goods. International shipments must withstand the rigors of handling as well as climatic variations. Potential savings in time and reduced damage outweigh the cost of using an export packager.

Ports

One of the most important decisions in the global logistics arena is *port selection*. The port a firm selects for a global shipment must be appropriate to the cargo, since selecting the wrong port can add extra time and expense to the shipment's overall cost. The logistics manager must consider many factors simultaneously when selecting the best port for a particular shipment.

port authority

The term *port authority* refers to any governmental unit or authority at any level that owns, operates, or otherwise provides wharf, dock, and other terminal facilities at port locations. These institutions, which provide access to the capital needed to develop and fund such operations, market the port to the shipping public and to other global logistics intermediaries.

port evaluation study

Figure 5–4 shows the factors that influence shippers' selection and evaluation of individual ports and port facilities. Over 90 percent of the shippers surveyed rated equip-

FIGURE 5–4 Port Evaluation Factors

Factor	Importance
Has equipment available	1
Provides low frequency of cargo loss/damage	2
Offers convenient pickup and delivery times	3
Allows large shipments	4
Offers flexibility in special handling needs	5
Has low freight handling charges	6
Provides information concerning shipments	7
Has loading/unloading facilities for large and/or odd-sized freight	8
Offers assistance in claims handling	9

Source: Paul Murphy, James Daley, and Douglas Dalenberg, "Some Ports Lack Shipper Focus," *Transportation & Distribution* (February 1991): 48.

ment availability as either important or very important. Factors such as cargo loss and damage frequency and pickup and delivery times also received high rankings.

Another important aspect of port selection is the type of domestic transportation available between inland points and the port facility. As with domestic shipments, the type of transportation a firm uses depends on factors such as the shipment's weight or quantity, the cargo's value, and the product's special handling requirements, if any. With a global/international shipment, a firm must decide whether or not to containerize the product for shipment.

After choosing the transport mode, the logistics manager must ensure that the inland carrier can get close enough to the overseas vessel to minimize handling and loading expenses. The manager must also consider these factors for the destination port. Such concerns particularly apply to less-developed areas, where advanced unloading equipment may be in short supply or even entirely absent.

Also important is the identity of the specific ocean carriers serving the origin port and the desired destination port. Logically, the logistics manager will wish to select ocean carriers that serve the origin-destination pair(s) of greatest interest to the shipper.

Once the consignment reaches the destination port, the shipper should load it into the vessel as quickly and as inexpensively as possible. This is where the availability of proper equipment and an adequate labor supply work to the customer's advantage. Containerized shipments require specialized equipment. Extra-large or outsize cargoes may also require heavy-lift cranes. These specific equipment types may be available only at certain ports.

Finally, the person making the port selection decision should consider the facility's potential effects on overall *door-to-door* transit time and variability. Defined as the transit time from the shipment's initial origin to its ultimate destination, this door-to-door measure will certainly be longer than the ocean crossing, or port-to-port time. Ports that help to minimize the time and variability of door-to-door logistics service are attractive to shippers who prefer a more comprehensive logistics approach.

Table 5–5 shows the ranking of U.S. ports based on the number of containers, tonnage, and value of commerce handled in 1999. The West Coast ports dominate in the number of containers and value of commerce handled because of the Pacific Rim trade. The Gulf and Atlantic Coast ports dominate in the tonnage handled.

TABLE 5–5 Ranking of U.S. Ports by Containers, Tons, and Cargo Value

By Containers	By Tons	By Cargo Value
Long Beach	Houston	Long Beach
Los Angeles	New Orleans	Los Angeles
New York/New Jersey	South Louisiana	New York/New Jersey
San Juan	New York/New Jersey	Houston
Oakland	Corpus Christi	Seattle
Seattle	Hampton Roads	Charleston
Charleston	Beaumont	Hampton Roads
Hampton Roads	Long Beach	Oakland
Tacoma	Philadelphia	New Orleans
Houston	Morgan City	Baltimore

Source: "Port Facts and Statistics," *American Association of Port Authorities* (2000).

Available from http://www.aapa-ports.org/port_facts_body.html

Storage Facilities and Packaging

Storage Facilities

containers

At several points during an international shipment, the goods being shipped may require storage. Storage may be necessary while the shipment waits for loading on an ocean vessel, after it has arrived at the destination port and is awaiting further transportation, or while customs clearance is being arranged for the merchandise. When packaged in a container, goods are protected from the weather, theft, and pilferage. A carrier or shipper can store containers outside between a journey's stages with little effect on the contents.

other options

Noncontainerized cargo, on the other hand, requires protection if it is to arrive in good order. Ports supply several types of storage facilities to fill this need. *Transit sheds,* located next to the piers or at the airport, provide temporary storage while the goods await the next portion of the journey. Usually, the port usage fee includes a fixed number of days of free storage. After this time expires, the user pays a daily charge. *In-transit storage areas* allow the shipper to perform some required operation on the cargo before embarkation. These actions may include carrier negotiations and waiting for documentation, packing, crating, and labeling to be completed. The carrier usually provides *hold-on-dock storage* free of charge until the vessel's next departure date, allowing the shipper to consolidate goods and to save storage costs.

bonded warehouse

When goods require long-term storage, the shipper uses a warehouse. *Public warehouses* are available for extended storage periods. The services and charges offered by these facilities are similar to those of public warehouses in the domestic sphere.

SUPPLY CHAIN TECHNOLOGY

GROWING UP

When a kid grows, he usually needs new clothes. When a company grows, it often needs new software. In the case of Mercedes-Benz U.S. International, a subsidiary of Daimler-Chrysler Corp., the needed software was a load configuration application to help it handle parts shipments to Graz, Austria.

Previously, Mercedes had built all its M Class sports utility vehicles at its headquarters in Tuscaloosa, Alabama. But it could not build enough, so the company signed a three-year contract to assemble M Class SUVs at a plant in Austria, mainly for the European market.

Parts come in to the Tuscaloosa plant from all over the world and are assembled into cars. The Tuscaloosa plant does no parts manufacturing. For the Graz plant, Mercedes consolidates much of the cars' parts in a warehouse in Bessemer, Alabama, a short distance from Tuscaloosa, and sends those larger shipments to Austria. The Bessemer warehouse is used solely for consolidation of parts being shipped to Austria.

Close to 70 percent of the parts for the M Class SUV are consolidated and shipped from Bessemer to Graz. Approximately 2,500 different kinds of parts, between 70 and 80 containers per day, are shipped to Graz. In addition, ten suppliers directly ship their parts to Graz without going through Bessemer.

Parts shipments to Europe are new for Mercedes and substantially harder to do than car shipments. Mercedes had nothing in place to handle parts shipments to Europe effectively. In particular, it did not have a process in place to reduce transportation costs and minimize inventory levels in Graz. Graz had a limited amount of storage space so it was important that they receive only what is needed.

In similar situations, most companies use a static system that sends the same configuration of parts, the same amount, every day. Although Mercedes already could dynamically determine amounts to send to Graz, it could not do dynamic load configuration—determining how best to fit those items into a sea container. Mercedes needed a dynamic cubing system to take the European loads and optimize them based on material coming into Bessemer. Each container holds parts of different sizes and shapes, perhaps fenders and seats, for example, so determining how to best load the container can be tricky.

Mercedes selected i2 Technologies' Load Configurator software to solve the problem. The software will monitor its suppliers, including themselves, and increase their efficiencies. The software will analyze daily forecasts to determine how many containers it needs to send to Graz each day and to plan repacking of sheet metal to be sent to Graz.

The software will determine how to pack the containers for maximum space efficiency. Currently, Mercedes has a 70 percent container fill rate (30 percent of the container is empty) and anticipates the fill rate to increase to 80 percent with the Load Configurator. Finally, the software will be used by the ten suppliers shipping direct to Graz to improve container utilization.

By using the load configuration, Mercedes will increase container utilization, thereby requiring fewer containers to be shipped and realizing lower transportation costs from Bessemer to Graz as well as from its suppliers direct to Graz.

Source: Kathleen Hickey, "Growing Up," *Traffic World, The Logistics News Weekly* (30 August 1999): 36–37.

Bonded warehouses, operated under customs supervision, are designated by the U.S. Secretary of the Treasury for the purpose of storing, repacking, sorting, or cleaning imported merchandise entered for warehousing without paying import duties while the goods are in storage. Only bonded carriers may move goods into and out of bonded warehouses.

One purpose of bonded warehouses is to hold imported goods for reshipment out of the United States. The owner can store items in a bonded warehouse for up to three years, allowing time to decide on the goods' ultimate disposition without having to pay import duties or taxes on them. If the owner does not reexport the goods before the three years elapse, they are considered imports and are subject to all appropriate duties and taxes.

Packaging

importance Export shipments moving by ocean transportation require more stringent packaging than domestic shipments normally do. An export shipment receives more handling: it is loaded at the origin, unloaded at the dock, loaded onto a ship, unloaded from the ship at port, loaded onto a delivery vehicle, and unloaded at the destination. This handling usually occurs under unfavorable condition—in inclement weather or with antiquated handling equipment, for example. If storage facilities are inadequate, the goods may remain exposed to the elements for a long time.

protection The shipper may find settling liability claims for damage to export goods very difficult. Usually, the freight handling involves many firms and these firms are located in different countries. Stringent packaging is the key to claims prevention for export shipments.

higher cost Stockout costs justify more protective packaging (increased packaging cost) for export shipments. The export distance is often so great that the time (two to four months) required to receive a reordered shipment may cause the buyer and seller extremely high stockout costs. The buyer may resort to an alternative supply source, and the seller may lose business.

The package size—weight, length, width, height—must conform to the customer's instructions. Packaging dimensions usually reflect the physical constraints upon transportation in the buyer's country. For example, the 40×8×8-foot containers common in the United States may be nontransportable in certain foreign countries. The container may not be compatible with some countries' existing transportation infrastructure, or it may exceed the height and lateral clearance of highways, bridges, and overpasses. If the package cannot be transported, the shipper must repackage the shipment. This additional handling adds costs, causes delay, and increases the risk of loss or damage to the shipment.

containers Sellers frequently use containers for international shipping. A containerized commodity receives considerably less handling. With reduced handling comes reduced risk of loss and damage as well as greater time efficiency in the transfer among modes. The decision to use containers must reflect the savings we noted earlier, as well as the container's added cost, return freight costs on it, and any additional handling and storing costs.

marking The package marking requirements for international shipments also differ from those for domestic shipments. On domestic shipments, package markings provide detail concerning things such as the shipment content and consignee. On export shipments, the package provides little information about the shipment. Large geometric symbols, numbers, letters, and various codes (see Figure 5–5) provide handling instructions to foreign materials handlers who often cannot read English. Using codes conceals the identity of the shipper, the consignee, and the goods so as to reduce the possibility of pilferage.

FIGURE 5–5 Some Symbols Used for Packing Export Shipments

Source: Courtesy of Air France.

Governmental Influences

As Figure 5–6 indicates, the export-import process can be quite complex in terms of the various intermediaries it may involve. In addition, export-import documentation is far more complicated than it is for domestic U.S. shipments. The topic of documentation is discussed in some detail in Chapter 10.

role of government

This section addresses issues relating to the role of government in international trade. As we discussed previously, an increasing number of governments are attempting to simplify international trade and to facilitate the flow of commerce.

There are several areas in which governments can exert power over the flow of international commerce. One method is through import tax and duties. Governments often set these at high rates to protect local firms from competition. Another approach is to place import quotas on certain goods. Quotas limit the physical amount of product that may be imported in a specific time period, usually a year.

FIGURE 5–6 Export-Import Flowchart

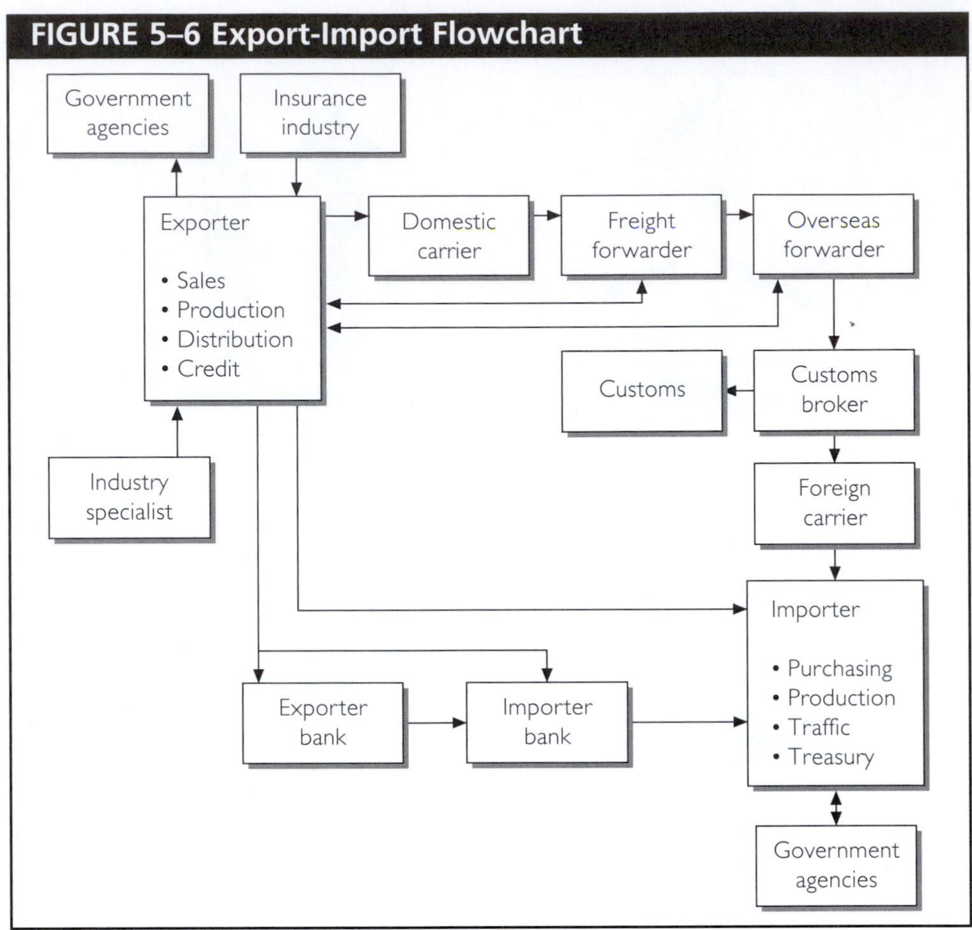

Source: John E. Tyworth, Joseph L. Cavinato, and C. John Langley, Jr., *Traffic Management: Planning, Operations and Control* (Reading, Mass.: Addison-Wesley, 1987), 388.

Individual nations may also enact regulations to prevent the import of dangerous items. For example, many nations restrict imports of animals and plants in order to prevent the spread of disease. The importing country may base still other restrictions on safety requirements.

A firm must take all possible restrictions into account before it can move goods internationally. Inadequate knowledge of current regulations may cause great losses in both time and money in terms of customer delays or extra import fees.

Customs Regulation

protection and revenue

National *customs regulations* have the greatest effect on the international movement of goods. Customs regulations fulfill two basic objectives: to protect domestic industry and to provide revenue.

Customs regulations protect national industries through high import duties, quotas, and restrictions on the items firms can import. If the companies involved research all of these factors before finalizing the sales contract, the shipment will encounter few problems at the actual time of entry.

import duties

Regulations raise revenue through the collection of *import duties.* These duties are set by national law and are determined in three different ways. *Ad valorem duties* are the most common type of import duty. They are stated as a percentage of the value of the imported goods. For example, if a good has a value of $1,000 and is subject to an import duty of 15 percent, the amount customs collects is $150 ($1,000 × 0.15 = $150). The value used in computing the import duty is usually the merchandise's *transaction value,* the total price paid or payable for the good. It includes the good's price at its origin, the packing costs the buyer incurred, any selling commissions, any royalty or license fees, and the cost of any modifications necessary to allow the importation of the item.

The next major type of import duty is based on a *cost per unit.* For example, $5 per pound or $100 per unit could be a duty. If the shipment's weight or number of items is known, this *unit duty* is easy to calculate.

The third type is the *compound duty.* This method combines the ad valorem and unit duties. Suppose that a company wishes to import 100 items with a value of $200 each, and that applicable rates for this shipment are 12 percent of the value and $25 per unit. We would calculate the total import duty as follows:

Ad valorem rate: 100 × $200 × 0.12	= $2,400
Unit rate: 100 units × $25	= $2,500
Compound rate: $2,400 + $2,500	= $4,900

duty drawback

If the owner decides to reexport a good after importing it and the applicable duties have been paid, he or she may apply for a *drawback.* Drawbacks return 99 percent of the duty paid during import. The customs service retains the other 1 percent as an administrative fee. To receive a drawback, one must file an application within three years of reexport.

Other Customs Functions

As well as collecting import duties, the customs service also inspects imported merchandise. These inspections, conducted before the goods may enter the country, perform the following functions:

- Determine that the goods' value is the same as that stated on the shipment's documentation. This value is used to determine the import duties.
- Ensure that the items have the correct markings. They must have all appropriate safety labels, instructions, or special marks, as well as identification of the country of origin.
- Find any items that are excluded from entry. These items include illegal drugs and weapons and articles that do not meet national standards.
- Ensure that the shipment is correctly invoiced and that the quantities stated are correct.
- Control quota amounts.

entry procedures

The customs service collects duties and performs inspections at *entry.* Entry includes all of the legal procedures a firm requires to secure possession of imported merchandise. Entry procedures must begin within five working days of a shipment's arrival. At entry, the customs service inspects the shipment's documentation for completeness and accuracy and inspects the items themselves to ascertain the value, to ensure that all import requirements are met, and to set the amount of any duties. The customs house broker is an essential intermediary for smooth flow through customs.

Customs procedures can be very time-consuming and expensive if a company does not conduct proper research before making a shipment. Knowing customs requirements beforehand is best. The U.S. Customs Service is striving to reduce import entry complications. The increasing use of electronic data transmission provides quicker entry times and improves the overall efficiency of customs procedures.

Foreign Trade Zones

Foreign trade zones (FTZs) are areas within a country that permit shippers to land, store, and process goods without incurring any import duties or domestic taxes. FTZs offer many advantages to parties engaged in international trade. Some of the major ones are as follows:

- Goods can be landed and stored without customs formalities, duty, or bond. FTZs offer excellent security for the merchandise because they are under customs control.
- Shippers can perform break-bulk operations on the goods before they are actually imported. Depending on the situation, this may lead to savings on duties and transportation costs.
- Imports can be processed, re-marked, or repackaged to meet local requirements before importation. This avoids any fines for importing improperly marked goods.
- FTZs can hold goods in excess of current quotas until the next quota period arrives.
- Buyers can test or sample products before import. This allows the buyer to ensure that the merchandise meets all contract stipulations before he or she accepts the goods and pays the import duties.
- The owner can reexport goods held in an FTZ at any time without having to pay any duties to the country where the FTZ is located.
- Goods can be stored indefinitely in an FTZ.

One very important aspect of a foreign trade zone is that a firm can use it for product manufacture. The manufacturer can purchase production process materials at the lowest price on the world market and bring them into the FTZ. The finished product can then be reexported or else imported paying the duty on either the components or the final product, whichever is more advantageous to the importer. In addition, the manufacturer pays no duties on waste or by-products from the production process, realizing even more savings.

SUMMARY

- Global business activity and global logistics activity are increasing. Businesses are relying on foreign countries to provide a source of raw materials and markets for finished goods. Logistics ties together these geographically distant sources and markets.

- As global trade barriers fall, global competition increases. This has led to global companies that formulate strategies on a worldwide basis.
- The global company attempts to satisfy common demands worldwide.
- Porter's "dynamic diamond" theory suggests that a country's global competitive advantage is related to four elements: factor conditions; demand conditions; related and support industries; and company strategy, structure, and rivalry.
- The critical changes in global logistics are a result of deregulation of the U.S. ocean liner industry, intermodalism, shipment control, trade policies, and currency fluctuations.
- The largest U.S. trading partners are Canada, Mexico, Japan, China, and Germany.
- The European Union (EU) has unified fifteen countries into a single trading block of 320 million consumers. The logistics impact of the EU is reduced documentation, simplified customs formalities, and common border posts.
- Eastern Europe, especially those countries that were once part of the USSR, represents a high-growth market potential for global companies.
- The North American Free Trade Agreement (NAFTA) joined the United States, Canada, and Mexico into the world's richest trading block. The logistics of moving products into and out of Canada poses minimal problems. But the logistics of trade with Mexico faces challenges in the areas of documentation, customs, transportation infrastructure, and labeling.
- A Maquiladora operation involves a U.S.-based company establishing a production or assembly facility in Mexico along the U.S.-Mexican border. The Maquiladora offers lower production (labor) costs, and U.S. import duties are limited to the value-added portion of the goods returning from Mexico.
- Asian and South American countries present sizable markets for goods and sources of raw materials and component parts.
- The primary global transportation system consists of ocean and air. For moves to bordering countries, rail and motor are used.
- The global logistics system relies heavily on intermediaries. The primary intermediaries are foreign freight forwarders, airfreight forwarders, non-vessel-operating common carriers, customs house brokers, and export management companies.
- The port used to exit and enter a country directly affects total logistics costs and service. Port authorities are governmental authorities that own, operate, or provide port facilities. Equipment availability is the most important port selection criterion.
- A bonded warehouse permits storage of an imported shipment without payment of duties on the goods until they are removed for sale or consumption.
- Packaging for global shipments is more stringent than for domestic.
- Customs regulations are designed to provide revenue to an importing country and to protect the country's industries.
- A foreign trade zone permits an importer to land, store, and process goods within the zone without incurring any import duties or domestic taxes.

Study Questions

1. What major trends do you see in world trade and in the significance of global logistics?
2. For global firms, describe the relationship between logistics strategy and other corporate strategies in the areas of technology, marketing, and manufacturing.
3. Discuss the importance of global logistics to both individual companies and to the United States as a whole.
4. What are the major elements of the *dynamic diamond* suggested by Michael Porter? Which do you feel are most important to the success of companies operating globally?
5. How have changes in the political, legal, and transportation environments affected global business and global logistics?
6. What is NAFTA? What impact has it had on global logistics systems for U.S. and European exporters?
7. Describe the role played by intermediaries in global logistics systems. Why are intermediaries not needed in domestic logistics systems?
8. What factors should be considered in selecting ports for global logistics operations?
9. What is a foreign trade zone? What is its significance to global logistics operations?
10. What is the role of customs regulations? How do they affect global logistics?

Notes

1. David L. Anderson, "Logistics Strategies for Competing in Global Markets," in *1985 Council of Logistics Management Annual Conference Proceedings* (Oak Brook, Ill.: CLM, 1985): 415.
2. Ibid.
3. Ibid., 416.
4. Martin Christopher, "Customer Service Strategies for International Markets," in *1989 Council of Logistics Management Annual Conference Proceedings* (Oak Brook, Ill.: CLM, 1989): 327–28.
5. Michael Porter, "Why Nations Triumph," *Fortune* (12 March 1990): 54–60.
6. Richard R. Young, "Europe 1992: The Logistics Perspective of a European-Based Multinational," *Proceedings of the R. Hadly Waters Logistics and Transportation Symposium* (University Park, Pa.: Penn State University, 1990): 13–26.
7. John D. Daniels and Lee H. Radebaugh, *International Business* (Reading, Mass.: Addison-Wesley, 1986), 465–99.
8. Evelyn A. Thomchick and Lisa Rosenbaum, "The Role of U.S. Export Trading Companies in International Logistics," *Journal of Business Logistics* 5, no. 2: 86.

CASE 5–1 ■ Sport Shoes, Inc.

Sport Shoes, Inc., (SS) is a well-established U.S. sport shoe retailer. It sells a complete line of tennis shoes for all major sports as well as a top-of-the-line sport shoe that has become a fashion symbol with young professionals.

All of SS's shoes are manufactured in the Pacific Rim and are transported to the United States in containers by water carriers. The containers arrive at the port of Long Beach, where they are transferred to a stack train for movement to its distribution center in Indianapolis, Indiana. From its distribution center in Indianapolis, SS ships direct to its 250 stores in the United States and sixty stores in Mexico. The total cycle time from Pacific Rim manufacturers to U.S. stores is four weeks, and to Mexican stores it is seven weeks.

SS has been doing business in Mexico since 1990. It started with three stores and has expanded the business to a current total of sixty stores in Mexico's Golden Triangle. The Golden Triangle is the region bounded by Mexico City, Guadalajara, and Monterrey. This area contains over half of Mexico's population.

The logistics of shoes in Mexico reached a critical stage during the period of 2000 to 2001. Considerable growth in the Mexican economy, coupled with the increased importation of U.S. goods, caused an explosion in the demand for SS sport shoes. As SS increased the number of retail outlets in Mexico, it continued to logistically support these stores from its Indianapolis distribution center. With the increased flow of goods into Mexico from the United States, the congestion at the border crossing points created longer cycle times and increased stockouts.

The growth in the Mexican economy was not matched by an equal growth in its logistics infrastructure. The border crossing points became very congested, with two to three days being the normal customs clearance time during peak periods. The Mexican highway system consists mostly of dirt roads (about 55 percent) and secondary roads (about 25 percent). The Mexican trucking system is dominated by many small, local companies. No U.S. trucking companies operate in Mexico, because Mexican law prohibits foreign ownership of Mexican trucking companies. Some U.S. trucking companies have developed strategic alliances with Mexican trucking companies, and this has helped. In the near future, NAFTA will permit 100 percent ownership by foreign investors of Mexican trucking companies that are hauling foreign commerce.

Given the growing demand for SS shoes in Mexico, top management has made a strategic commitment to remain in Mexico. Also, top management has made it a high priority to solve the long cycle time for shoes going to the stores in Mexico.

Case Questions

1. Describe the logistics supply chain for shoes distributed in the United States and in Mexico. What are the major similarities and differences?
2. What changes would you recommend to the logistics system supporting the Mexican market?
3. In 1995 the Mexican government devalued the peso by 50 percent against the U.S. dollar. This devaluation had a very negative impact on the demand for U.S. goods in Mexico. How would a similar monetary action affect your recommended logistics system for shoes in Mexico?

Suggested Reading

Chapter 1 Supply Chain Management

Bowersox, Donald J., David J. Closs, and Theodore P. Stank, "Ten Mega Trends That Will Revolutionize Supply Chain Logistics," *Journal of Business Logistics* 21, no. 2 (2000): 1–16.

Christopher, M., and L. Ryals, "Supply Chain Strategy: Its Impact on Shareholder Value," *International Journal of Logistics Management* 10, no.1 (1999): 1–10.

Handfield, Robert B., "Before You Build a B2B Network, Redesign Your Supply Chain," *Supply Chain Management Review* (July/August 2001): 18–27.

Mentzer, J. T., W. DeWitt, J. S. Keebler, S. Minn, N. W. Nix, C. D. Smith, and Z. G. Zacharia, "Defining Supply Chain Management," *Journal of Business Logistics* 22, no. 1 (2001): 1–26.

Maloni, Michael, and W. C. Benion, "Power Influences in the Supply Chain," *Journal of Business Logistics* 21, no. 1 (2000): 49–74.

Stank, T. B., S. B. Keller, and P. J. Daugherty, "Supply Chain Collaboration and Logistical Service Performance," *Journal of Business Logistics* 22, no. 1 (2001): 29–48.

Walker, B., D. Bovet, and J. Martha, "Unlocking the Supply Chain to Build Competitive Advantage," *International Journal of Logistics Management* 11, no. 2 (2000): 1–8.

Waller, M. A., P. A. Dabholkar, and J. J. Gentry, "Postponement, Product Customization and Market-Oriented Supply Chain Management," *Journal of Business Logistics* 21, no. 2 (2000): 133–160.

Chapter 2 Dimensions of Logistics

Bodegraven, A. V., "The State of Logistics in Cuba," *Journal of Business Logistics* 21, no. 2 (2000): 209–219.

Fernie, J., F. Pfaband, and Clive Marchant, "Retail Grocery Logistics in the UK," *International Journal of Logistics Management* 11, no. 2 (2000): 83–90.

Flint, Daniel J., and John T. Mentzer, "Logisticians as Marketers: Their Role When Customers' Desired Value Changes," *Journal of Business Logistics* 21, no. 2 (2000): 19–46.

Gammelgaard, B., and P. D. Larson, "Logistics Skills and Competencies for Supply Chain Management," *Journal of Business Logistics* 22, no. 2 (2001): 27–50.

Lambert, D. M., and R. Burduroglu, "Measuring and Selling the Value of Logistics," *International Journal of Logistics Management* 11, no. 1 (2000): 1–18.

Lynch, D. F., S. B. Keller, and John Ozment, "The Effects of Logistics Capabilities and Strategy on Firm Performance," *Journal of Business Logistics* 21, no. 2 (2000): 47–68.

Mollenkopf, D. A., A. Gibson, and L. Ozmant, "The Integration of Marketing and Logistics Functions: An Empirical Examination of New Zealand Firms," *Journal of Business Logistics* 21, no. 2 (2000): 89–112.

Rutner, J. M., and C. J. Langley, "Logistics Value: Definition, Process, and Measurement," *International Journal of Logistics Management* 11, no. 2 (2000): 73–82.

Weiss, A. D., "Crafting a Global Logistics Strategy: The Polaroid Experience," *Supply Chain Management Review* (Summer 1998): 46–55.

Zhao, M., C. Dröge, and Tp. P. Stank, "The Effects of Logistics Capabilities on Firm Performance," *Journal of Business Logistics* 22, no. 2 (2001): 91–100.

Chapter 3 Demand Management and Customer Service

Andersen Consulting, Stanford University, and Northwestern University, *Customer-Driven Demand Networks: Unlocking Hidden Value in the Personal Computer Supply Chain* (Andersen Consulting, 1997).

Bienstock, Carol C., John T. Mentzer, and Monroe Murphy Bird, "Measuring Physical Distribution Service Quality," *Journal of the Academy of Marketing Science* 25, no. 1 (1997): 31–44.

Blackwell, Roger D., and Kristina Blackwell, "The Century of the Consumer: Converting Supply Chains into Demand Chains," *Supply Chain Management Review* 3, no. 3 (Fall 1999): 24–25.

Bowersox, Donald J., John T. Mentzer, and Thomas W. Speh, "Logistics Leverage," *Journal of Business Strategies* 12 (Spring 1995): 36–49.

Copacino, William C., "Time to Review Order Management," *Traffic Management* (June 1993).

Ernst & Young, *Supply Chain Management in the Connected Economy,* Proceedings of "Advantage '99: Accelerating Supply Chain Innovations" (New York: Ernst & Young, 1999).

Forrester Research, Inc., *The Forrester Report: Online Supply Chain Realities* (Cambridge, Mass.: Forrester Research, Inc., 2000).

Francella, Kevin P., "Will CPFR Supplant ECR?" *Food Logistics* (September 1998): 10.

Kahn, Kenneth B., and John T. Mentzer, "Logistics and Interdepartmental Integration," *International Journal of Physical Distribution and Logistics Management* 26, no. 8 (1996): 6–14.

Langabeer II, Jim R., "Aligning Demand Management with Business Strategy," *Supply Chain Management Review* (May/June 2000): 66–73.

Mentzer, John T., Kenneth B. Kahn, and Carol C. Bienstock, *Sales Forecasting Benchmark Study: Executive Summary* (Knoxville, Tenn.: University of Tennessee Press, 1996).

Min, Soonhong, and John T. Mentzer, "The Role of Marketing in Supply Chain Management," *International Journal of Physical Distribution and Logistics Management* 30, no. 9 (2000): 765–787.

Pisharodi, R., Mohan, and C. John Langley, Jr., "Interset Association Between Measures of Customer Service and Market Response," *International Journal of Physical Distribution and Logistics Management* 21, no. 2 (1991): 32–44.

Ricker, Fred R., and Ravi Kalakota, "Order Fulfillment: The Hidden Key to E-Commerce Success," *Supply Chain Management Review* (Fall 1999): 60–71.

Voluntary Interindustry Commerce Standards (VICS) Association, White Paper #1, developed by the Collaborative Planning, Forecasting, and Replenishment VICS Subcommittee, 1997. Available at www.cpfr.org.

Chapter 4 Procurement and Supply Management

Bender, Paul S., "Debunking Five Supply Chain Myths," *Supply Chain Management Review* (March/April 2000): 52–58.

Dobler, Donald W., Lamar Lee Jr., and David N. Burt, *Purchasing and Supply Management,* 6th ed. (New York: McGraw-Hill, 1995).

Leenders, Michael R., Jean Nollet, and Lisa M. Ellram, "Adapting Purchasing to Supply Chain Management," *International Journal of Physical Distribution and Logistics Management* 24, no. 1 (1994): 40–42.

Leenders, M.R., and H.E. Fearon, *Purchasing & Supply Management,* 11th ed. (Irwin McGraw-Hill, 1997).

Monczka, Robert M., Robert J. Trent, and Thomas J. Callahan, "Supply Base Strategies to Maximize Supplier Performance," *International Journal of Physical Distribution and Logistics Management* 23, no. 4 (1993): 42–54.

Pickowitz, Steven J., and Jeffery P. Reekers, "Supply Chain Management: Get Ready and Approach Suppliers," *NAPM InfoEdge* 5, no. 2 (February 2000).

Sabath, Robert E., Chad W. Aurty, and Patricia J. Daugherty, "Automatic Replenishment Programs: The Impact of Organizational Structure," *Journal of Business Logistics* 22, no. 1 (2001): 91–105.

Taylor, David L., and Alyse D. Terhune, "Collaborative Business Communities: The Next Advantage," *Supply Chain Management Review* (March/April 2000): 36–43.

Venkatesan, Ravi, "Strategic Sourcing: To Make or Not To Make," *Harvard Business Review* 70, no. 6 (November-December 1992): 98–107.

Whyte, Cherish Karoway, "E-Procurement: The New Competitive Weapon," *Purchasing Today* (April 2000): 24–34.

Chapter 5 Global Logistics

Clarke, Richard L., "An Analysis of the International Ocean Conference System," *Transportation Journal* 36, no. 4 (Summer 1997): 17–29.

Hanback, Brandi, "Foreign Trade Zones Supply-Chain Impact," *Global Logistics & Supply Chain Strategies* (March 1999).

Harley, Stephen, "Transportation: The Cornerstone of Global Supply Chain Management," *Council of Logistics Management Annual Conference Proceedings* (1996): 635–641.

Maltz, Arnold B., James R. Giermanski, and David Molina, "The U.S.-Mexico Cross-Boarder Freight Market: Prospects for Mexican Truckers," *Transportation Journal* 36, no. 1 (Fall 1996): 5–19.

Minn, Hokey, and Sean B. Eom, "An Integrated Decision Support System for Global Logistics," *International Journal of Physical Distribution and Logistics Management* 24, no. 1 (1994): 29–39.

Morash, Edward A., and Steven R. Clinton, "The Role of Transportation Capabilities in International Supply Chain Management," *Transportation Journal* 36, no. 3 (Spring 1997): 5–17.

Porter, Michael E., "The Competitive Advantage of Nations," *Harvard Business Review* 68, no. 2 (March–April 1990): 73–93.

Rao, Kent, and Richard R. Young, "Global Supply Chains: Factors Influencing Outsourcing of Logistics Functions," *International Journal of Physical Distribution and Logistics Management* 24, no. 6 (1994): 11–19.

Skjoett-Larsen, Tage, "European Logistics Beyond 2000," *International Journal of Physical Distribution and Logistics Management* 30, no. 5 (2000).

Wood, Donald F., Anthony Barone, Paul Murphy, and Daniel L. Wardlow, *International Logistics* (New York: Chapman & Hall, 1995).

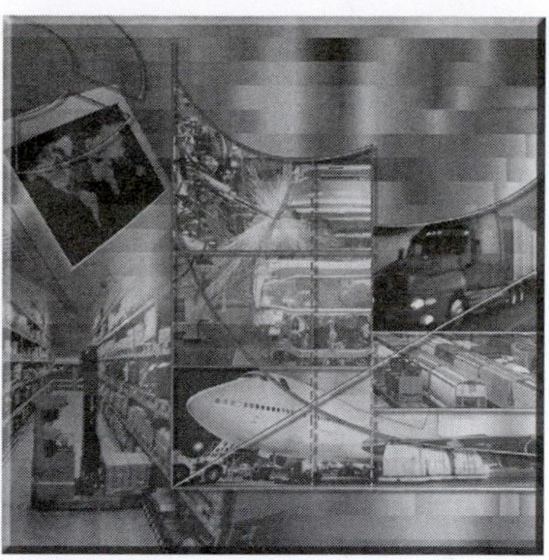

PART II

An understanding of the basic functional processes of the logistics system is critical in managing the logistics supply chain. Part II provides an in-depth discussion and analysis of the basic logistics processes of inventory, warehousing and transportation.

Chapters 6 and 7 in this section examine inventory, a critical activity for all logistics systems. In Chapter 6 a broad perspective is given for the rationale of having inventory in the supply chain and the costs associated with inventory. Chapter 7 builds on the inventory fundamentals presented in Chapter 6 by examining different approaches to managing inventory and presenting various inventory control techniques.

Chapter 8 discusses warehousing in logistics supply chains. The basic nature of and rationale for warehousing are presented, as well as the major decisions that need to be made for effective warehousing management and control. Chapter 8 also examines the related warehousing activities of materials handling and packaging that not only impact warehousing but also inventory.

The final two chapters in Part II address the critical logistics process of transportation, which is frequently the largest single cost in a logistics system. Chapter 9 provides an overview of all transportation alternatives available to a logistics supply chain manager. Emphasis is given to the advantages and disadvantages of the transportation alternatives. Chapter 10 considers the management of the transportation activity, with particular emphasis upon the strategic and operational aspects of transportation management.

CHAPTER 6

MANAGING INVENTORY FLOWS IN THE SUPPLY CHAIN

LEARNING OBJECTIVES

After reading this chapter, you should be able to do the following:

- Understand the importance of coordinated flows of inventory through supply chains.
- Appreciate the role and importance of inventory in the economy.
- Understand the major reasons for carrying inventory.
- Discuss the major types of inventory-related costs and their relationships to inventory decisions.
- Understand how inventory items (stock-keeping units) can be classified.
- Understand how companies can evaluate the effectiveness of their inventory management techniques.

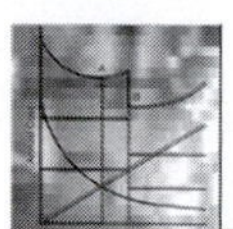

LOGISTICS PROFILE

Micros and More Case

"Inventory, inventory, inventory . . . , I am sick and tired of hearing the complaints about our inventory levels and the costs associated with carrying inventory," muttered Jim Gatto, COO and cofounder of Micros and More. "What am I supposed to do? We need inventory to operate our computer assembly operation, and we need inventory to satisfy our customer service requirements. I know that too much inventory increases our cost of goods sold (COGS), which means higher prices or lower profit margins. Ever since that article was published about Dell Computer in *Business Week*, which stated that they turned inventory fifty times a year and that they expected to reach seventy-five turns, some people around here have been casting disparaging looks in my direction. I can't wave a magic wand and make the inventory go away and reappear when we need it. The first time we are out of components for one of our computers that we are assembling in the plant, or we can't deliver parts in two or less hours to repair the computers that we sold to Penn State or Raytheon, I will be hung in effigy. I can't seem to win for losing, and I feel like everybody's scapegoat these days."

Jim Gatto was in his office alone, so no one heard the conversation that he was having with himself. Jim was being too sensitive about some comments that had been made at a recent board of directors meeting by several board members when the current financial data was being reviewed by Terry Edwards, CFO of Micros and More. Most vociferous was Dr. Roy Buck, a retired professor from Penn State and a major stockholder. He was the one that had distributed the *Business Week* article several months earlier and had been harping about excess inventory ever since. The problem was that several members of the board, especially Dr. Buck, did not really understand the role of inventory in a company. To them, inventory was an expense that increased the cost of goods sold and it should be minimized and ideally eliminated if Micros and More was going to continue to grow and be profitable.

COMPANY BACKGROUND

Micros and More was founded in Houtzdale, Pennsylvania, in 1985 by two friends who had complementary experiences and a common interest in being entrepreneurs. Jim Gatto had completed a degree in computer science at Penn State in 1982 and had worked in Fishkill, New York, for IBM in operations. Terry Edwards had been a finance major at Clarion University and had worked for Mellon Bank in Pittsburgh for several years where he specialized in assisting small local businesses with their banking and related financial issues.

Jim and Terry had competed against each other in high-school football and wrestling and had become friends through that process. They had worked together the summer after graduating from high school for a local highway construction company. They had maintained contact throughout college and during their first jobs. During the Christmas holidays in 1984, they had gotten together for a few beers and talked about wanting to work for themselves. They were both fascinated with computer technology and speculated about starting their own computer company in central Pennsylvania. They pooled their resources, borrowed money from a variety of sources, and opened up operations in an old textile plant in Houtzdale, Pennsylvania. Their business vision was to build customized computers for college students and small businesses; provide software to meet the unique requirements of individual customers; and provide outstanding customer service, which they defined as beyond anyone's expectations.

With a little luck and a lot of hard work, the company grew and prospered at a reasonable rate from 1985 to 1995. The plant in Houtzdale had been significantly expanded and now employed almost 200 people (a real boon for the local area). They had relocated their main office to State College, Pennsylvania, because of the proximity to Penn State and the growing number of small- to medium-size businesses developing in the immediate area. Penn State established a research park to sponsor and help small businesses. The Research Park was where Micros and More initially had their offices.

(*continued on next page*)

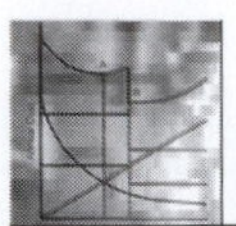

LOGISTICS PROFILE

Micros and More Case

continued

The company went public in 1995, and sold stock through a local brokerage firm. It became a relatively popular local stock and attracted numerous local investors. Their board included several large stockholders like Dr. Buck but also some local business executives such as Ralph Papa, president of the Central Region of Mellon Bank, and Ed Friedman, a local real estate developer.

CURRENT SITUATION

Micros and More had diversified its product line and expanded its customer base to continue to grow its market share. Its sales were expected to reach the $10 million level in the 2000 fiscal year. It had floated a large loan in 1999 from Mellon Bank to finance a new plant and warehouse in Clearfield, Pennsylvania, with the hope of selling computers to Walmart, which had a large warehouse near Clearfield. This was part of its modified vision statement to "grow" the business to the next level.

The fall of 2000 was a turning point for Micros and More. Technology companies were in a tailspin. Competition had become very intense from the larger manufacturers who had more scale and financial leverage. Computers were becoming a commodity and being sold on a price basis. The company was facing the possibility of its first negative profit margin. There was a real need to cut costs to maintain sales at competitive prices.

Jim Gatto realized that as COO he had a major role to play in whether the company would survive. Inventory was certainly one of the focal points, and an in-depth analysis had to be made of not only its managerial practices with respect to controlling inventory but also its relationships with vendors and customers who were a part of the overall supply chain for the company. As you read this chapter, consider Jim Gatto's challenges. Assume that you have to help him understand the role and rationale for inventory as well as the important trade-offs. He also needs some insight into understanding inventory costs.

INTRODUCTION

importance of inventory

As indicated in Chapter 1, effective management of the flow of inventory in supply chains is one of the key factors for success. In Chapter 2, it was suggested that one of the definitions that could be used for logistics was "management of inventory whether in motion or at rest." Inventory as an asset on the balance sheet of companies has taken on increased significance because of the strategy of many firms to reduce their investment in fixed assets, that is, plants, warehouses, office buildings, equipment and machinery, and so on. The reduction in fixed assets has been accomplished through leasing and other outsourcing practices, which has the effect of increasing variable cost. The end result is that the current asset section of the balance sheet has taken on increased relative importance, especially inventory.

impact on assets

Changes in inventory levels have an impact on return on assets (ROA), which is discussed in Chapter 14. ROA is an important financial metric from an internal and external perspective. Reduction in inventory usually improves ROA, which is a positive indicator of performance for current and potential investors. The opposite is obviously true if inventory investment goes up without offsetting increases in revenue. In the logistics profile at the beginning of this chapter, Jim Gatto of Micros and More is facing this very issue. When sales decline, inventory levels often increase, which has a double-edged effect on profits, that is, lower sales and more cost; but it also has a negative impact on ROA—in other words, ROA decreases.

balancing supply and demand

The ultimate challenge in managing inventory is balancing the supply of inventory with demand for inventory. In other words, a company would ideally want to have enough inventory to satisfy the demands of its customers for its products—no lost sales due to inventory stockouts. However, the company does not want to have too much inventory supply on hand because of the cost of carrying inventory. Enough but not too much is the ultimate objective. This chapter and the next chapter discuss the nature and role of inventory in a supply chain in order to address this challenge faced by logistics and supply chain managers.

In the next section, we examine inventory patterns and trends on a national/macro basis. The focus of this chapter is more micro in nature—that is, companies in a supply chain—but the examination of the macro data will provide some important insights into current inventory practices.

The major thrust of this chapter is to examine the general managerial issues related to inventory including providing a rationale for carrying certain types of inventory. An overview is provided of the basic types of inventory costs as well as classifications of inventory for more effective management.

Inventory in the Economy

It is safe to say that during the last two decades (1980s and 1990s) inventory was a focus of attention in many companies. It was recognized that many firms carried too much inventory, and, consequently, their costs or expenses to produce goods or services were inflated. The inventory practices of Japanese companies were well publicized, and U.S. companies did not compare favorably. Even earlier, in the 1970s, Ford Motor Company estimated that they were carrying fifteen times as much work-in-process (WIP) inventory as Toyota, which was a significant competitive disadvantage. The supply chain management orientation during the 1990s brought attention to the importance of reducing inventory levels in supply chains to reduce landed cost at the end of the supply chain.

inventory levels relative to GDP

The results of the "attack" on inventory cost can be demonstrated from the information provided in Table 6–1, which shows inventory costs relative to gross domestic product from 1985 through 2000. As you would expect, the level or value of inventory increases with growth in the economy—measured by gross domestic product (GDP). However, the important question is whether total inventory costs in the economy increase at the same rate as the growth in the economy. A lower rate of increase obviously indicates positive improvement in reducing inventory levels. Column 2 shows the total value of business inventories for each year from 1985 to 2000. Column 3 indicates the carrying cost rate for each year, which reflects interest rates and other factors that are discussed subsequently. Column 4 is the product of multiplying Column 2 by Column 3. Column 5 is the GDP as reported,

TABLE 6–1 Macro Inventory Cost in Relation to U.S. Gross Domestic Product

Year	Value of All Business Inventory $ Billion	Inventory Carrying Rate	Inventory Carrying Costs $ Billion	Nominal GDP $ Trillion	Inventory as a % of GDP
1985	847	28.6%	227	4.23	5.4
1986	843	25.7%	217	4.51	4.8
1987	875	25.7%	225	4.74	4.7
1988	944	26.6%	251	5.11	4.9
1989	1,006	28.1%	283	5.49	5.2
1990	1,041	27.2%	283	5.80	4.9
1991	1,030	24.9%	256	5.99	4.3
1992	1,043	22.7%	237	6.32	3.8
1993	1,076	22.2%	239	6.64	3.6
1994	1,127	23.5%	265	7.05	3.8
1995	1,211	24.9%	302	7.40	4.1
1996	1,240	24.4%	303	7.81	3.9
1997	1,280	24.5%	314	8.32	3.8
1998	1,323	24.4%	323	8.79	3.7
1999	1,379	24.1%	332	9.30	3.6
2000	1,485	25.4%	377	9.96	3.8

Source: Robert V. Delaney, "State of Logistics Report," presented on June 4, 2001, at the National Press Club in Washington, D.C., Cass Information Systems.

and Column 6 is inventory carrying cost as a percentage of GDP. If we compare 1985 with 2000, we see that there has been a significant change. Inventory as a percentage of GDP has decreased from 5.4 percent to 3.8 percent. So, while inventory carrying cost has increased from $227 billion to $377 billion, relatively, these costs have declined significantly. The conclusion that we have to draw is that the effort to reduce inventory has certainly paid off. It is easy to see, however, that there have been some ups and downs. For example, the percentage decreased to 4.9 percent in 1988 only to increase to 5.2 percent in 1989. Similarly, there was an increase from 1994 to 1995 (3.8 to 4.1) and from 1999 to 2000 (3.6 to 3.8) with the increase in carrying cost. While the trend is definitely down, the year-to-year changes indicate the element of volatility faced by many companies.

relative decline in inventory

Our focus should certainly be upon the trend, which clearly indicates a relative decline in inventory carrying cost—a positive metric for the economy and business organizations in general. As has been shown, inventory-related cost is a cost of doing business and is included in the price of products and services. Reductions in inventory cost, particularly if there is no decline in customer service, are beneficial to both buyer and seller.

inventory needed

As discussed in Chapter 2, not only has the relative cost of carrying inventory decreased during the last fifteen years, but also the relative cost of transportation has decreased. The combined impact of inventory and transportation efficiencies in the economy during the 1990s has been a positive factor promoting economic growth and prosperity and has helped make U.S. businesses more competitive on a global

ON THE LINE

INVENTORY TURNS

Think of *inventory turns* as a measure of how well a company's products are doing in the market and how well its inventory is managed. The term basically captures the number of times per year businesses such as retailers and manufacturers are able to sell off or use up their complete inventory of raw materials or finished goods. The more often a company is able to turn over its inventory, the better. The reason is simple: Businesses like to convert merchandise and materials into cash as quickly as possible. In addition, holding on to inventory costs a lot of money, both in terms of the capital tied up in unsold products and in the expenses associated with warehousing them; so, the quicker a company is able to push its inventory out the door, the higher the return on its inventory investment and the better its cash flow.

"Anytime you have products sitting in inventory, it means your resources are not producing cash flow," says Andy Chatha, an analyst at ARC Advisory Group, Inc., a manufacturing consultant in Dedham, Massachusetts. "Ideally, you want zero inventory" if you want to maximize cash flow, he adds.

The average number of inventory turns varies greatly by industry and by companies within industry segments. For instance, the ratio is particularly critical in industries that face significant pricing and competitive pressures, low margins, and fast obsolescence rates, Chatha says. These include companies in the automobile, consumer electronics, and computer industries, plus retailers of all types, say analysts. Companies in these sectors all have high inventory turnover rates because the cost of holding on to goods in hypercompetitive, fast-evolving areas can be unacceptably high. Some firms, like Dell Computer Corp.—considered by many experts to be one of the leaders in inventory management—have turnover rates that range from thirty to forty times per year.

Companies stand to benefit from improving inventory turns, even with relatively low-volume or slow-moving products, because of the same cost factors that drive companies with fast-moving products, says David Monroe, an analyst at PlantWide Research Group, a North Billerica, Massachusetts–based manufacturing consultant. "In fact, the only industries where it doesn't always help are in aerospace and defense," where the need to maintain inventories of parts for longer periods of time is part of the business model because of lower obsolescence rates, says Monroe.

GETTING BETTER ALL THE TIME

A study published in December 1999 by the management firm Pittiglio, Rabin, Todd, & McGrath in Waltham, Massachusetts, found that U.S. companies have dramatically improved their inventory turns during the past few years. U.S. inventory turns rose by more than 12 percent from 1994 through 1998 to an average of 5.4 annual turns, according to the report. During the same period, the average cash-to–cycle time—the number of days between paying for raw materials and getting paid for the product—improved by 10 percent to 100 days, the report stated.

Driving many of those inventory turns was the need to address falling margins and slowing annual growth, the report said. In addition, many big U.S. companies have also invested millions of dollars over the past several years to automate their inventory management processes using sophisticated supply chain management tools.

The continuing move away from traditional build-to-forecast manufacturing models to more flexible models such as build-to-demand, build-to-order, and flow manufacturing is also changing the way companies look at inventories, says Monroe. The increasing emphasis on a fully integrated supply chain means that inventories barely spend any time sitting unused.

Source: Jaikumar Vijayan, Computerworld, Framingham, Mass. (7 May 2001).

basis. Continued focus on reducing inventory levels is obviously important, and the supply chain analytical framework that we have been discussing should result in additional inventory efficiencies. However, note again that most organizations need to carry some inventory; more importantly, carrying inventory may in fact allow an organization to reduce costs in another related area, for example, transportation or manufacturing. The trade-off/total cost concept discussed in Chapter 2 is relevant for evaluating the need for carrying inventory. The next section explores the major reasons that companies carry inventory and the usual trade-offs in cost.

Inventory in the Firm: Rationale for Inventory

As indicated previously, inventory plays a dual role in companies. Inventory impacts the cost of sales, but it also supports order fulfillment (customer service). Table 6–2 reports total logistics for the economy and shows that inventory carrying cost is on average about 35 percent of the total logistics costs for companies.

consumer product companies

Consumer product companies and the wholesalers and retailers that are a part of their distribution channels face a special challenge in keeping inventory at accept-

TABLE 6–2 Total Logistics Costs—1999

	$ Billion
Carrying Costs—$1,376 Trillion All Business Inventory	
Interest	70
Taxes, obsolescence, depreciation, insurance	187
Warehousing	75
SUBTOTAL	332
Transportation Costs	
Motor Carriers	
Truck—intercity	300
Truck—local	150
SUBTOTAL	450
Other Carriers	
Railroads	36
Water (international 16, domestic 6)	22
Oil pipelines	9
Air (international 7, domestic 19)	26
Forwarders	6
SUBTOTAL	99
Shipper-Related Costs	5
Logistics Administration	35
TOTAL LOGISTICS COST	921

Source: Robert Delaney, Cass Information Systems, 2000.

able levels because of the difficulty of forecasting demand and expectations of customers about product availability. Both of these factors are exacerbated by the proliferation of their product lines. For example, if Kimberly-Clark estimated or forecasted aggregate demand for disposable diapers for the first quarter of next year at 5 million dozen diapers, they would have to break this number down by stock-keeping unit (SKU), color/design, package type, absorbancy, individual diaper design, and so on. Consequently, there would be over a thousand different stock-keeping units (SKUs) that required an individual forecast and some level of safety stock. Consumer preference can change quickly, which makes managing inventory levels a special challenge to meet customer service requirements.

example

To illustrate the cost side of the challenge, assume that Kimberly-Clark expects to carry an average monthly inventory during the first quarter of the year of 500,000 dozen diapers (remember that it will be producing diapers every day in its various plants). If each dozen diapers is valued at $5.00, the value of the inventory would be $2,500,000 ($5 × 500,000). If its cost of carrying inventory (to be explained in more detail) was 20 percent; its dollar cost of carrying inventory would be $500,000 on an annual basis. (Remember, this is only for diapers, not all of Kimberly-Clark's paper products). If the average inventory changed to 600,000 dozen, this would result in another $100,000 of inventory cost. If the increase in average inventory was not accompanied by an increase in sales, then Kimberly-Clark would face a reduced profit margin.

Hopefully, the point has been made that managing inventory is a critical factor for success in many companies. Surprisingly, perhaps, many companies have responded to the challenges, as indicated by the macro data in the previous section, and have reduced inventory levels while maintaining appropriate customer service levels. Their ability to achieve the twin goals of lower inventory (efficiency) and appropriate customer service (effectiveness) is based upon a number of factors discussed in this chapter and the next chapter. A good starting point is an understanding of why companies usually have to carry inventory and the corollary trade-offs and relationships.

Batching Economies/Cycle Stocks

Batching economies or *cycle stocks* usually arise from three sources—acquisition, production, and/or transportation. Scale economies are often associated with all three, which can result in the accumulation of stock that will not be used or sold immediately—which means there will be cycle stock or inventory that will be used up or sold over some period of time.

price discounts

In the acquisition or purchasing area, it is not unusual to have a schedule of prices that reflects the quantity purchased, that is, lower unit price for larger quantities. Purchase discounts are also prevalent for personal consumption items; for example, the larger box of soap or cereal often sells for a lower price per ounce. When we purchase the larger box, we have cycle stock. What we do not use immediately will have to be stored. When companies buy raw materials and supplies, particularly in our global economy, they are often offered discounts for larger quantities. The trade-off logic that was mentioned suggests that the discount savings have to be compared against the additional inventory carrying cost. This is a relatively straightforward analysis, which is discussed in the next chapter. In spite of the analytic framework available for analyzing discount trade-offs, there are instances when companies just focus on the price savings and do justify the discount against the additional inventory cost.

transportation rate discounts

A related discount situation occurs with transportation services. Transportation companies usually offer rate/price discounts for shipping larger quantities. In the motor carrier industry, a common example is the lower price/rate for a truckload shipment. The transportation company saves money in handling and related pickup costs, which are reflected in the rate to the shipper. The truckload rate is only one example for motor carriers; there are additional discount quantities available. The larger shipment quantities to justify the discount have the same effect as the purchase quantities—namely, cycle stocks. The trade-off requirement is the same. Does the cost savings more than offset the extra inventory carrying cost?

Note that acquisition or purchasing economies and transportation economies can be very complementary. That is, when companies buy larger quantities of raw materials or supplies, they can ship larger quantities, which can result in transportation discounts. Therefore, they are frequently the recipients of two discounts for the same item purchased, which can make the trade-off evaluation positive; but, nevertheless, it should still be analyzed. One of the big challenges, as is discussed subsequently, is that companies may not calculate their carrying costs accurately.

production economics

The third batching economy is associated with production or manufacturing. Many companies feel that their production costs per unit are substantially lower when they have long production runs of the same product. Long production runs or batches result in cycle stocks that must be stored until they are sold. Traditionally, companies rationalized long production runs to lower unit costs without really evaluating their inventory carrying cost, which can be high for finished goods. There is also the related concern about obsolescence of finished goods.

Most companies experience cycle stocks, even if they do not produce products, because of acquisition or purchase of supplies. Obviously, cycle stocks can be beneficial as long as the appropriate analysis is done to cost justify the inventory.

Uncertainty/Safety Stocks

reasons for uncertainty

All businesses are usually faced with uncertainty, which can arise from a variety of sources. On the demand or customer side, there is usually uncertainty about how much customers will buy and when. Forecasting demand is a common approach to help resolve uncertainty, but it is never completely accurate. On the supply side, there may be uncertainty about obtaining what is needed from vendors or suppliers and about how long it will take for fulfillment of the order. Uncertainty can arise from transportation in terms of getting reliable delivery. There are other sources of uncertainty. The net result of uncertainty is usually the same: companies accumulate safety stock to buffer themselves against uncertainty. The challenge and analysis are different for safety stock than for cycle stock; safety stock is much more complex and challenging to manage for many companies.

impact of information on uncertainty

As Jim Gatto exclaimed in the Micros and More Case, if the production line shuts down because of a supply shortage or a big customer does not get its delivery, it causes problems. Trade-off analysis is appropriate and can be accomplished using appropriate tools (to be discussed) to assess the risk and measure the inventory cost. In addition, companies today are taking a more proactive approach to reduce uncertainty, as indicated in Chapter 1 and Chapter 2—namely, using the power of information to reduce uncertainty and, consequently, the need for safety stock. You may recall that it was stated previously that information is a substitute for inventory. As is discussed in more detail in a later chapter, there has literally been an information revolution because of the technology now available to transmit information of high quality backward and forward in the supply chain. Collaboration in the sharing of information in some supply chains has had significant results in reducing inventory/cost and actually improving service at the same time. Collaborative planning and forecasting requirements (CPFR) is an excellent example of such an approach. Sophisticated bar codes, RF tags, EDI, the Internet, and so on have enabled companies to reduce uncertainty. However, it is not possible to eliminate uncertainty completely; so, tools of analysis need to be used to measure the trade-offs.

Time/In-Transit and Work-in-Process Stocks

The time associated with transportation, for example, vendor to manufacturing plant, and the time needed to assemble or produce a complex product (automobile or computer) mean that, even while goods or materials are in motion, there is an inventory cost associated with the time period. The longer the time, the higher the cost.

time-related trade-offs

The time period for in-transit inventory (inbound and/or outbound) and work-in-process (WIP) inventory should be evaluated in terms of the appropriate trade-offs. As is discussed in a later chapter, the transportation alternatives available for shipping freight may have different transit times as well as other service level differences, for example, reliability and damage rates. The rates/prices charged by the carriers usually reflect the service differences. For example, airfreight service is usually the fastest and often the most reliable but the price of airfreight service is considerably higher than motor or rail service. If there is overnight delivery from London, England, to New York City but surface transportation would require eight to ten days, is the higher air rate justified because of related inventory savings? The longer freight is in transit, the higher the inventory costs and, probably, the customer service related costs. It is possible to evaluate this trade-off, and it should be done to make rational decisions.

work-in-process inventory

Work-in-process inventory is associated with manufacturing/production. Significant amounts of inventory can be accumulated in production facilities, particularly in assembly operations such as those of automobiles and computers. The length of time work-in-process inventory sits in a production facility waiting to be included in the assembly of a particular product should be carefully evaluated in relationship to scheduling techniques and the actual production or assembly/technology. Some facilities operate with four to six hours of WIP inventory, while others may have ten to fifteen days of WIP inventory. A considerable difference in inventory carrying cost would exist between these two examples. Again, an evaluation of the trade-off alternative should be executed.

Seasonal Stocks

Seasonality can occur on the inbound side of a company's logistics system or the outbound side or both. Usually, companies that are faced with seasonality of supply and/or demand need to carefully analyze how much inventory they should accumulate.

perishable supply

Companies that process agriculture products are a good example of inbound supply seasonality; they may have to purchase the "raw" agriculture products during the harvest season. Since perishability is often a factor, the processing usually has to occur in a reasonably short period of time. The demand for the processed products (canned, frozen, etc.) is stable throughout the year. Therefore, the finished product usually has to be stored until it is sold. The other alternative may be to store the "raw" material in some instances, for example, grain such as wheat, rye, barley; cocoa beans; and so on.

Sometimes transportation can cause seasonality, particularly if water transportation is used. Rivers and lakes can freeze in the northern part of the hemisphere, which may interrupt the shipment of basic raw materials causing a need for accumulation of inventory during the period that the service is interrupted. The steel industry faced this problem in the past with iron ore moving across the Great Lakes or down the St. Lawrence Seaway.

seasonal demand

Many companies are faced with seasonality in their product demand, but some companies have significant seasonal demand, for example, Hallmark Cards and Hershey Foods. These companies may experience 60 percent of their annual sales in a ten- to fourteen-week period. Having the production capacity to meet the peak demand with much idle capacity the remainder of the year may not be very efficient. Companies with such significant seasonality usually find it more efficient to utilize smaller plants and produce products in advance of demand, which obviously means accumulation of inventory. The production cost (unit cost) would have to be traded off against the inventory cost to decide upon the appropriate balance between production capacity and warehousing space.

Anticipatory Stocks

A fifth reason for inventory arises when companies anticipate some unusual event, for example, strike, significant price increase, a major shortage of supply due to weather or political unrest, and so on. In such situations, companies may accumulate inventory to "hedge" against the unique event. Again, an analysis should be undertaken to assess the risk, probability, and cost of the inventory. Obviously, the analysis is more challenging in such circumstances because of the degree of uncertainty. However, there are analytical techniques available to help mitigate these challenges, which will be discussed in the next chapter.

Summary of Inventory Accumulation

Most companies have to accumulate some level of inventory. There are good reasons for such accumulation. In fact, the inventory cost may be more than offset by savings in other areas. The basic principle is that decisions to accumulate inventory need to be evaluated using a trade-off framework. In addition to the five reasons just discussed, there are other reasons for accumulating inventory—such as maintaining vendors or employees. For example, during periods when demand has decreased, a company may continue to buy from some vendors to maintain the relationship and/or to keep employees by producing to inventory. Again, an evaluation of the trade-offs is necessary.

As already discussed, several functional areas in most companies have an interest or stake in decisions that determine how much inventory should be held and related issues regarding timing and location. The next section examines some of the contrasting viewpoints of these functional areas.

The Importance of Inventory in Other Functional Areas

functional interfaces

As discussed in Chapter 2, logistics interfaces with an organization's other functional areas, such as marketing and manufacturing. The interface is usually more prominent in the inventory area. As background for analyzing the importance of inventory in the logistics system, we examine how logistics relates to other functional business areas with respect to inventory:

- *Marketing* desires high customer service levels and well-replenished inventory stocks to assure product availability and to meet customer needs as quickly and completely as possible.
- *Manufacturing* typically desires long production runs and the lowest procurement costs as well as early production of seasonal items to minimize manufacturing costs and to avoid overtime payments.
- *Finance* desires low inventories to increase inventory turnover, reduce current assets, and receive high capital returns on assets.

The preceding statements clearly show why other functional areas are interested in inventory. Also, finance area objectives may obviously conflict with marketing and manufacturing objectives. A more subtle conflict sometimes arises between marketing and manufacturing, although high inventory levels interest both areas. The long production runs that manufacturing may desire could cause shortages of some products needed by marketing to satisfy customer demand. For example, manufacturing may want to continue a particular production run up to 5,000 units at a time when marketing needs another product currently in short supply.

arbitrator role of logistics

Many companies can make a case for using a formal logistics organization to resolve these inventory objective conflicts. Inventory has an important impact on logistics, and, in many logistics organizations, inventory is the pivotal activity. The logistics manager is in an excellent position to analyze inventory trade-offs, not only with other logistics areas but also with the functional areas discussed here. In some instances, this can almost be an arbitrator's role.

Proper inventory management and control affects customers, suppliers, and the organization's major functional departments. In spite of the many possible advantages to having inventory in a logistics system, the inventory holding costs are a major expense, and the logistics system should emphasize reducing inventory levels.

INVENTORY COSTS

importance of inventory costs

Inventory costs are important for three major reasons. First, inventory costs represent a significant component of total logistics costs in many companies. Second, the inventory levels that a firm maintains at points in its logistics system will affect the level of service the firm can provide to its customers. Third, cost trade-off decisions in logistics frequently depend upon and ultimately affect inventory carrying costs.

This section provides basic information concerning the costs that logistics management should consider when making inventory policy decisions. The major types of costs include inventory carrying costs, order/setup costs, expected stockout costs, and in-transit inventory carrying costs.

Inventory Carrying Cost

There are four major components of inventory carrying cost: capital cost, storage space cost, inventory service cost, and inventory risk cost.[1] Each cost type has a unique nature, and the particular calculation for each includes different expenses or costs.

Capital Cost. Sometimes called the *interest* or *opportunity* cost, this cost type focuses upon what having capital tied up in inventory costs a company (in contrast to using capital in some other financially productive way). Stated differently, "What is the implicit value of having capital tied up in inventory, instead of using it for some other worthwhile project?"

The capital cost is frequently the largest component of inventory carrying cost. A company usually expresses it as a percentage of the dollar value of the inventory the company holds. For example, a capital cost expressed as 20 percent of a product value of $100 equals a capital cost of $100 × 20 percent, or $20. Similarly, if the product value is $300, then the capital cost is $60.

In practice, determining an acceptable number to use for capital cost is no small task. In fact, most firms find that determining capital cost may be more of an art than a science. One way of calculating capital cost for inventory decision making requires identifying the firm's *hurdle rate,* the minimum rate of return expected of new investments. In this way, the firm may make inventory decisions in much the same way as it decides to spend money for advertising, building new plants, or adding new computer equipment.

For example, assume that the average value of a company's inventory is $300,000. This inventory is a capital asset for the company, like a machine or any other capital investment. Therefore, if the company bases its capital cost on a 15 percent hurdle rate, then the capital cost is $45,000 ($300,000 × 15 percent) per year.

The inventory valuation method is critical to accurately determining capital cost and is subsequently critical to determining overall inventory carrying cost. According to Stock and Lambert, "the opportunity cost of capital should be applied only to the out-of-pocket investment in inventory. . . . This is the direct variable expense incurred up to the point at which inventory is held in storage."[2] Thus, the commonly accepted accounting practice of valuing inventory at fully allocated manufacturing cost is unacceptable in inventory decision making because raising or lowering inventory levels financially affects only the variable portion of inventory value and not the fixed portion of allocated cost. Including inbound transportation costs in inventory value, however, is consistent with this advice, and firms should include such cost measurements whenever possible.

A final suggestion on the topic of capital cost is to strive for accurate, comprehensive calculations of relevant cost elements. Although it is sometimes tempting, the inclination to use industry averages or percentage figures found in textbooks (such as 25 percent) not only will be misleading but may produce highly inaccurate results.

Storage Space Cost. Storage space cost includes handling costs associated with moving products into and out of inventory, as well as storage costs such as rent, heating, and lighting. Such costs may vary considerably from one circumstance to the next. For example, firms can often unload raw materials directly from railcars and store them outside, whereas finished goods typically require safer handling and more sophisticated storage facilities.

Storage space costs are relevant to the extent that they either increase or decrease as inventory levels rise or fall. Thus, firms should include variable rather than fixed expenses when estimating space costs as well as capital costs. Perhaps we can clarify the issue by contrasting public warehouse use with private warehouse use. When a firm uses public warehousing, virtually all handling and storage costs vary directly with the magnitude of stored inventory. As a result, these costs are all relevant to decisions regarding inventory. When a firm uses private warehousing, however, many storage space costs (such as depreciation on the building) are fixed and, as such, are not relevant to the inventory carrying cost.

insurance and taxes

Inventory Service Cost. Another component of inventory carrying cost includes insurance and taxes. Depending upon the product value and type, the risk of loss or damage may require high insurance premiums. Also, many states impose a tax on inventory value, sometimes on a monthly basis. High inventory levels resulting in high tax costs can be significant in determining specific locations where firms inventory product. Insurance and taxes may vary considerably from product to product, and firms must consider this when calculating inventory carrying costs.

risk and obsolescence

Inventory Risk Cost. This final major component of inventory carrying cost reflects the very real possibility that inventory dollar value may decline for reasons largely beyond corporate control. For example, goods held in storage for some time may become obsolete and thus deteriorate in value. Also, fashion apparel may rapidly deteriorate in value once the selling season is actively underway or over. This phenomenon also occurs with fresh fruits and vegetables when quality deteriorates or the price falls. Manufactured products may face similar risks, although typically not to the same degree. An extreme example would be the case of very high-value products such as computers and peripherals or semiconductors, which may experience relatively short product life cycles. In such instances, the cost of obsolescence or depreciation may be very significant.

Any calculation of inventory risk costs should include the costs associated with obsolescence, damage, pilferage, theft, and other risks to inventoried product. The extent to which inventoried items are subject to such risks will affect the inventory value and thus the carrying cost.

Calculating the Cost of Carrying Inventory

valuation of inventory

Calculating inventory carrying cost for a particular item stored in inventory involves three steps. The first is to identify the value of the item stored in inventory. According to traditional accounting practices, the three most widely recognized approaches include valuing inventory on first-in/first-out (FIFO) basis, last-in/first-out (LIFO) basis, or average cost. The most relevant value measure for inventory decision making is the cost of goods sold or the variable manufactured cost of product currently coming into the firm's logistics facilities. Again, this is because raising or lowering inventory levels affects only the variable portion of inventory value and not the fixed portion.

TABLE 6–3 Example of Carrying Cost Components for Computer Hard Disks

Cost	Percentage of Product Value
Capital	12%
Storage space	2
Inventory service	3
Inventory	8
Total	25%

carrying cost percentages

The second step is to measure each individual carrying cost component as a percentage of product value and to add the component percentages together to measure inventory carrying cost. Thus, carrying cost is typically expressed as a percentage of product value. In computing storage space, inventory service, and inventory risk costs, it may be helpful to first calculate these costs in dollar terms and then to convert to percentage figures.

calculation of carrying cost

The last step is to multiply overall carrying cost (as a percentage of product value) by the value of the product. This measures the annual carrying cost for a particular amount of inventory.

Example. Suppose that a company manufactures hard disks for personal computers at a variable manufactured cost of \$100 per unit. Table 6–3 lists the carrying cost components as a percentage of product value. The annual cost of carrying a single hard disk in inventory is calculated as follows:

$$\$100 \times 25\% = \$25 \text{ per year}$$

Nature of Carrying Cost

concept of average inventory

Items with basically similar carrying costs should use the same estimate of carrying cost per inventory dollar. However, items subject to rapid obsolescence or items that require servicing to prevent deterioration may require separate cost estimates. The estimate of carrying cost per inventory dollar expressed as a percentage of the inventory value carried during the year will reflect how carrying costs change with inventory value. Table 6–4 shows that as average inventory increases (i.e., as the inventory level increases), annual carrying cost increases, and vice versa. In other words, carrying cost is variable and is directly proportional to the number of average inventory units or the average inventory value.

Order/Setup Cost

A second cost affecting total inventory cost is *ordering cost* or *setup cost*. Ordering cost refers to the expense of placing an order for additional inventory and does not include the cost or expense of the product itself. Setup cost refers more specifically to the expense of changing or modifying a production or assembly process to facilitate product line changeovers, for example.

TABLE 6–4 Inventory and Carrying Cost Information for Computer Hard Disks

Order Period	Number of Orders per Year	Average Inventory* Units	Average Inventory* Value†	Total Annual Inventory Carrying Cost‡
1 week	52	50	$ 5,000	$ 1,250
2 weeks	26	100	10,000	2,500
4 weeks	13	200	20,000	5,000
13 weeks	4	650	65,000	16,250
26 weeks	2	1,300	130,000	32,500
52 weeks	1	2,600	260,000	65,000

*One week's inventory supply is 50 units.

†Value per unit is $100.

‡Percentage carrying cost is assumed to be 25%.

Order Cost. The costs associated with ordering or acquiring inventory have both fixed and variable components. The fixed element may refer to the cost of the information system, facilities, and technology available to facilitate order-placement activities. This fixed cost remains constant in relation to the number of orders placed.

activities affecting cost

There are also a number of costs that vary in relation to the number of orders that are placed for more inventory. Some of the types of activities that may be responsible for these costs include (1) reviewing inventory stock levels; (2) preparing and processing order requisitions or purchase orders; (3) preparing and processing receiving reports; (4) checking and inspecting stock prior to placement in inventory (although this activity should be minimized as part of a commitment to total quality management and "doing it right the first time"); and (5) preparing and processing payment. While the roles played by certain people and processes may seem trivial, they become very important when considering the total range of activities associated with placing and receiving orders.

production changeover

Setup Cost. Production setup costs may be more obvious than ordering or acquisition costs. Setup costs are expenses incurred each time a company modifies a production line to produce a different item for inventory. The fixed portion of setup cost might include use of the capital equipment needed to change over production facilities, while the variable expense might include the personnel costs incurred in the process of modifying or changing the production line.

Nature of Cost. Separating the fixed and variable portions of order/setup cost is essential. Just as calculations should emphasize the variable portion of inventory capital cost, calculations of order and setup costs should emphasize the variable portion of these expenses. As is discussed in Chapter 7, this emphasis becomes central to developing meaningful inventory strategies.

general relationship

When calculating yearly ordering costs, firms usually start with the cost or charge associated with each individual order or setup. Correspondingly, the yearly number of orders or setups affects the total order cost per year; this number is inversely related to individual order size or to the number of units manufactured (production run length) within a simple setup or changeover. Table 6–5 shows this general relationship.

TABLE 6–5 Order Frequency and Order Cost for Computer Hard Disks

Order Frequency	Number of Orders per Year	Total Annual Order Cost*
1 week	52	$10,400
2 weeks	26	5,200
4 weeks	13	2,600
13 weeks	4	800
26 weeks	2	400
52 weeks	1	200

*Assuming a cost per order of $200.

As we can see in Table 6–5, more frequent order placement results in customers placing a larger number of smaller orders per year. Since both small and large orders incur the variable expense of placing an order, total annual order cost will increase in direct relation to the number of orders placed per year. As long as yearly sales and demand remain the same, total annual order or setup cost will relate directly to the number of order or setups per year and will relate inversely to individual order size or individual production run length.

decreasing significance

Future Perspectives. Although an accurate, comprehensive statement of inventory cost must include the portion related to order/setup activities, the magnitude of these costs is likely to decrease in the future. Considering the move to highly automated systems for order management and order processing, and the streamlining of inventory receiving practices, the variable cost of handling individual orders is certain to lessen significantly. In firms where "vendor-managed inventory" programs are underway, the concept of placing orders itself loses significance, and there the concept of order cost loses relevance. Similarly, as firms improve their ability to quickly and efficiently change over production processes, the variable expense associated with this task will decrease as well. While there may always be a measurable element of order/setup cost, this expense is likely to become less relevant in the future than it is today.

Carrying Cost versus Order Cost

trade-off perspective

As shown in Table 6–6, order cost and carrying cost respond in opposite ways to changes in number of orders or size of individual orders. Total cost also responds to changing order size. Close examination indicates that order costs initially decrease more rapidly than carrying costs increase, which brings total costs down. In other words, a positive trade-off occurs, since the marginal savings in order costs exceed the marginal increment in inventory costs. However, at a certain point, this relationship begins to change, and total costs start to increase. Here a negative trade-off occurs because the marginal order cost savings are less than the marginal carrying cost increase. We can view this set of relationships in cost curve terms as shown in Figure 6–1.

TABLE 6–6 Summary of Inventory and Cost Information

Order Period	Number of Orders per Year	Average Inventory* (Units)	Total Annual Order Cost†	Change in Total Order Cost	Total Annual Inventory Carrying Cost‡	Change in Total Carrying Cost	Total Cost
1 week	52	50	$10,400		$ 1,250		$11,650
				–5,200		+1,250	
2 weeks	26	100	5,200		2,500		7,700
				–2,600		+2,500	
4 weeks	13	200	2,600		5,000		7,600
				–1,800		+11,250	
13 weeks	4	650	800		16,250		17,050
				–400		+16,250	
26 weeks	2	1,300	400		32,500		32,900
				–200		+32,500	
52 weeks	1	2,600	200		65,000		65,200

*Assume sales or usage at 100 units per week.

†Order cost is $200.

‡Value is $100 per unit and carrying cost is 25%.

FIGURE 6–1 Inventory Costs

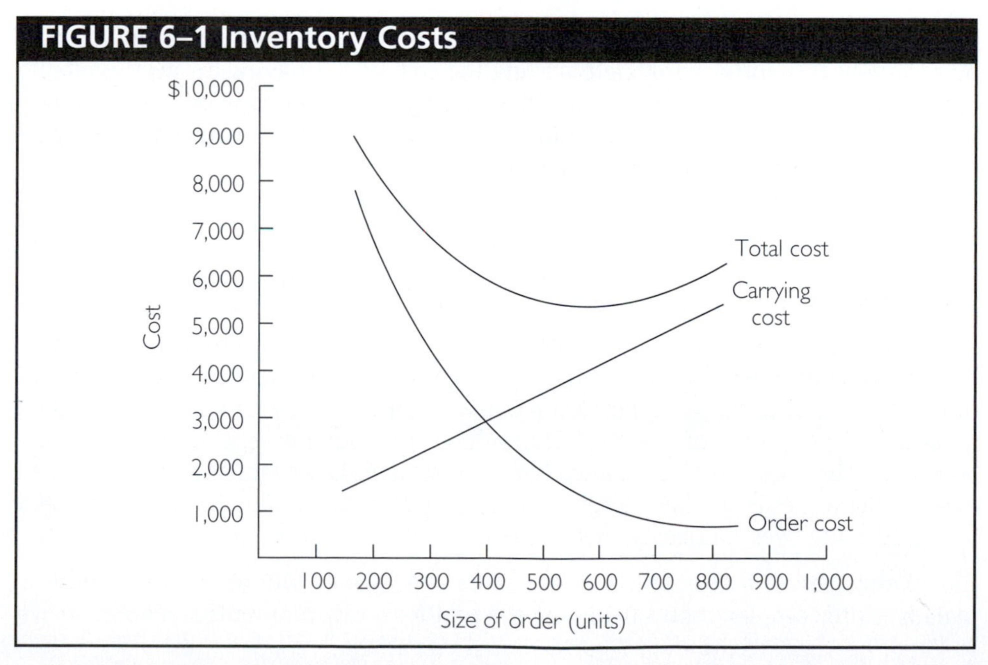

Expected Stockout Cost

Another cost critical to inventory decision making is *stockout cost*—the cost of not having product available when a customer demands or needs it. When an item is unavailable for sale, a customer may accept a back order for future availability of the needed product, or perhaps purchase (or substitute) a competitor's product, directly taking profit from the firm experiencing the stockout. If the firm permanently loses the customer to its competitor, the profit loss will be indirect but longer lasting. On the physical supply side, a stockout may result in no new materials or in semifinished goods or parts, meaning idle machine time or even shutting down an entire manufacturing facility.

Safety Stock. Most companies facing a stockout possibility will allow for *safety stock,* or buffer stock, to protect against uncertainties in demand or the lead time necessary for resupply. The inventory decision maker's difficulty is deciding how much safety stock to have on hand at any time. Having too much will mean excess inventory, whereas not having enough will mean stockouts and lost sales.

carrying cost

Developing information for deciding what level of safety stock to maintain is a difficult task. Measuring the carrying cost associated with different safety stock levels can be similar to measuring carrying cost in general. First determine a percentage carrying cost that includes capital cost, storage space cost, inventory service cost, and inventory risk cost. Then multiply this percentage figure by the dollar value per unit and the number of units involved.

We should make two points here. First, although the safety stock carrying cost is likely the same as the carrying cost for cycle stock, safety stocks are inherently riskier and implicitly more costly to carry than cycle stock. For simplicity, this text assumes that the same inventory carrying cost applies to both safety stock and cycle stock. Second, most decisions determining recommended safety stock levels involve probability analysis. The next chapter highlights this in a discussion of inventory decision making in the case of uncertainty.

stockout costs

Cost of Lost Sales. Determining the carrying cost for safety stock inventory may be relatively straightforward. Determining the cost of not having an item available for sale, however, may be much more challenging. For a company dealing with raw materials or supplies for a production line, a stockout may mean wholly or partially shutting down operations. Such operations cutbacks are particularly critical for firms involved in just-in-time manufacturing or assembly operations, as discussed previously on the topic of materials management.

To best decide how much safety stock to carry, a manufacturing firm should thoroughly understand the cost consequences of shutting down its operation if needed input parts or materials are unavailable. The firm should first determine the hourly or daily production rates and then multiply these by the profit loss on the number of units not produced. For example, if a plant with an hourly production rate of 1,000 units and a per-unit profit of $100 shuts down for four hours, the loss would be $400,000. This figure may be somewhat conservative, however, since the firm may need to pay wages to workers despite a temporary shutdown. The firm may also need to consider the overhead costs often assigned or allocated to each production unit.

Calculating how the cost of lost sales for finished goods will affect a customer is usually more complex than calculating the cost for a raw materials stockout. As we discussed earlier, the three principal results of a finished goods stockout are back orders, lost sales, and lost customers, ranked from best to worst in desirability.

In-Transit Inventory Carrying Cost

F.O.B. terms

Another possible inventory cost is that of carrying inventory in transit. This cost may be less apparent than the three discussed previously. However, under certain circumstances, it may represent a very significant expense. For example, a company selling its product "free-on-board" (FOB) destination is responsible for transporting the product to its customers, since title does not pass until the product reaches the customer's facility. Financially, the product, though still in the seller's inventory, will be contained in a transportation company vehicle or perhaps in the company's private truck.

trade-offs

Since this "moving" inventory is company-owned until delivered to the customer, the company should consider its delivery time part of its carrying cost. The faster delivery occurs, the sooner the transaction is completed and the company may receive payment for the shipment. Since faster delivery typically means higher-cost transportation, the company may want to analyze the trade-off between transportation cost and the cost of carrying inventory in transit. Appendix 7A specifically addresses this situation.

comparison with warehouse inventory

Determining Cost of In-Transit Inventories. An important question at this point is how to calculate the cost of carrying inventory in transit—that is, what variables should a firm consider? An earlier discussion in this chapter focused on four major components of inventory carrying cost: capital cost, storage space cost, inventory service cost, and inventory risk cost. While these categories are all valid, they apply differently to the cost of carrying inventory in transit.

First, the capital cost of carrying inventory in transit generally equals that of inventory in the warehouse. If the firm owns the inventory in transit, the capital cost will be relevant.

Second, storage space cost generally will not be relevant to inventory in transit, since the transportation service supplier typically includes equipment and necessary loading and handling within its overall price or rate.

Third, while taxes generally would not be relevant to inventory service costs, the need for insurance requires careful analysis. For example, liability provisions for using common carriers are fairly specific and a firm using a common carrier may not need to consider additional insurance (with the exception of certain "umbrella" coverages). Firms using private fleets or writing contracts with for-hire transportation suppliers may place greater value on making suitable arrangements for insurance.

Fourth, obsolescence or deterioration are lesser risks for inventory in transit, because the transportation service typically takes only a short time. Thus, this inventory cost is less relevant here than it is for inventory in the warehouse.

Generally, carrying inventory in transit typically costs less than carrying inventory in the warehouse. However, a firm seeking to determine actual cost differences most accurately should examine the details of each inventory matter in depth.

Supply Chain Technology

The Internet Positions Brick-and-Mortar Wholesalers to Help E-Businesses Succeed

The looming wave of distribution forces recognizes the factor of knowledge management as a central theme to attracting new customers and training the current set of profitable ones. Distributors realize tangible benefits in leveraging their Web sites to act as customer service portals by mixing the right details to keep their customers informed of product shipment delays, accounts receivable status, product specifications, pricing tables, and promotional offers. These represent just a few of the ways that knowledge ascends to service excellence. Invariably, customers once attracted by the lure of direct relationships with the manufacturer quickly become dissatisfied and return to distributors who meet their standards for service.

Collaboration Is the Future

Information is collated and analyzed in many different ways by businesses as they attempt to study distinct market segments. However, because information is often so voluminous, companies can only invest a small amount of time to analyze information they believe is accurate and, more importantly, relevant to their business. What many business leaders find is that collaboration can generate an enhanced understanding of their own target markets and other markets that are ripe for expansion.

Business-to-business (B2B) commerce is evolving into dynamic trading partnerships between businesses geared to more custom and complementary services. These partnerships are between those companies that already work together, such as Motorola and Apple, or Intel and IBM.

There are four main goals most B2B companies seek from their collaborative efforts: cost savings, control, cycle time, and customer satisfaction. Cost savings are realized through less costly processes for purchasing and overall lower costs of indirect (drop-ship) goods. Better management controls—as a result of embedded business rules in the procurement system—reduce off-contract buying and allow a company that engages in B2B commerce over the Internet to have more control of its operations. The Internet's speed delivers vastly improved cycle times. Company requisitioners increase customer satisfaction through better visibility of the procurement process and reduction of errors.

With the goals of collaboration understood, a number of pitfalls still exist in streamlining the B2B supply chain. The inability to transfer customer-specific information between intermediators and the ability to move this information seamlessly without a lot of repackaging are vital to reducing the overall costs. The second problem with the supply chain is philosophical, not technical, in nature. Many salespeople are paid on loading customers with product—many times, more than their customers can sell. This results in inventory peaks and valleys. Successful organizations, like the ones briefly profiled subsequently, are finding ways to overcome these potential shortcomings.

The phrase "brick and mortar" has come to symbolize the firm foundation upon which distribution rests. Without physical product inventories, how can the well-known CDNOW.com supply music to the world without the help of its distributor partnerships? Valley Media actively sources and ships music label products across the world for CDNOW.com and continues to leverage software as a key to its business solution inside its Woodland, California, warehouse. If you look behind the rows of product shelves, each order that leaves the Valley Media distribution center (DC) appears as if CDNOW.com fulfilled the order itself.

Bergen Brunswick, a major distributor of pharmacy items, wanted to start an Internet fulfillment center (IFC) to provide services for its clients. These clients—virtual pharmacies that ship thousands of over-the-counter health items to consumers—needed a distributor that could warehouse, box, and

(*continued on next page*)

SUPPLY CHAIN TECHNOLOGY *continued*

ship such products in a timely and efficient manner while retaining the identity of the virtual pharmacies on all invoices and shipping labels. Time-to-market and a multicompany functionality were also critical, and both were achieved. Bergen began shipping product within ninety days to its virtual clients.

Amidst the challenge of marketing a diverse product line to their customers, virtual stores have witnessed the difficulty of acting as a single point of integration—for products, service, and technical knowledge. This struggle, when contrasted with the role of distributors, lends a favorable position to those wholesalers who serve their customer channel as a one-stop shop. Keeping in mind the execution capability of distributors, most stand ready to meet the customer in all facets of the transactions—versus one or more of the missing service components of a virtual storefront.

A lesson in poor efficiency is learned when virtual storefronts struggle to process numerous orders with high transaction volumes. Pick selection becomes an encumbering process when single-quantity products fill the manifest and must reach multiple locations. Simply put, the scale of warehouse efficiency is greatly lessened because of the added effort required to complete each order.

But, for distributors, the consolidation of many small orders can lead to an efficient method of supplying the brick-and-mortar businesses with product flows to meet individual consumer demand; and, with the inherent knowledge of product movement, distributors can take advantage of inventory forecasting tools as a means to improve margins and operational profits. With wholesale benefits with multiple product lines on hand, wholesalers gain the additional benefits of wealth associated with functional diversity and the reach of products across separate markets for independence from single buyers. When possible, relationships with retailers emerge as specialty fulfillment and niche customers evolve from the repetitive buying habits of previous orders. To achieve E-business dominance, distributors will have to partner with their customers to better serve the supply chain and meet demand with extreme levels of efficiency.

The world of E-business dictates that technology requires distributors—as much as distributors require technology. The close relationships of E-commerce technology and wholesalers will change how B2B transactions take place on the front lines of an organization.

Virtual storefronts will continue to populate the Web; but, to succeed in product fulfillment, they will either need to continue to rely upon existing distribution networks or acquire their own. Eventually, the deficiencies of customer service and technical knowledge may require that these functions be outsourced to distributors who stand best positioned to aid the customer.

Source: Lowell Feil, Frontline Solutions, Duluth (April 2001).

CLASSIFYING INVENTORY

Multiple product lines and inventory control require companies to focus upon more important inventory items and to utilize more sophisticated and effective approaches to inventory management. Inventory classification is usually a first step toward efficient inventory management. While we could have saved classification for the next chapter, which deals with the tools of inventory control, we cover the topic now because it demonstrates an important aspect of most inventory decisions.

ABC Analysis

ranking system

The need to rank inventory items in terms of importance was first recognized in 1951 by H. Ford Dicky of General Electric.[3] He suggested that GE classify items according to relative sales volume, cash flows, lead time, or stockout costs. He used what we now refer to as ABC analysis for his particular classification scheme. This system assigns items to three groups according to the relative impact or value of the items that make up the group. Those thought to have the greatest impact or value, for example, constituted the A group, while those items thought to have a lesser impact or value were contained in the B and C groups, respectively.[4]

80-20 rule

Pareto's Law, or the "80-20 Rule." Actually, ABC analysis is rooted in Pareto's law, which separates the "trivial many" from the "vital few."[5] In inventory terms, this suggests that a relatively small number of items or stock-keeping units (SKUs) may account for a considerable impact or value. A nineteenth-century Renaissance man, Vilfredo Pareto suggested that many situations were dominated by a relatively few vital elements and that the relative characteristics of members of a population were not uniform.[6,7] His principle that a relatively small percentage of a population may account for a large percentage of the overall impact or value has been referred to as the "80-20 rule," which has been found to prevail in many situations.

examples

For example, marketing research might find that 20 percent of a firm's customers account for 80 percent of its sales; or a university might find that 20 percent of its courses generate 80 percent of its student credit hours; or a study might find that 20 percent of a city's people account for 80 percent of its crime. Although the actual percentages may differ somewhat from example to example, some variation of the 80-20 rule usually applies.

ABC inventories

Inventory Illustration. Figure 6–2 demonstrates ABC analysis as it applies to inventory management. The diagram indicates that only 20 percent of the items in the product line account for 80 percent of total sales. The items that make up this 20 percent are referred to as A items, due to the significant portion of sales for which they are responsible. The items in the B category account for approximately 50 percent of the items in the product line, yet make up only an additional 15 percent of total sales. Finally, the C items are represented by the remaining 30 percent of the items, which account only for approximately 5 percent of sales.

relative importance

In many ABC analyses, a common mistake is to think of the B and C items as being far less important than the A items and, subsequently, to focus most or all of management's attention on the A items. For example, a decision might be made to assure very high in-stock levels for the A items and little or no availability for the B and C items. The fallacy here relates to the fact that all items in the A, B, and C categories are important to some extent and that each set of items deserves its very own strategy to assure availability at an appropriate level of cost. This thinking has led some firms to differentiate inventory stocking policies by ABC category, making sure that the A items are available either immediately or through the use of express logistics services. The B and C items, while perhaps available at an upstream location in the logistics channel, could be available in a timely manner when needed.

There are a number of additional reasons not to overlook the importance of the B and C items. Sometimes, the use of B and C items may be complementary to the use of A items, meaning that the availability of B and C items may be necessary for the sale of A items; or, in some instances, the C items might be new products that

FIGURE 6–2 ABC Inventory Analysis

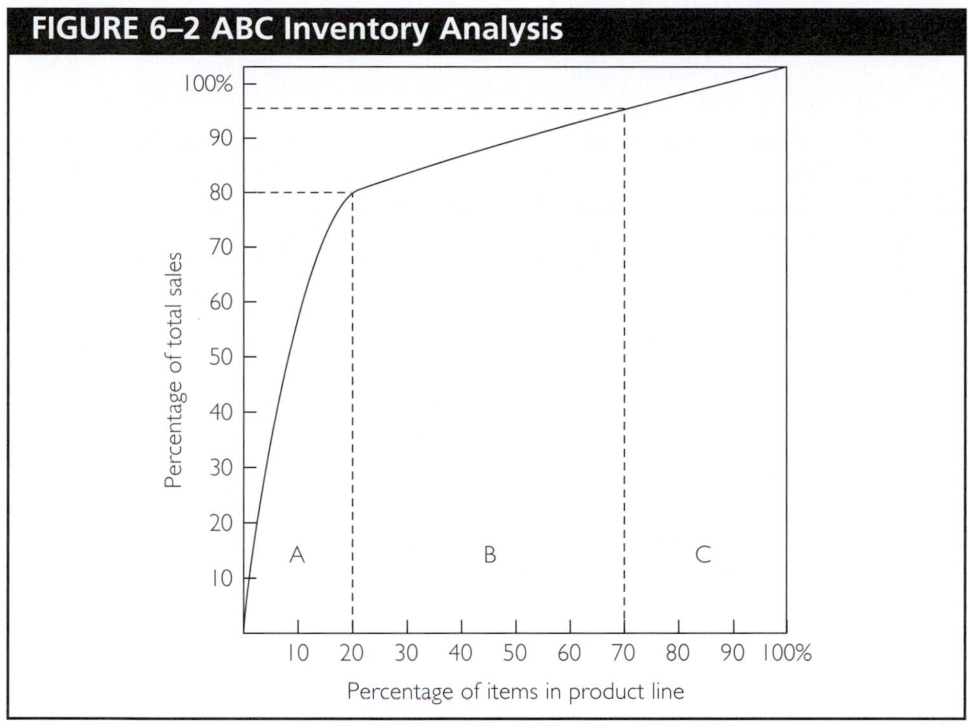

are expected to be successful in the future. In other cases, the C items may be highly profitable, despite the fact that they may account for only a small portion of sales.

steps in ABC analysis

Performing an ABC Classification. ABC classification is relatively simple. The first step is to select some criterion, such as sales revenue, for developing the ranking. The next step is to rank items in descending order of importance according to this criterion and to calculate actual and cumulative total sales revenue percentages for each item. This calculation should help to group the items into ABC categories.

Table 6–7 shows how to base an ABC inventory analysis on sales revenue generated per line item. The first column identifies the ten items in the Big Orange product line. The second and third columns show the annual sales and percentage of total annual sales represented by each item. The fourth and fifth columns show sales and items, respectively, as percentages of the total. From these columns emanate statements such as "20 percent of the items account for 80 percent of the sales." The last column places each item into ABC classification on the basis of annual item sales revenues.

This last step assigns the items into ABC groups. This step is the most difficult, and no simple technique is available. While the analysis is supported by data inputs that are presumably accurate, the ultimate decisions will require subjective judgment on the part of the decision maker. As one examines item rankings, significant natural "breaks" sometimes appear; but this is not always the case, and the decision maker will have to consider other variables such as the item's importance and the cost of managing individual item types. Also, note that the data in the fourth and fifth columns of Table 6–7 are the basic data points from which Figure 6–2 was constructed. This should bring our understanding of ABC inventory analysis full circle.

TABLE 6–7 ABC Analysis for Big Orange Products, Inc.

Item Code	Annual Sales ($)	Percentage of Annual Sales	Cumulative Sales	Percentages Items	Classification Category
64R	$ 6,800	68.0%	68.0%	10.0%	A
89Q	1,200	12.0	80.0	20.0	A
68I	500	5.0	85.0	30.0	B
37S	400	4.0	89.0	40.0	B
12G	200	2.0	91.0	50.0	B
35B	200	2.0	93.0	60.0	B
61P	200	2.0	95.0	70.0	B
94L	200	2.0	97.0	80.0	C
11T	150	1.5	98.5	90.0	C
20G	150	1.5	100.0	100.0	C
	$10,000	100.0%			

further insight

Moving beyond the simple ABC analysis based on total sales by line item, William C. Copacino suggests that a modified ABC analysis be performed using gross profit dollars per line item and line item order frequency as potential segmenting variables. He suggests using multiple measures of impact or value and then developing a weighting scheme to stratify items into the ABC categories.[8] This approach broadens the focus beyond just sales volume considerations and places attention on often overlooked issues such as item profitability (which affects overall profitability) and order frequency (which affects customer service performance). Furthermore, this more comprehensive approach allows users to examine the suitability of different criteria; different weightings of the criteria; and, ultimately, the impact of alternative classification policies on issues of strategic importance—sales volume, profitability, customer service, and inventory investment.

Quadrant Technique

As indicated in Chapter 4, not all items purchased and/or produced are the same in terms of value and risk. When developing procurement strategies, companies should take this into consideration, not only in purchasing products and services but also in managing products for inventory. As indicated in the discussion of ABC analysis, some items are much more important than others.

In the case of the *quadrant technique,* value is measured as the value contribution to profit. Risk is the negative impact of not having the product available. When needed, items with high value and high risk (critical items) need to be managed carefully to ensure adequate supply. Items with low risk and low value (generics or routine items) can be managed much less carefully. The other two categories deserve special consideration because of either their value or their risk (see Figure 4–3).

In the next section, we explore the topic of inventory visibility, which was mentioned in Chapter 1. Visibility has been receiving much attention in business publications.

Inventory Visibility

Inventory visibility can be interpreted simply as the ability of an organization to "see" inventory on a real-time basis throughout its logistics and/or supply chain system. Having knowledge of where inventory is in the system is not, however, sufficient to accomplish the objectives outlined previously. The concept of inventory visibility envisioned in this paper is much more comprehensive.

Inventory visibility implies having knowledge of not only "where" inventory (raw materials, supplies, work in progress, finished goods, etc.) is in the system (vendor locations, plants, warehouses, customer locations, in transit with carriers, etc.) but also how much is "there" (level), to whom it may be promised, what orders need to be fulfilled, when shipments can be delivered, and so on. Knowing the quality and the quantity of real-time data needed is a significant challenge, particularly when we consider the number of SKUs that some companies have in their product lines. Inventory sometimes disappears while it is in transit or while it is being held in a warehouse. Keeping inventory visible in the supply chain is a special challenge. Essentially, what is required is

- Tracking and tracing inventory status at the SKU/line item detail level for all orders (inbound from vendors, internal between locations, and outbound to customers) as all inventory is moved and stored through the logistics and supply chain systems
- Providing summary and detailed reports of shipments, orders, products, transportation equipment, location, and trade lane activity
- Notification of failures and potential delays in the flow of inventory throughout the system

The general benefits of inventory visibility include

- Improved customer service through on-time deliveries of complete orders to customers with visibility into order status at all stages of the supply chain
- Decreased cost-of-sales by lowering inventory holding costs, minimizing errors and back orders, and decreasing obsolete inventory
- Improvement of vendor/supplier relations and cost by providing accurate, timely information regarding requirements
- Increased return on assets (ROA) and shareholder value by lowering investment in inventory, reducing investment in fixed facilities necessary for holding inventory, and turning inventory faster
- Improved cash-to-cash and/or order-to-cash cycle by faster flow of inventory through the supply chain and by faster order fulfillment
- Ability to proactively respond and facilitate service recovery when delays and/or stockouts are probable by making adjustments in the system and responding quickly to service demands
- Improved performance metrics for overall supply chain, carriers, vendors, logistics service providers, and even customers by having timely accurate information available

Visibility can lower requirements for all types of inventory. We use safety stock to demonstrate this point. The keys to safety stock reduction are

- Better demand forecasts
- Reduction of uncertainty in lead time
- Reduction of lead time

For example, if lead time is normally distributed and averages 10 days with a standard deviation of 2 days, demand is 100 units per day, and a 90 percent service level is required, the safety stock required would be 256 units. If the standard deviation of lead time is reduced to one day, safety stock can be reduced to 128 units. Such a reduction in uncertainty can be achieved with inventory visibility through tracking the shipment in transit on a real-time basis. Better forecasts and lead-time reduction can also be improved with inventory visibility.

Let us examine another type of situation—in-transit inventory. Assume that there is a contracted delivery time for a given traffic lane of ten days, 80 percent of the shipments are on time, 15 percent are late by three days, and 5 percent are late by ten days. If a 90 percent service level is required, stockouts can only occur 10 percent of the time, which means thirteen days of inventory is required. If a tracking system can eliminate 50 percent of the late shipments, the inventory can be reduced to ten days to achieve 90 percent service. Depending on the value of the inventory, the bottom-line savings can be significant. The sophisticated tracking systems employed by some carriers, which allow real-time visibility of in-transit inventory, provide shippers with potential for this type of savings.

As suggested previously, inventory visibility can impact positively all three keys to reducing safety stocks and all three types of inventory mentioned earlier. If we add up the inventory savings, the cash flow benefit, and the improved customer service levels, the savings can easily reach $500,000 to $1,000,000 per month in larger companies. In one company that was studied, a savings of $250,000 per month was estimated by just improving visibility in several of its major trade lanes. Technology helps to provide the benefits discussed here.

Evaluating the Effectiveness of a Company's Approach to Inventory Management

A product buyer must be confident that suppliers and vendors have that product available when and where the buyer needs it. Similarly, a product seller's ability to manage inventory effectively should translate into a more satisfied customer base. Thus, both buyers and sellers should consider several questions when evaluating the effectiveness of a firm's inventory management approach.

customer satisfaction

The first question to raise is whether the company's customers are satisfied with existing levels of customer service. Insight into this issue can be gained by inquiring into matters such as customer loyalty, order cancellation experience, and stockouts and evaluating the company's general relationships with all channel partners. If there are areas where customer service levels need to improve, perhaps using more dependable transportation suppliers would help to enhance customer satisfaction.

backordering/ expediting

The second question is how frequently a need for back ordering or expediting occurs. The more frequently these occur, the less effective an inventory system is presumed to be. The company's inventory management approach may not respond promptly to signals for reordering and resupplying inventory levels; or, the company may need an ABC inventory system or faster and more dependable transportation services to see that inventory is available when and where the customer needs it.

inventory turnover

A third question involves inventory turnover measures calculated for an entire product line and for individual products and product groupings. Buyers and sellers should question whether these measures are increasing or decreasing and how they vary among different stocking points in the firm's distribution system.

Inventory turnover, sometimes referred to as inventory velocity, is calculated by dividing annual sales in dollars by average inventory measured in dollars. Assuming that the inventory valuation bases are equivalent (e.g., both are valued in terms of retail price or cost of goods sold), the resulting figure measures how many times per year average inventory turns over.

For example, assume that a firm values its yearly product sales at $50,000 and calculates its average on-hand inventory to be $10,000. The number of inventory "turns" per year would be $50,000 ÷ $10,000, or five. The firm could say either that average inventory turns five times per year or that, on the average, an inventory item stays on the shelf for one fifth of a year—or 10.4 weeks.

Inventory turnover varies widely among firms in different industries and also among firms in similar industries. Inventory turnover typically ranges from five to ten turns for many manufacturing firms and from ten to twenty turns for wholesale and retail firms, through whose systems inventory moves rapidly. In either case, buyers and sellers must have specific details about a firm and its logistics system before estimating inventory turnover. (We should view the percentages cited here not as industry standards but only as representing certain firms in the industries identified.)

While more inventory turns per year often imply more effective inventory management, customer service sometimes suffers if turnovers cause needed inventoried items to be unavailable. A firm interested in increasing its inventory turns while maintaining customer service levels should switch to faster and more reliable transportation services or improved order-processing systems, which will justify lowering its safety stock investment and therefore its overall inventory levels. Examining inventory turnover by individual products or facilities may help to identify trouble spots in a firm's logistics system.

As Table 6–8 indicates, as inventory turnover increases, both average inventory and the cost of carrying the average inventory will show decreases. These same relationships are shown in Figure 6–3. Also, according to studies by Cass Information Services and the Ohio State University, it is expected that inventories at plant warehouses and company-field warehouses will experience increased turns in the years ahead. The projections, based on survey research, are indicated in Figure 6–4.

TABLE 6–8 The Relationship among Inventory Turnover, Average Inventory, and Inventory Carrying Costs

Inventory Turnover	Average Inventory	Inventory Carrying Cost*	Incremental Savings in Carrying Cost	Cumulative Savings in Carrying Cost
1................	$20,000,000	$6,000,000	—	—
2................	10,000,000	3,000,000	$3,000,000	$3,000,000
3................	6,666,667	2,000,000	1,000,000	4,000,000
4................	5,000,000	1,500,000	500,000	4,500,000
5................	4,000,000	1,200,000	300,000	4,800,000
6................	3,333,333	1,000,000	200,000	5,000,000
7................	2,857,143	857,143	142,857	5,142,857
8................	2,500,000	750,000	107,143	5,250,000
9................	2,222,222	666,667	83,333	5,333,333
10................	2,000,000	600,000	66,667	5,400,000

*Assume that inventory carrying cost equals 30%.

FIGURE 6–3 Saving Inventory Dollars by Inventory Turns

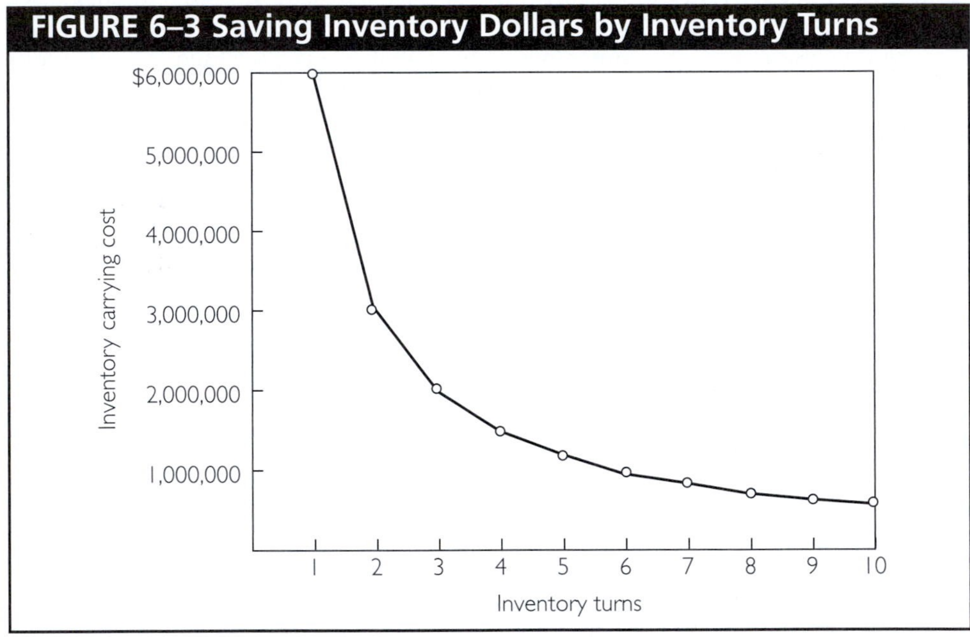

ratio of inventory to sales

A fourth question to raise is whether overall inventory as a percentage of sales rises or falls as a company's sales increase. Generally, given effective inventory management, this figure should decline as sales increase. If a firm's inventories are rising at a rate equal to or faster than its sales, the firm may need to reconsider its overall inventory policies. Commonly, many firms experiencing a growing demand for their products will "overinventory" those products where customers are concentrated. A more suitable alternative might be to centralize supplies of such items and to depend upon capable transportation suppliers and enhanced order-processing systems to provide timely product delivery to customers.

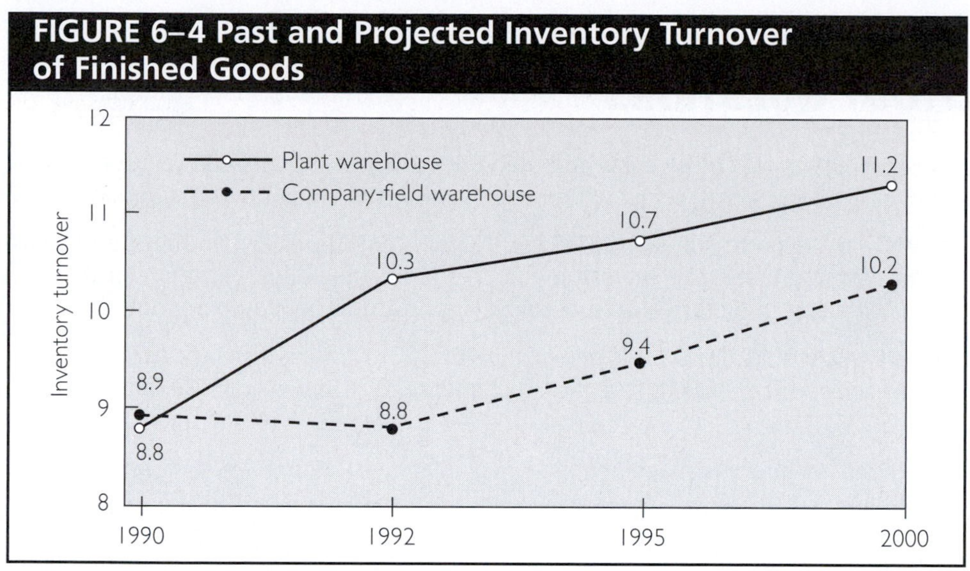

FIGURE 6–4 Past and Projected Inventory Turnover of Finished Goods

Source: Cass Information Services and The Ohio State University, 1993. Used with permission of Dr. Bernard J. LaLonde.

SUMMARY

This chapter discussed some important concepts and issues relating to inventory in the logistics system. The following key points summarize these concepts for a meaningful discussion of how inventory decisions are made in today's business environment:

- Inventory as a percent of overall business activity continues to decline. Explanatory factors include: greater expertise in managing inventory, innovations in information and communications technology, greater competitiveness in markets for transportation services, and emphasis upon reducing cost through the elimination of non-value-added activities.
- As product lines proliferate and the number of SKUs increase, the cost of carrying inventory becomes a significant expense of doing business.
- There are a number of principal reasons for carrying inventories. Types of inventory include: cycle stock, goods in process or goods in transit, safety stock, seasonal stock, anticipatory stock, and dead stock.
- Principal types of inventory cost are inventory carrying cost, order/setup cost, expected stockout cost, and in-transit inventory carrying cost.
- Inventory carrying cost is composed of capital cost, storage space cost, inventory service cost, and inventory risk cost. There are precise ways to calculate each of these costs.
- ABC analysis is a useful tool to improve the effectiveness of inventory management. Other tools include critical value analysis and supply segmentation.
- There are a number of key questions and issues that may be raised to evaluate the effectiveness of a company's approach to inventory management.
- Inventory visibility can result in significant benefits to companies including reduced costs, reduced stockouts, and so on.

Study Questions

1. Explain why inventory costs and inventory levels have declined relative to GDP over the last twenty years. Is this beneficial to the economy? Why, or why not?
2. Write a memo to Jim Gatto, COO of Micros and More, explaining the reasons for carrying inventory. In your memo, also indicate which of the major reasons for carrying inventory would be most important to his company and why.
3. As COO, would Jim Gatto's perspective on inventory be different than the chief financial officer (CFO) and the chief marketing officer (CMO)? Why or why not?
4. Why is inventory management such a challenge to companies such as Kimberly-Clark?
5. What are the major components of inventory carrying cost? How would you measure capital cost for making inventory policy decisions?
6. How can inventory carrying cost be calculated for a specific product? What suggestions would you offer for determining the measure of product value to be used in calculations of inventory carrying costs?
7. Explain the differences between inventory carrying costs and order costs.
8. Why is it generally more difficult to determine the cost of lost sales for finished goods than it is for raw materials inventories?
9. Discuss the cost of carrying inventory in transit.
10. What is meant by inventory visibility? What are the benefits of inventory visibility?
11. What key questions would you raise when judging the effectiveness of a company's inventory management approach? If the calculated value of inventory as a percentage of sales appears to be rising, would this concern you? Explain.
12. How is inventory turnover calculated? What is the nature of the relationship between inventory carrying cost and inventory turnover?

Notes

1. Douglas M. Lambert, *The Development of an Inventory Costing Methodology: A Study of the Costs Associated with Holding Inventory* (Chicago: National Council of Physical Distribution Management, 1976).
2. Douglas M. Lambert and James R. Stock, *Strategic Logistics Management*, 3d ed. (Homewood, Ill.: Irwin, 1993), 378–79.
3. Robert Goodell Brown, *Advanced Service Parts Inventory Control*, 2d ed. (Norwich, Vt.: Materials Management Systems, 1982), 155.

4. David P. Herron, "ABC Data Correlation," in *Business Logistics in American Industry,* ed. Karl Ruppenthal and Henry A. McKinnel Jr. (Stanford, Calif.: Stanford University, 1968), 87–90.

5. Thomas E. Hendrick and Franklin G. Moore, *Production/Operations Management,* 9th ed. (Homewood, Ill.: Irwin, 1985), 173.

6. Lambert and Stock, *Strategic Logistics Management,* 426–29.

7. Jay U. Sterling, "Measuring the Performance of Logistics Operations," Chapter 10 in *The Logistics Handbook,* ed. James F. Robeson and William C. Copacino (New York: The Free Press, 1994), 226–30.

8. William C. Copacino, "Moving Beyond 'ABC' Analysis," *Traffic Management* (March 1994): 35–36.

CASE 6–1 ■ Leola Milling Company

Jennifer Roberts, distribution manager for Leola Milling, has become increasingly aware that the company has a major problem as it continues to try to reduce inventories while maintaining the levels of service its customers have come to expect.

Company and Product

Founded in 1887, Leola Milling has provided high-quality bakery flours to commercial bakeries as well as to the consumer market. While commercial customers tend to have consistent buying patterns as well as brand loyalty, Leola has found that consumers have minimal loyalty but also generally prefer known names over the store brands. Demand is highly seasonal, with the annual peak occurring just before Thanksgiving and slacking off dramatically during January and February. To offset this, both Leola and its major supermarket chain accounts run special deals and sales promotions.

Production planning, located at the Leola, Pennsylvania, headquarters has responsibility for controlling inventory levels at the plant warehouse at Buffalo as well as at the three distribution centers located at Washington, Pennsylvania; Columbus, Ohio; and Pittsfield, Massachusetts. Planning has routinely been based on past history. No forecasting is performed, at least not in a formal sense. Distribution Centers (DCs) are replenished by rail from Buffalo; and lead times are typically seven days, with forty-eight to fifty-four pallets per car depending upon the type used. Should emergencies occur, eighteen pallets can be shipped by truck with a one-day transit time.

Recently Leola has experienced two major stockouts for its consumer-size five-pound sacks of bleached white flour. One of these was due to problems in milling operations; the other occurred when marketing initiated a "buy one, get one free" coupon promotion. Since these events, planning has become overly cautious and errs on the side of having excess inventories at the DCs. Additionally, two other events have affected DC throughput: (1) implementation of direct factory shipments for replenishing the five largest supermarket chains, and (2) a price increase making Leola flour more expensive than its national brand competitors, such as Pillsbury or Gold Medal.

Current Situation

Of the 1,500 pallets in the Pittsfield DC, Leola shows only 396 pallets for open orders. This has led the company to use outside overflow storage, where there are another 480 pallets. Flour is easily damaged; hence, Leola prefers to minimize handling. Overstocking at the DC alone costs $1.85 per pallet for outside storage, to which must be added $4.25 per pallet for extra handling and $225 per truckload for transportation. Similar scenarios are being played out at the other DCs as well.

Possible Solutions

Jennifer Roberts has been contemplating various approaches to solving the inventory issue. Clearly, product needs to be in place at the time a consumer is making a buying decision, but Leola cannot tolerate the overstocking situation and the stress that it is putting on facilities and cash flow.

Jennifer's first thought is that a better information system is needed, one that not only provides timely and accurate information but also extensively shares that information throughout the organization. Several questions immediately come to her mind; however, she needs additional information prior to coming to any solutions.

Case Questions

1. Evaluate the alternative solutions being considered by Jennifer Roberts.
2. What additional solutions do you propose? Why?

Source: Copyright 1996, Richard R. Young. The Department of Business Logistics, The Pennsylvania State University. Cases are examples of market or administrative situations. They are not presented as examples of good or bad practice.

CASE 6–2 ■ Casey-Lynn Corporation

The Casey-Lynn Corporation, a major producer of stereo receiver equipment, is currently faced with a rapidly growing product line and the inventory problems associated with a multiple product line. Casey-Lynn's president, Mary Lynagh, has decided to initiate a program to analyze the company's inventory requirements utilizing different inventory analysis tools. The first phase of this program consists of an ABC analysis of the company's product line (shown in the table). Ms. Lynagh has encountered difficulties in deciding on the appropriate criteria to use in the classification and in developing appropriate cutoff levels for each class of inven-

Sales Data (One-Year Period)

Product #	Units Sold	Price/Unit	Profit/Unit
SR101	12,386	$ 275	$ 82.50
SR103	784	1,530	459.00
SR105	1,597	579	173.30
SR201	48	2,500	975.00
SR203	2	3,000	1,200.00
SR205	9,876	450	149.00
SR301	673	600	180.00
SR303	547	725	200.00
SR305	3,437	917	240.00
SR500	78	1,000	312.00

tory. To solve her dilemma, Ms. Lynagh has contracted the services of a logistics consulting firm to perform the inventory analysis.

Case Questions

If you were employed by the consulting firm, how would you construct your method of analysis? What criteria would you use? What cutoff levels? Be sure to give explanations of the reasoning behind all of your decisions and methods.

CHAPTER 7

INVENTORY DECISION MAKING

LEARNING OBJECTIVES

After reading this chapter, you should be able to do the following:

- Understand the fundamental differences among approaches to managing inventory.
- Appreciate the rationale and logic behind the economic order quantity (EOQ) approach to inventory decision making, and be able to solve some problems of a relatively straightforward nature.
- Understand alternative approaches to managing inventory—JIT, MRP, and DRP.
- Realize how variability in demand and order cycle length affects inventory decision making.
- Know how inventory will vary as the number of stocking points decreases or increases.
- Recognize the contemporary interest in and relevance of time-based approaches to inventory management.
- Make needed adjustments to the basic EOQ approach to respond to several special types of applications.

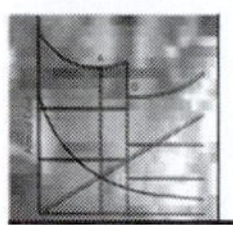

LOGISTICS PROFILE

Micros and More: The Sequel

Jim Gatto, COO, of Micros and More was sitting in his office talking to his recently hired manager of inventory, Don Warsing. Jim had spearheaded a major program to rationalize the inventory SKUs for Micros and More. The program lead to significant reduction in inventory levels and associated inventory carrying costs. Jim discovered, using *ABC analysis* to classify the company's inventory, that they had been carrying many SKUs that had very low turnover, which obviously increased their inventory costs. He was able to significantly reduce the *C* inventory items and some of the *B* items.

Instead of feeling satisfied, Jim decided that his company needed to improve its inventory situation even more, that is, further lowering inventory levels. Consequently, Jim decided to hire Don Warsing into the newly established position of inventory manager. Jim was impressed by Don's credentials, especially his education in quantitative analysis at North Carolina and working experience in logistics during the previous four years.

Jim asked Don the following question during their first official meeting: "What would you recommend to improve our efficiency in managing inventory?"

Don paused before making his reply. He was concerned that it might be a loaded question but decided to forge ahead. "Based upon my initial analysis, Mr. Gatto, I think that Micros and More has an opportunity to lower its inventory dramatically."

Jim Gatto was surprised since he expected a less-optimistic response. "Don, I am surprised that you think that we can reduce our inventory so significantly. Are you aware of the inventory rationalization program that we initiated last year?"

Don responded, "Mr. Gatto, I was informed about your inventory rationalization program and the savings by Mr. Edwards (CFO of Micros and More). That was certainly a successful program with important financial results, but from an economic perspective that was a one-time savings. I believe that we can build upon that successful implementation."

"Well Don, you have certainly caught my attention with that comment about significant additional reduction in inventory levels. But I must admit that I am surprised that you have such high expectations. Without giving me too much detail, can you describe what we can do to improve our inventory position so significantly?"

Don replied, "Mr. Gatto, I have completed a preliminary analysis of our inventory management practices. Our current practices for inventory replenishment appear to be inconsistent and based upon inaccurate forecasts. Consequently, we appear to have too much of some items, but not enough of others. I believe that we can improve by managing our order fulfillment more precisely and implementing a more advanced approach to our replenishment practices such as JIT or MRP/DRP. There are software packages available from various vendors that can really help us."

"Don, that's interesting, and I am excited about the possibility of additional reductions in inventory costs. But, do we have the talent or expertise among our current staff members to implement any of these advanced techniques?"

Don replied, "We have employees who can be trained to administer these systems using the guidelines that I will establish."

"Okay, you have convinced me, Don. What do we have to do next?"

"Well, Mr. Gatto, I will need about sixty days to review the inventory decision techniques and to evaluate some of the software packages as well as to talk to vendors. I will include several of my staff in the discussions and evaluations. Then, I should be able to present a comprehensive proposal to you with the benefits and disadvantages. Hopefully, you and Mr. Edwards will feel confident enough with my recommendation to move aggressively ahead."

INTRODUCTION

Chapter 6 developed the rationale for inventory in a logistics system and addressed several fundamental aspects of inventory management. An important part of that chapter analyzed major cost categories that are relevant to the inventory decision: inventory carrying costs, order/setup costs, and expected stockout costs.

This chapter places the content of Chapter 6 in an operational context by describing in detail how inventory management decisions are made. In addition, it focuses attention on a number of approaches to replenishment logistics. This chapter should help the student understand how companies make inventory decisions and how they develop overall strategies that can make significant reductions of inventory in the logistics pipeline.

FUNDAMENTAL APPROACHES TO MANAGING INVENTORY

basic issues

Historically, managing inventory involved two fundamental questions: *how much* to reorder from vendors and/or their plants and *when* to reorder. By performing a few simple calculations, an inventory manager could easily determine acceptable solutions to these issues. Today, questions regarding *where* inventory should be held and *what* specific line items should be available at specific locations challenge the creativity and analytical capabilities of inventory decision makers.

managing inventories

Each question is still relevant, but managing inventory in today's business environment is more challenging and usually involves selecting an overall strategy from a range of alternatives. At the same time that inventory decision making has become more complex, firms have placed more pressure on themselves to structure logistics systems to manage inventories more effectively and to lower cost and improve service as well. In practice, the difficulty of selecting an acceptable approach depends on the circumstances under which the company operates and the extent to which certain simplifying assumptions can be made. Generally, the more complex the circumstances, the more sophisticated the inventory approach required.

balancing cost with service

Regardless of the approach selected, inventory decisions must consider issues relating to cost and to customer service requirements. Figure 7–1, which illustrates the general relationship between inventory and customer service levels, suggests that increasing investments in inventory may result in higher levels of customer service. While there is some validity to this relationship, a high priority today is on identifying logistics solutions that will result in higher levels of customer service along with reduced investments in inventories. Several factors make this an achievable objective: (1) more responsive order-processing and order-management systems; (2) enhanced ability to strategically manage logistics information; (3) more capable and reliable transportation resources; and (4) improvements in the ability to position inventories so that they will be available when and where they are

FIGURE 7–1 Relationship between Inventory and Customer Service Level

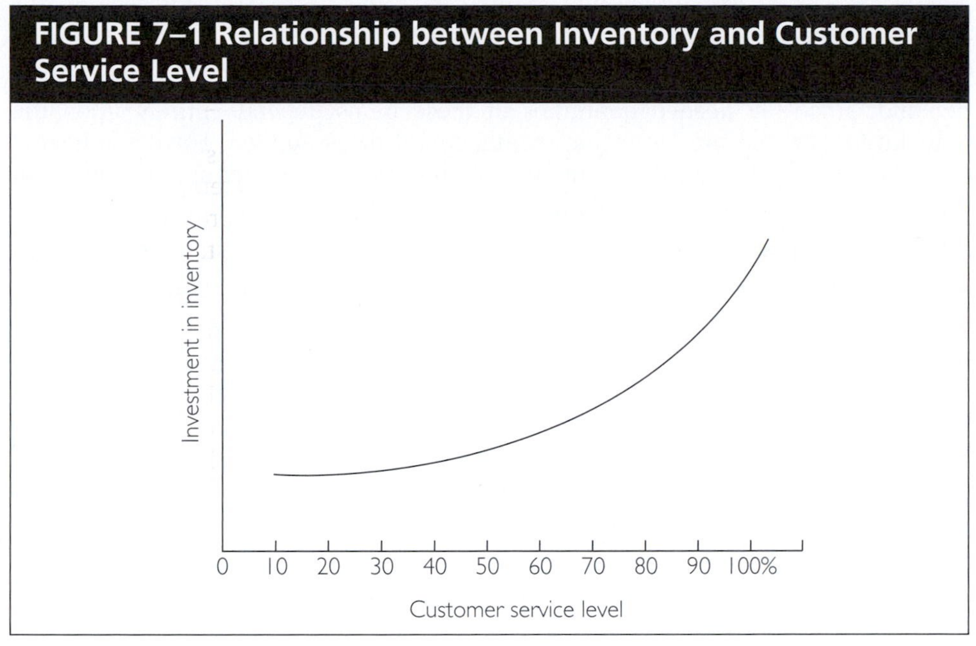

needed. Thus, the higher priority today is on identifying the total logistics solutions that will lead to increases in overall customer service levels and reductions in total logistics cost. Micros and More needs to move in the direction suggested here, namely, use inventory management proactively to lower cost and improve customer service.

Key Differences among Approaches to Managing Inventory

Given the various approaches to managing inventory that are available and used today, it is important to know the key ways in which they differ. These differences include dependent versus independent demand, pull versus push, and systemwide versus single-facility solutions to inventory management issues.

nature of demand

Dependent versus Independent Demand. This distinction is important to selecting an appropriate inventory management approach. "Demand for a given inventory item is termed 'independent' when such demand is unrelated to demand for other items—when it is not a function of demand for some other inventory item. . . . Conversely, demand is defined as 'dependent' when it is directly related, or derives from, the demand for another inventory item or product."[1] For example, the demand for finished automobiles is independent; the demand for tires is dependent on the desired quantity of finished automobiles. This dependency may be *vertical* (such as when a product's assembly requires a component part) or *horizontal* (for example, when an instruction booklet must accompany a finished product).

Thus, for many manufacturing processes, basic demand for most raw materials, component parts, and subassemblies *depends* upon demand for the finished product. In contrast, demand for many end-use items, which are typically warehoused and inventoried, is *independent* of the demand for any other higher-order manufactured item.

An important point to remember is that developing inventory policies for items exhibiting independent demand requires forecasting expected demand for these items. Alternatively, forecasting is less relevant for items having dependent demand, since the needed quantities of these items depend entirely upon the demand for the end product being manufactured or assembled. For items having dependent demand, needed quantity projections and receipts timing rely wholly on the forecast needs for the end product.

Of the approaches to inventory management that will be discussed, JIT, MRP, and MRPII are generally associated with items having dependent demand. In such instances, the demand for individual parts and items typically depends on the demand for the finished end product. Alternatively, DRP generally involves the movement and positioning of items having independent demand. The economic order quantity (EOQ) approach applies most frequently to items having demand that may be characterized as independent.

Pull versus Push.[2] Another important distinction between inventory management approaches is the issue of pull versus push. Sometimes called a "reactive" system, the pull approach relies on customer demand to "pull" product through a logistics system. In contrast, the "push," or proactive, approach uses inventory replenishment to anticipate future demand.

example

As an example, a fast-food system such as McDonald's basically runs on a pull system, while a catering service basically operates on a push system. McDonald's cooks hamburgers generally in response to current demand. In effect, individual purchases "trigger" more food item production. In contrast, the catering service tries to have a picture-perfect idea of what customers will need and when and pushes food items to where customers need them, at the right time and in the right quantity.[3]

hybrid system

While this distinction may seem simple enough, the McDonald's pull system may be quite effective in a downtown location with a steady stream of customers but may suffer in a high-traffic, peak-demand location such as a major airport concourse. In this instance, a pull and push system hybrid would be appropriate.

A principal attribute of pull systems is that they can respond quickly to sudden or abrupt changes in demand. Alternatively, a push system meets systemwide inventory needs in accordance with some master plan in an orderly and disciplined way. In general, the pull system applies more to independent demand and the push system to dependent demand. A deficiency of many pull systems is that product orders are typically triggered at individual stock-keeping locations; thus, the need for similar or identical items at parallel network facilities is uncoordinated. In contrast, push systems adapt better to the coincident needs of parallel logistics network facilities. Finally, pull systems sometimes involve only one-way communications between point of need and point of supply, while push systems tend to involve more two-way communications between point of need and point of supply.

environmental conditions

The pull, or reactive, approach would be most suitable when either order cycle time or demand levels are uncertain, or when market-oriented warehouses or distribution centers have capacity limitations.[4] The push, or planning-based, approach is most appropriate for highly profitable segments, dependent demand, scale economies, supply uncertainties, source capacity limitations, or seasonal supply buildups. In general, push systems are more prevalent among organizations having greater logistics sophistication.

Characteristically, JIT is a pull system, since firms place orders for more inventory only when the amount on hand reaches a certain level, thus pulling inventory through the system as needed. Having established the master production schedule, the MRP program develops a time-phased approach to inventory scheduling and inventory receipt. Because it generates a list of required materials in order to assemble or manufacture a specified number of finished products, the MRP and MRPII approaches are push based. Similar to these, but on the outbound or physical distribution side of logistics, DRP involves the allocation of available inventory to meet marketplace demands. Thus, it also is a push-based strategy.

The EOQ-based approach is generally pull based, but contemporary applications include elements of a push strategy as well. While this permits the EOQ technique to be reactive when necessary, it also allows the preplanning of certain inventory decisions in a proactive, or push, manner. In fact, many EOQ-based systems in evidence today are hybrid approaches that include elements of pull and push-based strategies.

Systemwide versus Single-Facility Solution. A final inventory management issue is whether the selected approach represents a systemwide solution or whether it is specific to a single facility, such as an individual warehouse or distribution center. Each approach has advantages and disadvantages. The principal factors associated with the *systemwide* approach are the time and expense of developing a truly comprehensive solution to a network's inventory problems, and also the question of whether or not it will work, once developed and implemented. The *single-facility* approach is less expensive and more straightforward in development terms. Its inherent risk is that it may produce optimal single-facility results that may be suboptimal from a systemwide perspective.

Essentially, the JIT and EOQ-based approaches are more applicable to single-facility decision making. The MRP and DRP approaches can deal more effectively with issues relating to the systemwide positioning of inventories and related decisions.

Overall, those choosing an approach must carefully consider its comprehensiveness. The two extremes offer very different perspectives on the problem. Those choosing must gain an early understanding of the specific advantages and disadvantages of each approach, given any specific inventory problem. Such understanding will reveal important trade-offs and provide information sufficient for a rational choice between the available alternatives.

Principal Approaches and Techniques for Inventory Management

In many business situations, the variables affecting the decision regarding the approach to inventory management are almost overwhelming. Therefore, models developed to aid in the decision process are frequently abstract or represent a simplified reality. In other words, models generally make simplifying assumptions about the real world they attempt to represent.

The complexity and accuracy of a model relate to the assumptions the model makes. Typically, the more the model assumes, the easier the model is to work with and understand; however, simple model output is often less accurate. The model developer or user must decide upon the proper balance between simplicity and

ON THE LINE

CANCER SOCIETY CURES INVENTORY CLOG

"What can we do to operate in a more business-like manner?" Even non-profit organizations find themselves under pressure to cut costs and find new revenue sources. Nelson Rivera, managing director, supply chain management and Bill Costa, director of logistics for the American Cancer Society (ACS), began by reviewing the practices of many for-profit companies. Even though a number of these for-profits did not offer much in the way of best practices, Rivera and Costa saw enough of what to do and what not to do to develop a plan. The lessons they learned apply to non-profit organizations as well as investor-owned companies.

Ten months after they began equipment implementation, the material handling and distribution operations were transformed from a decentralized, manual operation into a world-class automated centralized fulfillment system. The transformation went so well that the ACS Nationwide Distribution Center has extra capacity. The center may potentially offer its fulfillment services to other non-profit agencies, turning this extra capacity into a revenue stream.

The National Home Office is responsible for planning and coordinating public and professional educational material. Before the transformation, many of the brochures, posters, pamphlets and other material were stored in a 50,000-square-foot building in Atlanta. Each of 52 divisions replenished their material from this site, plus they stored material created for their local programs and specific language or culture needs. Most of the divisions housed up to 100 SKUs of the literature, some of which were decades old.

Because of the manual fulfillment methods, shipments to the divisions were usually in bulk quantities, and order cycle time could take up to six weeks. Storage organization was poor, inventory information was incomplete and inaccurate, and there were no measurement systems in place to gauge productivity.

The reorganization game plan they all developed resulted in:

- Turning the existing distribution center in Atlanta into a centralized fulfillment facility.
- Reducing order cycle time to five business days.
- Eliminating the need for additional storage locations throughout the organization and reducing obsolescence.
- Centralized fulfillment operations, allowing the center to negotiate higher carrier discount rates.

Part of the ACS transformation involved arranging storage and warehouse space more efficiently, often by going up. Shelves reach 20 feet high in many cases.

At the field offices, the online ordering system requires employees to provide a delivery date. The traffic module then schedules the carrier and factors in shipment time to meet that date.

Once the allocation plan is run, the WMS software requires all packages to be cubed and weighed, which is handled by the CubiScan system from Quantronix.

All orders are shipped in one of five cases sizes, based on the cube and weight information. The WMS prints out a label that gives the picker the appropriate case size for the order.

Ten months. That's what it took to install the equipment; train people in the field units; clean out, consolidate, and accurately count inventory, and move about 500 SKUs of material from field offices to the distribution center.

Payback was in two months, and the revamped distribution center saved the ACS $8 million in the first year.

Source: Leslie Langnau, *Materials Handling Management* (June 2001): 55–57.

accuracy. The best advice is to seek out models that are as simple and direct as possible but that do not assume away too much reality.

The remainder of this chapter contains an in-depth treatment of several approaches and techniques that are in common use today by inventory managers. Included are the fixed order quantity approach under conditions of certain and uncertain demand and lead time length (also known as the economic order quantity, or EOQ, approach) and the fixed order interval approach. These discussions should complement the coverage of techniques such as JIT, MRP, and MRPII, which relate to the physical supply side of logistics, and DRP, which is oriented more toward the outbound movement of finished product and related information. Following a discussion of how inventory will be affected as the number of distribution centers changes, the chapter discusses replenishment logistics. Although these approaches attempt to synchronize flows of product and information to be consistent with end-user or consumer needs, their implementation can be very comprehensive in terms of the overall supply chain.

Fixed Order Quantity Approach (Condition of Certainty)

As its name implies, the *fixed order quantity* model involves ordering a fixed amount of product each time reordering takes place. The exact amount of product to be ordered depends upon the product's cost and demand characteristics and upon relevant inventory carrying and reordering costs.

EOQ approach

Firms using this approach generally need to develop a minimum stock level to determine when to reorder the fixed quantity. This is usually called the *reorder point.* When the number of items in inventory reaches the predetermined level, the fixed order quantity (also called the economic order quantity, or EOQ) is "automatically" ordered. In a sense, the predetermined ordering level triggers the next order.

triggering orders for inventory

Sometimes firms call the fixed order quantity approach a *two-bin* system. When the first bin is empty, the firm places an order. The stock amount in the second bin represents the inventory quantity the firm needs until the new order arrives. Both notions (trigger and bin) imply that a firm will reorder or produce stock when the amount on hand decreases to some predetermined level. Again, the amount ordered depends upon the product's cost and demand, along with inventory carrying and reordering costs. The stock ordering level (number of units) depends upon the time it takes to get the new order and upon the product demand or sales rate during that time—such as how many units the firm sells per day or per week. For example, if a new order takes two weeks to arrive and a firm sells ten units per day, the reorder point will be 140 units (14 days × 10 units/day).

reorder point

Inventory Cycles

Figure 7–2 shows the fixed order quantity model. The figure shows three inventory cycles, or periods. Each cycle begins with 4,000 units, the fixed quantity ordered or produced, and reordering occurs when inventory on hand falls to a level of 1,500 units. Assuming that the demand or usage rate and the lead time length are

FIGURE 7–2 Fixed Order Quantity Model under the Condition of Certainty

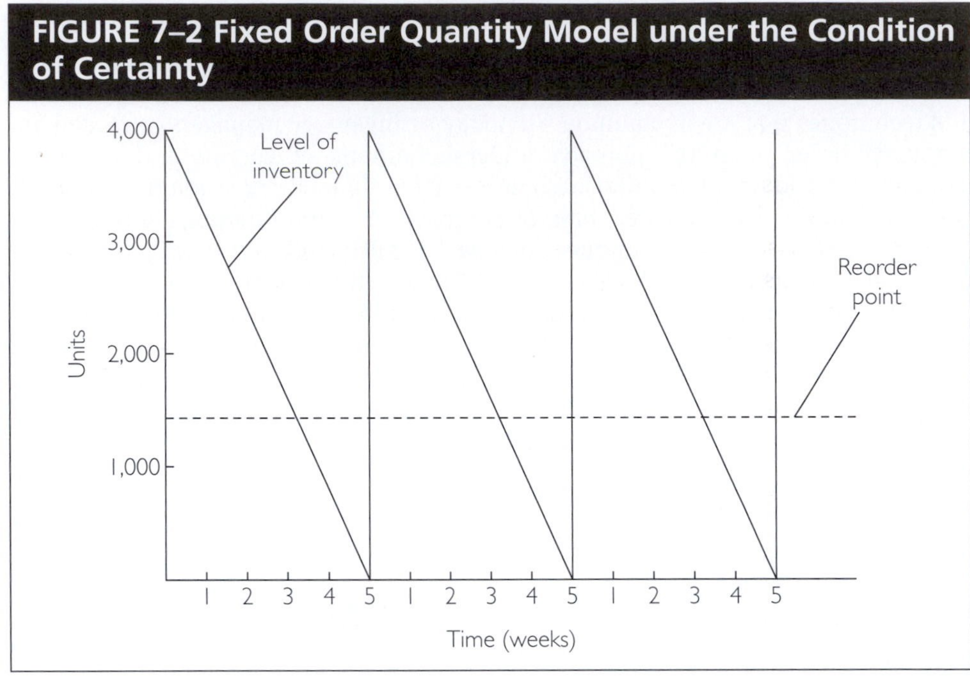

constant and known in advance, the length of each cycle will be a constant five weeks. This is an example of the application of the fixed order quantity model in the case of certainty.

As we suggested earlier, establishing a reorder point provides a trigger or signal for reordering the fixed quantity. For example, most people have reorder points for personal purchases such as gasoline. On a trip, one may customarily stop to fill the tank when the gauge indicates one-eighth of a tank. Or, similarly, one may wait until a dashboard light indicates that the gas supply has reached some minimum point.

sensitivity to demand changes

Business inventory situations base the reorder point upon lead time or replenishment time, the time it takes to replenish an order or manufacture the fixed quantity. The constant monitoring necessary to determine when inventory has reached the reorder point makes the fixed order quantity model somewhat expensive, although a computer can monitor inventory at little marginal cost per transaction. Generally, this approach can be sensitive to demand without carrying too much excess inventory.

Simple EOQ Model

assumptions

The following are the principal assumptions of the simple EOQ model:

1. A continuous, constant, and known demand rate
2. A constant and known replenishment or lead time
3. The satisfaction of all demand
4. A constant price or cost that is independent of the order quantity or time (e.g., purchase price or transport cost)

5. No inventory in transit
6. One item of inventory or no interaction between items
7. Infinite planning horizon
8. No limit on capital availability

certainty

The first three assumptions are closely related and basically mean that conditions of certainty exist. Demand in each relevant time period (daily, weekly, or monthly) is known, and usage rate is linear over time. The firm uses or depletes inventory on hand at a constant rate and knows the time needed to replenish stock. In other words, lead time between order placement and order receipt is constant. This means that neither demand nor the time it takes to produce or receive replenishment stock will vary. As a result, the firm has no need to be concerned about stockouts and, consequently, stockout costs.

Some individuals feel that the assumptions of certainty make the basic model too simplistic—and, consequently, the output decisions too inaccurate. Although this charge is true in certain cases, several important reasons justify using the simple model. First, in some businesses, demand variation is so small that making the model more complex is too costly for the extra accuracy achieved. Second, firms just beginning to develop inventory models frequently find the simple EOQ model convenient and necessary because of the limited data available to them. Some firms get caught up in sophisticated models with simple data, and the end results are probably no more accurate than they would have been if the firm had used the simple model. Third, simple EOQ model results are somewhat insensitive to changes in input variables. That is, such variables as demand, inventory carrying cost, and ordering cost can change without significantly affecting the calculated value of the economic order quantity.

The fourth assumption, regarding constant costs, essentially means that the firm offers no volume price discounts. It also means that the prices are relatively stable.

no in-transit inventory

The assumption that there is no inventory in transit means that the firm purchases goods on a delivered-price basis (purchase price includes delivery) and sells them FOB shipping point (the buyer pays transportation charges). On the inbound side, this means that title to the goods does not pass until the buyer receives them. On the outbound side, title passes when the product leaves the plant or shipping point. Under these assumptions, the company has no responsibility for goods in transit; that is, the company pays no in-transit inventory carrying costs.

Capital availability, the eighth assumption, may be important, but this decision is sometimes made outside the logistics area. If capital constraints do exist, they may result in an upper limit on inventory lot size.

inventory and order costs

Given the assumptions listed, the simple EOQ model considers only two basic types of cost: inventory carrying cost and order or setup cost. The simple model analyzes trade-offs between these two costs. If the model focused only on inventory carrying cost, which varies directly with increases in lot size, the order quantity would be as small as possible (see Figure 7–3). If the model considered only order cost or setup cost, large orders would decrease total order costs (see Figure 7–4). The lot size decision attempts to minimize total cost—that is, carrying cost plus setup or order cost—by reaching a compromise between these two costs (see Figure 7–5).

FIGURE 7–3 Inventory Carrying Cost

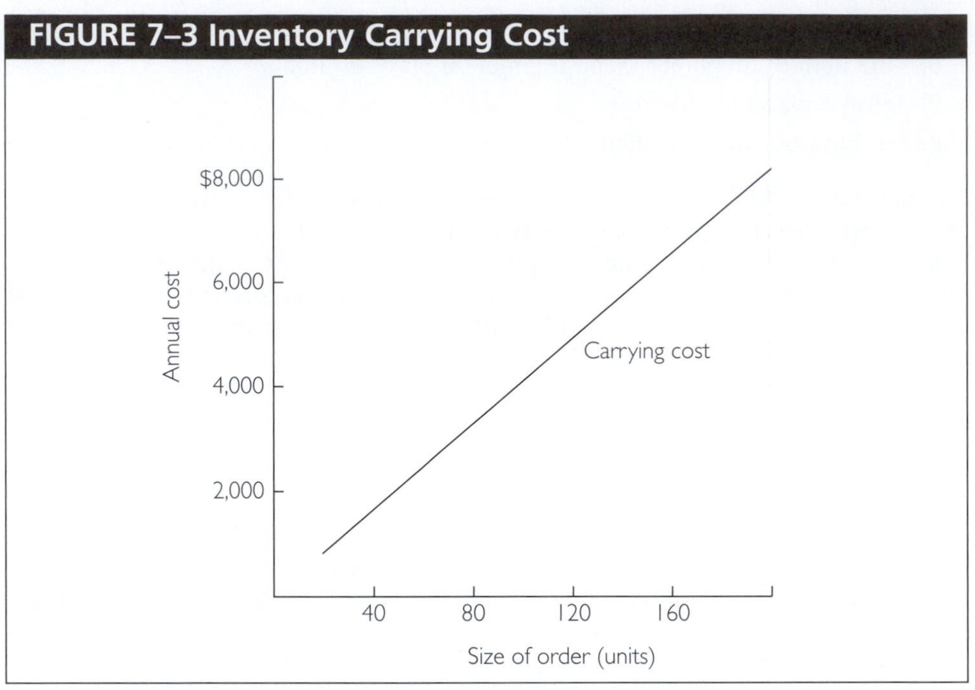

FIGURE 7–4 Order or Setup Cost

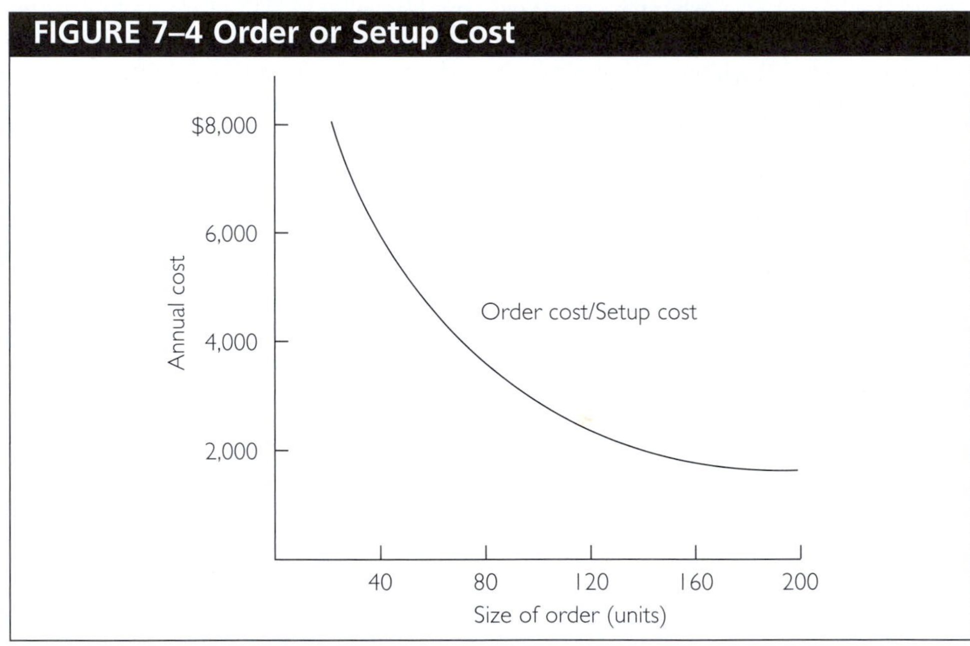

Mathematical Formulation. We can develop the EOQ model in standard mathematical form, using the following variables:

R = annual rate of demand or requirement for period (units)

Q = quantity ordered lot size (units)

A = cost of placing an order or setup cost ($ per order)

V = value or cost of one unit of inventory ($ per unit)

FIGURE 7–5 Inventory Costs

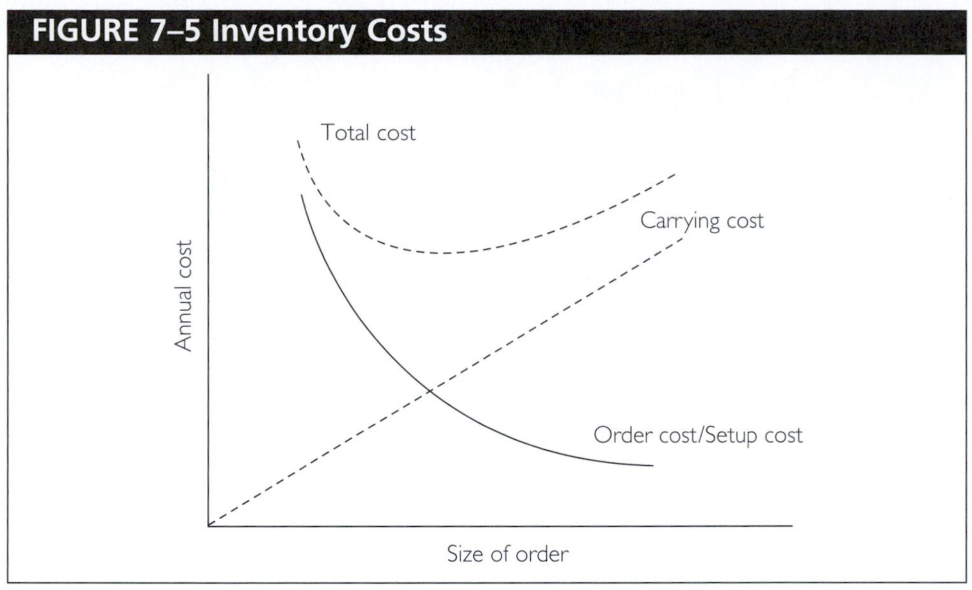

W = carrying cost per dollar value of inventory per year (% of product value)

$S = VW$ = storage cost per unit per year* ($ per unit per year)

t = time (days)

TAC = total annual cost ($ per year)

Given the previous assumptions, we can express the total annual cost in either of the following forms:

$$\text{TAC} = \frac{1}{2}QVW + A\frac{R}{Q}$$

or

$$\text{TAC} = \frac{1}{2}QS + A\frac{R}{Q}$$

inventory carrying cost

The first term on the right-hand side of the equation refers to inventory carrying cost; it states that these costs equal the average number of units in the economic order quantity during the order cycle (1/2 Q) multiplied by the value per unit (V) multiplied by the carrying cost (W). In Figure 7–6, called the sawtooth model, the equation's logic becomes more apparent. The vertical line labeled Q represents the amount ordered or produced at a given time and the amount on hand at the beginning of each order cycle. During the order cycle (t), a firm depletes the amount of product on hand at the rate represented by the slanted line. Demand is known and constant, and the firm uses inventory at a uniform rate over the period. The average number of units on hand during this period affects the inventory carrying cost. The average number on hand, given the constant demand rate, is simply one-half of

*When we substitute VW for S, storage cost becomes a function of price paid per unit bought—namely, volume.

FIGURE 7–6 Sawtooth Model

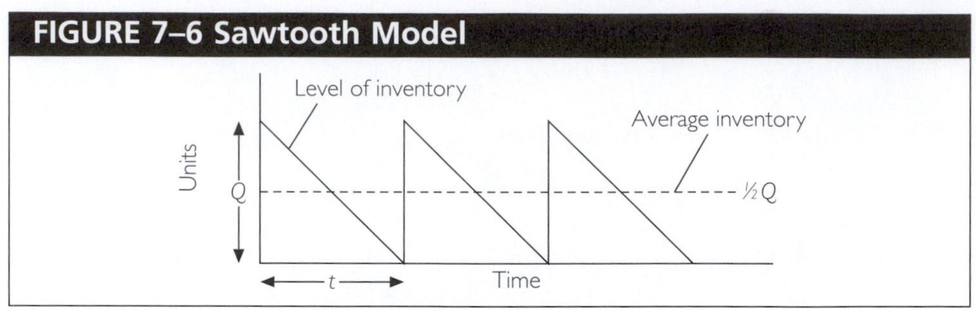

the initial amount (Q). The broken horizontal line in Figure 7–6 represents average inventory. The logic is very simple. Assuming that Q is 100 and that daily demand is 10 units, 100 units would last 10 days (t). At the period's halfway point, the end of the fifth day, 50 units would still be left, which is one-half of Q ($\frac{1}{2} \times 100$).

order size and inventory

Determining the average number of units is not enough, as the equation indicates. Knowing the value per unit, which depends upon the product, is still necessary. Knowing the percentage carrying cost, which depends upon the product and the firm's warehousing operations, is also necessary. The larger the Q amount, the higher the inventory carrying cost will be. We described this general relationship earlier: increasing carrying cost accompanies larger inventory lots or orders. As the present context shows, larger inventory order quantities will last longer, therefore increasing carrying costs. Given constant demand, average inventory will increase as the economic order quantity increases [see Figures 7–7 (a) and 7–7 (b)].

order cost

The second term in the equation refers to order cost or setup cost. Again, we assume order cost to be constant per order or setup. Therefore, if Q increases, the number of orders per year will be smaller, since annual demand is constant. It follows, then, that larger order quantities will lower annual order costs.

Although we have explained the general nature of carrying cost and order cost, we must still determine Q, the economic order quantity. As we indicated previously, this involves trading off inventory carrying cost and order cost. We can determine Q by differentiating the TAC function with respect to Q, as follows:

$$\text{TAC} = \frac{1}{2}QVW + A\frac{R}{Q}$$

$$\frac{d(\text{TAC})}{dQ} = \frac{VW}{2} - \frac{AR}{Q^2}$$

Setting $d(\text{TAC})/dQ$ equal to zero and solving for Q gives

$$Q^2 = \frac{2RA}{VW}$$

or

$$Q = \sqrt{\frac{2RA}{VW}}$$

or

$$Q = \sqrt{\frac{2RA}{S}}$$

FIGURE 7–7 Sawtooth Models

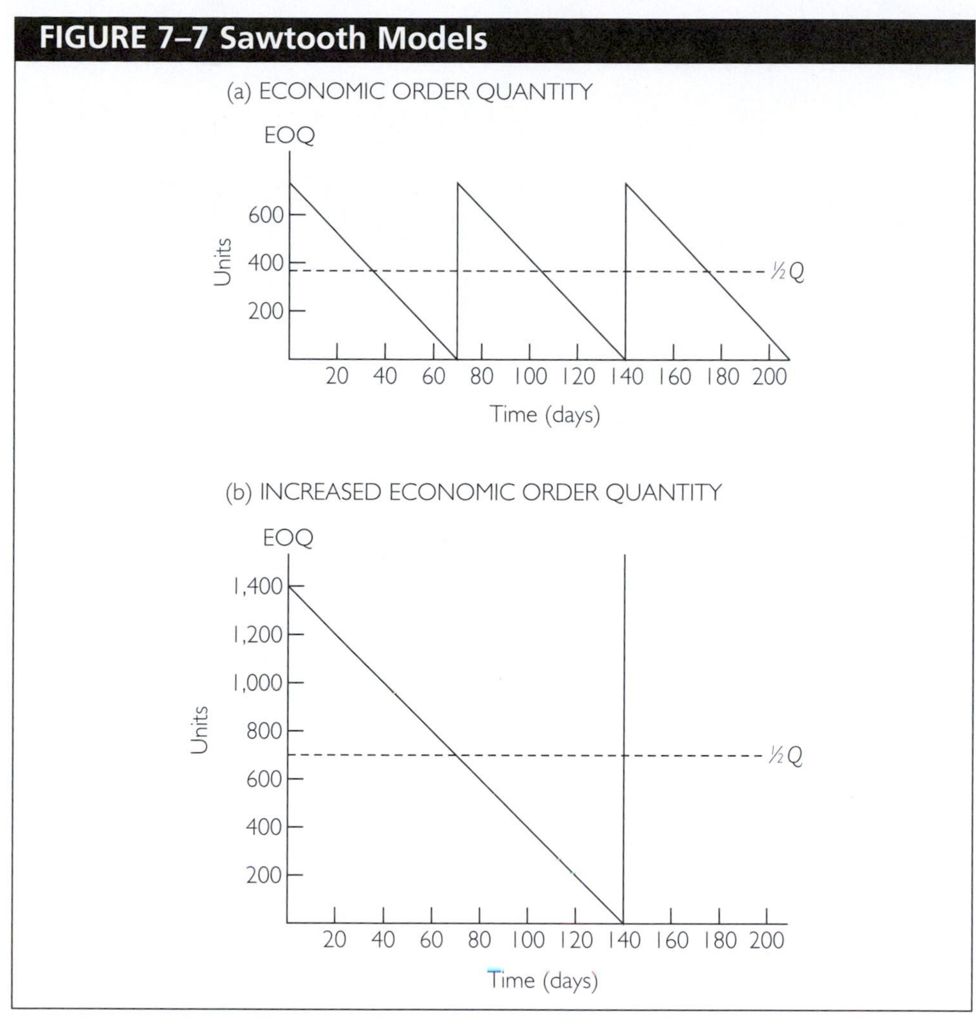

The following assumptions illustrate how the formula works in actual practice: **example**

V = \$100 per unit

W = 25%

S = \$25 per unit per year

A = \$200 per order

R = 3,600 units

To solve for Q, the example proceeds as follows:

$$Q = \sqrt{\frac{2RA}{VW}} = \sqrt{\frac{(2)(3,600)(\$200)}{(\$100)(25\%)}} = 240 \text{ units}$$

$$Q = \sqrt{\frac{2RA}{S}} = \sqrt{\frac{(2)(3,600)(200)}{\$25}} = 240 \text{ units}$$

TABLE 7–1 Total Costs for Various EOQ Amounts

Q	Order Costs *AR/Q*	Carrying Cost ½ *QVW*	Total Cost
100	$7,200	$1,250	$8,450
140	5,143	1,750	6,893
180	4,000	2,250	6,250
220	3,273	2,750	6,023
240	3,000	3,000	6,000
260	2,769	3,250	6,019
300	2,400	3,750	6,150
340	2,118	4,250	6,368
400	1,800	5,000	6,800
500	1,440	6,250	7,690

FIGURE 7–8 Graphical Representation of the EOQ Example

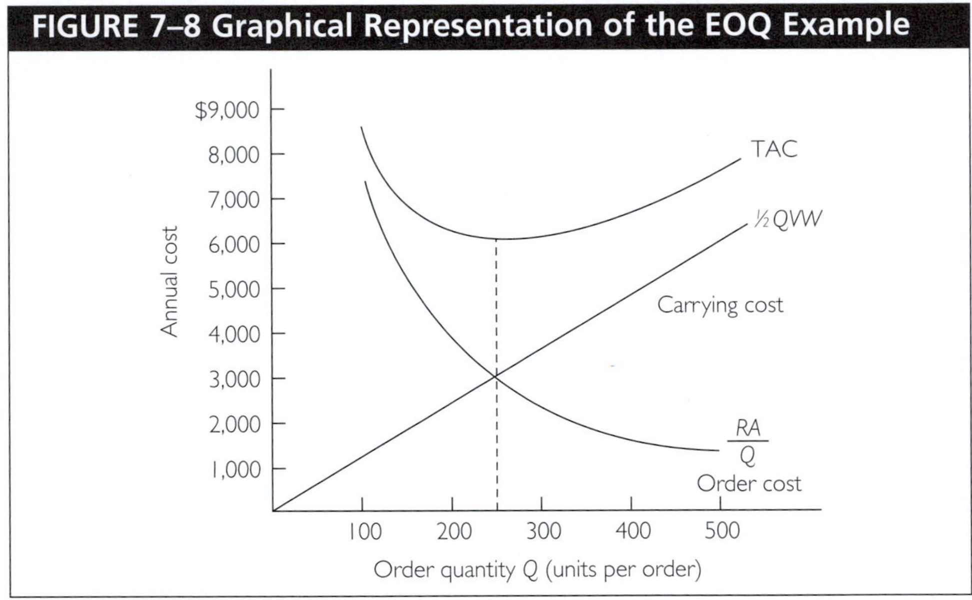

Analysis. Table 7–1 and Figure 7–8 show the preceding solution's trade-offs and logic. The illustrations show how inventory carrying cost and total cost vary as *Q* ranges from a low of 100 units to a high of 500 units.

quantity/cost relationships

As the table shows, the lower values for *Q* incur high order costs, as expected, but carrying costs are low. As *Q* increases to 240, ordering costs decrease because the number of orders per year decreases, but carrying costs increase because of the higher average inventories. Beyond 240 units, the incremental increase in carrying costs exceeds the incremental decrease in order costs, so total costs increase.

By defining the optimum *Q* in total cost terms, the information in Table 7–1 shows that a *Q* of 240 is optimal. Figure 7–8 also demonstrates this. Note, however, that the TAC curve between EOQ values of 180–200 and 300–320 is quite shallow. This means that the inventory manager can alter the EOQ considerably without significantly affecting TAC.

Reorder Point

A previous discussion indicated that knowing when to order was as necessary as knowing how much to order. The *when*, generally called a reorder point, depends on inventory level—that is, some number of units. Under the assumptions of certainty, a firm needs only enough inventory to last during the replenishment time or lead time. Therefore, given a known lead time, multiplying lead time length by daily demand determines the reorder point.

Replenishment time consists of several components: order transmittal, order processing, order preparation, and delivery. The time involved depends on factors such as the means of transmitting the order from buyer to seller, whether the vendor must produce the item being ordered or can fill it from available stock, and the transportation mode used. We discuss the many variables affecting lead time later in this chapter.

example calculation

Using the previous example, assume that order transmittal takes one day; order processing and preparation, two days; and delivery, five days. This results in a total of eight days for replenishment time or lead time. Given that demand is ten units per day (3,600 ÷ 360), the reorder point will be 80 units (8 days × 10 units per day).

A Note Concerning the Min-Max Approach

One widely used adaptation of the fixed order quantity approach is the *min-max* inventory management approach. With the traditional approach, inventory will implicitly deplete in small increments, allowing a firm to initiate a replenishment order exactly when inventory reaches the reorder point.

demand patterns

The min-max approach applies when demand may be larger and when the amount on hand may fall below the reorder point before the firm initiates a replenishment order. In this case, the min-max approach increments the amount ordered by the difference between the reorder point and the amount on hand. In effect, this technique identifies the *minimum* amount that a firm should order so that inventory on hand will reach a predetermined *maximum* level when the firm receives the order. While the min-max system is very similar to the EOQ approach, individual order amounts will tend to vary.

The min-max approach is most appropriate when demand is *lumpy,* or *erratic.* This type of demand is frequently, but not exclusively, limited to slow-moving items. Also, the lumpy demand characteristic may actually occur in up to 50 percent of the SKUs for many firms.[5]

Summary and Evaluation of the Fixed Order Quantity Approach

Traditionally, the EOQ-based approach has been a cornerstone of effective inventory management. While not always the fastest way to respond to customer demand, the fixed order quantity approach has been a useful and widely used technique.

recent emphasis on push systems

Recently, however, many companies have become more sophisticated in their use of EOQ-based approaches, adapting them to include a push as well as a pull orientation. As a result, many EOQ-based systems effectively blend both push and pull concepts. As indicated earlier, push, or proactive, inventory management approaches are far more prevalent in firms having greater logistics sophistication.

shortcomings

One principal shortcoming of the EOQ-based approach is that it suits inventory decision making at a single facility more than it suits decision making at multiple locations in a logistics network. Also, the EOQ approach sometimes encounters problems when parallel points in the same logistics system experience peak demands simultaneously. This happens, for example, when many consumers simultaneously stock up on groceries before a major snowstorm. The EOQ system alone, reacting only to demand levels as they occur, would respond too slowly to replenish needed inventory.

relaxing assumptions

We stated at the outset that the simple EOQ approach, though somewhat unrealistic because of the number of assumptions it requires, is still useful because it illustrates the logic of inventory models in general. Actually, firms can adjust the simple model to handle more complex situations. More than 200 variations now assist inventory-related decision making in various areas. Appendix 7A covers applications of the EOQ approach in four special instances: (1) when a firm must consider the cost of inventory in transit, (2) when volume transportation rates are available, (3) when a firm uses private carriage, and (4) when a firm utilizes in-excess rates.

independent demand

Typically, firms associate EOQ-based approaches with independent, rather than dependent, demand. The overall approach explicitly involves carrying calculated average inventory amounts; the trade-offs among inventory, order/setup, and expected stockout costs justify carrying these amounts. As we refine our ability to design flexible and responsive logistics systems and to significantly reduce marginal ordering and setup expenses, the value of this trade-off–based approach will diminish. Therefore, we will focus attention away from approaches such as EOQ and toward other techniques for managing inventory.

Fixed Order Quantity Approach (Condition of Uncertainty)

certainty

Under the assumptions used until now, the reorder point was based on the amount of stock remaining in the warehouse. We assumed that the usage or sales rate was uniform and constant. After selling the last unit of a particular EOQ amount, a firm received another order or batch, thus incurring no stockout costs (lost sales). Although assuming such conditions of certainty may be useful, these conditions do not represent the usual operating situation for most organizations.

demand variations

Most companies would not find conditions of certainty normal, for a variety of reasons. First, customers usually purchase products somewhat sporadically. The usage rates of many items vary depending on weather, social needs, psychological needs, and a whole host of other factors. As a result, sales of most items vary day by day, week by week, or season by season.

transit time variations

In addition, several factors can affect lead time or replenishment time. For example, transit times can and do change, particularly for distances over 500 miles, despite carrier efforts. In fact, for a firm deciding what transportation mode or agency to use or choosing a particular transportation company within a particular mode, the reliability of expected carrier transit times is an important factor.

order processing time variations

Another factor that can cause variations in lead time or replenishment time is order processing and transmittal. Mailed orders can cause delays. Clerks can overlook a particular order or develop undesirable backlogs. Problems in this area have led firms to develop and enhance computer systems for order processing and associated activities.

For a firm producing or manufacturing an item to order, production schedules can vary for a number of reasons. Other factors that could have an effect on lead time or replenishment time have been discussed throughout the preceding chapters.

damage

In addition to varying demand rates and replenishment times, the logistics manager can experience problems with merchandise lost in transit or damaged, in which case the firm would have to reorder the goods. Even though the carrier would usually be liable, the damage could cause a short-run stockout situation, resulting in lost sales. Figure 7–9 shows the fixed order quantity model under conditions of uncertainty.

probability distributions

Sometimes the inventory situation may seem hopeless. Fortunately, this is not the case. Statisticians refer to these variables as *stochastic,* or random, variables. Experience with a particular company and associated study will enable the manager to develop probability distributions for these variables and to apply expected-value analysis to determine the optimum reorder point.

safety stock

The manager may choose several approaches to solving the problem. An essential factor in any approach is the level of safety stock, or buffer stock, a firm requires to cover variations. Logistics managers must analyze requirements very carefully so as not to maintain too much safety stock, because it incurs excess inventory cost. On the other hand, a company without enough safety stock will experience a stockout, with consequent loss of sales.

FIGURE 7–9 Fixed Order Quantity Model under Conditions of Uncertainty

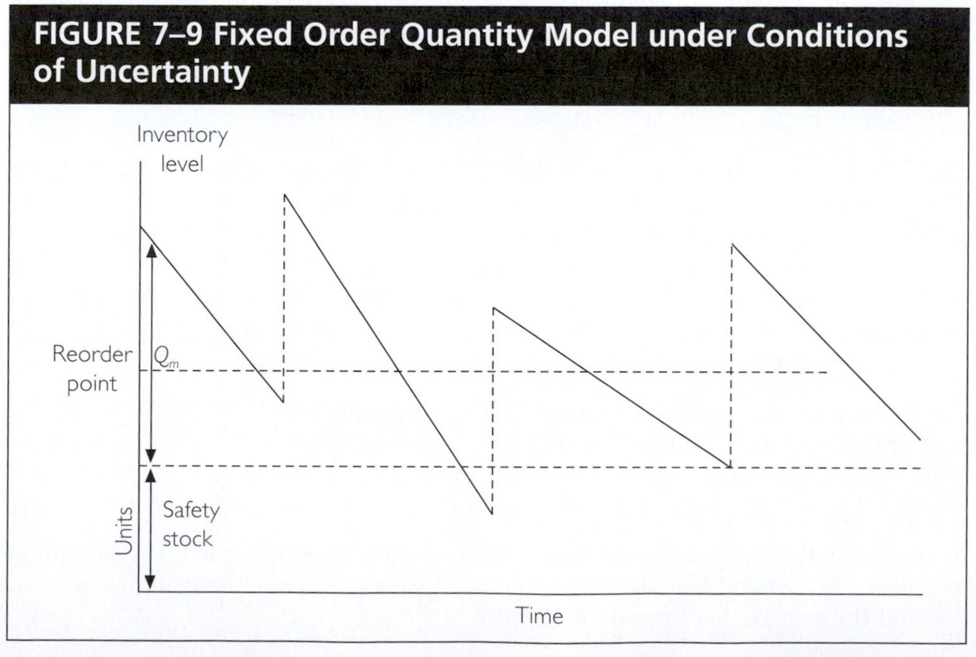

Reorder Point—A Special Note

reorder point with safety stock

As noted previously, the reorder point under the basic model is the inventory level sufficient to satisfy demand until the order arrives. Calculating the reorder point is straightforward, since demand or usage is constant, as is lead time. Therefore, a firm can multiply daily demand or usage by lead time in days and place an order for the determined quantity when inventory reaches the reorder point. Under uncertainty, the firm must reformulate the reorder point to allow for safety stock. In effect, the reorder point becomes the average daily demand during lead time plus the safety stock, as Figure 7–9 depicts. The following discussion clarifies this recalculation.

Uncertainty of Demand

Dealing first with only one factor that may cause uncertainty is easiest. The best and most common factor to examine is the sales rate or usage rate. As we focus on this variable, the following assumptions about the EOQ model still apply:

1. A constant and known replenishment or lead time
2. A constant price or cost that is independent of order quantity or time (e.g., purchase price or transport cost)
3. No inventory in transit
4. One item of inventory or no interaction between items
5. Infinite planning horizon
6. No limit on capital availability

balancing cost

In discussing uncertainty in sales, logistics managers emphasize balancing the cost of carrying safety stock against the cost of a stockout (lost sales).

In a fixed quantity model with an established reorder level, introducing uncertainty into the analysis initially affects the inventory level needed to cover sales during lead time. Recall that in the previous example, conditions of certainty resulted in an EOQ amount of 240 units and a reorder point of 100 units. In other words, the inventory period began with 240 units on hand, and reordering occurred when inventory reached a level of 100 units.

The fact that sales may vary—and that the time elapsing between a level of 240 units and 100 units may also vary—is not critical to the inventory problem when conditions of uncertainty exist. Determining whether 100 units is the best amount to have on hand at the start of the lead time or replenishment cycle *is* critical. Thus, raising the reorder level accounts for safety stock. However, raising it too high will leave too much stock on hand when the next order arrives. Setting it too low will cause a stockout.

example

Using the previous problem, assume that the hypothetical firm's demand during lead time ranges from 100 units to 160 units, with an average of 130 units. Furthermore, assume that demand has a discrete distribution varying in ten-unit blocks and that the firm has established probabilities for these demand levels (see Table 7–2).

In effect, the firm must consider seven different reorder points, each corresponding to a possible demand level listed in Table 7–2. Using these reorder points, we can develop the matrix that appears in Table 7–3.

TABLE 7–2 Probability Distribution of Demand during Lead Time

Demand	Probability
100 units	0.01
110	0.06
120	0.24
130	0.38
140	0.24
150	0.06
160	0.01

TABLE 7–3 Possible Units of Inventory Short or in Excess during Lead Time with Various Reorder Points

Actual Demand	Reorder Points: 100	110	120	130	140	150	160
100	0	10	20	30	40	50	60
110	−10	0	10	20	30	40	50
120	−20	−10	0	10	20	30	40
130	−30	−20	−10	0	10	20	30
140	−40	−30	−20	−10	0	10	20
150	−50	−40	−30	−20	−10	0	10
160	−60	−50	−40	−30	−20	−10	0

While Table 7–3 shows many of the possible situations confronting the hypothetical firm, it does not use information from the probability distribution of demand. Using the probability distribution of demand would permit the firm with seven possible reorder points to determine the expected units "short" or "in excess" at each point during lead time.

Assume that the firm experiences a stockout cost (k) of $10 per unit whenever a customer demands a unit that is not in stock. The profit lost on the immediate sale and future sales is an opportunity cost.

We calculate inventory carrying cost associated with safety stock in the same way as we calculated carrying cost for the simple EOQ model. We still assume the value per unit of inventory to be $100, and the percentage annual inventory carrying cost is 25 percent. Remember that the percentage figure is for the annual cost of inventory in the warehouse. Therefore, the $25 we derive by multiplying 25 percent by $100 is the annual cost per unit of inventory in the warehouse. The $25 contrasts

TABLE 7–4 Expected Number of Units Short or in Excess

Actual Demand	Probabilities	Reorder Points: 100	110	120	130	140	150	160	
100	0.01	**0.0**	0.1	0.2	0.3	0.4	0.5	0.6	
110	0.06	–0.6	**0.0**	0.6	1.2	1.8	2.4	3.0	
120	0.24	–4.8	–2.4	**0.0**	2.4	4.8	7.2	9.6	
130	0.38	–11.4	–7.6	–3.8	**0.0**	3.8	7.6	11.4	
140	0.24	–9.6	–7.2	–4.8	–2.4	**0.0**	2.4	4.8	
150	0.06	–3.0	–2.4	–1.8	–1.2	–0.6	**0.0**	0.6	
160	0.01	–0.6	–0.5	–0.4	–0.3	–0.2	–0.1	**0.0**	
Calculation of Lowest-Cost Reorder Point									
1. Expected excess per cycle (of values above diagonal line)		0.0	0.1	0.8	3.9	10.8	20.1	30.0	(e)
2. Expected carrying cost per year		0	\$ 2.50	\$ 20.00	\$ 97.50	\$270	\$502.50	\$750	(VW)
3. Expected shorts per cycle (of values below diagonal line)		30.0	20.1	10.8	3.9	0.8	0.1	0.0	(g)
4. Expected stockout cost per cycle		\$ 300	\$ 201	\$ 108	\$ 39	\$ 8	\$ 1	\$ 0	(gk) = G
5. Expected stockout costsper year		\$4,500	\$3,015	\$1,620	\$585	\$120	\$ 15	\$ 0	$\left(G\frac{R}{Q}\right)$
6. Expected total cost per year (2 + 5)		\$4,500	\$3,017.50	\$1,640	\$682.50	\$390	\$517.50	\$750	

with the \$10 stockout cost, which is a unit cost per cycle or order period. Therefore, as Table 7–4 shows, multiplying \$10 by the number of cycles or orders per year puts this cost on an annual basis.

Table 7–4 develops expected units short or in excess by multiplying the number of units short or in excess by the probabilities associated with each demand level. We can add the numbers below (shorts) and above (excesses) the horizontal line, as the lower portion of Table 7–4 shows, to find the number of units the firm expects to be short or in excess at each of the seven possible reorder points. The variables for this calculation are as follows:

e = expected excess in units

g = expected shorts in units

k = stockout cost in dollars per unit stocked out

$G = gk$ = expected stockout cost per cycle

$G\frac{R}{Q}$ = expected stockout cost per year

eVW = expected carrying cost per year for excess inventory

After performing the calculations indicated in Table 7–4, we may determine the total cost for each of the seven reorder levels. In this instance, the lowest total cost corresponds to the reorder point of 140 units. Although this number does not guarantee an excess or shortage in any particular period, overall it gives the lowest expected total cost per year: \$390.

Note that the number of orders per year used in Step 5 of Table 7–4 came from the preceding problem with conditions of certainty. That number was the only information available at that point. Now we can expand the total cost model to include the safety stock cost and stockout cost. The expanded formula would appear as follows:

$$\text{TAC} = \frac{1}{2}QVW + A\frac{R}{Q} + (eVW) + \left(G\frac{R}{Q}\right)$$

Solving for the lowest cost gives

$$\frac{d(\text{TAC})}{dQ} = \left[\frac{1}{2}VW\right] - \left[\frac{R(A+G)}{Q^2}\right]$$

Setting this equal to zero and solving for Q gives

$$Q = \sqrt{\frac{2R(A+G)}{VW}}$$

Using the expanded model and the computed reorder point of 140 units, we can determine a new value for Q as follows:

$$Q = \sqrt{\frac{2 \cdot 3{,}600 \cdot (200 + 8)}{100 \cdot 25\%}}$$

$$= 242 \text{ (approximately)}$$

Note that Q is now 242 units with conditions of uncertainty. Technically, this would change the expected stockout cost for the various reorder points in Table 7–4. However, the change is small enough to ignore in this instance. In other cases, recalculations may be necessary. The optimum solution to the problem with conditions of uncertainty is a fixed order quantity (EOQ) of 242 units, and the firm will reorder this amount when inventory reaches a level of 140 units (the calculated reorder point).

Finally, the situation requires a recalculation of total annual cost:

$$\text{TAC} = \frac{1}{2}QVW + A\frac{R}{Q} + eVW + G\frac{R}{Q}$$

$$= \left(\frac{1}{2} \cdot 242 \cdot \$100 \cdot 25\%\right) + \left(200 \cdot \frac{3{,}600}{242}\right) + (10.8 \cdot \$100 \cdot 25\%) + \left(8 \cdot \frac{3{,}600}{242}\right)$$

$$= \$3{,}025 + \$2{,}975 + \$270 + \$119$$

$$= \$6{,}389$$

The \$6,389 figure indicates what happens to total cost when we introduce conditions of uncertainty with respect to sales into the model. Introducing other factors, such as the lead time variable, would increase costs even more.

Uncertainty of Demand and Lead Time Length

This section considers the possibility that both demand and lead time may vary. It builds upon the preceding section in attempting to make this inventory approach more realistic. As expected, however, determining how much safety stock to carry will be noticeably more complex now than when only demand varied.

demand during lead time

As in the previous section, the critical issue is just how much product customers will demand during the lead time. If demand and lead time are constant and known in advance, calculating the reorder point (as we did in the section covering case of certainty) would be easy. Now that both demand and lead time may vary, the first step is to study the likely distribution of demand during the lead time. Specifically, we must accurately estimate the mean and standard deviation of demand during lead time.

normal distribution

Figure 7–10 illustrates three key properties of a normal distribution. The normal distribution is symmetrical, and its mean (average) equals its mode (highest point). Approximately 68.26 percent of the area under the normal curve lies within one standard deviation (1σ) from the mean, 95.44 percent within two standard deviations (2σ), and 99.73 percent within three standard deviations (3σ). Figure 7–10

FIGURE 7–10 Normal Distribution

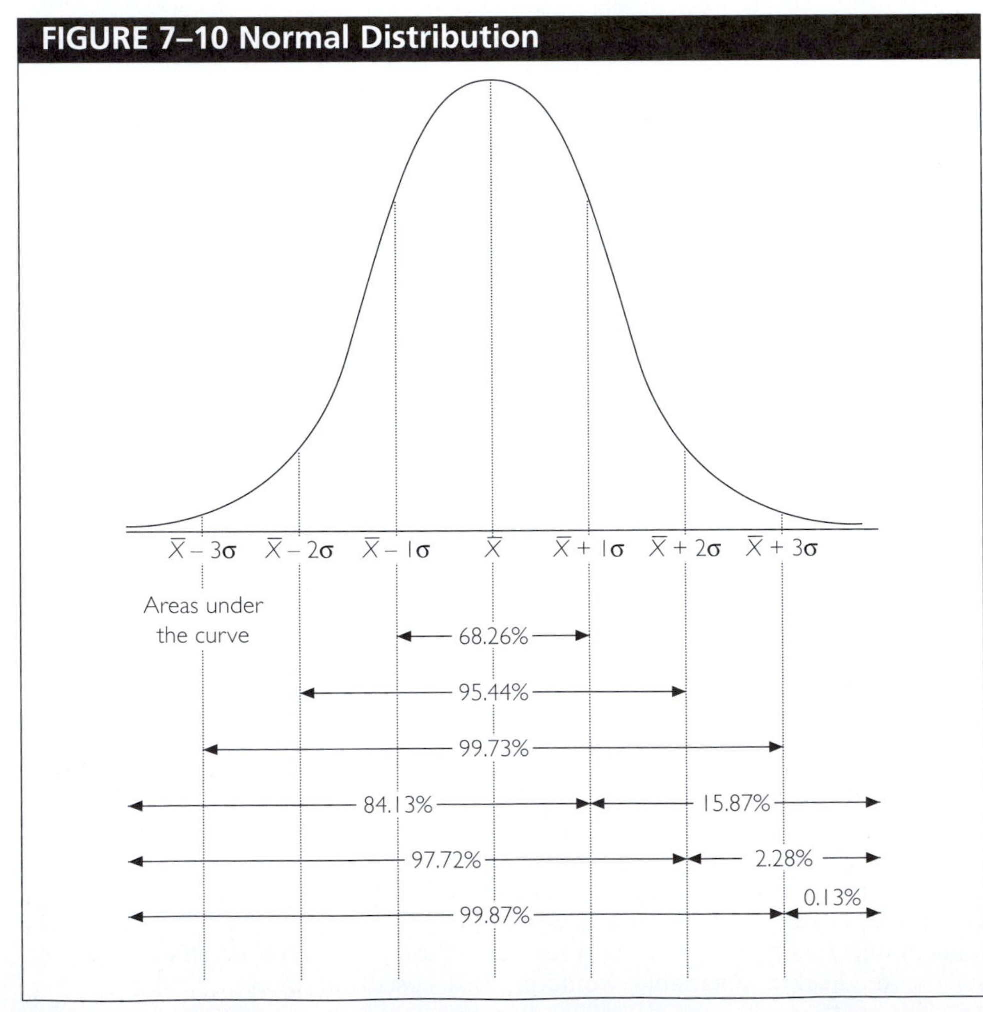

also shows the areas under the curve that lie to the left and right of one, two, and three standard deviations from the mean.

After calculating values for the mean and standard deviation of demand during lead time, we can describe the stockout probability for each particular reorder point. For example, imagine that Figure 7–10 represents demand distribution during lead time. Setting the reorder point equal to $\bar{X} + 1\sigma$ will result in an 84.13 percent probability that lead time demand will not exceed the inventory amount available. Increasing the reorder point to $\bar{X} + 2\sigma$ raises the probability of not incurring a stockout to 97.72 percent; reordering at $\bar{X} + 3\sigma$ raises this probability to 99.87 percent. Note that in the case of uncertainty, increasing the reorder point has the same effect as increasing the safety stock commitment. A firm must ultimately find some means to justify carrying this additional inventory.

calculations

We may calculate the mean and standard deviations for lead time demand using the following formula.[6]

$$\bar{X} = \bar{R}(\bar{X}_{LT})$$

and

$$\sigma = \sqrt{\bar{X}_{LT}(\sigma_R)^2 + \bar{R}^2(\sigma_{LT})^2}$$

where

$\bar{X}$ = mean (average) demand during lead time

σ = standard deviation of demand during lead time

$\bar{X}_{LT}$ = mean (average) lead time length

σ_{LT} = standard deviation of lead time length

$\bar{R}$ = mean (average) daily demand

σ_R = standard deviation of daily demand

example

For example, if the mean and standard deviations of daily demand are twenty and four units, respectively, and if the mean and standard deviations of lead time length are eight and two days, respectively, we calculate the mean and standard deviations of demand during lead time as follows:

$$\bar{X} = \bar{R}(\bar{X}_{LT}) = 20(8) = 160$$

$$\sigma = \sqrt{\bar{X}_{LT}(\sigma_R)^2 + \bar{R}^2(\sigma_{LT})^2} = \sqrt{8(4)^2 + 20^2(2)^2} = \sqrt{1{,}728} = 41.57, \text{ or } 42$$

Using the procedure suggested earlier, setting the reorder point at $\bar{X} + 1\sigma$, or 202 units, reveals an 84.13 percent probability that demand during the lead time will not exceed the inventory available. Stated differently, the probability of a stockout is only 100% – 84.13%, or 15.87%, when we set the reorder point at one standard deviation from the mean. Table 7–5 shows these figures and the ones computed for setting the reorder point at two and three standard deviations from the mean. A

TABLE 7–5 Reorder Point Alternatives and Stockout Possibilities

Reorder Point	Probability of No Stockout Occurring	Probability of a Stockout Situation
$\bar{X} + 1\sigma = 202$	84.13%	15.87%
$\bar{X} + 2\sigma = 244$	97.72%	2.28%
$\bar{X} + 3\sigma = 286$	99.87%	0.13%

firm should thoroughly compare the financial and customer service benefits of avoiding stockouts with the cost of carrying additional safety stock before choosing a reorder point.

FIXED ORDER INTERVAL APPROACH

The second form of the basic approach is the *fixed order interval* approach to inventory management, also called the *fixed period* or *fixed review period* approach. In essence, this technique involves ordering inventory at fixed or regular intervals; and generally the amount ordered depends on how much is in stock and available at the time of review. Firms customarily count inventory near the interval's end and base orders on the amount on hand at the time.

lower cost of monitoring inventory

In comparison with the basic EOQ approach, the fixed interval model does not require close surveillance of inventory levels; thus, monitoring is less expensive. A firm can order low-valued items infrequently and in large quantities, checking only infrequently to determine exactly how much is on hand at any particular time.

In other instances, delivery schedules or salespeople's visits necessitate this approach. This happens frequently in retail food stores, where deliveries may be daily for some items, weekly or biweekly for others, and monthly for still others. The store can determine a desired inventory level in advance and order enough each time to bring the number of units up to that level.

If demand and lead time are constant and known in advance, then a firm using the fixed order interval approach will periodically reorder exactly the same amount of inventory. If either demand or lead time varies, however, the amount ordered each time will vary, becoming a result of demand as well as lead time length. For example, as Figure 7–11 indicates, a company starting each period with 4,000 units and selling 2,500 units before its next order will have to reorder 2,500 units plus the units it anticipates selling during the lead time to bring inventory up to the desired beginning level of 4,000 units. Figure 7–11 shows an instance in which the amount ordered differs from one five-week period to the next.

Like the fixed order quantity approach to inventory management, the fixed order interval approach typically combines elements of both the pull and push philoso-

FIGURE 7–11 Fixed Order Internal Model (with Safety Stock)

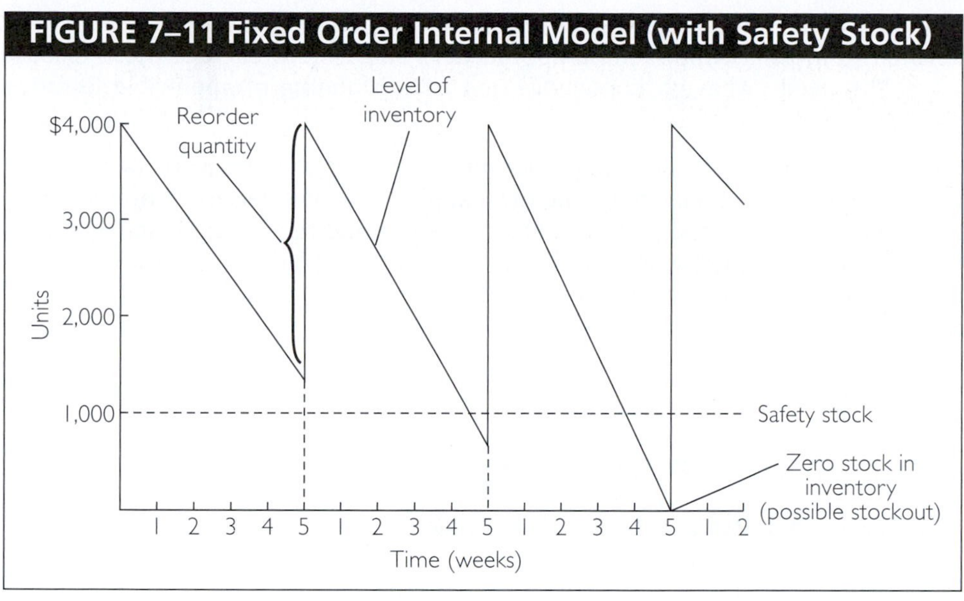

phies. This shows again how firms, in an effort to anticipate demand rather than simply reacting to it, are developing systems that incorporate the push philosophy.

Summary and Evaluation of EOQ Approaches to Inventory Management

relationship to ABC analysis

Some authors have argued that there are really four basic forms of the EOQ inventory model: fixed quantity/fixed interval, fixed quantity/irregular interval, irregular quantity/fixed interval, and irregular quantity/irregular interval. In a firm knowing demand and lead time length with certainty, either the basic EOQ or the fixed order interval approach will be the best choice (and would produce the same answer). If either demand or lead time varies, however, approach selection must consider the potential consequences of a stockout. In instances involving *A* items, a fixed quantity/irregular interval approach may be the best. The irregular quantity/fixed interval approach might be the best when *C* items are involved. Only under very restrictive circumstances could a firm justify using the irregular quantity/irregular interval approach to inventory management.

importance of trade-offs

The fixed order quantity (EOQ) and fixed order interval approaches have proven to be effective inventory management tools when demand and lead time are relatively stable, as well as when significant variability and uncertainty exist. Most importantly, studying these approaches requires us to gain familiarity with the inherent logistics trade-offs critical to inventory policy decision making.

new concepts

Firms in today's business environment that are expanding beyond the basic order quantity and order interval approaches have had considerable success with newer concepts such JIT, MRP, MRPII, and DRP, which are discussed in this chapter. Also, there is currently significant interest in the application of a number of contemporary approaches to replenishment logistics, including quick response and efficient consumer response. The remainder of this chapter is devoted to a discussion of these approaches. Throughout each of these discussions, the need to have a knowledge and understanding of applicable logistics trade-offs will be reinforced.

number of DCs

This issue of inventory at multiple locations in a logistics network raises some interesting questions concerning the most appropriate number of distribution centers, their location, the SKUs to be carried at each, and their overall strategic positioning. There is a growing priority on understanding the economics of facility location and inventory positioning, as firms search for lower-cost yet service-sensitive logistics alternatives.

Additional Approaches to Inventory Management

The management of inventory levels in the supply chain has often been the underlying rationale or "rallying cry" for the focus upon supply chain management. The interest in reducing inventory levels along the supply chain is indicative of the importance of inventory as a cost of doing business. In many companies, inventory is the first or second largest asset.

Companies, therefore, can reduce their costs of doing business and improve their return on investment or assets (ROI/ROA) in many cases by decreasing inventory levels. It should be noted, however, that the investment in inventory can add value by reducing costs in other areas, such as manufacturing and transportation, or enhance sales through better customer service. Therefore, a balanced view is necessary when making inventory decisions, one that recognizes both the cost implications and potential benefits of maintaining inventory in the supply chain.

In this section, we will examine several approaches to inventory control that have special relevance to supply chain management: JIT (Just–In–Time), MRP (Materials Requirements into Planning), and DRP (Distribution Resource Planning).

The Just-in-Time Approach

Perhaps the most widely discussed approach to inventory management is the *just-in-time,* or JIT, approach. In today's business environment people often refer to a JIT manufacturing process, JIT inventories, or a JIT delivery system. The commonsense phrase "just in time" suggests that inventories should be available when a firm needs them—not any earlier, nor any later. This section emphasizes additional factors that characterize a true just-in-time system.

Definition and Components of JIT Systems. Generally, just-in-time systems are designed to manage lead times and to eliminate waste. Ideally, product should arrive exactly when a firm needs it, with no tolerance for late or early deliveries. Many JIT systems place a high priority on short, consistent lead times. This may help to explain the recent popularity of "quick-response" systems for inventory decision making.

Kanban

The just-in-time concept is an Americanized version of the Kanban system, which the Toyota Motor Company developed in Japan. *Kanban* refers to the informative signboards attached to carts delivering small amounts of needed components and other materials to locations within Japanese plants. Each signboard precisely details the necessary replenishment quantities and the exact time when the resupply activity must take place.

JIT operations

Production cards (*kan* cards) establish and authorize the amount of product to be manufactured or produced; requisition cards (*ban* cards) authorize the withdrawal of needed materials from the feeding or supply operation. Given a knowledge of daily output volumes, these activities can be accomplished manually, without the need for computer assistance. Finally, an *Andon* system, or light system, is used as a means to notify plant personnel of existing problems—a yellow light for a small problem, and a red light for a major problem. Either light can be seen by personnel throughout the plant. In this way, workers are advised of the possibility of an interruption to the production/manufacturing process, if the problem warrants such action.[7]

fundamental concepts

Experience indicates that effectively implementing the JIT concept can dramatically reduce parts and materials inventories, work in process, and finished product. In addition, the Kanban and just-in-time concepts rely heavily on the quality of the manufactured product and components, and also on a capable and precise logistics system to manage materials and physical distribution.

Four major elements underpin the just-in-time concept: zero inventories; short lead times; small, frequent replenishment quantities; and high quality, or zero defects. JIT, a modern approach to distribution, production, inventory, and scheduling management, is an operating concept based on delivering materials in exact amounts and at the precise times that companies need them—thus minimizing inventory costs. JIT can improve quality and minimize waste and can completely change the way a firm performs its logistics activities. JIT, as practiced by the Japanese, is more comprehensive than an inventory management system. It includes a comprehensive culture of quality, vendor partnerships, and employee teams.

similarity to two-bin system

The JIT system operates in a manner very similar to the two-bin or reorder point system. The system uses one bin to fill demand for a part; when that bin is empty (the stimulus to replenish the part), the second bin supplies the part. Toyota has been very successful with this system because of its master production schedule, which aims to schedule every product, every day, in a sequence that intermixes all parts. Producing these products in small quantities through short production runs also creates a relatively continuous demand for supplies and component parts. In theory, the ideal lot size or order size for a JIT-based system is one unit. Obviously, this encourages firms to reduce or eliminate setup costs and incremental ordering costs.

reducing lead times

By adhering to extremely small lot sizes and very short lead times, the just-in-time approach can dramatically reduce lead times. For example, when manufacturing forklift trucks, Toyota experienced a cumulative material lead time of one month, top to bottom, including final assembly, subassembly, fabrication, and purchasing. American manufacturers of forklift trucks cited lead times ranging from six to nine months.[8]

In actuality, most individuals who have never studied inventory control systems do have exposure to JIT in their place of residence. The public water company and the electric company provide their "product" on a demand-responsive, just-in-time

TABLE 7–6 EOQ versus JIT Attitudes and Behaviors

Factor	EOQ	JIT
1. Inventory	Asset	Liability
Safety stock	Yes	No
2. Production runs	Long	Short
Setup times	Amortize	Minimize
Lot sizes	EOQ	1 for 1
3. Queues	Eliminate	Necessary
4. Lead times	Tolerate	Shorter
5. Quality inspection	Important parts	100% process
6. Suppliers/customers	Adversaries	Partners
Supply sources	Multiple	Single
Employees	Instruct	Involve

Source: Adapted from William M. Boyst, III, "JIT American Style," *Proceedings of the 1988 Conference of the American Production & Inventory Control Society* (APICS, 1988): 468.

basis that does not require us to hold inventory. Meters monitor what we use, and we are charged accordingly. On the other hand, if we use bottled water or bottled gas, we may not be able to get them on a JIT basis.

JIT versus EOQ Approaches to Inventory Management. Table 7–6 highlights key ways in which the JIT philosophy differs from customary inventory management in U.S. firms. This section discusses the critical differences.

reduce inventories

First, JIT attempts to eliminate excess inventories for both the buyer and the seller. Some people feel that the JIT concept simply forces the seller to carry inventory that the buyer previously held. However, successful JIT applications will significantly reduce inventory for both parties.

shorter production runs

Second, JIT systems typically involve short production runs and require production and manufacturing activities to change frequently from one product to the next. Historically, U.S. manufacturing operations have benefited from the economies associated with lengthy production runs. Controlling and minimizing the cost of frequent changeovers is critical to a JIT program's success.

minimize waiting lines

Third, JIT minimizes waiting lines by delivering materials and components when and where firms need them. U.S. automobile manufacturers using the JIT approach, for example, typically have replenishment inventory delivered exactly where the manufacturer needs parts for finished product.

short, consistent lead times

Fourth, the JIT concept uses short, consistent lead times to satisfy the need for more inventory in a timely manner. This is why suppliers tend to concentrate their facilities within a radius near manufacturing facilities planning to use the JIT approach. For example, once the Saturn Corporation, a wholly owned subsidiary of General Motors Corporation, decided to locate its plant in central Tennessee, many potential suppliers planned to locate new facilities in the surrounding area.

Fifth, JIT-based systems rely on high-quality incoming products and components and on exceptionally high-quality inbound logistics operations. The fact that JIT systems synchronize manufacturing and assembly with timely, predictable receipt of inbound materials reinforces this need.

quality

Sixth, the JIT concept requires a strong, mutual commitment between the buyer and seller, one that emphasizes quality and seeks win-win decisions for both parties. JIT success requires a concern for minimizing inventory throughout the distribution channel (or the supply channel); JIT will not succeed if firms only push inventory back to another channel member.

win-win relationships

Examples of JIT Successes. Implementing the JIT concept has resulted in notable successes in the United States.[9] One such success occurred at Apple Computer's Macintosh plant in Fremont, California, where the company's goal of achieving twenty-five annual inventory turnovers translated into a reduction in float from ten weeks to two weeks and a payback for the $20 million plant in just eighteen months. During the mid-1980s, General Motors Corporation credited JIT for the fact that its total raw material, work in process, and finished goods inventory increased by only 6 percent over two years, while production levels increased by 100 percent.

inventory savings

Other examples include a thirty-two minitrain that operated between a parts facility in Kalamazoo, Michigan, and a General Motors Oldsmobile plant in Lansing, Michigan.[10] The operation involved no railcar switching and successfully met its customers' pickup and delivery times.

rail example

Innovative motor carriers have designed supply systems that effectively fulfill JIT requirements. For example, Ryder Distribution Resources provides all inbound logistical support for direct materials moving into Saturn Corporation's plant in Spring Hill, Tennessee.[11] Similarly, Averitt Express, a Tennessee-based provider of high-quality regional and interregional freight transportation services, designed and operates a system for Saturn to ensure that indirect materials moving into the same plant meet JIT-based priorities.

motor carriers

Based on the availability of high-quality, dependable transportation services that can fit a JIT-based production system's precise demands, various automobile manufacturers have justified eliminating several previously significant freight consolidation systems. The functions of these centers have been replaced by the delivery of needed parts precisely when and where manufacturers need them.[12]

Figure 7–12 shows how a firm can use a transportation strategy known as the *orderly pickup concept* to meet JIT-based manufacturing needs. The diagram shows how a firm may use time-sequenced motor carrier pickup from suppliers in conjunction with rail-motor intermodal service to meet JIT requirements.

Some mention should also be made of the fact that not all JIT systems have been successfully implemented, nor can JIT be used in every situation. Successful implementation of JIT requires an integrated, coordinated effort among several functions in a company and members of the supply chain.

Summary and Evaluation of JIT. The just-in-time concept can enable logistics managers to reduce unit cost and to enhance customer service. A close examination of JIT-based approaches shows that they resemble the more basic reactive systems such as the economic order quantity (EOQ) and fixed order quantity approaches, since JIT is demand responsive.

FIGURE 7–12 The Orderly Pickup Concept

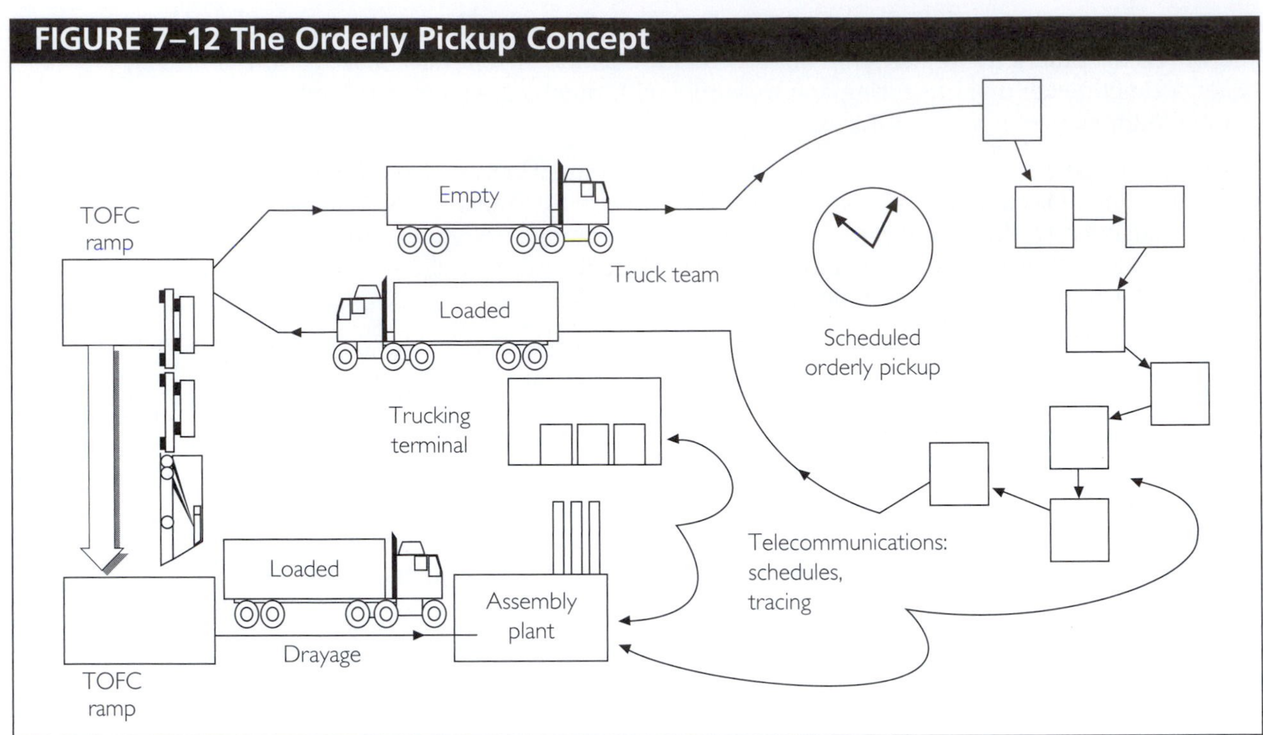

Source: Charles B. Lounsbury, Leaseway Transportation Corp., reprinted with permission.

comparison with traditional approaches

The principal difference between JIT and the more traditional approaches is the JIT commitment to short, consistent lead times and to minimizing or eliminating inventories. In effect, it saves money on downstream inventories by placing greater reliance on improved responsiveness and flexibility. Ideally, the use of JIT helps to synchronize the system so thoroughly that its functioning does not depend on inventories strategically located at points throughout the logistics system.

interface with manufacturing

Successful JIT applications also place a high priority on efficient and dependable production and manufacturing processes. Since JIT systems require the delivery of parts and subassemblies when and where the need arises, they rely heavily on the accuracy of the forecasting process used to anticipate finished product demand. In addition, timely JIT system operation demands effective and dependable communications and information systems, as well as high-quality consistent transportation services.

Business firms gaining additional experience with JIT-based approaches to manufacturing and logistics are sure to increasingly accept this concept. In fact, some companies, as indicated in the On-the-Line feature in this chapter, are expanding the JIT concept and referring to it as JIT II. The BOSE Corporation has been the prime proponent of this expanded role for vendors.

Materials Requirements Planning

Another inventory and scheduling approach that has received much recent attention is *materials requirements planning,* or MRP. Originally popularized by Joseph Orlicky, MRP deals specifically with supplying materials and component parts whose demand depends upon the demand for a specific end product. MRP's underlying concepts have existed for many years, but only recently have computers and information systems permitted firms to benefit fully from MRP and to implement such an approach.

computing net requirements

Definition and Operation of MRP Systems. A materials requirements planning (MRP) system consists of a set of logically related procedures, decision rules, and records designed to translate a master production schedule into time-phased net inventory requirements and the planned coverage of such requirements for each component item needed to implement this schedule. An MRP system replans net requirements and coverage as a result of changes in either the master production schedule, demand, inventory status, or product composition. MRP systems meet their objective by computing net requirements for each inventory item, time-phasing them, and determining their proper coverage.[13]

goals of MRP system

The goals of an MRP system are to (1) ensure the availability of materials, components, and products for planned production and for customer delivery; (2) maintain the lowest possible inventory level; and (3) plan manufacturing activities, delivery schedules, and purchasing activities. In so doing, the MRP system considers current and planned quantities of parts and inventory products, as well as the time used for planning.

exploding demand for component parts

MRP begins by determining how much end product customers desire and when they need it. Then MRP "explodes" the timing and need for components based upon the scheduled end-product need. Figure 7–13 shows how an MRP system operates by using these key elements:

- *Master production schedule.* Based on actual customer orders as well as demand forecasts, the master production schedule (MPS) drives the entire MRP system. The MPS details exactly what end products a company must manufacture or assemble and when the customers need them. In other words, the MPS will provide a detailed schedule of the various SKUs and when they must be produced.
- *Bill of materials file.* Just as a recipe specifies the ingredients needed to bake a cake, the bill of materials file (BMF) specifies the exact amount of raw materials, components, and subassemblies needed to manufacture or assemble the end product. Besides identifying gross requirements as needed quantities, the BMF tells when the individual inputs must be available. This file also identifies how the various inputs to one another relate and shows their relative importance to producing the end product. Therefore, if several components with different lead times need to be combined as a subunit, the BMF will indicate this relationship.
- *Inventory status file.* This file maintains inventory records so that the company may subtract the amount on hand from the gross requirements, thus identifying the net requirements at any time. The inventory status file (ISF) also contains important information on such things as safety stock needs for certain items and lead times. The ISF plays a critical role in support of maintaining the MPS and helping to minimize inventory.
- *MRP program.* Based on the end-product need specified in the master production schedule and on information from the bill of materials file, the MRP program first explodes the end-product demand into gross requirements for individual parts and other materials. Then the program calculates net requirements based on inventory status file information and places orders

FIGURE 7–13 An MRP System

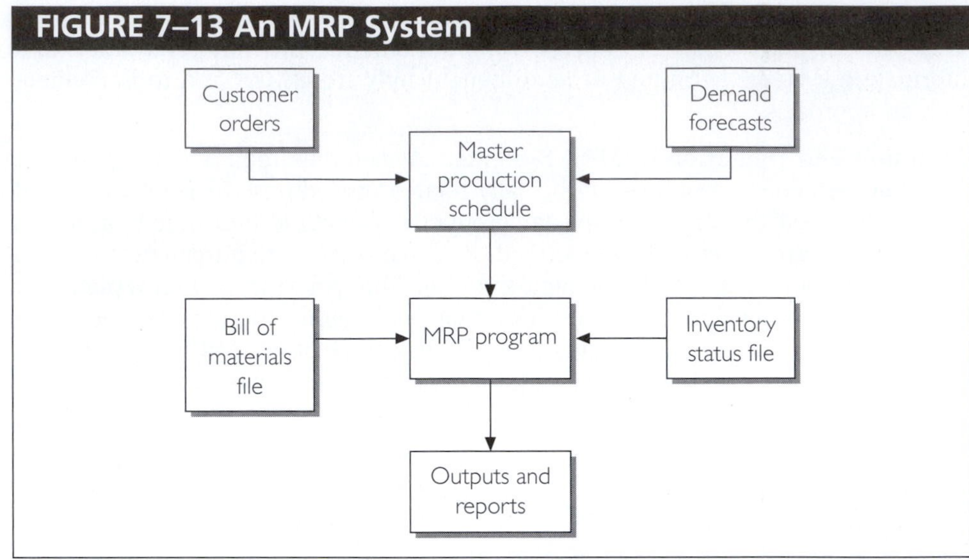

for the inputs necessary to the production/assembly process. The orders respond to needs for specific quantities of materials and to the timing of those needs. The example in the next section clarifies these MRP program activities.

- *Outputs and reports.* After a firm completes the MRP program, several basic outputs and reports will help managers involved in logistics, manufacturing, and assembly. Included are records and information related to the following: (1) quantities the company should order and when, (2) any need to expedite or reschedule arrival dates or needed product quantities, (3) canceled need for product, and (4) MRP system status. Those reports are key to controlling the MRP system and in complex environments are reviewed every day to make appropriate modifications and provide information.

Example of an MRP System. To understand the MRP approach more fully, consider a company that assembles egg timers. Assume that according to the master production schedule, the company desires to assemble a single, finished egg timer for delivery to a customer at the end of eight weeks. The MRP application would proceed as follows.

Figure 7–14 shows the bill of materials for assembling a single egg timer. The gross requirements for one finished product include two ends, one bulb, three supports, and one gram of sand. Figure 7–14 also shows that the company must add the gram of sand to the bulb before assembling the finished egg timer.

Table 7–7 displays the inventory status file for the egg timer example and calculates the net requirements as the difference between gross requirements and the amount of inventory on hand. The table notes the lead time for each component. For example, the lead time needed to procure supports and bulbs is one week, whereas sand needs four weeks and ends require five. Once all components are available, the time needed to assemble the finished egg timer is one week.

FIGURE 7–14 Relationship of Parts to Finished Product: MRP Egg Timer Example

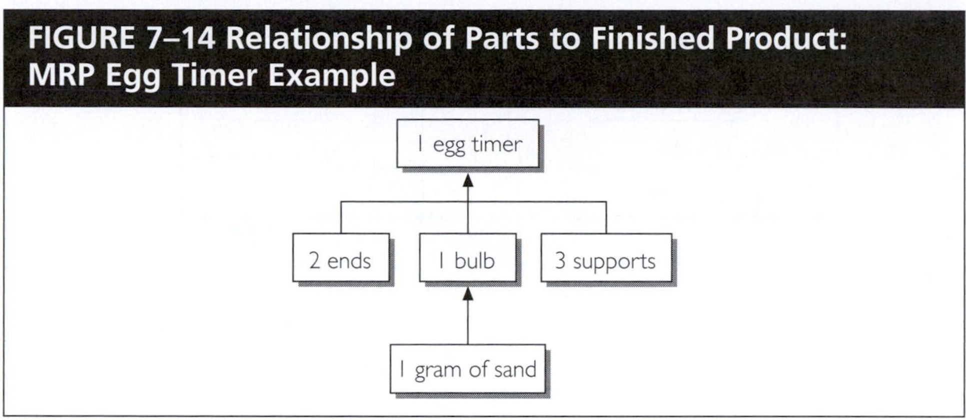

TABLE 7–7 Inventory Status File: MRP Egg Timer Example

Product	Gross Requirements	Inventory on Hand	Net Requirements	Lead Time (in Weeks)
Egg timers	1	0	1	1
Ends	2	0	2	5
Supports	3	2	1	1
Bulbs	1	0	1	1
Sand	1	0	1	4

Finally, Figure 7–15 is the master schedule for all activities relating to ordering and receiving components and assembling the finished egg timer. Because the company must have the single egg timer assembled and ready for customer delivery at the end of eight weeks, appropriate parts quantities must be available in the seventh week. The upper portion of Figure 7–15 shows this requirement.

Working backward from the need for parts in the seventh week, the lower portions of Figure 7–15 identify strategies for ordering and receiving component inventories. For example, for two ends requiring a lead time of five weeks, the company must place an order in the second week. For the one additional support requiring a lead time of a single week, the company should release an order during the sixth week. Finally, the company must order the bulb in the sixth week for delivery in the seventh, and order the sand in the second week for delivery in the sixth.

This example illustrates how the MRP-based approach relates to inventory scheduling and inventory control. In effect, the MRP program itself would perform the calculations involved in Figure 7–15. Once the program develops the master schedule, reports present this information in a format suitable for manager use. The company would place orders for needed parts in quantities and at times described.

In actual practice, MRP is exceptionally suitable for planning and controlling the ordering and receipt of large numbers of parts and products that may interact

FIGURE 7–15 Master Schedule: MRP Egg Timer Example

EGG TIMERS (LT=1)	1	2	3	4	5	6	7	8
Quantity needed								1
Production schedule							1	

ENDS (LT=5)	1	2	3	4	5	6	7	8
Gross requirements							2	
Inventory on hand	0	0	0	0	0	0	0	
Scheduled receipts							2	
Planned order releases		2						

SUPPORTS (LT=1)	1	2	3	4	5	6	7	8
Gross requirements							3	
Inventory on hand	2	2	2	2	2	2	2	
Scheduled receipts							1	
Planned order releases						1		

BULBS (LT=1)	1	2	3	4	5	6	7	8
Gross requirements							1	
Inventory on hand	0	0	0	0	0	0	0	
Scheduled receipts							1	
Planned order releases						1		

SAND (LT=4)	1	2	3	4	5	6	7	8
Gross requirements						1		
Inventory on hand	0	0	0	0	0	0		
Scheduled receipts						1		
Planned order releases		1						

during assembly or manufacture. With the exception of very simple problems such as the egg timer example, computerization is virtually a prerequisite to using MRP-based applications. Only through the processing speed and manipulative capabilities of modern computer systems can a firm perform MRP's inner workings cost-effectively.

Summary and Evaluation of MRP Systems. Having established the master production schedule, the MRP program develops a time-phased approach to inventory scheduling and inventory receipt. Because it generates a list of required materials in order to assemble or manufacture a specified number of finished products, MRP represents a "push" approach. Correspondingly, this encourages purchase order and production order development. Typically, MRP applies primarily when the demand for parts and materials depends upon the demand for some specific end product. MRP can deal with systemwide material supplies.

responsiveness

Since actual demand is key to the establishment of production schedules, MRP systems can react quickly to changing demand for finished products. Although some JIT proponents feel that a "pull" approach is inherently more responsive than a "push" approach such as MRP, the reverse is sometimes true. MRP systems can also help firms to achieve other typical JIT objectives, such as those pertaining to lead time management and elimination of waste. In short, MRP can achieve objectives more commonly associated with the JIT-based approaches, while at times decisions made through the pull concept do not reflect the future events for which the JIT policies are intended.

strengths

The principal advantages of most MRP-based systems include the following:

- They try to maintain reasonable safety stock levels and to minimize or eliminate inventories whenever possible.
- They can identify process problems and potential supply chain disruptions long before they occur and take necessary corrective action.
- Production schedules are based on actual demand as well as on forecasts of end-product needs.
- They coordinate materials ordering across points in a firm's logistics system.
- They are most suitable for batch or intermittent production or assembly processes.

limitations

Shortcomings of MRP-based approaches include the following:

- Their application is computer intensive, and making changes is sometimes difficult once the system is in operation.
- Both ordering and transportation costs may rise as a firm reduces inventory levels and possibly moves toward a more coordinated system of ordering product in smaller amounts to arrive when the firm needs it.
- They are not usually as sensitive to short-term fluctuations in demand as are order point approaches (although they are not as inventory intensive, either).
- They frequently become quite complex and sometimes do not work exactly as intended.[14]

advanced approaches

A Note Concerning MRPII Systems. In recent years, *manufacturing resource planning*, or MRPII, a far more comprehensive set of tools than MRP alone, has become available. Although MRP is a key step in MRPII, MRPII allows a firm to integrate financial planning and operations/logistics.

MRPII serves as an excellent planning tool, and it helps describe the likely results of implementing strategies in areas such as logistics, manufacturing, marketing, and finance. Thus, it helps a firm to conduct "what if?" analyses and to determine appropriate product movement and storage strategies at and between points in the firm's logistics system.

MRPII is a technique used to plan and manage all of the organization's resources and reaches far beyond inventory or even production control to all planning functions of an organization.[15] It is a holistic planning technique, one that can draw together all of the corporate functional areas into an integrated whole. The ultimate benefits of MRPII include improved customer service through fewer shortages and stockouts, better delivery performance, and responsiveness to changes in demand. Successfully implementing MRPII should also help to reduce inventory costs and the frequency of production line stoppages, and create more planning flexibility.[16]

Newer, more responsive approaches are developing rapidly. The integration of MRPII and JIT (known as MRPIII), for example, is a potentially-valuable development to logistics manufacturing and the whole firm.

Distribution Resource Planning

Distribution resource planning (DRP) is a widely used and potentially powerful technique for outbound logistics systems to help determine the appropriate level of inventory. In actuality, the success stories involving DRP indicate that companies can improve customer service (decrease stockout situations), reduce the overall level of finished goods inventories, reduce transportation costs, and improve distribution center operations. With this potential, it is no wonder that manufacturers are interested in implementing DRP systems.

DRP is usually used with an MRP (materials requirements planning) system, which attempts to manage and minimize inbound inventories, particularly where numerous items are needed, as is the case in the automobile industry. Items that need to be combined and used in the assembly of a finished product usually have varying lead times. Therefore, MRP is tied to the master production schedule, which indicates which items are to be produced each day and the sequence in which they will be produced. This schedule is then used as the basis to forecast the actual parts needed and when they will be needed. When the master production schedule is combined with the lead times necessary for each item, a schedule can be developed that indicates when each item has to be ordered. The quantity is determined by comparing inventory status with the total number of items needed to meet the production schedule.

MRP minimizes inventory to the extent that the master production schedule accurately reflects what is needed to satisfy customer demand in the marketplace. If the production schedule does not match demand, the company will have too much of some items and too little of others.

The underlying rationale for DRP is to more accurately forecast demand and to explode that information back for use in developing production schedules. In that way a company can minimize inbound inventory by using MRP in conjunction with production schedules. Outbound (finished goods) inventory is minimized through the use of DRP. Most DRP models are more comprehensive than standalone MRP models, and they also schedule transportation.

DRP develops a projection for each SKU and requires[17]

- Forecast of demand for each SKU
- Current inventory level of the SKU (balance on hand, BOH)

TABLE 7–8 DRP Table for Chicken Noodle Soup

Columbus Distribution Center—Distribution Resource Planning

Week	Jan. 1	2	3	4	Feb. 5	6	7	8	March 9
CHICKEN NOODLE:	Current BOH = 4,314 Q = 3,800 SS = 1,956 LT = 1								
Forecast	974	974	974	974	989	1,002	1,002	1,002	1,061
Sched. receipt	0	0	3,800	0	0	0	3,800	0	0
BOH-ending	3,340	2,366	5,192	4,218	3,229	2,227	5,025	4,023	2,962
Planned order	0	3,800	0	0	0	3,800	0	0	3,800
Actual order									

Q = Quantity
SS = Safety stock
LT = Lead time

Source: A. J. Stenger, "Distribution Resources Planning," Penn State University, class example.

- Target safety stock
- Recommended replenishment quantity
- Lead time for replenishment

This information is used to develop replenishment requirements. One of the key elements of a successful DRP system is the development of a DRP table, which consists of a variety of elements including the SKU, forecast, BOH, scheduled receipt, planned order, and so on. Table 7–8 illustrates the DRP table for chicken noodle soup at the Columbus Distribution Center. The table shows only nine weeks, but a DRP table would typically show fifty-two weeks and would be a dynamic document that would undergo continual change as the data, especially demand, changed. Individual tables provide useful information, but combining tables can lead to increased advantage. For example, combining all of the individual SKU tables of items shipped from one source can provide useful information about consolidation possibilities and when to expect orders to arrive at a warehouse. Essentially, the combining of tables helps to develop efficient production plans and shipping plans, as illustrated in Figure 7–16.

DRP, particularly when combined with MRP, is a powerful tool that can lead to better customer service and lower total logistics and manufacturing costs.

Inventory control is a special challenge in today's supply chains, and efforts such as efficient consumer response (ECR) focus primarily upon reducing inventory levels in the supply chain to reduce costs. Tools such as MRP can help, but it is also necessary to assess the true costs of inventory, especially stockouts.

FIGURE 7–16 Combining DRP Tables

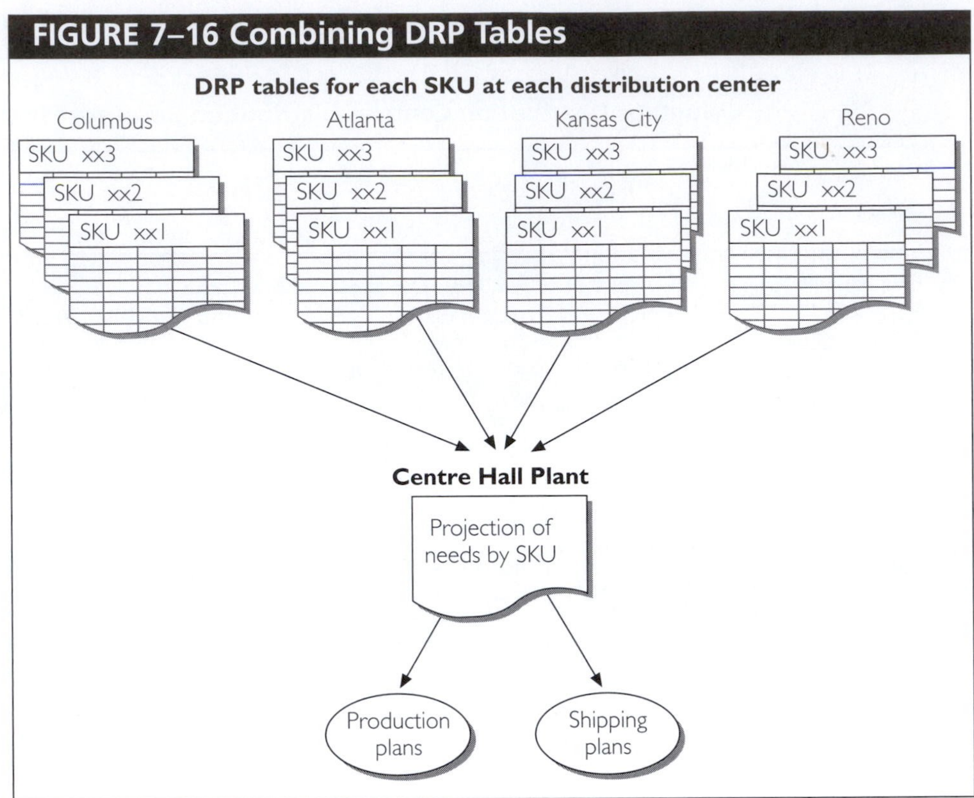

Source: Adapted from A. J. Stenger, "Distribution Resources Planning," *The Distribution Handbook* (New York: The Free Press, 1994).

Inventory at Multiple Locations—The Square Root Law

In their aggressive efforts to take cost out of logistics networks, firms are searching for new ways to reduce levels of inventory without adversely affecting customer service. A currently popular approach is to consolidate inventories into fewer stocking locations in order to reduce aggregate inventories and their associated costs. Correspondingly, this strategy requires the involvement of capable transportation and information resources to see that customer service is held at existing levels and is even improved whenever possible.

underlying principles

The square root law (SRL) helps determine the extent to which inventories may be reduced through such a strategy. Assuming that total customer demand remains the same, the SRL estimates the extent to which aggregate inventory needs will change as a firm increases or reduces the number of stocking locations. In general, the greater the number of stocking locations, the greater the amount of inventory needed to maintain customer service levels. Conversely, as inventories are consolidated into fewer stocking locations, aggregate inventory levels will decrease. The extent to which these changes will occur is understood through application of the square root law.[18]

The square root law states that total safety stock inventories in a future number of facilities can be approximated by multiplying the total amount of inventory at existing facilities by the square root of the number of future facilities divided by the number of existing facilities:

calculation

$$X_2 = (X_1)(\sqrt{n_2/n_1})$$

where

n_1 = number of existing facilities

n_2 = number of future facilities

X_1 = total inventory in existing facilities

X_2 = total inventory in future facilities

To illustrate, consider a company that presently distributes 40,000 units of product to its customers from a total of eight facilities located throughout the United States. Current distribution centers are located in Boston, Chicago, San Francisco, Los Angeles, Dallas, Orlando, Charlotte, and Baltimore. The company is evaluating an opportunity to consolidate its operations into two facilities, one in Memphis, Tennessee, and the other in Reno/Sparks, Nevada. Using the square root law, the total amount of inventory in the two future facilities is computed as follows:

example

n_1 = 8 existing facilities

n_2 = 2 future facilities

X_1 = 40,000 total units of product in the 8 existing facilities

Thus,

X_2 = total units of production in the 2 future facilities

$= (40,000)(\sqrt{2/8})$

$= (40,000)(0.5)$

$= 20,000$ units

Based on the results of this analysis, the two future facilities would carry a total inventory of 20,000 units. If the company designed them to be of equal size, and if market demand was equal for the geographic areas, each of these distribution centers would carry one-half of this total, or 10,000 units. Conversely, if for some reason the company considered increasing the number of distribution centers from 8 to, say, 32, total inventory needs would double from 40,000 to 80,000 units. (Use the formula to check this for yourself.)

Based on data from an actual company, Table 7–9 shows the total average units of inventory implied by specific numbers of distribution centers in the system. For example, as stocking locations increase from 1 to 25, the total average number of units in inventory increases from 3,885 units to 19,425 units. This is consistent with application of the SRL. Table 7–9 also shows the percentage change in inventories as the number of distribution centers in the system increases.

Although the square root law is simply stated, the model is based on several reasonable assumptions: (1) inventory transfers between stocking locations at the same level are not common practice; (2) lead times do not vary, and thus inventory centralization is not affected by rebound supply uncertainty; (3) customer

assumptions

TABLE 7–9 Example Impacts of Square Root Law on Logistics Inventories

Number of Warehouses (n)	$\sqrt{n}$	Total Average Inventory (Units)	Percent Change
1	1.0000	3,885	—
2	1.4142	5,494	141%
3	1.7321	6,729	173%
4	2.0000	7,770	200%
5	2.2361	8,687	224%
10	3.1623	12,285	316%
15	3.8730	15,047	387%
20	4.4721	17,374	447%
23	4.7958	18,632	480%
25	5.0000	19,425	500%

service level, as measured by inventory availability, is constant regardless of the number of stocking locations; and (4) demand at each location is normally distributed.[19] In addition, it has been shown that the potential for aggregate inventory reduction through consolidation of facilities will be greater when the correlation of sales between stocking locations is small to negative and when there is less sales variability at each of the stocking locations.[20]

A Special Note on Inventory for Outbound Systems

One definition that has been offered for logistics is that it is the management of inventory, whether in motion or at rest, for the purpose of satisfying customers. Nowhere is this description of logistics more appropriate than with outbound logistics, where inventory is the "glue" for the individual logistics system and even the supply chain and at the same time is the focus of constant scrutiny to reduce or eliminate it. This somewhat paradoxical role of inventory as both a problem and a solution can frequently make logistics managers paranoid as companies strive to increase market share and improve return on investment by lowering inventory cost.

The key to dealing with inventory is to recognize that it has to be managed from a systems perspective, in which the trade-offs are measured comprehensively and accurately. Decreasing or increasing inventory will affect not only direct inventory costs but also other areas of logistics such as warehousing, transportation, materials handling, customer service, and probably the manufacturing, marketing, and finance functions. Too frequently, the real costs of changes in inventory policy are not adequately measured; that is, firms use inappropriate measures or ignore certain costs. Chapter 6 provides a comprehensive analysis of the many dimensions of inventory to apprise the reader of the true cost of inventory. Two specific topics related to inventory are covered in this chapter: the cost of inventory stockouts and DRP systems. Some additional, more general observations are also offered.

The cost of stockouts is especially germane to our discussion of outbound logistics because it so directly affects customer service and the channels of distribution. We should have adequate measures to help us make good decisions.

DEMAND PULL APPROACHES TO MANAGING INVENTORY

As indicated previously, the supply chain or demand chain approach to managing inventory has placed increased emphasis upon demand-responsive fulfillment or replenishment. Traditional inventory techniques often pushed inventory in advance of demand. The demand pull approach focuses upon lowering cost while also improving service to customers, whereas the traditional, logistics analytical framework viewed customer service and logistics costs as trade-offs. For example, if a company wanted to improve customer service metrics, they could carry higher levels of inventory to improve order fill rates or reduce cycle time—increase cost to improve service. This approach was associated with the traditional inventory push strategies as opposed to the current demand pull strategies. The latter are sometimes referred to as *replenishment strategies.*

It should be noted, however, that it is almost impossible to operate the entire supply chain completely on a demand pull approach to inventory. For example, Dell Computer is a company that is frequently used as a reference or model for the demand pull approach to inventory management. There is no question that Dell places great emphasis on its demand pull, order-fulfillment system. The benefits to Dell are significant. For example, its average for daily sales inventory is four days, and it turns inventory about eighty-one times per year; but the most important outcome of this inventory velocity is that, on average, it has the cash from its customers from a sale for thirty days before it pays its vendors or suppliers for the components that are in that computer. Essentially, it has a negative cash flow, and the vendors are financing its inventory. It can operate on low profit margins because it can invest the cash before paying vendors.

When you dissect Dell's supply chain, however, you find that it is not a pure pull system. Inventory is pushed from its vendors to third-party logistics providers (3PLs) who hold the parts inventory. The parts inventory is pulled by Dell from the 3PL's warehouse when Dell receives an order for a computer. Dell does not own the inventory until it leaves the dock of the 3PL's facility. On the inbound and outbound sides of Dell's logistics system, it operates on a demand pull basis, but part of its supply chain operates on a more traditional push system. Dell maximizes efficiency for the 3PLs and its vendors through comprehensive information sharing related to orders and production schedules to reduce overall inventory in the supply chain because it realizes that its vendors and 3PL partners cannot survive unless they make a profit also.

Dell is somewhat unique as a manufacturer in being able to develop a time-based logistics strategy to minimize its inventory levels and increase its inventory turns. In some ways, it resembles a retailer since it sells directly to its customer; that is, it does not have a channel of distribution with wholesalers and/or retailers. In fact, retail industry companies have also been leaders in time-based logistics/supply chain strategies. Continuous-replenishment systems (Figure 7–17), quick response systems (Figure 7–18), and vendor-managed inventory systems (VMI) were developed to meet the requirements of the large retailers (Wal-Mart, Kmart, Target, Sears, etc.) who worked closely with their suppliers such as Proctor and Gamble, Nabisco, and Kimberly-Clark to develop demand-responsive strategies designed to lower their retail inventory requirements.

Efficient consumer response (Figure 7–19) is a more comprehensive, industrywide strategy developed by the grocery manufacturers to bring greater value to the grocery customer. ECR is based upon integrated EDI, continuous replenishment, computer-assisted ordering, and flow-through distribution. Overall, ECR is a time-based approach to replenishment logistics that emphasizes inventory visibility and velocity to achieve lower cost and better customer service.

Interest in the aforementioned time-based replenishment strategies in the retail industry has waned somewhat; but, nevertheless, they continue to be utilized in important segments of the consumer, packaged goods industry and by others. The current strategy that has been receiving increased attention is collaborative plan-

FIGURE 7–17 Four Directions for Replenishment Logistics

Direction	Objective	Key Programs
 Continuous-replenishment (CRP) inventory systems	Bring supply more in line with the rhythm of demand	Automated systems that enable distributors to stock and reorder goods based on actual consumer sales (i.e., point-of-sale transactions)
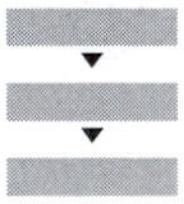 Flow-through distribution systems	Take every bit of wasted space, handling activities, time, and therefore costs out of the process	New methods that increase the speed of product flow by reducing inventory and relying on timely, coordinated, and dependable transportation and material handling
Pipeline logistics organizations 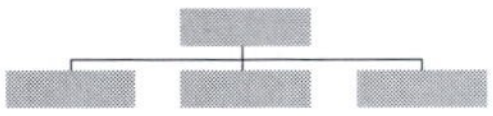	Institutionalize key product flow processes, cultivate "total pipeline view," and coordinate operations	New roles and responsibilities that remove barriers to communication, rationalize accountability, encourage coordination, and provide incentives for aggressive management of the logistics pipeline
Pipeline performance measures 	Establish objective tools for improving management control of processes and motivating appropriate decision making ("You can't manage what you can't measure")	Precise criteria, accurate decision rules, and consistent procedures that support management objectives and take into account total pipeline performance

Source: Mercer Management Consulting, *New Ways to Take Costs Out of the Retail Food Pipeline* (Atlanta, Ga.: Coca-Cola Retailing Research Council, 1994), 7. Used with permission.

ning and forecasting requirements (CPFR). As discussed in Chapter 4, CPFR places an emphasis on supply chain members developing a common forecast for individual SKUs to reduce uncertainty and, thereby, decrease inventory levels and improve customer service. In addition, velocity and visibility of inventory are a part of the effort to ensure lower cost and better customer service. In effect, they are incorporating the best of the old strategies with a new integrating strategy for their supply chains.

FIGURE 7–18 Basic Elements of Quick Response (QR)

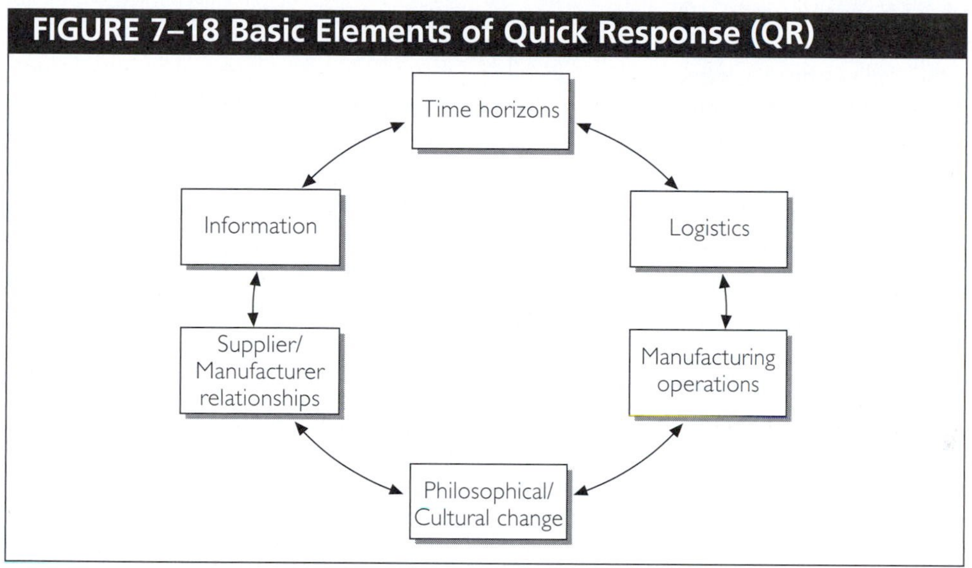

FIGURE 7–19 Efficient Consumer Response: Broad Operating Capabilities Tailored to Each Unique Partner

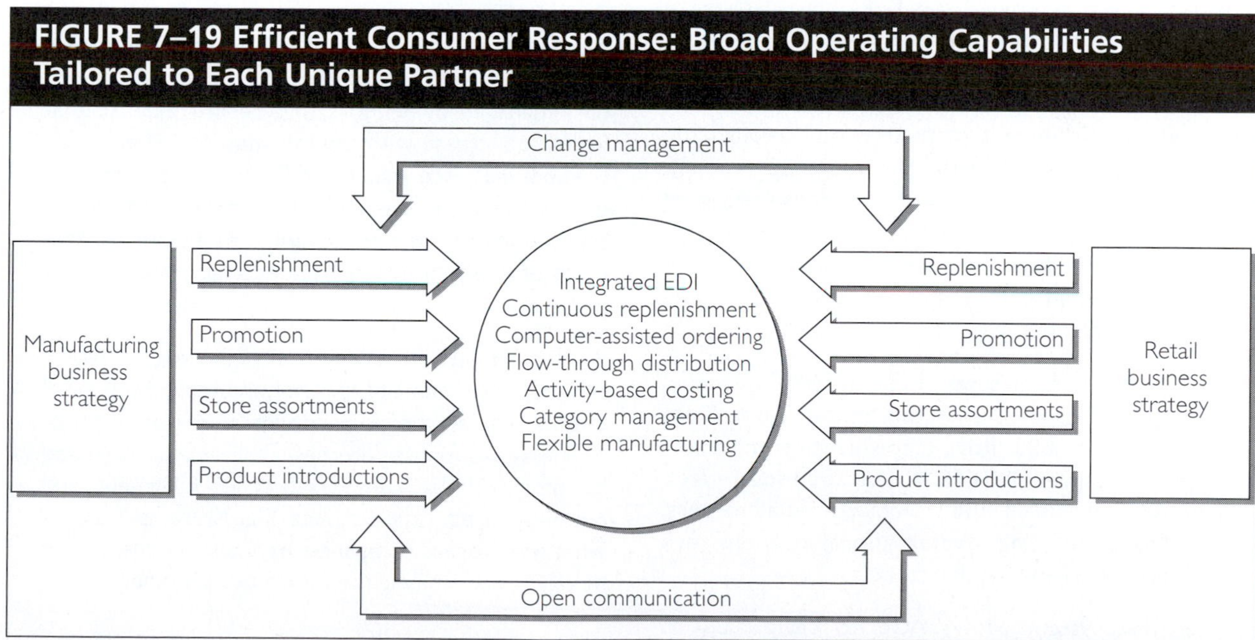

Source: Frederick A. Crawford, Computer Sciences Corporation, "Reengineering Consumer Goods Businesses: Seeking Smarter Solutions to Market Mandates," *Perspectives* (Cambridge, Mass.: Computer Sciences Corporation, 1995), page 3H.

Supply Chain Technology

Inventory Management: Balancing Act

Ace Hardware is the place for the helpful hardware folks—so says John Madden of the 5,100-store retail chain. And, if John says so, it must be true. The excitable and likable football celebrity has been touting the 4,200-employee, $2.8 billion retail chain since 1988. But, despite Madden's market appeal, it's probably safe to assume he knows more about football than hardware—and almost nothing about integrated solutions.

Nevertheless, the Oak Brook, Ill. - based retail giant has still managed to make integrated solutions an engine for its business—particularly in inventory management. Ace has to. It operates as an international cooperative. Unlike franchises, which mandate loyalty by their very nature, the cooperative structure allows retailers to purchase goods elsewhere if they so choose. This structure doubly motivates corporate Ace to keep its retailers happy.

"The retailers look to us for consistency in delivery, pricing, and advertising," says Greg Lenard, director of inventory control at Ace. Lenard should know. He's responsible for purchasing and replenishing all inventory for those retailers. "Retailers on average buy about 70 percent of their goods through the cooperative," notes Lenard. "We provide a two-step distribution process, so the dealer doesn't have to buy directly from the manufacturer. We used to call ourselves a wholesaler, but we are really a retail support company. Inventory is our second most important asset behind employees."

Ace has fifteen retail support centers (RSCs) located strategically across the United States. The facilities carry about 65,000 SKUs (shop keeping units) and range in size from 300,000 to 1,000,000 square feet. The RSCs fulfill all the company's retail orders, including those going to international locations such as Puerto Rico and Saudi Arabia.

The new system allows ACE to review up to 1,000,000 SKUs every night—an impossible feat with the old system. This review allows Ace to keep a current, daily picture of its inventory and purchase decisions. That is in stark contrast to the weekly overview that the company had with the mainframe system. TRIM also allows Ace to take advantage of forward buying procedures (purchasing large quantities of items at a discount), another feature that the old system never offered.

Ace also uses the system for gross profit buying, asset management, and getting a proper turnover. These key features alone have given Ace an edge that was unavailable with the old system. But, the crowning feature of Ace's new setup is the company's strengthened relationship with manufacturers.

The success of Ace's inventory management system supports the statistical improvement the company has seen since the installation. Ace calculates a "service to dealers ratio" based on the number of units ordered and sold to retailers. The average service figure was 95.4 percent. For example, if a retailer ordered 1,000 combined units (saws, hammers, drills, etc.), the warehouse would have shipped 954 of those items. With VMI relations, service levels are one to two points higher than that statistic—sometimes as high as 97.5 percent. Those small percentage increases are significant for a billion-dollar company. Ace also has about 20 percent of its inventory managed by vendors, and Lenard expects that figure to increase with the Internet implementation. Beyond that, Ace has turned weekly updates into daily reports and has shifted most of its inventory calculations to the new system. Clearly, the management of Ace's inventory has become more efficient and accurate.

By all accounts, Ace's focus on technology is paying off: heightened demand, forecast, and replenishment of inventory, strengthened vendor relationships through business-to-business Internet applications, increased business with back end Web-order fulfillment, and better-serviced retailers. Ace Hardware is learning what many other companies have also learned; technology is determining the future of all business.

Source: Douglas Weldon, *Integrated Solutions* (March 2000): 48–50.

SUMMARY

- Traditionally, inventory managers focused upon two important questions to improve efficiency, namely, how much to reorder from vendors and/or their own plants and when to reorder.
- The two aforementioned questions were frequently answered using the EOQ model, trading off inventory carrying cost against setup costs or order costs and then calculating a reorder point based upon demand or usage rates.
- The traditional EOQ model, particularly when using one of its adaptations, is still utilized in some parts of many supply chains. However, the complexity of today's business environment has necessitated the development of alternative models to address specific issues such as where to hold inventory, what SKUs should be held, and so on.
- Choosing the appropriate inventory model or technique should include an analysis of key differences that affect the inventory decision. These differences are determined by the following questions: (1) Is the demand for the item independent or dependent? (2) Is the distribution system based upon a push or pull approach? and (3) Do the inventory decisions apply to one facility or to multiple facilities?
- There are two basic forms of the EOQ model—the fixed quantity version and the fixed internal model. The former is the most widely used. Essentially, the relevant costs are analyzed (traded off) and an optimum quantity is decided. This reorder quantity will remain fixed unless costs change, but the intervals between orders will vary depending upon demand.
- The basic EOQ model can be varied or adapted to focus more specifically upon decisions that are impacted by inventory-related costs such as shipment quantities where there are rate discounts involved.
- Just-in-time (JIT) inventory management captured the attention of many U.S. businesses during the 1970s, especially the automobile industry. As the name implies, the basic goal is to minimize inventory levels with an emphasis upon frequent deliveries of smaller quantities and alliances with vendors or customers. To be most effective, JIT should also include quality management.
- Materials requirements planning (MRP) and distribution requirements planning (DRP) are typically used in conjunction with each other. In addition, a master production schedule (MPS) is utilized to help balance demand and supply of inventory. DRP is used on the outbound side of a logistics system. Demand forecasts of individual SKUs are developed to drive the DRP model. Then, an MPS schedule is developed to meet the scheduled demand replenishment requirements. The MRP schedule is developed to satisfy the replenishment requirements of the various MPS schedules. As implied, these models are usually used for multiple facility inventory decisions in complex environments where there are varying lead times.
- When companies are adding warehouses, a frequently asked question is, "How much additional inventory will be required?" The square root rule is a technique that can be used to help answer this question.

- One of the perplexing questions facing inventory managers is how to estimate the cost of a stockout for trade-off analysis. Using probability analysis, some insight can be gained to help answer that question.
- During the 1990s, a number of time-based strategies were developed to deal with demand pull replenishment in a complex, competitive environment. VMI, QR, CRP, and ECR are among the strategies that have been utilized.
- The latest strategy is usually referred to as collaborative planning forecasting requirements (CPFR). This strategy is a supply chain approach to developing a single forecast for each SKU at the final customer level and developing replenishment requirements at each level of the supply chain to satisfy these requirements.

Study Questions

1. Micros and More is considering whether it should use a demand pull approach to inventory control of its finished goods inventory or a more traditional approach. Explain the essential differences between a demand pull and a push strategy. What would you recommend for Micros and More? Why?
2. What is the difference between dependent demand and independent demand items? Why is this distinction important to inventory managers?
3. Compare and contrast the fixed quantity version of the EOQ model and the fixed interval version. What factors affect which version should be utilized?
4. Why has the JIT approach to inventory control become popular in some industries? How does the JIT approach compare to EOQ approaches to inventory management? Should JIT be adopted by all inventory managers? Why, or why not?
5. Explain the essential characteristics of MRP, MPS, and DRP. How do they operate in conjunction with each other to provide a systemic approach to managing inbound and outbound inventory?
6. Don Warsing of Micros and More is struggling with determining stockout costs in order to set appropriate customer service levels. He has developed the following information: 40 percent of stockouts will result in a back order with a cost of $5.00 per back order; 40 percent of the stockouts result in a lost sale and a profit of $50.00 per unit; and 20 percent of the stockouts result in a lost customer with an estimated loss of $100.00. What is its stockout cost?
7. Jim Gatto and Terry Edwards of Micros and More are considering consolidating into one warehouse in Tyrone, Pennsylvania, to take advantage of a newly constructed interstate highway (I99) and access to a major Wal-Mart warehouse in Clearfield, Pennsylvania. They need to estimate the change in inventory requirements. Mr. Edwards estimates that Micros and More is currently carrying about 5,000 computers in two warehouses in Bellefonte and Pleasant Gap. What will its new requirements be?
8. What are the major characteristics of the replenishment strategies utilized by Dell Computer to minimize its supply chain costs and maximize customer service levels?

9. "Demand pull replenishment strategies have made traditional push strategies obsolete." Critique this statement.
10. Compare and contrast the CRP, QR, and ECR approaches to inventory replenishment.

Notes

1. Joseph Orlicky, *Materials Requirements Planning* (New York: McGraw-Hill, 1975), 22.
2. Portions of the following discussion have been adapted from David J. Closs, "An Adaptive Inventory System as a Tool for Strategic Inventory Management," *Proceedings of the 1981 Annual Meeting of the National Council of Physical Distribution Management* (Chicago, Ill.: National Council of Physical Distribution Management, 1981): 659–79. Also, see John W. Hummel and Alan J. Stenger, "An Evaluation of Proactive vs. Reactive Replenishment Systems," *International Journal of Physical Distribution and Materials Management* 18, no. 4: 3–13.
3. This analogy has been drawn from Uday Karmarkar, "Getting Control of Just-in-Time," *Harvard Business Review* (September–October 1989): 122–31.
4. Donald J. Bowersox, David J. Closs, and Omar K. Helferich, *Logistical Management,* 3d ed. (New York: Macmillan, 1986), 227.
5. Ronald H. Ballou, *Business Logistics Management,* 3d ed. (Englewood Cliffs, N.J.: Prentice-Hall, 1992), 438–39.
6. Use of these formulas requires that demand and lead time length be independent, meaning *unrelated* in a statistical sense. If they are not independent, then the formula must be modified slightly to produce the statistical precision and accuracy desired. Note that we have simplified the discussion in this section. A recommended source for further study is Robert G. Brown, *Smoothing, Forecasting and Prediction of Discrete Time Series* (Englewood Cliffs, N.J.: Prentice-Hall, 1962), 366–67.
7. Walter E. Goddard, "Kanban or MRPII—Which Is Best for You?" *Modern Materials Handling* (5 November 1982): 42.
8. Ibid., 45–46.
9. "How Just-in-Time Inventories Combat Foreign Competition," *Business Week* Special Report (14 May 1984): 176E.
10. Joan M. Feldman, "Transportation Changes—Just in Time," *Handling and Shipping Management* (September 1984): 47.
11. Details concerning Ryder's involvement with Saturn Corporation may be found in Ray A. Mundy, Judy A. Ford, Paul E. Forney, and Jerry Lineback, "Innovations in Carrier Sourcing: Transportation Partnership," *1989 Council of Logistics Management Annual Conference Proceedings* (Oakbrook, Ill.: CLM, 1989): 109–14.
12. For additional ideas, see Daniel Goldberg, "JIT's Next Step Moves Cargo and Data," *Transportation & Distribution* (December 1990): 26–29.

13. Orlicky, *Materials Requirements Planning*, 22.
14. Denis J. Davis, "Transportation and Inventory Management: Bridging the Gap," *Distribution* (June 1985): 11.
15. John Gatorna and Abby Day, "Strategic Issues in Logistics," *International Journal of Physical Distribution and Materials Management* 16 (1986): 29.
16. For additional information regarding MRPII, see Oliver W. Wright, "MRPII," *Modern Materials Handling* (12 September 1980): 28.
17. A. J. Stenger, "Materials Resources Planning," *The Distribution Handbook* (New York: The Free Press, 1994), 89–97.
18. See D. H. Maister, "Centralization of Inventories and the 'Square Root Law'," *International Journal of Physical Distribution and Materials Management* 6, no. 3 (1976): 124–34; Walter Zinn, Michael Levy, and Donald J. Bowersox, "Measuring the Effect of Inventory Centralization/Decentralization on Aggregate Safety Stock: The 'Square Root Law' Revisited," *Journal of Business Logistics* 10, no. 1 (1989): 1–14; and David Ronen, "Inventory Centralization/Decentralization—The 'Square Root Law' Revisited Again," *Journal of Business Logistics* 11, no. 2 (1990): 129–42.
19. Zinn, Levy, and Bowersox, "Measuring the Effect of Inventory Centralization/Decentralization on Aggregate Safety Stock," 2.
20. Ibid., 14.

CASE 7–1 ■ Beierlein Distributors

For more than thirty years, Beierlein Distributors of Galesburg, Illinois, has experienced steady growth although it has had a few bumps along the road. About eight years ago, the Grocery Manufacturers Association (GMA) was promoting the ECR strategy to eliminate or reduce the number of end-of-quarter special promotions (read price discounts), which had been very beneficial to the Beirlein Company. It would buy sixty to ninety days of inventory of important SKUs at a discount, which provided the company with an assured source of supply at lower prices.

The GMA's rationale was that the end-of-the quarter promotions increased inventory in the supply chain (average of 104 days of inventory), which was suboptimal. They also led to other cost inefficiencies in manufacturing and logistics. It was conservatively estimated by the GMA that $30 billion per year could be saved initially.

Jim (CEO) and Julie (COO) Beierlein weathered the ECR initiatives and found that they could remain competitive without the end-of-the-quarter discounts. They had not measured their extra cost accurately for holding sixty to ninety days of inventory and were, therefore, surprised with the cost reductions that they experienced by buying SKUs on a weekly basis. In addition, they initiated value-added services to their top ten customers. Their most successful effort was a vendor-managed inventory (VMI) program for selected (top ten) customers. These selected customers had been able to reduce their "back room" inventory significantly. Overall, the supply chain was able to price more competitively.

Now, Beierlein was faced with another challenge, namely, to reduce stockouts and improve shelf availability of most SKUs. A number of its vendors, for example, Nabisco, Proctor and Gamble, and Kimberly-Clark wanted Beierlein to implement collaborative planning forecasting requirements (CPFR), which had been implemented by a number of the larger chains, such as Wal-Mart and Kmart. Beierlein was concerned about the cost of participating in such a strategy and the willingness of its customers to participate.

Case Questions

1. Prepare a rationale for Beierlein to use with its customers.
2. What are the advantages and disadvantages to Beierlein?

CASE 7–2 ■ Nittany Fans

Nittany Fans of Lewistown, Pennsylvania, is a distributor of industrial fans used in plants, warehouses, and other industrial facilities. Its market area encompasses most of Pennsylvania, Eastern Ohio, and New Jersey. The fans are manufactured in Neenah, Wisconsin, and currently shipped to Lewistown via rail transportation. LuAnn Jaworski, vice president of logistics, has asked her staff to evaluate using motor carrier service.

Rosi Greaser, director of distribution services, has developed the following information:

Annual demand: 36,000 fans
Fan value (price): $4,000
Inventory carrying cost: 25 percent
Order cost to replenish inventory: $200
In-transit inventory carrying cost: 15 percent
Order cycle time using rail: 4 days
Order cycle time using motor carrier: 2 days
Rail rate: $1.00/cwt
Motor rate: $1.25/cwt
Unit weight: 250 pounds per fan

Case Questions

1. What is the economic order quantity (EOQ) for Nittany Fans in units? In pounds?
2. What is the total cost (not considering transportation-related costs) of the EOQ?
3. What is the total cost using rail transportation?
4. What is the total cost using motor carrier transportation?
5. What alternative should Nittany Fans use?

Appendix 7A

SPECIAL APPLICATIONS OF THE EOQ APPROACH

Adjusting the Simple EOQ Model for Modal Choice Decisions—The Cost of Inventory in Transit

Chapter 1 mentioned the trade-off possibilities between inventory costs and transportation decisions regarding choice of mode. Implied in this discussion was the idea that longer transit times resulted in higher inventory costs. This is because in-transit inventory carrying costs will be incurred by the firms having ownership of the goods while they are being transported. In effect, the carrying costs of inventory in transit will be similar to the carrying costs of inventory in the warehouse. There are differences between inventory in transit and inventory in the warehouse, but basically the company is responsible for inventory in both instances. There is always some cost attached to having inventory, whether it is sitting in a warehouse or plant or moving to another point. Therefore, if modes of transportation have different transit times and different rates (prices) with other variables being equal, the trade-off between transportation rates and the inventory cost associated with the transit times should be examined. The transportation rates are usually easy to obtain. However, to calculate the cost of carrying inventory in transit, it will be necessary to modify the basic or simple EOQ model.

transit times

Recall that the simple EOQ model essentially considered only the trade-off between order or setup costs and the carrying cost associated with holding inventory in a warehouse. To consider how different transit times affect transportation and its cost, the company must relax one basic assumption of the EOQ model and adapt the model accordingly.

F.O.B. assumption

One assumption of the simple EOQ model was that inventory incurred no cost in transit, because the company either purchased inventory on a delivered-price basis or sold it FOB plant. If conditions change so that the company makes purchases FOB origin or sells products on a delivered-price basis, then it will be necessary to consider the cost of carrying inventory in transit. Figure 7A–1 depicts a modified sawtooth inventory model; the lower half shows the inventory in transit.

part of cycle period

The Sawtooth Model Adjusted. Comparing the lower half of Figure 7A–1 with the upper half, which depicts inventory in the warehouse, we can see two differences relevant for calculating the appropriate costs. First, inventory is usually in transit for only part of the cycle. Typically, the number of inventory shipping days would be less than the number of days that inventory from the preceding EOQ replenishment would be in the warehouse. Second, inventory in transit is not used up or sold; warehouse inventory may be used up or sold.

cost development

Since inventory in transit has these two distinctive characteristics, the cost of carrying inventory in transit will differ from that of storing inventory in the ware-

FIGURE 7A–1 Sawtooth Model Modified for Inventory in Transit

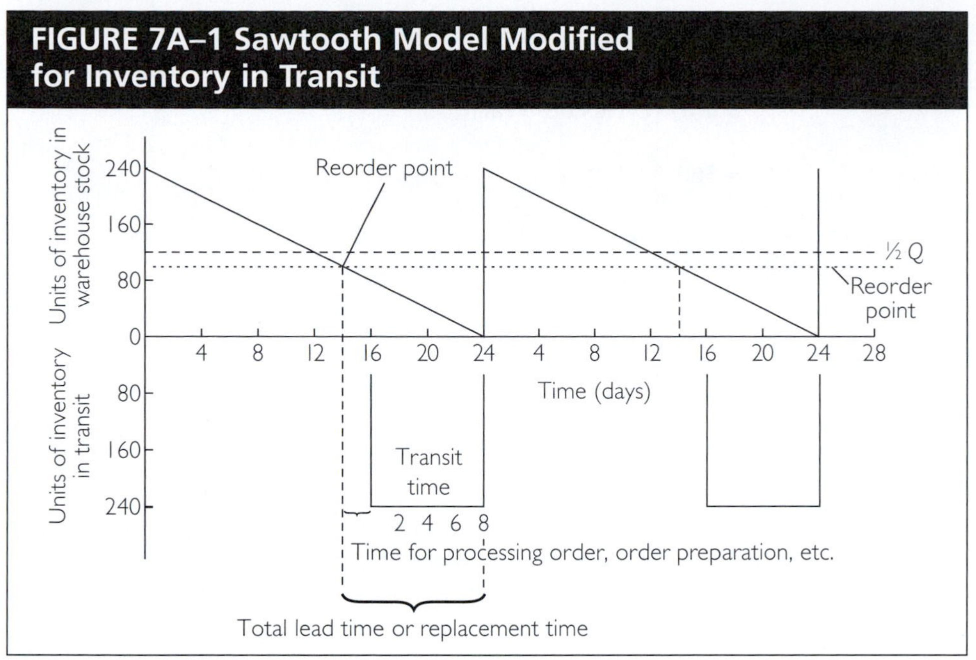

house. We can calculate this cost in several ways. If a daily inventory-in-transit carrying cost were available, we could multiply it by the number of days in transit. We could calculate this daily cost by multiplying the inventory-in-transit value by a daily opportunity cost. After multiplying this cost by the number of transit days, we could multiply it by the number of orders per year or cycles per year. This would give an annual cost of inventory in transit. In effect, this resembles the procedure we followed when calculating the cost of inventory in the warehouse.

Consider the following:

Y = cost of carrying inventory in transit

V = value/unit of inventory

t = order cycle time

t_m = inventory transit time

M = average number of units of inventory in transit

We calculate the value of M as follows:

$$\frac{t_m}{t} = \text{percentage of time inventory is in transit per cycle period}$$

Therefore,

$$M = \frac{t_m}{t} Q$$

We could rewrite this as follows:

$$t(\text{days in cycle}) = \frac{360 \text{ (days in year)}}{R/Q \text{ (cycles per year)}}$$

$$t = 360 \frac{Q}{R}$$

$$M = \frac{(t_m Q)}{360} \frac{R}{Q}$$

$$M = \frac{t_m}{360} R$$

The two approaches to calculating M give the same result, given the preceding assumptions. The second equation for M, however, is frequently more useful, since the variables are given in the problem.

Now that we have developed a way of calculating the average number of units in transit, all that remains is to multiply this figure by the value per unit and the percentage annual carrying cost of inventory in transit. The result will be a dollar cost for inventory in transit that compares to the dollar cost of inventory in the warehouse:

$$\frac{t_m}{t} QVY$$

We could write the new total inventory cost equation in either of the following forms:

$$\text{TAC} = \frac{1}{2} QVW + A \frac{R}{Q} + \frac{t_m}{t} QVY$$

or

$$\text{TAC} = \frac{1}{2} QVW + A \frac{R}{Q} + \frac{t_m}{360} RVY^*$$

Example of Modal Selection. We can measure the trade-off between transit times and transportation cost using the total cost formula developed in the preceding section. First review the information provided in the example in Chapter 6 to demonstrate the simple EOQ model:

R = 3,600 units (annual demand)

A = \$200 (cost of one order or setup)

W = 25% (cost of carrying inventory in warehouse)

V = \$100 (value per unit)

Q = 240 units (this would remain the same)

*Differentiating this equation and solving for Q with the expanded total cost formula results in the same equation as the previous one, since the last term added is not a function of Q; that is,

$$Q = \sqrt{\frac{2RA}{VW}}$$

Now consider that a hypothetical company is choosing between two transportation modes (rail or motor) and that the following information is available:

Rail: 8 days in transit time
$3 per hundred pounds
Motor: 6 days transit time
$4 per hundred pounds

Next assume that the company will ship the same mount, 240 units, regardless of mode. If each unit weighs 100 pounds, this represents 24,000 pounds, or 240 hundredweight (cwt). The cost of carrying inventory in transit (Y) is 10 percent. Given the preceding variables, we may examine the two alternatives using the formula developed previously.

The first step is to look at the product's total inventory cost if the company decides to ship by rail:

$$\begin{aligned}\text{Total inventory cost (rail)} &= \left(\frac{1}{2}\cdot 240\cdot \$100\cdot 25\%\right)+\left(\$200\cdot \frac{3,600}{240}\right)\\ &\quad+\left(\frac{8}{24}\cdot 240\cdot \$100\cdot 10\%\right)\\ &= \$3,000 + \$3,000 + \$800\\ &= \$6,800\end{aligned}$$

If we add the transportation cost to the inventory cost, the total cost would be

$$\begin{aligned}\text{Total cost (rail)} &= \$6,800+\left(\$3+240\cdot\frac{3,600}{240}\right)\\ &= \$6,800 + \$10,800\\ &= \$17,600\end{aligned}$$

The next step is to determine the total inventory cost if the company ships the items by motor:

$$\begin{aligned}\text{Total inventory cost (motor)} &= \left(\frac{1}{2}\cdot 240\cdot \$100\cdot 25\%\right)+\left(\$200\cdot \frac{3,600}{240}\right)\\ &\quad+\left(\frac{6}{24}\cdot 240\cdot \$100\cdot 10\%\right)\\ &= \$3,000 + \$3,000 + \$600\\ &= \$6,600\end{aligned}$$

Once again we should add the transportation cost to the inventory costs:

$$\begin{aligned}\text{Total cost (motor)} &= \$6,600+\left(\$4\cdot 240\cdot\frac{3,600}{240}\right)\\ &= \$6,600 + 14,400\\ &= \$21,000 \text{ by motor}\end{aligned}$$

trade-offs

Given these calculations, the rail alternative would be less costly and thus preferable. Before leaving this section, we should examine the trade-offs more closely. As you can see, the rail alternative has a higher inventory cost because of the slower transit time, but the transportation cost savings offset this. The net effect is an overall savings by rail.

Finally, we should note that the procedure suggested in this section is based on conditions of certainty. If transit times varied, we would need to establish probabilities and approach the solution in a more sophisticated manner.

Adjusting the Simple EOQ Model for Volume Transportation Rates

lower rate for larger volume

The basic EOQ model discussed previously did not consider the possible reductions in transportation rates per hundredweight associated with larger-volume shipments. For example, the hypothetical company in the previous illustration decided that 240 units was the appropriate quantity to order or produce. If we assume again that each unit weighed 100 pounds, this would imply a shipment of 24,000 pounds. If the rate on a shipment of 24,000 pounds (240 cwt) was $3 per hundred pounds (cwt) and the rate for a 40,000-pound shipment was $2 per cwt, knowing whether to ship 400 units (40,000 pounds) instead of the customary 240 units would be worthwhile.

total cost equation

Shippers transporting a specified minimum quantity (weight) or more commonly publish volume rates on carload (rail) and truckload (motor carrier)* quantities. Therefore, in inventory situations, the decision maker responsible for transporting goods should consider how the lower-volume rate affects total cost. In other words, in addition to considering storage (holding) cost and order or setup cost, the decision maker should consider how lower transportation costs affect total cost.

Cost Relationships. Sometimes the economic order quantity suggested by the basic model may be less than the quantity necessary for a volume rate. We can adjust the model to consider the following cost relationships associated with shipping a volume larger than the one determined by the basic EOQ approach.

- *Increased inventory carrying cost for inventory in the warehouse.* The larger quantity required for the volume rate means a larger average inventory ($1/2Q$) and consequently an increased inventory carrying cost.
- *Decreased order or setup costs.* The larger quantity will reduce the number of orders placed and the ordinary costs of order placement and/or order setup.
- *Decreased transportation costs.* The larger quantity will reduce the cost per hundredweight of transporting the goods, consequently lowering transportation costs.
- *Decreased in-transit inventory carrying cost.* Carload (CL) and truckload (TL) shipments usually have shorter transit times than less-than-carload (LCL) or less-than-truckload (LTL) shipments, and the faster time generally means a lower cost for inventory in transit.

Figure 7A-2 represents the cost relationships and considers possible transportation rate discounts (volume rates versus less-than-volume rates). The total cost function

---

*Motor carriers often publish different LTL rates and TL rates on quantities of 500, 2000, and 5000 pounds.

FIGURE 7A–2 EOQ Costs Considering Volume Transportation Rate

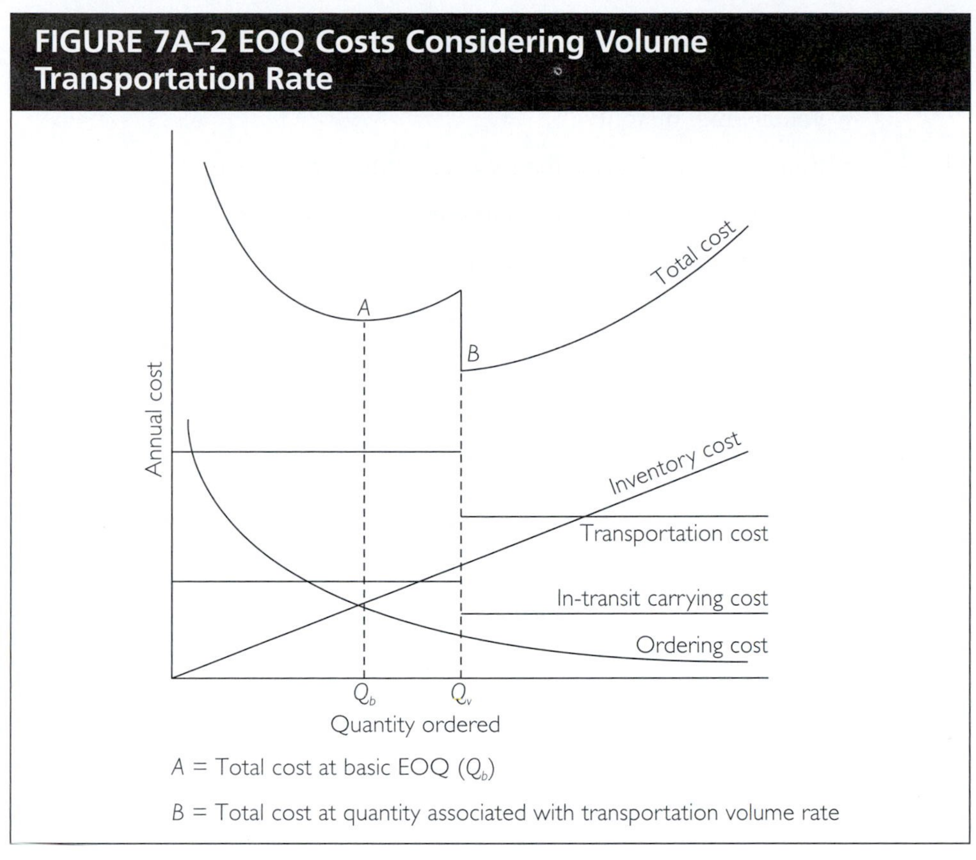

A = Total cost at basic EOQ (Q_b)

B = Total cost at quantity associated with transportation volume rate

sensitivity test

"breaks," or is discontinuous, at the quantity that permits a company to use the volume rate. Therefore, we cannot use the cost function for the transportation rate discount or discounts in the original EOQ formulation. Rather, we must use sensitivity analysis, or a sensitivity test, to determine whether total annual costs are lower if the company purchases a quantity larger than the basic EOQ amount. Note that although Figure 7A–2 indicates that using the volume rate will lower total cost, this does not necessarily have to be the case. For example, if the inventory dollar value was very high, then the increased storage (holding) costs could more than offset reductions in order and transport cost.

Mathematical Formulation

Although there are several ways to analyze opportunities for using volume transportation rates, a useful method is to calculate and compare the total annual costs of the EOQ-based approach with those of the volume-rate-based approach. The following symbols will be useful in this analysis:

TAC = inventory carrying cost + order cost + transportation cost + in-transit inventory carrying cost

TAC_b = total annual cost at basic EOQ

TAC_v = total annual cost at volume rate quantity

Q_b = basic EOQ

Q_v = volume rate quantity

t_m = time in transit for less-than-volume shipment

t_n = time in transit for volume shipment

H = less-than-volume rate (high rate)

L = volume rate (low rate)

We calculate each total annual cost as follows:

$$TAC_b = \frac{1}{2} Q_b VW + A \frac{R}{Q_b} + HQ_b \frac{R}{Q_b} + \frac{t_m}{t} Q_b VY$$

$$TAC_v = \frac{1}{2} Q_v VW + A \frac{R}{Q_v} + LQ_v \frac{R}{Q_v} + \frac{t_n}{t} Q_v VY$$

Noting that $HQ_b \frac{R}{Q_b}$ can be written simply as HR and that $LQ_b \frac{R}{Q_b}$ can be written simply as LR, we can reduce these equations to the following:

$$TAC_b = \frac{1}{2} Q_b VW + A \frac{R}{Q_b} + HR + \frac{t_m}{t} Q_b VY$$

$$TAC_v = \frac{1}{2} Q_v VW + A \frac{R}{Q_v} + LR + \frac{t_n}{t} Q_v VY$$

Transportation Rate Discount Example

An example that builds upon the previous problem will illustrate in this section how transportation rate discounts produce possible annual cost savings.

For this new example, assume the following variables:

H = \$3.00/cwt (assume each unit weighs 100 pounds)

L = \$2.00/cwt with a minimum of 40,000 pounds (with each unit weighing 100 pounds, this would be 400 units, or 400 cwt)

t_n = 6 days (time in transit for volume movement)

Y = 10% (carrying cost of inventory while in transit)

Q_v = 400 units

t_v = 40 days (length of a single inventory cycle for Q_v = 400 units)

From the previous problem, we know that

R = 3,600 units (3,600 cwt) (annual sales)

A = \$200 (cost of placing an order or cost of setup)

V = \$100/cwt/unit (value per unit)

W = 25%

Q_b = 240 units (240 cwt, or 240,000 pounds)

t_m = 8 days (time in transit for LTL movement)

t = 24 days (length of a single inventory cycle or period)

Solving for TAC_b and TAC_v:

$$\begin{aligned}\text{TAC}_b &= \left[\frac{1}{2} \cdot 240 \cdot \$100 \cdot 25\%\right] + \left[\$200 \cdot \frac{3,600}{240}\right] \\ &\quad + [\$3 \cdot \$3,600] + \left[\frac{8}{24} \cdot 240 \cdot \$100 \cdot 10\%\right] \\ &= \$17,600\end{aligned}$$

$$\begin{aligned}\text{TAC}_v &= \left[\frac{1}{2} \cdot 400 \cdot \$100 \cdot 25\%\right] + \left[\$200 \cdot \frac{3,600}{500}\right] \\ &\quad + [\$2 \cdot \$3,600] + \left[\frac{6}{40} \cdot 400 \cdot \$100 \cdot 10\%\right] \\ &= \$14,240\end{aligned}$$

Since TAC_b exceeds TAC_v by $3,360, the most economical solution is to purchase the larger quantity, 400 cwt. Reductions in ordering, transportation, and in-transit inventory carrying costs offset the increased cost of holding the larger quantity.

We may modify this analysis to consider potential volume discounts for purchasing in larger quantities. The same procedure of calculating and comparing total annual costs under the various alternatives applies, providing we make minor modifications to the equations.

Adjusting the Simple EOQ Model for Private Carriage

Many companies that use their own truck fleet or that lease trucks for private use assess a fixed charge per mile or per trip, no matter how much the company ships at any one time. In other words, since operating costs such as driver expense and fuel do not vary significantly with weight, and since fixed costs do not change with weight, many companies charge a flat amount per trip rather than differentiate on a weight basis. Therefore, since additional weight costs nothing extra, it is logical to ask what quantity the company should ship.

fixed cost per trip

The basic EOQ model can handle this analysis, since the fixed trip charge is comparable to the order cost or setup cost. Therefore, the decision maker must trade off the prospect of a smaller number of larger shipments against the increased cost of carrying larger average inventory amounts.

If T_c represents the trip charge, we can write the formula as follows:

$$\text{TAC} = \frac{1}{2}QVW + \frac{R}{Q}A + \frac{R}{Q}T_c$$

We can derive the basic model as

$$\text{EOQ} = \sqrt{\frac{2R(A + T_c)}{VW}}$$

From the previous example, we can add a charge of $100 per trip:

$$\text{EOQ} = \sqrt{\frac{2 \cdot \$3,600 \cdot (\$200 + \$100)}{\$100 \cdot 25\%}}$$
$$= \sqrt{\frac{\$2,160,000}{\$25}}$$
$$= \sqrt{86,400}$$
$$= 293.94$$

The EOQ size has been increased to 293.94 units because of additional fixed charges associated with private trucking costs.

Adjusting the Simple EOQ Model for the Establishment and Application of In-Excess Rates*

We can adjust the basic inventory analysis framework discussed in Chapter 6 to utilize an in-excess rate. Through in-excess rates, carriers encourage heavier shipper loadings. The carrier offers a lower rate for weight shipped in excess of a specified minimum weight. A logistics manager must decide whether the company should use the in-excess rate and, if so, the amount the company should include in each shipment.

Consider the following example: The CBL Railroad has just published a new in-excess rate on items that the XYZ Company ships quite often. CBL's present rate is $4/cwt with a 40,000-pound minimum (400 cwt). The in-excess rate just published is $3/cwt on shipment weight in excess of 40,000 pounds up to 80,000 pounds. The XYZ logistics manager presently ships in 400-cwt lots. The manager wants to know whether XYZ should use the in-excess rate, and, if so, what quantity the company should ship per shipment.

XYZ supplied the following data:

R = 3,200,000 pounds (32,000 cwt) (annual shipments)

V = $200 (value of item per cwt)

W = 25% of value (inventory carrying cost/unit value/year)

Each item weighs 100 pounds.

XYZ should use the in-excess rate as long as the annual transportation cost savings offset the added cost of holding a larger inventory associated with heavier shipments. That is, realizing the transportation cost savings of the in-excess rate will increase XYZ's inventory carrying cost. The optimum shipment size occurs when annual net savings are maximal, that is, when annual transport savings minus the annual added inventory carrying cost are the greatest.

In developing the savings and cost functions, we will use the following symbols:

S_r = savings per cwt between present rate and new in-excess rate

Q = optimum shipment quantity in cwt

Q_m = old minimum shipment quantity in cwt

*This section is adapted from James L. Heskett, Robert M. Ivie, and Nicholas A. Glaskowsky, *Business Logistics* (New York: Ronald Press, 1964), 516–20.

TABLE 7A–1 Annual Savings, Annual Cost, and Net Savings by Various Quantities Using Incentive Rates

Q	S_y	C_y	N_s
400	0	0	0
410	781	500	281
420	1,524	1,000	524
430	2,233	1,500	733
440	2,909	2,000	909
450	3,556	2,500	1,056
460	4,174	3,000	1,174
470	4,766	3,500	1,266
480	5,333	4,000	1,333
490	5,878	4,500	1,378
500	6,400	5,000	1,400
505	6,654	5,250	1,404
510	6,902	5,500	1,402
520	7,385	6,000	1,385
530	7,849	6,500	1,349
540	8,296	7,000	1,296
550	8,727	7,500	1,227
560	9,143	8,000	1,143
570	9,544	8,500	1,044
580	9,931	9,000	931
590	10,305	9,500	805
600	10,667	10,000	667
610	11,017	10,500	517
620	11,355	11,000	355

The annual net savings equals the annual transport savings minus the annual added inventory carrying cost, or $N_s = S_y - C_y$.

The annual transport savings equals the number of shipments per year times the savings per shipment, or

$$S_y = \frac{R}{Q} S_r(Q - Q_m)$$

where R/Q is the number of shipments per year, $Q - Q_m$ is the amount of shipment weight the company will ship at the lower in-excess rate, and $S_r(Q - Q_m)$ is the transportation savings per shipment. Rewriting the equation for S_r results in the following:

$$S_y = RS_r\left(1 - \frac{Q_m}{Q}\right)$$

The annual added inventory carrying cost, C_y, equals the added inventory carrying costs of the consignor (shipper or seller) and the consignee (receiver or buyer). The calculations must consider the consignee's added inventory, since the seller must pass these savings on as a price discount to encourage the buyer to purchase in larger quantities, or the seller will incur this cost if the shipment goes to the seller's warehouse or distribution center, for example.

FIGURE 7A–3 Net Savings Function for Incentive Rate

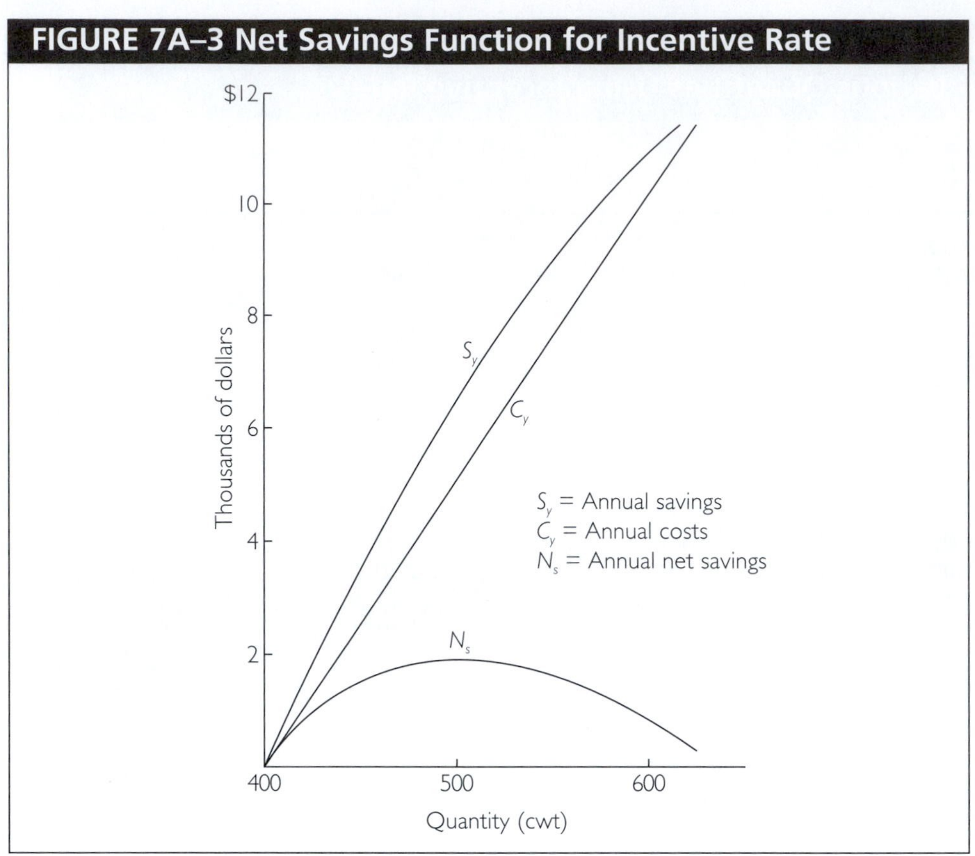

We calculate the added average inventory—the difference between the average inventories with the larger shipment quantity and the smaller (present) shipment quantity—as follows:

$$\text{Consignor's added inventory} = \frac{1}{2}Q - \frac{1}{2}Q_m$$

$$\text{Consignee's added inventory} = \frac{1}{2}Q - \frac{1}{2}Q_m$$

$$\text{Total added inventory} = 2\left(\frac{1}{2}Q - \frac{1}{2}Q_m\right) = Q - Q_m$$

$C_y = WV(Q - Q_m)$, where $V(Q - Q_m)$ equals the value of added inventory and W equals the inventory carrying cost per dollar value. Table 7A–1 and Figure 7A–3 show the savings and cost relationships developed here.

The function that maximizes annual net savings is

$$N_s = S_y - C_y = RS_r\left(1 - \frac{Q_m}{Q}\right) - WV(Q - Q_m)$$

Taking the first derivative, setting it equal to zero, and solving for Q results in the following:

$$\frac{d(N_s)}{dQ} = RS_r \frac{Q_m}{Q^2} - WV = 0$$

$$WV = \frac{RS_r Q_m}{Q^2}$$

$$Q^2 = \frac{RS_r Q_m}{WV}$$

$$Q = \sqrt{\frac{RS_r Q_m}{WV}}$$

Now, taking the data from the problem posed in this example, we find the solution as follows:

$$Q = \sqrt{\frac{(32,000)(\$1.00)(400)}{(0.25)(\$200)}} = \sqrt{256,000} = 506 \text{ cwt}$$

The conclusion is that the XYZ Company should use the in-excess rate and should ship 50,600 pounds in each shipment.

Summary

The four adjustments to the basic EOQ approach discussed in this appendix all relate to decisions important to the logistics manager—modal choice, volume rates, private trucking, and in-excess rates. We could include other adjustments, but these four should be sufficient in most cases. While all of the adjustments discussed here assume a condition of certainty, other adjustments may require modifying the model for conditions for uncertainty.

CHAPTER 8

WAREHOUSING DECISIONS

LEARNING OBJECTIVES

After reading this chapter, you should be able to do the following:

- Discuss the strategic value-adding role warehousing plays in the logistics system.
- Develop an analytical framework for basic warehousing decisions.
- Discuss the major principles of warehouse layout design.
- Compare the use of private versus public warehousing.
- Explain public warehousing services, regulations, and pricing.
- Describe the decision-making approach used to determine the number of warehouses in the logistics system.
- Discuss the different types of materials-handling equipment and the criteria used to select this equipment.
- Explain the cross-functional role of packaging in a company.
- Discuss the role of packaging in the logistics system.

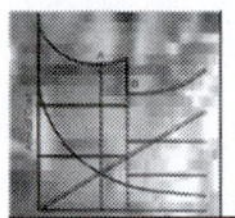

LOGISTICS PROFILE

Redesigning Distribution Centers

When William W. Grainger took his eight-page catalog (the original Grainger Red Book) to the streets of Chicago in 1927, the Web was a wide world away from creation. Grainger's goal was to give customers convenient and quick access to electric motors. And that is exactly what he did—and he did it well. After only six years, sales grew to $250,000. That growth, it seems, was due largely to Grainger's dedication to impeccable customer service.

The same dedication is still evident in W. W. Grainger of today. Although much bigger and seemingly more imposing, the organization still prides itself on excellent customer satisfaction. Some of those satisfied customers include Campbell Soup Co., Abbott Laboratories, Ford Motor Co., and the U.S. Postal Service. These are only a few of Grainger's 1.5 million active customers.

Grainger's product line now exceeds more than 220,000 SKUs. Its diverse lineup ranges from A-coils and Zip screws to electric motors. Customers can access these products via the company's Web site, Grainger.com, and at a network of local branches. Such a setup is designed to make accessibility simple for Grainger's customers.

Aside from the convenience of the Internet, Grainger has 373 branches located throughout the United States and Puerto Rico and 190 branches in Canada and Mexico. According to the company, 70 percent of all U.S. businesses are located within twenty minutes of a Grainger branch. These branches average 21,000 square feet and carry an average inventory of 15,000 products totaling $2 million. The proof of Grainger's seventy-year success is in its bottom line. In 1999, Grainger touted sales of $4.5 billion.

With a boatload of ingenuity and dedication to customer service, this distributor of maintenance, repair, and operating supplies and services has carved itself a huge niche in the on-line arena. But it has not done so without an effective network of warehouses that get products to its branches—and the customer—on time.

So, how does all this success come to pass? Via a streamlined and consistently evolving distribution process and approximately 13.6 million square feet of North American warehouse space. Currently, Grainger's distribution system is segmented into three levels: a national distribution center, regional and zone distribution centers, and local branches.

Located in Chicago, Grainger's national DC ships directly to customers and replenishes regional and zone DCs. According to Rick Adams, Grainger's vice president of logistics, the national DC is also used to house slow-moving products. Grainger's regional and zone DCs are responsible for replenishing Grainger's 373 branches. In addition to providing twenty-four-hour product replenishment, zone DCs also ship products directly to customers. Regional DCs are located in Greenville County, South Carolina, and Kansas City, Missouri. The zone DCs, which average 220,000 square feet, are located in Atlanta; Chicago; Cleveland; Cranbury, New Jersey; Dallas; and Los Angeles.

Grainger's zone DCs handle a total of 60,000 to 80,000 customer orders per day. Through this distribution network, Grainger is able to provide immediate pickup or same-day shipment or delivery for most products. "We are able to fill customer orders in minutes," notes Adams. "They are either shipped that day or the next."

Grainger Industrial Supply has also begun the rollout of Smart Linq, a computer program enhancement to its SAP system. Smart Linq helps Grainger branch personnel reduce shipping costs and excess inventory by identifying products to ship based on inventory quantity and distance.

In addition to its extensive line of new products, Grainger also provides more than 285,000 repair and replacement parts to its customers. From more than 550 suppliers, Grainger is able to ship in-stock parts 24 hours a day.

(continued on next page)

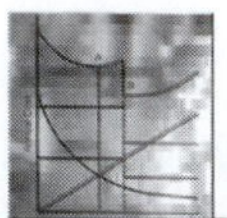

Logistics Profile

Redesigning Distribution Centers *continued*

Let's face it—the Internet is still a relatively new phenomenon. When it comes to conducting E-commerce, many organizations are stumbling around trying to determine how to handle day-to-day business generated by the Internet. Unfortunately, however, it is their supply chains that are often required to pick up the slack—and take the flack if something goes awry.

Grainger realizes these challenges and actually welcomes them. In fact, the company has uncovered myriad opportunities on the Internet and has invested approximately $6 million in the process. Most importantly, it has built a sound distribution network that has been able to support these new opportunities and demands.

Grainger first stepped into the Web in 1995 with Grainger.com, where customers have instant, 24-hour access to the company's 220,000 products, including real-time prices as well as local availability and shipping information. Although there is no minimum order requirement, the average order size on Grainger.com is almost twice the average order size of those in Grainger's physical stores. Why? Simply stated, customers can shop twenty-four hours a day, seven days a week; and, perhaps most importantly, they can spend as much time as they want shopping on the Web site.

Early in 2000, Grainger.com reached a milestone—a million dollar sales day. The company expects to do $300 million in sales on the Internet in 2000.

Source: Colleen Gourley, "Redefining Distribution," *Warehousing Management* (October 2000): 28–29. Reprinted with permission.

Introduction

Warehousing in the 2000s has a different focus than in the recent past. Traditionally, warehousing served the strategic role of long-term storage for raw materials and finished goods. Manufacturers produced for inventory and sold out of inventory stored in the warehouse. Warehouses had to support inventory levels of sixty to ninety days supply. Most facilities had a nominal activity level.

With the arrival of just-in-time, strategic alliances, and logistics supply chain philosophies in the 1990s, the warehouse has taken on a strategic role of attaining the logistics goals of shorter cycle times, lower inventories, lower costs, and better customer service. The warehouse of today is not a long-term storage facility; the activity level in the facility is fast paced. Attention is given to the speed with which a product moves through the facility. In many companies, the product is in the warehouse for just a few days or even a few hours.

To meet customer demands for shorter cycle times and lower prices, logistics managers are examining the warehouse process for productivity and cost improvements. Warehouses are being redesigned and automated to achieve order-processing and cost goals and are being relocated to achieve overall supply chain customer service goals.

As indicated in the opening Logistics Profile, W. W. Grainger's success is attributable to providing impeccable customer service to its 1.5 million active customers. Grainger provides this demanding customer service with a network of 382 warehouses totaling 13.6 million square feet of space. The network of 1 national, 2 regional, 6 zone, and 373 local warehouses receives stores, picks, and ships over 220,000 SKUs and fulfills orders on the same day received or the next day.

THE NATURE AND IMPORTANCE OF WAREHOUSING

We often define *warehousing* as the storage of goods. Broadly interpreted, this definition includes a wide spectrum of facilities and locations that provide warehousing, including the storage of iron ore in open fields; the storage of finished goods in the production facility; and the storage of raw materials, industrial goods, and finished goods while they are in transport. It also includes highly specialized storage facilities such as bean and grain elevators, tobacco warehouses, potato cellars, and refrigeration facilities. Every product manufactured, grown, or caught is warehoused at least once during its life cycle (from creation to consumption). Given this fact, we can easily understand why warehousing is of national economic importance. In 1999, warehousing cost amounted to $75 billion, or 0.81 percent of GDP. The total supply of U.S. warehousing space in 1999 was 6.1 billion square feet, an increase from 1990 of 700 million square feet of space.[1]

creating time utility

In a macro-economic sense, warehousing performs a very necessary function. It creates time utility for raw materials, industrial goods, and finished products. The proximity of market-oriented warehousing to the customer allows a firm to serve the customer with shorter lead times. More important, warehousing increases the utility of goods by broadening their time availability to prospective customers. In other words, by using warehouses, companies can make goods available *when* and *where* customers demand them. This warehousing function continues to be increasingly important as companies and industries use customer service as a dynamic, value-adding competitive tool.

THE ROLE OF THE WAREHOUSE IN THE LOGISTICS SYSTEM: A BASIC CONCEPTUAL RATIONALE

The warehouse is a point in the logistics system where a firm stores or holds raw materials, semifinished goods, or finished goods for varying periods of time. Holding goods in a warehouse stops or interrupts the flow of goods, adding cost to the product or products. Some firms have viewed warehousing cost very negatively; in short, they sought to avoid it if at all possible. This view is changing due to the realization that warehousing can add more value than cost to a product. Other firms, particularly distributors or wholesalers, went to the opposite extreme and warehoused as many items as possible. Neither end of the spectrum is usually correct. Firms should hold or store items only if possible trade-offs exist in other areas.

transportation consolidation

The warehouse serves several value-adding roles in a logistics system (see Table 8–1). As Figure 8–1 demonstrates, companies will sometimes face less-than-truckload (LTL) shipments of raw materials and finished goods. Shipping goods long distances at LTL rates is more costly than shipping at full truckload or carload rates. By moving the LTL amounts relatively short distances to or from a warehouse, warehousing can allow a firm to *consolidate* smaller shipments into a large shipment (a carload or truckload) with significant transportation savings. For the inbound logistics system, the warehouse would consolidate different suppliers' LTL shipments and ship a volume shipment (TL) to the firm's plant. For the outbound logistics system, the warehouse would receive a consolidated volume shipment from various plants and ship LTL shipments to different markets.

product mixing

A second warehousing function may be customer order *product mixing*. Companies frequently turn out a product line that contains thousands of "different" products,

TABLE 8–1 Warehouse Value-Adding Roles

Value-Adding Roles	Trade-Off Areas
Consolidation	Transportation
Product mixing	Order filling
Service	Lead times, stockouts
Contingency protection	Stockouts
Smooth operation	Production

FIGURE 8–1 Transportation Consolidation

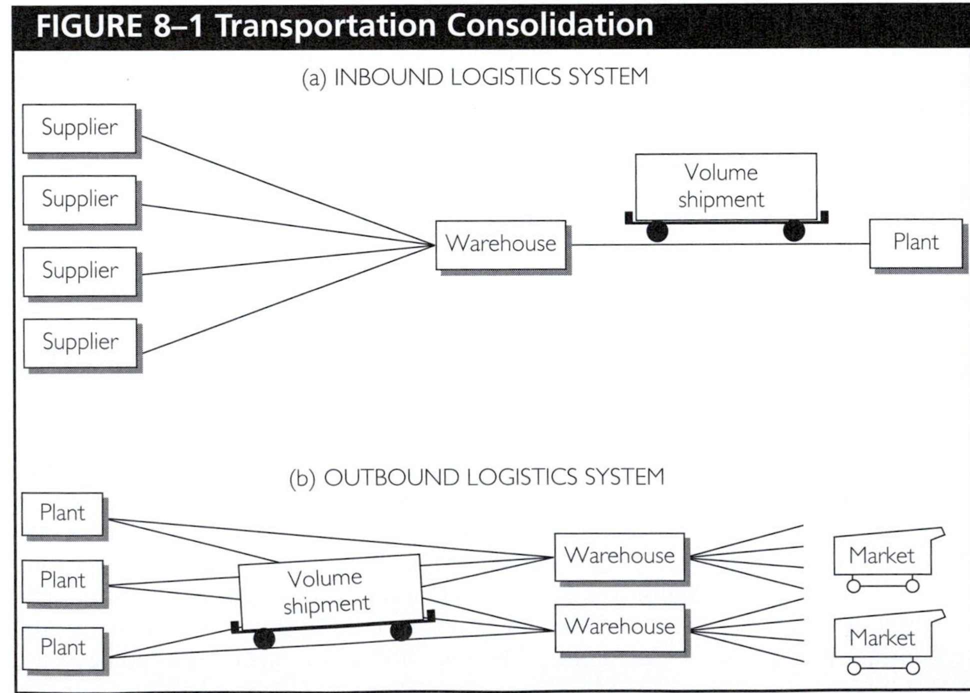

if we consider color, size, shape, and other variations. When placing orders, customers often want a product line mixture—for example, five dozen four-cup coffee pots, six dozen ten-cup coffee pots with blue trim and ten dozen with red trim, and three dozen blue salad bowl sets. Because companies often produce items at different plants, a company that did not warehouse goods would have to fill orders from several locations, causing differing arrival times and opportunity for mix-ups. Therefore, a product-mixing warehouse for a multiple-product line leads to efficient order filling (see Figure 8–2). By developing new mixing warehouses near dense urban areas, firms can make pickups and deliveries in smaller vehicles and schedule these activities at more optimum times to avoid congestion.

In addition to product mixing for customer orders, companies using raw materials or semifinished goods (e.g., auto manufacturers) commonly move carloads of items mixed from a physical supply warehouse to a plant (see Figure 8–2). This strategy not only reduces transportation costs from consolidation but also allows the company to avoid using the plant as a warehouse. This strategy will become

FIGURE 8–2 Supply and Product Mixing

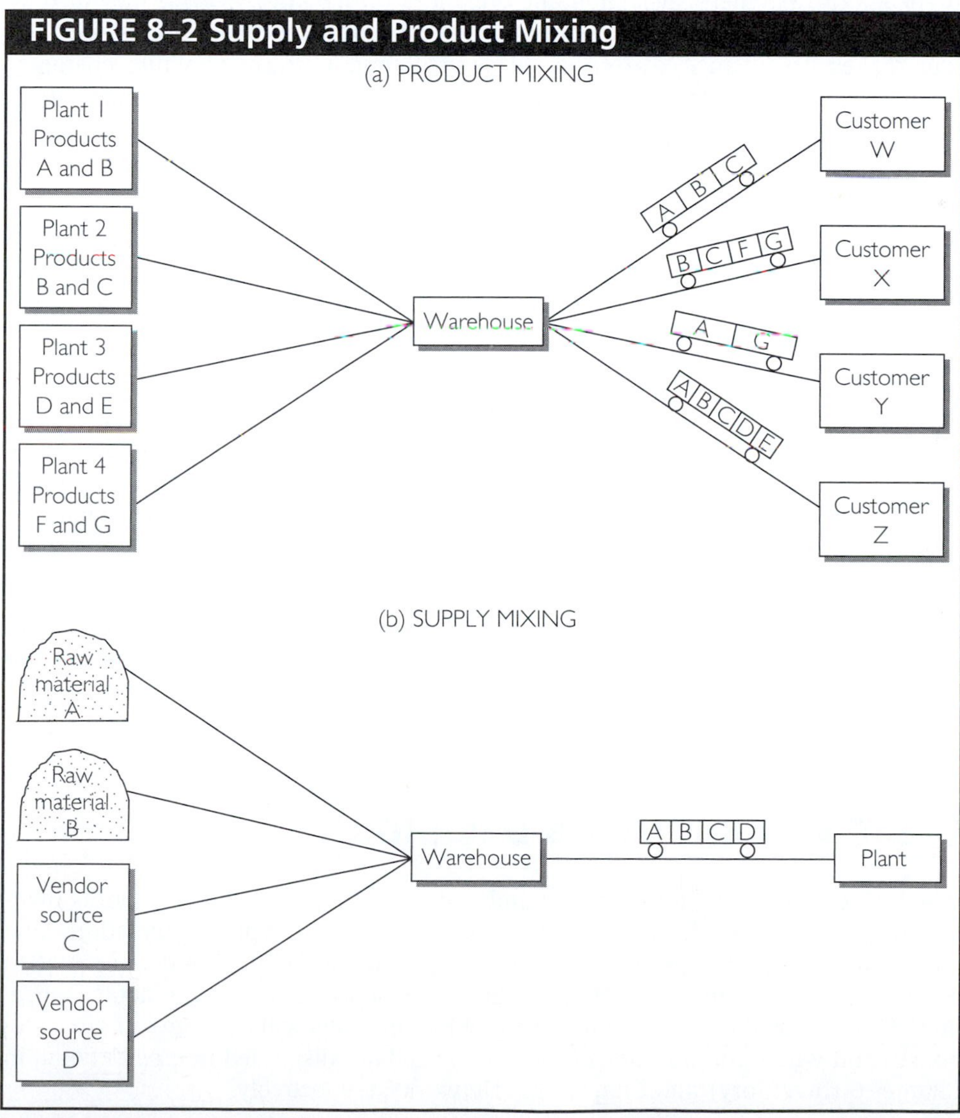

increasingly popular as increased fuel expenses raise transport costs and firms increase the use of sophisticated strategies such as materials requirements planning (MRP) or just-in-time (JIT) systems.

cross-docking *Cross-docking* is an operation that facilitates the product-mixing function. In a cross-docking operation, products from different suppliers arrive in truckload lots, but instead of being placed into storage for later picking, they are moved across the warehouse area to waiting trucks for movement to particular customers. The incoming materials are picked from the delivering truck or from temporary storage locations to fill a specific order and moved across the dock to a truck destined for the customer. The whole process is completed in a matter of hours. Excess product and small items are stored temporarily to await scheduled deliveries and to permit sorting of inbound loads of mixed products.

service A third warehouse function is to provide *service.* The importance of customer service is obvious. Having goods available in a warehouse when a customer places an order, particularly if the warehouse is in reasonable proximity to the customer, usually leads to customer satisfaction and enhances future sales. Service may also be a factor for physical supply warehouses. However, production schedules, which a firm makes in advance, are easier to service than customers: while customer demand is often uncertain, physical supply stockout costs sometimes seem infinite.

contingencies A fourth warehousing function is *protection against contingencies* such as transportation delays, vendor stockouts, or strikes. A potential trucker's strike will generally cause buyers to stock larger inventories than usual, for example. This particular function is very important for physical supply warehouses in that a delay in the delivery of raw materials can delay the production of finished goods. However, contingencies also occur with physical distribution warehouses—for example, goods damaged in transit can affect inventory levels and order filling.

smoothing A fifth warehousing function is to *smooth* operations or decouple successive stages in the manufacturing process. Seasonal demand and the need for a production run long enough to ensure reasonable cost and quality are examples of smoothing—that is, preventing operations under overtime conditions at low production levels. In effect, this balancing strategy allows a company to reduce its manufacturing capacity investment.

As we can see, warehousing functions can make important contributions to logistics systems and company operations. However, we must also view warehousing in a trade-off context; that is, warehousing's contribution to profit must be greater than its cost.

BASIC WAREHOUSING DECISIONS

Warehouse management involves a number of important decisions, including ownership, number, size, stocking, and location, that is, what type, organization, how many, what size, what products, and where (see Figure 8–3). The decisions as to warehouse ownership, number, and size are discussed in greater detail subsequently, whereas the questions relating to what products will be stored in the warehouses and where the warehouses will be located are discussed in greater detail in Chapter 6 (Inventory) and Chapter 14 (Network), respectively.

FIGURE 8–3 Basic Warehousing Decisions

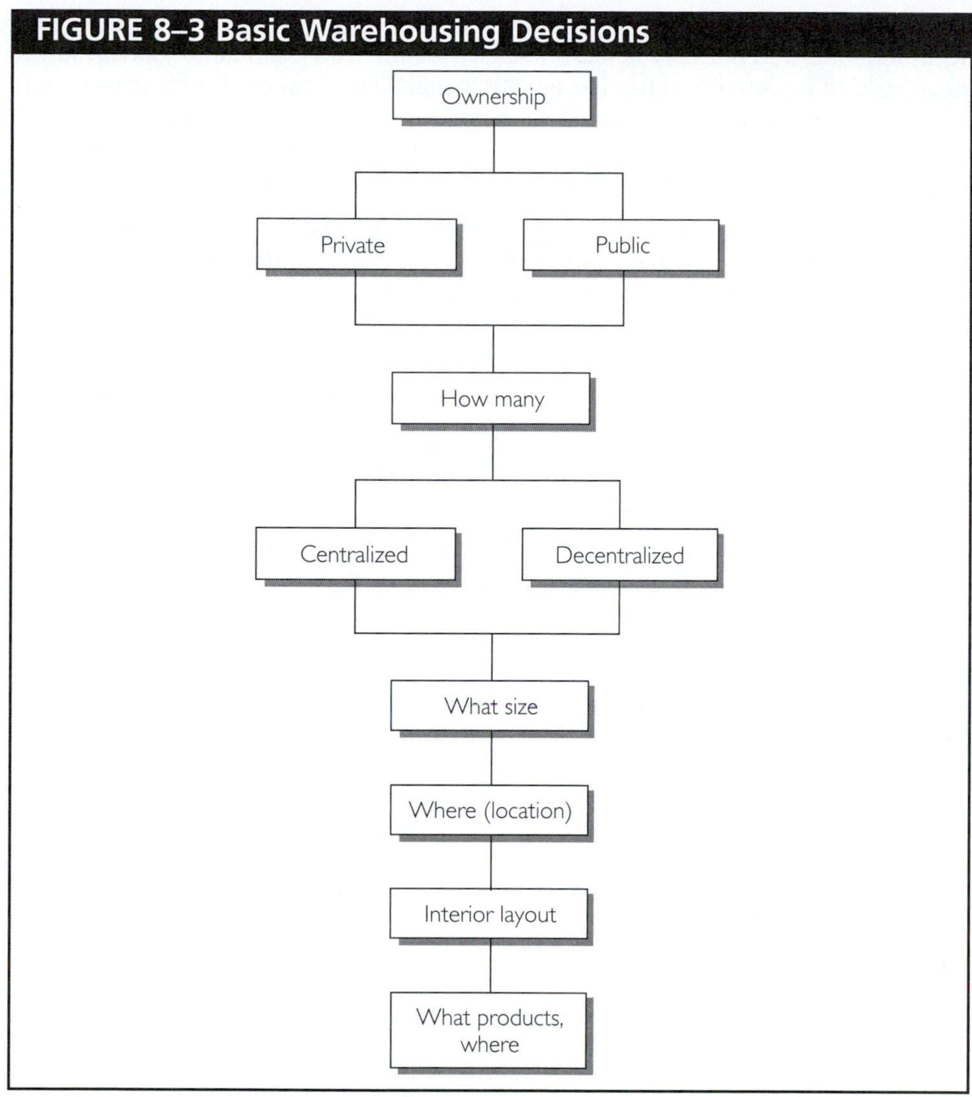

cost trade-off

These basic warehouse decisions are made in a trade-off framework. The total cost, including the service impact on lost sales, is the criterion used to make the decisions. For example, having many warehouses increases service provided to the consumer because the product is located closer to the customer. However, the trade-off is higher warehousing, inventory, and, possibly, transportation costs. The total cost will be the determining factor.

ownership

In arranging warehousing space, a company has two basic alternatives: private (or leased) ownership of facilities or use of public warehouses. The choice between the two is a major warehousing decision impacting both the company's balance sheet (facility investment) and income statement (warehousing cost). Many companies combine public and private warehousing because of varying regional market conditions and other factors, such as seasonality of demand or supply.

how many

Another important decision is whether to centralize or decentralize warehousing. This decision essentially concerns how many warehouses will be in the supply chain network. Small- and medium-size companies with a regional market area often will need only one warehouse, whereas large companies with national or global market areas need to examine the question in great detail. The number of warehouses must be examined in light of transportation alternatives, such as the use of airfreight with one or two warehouses instead of five or six warehouses. The high cost of airfreight is traded off against lower costs of inventory and warehousing.

location Along with the question of how many warehouses should be in the network is the question of where, or location. As with other warehouse decisions, a firm must examine location in a trade-off perspective. By analyzing the warehouse's intended function, general locations can be determined, such as high-service facilities near markets and raw materials mixing close to suppliers. The firm must achieve a desired level of customer service at the least possible logistics cost.

size If the company is using public warehousing, the question of what size facility is less important because the public warehousing firm can make more or less space available to meet the warehousing needs at different times. For firms using private warehousing, the size decision is more important because the private facility size, once designed and built, is fixed and cannot be modified without considerable expense.

layout In addition to the preceding basic warehousing decisions, a company using private warehousing is faced with the question of how to lay out the warehouse's interior. The company must make decisions regarding aisle space, shelving, material-handling equipment, and all the physical dimensions of the interior warehouse. When using a public warehouse, the public warehousing company makes the layout decision.

item stocking Finally, inventory decisions are required as to what products in what amounts will be stored in which warehouses. These item-stocking decisions are relevant only for firms with multiple warehouses. The firms must decide if all items will be carried at all warehouses, whether each facility will carry only specific items, or whether the warehouses will combine specialization and general stocking. As the Logistics Profile indicates, W. W. Grainger holds slow-moving items at only the national warehouse.

Warehousing decisions are important and require close attention. Improving efficiency and productivity is a major management focus in warehousing operations. Properly utilizing space through carefully planned inventory management and distribution operations will be more important in the future than building additional facilities. Moreover, warehouse decisions interact very closely with other areas of the logistics system. We explore some of these decisions in detail in this chapter.

The Ownership Decision

As stated earlier, one of the basic warehousing decisions is whether to use private or public warehousing. In other words, should the company purchase, build, or lease its own warehouse(s) or should it rent public warehouse space on an as-needed basis? Both approaches have advantages and disadvantages.

Figure 8–4 shows a general cost comparison between a public warehouse and a private warehouse. As we can see, the public warehouse is all variable cost. As the throughput volume in the warehouse increases, the company has to rent more

FIGURE 8–4 Cost Comparison between Private and Public Warehousing

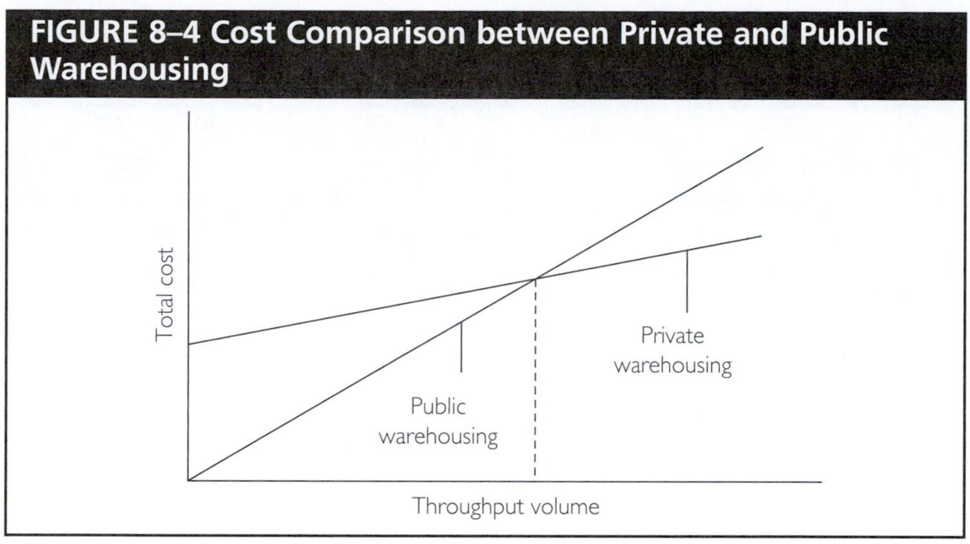

space. This space is available at a specific charge per square foot or per cubic foot. As the company uses more space in the public warehouse, the cost will rise proportionately; that is, the cost is linear in this instance. In reality, the public warehouse rates are discounted with larger usage, making the cost per square or cubic foot less than proportional.

fixed cost

The private warehouse, on the other hand, has a fixed cost element, which we can attribute to elements such as property taxes and depreciation in its cost structure. The variable portion of the warehouse operating cost would usually increase more slowly than the cost of the public warehouse because of the profit and the cost of marketing the public facility. Consequently, at some point, the two cost functions will meet, or be equal. Generally, at lower output volumes, the public warehouse is the best alternative. As volume increases, companies are able to use private facilities more efficiently; that is, they can spread the fixed costs over the large output volumes.

This is a somewhat simplistic view of the situation confronting many firms, particularly large multiple-product-line companies that may be involved with anywhere from 5 to 100 warehouses. However, for two reasons, such a simplistic perspective may be fairly realistic even for more complex situations. First, companies often add warehouses one at a time, and, because of different market and cost circumstances, the choice in each new instance could be between private and public. Second, even when a company is adding more than one warehouse, the locational circumstances are often quite different and require the company to analyze each warehouse in terms of the ownership question.

At this point, it is appropriate to investigate some characteristics of firms and their products that result in their using private or public warehousing. Table 8–2 summarizes these characteristics or factors.

throughput volume

Because of fixed costs, the private warehouse situation requires a relatively high throughput volume to make the warehouse economical. Since the fixed costs occur irrespective of use, the company must have a volume sufficient to "spread out" the fixed cost so that the private warehouse's average cost (fixed plus variable) is lower

TABLE 8–2 Firm Characteristics Affecting the Ownership Decision

Firm Characteristics	Private	Public
Throughput volume	High	Low
Demand variability	Stable	Fluctuating
Market density	High	Low
Special physical control	Yes	No
Customer service required	High	Low
Security requirements	High	Low
Multiple use needed	Yes	No

than the public facility's. This analysis implies two assumptions. One assumption, as Figure 8–4 indicates, is that the variable cost per unit (the slope of the function) for the private warehouse is less than the variable cost per unit for the public warehouse. Otherwise, the private warehouse would never be less expensive. The other assumption is that the usage rate or throughput is stable throughout most of the year. If this is not true, then the company will have problems with the size decision and will be unable to utilize its space efficiently.

stable demand

Stability of warehouse demand must be examined over multiple products. Many large firms and some smaller firms have multiple-product lines, and this helps to stabilize the warehouse throughput to build the volume necessary for an economical private warehouse. Examples would be companies like General Foods or General Mills. When coffee sales drop off in the summer, they sell more tea for iced-tea drinkers.

dense market area

Another factor conducive to private warehousing is a dense market area relatively close to the warehouse or numerous vendors relatively close to a physical supply warehouse. As a previous section indicated, rates for small shipments (LTL) are relatively high per mile. Therefore, paying the relatively high small-shipment rates quickly uses up the savings that usually accrue by shipping in bulk (TL) to a warehouse. Consequently, in low-population-density areas, firms often find using several public warehouses in different locales more economical than "putting together" enough volume for a private warehouse and having to serve a rather broad geographical area.

control

An additional reason that a private warehouse might benefit a firm more is for control purposes. This can encompass physical control for such things as security or refrigeration and service control for customers and plants. Certain raw materials and finished goods are highly susceptible to theft or to loss of value from damage or spoilage. Although public warehouses are usually reputable firms and must exercise care in storing goods, the chances of loss may be higher than with private warehouses. Even if the public warehousing company pays for losses, the loss of customer goodwill or production efficiencies may be too great. In some regions, public warehousing firms will not store particular products because of their hazardous nature or for some other reason. If a firm manufacturing such products decides that storage in that region is important, the only option is to use a private facility. Customer service competition is another control factor favoring private warehousing. Although this rationale can lead to too much private warehousing, it nevertheless has become an increasingly important justification for private warehousing. This is particularly true with more sophisticated information system software that coordinates inventory control and order processing.

multiple use

One final justification for private warehousing may be combining this facility's use with the firm's other regional needs. For example, sales representatives and customer service representatives can have offices in the same building, with a lower total cost than having offices in two local facilities. The firm would have to combine this consideration with other cost justifications.

Companies currently using or contemplating using private warehousing find that the preceding characteristics interact to justify their use of private warehousing. Because they have volume, stability, dense markets, and the need to exercise control, firms with multiple-product lines often find private warehousing particularly economical for physical distribution; and, because they usually have multiple plant operations, they also find private warehousing most economical for physical supply.

At this point, we might ask if public warehousing is ever economical. The answer is yes. In fact, if we reflect on the characteristics that make private warehousing economical, we can find many firms for whom public warehousing is most economical. A firm wishing to use public warehousing should know the various services such warehousing offers, as well as such things as regulation and pricing practices. Before covering these topics, the next two sections examine the importance of public warehousing.

Public Warehousing

The previous section mentioned the growth of private warehousing in conjunction with customer service competition. This does not mean that public warehousing has declined or even maintained the status quo. Instead, public warehousing has grown and prospered and has been a very dynamic and changing industry. In particular, public warehousing for general merchandise, which most companies would use most frequently, has grown rapidly.

A company with no large inventory accumulations or a very seasonal need for warehousing space could not utilize a private warehouse consistently and efficiently. A company shipping in small quantities for long distances (to dispersed customers or plants) would also usually find a public warehouse more economical, as would a firm entering a new market area where the sales level and stability are uncertain. Such conditions usually necessitate using a public warehouse until the firm effectively penetrates the market. If the market venture is successful and experience shows the necessary volume and stability, then the firm can institute private warehousing.

limited capital investment

The first and most significant reason for using public warehousing is financial; it requires no or limited capital investment by the company. When a company builds, it establishes a long-term financial commitment. Therefore, the firm incurs capital payback risks through continued profitable use or sale of the facility. For automated warehouses, the consideration of facility obsolescence becomes even more acute. By using public warehousing, companies can avoid the capital investment and financial risks of owning their own warehouses.

flexibility

A second advantage of public warehousing is flexibility. A firm can rent space for thirty-day periods, enabling the firm to react quickly to movements in demand or changes in the quality of transportation services. Exploring new markets requires location flexibility. Public warehousing enables a firm to immediately launch in, expand in, or pull out of new, untried markets without lingering distribution costs.

Public Warehousing Services. Public warehouse personnel can perform such tasks as testing, assembly, price marking, and lot number marking. In addition, they offer packaging, order picking, stretch wrapping, order fulfillment, and EDI or Internet transmissions. Contract warehousing, a public warehousing subgroup, provides these highly specialized services only to major or special accounts. Contract warehousing can offer a feasible alternative to private warehousing. Public warehousing can provide, at the right price, almost all of the services that are available in private warehousing.

In addition, a public warehouse or a public warehouse manager at a private facility can offer two traditional public warehousing services: a bonding service and field warehousing. In both instances, the public warehouse manager is responsible for goods, issues a receipt for them, and cannot release the goods unless the requester meets certain conditions.

bonded warehousing

In bonded warehousing, the user is usually interested in delaying the payment of taxes or tariffs, or even avoiding their payment altogether. Because taxes are relatively high on certain items such as cigarettes and liquor, the seller, who is liable for the taxes, may want to postpone paying them until the goods are immediately ready for sale. The same may be true of imported items that a seller needs to hold in inventory before sale. If a public warehouse holds the items in bonded custody, the seller does not have to pay the tax or duty until the warehouse releases the items.

field warehouse

A field warehouse situation occurs when a firm requests a receipt for goods stored in a public warehouse or under a public warehouse manager's supervision in a private warehouse. The firm usually plans to use the warehouse manager's receipt as collateral for a loan. The receipt is a negotiable instrument whereby title to the goods is transferable. This service is attractive to individuals or companies that have accumulated inventory and that need working capital. While most attractive to small- and medium-size companies, it is a potentially valuable service for all companies.

All in all, public warehousing today offers many valuable services, from the traditional storage function to complete inventory management and associated customer services. A dynamic dimension of the logistics industry, public warehousing offers the logistics manager many possible alternatives. An additional public warehousing area is legal control, which we consider in the next section.

Public Warehousing Regulation. In spite of public warehousing's for-hire or public nature, the government has exercised very little control over this industry's affairs. This is in sharp contrast to the transportation industry's for-hire segment, particularly the common carrier. There are probably a number of reasons for the difference in regulatory control, but the underlying cause is that the warehousing industry has never caused public clamor for regulation by discriminating against its users, as was the case in the nineteenth-century rail industry.

liability

Several regulatory acts have affected public warehousing. The most comprehensive and important was the *Uniform Warehouse Receipts Act of 1912*. This act did several things. First, it defined the warehouse manager's legal responsibility. The public warehouse operator is liable only for exercising *reasonable* care. So if the public warehouse manager refused to pay for damages he or she felt were basically beyond his or her control, the user would have the *burden of proof* to attempt to show that the warehouse manager was liable.

receipts

In addition to establishing the public warehouse manager's legal responsibility, the Uniform Warehouse Receipts Act defined the types of receipts that the public warehouse manager can issue for items stored. The act recognized two basic types of receipts—negotiable and nonnegotiable. If the receipt is negotiable, then the title to the goods the public warehouse manager holds is transferable. So, in effect, the "holder" of the receipt owns the goods; in other words, the holder can sign over the receipt like a check.

The act also set forth certain receipt information requirements. Required information included the warehouse location, the receipt's issuance date, the warehousing service rate, a description of the goods, signatures of the parties, and the instrument type. These requirements primarily protect the public warehousing user and anyone taking advantage of the receipt's negotiable aspects.

While public warehouse regulation and service is important, the logistics manager is also very much interested in public warehousing rates or charges, which is the topic of the next section.

Public Warehousing Rates. The public warehouse sells service in terms of a facility with fixed dimensions. The warehouse usually sells the service on a space basis per time period—for example, dollars per square foot per time period. Although the warehouse company in a sense has a less complicated pricing structure than a transportation company does, the logistics manager should understand the basic factors affecting rates, keeping in mind that rates are negotiable.

Value. As indicated previously, a public warehouse has a certain legally defined liability for goods stored. The risk increases with higher-valued goods, and rates generally reflect the higher risk of higher-valued goods.

Fragility. Warehouse rates must consider commodities' general susceptibility to damage because of the risk to the warehouse company. The logistics manager may reduce the risk of damage by using protective packaging and, consequently, reduce the warehouse rates. Once again, the trade-off is between the warehouse rate reduction and the increased packaging cost.

Damage to other goods. In a public warehouse setting, incompatible stored goods always run the risk of damaging each other. In a sense, this is a two-way risk. Your product may damage another, or your product may be particularly susceptible to damage from some other product. Chemicals and food are obvious examples, but other more subtle ones exist. For example, automobile tires may have an adverse effect on certain products, even causing color change in some instances. Using proper packaging may reduce the risk; but, once again, the logistics manager should view this in a trade-off context.

Volume and regularity. While the cost of using a public warehouse is generally variable, the warehouse company itself will experience fixed costs. Therefore, use volume and regularity will influence the rates, since the company can "spread" its fixed costs; that is, volume and regularity will help achieve efficiencies in terms of lower per-unit costs.

Weight density. Warehouses generally set rates in terms of space, usually square footage. However, warehouses sometimes base charges on weight density. In other words, like transportation carriers, warehouses assess charges on a hundredweight basis. Therefore, the warehouse manager has to assess higher charges for light and bulky items. Even users whose charges the warehouse does not assess in this fashion should be concerned about weight density because it affects their ability to use the space they rent efficiently. For example, lightweight assembled items use up a lot of space per unit of weight. Perhaps the seller could store the same number of items in a smaller space if the items were packaged unassembled.

Services. Public warehousing is a comprehensive and sophisticated industry today, willing and able to offer a variety of services beyond the general storage function. Such services have associated charges—and the more service, usually the higher the charge. However, having the public warehouse provide the services may be less costly, particularly in low-sales-density areas, than providing them privately.

As the preceding discussions show, logistics managers can influence the rates they pay for public warehouses. While these rate-influencing opportunities require analysis to prove their economic justification, the logistics manager should explore the options nevertheless.

Contract Warehousing

A growing public warehousing trend is the use of contract or third-party warehousing. Contract warehousing expenditures for 2000 were $20.4 billion and growing at a rate of 23 percent per year.[2] Contract warehousing is a customized version of public warehousing in which an external company provides a combination of logistics services that the firm itself has traditionally provided. The contract warehousing company specializes in providing efficient, economical, and accurate distribution services.

The logistics manager must differentiate contract warehousing from general public warehousing. Firms desiring "above average" quality and service should use contract warehousing. These warehouses are designed to adhere to higher standards and specialized handling needs for products such as pharmaceuticals, electronics, and high-value manufactured goods. On the other hand, firms desiring average product handling service levels should use public warehousing. In essence, contract warehousing is a partnership between the manufacturer and the warehousing firm. Because of these partnerships, contract warehousing companies service a smaller client base than traditional public warehousing companies do. The contract warehouse provides space, labor, and equipment tailored to handle a client's specific product needs.

customized services

The contract warehousing company makes a market basket of customized logistics services available to a limited number of warehouse users. Examples of these services include storage, break-bulk, consolidation, order assortment, spot stocking, in-transit mixing, inventory control, transportation arrangement, logistics information systems, and any additional logistics support services a user requires. Rather than providing only storage, the contract warehousing firm provides the logistics services package the user requires to support a firm's logistics channel.

Even though contract warehousing and distribution have grown substantially, the concept is still in its infancy in terms of overall understanding and use. In the past, companies needing to cut costs turned to the manufacturing operations. Companies contracted out component or subassembly production or outsourced overseas where labor costs were lower. Presently, companies are turning to logistics operations for potential cost reductions. By using contract warehousing services, a company can also outsource its logistics operations. By contracting out their secondary business functions, firms can concentrate on manufacturing and marketing.

Contract warehousing has many strategic, financial, and operational advantages over private or traditional public warehousing. The main advantages are cost reduction and focusing on core competencies such as manufacturing and marketing. These issues are discussed in Chapter 11.

The Number of Warehouses

One of the logistics manager's most important tasks is to decide how many warehouses to have in the system. As was the case when examining private versus public warehousing, evaluating the general cost trade-offs in such decisions would probably be best.

increasing the number of warehouses

Figure 8–5 depicts how increasing the number of warehouses in a logistics system affects important physical distribution costs. As the number of warehouses increases, transportation cost and the cost of lost sales decline, whereas inventory cost and warehousing cost increase.

Consolidating shipments into carload or truckload lots with lower rates per hundredweight decreases transportation costs. On the outbound side, increasing the number of warehouses brings the warehouses closer to the customer and market area, reducing both transportation distance and costs.

Warehousing costs increase because the total amount of space always increases with a larger number of warehouses. For example, a firm with only one warehouse that has 200,000 square feet would not be able to operate at the same sales level

FIGURE 8–5 Logistics Cost Related to Number of Warehouses

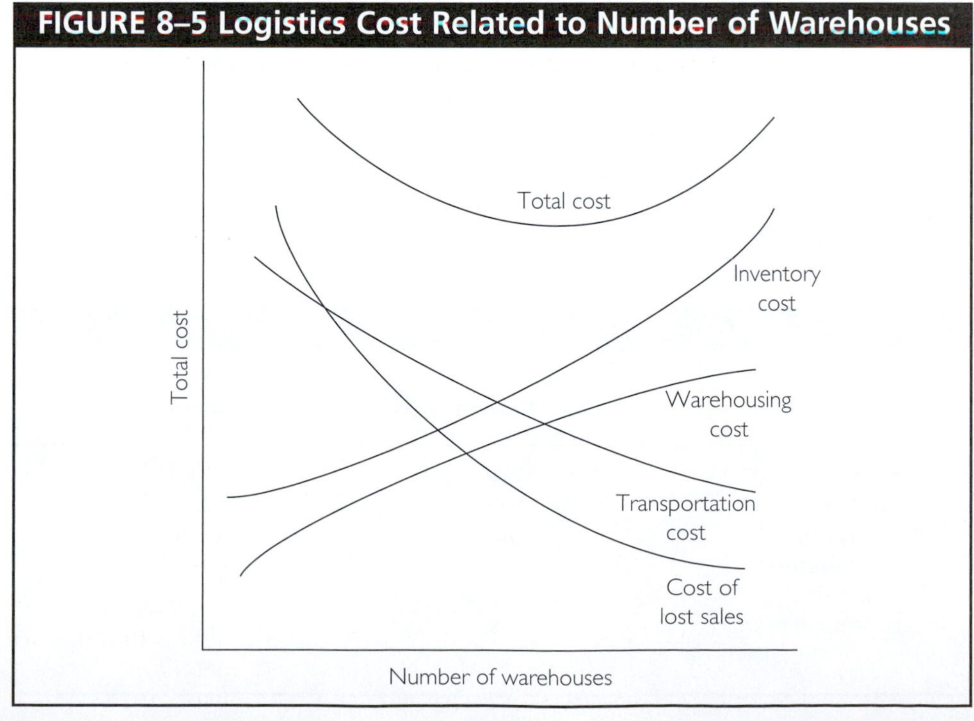

with two facilities having 100,000 square feet each. Maintenance, offices, lavatories, lunchrooms, and other facilities need a certain, almost fixed amount of space. Also, aisles use up a higher proportion of space in smaller warehouses.

In addition, since a company increasing its number of warehouses carries more total inventory, inventory cost increases. The larger amounts of inventory require more total space. More inventory is necessary because the difficulty of predicting demand may force a company with two or more warehouses to maintain overly high levels of a product line's slower-moving items at each facility. Moreover, as companies increase their number of warehouses, growing product lines will likely require more total space, even at the same sales volumes.

As Figure 8–5 indicates, as the number of warehouses increases, total cost will generally decline. However, total costs begin to rise as increasing inventory and warehousing costs offset decreasing transportation costs and the cost of lost sales. Of course, the total cost curve and the range of warehouses it reflects will be different for each company.

decreasing the number of warehouses

Companies often increase their number of warehouses to improve customer service, to reduce transportation costs, and to provide storage for increased product volumes. Surprisingly, decreasing a system's number of warehouses is becoming the preferred way to meet the same needs. Warehouse building and operating costs are great. In contrast, by reducing the number of warehouses, a company can eliminate those unproductive facilities that incur wasteful costs. Combining the utilization of fewer warehouses with a reliable transportation system can improve customer service and lower transportation costs through consolidation opportunities. With fewer warehouses and greater volumes of products to move, a company must increase throughput rates or inventory turns. By increasing its number of inventory turns, a company will lower its inventory carrying costs.

As noted in an earlier section, the question of the number of warehouses in the network can be viewed as a centralized versus a decentralized system. With a centralized warehouse system, the company has fewer facilities; and, conversely, it has more facilities with a decentralized system. Table 8–3 provides a summary of the factors affecting warehouse centralization or decentralization, the number of facilities in the network.

decentralize

If product substitutability is high (i.e., there are many substitutes available), a decentralized warehouse system is indicated so as to reduce lost sales resulting from stockout or long lead times. The need for high customer service in local mar-

TABLE 8–3 Factors Affecting the Number of Warehouses

Factor	Centralized	Decentralized
Substitutability	Low	High
Product value	High	Low
Purchase size	Large	Small
Special warehousing	Yes	No
Product line	Diverse	Limited
Customer service	Low	High

ket areas usually correlates with high product substitutability. Another customer service factor suggesting decentralization is inadequate transportation service resulting in longer lead times; if inadequate transportation service is available, more warehouses will be added to the network to reduce customer lead time.

W. W. Grainger, a national distributor of maintenance, repair, and operating supplies, utilizes a system of 373 local warehouses to provide the required customer service levels (see Logistics Profile). The products have many substitutes, and there are many competing suppliers/distributors. To ensure meeting the logistics requirements of its customers, Grainger has placed local warehouses within 20 minutes of 70 percent of all U.S. businesses.

Another factor favoring decentralized warehousing is small-quantity purchases. The cost of shipping many LTL shipments from a centralized warehouse to customers would be much higher than that of shipping TL shipments to the decentralized warehouses and then shipping LTL shipments to customers in the local market. Retailers and wholesalers, increasingly conscious of inventory costs, tend to buy in smaller quantities and more frequently. To maintain acceptable lead times and to control freight costs, many sellers add warehouses to store the goods closer to the buyers who purchase in small quantities.

centralize

If the value of the products stored is high, this suggests the use of centralized warehousing. By reducing the number of warehouses used, a firm will reduce the inventory level, which, for high valued goods, results in a greater inventory carrying cost reduction. Similarly, a firm with a very diverse product line (i.e., a large number of items) will find that centralized warehousing will reduce overall inventory levels and inventory carrying cost. Lastly, special warehousing requirements, such as controlled temperature and humidity, suggest the use of fewer warehouses to reduce investment in facilities and equipment.

The preceding discussion provides a general overview of the cost impact of the factors affecting the number of warehouses, but it does not lead to an optimal solution. For example, suppose the company has a very diverse product line that is highly substitutable product, is high in value, is purchased in small quantities, requires specialized warehousing, and has high customer service requirements. Three of the factors indicate centralized warehousing, and three indicate decentralized warehousing. To determine the optimum number of warehouses in the network, the logistics manager must conduct a total cost analysis for different numbers of warehouses in the network.

Basic Warehouse Operations

movement

The basic warehouse operations are movement and storage. Storage is probably the most obvious warehouse operation, whereas movement may seem incongruous. However, short-distance movement is a very vital aspect of warehousing. The movement function characterizes a distribution and cross-docking warehouse for finished goods. Goods brought to cross-docking or distribution warehouses *move* through the warehouse rapidly; that is, there is rapid inventory turnover. The reasons for rapid finished goods stock turnover is the high cost of holding finished goods inventory; the need for more sophisticated storage facilities; and the greater risk of loss, damage, or obsolescence. So, moving goods quietly and efficiently through a distribution or cross-docking warehouse is almost mandatory.

As shown in Figure 8–6, product movement occurs at four operations: (1) receiving—receiving goods into the warehouse from the transport network; (2) put-away—transferring goods into a particular location in the warehouse; (3) order picking—selecting particular combinations of goods for customer orders or raw materials for production; and (4) shipping—loading goods for shipping to the customer or to the production line. All four involve short-distance movement.

receiving

At the *receiving* operation, the inbound carrier is scheduled to deliver the goods at a specific time so as to improve warehouse labor productivity and unloading efficiency. The goods are physically moved from the transport vehicle to the receiving dock. Once on the dock, the goods are inspected for damage; any damage is noted on the carrier's delivery receipt, and the receipt is signed. Prior to putting the goods into storage, the items are checked against the purchase order (P/O) to verify that the items received were the same as those ordered.

FIGURE 8–6 Basic Warehouse Operations

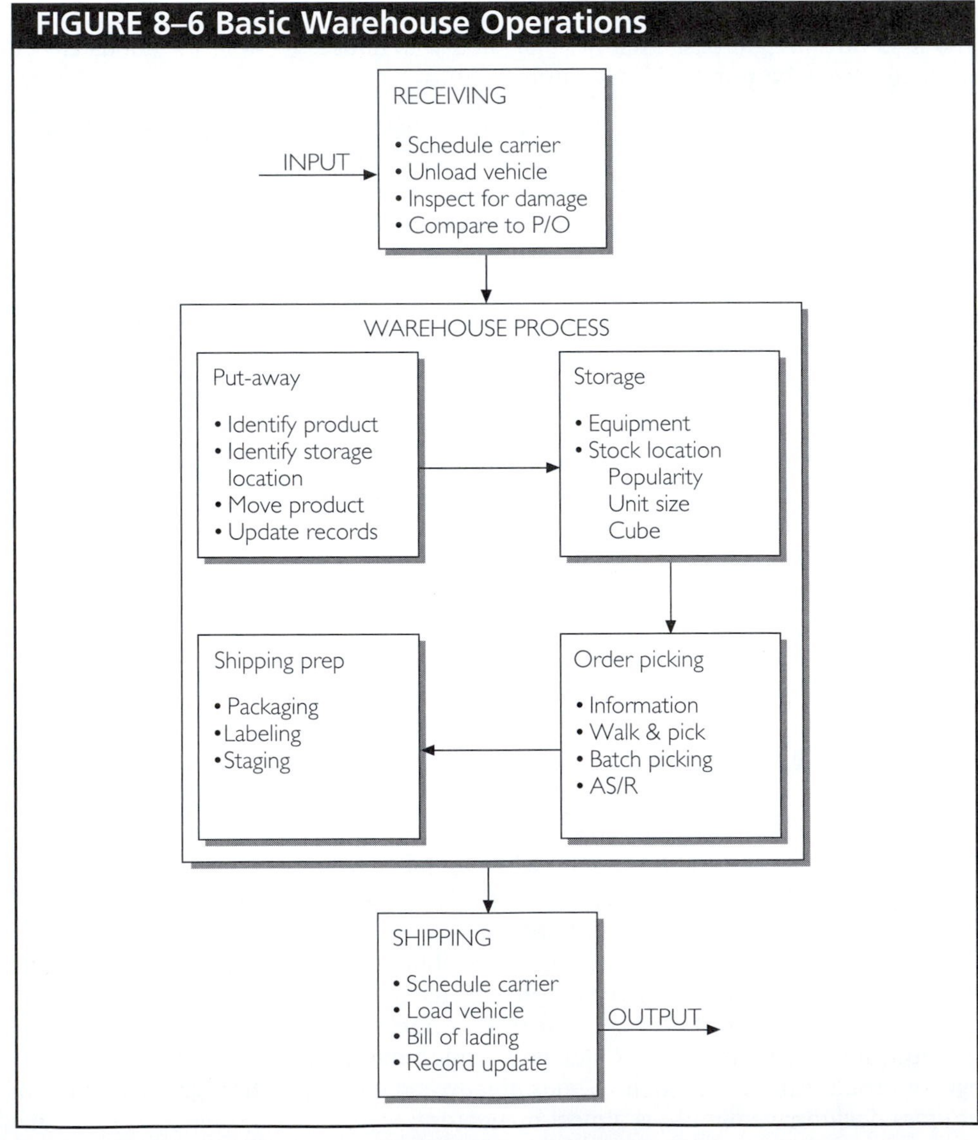

put-away

The *put-away* operation physically moves the items from the receiving dock to the storage area of the warehouse. This process involves identifying the product, typically scanning the product's bar code, identifying a location for the item, and moving the product to the proper location. Finally, the warehouse inventory records are updated to reflect receipt of the item and its location in the warehouse.

order-picking

The *order-picking* process requires warehouse personnel to select from the storage area the items ordered by the customer or manufacturing operation. The order information is given to the warehouse personnel on a *pick slip*. In some operations, the items on the pick slip are arranged so as to maximize the order-picking efficiency by minimizing the distance the order picker walks from item to item to shipment preparation area. In the batch-picking process, the total number of units of a given product on all orders are picked at one time and sent to the shipment preparation area. The *AS/R* process is an automated storage and retrieval materials-handling system that will do the picking process (for example, the picking of ice cream from a frozen foods warehouse).

When the order arrives at the shipping preparation area, the items are placed in an exterior (shipping) package or placed on a pallet. When a pallet is used, the items are secured onto the pallet by means of strapping or plastic wrap (shrink or stretch). Then, a shipping label indicating the ship-to person/firm and address is attached to the package. Finally, the complete customer order is staged (placed on the floor or in storage racks) for loading into the transport vehicle.

shipping

The final movement process occurs at the *shipping* operation. After the outbound carrier arrives at the loading dock, the goods are moved from the staging area to the loading dock and into the carrier's vehicle. The carrier indicating receipt of the goods from the shipper signs a bill of lading. Lastly, the warehouse information system is updated to reflect removal of the item from the warehouse inventory and shipment of the goods to the customer.

storage

The other major warehouse operation is storage. In cross-docking warehouses, the storage function is very temporary or short term. In fact, many items will "turn" in twenty-four hours or less. Long-term storage (over ninety days) is often associated with raw materials or semifinished goods, because they have a lower value, involve less risk, require less-sophisticated storage facilities, and may involve quantity purchase discounts. Finished goods may be held for long-term storage because of erratic demand, seasonal demand (Christmas items), or final processing (aging of wine).

The storage operation utilizes various types of materials-handling equipment, such as forklift trucks, conveyors, and racks to move and hold the goods. Since materials handling is discussed in more detail in a subsequent section of this chapter, we focus our attention here on the location of stock in the storage area.

stock location

Figure 8–6 indicates the three stock location criteria commonly used to locate stock: popularity, unit size, and cube. The *popularity* criterion locates popular items (most units ordered in a given time period) near the shipping area and the unpopular items (fewer units ordered) away from the shipping. By this method, the order pickers travel a shorter distance to pick the most popular items being ordered, thereby reducing the time required to pick orders.

The *unit size* criterion suggests that small-size items (item cubic dimensions) be located near the shipping area and larger-size items be placed farther away from the shipping area. By locating smaller-size items near the shipping area, more items can be stored near the shipping area, which reduces the order picker travel distance and order-picking time. The *cube* criterion is a variation of unit size in that the items

FIGURE 8–7 The Computerized Warehouse

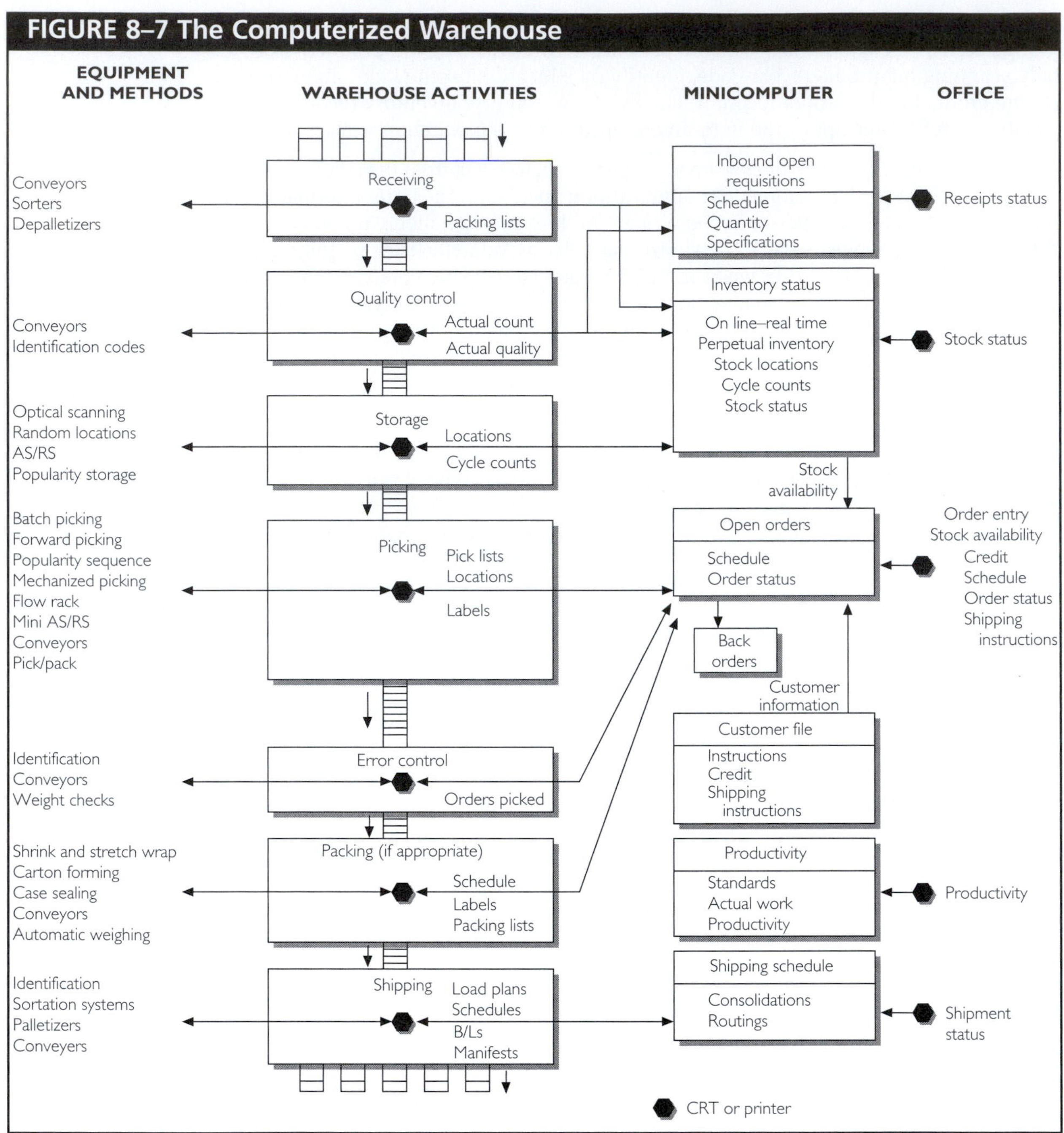

with smaller total cubic space requirements (item cube times number of items held) are located near the shipping area. The logic is the same as that used for unit size.

WMS Many companies are implementing *warehouse management systems* (WMS) that assist the warehouse manager in controlling the various warehouse operations. These computer software systems assist in the accurate management of the receiving, put-away, picking, packing, shipping, storage location, work planning, warehouse layout, and analysis activities. The typical WMS begins at the receiving dock where the item bar code is scanned into the system (see Figure 8–7). From this point, the WMS ver-

On The Line

Homemade Warehousing

It's rare these days that you hear of successful warehouses that do business "the old-fashioned way," sans all the high-tech gadgetry available today. Yet, that's exactly the type of warehouse Sue Kriegel, distribution center manager at Starlight International, oversees. And she does it while maintaining a 99.98 percent inventory accuracy rate.

"We have no WMS, no pick-to-light, no RF (radio frequency)—none of the really high-tech tools you see in many warehouses today," she says of the Monterey, California–based company. "We have a homemade location system and use bar coding for receiving and shipping."

So what's Kriegel's secret? "When we receive something, we check and double-check it," she says. "Nothing goes into the operating system without being pick-ready."

In addition, on the outbound side, every item is scanned as it is compiled into an order. No shipping label is printed until the order is filled to completion. And, Kriegel has implemented a daily cycle count process to help maintain that high inventory accuracy level.

The formula works for this young business. Starlight was founded six years ago by a former Hollywood producer as a direct-to-consumer business offering a variety of weight-loss and nutritional products. Currently, the company offers 250 SKUs, and the number is growing.

You might think that with so little technology, Starlight's operations would require a big staff. Not so: at its busiest times, Starlight's staff consists of twenty-six people. Just three of those staff members make up the receiving department, and the staff turns out three full truckloads plus several LTL shipments per week.

Starlight ships to a network of 70,000 independent distributors who sell directly to customers and/or sign on additional distributors to work underneath them. The DC prepares shipments for these distributors or their customers, depending on the distributor's preference. Because of this style of doing business, Kriegel says the company's reputation means everything. "We're in partnership with our distributors so that they can do business," she says. "We have to make sure we ship the right thing in pristine condition. It's our reputation to the distributors that counts."

To ensure those distributors are happy, Kriegel sees to it that 75 percent to 80 percent of shipments go out the same day orders are placed. The DC can ship up to 8,000 orders per week, and figures that of every 8,000 orders, there are generally about six mistakes. "We have a saying here," she says, "We do things with 'Starlight style,' which means that everything is done just right, at a five-star level."

Kriegel keeps her staff motivated to maintain that style by leading by example. "I'm a working manager," she says. "I'm out there with them all the time. I also ask for the staff's input and discuss changes with them. Nothing is written in stone here—I'm very flexible."

Kriegel also credits her success in management with the fact that she started on the DC floor and worked her way up. "I've walked in my staff's shoes," she says. "I know where they're coming from."

Source: "Homemade Warehousing," *Warehousing Management* (January/February 2000): 27. Reprinted with permission.

ifies the item against the purchase order, adds the item to inventory, determines the stock location in the warehouse, keeps track of the item's location following subsequent moves in the warehouse, determines the item-picking arrangement on the pick slip, and determines and keeps track of the staging location of the completed orders. More advanced WMS software will enable integration with materials-handling equipment, picking systems, and sorting systems (e.g., notifying forklift operators, via radio frequency devices, where items are located or providing order and item location information to automated picking systems). As the Supply Chain Technology article indicates, Hasbro has realized significant benefits with the use of radio frequency technology in conjunction with WMS.

The benefits of WMS are significant. Improved warehouse productivity, efficiency, and accuracy are the obvious benefits. By keeping track of item locations in the warehouse, the WMS reduces wasted efforts associated with warehouse personnel "hunting" for an item. This improves labor's productivity, reduces the number of personnel required, and improves the order-picking accuracy. In addition, WMS technology provides improved managerial control and effectiveness through point-of-work confirmation, accountability, performance measurement, and what-if scenario planning.

WAREHOUSE LAYOUT AND DESIGN

To understand warehouse layout and design, some background information on a typical warehouse's basic space requirements is necessary (see Figure 8–8). This discussion of space requirements relates quite closely to the discussion of basic warehouse operations. Before looking specifically at the types of space a firm needs, we comment briefly about determining how much space a firm requires.

The first step in determining warehouse space requirements is to develop a demand forecast for a company's products. This means preparing an estimate in units for a relevant sales period (usually thirty days) by product category. Then the company will need to determine each item's order quantity, usually including some allowance for safety stock. The next step is to convert the units into cubic footage requirements, which may need to include pallets and which usually include an allowance of 10 to 15 percent for growth over the relevant period. At this point, the company has an estimate of basic storage space requirements. To this the company must add space needs for aisles and other needs such as lavatories and meeting rooms. Warehouses commonly devote one-third of their total space to nonstorage

FIGURE 8–8 Warehouse Space Requirements

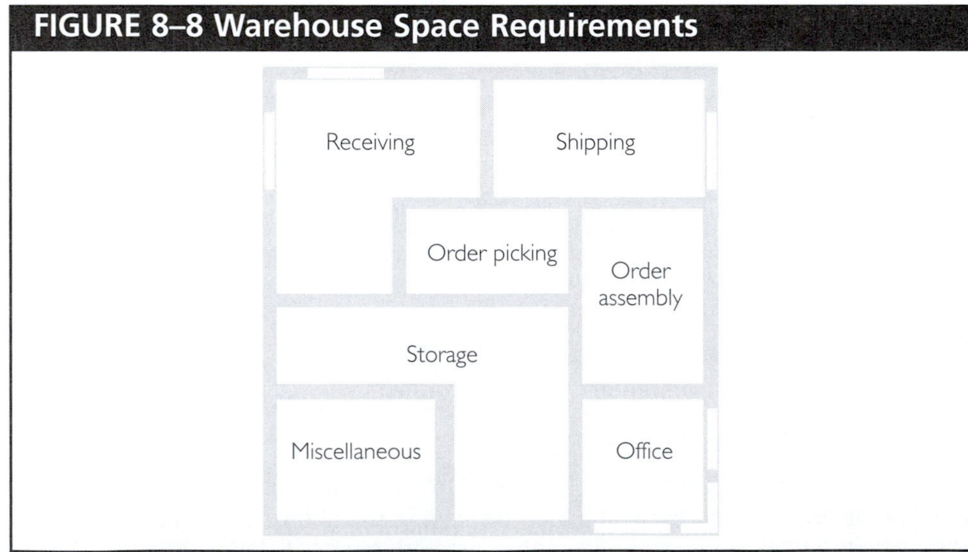

functions. Many companies make these space decisions through computer simulation. The computer can consider a vast number of variables and can help predict future requirements; good software packages are available.

transportation interface

One additional warehouse space requirement provides an interface with the transportation part of the logistics system—*receiving and shipping.* While this can be one area, efficiency usually requires two separate areas. In considering these space needs, a firm must choose whether to use the dock area outside the building or to unload goods out of the vehicle directly into the warehouse. The firm has to allow for turnaround space and possibly for equipment and pallet storage. Also important are areas for staging goods before transportation and for unitizing consolidated shipments. In addition, this area may need space for checking, counting, and inspecting. The volume and frequency of the throughput are critical in determining receiving and shipping space needs.

order-picking space

Another space requirement in physical distribution warehouses is for *order picking* and *assembly.* The amount of space these functions need depends upon order volume and the product's nature, along with the materials-handling equipment. This area's layout is critical to efficient operations and customer service.

storage space

A third type of space is the actual *storage* space. In a warehouse, a firm must use the full volume of the cubic storage space as efficiently as possible. A firm can derive the amount of storage space from the analysis described earlier in this section, and it will be the largest single area in the warehouse. As with the order-picking area, a firm has to consider storage area layout in detail. We cover this topic in a subsequent section.

office, recouping, miscellaneous space

Finally, a firm must consider three additional types of space. First, many physical distribution warehouses have space for *recouping*—that is, an area to salvage undamaged parts of damaged cartons. Second, administrative and clerical staff generally require *office* space. Finally, rest rooms, an employee cafeteria, utilities, and locker rooms require *miscellaneous* space. The amount of space these last three categories require depends upon a number of variables. For example, the average amount of damaged merchandise and the feasibility of repacking undamaged merchandise determine recouping space needs. The space requirement for a cafeteria and locker rooms depends on the number of employees.

Layout and Design Principles

While the discussion thus far has delineated a typical warehouse's various space needs, we need to consider layout in more detail. We first consider some general layout design principles (see Figure 8–9) and then examine layout in the context of the space categories discussed previously.

The most commonly accepted warehouse design and layout principles are as follows: First, use a one-story facility wherever possible, since it usually provides more usable space per investment dollar and usually is less expensive to construct. Second, use straight-line or direct flow of goods into and out of the warehouse, as Figure 8–10 illustrates, to avoid backtracking and inefficiency.

A third principle is to use efficient materials-handling equipment and operations. The next section explores materials-handling fundamentals. Among other benefits, materials-handling equipment improves efficiency in operations.

FIGURE 8–9 Principles of Warehouse Layout Design

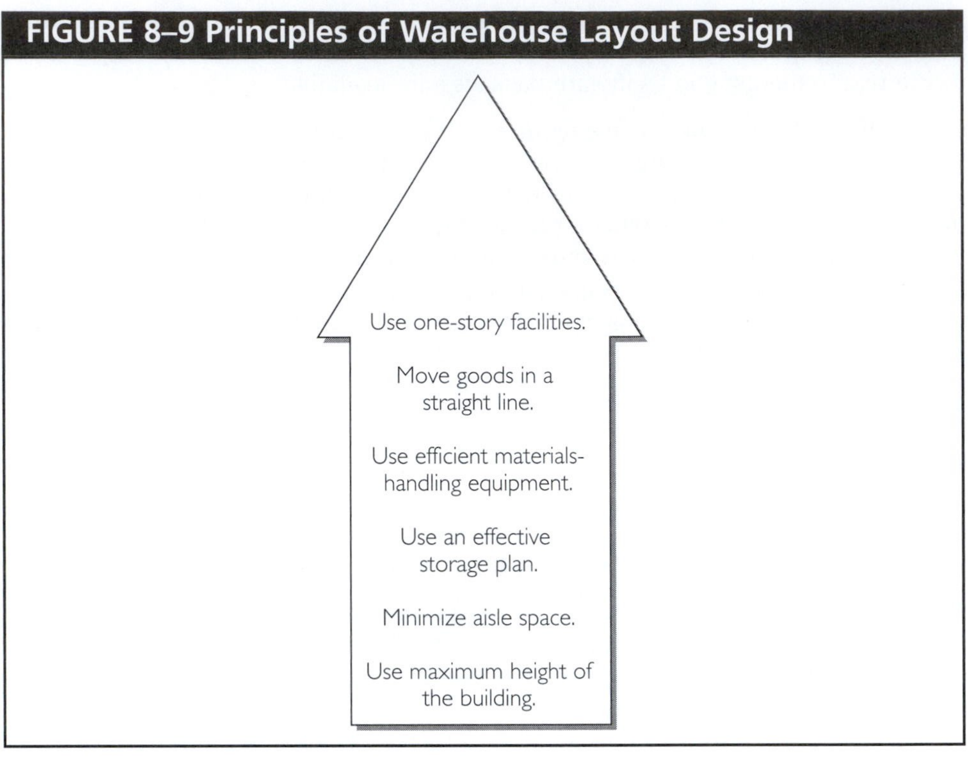

FIGURE 8–10 Basic Warehouse Configuration

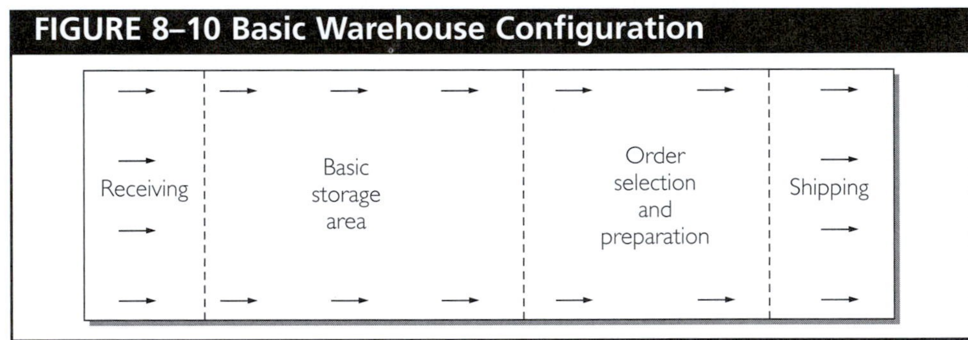

A fourth principle is to use an effective storage plan in the warehouse. In other words, the firm must place goods in the warehouse in such a way as to maximize warehouse operations and avoid inefficiencies. Stated simply, we are trying to utilize existing space as completely and effectively as possible while providing both adequate accessibility and protection for the goods we are storing.

A fifth principle of good layout is to minimize aisle space within the constraints that the size, type, and turning radius of materials-handling equipment impose. We must also consider the products and the constraints they impose.

A sixth principle is to make maximum use of the building's height—that is, to utilize the building's cubic capacity effectively. This usually requires integration with materials handling. Though vehicles capable of maneuvering in small aisles and stacking higher-than-conventional materials can be very expensive, such equipment offers potentially large overall systems savings because using height costs only one-fifth the cost of building the same cubic footage horizontally. Additionally, a high-rise building (forty to fifty feet high) attains almost the same cubic footage as a building twenty-five feet high, with less than half of the floor space, thus cutting land costs.

With these general principles in mind, we can focus upon the design requirements of some of the warehouse's basic space areas. With regard to the shipping and receiving areas, a firm has to consider whether to place stock temporarily in these areas and whether to store equipment here. The turning requirements of materials-handling equipment will also influence needs in this area. The firm must also analyze the number of bays, as well as their size and shape. The type of carrier the firm utilizes, product characteristics, and materials-handling equipment influence the bay requirements.

In regard to the order-picking and preparation area, we must keep in mind that, in a physical distribution warehouse, nearly constant movement characterizes this section. Utilizing cubic space effectively is difficult because of the need to keep items within order pickers' reaching distance. While utilizing materials-handling equipment can overcome this problem to some extent, a firm will never completely resolve the problem, because constant movement requires more open space.

Layout and Design Objectives

cubic capacity utilization

As stated previously, an underlying principle of layout design in the warehouse's storage area is to fully use the cubic capacity. One storage area design feature that lends itself to this objective is the use of larger storage bays having more limited access. The turnover or throughput level will affect the storage bays' actual size. For example, when turnover is very low, as in physical supply warehouses, the bays can be wide and deep, with limited access, and the aisles can be narrow. Increased turnover necessitates better access and, consequently, smaller bays and wider aisles. The customer service requirements of the physical distribution warehouse necessitate quick access.

protection

Warehouse layout's protection and efficiency objectives provide a good framework for determining the use of warehouse space. Looking first at the protection aspect, we can develop some general guidelines. First, warehouse space utilization should separate hazardous materials such as explosives, flammable items, and oxidizing items from other items so as to eliminate the possibility of damage. Second, the firm should safeguard products requiring special security against pilferage. Third, the warehouse should properly accommodate items requiring physical control such as refrigeration or heat. Fourth, warehouse personnel should avoid stacking or storing light or fragile items near other items that could cause them damage.

efficiency

The efficiency aspect has two dimensions. One is the effective *utilization of space* in the warehouse, which means utilizing the facility's height and minimizing aisle space. The second efficiency dimension is the *placement of stock* in the warehouse so as to minimize labor costs or handling costs.

mechanization

Though mechanized systems are not the solution for every warehouse, these systems frequently offer great potential to improve distribution efficiency. Careful planning should include consideration of all the risks of investing in automation. These risks include obsolescence due to rapid technological change, market fluctuations, and return on the large investment. Mechanization generally

TABLE 8–4 Warehouse Productivity Metrics

Pounds or units per day
Employees per pound moved
Pounds unloaded per hour
Pounds picked per hour
Pounds loaded per hour
Percentage of orders correctly filled

$$\text{Productivity ratio} = \frac{\text{pounds handled/day}}{\text{labor hours/day}}$$

Throughput = amount of material moved through system in a given time period

works best when items are regularly shaped and easily handled, when order selection is the middle range of activity, and when product moves in high volumes with few fluctuations.

productivity

A company should not make warehousing decisions once and then take them for granted; rather, the company should monitor productivity regularly during warehouse operations. While monitoring methods vary widely, the company should set goals and standards for costs and order-handling efficiency and then measure actual performance in an attempt to optimize the warehouse's productivity. By improving productivity, a company can improve its resource use; increase cash flow, profits, and return on investments; and provide its customers with better service. Table 8–4 contains examples of warehouse productivity metrics.

To begin a productivity program, a company should divide warehouse operations into functional areas and measure each area's productivity, utilization, and performance, focusing on improvements in labor, equipment, and facilities and making comparisons with standards if they exist. Repeating measurements can show relative trends. There is no single measure of warehouse productivity, but the method the company chooses must have the following attributes: validity, coverage, comparability, completeness, usefulness, compatibility, and cost-effectiveness.

MATERIALS HANDLING

definition

Materials handling is very important to any warehouse's efficient operation, both in terms of transferring goods in and out and in moving goods to various locations in the warehouse. The term *materials handling* is somewhat difficult to define. Some people picture elaborate equipment designed to move goods in a warehouse, such as forklift trucks or conveyor equipment. Others visualize the actual manual handling of the goods. In fact, elaborate mechanical equipment, manual labor, or a combination can perform materials handling. We can think most conveniently of materials handling as *efficient short-distance movement that usually takes place within the confines of a building such as a plant or a warehouse and between a building and a transportation agency.* Appendix 8A discusses the different types of materials-handling equipment.

In a modern logistics system, specially designed equipment most often performs this short-distance movement; hence, thinking of materials handling from an equipment perspective is not unusual. However, manual movement is also materials handling. The key factor is efficiency, whether the movement is mechanical, manual, or both. Most systems are a combination.

movement

Materials handling has four dimensions: movement, time, quantity, and space. The *movement* aspect of materials handling involves the conveyance of goods into and out of storage facilities, as well as within such facilities. Efficient materials handling, then, means efficient movement of goods to, from, and within the storage facility.

time

The *time* dimension of materials handling is concerned with readying goods for production or for customer order filling. The longer it takes to get raw materials to production, the greater the chance of work stoppage, higher inventories, and increased storage space. Likewise, the longer it takes to move finished goods to the shipping area, the longer the order cycle time and the lower the customer service.

quantity

The *quantity* issue addresses the varying usage and delivery rate of raw materials and finished goods, respectively. Material-handling systems are designed to assure that the correct quantity of product is moved to meet the needs of production and customers.

space

Materials-handling equipment consumes *space* in the warehouse and plant. This space in a facility is fixed, and the materials-handling system must utilize this space effectively. Forklifts adapted with extensions can reach twenty-five to thirty feet, thereby increasing the capacity utilization of the warehouse.

coordination

Most often, the logistics manager's materials-handling responsibility occurs in and around warehouses or plants' warehousing sections. Materials handling may require some coordination with individuals, such as the production manager, at least in the purchase of equipment and perhaps maintenance. Manufacturing and logistics may also need to interchange equipment. In designing or purchasing materials-handling systems, a firm must look not only at the technology available but also at the entire organization's long-range plans.

Objectives of Materials Handling

The general objectives of materials handling, listed in Figure 8–11, apply to areas besides logistics and have varying importance for the logistics manager.

increase effective capacity

One basic materials-handling objective is to increase the warehouse facility's usable capacity. A warehouse has fixed interior length, width, and height—that is, cubic capacity. Utilizing as much of this space as possible minimizes the warehouse's operating cost.

The use of warehouse space usually has two aspects. One is the ability to use the building's height as much as possible. Many warehousing facilities waste much space by not storing goods as high as possible. Figure 8–12 illustrates the importance of a warehouse's vertical space. Horizontal warehouse space is usually the most obvious and easiest to fill. But the vertical dimension is also a cost factor, and a warehouse operation must utilize this space effectively in order to be efficient. The vertical dimension is, therefore, the biggest challenge. Warehouse managers must focus on cubic space, not just on floor space.

FIGURE 8–11 General Objectives of Materials Handling

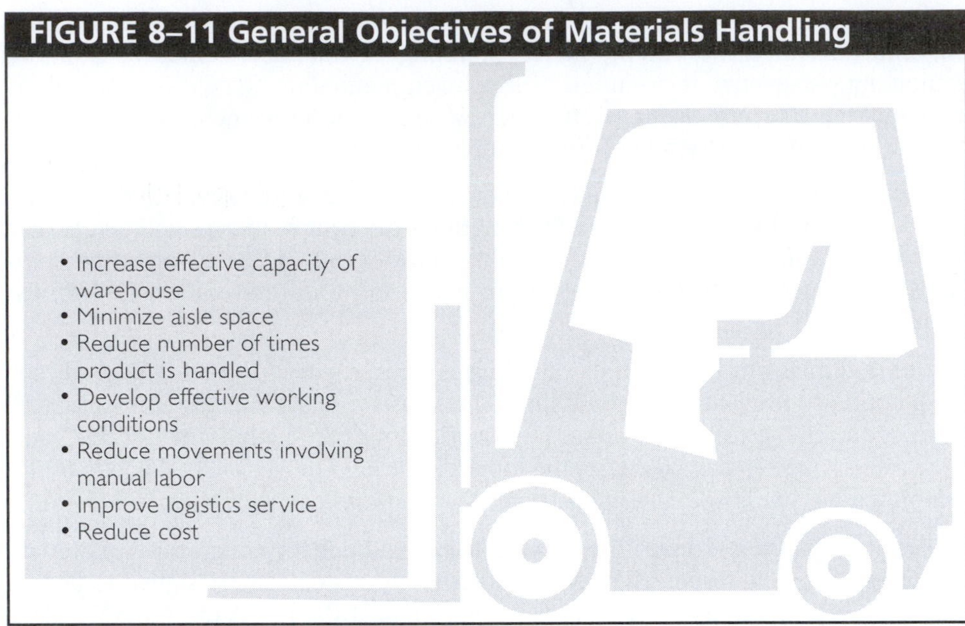

FIGURE 8–12 Utilization of a Warehouse's Cubic Capacity Principles of Warehouse Layout Design

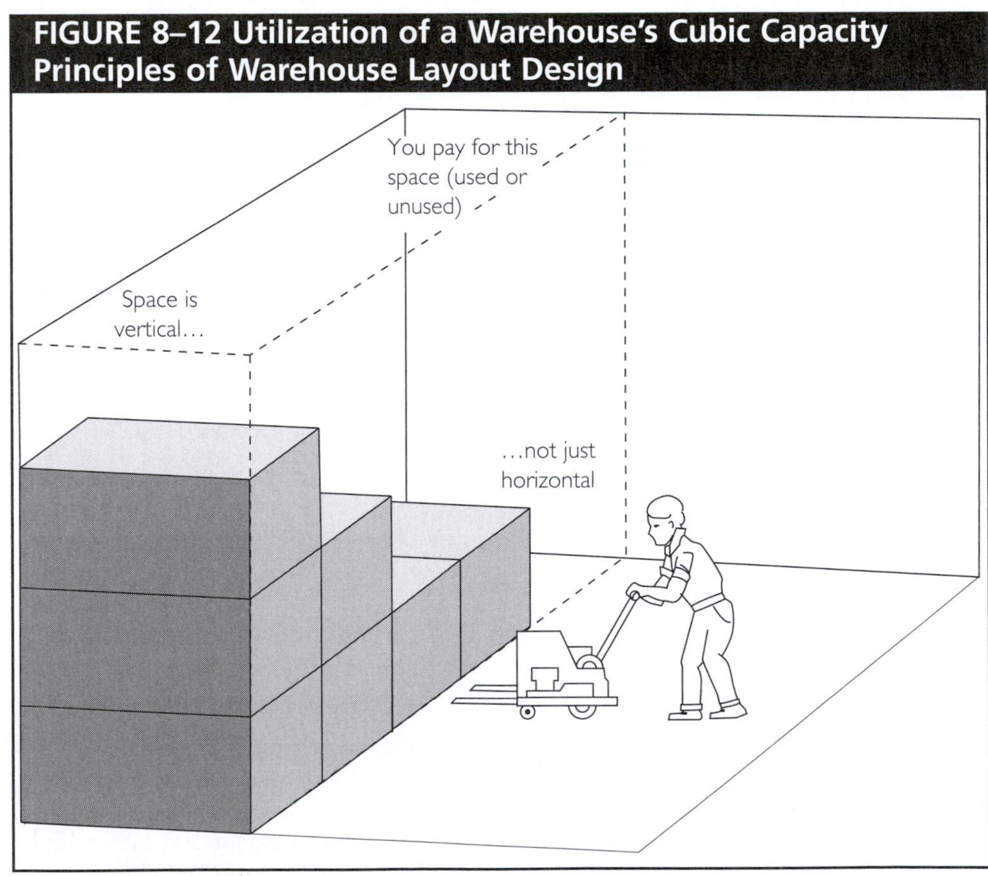

A second aspect of space utilization is to minimize aisle space while avoiding aisles narrow enough to impede movement in the warehouse facility. The type of materials-handling equipment a company uses will affect aisle width. Forklift trucks, for example, very often require turning space, and they may necessitate much wider aisles than required by other types of materials-handling equipment.

improve operating efficiency

Another materials-handling objective is to reduce the number of times a company handles goods. As we noted in our discussion of warehousing, a company usually moves products into a warehouse and places them in a storage area, then moves them to an order selection area to be "picked" and made up into orders, and finally moves the products again to ready them for shipment to customers. This process necessitates several unavoidable movements. In some warehouses, however, a company may move goods several times in each area. The company must avoid this additional handling if a warehouse is to operate efficiently. Therefore, the design of any materials-handling system and its associated activities should minimize movements to, within, and from a warehouse.

At times, extra movement is unavoidable. Because of overcrowding, any firm may have to temporarily store and then move products. However, an efficiently designed materials-handling system should minimize the number of movements and allow products to flow through the warehouse rapidly and efficiently.

develop effective working conditions

The objective of effective working conditions has a number of significant dimensions in the logistics area, including safety. All materials-handling systems, whether in connection with logistics or manufacturing, should minimize danger to nearby workers while enhancing productivity.

As stated previously, materials handling usually combines automation and manual labor. Most manual effort usually occurs in the order-picking area. Therefore, a company has to create an environment that motivates people to get the job done.

reduce heavy labor

Another part of this objective is to eliminate as much as possible short-distance warehouse movements, which are monotonous and involve heavy manual labor. While completely eliminating all routine movements or boring warehouse work is difficult, the materials-handling system should perform as much of this work as possible.

Taken to its logical conclusion, this objective suggests that companies should automate warehouses as much as possible. For a variety of reasons, including cost efficiencies, firms have attempted to eliminate warehouse labor personnel. Firms may encounter difficulty in minimizing or eliminating order selection personnel in physical distribution warehouses because some companies often receive orders for a small number of a stock-keeping unit (SKU). Consider, for example, Hallmark cards, where the typical order requires only one to three boxes of a certain card. Companies will usually handpick orders requiring small numbers of a large variety of items. This is also true of Kinney Shoes, where each shoe length and width is an SKU. In contrast, some companies receive orders for individual SKU pallet loads; these companies find automation quite feasible. Robots are a potential alternative to handpicking small numbers of items from different SKUs.

improve logistics service

Materials handling improves efficiency by making the logistics system respond quickly and effectively to plant and customer requirements. Materials handling plays a key role in getting goods to customers on time and in the proper quantities. By efficiently moving goods into the warehouse, locating stock, accurately filling orders, and rapidly preparing orders for shipment to customers, materials handling is very important to outbound logistics. In inbound logistics terms, materials handling serves company plants in much the same way.

The service objective receives much attention from the logistics manager. He or she must constantly ensure that the materials-handling system will respond quickly and efficiently to customers' orders and to a production schedule's requirements. Some companies spend a lot of time and effort trying to reduce transportation time by twelve or twenty-four hours. At the same time, their materials-handling systems may be adding several days to the time elapsing after a customer places an order. Customer service improvements that may be possible through improvement in materials handling are easy to overlook.

Many firms recognize the need for flexible materials handling within their customer service program. Firms need to integrate materials-handling requirements not only with the company's departmental needs but also with customers' needs.

reduced cost

Effective materials handling can contribute to a cost minimization program by increasing productivity (by providing more and faster throughput). Also, utilizing space more efficiently and misplacing items less frequently will lead to decreased cost.

All of these objectives are important and interrelated. In the 2000s, materials handling helps companies to minimize warehouse investment and to achieve higher inventory turns.

Guidelines and Principles for Materials Handling

Materials handling requires detailed analysis that can incorporate sophisticated mathematical techniques or modeling. This dimension of materials handling involves complex concepts that are beyond the scope of this textbook. In practice, the logistics manager can ask experts to provide detailed analysis. Therefore, logistics managers do not have to provide such analysis themselves.

However, in order to effectively plan and control materials handling, the logistics manager should recognize some guidelines and principles. Table 8–5 lists twenty of the most commonly accepted principles of efficient materials handling. Asterisks denote principles that deserve special emphasis.

The distances materials are moved in a warehouse should be as short as possible. This will minimize labor and equipment costs. A company should give the popularity principle some consideration, storing high-volume items at the shortest distance from the shipping area. Once items are in motion, they should stay in motion as long as possible. Stopping and starting are expensive for labor and equipment. Also, routes of materials should be on the same level as much as possible given a particular building configuration. Moving items up and down contributes to higher labor and equipment costs. In addition, a company should minimize the number of times and the length of time it handles an item.

TABLE 8–5 Principles of Materials Handling

1. *Planning Principle.* Plan all materials-handling and storage activities to obtain maximum overall operating efficiency.
2. *Systems Principle.* Integrate as many handling activities as is practical into a coordinated operations system covering vendor, receiving, storage, production, inspection, packaging, warehousing, shipping, transportation, and customer.
*3. *Materials Flow Principle.* Provide an operation sequence and equipment layout that optimize materials flow.
*4. *Simplification Principle.* Simplify handling by reducing, eliminating, or combining unnecessary movements and/or equipment.
*5. *Gravity Principle.* Utilize gravity to move material wherever practical.
*6. *Space Utilization Principle.* Make optimum use of the building cube.
7. *Unit Size Principle.* Increase the quantity, size, or weight of unit loads or their flow rates.
8. *Mechanization Principle.* Mechanize handling operations.
9. *Automation Principle.* Provide automation that includes production, handling, and storage functions.
*10. *Equipment Selection Principle.* In selecting handling equipment, consider all aspects of the material handled—the movement and the method to be used.
*11. *Standardization Principle.* Standardize handling methods, as well as types and sizes of handling equipment.
*12. *Adaptability Principle.* Use methods and equipment that adapt to the widest variety of tasks and applications, except where special-purpose equipment is justified.
13. *Deadweight Principle.* Reduce ratio of mobile handling equipment deadweight to load carried.
14. *Utilization Principle.* Plan for optimum utilization of handling equipment and labor.
15. *Maintenance Principle.* Plan for preventive maintenance and scheduled repairs of all handling equipment.
16. *Obsolescence Principle.* Replace obsolete handling methods and equipment when more efficient methods or equipment will improve operations.
17. *Control Principle.* Use materials-handling activities to improve control of production, inventory, and order handling.
18. *Capacity Principle.* Use handling equipment to improve production capacity.
19. *Performance Principle.* Determine handling performance effectiveness in terms of expense per unit handled.
20. *Safety Principle.* Provide suitable methods and equipment for safe handling.

*Principles that deserve particular emphasis.

Source: Adapted from College-Industry Committee on Materials Handling (Pittsburgh, Pa.: Materials Handling Institute, 1990).

Companies should use mechanical and automated equipment for materials whenever travel routes, volume, and cost trade-offs justify this investment. In other words, mechanization and automation are not a panacea for low cost and efficiency. Some very effective materials-handling systems utilize a fairly high ratio of labor to equipment.

Materials-handling equipment should be as standard as possible and as flexible as possible to lower cost; the equipment should use gravity as much as possible and should minimize the ratio of deadweight to payload.

A fundamental element impacting materials handling and warehouse operations is the package, the topic of the next section.

Supply Chain Technology

RF Helps Hasbro Get Ahead of the Game

What is the best way to manage the complex operations of a large manufacturing and storage facility? For toy and game manufacturer Hasbro, Inc., installing a warehouse management system was part of the answer. But not until the company linked radio frequency (RF) technology to its system last year did things really take off.

Hasbro, Inc., headquartered in Pawtucket, Rhode Island, reported net earnings of $4.2 billion in 1999 from the worldwide sales of toys, board games, and interactive software. The toy maker operates a plant in East Longmeadow, Massachusetts, where it manufactures some of its merchandise. Also located at that site are a raw materials receiving warehouse that handles inbound shipments and a work-in-process warehouse that supports a manufacturing plant. Both warehouses—which together take up 250,000 square feet of space—are actually housed in the same building as the plant. More than fifty employees work in those two distribution operations.

To oversee its manufacturing process, the company in July 1998 implemented an enterprise resource planning (ERP) system from German software vendor SAP. About six months later, the toy maker also installed SAP's warehouse module in its raw materials and work-in-process warehousing operations.

But the most sophisticated warehousing system in the world cannot operate very effectively without real-time data. So Hasbro retained Teklogix, Inc., to connect that software with an RF system. Teklogix used its TekRF front-end software to enable the SAP warehousing module to communicate with RF terminals located on vehicles, as well as with the workers' handheld units.

With the new system, workers can update inventory counts in real time via RF transmissions. As they scan bar codes on items placed into or removed from storage, the RF system simultaneously updates information on available stock in the WMS and inventory management systems.

The paperless system has boosted the efficiency of the inbound warehouse operation. In the past, forklift truck drivers used a paper pick list as a guide for retrieving items from storage. After the items were selected and removed for manufacturing, the forklift driver would bring that pick list to a clerical worker, who, in turn, typed in the information on picked items to update the inventory.

"Now the forklift driver goes to a location, scans the material, and the inventory gets updated, with a push of a button," says Don Lacharite, a division supervisor at Hasbro. He estimates that the paperless process has saved sixteen man-hours of labor per shift. In fact, the RF system combined with the WMS has allowed Hasbro to manage the movement of 3,000 skids in and out of storage each day.

Lacharite credits Teklogix's training and field support with getting the warehouse system up and running quickly. "Teklogix provided us with trainers," he says. "We had our staff fully operational in less than thirty days." Lacharite adds that designating and training a small number of workers to become in-house experts on the new system were keys to the successful installation.

Other factors that contributed to the installation's success were Teklogix's decision to implement the project in phases, adding functions one at a time over a three-week period, and Lacharite's decision to devote adequate human resources to the project in the early stages. "Someone advised me to dedicate enough resources," he says. "I chose to suffer up front. But the reward for doing that is that (workers) quickly become proficient in the new system."

Source: Doug MacLaughlin, "RF Helps Hasbro Get Ahead of the Game," *Logistics Management* (May 2000): 87. Reprinted with permission.

PACKAGING

logistics impact

Packaging interacts with the logistics system in a number of different and important ways. The size of and protection afforded by the package affect the type of materials-handling equipment used and the level of product damage incurred. The package has an impact on the stacking height of the product in the warehouse and thereby on the utilization and cost of the warehouse. Also, from a logistics manager's point of view, packaging is quite important for effective damage protection, not only in the warehouse but also during transportation. Packaging may contribute nothing to a product's value, but its influence on logistics costs is considerable.

size

Package size may affect a company's ability to use pallets or shelving or different types of materials-handling equipment. Many companies design packages that are too wide or too high for efficient use of either a warehouse or transportation carrier. So, coordinating packaging with warehousing and with transportation is quite important. Also, poor packaging can contribute to higher handling costs and result in lower future sales if the goods arrived damaged.

Although packaging is important to logistics and supply chain managers, it is also of great importance to other functional areas of the company. Like materials handling, packaging connotes different things to different people. Since packaging involves a number of organizational areas, these functional entities will need to coordinate their packaging concerns.

marketing

production

legal

Packaging is a concern to marketing, production, and legal. To the marketer, packaging may be a method of selling or at least a method of providing product information. As a sales tactic, the package acts as a silent salesperson by attracting attention because of its color, design, or functionality. Production managers are concerned with the cost of placing goods into the package; and the package's size, shape, and type will very often affect labor efficiency. Lastly, the legal section gets involved with the information provided on the package as well as compliance with various transportation and environmental packaging rules and regulations.

The Role of Packaging

identify product and provide information

A very important packaging function is to provide information about the product the package contains. Looking at this from the perspective of a marketing manager who is trying to sell a product in competition with other products on a supermarket shelf might be easiest. The package should provide information that would make the product more appealing to the customer. The package must also provide handling information. For example, if the package is easily damaged, or if it should be set in only one position, the package should say so.

Information provision is also important to logistics people. Goods stored in a warehouse must bear the proper identification so that warehouse personnel can locate them easily and correctly. When designing a package, firms may spend a lot of time and effort making sure that it provides information to warehouse personnel. Companies can use color codes for placing goods in a warehouse. The company should note the weight on the package in order to inform people lifting the package or to determine what can rest on top of it.

Techniques for providing information include color coding, universal product codes, heat transfers, computer-readable tables, symbols, and number codes. A firm's technique or combination of techniques will depend on the organization's particular circumstances.

improve efficiency in handling and distributing packages

A major packaging concern is the ease of handling in conjunction with materials handling and transportation. Large packages, for example, may be desirable from a production perspective, but the contents' size and weight might cause problems for materials-handling equipment or for transfer into and out of transportation equipment; so any packaging design should try to maximize handling ease in the warehouse and during transportation. Handling ease is also quite important to the production manager, who places the goods in the package.

The important considerations of package design fall into three areas. The first is the package's physical dimensions. The design must consider space utilization in terms of the warehouse, transport vehicle, and pallets. The product's physical dimension must also take into account the company's materials-handling equipment. The second consideration is the package's strength. The package designer must analyze the package's height, handling, and the type of equipment that will handle the package. The final consideration is package shape.

customer interface

With customer service playing an ever-increasing role in logistics planning, companies need to integrate their packages with customers' materials-handling equipment. A special package that can interface with a company's innovative equipment may move products inexpensively through its system; however, a customer's incompatible equipment will impair its ability to receive and store those goods. In this situation, customer service value may be lost.

protect product

A logistics manager's major concern is protecting the goods in the package. In the warehouse, for example, where moving goods could drop from a conveyor or be hit with a forklift truck, the package must provide the product adequate protection. Protection is also important when a transportation agency handles the product. Protection can also mean protecting products from contamination resulting from contact with other goods, water damage, temperature changes, pilferage, and shocks in handling and transport. Sometimes packaging must support the weight of products stacked above it, or provide even weight distribution within the package to facilitate manual and automatic materials handling.

Changes in federal and state regulations have also affected packaging's protection aspect, especially in food and drug product areas, where companies must design packaging to reduce consumer anxieties about tampering.

What Is Packaging?

We generally discuss two types of packaging: *consumer packaging,* or *interior packaging;* and *industrial,* or *exterior packaging.* The marketing manager is usually most concerned about the former because consumer or interior packaging provides information important in selling the product, in motivating the customer to buy the product, or in giving the product maximum visibility when it competes with others on the retail shelf. Marketing personnel often refer to consumer packaging, which has to appeal to the customer, as a silent salesperson.

On the other hand, industrial or exterior packaging is of primary concern to the logistics manager. This packaging protects goods that a company will move and store in the warehouse and also permits the company the effective use of transportation vehicle space. It also has to provide information and handling ease, as our discussion of the role of packaging indicated.

Although talking about packaging as a dichotomy is convenient—and quite often we can divide packaging in this way—the two areas do overlap. We cannot design the interior (consumer) package without considering the exterior or industrial package. Spending a lot of time and effort trying to minimize damage through an exterior package makes no sense if a company does not provide interior protection. Therefore, marketing and logistics have to coordinate packaging's consumer and industrial dimensions. These areas must also interact with production area people, since they typically join the two packaging types.

Packaging Materials

Many different exterior packaging materials are available to the logistics manager. In fact, as in materials handling, a packaging materials revolution has occurred in the last decade. At one time the use of harder materials, such as wood or metal containers, was widespread. But these added considerable shipping weight, which increased transport costs since transportation companies bill customers for total weight, including packaging.

softer materials

In recent years, companies have tended to use softer packaging materials. Corrugated materials have become popular, particularly with respect to package exterior. However, the plastic materials companies use to cushion the product inside the box have possibly done the most to revolutionize packaging. These materials enable manufacturers to highly automate the packaging area and to maximize protection while minimizing costs. In addition, plastic provides the lowest weight-to-protection shipping ratio.

Cushioning materials protect the product from shock, vibration, and surface damage during handling. Cushioning materials include shrink-wrap, air bubble cushioning, cellulose wadding, corrugated paper, and plastics. We can divide the plastics into expanded polystyrene, polyurethane, foam-in-place, and polyethylene. Table 8–6 shows a comparison of the various cushioning materials.

plastic

Companies often use shrink-wrap for consumer package goods, either alone or in conjunction with containers and slipsheets. It provides protection and stability, helps to reduce pilferage, and deters product tampering while items are in a warehouse. Shrink-wrap allows companies to stop using corrugated paper boxes. Warehouse personnel place the interior package directly on a pallet and shrink-wrap it. This also displays the item prominently for identification and helps to reduce overall logistics costs. In large warehouse-type retail operations, stores receive pallet loads directly and remove the shrink-wrap, making the product immediately accessible to the consumer. Since removing items from a box and placing them on a shelf is unnecessary, the retailer also saves money.

Air bubble cushioning is made of plastic sheets that contain air pockets. Cellulose wadding is composed of tissue paper layers. By forming upright columns in a box, corrugated inserts help prevent a product from getting crushed. Expanded polystyrene (EPS), the most popular cushioning material, is also recyclable. The loose-fill EPS commonly appears as foam peanuts or shells. Polyurethane (PU), the softest foam, provides cushioning for lightweight products. Foam-in-place polyurethane

TABLE 8–6 Comparison of Cushioning Materials

Material	Material Cost	Static Loading	Resiliency	Typical Applications
Air bubble	Low	Light to medium	Good	Void fill Wrapping Keyboards Plastic and metal parts Service centers
Cellulose wadding	Low	Light to medium	Fair	Surface protection Furniture Plastic parts
Corrugated	Low	Light to heavy	Fair	Blocking and bracing Rugged parts
Expanded polystyrene:				
Loose fill	Low	Light to medium	Fair	Void fill Books Plastic and metal parts
Molded	Low	Light to medium	Fair	Appliances Computers Electronic hardware
Polyurethane	High	Light to medium	Excellent	Computers Electronics Medical instruments
Foam-in-place	Medium	Medium to heavy	Good	Electronics Service centers Spare parts
Polyethylene	High	Medium to heavy	Excellent	Disk drives Fragile electronics Printers

Source: "Playing the Protective Packaging Game," *Modern Materials Handling* (April 1989): 65.

is a mixture of two chemicals that produce a foam that expands and molds to a product's exact shape. Polyethylene (PE) provides lightweight cushioning for heavy products.

These materials are inexpensive and highly protective. In addition, their light weight helps to minimize transportation costs. If a packaging revolution has occurred, we can probably attribute it to the development of these materials.

environment

When selecting packaging materials, companies today must consider environmental protection. Consumer advocates as well as government regulations have affected distribution planning. Examples include Food and Drug Administration restrictions on food product packaging.

recycling

One way to reduce this waste is to reduce the overall packaging a company uses. Another way is to recycle packaging materials. State and local governments have proposed and implemented much legislation to enforce business and community recycling.

Bar Coding

A discussion of packaging would be incomplete without a discussion of bar coding. Lineal bar code symbols that an optical scanner can read are having a major impact upon distribution logistics. The use of bar code technology caught on in the 1970s and took a huge leap in the 1980s and 1990s.

A *bar code* is a series of parallel black and white bars, both of varying widths, whose sequence represents letters or numbers. This sequence is a code that scanners can translate into important information such as a shipment's origin, the product type, the place of manufacture, and the product's price. Bar code systems are simple to use, accurate, and quick; and they can store large amounts of information.

Different industries use different bar code standards. A *bar code standard* states the language the code uses, the print quality companies expect on the label, the type of information the label contains, and the information format. Over thirty major U.S. industries have developed written standards for bar coding in manufacturing and warehouse operations.[3] For example, different standards include the Automotive Industry Action Group (AIAG) standards and the Universal Product Code that the grocery industry uses. With one bar code language standard, suppliers and vendors in a particular industry can easily read each other's package labels.

scanners

Bar code scanners fall into two main categories: automatic and handheld. Automatic scanners are in a fixed position and scan packages as they go by on a conveyor belt. In contrast, a worker can carry the portable handheld scanner or wand throughout the warehouse. To read bar codes, these optical scanners emit light beams and translate the reflections bouncing off the black and white bars into electrical signals. These electrical signals, which the scanner records as binary digits of 1s and 0s, form the code.

Most of us encounter bar coding in large retail outlets like supermarkets, where clerks now scan individual package bar codes at the cash register. Supermarkets have almost eliminated the practice of labeling every item with a price tag. More important, the bar code contributes to much more effective retail inventory control. The scanner and cash register, along with a backup computer system, enable the retail outlet to closely monitor sales and, therefore, inventory levels. The instantaneous transmission of information has allowed companies greater central control and inventory reduction in many retail locations.

Bar coding had its initial logistics impact when companies used it on cartons and monitored or scanned the codes as the cartons flowed into a warehouse. Bar coding at the warehouse improves data collection accuracy, reduces receiving operations time and data collection labor, and helps to integrate data collection with other areas, leading to better database and inventory controls. Companies can assign items more quickly into the warehouse, and warehouse personnel can select and prepare orders much more rapidly.

SUMMARY

- Warehousing plays a strategic role in attaining overall logistics cost and service goals.
- The value-adding roles of warehousing include transportation consolidation, product mixing, service, contingency protection, and smoothing.

- The basic warehousing decisions involve ownership, centralization versus decentralization, number, size, location, interior layout, and items stocked.
- Movement and storage are the primary warehouse operations.
- The decision to use private or public warehousing examines total cost and is affected by throughput volume, demand variability, market density, special physical control requirement, customer service needs, security, and multiple-use needs.
- Public warehousing is a variable component in the logistics system; provides a wide array of services; and is regulated as to rates, liability, and receipts.
- The greater the number of warehouses in a logistics system, the lower the transportation and lost sales cost, but the higher the warehousing and inventory cost.
- The space requirements of a warehouse include space for receiving, shipping, order picking, order assembly, storage, offices, and miscellaneous activities.
- The major principles of warehouse layout design are: use one-story facilities, move goods in a straight line, use efficient materials-handling equipment, use an effective storage plan, minimize aisle space, and use the maximum height of the building.
- Materials handling is the short-distance movement of goods that takes place within the confines of a building such as a plant or warehouse and between a building and a transportation vehicle.
- Materials handling has four dimensions: movement, time, quantity, and space.
- The objectives of materials handling are to increase the effective capacity of facilities, improve operating efficiency, develop effective working conditions, improve logistics service, and reduce cost.
- The logistics concern with packaging involves product identification, ease of handling, efficient use of storage facilities and transportation vehicles, the environment, and product protection.
- Packaging affects marketing, production, warehousing, and transportation.
- New packaging materials offer greater protection with lesser weight.
- Bar coding is an electronic method of identifying the package and its contents, and it enhances the efficiency of product storage and retrieval.

Study Questions

1. During the 2000s, many companies are focusing upon the logistics pipeline to meet their customers' needs for shorter lead times or response times. How can warehousing help companies to achieve quicker response times?
2. Some managers argue that warehousing can aid companies in providing value-added service for their customers. What is your view of this statement?
3. The trend in private warehousing is to use fewer but larger facilities in the network. Discuss the underlying economic rationale for this strategic shift in the number and size of private warehouses.
4. Public warehousing use is increasing among many large manufacturers in the 2000s. Why would a company such as Proctor & Gamble, which produces a wide variety of consumer goods, move toward public warehousing?

5. Movement and storage are the two basic functions of warehousing. Discuss the emphasis placed on these two basic functions in cross-docking, distribution, and basic raw material warehouses. What is the rationale for the similar or different emphasis?
6. How is the trend toward JIT inventory control systems likely to affect the number of warehouses companies operate? Why?
7. We frequently define materials handling as short-distance movements. What exactly does that mean? Where does this short-distance movement take place? Why are logistics managers concerned about materials handling?
8. One objective of materials handling is to increase effective capacity, that is, to improve space utilization. How does materials handling help to achieve this objective?
9. What functional areas in a company are interested in packaging? What is the nature of their respective interests? What types of disagreements may arise because of these varying interests?
10. How has bar coding affected packaging, materials handling, and inventory control?

NOTES

1. Robert V. Delaney and Rosalyn Wilson, "11th Annual State of Logistics Report," Cass Information Systems and ProLogis (2000), 12.
2. Armstrong & Associates, Inc., "Who's Who in Logistics?—Armstrong's Guide to Third Party Logistics Service Providers." Reprinted in Robert V. Delaney and Rosalyn Wilson, "Managing Logistics in a Perfect Storm—12th Annual State of Logistics Report," Cass Information Systems and ProLogis, Inc. (2001), Figure 14.
3. Gary Forger, "Bar Code Label Standards," *Modern Materials Handling* (November 1990): 43.

CASE 8–1 ■ Vanity Products

John Vance, president of Vanity Products, is reading the latest financial results reported in the company newsletter. Every time he reads this year's financials, he recalls the company's early days and the struggle to get retailers to stock his new line of bathroom vanities, mirrors, and light fixtures. Today, the company is straining to produce enough product to meet retailer demand.

Vanity Products (VP) manufactures a variety of bathroom accessories, including vanities (medicine chests), mirrors, lighting fixtures, and shelving. The products are made of rust- and chip-resistant molded plastic and come in a variety of modern designs and colors. The plastic construction permits VP to produce a high-quality bathroom accessory at an affordable price.

In the middle 1990s, John focused the company's marketing attention on the large home center chain stores: Home Depot, Walmart, Sears, and so on. Today, more than 80 percent of VP's sales are to these retail chains, and they account for 95 percent of its growth. Without these chain store customers, VP would still be a small, struggling manufacturer.

John's pleasant memories quickly fade to the realities of dealing with these large chain retailers. In the past two years, VP has been required to install EDI software that permits the buyers to assess VP's inventory data file to determine availability, to place orders, and to verify shipment status. The latest demand from one of the chains, which is a precursor of what the others will want, is for VP to reduce cycle time by shipping orders directly to the stores.

Currently, VP receives an order that is a consolidation of store orders to be served from a chain distribution warehouse. The order is sent in truckload quantity to the distribution warehouse, where the individual store order is broken out and sent to the store. Now, each store will be ordering separately, and VP is to deliver the order within five working days.

When John approached Tom White, manager of logistics, with the latest demand, Tom was not very comforting. He indicated that freight costs would certainly increase because VP would be shipping less-than-truckload quantities at higher freight rates. This higher freight cost could be offset with freight consolidation software that combines store shipments into truckload quantities for peddle runs. John liked the idea of keeping freight costs down, because VP would have great difficulty increasing prices because of competition.

However, the freight consolidation strategy would increase the shipment holding time prior to dispatch, thereby making it difficult for VP to meet the requirement that orders be delivered in five working days. Since cycle time reduction is the primary objective of the chain store's demand, any process adding to the delivery time would not be acceptable.

Tom is working on an idea to establish a series of distribution warehouses in the market areas where the chain stores are located. Tom's vision includes truckload shipments from the plants to the distribution centers, and cross-docking of products from incoming trucks to trucks delivering orders to specific stores. In addition, each distribution warehouse would maintain a minimal level of inventory to meet emergency orders placed by local stores.

John is skeptical of Tom's distribution warehouse idea because he feels it would increase capital costs, inventory levels, and transportation costs. He is not even certain it would meet the delivery time requirements.

Case Questions

1. Analyze the logistics service and cost constraints imposed on VP by the chain store's latest demand.
2. What is your opinion of Tom White's proposal for establishing a series of distribution warehouses?
3. What ownership and management structures would you recommend for the distribution warehouses?
4. Develop a process map depicting the information and product flows in Tom's proposal.

APPENDIX 8A

MATERIALS-HANDLING EQUIPMENT

In this appendix we explore the different types of materials-handling equipment available to the logistics manager, including dock, conveyors and cranes, guided vehicles, and order-picking and storage equipment. In addition, the materials-handling equipment selection decision is examined from a design perspective, as well as from a pragmatic viewpoint of the factors utilized in the selection decision.

Dock Equipment

The proliferation of products on the market today makes materials-handling selection a very dynamic process. We now discuss the various equipment categories companies could use in designing a materials-handling system. Our objective is to appreciate how and when a company might use such equipment in a logistics system. Keep in mind, however, that because of many new technological advances, logistics managers need much information when making a decision in this area.

Materials handling begins at the loading dock when a truck containing the goods arrives and needs to be unloaded. The faster the warehouse unloads the goods, the greater its throughput capability. Due to the constant activity, both the receiving and shipping dock activities need to be efficient. To load or unload the goods safely and quickly, the warehouse should utilize the necessary dock equipment. The following section describes important dock equipment such as forklifts, dock bumpers, dock levelers, dock seals, trailer restraint systems, and pallets.

Forklifts. One type of dock equipment common to many materials-handling systems is the forklift truck (see Figure 8A–1), a very versatile piece of equipment that a company can provide at a very reasonable cost. Able to perform several useful materials-handling tasks, the forklift is individually powered and is available with various lift arrangements. Warehouses usually use forklifts in conjunction with pallets.

The forklift truck operates very efficiently, and companies can use it in a variety of ways. Its major disadvantage is that it requires an operator, who may very often be idle when the forklift is not in use. But, all things considered, it is probably the most popular and most common type of materials-handling equipment in existence. Even the smallest firm with the simplest materials-handling system can often afford a forklift truck. Its biggest advantage is its versatility in moving goods from one warehouse section to another or in transferring goods into and out of transportation equipment.

In selecting forklift trucks, a company should consider normal equipment variations such as lifting capacity, lifting height, power source (gasoline, battery, or propane gas), the aisle space the forklift needs, and speed. Manufacturers today offer a wide selection of forklift trucks, including trucks that handle slipsheets instead of pallets, electric trucks, narrow-aisle high-stacking trucks, compact forklifts, and trucks with greater lifting capacity. Computer-controlled lift trucks, designed for use with or without a driver, are also becoming popular for use in the dark, in extreme temperatures, or with hazardous materials.

FIGURE 8A–1 Forklift Truck

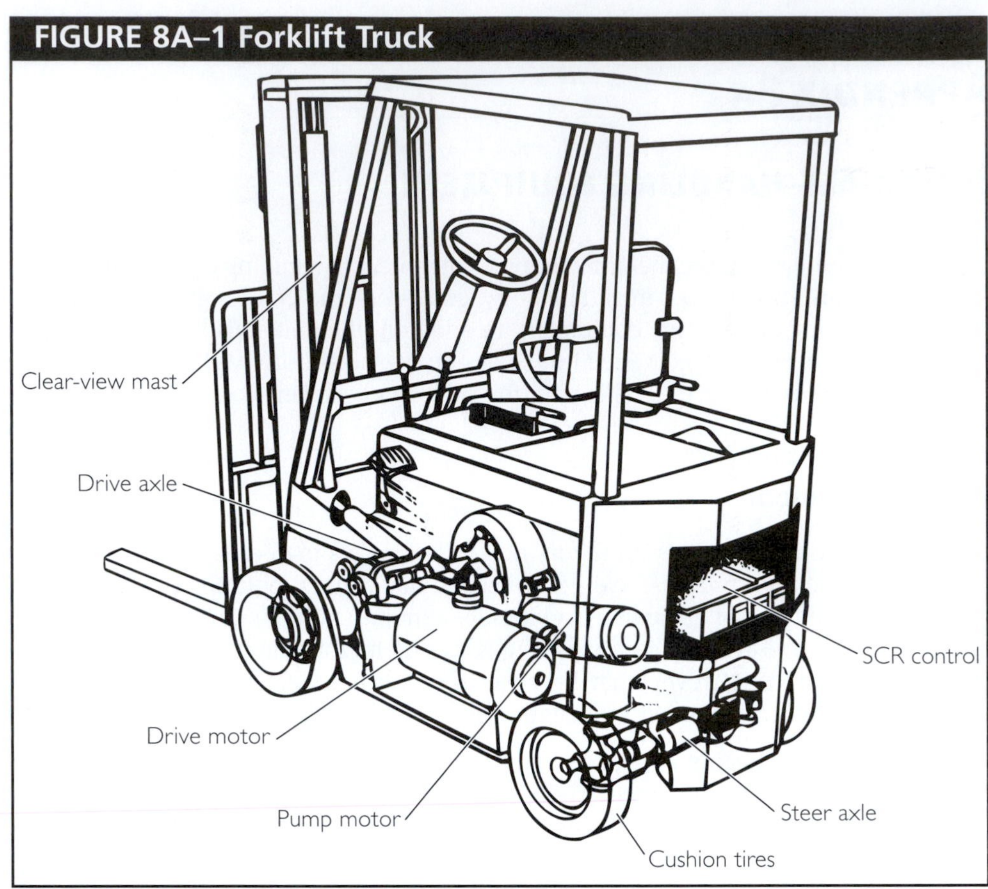

Source: Modern Materials Handling (March 1989): 69.

Dock Bumpers. Dock bumpers are molded rubber pieces that protect the building from the impact of a docking trailer backing into it and from a trailer shifting in weight during loading or unloading.

Dock Levelers. Dock levelers level out the angle between the dock and the trailer by providing a ramp that enables the forklift to drive into the trailer safely. The greater the ramp angle, the greater the chance of an accident.

Dock Seals. A dock seal is a cushioned frame around the dock door opening that connects the trailer to the dock. Its purpose is to create a seal blocking any outside weather, smoke, and fumes from entering the warehouse.

Trailer Restraint Systems. Vehicle restraints prevent the trailer from drifting away from the dock during loading or unloading. Since this drifting causes many dock accidents, the Occupational Safety and Health Administration (OSHA) must approve a warehouse's restraining system. While a company can use wheel chocks or wedge molded rubber under a truck's tires, these methods are ineffective on ice, snow, or gravel. The best system is an automated one that uses a lighting or sound system to communicate the trailer's safety status between the dock worker and the truck driver.

Pallets. Pallets are both basic and essential to materials-handling operations. A pallet's main function is to provide a base to hold individual items together (see Figure 8A–2). Once the items are stacked on the pallet, materials-handling equipment,

FIGURE 8A–2 Pallet Types

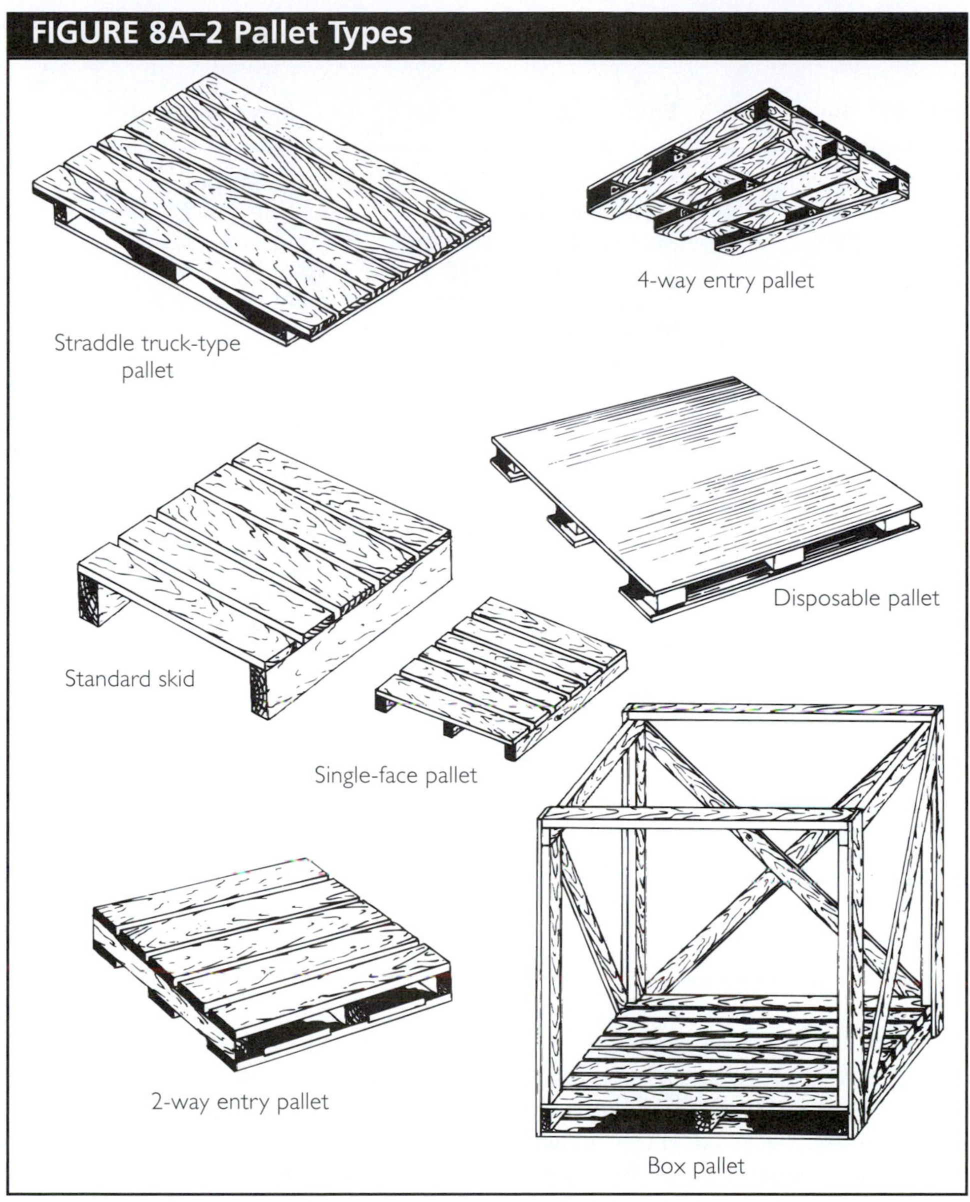

Source: General Services Administration, Warehouse Operations (Washington, D.C.: Government Printing Office).

most often a forklift, can move the pallet to the proper storage location. Companies also use pallets when shipping products from the warehouse to the customer.

Although pallets play an integral distribution role, their use has one important problem. Most companies do not recycle pallets, even though they can; and many used or unusable pallets go to the landfill. This issue is of growing concern to both environmentalists and logistics managers who must find ways of reducing this waste. Table 8A–1 shows the alternative pallet materials and their environmental effects. Wood pallets continue to serve about 85 to 90 percent of pallet users' needs. Wood is both biodegradable and recyclable. Shredded wood pallets can be

TABLE 8A–1 Pallet Type Comparison

Material	Durability*	Repairable?	Environmental Impact	Typical Application
Wood	Medium	Yes	Material is biodegradable and recyclable	Grocery; automotive; durable goods; hardware
Pressed wood fiber	Medium	Yes	Material is recyclable and can be burned without leaving fuel residues	Printing metal stampings; plumbing fixtures; building materials
Corrugated fiberboard	Low	No	Material is biodegradable and recyclable	One-way shipping applications in grocery; lightweight paper products; industrial parts
Plastic	High	No	Material is recyclable	Captive or closed-loop systems; FDA, USDA applications; automotive
Metal	High	No	Material is recyclable	Captive or closed-loop systems; FDA, USDA applications; military

*We define durability as a pallet's expected number of trips.

Source: Modern Materials Handling (April 1990): 53.

used for mulch, animal bedding, and packaging material; however, the market for these products is still limited. In addition, damaged wooden pallets are easy to fix.

For example, grocery products manufacturers, the largest users of wooden pallets, currently repair about 68 million pallets each year. Pressed wood fiber pallets, a recyclable alternative to wood pallets, are nail-free, which helps protect products from damage. Corrugated fiberboard pallets reduce weight in the trailer and provide better shock absorbency than wood, and companies can sell the used pallets as recyclable paper scrap. The pharmaceutical, food-processing, and chemical industries use plastic and metal pallets because these pallets are easy to clean and keep sanitary. Recycled plastic pallets become products such as orange highway construction barriers or compact discs. All pallet materials have recycling potential. By recycling pallets, the warehouse will receive salvage value from recycling firms instead of paying disposal costs.

Home Depot has switched from using pallets to plastic slipsheets. The plastic slipsheet eliminates the problem of pallet disposal and return, thereby lowering disposal costs. At the same time, Home Depot is experiencing a reduction in the amount of product damage. The plastic slipsheet is being reused four to five times, with the final trip being to a plastic recycler who turns the spent slipsheet into a new one for another four to five trips.

Another method used extensively in the grocery industry is pallet rental. The leading pallet rental company is Chep USA. Under the Chep plan, a grocery manufacturer rents the pallet for a one-way trip to the wholesaler or retailer. When the product is removed from the pallet, the wholesaler or retailer sends the empty pallet to one of Chep's regional depots.

Other Materials-Handling Equipment

Conveyors. Conveyors, a very popular form of materials-handling equipment, play an important role in advancing productivity and improving bottom-line operating results, particularly in the mechanized distribution center or warehouse. These systems decrease handling costs, increase productivity of workers and equipment, and provide an interface with management information systems.

roller versus belt conveyor

There are two basic types of conveyors (see Figure 8A–3). The first, a *roller conveyor,* basically uses the gravity principle. The conveyor is inclined, and goods move down the conveyor by force of their own weight, typically at a slow pace depending on the conveyor's incline. The other type is the *wheel conveyor,* or *belt* or *towline conveyor,* which requires power equipment. Such conveyors move goods either on a level or up inclines to a warehouse section. Companies use a roller conveyor wherever possible to minimize their operating costs.

Many companies consider conveyors advantageous because they can be highly automatic and, therefore, can eliminate handling costs. They also may save space since they can use narrow aisles and can operate on multiple levels in the same area. Conveyor systems often have low operating costs.

advantages

Conveyors equipped with scanners and other automatic devices enable companies to move goods very efficiently and quickly from one warehouse area to another. Scanners can keep inventory records by recording packages moving on conveyors, and can track storage locations. Finally, scanners enable managers to use computers to rapidly locate goods.

A modern conveyor system is very expensive and requires a large capital investment. It is also fixed in location; that is, it lacks versatility. Designing a conveyor system requires much time and effort, particularly with reference to a company's future needs. If conditions change, changing the conveyor system may be necessary, often at a very high cost. Organizations that invest in complex conveyor systems are usually large and successful manufacturing firms. Using conveyors to automate a large distribution warehouse, for example, generally requires a significant investment of funds in a very complex and sophisticated conveyor system. However, companies can install some very simple conveyors at a very reasonable cost.

capital-intensive

In analyzing the possibility of using warehouse conveyor systems, an organization must decide whether its materials-handling approach should be capital-intensive or labor-intensive. Many large companies with sophisticated logistics requirements find capital-intensive systems such as elaborate conveyors to be extremely worthwhile because of reduced labor costs and possible improvements in distribution time. However, such approaches are not necessarily right for all companies. More labor-intensive approaches may be much more appropriate. Comparing labor-intensive and capital-intensive materials-handling methods is analogous to comparing private and public warehousing. In other words, conveyor systems have a very important fixed cost segment, and a company must have throughput volume sufficient to defray or spread the fixed costs.

One disadvantage of conveyors is the possibility of equipment malfunction, which could cause logistics system delays. However, conveyor users can minimize operational problems. To avoid exceeding the equipment's capacity and causing breakdowns, the company using conveyors must consider the dimensions and weight of

FIGURE 8A–3 Materials-Handing Equipment Top-running

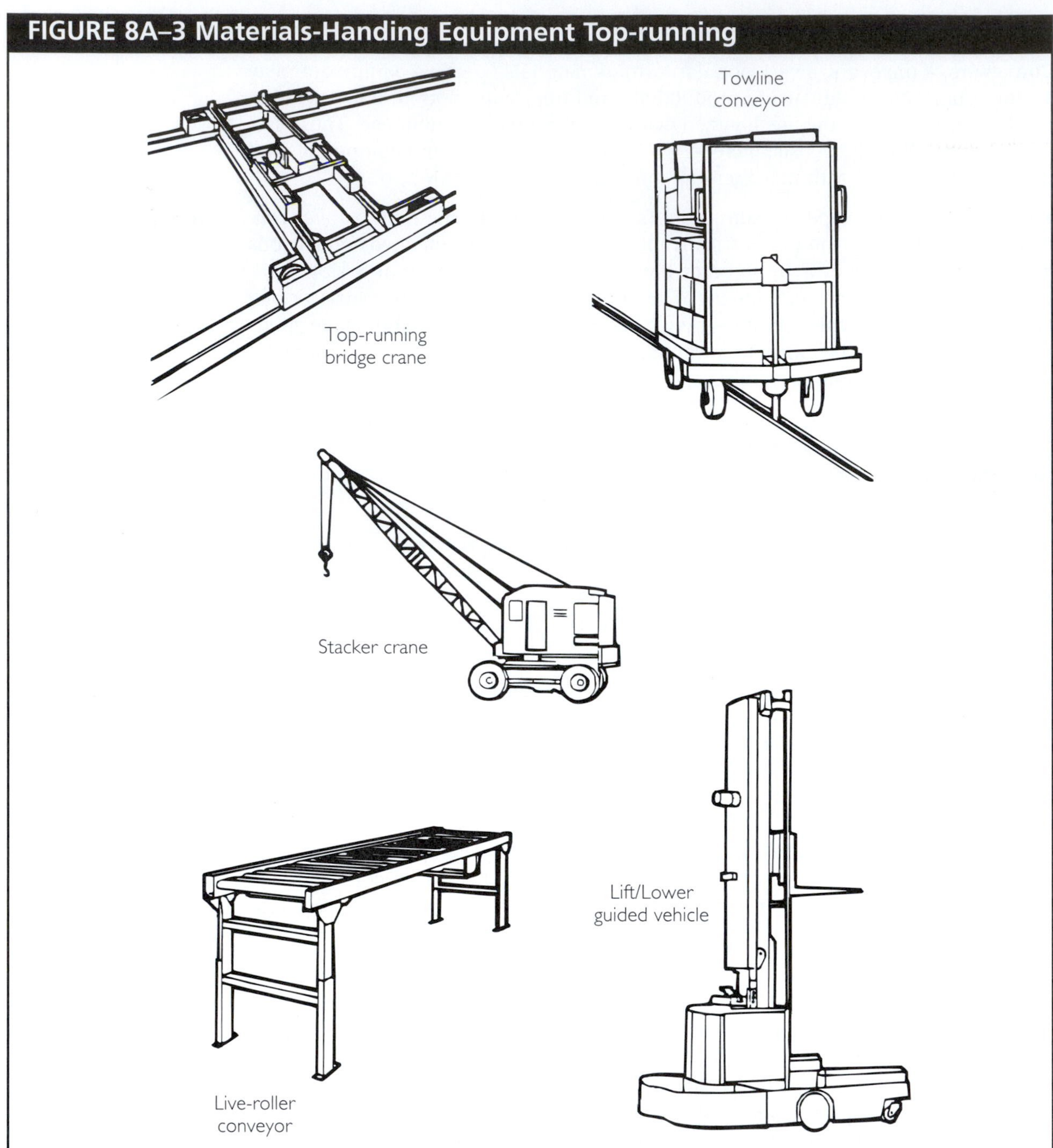

Source: Modern Materials Handling (1987): 107, 381.

each unit the conveyors will carry. The company must consider the load's center of gravity when loads travel on inclined or declined conveyors, are handled in start-stop operations, or are transferred while in motion. To avoid problems, a company must operate a conveyor at the rate for which the company intended it. This rate may vary, depending on unit sizes; and these sizes will be mixed.

Conveyors can handle loads of almost any size, shape, weight, or fragility. However, users must determine, before they purchase equipment, the items a specific conveyor will handle and its expected functions—sortation, for example. Following the guidelines this section suggests will contribute to an effective conveyor system.

Trends show that conveyor usefulness will continue to increase as automation technologies develop. Already, conveyors can be valuable tools in data generation and product-monitoring systems, and their use in computerized inventory control is quite common.

Cranes. Companies can utilize a variety of cranes in warehouses (see Figure 8A-3). The two basic types are *bridge cranes* and *stacker* or *wagon cranes*. Bridge cranes are more common in physical supply warehouses or where companies have to move, store, and load heavy industrial goods such as steel coils or generators.

Stacker cranes have become increasingly popular in physical distribution warehouses because they can function with narrow aisles, effectively utilizing a warehouse's cube capacity. This equipment is also very adaptable to automation. Fully automated stacker cranes on the market today can put stock into and take it out of storage areas without an operator. The computer equipment such systems utilize can select the best storage placement and recall this placement later. Stacker cranes are commonly used in conjunction with elaborate shelving systems.

Though not usually as expensive as conveyor systems, cranes are also capital-intensive equipment. Handling very heavy items may require bridge cranes; a company should justify stacker cranes on a cost basis. The advantage of bridge cranes is the ability to lift heavy items quickly and efficiently. The advantages of stacker cranes are the effective use of space and the possibility for automation.

Automatic Guided Vehicle Systems. Automatic guided vehicles (AGVs) are machines that connect receiving, storing, manufacturing, and shipping. Firms can track these vehicles, either roaming freely or on a fixed path, with computers that make traffic control decisions. Essentially, AGVs travel around the warehouse or manufacturing plant carrying various items to a particular programmed destination. Since these AGVs do not require a driver, labor costs are reduced.

The double-pallet jack, another vehicle that does not require a driver, can transport two pallet loads between warehouse areas. As with AGVs, a computer can guide the double-pallet jack to its destination along a floor-wired guide.

Also available is a variety of other, more specialized equipment, including draglines that pull carts in a continuous circle in a warehouse, elevators, hoists, and monorails.

Order-Picking and Storage Equipment

One of the main functions of a physical distribution warehouse is order picking, the process of identifying, selecting, retrieving, and accumulating the proper items for customer orders. Although order picking by nature is labor-intensive, an effectively designed order-picking and storage system can enhance the speed, accuracy, and cost-effectiveness of the order-picking process. Most storage systems primarily try to use warehouse space effectively. Because the cost of labor, equipment, and space for order picking equals about 65 percent of total warehouse operating costs, any improvement that reduces these costs is greatly important. This section covers two main equipment types: picker-to-part and part-to-picker. Picker-to-part systems include bin shelving,

FIGURE 8A–4 Order-Picking Equipment

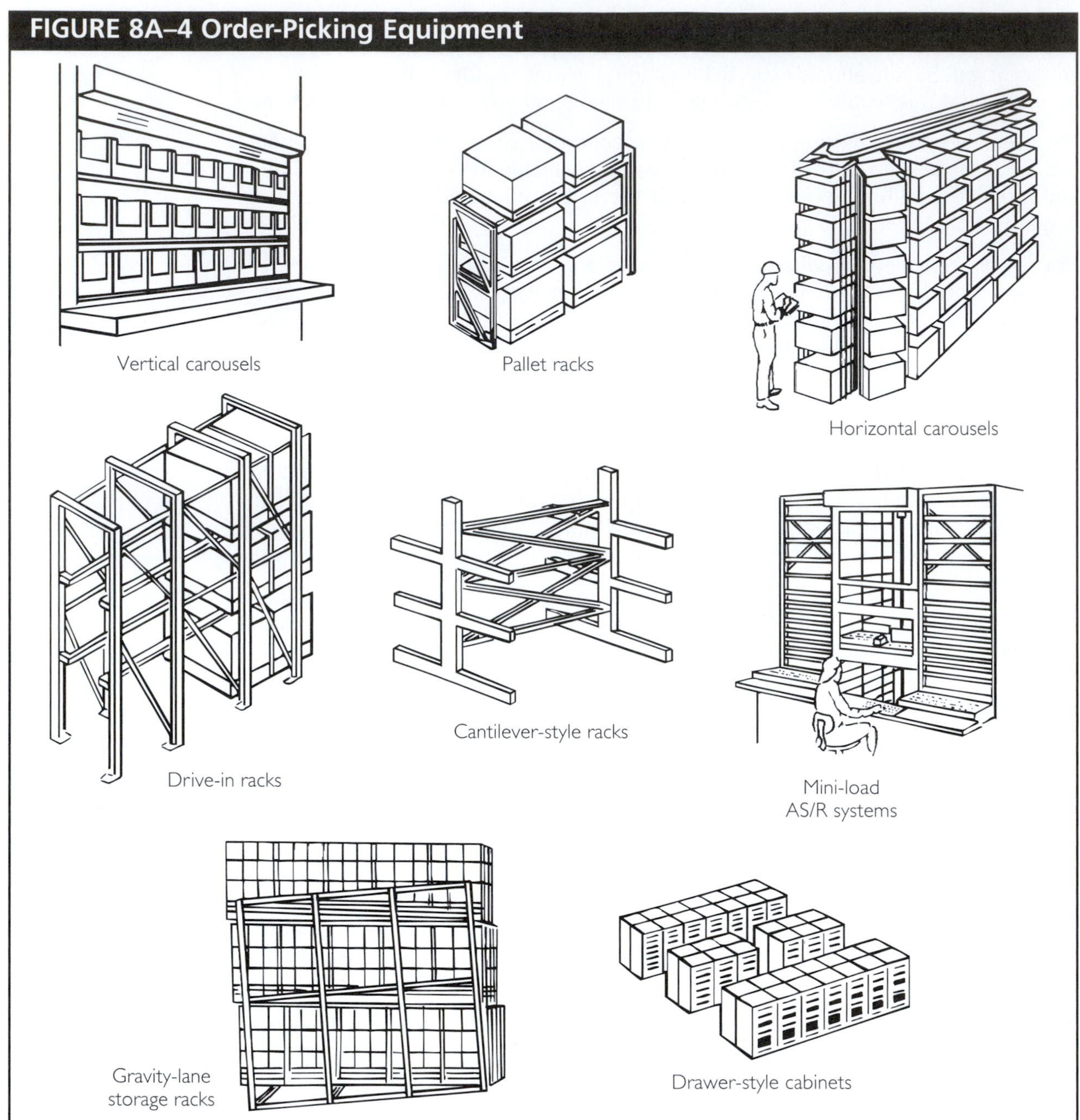

Source: Modern Materials Handling, 1992 Casebook Reference Issue (September 1991): 97.

modular storage drawers, flow racks, mobile storage systems, and order-picking vehicles. Part-to-picker systems include carousels and miniload automated storage and retrieval systems (AS/RS). Figure 8A–4 illustrates these systems.

Picker-to-Part Systems. In picker-to-part systems, the order picker must travel to the pick location within the aisle:

- *Bin shelving.* Bin shelving is the oldest and most basic storage system available for storing small parts. The main advantages of bin shelving are the low initial cost and the ability to divide units into various compartments. However, the system underutilizes cubic space by not using a bin's full size and by requiring shelf height to be within a person's reach.

- *Modular storage drawers.* Modular storage drawers are cabinets that are divided into drawers and further subdivided into compartments. Their main advantage is their ability to hold a large number of SKUs. Their main drawback is height: the drawers cannot be more than approximately five feet high because the order picker must look into them when picking an order.
- *Flow racks.* Flow racks store items in cartons having a uniform size and shape. The cartons, which warehouse personnel replenish from the rack's back end, flow on rollers, by gravity, to the rack's front or aisle end for order picking. A main advantage to this system is that the back-to-front item movement ensures first-in/first-out (FIFO) inventory turnover. Flow racks can also hold full pallets of items.
- *Mobile storage systems.* Mobile storage systems need only one order-picking aisle because a motorized system can slide the racks, shelves, or modular drawers to the left or right. The order picker can slide the racks apart to expose the aisle in which he or she needs to pick an order. Slower picking speed due to the shift time offsets the advantage of high storage density.
- *Order-picking vehicles.* Order-picking trucks and person-aboard storage and retrieval (S/R) vehicles increase order-picking rates and maximize cubic space utilization. The order picker rides or drives the vehicle horizontally or vertically to the pick location. Some of these vehicles move automatically, allowing the order picker to perform another task while traveling.

Part-to-Picker Systems. In part-to-picker systems, the pick location travels through an automated machine to the picker. These systems have a higher initial cost than picker-to-part systems, but utilizing automated storage and retrieval equipment speeds up order-picking operations, improves inventory control, and increases profits. Part-to-picker systems minimize travel time. By comparison, in static shelving systems, workers spend up to 70 percent of their time traveling:

- *Carousels.* Carousels are shelves or bins linked together through a mechanical device that stores and rotates items for order picking. The two main types of carousels are horizontal and vertical.

  Horizontal carousels are a linked series of bins that rotate around a vertical axis. A computer locates a needed part and rotates the carousel until the part location stops in front of the order picker's fixed position. Automated systems attempt to minimize wait times and maximize order-picking times. For this reason, an order picker usually works two carousels. In this way, the picker can pick from one carousel while waiting for the other carousel to rotate to a needed item. Industries that use horizontal carousels include aviation, electronic, paper, and pharmaceutical.

  Vertical carousels differ from horizontal ones in two ways: the bins are enclosed for cleanliness and security, and the carousel rotates around a horizontal axis. The vertical carousel operates on a continuous lift principle, rotating the necessary items to the order picker's work station. This vertical storage approach cuts floor space use by 60 percent and increases picking productivity by up to 300 percent over racks and shelving of equal capacity. Some industries that use vertical carousels include electronic, automotive, aerospace, and computer.

- *Miniload automated storage and retrieval systems (AS/RS).* The most technically advanced order-picking system is the miniload AS/RS, which efficiently uses storage space and achieves the highest accuracy rate in order picking. The AS/RS machine travels both horizontally and vertically to storage locations in an aisle, carrying item storage containers to and from an order-picking station at the end of the aisle. At the order-picking station, the order picker programs the correct item-picking sequence. The AS/RS machine retrieves the next container in the sequence while the order picker obtains items from the present container. The miniload AS/RS utilizes vertical space and requires few aisles, but this system is very expensive.

Mezzanines. Mezzanines are double-layered storage systems that utilize a second level of bin shelving, modular storage cabinets, flow racks, or carousels above the first storage level. Instead of using up square footage space, the mezzanine adds a second level to utilize the warehouse's cubic capacity more efficiently. A steel grating usually divides the two levels, which workers access by stairs. The mezzanine is not part of the building's actual construction, so its location is flexible (see Figure 8A–5).

FIGURE 8A–5 Mezzanines

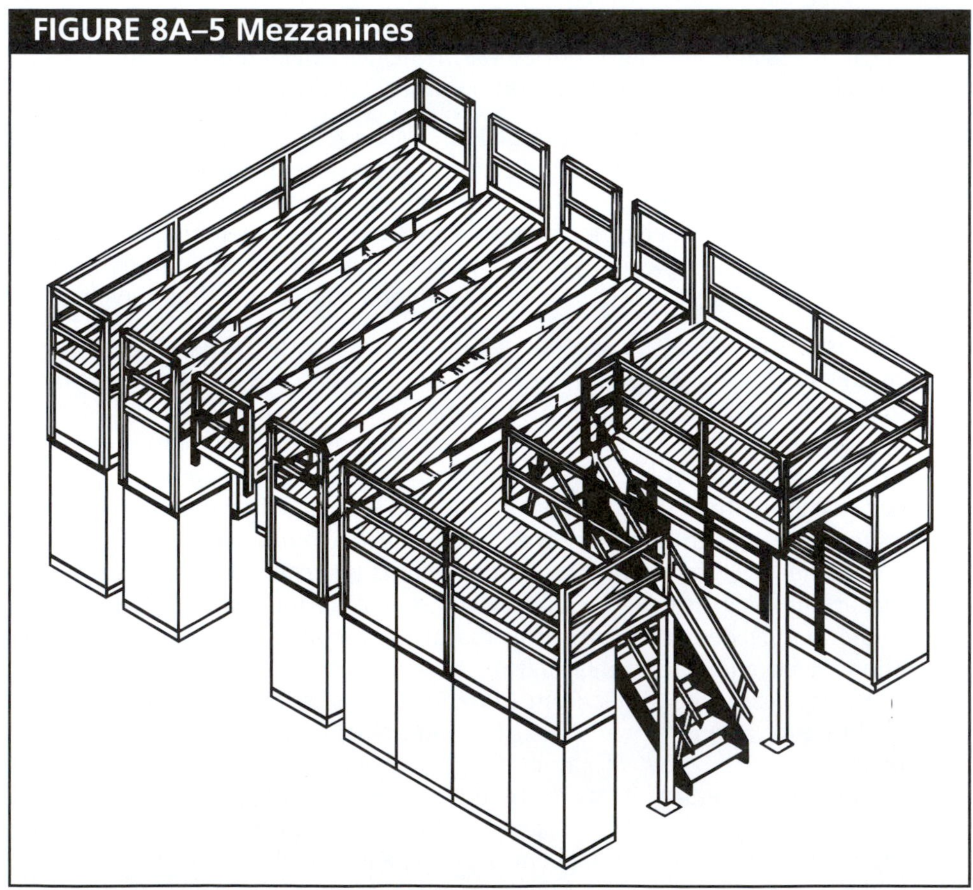

Source: Plant Engineering (8 March 1980): 81.

Types of Materials-Handling Equipment—A Design Perspective

flexible path

Companies often divide materials-handling equipment into three design categories. The first category is *flexible-path equipment,* which includes manual hand trucks, all forklift trucks, and some other picking equipment. Its design advantages are versatility and flexibility. However, it is customarily more labor-intensive.

continuous-flow fixed path

The second category is *continuous-flow fixed-path equipment,* which includes conveyors and draglines. These are usually very efficient and highly automated. However, the investment is high; often specializing in certain products, they usually have limited versatility; and they have limited flexibility. For a company with volume flow and uniform product size, this approach has many cost advantages.

intermittent-flow fixed path

A third type is *intermittent-flow fixed-path equipment.* Including cranes, monorails, and stacker crane equipment, this category combines the efficiency of continuous-flow equipment with the ability to stop unneeded equipment.

By recognizing the need for equipment able to efficiently move goods within, into, and out of the warehouse, manufacturing firms and equipment manufacturers have revolutionized the whole materials-handling area. The number of equipment types available today could overwhelm a materials-handling system designer. But these equipment choices also represent an important challenge because of their potential for improving a logistics system.

An interesting question is whether logistics managers should be actual experts in the design of materials-handling equipment. This is very unlikely. Usually, the logistics manager depends on the advice of the organization's engineering staff or various equipment managers. However, logistics managers should know about their own systems and their particular needs. This enables logistics managers to establish general parameters for a materials-handling system and provides a framework for choosing the best system for a particular company or firm. In the next section, we discuss some of the logistics manager's criteria for selecting equipment.

Equipment Selection Factors

Several factors affect the type of materials-handling equipment a company should use. These factors offer the logistics manager guidelines for analyzing company requirements. The manager must approach this analysis in trade-off terms, measuring benefits against costs.

physical attributes of product and packaging

United States firms produce a vast array of products. Even individual companies sometimes produce numerous different products. A materials-handling system that moves books in or around a warehouse is quite distinct from one that stores automobile tires or chain saws. Therefore, the physical attributes of the product or product group handled affect the type of materials-handling equipment used.

For example, item weight will influence a system's design. Large pieces of equipment that a firm must store in a warehouse may negate the use of something like a conveyor system and may require overhead bridge cranes. If a product is small and lightweight, usually a firm can use any of several categories of materials-handling equipment. The product and its weight, size, packaging, value, handling ability, and susceptibility to damage all influence the type of equipment a company uses. Therefore, the logistics manager should first consider the product and its dimensions when deciding which equipment options are available and most appropriate for a firm's materials-handling system. Because of his or her transportation and inventory experience, the logistics manager will know the company's product or products and the factors that will affect materials-handling equipment use.

Since the 1970s, the government has become increasingly interested in the movement of hazardous materials, including radioactive materials and other chemicals. A materials-handling setting must take this into account. For example, certain raw materials with unique handling characteristics require loose, rather than packaged, movements. Lately, companies have debated the use of slurry systems versus dry bulk systems to move bulk products.

characteristics of physical facility

A warehouse facility's physical characteristics also influence the use of materials-handling equipment. Very often we visualize a large, well-lit, one-story facility with very few obstacles, which is conducive to the use of conveyors, forklift trucks, shelves, or any type of materials-handling equipment discussed here. Sometimes, however, this type of facility is not possible. A company may have to use a mobile storage facility where conveyors, for example, would not be feasible. Or it may be using an old warehouse that has low ceilings, negating the use of shelving or containers, or one with floors that are unable to support a heavy-duty forklift truck. Firms do not always have the option of using the best type of facility, and the facility itself will affect the type of equipment a firm can use.

If the company is designing a brand-new warehousing facility, then all the equipment options described here are probably available. If it is dealing with an existing facility, particularly if it is old, then the company faces some constraints on the type of equipment it can use.

time requirements

Time is a logistics system factor in various ways, and it does affect materials handling. Because customers expect to receive orders in a reasonable time period, time is critical in a market or distribution warehouse where a firm stores its valuable finished goods. These companies select materials-handling equipment that enables them to move goods into, around, and out of the warehouse as fast as possible.

Rapid movement characterizes the distribution or transit warehouse, and we often find the most sophisticated and largest variety of materials-handling equipment in these facilities. These warehouses, usually automated, utilize elaborate and sophisticated conveyor systems, automatic storage placers, and all of the materials-handling equipment we have discussed here.

On the other hand, if we are talking about a storage warehouse or one that a firm uses primarily in conjunction with the manufacturing facility to store semifinished goods and perhaps basic materials, then time is not usually as critical. The equipment would be more basic, and automating such a facility might be unnecessary.

Because of trade-off possibilities, a firm for whom time is critical may be much more willing to invest large amounts of money in sophisticated materials-handling equipment. Investing more in a materials-handling system enables the firm to increase sales or have savings in other areas.

These factors will provide the logistics manager a basic framework for analyzing the company's particular needs and the materials-handling equipment options available to the company. After this analysis, the manager can look at what the most likely equipment manufacturers can offer in each category. The logistics manager can also get additional engineering information from the company's own staff, which will help further in designing the system that will best meet the company's particular needs. Although the final selection of a system and its equipment will require a lot of detail, knowing the equipment available and the factors the selection involves provides the basis for developing an efficient system for any organization.

Sources of Information. In evaluating materials-handling equipment alternatives, a number of sources provide help and insight.

Computers can estimate storage/retrieval requirements. One recently developed program estimates net cube requirements, storage location requirements, and activity and storage/retrieval configuration and runs a sensitivity analysis. Often, switching to an expensive system is unnecessary. Rather, a firm should try to reduce picking time by increasing the accuracy of storage and inventory information and by optimizing the goods placement for manual retrieval.

Many large companies and some small ones have staff engineers who can help the logistics manager analyze the situation. These individuals can provide detailed guidance once the logistics manager has completed an initial analysis.

Equipment manufacturers maintain a staff of engineers who can provide their company cost data on possible alternatives. Equipment has become so specialized today that this may be the best way to get detailed cost information.

Another possibility is to use consultants to analyze need and select the best equipment. Although such organizations are sometimes expensive, they often provide a very reasonable analysis based upon the costs of using alternative resources.

In addition to these, companies can use sources such as trade associations and self-study. While both of these usually provide only simplified data, they often provide a convenient starting place.

CHAPTER 9

THE TRANSPORTATION SYSTEM

LEARNING OBJECTIVES

After reading this chapter, you should be able to do the following:

- Explain the economic role transportation plays in the economy.
- Discuss the economic and service characteristics of the basic modes.
- Discuss the economic effect of rates, transit time, reliability, capability, accessibility, and security in the carrier selection decision.
- Compare the advantages and disadvantages of using common, regulated, contract, exempt, and private carriers—the five legal classes of carriers.
- Discuss the economic and service characteristics of intermodal transportation and explain the dominance of rail-truck (piggyback) intermodal service.
- Discuss the economic and service characteristics of indirect and special carriers.

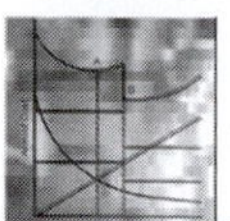

LOGISTICS PROFILE

Victoria's Secret for Success

Intimate Brands, Inc., is a leading specialty retailer of intimate apparel and beauty and personal care products through the Victoria's Secret and Bath & Body Works brands. In 1999, net sales for the Victoria's Secret brand, including stores, catalog and E-commerce, were $2.9 billion. Catalog and E-commerce accounted for 18 percent of the business, or $799 million.

According to Kurt Kravchuk, director of Parcel Transportation for Victoria's Secret catalog and E-commerce, "Victoria's Secret catalog is using cutting-edge technology partners to provide the excellent brand experience Victoria's Secret customers have come to expect—through on-time delivery and efforts to keep shipping costs down."

For shipments under one pound, about 33 percent to 35 percent, Victoria's Secret ships via the U.S. Postal Service. With products including clothing, shoes, accessories, and bath and beauty products, in addition to lingerie, orders can vary from a few ounces for a single item to several pounds. "We've always used some form of postal service," Kravchuk says, "because they provide a good service at a good price and because of customer requests or orders that go to post office boxes." Kravchuk continues, "The USPS offers us a cost benefit in certain areas, and we take advantage of that." However, he says even though cost is always one consideration, it is not the primary one. "Service to customers is always primary."

Although there are requests for expedited service, with which Victoria's Secret complies, many customers are happy with the company's pledge to deliver orders in seven to ten business days. It works hard to stay within that time frame and monitors performance on a weekly basis to ensure that service level. The majority of orders come in by phone but also fax and mail, with increasing activity via http://www.VictoriasSecret.com. Contrary to what might be expected, Kravchuk says customer delivery requirements on Internet orders closely mirror phone orders. He has not seen a dramatic surge in requests for expedited delivery of Internet orders.

For the past three years, Victoria's Secret has used Global Logistics, a package expeditor, to service its USPS shipments in the southeast. Bob Thatcher, Global Logistics' president, makes the distinction himself between being a consolidator and an expeditor. He describes the company as a regional expeditor because he focuses more on service and performance than price. Global Logistics focuses on serving major catalogers that focus on quality of service. His goal is to provide three- to five-day service from the time an order is shipped to the time it is delivered to the household. This obviously fits well with the Victoria's Secret promised delivery. Intimate Brands provides linehaul from its Columbus, Ohio, distribution center to Global Logistics' facility in Stone Mountain, Georgia. Global then sorts, palletizes, and manifests loads for delivery. Victoria's Secret sends an average of one trailer every day, five days a week. This may increase two trailers a day during the peak holiday season in December, as well as a sales period in January.

Among the services Global Logistics offers is serving as its customers' eyes in the field. For example, Global Logistics is always on the alert for area-specific issues that may affect delivery such as weather or other events and determines which ZIP codes will be affected. Sharing this information with Victoria's Secret helps Global Logistics keep delivery schedules on track. According to Thatcher, "We look at every opportunity to reduce time, either in transit or in steps, to ensure quick delivery."

One of the time-saving techniques it uses is taking orders processed on Fridays and getting them to the post office on Sunday and Monday. This can cut up to a day off delivery times. In reducing steps, Global Logistics does not over label. The shipper is responsible for applying all markings (including the postage indicia) on its labels. As a result, when Global Logistics receives the shipment, it just scans the five-digit bar code, sorts, palletizes, and manifests.

(continued on next page)

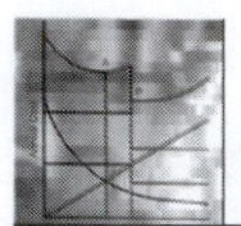

LOGISTICS PROFILE

Victoria's Secret for Success *continued*

All deliveries are palletized for ease of handling. Thatcher is quick to point out that all of Global Logistics' deliveries to the bulk mail centers are standing appointments and live unloads. The alternative, Thatcher says, is drop and pick, where a trailer is dropped at the bulk mail center and the postal service personnel have up to twenty-four hours to unload it. Although it typically does not take the full twenty-four hours, it is a variable Thatcher does not want in his schedule.

According to Kravchuk, visibility of products at this point does not play a role in their distribution. He would, however, like to work more closely with the USPS to get delivery information in real time. Because Victoria's Secret does not apply a tracking number, Global Logistics tracks performance through the postal system with an 8125 (Mailing Form) to ensure proper service.

Source: Bert Moore, "Victoria's Secret For Success," *Parcel Shipping & Distribution* (Fall 2000): 32–34. Reprinted with permission.

INTRODUCTION

The transportation system is the physical link connecting a company's customers, raw material suppliers, plants, warehouses, and channel members—the fixed points in a logistics supply chain. The fixed points in the logistics system are where some activity temporarily halts the flow of goods in the logistics pipeline. The transportation companies utilized to connect these facilities affect not only the transportation costs but also the operating costs at these facilities.

This chapter is concerned with the transportation system in the logistics system. We focus on the fundamental relationship between transportation and the logistics supply chain, the carrier selection decision, and the characteristics of alternative transportation providers.

THE ROLE OF TRANSPORTATION IN LOGISTICS

bridge over buyer-seller gap

Conceptually, a company's logistics supply chain is a series of fixed points where the goods come to rest and transportation links. The transportation link permits goods to flow between the various fixed points and bridges the buyer-seller gap. The transportation carrier a company utilizes to perform the link service is a decisive factor in determining the efficiency of operating the supply chain facility and partially determines the company's competitive edge and product demand in a given market area.

As the Logistics Profile points out, on-time delivery and low shipping costs provide Victoria's Secret with a competitive edge. The goal is to have all orders delivered within seven to ten days from the date the customer places the order. The transit time goal is to have the order delivered to the customer within three to five days from the time the order is shipped. Various tactics are used to eliminate time delays such as using a package expeditor, palletizing loads, and using delivery time appointments at the bulk mail centers. Transportation, in this case the U.S. Postal Service, plays a key role in assuring that Victoria's Secret provides the delivery service the customer expects.

value added

Knowledge of the transportation system is fundamental to the efficient and economical operation of a company's logistics function. Transportation is the physical thread connecting the company's geographically dispersed operations. More specifically, transportation adds value to the company by creating time and place utility; the value added is the physical movement of goods to the place desired and at the time desired.

For a firm to function without the aid of transportation is virtually inconceivable in today's global economy. Most companies are geographically divorced from their supply sources, thereby making them dependent upon transportation to connect the supply source to the consumption point. Labor specialization, mass production, and production economies normally do not coincide with the area where demand for the good exists. Thus, transportation is necessary to bridge this buyer-seller spatial gap.

global impact

As supply chains become increasingly longer in our global economy, the transportation function is connecting buyers and sellers that may be tens of thousands of miles apart. This increased spatial gap results in greater transportation costs. In addition, operations within this international marketplace require more transportation time, which necessitates higher inventories and resulting higher storage costs. Therefore, the greater the buyer-seller gap, the greater the transportation and storage costs.

importance in economy

The total dollars spent in the United States to move freight reveal the importance of transportation in the economy. In 1999, the United States spent an estimated $554 billion to move freight or 9.9 percent of the GDP.[1] This total expenditure included shipper costs of $5 billion for loading and unloading freight cars and for operating and controlling the transportation function.

importance in company

As an example of transportation's relative importance in a company, a study of 1999 physical distribution (outbound only) costs revealed that total logistic costs represented 7.34 percent of sales and that the outbound transportation cost amounted to 3.24 percent of sales, or 30.1 percent of total distribution costs. Warehousing cost was 1.84 percent of sales; customer service and order processing accounted for 0.48 percent of sales; administration was 0.38 percent of sales; and, inventory carrying cost was 1.52 percent of sales.[2] Outbound transportation was clearly the largest component of total physical distribution costs.

To say that transportation is logistics implies that transportation operates independently of other logistics functions. Nothing could be further from the truth, because transportation directly affects a facility's operation. The quality of the transportation service provided bears directly upon inventory costs and stockout costs at a facility as well as upon the cost of operating the facility.

cost-service trade-off

For example, if a company switches from rail to air transportation to move raw materials from a vendor to the plant, the air carrier's increased speed, or lower transit time, permits the company to hold lower inventories to meet demand during transit time and to use less warehousing space and less-stringent product packaging; but the company realizes these advantages at the expense of higher transportation costs. Thus, a firm cannot make the transportation decision in a vacuum; applying the total cost or systems approach requires a company to consider how the transport decision will affect other elements of the logistics system.

THE TRANSPORT SELECTION DECISION

As has been indicated, the transportation expenditures companies incur involve significant dollar amounts; and the carrier's service quality affects other logistics operating costs and the demand for the company's product. The company controls these expenditures and service levels through the transportation decision.

This section focuses on the process of selecting a carrier and factors relevant to that decision. The carrier selection decision process provides the framework for the discussion of the different types of transportation providers that follows this section.

The Transportation–Supply Chain Relationship

The carrier selection decision is a specialized purchasing process whereby a firm purchases the services of a carrier to provide the necessary link among logistics facilities. The carrier selected directly affects the operation of the logistics facility and other logistics system functions.

scope of transport selection decision

The carrier selection decision, then, entails more than merely evaluating the prices of different transportation methods. It must also consider the other costs associated with how the transport method's service affects the facility operation. The transit time different methods incur will affect the inventory level; that is, the longer the transit time, the greater the inventory level the company requires to protect against stockouts until the next shipment arrives. The transport method's dependability and the degree of safe delivery also affect the inventory levels held at a facility, the utilization of materials-handling equipment and labor, and the time and cost of communicating with the carrier to determine shipment status or to seek reparations for goods damaged in transit.

A company's knowledge of carrier prices and pricing practices can simplify the carrier selection decision. Measuring and evaluating the logistical implication of the carrier cost determinant is much easier than measuring carrier service performances; logistics personnel know carrier rates and can easily compute an alternative's direct transportation cost. However, basing transport method selection upon lowest transport costs does not guarantee the least-cost decision for the whole logistics supply chain.

The Carrier Selection Decision

specialized purchasing process

As we have noted, the carrier selection decision is a specialized purchasing process. As with any procurement decision, vendor price (carrier rate) is not the only selection criterion the firm considers. True, the carrier rate is an important factor in the decision, but the firm must consider the quality of the service and how this service affects facility operating costs.

modal choice

Carrier selection is a twofold process, as Figure 9–1 indicates. First, the firm selects a transportation mode. The choices include the basic modes of rail, water, truck, air, and pipeline. In addition, intermodal transportation, which uses two or more modes to provide service over a given traffic lane, is available. The most common forms of intermodal transportation include rail-truck (piggyback), truck-air, and rail-water.

specific carrier choice

The second step in the decision is to select a specific carrier from within the chosen mode or intermodal form. The specific carrier selection requires the firm to choose the legal carrier type: common, regulated, contract, exempt, or private. The number of alternative carriers is much greater in the specific carrier selection phase than in the modal phase. For example, while the basic modal choice is limited to five alternatives, the number of for-hire motor carriers from which a firm may choose is approximately 400,000.

repetitive decision

Generally, a firm considers the carrier selection decision a repetitive purchase decision. That is, a company deciding to use motor carriers does not review this decision every time it selects a carrier to provide link service. The decision to use trucks remains in effect until the firm makes a major review of overall transportation costs and/or makes a major change in its logistics system. This repetitive decision characteristic also applies to the specific carrier decision. The firm uses the selected carrier repeatedly until the carrier's service level or rate becomes unacceptable.

The modal selection phase has received a great deal of attention. This usually involves evaluating the rates and service levels of alternative modes and intermodal forms. The firm selects the mode or intermodal form that occasions the lowest total logistics costs and then applies this analysis to the specific carriers within the selected mode (or intermodal). Given today's deregulated transportation environment, carrier rates and service performance do vary among carriers within the same mode.

FIGURE 9–1 The Carrier Selection Decision

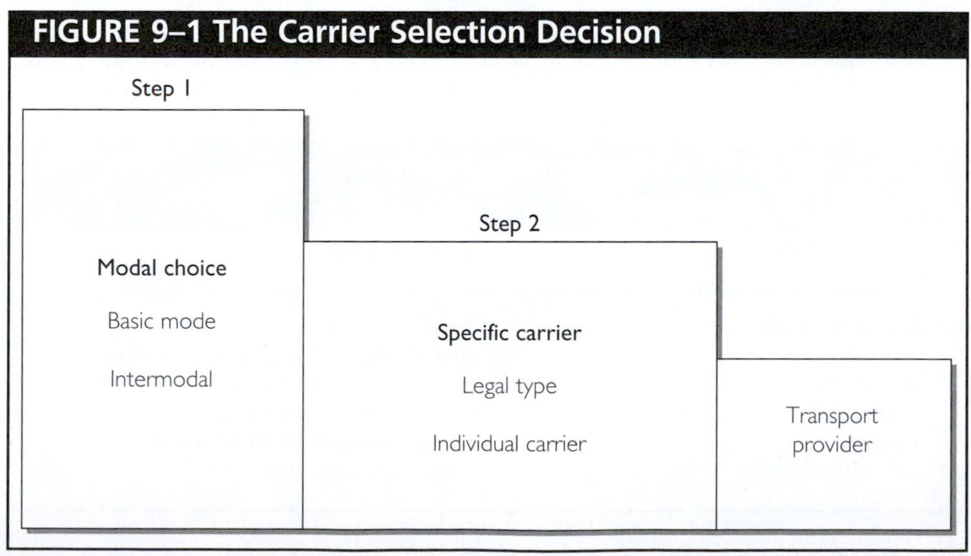

service Most carriers in a given mode have the technical characteristics to provide the same level of service, but these service levels can and do vary greatly from one carrier to another. Also, since the cost structures are essentially the same for carriers in a given mode, the rates of alternative carriers in that mode are quite similar for a given movement. But, given the market and operating conditions different carriers face, the rates carriers within a given mode charge may vary somewhat. Thus, allowing for slight rate disparities, the transport rate is not the most important criterion in selecting a specific carrier; but the rate is important in modal selection. Carrier service performance, then, becomes the relevant determinant for selecting a specific carrier from one mode.

Carrier Selection Determinants

What, then, are the criteria firms use to evaluate the alternative modes and carriers? According to the carrier selection literature, the salient selection determinants are carrier costs and service performance. The relevant service performance determinants are transit time, reliability, capability, accessibility, and security (see Figure 9–2). We now discuss how carrier cost and service determinants interact in the firm's logistics function.

transportation cost *Transportation cost* was the predominant carrier selection determinant in early carrier selection works. The transportation cost includes the rates, minimum weights, loading and unloading facilities, packaging and blocking, damage in transit, and special services available from a carrier—for example, stopping in transit.

Transportation cost analysis is oriented toward evaluating alternative modes, since the rates, minimum weights, loading and unloading facilities, packaging, and blocking will vary from one mode to another. However, the importance of transportation costs has receded somewhat with the advent of the business logistics concept, which now focuses attention upon the cost trade-offs existing between the service a carrier provides and facility operation costs. Even so, the transportation cost disparities prevalent in today's deregulated environment remain an important criterion in the carrier selection decision.

transit time and reliability *Transit time* is the total time that elapses from the time the consignor makes the goods available for dispatch until the carrier delivers same to the consignee. This includes the time required for pickup and delivery, for terminal handling, and for

FIGURE 9–2 Carrier Selection Determinants and User Implications

Selection Determinants	User Implication
Transport cost	Landed costs
Transit time	Inventory, stockout costs, marketing
Reliability	Inventory, stockout costs, marketing
Accessibility	Transit time, freight costs
Capability	Meet physical/marketing needs
Security/Safety	Inventory, stockout costs

movement between origin and destination terminals. *Reliability* refers to the consistency of the transit time a carrier (the link supplier) provides.

inventory and stockout costs

Transit time and reliability affect inventory and stockout costs (which take the form of lost sales or forgone productivity). Shorter transit times result in lower inventories, while more dependability causes lower inventory levels or stockout costs. With a given level of lead time, a firm can minimize inventories and consequently inventory carrying costs. But if the transit time is not consistent, the firm must increase inventories above the level that a consistent transit time would require. More specifically, a facility now must hold larger amounts of inventory as a safety factor against stockouts that could arise from inconsistent service.

product differentiation

The marketing implications of reliable transit time are product differentiation and a competitive advantage in the marketplace. (See, for example, Victoria's Secret transit time advantage in the Logistics Profile.) Thus, if your firm can provide a customer with a shorter and more dependable transit time than your competitor, the customer can reduce inventory or stockout costs and your firm can increase sales. Sales are quite sensitive to consistent service, and the logistics manager must concentrate on carrier transit time and reliability to differentiate a firm's product in the marketplace.

capability and accessibility

Capability and accessibility determine whether a particular carrier can physically perform the transport service desired. *Capability* refers to the carrier's ability to provide the equipment and facilities that the movement of a particular commodity requires. Equipment that can provide controlled temperatures or humidity and special handling facilities are examples of capability factors. *Accessibility* considers the carrier's ability to provide service over the route in question. Accessibility refers to a carrier's physical access to facilities. The geographic limits of a carrier's route network (rail lines or waterways) and the operating scope that regulatory agencies authorize constrain a carrier's accessibility. A carrier's inability to meet the desired capability and availability service requirements can eliminate the carrier from consideration in the carrier selection decision.

security

Security concerns the arrival of goods in the same condition they were in when tendered to the carrier. Although the common carrier is held liable for all loss and damage, with limited exceptions, the firm does incur costs when the carrier loses goods or delivers them in a damaged condition. Unsafe service results in opportunity costs of forgone profits or productivity because the goods are not available for sale or use. To guard against these opportunity costs, a firm will increase inventory levels, with resulting increased inventory costs. The continued use of an unsafe carrier will adversely affect customer satisfaction and, consequently, sales.

A firm using a common/regulated carrier holds the carrier liable for damage to the lading. To recover the damage value, the shipping firm must file a claim with the carrier. This entails a claim preparation and documentation cost, as well as legal fees if the firm has the claim settled through the courts. Therefore, frequent damage to the commodities also aggravates the cost associated with claim settlement.

The Pragmatics of Carrier Selection

transit time reliability

Figure 9–3 gives the relative importance of the carrier selection determinants for firms selecting motor carriers in today's deregulated environment. The most

FIGURE 9–3 Importance Ranking of Carrier Selection Determinants

Determinant	Rank
Transit time reliability or consistency	1
Door-to-door transportation rates or costs	2
Total door-to-door transit time	3
Willingness of carrier to negotiate rate changes	4
Financial stability of the carrier	5
Equipment availability	6
Frequency of service	7
Pickup and delivery service	8
Freight loss and damage	9
Shipment expediting	10
Quality of operating personnel	11
Shipment tracing	12
Willingness of carrier to negotiate service changes	13
Scheduling flexibility	14
Line-haul services	15
Claims processing	16
Quality of carrier salesmanship	17
Special equipment	18

Source: Edward J. Bardi, Prabir Bagchi, and T. S. Raghurathan, "Motor Carrier Selection in a Deregulated Environment," *Transportation Journal* 29, no. 1 (Fall 1989): 4–11.

important criterion is the quality of the service the carrier provides, that is, transit time reliability. The impact of reliable transit time and total transit time (importance rank 3) on inventory and stockout costs and customer service is of paramount importance today.

carrier rates

limited carriers

Transportation deregulation has provided transportation users with increased opportunity to negotiate both rates and services with carriers. This greater reliance on the marketplace has increased interest in the rate the carrier charges. Shippers are generally utilizing fewer carriers in order to become more important to the carrier and thereby to increase their negotiating power with the carrier.

financial stability

Transportation rates, the carrier's willingness to negotiate rate changes, and the carrier's financial stability reflect the negotiating strategy inherent in the deregulated environment. Today's shippers utilize their economic buying power in the marketplace to realize lower transportation rates from carriers; but this highly competitive motor carrier industry has experienced thousands of bankruptcies since deregulation began in 1980. The heightened possibility of bankruptcy increases the service disruption risk; and the magnitude of this risk increases as firms implement a reduced carrier strategy.

sales rep

Shippers give capability and accessibility average importance, as the factors ranked from 6 to 15 show. The security criterion of freight loss and damage ranks ninth in importance, and the claims-processing factor ranks sixteenth.

special equipment

Less important selection determinants are the quality of carrier salesmanship and special equipment. Shippers making the carrier selection decision give little importance to the quality of the carrier sales representative. Special equipment is not an important selection determinant for shippers who require standard equipment, but for those requiring special equipment the carrier who has it is the only one the shipper will use.

THE BASIC MODES OF TRANSPORTATION[3]

The basic modes of transportation available to the logistics manager are rail, motor, water, pipeline, and air. Each mode has different economic and technical structures, and each can provide different qualities of link service. This section examines how each mode's structure relates to the cost and quality of link service possible with the basic modes—the basis for the modal selection analysis.

Distribution of *ton-miles* (an output measurement combining weight and distance, or tonnage multiplied by miles transported) among the modes shows each mode's relative importance. Table 9-1 shows this distribution. These data suggest that the relative importance of rail and water transport has lessened and that the importance of motor, air, and multimodal transport has increased. Air transport has continued to advance in property movement, an increase of 55.5 percent from 1993 to 1997. On the surface, these data suggest that shipping firms increasingly use "premium" transportation—motor, air, and multimodal—to provide a desired level of customer service by trading off higher transportation costs (motor and air, as compared with rail and water) for lower facility costs.

In 1999, motor carriers received 82.0 percent of the U.S. freight expenditures; rail, 6.6 percent; air, 4.7 percent; water, 4.0 percent; and oil pipeline, 1.6 percent.[4] The bulk of the U.S. freight bill goes for the purchase of truck transportation.

TABLE 9–1 Modal Distribution of Ton-Miles

	1997		1993		% Change
Mode	**(Bil)**	**%**	**(Bil)**	**%**	**1997–1993**
Truck	1023	40.6	870	38.2	17.7
Rail	1022	40.6	943	41.4	8.5
Water	261	10.4	271	11.9	(3.8)
Air	6	0.3	4	0.2	55.5
Pipeline	NA	—	NA	—	—
Multiple mode	204	8.1	191	8.4	6.8
Total	2516		2279		10.4

Source: U.S. Census Bureau, 1997 Commodity Flow Survey (1999), 9.

Railroads

capability

All for-hire railroads in the United States are classified as common carriers[5] and are thus subjected to the legal service obligations we discuss later. Since the Surface Transportation Board (STB) imposes no legal restraints or operating authority regulations regarding the commodities railroads may transport, railroads have a distinct advantage in availability and in the ability to provide service to "all" shippers. This is not to imply that railroads can transport any product anywhere, for the accessibility of rail transportation does have limitations. Railroads are not restricted as to the cargo type they may transport; rather, all railroads are legally, as well as physically, capable of transporting all commodities tendered for transportation.

limited number of carriers

The railroad industry consists of a small number of large firms. There are about 360 railroads, of which fewer than 10 have revenues exceeding $250 million per year, with the remainder having less than $250 million in revenues. This rather limited number of carriers may suggest limited rail service availability, but the railroads are required to provide through service, which makes rail service available to points beyond a particular carrier's geographic limits.

market structure

This mode's economic structure partly accounts for the limited number of rail carriers. Railroads, which fall within that infamous group of business undertakings labeled as "natural monopolies," require a large investment in terminals, equipment, and trackage to begin operation; and the accompanying huge capacity allows the railroads to be a decreasing-cost industry. As output (ton-miles) increases, the average per-unit production cost decreases. Thus, having fewer railroads in operation in a given area and permitting those few firms to realize inherent large-scale output economies are economical and beneficial to society.

Through mergers, four railroads—Burlington Northern Santa Fe, CSX Transportation, Norfolk Southern and Union Pacific—have evolved as the dominant carriers in the industry. Many of these carriers have acquired nonrail transportation companies such as trucking and water carriers, permitting one organization to provide multimodal transportation service to shippers.

long distance and large volume

Railroads are primarily long-distance, large-volume movers of low-value, high-density goods. The reason for these long-distance, large-volume rail movements is ingrained in the mode's economic and technical characteristics. The railroad's decreasing cost structure suggests that large-volume, long-distance movements lower the average production cost by increasing output (ton-miles) and thereby spreading the fixed costs over a greater output base.

A major advantage of using railroad transportation is the long-distance movement of commodities in large quantities at relatively low rates. Products of forests, mines, and agriculture are the major commodities railroads transport. For these low-value, high-density products, transportation costs account for a substantial portion of their selling price. Railroads tend to serve the inbound portion of the logistics supply chain; however, railroads transport about 70 percent of the vehicles from domestic automobile manufacturers. Rail transportation has one of the lowest revenue per ton-mile of all modes, and it has the lowest revenue per ton-mile of the modes capable of transporting general commodities domestically—rail, motor, and air.

low accessibility

Low accessibility is one primary disadvantage of rail transport. Accessibility refers to the carrier's ability to provide service to and from the facilities in a particular situation. The rail carrier cannot deviate from the route that the rail trackage follows. If a shipper or consignee is not adjacent to the rail right-of-way, rail transport is not easily accessible. To use rail service, a shipper or consignee not adjacent to the track must utilize another transport mode—namely, truck—to gain access to the rail service. Thus, rail service may not be advantageous in logistics situations such as the ultimate delivery of consumer goods to retail outlets.[6]

long transit times

Rather long transport time is another disadvantage of rail transport. The problem occurs in the classification yard, where the carrier *consolidates* boxcars, or marshalls them into train units. This huge physical task, which requires consolidating boxcars going in a similar direction and breaking out cars that have reached their destination or that the carrier must transfer to another train unit, adds to the overall slow speed of rail transport.

reliability and safety

Railroads favorably provide other service qualities important to the logistics manager—reliability and safety. Weather conditions disrupt rail service less than they disrupt the service of other modes; such conditions cause only minor fluctuations in rail transit time reliability. Rail safety incurs greater costs. Moving goods by rail requires considerable packaging and resultant packaging costs. This stems from the car classification operation, in which the carrier couples cars at impacts ranging from one to ten miles per hour, and from the rather rough ride that steel wheels running on steel rails provide. But these service qualities differ among particular carriers, and the logistics manager must research such qualities carefully.

Today's railroad industry is changing considerably in response to the economy, deregulation, and the logistics approach of business. The traditional markets of low-value, high-density, high-volume products (grain, steel, coal, etc.) are stagnant or declining. Deregulation has increased the competitive pressures for railroads to lower rates, and the railroads have responded through the contract ratemaking provisions of the Staggers Act of 1980. Finally, the railroads are experiencing pressures from logistics managers to improve service (see the On the Line article: "It's the Service, Stupid") and to integrate with other modes (primarily trucking).

During the past ten years, the railroads have made considerable improvements in productivity. They have abandoned unused tracks, sold off unprofitable lines (regional railroads), reduced the workforce, and modified labor work rules. Increased computer use is enabling the industry to improve train movement efficiency, saving fuel and labor costs.

Railroad mergers are another possible strategy for improving productivity. Larger companies offer the opportunity for economies of scale and lower rates to the shipping public. Recent mergers have resulted in four major railroads serving the United States.

intermodal

New market penetration is another railroad strategy that has improved profitability. The major new market being entered is intermodal freight. During the last few years, intermodal traffic has increased dramatically. Railroads have developed the stack train that hauls two containers on one specially designed flatcar. This service is used primarily by international shippers who integrate water carriage to and from foreign countries with rail domestically to form an integrated transportation process.

IMC

Additionally, railroad intermodal traffic is growing because of a new type of transportation company, the intermodal marketing company, or IMC. The IMC is an

ON THE LINE

IT'S THE SERVICE, STUPID

It is difficult to assess the state of the railroad industry without getting into the subject of service—shippers complain about it, rail carriers say they are trying to improve it, and Wall Street maintains more of it will be expected of the railroads if the industry is to grow.

Ed Emmett, president of the National Industrial Transportation League (NITL), took issue recently with Union Pacific Railroad President Dick Davidson's position that it is not poor service that shippers are fed up with but the fact that the railroads engage in differential pricing. "What shippers are hoping for, Dick, is that their railcars get delivered when you say they're going to get delivered. That's what the railroad industry has to understand," Emmett said.

Even Wall Street—which is not interested in how the railroads grow long term as long as they achieve it—says that improving service is imperative. "It is clear that the cost-cutting theme that drove rail stocks in the decade following deregulation is over," said independent rail analyst Tony Hatch. "What is really going to move the stocks now has got to be top-line growth. And the only thing that can drive that is improved service."

After a period of significantly improved service in the early 1990s, service has clearly declined, Hatch said. "And what's doubly unfortunate about this is that it's declined at a period where customers are demanding ever higher levels of service. They don't want service to be 'X,' they want it to be 'X plus 1' every year," he said.

On the regulatory side, industry observers do not see any real movement on issues such as reauthorization of the Surface Transportation Board or reregulation. "One of the reasons for that is because railroads don't have an incentive to move," said NITL's Emmett. "If there's no reauthorization, the agency is reappropriated under the old authorization. Status quo rules, and railroads are happy with the status quo so why should there be a big push?" In addition, Emmett says, members of Congress are not getting beat up by their constituents over STB reauthorization, so it is not an issue they feel like they have to deal with.

And then there are the problems Norfolk Southern and CSX are having integrating Conrail into their systems—a subject difficult to avoid in assessing the industry at this point. "I've been in this racket forty-seven years, and I have never seen the frustrations with the railroad service that we have right now," said Ken Enzor, director of logistics for chemical manufacturer Omya, Inc. "The railroads are trying to do something in developing a service that (shippers) have always pleaded for but have never gotten. It seems service was better when we were tracing cars over the telephone. At least back then we got some answers and we knew how to prepare."

Emmett is more optimistic. "It was almost unavoidable that there were going to be service problems; one can only try to minimize them and hopefully be more responsive than the carriers were in the West," he said. "Actually that's the silver lining of the Eastern clouds. The railroads have been extremely responsive to this. They're highly cognizant that it's going on, and they're not in any sense of denial."

In a word, says Hatch, the state of the rail industry is in flux. "But there are more good signs than bad," he said. "In the West I think UP is really doing well. The East is worrisome but it doesn't cause me to panic. If you look at the headlines right now you say, 'How could anyone possibly be optimistic?' That's because I can look back just a few years before this current merger issue and see where the railroads were."

"The goals in the industry haven't changed: improve service across the board, which will improve their reputation among customers, and therefore help grow their business while decreasing pressure from the government to reform. These are the two issues facing them. And as long as they continue to focus on improving service in the West and get through these initial service issues in the East, they'll be fine. But we're in the middle of it; we can't say it's done."

Source: John Gallagher, "It's the Service, Stupid," *Traffic World* (5 July 1999): 31–32. Reprinted with permission of *Traffic World, The Logistic News Weekly.*

intermediary who solicits intermodal traffic from shippers and gives it to the railroad to transport. The IMC initially started as a marketing effort to seek freight to fill empty containers moving back to the West Coast and on to Pacific Rim countries. Now the IMCs have contracted with railroads to ship a given number of containers per train over specific traffic lanes.

Motor Carriers

The motor carrier is very much a part of any firm's logistics supply chain; almost every logistics operation utilizes the motor truck, from the smallest pickup truck to the largest tractor-semitrailer combination, in some capacity. The United States' sophisticated highway network permits the motor carrier to reach all points of the country. Therefore, the motor carrier can provide transportation service to virtually all shippers. Table 9–1 points out that motor carriers have made great inroads into the number of ton-miles that carriers transport in the United States; they realize 82 percent of the U.S. freight enpenditures. Figure 9–4 offers an overview of the motor carrier industry.

types of legal carriers

The motor carrier industry, unlike the railroad industry, consists of for-hire and private carriers. Private motor carriers transport freight that is owned by the firm that owns/leases and operates the trucks. The for-hire carriers are classified as regulated, contract, or exempt. The regulated carriers are not subject to the common carrier obligations, except they are held liable for damage to the shippers' goods. Contract carriers are governed by the terms and conditions of the contract signed by the carrier and the shipper. Exempt carriers are specifically excluded from federal economic regulations.

The exempt carrier primarily transports agricultural, fish, and horticultural products—the exempt commodities to which the next section refers. While private carriers transport a variety of products, private truck transportation most commonly moves high-value, high-rated traffic and commodities requiring "personalized" service such as driver-salesperson operations.

FIGURE 9–4 Overview of Interstate Motor Carrier Industry

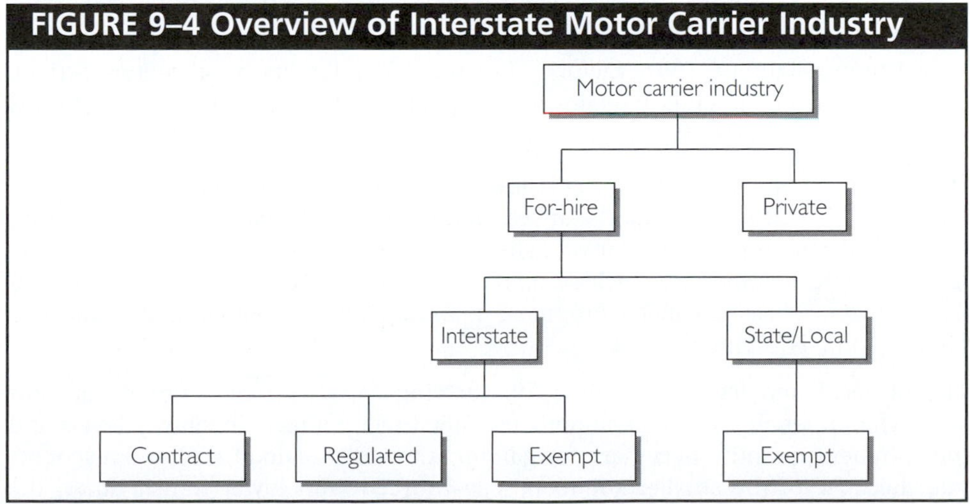

Source: Adapted from John J. Coyle, Edward J. Bardi, and Robert A. Novack, *Transportation,* 5th ed. (Cincinnati, Ohio: South-Western College Publishing, 2000), 102.

large number of small carriers

The motor carrier industry is characterized by a large number of small carriers. In 1999, there were approximately 505,000 motor carriers (for-hire and private) registered with the U.S. Department of Transportation. Of the approximate 12,500 regulated motor carriers, 850 (7 percent) have annual revenues greater than $10 million (Class I); 2,100 (17 percent) have revenues of $3 million to $10 million; and 9,500 (76 percent) have revenues of less than $3 million.

This large number of carriers is due in part to the low capital that entering the trucking business requires. High variable cost and low fixed cost characterize the cost structure. The motor carrier does not require extensive terminal and equipment investment and does not invest in its own highway. The government builds and maintains the highway, and the carrier pays for highway use through fees such as use taxes and licensing charges. These variable expenses contribute to the high-variable-cost structure.

availability and operating authority

The large number of motor carriers suggests a high availability. For example, many more motor carriers than railroads are available in an area. However, the operating authorities granted carriers have limited motor carrier availability somewhat. These operating grants limit the type of commodity a carrier may transport and the area within which the carrier may provide service. A regulated motor carrier of property may have operating authority to transport only general commodities, household goods, heavy machinery, liquid petroleum products, building materials, or explosives, for example.

high accessibility

The major advantage of motor transport over other modes is its inherent ability to provide service to any location. Truck transportation need not provide service only to customers located adjacent to a track, waterway, or airport. For the logistics manager, the motor carrier is the most accessible transportation mode existing to serve domestic markets today.

transit time

Motor carrier operations do not involve coupling trailers together to form long "train" units, because each cargo unit (trailer) has its own power unit and can be operated independently. Thus, on truckload movements, the shipment goes directly from the shipper to the consignee, bypassing any terminal area and consolidation time. Such technical and operational characteristics enable the motor carrier to provide transit times lower than those for rail and water but higher than that for air.

reliability

Weather conditions and highway traffic can disrupt motor service and thus affect transit time reliability. These factors affect the dependability of all motor carriers. A specific carrier's reliability relates to the operating efficiency the carrier achieves for a given link; this reliability may vary among the given carrier's links.

manufactured goods

While some motor carriers transport low-value products, such as coal and grain, and move products over long distances, motor carriers primarily transport manufactured commodities over relatively short distances. Characterized by high value, manufactured commodities include textile and leather products, rubber and plastic products, fabricated metal products, communication products and parts, and photographic equipment.

small shipment size

The physical and legal constraints[7] on carrying capacity make motor transport somewhat amenable to small shipments. This directly affects inventory levels and the shipment quantity necessary for gaining a lower truckload (volume discount) rate. Because of the smaller shipment size coupled with lower transit times, the logistics manager can reduce inventory carrying costs while maintaining or improving customer service levels.

safety

Generalizing the other relevant service attribute, safety, is difficult for motor carriers. The packaging required for motor carrier movements is less stringent than that required for rail or water; pneumatic tires and improved suspension systems make the motor carrier ride quite smooth. Again, the degree of safety for a given link depends upon the actual operations of individual carriers.

high cost

The logistics manager must consider the relatively high cost of using a motor carrier. The average truck revenue per ton-mile is higher than that of rail and water. This again suggests that commodities shippers move by truck must be of value high enough to sustain the transportation costs, or that trade-offs in inventory, packaging, ware-housing, or customer service costs must warrant the use of this higher-cost mode.

Since deregulation, competition in the for-hire motor carrier industry has increased tremendously. The easing of regulatory entry controls has permitted thousands of new carriers to enter the industry and to compete for existing freight. To gain a market share, the new carriers, as well as the existing carriers, offer lower rates and improved service. Rate discounts are the norm today; some LTL carriers offer shippers discounts as high as 60 to 70 percent.

The competitive environment has been a mixed blessing to shippers. On the positive side, lower motor carrier rates have enabled shippers to reduce transportation costs and improve profitability. On the negative side, the downward pressure on rates has contributed to over 10,000 carrier bankruptcies since 1980. These have caused logistics disruptions ranging from minor delivery delays for freight caught in the bankrupt carrier's system to temporary halting of a firm's transportation function until the firm can find a carrier to replace a key link provider.

Many trucking companies have established nonunion subsidiaries to combat low profitability, such as the ConWay carriers, which are nonunion trucking subsidiaries of Consolidated Freightways, Inc. They have made substantial growth and are a major supplier of trucking service today. Finally, most large trucking companies have created logistics outsourcing companies. These logistics outsourcing firms provide multiple logistics services for clients.

Water Carriers

Water transportation, a major factor in U.S. development, remains an important factor in today's economy. In the early stages of U.S. development, water transportation provided the only connection between the United States and Europe, the market area for U.S. agricultural production and the source of manufactured goods. Thus, many larger industrial cities in both the United States and Europe are located along major water transport routes.

Domestic. Domestic commodity movements take place along the Atlantic, Gulf, and Pacific coasts, as well as inland along internal navigable waterways such as the Mississippi, Ohio, and Missouri Rivers and the Great Lakes. As Figure 9–5 indicates, water carriers are classified as internal water carriers, Great Lakes carriers, and coastal and intercoastal carriers. Internal water carriers operate on the internal navigable waterways. Great Lakes carriers operate on the Great Lakes and provide service to shippers along the northern border of the United States. Coastal carriers operate between points on the same coast, whereas intercoastal carriers operate between points on the Atlantic and the Pacific via the Panama Canal.

FIGURE 9–5 Overview of the Domestic Water Carrier Industry

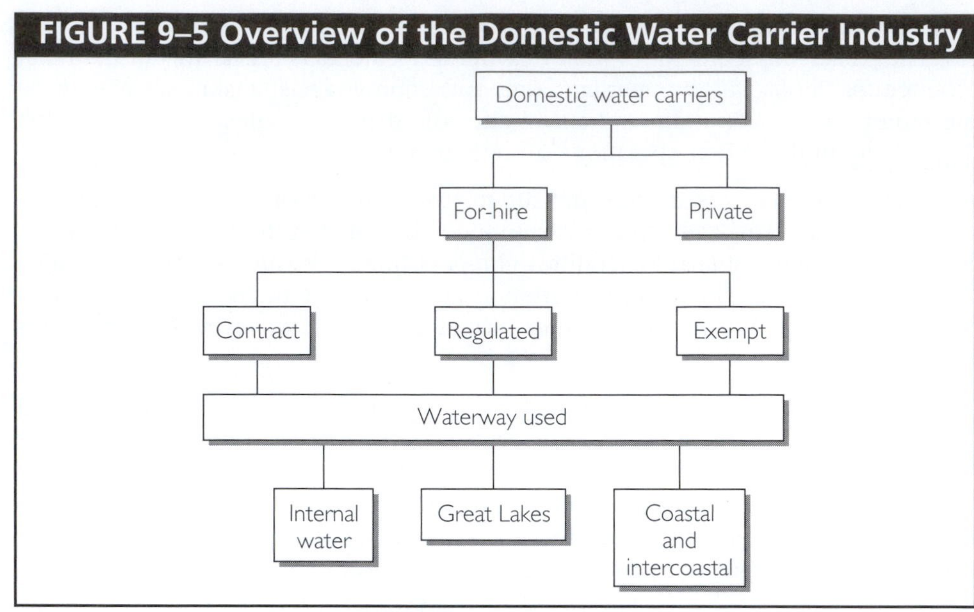

Source: John J. Coyle, Edward J. Bardi, and Robert A. Novack, *Transportation,* 5th ed. (Cincinnati, Ohio: South-Western College Publishing, 2000), 151.

legal carrier types

Four legal classifications of carriers exist in water transportation. Regulated for-hire and contract carriers transport approximately 5 percent of the intercity ton-miles for water-transported freight, and exempt and private carriers transport the remaining 95 percent.

cost structure

Rather low capital entry restraint and operations exempt from federal economic regulation account partly for a large portion of the unregulated domestic traffic transported by water. To begin operation, a water carrier requires no investment for the right-of-way—nature provides the "highway," and public expenditures maintain the facility. The water carrier requires only the entry capital necessary for equipment. Thus, the investment does not preclude private water transport as it does private rail transport. Exemption exists for the transportation of bulk commodities or bulk oil products, and these are the major commodities shippers transport by water.

service characteristics

Water carriers are primarily long-distance movers of low-value, high-density cargoes that mechanical devices easily load and unload. Mineral, agricultural, and forest products are the major commodities transported. Carriers move these products in large quantities: one barge can transport about 1,500 tons.

The principal advantage of using water transport is its low cost. The average revenue per ton-mile for water carriage is lower than that for rail, motor, and air. Thus, water transport is most advantageous for commodities with a low value-to-weight relationship or for commodities in which the transportation cost is a significant portion of the selling price.

long transit time

In return for this low rate, the shipper receives a slow movement method. Water transport possibly provides the highest transit time of all modes. Weather conditions affect internal and Great Lakes operations—ice and low water levels disrupt service.

low accessibility

In addition, water transport has greatly restrained accessibility. Only shippers adjacent to the waterway can use water transport directly. In other situations, water carriage use requires a prior or subsequent land transport movement. Thus, the major disadvantages of water transport are long transit times and low accessibility.

International. As was indicated previously, transport by ship is by far the most widely used international shipment method. In 1999, ocean carriage accounted for approximately 70 percent of U.S. international freight movements. Companies ship almost any conceivable cargo type by sea, but most ocean cargo consists of low weight-to-value commodities such as petroleum, minerals, and dry bulk items.

general cargo ships

Types of Ships. The most common type of ocean vessel in use today is the *general cargo ship.* These ships, usually engaged to transport shipload cargoes on a contract basis, have large cargo holds and are equipped to handle a large variety of cargo. Many of these ships also have what is called a *tween deck,* a deck between the main deck and the main holds in which the carrier commonly stows palletized cargo. Some carriers equip cargo ships with large side doors, which allow easy access for forklifts loading pallets. Most carriers equip cargo ships with derricks, which allow them to load and discharge cargo at ports that lack up-to-date cargo-handling equipment. This feature is very important for ships transporting goods to less-developed portions of the world.

bulk carriers

Bulk carriers carry cargoes with low value-to-weight ratios, such as ores, grain, coal, and scrap metal. Very large openings on these ships' holds allow easy loading and unloading. Watertight walls dividing the holds allow a ship to carry more than one commodity at a time.

tankers

Tankers carry the largest amount of cargo by tonnage. These ships range in size from World War II–era tankers of 18,000 tons to VLCCs (very large crude carriers), some of which top 500,000 tons. Tankers are constructed in much the same way as bulk carriers, but with smaller deck openings. Considering the oil spill problem, the use of double-hulled tankers has become preferable to more conventional single-hulled tankers. Another, less common type of tanker ship, referred to as an LNG ship, carries liquified natural gas. The largest of these vessels can carry enough natural gas to heat New York City for a winter week.

container ships

Container ships are becoming increasingly more important in today's market. These ships are specially designed to carry standardized containers, which are commonly rated in TEUs (twenty-foot equivalent units) or FEUs (forty-foot equivalent units). Some of the larger container ships today carry upwards of 5,000 TEUs on board a single vessel. Also, container ships can carry a wide variety of cargo, including many products that require special handling, temperature control, and so on.

The containers are preloaded at their origin and then placed aboard ship, allowing lower port loading and unloading costs. Containers allow direct access to inland points through intermodal arrangements but require specially designed heavy-lift derricks for loading and unloading. Many smaller ports cannot afford the investment required to handle this type of cargo.

RO–RO

Roll-on–roll-off (RO–RO) vessels are another type of ship proving its value in international trade. RO–ROs are basically large ferry ships. The carrier drives the cargo directly onto the ship using built-in ramps and drives or tows it off at its destination. Toyota currently operates several RO–RO ships to carry automobiles from Japan to the United States and Europe. Each ship can transport 2,000 or more cars at a time. On the return trip, the vessels carry grain or coal for use in Japan.

RO–ROs allow carriers to use standard highway trailers to transport cargo. This can be an advantage in less-developed areas where ports lack container-handling facilities. RO–ROs can also carry oversized cargoes such as large earth-moving equipment or cranes, which carriers can drive directly onto the ship.

Combination RO–RO/container ships are also becoming common. The rear of these ships has built-in ramps. They also have movable decks and inner partitions. The carrier can change the ship configuration so that it may carry various combinations of containers and RO–RO cargo.

OBO *Oil-bulk-ore (OBO) vessels* are multipurpose bulk carriers that are able to carry both liquid and dry bulk products. The development of these vessels allowed the shipowner to carry cargoes on most legs of a voyage, whereas previously the vessel may have had to transit in ballast (empty) due to the trade patterns of the products shipped.

barges *Oceangoing barge vessels* are prominent in the United States-to-Puerto Rico trade and in the Hawaiian interisland trade. In practice, these vessels are towed by an oceangoing tug, as opposed to being pushed like barges on the inland waterways. Compared to the RO–RO vessels, the oceangoing barge is very inexpensive. Currently, the largest of these barges measures 730 feet long and 100 feet wide and has a capacity of 512 trailers on three decks.

Air Carriers

Passenger movement is the air carrier's principal business; passenger revenue accounts for the majority of air carrier business. In the movement of freight, air transport is somewhat nascent, accounting for less than 1 percent of the total intercity ton-miles of freight, and 4.7 percent of the U.S. freight expenditure.

The air carrier industry is highly concentrated in a limited number of carriers. The major carriers earn nearly 90 percent of the industry's revenue; the revenue these carriers generate is primarily from passenger transport.

The type of designations used for air carriers differ somewhat from those used for rail and motor. For-hire air carriers are classified as follows:

- *Certificated:* carrier holding a certificate to operate large aircraft
- *Noncertificated:* carrier that does not hold a certificate to operate because it operates aircraft with a maximum payload of 18,000 pounds and sixty seats
- *All-cargo:* carrier that transports cargo only
- *International:* certificated carrier that operates between the United States and a foreign country
- *Air taxi:* noncertificated carrier that will fly anywhere on demand with a maximum payload of 18,000 pounds and sixty passengers
- *Commuter:* noncertificated carrier that operates with a published timetable
- *Major:* carrier with annual revenues greater than $1 billion
- *National:* carrier with annual revenues between $75 million and $1 billion
- *Large regional:* carrier with annual revenues between $10 million and $75 million
- *Medium regional:* carrier with annual revenues less than $10 million

The logistics manager may use any of the preceding air carrier classes to transport freight.

cost characteristics

The air carrier cost structure consists of high variable costs in proportion to fixed costs, somewhat akin to the motor carrier cost structure. Like motor and water carriers, air carriers do not invest in a highway (airway). The government builds terminals, and carriers pay variable lease payments and landing fees for their use. The equipment cost, though quite high, is still a small part of the total cost.

Major commercial air carrier freight movement started as a passenger business by-product. Excess capacity existed in the plane's "belly," offering potential room for freight movement. As cargo demand grew, the carriers began to seriously consider this business arena. Now the scheduled carriers have dedicated equipment specifically to freight movement and operate freight service to meet freight shippers' ever-growing needs. The all-cargo lines have always concentrated upon cargo transportation.

low transit time

The major advantage of using air transportation is speed. Air transport affords a distinct advantage in low transit time over long distances. Thus, air transport is necessary for moving emergency shipments or shipments that are highly perishable in terms of both spoilage and lost sales or productivity.

high cost

Cost is the major disadvantage of using air transportation, and it precludes many shippers from utilizing this mode. The average revenue per ton-mile for air carriers is higher than that of rail and motor transport. Commodities with a high value-to-weight relationship can sustain this high transport cost because transportation is a smaller portion of the commodity's selling price than is inventory holding cost. In this shipping situation, the logistics manager can reduce inventory levels and inventory costs and can rely upon air transport speed to meet demand.

limited accessibility

Air transport accessibility is somewhat limited. Most firms using air carriers must rely upon land carriers to transport freight to and from the airport. The most common and feasible mode is the motor carrier; firms utilize both local for-hire and private motor carriage to overcome air carrier inaccessibility.

reliability

Air transport reliability is also somewhat of a disadvantage. Weather conditions interrupt air service. These conditions result in increased transit time and adjusted higher inventory levels; but the advent of instrument flying and the adoption of these devices at a greater number of airports are minimizing this service interruption.

international

Air transport has become a very viable alternative to water (ocean) transport for international shipments. The reduced air transit time, reduced delays and port handling costs, and reduced packaging costs enable exporters and importers to reduce overall logistics costs and improve customer service. Again, the logistics manager must trade off the high air transport rate against other logistics cost reductions to justify using this method.

Pipelines

The pipeline industry refers to oil pipelines, not natural gas pipelines. However, the Federal Energy Regulatory Commission, which regulates approximately 140 oil pipelines, also regulates natural gas pipelines just as it regulates any other public utility.

TABLE 9–2 Performance Rating of Modes by Selection Determinant

Selection Determinants	Modes: Railroad	Motor	Water	Air	Pipeline
Cost	3	4	2	5	1
Transit time	3	2	4	1	—
Reliability	2	1	4	3	—
Capability	1	2	4	3	5
Accessibility	2	1	4	3	—
Security	3	2	4	1	—

1 = Best, lowest; 5 = Worst, highest.

limited capability Pipeline transportation is not suitable for general commodity transportation; rather, its use is restricted to the movement of liquid petroleum products. Some firms have attempted to move commodities such as coal in a slurry form, but moving such commodities by pipeline has not been a viable alternative to other modes—namely, water and rail.

limited accessibility Pipeline accessibility is limited. Only shippers adjacent to the pipeline can use this mode directly. Shippers not located adjacent to the pipeline require another, more accessible mode such as water, rail, or truck to transport products to or away from the pipeline. The speed is quite slow, typically less than ten miles per hour, resulting in long transit times; however, weather conditions do not disrupt pipeline service.

cost characteristics The pipeline cost structure is one of high fixed costs and low variable costs, quite similar to that existing for the railroads. The investment in the line, terminals, and pumping stations contributes most to this cost structure.

low cost Low cost, as compared with other modes, is the major advantage to using oil pipelines. However, the inability to transport solids limits its usefulness in the logistics system of a firm manufacturing durable goods.

Performance Rating of Modes

The logistics manager bases the transportation mode decision upon cost and service characteristics. Table 9–2 summarizes each mode's relative advantages and disadvantages. Note that the ratings in this table are generalizations; the exact relationship among specific carriers of different modes may vary.

LEGAL CLASSIFICATIONS OF CARRIERS

The signing into law of the Interstate Commerce Commission (ICC) Termination Act of 1995 abolished the ICC, created the Surface Transportation Board (STB), and drastically altered the federal economic controls exercised over interstate transportation companies. Most of the economic regulations imposed over motor carriers and water carriers are eliminated or greatly reduced, while the majority of the traditional railroad economic regulations still exist. The STB is charged with administering the remaining regulations imposed on railroads, motor carriers, air carriers, pipelines, freight brokers, and freight forwarders.

As a result of the ICC Termination Act, interstate freight carriers are classified into five categories: common, regulated, contract, exempt, and private. The first four are for-hire carriers; the last is not. The common carrier is found in the railroads and pipelines. The regulated, contract, and exempt carriers are found in motor, water, and air transportation. The firm wishing to move its goods in its own vehicles provides private transportation; private trucking is the dominant form of private transportation.

Common Carrier

definition

The *common carrier* is a for-hire carrier that serves the general public at reasonable charges and without discrimination. Economically, the common carrier is the most highly regulated of all the legal carrier types. The economic regulation imposed upon these carriers (railroads and pipelines) acts to protect the shipping public and to ensure sufficient transport service within normal limits.

service requirements

The essence of this regulation is located in the legal service requirements under which the common carrier operates: to serve, to deliver, not to discriminate, and to charge reasonable rates. These service requirements contain the underlying principle of public protection, for the common carrier is a business enterprise affecting the public interest. To guarantee the transportation service the economy requires, the federal government has imposed regulatory controls on common carriers. The government does not impose all of these legal service requirements upon the other types of carriers.

serve the public

To meet its public service requirement, the common carrier must transport all commodities offered to it. The common carrier cannot refuse to carry a particular commodity or to serve a particular point within the carrier's scope of operation. The logistics manager's supply of transportation services seems assured, since the common carrier cannot refuse to transport the firm's commodities, even if the movement is not profitable for the carrier.

liability for damage

The delivery requirement refers to the common carrier's liability for the goods in its care. The common carrier must deliver goods in the same condition they were in when the carrier received them at the shipment's origin. More specifically, the common carrier is liable for all goods lost, damaged, or delayed while in its care. This absolute level of liability has limited exceptions: acts of God, acts of public enemy, acts of public authority, acts of the shipper, and defects inherent in the goods. The logistics manager, then, can transfer the risk of cargo damage, or the bearing of this risk, to the carrier when using a common carrier.

no discrimination

The shipping public finds additional protection in the requirement that the common carrier not discriminate among shippers, commodities, or places. *Discrimination* is when a carrier charges different rates or provides different service levels for essentially similar movements of similar goods. There are, however, permissible forms of discrimination. For example, common carriers may favor larger-volume shippers by charging lower rates for volume movements and higher rates for less-than-volume movements. Cost difference justifies quoting different rates for volume and less-than-volume movements.

charge reasonable rates

Finally, the duty to charge reasonable rates constrains the carrier from charging excessively high or low rates. This requirement has two protective dimensions: it protects the shipping public from rates that are too high, and it protects the carrier from charging rates that are too low. The second protective dimension ultimately protects the public by ensuring continued transportation service.

In summary, the common carrier makes itself available to the public, without providing special treatment to any one party, and operates under rate, liability, and service regulations.

Regulated Carrier

minimal economic regulation

The *regulated carrier* is found in motor and water carriage. The ICC Termination Act eliminated most of the common carrier economic regulations for these two modes, including entry controls, reasonable rates, and nondiscrimination provisions. Regulated carriers are not required to file tariffs containing their rates and are not subject to rate controls.[8] However, regulated carriers must provide tariffs to shippers upon request and these carriers have antitrust immunity for collective ratemaking, such as publishing the national motor freight classification.

carrier obligations

Regulated carriers are required to provide safe and adequate service, equipment, and facilities upon reasonable request, but this is not the same common carrier duty to serve. Regulated motor and water carriers are held liable for damage to cargo in the carrier's care, but the carrier can establish limits upon the value of the liability through the use of tariff rules or released value rates. Thus, regulated carriers must provide safe and adequate service upon reasonable request and are liable for cargo damage up to the limits established by the carrier. Finally, all regulated carriers can contract with shippers and, when doing so, the regulated carriers are not subject to the STB economic regulations for the shipments governed by the contract.

In summary, the regulated carrier is subject to minimal federal economic controls. The logistics manager realizes common carrier benefit of cargo liability when utilizing the regulated carrier, but this benefit is minimized by the valuation limits imposed on liability by the regulated carrier. Since the motor carrier is a significant transportation mode in most logistics systems, the regulated carrier impacts most, if not all, logistics managers.

Contract Carrier

definition

The *contract carrier* is a for-hire carrier that does not serve the general public but, rather, serves one or a limited number of shippers with whom it is under specific contract. The contract carrier, available in all modes, has no legal service obligations imposed upon it. The contract contains terms pertaining to the carrier's rates, liability, and type of service and equipment. Usually, a contract carrier's rates are lower than those of common or regulated carriers.

tailored service

The contract carrier provides a specialized type of service to the shipper. Because the carrier does not serve the general public, it can tailor its services to meet specific shippers' needs by utilizing special equipment and arranging special pickups and deliveries. In general, the logistics manager may assume that contract carriage is essentially similar to private transportation, at least in service level terms.

Use of the contract carrier greatly increased in the 1990s. Logistics managers are using contract carriage to assure service levels and rates. Contract carriage enables the shipper to protect against unilateral decisions by common carriers to change rates and rules.

Exempt Carrier

definition

The *exempt carrier* is a for-hire carrier exempt from economic regulation regarding rates and services. The laws of the marketplace determine the rates, services, and supply of such carriers. The only controls over entry into this transport industry sector are capital requirements, which do not seriously restrict some modes.

service

An exempt carrier gains this status by the commodity it hauls or by the nature of its operation. For example, a motor carrier is an exempt carrier when transporting agricultural products, newspapers, livestock, and fish; and a rail carrier is exempt when hauling fresh fruit. Carriers whose operation type provides exemption include motor carriers whose operations are primarily local; water carriers that transport bulk commodities such as coal, ore, grain, or liquid; air carriers that haul cargo; and rail carriers that transport piggyback shipments.

The limited number of exempt carriers—that is, the limited number of situations in which carrier exemption is possible—restricts the availability of such service; but, for moving commodities such as agricultural products, where exempt carriage is possible, firms make significant use of these carriers. The primary reason for using an exempt carrier is lower transport rates. For the movement of industrial commodities, the exempt carrier does not provide viable link service.

Private Carrier

definition

A *private carrier* is essentially a firm's own transportation. The private carrier is not for-hire and not subject to federal economic regulations. More specifically, private carriage involves any person who transports in interstate or foreign commerce property of which such person is the owner, lessee, or bailee, when such transportation is for the purpose of sale, lease, rent, or bailment, or in furtherance of any commercial enterprise. A private carrier's crucial legal distinction is that transportation must not be the controlling firm's primary business; stated differently, the carrier owner's primary business must be some commercial endeavor other than transportation. Private motor carriers may charge 100-percent-owned subsidiaries an intercorporate hauling fee.

primary business

The most prevalent private transportation type is by motor vehicle; private carrier is nearly synonymous with private motor carrier. The relative ease of meeting motor transport capital entry requirements and the high degree of accessibility by motor vehicle have made this mode most advantageous to shippers wishing to provide their own transportation. We should point out that private transportation by water primarily moves bulk raw materials. To a much lesser extent, private rail carriers move bulk products short distances within a plant, between plants, or from plants to rail sidings. Firms use private aircraft extensively to move company personnel and, to a lesser degree, to move emergency property shipments.

rationale

The basic reasons for a firm to enter into private transportation are cost and service. When for-hire carrier rates increase, many firms find private transport a means of controlling transportation costs. Basically, a firm can reduce private transportation costs by conducting the private carrier operation as efficiently as a for-hire operation. If this same efficiency is possible, private transport theoretically should cost less, since the firm pays no for-hire carrier profit. However, one major operational problem, the empty backhaul,[9] may actually elevate profit.

advantages

By using private transportation, a firm gains greater control and flexibility in responding to buyer and plant demands. This increased control and flexibility may result in lower inventory levels, greater customer satisfaction, and greater efficiency at the loading and unloading docks. The firm can also use private equipment as an advertising medium.

disadvantages

Private transportation does have some disadvantages. The main ones are large capital requirements and problems in labor and management. The capital the firm invests in the transport fleet has alternative uses in other firm operations, and this capital must provide a return that at least equals other investment opportunities. The labor problems arise from the firm's dealing with a new labor union. Administrative problems may arise when the firm utilizes existing managers to manage a private transport operation. Finally, the current deregulated environment has produced substantially lower for-hire carrier rates, occasionally making long-haul private transportation more costly.

INTERMODAL TRANSPORTATION

definition

Intermodal transport services refers to the use of two or more carriers of different modes in the through movement of a shipment. Carriers offer such services to the public by publishing a rate from origin to destination for one carrier of each available mode. In other situations, the logistics manager, through routing, uses different modes to get a product to its final destination.

rationale

The logistics manager often must utilize different transport modes to service a given link. While intermodal services are necessary for numerous reasons, the basic reasons are the various modes' service characteristics and costs. For example, the limited accessibility of air transport requires coordination with a land carrier to make the pickups and deliveries. Similar inaccessibility applies to rail, water, and pipeline, but not to motor, which has a definite advantage here. By manipulating the modes, a logistics manager can overcome a given mode's service disadvantages and retain the mode's basic advantage, usually low cost. This is the primary motivation for combining rail and water to move coal or grain: the rail segment improves water transport's accessibility, and the water portion permits savings by providing low-cost service for the long-distance portion of the move.

Intermodal services maximize the primary advantages inherent in the combined modes and minimize their disadvantages. The combined services will have both the good and the bad aspects of the utilized modes. For example, the coordination of rail and water will have a lower total cost than an all-rail movement but a higher cost than all-water. Likewise, the combined system's transit time will be lower than

SUPPLY CHAIN TECHNOLOGY

THE VIRTUAL FREIGHT MARKETPLACE

Marketplace is a term that brings to mind a physical location where buyers and sellers come together to finalize the exchange process. One often associates the term *marketplace* with a farmers' market that brings together at one location many local farmers and buyers. The buyers stroll up and down the aisles lined with farmers offering their harvest for sale. The buyers are able to view the quality and price of the sellers' products and select the products that offer the best quality for the price. After some negotiation, the buyer and seller agree on a price and the exchange takes place.

In transportation, this marketplace concept of bringing together many shippers and carriers at one place has been functioning through the auspices of the freight broker. The freight broker acts as the marketplace facilitator by contacting shippers with loads to be moved and carriers with available equipment in the area. Using the telephone as the technological mainstay, the typical freight broker calls local shippers to ascertain the availability loads and to obtain specific load information such as shipment date, origin, destination, and commodity. When a carrier has equipment in the freight broker's area, it calls the broker to ascertain the availability of loads. With the freight broker acting as the intermediary, the carrier and shipper negotiate a rate for the shipment. Following agreement on the rate, the shipment is transported, the shipper pays the broker, and the broker pays the carrier less a broker's fee of about 8 to 10 percent.

This freight broker marketplace is being created in the virtual world through the electronic freight matching service. Typically, a third-party company will build an electronic auction system that permits many carriers and many shippers to come together in the electronic world to facilitate the exchange process for freight shipments. The shippers place shipments on the electronic auction market for carriers to review for possible movement. If the carrier and shipper agree on a price, the shipper electronically tenders the load to the carrier, the carrier transports the shipment, the shipper pays the carrier, and the third-party electronic firm collects a fee, usually a minimal (less than $15.00) fixed fee per transaction.

In theory, the carrier benefits from this virtual marketplace by gaining knowledge of a shipment and potential revenue source. The carrier can select loads that offset its empty backhaul, incurring a lower load sourcing cost than via the freight broker, thereby making the carrier more efficient. The shipper benefits with lower freight rates offered by carriers that bid down the rate in an attempt to eliminate the empty backhaul. The ultimate beneficiaries are the consumers because the electronic freight matching service can reduce transportation excess capacity, empty backhauls, and lower overall transportation costs.

In reality, the public electronic freight matching services have not faired well. The companies offering this service to the general carrier and shipper public have had some difficulties generating the transaction volume necessary to make the operation viable. Shippers are reluctant to offer loads on the virtual marketplace because of concerns over the lack of knowledge regarding the carrier and its service. Carriers view the virtual marketplace as merely a methodology for bidding down the freight rates that already are too low. Thus, many of these electronic marketplaces have closed.

However, the concept of electronic freight matching has found success in the private auction arena, that is, a limited number of shippers and carriers participating in the electronic auction. Typically, the carriers are under contract with the shippers in the private auction so the shipper knows the carrier and its service. With loads posted on the private auction, the carriers can select those loads that will improve their operating efficiencies and the shippers benefits from the lower rates associated with elimination of the empty backhaul.

The virtual freight marketplace has hit some snags in its early introduction, but the concept of electronically matching shipments with carriers having empty backhauls is grounded in sound economic rationale. Future supply chain managers will be using some form of virtual freight marketplace to buy transportation service.

that of an all-water movement but higher than that of all-rail. The decision to use combined modes must consider the effect on total logistics costs.

types

Various types of intermodal service exist, as Figure 9–6 shows. The most prevalent forms have been truck-rail, truck-water, and truck-air. However, rail-water, pipeline-water, and pipeline-truck also occur.

We can attribute extensive motor carrier use in intermodal service to the extremely high accessibility motor transport allows. Birdyback, fishyback, and piggyback services are examples of coordination in which a carrier physically transfers the motor carrier trailer, with the cargo intact, in another mode. Birdyback combines the accessibility of motor with the speed of the airline; fishyback couples motor accessibility with the low cost of water carriage; and piggyback adds the truck's accessibility to the low cost of rail service. In each case, the combined service suffers the disadvantages of one of the modes involved; for example, birdyback has the disadvantage of air transport's high cost.

transportation company

The ultimate intermodal service is the transportation company, which provides all modal services. That is, it makes rail, motor, water, air, and pipeline transportation services available to the public. The advantages of such a transportation company lie in its ability to utilize the most efficient and economical modal services to meet shipper needs. A number of companies offer different modal services. CSX Corporation operates a railroad, water carrier, and trucking company. Consolidated Freightways offers through its subsidiaries trucking, air, and intermodal services.

limitations

One substantial stumbling block to intermodal service is that carriers are reluctant to participate. The carriers coordinate willingly, even eagerly, to move a product that any one carrier could not transport in its entirety; but when one carrier can transport the commodity the entire distance over its own lines, the carrier is hesitant to coordinate with other carriers.

Another problem with intermodal services is the transfer of freight from one mode to another. This creates time delays and adds to transportation costs. Some forms of coordination eliminate this problem by transferring a motor carrier trailer to another transport mode. The motor carrier trailer's transferability is a special coordination form termed *containerization,* the trailer being a container.

FIGURE 9–6 Types of Intermodal Services

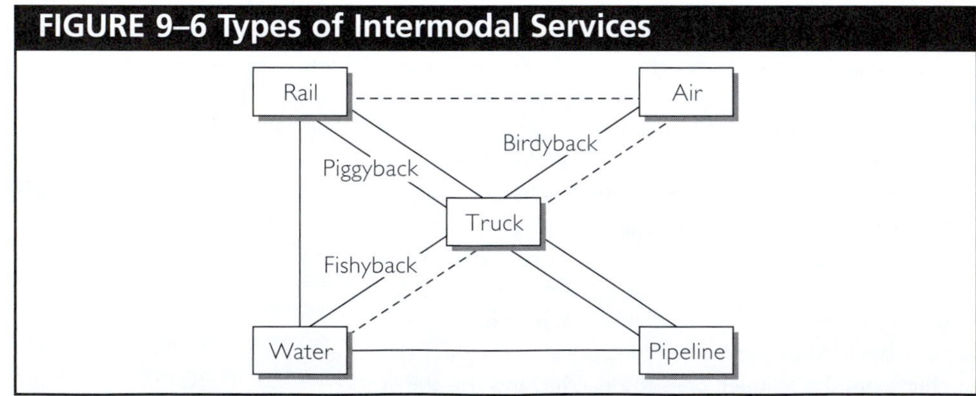

Containerization

Simply stated, a container is a large rectangular box into which a firm places commodities to be shipped. After initial loading, the commodities themselves are not rehandled until they are unloaded at their final destination. Throughout the movement, the carrier handles the container, not the commodities; the shipper can transfer the container from one mode to another, eliminating the need to handle the commodities each time. Reducing commodity handling reduces handling costs, damage costs, theft and pilferage, and the time required to complete the modal transfer.

Containerization changes materials handling from a labor-intensive to a capital-intensive operation. Handling containerized freight requires less labor because the container is too large and too heavy for manual movement. Many firms that modify their materials-handling systems to include cranes, forklift trucks, and other equipment capable of handling the large, heavy containers have found containerization to be a desirable avenue for increasing productivity and controlling materials-handling costs, especially in periods of continually increasing labor costs.

Containerization has gained notable acceptance in international distribution. The service reduces the time and cost associated with shipment handling at ports and curtails damage and theft. Some firms containerizing shipments to foreign markets have reduced costs by from 10 to 20 percent and have increased the service level they provide to these markets.

land bridge

As discussed earlier, a unique type of intermodal service using the container is the *land bridge,* which utilizes rail transportation to link prior and subsequent container moves by water transportation. For example, containers destined for Europe from the Far East move to the West Coast of the United States by water transportation. The containers move by rail to the East Coast, where a carrier loads them onto an oceangoing vessel for the final transportation to Europe. The rail movement provides the intermodal bridge between the two water moves and permits an overall transit time shorter than that of an all-water shipment.

Piggyback

Piggyback, or trailer-on-flatcar (TOFC), is a specialized form of containerization in which rail and motor transport coordinate. In piggyback, the carrier places the motor carrier trailer on a rail flatcar, which moves the trailer by rail for long distances. A motor carrier then moves the trailer for short-distance pickups and deliveries. This service combines the long-haul, low-cost advantage of rail with the accessibility of motor.

Since it is deregulated, piggyback service mostly moves under contract. Generally, five basic piggyback plans are available. The groups able to utilize each plan are restricted as follows:

- *Plan I:* All motor carrier
- *Plan II:* All rail
- *Plan III:* Shipper provides trailer
- *Plan IV:* Shipper provides trailer and rail flatcar
- *Plan V:* Joint railroad and motor carrier

The vast majority of piggyback shipments move under Plan II. Since Plans III and IV require an investment in or lease of equipment, shippers do not use these plans to any great extent. Motor carriers use Plan I to reduce load pattern imbalances. Plan V generates very little volume since it requires the joint efforts of a railroad carrier and a motor carrier. If the shipment does not require this coordination, it will occur only when both parties benefit.

International Shipments

Almost every international shipment travels on more than one mode from its origin to its destination. Recent efforts have attempted to reduce shipping times and costs by increasing the various modes' compatibility and by trying new mode combinations.

In the early 1950s, Sea-Land's introduction of containers that trucks as well as ships could carry began the current revolution in shipping. Containers now come in several sizes and supply the major portion of break-bulk overseas shipping.

advantages

Containerized shipments have several advantages. Reduced loading times allow carriers to utilize their equipment more efficiently. Shippers benefit from shorter transit times and the reduced risk of pilferage and damage during loading and unloading. Savings may also result from reductions in required packing materials and insurance.

disadvantages

Containers also have several disadvantages. Not every port is equipped to handle containers, limiting the number of shipping routes available. Finding cargo for the container's backhaul may be difficult. Additionally, the carriers at the origin and destination are not always able to take advantage of the speed available in loading and unloading containers, decreasing the mode's efficiency.

land bridge

Maritime bridges are prime examples of the savings available by combining modes. Using *double-stack* trains, which stack containers two high on railway flatcars, allows the railroads to operate their equipment more efficiently and to pass these savings on in the form of special intermodal rates, reducing overall shipping costs.

A very recent innovation is the *air/sea combination,* where carriers combine ocean and air transport to move a shipment. This method is most commonly used to ship high value-to-weight items from the Far East to Europe by way of the West Coast of the United States.

Shipping air/sea has two advantages. One, the cost of the combined modes is less than that of an all-air movement. Two, it is much faster than any of the available all-surface modes. Modern container ships can make the Pacific crossing from Japan to Seattle in ten days. When we combine this with the air leg from Seattle to Europe, total transit time will range from ten to fourteen days. This is approximately one-third of the all-ocean transit time and one-half of the land bridge time. The in-transit inventory savings will outweigh the increased cost of the premium modes.

Carriers also commonly use *roll-on–roll-off* in international trade. RO–RO is very similar to container shipping, except that the carrier uses standard truck trailers instead of containers, towing them onto the vessel at the port of origin and off at the destination. RO–RO, which transports automobiles and large mobile equipment such as tractors, has proven extremely useful for shipments to less-developed areas of the world where modern port facilities are unavailable. While RO–RO's advantages are basically the same as those of container shipping, RO–RO does not require special loading equipment.

INDIRECT AND SPECIAL CARRIERS

Another category of carriers offers specialized or intermediary transportation service. In some cases, these carriers have line-haul equipment; in others, they merely provide pickup and delivery and consolidate the service.

Moving shipments of less than 500 pounds creates serious operational problems for the major modes. To make the move economical, the carrier must consolidate the small shipments into larger ones, adding time and cost for the carrier and increasing transit times and transportation charges.

Small-Package Carriers

A number of transportation companies—namely, bus, express, and package carriers—have concentrated upon small freight movements. Bus lines move small packages in their vehicles' luggage compartments. These carriers have cargo capacity only in the space passenger luggage does not require, and therefore they do not require large shipments to make this service profitable. Coupled with frequent schedules, the bus lines offer a viable alternative to the logistics manager who must distribute many small-package shipments.

United Parcel Service (UPS)

A regulated motor carrier, United Parcel Service (UPS), has made great strides in the efficient movement of small shipments. (Another carrier of this type is FedEx Ground.) UPS, an innovator in terminal handling and in pickup and delivery scheduling, can transport small shipments profitably while providing better service and lower transit time than other major modes. Regulations limit the type of package a shipper can transport by UPS; at present, these restrictions are (1) a maximum weight of 150 pounds per package and (2) a maximum length and girth of 130 inches.

hub

Other express companies offer air transportation. Federal Express, the largest air express package delivery firm, utilizes a fleet of aircraft and ground vehicles to provide next-day delivery of small packages and envelopes throughout the United States and internationally. Its operation, like that of most air express companies, centers around a *hub* package distribution center. Typically, Federal Express picks up packages in the late afternoon, delivers them to the local airport, and flies them to the Memphis hub airport, where they arrive in the late evening hours. Federal Express then sorts the packages according to destination and reloads them onto aircraft scheduled for predawn arrival at the destination airport, where the service loads the packages onto ground vehicles for morning delivery to the consignee.

The major advantage of using air express companies is speed—the speed required to get needed parts, equipment, documents, sales literature, and specimens to their destinations the next day. But the high cost of such service generally prohibits the nonemergency shipment of low-value, high-density commodities.

Consolidators

lower freight cost

The advent of B2C (business to consumer) E-commerce created a need for a new indirect carrier, the *consolidator.* B2C business generates many small shipments, and the freight cost for a small shipment is very high. If the B2C landed cost of an item is higher than the cost at a local brick-and-mortar store, then the consumer may decide to buy the item locally rather than via the Internet. The consolidator assists file shipper of small shipments in reducing freight costs by consolidating many small shipments and shipping the consolidated load at a lower freight rate.

For example, a freight consolidator was used to consolidate small packages from a catalog retailer, combine these packages with those or other shippers, drop-ship the combined shipment to U.S. Postal Service sectional center facilities, and place them into the U.S. Postal Service system closer to the buyer's location. The use of the consolidator resulted in a 35 percent reduction in shipping (postage) cost.

The consolidator is not considered a carrier and is not subject to regulations. Consequently, the consolidator is not liable for in-transit cargo damage.

Freight Forwarders

consolidator

The domestic surface *freight forwarder* is a consolidator that collects small shipments from shippers, consolidates these shipments into large loads, and presents the consolidated shipments to railroads or motor carriers for intercity movement. At destination, the freight forwarder breaks the load down into individual shipments and delivers them to the correct consignee. The domestic freight forwarder realizes its revenue from the difference between the high less-than-volume rate the shipper pays and the lower volume rate the for-hire carrier charges the freight forwarder. The main advantage of using a freight forwarder is lower transit time for small shipments. The freight forwarder is a regulated carrier and is liable for cargo damage.

Shippers Associations

An indirect form of transportation known as the *shippers association* moves small shipments for shipper members. The shippers association consolidates shipments, presents the larger loads to for-hire carriers, and pays a lower rate for the larger-volume movement. The association passes on the lower-volume rate to its members.

Brokers

intermediary

The freight *broker* is a person or firm that acts as an intermediary between the shipper and carrier. The broker acts as the carrier's sales agent and as the shipper's traffic manager. That is, the broker represents a number of carriers that need loads to move in given directions. With this knowledge of carrier capacity, the broker contacts the shippers and solicits freight to meet the carriers' needs. The broker typically charges the shipper the carrier's published rate, deducts 7 to 10 percent, and then remits the net amount to the carrier. (See the Supply Chain Technology article for an example of an E-commerce form of freight brokerage.)

types

There are two types of brokers: licensed and unlicensed. The *licensed* broker is licensed by the STB and may arrange freight transportation with STB-regulated carriers. The licensed broker operates under STB-administered regulations. An *unlicensed* broker, who does not require STB licensing, may arrange freight transportation for exempt transportation such as local distribution, agricultural commodities, and piggyback. Many private fleet managers utilize broker services, seeking exempt commodity movement to eliminate the empty backhaul.

Since deregulation, the number and use of brokers have dramatically increased. The Motor Carrier Act of 1980 reduced the entry requirements for brokers and motor carriers. The broker provides new, small trucking companies a marketing channel with a salesforce capable of generating shipments from local shippers. At the same time, the broker offers the shippers access to these new, generally lower-cost carriers. In addition, brokers may offer consolidation services that afford the shipper additional savings.

selection criteria

A logistics manager selecting a broker should consider the broker's authority, liability, and billing. First, the manager should review the STB broker license to make certain the broker is in fact licensed and subject to STB regulations. Second, since the broker is not legally liable for cargo damage a carrier causes while transporting goods, the logistics manager must determine whether the broker will assist in filing claims with the carrier and whether the carrier the broker uses can pay damage claims. Finally, the manager should determine if the broker's fees are included in or are in addition to the carrier's rate.

Intermodal Marketing Companies

The *intermodal marketing company* (IMC) is an intermediary that solicits freight for movement by intermodal rail. At the outset, the IMC acted as a sales representative for the railroad or steamship company seeking to fill empty containers moving back to origin. Today the IMC is more representative of the shipper's interests and seeks to improve intermodal service to meet shipper needs.

The largest IMCs include The Hub Group; C. H. Robinson; Landstar Logistics; and GST Corporation. These companies represented a major component of the intermodal transportation system in 2001.

advantages

The prime advantages of using an IMC are cost savings, consolidation, and improved transit time. The IMC normally consolidates enough freight to fill two piggyback trailers (the number of trailers loaded onto one flatcar), thereby reducing the time the carrier holds the freight before moving it. Some IMCs have contracted with railroads to provide sixty to eighty piggyback trailers per week. The IMCs then solicit freight with lower rates and a delivery guarantee, making piggyback more advantageous.

disadvantages

A disadvantage of using an IMC is liability for freight charges. The shipper normally pays the freight charge to the IMC. Should the IMC fail to pay the carrier, the shipper may be liable for paying the charges to the carrier. Another disadvantage is liability for damage. The IMC is not a carrier and is not legally liable for damage claims. Some IMCs provide claim liability protection, but the shipper should investigate the IMC before use.

international intermediaries

In addition to the indirect and special carriers discussed in this section, there are several types of intermediaries that are more closely related to the international shipping industry. Chapter 5 contains a description of the nature and importance of the foreign freight forwarder, non-vessel-owning common carriers, export management companies, export trading companies, customs house brokers, and ports.

SUMMARY

Typically, transportation represents the major cost component of the logistics supply chain. Transportation provides the bridge between the producer and the consumer, and the quality of the transportation service enables a firm to differentiate its product in the marketplace.

- The transportation system available to the logistics manager consists of the basic modes, intermodal, and indirect and special carriers.
- The carrier selection is twofold: selection of the mode and selection of the specific carrier.
- Factors determining carrier selection include transportation rate, transit time, reliability, capability, accessibility, and security.
- Railroads offer low cost for long hauls of large volumes, but they have accessibility limitations and long transit time.
- Motor carriers are very accessible and move products in small quantities with low, consistent transit times. However, their costs are higher than the other modes, except air.
- Water transportation is relatively low cost and is desirable for moving large volumes over long distances. The prime disadvantage is long transit times and service disruptions caused by weather.
- Air carriers have very low transit times but very high rates.
- Pipelines offer very low rates for the movement of liquids but are not a viable option for manufactured goods.
- There are five legal classes of carriers: common, contract, regulated, exempt, and private.
- Intermodal transportation is the combination of two or more basic modes to provide through movement. The dominant form is rail-truck, or piggyback.
- Containerization is the shipping of freight in a large box, or container, that is subsequently transferred from one carrier to another. It reduces freight handling and damage while improving transit time.
- The transportation system includes a number of indirect and special carriers, such as small package carriers, consolidators, freight forwarders, shippers associations, brokers, and intermodal marketing companies.

STUDY QUESTIONS

1. When purchasing transportation services, the carrier with the lowest rate is usually not the carrier offering the lowest total cost. Explain.
2. What are the major advantages and disadvantages of each of the basic modes?
3. Normally, a firm delivers a low-cost part to its assembly plant via railroad; but when the plant is facing a stockout, the firm sends the part via airplane. What cost justification can the firm give for using air?
4. Compare the advantages and disadvantages of using common, regulated, contract, exempt, and private carriage in the logistics system.

5. Under what conditions is intermodal transportation advantageous?
6. Using the Internet, compare the services offered by the following motor carriers:
   Consolidated Freightways (http://www.cfwy.com)
   Yellow Freight (http://www.yellowfreight.com)
   Roadway (http://www.roadway.com)
   J.B. Hunt (http://www.jbhunt.com)
7. What role does the container play in domestic and international shipments?
8. Under what circumstances would a firm utilize indirect or special carrier services?
9. Using the Internet, compare the services offered by the following railroads:
   CSX (http://www.csx.com)
   NorfolkSouthern (http://www.nscorp.com)
   Burlington Northern Santa Fe (http://www.bnsf.com)
10. Compare the services offered by the following expedited/package carriers:
   BAX Global (http://www.baxglobal.com)
   Federal Express (http://www.fedex.com)
   UPS (http//www.ups.com)
   United States Postal Service (http://www.usps.gov)

Notes

1. Rosalyn Wilson and Robert V. Delaney, "11th Annual State of Logistics Report," Cass Information Systems and ProLogis (2000).
2. *Logistics Cost and Service 1999* (Fort Lee, N.J.: Herbert W. Davis and Company, 1994), 2.
3. For an in-depth discussion of the basic modes, see John J. Coyle, Edward J. Bardi, and Robert A. Novack, *Transportation,* 5th ed. (Cincinnati, Ohio: South-Western College Publishing, 2000), chapters 3–8.
4. Wilson and Delaney, "11th Annual State of Logistics Report."
5. Several years ago, the ICC exempted from economic regulation railroad movement of fresh fruits and vegetables, piggyback freight, and boxcar traffic.
6. Railroads are using *piggyback* (trailer-on-flatcar) service to overcome inaccessibility. A rail flatcar moves a motor truck trailer between origin and destination terminals, but a truck transports the trailer over the highways to the consignor and consignee. We discuss piggyback service in greater detail in a later section of this chapter.
7. Maximum gross vehicle weight for a five-axle tractor trailer operating on an interstate highway is 80,000 pounds.
8. There are two freight operations that remain subject to rate regulation administered by the STB: household goods motor carriers and noncontiguous trade (trade between the continental United States and Hawaii, for example).
9. The *empty backhaul* refers to a vehicle going from origin to destination loaded, and returning empty.

CASE 9–1 ■ Double D Trucking

Double D Trucking was started by Douglas Dean in 1981 and has grown from a one-truck operation to a 550-tractor-trailer fleet serving shippers in a five-state region in the upper Midwest. Double D serves the automotive industry by providing inbound transportation to the assembly plants. It has a strategic alliance relationship with the Big Three auto makers and is the exclusive trucking company for a number of the auto suppliers.

From its inception, Double D has been an innovator in the trucking industry. Douglas Dean is widely known for his willingness to adopt new equipment technology, computer systems, and management techniques. This cutting-edge strategy has resulted in customer loyalty and employee allegiance. Double D promotes itself as a trucking company that has never lost a customer and never lost a day to labor disputes.

As Douglas Dean was preparing for a strategic planning meeting with top executives, he was mulling over recent trends in the trucking industry as well as the logistics field. Dean knew Double D was a profitable regional trucking company and registered high in customer satisfaction surveys. He also knew that to retain this enviable position he must continue to be innovative and provide the services customers need.

During the past two years, Double D has witnessed increased competition. Long-haul trucking has come under severe competitive pressure from rail piggyback, and the long-haul truckers see regional trucking as a profitable marketplace. Expediting carriers, trucking companies that provide rush deliveries, have made significant inroads into the automotive industry, where just-in-time management systems mandate minimal raw material inventories, guaranteed deliveries, and vendor penalties for late deliveries that result in production line stoppage.

The most perplexing trend to Dean is the growing vertical integration of trucking companies into other logistics services. A number of regional trucking companies have started warehousing divisions to provide sorting, kitting (putting pieces together to make up a kit), and cross-docking (moving freight across a dock to a waiting truck). Other carriers are adding third-party logistics divisions to manage a shipper/receiver's transportation and storage activities. Finally, a few trucking companies have started air carrier divisions, freight-forwarding services, and logistics information services.

Dean also recognizes that this vertical integration of trucking companies is a result of customer demands. As manufacturers move to an integrated logistics supply chain approach, they are demanding that transportation suppliers provide other logistics services. In addition, shippers are reducing the number of vendors, including transportation suppliers, being used and asking the few vendors to provide a wider range of products and value-added services.

After considerable thought, Dean decides that the only viable, long-term strategy for Double D is to become a full-service logistics provider. Being only a trucking company will greatly impair the growth and profit potentials of Double D. The only question remaining for Dean is, what other logistics services are appropriate for Double D?

Case Questions

1. Assess the conclusion reached by Douglas Dean regarding the nature of today's trucking industry and shipper demand characteristics.
2. Do you agree that the logical strategic thrust for Double D is to vertically integrate and provide other logistics services? Why or why not?
3. Describe the analytical process you would use to evaluate alternative logistics services being added to Double D's market offering.
4. Describe the value-added services you would recommend that the strategic planning team consider for Double D.

CHAPTER 10

TRANSPORTATION MANAGEMENT

LEARNING OBJECTIVES

After reading this chapter, you should be able to do the following:

- Define proactive transportation management.
- Discuss the five transportation management strategies: reducing the number of carriers, negotiating with carriers, contracting with carriers, consolidating shipments, and monitoring service quality.
- Explain the current economic regulation (deregulation) of transportation.
- Distinguish among the transportation documents: bill of lading, freight bill, and freight claims.
- Compare the domestic terms of sale with international Incoterms.
- Explain cost of service and value of service ratemaking and the effect of shipment weight and distance on freight rates.
- Discuss terminal and line-haul services offered by carriers.

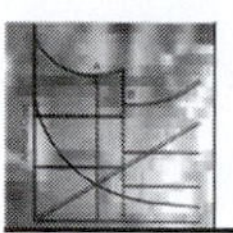

LOGISTICS PROFILE

Mastering the Art of Advance Planning

Intensive advance planning, painstaking attention to detail, and constant communication—these are without doubt the most important factors in the success of NBC Olympics' effort to ship television broadcasting equipment and supplies to Sydney, Australia, for the 2000 Summer Olympics.

Both NBC and Fritz Cos., which handles the broadcaster's freight forwarding and customs brokerage, have staff members dedicated full time to the Olympics effort. In addition to daily, ad hoc telephone communications, there are weekly conference calls between NBC Technical Logistics, staff members in the United States and Sydney, Fritz's managers in the United States, and the Olympics project team at Fritz's Sydney office. During those calls, the four groups update each other on the past week's activities and plan for upcoming shipments. Staff members also enter updated information into Fritz's customer-service "Response Tracking" software, Microsoft Excel spreadsheet files, or Microsoft Access database files; these are quickly and easily shared with all parties in both countries when sent as E-mail attachments.

Advance planning occupied much of the groups' time. Every one of the thousands of items that NBC brought into Australia over a ten-month period must leave the country within a few weeks after the Games end. And items in each departing shipment must be matched with their original import documentation. The shipments, moreover, must be consolidated with others that are headed for the same destination. And they have to leave by certain dates to ensure that they arrive at their destinations before they are needed at other events.

To make all that happen, NBC and Fritz planned the exact order in which every item and piece of equipment must be shipped back from Sydney. The logistics service provider booked space with air and ocean carriers long in advance. And Fritz's customs brokers made sure when the original shipments were exported that all of the import documentation needed for re-entry into the United States was ready to go.

Nothing in this enormous program was left to chance. When NBC and Fritz began their collaboration, says Fritz Client Relations Manager Dave Smith, the shipper and forwarder wrote a 150-page operations manual to ensure that there would be no "holes." "A lot of thought went into this," he says. "Very talented people at both NBC and Fritz recognized the magnitude of this project and made sure there was a process in place for each item that needed to be there. . . . When we turned on the TV to watch the Olympics, we felt proud to say, 'I was a part of that.' "

Source: "Mastering the Art of Advance Planning," *Logistics Management* (September 2000): 55.

INTRODUCTION

Transportation costs, which represent approximately 40 to 50 percent of total logistics costs and 4 to 10 percent of the product selling price for many companies, may represent logistics management's major concern. Transportation decisions directly affect the total logistics costs, costs in other functional areas of the firm, and costs within other logistics channel members. This chapter focuses on the daily transportation management activities in today's deregulated transportation environment, concentrating specifically on carrier pricing, services, and documentation. We first direct our attention toward transportation management strategy.

MANAGEMENT STRATEGY

seeking parity

The passage of the transportation deregulation acts in 1977 and 1980 drastically changed the business climate within which the transportation manager operates. Before those acts, the climate emphasized the ability to operate effectively within regulation confines. Good transportation managers were those who worked within the system to ensure that competitors were not getting better rates or services, that is, who sought to achieve regulatory parity among transportation users.

The bureaucratic red tape of transportation regulation placed a stranglehold on management initiative. Innovative transportation management was difficult to develop because of regulatory constraints. By necessity, transportation managers armed themselves with a list of "thou shalt nots" that would squelch any and all suggestions company managers put forth.

Today, the transportation environment has changed and the regulations shackling management decisions are gone. A transportation manager can no longer utilize the regulatory constraints to prevent a competitor from gaining a competitive advantage when a carrier offers the competitor better rates and services. In fact, contracting, the elimination of tariff-filing requirements, and the publication of individual carrier tariffs prevent the transportation manager from knowing what rates and services a carrier is providing to competitors.

Proactive Management Approach

With the regulatory safety net gone, today's transportation manager must rely on traditional management techniques, using a proactive approach to identify and solve transportation problems and to provide the company with a competitive advantage in the marketplace. (See the Logistics Profile for an example of transport planning.)

A proactive management approach seeks to identify transportation problems and to postulate solutions that benefit the whole company. Without a regulatory rule book, transportation management is free to concentrate on innovative solutions to today's logistics and transportation challenges. Only managers' abilities and creativity and normal business law constraints limit the benefits of this proactive business strategy.

For example, suppose that a firm's sales decline in a particular market results from longer and less-dependable lead times than those provided by the competition in that market. If the firm makes a modal switch from rail to truck, the increased cost of truck service would force the firm to increase prices or to incur a loss, neither of which is acceptable. Negotiating with carriers, establishing carrier contracts with prescribed service levels, and modifying loading procedures are alternatives that the transportation manager may explore to improve services and sales while maintaining acceptable costs.

negative versus positive approach

Today, the transportation manager actively participates in solving company problems. Companies no longer look upon transportation as a necessary evil; rather, transportation contains fundamental solutions to problems that plague a company's functional areas. Thus, today's transportation manager must understand other functional areas, as well as the entire company, so as to seek logistics strategies that support other departmental and corporate strategies.

Reducing the Number of Carriers

market power

By reducing the number of carriers it uses, a shipping firm increases the freight volume and freight revenue that it gives to a carrier, thereby increasing its ability to have the carrier provide the rates and services the shipper needs. As the shipper concentrates its freight business in a limited number of carriers, the shipper becomes more important to each carrier; and each carrier, in becoming more dependent on the shipper's business, is more willing to negotiate with the shipper.

Being one of the carrier's largest customers gives the shipper significant negotiating power: the fear of losing the shipper's business motivates the carrier to comply with the shipper's demands for better rates and service levels. In essence, the shipper who is one of the carrier's A customers (part of the 20 percent of the carrier's customers who provide 80 percent of the carrier's sales revenue) possesses market power with the carrier.

strategic alliance

This concentration of freight in a limited number of carriers not only increases market power but also permits a company to develop a strategic alliance with the carriers it uses. In a strategic alliance, the shipper and the carrier, recognizing their mutual dependency, strive to be efficient so that both can survive and prosper. In addition to reducing transportation costs, the improved working relations within the strategic alliance reduce other logistics costs such as information processing, inventory, and warehousing.

Reducing the number of carriers a firm uses may also increase the possibility of providing a carrier with balanced loads of raw materials inbound and finished goods outbound. By reducing excess capacity, a balanced-load pattern enables the carrier to reduce its costs and to offer lower rates. In addition, providing the carrier with balanced loads may increase the carrier's service level.

risks

A negative risk associated with concentrating business in a limited number of carriers is the firm's increased dependency on the carrier it uses. A shipper who uses only ten carriers is much more vulnerable to shipment disruptions and resulting customer service declines than is a shipper who uses 100 carriers. With the 100-carrier strategy, losing one carrier requires the shipper to reallocate only 1 percent of its freight volume among the remaining ninety-nine carriers, which should pose no problem to carrier capacity and customer service levels. In the ten-carrier scenario, however, losing one carrier requires the shipper to secure shipping capacity equivalent to 10 percent of the shipper's volume, which the remaining nine carriers may not have the capacity to handle. This will force the shipper to use carriers unfamiliar with the shipper's freight, shipping procedures, and customer service requirements; will normally disrupt operating systems and customer service levels; and, possibly, will lead to higher transportation costs, since crisis stage allows the shipper little market power to negotiate favorable rates.

Single sourcing is the ultimate concentration of market power. By using one carrier, the shipper realizes the maximum market power for the freight dollars spent. Corporate-wide single sourcing poses a substantial risk of complete disruption of transportation operations if the carrier fails. However, single sourcing occurs at one facility or for one product (inbound or outbound).

Negotiating with Carriers

Today, carrier negotiation is the norm, and, in some situations, a daily function. The transportation manager must possess negotiating skills sufficient to secure the desired service level at the least cost. Successful carrier negotiation has enabled many companies either to remain competitive in the market or to increase competitive advantage through improved carrier service levels.

negotiating constraints

Market forces and regulatory constraints determine the negotiable factors between the carrier and the shipper. Generally, the negotiated factors revolve around the rates and services the carriers provide. The remaining economic regulations, the STB (see the following section), and antitrust scrutiny imposed upon the truck and rail common carriers govern the negotiated rates and services; air carrier negotiations are subject to antitrust scrutiny only.

The marketplace determines the negotiable factors, assuming that these factors violate no regulatory constraints. The shippers' operational needs, customer demands, and company objectives determine the areas where negotiations will begin. The shipper brings these needs to the carrier, who decides (negotiates) whether these needs are realistic. More than likely the carrier will respond with a counterproposal that offers something less than what the shipper requested.

At other times the carrier will initiate negotiations. The carrier, who may have a specific need to eliminate an empty backhaul, specify pickup times, or increase tonnage, entices a shipper to respond, usually by offering a concession, such as a reduced rate. The shipper will analyze the carrier proposal and either accept or reject the offer or request a greater concession.

market power

Throughout this negotiation, the market power each party enjoys influences the outcome. The shipper possesses market power in terms of the transportation business available in a given time period and can increase this market power by limiting the number of carriers it uses. The carrier possesses market power in terms of the carrier's importance to the shipper—that is, the availability of equal or better-quality service substitutes.

Contracting with Carriers

The Motor Carrier Act of 1980, the Staggers Act of 1980, and the ICC Termination Act of 1995 increased shippers' ability to enter into contracts with carriers. Contracting enables the shipper to eliminate the uncertainties in rates and services that common carriers provide. Through the contract terms, the shipper can specify the rate and level of service that the carrier will provide and can dictate noncompliance penalties, thereby fixing service levels during the contract period.

tailored service

Contracting permits shippers that desire specialized services to purchase a unique or tailored service level that may not be available from the regulated or common carrier. The common carrier must provide service to all shippers without discrimination or preferential treatment, whereas the regulated carrier, which does not have the same regulatory requirement, provides a generic level of service to the shipping public. The regulated carrier service is a unilateral agreement in which the carrier, through its rate and rules tariffs, specifies the level of service that will be provided. The shipper has no input into the service decision, and the carrier can make changes without the shipper's approval or knowledge in some cases.

In contrast to the unilateral agreement of the regulated carrier, the contract is a bilateral agreement whereby the shipper and the carrier define the level of service and rates. When the two parties agree, a contract containing the mutually agreed-upon terms is implemented. Changes to the contract can be made only with the consent of both parties, in contrast to the unilateral carrier actions with regulated carrier service.

examples

Shippers using motor transportation have adopted contracting to cover all types of shipments including TL, LTL, small package, and local delivery. As noted earlier, a current shipper strategy is to reduce the number of carriers used, with many shippers using a core carrier approach. The core carrier tactic utilizes a limited number of carriers—eight or ten carriers—to provide the bulk of the transportation service to the shipper. The core carriers are under contract to the shipper, and the contract specifies special services required, the rates associated with these special services, and a penalty clause for nonperformance.

Rail transportation has widely adopted contracting. A railroad negotiation normally establishes a contract rather than the rate discount common to motor carrier negotiations. Rail contracts normally specify a rate, the type of equipment the carrier will provide, and the service level the shippers expect (a fifteen-day maximum transit time on shipments from Chicago to Seattle, for example). The contract also dictates a minimum or guaranteed quantity that the shipper will tender to the carrier during the contract life.

JIT

Companies implementing the just-in-time (JIT) system use contracting to ensure safe, consistent, and fast service. The JIT system emphasizes low inventory levels and a reliance upon transportation to deliver goods as customers and logistics nodes need them. Transportation delays decrease production, increase inventory costs, and disrupt operations, which defeats JIT's objectives. Contracting with all transportation modes ensures the required transportation service level.

Consolidating Shipments

The freight volume a shipper tenders to a carrier directly relates to the freight rate the carrier charges. By consolidating shipments, the transportation manager can reap the benefits of the lower rates carriers charge for larger shipment volumes. That is, the manager may increase the weight of the shipment the shipper tenders to the carrier to the level that will enable the carrier to use TL (truckload) or CL (carload) rates. In addition, the motor carrier tariffs provide rate discounts at multiple weight levels such as 1,000 pounds, 2,000 pounds, and 5,000 pounds, thus encouraging shippers to consolidate small shipments into larger ones.

shipment size and rates

As a general rule, carriers charge lower rates for shipping larger quantities. Carrier cost per weight unit transported (pound, hundredweight, or ton) decreases as the shipment weight increases. For example, the carrier pickup cost does not vary with shipment size. The per-pound carrier pickup cost for a 2,000-pound shipment is 50 percent of that for a 1,000-pound shipment. (If the pickup cost is $50, the pickup cost per pound is $0.05 for the 1,000-pound shipment and $0.025 for the 2,000-pound shipment.) TL rates requiring 25,000-to 30,000-pound shipments may be 30 to 60 percent lower than LTL rates.

quantity discounts

A shipper may utilize freight consolidation to support a competitive price marketing strategy. By consolidating shipments, the transportation manager realizes a lower carrier rate; and the shipper can translate this lower transportation cost per unit into a lower price for buyers purchasing the larger quantity. Thus, shippers can coordinate the quantity discounts they offer buyers with the rate reductions possible with consolidated shipment sizes.

Freight consolidation is also being used to control the shipping cost of B2C E-commerce. The typical B2C shipment is small, moves to residential destinations, and is delivered by the U.S. Postal Service (USPS), a major carrier providing the residential delivery service. USPS rates are based on weight and distance (zones); the greater the distance (zones traversed), the higher the rate. By consolidating B2C shipments, the shipper can move the consolidated load at lower TL rates to a postal station near the customer's residence, thereby minimizing the distance (zones) the shipment is moved and the USPS rate. The new USPS plus the TL rate and consolidation costs must be lower than the all USPS rate to make the freight consolidation of B2C shipments economical. However, customer service may dictate the use of a higher freight cost freight consolidation program because the transit time may be lower than an all USPS system.

Monitoring Service Quality

product differentiation

Transportation service quality can differentiate a company's product, thereby providing the company with a competitive market advantage. An ability to get the product to the customer on a consistent, timely, and undamaged basis reduces the buyer's inventory and stockout costs. Thus, product differentiation through the transportation service a company provides is a significant nonprice marketing strategy.

service/cost trade-off

However, a trade-off exists between transportation service quality and cost. The transportation manager must compare the quality of service required by buyers of the finished product against the level the shipper currently provides. If the buyers require three-day transit time and the shipper provides two-day transit time, the transportation manager is providing a better and more costly service level than the buyers demand. The transportation manager might correct the service level by negotiating a lower rate with the carrier in return for a longer transit time (three-day delivery instead of two-day delivery) or utilizing a slower but lower-cost mode of transportation.

A fundamental element for implementing service quality monitoring is information. The transportation manager must have information regarding the customer service demands and the service level that current carriers provide. Without this information, the transportation manager cannot make a rational transportation service/cost decision that meets the shipper's established logistics and corporate goals.

Normal transportation documentation—the bill of lading, freight bill, customer shipping document, and so on—does not contain transportation service data. These source documents do not indicate the number of days the shipment is in transit, the transit time consistency, or the frequency and extent of shipment damage. The transportation manager must obtain these data directly from the shipment's receiver.

transit time

The bill of lading, freight bill, and customer shipping document indicate the date the shipper dispatched the shipment to the carrier, but not the date the consignee received it. Many carriers offer electronic notification of delivery and can provide transit time data by shipment.

Figure 10–1 is an example of a carrier evaluation report that bases its evaluation criteria upon the carrier selection factors discussed in Chapter 9. The figure assigns

FIGURE 10–1 Carrier Evaluation Report

Carrier: ______________________ Time period: ______________

Maximum Rating	Evaluation Criteria	Carrier Rating	Comments
	Meets pick-up schedules		
	Meets delivery		
	Transit time		
	Overall		
	Consistency		
	Claims		
	Frequency		
	Timely settlement		
	Equipment		
	Availability		
	Condition		
	Driver		
	Customer acceptance		
	Courtesy		
	Attitude		
	Scope of operations		
	Operating authority		
	Computer		
	Electronic billing		
	Billing		
	Errors		
	Timeliness		
	Tracing capabilities		
	Problem solving		
	Innovativeness		
	Management		
	Attitude		
	Trustworthiness		
	Financial		
	Operating ratio		
	Cash flow		
	Profitability		
	Rates		
	Accessorial charges		
	Handles rush shipments		
100	Total weighted rating		

Evaluator: ______________________ Date: ______________

each criterion a maximum rating totaling 100 and gives the carrier's performance in each service and financial area a numerical rating. The sum of the weighted ratings provides an evaluation score for each carrier.

Using a carrier evaluation system like the one Figure 10–1 depicts provides the transportation manager with information that is vital to the achievement of the transportation, logistics, and corporate customer service strategies and goals.

FEDERAL REGULATION[1]

Federal regulation of transportation has been with us since the Act to Regulate Commerce passed in 1887. The years immediately preceding the enactment of this law were full of turmoil, for both shippers and carriers. Inland transportation was basically by railroad, and the carriers charged high rates when possible and discriminated against small shippers. Control over the transportation industry was important to U.S. economic growth and to assure a stable transportation service supply compatible with the needs of an expanding society.

public interest

We find the basis for federal economic regulation of transportation in transportation's significance to the overall economy of the United States. Transportation enables business to accomplish the very foundation of economic activity—the exchange of commodities from areas of oversupply to areas of undersupply. The transportation activity benefits all citizens; thus, we could argue that the government should provide transportation, just as it provides public interest functions such as the court system and national defense.

Traditionally, however, private enterprise has provided freight transportation. Through the dollars shippers spend, the marketplace identifies the resources that transportation companies commit to various transportation services and considers this resource allocation to be more efficient than that a governmental, political allocation could produce. Since the free enterprise marketplace has imperfections that may allow monopolies to develop, government control of transportation attempts to allocate resources in the public's interest by maintaining and enforcing the competitive market structure.

marketplace controls

Current federal economic regulation of transportation is very minimal, and the forces of the marketplace are the major controls used to enforce a competitive market structure. The lessening of federal regulatory controls over transportation began in 1977 with the deregulation of air transportation and followed in 1980 with reduced regulation over trucking and rail transportation. Virtual deregulation occurred with the enactment of the ICC Termination Act of 1995, which eliminated the Interstate Commerce Commission, reduced or eliminated most economic regulation over motor and water carriers, and established the Surface Transportation Board (STB) to administer the remaining railroad regulations. The current status of federal regulation of the modes follows:

- *Motor and Water Carriers.* All rate and tariff-filing regulations are eliminated except for household goods and noncontiguous trade (continental United States and Alaska, for example). The common carrier concept is eliminated, but the carriers are held liable for damage. All carriers may contract with shippers. Antitrust immunity is granted carriers for collective ratemaking (for

On The Line

Transportation: The Forgotten Factor

The talk at supply chain management events and in supply chain management articles covers a wide spectrum—how to design a supply chain; how to synchronize supply with demand; how to form alliances with your suppliers; how to select the right technology; and, of course, the hottest topic of all, how to understand—and then leverage—the power of the Internet.

Now, all of these issues are important and rightly deserve a prominent position on conference agendas and in books and periodicals. The problem, however, is that in most of the discussions about effective supply chain management, one element is conspicuously missing, or at least underrepresented. And that is transportation.

The move to the E-economy has brought about many changes in the way we move goods and information through the supply chain. But one reality has not changed. The customer's most direct—and often most lasting—impression of you is based on how your product is physically delivered to its place of business.

The quality of the product's packaging and its condition upon arrival are crucial, though often overlooked, factors in the overall business transaction. The timeliness of delivery is absolutely essential, too, because more and more companies are operating on strict delivery schedules. How fast claims are processed or shipment problems are resolved are central parts of the total supply chain experience. So are the attitude, appearance, and professionalism of the driver who delivers the freight. (And no, it is not too much of a stretch to assert that the driver helps create the customer's overall impression of you and your product—whether we are talking about your private fleet or a for-hire carrier.)

Logistics managers need to keep these considerations in mind as they investigate the various electronic exchanges and dot-com marketplaces that are proliferating today. Certainly, these technologies have a place in the new economy—and anyone who would foreclose on using them probably does a disservice to his or her company.

Yet, transportation remains the final and most direct link to the customer. For this reason, transportation management and carrier selection cannot be an afterthought or a secondary responsibility assigned to someone with no real experience. And the idea of going out blindly into the electronic market and making transportation decisions based on price alone is an invitation to disaster.

Companies expend tremendous amounts of time and resources determining the right configuration for their distribution network or evaluating the right supply chain technology. The same type of rigorous analysis should be applied to the evaluation and selection of transportation options for actually moving the freight to the customer. This is the last link in a supply chain that stretches all the way back to the sourcing of the raw material. If there is a problem at this critical juncture, then all of the excellent planning and executing that went before could go for naught.

Source: Francis J. Quinn, "Transportation: The Forgotten Factor," *Logistics Management* (September 2000): 45. Copyright Cahners Business Information. Reprinted by permission.

example, joint publishing of a freight classification), and the carriers must provide tariffs (containing rates and rules) to shippers upon request. In essence, there is little federal economic control exercised over these modes.

- *Railroads.* In theory, rail economic regulation still exists. The STB has jurisdiction over rail rates and rules, as well as routes, services, facilities, and mergers. The railroads are subject to the common carrier obligations to provide service to all shippers; to not discriminate against persons, places, or commodities; to charge reasonable rates; and to be liable for damage to the goods. The filing of rail tariffs and contracts is not required. The railroad industry remains the most highly regulated transportation mode, but complete rate deregulation exists over certain types of rail traffic—piggyback and fresh fruits, for example.

- *Air Transportation.* In 1977, economic regulation of air transportation was eliminated; the marketplace determines rates and services. Safety regulation, however, remains a major thrust of federal controls over air carriers. Such safety regulations as the controls over the number of landings and takeoffs permitted at an airport indirectly determine the level of service provided by an air carrier and whether an air carrier can provide service to a particular airport (availability of landing slots).
- *Freight Forwarders and Brokers.* Both forms of transportation are required to register with the STB, and the broker must post a $10,000 surety bond to ensure the carrier used will receive payment from the broker. However, there are no federal economic controls over the rates or services provided by these two intermediaries. A freight forwarder is considered a carrier and is held liable for freight damage, whereas the broker is not considered a carrier and is not liable for freight damage.

Documentation—Domestic

Domestic transportation utilizes a number of different documents to govern, direct, control, and provide information about a shipment. This section focuses on the bill of lading, freight bill, claims, and F.O.B. terms of sale—the documentation that is most prevalent in interstate transportation.

Bill of Lading

contract receipt

The *bill of lading* is probably the single most important transportation document. It originates the shipment, provides all the information the carrier needs to accomplish the move, stipulates the transportation contract terms, acts as a receipt for the goods the shipper tenders to the carrier, and, in some cases, shows certificate of title to the goods. Figure 10–2 shows a typical bill of lading.

All interstate shipments by common carriers begin with the issuance of a properly completed bill of lading. The information on the bill specifies the name and address of the consignor and consignee, as well as routing instructions for the carrier. The bill also describes the commodities in the shipment, the number of items in each commodity description, and the commodity's class or rate. Many shippers provide their own bills of lading (short form), which show the shipper's preprinted name and describe the commodities the company most commonly ships. This reduces the time required to fill out the bill, thereby eliminating delays at the shipper's loading facilities. Electronic bills of lading are being used in situations where the carrier and shipper have a strategic alliance established.

nonnegotiable

Straight Bill of Lading. The *straight bill of lading* is a nonnegotiable instrument, which means that endorsement of the straight bill cannot transfer title to the goods the straight bill names. For firms using the straight bill of lading, the terms of sale

FIGURE 10–2 Bill of Lading

THIS MEMORANDUM is an acknowledgment that a Bill of Lading has been issued and is not the Original Bill of Lading, nor a copy or duplicate, covering the property named herein, and is intended solely for filing or records.

Received subject to the classifications, lawfully filed tariffs, and contracts in effect on the date of the receipt by the carrier of the property described in the Original Bill of Lading the property described below, in apparent good order, except as noted (contents and condition of contents of packages unknown), marked, consigned, and destined as indicated below, which said carrier being understood throughout this contract as meaning any person or corporation in possession of the property under the contract) agrees to carry to its usual place of delivery at said destination, if on its route, otherwise, to deliver to another carrier on the route to said destination. It is mutually agreed as to each carrier of all or any of said property over all or any portion of said route to destination, and as to each party at any time interested in all or any of said property, that every service to be performed hereunder shall be subject to all the terms and conditions of the Uniform Domestic Straight Bill of Lading set forth (1) in Uniform Freight Classification in effect on the date hereof, if this is a rail or a rail-water shipment, or (2) in the applicable motor carrier classification or tariff if this is a motor carrier shipment.

Shipper hereby certifies that he is familiar with all the terms and conditions of the said bill of lading, including those on the back thereof, set forth in the classification or tariff which governs the transportation of this shipment, and the said terms and conditions are hereby agreed to by the shipper and accepted for himself and his assigns.

*If the shipment moves between two ports by a carrier by water, the law requires that the bill of lading shall state whether it is "carrier's or shipper's weight." NOTE: Where the rate is dependent on value shippers are required to state specifically in writing the agreed or declared value of the property. The agreed or declared value of the property is hereby specifically stated by the shipper to be not exceeding Per

BILL OF LADING NO.	950980R2

FROM ANDERSONS INDUSTRIAL PROD DIVISION
MAUMEE, OHIO

Subject to Section 7 of conditions of applicable bill of lading, if this shipment is to be delivered to the consignee without recourse on the consignor. The consignor shall sign the following statement.
The carrier shall not make delivery of this shipment without payment of freight and all other lawful charges.

THE ANDERSONS
(Signature of consignor)

If charges are to be prepaid, write or stamp here, "TO BE PREPAID"
TO BE PREPAID

SHIP TO
EMPIRE BEARING & TRANS
165 BROAD AVENUE
FAIRVIEW NJ 07022

CUSTOMER NUMBER	CUSTOMER P.O. NO.	ORDER NO.	ORDER DATE	SHIP DATE	SHIP VIA
7132701	1619	950980	02/27/95	03/01/95	YELLOW FREIGHT TRUCK

	WAREHOUSE	PALLETS	PRODUCT CODE	DESCRIPTION	UNIT WGT.	NO. OF UNITS	WEIGHT
1	1		SK191	LG. O.P. SK (95GAL)NON-AGRSV.	118.00	1	118
2	1		DP41	5 DRIP PANS W/40 PILLOWS O.D.	25.00	1	25
3	2		RP12	REPAIR PUTTY 12/CS	5.00	2	10
4	10		5100	18" X 18" H.WGT. PADS (100)	19.00	10	190
5	20		SW46	46"SLIKWIK SOC ABSORBENT 40/CS	63.00	20	1260

UNITS	TYPE	HM	DESCRIPTION AND NMFC ITEM	WEIGHT
20	CS		BOOMS, PADS, SWEEPS OR FORMS, DENS 10-12# PCF, ITEM 14926557, CL 92.5	1260
12	CS		BOOMS, PADS, SWEEPS OR FORMS, DENS 6-8# PCF, ITEM 14926555, CL 125	200
2	EA		BOOMS, PADS, SWEEPS OR FORMS, DENS 6-8# PCF, ITEM 14926555, CL 125	143

34 ← TOTAL UNITS

CUST PHONE: 201 945 7850

PRODUCT WEIGHT	1603
CONTAINER WEIGHT	0
PALLET WEIGHT	110
TOTAL WEIGHT	1713

EXTRA PALLT WGT________
ADJUSTED WEIGHT________

THIS IS TO CERTIFY THAT THE ABOVE-NAMED MATERIALS ARE PROPERLY CLASSIFIED, DESCRIBED, PACKAGED, MARKED AND LABELED AND ARE IN PROPER CONDITION FOR TRANSPORTATION ACCORDING TO THE APPLICABLE REGULATIONS OF THE DEPARTMENT OF TRANSPORTATION.

SIGNATURE: TITLE:
X

*SEND PREPAID FREIGHT BILL WITH BILL OF LADING TO:
TRAFFIC DEPARTMENT
P.O. BOX 119
MAUMEE, OHIO 43537

LOAD NO. 95 09 80 TOT DELVY 1 STOP NO. 1 TOT PALLETS________ & LOOSE PIECES________

SHIPPER PER X	CUSTOMER PER X	NOTE IF SHIPMENT IS OVER, SHORT, OR DAMAGED DATE	CARRIER PER X

PERMANENT POST OFFICE ADDESS- BOX 119, MAUMEE, OH 43537

Source: Courtesy of The Andersons Management Corporation. Used with permission.

upon which the buyer and seller agreed, the buyer and seller generally dictate where title to the goods passes. The carrier does not require presentation of the straight bill's original copy to effect delivery; the carrier must simply deliver the goods to the person or firm the straight bill of lading names as consignee.

negotiable

Order Bill of Lading. The *order bill of lading* is a negotiable instrument showing certificate of title to the goods it names. Using the order bill of lading enables the consignor to retain security interest in the goods.[2] That is, the consignee must pay the goods' invoice value to obtain the original copy of the order bill of lading that must be presented to the carrier for delivery.

Contract Terms. The bill of lading contains the *terms of contract* for movement by common carrier. The contract is between the shipper and the common carrier for the movement of the freight that the bill of lading identifies to the consignee that the bill identifies. The bill of lading contract contains nine sections. Section 1, delineating the extent of the carrier's liability, is a primary contract term.

exceptions to liability

The major terms of the common carrier's contract of carriage as found in the bill of lading sections are as follows:

1. *Common carrier liability.* The carrier is held liable for all loss, damage, or delay to the goods except for the following:

   Act of God—loss resulting from any unavoidable natural catastrophe. If the carrier had sufficient opportunity to avoid the catastrophe, the carrier is liable and cannot use this exception.

   Act of public enemy—loss resulting from armed aggression against the United States.

   Act of shipper—loss resulting from shipper's improper loading, packaging, or concealment of goods being shipped.

   Act of public authority—loss resulting from public agencies taking or destroying goods by due process of law.

   Inherent nature of the goods—the normal or expected loss of the products (e.g., evaporation).
2. *Reasonable dispatch.* The shipper holds the carrier liable for the actual loss or damage that results from an unreasonable delay in transit. No specific rule exists for determining reasonable time. The shipper examines the shipment's specifics to see if the delay was unreasonable under given circumstances.
3. *Cooperage and baling.* The owner pays such costs. The carrier may compress cotton or cotton linters and may commingle bulk grain shipments destined to a public elevator with other grain.
4. *Freight not accepted.* The carrier may store at the owner's cost any property the consignee does not remove within the free time. After notifying the consignor, the carrier may sell at public auction property the consignee refuses.
5. *Articles of extraordinary value.* The carrier is not obligated to carry documents or articles of extraordinary value unless the classification or tariff specifically rates such items. This is one area where a common carrier can refuse to provide service.
6. *Explosives.* The shipper shall give the carrier full written disclosure when shipping dangerous articles. If there is no disclosure, the shipper is held liable for any damage such goods cause.

7. *No recourse.* The carrier has no legal recourse back to the shipper for additional charges after making delivery. If the shipper signs the no recourse clause and the carrier delivers the shipment, the carrier has recourse only to the consignee for additional freight charges for the shipment.
8. *Substitute bill of lading.* When a bill of lading is an exchange or substitute for another, the subsequent bill of lading shall encompass the prior bill's statements regarding shipment value, election of common law liability, and consignor's signature.
9. *Water carriage.* If water transportation is involved, the water carrier is liable for negligence in loading, and is responsible for making the vessel seaworthy and for outfitting and manning the vessel.
10. *Alterations.* The carrier's agent must note any changes, additions, or erasures to make such alterations enforceable.

liability limits

The discussion of the bill of lading contract terms describes the contract of carriage with a common carrier, railroad. Many contracts signed with motor carriers hold the carrier to these liability terms. Current regulations hold regulated motor carriers liable for cargo damage, but the regulations permit the motor carrier to limit its liability through released value rates (to be discussed subsequently) and maximum liability rules found in the carrier's rules tariff. Examples of the motor carrier liability limits include a maximum liability of $50,000 if the entire shipment is damaged or a maximum liability limit of $2.50 per pound. Freight claims are discussed in a subsequent section.

Freight Bill

definition

The *freight bill* is the carrier's invoice for the charges the carrier incurs in moving a given shipment. The freight bill lists the shipment, the origin and destination, the consignee, the items, total weight, and total charges. In addition, the freight bill specifies the credit time period for payment. Note that the carrier is not obligated to extend credit to the shipper and the carrier may require prepayment of the charges if, in the opinion of the carrier, the commodity's value is less than the freight charge.

credit terms

A brief description of the carrier's credit payment terms is typically found on the freight bill, but the carrier's rules tariff contain the credit payment terms in detail. The transportation manager should have a working knowledge of the carrier's credit payment terms because some carriers have excessive penalties for not paying within the allowed credit period and/or discounts for paying early.

For example, some carriers provide a credit payment period of thirty days. Shippers who pay promptly (within ten days) are afforded a discount (2 percent, for example). However, if payment is not received within thirty days, the carrier's penalty may be loss of all discounts (average of 55 percent for LTL shipments) plus a 10 percent late charge fee.

prepaid or collect

Freight bills may be either prepaid or collect. The prepaid or collect basis determines when the carrier will present the freight bill, not necessarily whether the shipper will pay the charges in advance or after the movement's completion. On a *prepaid* shipment, the carrier presents the freight bill on the effective day of shipment. On a *collect* shipment, the carrier presents the freight bill on the effective day of delivery. In both cases, the shipper must pay the bills within the maximum days of credit from presentation; but, on the collect basis, the carrier extends the payment due date by the length of the transit time.

freight bill auditing

Freight bill auditing can be performed either internally or externally. The trend today is for shippers to outsource the freight bill auditing function because most shippers lack the expertise and resources for economical and efficient freight bill auditing. With the advent of computerized tariffs and the use of simpler rate structures, especially in conjunction with contracting, freight bill auditing involves matching the computer-generated charge with the carrier's freight bill. If the two do not match, the freight bill is given to a transportation manager to resolve. Often times, the audit occurs prior to payment of the freight bill.

Claims

time limits

The *freight claim* is a document (with no prescribed format) that the shipper files with the carrier to recoup monetary losses resulting from loss, damage, or delay to the shipment or to recover overcharge payments. The shipper must file in writing freight claims with the carrier (originating, delivering, or on whose line damage occurred) within nine months of delivery or, in the case of loss, within nine months of reasonable delivery. If a contract of carriage governs, the contract may stipulate a different filing time period. Air carrier claim filing times are generally less than nine months and vary by carrier.

Damage may be either visible or concealed. *Visible damage,* usually discovered at delivery, is damage that the consignee detects before opening the package. *Concealed damage* is not detected until the consignee opens the package. A problem arises with determining whether concealed damage occurred while the goods were in the carrier's possession or in the consignee's possession. Many carriers stipulate that the shipper must file concealed damage claims within fifteen days of delivery. This does not overrule the nine-month limitation, but the carrier will look more favorably upon the claim if the shipper files it within the stated policy period.

claim value

The following principle establishes the damage claim's value: The claim shall restore the claimant to a condition as good as that in which the claimant would have been had the carrier safely delivered the goods. To determine this value, the claimant utilizes the original invoice, price catalog, and other factors to show the commodity's market value at destination. For commodities that do not have a ready market value, such as one-of-a-kind items, the claimant may use cost accounting records to determine value.

A *released value* is an exception to the full value liability obligation. At the time of shipment, the shipper may elect to release the value of the shipment to something less than its full value. This election reduces the carrier's liability in case of damage to the amount stipulated by the shipper. In return, the shipper usually receives a lower freight rate.

Another exception to the full value liability is the automatic released-value rules that some carriers place in their rules tariffs. The automatic released value states that the value of the product is automatically reduced (released) to that stipulated in the tariff unless the shipper states otherwise on the bill of lading at the time of shipment. Finally, some carriers have limits on the maximum liability for a shipment.

F.O.B. Terms of Sale

transportation responsibility

The *F.O.B. terms of sale* determine the logistics responsibility that the buyer and seller will incur. Originally, F.O.B. referred to the seller's making the product free of transportation charges to the ship, or "free on board." More specifically, the F.O.B. terms of sale delineate (1) who is to incur transportation charges, (2) who is to control movement of the shipment, and (3) where the title passes to the buyer.

The F.O.B. term specifies the point to which the seller incurs transportation charges and responsibility and relinquishes title to the buyer. For example, *F.O.B. delivered* indicates that the seller incurs all transportation charges and responsibility to the buyer's destination and that title passes to the buyer at delivery. *F.O.B. origin* means the opposite: the buyer incurs all transportation charges and responsibility, and title passes to the buyer at the shipment's origin.

The terms a firm utilizes to sell its products or to purchase its raw material directly affect the magnitude of the transportation function. A firm that purchases raw materials F.O.B. origin and sells its finished product F.O.B. delivered would require extensive transportation management. In such a situation, the firm controls carrier selection and warehousing and also incurs transportation charges for all commodity movements. The firm can pass this responsibility on to the buyer or supplier by altering the terms of sale, thereby lessening its transportation management requirements.

The F.O.B. term also defines the party responsible for filing a damage claim. The party that possesses title to the goods must file the claim. If damage occurs after the shipment reaches the named point, the buyer would be responsible for filing the claim. Conversely, if damage occurs before the shipment reaches the named point, the seller would file the claim.

DOCUMENTATION—INTERNATIONAL

Export documentation is far more complicated than the documentation that domestic shipments require. Since the transaction involves different nations, political as well as economic considerations affect the documentation required. Specific documentation requirements vary widely from country to country. It is necessary to complete each document accurately, for a mistake may delay the shipment's delivery.

For discussion purposes, we group the various documents into two categories: sales and transportation. Much of the information the documents require is similar, but each document serves a different purpose.

Sales Documents

sales contract

The *sales contract* is the initial document in any international business transaction, and export sales contracts exhibit little uniformity. To reduce time and cost, the export sales contract should completely and clearly describe the commodities, price, payment terms, transportation arrangements, insurance requirements, the carriers, and any special arrangements the agreement may require.

letter of credit

After negotiating the sales contract, the parties involved must determine the method of payment. The *letter of credit,* the most common payment method, provides a high degree of protection. Other forms of payment include cash, consignment, and open account. The letter of credit is a bank's assurance that the buyer will make payment as long as the seller meets the sales terms (export sales contract terms) to which the parties have agreed. When the seller complies with the sales conditions that the letter of credit states and presents a draft drawn in compliance with the letter of credit, the buyer makes payment to the exporter.

A letter of credit is drawn up and used in the following manner:

1. The buyer and seller make a contract for the sale of goods.
2. The buyer arranges for its bank to issue the seller a letter of credit in the sale amount.
3. The buyer's bank places the amount in the seller's bank.
4. The seller prepares a draft against the deposit and attaches the draft to the following documents:
   —Clean, negotiable bill of lading
   —Certificate of insurance
   —Seller's invoice
   —Letter of credit
5. The seller endorses the order bill of lading to the bank and receives the money.
6. The seller's bank endorses the bill of lading to the buyer's bank.
7. The buyer's bank endorses the bill of lading to the buyer.
8. The buyer takes the bill of lading to the carrier and picks up the shipment.

Terms of Sale

The international terms of sale are known as *Incoterms.* Unlike domestic terms of sale, where the buyers and sellers primarily use F.O.B. origin and F.O.B. destination terms, there are thirteen different Incoterms. Developed by the Paris-based International Chamber of Commerce in 1936, these Incoterms are internationally accepted rules defining trade terms.

The Incoterms define responsibilities of both the buyer and the seller in any international contract of sale. For exporting, the terms delineate buyer or seller responsibility for:

- Export packing cost
- Inland transportation (to the port of export and from port of import)
- Export clearance
- Vessel or plane loading
- Main transportation cost
- Cargo insurance
- Customs duties
- Risk of loss or damage in transit

departure contract

E terms. The *E terms* consist of one Incoterm, *Ex Works* (EXW). This is a departure contract that means the buyer has total responsibility for the shipment. The seller's responsibility is to make the shipment available at its facility. The buyer agrees to take possession of the shipment at the point of origin and to bear all of the cost and risk of transporting the goods to the destination. (See Table 10–1 for additional responsibilities of the E terms.)

TABLE 10–1 Summary of Incoterms Cost Obligations

Cost or Activity	EXW	FCA	FAS	FOB	CFR	CIF	CPT	CIP	DAF	DES	DEQ	DDU	DDP
Export packing	B	S	S	S	S	S	S	S	S	S	S	S	S
Export clearance	B	S	S	S	S	S	S	S	S	S	S	S	S
Inland transport (domestic)	B	S	S	S	S	S	S	S	S	S	S	S	S
Vessel/plane loading	B	B	B	S	S	S	S	S	S	S	S	S	S
Main transport	B	B	B	B	S	S	S	S	S	S	S	S	S
Cargo insurance	B	B	B	B	B	S	B	S	S	S	S	S	S
Customs duties	B	B	B	B	B	B	B	B	B	B	S	B	S
Inland transport (foreign)	B	B	B	B	B	B	B	B	B	B	B	B	S
Mode applicability	X	X	W	W	W	W	X	X	X	W	W	X	X

B = buyer; S = seller; W = water carrier; X = air, motor, rail, intermodal.

F Terms. The three *F terms* obligate the seller to incur the cost of delivering the shipment cleared for export to the carrier designated by the buyer. The buyer selects and incurs the cost of main transportation, insurance, and customs clearance. *FCA,* Free Carrier, can be used with any mode of transportation. Risk of damage is transferred to the buyer when the seller delivers the goods to the carrier named by the buyer.

FAS, Free Alongside Ship, is used for water transportation shipments only. Risk of damage is transferred to the buyer when the goods are delivered alongside the ship. The buyer must pay the cost of "lifting" the cargo or container on board the vessel. *F.O.B.,* Free on Board, is used only for water transportation shipments. The risk of damage is transferred to the buyer when the shipment crosses the ship's rail (when the goods are actually loaded on the vessel). The seller pays the lifting charge. (See Table 10–1 for additional responsibilities of the F terms.)

shipment contract

C Terms. The four *C terms* are shipment contracts that obligate the seller to obtain and pay for the main carriage and/or cargo insurance. *CFR,* Cost and Freight, and *CPT,* Carriage Paid To, are similar in that both obligate the seller to select and pay for the main carriage (ocean or air to the foreign country). *CFR* is used only for shipments by water transportation, while *CPT* is used for any mode. In both terms, the seller incurs all costs to the port of destination. Risk of damage passes to the buyer when the goods pass the ship's rail (CFR) or when delivered to the main carrier (CPT).

CIF, or Cost, Insurance, Freight, and *CIP,* Carriage and Insurance Paid To, require the seller to pay for both main carriage and cargo insurance. The risk of damage is the same as that for CFR and CPT. (See Table 10–1 for additional responsibilities of the C terms.)

arrival contract

D Terms. The *D terms* obligate the seller to incur all costs related to delivery of the shipment to the foreign destination. There are five D terms; two apply to water transportation only, and three apply to any mode used. All five D terms require the seller to incur all costs and the risk of damage up to the destination port.

DAF, Delivered at Frontier, means that the seller is responsible for transportation and incurs risk of damage to the named point at the place of delivery at the frontier of the destination country. For example, DAF Laredo, Texas, indicates that the seller is responsible for making the goods available at Laredo, Texas. The buyer is responsible for customs duties and clearance into Mexico. DAF can be used with all modes.

DES, Delivered Ex Ship, and *DEQ,* Delivered Ex Quay (wharf), are used with shipments by water transportation. Both terms require the seller to select and pay for the main carriage. Under DES, the risk of damage is transferred when the goods are made available to the buyer on board the ship, uncleared for import at the port of destination. The buyer is responsible for customs clearance. With DEQ, risk of damage is transferred to the buyer when the goods, not cleared for import, are unloaded onto the quay (wharf) at the named port of destination.

DDU, Delivered Duty Unpaid, and *DDP,* Delivered Duty Paid, are available for all modes. DDU requires the seller to incur all costs, except import duties, to the named place in the country of importation. Risk of damage passes to the buyer when the goods are made available, duties unpaid, at the named place. (DDU is similar to DES.) DDP imposes the same obligations on the seller as DDU plus the additional responsibility of clearing the goods for import and paying the customs duties. (DDP is similar to DEQ.) (See Table 10–1 for additional responsibilities of the D terms.)

Transportation Documents

export declaration

After the buyer and seller reach an agreement as to sales and credit terms, the exporter files with exit port customs an *export declaration* (see Figure 10–3), which provides the Department of Commerce with information concerning the export shipment's nature and value. The required information usually includes a description of the commodity, the shipping weight, a list of the marks and numbers on the containers, the number and dates of any required export license, the place and country of destination, and the parties to the transaction.

export license

A company requires an *export license* to export goods from the United States. These licenses fall into one of two categories. The *general license* allows the export of most goods without any special requirements. The commodities this license covers are general in nature and have no strategic value to the United States. On the other hand, certain items whose export the government wishes to control require a *validated export license.* Commodities requiring this type of license include military hardware, certain high-tech items such as microprocessors and supercomputers, and other goods for which control is in the national interest.

invoices

The *commercial invoice,* which the seller uses to determine the commodity's value less freight and other charges is basically the seller's invoice for the commodities sold. The letter of credit and companies or agencies often require this invoice to determine the correct value for insurance purposes and for assessing import duties. Some countries have special requirements (language, information requested, etc.) for the commercial invoice. Many countries also require a special form called a *consular invoice* for any incoming shipments. The consular invoice, which allows the country to collect import statistics, is usually written in the importing nation's language.

FIGURE 10–3 Shipper's Export Declaration

U.S. DEPARTMENT OF COMMERCE - BUREAU OF THE CENSUS - INTERNATIONAL TRADE ADMINISTRATION

FORM **7525-V** (1-1-88) **SHIPPER'S EXPORT DECLARATION** OMB No. 0607-0018

1a. EXPORTER *(Name and address including ZIP code)*

ZIP CODE

2. DATE OF EXPORTATION

3. BILL OF LADING/AIR WAYBILL NO.

b. EXPORTER'S EIN (IRS) NO.

c. PARTIES TO TRANSACTION

☐ Related ☐ Non-related

4a. ULTIMATE CONSIGNEE

b. INTERMEDIATE CONSIGNEE

5. FORWARDING AGENT

6. POINT (STATE) OF ORIGIN OR FTZ NO.

7. COUNTRY OF ULTIMATE DESTINATION

8. LOADING PIER *(Vessel only)*

9. MODE OF TRANSPORT *(Specify)*

10. EXPORTING CARRIER

11. PORT OF EXPORT

12. PORT OF UNLOADING *(Vessel and air only)*

13. CONTAINERIZED *(Vessel only)*

☐ Yes ☐ No

14. SCHEDULE B DESCRIPTION OF COMMODITIES,
15. MARKS NOS., AND KINDS OF PACKAGES. *(Use columns 17—19)*

D/F (16)	SCHEDULE B NUMBER (17)	CHECK DIGIT	QUANTITY – SCHEDULE B UNIT(S) (18)	SHIPPING WEIGHT *(Kilos)* (19)	VALUE (U.S. dollars, omit cents) *(Selling price or cost if not sold)* (20)

21. VALIDATED LICENSE NO./GENERAL LICENSE SYMBOL

22. ECCN *(When required)*

23. Duly authorized officer or employee

The exporter authorizes the forwarder named above to act as forwarding agent for export control and customs purposes.

24. I certify that all statements made and all information contained herein are true and correct and that I have read and understand the instructions for preparation of this document, set forth in the "**Correct Way to Fill Out the Shipper's Export Declaration.**" I understand that civil and criminal penalties, including forfeiture and sale, may be imposed for making false or fraudulent statements herein, failing to provide the requested information or for violation of U.S. laws on exportation (13 U.S.C. Sec. 305; 22 U.S.C. Sec. 401; 18 U.S.C. Sec. 1001; 50 U.S.C. App. 2410).

Signature

Confidential - For use solely for official purposes authorized by the Secretary of Commerce (13 U.S.C. 301 (g).

Title

Export shipments are subject to inspection by U.S. Customs Service and/or Office of Export Enforcement.

Date

25. AUTHENTICATION *(When required)*

The "Correct Way to Fill Out the Shipper's Export Declaration" is available from the Bureau of the Census, Washington, D.C. 20233.

carnet When a seller makes a shipment in a sealed container, a *carnet* is often issued. A carnet indicates that the shipment has been sealed at its origin and will not be opened until it reaches its final destination. The container may then pass in transit through intermediate customs points without inspection. Carnets are very useful for intermodal shipments and for containers crossing several national boundaries between origin and destination. Much of the overland shipping in Europe travels under carnet.

A destination country that has made a treaty agreement to give favorable import duty treatment to certain U.S. goods often requires a *certificate of origin,* which certifies that the goods' origin is the United States. This prevents a shipper from applying the favorable import duty to foreign goods that the shipper merely reshipped from the United States.

bill of lading The initiating document for any international shipment is the bill of lading (B/L). One bill of lading, the *export bill of lading,* could govern the domestic portion of the move (from plant to port of exit), the intercountry portion (by ocean or air), and the foreign portion (from port of entry to final destination in a foreign country). In practice, most shipments move under a combination of domestic and ocean (or air) bills of lading.

The *ocean bill of lading* is similar to the domestic bill of lading discussed earlier. The ocean bill of lading serves as the contract of carriage between the carrier and the shipper. It sets down the terms of shipment and designates the origin and destination ports. It also supplies shipment information, such as the quantity and weight, the freight charges, and any special handling requirements. The ocean bill of lading is hardly uniform. The carrier is able to add conditions to the bill of lading as long as the additions are not contrary to law.

As discussed earlier, *order bills of lading* also provide evidence of ownership. Sellers can use these negotiable documents to transfer title of the goods.

The carrier issues a *clean bill of lading* when the cargo arrives aboard ship in good condition. If the goods show evidence of damage, the carrier will note this on the bill of lading and will not issue a clean B/L. After processing all the bills of lading, the carrier prepares a *ship's manifest,* which summarizes the cargo aboard the ship, listed by port of loading and destination.

liability The primary bill of lading contract terms concern the ocean carrier's liability. The Carriage of Goods by Sea Act of 1936 states that the ocean carrier is required to use due diligence to make its vessel seaworthy and is held liable for losses resulting from negligence. The shipper is liable for loss resulting from perils of the sea, acts of God, acts of public enemies, inherent defects of the cargo, or shipper negligence. Thus, the liability of the ocean carrier is less than that imposed upon a domestic carrier.

The terms of sale may also require a *certificate of insurance.* This certificate will state that the buyer or seller has obtained insurance adequate to cover any losses resulting during transit.

dock receipt After the carrier has delivered the goods at the dock, the steamship agent issues a *dock receipt* indicating that the domestic carrier has delivered the shipment to the steamship company. This document can be used to show compliance with a letter of credit's payment requirements and to support damage claims.

airway bill Another increasingly important document is the *universal airway bill,* a standardized document that air carriers use on all international air shipments. By reducing required paperwork to one document, the carrier reduces processing costs. Having a standardized document also helps to speed shipments through customs.

Improving Documentation

It has been said that international trade moves on paper and without the proper paperwork, documentation, the shipment will stop. To say the least, international documentation is very cumbersome, costly, and time consuming. Efforts are being made to reduce the reliance on paper documents and to move toward the use of electronic documents. This is true of the industrialized nations, but many of the developing nations of the world are not technically advanced and the paper document will remain the mainstay in these countries.

electronic filing

Electronic data interchange (EDI) and the Internet hold much promise in achieving the goal of less international documentation. Importers and exporters, as well as carriers and intermediaries, are beginning to exchange international documentation data via the Internet and EDI. The U.S. government has developed the Automated Brokerage System (ABS) to automate the import documentation process for customs house brokers. For exports, the Bureau of the Census has developed the Automated Export System, an EDI-based system for electronic filing of the Shipper's Export Declaration (SED), and it expects by 2002 to have paperless reporting of SED export information.

Computer software programs are available to produce the international document required for a shipment to/from a specific country. These programs can produce the document in the specified language and make as many copies as necessary. The completed documents can then be sent electronically to the importing country, carriers, intermediaries, and financial institutions. For companies that are long-standing trading partners, such software provides substantial savings in paper cost, personnel time, errors, and shipping delays.

Harmonized Code

Finally, an international classification system, the *Harmonized Commodity Description and Coding System,* has been developed to identify specific products with an internationally accepted identification number. The Harmonized Code permits consistent classification for transportation elements such as documentation and duties.

Bases for Rates

This section directs attention toward the bases carriers use or the factors they consider in determining rates. The following factors usually affect the rate: (1) the cost and value of service, which affect the different rates the carrier establishes for different commodities; (2) distance; and (3) the volume or weight of the shipment.

Cost of Service

Basing rates upon the *cost of service* considers the supply side of pricing. The cost of supplying the service establishes the floor for a rate; that is, the supply cost permits the carrier's viability by providing the rate's lower limit (see Figure 10–4).

FIGURE 10–4 Limits on Rates

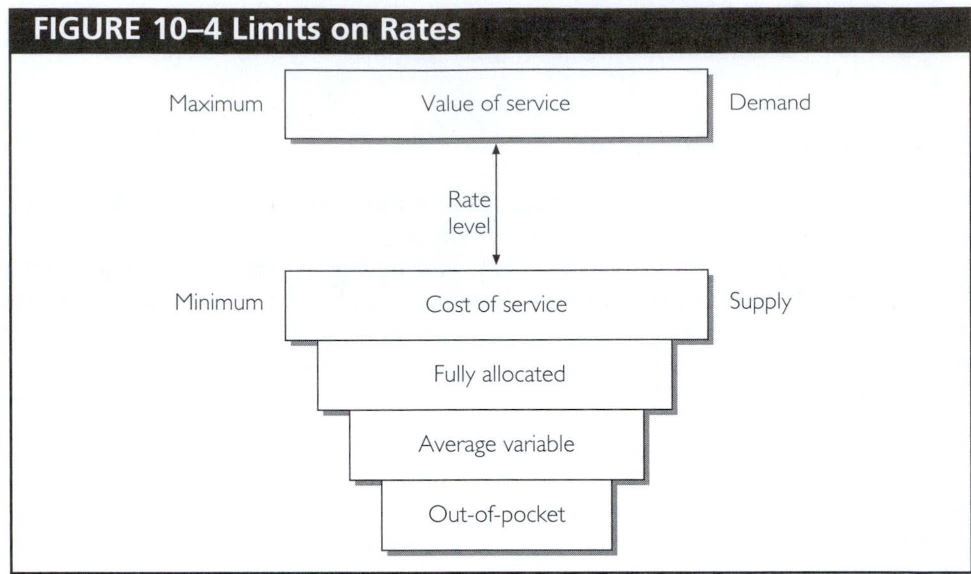

cost concepts

A continual problem of what cost basis to use has plagued this area. Carriers have used fully allocated (average total) costs, as well as average variable costs and out-of-pocket (marginal) costs. In essence, this problem sets up subfloors to the lower rate limit: the carrier will base the higher limit upon fully allocated costs and will base the lower limit upon out-of-pocket costs.

common costs
joint costs

Common and joint costs also increase the problem of using service cost as a basis for rates. The carrier incurs common and joint costs when producing multiple units of output; the carrier cannot directly allocate such costs to a particular production unit. (*Joint cost* is a particular type of common cost in which the costs a carrier incurs in producing one unit unavoidably produce another product. For example, moving a commodity from A to B unavoidably produces the movement capacity and cost from B to A—the backhaul.) The procedure the carrier uses to assign these costs determines the cost basis, permitting latitude for cost variations and, consequently, for rate variations.

Value of Service

Value of service pricing considers the demand side of pricing. We may define value of service pricing as "charging what the traffic will bear." This basis considers the transported product's ability to withstand transportation costs. For example, in Figure 10–5, the highest rate a carrier can charge to move producer A's product to point B is fifty cents per unit. If the carrier assesses a higher rate, producer A's product will not be competitive in the B market area. Thus, value of service pricing places the upper limit upon the rate.

rationale

Generally, rates vary by transported product. The cost difference associated with various commodity movements may explain this, but this difference also contains the value of service pricing concept. For higher-value commodities, transportation charges are a small portion of the total selling price. From Table 10–2, we can see that the transportation rate for diamonds, for a given distance and weight, is 100 times

FIGURE 10–5 Example of Value of Service Pricing

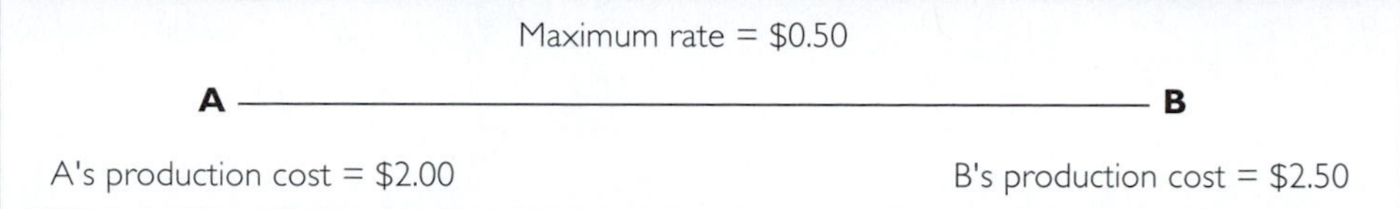

Maximum rate = $0.50

A ——————————————————————— B

A's production cost = $2.00 B's production cost = $2.50

TABLE 10–2 Transportation Rates and Commodity Value

	Coal	Diamonds
Production value per ton*	$30.00	$10,000,000.00
Transportation charge per ton*	10.00	1,000.00
Total selling price	$40.00	$10,001,000.00
Transportation cost as a percentage of selling price	25%	0.01%

*Assumed.

greater than that for coal; but transportation charges amount to only 0.01 percent of the selling price for diamonds, as opposed to 25 percent for coal. Thus, high-value commodities can sustain higher transportation charges; and carriers price the transport services accordingly—a specific application of demand pricing.[3]

Distance

Rates usually vary with respect to *distance;* that is, the greater the distance the commodity moves, the greater the cost to the carrier and the greater the transportation rate. However, certain rates do not relate to distance. One example of these is a *blanket rate.*

blanket rate

A blanket rate does not increase as distance increases; the rate remains the same for all points in the blanket area the carrier designates. The postage stamp rate is one example of a blanket rate. No matter what distance you ship a letter, your cost as shipper (sender) is the same. In transportation, carriers have employed blanket rates for a city's commercial zone,[4] a given state, region, or a number of states, for example. In each case, the rate into (out of) the blanket area will be the same no matter where the destination (origin) is located in the blanket area.

tapering rate

Most transportation rates do increase as distance increases, but the increase is not directly proportional to distance. This relationship of rates to distance is known as the *tapering rate principle.* As Figure 10–6 shows, the rate increases as distance increases, but not linearly. The rate structure tapers because carriers spread terminal costs (cargo handling, clerical, and billing) over a greater mileage base. These terminal costs do not vary with distance; as the shipment's movement distance increases, the terminal cost per mile decreases. The intercept point in Figure 10–6 corresponds to the terminal costs.

FIGURE 10–6 Example of the Tapering Rate Principle

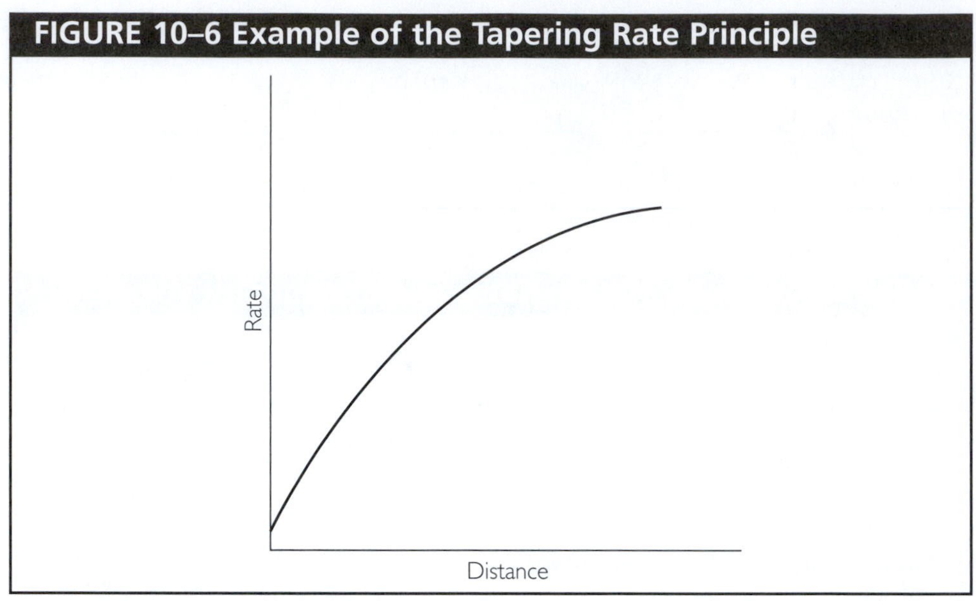

Weight of Shipment

Carriers quote freight rates in cents per hundredweight (actual weight in pounds divided by 100 = hundredweight, or cwt) and determine the total transportation charge by the total weight of the shipment in cwt, and the appropriate rate per cwt. The rate per cwt relates to the shipped volume: carriers charge a lower rate for volume shipments and a higher rate for less-than-volume quantities. In essence, carriers offer a quantity discount for shipping large volumes (buying service in a large quantity).

quantity discount

Railroads term these quantity discounts carload (CL) and less-than-carload (LCL); motor carriers call them truckload (TL) and less-than-truckload (LTL). The CL and TL rates represent the lower, volume rates; and the LCL and LTL rates denote the higher, less-than-volume rates.

One noteworthy exception to the rate-volume relationship is the any-quantity (AQ) rate, which bears no relationship to volume shipped. The rate per cwt remains constant regardless of the volume a firm tenders to the carrier for shipment; that is, no quantity discount is available.

The pragmatics of carrier pricing are presented in Appendix 10A, following this chapter.

Transportation Services

The preceding material does not entirely delineate the nature of the transportation service. Carriers may seem merely to provide commodity movement service between two facilities; in reality, the carrier provides terminal and line-haul services as well as basic transport service. For some services, but not all, the carrier charges no additional fee. The transportation manager must recognize and take advantage of these "extra" services.

Terminal Services

Although carrier terminal operations fall outside the logistics manager's direct control, exploring the nature of this operation provides the logistics manager with some knowledge of the constraints that carrier terminals impose upon the provision of transportation service.

Terminal Functions. Essentially, the carrier's terminal performs five basic functions: consolidation, breakbulk, shipment service, vehicle service, and interchange. Performing these functions requires time and, therefore, affects the total transit time a carrier provides.

consolidation

Consolidation is the combining of many less-than-volume shipments into one large shipment that the carrier can transport economically. Thus, if a shipper tenders a 2,000-pound shipment, the carrier will combine this shipment with other small shipments before dispatching it on toward destination. *Breakbulk* is just the opposite; when a consolidated shipment arrives at the destination terminal, the carrier must break down the many shipments in the vehicle for dispatch to the individual consignees.

breakbulk

Through *shipment service,* the carrier provides freight-handling services for consolidation and dispersion and performs the clerical, billing, routing, and other functions for the shipment. *Vehicle service* essentially maintains a sufficient vehicle supply. The carrier must constantly review vehicle distribution among terminals to ensure a supply sufficient to provide the transport service the shipping public and regulatory requirements demand. Finally, *interchange* provides freight-exchange facilities for carriers coordinating to provide through service.

In addition to the preceding functions, the carrier's terminal provides pickup and delivery service. Pickup and delivery involve picking up movement-ready freight at the shipper's plant or making ultimate shipment delivery at the consignee's plant. Carriers may or may not charge for this service; the shipper must consult the carrier's rules and accessorial tariffs.

Loading and Unloading. The consolidation function embraces the carrier's obligation to load and unload small shipments. For TL- and CL-size shipments, the shipper is required to load the vehicle and the consignee is required to unload it; but, if a firm wishes, the carrier will perform these services at an added cost. The shipper must consult the carrier's rules to determine loading (or unloading) requirements.

demurrage and detention

The carrier grants the shipper or consignee a specified amount of free time to load or unload a vehicle and assesses charges for holding the vehicle beyond the free time; these are known as *demurrage* (rail) and *detention* (motor) charges. For railroads, the free time for loading or unloading a boxcar is twenty-four to forty-eight hours, Saturdays, Sundays, and holidays excluded. The demurrage charge per railcar per day held varies by carrier.

The motor carrier industry has no standard detention rules and charges. Consequently, a shipper must consult each carrier's rules tariff to determine free time and detention charges. As a general rule, detention charges for holding the power unit and driver beyond the free time are higher than for holding the trailer only.

weighing

Shipment Monitoring. As noted earlier, carriers quote transportation rates in terms of cents per cwt. Thus, the carrier needs the shipment's exact weight determined so that the carrier realizes the appropriate revenue and the shipper pays the correct charges. The carriers maintain weighing devices that the regulatory commissions control. A shipper may request a carrier to reweigh a vehicle and its contents if the shipper feels the original weight is in error. For some commodities, the carrier and shipper use an agreed weight per package, case, carton, or other container. If an agreed weight is in effect, the number of shipped packages times the agreed weight determines the total shipment weight.

tracing

In many situations, the transportation manager must know where a shipment is or when it will arrive at its destination. Such information eliminates customer ill will and stockouts and improves the utilization of materials-handling equipment and labor. Carriers provide this monitoring function, known as tracing and expediting. *Tracing* is tracking a shipment's movement to determine its location in the transportation pipeline. *Expediting,* which utilizes the same procedure as tracing, has the objective of getting the shipment to its destination quicker than normal. Some motor carriers use satellites to monitor a vehicle's exact location.

expediting

electronic tracing

Technology has drastically improved the tracing and expediting functions. Many carriers have Internet-based information systems that enable the shipper to trace the location of the shipment by using the shipment's bill of lading or airway bill number. Depending on the system configuration, the shipper can trace the progress of the shipment in the carrier's system. As the shipment traverses a system checkpoint (terminal), the carrier's information system updates the status of the shipment. Motor carriers and ground expedited and air express carriers have made great strides in the use of Internet-based tracing systems.

global positioning system

The motor carriers have been adopting the use of the Global Positioning System (GPS) that can pinpoint the location of a vehicle within a matter of feet. The GPS utilizes a system of satellites that triangulates the position of the vehicle to give the shipper and carrier an exact location of the shipment in real time. And, with the addition of a computer terminal in the vehicle, the carrier can communicate to the driver any delivery or routing changes required.

Line-Haul Services

Carriers also provide line-haul services that permit the logistics manager to effect changes in the original shipping order and to realize savings in transportation costs. The line-haul services are reconsignment and diversion, pool car (or truck) service, stopping in transit, and transit privilege.

Reconsignment and Diversion. Carriers use *reconsignment and diversion* interchangeably to mean a change in the shipment's destination and/or consignee with the shipper paying the through rate from origin to final destination. There is, however, a technical difference between the two. Reconsignment permits the shipper to change the destination and/or consignee after the shipment has reached its original destination but before the carrier has delivered it to the original consignee. Diversion enables the shipper to effect the same changes while the shipment is en route and before it reaches the original destination.

benefit

Shippers use reconsignment and diversion extensively in the movement of perishable products (fruits, etc.) and movements in which the original consignee refuses the shipment or cancels the order. Shippers may start perishable products in movement before they have a buyer, using the time in transit to obtain a buyer. Having found a buyer, the shipper issues a reconsignment or diversion order with the buyer named as consignee. Or, when an original buyer decides not to accept an

Supply Chain Technology

The Home Delivery Portal

Obviously, the home delivery of goods and services is a tremendous E-commerce target market, but receipt of those goods and services also presents one of the biggest challenges. While many of the dot-com companies schedule home deliveries around the needs of the customer, other clients may require goods to be left when they are not home. However, the millions of Americans who use the latest technology to buy and receive over the Internet typically do not have a technologically advanced "mailbox" capable of receiving those purchases. With this market in mind, companies like Deliverybox.com and mentalPhysics.com (formerly Smart Box) have moved beyond the concept stage and have experimented with "receptacle" designs and some are seeking design patents.

To meet the diverse containerization needs of home-delivered goods, the designs vary in size and may be temperature controlled. For security purposes, some designs have access codes that only the owner and approved delivery company know. Streamline.com provides its customers with free refrigerators and fits their garages with keypad entry systems for delivery when the customers are not home. An independent receptacle, however, may be required if carriers are unwilling to commingle their delivered goods with another carrier's.

There are several physical challenges with these new mailboxes, including the size, which is about the size of a small hotel honor-bar refrigerator, and placement. Placement of the receptacle will be relatively easy if you live in a house with a two-car garage; however, it becomes a problem if you are an apartment dweller. Regardless of the physical challenges associated with these receptacles, this new age of Internet home shopping presents the case for an apparent need for the "home delivery portal." Consumers have computer access to place orders day or night, and package carriers like FedEx and UPS, as well as the new dot-com delivery companies, could drive efficiencies further if they have the opportunity to leverage their networks and infrastructures to operate twenty-four/seven, utilizing current unused capacity.

Source: "The Home Delivery Portal," *Parcel Shipping & Distribution* (March 2000): 28. Reprinted by permission.

order, the shipper can utilize a reconsignment or diversion order to change the shipment's destination to a new buyer location or to have the shipment stopped and returned to the seller's location. These services permit the shipper to amend the original contract (bill of lading) with the carrier and to realize the benefits of the lower through rate (the tapering rate principle) from origin to new destination.

Pooling. *Pool car or pool truck service* permits the shipper to combine many LCL or LTL shipments into one CL or TL shipment and to send it to one destination and one consignee. The lower CL or TL rate applies to the combined shipments and thus effects savings for the shipper. Since the service requires one destination and one consignee, the shipper usually sends the shipment to a warehouse or drayage firm,[5] which breaks down or disperses the consolidated shipment into individual shipments and delivers them to the appropriate consignees. The warehouse manager or drayage firm assesses a fee for this service. For inbound movements, the opposite is possible: the warehouse manager can combine small shipments from a firm's suppliers and present them to a carrier, who delivers them to the firm's plant under a lower high-volume rate.

Stopping in Transit. Another service, *stopping in transit* (also known as *drop shipping*), allows the shipper to complete loading or to partially unload freight, and to pay on the highest weight in the vehicle at any time the lower TL or CL rate

FIGURE 10–7 Example of Stopping-in-Transit Service

Toledo	Chattanooga	Atlanta
45,000 lb. (Total shipment)	25,000 lb.	20,000 lb.

Rates per cwt

	LTL	TL	Minimum Weight
Toledo to Chattanooga	$7.50	$5.00	45,000 lb.
Toledo to Atlanta	$8.00	$5.50	45,000 lb.

Stop-off charge = $55.00 per stop-off

between the most distant destination and the origin. The shipper assesses a stop-off charge for each intermediate stop, but not for the final destination.

Figure 10-7 shows an example of stopping-in-transit service. The shipper at Toledo has two customers, located at Chattanooga and Atlanta, that have purchased 25,000 and 20,000 pounds respectively. The shipper has two shipping options for these two shipments: (1) as two LTL shipments and (2) as one stopping-in-transit shipment. The cost of each is as follows:

1. Two LTL shipments:
   Toledo to Chattanooga = 250 cwt @ $7.50 = $1,875.00
   Toledo to Atlanta = 200 cwt @ $8.00 = 1,600.00
   Total cost = $3,475.00
2. Stopping-in-transit shipment:
   450 cwt @ $5.50 = $2,475.00
   Stop-off charge = 55.00
   Total cost = $2,530.00

Use of the stopping-in-transit service saves $945.00.

Transit Privilege. The final line-haul service is the *transit privilege,* which permits the shipper to stop the shipment in transit and to perform some function that physically changes the product's characteristics. With this privilege, carriers charge the lower through rate (from origin to final destination) rather than the higher combination of rates from origin to transit point and from transit point to final destination. Carriers have established the transit privilege for grain milling, steel fabrication, lumber processing, and storage of various commodities for aging.

SUMMARY

Transportation management encompasses the day-to-day functions of the transportation process. Considerable knowledge is required of transportation pricing, services, and regulation, both domestic and international, to manage the transportation process and to operate the logistics system efficiently.

- Transportation management embraces a proactive philosophy to identify and solve transportation problems.

- To increase negotiating power and facilitate partnerships, shippers are using a limited number of carriers.
- Carrier negotiating and contracting are a natural outgrowth of carrier deregulation. Both activities result in lower freight costs and improved services.
- Shipment consolidation is a strategy that combines smaller shipments into a larger shipment to realize lower freight rates inherent in carrier pricing.
- Economic regulation of transportation placed controls over carrier entry, prices, and services. Today, economic deregulation of transportation emphasizes the marketplace, not government, as the mechanism for control.
- Carrier performance quality is measured with a carrier evaluation technique that uses a rating scale to rate carrier performance.
- Domestic documentation includes the bill of lading, freight bill, and freight claim. The bill of lading is the contract of carriage and a receipt for the goods tendered to the carrier. The freight bill is the carrier's invoice, and the freight claim is a shipper request for reimbursement for freight loss and damage.
- Common carriers are liable for all loss and damage, with limited exceptions.
- International documentation consists of financial, customs, and transportation documents.
- For domestic trade there are basically two terms of sale, whereas for international trade there are thirteen.
- Transportation rates are based on either cost of service or value of service. Cost of service reflects the carrier's cost, while value of service considers how much the shipper is willing to pay.
- Freight rates vary with distance and weight. Rates increase with distance and weight shipped.
- In addition to basic movement service, carriers offer terminal and line-haul services. Terminal services include the terminal functions, loading and unloading, and shipment monitoring. Reconsignment and diversion, pooling, stopping in transit, and transit privilege are line-haul services.

Study Questions

1. Describe the transportation management philosophy existing today, pointing out the major strategies firms use.
2. Discuss the concept of market power and show how it relates to carrier negotiation and carrier contracting.
3. How would a transportation manager monitor the quality of service provided by the carriers used?
4. What is the basis of economic regulation of transportation? Explain the rationale for economic deregulation of transportation.
5. How has economic deregulation of transportation impacted shippers?
6. Describe the function of the following documents: bill of lading, freight bill, freight claim, certificate of origin, letter of credit, carnet, dock receipt, and airway bill.

7. Discuss the cost implications to the buyer of the thirteen Incoterms.
8. What is the economic implication of cost of service, value of service, shipment weight, and shipment distance in carrier pricing?
9. Discuss the economic and operation impact of a carrier's terminal services upon the shipper and carrier rates.
10. Describe the circumstances under which a company would utilize the line-haul services of reconsignment and diversion, pooling, stopping in transit, and transit privilege.

NOTES

1. For a thorough discussion of transportation regulation, see John J. Coyle, Edward J. Bardi, and Robert A. Novack, *Transportation,* 5th ed. (Cincinnati, Ohio: South-Western College Publishing, 2000), Chapter 2.
2. When using a straight bill of lading, the shipper can retain security interest in the goods by using the C.O.D. (cash on delivery) service carriers offer. With a C.O.D. shipment, the carrier collects the invoice price of the shipment before delivering the shipment to the consignee.
3. We could argue that for high-valued goods the carrier bears a higher cost because of the increased liability risk in case of damage.
4. We define the commercial zone as the city proper plus surrounding points, determined by population, and the rates to the city apply to the surrounding points within this limit.
5. A *drayage firm* is a motor carrier specializing in providing pickup and delivery service.

CASE 10–1 ■ Specialty Metals Company

During the past two months, Thomas Train, vice president of transportation for Specialty Metals Company, a metals servicing company with operations in ten midwestern states, has been soliciting bids for the movement of tool steel, a specialty steel used for manufacturing tools and related products. Tom's goal is to reduce the shipping cost of this high-value steel. The supplier is located in Weirton, West Virginia, 350 miles from Specialty's Toledo, Ohio, service center. Steel Haulers, Inc., a regional contract motor carrier, currently moves the tool steel under contract. Steel Haulers' current rates are incremental: $2.80/cwt for shipments weighing less than 150 cwt, $2.60/cwt for shipments between 150 and 250 cwt, $2.40/cwt for shipments between 250 and 400 cwt, and $2.25/cwt for shipment weights in excess of 400 cwt up to a maximum of 450 cwt. The carrier submitted a rate of $2.25/cwt for weights in excess of 400 cwt two hours before the submission deadline for the carrier proposals.

For various equipment, financial, and/or management reasons, Tom has eliminated all but two carrier proposals. One of the two remaining carrier proposals is from Flatbed, Inc., a contract motor carrier that has an excellent reputation for providing specialized steel hauling service. Flatbed submitted a rate of $2.60/cwt with a minimum weight of 100 cwt; the carrier gives no discounts for larger shipments. The second carrier under consideration is the Middlewest Railroad, which submitted a piggyback rate of $2.45/cwt with a minimum of 200 cwt; the rate is for Plan 2, door-to-door piggyback service with a maximum shipment weight of 400 cwt per load. Both motor carriers will provide one-day transit time, while the piggyback transit time is three days.

The final proposal Tom is considering is a private trucking proposal submitted by the transportation department. The estimated total operating cost for the private fleet (including overhead and depreciation) is $50,000 per year; the investment the vehicles require is $85,000. This annual operating cost equates to $2.50/cwt with a minimum of 400 cwt per shipment and fifty shipments per year. The private truck proposal recognizes Specialty's inability to provide a load for the backhaul from Toledo to Weirton. But, given today's deregulated environment, the proposal assumes the private fleet will be able to solicit return loads from other Toledo shippers 30 percent of the time and generate $15,000 in annual backhaul revenue.

Specialty has a contract with the steel mill to purchase two million pounds of tool steel per year. Last year, tool steel shipments averaged 250 cwt per order. Tool steel has a purchase value of $250/cwt. Unloading costs would be the same under each proposal. The chief financial officer estimates Specialty's annual inventory carrying cost per dollar of average inventory stored to be 20 percent (15 percent for the cost of money and 5 percent for the cost of insurance, taxes, and handling); he estimates the cost to place an order to be $75. The inventory-in-transit cost is 15 percent per year.

Case Question

Tom indicated that he would decide on the bid proposals today. Given the facts of the different proposals, what would you advise Tom to do?

APPENDIX 10A

THE PRAGMATICS OF CARRIER PRICING

One of the most difficult and confusing responsibilities of a logistics manager is determining the prices of various transportation services available for a logistics system's use. Determining how much it will cost to move a barrel of pickles from Toledo, Ohio, to New York City is not always easy.

To appreciate the problem, consider the nature of a transportation service. It would be simple if carriers sold all transportation service on the basis of ton-miles; that is, if we had to pay *X* dollars to move one ton of a product one mile. But carriers do not sell transportation services in ton-miles; rather, carriers sell transportation services for moving a specific commodity (pickles) between two specific points (Toledo and New York City). This fact gives us a glimpse of the enormous magnitude of the transportation pricing problem. There are more than 33,000 important shipping and receiving points in the United States. Theoretically, the number of different possible routes would be all the permutations of the 33,000 points. The result is in the trillions of trillions. In addition, we must consider the thousands and thousands of different commodities and products that firms might ship over any of these routes. On top of that, we must consider the different modes and different companies within each mode. We may also need to consider each commodity's specific supply-and-demand situation over each route.

Class Rates

Since quoting trillions and trillions of rates is impossible, the transportation industry has taken two major steps toward simplification.

shipping points

The first step was to consolidate the 33,000 shipping points into groups by dividing the nation into geographic squares. The most important shipping point (based on tonnage) in each square serves as the *rate base point* for all other shipping points in the square, reducing the potential number of distance variations for ratemaking purposes. The carriers determined the distances from each base point to every other base point and published them in the National Rate Basis Tariff. The distance between any two base points is called the *rate basis number.* This first simplifying step reduced the number of possible origins and destinations for pricing purposes.

rate basis number

The second step deals with the thousands and thousands of different items that firms might ship between any two base points. The railroads have established a national scale of rates, which gives a rate in dollars per hundredweight (cwt) for each rate basis number. (Motor carriers have individual rate scales.) These rate scales are the basis for a simplified product classification system.

classification procedure

Classification simply means grouping together products with similar transportation characteristics so that one rating can be applied to the whole group. The four primary classification characteristics are density, stowability, ease or difficulty of handling goods, and liability. High-demand and high-value items might be placed in class 100, which means that carriers will charge them 100 percent of the *first class rate.* Low-value items, such as coal, might be placed in class 50, which means carriers will charge them 50 percent of the first class rate. This percentage number is a *class rating,* the group into which carriers place a commodity for ratemaking purposes.

Now the number of possible pricing situations is small enough to allow the formation of a transportation pricing system. We determine the price of moving a particular item between two particular points as follows: First, look up the rate basis point for the origin and for the destination. Then determine the rate basis number between the two base points. Next, determine the classification rating (class rating) for the particular product to be shipped. Then find the rate in the class rate tariff that corresponds to the appropriate rate basis number and class rating. Finally, multiply this rate, which is in cents per cwt, by the total shipment weight in cwt to determine the cost to move that specific product between those two points.

tariff

The word *tariff* commonly means almost any publication that a carrier or a tariff publishing agency produces that concerns itself with the pricing or service the carrier performs. All the information a shipper needs to determine the cost of a move is in one or more tariffs.

example

Now look at an example of the mechanics involved in determining the class rate charges for a motor carrier shipment. A firm wishes to ship 4,000 pounds of putty in steel-lined drums with metal covers from Reading, Pennsylvania, to Washington, D.C.:

1. The rate basis number in Table 10A–1 is 98 (at the intersection of Reading, Pennsylvania, and Washington, D.C., in the vertical and horizontal portions of the tariff, respectively).
2. The class ratings and minimum weight, found in the classification for putty in steel-lined drums with metal covers (see Table 10A–2), are LTL = 55, TL = 35, and minimum weight = 36,000 lb. For interstate shipments we use the LTL rating of 55.

TABLE 10A–1 Table of Rate Basic Numbers

	From Rate Groups (All Cities in Pennsylvania)							
	Allentown	Altoona	Bellefonte	Reading	Scranton	State College	Williamsport	York
To Rate Groups	**Apply Rate Basis Numbers**							
Baltimore . . . . MD	84	73	86	62	64	92	76	98
Barnesville . . . MD	103	94	122	96	95	132	102	117
Newark . . . . . . NJ	98	90	96	101	92	113	84	76
Newark . . . . . . NY	61	76	60	76	76	76	60	77
New York . . . . NY	96	92	92	101	96	111	87	73
Washington. . . DC	109	96	111	98	90	118	103	122
Wilmington . . . DE	98	66	98	84	66	107	83	101

Source: MAC Tariff 2-M.

TABLE 10A–2 National Motor Freight Classification

Item		Articles	Classes LTL	TL	MW
149500		PAINT GROUP, Articles consist of Paints, Paint Material, or Putty, as described in items subject to this grouping, see Note, item 149502.			
149502		NOTE—Commodities listed under this generic heading when tendered for shipment in Package 2452 are to be classified under the same provisions that apply when tendered to the carrier in boxes.			
149520		Aluminum, or Bronze Powders, or Filters, in barrels, boxes, or Package 2258	60	40	30
149580		Blue, ultramarine, forms or shapes, in barrels or boxes or in double bags	70	40	30
149590		Blue, ultramarine, lumps or powdered, see item 600000 for classes dependent upon agreed or released value:			
	Sub 1	In containers in barrels or boxes	70	40	30
	Sub 2	In bulk in double bags, double-wall paper bags, barrels, or boxes	55	35	36
150110		Putty in containers in barrels, boxes, or crates or in bulk in barrels, steel putty drums, kits, pails, or tubs, or steel-lined drums or tubs with metal or wooden covers	55	35	36

Source: National Motor Freight Classification 100-P.

3. The table of class rates gives the applicable rate (see Table 10A–3); the intersection of the horizontal line of rate basis number 98 (the 92 to 99 group) and the vertical line of class 55 determine this rate. Since the 4,000-pound shipment falls between weight groups 2,000 and 5,000, we must compute the charges under both weight groups to determine the lowest cost. The appropriate rates are \$2.33/cwt for 2,000 pounds and \$1.77/cwt for 5,000 pounds.
4. We find the transportation charge by multiplying the rate per cwt by the number of cwt in the shipment, or

   $$4{,}000 \text{ lb} = \frac{4{,}000}{100} = 40 \text{ cwt}$$

   The firm could ship the 40 cwt under the 2,000-pound rate of \$2.33 or under the 5,000-pound rate of \$1.77 as follows:

   40 cwt @ \$2.33 = \$93.20
   50 cwt @ \$1.77 = \$88.50

   In this case, the shipper would elect the 4,000-pound shipment as a 5,000-pound shipment—in essence, shipping 1,000 pounds of phantom weight—and pay \$88.50 rather than \$93.20.

weight break

We can compare the cost of shipping at a volume higher than actual weight to realize a lower rate and lower shipping cost with the cost of shipping at the actual weight by determining the *weight break*. The weight break is the shipment size that equates the transportation charges for different rates and weight groups. That is,

TABLE 10A–3 Class Tariff

Rate Basis No.	Weight Group	100	85	70	60	55	50	45	40	35
		Rates in Cents per 100 Pounds								
60 to 67	500 LTL	408	358	312	273	256	239			
	1,000 LTL	361	314	268	236	223	207			
	2,000 LTL	297	255	216	189	175	161			
	5,000 LTL	216	184	151	130	119	108			
	Truckload	169	144	120	103	95	89	82	73	64
76 to 83	500 LTL	470	410	355	311	291	270			
	1,000 LTL	421	365	310	273	256	238			
	2,000 LTL	356	304	256	223	208	191			
	5,000 LTL	271	230	190	163	149	136			
	Truckload	223	191	158	135	125	116	107	97	84
	TL 30,000	221	189	156	133	123	114	101	90	80
84 to 91	500 LTL	496	432	374	325	304	282			
	1,000 LTL	449	388	330	288	271	251			
	2,000 LTL	385	329	278	241	223	205			
	5,000 LTL	304	258	213	182	167	152			
	Truckload	263	223	187	159	147	136	125	113	98
	TL 30,000	261	221	185	157	145	134	118	105	93
92 to 99	500 LTL	514	448	386	336	314	291			
	1,000 LTL	467	404	342	299	281	260			
	2,000 LTL	403	345	290	252	233	214			
	5,000 LTL	322	274	225	193	177	161			
	Truckload	285	242	201	171	158	147	136	122	106
	TL 30,000	283	240	199	169	156	145	129	114	101
100 to 109	500 LTL	566	492	423	367	343	317			
	1,000 LTL	519	448	379	330	310	286			
	2,000 LTL	455	389	327	283	262	240			
	5,000 LTL	374	318	262	224	206	187			
	Truckload	342	290	240	206	188	170	165	149	130
	TL 30,000	342	290	240	206	188	170	156	139	121
110 to 125	500 LTL	598	519	444	387	361	334			
	1,000 LTL	549	474	399	349	326	302			
	2,000 LTL	484	413	345	299	278	255			
	5,000 LTL	399	339	279	239	219	200			
	Truckload	365	310	254	219	200	185	177	159	138
	TL 30,000	365	310	254	219	200	185	168	152	131

(Columns 100 through 35 are Classes.)

Application of weight groups: 500 LTL: Applies on LTL or AQ shipments weighing 500 pounds or more but less than 1,000 pounds. 1,000 LTL: Applies on LTL or AQ shipments weighing 1,000 pounds or more but less than 2,000 pounds. 2,000 LTL: Applies on LTL or AQ shipments weighing 2,000 pounds or more but less than 5,000 pounds. 5,000 LTL: Applies on LTL or AQ shipments weighing 5,000 pounds or more. Truckload: Subject to minimum weights in NMFC (Note A). 30,000: Applies on truckload shipments where actual or billed weight is 30,000 pounds or more (Note A).

Note A: Where the charge under the rates for TL 30,000 pounds is lower than the charge under the rates for TL shipments subject to minimum weights of less than 30,000 pounds.

$$\text{LV rate} \times \text{WB} = \text{HV rate} \times \text{MW}$$

where

LV rate = lesser-volume rate
WB = weight break
HV rate = higher-volume rate
MW = minimum weight for higher-volume rate

Plugging in the numbers from the example used here, we find the weight break to be

$$\$2.33 \times \text{WB} = \$1.77 \times 50 \text{ cwt}$$
$$\text{WB} = 37.98 \text{ cwt}$$

Next, we can establish a simple decision rule for shipping clerks to use to determine when it is economical to ship a shipment at a volume higher than the volume a firm is actually shipping. In this example, the decision rules are:

shipping decision rules

1. If the shipment weighs between 2,000 and 3,798 pounds, ship the actual weight at the 2,000-pound rate of \$2.33/cwt.
2. If the shipment weighs between 3,798 and 5,000 pounds, ship at 5,000 pounds (minimum weight) at the 5,000-pound rate of \$1.77/cwt.
3. If the shipment weighs more than 5,000 pounds but less than the truckload minimum weight, ship the actual weight at the 5,000-pound rate of \$1.77/cwt. (*Note:* a weight break exists between the 5,000-pound rate and the truckload rate.)

Exception Ratings (Rates)

Carriers publish exception ratings when the transportation characteristics of an item in a particular area differ from those of the same article in other areas. For example, large-volume movements or intensive competition in one area may require the publication of an exception rating; the exception rating supersedes the classification. The same procedures described earlier apply to determining the exception rate, except now we use the exception rating (class) instead of the classification rating. Table 10A–4 gives an example of an exception tariff.

Continuing with the earlier example, an exception rating is available under item number 150110 of the exception tariff for the putty moving from Reading, Pennsylvania, to

TABLE 10A–4 Exception Tariff

Exceptions to National Motor Freight Classification

	Classes (Ratings)			
Item	**Articles**	**LTL**	**TL**	**MW**
150110	Putty, in containers in steel-lined drum or tubs with metal or wooden covers	50	35	36

Washington, D.C. It lists a class rating for LTL quantities of 50. The exception rating of class 50 takes precedence and results in a rate of $2.14 for 2,000 to 5,000 pounds and $1.61 for 5,000 pounds to a truckload (see Table 10A–3).*

Using the exception rating, we find that the cost to ship 4,000 pounds of putty is 50 cwt @ $1.61 = $80.50. The exception rate produces a savings of $8.00, or 9.0 percent of the class rate.

Commodity Rates

commodity specific

direction specific

O-D (origin-destination) specific

Carriers can construct a commodity rate on a variety of bases. The most common is a specific rate concerning a specific commodity or related commodity group between specific points and generally by specific routes. Commodity rates are complete in themselves and are not part of the classification system. If the rate does not specifically state the commodity you are shipping, or if the origin-destination (O-D) is not one that the commodity rate specifically spells out, then the commodity rate does not apply for your particular movement. A published commodity rate takes precedence over the class rate or exception rate on the same article between the specific points.

Carriers offer this type of rate for commodities that firms move regularly and in large quantities. But such a pricing system, which completely undermines the attempts to simplify transportation pricing through the class rate structure, has caused transportation pricing to revert to the publishing of a multiplicity of rates and adds greatly to the pricing system complexity.

Table 10A–5 gives an example of a commodity tariff. Using the putty shipping example, we find that a commodity rate exists in item 493 in Table 10A–5. Item 493, which applies to classification items 149500 to 150230, includes putty, as shown in Table 10A–2. Note that the commodity rate specifies a route from Reading, Pennsylvania, to Washington, D.C., the example problem's origin and destination. However, Table 10A–5 lists only a TL rate with a minimum weight of 30,000 pounds.

*We find the exception rates for class 50 in Table 10A–3 at the intersection of class 50 and rate basis 92 to 99 for 2,000 LTL and 5,000 LTL.

TABLE 10A–5 Commodity Tariff

Commodity Rates in Cents per 100 Pounds

Item	Commodity	From	To	TL Rate	Min. Wt.
493	PAINTS GROUP, as described in NMFC Items 149500 to 150230, rated Class 35	Reading . . . PA	Baltimore . . . . . MD	79	23M
			Beltsville . . . . . . MD	82	30M
			Washington . . . DC	82	30M

We can compare the class, exception, and commodity rates for the movement of putty from Reading, Pennsylvania, to Washington, D.C., in truckload quantities (36,000 pounds or more) as follows:

Class rate = $1.01/cwt
Exception rate = $1.01/cwt
Commodity rate = $0.82/cwt

zip code

As we can see from this comparison, the commodity rate is the lowest, 18.8 percent less than the class rate and the exception rate.

Many LTL and express carriers use U.S. Postal Service zip codes to identify origins and destinations. The *zip code commodity rates* specify rates for named commodities from a specific origin to multiple destinations identified by a zip code.

Other Rates

In addition to class rates, exception rates, and commodity rates, many special rates have developed over the years to meet very specific situations. The most prevalent and most important of these special rates are all-commodity, released-value, actual-value, deferred, multiple-vehicle, incentive, and innovative rates.

All-Commodity Rates. All-commodity rates, also known as freight-all-kinds (FAK) rates, are a recent development in which the carrier specifies the rate per shipment either in dollars per hundredweight or in total dollars per shipment with a specified minimum weight. The shipped commodity or commodities are not important. These rates tend to price transportation services by cost rather than by the value of service and are used mostly by shippers who send mixed-commodity shipments to a single destination.

released value

actual value

Value Rates. Of a whole host of value rates, released-value rates and actual-value rates are the most important. The degree of liability (commodity value) the carrier assumes determines these rates. Generally, a common carrier is liable for the actual value of any goods lost or damaged while in the carrier's custody. Carriers base a released-value rate on the assumption of a certain fixed liability, usually stated in cents per pound. Usually this fixed liability is considerably less than the actual value of the goods. As a result of this limited liability, the shipper receives a lower rate.

Carriers use released-value rates extensively in the shipment of household goods and use actual-value rates when goods considered to be the same commodity—jewelry, for example—vary greatly in value. In these cases, a single rate is not desirable because some shipments have a high-liability potential whereas other shipments have a low liability potential. The actual-value rates make allowances for this potential difference, and the rate the carriers charge reflects the liability difference. The 1980 deregulation acts reduced the ICC constraints on motor carrier and railroad use of value rates. Today, motor carriers may offer value rates without STB approval.

Deferred Rates. Deferred rates are most common in air transportation. In general, they allow the carrier to charge a lower rate for the privilege of deferring a shipment's arrival time. For example, Federal Express offers a two-day two-pound package delivery rate that is 42 percent lower than the rate for priority, 10:00 A.M. next-day delivery. A deferred rate allows the carrier to move shipments at the carrier's convenience as long as the shipment arrives within a reasonable time or by the scheduled deferred delivery date. This allows the carrier to use the deferred-rate shipments as "filler freight" to more fully load its vehicles.

Multiple-Vehicle Rates. Carriers offer multiple-vehicle rates as a special incentive rate to firms shipping multiple-vehicle loads of a particular commodity at one time to a single destination. Motor carriers first used these rates to overcome the fact that a railcar holds more than a truck. By publishing lower multiple-vehicle rates, the motor carriers competed more effectively with the railroads. Multiple-vehicle rates also reduce commodities' transportation costs, thus allowing those commodities to move to more distant markets. The savings that carriers achieve by economies of scale justify lower rates. The railroads can often demonstrate savings in multiple-vehicle pickups. Multiple-vehicle rates have progressed to the unit train rates that rail carriers give for whole trainloads of commodities such as coal, ore, and grain.

Incentive Rates. A carrier publishes incentive rates, or in-excess rates, to encourage heavier loading of individual vehicles so that the carrier can improve its equipment utilization. One rate covers all cargo up to a certain minimum weight, and a lower rate covers all cargo in excess of the minimum weight.

in-excess rates

Innovative Rates. Shippers commonly negotiate rates with carriers. The negotiated rate could take the form of (1) a discount from the prevailing rate, a situation common to shippers that ship small shipments under class rates; (2) a commodity rate for TL shipments that move in large volumes on a regular basis—for example, 40,000 pounds per day, seven days per week; and (3) a contract rate (rail) for very large freight volumes—for example, 800 carloads (80,000 tons) per year.

The following are examples of the rates that shippers and carriers have negotiated in recent years:

- *Density-based rating.* A lower rating (classification or exception) is possible when the shipper increases product density; the increased product density permits heavier loading of the carrier's vehicle, thus spreading the cost over a larger number of weight (pricing) units.
- *Specific description.* Shippers seek a specific commodity description for a commodity that does not fit an existing classification description; for example, defective goods being returned to the plant have a lower value, liability, and so forth than if perfect, and thus should receive a lower rating.
- *Loading and unloading allowance.* The carrier is responsible for loading and unloading LTL-size shipments. If the shipper and consignee perform this function, the carrier realizes a lower cost and passes it on to the shipper and consignee.
- *Aggregate tender rate.* The carrier gives a lower rate to the shipper who presents multiple shipments at one time. The carrier realizes a lower pickup cost per shipment, while the shipper delays delivery by aggregating shipments before dispatch.
- *Mileage rate.* This rate is quite common for truckload-type freight; carriers base it upon the number of miles the shipment moves, regardless of the commodity or the shipment's weight.
- *Contract rate.* Railroads may negotiate a specific rate with a shipper for moving a given commodity volume between specified points. These rates, which require large volumes, 600 cars or more per year, are appropriate for the

movement of bulk commodities or manufactured products that move regularly between specific points in large volumes. The shipper may specify service constraints and penalties for noncompliance.

Ocean Freight Rates. Carriers set ocean freight rates at a level that will cover all the expenses of operating the ship, the ship's capital cost, and any charges specific to the voyage. The rates cover items such as fixed costs for crew, maintenance, repair, and insurance, and variable costs such as fuel, port fees, dockage, and cargo handling. The carrier and the shipper balance these factors against the cargo type, as well as the voyage's length and special requirements, to arrive at an agreeable price.

Ocean freight rates are typically quoted on a weight-ton or measurement-ton basis. There are three weight tons: short = 2,000 pounds; long = 2,240 pounds; and metric = 2,205 pounds. The measurement ton is 40 cubic feet. The carrier will use whichever ton generates the greatest revenue. For example, a 100-cubic-foot shipment weighing 3,500 pounds will be charged for 2.5 measurement tons (100 cubic feet divided by 40 cubic feet per measurement ton) rather than 1.563 metric tons (3,500 pounds divided by 2,205 pounds).

Container rates are quite common for shipping manufactured products. The container rate does not vary by the weight shipped in the container. Generally, container rates are quoted from port to port, not shipment origin to shipment destination. Land transportation costs are added to the container rate to get the through rate.

Finally, ocean carriers add numerous surcharges to the basic rate. Example surcharges include fuel, currency, port congestion, out-of-port differential, trans-shipment, and terminal handling.

As the following example indicates, the container rate for moving a container from Charleston, South Carolina, to Antwerp, Belgium, is only 54.8 percent of the total ocean freight charge.

Rate per 40-foot container	$1,201
Currency adjustment factor	408
Terminal handling charge	500
Fuel adjustment factor	80
Total container rate	$2,189

Study Questions

1. Determine the cost of shipping 8,500 pounds of blue, ultramarine, powdered paint in bulk in double bags to Newark, New York, from State College, Pennsylvania.

2. What is the freight cost to move 22,000 pounds of putty from Reading, Pennsylvania, to Baltimore, Maryland? The putty is in a container in a steel-lined tub with a wooden cover.

3. Calculate the shipping cost to move 1,500 pounds of aluminum powders in Package 2452 to Baltimore, Maryland, from Reading, Pennsylvania.

4. You are shipping a ten-pound box (12″ × 12″ × 12″) of dry roasted peanuts in the shell from Atlanta, Georgia, 30001, to Chicago, Illinois, 60601. Comparing the charges for this shipment by FedEx (http://www.fedex.com), UPS (http://www.ups.com), and the U.S. Postal Service (http://www.usps.gov), which carrier would you use for: (1) next-day delivery, (2) second-day delivery, and (3) third- or fourth-day delivery?

Suggested Reading

Chapter 6 Managing Inventory Flows in the Supply Chain

Cattani, K. D., "Supply Chain Planning for Demand Uncertainties," *Supply Chain Management Review* (Winter 2000): 25–28.

Cooke, J. A., "Logistics Ropes in Inventory," *Logistics Management and Distribution Report* (July 2000): 49–62.

Cunningham, R., "Balancing Inventory and Service Levels," *APICS Journal* (August 1998): 42–47.

Hoffman, K. C., "Clarity Brought to Window Maker's Supply Chain," *Global Logistics and Supply Chain Management* (May 2001): 40–44.

LaLande, B., "Why So Much Inventory," *Supply Chain Management Review* (Summer 1999): 7–8.

Lindhart, J. A., "The Peaks and Valleys of Inventory Record Accuracy," *APICS Journal* (July 1998): 34–38.

Murphy, J. V., "Customer Driven Supply Chains," *Global Logistics and Supply Chain Strategies* (April 2001): 40–49.

Sankar, R., "Inventory Management Across the Retail Supply Chain," *Supply Chain Management Review* (Winter 2000): 56–63.

Waller, M., M. E. Johnson, and T. Davis, "Vendor-Managed Inventory in Retail Supply Chains," *Journal of Business Logistics* 20, no. 1 (1999): 183–204.

Chapter 7 Inventory Decision Making

Ballou, R. M., "Evaluating Inventory Management Performance Using a Turnover Curve," *International Journal of Physical Distribution and Logistics Management* 30, no. 1 (2000): 72–85.

Claycomb, C., C. Dröge, and R. Germain, "The Effect of Just-in-Time with Customers on Organizational Design and Performance," *International Journal of Logistics Management* 10, no. 2 (1999): 37–58.

Das, C., and R. Tyagi, "Effect of Correlated Demands on Safety Stock Centralization," *Journal of Business Logistics* 20, no. 1 (1999): 205–214.

Dröge, C., and R. Germain, "The Just-in-Time Inventory Effect," *Journal of Business Logistics* 20, no. 1 (1999): 53–72.

Pfol, H. C., O. Cullmann, and W. Stolzle, "Inventory Management with Statistical Process Control," *Journal of Business Logistics* 20, no. 1 (1999): 101–120.

Schuster, Edmund W., Stuart J. Allen, and Michael P. D'Itri, "Capacitated Materials Requirements Planning and Its Application in Process Industries," *Journal of Business Logistics* 21, no. 1 (2001): 169–186.

Schwarz, L. B., and Z. K. Wong, "The Design of a JIT Supply Chain," *Journal of Business Logistics* 20, no. 1 (1999): 141–164.

Tracey, M., "The Importance of Logistics Efficiency to Customer Service and Firm Performance," *International Journal of Logistics Management* 9, no. 2 (1998): 65–82.

Tyagi, R., and C. Das, "Extension of the Square Root Law for Safety Stocks to Demands with Unequal Variances," *Journal of Business Logistics* 19, no. 2 (1998): 197–203.

Vokurka, R. J., and R. R. Lummas, "The Role of Just-in-Time in Supply Chain Management," *International Journal of Logistics Management* 11, no. 1 (2000): 38–98.

Chapter 8 Warehousing Decisions

Ackerman, Kenneth B., *Practical Handbook of Warehousing*, 4th ed. (New York: Chapman & Hall, International Thomson Publishing, 1999).

Ackerman, Kenneth B., *Warehousing Profitability: A Manager's Guide* (K.B. Ackerman Co., 1999).

Foger, Gary, "Productivity Climbs with Real-Time Warehouse Control," *Modern Materials Handling* 49, no. 3 (April 1994): 38–40.

"Hot New Trends in Packaging," *Modern Materials Handling* (October 2001).

James, Aaron, "Re-Inventing the Public Warehouse," *Logistics Management Distribution Report* (May 1, 2000).

Jedd, Marcia, "Trends in Selecting Distribution Centers Are All Over the Map," *Global Logistics & Supply Chain Strategies* (March 2001).

Kulwiec, Ray, "Materials Handling and the Supply Chain," *Modern Materials Handling* (March 21, 1999).

Murphy, Paul R., and Richard F. Poist, "In Search of Warehousing Excellence: A Multivariate Analysis of HRM Practices," *Journal of Business Logistics* 14, no. 2 (1993): 145–164.

Thompkins, James A., Yavuz A. Bozer, Edward Frazelle, Joe Tanchoco, and John White, *Facilities Planning* (New York: John Wiley & Sons, 1996).

Towle, William H., *Warehousing Law* (Cawley Press, LTD, 1988).

Chapter 9 The Transportation System

Bowman, Robert J., "Are Bigger Ocean Carriers Better? Shippers and Lines Don't See Eye to Eye," *Global Logistics & Supply Chain Strategies* (March 2000).

Clott, Christopher B., "Ocean Freight Intermediaries: An Analysis of Non-Vessel Operating Common Carriers (NVOCC's) and Maritime Reform," *Transportation Journal* 40, no. 2 (Spring 2001): 17–26.

Contrill, Ken, "Air Express Carriers Stress Time-Definite Service in U.S.-Europe Trade," *Global Sites and Logistics* (October 1998): 28–35.

Cooke, James A., "Logistics Exchanges and ASPs: On the Evolutionary Path," *Logistics Management Distribution Report* (December 2000).

Coyle, John J., Edward J. Bardi, and Robert A. Novack, *Transportation*, 5th ed. (Cincinnati, Ohio: South-Western College Publishing, 2000).

Crum, M.R., D. A. Johnson, and B. J. Allen, "A Longitudinal Assessment of EDI Use in the Motor Carrier Industry," *Transportation Journal* 38, no. 1 (Fall 1998): 15–28.

Evers, Philip T., and Carol J. Johnson, "Performance Perceptions, Satisfaction, and Intention: The Intermodal Shipper's Perspective," *Transportation Journal* 40, no. 2 (Spring 2001): 27–39.

Hoffman, Kurt C., "Tight Supply Chains Respond to Guaranteed Truck Service," *Global Logistics & Supply Chain Strategies* (February 2000).

Milligan, Brian, "Transportation Can Provide a Competitive Edge—Or Take It Away," *Purchasing* (January 13, 2000).

"Will Tomorrow's Transportation System Be Viable?" *Logistics Management Distribution Report* (April 2001).

Chapter 10 Transportation Management

Bardi, Edward J., Prabir K. Bagchi, and T. S. Raghunathan, "Motor Carrier Selection in a Deregulated Environment," *Transportation Journal* 29, no. 1 (Fall 1989): 4–11.

Bardi, Edward J., and Michael Tracey, "Transportation Outsourcing: A Survey of U.S. Practices," *International Journal of Physical Distribution & Logistics Management* 15, no. 1 (1985): 15–21.

Bradley, Peter A., Mary Collins Holcomb, Karl B. Manrodt, and Richard H. Thompson, "Trends and Issues in Logistics: Ninth Annual Survey of the Giants of Shipping," *Council of Logistics Management Annual Conference Proceedings* (2000): 99–110.

Con, Larry A., "Establishing Effective Transportation Controls in a Decentralized Company," *Council of Logistics Management Annual Conference Proceedings* (1995): 391–398.

Cooke, James A., "Logistics Exchanges and ASPs: On the Evolutionary Path," *Logistics Management Distribution Report* (December 2000).

"Driving Shipper and Transport Provider Networks to Optimal Performance, While Improving the Bottom Line for Both," *Logistics Management Distribution Report* (March 2001).

LaLonde, Bernard J., James M. Masters, Arnold B. Maltz, and Lisa R. Williams, *Evolution Status and Future of the Corporate Transportation Function* (American Society of Transportation and Logistics, 1991).

Liberatore, Matthew J., and Tan Miller, "A Decision Support Approach for Transport Carrier and Mode Selection," *Journal of Business Logistics* 16, no. 2 (1995): 85–116.

Manrodt, Karl, "Trading Exchanges in Transportation," *Logistics Management Distribution Report* (December 2000).

Murphy, Paul R., and Patricia K. Hall, "The Relative Importance of Cost and Service in Freight Transportation Choice Before and After Deregulation: An Update," *Transportation Journal* 35, no. 1 (Fall 1995): 30–38.

Part III

Strategic Issues for Logistics and Supply Chain Management

Achieving the desired objectives is a challenging and formidable task for any logistics or supply chain manager. Successful firms will be those that identify and utilize the new, innovative, and value-added approaches to logistics and supply chain management.

Chapter 11 addresses contemporary issues relating to logistics relationships and the use of third party logistics services. New emphasis is placed on the move to collaborative logistics relationships as a means to creating additional logistics and supply chain value.

Chapter 12 focuses on logistics and supply chain information systems. Topics covered include: information systems architecture; how information technologies are impacting logistics and supply chain management; the logistics information system; and E-commerce.

Chapter 13 provides an overview of logistics performance measurements and metrics. This chapter highlights a number of useful techniques to improve the efficiency and effectiveness of logistics and supply chain operations.

Chapter 14 examines issues relating to network design and facility location. Considering the need to keep today's logistics and supply chain systems up-to-date, an understanding of analytical approaches proves to be of value.

Chapter 15 is new to this 7th edition, and focuses on the value of financial techniques to the logistics and supply chain areas. The use of appropriate financial approaches helps to improve decisions made by logistics and supply chain managers.

Chapter 16, the book's final chapter, addresses strategies that progressive firms must utilize to gain a competitive advantage. This chapter also discusses a number of macro trends that will impact the future of logistics and supply chain management.

CHAPTER 11

LOGISTICS RELATIONSHIPS AND THIRD-PARTY LOGISTICS

LEARNING OBJECTIVES

After reading this chapter, you should be able to do the following:

- Understand the types of logistics relationships and their importance.
- Be knowledgeable of a process model that will facilitate the development and implementation of successful supply chain relationships.
- Define what is meant by *third-party logistics* (3PL), and know what types of firms provide 3PL services.
- Know what types of 3PL services are used by client/customer firms, and know what types of 3PL providers are used.
- Appreciate the role and relevance of information technology–based services to 3PLs and their clients/customers.
- Know the extent to which customers are satisfied with 3PL services, and understand where improvement may be needed.
- Recognize the importance of "collaborative" supply chain relationships.

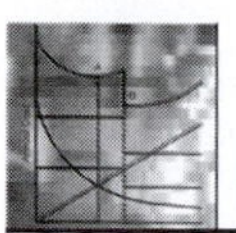

LOGISTICS PROFILE

UPS Inks $150 Million Deal with Chip Maker

United Parcel Service's UPS Logistics Group was awarded a five-year, $150 million deal to manage National Semiconductor Corp.'s global supply chain distribution center in Singapore. The Logistics Group was awarded responsibility for managing the movement of National's chips from manufacturing plants in Malaysia and Singapore to the new global distribution center and then to customers worldwide. Prior to the award to UPS Logistics Group, the National Semiconductor business had been handled by Federal Express, who was responsible for the centralization of National's distribution, as well as significant streamlining and improvement of its logistics processes.

Proprietary information systems developed by the UPS Logistics Group enable it to monitor receipt, storage, shipment, and delivery of chips to carriers or to customer destinations. The company uses carrier-neutral transportation, closed-loop security, and online information systems to manage the supply chain.

National's distribution center uses radio frequency, bar-code scanning, and Web-based technologies to fill more than 450,000 orders for semiconductors a year and has an average delivery time of 48 hours worldwide. It has the capacity to receive 12 million inbound chips daily. Its chips are sold to the personal computer, communications, and consumer markets. Construction of the center was part of National's growth plan, as the company had planned to ship four billion products in 2000, a figure that is twice that of the previous year. National Semiconductor's sales in 1999 totaled $2.1 billion.

Source: Adapted from *Logistics Management and Distribution Report* (September 2000): 25. Copyright Cahners Business Information. Reprinted by permission.

INTRODUCTION

As indicated throughout this book, many firms have directed significant attention toward working more closely with supply chain partners, including not only customers and suppliers but also various types of logistics suppliers. Considering that one of the fundamental objectives of effective supply chain management is to achieve coordination and integration among participating organizations, the development of more meaningful "relationships" through the supply chain has become a high priority.

This chapter focuses on two, highly related topics. The first is that of logistics relationships in general, with an emphasis on the types of relationships, the processes for developing and implementing successful relationships, and the need for firms to collaborate to achieve supply chain objectives. The second is that of the third-party-logistics (3PL) industry in general and how firms in this industry create value for their commercial clients. The 3PL industry has grown significantly over recent years and is recognized as a valuable type of supplier of logistics services.

interest in 3PL industry

As suggested by Robert V. Delaney in his *11th Annual State of Logistics Report*,[1] relationships are what will carry the logistics industry into the future. In commenting on the current rise of interest in E-commerce and the development of electronic markets and exchanges, he states, "We recognize and appreciate the power of the new technology and the power it will deliver, but, in the frantic search for space, it is still about relationships." This message not only captures the importance of developing logistics relationships but also suggests that the ability to form relationships is a prerequisite to future success. Also, the essence of this priority is captured in a quote from noted management guru Rosabeth Moss Kanter,[2] who stated that "being a good partner has become a key corporate asset; in the global economy, a well-developed ability to create and sustain fruitful collaborations gives companies a significant leg up."

LOGISTICS RELATIONSHIPS

Types of Relationships

"vertical" versus "horizontal"

Generally, there are two types of logistics relationships. The first is what may be termed *vertical* relationships; these refer to the traditional linkages between firms in the supply chain such as retailers, distributors, manufacturers, and parts and materials suppliers. These firms relate to one another in the ways that buyers and sellers do in all industries, and significant attention is directed toward making sure that these relationships help to achieve individual firm and supply chain objectives. Logistics service providers are involved on a day-to-day basis as they serve their customers in this traditional, vertical form of relationship.

The second type of logistics relationship is *horizontal* in nature and includes those business agreements between firms that have "parallel" or cooperating positions in the logistics process. To be precise, a horizontal relationship may be thought of as a service agreement between two or more independent logistics provider firms based on trust, cooperation, shared risk and investments, and following mutually agreeable goals. Each firm is expected to contribute to the specific logistics services in which it specializes, and each exercises control of those tasks while striving to integrate its services with those of the other logistics providers. An example of this may be a transportation firm that finds itself working along with a contract warehousing firm to satisfy the needs of the same customer. Also, cooperation between a third-party logistics provider and a firm in the software or information technology business would be an example of this type of relationship. Thus, these parties have parallel or equal relationships in the logistics process and likely need to work together in appropriate and useful ways to see that the customer's logistics objectives are met.

Intensity of Involvement

vendor

As suggested by Figure 11–1, the range of relationship types extends from that of a vendor to that of a strategic alliance. In the context of the more traditional "vertical" context, a *vendor* is represented simply by a seller or provider of a product or service, such that there is little or no integration or collaboration with the buyer or purchaser. In essence, the relationship with a vendor is "transactional," and parties to a vendor relationship are said to be at "arm's length" (i.e., at a significant distance). The analogy of such a relationship to that experienced by one who uses

FIGURE 11–1 Relationship Perspectives

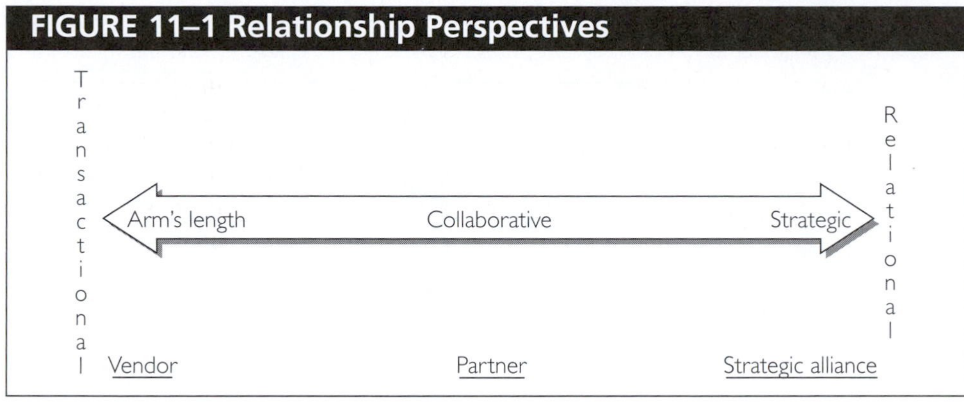

a "vending" machine is not inappropriate. While this form of relationship suggests a relatively low or nonexistent level of involvement between the parties, there are certain types of transactions for which this option is desirable. One-time or even multiple purchases of standard products and/or services, for example, would suggest that an "arm's length" relationship would be appropriate.

strategic alliance

Alternatively, the relationship suggested by a *strategic alliance* is one in which two or more business organizations cooperate and willingly modify their business objectives and practices to help achieve long-term goals and objectives. The strategic alliance by definition is more strategic in nature and is highly relational in terms of the firms involved. This form of relationship typically benefits the involved parties by reducing uncertainty and improving communication, increasing loyalty and establishing a common vision, and helping to enhance global performance. Alternatively, the challenges with this form of relationship include the fact that it implies heavy resource commitments by the participating organizations, significant opportunity costs, and high switching costs.

partnership

Leaning more toward the strategic alliance end of the scale, a *partnership* represents a customized business relationship that produces results for all parties that are more acceptable than would be achieved individually. Partnerships are frequently described as being "collaborative," which is discussed further at a later point in this chapter.

Note that the range of alternatives suggested in Figure 11–1 is limited to those that do not represent the ownership of one firm by another (i.e., vertical integration) or the formation of a *joint venture,* which is a unique legal entity to reflect the combined operations of two or more parties. As such, each represents an alternative that may imply even greater involvement than the partnership or strategic alliance. Considering that they represent alternative legal forms of ownership, however, they are not discussed in detail at this time.

Regardless of form, there are numerous ways that relationships may differ. A partial list of these differences follows:

- Duration
- Obligations
- Expectations
- Interaction/Communication

FIGURE 11–2 Effectiveness of Supply Chain Relationships

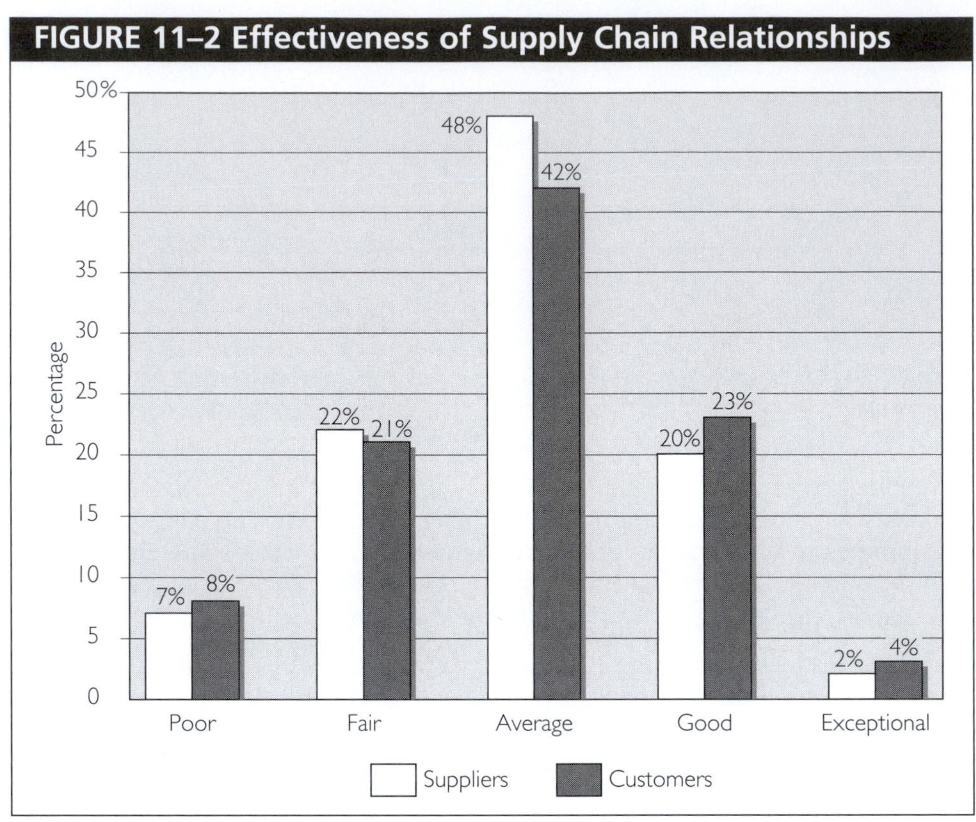

Source: Adapted from *Supply Chain Yearbook 2000* (Newton, Mass.: Cahners Publications, 2000), 60. Reprinted with permission of Cahners Business Information.

- Cooperation
- Planning
- Goals
- Performance analysis
- Benefits and burdens

Figure 11–2 is somewhat of a "report card" indicating the success that logistics organizations have had with the formation of successful supply chain relationships. As indicated in this figure, nearly 50 percent of suppliers and customers feel that their relationships should receive a rating only of *average* on a scale of *poor* to *exceptional.*

Model for Developing and Implementing Successful Supply Chain Relationships

relationship process model

Figure 11–3 outlines the steps in a process model for forming and sustaining supply chain relationships. For purposes of illustration, let us assume that the model is being applied from the perspective of a manufacturing firm, as it considers the possibility of forming a relationship with a supplier of logistics services (e.g., transport firm, warehouseman, etc.).

FIGURE 11–3 Process Model for Forming Logistics Relationships

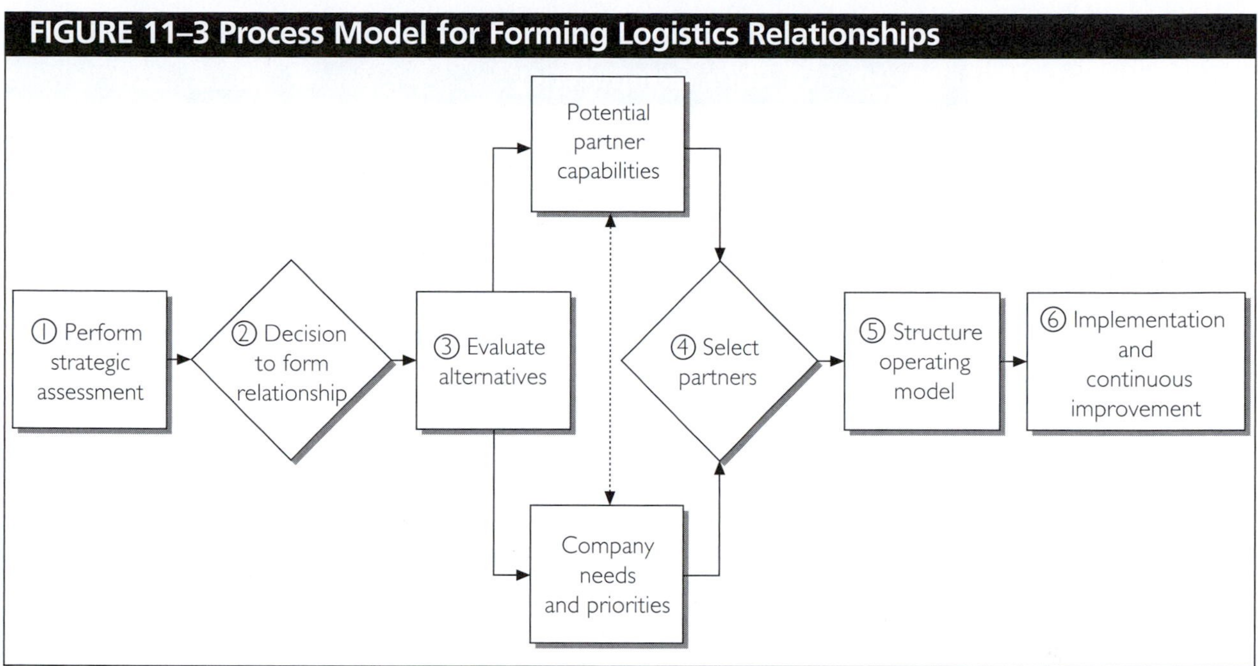

Source: Copyright © 2001, C. John Langley Jr., Ph.D., used with permission.

logistics audit information

Step 1: Perform Strategic Assessment. This first stage involves the process by which the manufacturer becomes fully aware of its logistics and supply chain needs and the overall strategies that will guide its operations. Essentially, this is what is involved in the conduct of *logistics audit,* discussed in detail in Chapter 14. The audit provides a perspective on the firm's logistics and supply chain activities, as well as developing a wide range of useful information that will be helpful as the opportunity to form a supply chain relationship is contemplated. Some of the types of information that may become available as a result of the audit include:

- Overall business goals and objectives, including those from a corporate, divisional, and logistics perspective
- Needs assessment to include requirements of customers, suppliers, and key logistics providers
- Identification and analysis of strategic environmental factors and industry trends
- Profile of current logistics network and the firm's positioning in respective supply chains
- Benchmark, or target, values for logistics costs and key performance measurements
- Identification of "gaps" between current and desired measures of logistics performance (qualitative and quantitative)

Given the significance of most logistics and supply chain relationship decisions, and the potential complexity of the overall process, any time taken at the outset to gain an understanding of one's needs is well spent.

FIGURE 11–4 What Does It Take to Have an Area of Core Competency?

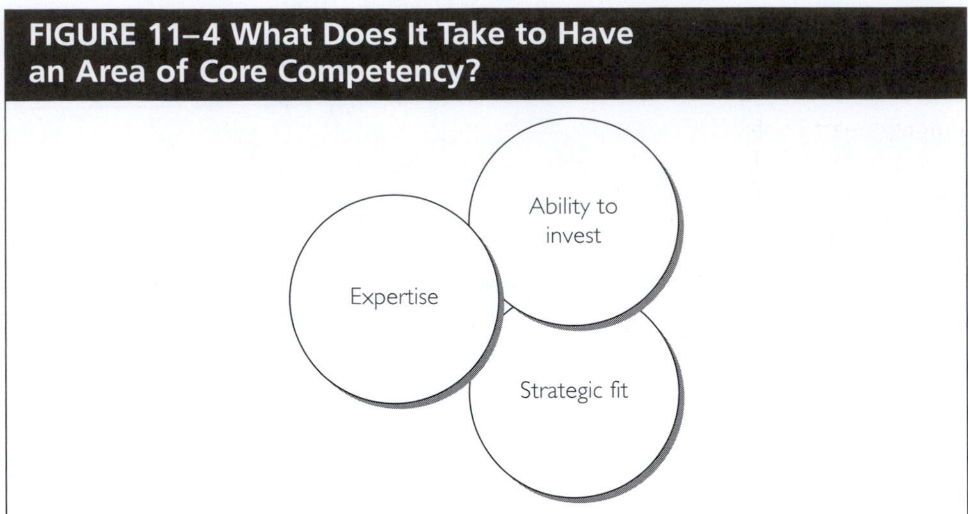

Source: Copyright © 2001, C. John Langley Jr., Ph.D., used with permission.

Step 2: Decision to Form Relationship. Depending on the type of relationship being considered by the manufacturing firm under consideration, this step may take on a slightly different decision context. When the decision relates to using an external provider of logistics services (e.g., trucking firm, express logistics provider, third-party logistics provider), the first question is whether or not the provider's services will be needed. A suggested approach to making this decision is to make a careful assessment of the areas in which the manufacturing firm appears to have core competency. As indicated in Figure 11–4, for a firm to have core competency in any given area, it is necessary to have expertise, strategic fit, and ability to invest. The absence of any one or more of these may suggest that the services of an external provider are appropriate.

If the relationship decision involves a channel partner such as a supplier or customer, the decision does not focus so much on whether or not to have a relationship but on what type of relationship will work best. In either case, the question as to what type of relationship is most appropriate is one that is very important to answer.

Lambert, Emmelhainz, and Gardner have conducted significant research into the topic of how to determine whether a partnership is warranted and, if so, what kind of partnership should be considered.[3] Their partnership model incorporates the identification of "drivers" and "facilitators" of a relationship; it indicates that for a relationship to have a high likelihood of success, the right drivers and facilitators should be present.

reasons to partner

Drivers are defined as "compelling reasons to partner." For a relationship to be successful, the theory of the model is that all parties "must believe that they will receive significant benefits in one or more areas and that these benefits would not be possible without a partnership." Drivers are strategic factors that may result in a competitive advantage and may help to determine the appropriate type of business relationship. Although there certainly are other factors that may be considered, the primary drivers include the following:

- Asset/Cost efficiency
- Customer service

- Marketing advantage
- Profit stability/Growth

Facilitators are defined as "supportive corporate environmental factors that enhance partnership growth and development." As such, they are the factors that, if present, can help to ensure the success of the relationship. Included among the main types of facilitators are the following:

supporting factors

- Corporate compatibility
- Management philosophy and techniques
- Mutuality of commitment to relationship formation
- Symmetry on key factors such as relative size, financial strength, and so on

In addition, a number of additional factors have been identified as keys to successful relationships. Included are factors such as: exclusivity, shared competitors, physical proximity, prior history of working with a partner or the partner, and a shared high-value end user.

Step 3: Evaluate Alternatives. Although the details are not included here, Lambert and his colleagues suggest a method for measuring and weighting the drivers and facilitators we have discussed.[4] Then, they suggest a methodology by which the apparent levels of drivers and facilitators may suggest the most appropriate type of relationship to consider. If neither the drivers nor the facilitators seem to be present, then the recommendation would be for the relationship to be more transactional, or "arm's length" in nature. Alternatively, when all parties to the relationship share common drivers, and when the facilitating factors seem to be present, then a more structured, formal relationship may be justified.

evaluate drivers and facilitators

In addition to utilization of the partnership formation process, it is important to conduct a thorough assessment of the manufacturing company's needs and priorities in comparison with the capabilities of each potential partner. This task should be supported with not only the availability of critical measurements and so on but also the results of personal interviews and discussions with the most likely potential partners.

Although logistics executives and managers usually have significant involvement in the decision to form logistics and supply chain relationships, it is frequently advantageous to involve other corporate managers in the overall selection process. Representatives of marketing, finance, manufacturing, human resources, and information systems, for example, frequently have valuable perspective to contribute to the discussion and analysis. Thus, it is important to assure a broad representation and involvement of people throughout the company in the partnership formation and partner selection decisions.

Step 4: Select Partners. While this stage is of critical concern to the customer, the selection of a logistics or supply chain partner should be made only following very close consideration of the credentials of the most likely candidates. Also, it is highly advisable to interact with and get to know the final candidates on a professionally intimate basis.

partner selection

As was indicated in the discussion of Step 3, it is likely that a number of executives will play key roles in the relationship formation process. It is important to achieve consensus on the final selection decision to create a significant degree of "buy-in" and agreement among those involved. Due to the strategic significance of the decision to form a logistics or supply chain relationship, it is essential to ensure that everyone has a consistent understanding of the decision that has been made and has a consistent expectation of what to expect from the firm that has been selected.

operating model

Step 5: Structure Operating Model. The *structure* of the relationship refers to the activities, processes, and priorities that will be used to build and sustain the relationship. As suggested by Lambert and his colleagues, components "make the relationship operational and help managers create the benefits of partnering."[5] A suggested list of components of the operating model include:[6]

- Planning
- Joint operating controls
- Communication
- Risk/Reward sharing
- Trust and commitment
- Contract style
- Scope of the relationship
- Financial investment

start-up operation

Step 6: Implementation and Continuous Improvement. Once the decision to form a relationship has been made and the structural elements of the relationship identified, it is important to recognize that the most challenging step in the relationship process has just begun. Depending on the complexity of the new relationship, the overall implementation process may be relatively short or it may be extended over a longer period of time. If the situation involves significant change to and restructuring of the manufacturing firm's logistics or supply chain network, for example, full implementation may take longer to accomplish. In a situation where the degree of change is more modest, the time needed for successful implementation may be abbreviated.

Finally, the future success of the relationship will be a direct function of the ability of the involved organizations to achieve both continuous and breakthrough improvement. As indicated in Figure 11–5, there are a number of steps that should be considered in the continuous improvement process. In addition, efforts should be directed to creating the breakthrough, or "paradigm-shifting," type of improvement that is essential to enhance the functioning of the relationship and the market positioning of the organizations involved.

Third-Party Logistics—Industry Overview

As indicated throughout this book, firms have directed considerable attention toward working more closely with other supply chain participants, including customers, suppliers, and various types of logistics suppliers. In essence, this has resulted in the development of more meaningful relationships among the companies involved in overall supply chain activity. As a result, many companies have

FIGURE 11–5 Implementation and Continuous Improvement

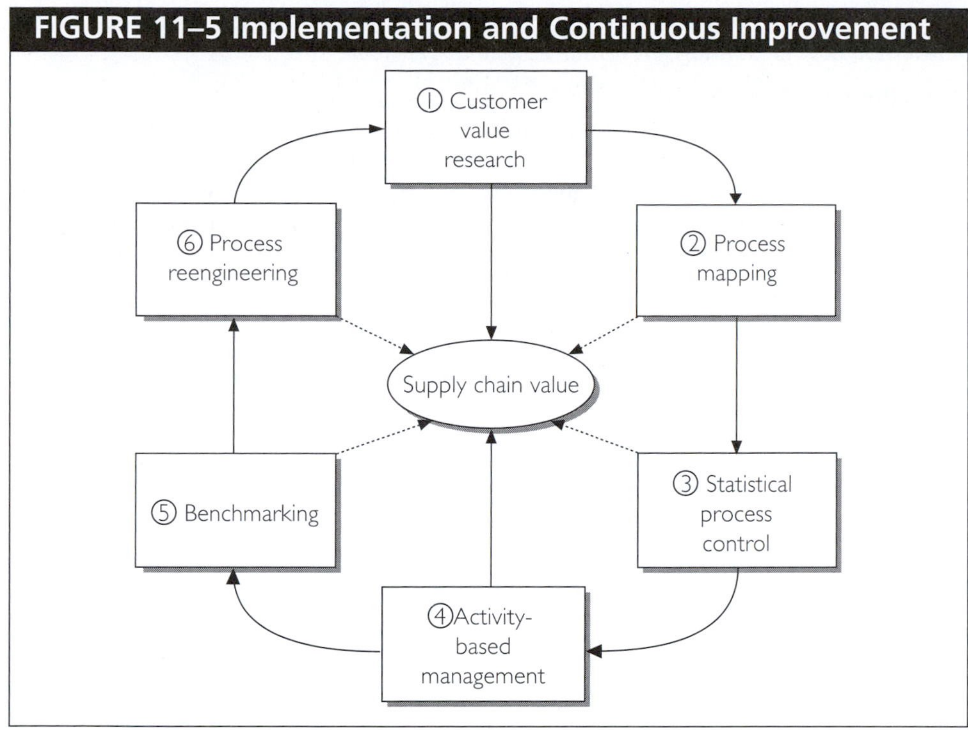

Source: Ray A. Mundy, C. John Langley Jr., and Brian J. Gibson, *Continuous Improvement in Third-Party Logistics* (forthcoming).

been in the process of *extending* their logistics organizations into those of other supply chain participants and facilitators.

One way of extending the logistics organization beyond the boundaries of the company is through the use of a supplier of third-party or contract logistics services.[7] While the emergence and growth of the 3PL industry was a major phenomenon of the 1990s, thoughts differ as to how to best define this type of logistics provider and what services might be included. These issues are dealt with next.

Definition of Third-Party Logistics

"true" 3PL

Essentially, a third-party-logistics firm may be defined as an external supplier that performs all or part of a company's logistics functions. This definition is purposely broad and is intended to encompass suppliers of services such as transportation, warehousing, distribution, financial services, and so on. As is discussed later, there are other desirable characteristics of a "true" 3PL. Among these, multiple logistics activities are included; those that are included are "integrated" or managed together, and they provide "solutions" to logistics/supply chain problems.

Recently, there have been significant increases in the number of firms offering such services, and this trend is expected to continue. While many of these firms are small, niche players, the industry has a number of large firms as well. Examples of the latter include Ryder, FedEx, UPS Worldwide Logistics, Exel, Menlo Logistics, Schneider Logistics, and Caterpillar Logistics Services.

contract logistics

Depending on the firm and its positioning in the industry, the terms *contract logistics* and *outsourcing* are sometimes used in place of *third-party logistics.* While some industry executives take care to distinguish among terms such as these, the terms refer to the use of external suppliers of logistics services. Except for the suggestion that the term *contract logistics* generally includes some form of contract, or formal agreement, this text does not suggest any unique definitional differences between these terms.

Types of 3PL Providers

Although most 3PL firms promote themselves as providers of a comprehensive range of logistics services, it is useful to categorize them in one of several ways. Included are transportation-based, warehouse/distribution-based, forwarder-based, shipper/management-based, financial-based, and information-based firms. Each of these is discussed briefly in the following paragraphs.

transport based

Transportation Based. Included among the transportation-based suppliers are firms such as Ryder, Menlo Logistics, Schneider Logistics, FedEx Logistics, and UPS Logistics, most of which are subsidiaries or major divisions of large transportation firms. Some of the services provided by these firms are *leveraged,* in that they utilize the assets of other companies; and some are *nonleveraged,* where the principal emphasis is on utilizing the transportation-based assets of the parent organization. In all instances, these firms extend beyond the transportation activity to provide a more comprehensive set of logistics offerings.

In early 2000, Transplace was formed through the merger of the logistics business units of several of the largest publicly held truckload carriers in the United States. While this new company is transportation based in that major elements of its corporate heritage do involve the commercial transportation industry, its approaches to operations, management, and planning significantly utilize and leverage information technologies. For this reason, a more comprehensive description of this company is found later in this section under the topic of information-based providers.

Warehouse/Distribution Based. Traditionally, most warehouse/distribution-based logistics suppliers have been in the public or contract warehousing business and have expanded into a broader range of logistics services. Examples of such firms include DSC Logistics, USCO, and Exel. The latter firm, Exel, has a much broader range of expertise, considering the 2000 merger of the former Exel Logistics (predominantly a warehousing/distribution-based firm) and MSAS (having strength in the forwarding and ocean shipping areas).

distribution based

Based on their traditional orientation, these firms have already been involved in logistics activities such as inventory management, warehousing, distribution, and so on. Experience has indicated that these facility-based operators have found the transition to integrated logistics services to be less complex than have the transportation providers.

This category also should include a number of 3PL firms that have emerged from larger corporate logistics organizations. Prominent among these are Caterpillar Logistics Services (Caterpillar, Inc.), Intral Corporation (Gillette), and IBM (IBM Corporation). These providers have significant experience in managing the logistics operations of the parent firm and, as a result, prove to be very capable providers of such services to external customers.

Forwarder Based. This category includes companies, such as Kuehne & Nagel, Fritz, C. H. Robinson, and Hub Group, that have extended their middleman roles as forwarders and/or brokers into the broader range of 3PL services. Essentially, these firms are non–asset owners, are very independent, and deal with a wide range of suppliers of logistics services. They have proven quite capable at putting together packages of logistics services that meet customers' needs.

forwarder based

Financial Based. This category of 3PL provider includes firms such as Cass Information Systems (a division of Cass Commercial Corporation), CTC (Commercial Traffic Corporation), GE Information Services (General Electric), and FleetBoston Financial Corporation. These firms provide services such as freight payment and auditing; cost accounting and control; and logistics management tools for monitoring, booking, tracking, tracing, and managing inventory.

financial based

Information Based. At the time of the writing of this text, there existed significant growth and development of Internet-based, business-to-business, electronic markets for transportation and logistics services. Since these resources effectively represent alternative sources for those in need of purchasing transportation and logistics services, they may be thought of as a newer, innovative type of third-party provider. Examples of two firms that would be representative of this category follow:

information based

- *Transplace* is an Internet-based company that represents the merger of the 3PL business units from six of the largest publicly held truckload carriers in the United States. The founding carriers are Covenant Transport, Inc.; J. B. Hunt Transport Services, Inc.; M. S. Carriers, Inc. (since merged with Swift Transportation Co., Inc.); Swift Transportation Co., Inc.; U.S. Xpress Enterprises, Inc.; and Werner Enterprises, Inc. Transplace offers a Web-enabled platform to bring together shippers and carriers worldwide to collaborate on their transportation logistics planning and execution in the most efficient and effective manner.
- *Nistevo* is a leading provider of an Internet-based, collaborative logistics network. Nistevo's collaborative network is an Internet service that allows shippers and carriers to collaborate to improve profitability and performance. Among the results experienced by both shippers and carriers through use of Nistevo's capabilities are: improved operating performance through on-line, real-time network visibility; management of the entire procurement, service, and delivery cycle from a single application; and improved contract and relationship management.

Further details concerning information technologies and their applicability to logistics and supply chain management are discussed in Chapter 12: Logistics and Supply Chain Information Systems.

ON THE LINE

EXEL AND BASS—TRADE TEAM RELATIONSHIP

The U.K. beer market had been in long-term decline with pub consumption shrinking at approximately 1 percent per annum and the overall industry suffering from excess capacity and lower margins. On top of this, the government had required brewers to divest themselves of their interest in pubs, which had significant marketplace implications. For example, between 1992 and 1999, pub ownership by regional and national brewers declined from 74 percent to 33 percent. The end result was that, typical of low-growth industries, the brewers had been consolidating and repositioning and were in need of a fresh approach to marketing and distribution.

As the largest provider of brewery distribution services in the United Kingdom, Exel Logistics had a significant interest in protecting a business that was under pressure from individual brewers and emerging pub ownership groups. Thus, one of Exel's preferred strategies was the idea of taking over a brewer's existing distribution infrastructure with the "critical mass" of one brewer's market share. Thus, this priority led to the formation of a joint venture between Exel Logistics and Bass, already the industry's low-cost producer. The features of this "Trade-Team" relationship included its ability to achieve significant further cost reduction; revenue increases through market expansion; and, overall, a superior cost/service structure for a capable third-party-logistics entity in the brewing industry.

Currently, TradeTeam is the United Kingdom's leading independent logistics provider to the beverage industry. It has annual revenues of U.S. $200 million and currently delivers around 280 million gallons of beer and other beverages annually to over 27,000 retail customers on behalf of a number of beverage suppliers. Uniquely situated between the consumer and the supplier as a multi-user distributor, TradeTeam has revolutionized the beverage industry supply chain. Results to date are very encouraging, in that market share for this joint venture is in the 40 to 50 percent range. Thus, this initiative represents the largest outsourcing initiative ever. Additionally, the logistics infrastructure that has been developed is capable of moving other types of products to market, and this opportunity is being carefully analyzed.

Source: Exel (2000).

THIRD-PARTY-LOGISTICS RESEARCH STUDY—INDUSTRY DETAILS

3PL study objectives

One significant research study, "Third-Party-Logistics Study: Views from the Customers," is conducted on an annual basis by Dr. C. John Langley Jr., in conjunction with Cap Gemini Ernst & Young and Ryder System, Inc.[8] This study provides a comprehensive look at the third-party-logistics industry from the perspective of the customers and users of third-party services. Specific study objectives follow:

- Measure the development, growth, and utilization of 3PL services across major industry markets, and deepen the knowledge of the services they provide.
- Identify customer needs for information technology–based services, and evaluate how well 3PLs are responding to those needs.
- Understand how customers purchase and manage 3PL services and how they structure relationships with 3PL providers. Also, see how 3PLs relate to global

FIGURE 11–6 3PL User/Nonuser Experience, 1996–2001

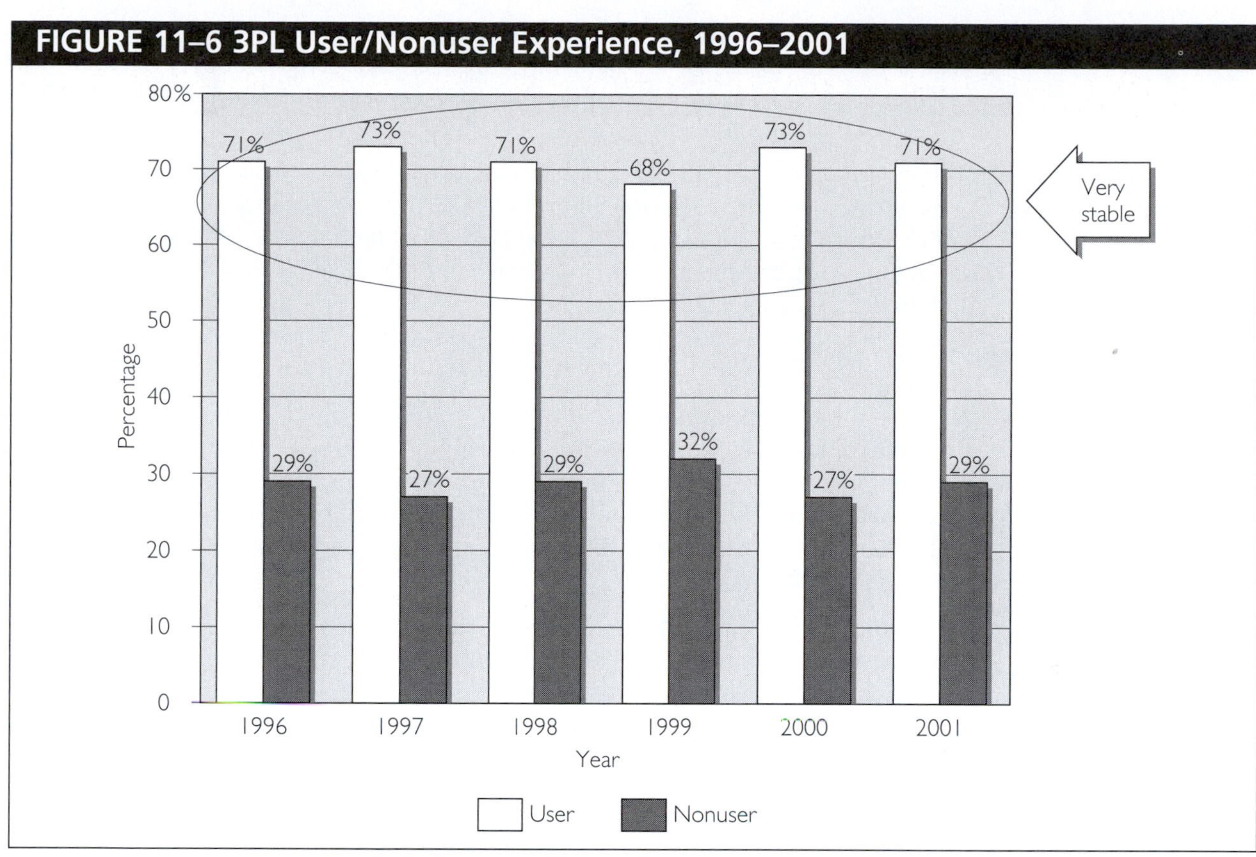

Source: C. John Langley Jr., Gary R. Allen, and Gene R. Tyndall, *Third-Party-Logistics Services: Views from the Customers* (Atlanta, Ga.: Georgia Institute of Technology, Cap Gemini Ernst & Young and Ryder System, Inc., 2001).

needs of their customers and how customers may involve management consultants with the third-party-logistics process.

- Examine the overall customer value framework as it relates to the use of 3PL services. Included is an understanding of customers' satisfaction with 3PL services, problems they have experienced, and how 3PLs are viewed by customers.

The principal vehicle for gathering logistics customer perspectives was a survey sent via the Internet to the chief logistics executives at prominent companies in the following industries: automotive, chemical, computers and peripherals, consumer products, electronics, medical supplies and devices, retail, and telecommunications.[9] These industries were selected because they view logistics as strategically important and are making purposeful moves toward integrated supply chain management. The total number of surveys sent by E-mail to companies in these industries was 725.[10] Of these, a total of ninety-three usable responses was received, for an overall response rate of 13 percent.

Profile of Logistics Outsourcing Activities

Of the ninety-three responding executives, 71 percent indicate their companies currently use or are considering the use of 3PL services. As indicated in Figure 11–6, the percentage of respondents indicating their firms use 3PL services has remained relatively consistent during the years this study has been conducted. Over the six-year period, for example, the percentage of users has ranged from a reported low of 68 percent (1999) to reported highs of 73 percent (1997 and 2000). In 2001, 29 percent of the respondents indicated that their companies did not use 3PL services.

user firm characteristics

Although the overall percentage of companies using 3PL services remains relatively constant from year to year, the use of 3PL services is seen to vary by firms in the industries studied. For example, two industries that tend to exhibit higher use of 3PL services are (1) computers and peripherals and (2) consumer products (90 percent and 85 percent, respectively). Among those industries typically indicating less use of 3PL services are automotive, chemical, and retail. In the current study, firms in these industries exhibited 3PL use in the range of approximately 50 percent to 60 percent.

A new metric resulting from the 2001 3PL study was the percentage of total logistics expenditures that are directed to outsourcing at the respondent firms. Based on the results of this year's study, the average current figure is 35 percent, and respondents project that this figure will increase to 50 percent within the next five years. If this increase is realized, it will result in significantly increased revenues for the overall 3PL industry.

Table 11–1 contains a summary of specific shippers who were identified in another study as utilizing multiple 3PLs. Based on the information in that table, General Motors was observed to have used twenty-five third-party providers. Other representative shippers using multiple 3PLs are also indicated in that table.

Indicated in Table 11–2 are estimates of the U.S. 3PL industry revenues for the year 2000. As is evident, there are several ways to categorize 3PL services for revenue purposes, and the total market was estimated to be approximately $56.4 billion. After deducting the cost of purchased transportation services, the estimated net third-party-logistics revenues would be approximately 55 to 60 percent of this total.

activities outsourced

Logistics Activities Outsourced. Table 11–3 summarizes the use of specific logistics services that were reported as being outsourced by respondents in 2001. According

TABLE 11–1 Shippers Using More than Five 3PLs

Rank	Shippers	Number of 3PLs Used
1	General Motors	25
2	Ford	19
3	IBM, Wal-Mart	15
4	Hewlett-Packard, Procter & Gamble, Sears	14
5	E. I. DuPont	11
6	Chrysler	10
7	Allied Signal, Coca-Cola, Compaq, General Electric, Kimberly-Clark, Motorola, Philips, Pillsbury, Toyota, Xerox	8
8	3M, Anheuser-Busch, Goodyear, Honda, Kmart, Kraft, Nabisco, Nestle, Sun Microsystems	7
9	Colgate-Palmolive, Georgia-Pacific, Monsanto, Nissan, Quaker Oats, Reynolds Metals, Sam's Club	6

Source: Copyright © 1999, *Armstrong & Associates, Inc.*

to the 2001 study, the activities most frequently outsourced to 3PLs are warehousing (73.7 percent), outbound transportation (68.4 percent), freight bill auditing/payment (61.4 percent), inbound transportation (56.1 percent), freight consolidation/distribution (40.4 percent), and cross-docking (38.6 percent). In contrast, the activities outsourced least frequently include product returns and repair (22.8 percent), inventory

TABLE 11–2 Third-Party Revenues Estimated at $56.4 Billion in 2000

Third-Party Service Providers	Gross Revenues ($ Billions)
Dedicated contract carriage	8.7
Domestic transportation management	10.0
Value-added warehouse/distribution	20.4
U.S.-based with international operations	13.8
3PL software	3.5
Total Third-Party-Logistics Market	**$56.4**

Source: Copyright © 2001, *Armstrong & Associates, Inc.*

TABLE 11–3 Outsourced Logistics Services: 2001

	Percent Outsource
Warehousing	73.7%
Outbound transportation	68.4
Freight bill auditing/payment	61.4
Inbound transportation	56.1
Freight consolidation/distribution	40.4
Cross-docking	38.6
Product marking/labeling/packaging	33.3
Selected manufacturing activities	29.8
Product returns and repair	22.8
Inventory management	21.0
Traffic management/fleet operations	19.3
Information technology	17.5
Product assembly/installation	17.5
Order fulfillment	15.8
Order entry/order processing	5.3
Customer service	3.5

Note: Figures refer to percentages of users indicating use of specific 3PL services.

Source: C. John Langley Jr., Gary R. Allen, and Gene R. Tyndall, *Third-Party-Logistics Services: Views from the Customers* (Atlanta, Ga: Georgia Institute of Technology, Cap Gemini Ernst & Young and Ryder System, Inc., 2001).

management (21.0 percent), traffic management/fleet operations (19.3 percent), information technology (17.5 percent), product assembly and installation (17.5 percent), order fulfillment (15.8 percent), order entry/order processing (5.3 percent), and customer service (3.5 percent).

breadth of service offerings

A strategic issue is how customers feel that 3PLs should position themselves in terms of depth and breadth of service offerings. Overall, and consistent with findings reported in earlier years' studies, respondents indicated significant agreement with the statement that "third-party suppliers should provide a broad, comprehensive set of service offerings" and disagreement with the statement that "third-party suppliers should focus on a limited range of service offerings." This implies that there may be increased interest and desire at the client level for a single-source solution or a "lead logistics manager" role to the provision of integrated logistics services.

noncustomer views

Views of Noncustomers. To help better understand those who were not among the users of 3PL services, the study asked a number of questions regarding their choice not to be so involved. Figure 11–7 profiles their responses for the 2001 study. This year, there were two reasons that seemed to generate the most response in terms of explaining why firms choose not to outsource: "control over outsourced functions would diminish," and "costs would not be reduced." Also reported were several other reasons, including: "service commitments would not be met," "logistics is a core competency," "we have more expertise," and "logistics too important to outsource."

Interestingly, and as reported in earlier years, there are many existing customers of 3PLs who have been satisfied with such relationships because they help to *improve*

FIGURE 11–7 Nonuser Respondents: Rationale for Not Using 3PL Services

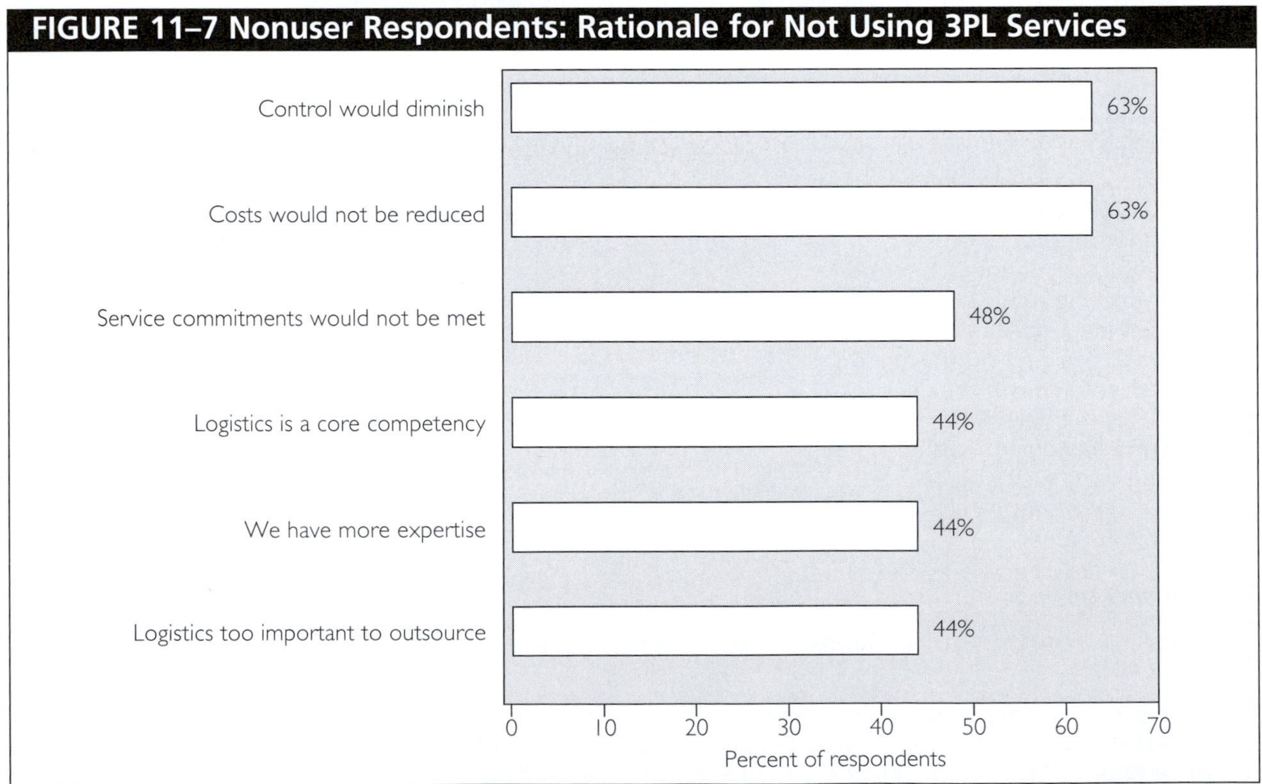

Source: C. John Langley Jr., Gary R. Allen, and Gene R. Tyndall, *Third-Party-Logistics Services: Views from the Customers* (Atlanta, Ga.: Georgia Institute of Technology, Cap Gemini Ernst & Young and Ryder System, Inc., 2001).

(rather than diminish) control over certain outsourced activities. Also prevalent among the reasons not to outsource is the belief that firms can perform internally at least as effectively as would be expected of a 3PL. If this assertion is true, then the choice of not using a 3PL is understandable. The results from user firms, however, document that, although there is room for improvement, users historically have been satisfied with 3PLs, both from a cost and from a service viewpoint.

Strategic Role of Information Technology

A major objective of the 2000 study was to gain insight into customer needs for information technology–based services, as well as evaluating how 3PLs are responding. Considering the importance of information technology to supply chain management in general, this topic also is of revelance to the use of 3PLs.

importance of technology

Information Technology–Based Services. Results of the 2001 study suggest that there is significant interest in the development and utilization of 3PL-provided information technologies. While this observation is encouraging, the study respondents felt that 3PL firms were not providing sufficient leadership in this area. When asked about their extent of agreement with the statement, "we rely on our 3PL providers for leadership in information technology," 66 percent responded with a response in the category of either "yes" or "somewhat." Also, while 72 percent felt that "E-commerce capabilities were a necessary element of 3PL expertise," only 40 percent felt that "3PLs were providing a leadership role with regard to E-commerce." Thus, further involvement in the IT area by 3PLs represents a prominent area for improvement.

technology requirements

Table 11–4 summarizes the current availability and projected future requirements for a number of information technology–based services that may be provided by

TABLE 11–4 Information Technology-Based Services: Current versus Future

	Currently Available	Future Requirement
Warehouse/distribution center management	70.3%	7.4%
Shipment tracking/tracing	68.5	18.5
Transportation management	66.7	11.1
Export/import/freight forwarding	66.7	9.3
Web-enabled communication	48.1	35.2
Customer order management	20.4	27.8
Transportation-logistics electronic markets	20.4	37.0
Supplier management systems	9.3	44.4
Supply chain planning (forecasting, etc.)	1.9	33.3
Product-specific industry electronic markets	0.0	18.5

Note: Figures refer to percentages of users indicating current availability and future requirements for the information technology–based services indicated. Respondents were asked not to place check marks in both columns.

Source: C. John Langley Jr., Gary R. Allen, and Gene R. Tyndall, *Third-Party-Logistics Services: Views from the Customers* (Atlanta, Ga.: Georgia Institute of Technology, Cap Gemini Ernst & Young and Ryder System, Inc., 2001).

3PLs. The most frequently available technologies are: warehouse/distribution center management (70.3 percent); shipment tracking/tracing (68.5 percent); transportation management (66.7 percent); export/import/freight forwarding (66.7 percent); and Web-enabled communication (48.1 percent). Interestingly, an additional 35.2 percent of the respondents suggest that the availability of Web-enabled communication will be a future requirement as well.

Looking further at future requirements for IT-based capabilities, other types of services will be needed by 3PL users. Two striking examples are supply chain planning and supplier management systems technologies, where future requirements were indicated by 33.3 percent and 44.4 percent of the respondents, respectively. Significant increases in requirements are also projected for capabilities, such as customer order management, transportation-logistics electronic markets, and product-specific industry electronic markets.

sources of technology

Sources of Technology. Looking at the utilization of technology from the customers' perspective, an interesting question in the study was "do you utilize your 3PL to gain access to information technology, or do you go directly to a technology provider?" Examples of technology providers would be companies such as Manugistics, i2 Technologies, Manhattan Associates, Optum, EXE Technologies, Insight, and so on. Figure 11–8 indicates that the customer-reported sources of technology are: 3PL (20 percent of the time), technology provider (69 percent), and internal (11 percent).

FIGURE 11–8 Sources of Information Technology

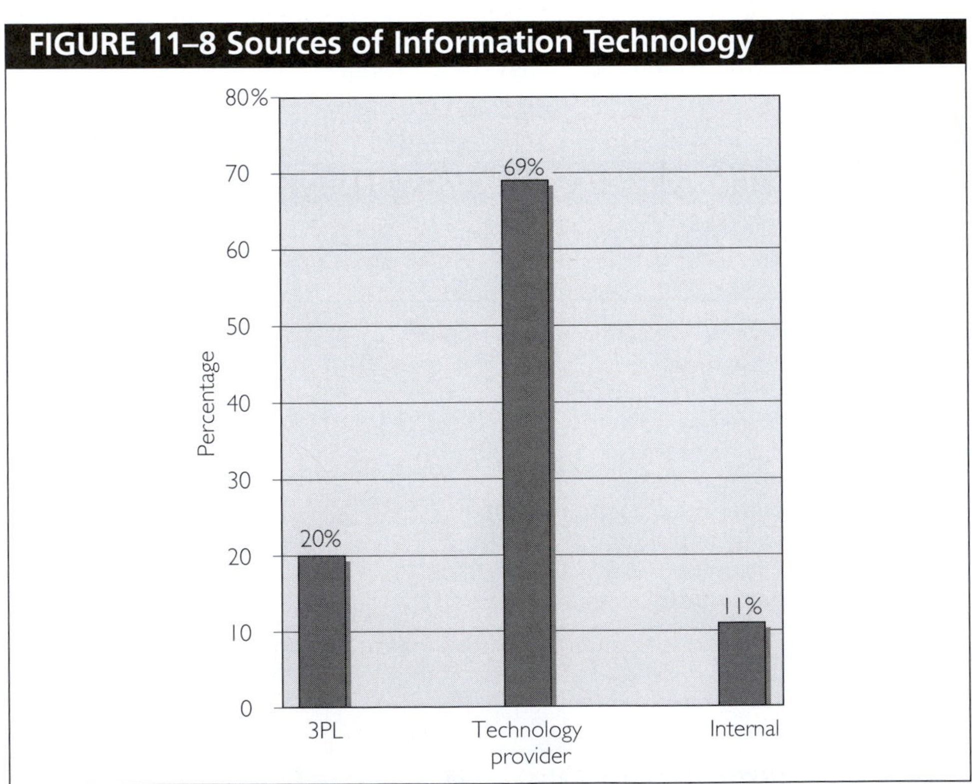

Source: C. John Langley Jr., Gary R. Allen, and Gene R. Tyndall, *Third-Party-Logistics Services: Views from the Customers* (Atlanta, Ga.: Georgia Institute of Technology, Cap Gemini Ernst & Young and Ryder System, Inc., 2001).

Use of Internet and Independent Electronic Markets. Clearly, the years 2000 and 2001 were challenging for the technology sector in general and for Internet-based capabilities including independent electronic markets. One of the areas of questioning first introduced in the year 2000 study was the current and projected use by respondents of independent trading exchanges. The types of greatest interest here are industry vertical procurement (e.g., ShipChem, Steel.com, Converge, Transora, Covisint) and transportation/logistics services (e.g., Nistevo, elogex, NTE, Logistics.com).

Figure 11–9 and Figure 11–10 summarize responses to the questions relating to independent trading exchanges that were included in the 2000 and 2001 3PL studies. Looking back to 2000, there was a great sense of optimism and enthusiasm about the future use of these electronic market capabilities. In the case of electronic markets for industry vertical procurement, Figure 11–9 shows that reported usage declined from 14 percent in 2000 to 11 percent in 2001, while projected future use declined from 60 percent to 28 percent over this same time interval. In the case of transportation/logistics electronic markets (see Figure 11–10), although reported usage increased somewhat from 10 percent in 2000 to 13 percent in 2001, projected future use declined from 71 percent to 50 percent. Although most respondents probably would agree with an observation from the 2000 study that "the Internet will ultimately enhance their company's ability

FIGURE 11–9 3PL Customer Use of Industry Vertical Procurement Markets

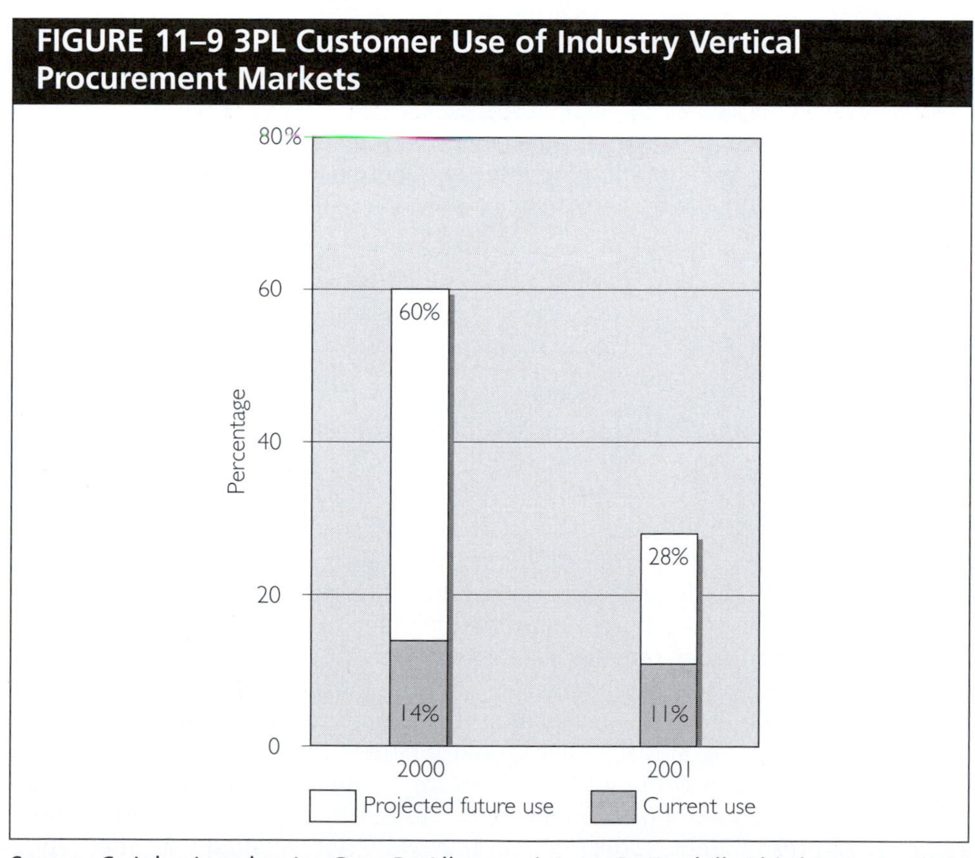

Source: C. John Langley Jr., Gary R. Allen, and Gene R. Tyndall, *Third-Party-Logistics Services: Views from the Customers* (Atlanta, Ga.: Georgia Institute of Technology, Cap Gemini Ernst & Young and Ryder System, Inc., 2001).

FIGURE 11–10 3PL Customer Use of Transportation/Logistics Electronic Markets

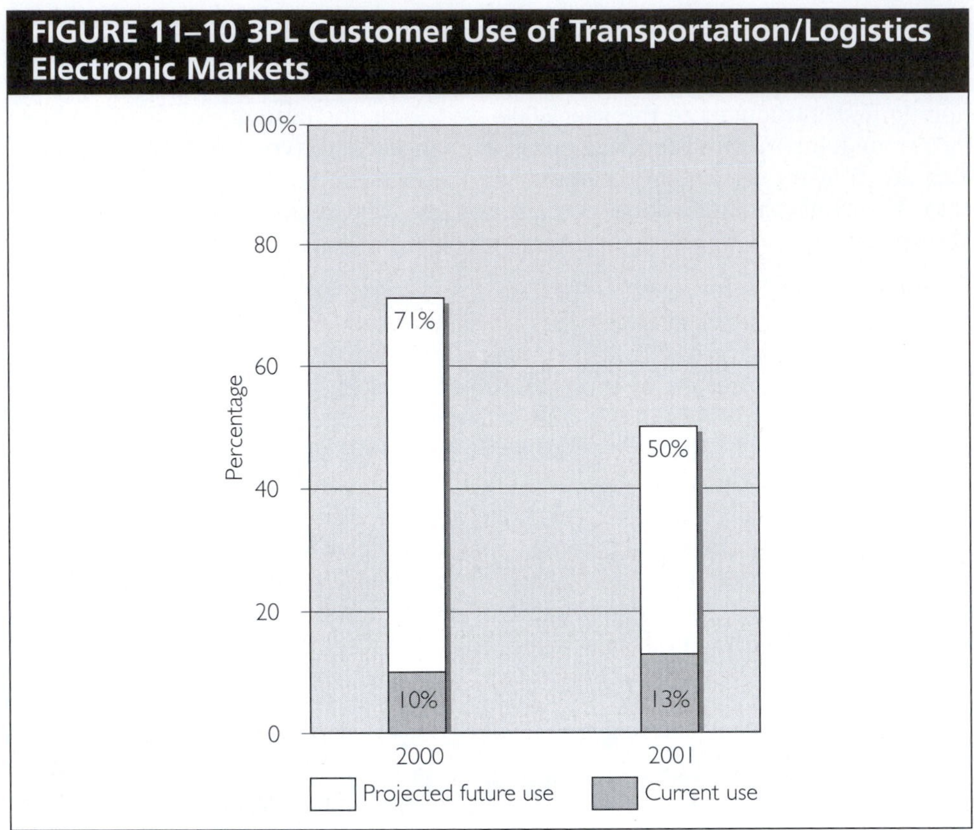

Source: C. John Langley Jr., Gary R. Allen, and Gene R. Tyndall, *Third-Party-Logistics Services: Views from the Customers* (Atlanta, Ga.: Georgia Institute of Technology, Cap Gemini Ernst & Young and Ryder System, Inc., 2001).

to create sustainable competitive advantage through supply chain management," the path to this objective is likely more methodical and structured than originally anticipated.

customer satisfaction

Overall 3PL Customer Satisfaction with Technology. Although it is evident that customers generally do not look to their 3PLs for leadership in information technology, this may be due to the fact that they do not perceive the 3PL sector to be as involved or as strong in this area as the technology providers themselves. While this may be true in certain instances, many 3PLs are using the technology area to distinguish themselves from their competitors. For example, the availability of competent transportation management software and/or warehouse management software from 3PLs is something that may be expected. This is particularly relevant, considering a finding of the 2001 study that 84 percent of the respondents felt that "having the 'right' software" is a major competitive advantage for a 3PL. When asked whether they agree with the statement "we are satisfied with our 3PL's software," only 12 percent of respondents indicated "yes" and another 50 percent "somewhat." Thus, the remaining 38 percent of respondents indicated that they were not satisfied with their 3PL's software.

SUPPLY CHAIN TECHNOLOGY

HARRY POTTER'S LOGISTICS DILEMMA

Never before had so many children waited so excitedly to see a FedEx truck pull into their driveway. On Saturday, July 8, 2000, FedEx Express and FedEx Home Delivery provided delivery of J. K. Rowling's new book, *Harry Potter and the Goblet of Fire,* to the first 250,000 people that ordered it on Amazon.com. Amazon.com had agreed to absorb the extra delivery charges above the normal shipping charges paid by customers for delivery via the U.S. Postal Service. Referred to by Amazon.com as the "largest E-commerce distribution event to date," the event was indicative of the ways in which the Internet was beginning to revolutionize supply chain management.

To accomplish this objective, FedEx moved the books from Amazon's six distribution centers in New Castle, Delaware; Seattle, Washington; Fernley, Nevada; Coffeyville, Kansas; McDonough, Georgia; and Campbellsville, Kentucky, through approximately 25 FedEx facilities using more than 100 scheduled flights. The book's size is not kid's stuff, as its 752 pages weigh a hefty 2.7 pounds. As part of the deal, FedEx would not deliver more than nine books to any one address. FedEx had expected more than 30,000 employees to participate in the one-day move, likely to be the largest business-to-consumer distribution in the Internet shopping history.

Apparently, the logistics strategy was at least partly responsible for the book's exceptional sales figures. One week prior to the book's official release, for example, more than 253,000 books had been preordered for delivery on the July 8 release date, at the time breaking all Amazon.com records for prerelease book orders.

Source: Adapted from Ken Cottrill, "Web Wizardry," *Traffic World* (3 July 2000): 17; and Kristin S. Krause, "Muggles Mania," *Traffic World* (3 July 2000): 17.

Management and Relationship Issues

The need for competency as it relates to the formation and continuation of successful relationships has become critical in today's 3PL industry. Although both providers and users of 3PL services have been improving in their ability to create more productive, effective, and satisfying business relationships, the media is replete with examples of failed relationships. Then, the important question is "what can we do to improve in this area?"

executive involvement

An interesting finding from the year 2000 third-party-logistics study[11] was that the chief executive in the logistics area is the one who clearly is most aware of the need for 3PL services. While evidence supported the fact that the president or CEO and the finance executive are many times involved with the identification of the need for such services, executives from other areas such as manufacturing, human resources, marketing, and information systems are also aware of such needs but to a lesser degree. Looking specifically at the task of implementing a 3PL relationship, however, it was apparent that information systems executives are becoming increasingly involved. This is not surprising, considering the key role of IT in many of today's logistics and supply chain processes. Further perspective on this issue is provided in Figure 11–11.

3PL Relationship Processes. In a number of areas, the 2001 study attempted to provide insight into the elements of the relationships between 3PLs and their customers.

FIGURE 11–11 Involvement in Outsourcing: Who Is Responsible for Implementation?

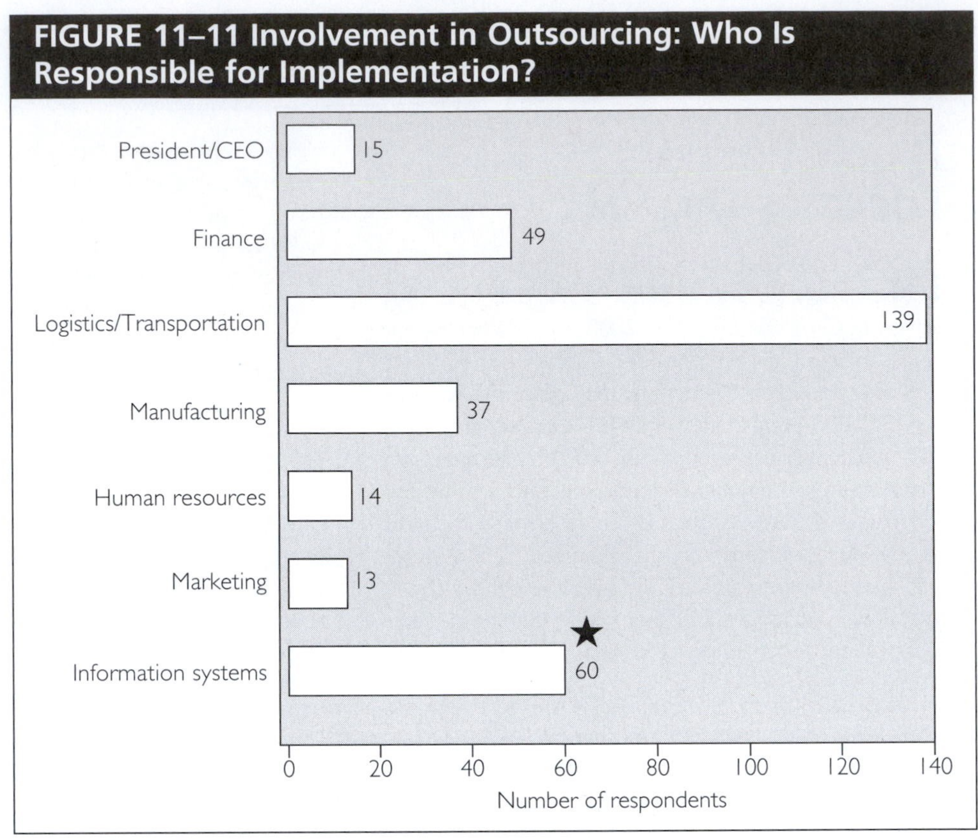

Source: C. John Langley Jr., Brian F. Newton, and Gary R. Allen, *Third-Party-Logistics Services: Views from the Customers* (Knoxville, Tenn.: University of Tennessee, Exel and Cap Gemini Ernst & Young, 2000).

When asked whether "using 3PL(s) is a key to satisfying our company's customers," 80 percent of the respondents responded "yes" or "somewhat." Also, 82 percent responded similarly to the question of whether they feel they have a "collaborative" relationship with their 3PLs. These two findings suggest a concern by the customers for developing and benefiting from improved relationships with their 3PL providers.

"hybrid" management structure

Successful 3PL relationships establish appropriate roles and responsibilities for both 3PLs and client firms. While sometimes the use of a 3PL is interpreted simply as "turning over all logistics activities" to an outsourced provider, respondents to the 2001 study suggested that a "hybrid" management structure represents a highly effective way to manage 3PL relationships. Essentially, this reflects a desire on the part of the client firm to have sufficient power over operations for a track record of performance or "trust" factor to be built up. Although most client firms (appropriately) retain control over strategy formulation and direction setting for the logistics areas of responsibility, this hybrid approach to the management of operations is an innovative response to the challenge of successfully managing 3PL-client relationships.

Customer Value Framework

success of 3PL relationships

Customer Satisfaction Indicators. Figure 11–12 provides a six-year summary of the percentages of 3PL users indicating overall success with their outsourcing

FIGURE 11–12 Customer Evaluation of Outsourcing (Yearly Comparisons)

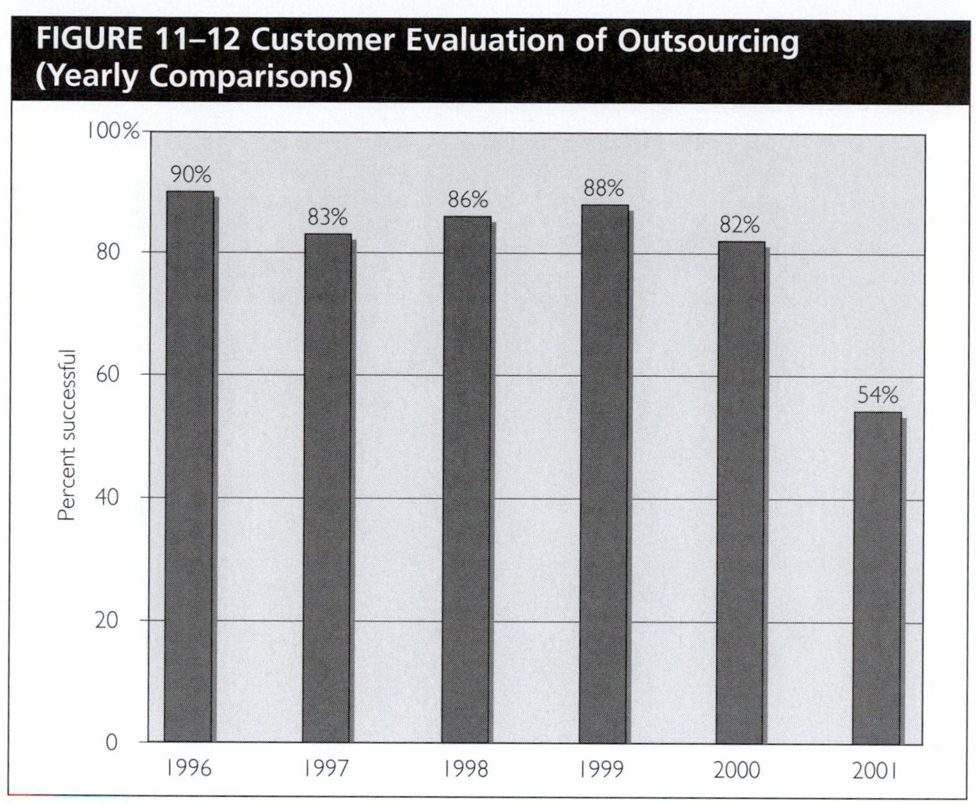

Source: C. John Langley Jr., Gary R. Allen, and Gene R. Tyndall, *Third-Party-Logistics Services: Views from the Customers* (Atlanta, Ga.: Georgia Institute of Technology, Cap Gemini Ernst & Young and Ryder System, Inc., 2001).

efforts. The 2001 results are strikingly different from those of previous years, in that only 54 percent of the respondents rated their 3PL services as being either "extremely" or "somewhat" successful. Interestingly, the percentage figure for 2000 (82 percent) was reported as "suggesting a modest decline from the increasing trend of the (then) two most recent years." Looking more closely at the actual responses, it is apparent that the percentage of 3PL users indicating "extremely" successful declined significantly. While this should be interpreted as an area of concern, it also may be indicative of increasing expectations by users of 3PL services. When the standards for success are increased, it would be expected that fewer provider relationships would be viewed as extremely successful.

Figure 11–13 provides information concerning the relative importance of cost, performance, and value creation as determining factors for evaluating and selecting 3PLs.[12] While cost and performance were cited as the most prevalent current factors for evaluation and selection, the data suggested that future selection processes will increasingly emphasize value creation. If this occurs, it would suggest that 3PL customers are moving beyond criteria that are easily measurable, such as cost and performance, and that they are becoming increasingly interested in assessing the overall value derived from their logistics outsourcing.

measures of success

Quantifiable Measures of 3PL Success. On a more positive note, respondents were asked about the types of improvements that are being experienced as a result

FIGURE 11–13 Factors for Selecting and Evaluating 3PLs

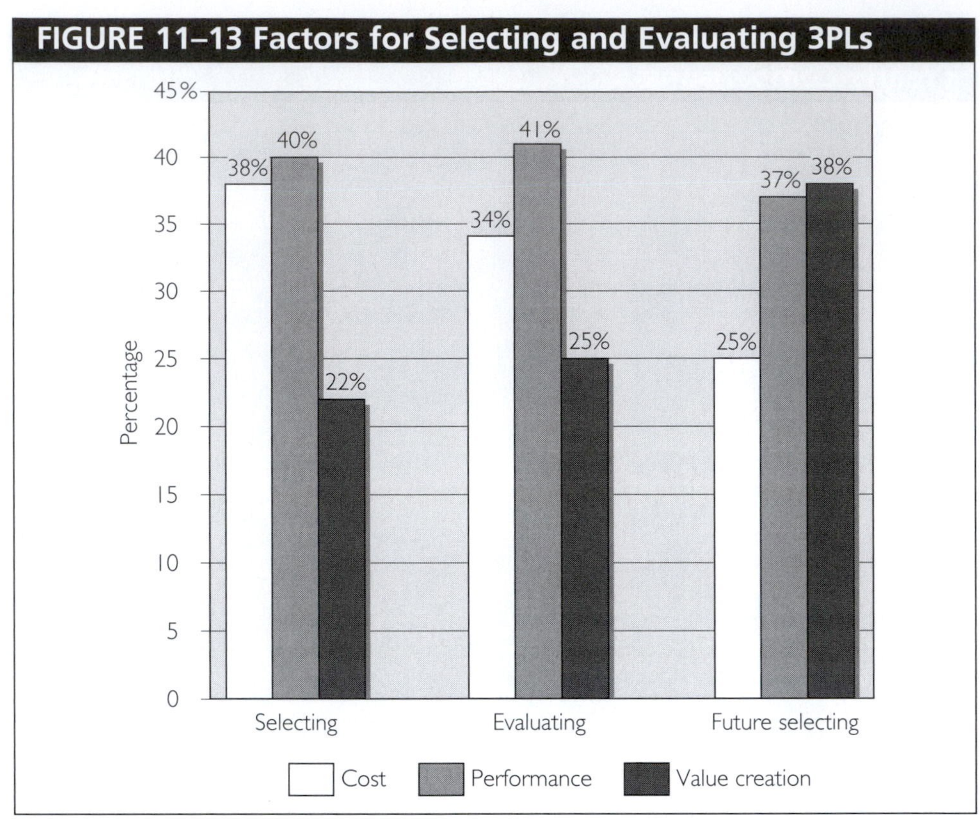

Source: C. John Langley Jr., Brian F. Newton, and Gary R. Allen, *Third-Party-Logistics Services: Views from the Customers* (Knoxville, Tenn.: University of Tennessee, Exel and Cap Gemini Ernst & Young, 2000).

of using a 3PL provider. The following averages were calculated based on individual responses:

- Logistics costs reduced by 8.2 percent
- Logistics assets reduced by 15.6 percent
- Average order cycle length changed from 10.7 to 8.4 days
- Overall inventories reduced by 5.3 percent

problems experienced

Reported Problem Areas. Respondents to the 2000 study reported experiencing a number of problems. Categorically, their responses tended to focus on several key areas of concern:

- Service level commitments have not been realized.
- Strategic management skills are lacking.
- Cost reductions have not been realized.
- Costs "creep" and price increases occur once relationship has commenced.
- Continuous, ongoing improvements and achievements in offerings are lacking.
- Control over the outsourced function(s) has diminished.
- Consultative, knowledge-based skills are lacking.
- Technology capabilities are available but are not being delivered to the client.
- Time and effort spent on logistics have not been reduced.

FIGURE 11–14 How Respondents View Providers of Third-Party-Logistics Services

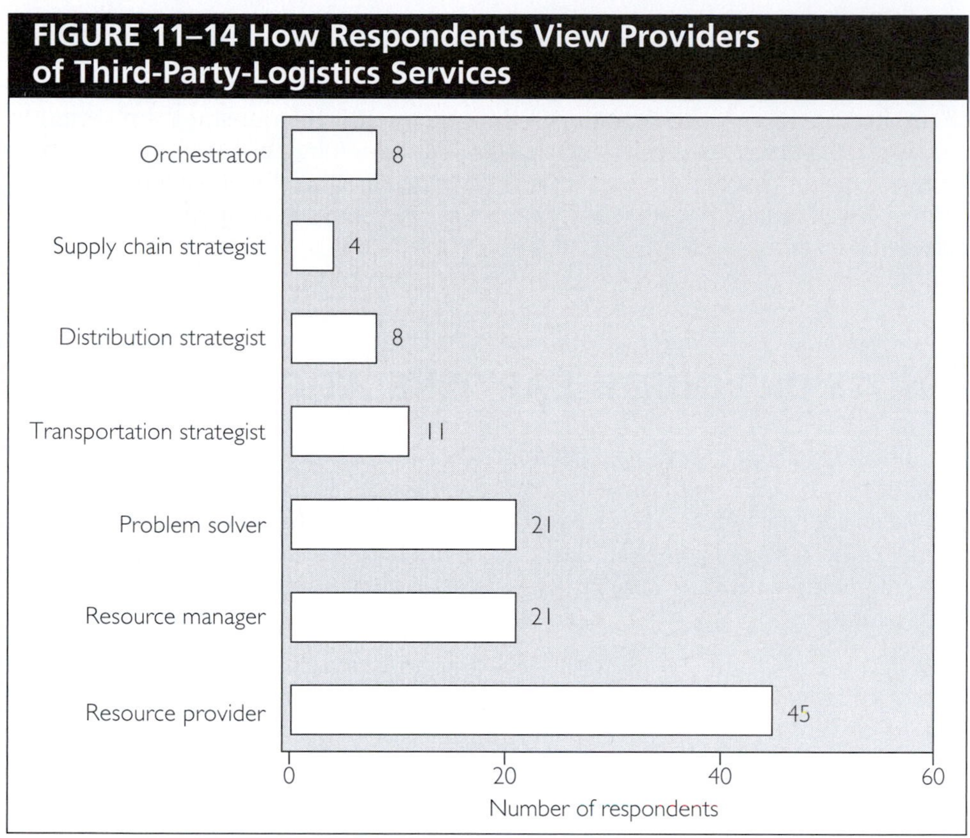

Source: C. John Langley Jr., Gary R. Allen, and Gene R. Tyndall, *Third-Party-Logistics Services: Views from the Customers* (Atlanta, Ga.: Georgia Institute of Technology, Cap Gemini Ernst & Young and Ryder System, Inc., 2001).

This list should be viewed as a starting point for continuous improvement by 3PL providers. Overall, it suggests a need to meet service level and cost objectives and to avoid unnecessary increases in price to the customer once the relationship has commenced. Also, it appears that some 3PLs need to improve in the areas of strategic management, technology, and knowledge-based skills. These suggest expectations by the customers that currently are not being met. Finally, there are users of 3PL services who feel that the time and effort spent on logistics have not decreased, and that their control over the outsourced function may have lessened. In the latter instance, the move to "hybrid" management of the 3PLs responsibilities may be a useful alternative.

strategic value

Logistics Strategic Value and the Role of 3PLs. Of the companies indicating current or intended use of 3PL services, 93 percent indicated their feeling that "logistics represents a strategic, competitive advantage for our company," and an equal number felt that "customers are placing greater emphasis on logistics customer service." As suggested in each of the earlier studies, these figures imply that the use of 3PL services is not necessarily inconsistent with logistics being an area of strategic importance to the company. Thus, it is apparent that there are a significant number of firms that view logistics as a core competency and a source of competitive advantage, but that also have elected to outsource certain portions of their logistics and supply chain processes.

The 2001 study also included a question relating to how respondents think of 3PLs. As shown in Figure 11–14, most users currently think of their 3PL firm as a "resource provider," while about one-half of this total view the 3PL as a "resource manager" and a "problem solver." To a lesser extent, 3PL firms are thought of as a "transportation strategist," "distribution strategist," "supply chain strategist," or "orchestrator." While many 3PL relationships are certainly deeper and more strategically focused than these characterizations would suggest, it appears that a valid objective is for more firms to be considered in these "higher-level" categories that imply a more meaningful, strategic relationship between a user and a 3PL.

A Note on Fourth-Party Relationships

4PL relationships

Beyond the concept of a third-party-logistics provider, the next evolution may be thought of as a 4PL, or a provider of "fourth-party-logistics"[13] services. Essentially a supply chain integrator, a 4PL is thought of as a firm that "assembles and manages the resources, capabilities, and technology of its own organization with those of complementary service providers to deliver a comprehensive supply chain solution."[14]

As suggested by Figure 11–15, a 4PL leverages the capabilities of 3PLs and suppliers of technology services through a centralized point of contact. In one sense, an important role of the 4PL is to manage and direct the activities of multiple 3PLs. In another, more strategic role, the 4PL serves as the integrator that brings together the needs of the client and the resources available through the 3PL providers, the IT providers, and the elements of business process management.

Need for Collaborative Relationships[15]

Whether the relationship may or may not be with a provider of logistics services, today's supply chain relationships are most effective when collaboration occurs among the participants who are involved. Collaboration may be thought of as a "business practice that encourages individual organizations to share information and resources for the benefit of all."[16] According to Dr. Michael Hammer, collaboration allows companies to "leverage each other on an operational basis so that together they perform better than they did separately."[17] He continues by suggesting that collaboration becomes a reality when the power of the Internet facilitates the ability of supply chain participants to readily transact with each other and to access each other's information.

collaboration defined

While this approach creates a synergistic business environment in which the sum of the parts is greater than the whole, it is not one that comes naturally to most organizations, particularly those offering similar or competing products or services. In terms of a logistics example, consider that consumer products manufacturers sometimes go to great lengths to make sure that their products are not transported from plants to customers' distribution centers with products of competing firms. While this practice does have certain logic, a willingness of the

FIGURE 11–15 Fourth-Party Logistics (Registered Trademark of Accenture, Inc.)

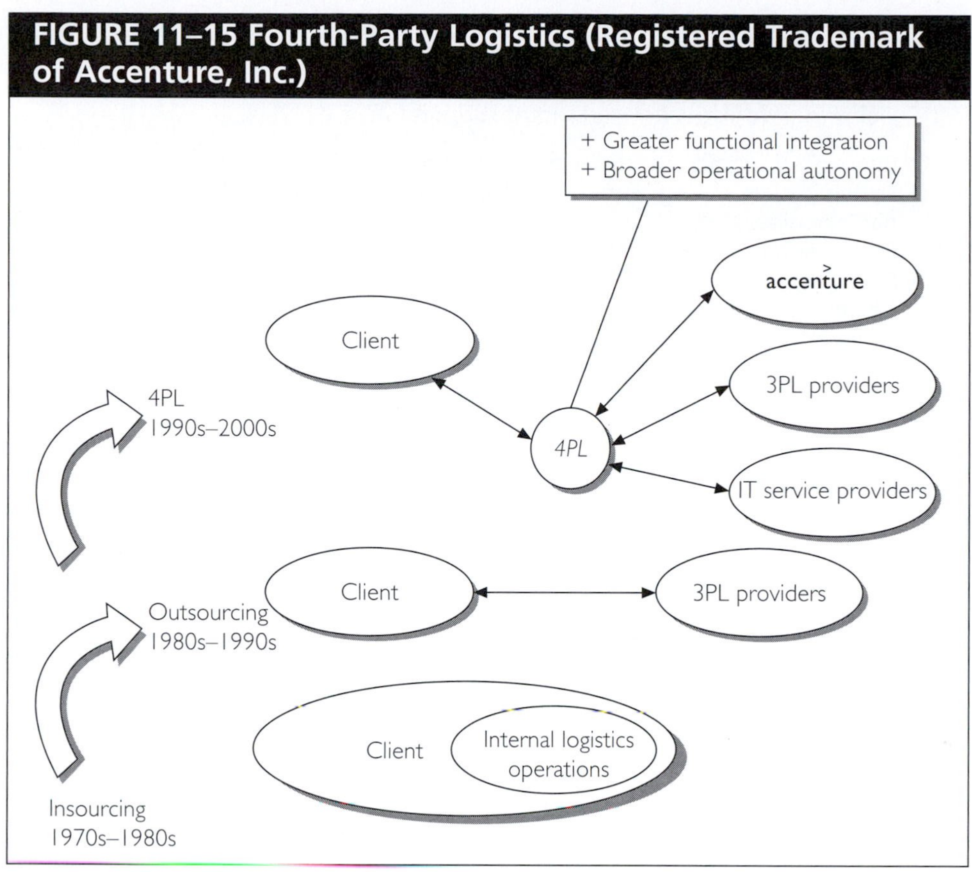

Source: Accenture, Inc.

involved parties to collaborate and share resources can create significant logistical efficiencies. Also, it makes sense, considering that retailers routinely commingle competing products as they are transported from distribution centers to retail stores. When organizations refuse to collaborate, real losses may easily outweigh perceived gains.

As discussed before, Nistevo is a leading provider of an Internet-based, collaborative logistics network. Essentially, Nistevo's information-based capabilities allow shippers and carriers to manage their relationships to improve effectiveness and efficiency for all. Aside from its operational capabilities, Nistevo's positioning as being both "shipper- and carrier-neutral" helps to identify opportunities and solutions that will be best for the overall relationship, rather than the possibility that they may be biased toward either shipper or carrier.

While there are numerous sources of suggestion and insight as to how to most effectively create successful, collaborative relationships, Table 11–5 lists each of the "Seven Immutable Laws of Collaborative Logistics." The collective impact of these principles is that they represent a course of action that, if followed, should enhance the success and benefits to be derived from truly collaborative relationships.

TABLE 11–5 Seven Laws of Collaborative Logistics

Collaborative logistics networks must support:

- Real and recognized benefits to all members
- Dynamic creation, measurement, and evolution of collaborative partnerships
- Co-buyer and co-seller relationships
- Flexibility and security
- Collaboration across all stages of business process integration
- Open integration with other services
- Collaboration around essential logistics flows

Source: Copyright © 2000, C. John Langley Jr., Ph.D., used with permission.

SUMMARY

- The two most basic types of supply chain relationships are "vertical" (e.g., buyer-seller) and "horizontal" (e.g., parallel or cooperating).
- In terms of intensity of involvement, interfirm relationships may span from transactional to relational and may take the form of vendor, partner, and strategic alliances.
- There are six steps in the development and implementation of successful relationships. These six steps are critical to the formation and success of supply chain relationships.
- Third-party logistics may be thought of as an "external supplier that performs all or part of a company's logistics functions." It is desirable that these suppliers provide multiple services and that these services are integrated in the way they are managed and delivered.
- The several types of 3PLs are transportation-based, warehouse/distribution-based, forwarder-based, financial-based, and information-based suppliers.
- Based on the results of a comprehensive study of users of 3PL services in the United States, over 70 percent of the firms studied are, to some extent, users of 3PL services.
- User experience suggests a broad range of 3PL services utilized; and the most prevalent are warehousing, outbound transportation, and freight bill payment and auditing.
- While nonusers of 3PL services have their reasons to justify their decision, these same reasons are sometimes cited by users as justification for using a 3PL.
- Customers have significant IT-based requirements of their 3PL providers, and they feel that the 3PLs are attaching a priority to respond to these requirements.
- Approximately two-thirds of the customers suggest 3PL involvement in their global supply chain activities.
- Although most customers indicate satisfaction with existing 3PL services, there is no shortage of suggestions for improvement.

- Customers generally have high aspirations for their strategic use of 3PLs and consider their 3PLs as keys to their supply chain success.
- There is a growing need for fourth-party-logistics[18] relationship that provide a wide range of integrative supply chain services.
- Collaborative relationships have been identified as highly useful to the achievement of long-term supply chain objectives. The "Seven Immutable Laws of Collaborative Logistics" provide a framework for the development of effective supply chain relationships.

STUDY QUESTIONS

1. What are the basic types of supply chain relationships, and how do they differ?
2. How would you distinguish between a vendor, a partner, and a strategic alliance? What conditions would favor the use of each?
3. What does it take to have an area of "core competency"? Provide an example.
4. Describe the steps in the process model for forming and implementing successful supply chain relationships. What step(s) do you feel is (are) most critical?
5. What are some of the more common "drivers" and "facilitators" of successful supply chain relationships?
6. What are the basic types of 3PL firms, and which are in most prevalent use?
7. What are some of the more frequently outsourced logistics activities? Less frequently outsourced?
8. Why do some firms choose not to use the services of 3PL firms?
9. In what ways are clients/customers counting on 3PLs for involvement with information technology–based services?
10. To what extent are clients/customers satisfied with 3PL services? What is the relative importance of cost, performance, and value creation as determining factors for evaluating and selecting 3PLs?
11. To what extent do clients/customers think of their 3PL providers in a strategic sense? What evidence suggests that this may change in the future, and what kind of change may be expected?
12. What is meant by "collaborative" relationships, and how are they relevant to supply chain issues?

NOTES

1. Robert V. Delaney, *11th Annual State of Logistics Report©* (St. Louis, Mo.: Cass Information Systems, 5 June 2000), 25.
2. Rosabeth Moss Kanter, *Harvard Business Review* (July–August 1994).
3. Douglas M. Lambert, Margaret A. Emmelhainz, and John T. Gardner, "Developing and Implementing Supply Chain Partnerships," *The International Journal of*

Logistics Management 7, no. 2 (1996): 1–17. The content of this section relating to drivers and facilitators has been quoted from this excellent research article.

4. Ibid., 4–10.
5. Ibid., 10.
6. Ibid., 10–13.
7. For further information, see Robert C. Lieb and Arnold Maltz, "What's the Future for Third Party Logistics?" *Supply Chain Management Review* (Fall 1999): 85–95; Leslie Hansen Harps, "Managing 3PL Relationships: Partnering for Performance," *Inbound Logistics* (July 1998): 26–40; Armstrong & Associates, Inc., *Armstrong's Guide to Third-Party-Logistics Services Providers*, 8th ed. (2000); Donald J. Bowersox, "The Strategic Benefits of Logistics Alliances," *Harvard Business Review* 90, no. 4 (July–August 1990): 36–45; Harry L. Sink, C. John Langley Jr., and Brian J. Gibson, "Buyer Observations of the U.S. Third-Party-Logistics Market," *International Journal of Physical Distribution and Logistics Management* 26, no. 3 (1996): 38–46; Harry L. Sink and C. John Langley Jr., "A Managerial Framework for the Acquisition of Third-Party-Logistics Services," *Journal of Business Logistics* 18, no. 2 (1997): 163–90; and C. John Langley Jr., Brian F. Newton, and Gene R. Tyndall, "Third-Party Logistics: Has the Future Already Arrived?" *Supply Chain Management Review* 3, no. 3 (Fall 1999): 85–94.
8. C. John Langley Jr., Gary R. Allen, and Gene R. Tyndall, *Third-Party-Logistics Services: Views from the Customers* (Atlanta, Ga.: The Georgia Institute of Technology, Cap Gemini Ernst & Young and Ryder System, Inc., 2001). This report provides details concerning the results and findings from this sixth annual study. Included in this chapter is relevant information that pertains to the use of 3PL services in the U.S.
9. In addition to the study authors, others who significantly contributed to the conduct and analysis of this year's study were Teresa McCarthy, Susan Golicic, and Duke Leingpibul, all Ph.D. students at the University of Tennessee; and Kevin Bott and Kevin Hagerty, executives at Ryder System, Inc.
10. This figure (725) reflects the deletion of approximately 10 percent of the e-mail addresses that resulted in delivery failures.
11. C. John Langley Jr., Brian F. Newton, and Gary R. Allen, *Third-Party-Logistics Services: Views from the Customers* (Knoxville, Tenn.: University of Tennessee, 2000). This report includes the results and findings from the fifth annual version of this comprehensive study.
12. The results reported in this section are from C. John Langley Jr., Brian Newton, and Gary R. Allen, op. cit.
13. 4PL and fourth-party logistics are registered trademarks of Accenture, Inc.
14. Accenture, Inc., by permission.
15. For an overview of collaborative logistics, see C. John Langley Jr., "Seven Immutable Laws of Collaborative Logistics" (2000), available at http://www.nistevo.com

16. Ibid., 4.
17. Ibid., 2.
18. Trademark, Accenture, Inc.

CASE 11–1 ■ Ocean Spray Cranberries, Inc.

August is typically a challenging month for Ocean Spray Cranberries, Inc., when the Lakeville, Massachusetts-based firm has to pump up volume to meet the surge in demand for the upcoming holiday season. Ocean Spray is an agricultural co-op owned by more than 750 citrus growers in the United States and Canada. The company produces canned and bottled juice, juice drinks, and food products at distribution centers in Bordentown, New Jersey; Kenosha, Wisconsin; Sulphur Springs, Texas; and Henderson, Nevada.

Ocean Spray was managing its transportation operations internally, but the company decided it wanted to focus on its core competency, which, according to its director of logistics, is "maintaining our leadership in the shelf-stable juice drink category." The company also wanted to centralize its transportation operations. Looking carefully at the issue of overall performance in the logistics and transportation areas, it was found that there was a significant amount of variability in its operations. For purposes of uniformity and control, a major priority was attached to centralization of its logistics operations.

In addition, Ocean Spray wanted to be able to reach markets that it did not already have access to, which would require expansion of its logistics network. According to the director of logistics, an analysis was undertaken to study how long it would take and what it would cost to build up Ocean Spray's transportation capabilities to be able to support such a network. As a result, a recommendation had been made to seriously investigate the use of a third-party-logistics (3PL) provider.

Case Questions

1. What rationale is offered by Ocean Spray in support of the idea of using a 3PL? Do you agree with the reasons cited for the interest in a 3PL?
2. Based on your understanding of Ocean Spray and its business needs, what type of 3PL firm do you feel might be of greatest potential value in terms of a relationship?
3. What steps would you suggest be considered by Ocean Spray as it begins to analyze the feasibility of forming a relationship with individual 3PL providers?
4. Once the selection process is complete, what kind of relationship do you feel would be most appropriate: vendor, partner, strategic alliance, or some other option?

Source: Adapted from Adrienne Breiner, "Outsourcing Helps to Take Squeeze Out of Surge," *Food Logistics* (15 April 1999): 62.

CHAPTER 12

LOGISTICS AND SUPPLY CHAIN INFORMATION SYSTEMS

LEARNING OBJECTIVES

After reading this chapter, you should be able to do the following:

- Understand the overall importance of information systems to logistics and supply chain management.
- Recognize key issues in information systems.
- Know what is meant by the quality of information, and know what to measure to assure that this quality exists.
- Understand the architecture and objectives of information systems in general, and the structural components of the logistics information system.
- Appreciate the role of logistics in the "connected" economy, and appreciate how evolving technologies are impacting logistics and logistics processes.

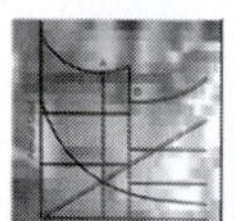

LOGISTICS PROFILE

Applebee's Looks for Greater Control of Information

According to experienced restaurant operators, much has changed over the years in the ways Applebee's and other stores run their businesses. In the earlier days, a phone call every couple of days or so was used to verify specific items that were to be delivered to individual stores by the food service distributor. Then, more progressive practices resulted in store operators faxing in their orders. Now, products are ordered on a regular basis over the Internet. In addition to facilitating the order-entry process, capable Internet interfaces provide real-time pricing, inventory availability, and fulfillment visibility.

One advantage of such capabilities is that it helps operators to "flag" prices that seem out of line. When a restaurant chain negotiates a specific price for a certain type of commodity, for example potatoes at thirty-two cents per pound, it is important to make sure that every distributor is honoring that price. Complicating matters is that the invoice may indicate a base price for the product plus a "markup" of 8 or 9 percent for shipping.

Considering that a typical invoice may consist of 200 to 300 individual items from a distributor, it is very challenging for an operator such as Applebee's to go through all the items to make sure it is receiving the negotiated price. Currently, an Applebee's associate in the accounting office spot-checks bills from various franchisees and company stores for inconsistencies. The software behind the Internet interface has helped to flag prices that vary more than 2 or 3 percent from the agreed-upon price. Also, the software can help to assure consistency across the stores in a restaurant chain in the matter of "rebates," where, for example, a chain may receive a rebate of fifty cents a case on its purchases of ketchup, assuming a minimum aggregate of orders.

Most importantly, Internet interfaces can help Applebee's to do a better job at tracking inventory. For example, if the chain comes up with a Tequila Lime Marinated Chicken as a promotional item and forecasts sales of 30,000 units during the four-week promotion, it is useful to have an accurate knowledge of actual sales plus how much inventory of the item is in the pipeline. This will help to make a determination as to whether it wants the manufacturer to ramp up and make some more product in the case that demand may have been underestimated—or to discontinue the item if it did not sell as well as planned.

Overall, the utilization of Internet-enabled systems has great potential to improve the efficiency and effectiveness of supply chain activity as it applies to businesses such as Applebee's. To the extent that it facilitates the business relationship between restaurant chains and their food service distributors, it represents a significant improvement over traditional practices. In the end, the consumer in the store is the one who benefits most from this type of innovation and creativity.

Source: Adapted from "Applebee's Looks for Greater Control of Information," *Food Logistics* (July/August, 2000) Supplement: 54–55.

INTRODUCTION

Many firms today view effective management of logistics and supply chain activities both as a prerequisite to overall cost efficiency and as a key to ensuring their ability to competitively price their products and services.[1] It is typical that high-level corporate and marketing executives consider their firm's logistics competencies to be among the unique ways in which the firm is able to differentiate itself in the marketplace. Also, research conducted at Michigan State University suggests that information technology is being used by leading-edge firms to increase competitiveness and develop a sustainable competitive advantage.[2] Although capabilities relating to information systems and information technologies have traditionally been regarded also as key strategic resources, expertise in these areas is now thought to be among the most valuable and essential of all corporate resources. Considering the need for effective management of corporate information systems and technologies, and their exceptional relevance and importance to logistics and supply chain management, it is useful to devote an entire chapter to coverage of this important topic.

customer needs

Effective information management also can help ensure that a firm meets the logistical needs of its customers. Studies have shown that firms should place priority on logistical elements such as on-time delivery, stockout levels, order status, shipment tracing and expediting, order convenience, completeness of orders, creation of customer pickup and backhaul opportunities, and production substitution.[3] These activities are within the logistics manager's domain, and their successful implementation depends heavily upon a timely and accurate flow of meaningful information. The logistics area can assist significantly in meeting customer needs, and a first-class information system can facilitate the logistics mission.

According to author David J. Closs, "Logistics information systems combine hardware and software to manage, control, and measure logistics activities."[4] These activities occur within specific firms as well as across the overall supply chain. Hardware includes computers and servers, Internet technologies, input and output devices, communications channels, ancillary technologies such as bar code and RF devices, and storage media. Software includes system and applications programs used for logistics and supply chain activities. Although there is a growing range of information technologies that are utilized by and applicable to logistics and supply chain processes, it is the ability to integrate and, thus, leverage the power of these technologies that distinguishes the successful firms from those that are less successful.

A year 2000 research study reported by Gustin, Rutner, and Gibson identified a number of areas as "high priority" in terms of the need for better information.[5] According to this research, companies most needed information on their customers, such as customer service and sales forecasting. This was followed closely in importance by the need for information on their suppliers, such as production planning and sourcing, and purchasing. Areas where technology systems were not delivering needed information included decision support systems/information technology and logistics management activities, especially data required for strategic decision making. Results varied by industry and company size, with larger companies having better logistics support than smaller ones.

This chapter first identifies a number of contemporary issues that apply to information systems in general and then discusses the functional areas affected by significant corporate investments in information technology. Also, attention is directed to the issue of quality in information. Second is a discussion of major drivers of the "connected" economy, with special coverage of the Internet environment as it applies to logistics and supply chain management. Third, attention is directed toward the architecture and objectives of information systems; and, fourth, an overview is provided of a number of contemporary logistics and supply chain information technologies. Fifth, the concept of a logistics information system is defined and discussed. This is followed by coverage of IT advances in procurement and strategic sourcing, and further detail concerning the relevance of collaborative supply chain relationships to the development of effective logistics and supply chain strategies.

Contemporary Issues in Information Systems

Results from Annual CSC Study on Information Systems Management

The authors of the "13th Annual Critical Issues in Information Systems Management Survey," conducted in 2000 by Computer Sciences Corporation (CSC), suggest that the highest priorities are on customers, productivity, and performance. The study is broad-based geographically—executives from twenty-six countries participated in 2000—and included 822 respondents. Their overall observation is that "connecting for results" is the focal point for IS executives, past, present, and future.[6]

top technology issues

In its report, CSC identifies the top ten issues relating to information systems for 2000. These are listed in Table 12–1, along with the percentage of global respondents indicating that each was of major concern. The area of greatest concern is "connecting to customers, suppliers, and/or partners," with 65.9 percent of the respondents in agreement. The remainder of the top five are "optimizing organizational effectiveness," "optimizing enterprise-wide IS services," "developing an

TABLE 12–1 Top Information Systems Issues for 2000 (Global Responses)

Rank	Issue	Percentage of Respondents
1	Connecting to customers, suppliers, and/or partners	65.9
2	Optimizing organizational effectiveness	62.8
3	Optimizing enterprise-wide IS services	59.9
4	Developing an E-business strategy	59.3
5	Organizing and utilizing data	57.7
6	Aligning IS and corporate goals	52.7
7	Integrating systems with the Internet	52.1
8	Using IT for competitive breakthroughs	51.6
9	Using obsolete systems	51.3
10	Instituting cross-functional information systems	46.1

Source: Computer Sciences Corporation, *13th Annual Critical Issues of Information Systems Management Survey* (Cambridge, Mass.: Computer Sciences Corporation, 2001). Available at http://www.csc.com

TABLE 12–2 Critical Business Processes (North American Responses)

Business Process	Percentage of Respondents
1. Customer service	48.4%
2. Order processing	38.8
3. Delivery/logistics	27.7
4. Sales	24.4
5. Accounting/billing/finance	22.6

Source: Computer Sciences Corporation, *Critical Issues of Information Systems Management for 1995,* CSC News Release (Cambridge, Mass.: Computer Sciences Corporation, 1995), page 3H.

E-business strategy," and "organizing and utilizing data." Looking through the issues identified in Table 12–1, it is clear that Internet and E-commerce issues have become recognizable and critical, as judged by the survey respondents.

Reported in an earlier version of this same study were responses to a question that asked North American respondents to identify the three business processes most critical to their business. The results are shown in Table 12–2, which indicates that the top three issues are all directly related to logistics and supply chain management (customer service, order processing, and delivery/logistics).[7] In fact, the processes ranked fourth and fifth, respectively, sales and accounting/billing/finance, have significant areas of interaction with logistics. Thus, all of the top five critical business processes have at least some, and in most cases a very significant, relationship to logistics and supply chain management. These areas are all excellent candidates to be aggressively funded by companies in their future efforts to leverage IS capabilities into greater profitability and improved service to customers.

Quality of Information[8]

Three issues characterize information quality. First is the availability of the information required to make the best possible decisions. Second is the accuracy of the information. Third is the effectiveness of the various means that are available to communicate needed information.

relevance of information

Availability of Information. Unfortunately, logistics managers do not always have the information they need to make effective decisions. Perhaps the most common reason is that many managers are uncertain of their information needs and, thus, have difficulty conceptualizing and verbalizing those needs. This sometimes occurs with customers, who may not have a sound understanding of their needs or who may have difficulty in terms of expressing or articulating those needs.

Another reason for not having the right information is that staff people charged with securing information give the logistics manager what they think is needed or what they find convenient or cost-effective to provide. Many times, this is quite different from what the logistics manager truly needs.

Logistics managers need to know more about information systems, technologies, and their management. Conversely, many information systems managers (such as the director of corporate MIS, the chief information officer, etc.) could benefit from a better understanding of logistics management and business in general. This indicates a need for a two-way educational process in which managers in these areas become far more aware of and sensitive to one another's needs and capabilities.

information accuracy

Accuracy of Information. Information available to logistics managers often leaves much to be desired and, as a result, tends to cause suboptimal management decision making. This sometimes occurs because many companies use cost accounting and management control systems that were developed years ago in very different corporate and competitive environments. Many of these systems distort product-cost information and do not produce the information that logistics managers need to make the best decisions. Although vendors of state-of-the-art ERP (enterprise resource planning) systems suggest that their products will help to eliminate this type of problem, rarely is this such as simple matter.

For example, many logistics managers have approved capital investments in equipment and systems to facilitate operations in areas such as warehousing, transportation, and inventory control. As a result, some have seen dramatic increases in the labor component of total logistics cost. If firms continue to allocate overhead expenses on the basis of direct labor hours, as is the case in many standard cost accounting systems, the cost figures produced will not be very helpful for management decision making.[9] The information needs of the whole company—its functional areas and key processes, not the external reporting requirements of various industry and regulatory groups—need to drive each company's internal accounting practices.

Data accuracy sometimes proves to be a critical concern for retailers, who sometimes levy penalties on suppliers who routinely provide inaccurate data. One of these retailers has instituted a "three strikes and you're out" program: any supplier providing inaccurate data on three or more occasions loses its "preferred supplier" status. Another example illustrating the need for accurate data is that of the mass merchant in a "do-it-yourself" chain. Because a case of padlocks was incorrectly labeled by the manufacturer, the merchant's computer charged for a single lock when an entire case was purchased. The inaccurate data was also responsible for erroneous inventory counts and costly stock outages.[10]

The logistics literature has raised the need for customization of accounting practices to accommodate logistics needs.[11] Although considerable progress is yet to be made, the principles of *activity-based costing* (ABC) and *activity-based management* (ABM) have helped to improve the accuracy of information at many firms.

communication

Effectiveness of Communication. To be useful to managers, information needs to be communicated effectively.[12] This in turn requires that it be communicated in the language of the intended recipient. Otherwise, perceiving the information may be difficult for whom it is intended. Also, communication is sometimes thwarted when people ignore unexpected information. This is sometimes referred to as *selective perception*. Finally, communication takes place only if the information keys into a person's values and pertains directly to the management decisions the recipient needs to make. In short, effective communication requires knowledge of what the recipient can perceive, what that person expects to perceive, and what the person intends to do with what is perceived. If the communicator misses any of these targets, effective communication is more challenging.

ARCHITECTURE AND OBJECTIVES OF INFORMATION SYSTEMS[13]

Information System Building Process

designing information systems

IBM Corporation has expended significant resources to provide companies with a comprehensive direction for integrating information in a consistent, effective manner across the business enterprise and the supply chain. The objectives are to utilize a computer integrated logistics/information system (CIL/IS) architecture to help design and implement systems to improve resource utilization, provide better customer service, and increase the effectiveness of inter-enterprise information flow. The objective of a CIL/IS is to integrate, manage, and provide access to the information associated with the positive control of end-to-end freight movement to ensure satisfaction of customer commitments consistent with desired levels of resource allocation.

Figure 12–1 illustrates the building process as it relates to the information system. The technique begins with a snapshot of a company or organization as it exists, an *enterprise model* (a). This indicates the overall organization and a general description of functions. Following determination of the organization's requirements, goals, objectives, and critical success factors, the *business process model* (b) shows what each area of the company does. The *data model* (c) shows the data and the data flow required to support these processes.

Following a decision as to the specific process(es) on which to focus attention, the detailed *process description* (d) and *data description* (e) steps must be completed. Either through use of a programmer or a software engineering tool, the *applications programs* (f) and *database descriptions* (g) are produced.

Finally, a systems programmer looks at the work to be done and builds a *system platform* (h) that not only supports the operational system but also has tools, conveniences, and enablers to help the programmer do the job.

Overall, three key types of people are involved in the building process:

- *Architect.* Involved in designing the process and specifying some standards and rules for certain processes, such as using EDI or XML for communications. The architect specifies the size of the platforms (workstation or mainframe), physical data requirements, and the network to link users of the technology (Internet-based, servers, etc.).
- *Systems programmer.* Assembles hardware and system software products.
- *Data manager.* Uses database products to build a directory or repository that describes what data exists, where it is stored, and how it will be used. The applications programmer uses this system platform and database to produce the operational application code.

Once an initial information system is complete, subsequent systems are easier to build because the system platform and database structure exist, the business

FIGURE 12–1 Information System Building Process

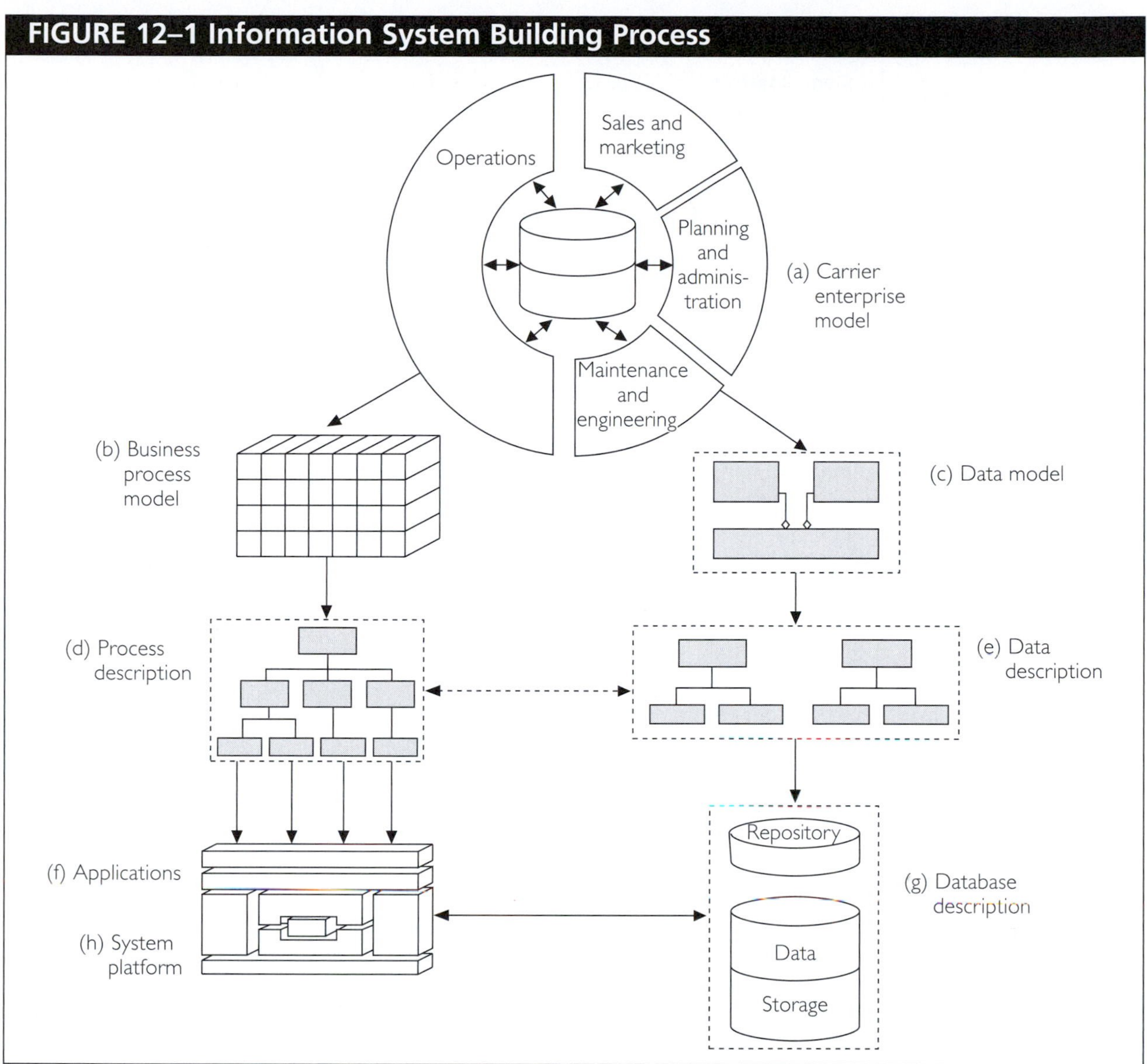

Source: Stanley Scheff and David B. Livingston, *Computer Integrated Logistics: CIL Architecture in the Extended Enterprise* (Southbury, Conn.: IBM Corporation, U.S. Transportation Industry Marketing, 1991), 7.

process model and data model disciplines are understood, and the next business area information system will be integrated with the one previously developed.

Positioning Information in Logistics

critical information flows

According to Closs, logistics information systems include two types of flows, incorporating coordination and operational activities.[14] The key activities within each type of flow are indicated in Figure 12–2. Those that make up the coordination flow include those that are related to scheduling and requirements planning throughout the firm. Operational flow activities relate to the initiation and tracking of receipts,

FIGURE 12–2 Logistics Information Flow

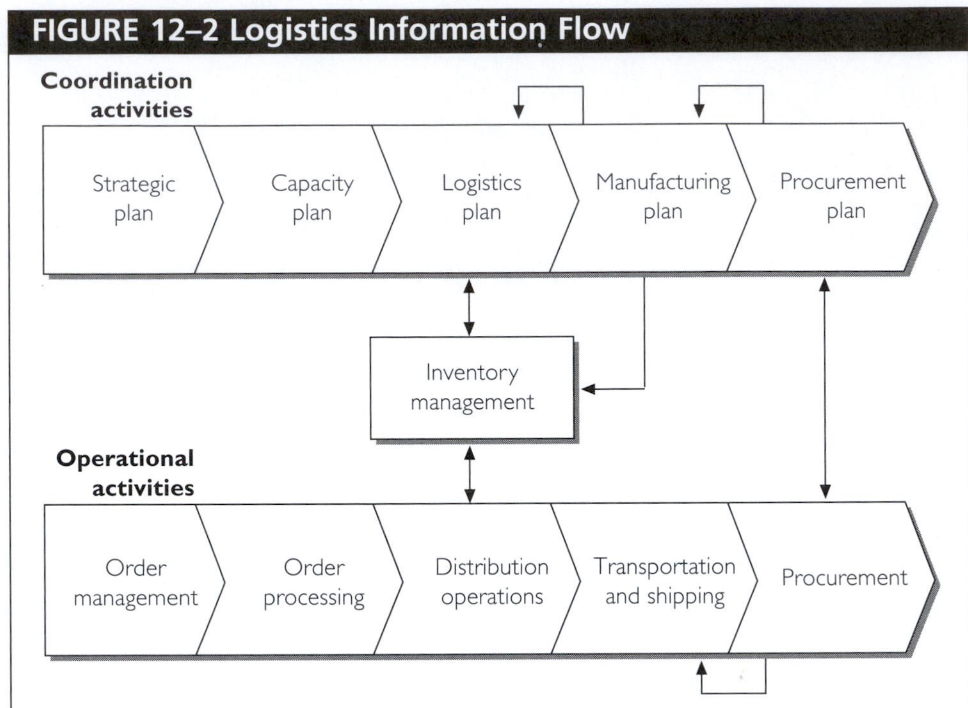

Source: Reprinted with the permission of The Free Press, a division of Simon & Schuster, Inc., from *The Logistics Handbook,* James F. Robeson and William C. Copacino, Editors-in-Chief. Copyright © 1994 by James F. Robeson and William C. Copacino.

inventory assignment, and shipment of replenishment and customer orders. *Replenishment orders* are those that resupply distribution centers from manufacturing facilities; *customer orders* relate to the movement of product from DCs to customer locations. In either instance, order fulfillment requires a series of activities such as order placement, order processing, order preparation, and order shipment. These activities were discussed in greater detail in Chapter 3 of this text. The role of the inventory management component as it appears in Figure 12–2 is to assure that the operational activities are conducted in a manner consistent with the coordination activities. This involves synchronization of product and information flow both upstream and downstream in the order-fulfillment process.

While it is essential to recognize the role to be played by both of these flows, Closs suggests three types of change that are needed in the future.[15] The first is to make sure that there is a significant interchange of data between the two flows. At present, it is not unusual for different data to be used for planning and operations activities. The second is the need to integrate coordination activities into operational modules. An example of this is to assign customer orders to alternate distribution facilities when an out-of-stock situation exists at the primary shipping location. The third type of change is to think of these flows as flexible, not linear as depicted in Figure 12–2. This provides added versatility and responsiveness to overall logistical needs.

FIGURE 12–3 Examples of Information Flows

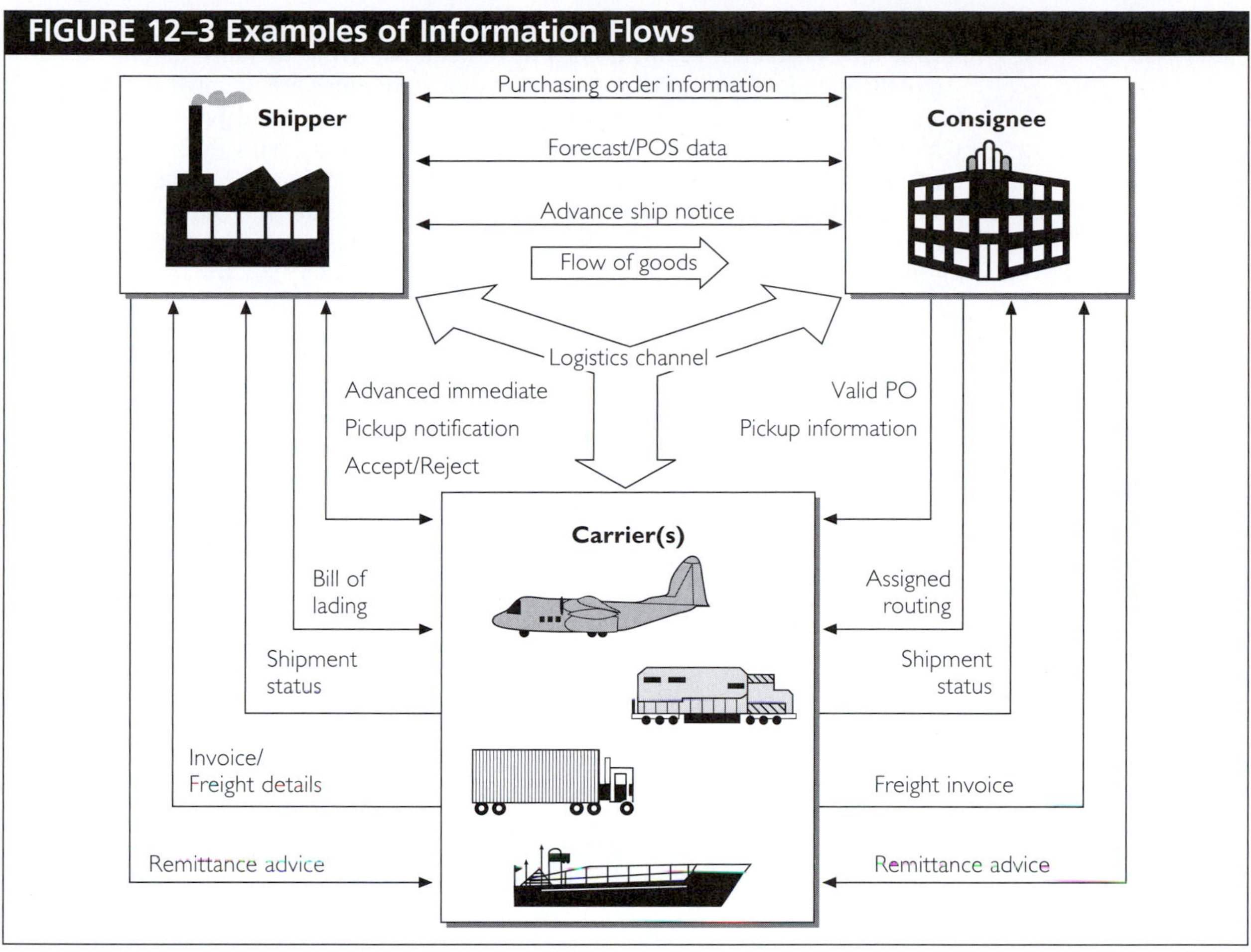

Source: Stanley Scheff and David B. Livingston, *Computer Integrated Logistics: CIL Architecture in the Extended Enterprise* (Southbury, Conn.: IBM Corporation, U.S. Transportation Industry Marketing, 1991), 9.

proprietary versus shared data

Figure 12–3 is an example of the logistics information flows that support both proprietary and shared data.[16] Being needed to manage the company, the proprietary data is accessible only to those employees having a legitimate internal business need. The shared data is available through appropriate information interfaces to customers, logistics suppliers, or any other party having a need to know through a contract or standard to which all parties agree. The data is kept physically in the database of the individual company but can be accessed when needed by other firms through use of suitable information technologies such as a company Web site that may be accessed via the Internet and so on.

MAJOR DRIVERS OF THE CONNECTED ECONOMY[17]

technology drivers

The World Wide Web is responsible for a transformation of the global economy and, with it, supply chain management practices. In increasingly competitive business environments, driven by customers' growing demands for service, speed, and customization, the ability to deliver (i.e., fulfillment) becomes the key differentiator. In fact, customers' expectations have been shown to increase as their level of sophistication increases. The net result is that companies are paying far more attention to their customers' needs than ever before. A second driver is technology, which has enhanced the ability of companies to connect with their suppliers and customers. Leveraging the power of technology has facilitated a move toward real-time visibility and optimization of the supply chain. The overriding objective for all companies should be to reach a point where efficiency and effectiveness are at an optimal balance from a total supply chain perspective.

The velocity of the Internet revolution, along with the resulting transformation of related operating rules, has created new challenges and opportunities that companies must consider as they evaluate their business and supply chain strategies. In response to a major mail survey, participants revealed that transformation of operating rules is affecting the way they view their supply chains. These changes are putting pressure on the customers' ability to manage their logistics networks effectively, and impact traditional operating characteristics. Those who are successful at managing logistics and supply chain processes within the shifting business environment will likely survive the evolving ways in which firms relate to and communicate with each other. Overall, the connected economy is creating a shift from predictable, scheduled, bulk-type shipments to variable, real-time, smaller-size shipments, which, for most companies, drive significant change and complexity in the logistics and supply chain areas. Table 12–3 indicates a number of key ways in which logistics matters in the "connected" economy differ from those of the traditional economy.

TABLE 12–3 The Shift of Logistics Operations in the Connected Economy

	Traditional Logistics	E-Logistics
Orders:	Predictable	Variable, small lots
Order Cycle Time:	Weekly	Short OTD/daily or hourly
Customer:	Strategic	Broader base
Customer Service:	Reactive, rigid	Responsive, flexible
Replenishment:	Scheduled	Real-time
Distribution Model:	Supply-driven (push)	Demand-driven (pull)
Demand:	Stable, consistent	More cyclical
Shipment Type:	Bulk	Smaller lots
Destinations:	Concentrated	More dispersion
Warehouse Reconfiguration:	Weekly/monthly	Continual, rules-based
International Trade Compliance:	Manual	Automated

Source: Cap Gemini Ernst & Young and The University of Tennessee, *Logistics @ Internet Speed: The Impact of E-Commerce on Logistics* (Knoxville, Tenn.: University of Tennessee, 2000), 10.

Customer-Centric Value Web® Model[18]

The power of the Internet to deliver convergence, speed, and connectivity has changed many customers' expectations toward suppliers. Customers of all types are demanding more, at faster speeds, and with improved reliability. Figure 12–4 is a representation of this phenomena, the "Customer-Centric Value Web Model." This model reveals that the Internet has the ability to connect everyone, everywhere, in real time.

customer-centric approaches

The emergence of new, dynamic customer requirements have been responsible for the emergence of innovative, contemporary logistics networks. As a result, traditional supply chain boundaries are disappearing, to be replaced by a merging of activities and processes in areas such as manufacturing, distribution, and transportation. The end result is that the traditional, linear supply chain model is being replaced by new, customer-centric approaches such as suggested in Figure 12–4. This approach stresses the need for integration and transformation to achieve relevant supply chain objectives. In fact, this customer-centric supply chain model enables:

- Global visibility of customer, product, or supply information throughout the supply chain
- Enhanced customer relationships leading to repeat business through fast, accurate product delivery and professional customer response services
- Efficient transactions through seamless integration of internal and external flows of information and materials
- Flexible infrastructure and partnering

FIGURE 12–4 Customer-Centric Value Web® Model

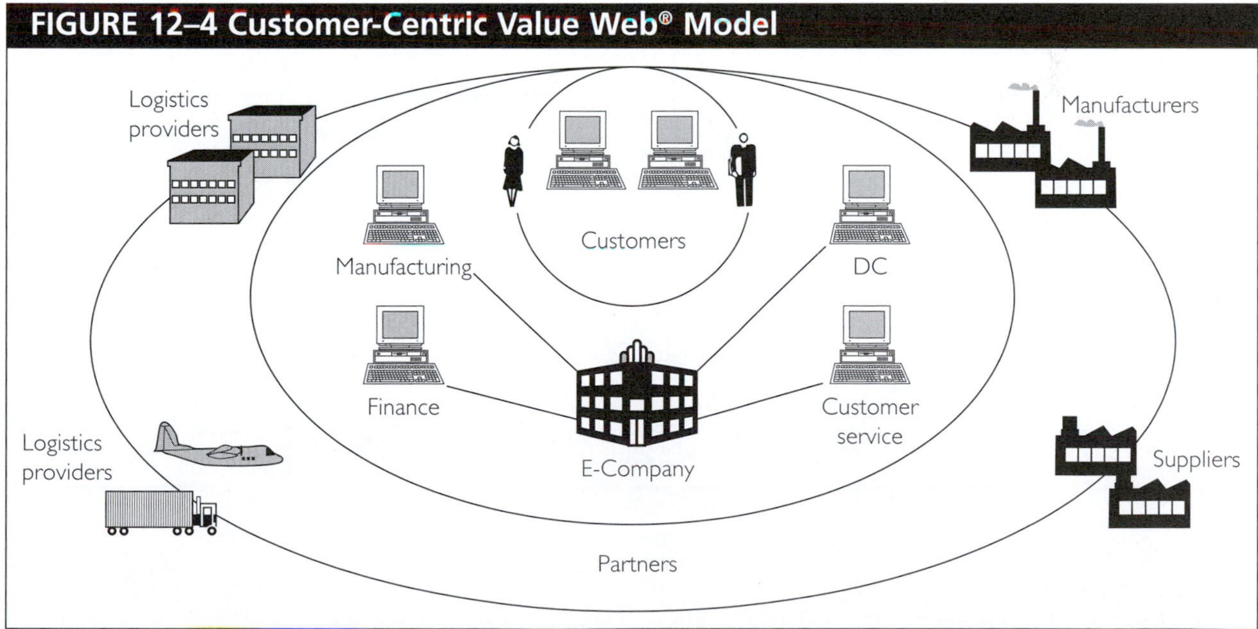

Source: Cap Gemini Ernst & Young and The University of Tennessee, *Logistics @ Internet Speed: The Impact of E-Commerce on Logistics* (Knoxville, Tenn.: University of Tennessee, 2000), 14.

- Analytical assessment and optimization of material movement, price, and placement actions on demand
- Coordinated, rapid decision-making environment that synchronizes the global supply chain

Technology Impacts on Supply Chain Disintermediation

disintermediation

The availability of improved information technologies quickly leads to improved abilities of firms to communicate with one another and to establish meaningful relationships. Traditionally, we would think of typical supply chain relationships as occurring between customers and retailers, retailers and distributors, distributors and manufacturers, and so on. Leveraging the power of technology and Web-based connectivity, however, it is becoming more common for manufacturers to deal directly with customers, thus *disintermediating* the distributors and retailers who previously may have been "in between." These alternatives are pictured in Figure 12–5.

While disintermediation may diminish the involvement of certain traditional firms in the supply chain, it should be viewed as a new and innovative logistics channel that helps to move product from manufacturer to ultimate customer. This phenomenon is exemplified by the emergence of a number of business-to-business electronic markets, which shorten and simplify relationships between customers and manufacturers. As a result, many traditional retail and distribution firms have

FIGURE 12–5 Technology Impacts on Supply Chain Disintermediation

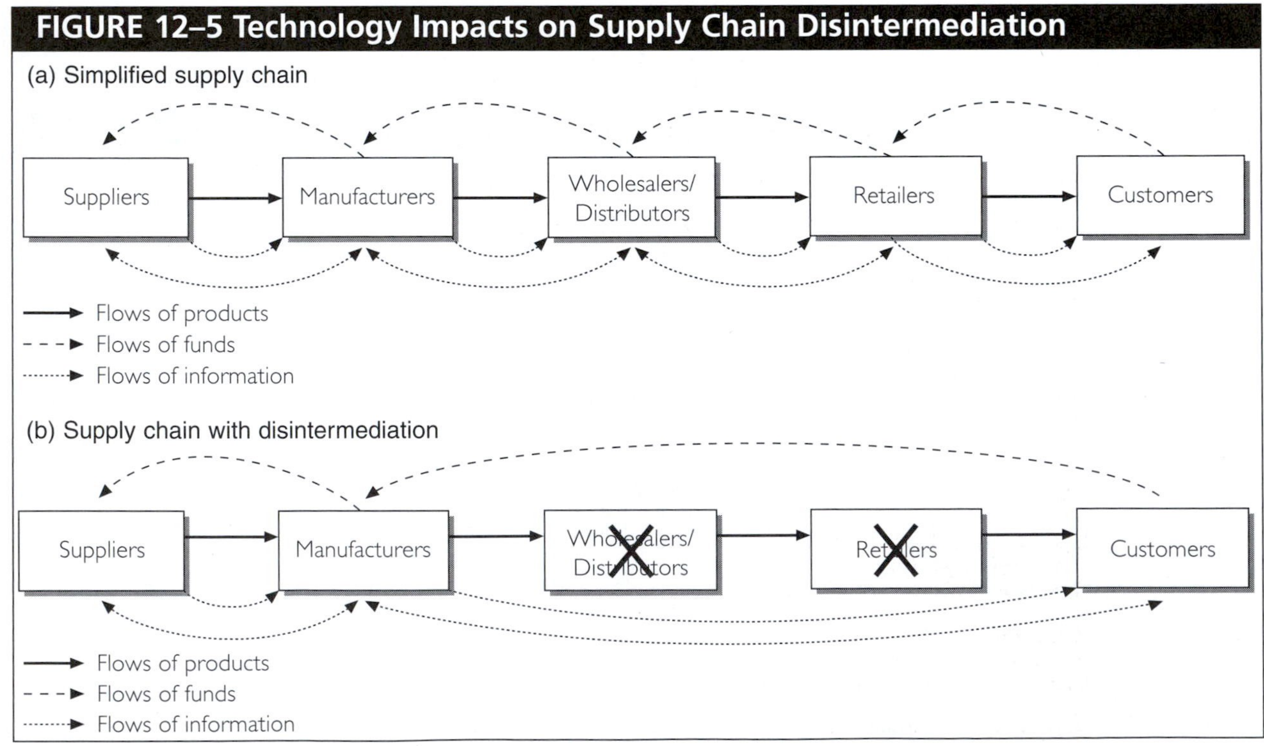

developed Web-enabled technologies to retain access to their customers who now have alternative ways to procure needed products and materials.

Evolving Technological Changes

technological advances

Figure 12–6 provides a perspective on the technological advances that are leading to the development of significant intelligent marketplaces. Beginning with basic Web-site capabilities, the progression grows through exchanges, communities, and intelligent marketplaces. These are described briefly in the following paragraphs.

Web site. The experience of both stand-alone Web-based firms (e.g., Amazon.com; eBay.com, etc.) and those that extended their traditional businesses into Web-based capabilities has been the same—building the infrastructure and managing the processes needed to move the actual order through the entire supply chain proved to be very challenging.

Exchanges. This enhancement provided electronic opportunities for supply chain participants to buy and sell products and services that were needed. By their very nature, *exchanges* did not facilitate the kinds of coordination and collaboration between buyers and sellers of supply chain services that would create the needed levels of efficiency and effectiveness.

Trading Communities. Trading communities essentially are hubs of suppliers, customers, manufacturers, distributors, and wholesalers brought together with a common data interchange platform—the Internet. From an information flow and redundancy perspective, this *community* of companies forms a Web, thus replacing the traditional, linear supply chain.

The objective of trading communities is to bring efficiency to many traditional business and delivery functions. These efficiencies take the form of reduced transaction costs, improved asset utilization from the perspective of the service provider,

FIGURE 12–6 Chronicle of Internet Milestones

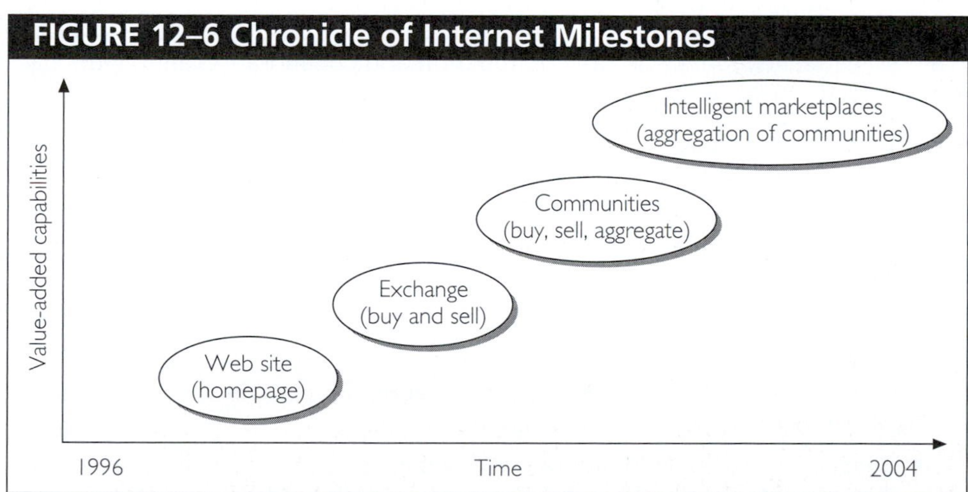

Source: Cap Gemini Ernst & Young and The University of Tennessee, *Logistics @ Internet Speed: The Impact of E-Commerce on Logistics* (Knoxville, Tenn.: University of Tennessee, 2000), 7.

FIGURE 12–7 Logistics Trading Exchanges

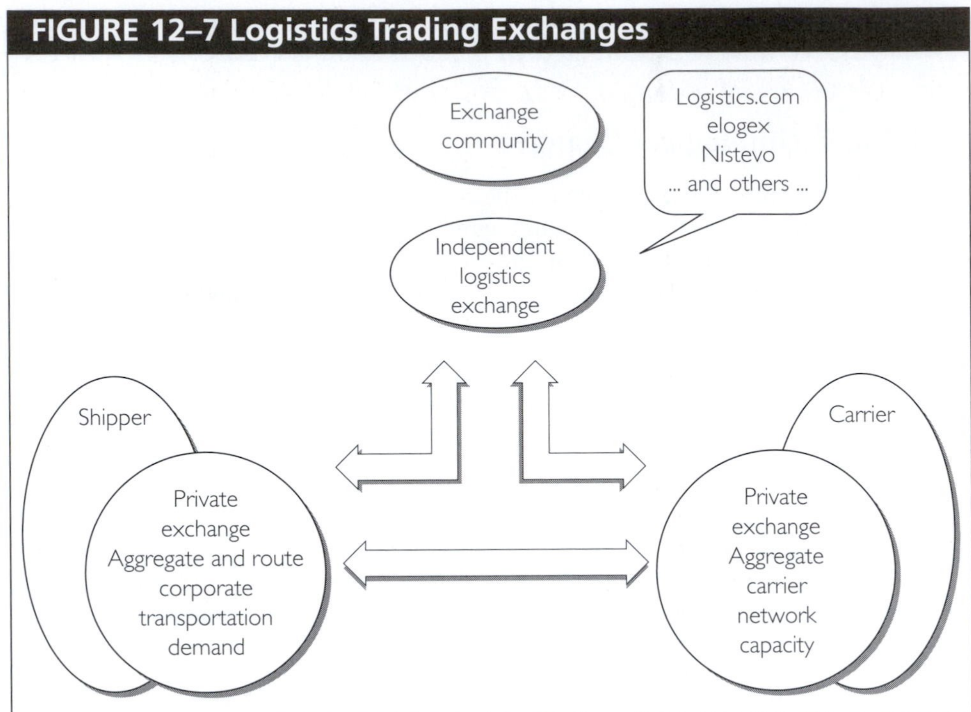

Source: Adapted from AMR Research, John Fontanella (2000).

increased working capital, and reduced operating costs. From a technology perspective, the sharing of resources among members helps to diffuse the overall cost throughout the full range of participating firms.

Figure 12–7 provides a perspective on trading exchanges and trading communities that is relevant to transactions involving logistics services. The key participants are the shipper, the carrier, and the exchange community. In addition to desired improvements in terms of overall efficiency and effectiveness, a high priority is attached to meaningful coordination and collaboration among the parties involved.

Intelligent Marketplaces. This step is the most sophisticated in terms of those suggested by Figure 12–6 and represents a logical extension of the trading communities. It is anticipated that these marketplaces, led by innovative software providers, consultancies, and service providers, will be characterized by four elements:

- *Tools.* Increased reliance on software tools will enable members to optimize the entire network.
- *Technology.* Intelligent marketplaces will equip all participants with sophisticated tools that facilitate collaboration.
- *Integration.* These communities will experience greater collaboration and seamless integration of key supply chain processes.
- *Flexibility.* Trades, transactions, and solutions will consider operational flexibility components such as equipment availability. This will help to dampen the primary, overriding concern for price that is frequently observed.

On The Line

ShipChem—How E-Commerce Is Changing Supply Chain Relationships

Sometimes, the "whole is greater than the sum of its parts." Take for example, the Internet logistics company ShipChem, formed by Eastman Chemical and Global Logistics Technology (a.k.a. G-Log). Essentially, the company represents the result of Eastman Chemical outsourcing its entire logistics operation. This is an exceptionally significant initiative by one of the world's largest chemical companies, a firm with approximately $5 billion in sales that already is a recognized industry leader in supply chain management. In fact, the creation of ShipChem represents an innovative integration of traditional business capabilities with the power of true, business-to-business electronic commerce. Representing a global logistics portal for chemicals shippers, ShipChem manages all orders and shipments as a single, integrated global logistics process across the multi-enterprise supply chain.

With reference to the "sum of its parts," a competency of ShipChem is its ability to integrate the capabilities of multiple partnerships with a variety of software packages to meet the needs of its customers. In addition to the G-Log functionality with a ShipChem interface, other capabilities include international trade logistics capabilities, international document management, technical support, and activities such as freight forwarding, customs brokerage, warehousing, and distribution.

Beyond the needed logistics services that ShipChem is able to offer to chemicals shippers, it also would like to take over entire shipping departments. In fact, this is what already has been done, as Eastman Chemical has outsourced the full range of its logistics needs to ShipChem. Also, since this responsibility will involve the management by ShipChem of Eastman's relationships with third party logistics providers, the company is essentially a provider of 4PL services.[1]

Clearly, ShipChem is not a typical Internet start-up company. While many firms in today's marketplace may be looking for the "quick hits," Eastman's commitment to the success of this venture is evidence of how serious companies have become in terms of leveraging the power of the Internet. Using the ShipChem model, Eastman and G-Log believe they will be able to solve many of the logistics problems that chemicals logistics shippers have been facing for years. Following its start-up, ShipChem's intention was to expand its offerings through an all-Internet-based product, "with no fancy IT integration." This is consistent with ShipChem's highest priority which is to serve its chemical industry customers, and to be viewed as a "neutral logistics portal." This initiative is one that combines traditional and electronic methods of doing business in a meaningful and effective manner.

[1]4PL and Fourth Party Logistics are registered trademarks of Accenture, Inc.

Source: Adapted from Kathleen Hickey, "ShipChem, G-Log Work Together and With Others to Create a Tasty Ensemble," *Traffic World* (18 September 2000): 54.

Contemporary Logistics Information Technologies

contemporary technologies

Aside from the Internet-based technologies just discussed, there are a number of information technologies that are in common use throughout the logistics and supply chain areas. Several of the more prominent ones are listed here, along with a brief description of each:

- *Bar coding.* Represents the most commonly used automatic identification technology. Considering that there are numerous bar-code symbologies, or standards, in use today, consistency of technologies is essential for moving product effectively and efficiently throughout supply chains.

- *Electronic data interchange.* EDI is the organization-to-organization, computer-to-computer exchange of business data in a structured, machine-processable format. The purpose of EDI is to eliminate duplicate data entry and to improve the speed and accuracy of information flow by linking computer applications between companies.[19] Figure 12–8 contrasts the use of EDI versus more traditional methods of information flow.
- *XML.* Short for *extensible markup language,* XML is a method of packing information for movement on the Internet. This is a highly efficient way to package information, such that it can be readily accessible to any person or company having Internet or Web-based capabilities. The potential of XML is that over time it will prove to be a preferred substitute to the use of electronic data interchange.

data management

- *Data management.* The use of handheld devices for data management is popular today, as is the use of devices for optical scanning. Also, the use of CD-ROM has emerged as a significant factor in data management activity.
- *Imaging.* Another technology that significantly impacts logistics is image processing, which allows a company to scan, or take electronic photographs of, essential documents. These images then may be communicated as may be needed or stored centrally until their use is necessary. This technology is used frequently by transportation firms that are asked to provide proof of delivery by many of their customers. By having a consignee sign an electronic pad, a facsimile of the signature is automatically digitized and stored for

FIGURE 12–8 EDI versus Traditional Methods

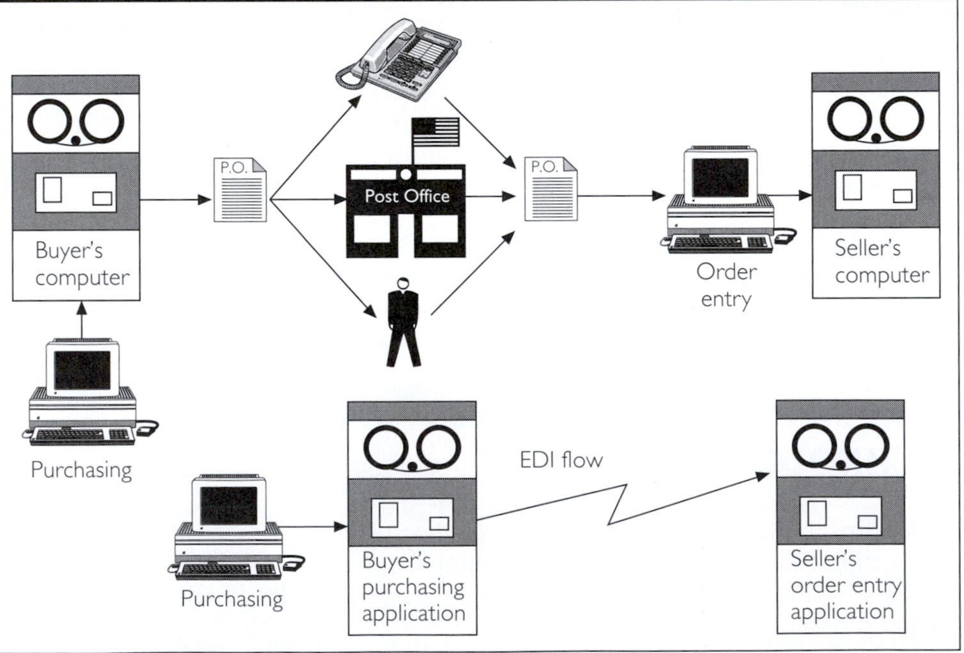

Source: Margaret A. Emmelhainz, *Electronic Data Interchange: A Total Management Guide* (New York: Van Nostrand Reinhold, 1990), 5. Used with permission.

future reference. When necessary, a copy of the signature can easily be downloaded to provide proof of delivery.

- *Artificial intelligence/expert systems*. The use of *artificial intelligence* (AI) and expert systems is becoming increasingly prevalent in logistics today. AI has been described as the portion of computer science that is concerned with making machines do things that would require intelligence if done by humans, and also as the "development of computers that perform functions that people perform."[20] An *expert system* is a computer program that "mimics a human expert"; by studying the methods and information used by human experts, an expert system can help to solve problems, identify alternatives, and provide advice that is comparable to that of the human expert.
- *RF technology.* Particularly useful in the warehouse or distribution center, radio frequency, or RF, "allows users to relay information via electromagnetic energy waves from a terminal to a base station, which is linked in turn to a host computer. The terminals can be placed at a fixed location, mounted on a forklift truck, or carried in a worker's hand."[21] When combined with a bar-code inventory system for identifying inventory items, an RF system can update inventory records in "real time." This results in significant improvement to the quality of order-picking and shipping accuracy.

  The experience of Microsoft Corporation, in Redmond, Washington, for example, was that implementation of an RF-based bar-code system for tracking stored product improved inventory accuracy from 95 percent to well over 99 percent.[22]

remote access

- *Computers on board and satellite tracking.* In essence, the principles of RF technology sometimes translate into "on-board" communications and computer capabilities. A major difference, however, is that communications are facilitated by two orbiting satellites, one that serves as a communications link between driver and dispatcher, for example. The other serves as a resource to track the vehicle, which provides the dispatcher with continuous knowledge of the whereabouts of the vehicle and, thus, the ability to determine whether or not a shipment is on time. Through this same on-board capability, the driver has access to computerized capabilities, such as "global positioning" that provides the driver with a real-time knowledge of the truck's current location and directions to intended destinations.

LOGISTICS INFORMATION SYSTEM

The logistics information system may be defined as:

> An interacting structure of people, equipment, and procedures that together make relevant information available to the logistics manager for the purposes of planning, implementation, and control.[23]

LIS subsystems

Figure 12–9 highlights the relationships among the logistics information system (LIS), the elements of the logistics environments, and the logistics decision-making process. The diagram shows four principal subsystems, or modules, that constitute the logistics information system: planning, execution, research and intelligence, and reports and outputs. Collectively, these systems should provide the logistics manager with timely and accurate information for the basic management

FIGURE 12–9 Logistics Information System

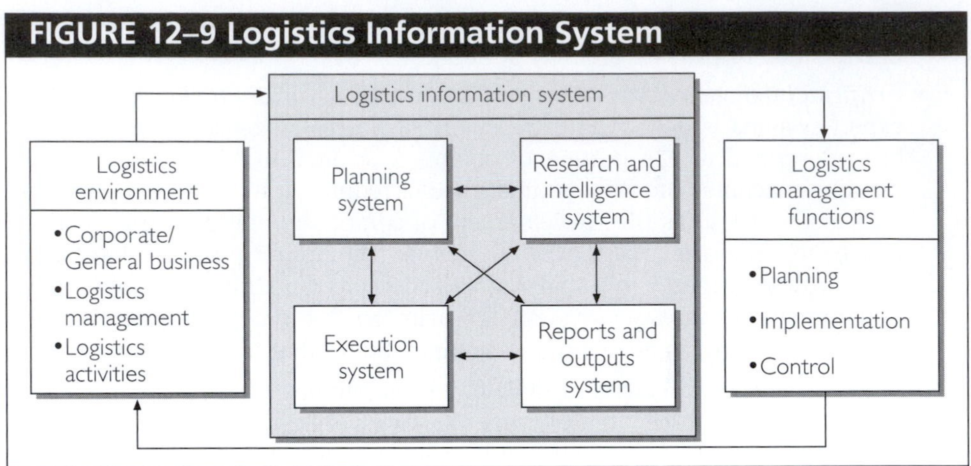

Source: Adapted from Philip Kotler, *Marketing Management: Analysis, Planning, and Control,* 5th ed. (Englewood Cliffs, N.J.: Prentice-Hall, 1984), 189.

functions of planning, implementation, and control.[24] These modules are discussed in the sections that follow.

Planning System

Figure 12–10 overviews the functional scope of information technologies for supply chain planning and supply chain execution. In addition to identifying example technologies that characterize each of these important elements of the logistics information system, the figure suggests the decision scope and likely time horizons that are relevant to each.

decision support

In earlier editions of this text, the technologies that comprise the *planning system* were referred to as *decision support* technologies, where the decision support system was defined as an "interactive, computer-based system that provides data and analytic models to help decision makers solve unstructured problems—those with many difficult-to-define variables." Essentially, this system represents a comprehensive set of computer-oriented tools designed to help managers make better decisions and gain broader insight into issues that are strategic to the conduct of logistics and supply chain activities.

As suggested in Figure 12–10, the planning technologies relate to such needs as network design, demand planning and forecasting, strategic sourcing, production planning and scheduling, and distribution planning. Several of these are discussed more fully in chapters of this text that relate more directly to the types of decisions to be made.

Logistics Functional Databases. Effective utilization of systems for logistics and supply chain planning requires a comprehensive database that contains the types of information that logistics managers need most to make effective decisions. Table 12–4 identifies some of the major trends in logistics data computerization that occurred between 1975 and 2000. A quick scan of this information suggests that the greatest recent increases in computerization of logistics data have occurred

FIGURE 12–10 Supply Chain Functional Scope: Planning and Execution

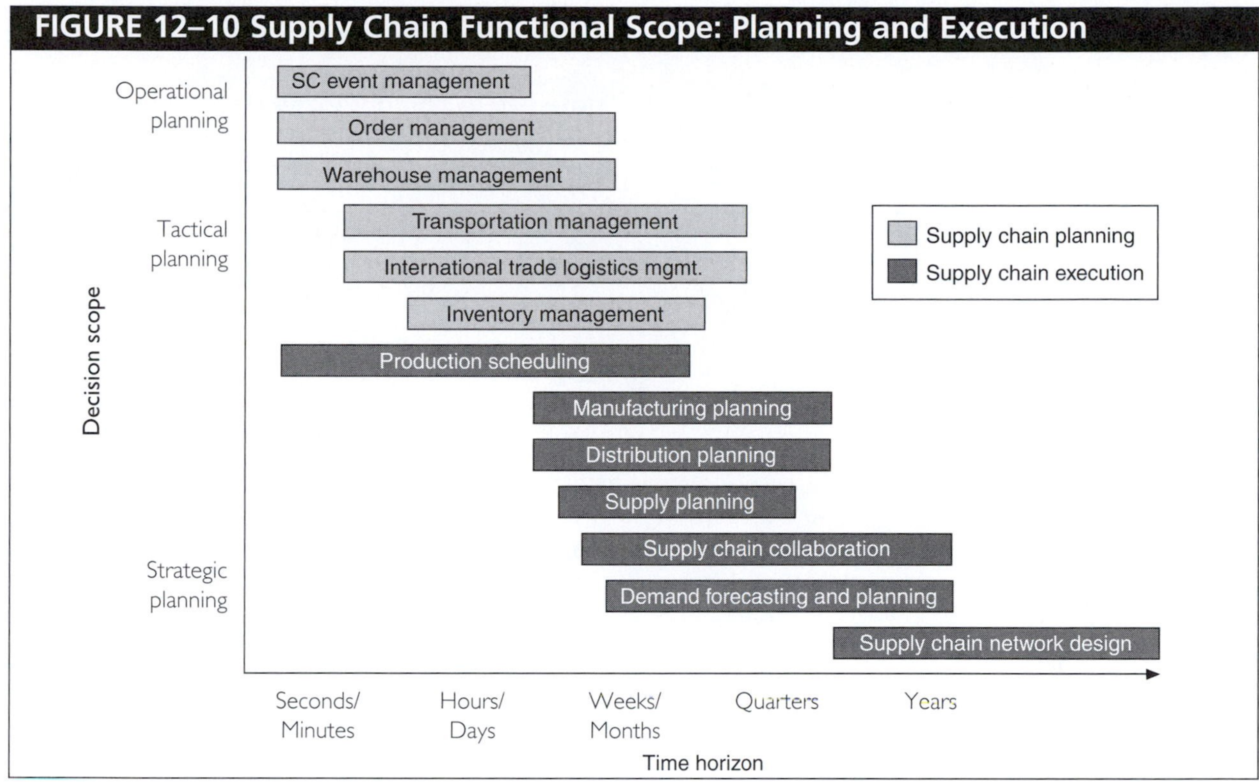

Source: Adapted from AMR Research, Inc. (2000).

in the transportation, inventory, and product areas, with the warehousing and customer areas showing less progress.

relational database management

Once priorities have been established for data acquisition, plans should be made so that the data files will be available for use in various types of analyses, as well as for manager inquiry. The database management approach used should first identify the logical relationships among the individual data elements and then recapture these elements into a logical database. Thus, the term *relational database management* has become a very popular and descriptive term that is in common use today.

modeling approaches

Types of Modeling Approaches. As is discussed in greater detail in Chapter 14, models can be classified generally as optimization, simulation, or heuristic. Simply stated, *optimization* approaches search for "best" solutions, *simulation* models replicate the functioning of the logistics network, and *heuristic* techniques are able to accommodate broad problem definitions but do not provide optimum solutions.

Table 12–5 arrays three logistics time horizons (strategic, tactical, and operational) against several functional areas of logistics. This diagram shows that virtually every logistics area requires significant decisions in each of the three time frames. Logistics modeling needs flexible, capable approaches. The approaches and technologies that comprise the LIS planning system can be effective in helping to analyze problems such as those suggested in Table 12–5.

TABLE 12–4 Trends in Logistics Data Computerization

Logistics Data Element	% Contained in Computerized Database				
	1975	1982	1987	1992/3	2000
Transportation					
Shipping open order files	84	85	89	92	94
Shipped manifest/bill of lading	49	55	70	71	83
Carrier files	57	53	64	66	75
Freight bill payment	51	56	62	63	71
Freight rates	45	36	61	63	71
Shipment schedules	34	51	57	59	70
Transit times	35	30	35	37	52
Warehousing					
Handling costs	30	31	42	41	47
Storage costs	29	28	39	39	41
Inventory					
Inventory levels	84	93	94	93	97
Purchasing open order files	51	71	80	88	95
Deleted order files	41	69	71	80	81
Back orders	74	74	75	78	85
Forecasted sales	65	67	72	68	69
Carrying costs	29	38	43	43	42
Stockout costs	7	10	15	17	14
Customer					
Names and locations	92	97	97	98	98
Financial limits	60	72	77	77	80
External market data	28	25	33	32	31
Product					
Master order files	24	89	90	93	97
Product descriptions	83	94	94	90	95
Production costs	60	71	70	69	71
Packaging costs	34	41	45	47	56

Source: Craig M. Gustin, "Logistics Information Systems: Progress Made During the Last Decade," *1993 Council of Logistics Management Annual Conference Proceedings* (Oak Brook, Ill.: Council of Logistics Management, 1993), 166; and Craig M. Gustin, Stephen M. Rutner, and Brian J. Gibson, "An Overview of Current Supply Chain Information Systems," presentation at 2000 Annual Conference of the Council of Logistics Management, New Orleans, La.

Execution System

The technologies included in the LIS *execution system* are those that are responsible for the short-term, day-to-day functioning of the logistics system. Included are technologies that help to manage activities in areas such as warehousing, transportation, international trade, and inventory. Also included are the range of capabilities needed

TABLE 12–5 Logistics Decisions

Subjects of Descriptions	Nature of Decisions		
	Strategic	**Tactical**	**Operational**
Forecasting	• Long range • New products • Demographic shifts	• 6–12 months • Seasonality • Marketing impacts	• 12–16 weeks • Promotions • Trends
Network design/analysis	• Plant and DC locations • Sourcing alternatives	• Public warehouses—usage and assignments • Inventory positioning	• Customer reassignments • Contingency planning
Production planning	• Production mix • Equipment required • Equipment location	• Production mix • Inventory vs. overtime • Crew planning	• Contingency planning
Materials planning	• Materials and technology alternatives	• Stockpiling & contracts • Shortage analyzer • Distribution plans	• Purchasing • Inventory levels • Material releases
Production scheduling	• Economic analyses—dedicated lines vs. multiproduct	• 6–12 month production schedules	• Daily/weekly production schedules
Dispatching	• Fleet sizing and configuration	• Carrier contracts • Equipment location	• Daily/weekly loading and delivery plans • Billing

Source: Richard F. Powers, "Optimization Models for Logistics Decisions," *Journal of Business Logistics* 10, no. 1 (1989): 108. Used with permission.

to effectively manage the customer orders that should be responsible for the initiation of supply chain activities. Further detail concerning order-processing and order-management processes was included earlier in Chapter 3.

advances in technology

There have been recent, significant advances in the development and utilization of technologies for logistics and supply chain execution. In many cases, these technologies have been Web-enabled and are accessible through a number of exchanges, communities, and applications service providers. In the transportation management area, for example, a number of Web-enabled resources have emerged to help with this important responsibility. Included among these are companies such as Nistevo, Logistics.com, elogex, and so on.

Overall, industry estimates suggest significant increases in on-line purchasing of direct materials needed by manufacturing firms. Essentially, this activity is representative of those in the category of supply chain execution. Referring to Figure 12–11, it is apparent that companies anticipate significant increases in the extent to which the Internet facilitates the purchasing of parts and materials used directly in manufacturing processes.

FIGURE 12–11 Direct Materials Purchasing Moves On-Line

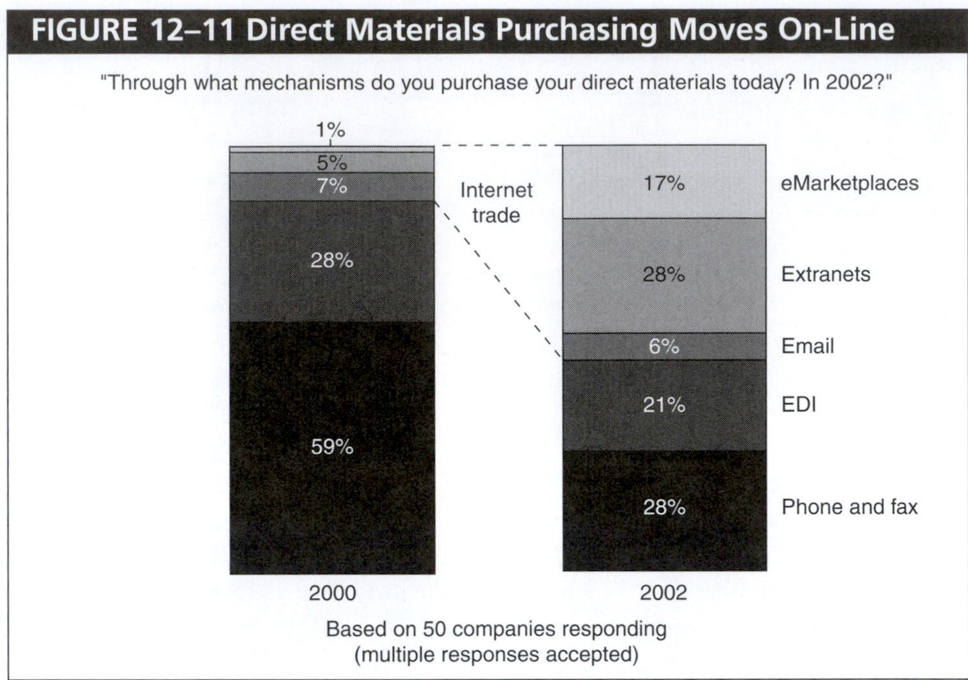

Source: On-Line Supply Chain Realities (Cambridge, Mass.: Forrester Research, Inc., 2000), 3.

Research and Intelligence System

To effectively manage activities within the logistics manager's responsibility, the logistics manager must have useful information relating to three distinct, yet related, environments. These include (1) the macro, or external, environment; (2) the interfirm environment, as characterized by a firm's distribution channels; and (3) the micro, or interfirm, environment. The LIS *research and intelligence system* scans the environment and makes observations and conclusions available throughout the logistics area and the whole firm.

approaches

Environmental Scanning. The logistics manager may properly scan the environment in four recognized ways:[25]

- *Undirected viewing.* General exposure to information where the manager has no specific purpose in mind
- *Conditioned viewing.* Directed exposure, not involving active search, to a more or less clearly identified area of information type
- *Informal search.* A relatively limited and unstructured effort to obtain specific information or information for a specific purpose
- *Formal search.* A deliberate effort—usually following a preestablished plan, procedure, or methodology—to secure specific information or information relating to a specific issue

Also, we can consider the environmental scanning process to be *irregular* (focusing on historical events typically in a reactive manner); *regular* (basically anticipatory, including approaches such as customer surveys); or *continuous* (generally

SUPPLY CHAIN TECHNOLOGY

HEINEKEN REDEFINES COLLABORATIVE PLANNING

Heineken USA, the largest beer importer in the United States, is a subsidiary of Heineken NV, the world's second-largest brewer. Heineken recognized the need to efficiently process sales forecasts and orders. As a global company, Heineken traditionally had a long lead time in getting forecasts in and product distributed throughout the United States and the world. The company's objective was to reduce the time between when an order is placed and when it is delivered (i.e., the order cycle) from ten to twelve weeks to between four and six weeks.

Heineken decided to implement a supply chain management system to replace the old way of dealing with its distributors. In the past, district managers would sit down with distributors to plan orders three months in advance. The district manager then would fax orders over to Heineken's U.S. headquarters, where the order would be transmitted to the company's brewery and world headquarters in Amsterdam, the Netherlands. As a result, it frequently took ten to twelve weeks for a distributor to receive an order that had been placed—an unacceptable length of order cycle.

To counter this problem, Heineken decided to implement an *Extranet,* a private network that connects Heineken with its customers and/or suppliers using an Internet technology. The system also can be used as an Intranet, connecting salespeople to the central database. Calling the system HOPS (Heineken Operational Planning System), Heineken can do real-time forecasting and ordering interaction with its distributors. This Internet-enabled, collaboration solution adopted by Heineken eliminates order taking via telephone, hand calculations, or faxing, all of which can lead to human error. Distributors log on to the customized Web pages using a standard browser and Internet connection. Once they are on-line, they can view their sales forecast, modify their order, and submit their order to Heineken. Order submissions are available in real time at the Heineken brewery in Europe, which can make any needed adjustments to its brewing and shipment schedules. Also, the Internet interface can facilitate the sending of E-mail to send out broadcasts of problems, new products, or company newsletters. Other benefits of on-line collaborative planning are lower procurement costs, smaller inventories, and shorter cycle times.

Heineken's new collaborative planning has reduced order cycle times from three months to four weeks, cut inventory overall by 40 percent, and simplified planning for its distributor customers. According to a company official, "because we have reduced lead time, we can produce our product closer to the time when we will need to get it to the customer, so that the product in the market will be much fresher." Heineken anticipated payback from this initiative within half a year, and that is what they experienced.

Source: Adapted from "Heineken Redefines Collaborative Planning," *Supplement to Food Logistics* (July/August 2000) Supplement: 44–45.

longer lasting and representing an ongoing process, such as the use of customer advisory boards).[26]

knowledge management

Knowledge Management. To maximize the results of an environmental scanning process, the logistics manager should include several key information sources in a comprehensive monitoring system. First are logistics area employees, as well as other people employed throughout the firm. Sales/account executives, for example, are in an excellent position to gather strategically valuable customer-related and competitive information, once the logistics manager tells them exactly what it needed. Similarly, fleet drivers can frequently gather valuable information on the loading dock, if they simply know what to look for. Second, channel partners such as suppliers, customers, carriers, and warehouse managers represent valuable sources of additional environmental information. These firms are usually very willing to share their environmental observations and perceptions, once asked to do so. Third, either an internal function or an outside consultant or advisory firm should perform some type of ongoing environmental monitoring and evaluation. Many firms find that the selective use of external firms to assist in this process can provide an extremely objective and thorough environmental scanning and evaluation.

In addition to these ideas, it is also advisable to identify, in a retrievable format, details concerning logistics and supply chain initiatives that have been implemented elsewhere in the firm. This is particularly helpful for firms that are multidivisional and that operate in a number of disparate geographical areas of the world.

It is becoming increasingly popular for firms to dedicate an information resource, such as a Web site, to provide access to the types of information just discussed. At Coca-Cola, for example, the ASK System (*always seeking knowledge*) is an internal capability that captures and disseminates such information on a firm-wide basis.[27]

Discussed earlier in Chapter 3, and included among the types of planning systems outlined earlier in this chapter, the firm's forecasting abilities are a key element of its research and intelligence system. Considering today's objective of moving to customer-responsive, "pull-based" replenishment systems, the availability of accurate forecast information is of increasing significance.

Reports and Outputs System

types of reports

The *reports and outputs system* is the fourth major component of the logistics information system. Many logistics managers believe that most reports and other forms of output do not communicate effectively. As a result, many good ideas, many useful research reports, and many managerial recommendations simply go unnoticed for lack of proper communication.

Reports may serve purposes such as planning, operations, and control. For example, *planning reports* may include information such as sales trends and forecasts, other market information, and economic projections of cost factors. Planning reports include both historic and future-based information.

Operating reports inform managers and supervisors about matters such as current on-hand inventories, purchase and shipping orders, production scheduling and control, and transportation. Typically, these reports make information available to managers on a real-time basis.

Control reports may summarize cost and operating information over relevant time periods, compare budgeted and actual expenses, and provide direct transportation costs. They serve as a basis for strategically redirecting operating approaches and tactics.

Considering the current emphasis on integration, collaboration, and synchronization of activities among firms comprising the supply chain, there is significant interest in assuring the availability of relevant information at points throughout the supply chain when and where it may be needed. As would be expected, there is a high priority on the development of suitable information technologies to see that this is accomplished.

Overall, it is important to remember that communication occurs only if the communicated information keys into a person's (or business's) values and responds directly to the decisions that managers need to make. In actual business practice, the molding of people's expectations about the information contained in reports and outputs is essential. Incorporating the time-honored features of effective business communications—brevity, exception reporting, and getting to the "heart of the matter"—is also important. People have neither the time nor the inclination to deal with ineffective communication. In the firm's logistics and supply chain areas, high-quality communication through appropriate reports and outputs should be the standard, not the exception.

Whether the underlying information relates to managerial planning, operations, or control, the effectiveness of communications significantly impacts how well the firm's logistics function achieves its mission.

Adapting to New Information Technologies

search for new technologies

At many firms, a relentless search is underway for information technologies that will lead to efficiency, effectiveness, and differentiation. According to the 1999 Survey of Career Patterns conducted for the Council of Logistics Management, new technologies have become critical to compete and certain new technologies may help to create competitive advantages.[28] Respondents to the survey were asked to identify and rank the most critical "emerging" technologies that need to be adopted by their companies in the next five years to remain competitive. Figure 12–12 identifies the six emerging technologies that were thought to be most critical by study respondents.

Among the technologies listed, it is apparent that E-commerce and the Internet/WWW were viewed as most essential. Ranking just after these was *groupware*, which refers to a growing set of information technologies that enhance people's interactions. Examples of groupware are E-mail, videoconferencing, electronic bulletin boards, LotusNotes, and so on. These are a welcome addition to existing technologies such as fax and voice mail.

As is the case with a move to any innovative technology, there is no shortage of challenges and opportunities. The following considerations are relevant to the process of adapting to new information technologies such as those we have discussed:

- It is important to have a scientific as well as an intuitive understanding of *customer and supplier information requirements*, as well as those of all supply chain participants. It is necessary for information technologies to be flexible and adaptable, depending on the specific set of needs being served.
- It is necessary to recognize that implementation delays can result from *a lack of coordination and integration among key logistics and supply chain processes*. Inconsistencies and lengthy order cycles can result, for example, from the failure to synchronize logistics operational versus coordination activities.
- It is important to see that the *logistics organizational strategies move from a functional to a process orientation*. Emphasis on the latter assures a more meaningful measurement of relevant processes and assures more timely and accurate process feedback and process knowledge.

FIGURE 12–12 Critical Emerging Technologies

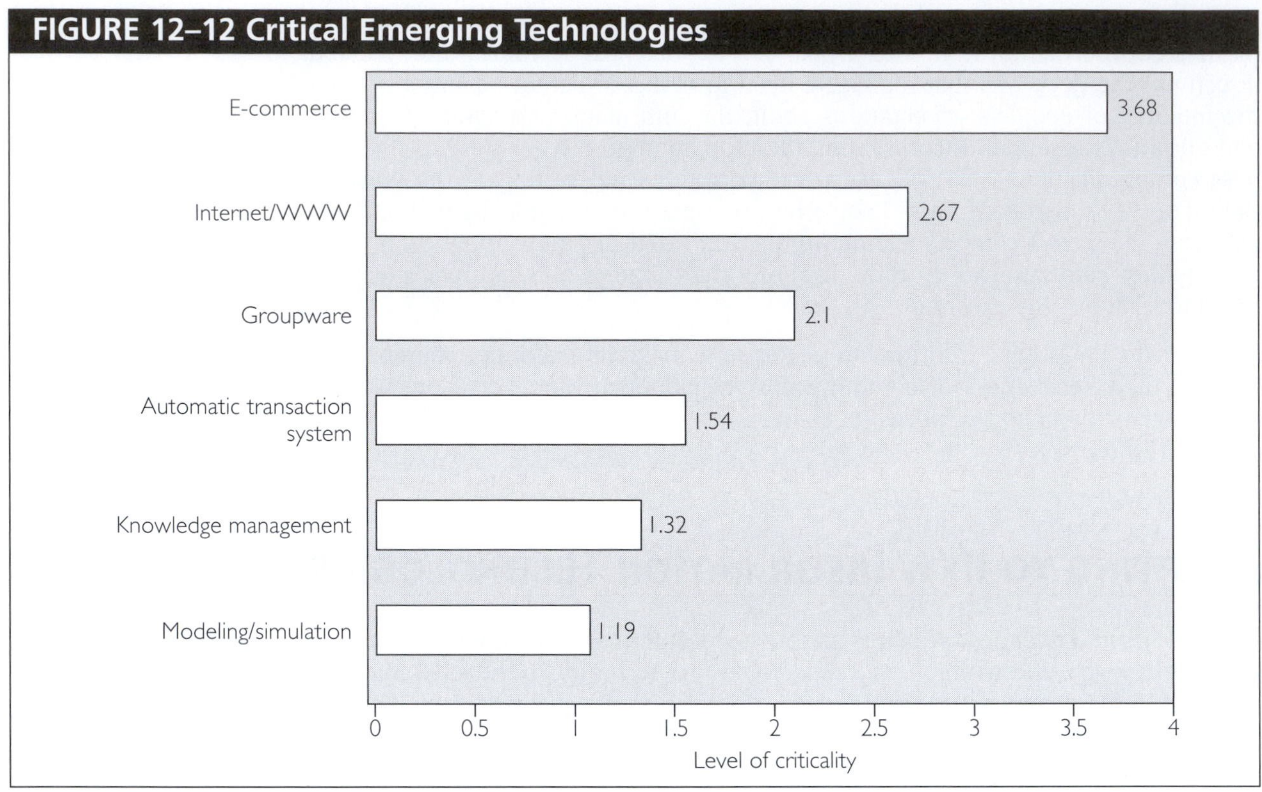

Source: The Ohio State University, *1999 Survey of Career Patterns in Logistics* (Columbus, Ohio: The Ohio State University, Supply Chain Management Research Group, 1999).

- Inevitably, early implementation efforts may suffer due to *poor data or the nonavailability or nonsharing of future data* pertaining, for example, to future orders, forecasts, and target production schedules.
- It is important that the organization have the *financial resources* needed to assure a smooth, full implementation. Also, a *willingness among employees to accept and make use of new technologies* is critical to this process. A recent trend among firms has been to develop business strategies designed to make employees more enthusiastic and less resistant to change.
- It is necessary for firms to create opportunities for *interaction and team efforts among logistics managers and those others most knowledgeable about information technologies.* Logistics managers need to know more about the art and science of information systems, and information systems specialists must develop greater insight into the types of problems faced on a daily basis by those involved in managing the logistics process.

Overall, firms must recognize the strategic value of having timely and accurate logistics information. Companies must consider the logistics information system as strategically important to the overall firm. As a result, efforts at integrating logistics information needs with the capabilities of ERP systems must be successful. Also, corporate management should agree that it is important to develop logistics information strategies, just as they would develop strategies relating to new products or capital expenditures.

Summary

- The effectiveness of information management is central and critical to the successful execution of logistics and supply chain responsibilities and processes.
- The most important information need relates to customers.
- Based on the results of a current study, the most critical information systems issue is "connecting to customers, suppliers, and partners electronically."
- Quality of information depends on three factors: availability of information, accuracy of information, and effectiveness of communication.
- There are identifiable steps in the process of building an effective information system, and there are a number of key types of people and processes that are involved.
- The emergence of new, dynamic customer requirements has been largely responsible for the emergence of innovative, contemporary logistics networks.
- Effective use of available information technologies may result in supply chain "disintermediation," which may lead to improved supply chain operations.
- Changes and advances in available information technologies have had significant impacts on logistics and supply chain management. In addition to a number of new and innovative logistics information technologies, significant benefits have been derived from Web sites, exchanges, trading communities, and intelligent marketplaces.
- The logistics information system consists of four modules or systems: planning, execution, research and intelligence, and reports and outputs.
- There are a number of considerations that can facilitate the adaptation of new information technologies. Critical among these is for all involved to have a sound understanding of both information technologies and relevant logistics and supply chain processes.

Study Questions

1. In what ways are the availability of capable information systems related to the effective management of logistics and supply chain processes?
2. What are some of the most prevalent issues involving information systems today? Which are of greatest concern to companies?
3. What is meant by "quality" of logistics information?
4. Discuss how an "information systems architecture" can be used to build an information system.
5. What impacts on logistics and supply chain activity are being created by the "connected" economy?
6. How does the "Customer-Centric Value Web Model" relate to the availability of new and innovative information technologies?

7. Explain what is meant by supply chain "disintermediation" and how it may occur?
8. What information technologies are recognized as being particularly useful and relevant to the logistics process?
9. Discuss a logistics information system in terms of its purpose and components.
10. What is the objective of the research and intelligence subsystem of the LIS? What activities are performed by this subsystem?
11. What are some of the key challenges to be faced by those individuals and firms involved with implementing new and innovative logistics information technologies?

NOTES

1. Portions of this discussion have been adapted from C. John Langley Jr., "Information-Based Decision Making in Logistics Management," *International Journal of Physical Distribution and Materials Management* 15, no. 7 (1985): 41–42.
2. Donald J. Bowersox, Patricia J. Daugherty, Cornelia L. Droge, Dale S. Rogers, and Daniel L. Wardlow, *Leading Edge Logistics: Competitive Positioning for the 1990s* (Oak Brook, Ill.: Council of Logistics Management, 1989).
3. For example, see Bernard J. LaLonde, Martha C. Cooper, and Thomas G. Noordewier, *Customer Service: A Management Perspective* (Oak Brook, Ill.: Council of Logistics Management, 1988), 37–70.
4. See David J. Closs, "Positioning Information in Logistics," Chapter 31 in *The Logistics Handbook* (New York: The Free Press, 1994), 699–713.
5. Craig M. Gustin, Stephen M. Rutner, and Brian J. Gibson, "An Overview of Current Supply Chain Information Systems," presentation at 2000 Annual Conference of the Council of Logistics Management. An overview of the study results is contained in Kathleen Hickey, "The Way We Are: Logistics Technology Trends . . . Highlighted by Study," *Traffic World* (9 October 2000): 39–41.
6. Computer Sciences Corporation, *13th Annual Critical Issues in Information Systems Management Survey* (Cambridge, Mass.: Computer Sciences Corporation, 2001). Available at http://www.csc.com
7. Computer Sciences Corporation, *Critical Issues in Information Systems Management for 1995* (Cambridge, Mass.: Computer Sciences Corporation, 1995).
8. Contents of this section are adapted from Langley, "Information-Based Decision Making in Logistics Management," 41–42.
9. Robert S. Kaplan, "Yesterday's Accounting Undermines Production," *Harvard Business Review* 62, no. 4 (July–August 1984): 95–101.
10. For example, see the following: Douglas M. Lambert and Howard M. Armitage, "Distribution Costs—The Challenge," *Management Accounting* (May 1979): 33-38; John L. Boros and R. E. Thompson, "Distribution Cost Accounting at PPG Industries," *Management Accounting* (January 1983): 54–60; and

Howard M. Armitage, "The Use of Management Accounting Techniques to Improve Productivity Analysis in Distribution Operations," *International Journal of Physical Distribution and Materials Management* 14, no. 1 (1984): 41–51. Although not specifically oriented to logistics and supply chain management, also see Robin Cooper and Robert S. Kaplan, "Measure Costs Right: Make the Right Decisions," *Harvard Business Review* 66, no. 5 (September–October 1988): 96–103.

11. Joseph Bonney, "More Logistics Tools Than They Can Use," *American Shipper* (October 1994): 58.

12. The issue of managerial communication in general is treated effectively in Peter F. Drucker, *Management: Tasks, Responsibilities, Practices* (New York: Harper & Row, 1974). This paragraph draws particularly on the content of Chapter 38, "Managerial Communications," 481–93.

13. Major portions of this section are contained in IBM Corporation, *Computer Integrated Logistics: CIL Architecture in the Extended Enterprise* (Southbury, Conn.: IBM Corporation, U.S. Transportation Industry Marketing, 1991), 6–7.

14. Portions of this section have been adapted from Closs, "Positioning Information in Logistics," 699–707.

15. Closs, "Positioning Information in Logistics," 706–07.

16. For additional detail, see IBM Corporation, *Computer Integrated Logistics: CIL Architecture in the Extended Enterprise* (Southbury, Conn.: IBM Corporation, U.S. Transportation Industry Marketing, 1991), 9–11.

17. Portions of this section have been adapted from Richard H. Thompson and Karl B. Manrodt, *Logistics @ Internet Speed: The Impact of E-Commerce on Logistics* (Knoxville, Tenn.: Cap Gemini Ernst & Young and The University of Tennessee, 2000).

18. "Customer-Centric Value Web® Model" is a registered trademark of Cap Gemini Ernst & Young.

19. Margaret A. Emmelhainz, "Electronic Data Interchange in Logistics," Chapter 33 in *The Logistics Handbook* (New York: The Free Press, 1994), 737.

20. James M. Masters and Bernard J. LaLonde, "The Role of New Information Technology in the Practice of Traffic Management," *The Logistics Handbook* (New York: The Free Press, 1994), 490.

21. James Aaron Cooke, "Technology Ups the Ante in the Technology Game," *Traffic Management* (April 1994): 66.

22. Ibid., 65–66.

23. This definition has been adapted from a definition of a marketing information system suggested in Philip Kotler, *Principles of Marketing,* 3d ed. (Englewood Cliffs, N.J.: Prentice-Hall, 1986), 87.

24. For an interesting discussion of logistics information systems, see Alan J. Stenger, "Information Systems in Logistics Management: Past, Present, and Future," *Transportation Journal* 26, no. 1 (Fall 1986): 65–82. In this discussion, logistics information is viewed as consisting of four groups: transaction systems, short-term scheduling and inventory replenishment systems, flow planning systems, and network planning systems.

25. Philip Kotler, *Marketing Management: Analysis, Planning, and Control,* 5th ed. (Englewood Cliffs, N.J.: Prentice-Hall, 1984), 192.

26. Liam Fahey and William R. King, "Environmental Scanning for Corporate Planning," *Business Horizons* 20, no. 4 (August 1977): 61–71.

27. ASK® is a registered trademark of Coca-Cola Corporation.

28. Bernard J. LaLonde and Terrance Pohlen, *1999 Survey of Career Patterns in Logistics* (Columbus, Ohio: Logistics Research Group, The Ohio State University, 1999).

CASE 12–1 ■ Peninsula Point, Inc.

In recent years, Peninsula Point, Inc., has emerged as a very successful merchandiser of contemporary fashion apparel for men and women. The company publishes a high-quality catalog that it sends to prospective customers, who then place orders by mail or by using a toll-free telephone number. The customer base consists principally of young couples with two incomes and no children. These customers typically receive catalogs from competitor firms such as L.L. Bean, Land's End, Eddie Bauer, and Orvis.

Although the catalog business is fiercely competitive, the catalog business is growing. People who are "just too busy" to shop in retail stores regard it as an appealing alternative. Purchasing apparel merchandise by catalog also seems to have an element of prestige in certain social circles.

To further connect with today's consumers, the company has developed an Internet-based capability, PeninsulaPoint.com that provides full catalog and ordering services for on-line customers. The breadth of product line is identical to that of the traditional catalog; the company's Web site offers a new and effective way to interact with customers.

Among companies of its kind, Peninsula Point is thought to offer the best product assortment, product quality, and customer service. Two critical customer service elements at Peninsula Point are that the company receives, packs, and ships orders in a timely manner and that product returns procedures are "customer friendly." Although the company accommodates product returns with little or no bother to the customer, this practice is expensive and of growing concern to upper-level management.

Peninsula Point does not produce any of the merchandise it sells. Instead, it contracts with manufacturers in Korea, Hong Kong, Taiwan, and Singapore to meet its largely seasonal product line needs. The company ships containerloads of labeled and pretagged merchandise by combination of ocean transportation and domestic inland motor freight to a centralized distribution center in Nashville, Tennessee. Subsequent movements to individual customers are made by UPS and Federal Express.

Peninsula Point executives consider themselves to be in the "logistics business." They feel that the company's logistical capabilities are a key to its excellent reputation in the marketplace. An area of nagging concern to Peninsula Point managers, however, is that consumer tastes and company product preferences are beginning to change very quickly, sometimes in the middle of a selling season. Only a continued ability to react quickly to changing marketplace needs will separate market leaders from the others.

Case Questions

1. In what ways should we consider the components of the logistics information system (as discussed in the chapter) important to Peninsula Point? What suggestions do you have for improving the company's logistics information system?
2. What types of logistics challenges do you feel may be associated with the use by customers of the company's on-line capability, PeninsulaPoint.com?
3. What macroenvironmental factors will be critical to Peninsula Point's future success? In what specific ways can the company develop logistics capabilities to address these factors?

CHAPTER 13

SUPPLY CHAIN PERFORMANCE MEASUREMENT

LEARNING OBJECTIVES

After reading this chapter, you should be able to do the following:

- Understand the scope and importance of performance measurement.
- Explain the characteristics of good performance measures.
- Discuss cost and service performance measurement and quantification.
- Understand transaction and revenue measurement and quantification.
- Explain supply chain channel measurement.
- Discuss overall supply chain metrics.

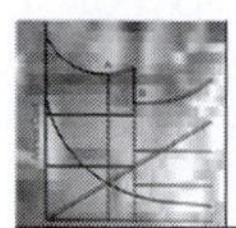

Logistics Profile

Micros and More: A Final Sequel

It was late on Friday afternoon, and Jim Gatto, COO, and Terry Edwards, CFO, were sitting in the conference room of Micros and More's office suite in a new office building in Port Matilda, Pennsylvania. Jim and Terry were tired since it had been another long week of twelve-hour days. Jim remarked to Terry, "We should feel good about the past fifteen months. We have surpassed our quarterly sales goal for the third quarter in a row and we seem to have resolved our problems with inventory. However, I must be getting paranoid in my old age because I am still concerned about our future viability."

Earlier in the year, Jim had been under great pressure from certain members of the board of directors to reduce inventory levels and to improve inventory turnover. Jim had attacked this problem with a group of Penn State interns who rationalized inventory based upon certain categories—cycle stock, seasonal stock, safety stock, etc. and had also developed an ABC classification and analysis of SKUs. The latter had proved to be particularly insightful because it clearly identified the slow moving SKUs that could be minimized or even eliminated from inventory.

The second major endeavor was undertaken by Don Warsing, a newly employed manager who instituted a thorough evaluation of the company's inventory. Don found that traditional EOQ techniques were being utilized without appropriate adjustments. Don also determined that the forecasting techniques being used by Micros and More were inadequate and contributed to the inventory problems. He recommended a demand planning approach with an emphasis upon a demand pull distribution system whereby computers were customized for customers after orders had been placed. Essentially, the system was based upon the approach that Dell Computer had made famous. Alliances with key vendors enabled the company to implement a JIT inventory approach on the inbound side of their manufacturing facilities. Vendors were provided real time order information that gave them advanced lead time on parts requirements. Components for popular computer models were assembled in advance by their vendors to reduce total lead time for customers.

Jim indicated to Terry that much had been accomplished during the past year and they should feel good about it. However, he admitted that he was frustrated because he was not certain how much improvement the company had really made. "Terry," he said, "we know that our sales are up, our profits have improved and our inventory turns have increased." Terry replied, "Well, what's the problem, Jim? The Board is pleased and the employees liked their recent bonus." "I know, I know," replied Jim, "but if the truth be known, we need more comprehensive performance measures. We need to have more detailed information to really understand our efficiency and effectiveness and to gauge our improvement more specifically. I remember my management professor at Penn State saying, 'If you can't measure it, you can't manage it.' We really do not know how good we are and what buttons to push to make significant improvements."

"Jim, this sounds like another study by several staff members," stated Terry. Jim nodded, "You are reading my mind again, Terry, and you are right on target. I read an interesting article in the *Harvard Business Review* about performance metrics on my last trip to Memphis. I feel that the euphoria we are feeling about our accomplishments over the past year is more subjective than objective. We need to be more precise about 'where we are' and 'where we have been' in order to chart a course for the future and measure our performance along the way. In particular, we need better metrics for logistics performance, but they have to be more comprehensive to evaluate not only our external customers but also our internal customers."

Terry agreed. "Okay, Okay, Jim. Let's pull in Lauren and Matt Weber to work with us, and make it an internal task force of four." Terry continued, "As a first step I will ask our friends at Penn State's Center for Supply Chain Research to put together a selection of readings on performance measures with an emphasis on logistics and supply chain management. We may want to consider bringing in Professor Novack to facilitate a brainstorming session and help us make a first cut at a set of appropriate metrics for success."

Introduction

The Micros and More logistics profile points out very important issues for all organizations irrespective of whether they are private or public, profit or non-profit. All organizations need performance measurements or metrics. Terry Edwards, the COO of Micros and More refers to a popular management principle—if you can't measure it, you can't manage it. Most organizations want to achieve efficiency in operations and effectiveness in dealing with their customers. But simply stating those two objectives is not adequate unless they have specific performance metrics that enable them to gauge their success in achieving these objectives.

For example, if you are a student and your parent or guardian indicates that they want you to achieve good grades while in college, what does that standard really mean? Is a "C" average good enough? It may be acceptable to the student but not to the parent or guardian. A more specific metric might be the expectation to maintain at least a "B" average. Obviously, grades are one metric that can be utilized to measure appropriate academic performance.

Dimensions of Performance Metrics

Performance measurement is more complex than it may appear initially. There is another management principle—metrics drive behavior, or, stated another way—what you measure is what you get. In other words, some seemingly good metrics could lead to an inappropriate outcome. For example, if a company established a metric of 'complete orders shipped' as their measure of performance for order fulfillment or customer service, they may find that orders are delayed until all of the items (SKUs) are available. Therefore, the orders may have an unacceptable lead time or replenishment time. However, the manager may be achieving an SKU order fill rate of 100%. The orders are complete, but the customers are not satisfied because it takes too long to fill their orders.

Also important to note is that performance measurements need to change over time; not only the performance standard, for example 85 percent, but also the individual metric, for example, percentage of orders shipped on time. With regard to the first example, the standard may change to 90 percent as new processes and/or technologies are introduced that enable the organization to consistently surpass the old 85 percent standard. The advocates of Total Quality Management (TQM) have taught us to focus upon continuous improvement, which should result in raising performance expectations over time.

The second aspect, indicated previously, regarding changing standards is also very important. Namely, the specific metric may have to change. Orders shipped on time and orders shipped complete were frequently used for performance metrics in logistics. However, as customer service received more and more attention, the metric was changed in many of the best companies to "orders delivered on time" and "orders delivered complete" which emphasized the more intense customer focus. In other words, the customer was more concerned about delivery than when the order left the warehouse or plant. These new standards also indicate an increased assumption of responsibility on the part of the seller. Another related example is the changes required by the supply chain approach. The logistics cost for an individual company in a supply chain may not be as important as the total supply chain logistics costs since global supply chains compete against each other.

We can expect that metrics will continue to evolve because of the change drivers that were discussed in Chapter 1. Expectations will increase for lead-time, inventory turns, etc. New standards will evolve to provide better measurement of the supply chain in its entirety and the role and relationships among companies in a supply chain. The evolution of supply chain management discussed in Chapter 1 is an indication of the type of change required. The migration from physical distribution (outbound) management to logistics (inbound and outbound) management to supply chain management has necessitated changing metrics. The supply chain approach, because of its boundary spanning coordination and integration, has presented some special challenges for developing appropriate metrics. We will discuss the special challenges of supply chain metrics later in this chapter.

One might ask the question of whether the focus on performance measurement is a recent event, and the answer to that question is a definite "no." Recall from Chapter 2 that the development of the physical distribution and logistics concepts was based upon systems theory with the specific application focused upon total cost analysis. Total cost is a measure of efficiency, and was the rationale supporting physical distribution management. Total cost was later used to support the logistics management approach.

The focus upon a total system cost required measuring the trade-off costs when a suggested change was made in one of the components or elements of the system, for example, switching from rail to motor transportation or adding a warehouse to the distribution system. Cost has long been recognized as an important metric for determining efficiency. However, as we have noted, there are some special challenges in determining which costs to measure and how to accurately determine these costs. The existence of fixed costs and common or overhead costs make specific measurement a daunting task in some instances.

Evolving from the lowest functional cost, for example, transportation to the lowest logistics system cost to the lowest pipeline or supply chain cost may seem complex. However, we also need to examine measures of effectiveness both internally and externally. The important message here is that performance measurement requires a comprehensive set of metrics and the importance of these measures will increase over time. Essentially, the supply chain manager needs a "dashboard" to check how the supply chain engine is performing. The "dashboard" should have multiple measures with no one measure being a single determinant of success. Also, there will exist trade-offs among the dashboard metrics and the processes that support them.

Figure 13–1 further explicates how the dimensions and importance of performance measurement has expanded. The figure clearly indicates that expectations have increased since the 1960s and 1970s and that in each of the decades identified there have been important drivers for better performance. Each new decade, however, built upon the improvements in the previous decade(s).

Figure 13–2 provides some additional perspectives on the complexity issue discussed previously. There are many measures or metrics that are and can be used to measure performance in logistics and supply chain systems. Figure 13–2 provides some insight into the various metrics utilized as well as their popularity among the

FIGURE 13–1 Raising the Performance Bar

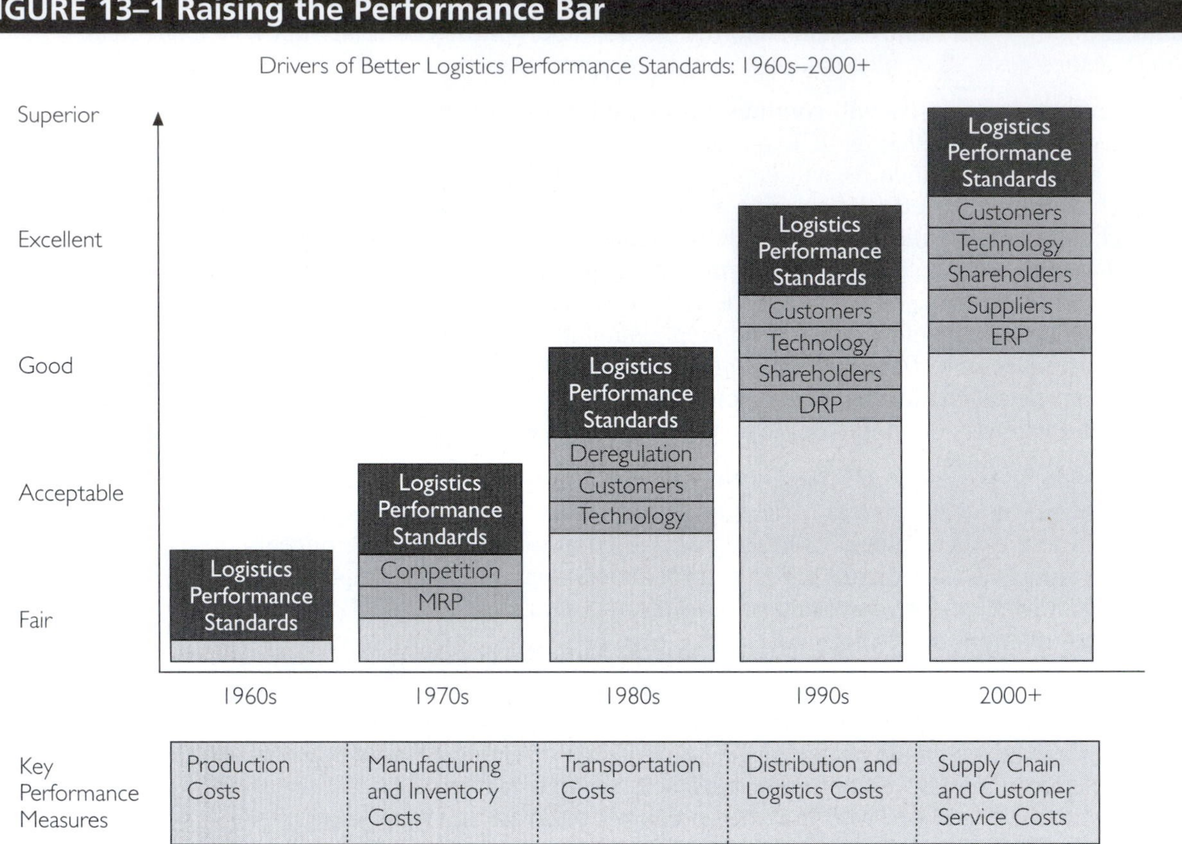

Source: J. S. Keebler, D. A. Durtsche, K. B. Manrodt, D. M. Ledyard, *Keeping Score*, Council of Logistics Management, 1999.

companies who replied to the survey. It is important, as a part of the discussion of performance measurement, to provide some more specific insights into how such metrics can be evaluated. This will be covered in the next section. Companies need to select metrics that are appropriate to their organization. Both the quality and the quantity of the metrics are important for performance measurement.

Overview of Performance Measurement[1]

Knowing what metrics to use is an important issue for performance measurement. Figure 13–2 provides a list of measures that have varying degrees of utilization among companies. The utilization rates indicate the popularity of the metrics but not necessarily their value or utility. Some better insights into the characteristics of good measures are needed. For example, some companies use metrics because they are easy to capture. Outbound freight cost, which is first on the list in Figure 13–2, is a good example of a measurement that is usually straight forward and easily obtainable. But what is the value of this metric? Does it drive appropriate decision making? If a manager decreases outbound freight cost, does it result in increased warehousing and/or inventory costs?

FIGURE 13–2 Measures Captured on a Regular Basis Within the Company

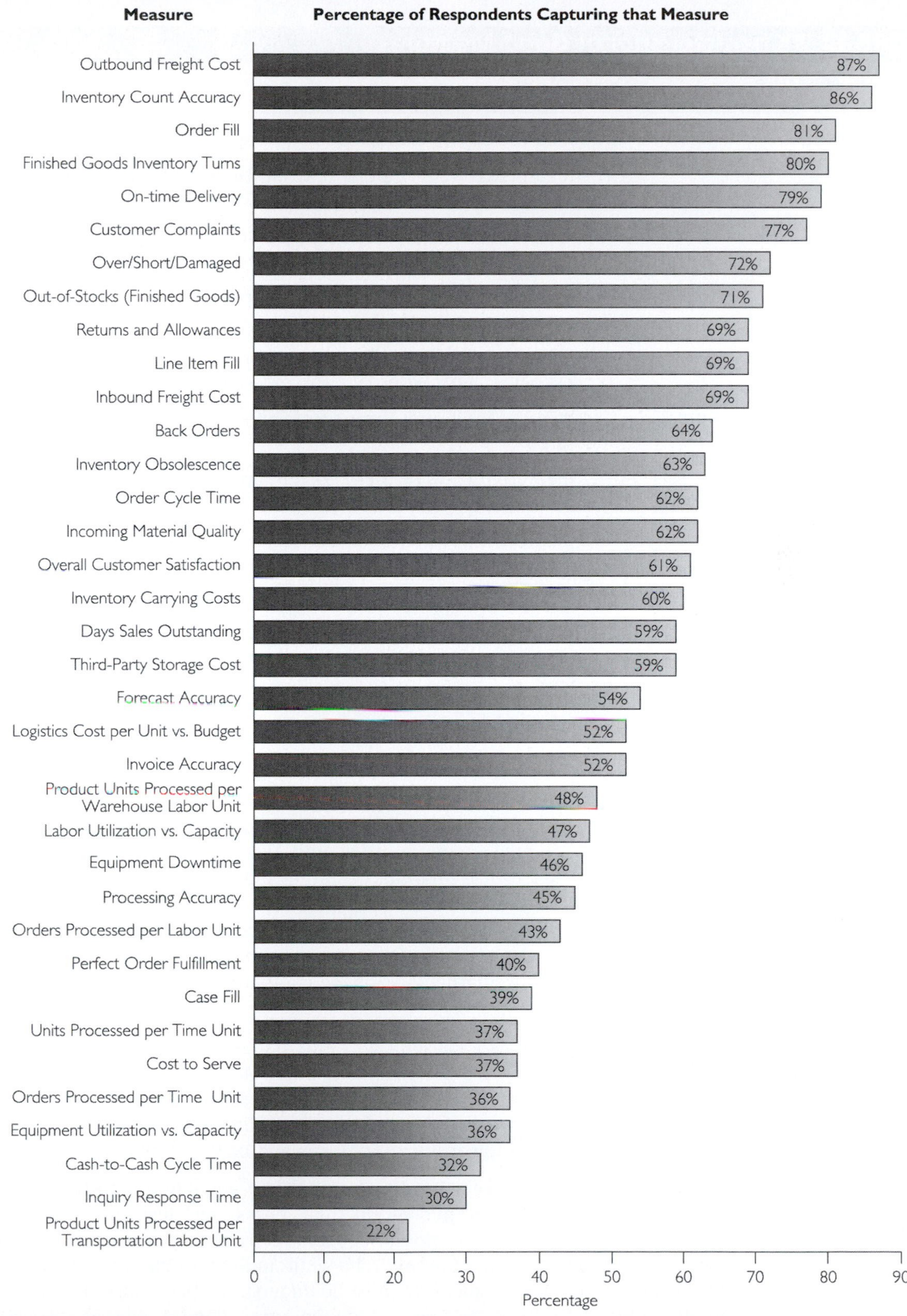

Source: CSC/University of Tennessee Logistics Survey, 1998.

FIGURE 13–3 Characteristics of Good Measures

A Good Measure	Description
• is quantitative	• The measure can be expressed as an objective value.
• is easy to understand	• The measure conveys at a glance what it is measuring, and how it is derived.
• encourages appropriate behavior	• The measure is balanced to reward productive behavior and discourage "game playing."
• is visible	• The effects of the measure are readily apparent to all involved in the process being measured.
• is defined and mutually understood	• The measure has been defined by and/or agreed to by all key process participants (internally and externally).
• encompasses both outputs and inputs	• The measure integrates factors from all aspects of the process measured.
• measures only what is important	• The measure focuses on a key performance indicator that is of real value to managing the process.
• is multidimensional	• The measure is properly balanced between utilization, productivity, and performance, and shows the trade-offs.
• uses economies of effort	• The benefits of the measure outweigh the costs of collection and analysis.
• facilitates trust	• The measure validates the participation among the various parties.

Source: Keeping Score: Measuring the Business Value of Logistics in the Supply Chain, CSC, University of Tennessee, CLM, 8.

Figure 13–3 provides some important insights into the characteristics of a good metric. While not all measurements are quantitative, it is usually a requirement for comparison purposes to use quantitative rather than qualitative measures. Qualitative statements of performance are subject to different interpretations. Quantitative measures are also consistent with the second characteristic in the figure; namely, it is easy to understand. Quantitative measures usually convey immediately what is happening, particularly as we compare them over time or use them for benchmarking.

The third characteristic is consistent with the management principle stated previously; namely, metrics drive behavior. The important aspect is having the appropriate metric in place so as not to encourage the wrong outputs. For example, if a warehouse manager is measured by cubic space utilization, she will keep the warehouse filled, which will lower inventory turns and drive up inventory costs.

The fourth characteristic of a good metric is that it should be readily apparent or visible to those individuals involved in the process. The fifth item supports the fourth. If employees help to define or develop metrics, they will understand them and be more likely to have "buy in." The sixth and eighth characteristics are also interrelated. While a good measure must be understandable, it also needs to incorporate inputs and outputs and be multidimensional. The last characteristics listed is also related since it indicates that the employees have "buy in." A good metric is believed to be valid. If there is "buy in" and credibility, the appropriate outcomes will follow.

The seventh characteristic relates to a previous statement; that is, do not use measures just because they are easy to develop. You need to measure the important aspects of the processes. This is also necessary to drive appropriate behavior. The ninth characteristic is also very important since it indicates that the benefits of the metric must be greater than the costs.

The characteristics that have been discussed are all interrelated and highly synergistic. They are a good reference to use for new and old metrics to try to determine if the metrics that have been identified have any shortcomings. They are high level and not specific but nevertheless very useful as a frame of reference for developing good performance metrics.

Another set of useful guidelines for logistics and supply chain performance is as follows:[2]

- *The metrics must be consistent with overall corporate strategy.* If the overall organizational strategy is based upon effectiveness in serving customers, a logistics strategy which emphasizes low cost or efficiency could be in conflict with expected corporate outcomes.
- *The metrics must focus upon customer needs and expectations.* For example, customers are not typically concerned about when orders are shipped from a warehouse. They are more likely to be interested in when the order arrived at the expected delivery point and whether the delivery time was consistent with their expectation. So measuring when the order was shipped may not be an effective metric.
- *Prioritize your metrics.* There are hundreds of performance measures associated with logistics and supply chain management. Companies need to select those metrics which are significant for their organization and their supply chain.
- *Focus upon processes not functions.* Logistics and supply chain metrics should be focused upon several key processes: planning, sourcing, making, and fulfilling. The metrics used should allow the organization to monitor the performance of these key processes. Ideally, this should happen across the boundaries of supply chain members to permit effective supply chain measurement.
- *Use a balanced approach in selecting and developing metrics.* In today's global environment with an emphasis upon supply chains, both internal and external measures are needed to gauge successful performance.
- *Precise cost measurement is an important aspect for gauging improvement.* Managing logistics and supply chain activities requires evaluating alternate scenarios with different cost trade-offs. Cost measurement accuracy is a must to allocate resources among competing needs in a company.
- *Use technology to enhance efficient performance measurement.* The explosion of technology during the 1990s has provided an opportunity for organizations to overcome some of the barriers, including cost, to effective performance measurement. Real time, data of high integrity, is an achievable goal with 21st century logistics related technology. Externally, customers are a primary focus as indicated in Chapter 4, but vendors may also be included. Internally, it is not sufficient just to focus upon logistics. The other major functional areas must be included, especially marketing, operations, and finance.

ON THE LINE

The current economic slowdown has sent many companies into a tailspin as they look for ways to cut costs and improve productivity without increasing resources. Indeed, as many businesses have been forced into bankruptcy the pressure has never been greater to closely examine internal operations, monitor performance, and find hidden inefficiencies throughout the supply chain.

It is during times such as these that marketplace conditions offer the perfect opportunity for companies to affect business change and ensure objectives are being met. A number of methods, tools and techniques are available for those wishing to pinpoint where problems may exist in their enterprise, as well as outside the four walls. By establishing performance measurements or metrics throughout the supply chain, companies are more likely to reach overall corporate goals and business strategies.

Measuring performance is not a new concept, but the key players, critical issues and data complexity involved has altered dramatically how companies approach supply-chain metrics. The traditional challenge of blending operational and strategic goals in a comprehensive enterprise-wide business strategy has been complicated further by the universal reliance on operating within independent functional silos. Plus, the inter-enterprise nature of supply-chain management has prompted many organizations to find ways and tools to track and measure trading partner performance.

Common methods for measuring critical performance issues include establishing key performance indicators (KPIs), balanced scorecards, and supply-chain metrics. "The classic approach is to say, if you want more of something, measure it, but at the same time, companies must be careful what they measure," cautions Kent McSparran, for Boston-based Keane, an IT consulting firm. "Unintended behavior from a specific metric is a common problem. In many cases, metrics result in unplanned consequences that may cause short-term successes, but don't solve the problem."

For example, one Keane client wanted to move inventory faster throughout the supply-chain pipeline, and created a metric to reach that goal. While internal results were good and the company celebrated its improvements, in reality, it actually pushed an inventory cushion back onto its distributors. "Inventory moved faster through their own internal pipeline, but in the end, the cost flowed back to them," says McSparran.

Another common mistake is to choose only one metric, such as creating the "perfect order" or "perfect shipment," which needs more measurements surrounding it for counterbalance. A perfect order usually means ensuring every order is 100 percent accurate and delivered on time. "The concept of the perfect order is a good metric, but used alone, it is too one-sided," says McSparran. "The metric is particularly valuable because it is cross-functional and does not discriminate. If there is a breakdown in this metric, it could be due to errors in any department or with any person."

The e-SCOR system from Gensym, Cambridge, Mass., is one of only a few software solutions specifically designed around the SCOR model, providing modeling, simulation, and decision support for supply chains. The e-SCOR solution standardizes the way supply chains are described, builds models to simulate their operations, and cracks SCOR's array of 200 metrics. "Inventory control is a function that everyone performs, but one company may perform it by manually sending out someone to count product, while another may use an electronic database," says Mark Whitworth, vice president of sales for e-SCOR.

Similar to SCOR, the e-SCOR system is hierarchical, consisting of three levels of need. The first level allows users to describe supply-chain players, and their relationships with one another. Level two outlines the operations strategy of each player, taking into account the type of product and manufacturing mode such as make-to-stock or make-to-order. Level three maps the physical and virtual elements of the SCOR model, describing tasks used to carry out management functions, such as how to take an order, and how to manage inventory.

Source: K. A. Dilger, "Say Goodbye to the Weakest Link with Supply Chain Metrics," *Global Logistics & Supply Chain Strategies* (June 2001): 39–41.

These guidelines offer some important insights into the challenges of performance measurement. Like most endeavors that are worthwhile, diligent effort has to be put forth in the planning stage to ensure that appropriate metrics are developed. The discussion in this section addressed that issue. Once the metrics are in place, the information or data has to be accurately recorded and made available to all relevant parties. The ongoing process will require proper monitoring and analysis to achieve the desired outcomes—improved efficiency (lower cost) and increased effectiveness (better service to internal and external customers). The next section will discuss the evolution of the utilization of performance metrics.

Evolution of Metrics Utilization

Most organizations go through several phases on the path to develop the most meaningful metrics internally as well as externally.[3] The first stage is awareness or recognition of the importance and potential for improvement associated with the development and utilization of appropriate performance measurement. Within an organization, the focus may be upon logistics and related functions including areas such as marketing and operation or manufacturing. Externally, the recognition of the potential benefits of supply chain management, as indicated in previous chapters of this text, leads to an awareness of the importance of metrics to manage activities which span the boundaries of organizations.

The second stage is delineating and developing the actual metrics which will be utilized in the organization to track performance. This will usually require reconciling definitions and reaching general agreement on which metrics are most appropriate and comparing to best-in-class organizations to gauge success. Externally, the supply chain approach will require a similar approach but agreement may be more challenging. The development of the SCOR Model by the Supply Chain Council has aided inter-organizational agreement on metrics. The SCOR Model, which will be discussed subsequently, provides a common metrics platform that companies can use for measuring supply chain performance.

The third stage is performance improvement. The development of appropriate metrics followed by comparison to comparable best-in-class organizations usually provides insight into how performance can be enhanced. Understanding the underlying processes driving performance will lead to estimating the costs and benefits of making changes and then in implementing the change(s) to achieve the desired results. Essentially, the supply chain approach requires similar action with the same cavort mentioned previously—inter-organizational changes are more difficult to achieve.

The integration stage is the final step for performance measurement. Internally, this stage requires cross functional coordination with special emphasis upon the financial aspects of performance improvement. Increasingly, logistics professionals have recognized that understanding the impact of their activities on familiar financial metrics such as ROA and ROI are very important. The integration of the financial metrics internally and across the supply chain enhances the creditability and awareness of the contributions of logistics to gaining market share and improving profits. Chapter 14 discusses this relationship in some detail and provides important insights into various financial metrics that are important for logistics and supply chain managers. The following section will discuss how performance can be classified or categorized to help logistics and supply chain managers.

PERFORMANCE CATEGORIES

There are a number of approaches one could use to classify performance metrics. Figure 13–4 identifies four principal categories with examples that provide a useful way of examining logistics and supply chain performance: time, quality, cost, and supporting measures.

Time has traditionally been accorded attention as an important barometer of logistics performance, especially with regard to measuring effectiveness. Figure 13–4 lists five widely used time measures. The metrics capture two elements of time—the elapsed time for the activity and the reliability or variability. For example, it may be possible to have a five-day cycle time, but does the company achieve this 100 percent of the time or 50 percent of the time? If the latter is true and customers are told to expect a five-day order cycle, they will be disappointed half of the time. They will have to hold safety stock to protect against stock outs. The important point is that time metrics need to include both the absolute time measurement and variability measures.

The second category indicated in Figure 13–4 is cost, which is the measurement for efficiency. Most companies focus on cost since it is so crucial to their ability to

FIGURE 13–4 Process Measure Categories

Time	**Cost**
On-time Delivery/Receipt Order Cycle Time Order Cycle Time Variability Response Time Forecasting/Planning Cycle Time	Finished Goods Inventory Turns Days Sales Outstanding Cost to Serve Cash-to-Cash Cycle Time Total Delivered Cost • *Cost of Goods* • *Transportation Costs* • *Inventory Carrying Costs* • *Material Handling Costs* All Other Costs • *Information Systems* • *Administrative* Cost of Excess Capacity Cost of Capacity Shortfall
Quality	**Other/Supporting**
Overall Customer Satisfaction Processing Accuracy Perfect Order Fulfillment** • *On-time Delivery* • *Complete Order* • *Accurate Product Selection* • *Damage-free* • *Accurate Invoice* Forecast Accuracy Planning Accuracy • *Budgets and Operating Plans* Schedule Adherence	Approval Exceptions to Standard • *Minimum Order Quantity* • *Change Order Timing* Availability of Information

** Contains a time component.
* Indicates a component of a process measure.
Source: J. S. Keebler et al., *Keeping Score,* Council of Logistics Management, 1999.

compete in the market, and make adequate profit and sufficient return on assets and/or investment. There are a number of cost metrics related to logistics and supply chain management that are important to organizations.

Some of the cost metrics indicated in Figure 13–4 are straightforward and obvious. For example, total delivered cost or landed cost will have a direct impact on the prices that will have to be charged in the market. Total delivered cost is multidimensional and includes the cost of the goods, transportation, inventory, and material handling. Inventory turns and days of sales outstanding are not as obvious. Inventory turns reflects how long a company holds inventory that impacts their carrying cost. Days of sales outstanding impacts service levels to customers and can lead to order cancellations. The cash-to-cash cycle is receiving increased attention in companies because it measures cash flow. Companies are interested in getting their money back as quickly as possible in order to enhance their financial viability. Chapter 14 will explicate this point more completely.

Quality is the third category or general type of metric mentioned in Figure 13–4. There are a number of dimensions to the Quality category that are important to logistics and supply chain management as pointed out in Chapter 4. The perfect order concept is a good example of the increased emphasis being placed upon customer service because it simultaneously measures five components that must be met to get a positive metric. Overall, quality metrics have become increasingly important for logistics and supply chain management. The fourth component considers some supporting metrics such as approval of exceptions to standards.

Figure 13–5 is interesting because it shows various customer service metrics and indicates whether customers use the measure and how important they think it is.

FIGURE 13–5 Do Customers Use These Measures to Evaluate Your Performance?

Measure	Percent of Customers Using Measure	Percent Say Important or Very Important	How are measures defined? Jointly	By Customer	Total Defined
On-time Delivery	86	91	31	29	60
Order Fill	75	88	25	33	58
Invoice Accuracy	69	77	28	30	58
Performance to Request Date	66	82	22	32	54
Order Cycle Time	63	78	25	25	50
Customer Service Performance	63	79	24	28	52
Stockouts/Back Orders	62	84	26	29	55
Over/Short/Damaged	61	73	25	32	57
Performance to Commit Date	55	84	22	30	52
Line Item Fill	55	84	29	29	58
Returns and Allowance Handling	44	63	24	26	50
Freight Cost	44	68	31	21	52
Inquiry Response Time	36	63	25	27	52
Case Fill	32	77	24	29	53
Forecast Accuracy	16	55	25	19	44

Source: CSC/University of Tennessee Logistics Survey, 1998.

FIGURE 13–6 Logistics Quantification Pyramid

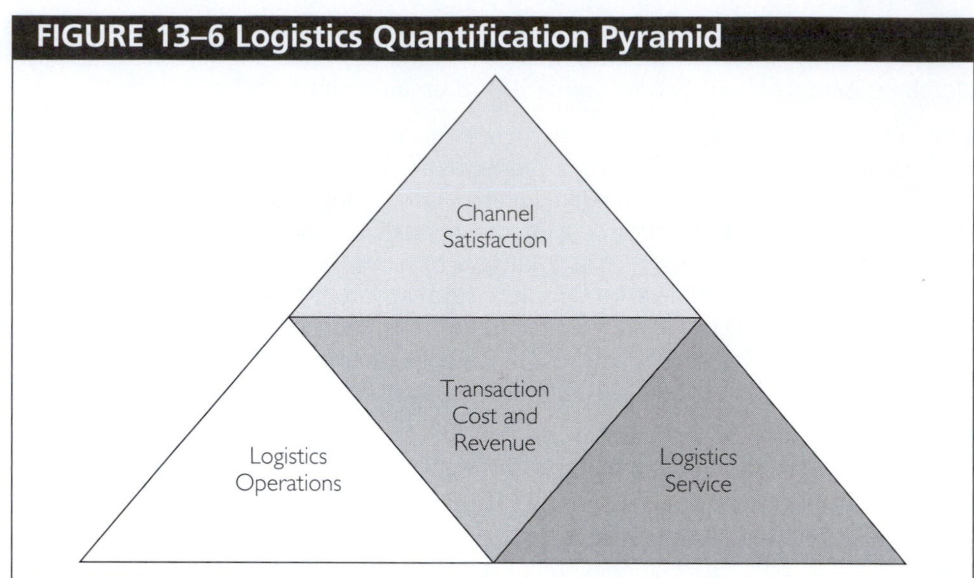

Source: R. A. Novack, Center for Supply Chain Research, Penn State University.

Also, the exhibit indicates how the measure was defined—jointly or by the customer. The percentages indicated in Figure 13–5 have increased over time. This demonstrates the increased attention being paid to metrics and, especially, customer service metrics.

Another Approach to Metric Classification

From another perspective (see Figure 13–6), it could be stated that the performance metrics for logistics should include logistics operations costs, logistics service metrics, transaction cost and revenue quantification, and channel satisfaction metrics.

In terms of logistics operations cost, a good example is inventory cost. By calculating the cost of carrying one unit of inventory (see Figure 13–7) and the impact of inventory turns on total inventory investment (see Figure 13–8), a company could evaluate the savings associated with eliminating obsolete and slow moving items from their inventory. In addition, by using the strategic profit model (discussed in Chapter 14) a company could determine the increase in net profit margin; the improvement in asset turnover; the increase in the return on assets (ROA); and the increase in return on net worth.

An important point here is that many of the metrics can be used to analyze tradeoffs, alternative scenarios, and financial impact, which is very powerful for logistics and supply chain managers. For example, from the information provided in Figures 13–7 and 13–8, a company determined that by eliminating obsolete inventory items (SKUs) and slow movers ("C" items), they could reduce inventory carrying cost by $4 million per year (variable operating expense reduction) and inventory investment (current asset) by $13 million. Both reductions had a very positive impact upon their ROA.

FIGURE 13–7 Distribution Inventory Costs

Case Example: ABC Power Tools
What does it cost to hold one unit of inventory?

Item 1		**Average Value Per Units = $ 647.00**	
Cost Element		*Computation*	*Annual Cost*
Interest		614.65/Unit × 10% interest	
Freight Inbound	+	32.35/Unit	64.70 each
		647.00 × 10% interest	
Labor		16.18/Unit received	16.18
		1.29/Unit/month upkeep × 12 months 15.48 total	31.66
Space		0.30/Sq. ft/Month × 8 sq. ft/Unit × 12 months	28.80
Insurance		3.23/Year/Unit	3.23
Taxes		10.00/100 assessment @ 25% valuation	16.18
Loss & Damage		2%/Year × 647.00/unit	12.94
Obsolescence		1%/Year × 647.00/Unit	6.47
Total Annual Carrying Cost			196.33
Inventory Carrying Cost %		196.33/647.00	30.3%

Source: R. A. Novack, Center for Supply Chain Research, Penn State University.

FIGURE 13–8 Distribution Inventory Management

Case Example: ABC Power Tools
Increase Turns
How do inventory turns impact ABC Power Tools' inventory investment?

Turns	Average Inventory	Inventory Carrying Cost*	Incremental Savings in Carrying Costs	Cumulative Savings in Carrying Costs
1	150,000,000	45,000,000	—	—
2	75,000,000	22,500,000	22,500,000	22,500,000
3	50,000,000	15,000,000	7,500,000	30,000,000
4	37,500,000	11,250,000	3,750,000	33,750,000
5	30,000,000	9,000,000	2,250,000	36,000,000
6	25,000,000	7,000,000	1,500,000	37,500,000
7	21,428,571	6,428,571	1,071,429	38,571,429
8	18,750,000	5,625,000	803,571	39,375,000
9	16,666,667	5,000,001	624,999	39,999,999
10	15,000,000	4,500,000	500,001	40,500,000

* Assume ICC = 30%
Source: R. A. Novack, Center for Supply Chain Research, Penn State University.

FIGURE 13–9 Logistics Outputs That Influence Customer Service

- Product availability
- Order cycle time
- Logistics operations responsiveness
- Logistics system information
- Postsale logistics support

Source: R. A. Novack, Center for Supply Chain Research, Penn State University.

Figure 13–9 shows basic logistics service outputs or service performance for metrics development. Product availability is a logistics metric which is used frequently because it is a good indicator of supply chain performance and its influence on customer inventory requirements, order fill rates, and seller revenue. It is important to note that when using this metric you must define where the supply chain availability will be measured in order to be consistent.

Order cycle time (OCT) is another very important service metric. OCT influences product availability, customer inventories, and seller's cash flow and profit. Once an expected order cycle time is established for customers, service failures can be measured, for example, how many late deliveries per 100 shipments. From a revenue on cash flow perspective, a company can calculate the impact of late deliveries on revenue, profit, and cash flow.

All of the logistics outputs listed in Figure 13–9 can be utilized in some form to develop metrics for service performance. As indicated previously, the service output metrics reflect the quality of service being provided to customers, which is important to sustain and, hopefully, increase revenue/sales and cash flow. Also, the metrics for service outputs can be utilized to analyze and evaluate the financial implications of changes in logistics operations.

Transaction cost and revenue relates to the value added by logistics. In other words, what is the service and price relationship and what specifically is the customer's perception? From the sellers perspective there are three basic alternatives:

- Increased service with constant price
- Constant service with reduced price
- Increased service with reduced price

The basic logistics outputs delineated in Figure 13–9 represent the dimensions service that can add value for customers through lowering their cost of doing business and or increasing their sales revenue. Figure 13–10 indicates the results of a 1999 survey of the percentage of companies that measure performance of each of the five service outputs as well as the percentage that measures value. If we compared the survey results indicated in Figure 13–10 with previous surveys you would see important increases. The level of interest will continue to grow for the use of these metrics.

The final category is channel satisfaction. This essentially looks at how logistics service changes impact channel member firms. The research in this area is

FIGURE 13–10 Service Measurement

	1994 (%)	1999 (%)
Product availability	89.8	94.9
Order cycle time	77.4	79.3
Logistics operations response	63.9	59.7
Logistics system information	40.8	39.0
Postsale customer support	40.9	32.3

Source: R. A. Novack, Center for Supply Chain Research, Penn State University.

limited. Most of the focus on measurement has been on immediate or direct customers in the channel and not further downstream. However, as we will discuss in the next section, the channel perspective encompassed in the supply chain is receiving much attention in terms of the metrics discussed above.

Overall, much progress has been made during the 1990s toward developing appropriate metrics and using them proactively to measure performance in terms of the impact upon the financial results in the organization. However, as several of the figures have indicated, there is much more to be accomplished. The next section will focus specifically on supply chain metrics. These are the most challenging since they are intercompany and boundary spanning.

Supply Chain Metrics

Supply chain metrics are, by their nature, different from traditional logistics metrics since they are inter-company or boundary spanning. Supply chain metrics focus on common processes and there must be agreement among the supply chain members in terms of the processes and their definitions. It is important to try to capture all aspects of supply chain performance and attempt to quantify profit from success or the impact on revenues of the cost of failure.

SCOR Model

The Supply Chain Operations Reference (SCOR) model was developed initially under the auspices of Pittiglio, Rabin, Todd, and McGrath (PRTM) and AMR Research in conjunction with about 70 voluntary companies and three universities. The group of organizations established the Supply Chain Council (SCC), an independent not-for-profit corporation, to continue to develop and administer the SCOR model. The SCC is now open to all organizations and companies who have an interest in applying the model to their supply chain and advancing supply chain management best practices.

SUPPLY CHAIN TECHNOLOGY

By now every supply-chain executive has gotten the message: Success in business today is all about satisfying the customer. All else is secondary.

Their vision can be summed up in three words: cash to cash. The term defines the time between a manufacturer paying for raw materials, and getting paid for finished product. Appealing in both its breadth and evident simplicity, it's a devilishly hard concept to adopt.

Current business conditions are forcing companies to try. The slowing economy has them casting about for new ways of streamlining the supply chain. Shorter product lifecycles demand a faster return on investment from new systems and business processes. Outsourcing calls for better integration among business partners, not just within the enterprise. The hunger for new product requires greater flexibility in manufacturing.

Until now, managers have tackled the problem from the standpoint of physical goods and information. The third major drain on working capital, finance, has largely been ignored. Yet it's the one with the greatest potential for savings today.

Companies are beginning to change their perspective, and the high-tech sector is leading the way. Few industries are so consumed by the need for speed, flexibility and cost control. Personal computers today have a marketing life of around 26 weeks. Semiconductors can be sold for nine months, versus three years just a couple of years ago.

Even a single model of computer or high-tech component undergoes multiple versions. Dell computer initiates up to 300 product changes a day. Yet its supply chain is extremely sensitive to error. Dell aims to ship product within five days of receiving an order. By stretching that period to 15 days, it would suffer 20 percent order cancellations.

Outsourcing is the order of the day among high-tech producers, creating the need for common processes and better communications between equipment sellers and those who actually make and move the goods. Forecasts, designs, specifications, and change orders must flow effortlessly among partners. In such an environment, companies are forced to acquire a broader view, with an emphasis on how cash is moving all the supply chain.

Some of the most obvious solutions, such as cutting down on accounts receivable, may be the best ones. Of critical importance is the ability to combine lagging with leading indicators—embracing both fulfillment and forecasting—to measure total supply-chain performance. Only then can a company capture information at multiple stages o the chain, even at the level of tier two or three suppliers.

Electronic procurement is another good place to start. In place of expensive, full-blown software solutions on the procurement side, companies can set up intranet hubs with suppliers to facilitate better communications. But no systems-oriented approach will work unless underlying business processes are reengineered at the same time.

Many companies let receivables age because they fail to address customer service problems. Faster payment can come from the alignment of performance metrics between sales and finance departments, leading to overall cycle-time reductions of between 10 percent and 20 percent. At the very least sales should know when problems crop up, which isn't always the case today.

Thinking cash-to-cash means scrapping the notion of a linear supply chain and embracing collaboration across the network, especially when it comes to planning. Under the old system, physical product was like cash today: There was too much of it, in too many places.

For most companies, even those claiming enlightenment, the walls still stand. Cash-to-cash is a familiar concept to many managers; measuring it accurately is another matter entirely. They tend to focus on cutting out time in obvious areas such as transportation, which accounts for only a small part of the cycle. They shy away from wider-ranging processes, such as information sharing, that require the cooperation of multiple players in the chain.

Source: R. J. Bowman, "From Cash to Cash: The Ultimate Supply Chain Measurement Tool," *Global Logistics & Supply Chain Strategies* (June 2001): 44–48.

FIGURE 13–11 Five Distinct Management Processes of SCOR

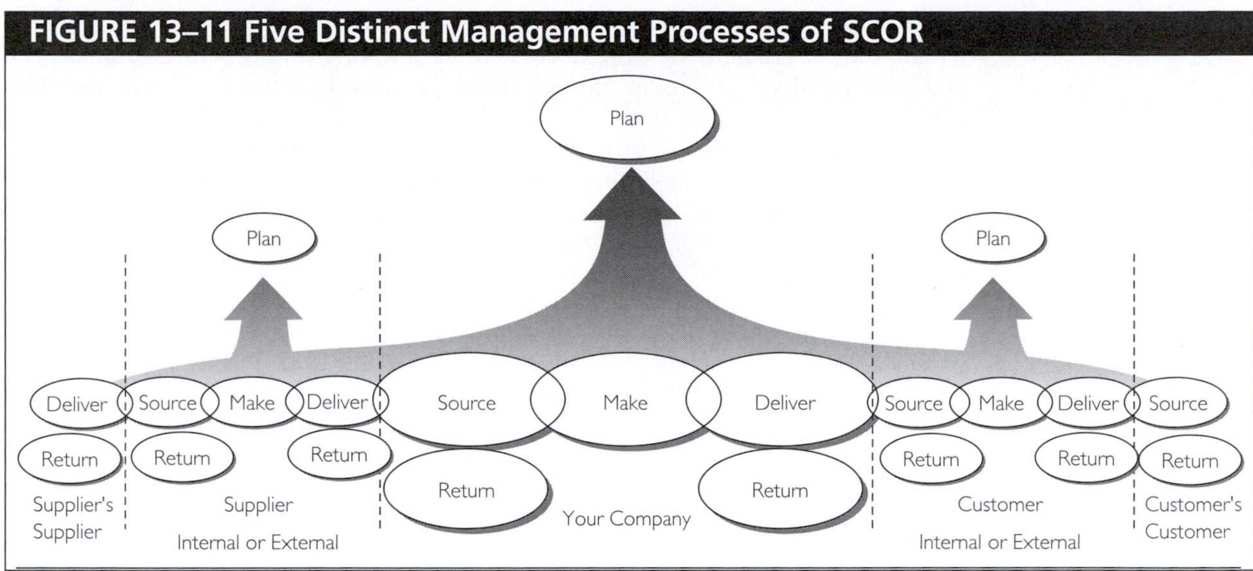

Source: Supply Chain Council.

In general, process reference models integrate the well-known concepts of business process reengineerings, benchmarking, and process measurement into a cross functional relationship. Consequently, the process reference model attempts to

- Capture the "as is" state of a process and derive the desired "to be" future state (reengineering)
- Quantify the operational performance of similar companies and establish internal targets which are based upon "best-in-class" performance of member companies (bench marking)
- Characterize and describe the management practices and software solutions that will result in "best-in-class" performance (best practice analysis)

The underlying tenet of the SCOR model is, obviously, to help member organizations to improve their supply chain efficiency and effectiveness. The Supply Chain Council is dedicated to improving the SCOR Model as a management tool. The current version is 5.0.

As indicated previously, good supply chain metrics require agreement on common processes and comprehensive measurement across the supply chain. The SCOR model meets these requirements since it provides standard descriptions of the relevant management processes; a framework of the relationships among the standard processes; standard process performance metrics; and standard alignment to features and functionality. The ultimate aim is to produce best-in-class supply chain performance.

Figure 13–11 provides an overview of the SCOR model. The model focuses upon five key processes for supply chains: plan, source, make, deliver, and return. Each of these five processes deserves separate attention.

The *plan* process encompasses demand and supply planning and management which requires balancing resources with requirements and the establishment and communication of plans for all other processes in the supply chain. The planning would include management of business rules, supply chain performance, data collection, inventory, capital assets, transportation, etc. It would also include aligning the supply chain unit plan with the financial plan. Essentially, it encompasses the processes that balance aggregated demand and supply to develop a course of action which best meets sourcing, production, and delivery requirements.

The *source* process encompasses sourcing stocked, make-to-order and engineer-to-order products or materials. More specifically, the process would include scheduling deliveries, receiving, verifying, transferring, and authorizing vendor payments. It could include the identification and selection of new supply sources. The source process covers managing the source business rules, assessing supplier performance, and maintaining appropriate data, as well as managing inventory, capital assets, incoming product, the supplier network, import/export requirements, and supplier agreements. Essentially, sourcing includes those processes that procure goods and services to meet planned or actual demand.

The *make* process encompasses make-to stock, make-to-order, and engineer-to-order production. The process includes scheduling production activities, issuing product, producing and testing, packaging, staging, and releasing. It would also include finalizing the engineering for an engineer-to-order product. Essentially, "make", includes those processes that transform product to a finished state to meet planned or actual demand.

The *deliver* process encompasses ordering, warehousing, transporting, and installation of stocked, made-to-order and engineered-to-order products. It would include all order management activities, warehousing activities, invoicing, and managing transportation-related activities necessary to meet planned or actual demand.

The *return* process encompasses the return of raw materials (to vendors) and receipt of finished goods (returns from customers). It would include authorizing, scheduling, receiving, verifying, and disposing of returns to maximize recapture of revenues for the organization.

The SCOR model contains three levels of process detail: top level (process types), configuration level (process categories), and process element level (decompose processes). Level 1 defines the scope and content for the model and it is here that the competition performance targets are set. Level 2 provides the opportunity to configure to order a specific company's supply chain. It is here that companies can implement their operations strategy. Level 3 defines a company's ability to compete in its markets and would include process elements—definitions, information about inputs and outputs, performance metrics, best practices, system capabilities to support best practices, and systems and tools. Companies can fine tune their operations strategy at level 3.

It is probably very obvious that the SCOR model is relatively simple at the conceptual level but complex and comprehensive at the implementation level. As an industry standard using standard language, the SCOR model has the potential to provide needed metrics and communication among supply chain partners.

SUMMARY

- Performance measurement for logistics systems and, especially, for supply chains is necessary but challenging because of their complexity and scope.
- Performance metrics are needed to effectively manage organizations over time and to drive expected outcomes and behavior.
- Performance metrics need to be adjusted over time to reflect both internal and external changes. In some instances, the metrics have to be significantly modified or replaced if they become obsolete.
- Performance measurement is not a new interest or focus of logistics and supply chain managers. The development of the physical distribution concept in the 1960s and 1970s was based on measures of efficiency with its emphasis on total system cost. In each decade since the 1960s, there have been different change drivers impacting logistics and supply chain metrics.
- Certain characteristics should be incorporated into good metrics—quantitative, visible, easy to understand, involve employee input, multi-dimensional and the benefits outweigh the costs.
- Important guidelines for metric development for logistics and supply chains include: consistency with overall corporate strategy; focus on customer needs and expectations; careful selection and prioritization of metrics; focus on processes; use of a balanced approach; emphasis on accuracy in developing metrics; and use of technology to improve measurement effectiveness.
- Typically, organizations go through several phases on the path to developing effective metrics: awareness; metric delineation and development; performance improvement; and internal and external integration.
- There are four principal categories for performance metrics: time, quality, cost, and miscellaneous or support. Another classification for logistics and supply chains suggests the following categories for metrics: operations cost, service, revenue or value, and channel satisfaction.
- The SCOR model is being utilized by a growing number of organizations to develop their supply chain metrics, benchmark their performance, and to make appropriate changes to improve performance.

STUDY QUESTIONS

1. Two principles associated with performance measurement state: "If you can't measure it, you can't manage it" and "metrics drive behavior." Explain these two principles. How do they apply to the Micros and More case?
2. Why do performance metrics change over time? Will this be an issue for Micros and More? Why or why not?
3. What factors cause performance metrics to change over time? Are these factors external or internal to the organization or both? Which of the factors that you have identified are likely to have the biggest impact upon Micros and More?

4. "Performance measurement for logistics managers is relatively recent. Their focus was directed toward other managerial activities." Agree or disagree with this statement? Explain your position.
5. What role should employees, in general, play in the development of performance metrics? Why is this role important?
6. "Metrics must focus upon customer needs and expectations." Explain the meaning of this statement? Why have customers become more important for performance measurement? What role, if any, should customers play in developing supply chain metrics?
7. It is generally recognized that organizations go through several phases on the path to developing appropriate supply chain metrics. Discuss the stages of supply development for supply chain metrics. Choose which of the stages of evolution you think would be most challenging for an organization. Explain your choice.
8. Discuss the two basic dimensions of time when time is used as a logistics or supply chain performance metric. Why are both dimensions important and why should they be used together?
9. Discuss the various categories of performance measurement. Which category do you think usually gets the most attention? Why? Do you agree with this priority? Why or why not?
10. Define the SCOR model. What are its objectives? List the basic processes covered in the SCOR model. Why has the SCOR model captured so much attention?

NOTES

1. This section is adapted from J. S. Keebler, K. B. Manrodt, D. A. Durtsche, and D. M. Ledyard, *Keeping Score* (Oakbrook, Ill.: Council of Logistics Management, 1999), 4–10.
2. Ibid., 126–135.
3. Ibid., 12–23.
4. This section is adapted from Anonymous, *Supply Chain Operations Reference—Model: Overview of SCOR Version 5.0* (Pittsburgh, Pa.: Supply Chain Council, Inc., 2001).

CASE 13–1 ■ CPDW

Harry Groves, CEO of Central PA Distribution and Warehouse (CPDW), had just called the monthly meeting of the Board of Directors of CPDW to order. Harry looked tired and grim, thought Joe Zimmerman (a local entrepreneur and board member). Harry's opening statement gave reason for the body language. CPDW had another dismal month that was delineated in the monthly financial statements and Harry's description of monthly activities.

Company Backround

CPDW is located in Milroy, Pennsylvania adjacent to an interchange on a major east-west roadway in central Pennsylvania. The company was founded five years ago by a group of individuals who owned local businesses or held management positions in local companies. The board members were all limited partners in the venture so they had a very special interest in the financial viability of the organization.

The partners, under the leadership of Harry Groves, had purchased a building (120,000 square feet) and parcel of land (32.6 acres) from the Sanyo Corporation. The building had been used primarily as a manufacturing facility by Sanyo. The partners purchased the building with the express purpose of utilizing it as a distribution facility for providing logistics services for companies within central Pennsylvania. While the building was not ideal for storage because of the ceiling height, the partners believed that it was versatile enough to be used for various logistics activities including repackaging, order fulfillment, reverse logistics, etc.

The paradox of the situation was that the facility was completely filled with pallet loads of glass from a local glass manufacturer. In fact, the original estimate on useable storage space, excluding aisles, offices, restrooms, etc., was 99,500 square feet. However, Jon Parton, C.O.O. of the company had pushed and squeezed until they were utilizing 110,000 square feet.

Board Meeting

After reviewing the useage rate, Jay Lenard asked Harry for some additional insight into their situation. He prefaced his question with the comment "I thought that we wanted to fill the facility and in doing so, we would be profitable. When I look at square foot utilization, which I thought was our best performance metric, I'm pleased, but you are telling us that this is a problem. I just don't understand our financial situation based upon this metric."

Harry let out a sigh and said, "Jay, I really wish that it was that easy. I have come to realize that our base metric for pricing square feet of space utilized is too narrow. With our current situation, even though we are using more square feet than I thought we had available, thanks to Jon, we are not breaking even. When the building is full and nothing is moving in or out, we are in trouble. We need to change our metrics and align them with a new pricing strategy."

Case Questions

1. Describe the nature of CPDW's problem.
2. What metrics would you recommend that CPDW use to enhance their pricing strategy? Provide a rationale for your recommendations.

CHAPTER 14

NETWORK DESIGN AND FACILITY LOCATION

LEARNING OBJECTIVES

After reading this chapter, you should be able to do the following:

- Identify factors that may suggest a need to redesign a logistics network.
- Structure an effective process for logistics network design.
- Be aware of key locational determinants and the impact they may have on prospective locational alternatives.
- Understand the different types of modeling approaches that may be used to gain insight into logistics network design and facility location.
- Apply the simple "grid" or center-of-gravity approach to facility location.
- Have knowledge of certain ways in which transportation and transportation costs affect the location decision.

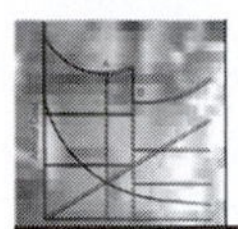

LOGISTICS PROFILE

Need for Speed Turns Guadalajara into a High-Tech Hub

On trips back home to California, Brad Knight likes to pop into the local Circuit City store. He strides down the aisles, stopping in front of a stack of Sony Web TV set-top boxes. He pauses at a counter full of PalmPilots. Then, he checks out the Hewlett-Packard printers to see how they are selling. On his way out, he might straighten a rack of Johnson & Johnson blood-glucose monitors. And he does it all with a sense of pride: that is because all these products came out of his Guadalajara, Mexico, factory.

Mr. Knight opened the one-million-square-foot facility in Guadalajara in 1997 for his employer, Flextronics International, Ltd. In its first eight months of operation, the plant had $12 million in sales. . . . Revenue is currently 140 million a quarter and is growing at 68 percent annually.

Actually, a revolution has swept the nuts-and-bolts end of the technology business, as companies such as Flextronics; Solectron Corp.; Jabil Circuit, Inc.; and SCI Systems, Inc., barely known just a few years ago, have emerged as highly efficient manufacturers and supply chain managers that operate factories around the globe. The electronics giants whose names their products carry—such as Compaq, 3Com, Ericsson, and Cisco—are just as quickly getting out of the business of making things, concentrating instead on developing new products and persuading consumers to buy them. According to Mr. Knight, "the standard manufacturing model for the high-tech industry isn't standard anymore."

Ground zero of this structural shift is Guadalajara, a graceful city of 3.3 million known more for its fiery tequila and mellifluous mariachis. Since the North American Free Trade Agreement took effect in 1994, contract manufacturers, their suppliers, and some of their customers have made decisions to locate there. As a result, Mexico's No. 2 city is on its way to supplanting China and other Asian countries as the principal manufacturing center for products sold in the United States.

Globalization was supposed to mean that most of the world's manufacturing jobs would gravitate to low-cost locations in Asia. But, nowadays, technology companies cannot afford the two weeks it takes to deliver their products from Asia to the United States, or vice versa, by ship, and airfreight on such long hauls is prohibitively expensive. That means locating factories close to customers, and that is why the old wisdom of "locating in the lowest-cost part of the globe just doesn't apply anymore." In addition to customer proximity, the decision of firms to locate in Mexico was facilitated by a number of factors including tax breaks, availability of low-cost state land for new investors, and a friendly governmental attitude toward companies who considered location in the area.

Source: Adapted from Jonathan Friedland and Gary McWilliams, "How a Need for Speed Turned Guadalajara into a High-Tech Hub," *Wall Street Journal* (2 March 2000): 1.

INTRODUCTION

strategic importance

As firms search for new ways to lower costs and improve service to their customers, the issue of where to locate logistics and manufacturing facilities has never been more complex or critical. In addition to enhancing the efficiency and effectiveness of a logistics operation, the redesign of a firm's logistics network can help to differentiate a firm in the marketplace. Several examples illustrate this type of success:

- A leading pharmaceutical distributor with nationwide service recently reduced its logistics network from more than sixty to twenty distribution centers, while offering its customers a selection of service responses from which to choose (for example, same-day delivery, regular service, and so on).
- A prominent office products company reduced its network of distribution facilities from eleven to three, while substantially increasing the level of cross-docking activity with its customers and significantly improving logistical customer service.
- A direct-selling company with a national distribution capability reengineered its customer service operation and eliminated a major distribution point, which resulted in significant reductions to its fixed assets and operating expenses, at the same time differentiating its services to meet a recognized range of customer requirements.
- As a result of the merger of two large grocery industry manufacturers, the combined logistics network consisted of fifty-four distribution centers across the United States. Following careful study and analysis, with a look to the future, the company consolidated its network into fifteen strategically located facilities. This move significantly reduced the company's overall logistics costs and improved service levels to its customers.
- A major manufacturer of semiconductor products recently consolidated its logistics network into a single, global distribution center in Singapore, and engaged a third-party supplier of express logistics services to manage its overall distribution activity. The end results included lower cost, improved service, and a new way for the firm to differentiate itself in the marketplace.

While there are also examples of the opposite situation, in which firms have justifiably expanded their logistics networks and increased the number of distribution facilities, the move to consolidate existing systems is far more common. Assuming that a firm considers the impact of such a decision on total logistics cost, it is not unusual for the inventory cost savings associated with consolidating facilities to outweigh any additional transportation expense involved with moving product to the customer. Also, the use of currently available information technology, coupled with the time-sensitive capabilities of many suppliers of transportation service, can mean that such a move enhances responsiveness and the levels of service experienced by customers.

change process

This chapter first looks at several strategic aspects of logistics network design. While it may sometimes be that "change for the sake of change" is needed, a number of prominent factors may suggest that a redesign of the logistics network may be appropriate. Next, the process of logistics network redesign is examined in detail. This content provides a useful framework for understanding the key steps that must be included in a comprehensive approach to logistics network design and facility location.

locational determinants

Following these discussions, attention shifts to several major locational determinants. These factors may be either regionally focused or site-specific. Also included is a summary of current trends governing site selection. The chapter concludes with coverage of several modeling approaches that can be used to provide insight into the issues of logistics network design and facility location. Several examples of transportation-specific factors are also included.

The Need for Long-Range Planning

In the short run, a firm's logistics network and the locations of its key facilities are givens, and the logistics manager must operate within the constraints imposed by the facility locations. Site availability, leases, contracts, and investments make changing facility locations impractical in the short run. In the long run, however, the design of the logistics network must be thought of as variable. Management decisions can and should be made to change the network to meet the logistics requirements imposed by customers, suppliers, and competitive changes.

future implications

In addition, the decisions as to network design and facility location that are made today will have implications far into the future. A facility properly located under today's economic, competitive, and technological conditions may not be at an optimum location under future conditions. Today's facility location decision will have a significant effect on future costs in such areas as logistics, marketing, manufacturing, and finance. Thus, the facility location decision must seriously consider anticipated business conditions and acknowledge a critical need to be flexible and responsive to customer needs as they may change in the future. This latter concern heightens the attractiveness of the third-party-logistics option for many logistics operations today.

The Strategic Importance of Logistics Network Design

Why analyze the logistics network? In essence, the answer lies in the fact that all businesses operate in a very dynamic environment in which change is the only constant. Characteristics of consumer and industrial-buyer demand, technology, competition, markets, and suppliers are constantly changing. As a result, business must redeploy its resources in response to and in anticipation of this ever-changing environment.

network redesign

Considering the rate at which change is occurring, it is questionable whether any existing logistics network can be truly current or up to date. Any logistics network that has been in existence for a number of years is certainly a candidate for reevaluation and potential redesign. Even if the existing system is not functionally obsolete, an analysis of the existing network will probably uncover new opportunities to reduce cost and/or improve service.

This section focuses attention on several types of change that may suggest a need to reevaluate and/or redesign a firm's logistics network. While not all of these factors will affect any single firm at the same time, they represent some of the more frequently changing elements of the business environment that affect logistics and supply chain management.

Changing Customer Service Requirements

changing requirements

As was discussed in Chapters 1 through 4, the logistical requirements of customers are changing in numerous ways. As a result, the need to reevaluate and redesign logistics networks is of great contemporary interest. While some customers have intensified their demands for more efficient and more effective logistics services, others are seeking relationships with suppliers who can take logistical capabilities and performance to new, unprecedented levels.

examples

While customer service requirements may experience change, the types of customers served may also evolve over time. Consider, for example, the case of food manufacturers who have distributed their product to independent stores and regional retail chains for many years and who have recently added mass merchants to their list of customers. Another example is manufacturers of stationery who traditionally served a multitude of customers, from small retail to club stores, but who now focus primarily on distributors of office supply products. In both of these examples, change has occurred at both the customer and supply chain level, with significant impacts on lead times, order size and frequency, and associated activities such as shipment notification, marking and tagging, and packaging.

Shifting Locations of Customer and/or Supply Markets

dynamic marketplace

Considering that manufacturing and logistics facilities are positioned in the supply chain between customer and supply markets, any changes in these markets should cause a firm to reevaluate its logistics network. When the U.S. population shifted to the Southeast and Southwest, for example, new warehouses and distribution facilities followed the changing geo-location trends. As a result, cities such as Atlanta, Houston, and Reno/Sparks have become popular distribution center locations for companies serving these increasing population centers.

On the supply side, the service and cost requirements of the automobile industry's movement to JIT-based manufacturing have forced companies to examine the locations of logistics facilities. Many suppliers to Saturn Corporation in Spring Hill, Tennessee, for example, have selected nearby points for manufacturing and/or parts distribution facilities.

global examples

On the global scene, the collapse of economic and political walls in Eastern Europe, plus the unification initiatives of the European Union, have forced many U.S. companies to examine facility locations in terms of their suitability for competition in these rapidly developing markets. In addition to reconfiguring their logistics networks, firms facing these challenges have taken steps such as establishing European branch operations and entering into joint agreements with European-based companies to gain a presence in this potentially significant marketplace.

Sourcing of raw materials from offshore suppliers is another reason to analyze the location of existing facilities. Using Pacific Rim suppliers makes the western United States a desirable location for a distribution center, whereas an East Coast location would be more desirable for a company receiving similar materials from Europe. Also, as described in the Logistics Profile for this chapter, Guadalajara, Mexico, has become a very popular location for manufacturers serving U.S.-based markets for high-tech and consumer electronics products. As world economies become more interdependent, these types of facility location decisions will become more common.

Change in Corporate Ownership

A relatively common occurrence today is for a firm to experience an ownership-related change associated with a merger, acquisition, or divestiture. In such instances, many companies choose to be proactive and to conduct a formal evaluation of new versus previous logistics networks in advance of such a change. This is very helpful in terms of making sure that the newly merged or newly independent firm will have fully anticipated the logistics impacts of the change in corporate ownership. In other instances, the logistics manager may be the last one to find out about the impending change, and the role of logistics network design immediately takes on a defensive posture.

Even if the logistics impacts are not part of the planning process, it is critical for firms to reassess their logistics networks following ownership-related changes such as those identified in the preceding paragraph. Such changes increase the likelihood that the new operation is duplicating effort and incurring unnecessary logistics expense.

Cost Pressures

sources of cost savings

A major priority for many firms today is to figure out new and innovative ways to take cost out of their key business processes, including those relating to logistics. In such instances, a reevaluation of the logistics network and the functioning of the overall supply chain can frequently help to uncover new sources of such savings. Whether the answer lies in reducing cost in transportation, inventory, warehousing, or another area, a detailed examination of the current system versus alternative approaches can be exceptionally useful.

For example, labor issues have caused many firms to analyze a facility's location. High labor costs or restrictive union work rules have caused companies to move production and logistics facilities from the Northeast to the South, as well as to Mexico and the Pacific Rim countries. Companies balance the lower labor costs in these areas against what may be higher costs for transportation, inventory, and communications. For example, it was reported that footwear giant Nike, Inc., in Beaverton, Oregon, raised its monthly minimum wage for Indonesian workers from $28.01 to $29.69. With housing and other allowances, no worker made less than $37.19 per month.[1]

Companies considering plant modernization needs also sometimes benefit from a comprehensive cost analysis, which might accompany a reevaluation of the logistics network. A firm considering an investment of millions of dollars in an existing plant must ask, "Is this the proper location for a plant, given the current and future customer and vendor locations?"

Competitive Capabilities

Another factor relates to competitive pressures that may force a company to examine its logistics service levels and the costs generated by its network of logistics facilities. To remain competitive in the marketplace or to develop a competitive advantage, a company should frequently examine the relative locations of its facilities toward the goal of improving service and/or lowering costs. Companies often conduct this network review in light of newly developed transport alternatives.

time-critical services

For example, many firms locate distribution facilities near the hub operations of companies such as Federal Express, UPS, Airborne, Emery, and DHL so that access to time-critical, express transportation services will be facilitated. This strategy is particularly appropriate for inventories of high-value, time-sensitive products that may need to be shipped on a moment's notice. The resulting service level is higher, and the total cost of the comprehensive, express logistics services is lower than the total cost would be of warehousing the needed inventories at various locations throughout the company's logistics network. Essentially, the centralization of such inventories at strategically selected locations reduces the overall cost of logistics and significantly improves responsiveness in terms of delivery times.

Corporate Organizational Change

downsizing

It is not unusual for logistics network design to become a topic of discussion at the same time that a firm considers any major corporate organizational change, such as downsizing. In such instances, the strategic functioning of the firm's logistics network is viewed as something that must be protected and even enhanced through the process of organizational change.

reengineering

Considering the current popularity of corporate reengineering efforts, the logistics process is frequently a prime candidate for attention. For example, many firms today have become involved in the reengineering of their order-fulfillment process, which has significant implications for the firm's logistics function. An important component of the overall effort will include a systematic evaluation of and recommendations for change to the firm's logistics network.

LOGISTICS NETWORK DESIGN

complex process

A firm must consider many factors as it approaches the task of determining the optimum design of its logistics network. These factors are identified and discussed at a later point in this chapter. At the outset, however, it is important to realize that the task of designing an appropriate logistics network should be coordinated closely with the identification and implementation of key corporate and overall business strategies. Since the process of designing or redesigning a firm's logistics network can be complex, it is discussed in the context of a major corporate reengineering process.

Figure 14–1 identifies the six major steps that are recommended for a comprehensive logistics network design process. Each of these steps is discussed in detail in the following paragraphs.

Step 1: Define the Logistics Network Design Process

logistics network reengineering team

Of initial importance is the formation of a logistics network reengineering team to be responsible for all elements of the logistics network design process. This team will first need to become aware of overall corporate and business strategies and the underlying business needs of the firm and the supply chains in which it is a participant.

design process objectives

Also in this step, it is important to establish the parameters and objectives of the logistics network design or redesign process itself. An awareness of the expectations of senior management, for example, is essential to the effective progress of

FIGURE 14–1 Key Steps in the Logistics Network Design Process

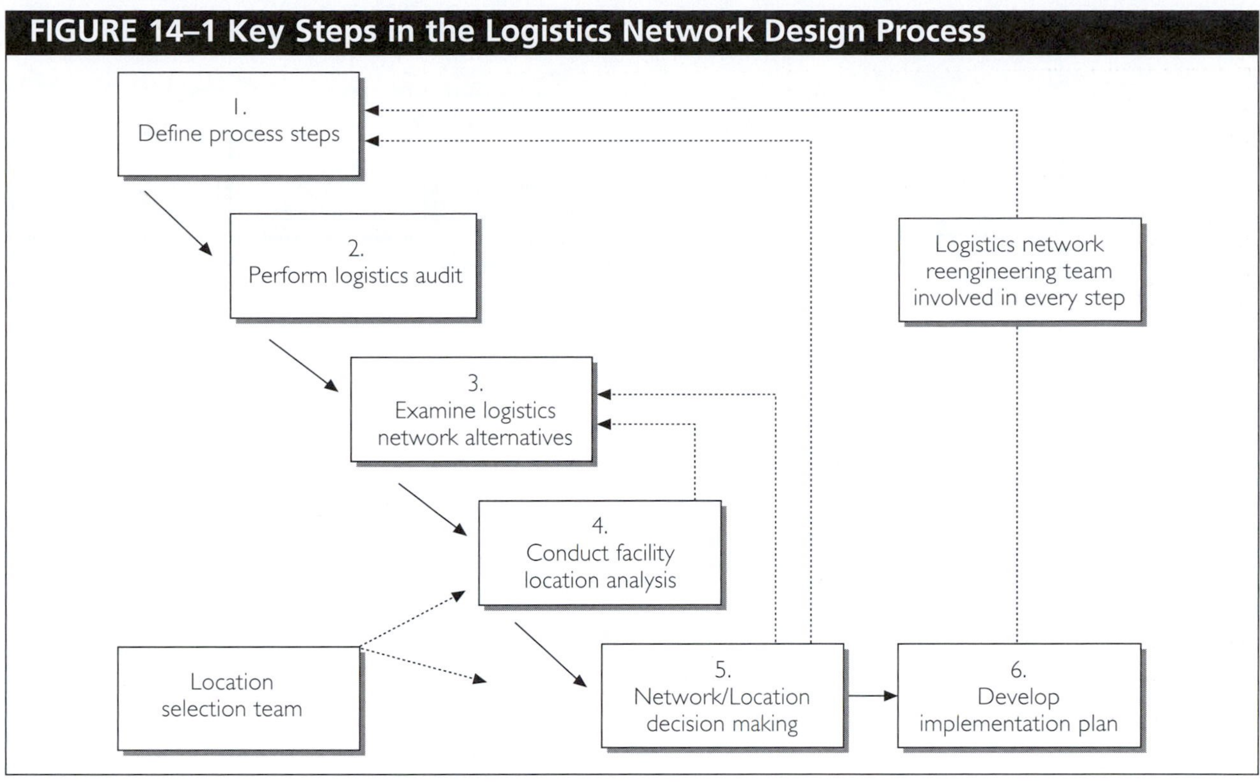

the overall reengineering process. Issues pertaining to the availability of needed resources in the areas of funding, people, and systems must be understood at an early stage in the process.

third-party suppliers

An additional topic to be addressed early on is the potential involvement of third-party suppliers of logistics services as a means of achieving the firm's logistics objectives. This consideration is critical, since it will expand the mind-set of the network design team to include a consideration of logistics network solutions that may involve externally provided as well as proprietary logistics resources.

Step 2: Perform a Logistics Audit

audit steps

The logistics audit provides members of the reengineering team with a comprehensive perspective on the firm's logistics process. In addition, it helps to gather essential types of information that will be useful throughout future steps in the redesign process. Figure 14–2 indicates a number of key steps that should be included in a logistics audit. Listed here are examples of the types of information that should become available as a result of this audit:

important information

- Customer requirements and key environmental factors
- Key logistics goals and objectives
- Profile of the current logistics network and the firm's positioning in respective supply chain(s)
- Benchmark, or target, values for logistics costs and key performance measurements

FIGURE 14–2 Key Steps in a Logistics Audit

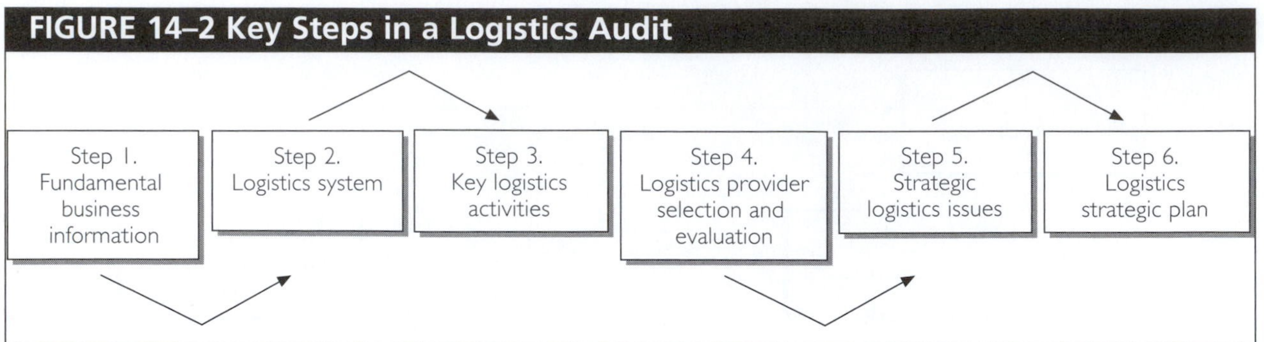

- Identification of gaps between current and desired logistics performance (qualitative and quantitative)
- Key objectives for logistics network design, expressed in terms that will facilitate measurement

Step 3: Examine the Logistics Network Alternatives

basic modeling alternatives

The next step is to examine the available alternatives for the logistics network. This involves applying suitable quantitative models to the current logistics system as well as to the alternative systems and approaches under consideration. The use of these models provides considerable insight into the functioning and cost/service effectiveness of the various possible networks. As already discussed in Chapter 12, the principal modeling approach will be optimization, simulation, or heuristic. These approaches are explored in detail later in this chapter. Briefly, optimization approaches search for "best" solutions, simulation models replicate the functioning of the logistics network, and heuristic techniques are able to accommodate broad problem definitions but do not provide optimum solutions.

insight, not answers

Once an appropriate modeling procedure has been selected, it should be used to help identify a logistics network that is consistent with the key objectives identified during the logistics audit. Although, at first, reengineering teams often look to the model to suggest answers to the key questions that have been raised, they quickly realize that the modeling effort is likely to produce more insight than answers.

Once preliminary design solutions have been identified, subsequent "what if" types of analysis should be conducted to test the sensitivity of recommended network designs to changes in key logistics variables. The results of this step should provide a valuable set of recommendations for the number and general location of logistics facilities that will help to meet the desired objectives.

Step 4: Conduct a Facility Location Analysis

qualitative and quantitative

Once a general configuration of the desired logistics network has been recommended, the next task is to carefully analyze the attributes of specific regions and cities that are candidates for sites of logistics facilities. These analyses will have both quantitative and qualitative aspects. Many of the quantitative elements have already been incorporated into Step 3 of the modeling effort. The qualitative aspects, to be discussed in a later section of this chapter, include such considerations as labor climate, transportation issues, proximity to markets and customers, quality of life, taxes and industrial development incentives, supplier networks, land costs and utilities, and company preference.

location selection team

The effort in this step will be facilitated by the formation of a location selection team, which will collect information on specific attributes such as those identified earlier. In addition, this team should be able to examine potential sites in terms of topography, geology, and facility design. To supplement internally available resources, the firm may wish to engage the services of a consulting firm that specializes in assisting clients with the process of selecting a location.

initial screening

The first screening by the location selection team usually eliminates areas that are uneconomical from a logistics perspective, thereby reducing the number of alternatives. For example, consider the number of potential distribution center sites in the southeastern United States. Applying the logistics location determinant, the team may find that the logistically optimum location is in the Tennessee/Georgia area. This definitely reduces the number of potential sites and enables the team to direct the location analysis toward a specific area.

Step 5: Make Decisions Regarding Network and Facility Location

compare recommendations with criteria

Next, the network and specific sites for logistics facilities recommended in Steps 3 and 4 should be evaluated for consistency with the design criteria that were identified in Step 1. This step should confirm the types of change that are needed to the firm's logistics network and should do so in the context of overall supply chain positioning. Although the feasibility of involving third-party suppliers should have been incorporated into the alternatives that were evaluated in the two preceding steps, the decision to involve external suppliers will have cost and service implications as well as strategic ones.

Step 6: Develop an Implementation Plan

strategic implementation

Once the overall direction has been established, the development of an effective implementation plan, or "blueprint for change," is critical. This plan should serve as a useful road map for moving from the current logistics network to the desired one. Since it was known from the beginning that this reengineering process was likely to produce recommendations for significant change, it is important that the firm commit the resources necessary to assure a smooth, timely implementation.

MAJOR LOCATIONAL DETERMINANTS

The focus of Step 4 in the logistics network redesign process is on analyzing the attributes of specific regions and areas that are candidates for sites of logistics facilities. Table 14–1 lists a number of major locational determinants for both regional and site-specific locations. While these factors are listed in general order of importance, the relative weighting applied to each depends on the details of the specific location decision under consideration.

TABLE 14–1 Major Locational Determinants

Regional Determinants	Site-Specific Determinants
Labor climate	Transportation access
Availability of transportation	• Truck
Proximity to markets and customers	• Air
Quality of life	• Rail
Taxes and industrial development incentives	• Water
Supplier networks	Inside/Outside metropolitan area
Land costs and utilities	Availability of workforce
Company preference	Land costs and taxes
	Utilities

variation by industry and company

The importance of major locational determinants varies among industries and among individual companies within specific industries. For example, labor-intensive industries such as textiles, furniture, and household appliances place significant emphasis on the availability and cost of labor in both regional and local market areas. Alternatively, manufacturers of high-tech products such as computers and peripherals, semiconductors, and engineering and scientific instruments place great emphasis on assuring the availability of a highly qualified workforce with very specific technical skills and, as discussed earlier, proximity to customer markets. For industries such as drugs, beverages, and printing and publishing, in which competition or logistics costs are significant, other logistics variables are very important.

Key Factors for Consideration

This discussion focuses attention on the regional determinants shown in Table 14–1. Because the site-specific determinants cannot be generalized as readily, this level of detail should be acquired and evaluated through the efforts of the location selection team.

Labor Climate. Location decision makers consider a number of factors in determining an area's labor climate. Given the typically labor-intensive nature of many logistics operations, the cost and availability of labor are major issues of concern. Other factors to be considered include the workforce's degree of unionization, skill level, work ethic, productivity, and the enthusiasm of local public officials. The existence of state right-to-work laws (which prohibit union membership as a condition of employment), and the unionization of major area employers reveal the area workforce's degree of unionization. Government information regarding work stoppages, productivity (value added per employee), and skill levels is available for most areas. Data regarding hourly earnings by industry and occupation are available from governmental agencies.

Another labor-related factor to be considered is the rate of unemployment in the local areas under consideration. While many other factors may seem to be quite acceptable, low levels of unemployment may require a firm to significantly increase its projected hourly wage scales to attract qualified workers. This sometimes unexpected increase may affect the overall attractiveness of a particular local area under consideration. The location study team will need to visit areas of potential interest to gather impressions and study attitudes regarding work ethic, absenteeism, potential labor-management issues, and the cooperativeness of state and local public officials.

transport services and cost

Availability of Transportation. Given the need by many firms for high-quality, capable transportation services, this factor is of great significance in many location decisions. Depending on the product type and industry to be served, a suitable location may require one or more of the following features: interstate highway access, availability of intermodal or local rail facilities, convenience of a major airport facility, proximity to inland or ocean port facilities, and so on. The number of serving carriers, as well as the breadth of overall transport capabilities, are factors that may need to be evaluated.

Considering the significant service improvements that have been made in recent years by many transportation firms, most regional and local areas are strong in at least one or more areas related to transportation. For certain high-value, low-weight products, such as computers, semiconductors, and electronic equipment, it may be that the location decision will focus on identifying a single national or international geographical area from which to distribute the company's entire manufactured output. Given the time-sensitive logistics services available today from firms such as FedEx, UPS, Emery, DHL, and Airborne, this strategy is becoming more prevalent.

market oriented

Proximity to Markets and Customers. The nearness-to-market factor usually considers both logistics and competitive variables. Logistics variables include the availability of transportation, the freight cost, and the geographical market size that can be served, for example, on a same-day or next-morning basis. The greater the number of customer firms within the market area, the greater the competitive advantage offered by the proposed location.

Although many companies place a high priority on locating logistics facilities near markets and customers, an overly complex logistics network can be disadvantageous from a cost perspective. Also, the availability of high-quality transportation services and capable information technologies has resulted in an expansion of the geographical areas that can be served in a timely manner from key logistics facilities.

Quality of Life. A particular region's or area's quality of life is difficult to quantify, but it does affect the well-being of employees and the quality of the work they are expected to perform. The quality-of-life factor is more important to companies that must attract and retain a mobile professional and technical workforce capable of moving to any location. Such a situation is common in the high-tech industry, especially in a company's research and development operations. The *Places Rated Almanac*[2] rates the quality of life in metropolitan areas in terms of climate, housing costs, health care and environment, crime, passenger transportation, education, recreation, the arts, and economic opportunities.

financial considerations

Taxes and Industrial Development Incentives. It is important to have advance knowledge of state and local taxes that apply to businesses and individuals. Prevailing business taxes, including revenue or income taxes, inventory taxes, property taxes, and so on will have a significant impact on the cost of operating a business in the area under consideration. Personal taxes that may affect the attractiveness of a particular region or local area include taxes on income and property, as well as applicable sales taxes, excise taxes, and so forth.

Another significant factor is the availability of industrial development incentives, which are used by some states and communities to entice companies to locate in their area. Examples include tax incentives (reduced rates or tax abatements on things such as property, inventory, or sales), financing arrangements (state loans or state-guaranteed loans), reduced water and sewage rates, and rent-free buildings that are built by the community to the company's specifications. Most states have an industrial development commission that provides information about state and local inducements. In addition, early contact and discussions with representatives of the state and local-area banking institutions and financial communities will provide a wide range of useful information, as well as commitments regarding financing and other services.

Mercedes-Benz example

As an example, in 1993, the State of Alabama offered numerous incentives in its successful effort to be selected as the site for Mercedes-Benz AG's first U.S. car plant.[3] Among the incentives offered were an agreement to build a $35 million training center at the company's plant and to pay employees' salaries while they studied; a willingness to purchase more than 2,500 Mercedes vehicles for state use; and prominent placement of the distinctive Mercedes emblem in a football stadium in which the big, televised Alabama-Tennessee football game was scheduled to be played. Overall, it was estimated that Alabama would provide Mercedes with well over $300 million in industrial development incentives in return for being selected as the site for the new facility.

supply oriented

Supplier Networks. In the case of a manufacturing facility, the availability and cost of raw materials and component parts, as well as the cost of transporting these materials to the proposed plant site, are of significance. For a distribution center, it is important to know how the proposed facility sites will fit with the geographic locations of key supplier facilities. In either instance, the cost and service sensitivity of the inbound movements from suppliers will be important to consider.

As an example, consider the case of Lear Corporation, a company that is a supplier of seats for two Ford Motor Company truck plants. Essentially, the seats are manufactured in sequence so that they can go right off the delivery vehicle onto the Ford assembly line in the order in which they will be installed. Faced with the need to expand, and knowing that its existing plant was landlocked, Lear chose a new plant site that was ten minutes away from one plant and twenty minutes from the other. As a result, for twenty hours per day, trucks loaded with seats leave the Lear factory every fifteen minutes. According to Lear company officials, the location is about as far away from the customer as they can afford and still deliver true, JIT (just-in-time) deliveries.

Land Costs and Utilities. Depending on the type of facility under consideration, issues relating to the cost of land and the availability of needed utilities are more or less critical. In the case of a manufacturing plant or distribution center, for example, it may be that a certain minimum acreage or parcel size is needed for current use as well as future expansion. This represents a potentially significant expense. Factors such as local building codes and cost of construction are important to consider. Also, the availability and expense of utilities such as electrical

ON THE LINE

TENNESSEE—SITE FOR EXPANDED MANUFACTURING CAPACITY

After evaluating more than twenty cities in other geographical areas of the United States, Dell Computer chose Nashville, Tennessee, as the site for an expansion of its personal computer manufacturing operations. This location represented the first move for this company beyond its operations in the state of Texas. Following consideration of other locations in the Southeast, Southwest, and Western United States, Dell's selection of Tennessee was based on a number of factors, including: proximity to Dell customers, access to a capable logistics network, general business climate, telecommunications capabilities, and the availability of skilled workers.

While this is the first time a major computer manufacturer selected Tennessee as a site for manufacturing, sales, and technical support, the state has for many years been a popular choice for automotive manufacturing and supplier locations. For example, in the 1980s the State of Tennessee invested approximately $100 million to lure Nissan (manufacturing plant in Smyrna) and Saturn (manufacturing plant in Spring Hill) to locate in the state. More recently, Tennessee ranked fourth in the United States in terms of auto production, with about 140,000 residents working either for auto makers or for the 829 automotive suppliers that operate across the state. Figures compiled by the Tennessee Department of Economic and Community Development suggest that the state's automotive industry is responsible for approximately $6 billion annually in payroll.[1]

Looking more closely at the Dell decision to open a new manufacturing plant along I–40, approximately twelve miles east of the Nashville International Airport, the 260,000-square-foot facility was expected to involve an employee population of more than 1,000. Also, Dell constructed additional manufacturing space on its Nashville campus near the airport. This second plant occupies 300,000 square feet of space to support manufacturing of additional lines of notebook computers. Clearly, Dell's investment in its Tennessee facilities represented a significant, strategic element of its overall manufacturing, sales, and technical support capabilities. From the perspective of Nashville and the State of Tennessee, the overall positive economic impact of having Dell locate in Tennessee was worth the estimated $25 million they planned to spend on infrastructure improvements, worker training, and tax credits.[2]

Source: Portions have been developed from information available on the Dell Computer Web site, www.dell.com. Used with permission.

[1]Details relating to the automotive industry presence in Tennessee have been drawn from Kathy Brister, "Ripple Effect," *Knoxville News Sentinel* (15 July 1999).

[2]Ibid.

power, sewage, and industrial waste disposal need to be factored into the decision-making process.

Company Preference. Aside from all of the preceding types of factors, it may be that a company, or its CEO for that matter, prefers a certain region and/or local area for the location of a logistics facility. For example, a company may prefer to locate all new facilities in rural areas within fifty miles of a major metropolitan area. Or a company may wish to locate its facilities in areas where competitors already have a presence. In other instances, a firm may wish to locate facilities in an area where it may enjoy common access with other firms to benefits such as a skilled labor supply, excellent marketing resources, or proximity to key supplier industries. This determinant is referred to as *agglomeration,* a phenomenon that sometimes explains why certain firms tend to co-locate facilities.

Current Trends Governing Site Selection

There are a number of trends in today's logistics environment that may have significant effects on decisions involving logistics facility location. Included among these are the following.

location trends

- Strategic positioning of inventories, such that fast-moving, profitable items may be located at "market-facing" logistics facilities. Slower-moving, less-profitable items may be located at more regional, or national, facilities. These examples are consistent with implementation of effective, inventory segmentation strategies.
- Aside from a general trend toward "disintermediation" of many wholesaler/distributor operations, companies are moving to greater use of "customer-direct" delivery from manufacturing and other upstream supply chain locations. Many times, this bypasses and diminishes the need for complete networks of distribution facilities. Increased use of "drop" shipments provides deliveries of product direct from manufacturing to the customer, thus eliminating the need for intermediate distribution capabilities.
- There is a growing use of and need for strategically located "cross-docking" facilities that serve as transfer points for consolidated shipments that need to be disaggregated or mixed into typically smaller shipments for delivery to individual customers. An example of this would be the consolidation of multiple-vendor shipments into full trailerloads being shipped to retail stores or points of use. Applied to inbound movements, this concept can significantly reduce the need for inbound consolidation facilities.
- Greater use of providers of third-party-logistics services, who may assume part or all of the responsibility for moving a firm's products to its customers, and/or moving its inbound parts and materials to its manufacturing process.

MODELING APPROACHES

This section focuses broadly on the topic of modeling approaches that can provide insight into the choice of a logistics network design. As such, the techniques discussed here are applicable to a wide range of issues pertaining to the locations of plants, distribution centers, and customers and to the flows of product and information to support the functioning of the logistics network. The principal modeling approaches to be covered are optimization, simulation, and heuristic models. Detailed coverage of the grid method for facility location is included as part of the discussion of heuristic modeling approaches.

use of techniques

As was indicated previously, the use of appropriate modeling techniques will facilitate a comparison of the functioning and cost/service effectiveness of current versus proposed logistics networks. Once an appropriate modeling procedure has been selected, it should be used to help identify a logistics network that is consistent with the key objectives identified earlier in the logistics network redesign process. After preliminary solutions have been identified, subsequent "what if" types of analyses should be conducted to test the sensitivity of the recommended network designs to changes in key logistics variables.

Optimization Models

The *optimization model* is based on precise mathematical procedures that are guaranteed to find the "best," or optimum, solution, given the mathematical definition of the problem under evaluation. This means that it can be proved mathematically that the resulting solution is the best. The simple EOQ model, discussed earlier, is an example of a technique that produces an "optimum" solutions.

search for optimum solutions

While recognizing relevant constraints, optimization approaches essentially select an optimal course of action from a number of feasible alternatives. The optimization models in use today incorporate such techniques as mathematical programming (linear, integer, dynamic, mixed-integer linear, etc.), enumeration, sequencing, and the use of calculus.[4] Many of these have been incorporated into software packages that are commercially available.

Figure 14–3 lists the types of issues that may be addressed through the use of optimization techniques. Several advantages of this overall type of approach are as follows:

key issues

- The user is guaranteed to have the best solution possible for a given set of assumptions and data.
- Many complex model structures can be handled correctly.
- The analysis and evaluation of all alternatives that are generated result in a more efficient analysis.
- Reliable run-to-run comparisons can be made, since the "best" solution is guaranteed for each run.
- Cost or profit savings between the optimum and heuristic solution can be significant.[5]

One of the optimization techniques that has traditionally received significant attention is linear programming, or LP. This approach is most useful for linking facilities in a network where supply and demand limitations at plants, distribution centers, or market areas must be treated as constraints. Given an objective function that focuses attention on, for example, minimizing total cost, LP defines the optimum facility distribution pattern consistent with the problem's demand-supply constraints. Although this technique is actually quite useful, its applicability is limited due to the need for the problem formulation to be deterministic and capable of linear approximation. Also, the use of LP itself does not allow for consideration of fixed as well as variable costs of operating logistics facilities.

linear programming

The use of mixed-integer linear programming permits the model to deal with issues such as fixed and variable costs, capacity constraints, economies of scale, cross-product limitations, and unique sourcing requirements. One of the leading models of this type is SAILS (Strategic Analysis for Integrated Logistics Systems), developed by Insight, Inc. Figure 14–4 illustrates the supply chain complexity that may be addressed by a capable network optimization model such as SAILS. In brief, SAILS answers the question, "Given demand for a set of products, either historical or forecast, what is the optimal configuration of the production/distribution network to satisfy that demand at specified service levels and lowest cost?"

Once a modeling database, either simple or complex, has been created, the use of SAILS facilitates the rapid generation and evaluation of many alternate scenarios

SAILS

FIGURE 14–3 Strategic Issues Relevant to Logistics Network Modeling

Network rationalization issues

- Customer service levels to be maintained
- Assignments of customers to distribution centers (DCs)
- Number and locations of DCs
- Mission of each DC—inventories and service territory
- Assignments of DCs to plants by product
- Number and locations of plants
- Mission of each plant—production to product, inventories, and service territory

"What if" questions

- Environmental issues
  —Market shifts
  —Strikes, natural disasters, energy shortage
  —Global economic conditions
- Logistics system decisions
  —Impacts of changes in mode choice and/or carrier selection
  —Use of company-operated versus contract versus third-party-logistics operations
  —Incorporation of plant-direct to customer shipments
- Business decisions and policy issues
  —Plant capacity expansion
  —New product introduction
  —Shipment planning policy analysis
  —DC capacity expansion or elimination
  —Multidivision distribution system merger
  —Merger/Consolidation with other businesses

Cost and service sensitivity issues

- Total production/Logistics system cost
- Logistics cost versus customer service
- Logistics cost as function of number of DCs
- Demand forecasts

Source: Adapted from SAILS™ (Strategic Analysis for Integrated Logistics Systems), (Manassas, Va.: Insight, Inc., 2001). Used with permission.

FIGURE 14–4 Supply Chain Scenario for Network Analysis

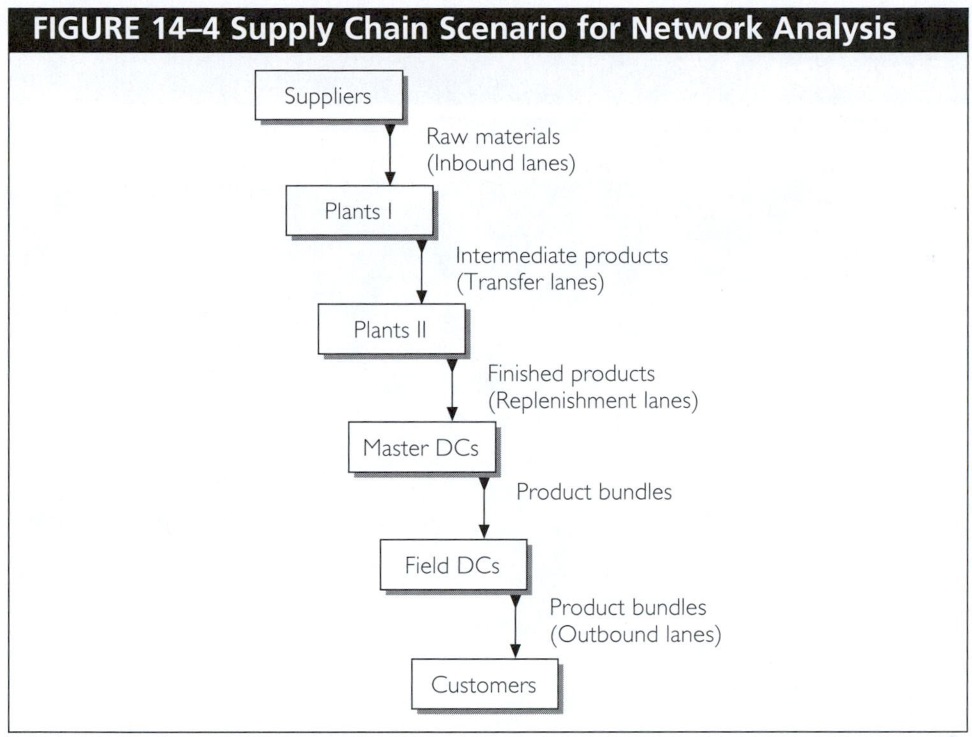

Source: SAILS™ (Manassas, Va.: Insight, Inc., 2001). Used with permission.

for analysis.[6] There are also numerous shipment planning controls that permit the user to evaluate the network impact of various shipment planning options such as pooling, stop-offs, pickups, and direct plant shipments. SAILS is a highly flexible logistics modeling tool that can be used for a range of problems from the very simple to ones in which data may exist in the form of millions of shipment transactions. When a given modeling scenario has been generated, SAILS utilizes mixed-integer linear programming, along with an advanced technique called network factorization, to produce an optimum solution. Typical data inputs to SAILS include: Customer demand (either forecast or historical); aggregated product and customer identification; facility data for plants and DCs; transportation options and rates; and policy considerations such as shipment planning rules, DC inventory constraints, and customer service requirements.

Although optimization approaches typically require significant computer resources, the availability of capable systems today has greatly facilitated their ease of use. Along with improvements in model design and solver technologies, future approaches should be even more convenient for general use by those involved with the design and analysis of logistics networks.

In addition to improved analytical techniques, the availability of insightful visual representations of logistics networks has enhanced our ability to gain insight into network alternatives. Figure 14–5 is an example of the types of "geo-mapping" alternatives that are currently available.

FIGURE 14–5 Example "Geographical-Mapping" Representation

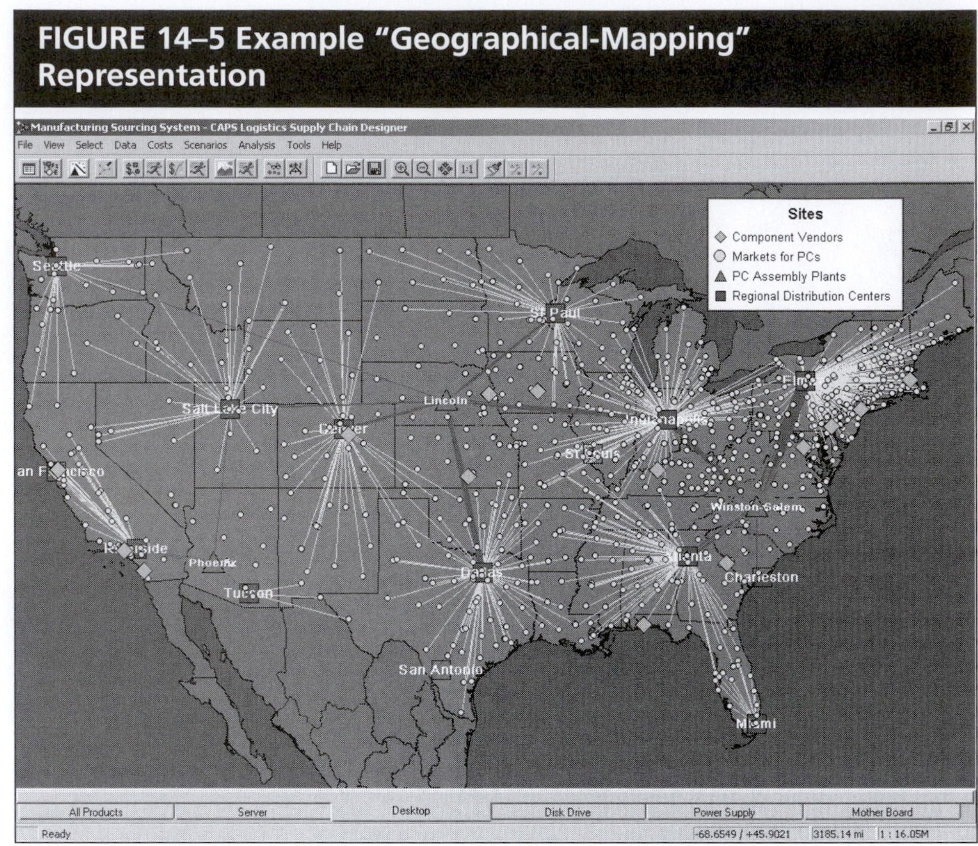

Source:

Simulation Models

The second approach to logistics network design includes the development and use of *simulation models.* Simulation is defined as "the process of designing a model of a real system and conducting experiments with this model for the purpose either of understanding the behavior of the system or of evaluating various strategies within the limits imposed by a criterion or set of criteria for the operation of the system."[7] Network simulation involves developing a computer representation of the logistics network and then observing the cost and service characteristics of the network as cost structures, constraints, and other factors are varied. It has been stated that the process of simulation is "nothing more or less than the technique of performing *sampling experiments* on the model of the system."[8]

sensitivity analysis

For location analysis, the use of simulation allows the decision maker to test the effect of alternative locations upon costs and service levels. The modeling requires extensive data collection and analysis to determine how system factors such as transportation, warehousing, inventory, materials handling, and labor costs interact. The simulation process evaluates the decision maker's selected sites to determine respective costs. Simulation does not guarantee an optimum solution but simply evaluates the alternatives that are fed into it.[9] A critical characteristic of a simulation tool is whether it is static or dynamic in nature. A dynamic tool will not

static versus dynamic

only incorporate a multiperiod time perspective but also update system status for each time period based on the results of the previous time periods.

According to Ballou, simulation has value in business network planning.[10] Although it does not search directly for the best warehouse configuration, its problem description can be very rich, including cost functions that are nonlinear (inventory), stepwise (labor costs), and discontinuous (quantity discounts). Simulation continues to be used as a stand-alone approach but also is used as a supplemental methodology within other search-oriented approaches. If for no other reason, simulation is needed to replicate, or cost out, the current logistics network of a firm so that potential improvements from location analysis can be compared to it.

Although simulation models are not designed to produce optimum solutions, they are very capable in terms of their ability to incorporate relatively comprehensive and detailed problem descriptions. Sometimes an optimization approach is used first to identify and evaluate feasible network design alternatives, and then highly customized simulation models are used to focus on the exact logistics network that will best meet the desired objectives.

Heuristic Models

Heuristic models are able to accommodate broad problem definitions, but they do not provide an optimum solution. The use of a heuristic approach can help to reduce a problem to a manageable size and search automatically through various alternatives in an attempt to find a better solution. As is indicated in the discussion of the grid technique that follows, heuristic approaches can provide a good approximation to the least-cost location in a complex decision problem. To reduce the number of location alternatives, the decision maker should incorporate into the heuristic program site characteristics considered to be optimal.

For example, the location team may consider an optimum warehouse site to be (1) within twenty miles of a major market area, (2) at least 250 miles from other company distribution centers, (3) within three miles of an interstate highway, and (4) within forty miles of a major airport facility. The heuristic model searches for sites with these characteristics, thus reducing the number of alternative sites to those the decision maker considers practical.

Additionally, heuristic decision rules are sometimes incorporated into the decision-making process in what may appear to be "rules of thumb." Examples might include requirements to locate distribution centers at or near points of demand, to supply customers from the nearest distribution facility, to choose as the next distribution site the one that will produce the greatest cost savings, or to serve all customers within a twenty-four-hour delivery time.[11]

powerful heuristic approaches

As we are reminded by Ratliff and Nulty,[12] sometimes the word *heuristics* implies a "seat-of-the-pants" solution approach, involving little or no intelligence or sophistication. They suggest that this is unfortunate, as many times, analytical heuristics can be as technically sophisticated as mathematical optimization approaches. Many heuristics are based on mathematical optimization models and algorithms, such as using practical rules to formulate a mathematical optimization model. A powerful heuristic approach is to modify a mixed-integer program by temporarily assuming the integer variables to be linear in nature, thus creating an approximate but much more solvable model. Then, the solution to this model is used as a basis for constructing a solution to the integer problem.

Potential Supply Chain Modeling Pitfalls to Avoid

According to Bender, there are a number of common pitfalls that should be avoided in designing and implementing an optimum worldwide supply chain.[13] To recognize these in advance should help to maximize the value to be achieved through use of appropriate mathematical techniques for supply chain network design.

pitfalls to avoid

- *Short-term horizon.* Unless modeling features are designed, implemented, and used with a long-term perspective, significant suboptimization is likely to occur.
- *Too little or too much detail.* Too little detail can make it difficult to implement results due to insufficient information; too much detail can create unnecessary complexity, making it difficult to understand the results and more difficult to implement effectively.
- *Thinking in two dimensions.* While the use of two-dimensional maps certainly helps to provide insight into supply chain problems, the geometry of the networks may ignore cost and geographical dispersions of demand. Over significant distances, and particularly for global supply chain analyses, the curvature of the earth may distort distance calculations, in which case needed adjustments must be made.
- *Using published costs.* Many "published" costs tend to represent "list" prices that need to be modified to reflect what may result after significant negotiations occur between buyers and sellers of transport services.
- *Inaccurate or incomplete costs.* Analyses based on insufficiently accurate information lead to invalid results; inaccurate cost forecasts result in suboptimal allocations of resources, typically leading to seriously flawed strategies.
- *Use of erroneous analytical techniques.* The selected techniques and approaches should be matched with the level of precision desired; the identification of modeling objectives is an important forerunner to the selection of the techniques to be utilized.
- *Lack of appropriate robustness analysis.* Since most or all model inputs have at least an element of uncertainty, it is important to understand the consequences that could result from variation in actual behavior of key model inputs; robustness analysis can help to assure the practicality and validity of the results from the selected analyses.

Example of a Heuristic Modeling Approach: The Grid Technique

Although other factors are also important, the availability and expense of transportation service are factors that are commonly included in location analyses. While transportation itself can represent a significant cost, decision makers should strive to make the final decision on the basis of the full range of relevant cost factors, as well as on the customer service implications of the network alternative being evaluated.

grid technique

The grid technique is a simplistic, but well-known, heuristic approach to help companies with multiple markets and multiple supply points determine a least-cost

SUPPLY CHAIN TECHNOLOGY

TOYOTA MOTOR SALES USA, INC.

In 1999, Toyota Motor Sales USA, Inc., decided that its U.S. distribution network was due for a tune-up. The three-decade-old system of warehouses had been established at a time when the Japanese automaker sourced most of its parts from overseas to serve a small network of U.S. dealerships.

Under the existing system, the Torrance, California-based company has been providing U.S. after-sales support to 1,200 car dealerships, 200 Lexus luxury car dealers, and 100 forklift dealers via a two-tiered system. Toyota had not undertaken a strategic network analysis since 1978, but its operations had changed significantly since that time. Key areas in which change has occurred include the following: explosion of the dealership network, shifting customer base and geographical concentration, greater parts sourcing in North America rather than from Japan, and added responsibility for Lexus parts distribution.

A major question to be answered by Toyota was "what would be the optimal network for an organization that moves more than eight million parts and accessories around the country each month?" To answer that question, Toyota turned to computer modeling and, specifically, to the use of network optimization software. When the computer model was run for the first time, it showed that Toyota needed another DC in the Texas area to serve its Lexus car dealerships. Although Lexus parts support had been handled by the Kansas City facility, issues relating to overcapacity made this an inferior situation from a cost and service perspective. Modeling results indicated that Toyota could realize \$2 million in savings by cutting back on expedited ground transportation and on emergency air shipments of Lexus parts. Also, a dedicated Lexus parts facility would improve customer service to Lexus dealerships by speeding up parts delivery so that 88 percent of parts orders would be delivered in one day and the remaining 12 percent in two days.

Overall, this Toyota parts distribution system redesign initiative produced a number of highly desirable results. Also, the company reports gaining knowledge that "customers with newer cars might have different parts-replacement service expectations from those of customers owning older vehicles." Although the company has decided on the Texas location, a yet-to-be-made decision was whether to operate the 60,000-square-foot facility itself or outsource the operation to a third-party-logistics concern.

In addition, the overall examination of the existing parts distribution system, using state-of-the-art modeling, helped to make Toyota executives aware of the possible benefits of reconfiguring the company's U.S. distribution network. The project's main selling point was that customer service and responsiveness would be significantly improved—and that objective was met.

Source: Adapted from material in James A. Cooke, "Toyota Tunes Up Its Distribution Network," *Logistics Management and Distribution Report* (1 March 2001). Copyright Cahners Business Information. Reprinted by permission.

facility location. Essentially, the grid technique attempts to determine a fixed facility (such as a plant or distribution center) location that represents the least-cost center for moving inbound materials and outbound product within a geographic grid. The technique determines the low-cost "center of gravity" for moving raw materials and finished goods.

This technique assumes that the raw materials sources and finished goods markets are fixed and that a company knows the amount of each product it consumes or sells. The technique then superimposes a grid upon the geographic area containing the raw materials sources and finished goods markets. The grid's zero point

approach

FIGURE 14–6 Grid Locations of Sources and Markets

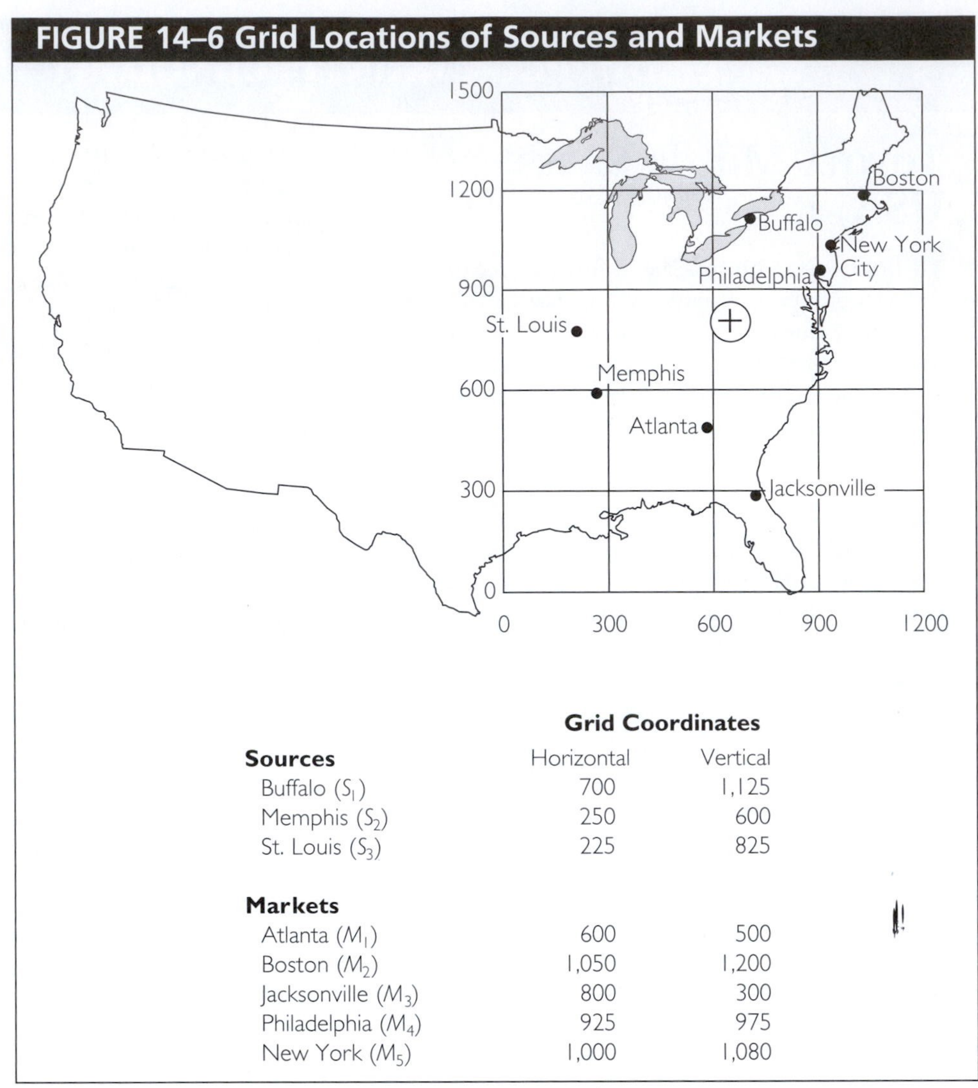

	Grid Coordinates	
Sources	Horizontal	Vertical
Buffalo (S_1)	700	1,125
Memphis (S_2)	250	600
St. Louis (S_3)	225	825
Markets		
Atlanta (M_1)	600	500
Boston (M_2)	1,050	1,200
Jacksonville (M_3)	800	300
Philadelphia (M_4)	925	975
New York (M_5)	1,000	1,080

corresponds to an exact geographic location, as do the grid's other points. Thus, the company can identify each source and market by its grid coordinates.

Figure 14–6 is an example of a supply source and market environment for a company that is deciding where to locate a plant. The company, which has located supply sources and markets on the map and has superimposed a grid system over the source-market area, purchases raw materials from sources in Buffalo, Memphis, and St. Louis—S_1, S_2 and S_3, respectively. The new plant will serve five markets: Atlanta, Boston, Jacksonville, Philadelphia, and New York—M_1, M_2, M_3, M_4, and M_5, respectively.

grid location

The technique defines each source and market location in terms of its horizontal and vertical grid coordinates. For example, the Jacksonville market (M_3) has a horizontal grid coordinate of 800 and a vertical grid coordinate of 300. The Buffalo source is located at grid coordinates 700 horizontal and 1,125 vertical.

strings, weights, and knot

We can visualize this technique's underlying concept as a series of strings to which are attached weights corresponding to the weight of raw materials the company consumes at each source and of finished goods the company sells at each market. The strings are threaded through holes in a flat plane; the holes correspond to the source and market locations. The strings' other ends are tied together, and the weights exert their respective pulls on the knot. The strings' knotted ends will finally reach an equilibrium; this equilibrium will be the center of mass, or the ton-mile center.

ton-mile center

We can compute this concept mathematically, finding the ton-mile center, or center of mass, as follows:

$$C = \frac{\sum_{1}^{m} d_i S_i + \sum_{1}^{n} D_i M_i}{\sum_{1}^{m} S_i + \sum_{1}^{n} M_i}$$

where

C = center of mass, or ton-mile center

D_i = distance from 0 point on grid to the grid location of finished good i

d_i = distance from 0 point on grid to the grid location of raw material i

M_i = weight (volume) of finished goods sold in market i

S_i = weight (volume) of raw material purchased at source i

location and transportation rate

This equation will generate the least-cost location if transportation rates for raw materials and finished goods are the same. But transportation rates vary among commodities, and the ton-mile center equation does not reflect differences in the costs of moving commodities. The transportation rate pulls the location toward the location of the commodity with the higher rate. Thus, the higher rates of finished goods will draw the least-cost location toward the finished goods market and thereby reduce the distance the company moves these higher-rated goods. This will increase the distance the company transports lower-rated raw materials.

Thus, we must incorporate into our analysis the transportation rates of different products. This modification is as follows:

$$C = \frac{\sum_{1}^{m} r_i d_i S_i + \sum_{1}^{n} R_i D_i M_i}{\sum_{1}^{m} r_i S_i + \sum_{1}^{n} R_i M_i}$$

where

R_i = finished good transportation rate/distance unit for finished good i

r_i = raw material rate/distance unit for raw material i

linear rates

R_i and r_i are the transportation rates per distance unit, and we assume them to be linear with respect to distance. This assumption does not correspond to the tapering principle of rates (to be discussed later), but it does simplify the analysis.

Plant Location Example. Table 14–2 presents relevant data for a plant location example, as well as the grid technique solution using a computer spreadsheet

TABLE 14–2 Grid Technique Analysis of Plant Location Example

Sources/Markets	Rate $/Ton-Mile (A)	Tons (B)	Grid Coordinates Hor.	Grid Coordinates Vert.	Calculations (A) ∗ (B) ∗ Hor.	Calculations (A) ∗ (B) ∗ Vert.
Buffalo (S_1)	$0.90	500	700	1,125	315,000	506,250
Memphis (S_2)	$0.95	300	250	600	71,250	171,000
St. Louis (S_3)	$0.85	700	225	825	133,875	490,875
		1,500			520,125	1,168,125
Atlanta (M_1)	$1.50	225	600	500	202,500	168,750
Boston (M_2)	$1.50	150	1,050	1,200	236,250	270,000
Jacksonville (M_3)	$1.50	250	800	300	300,000	112,500
Philadelphia (M_4)	$1.50	175	925	975	242,813	255,938
New York (M_5)	$1.50	300	1,000	1,080	450,000	486,000
	TOTALS	1,100			1,431,563	1,293,188

	Horizontal	Vertical
Numerator: $\Sigma\,(r * d * S)$ =	520,125	1,168,125
$+\Sigma\,(R * D * M)$ =	1,431,563	1,293,188
Sum	1,951,688	2,461,313
Denominator: $\Sigma\,(r * S)$ =	1,330	1,330
$+\Sigma\,(R * M)$ =	1,650	1,650
Sum	2,980	2,980
Grid Center	655	826

program. The grid coordinates of the raw materials sources and markets correspond to their locations on the grid in Figure 14–6. For simplicity, we will assume that this company produces only one type of finished good, so that each finished good's transportation rate is the same.

compute two coordinates

To determine the least-cost center on the grid, we must compute two grid coordinates, one for moving the commodities along the horizontal axis and one for moving them along the vertical axis. We compute the two coordinates by using the grid technique formula for each direction.

Table 14–2 provides this example's computations. The two columns at the far right contain the calculations that the grid technique equation indicates. The first calculations column contains the calculations for the horizontal numerator, or the sum of the rate times the horizontal grid coordinate times the tonnage for each raw material source and market. The calculations at the bottom of Table 14–2 indicate the numerator and denominator of the grid technique equation.

As Table 14–2 indicates, the plant location's least-cost center in this example is 655 in the horizontal direction and 826 in the vertical direction. We measure both distances from the grid's zero point. Figure 14–6 indicates the least-cost center as point +. The least-cost location for the plant is in southeastern Ohio or northwestern West Virginia in the Wheeling-Parkersburg area.

The preceding example applied the grid technique to a plant location. Companies can use the technique to solve warehousing location problems as well. The company follows the same procedure, but the company's plants are the raw material sources.

warehouse application

Advantages. The grid technique's strengths are in its simplicity and its ability to provide a starting point for location analysis. Computationally, the technique is relatively easy to use. A company can generate the necessary data from sales figures, purchase records, and transportation documents (either the bill of lading or the freight bill). More exact market and source location coding is possible, as is modifying the rate-distance relationship quantification. A computer can easily handle such refinements.

simplicity

The grid technique also provides a starting point for making a location decision. As we suggested earlier, transportation cost is not the only locational determinant. Using the grid technique can eliminate certain areas, permitting the decision maker to focus on an area that is logistically advantageous. For example, the grid technique may suggest Toledo, Ohio, as the least-cost location for a plant to serve the Ohio, Michigan, Indiana, and Illinois market area. This eliminates consideration of Chicago, Indianapolis, and other regional cities and permits the decision maker to concentrate the location analysis in northwestern Ohio and southeastern Michigan. This is a tremendous step forward in the location decision process.

starting point

eliminates sites

Limitations. The grid technique has limitations that the decision maker must recognize. First, it is a static approach, and the solution is optimum for only one point in time. Changes in the volumes a company purchases or sells, changes in transportation rates, or changes in raw materials sources or market locations will shift the least-cost location. Second, the technique assumes linear transportation rates, whereas actual transportation rates increase with distance but less than proportionally. Third, the technique does not consider the topographic conditions existing at the optimum location; for example, the recommended site may be in the middle of a lake. Fourth, it does not consider the proper direction of movement; most moves occur along a straight line between two points, not "vertically" and then "horizontally."

static

linear rates

topography

direction

Sensitivity Analysis. As mentioned in the preceding paragraph, the grid technique is a static approach; the computed location is valid only for the situation analyzed. If the transportation rates, market and source locations, and volumes change, the least-cost location changes.

Sensitivity analysis enables the decision maker to ask "what if" questions and measure the resulting impact on the least-cost location. For example, the decision maker may examine the least-cost location in light of a five-year sales projection by inserting the estimated market sales volumes into the grid technique equation and determining the least-cost location. Other "what if" scenarios could include adding new markets and/or sources, eliminating markets and/or sources, and switching transportation modes, thereby changing rates.

"what if"

Tables 14–3 and 14–4 perform two sensitivity analyses for the original problem in Table 14–2. The first "what if" scenario considers switching from rail to truck to serve the Jacksonville market; the switch entails a 50 percent rate increase. The data in Table 14–3 shows that the rate increase shifts the least-cost location toward Jacksonville; that is, the new location grid coordinates are 664 and 795, or east and south of the original location (655, 826). Therefore, a rate increase will pull the least-cost location toward the market or supply source experiencing the increase.

rate increase

TABLE 14–3 Impact of Rate Change on Least-Cost Location

Sources/Markets	Rate $/Ton-Mile (A)	Tons (B)	Grid Coordinates Hor.	Vert.	Calculations (A) ✱ (B) ✱ Hor.	(A) ✱ (B) ✱ Vert.
Buffalo (S_1)	$0.90	500	700	1,125	315,000	506,250
Memphis (S_2)	$0.95	300	250	600	71,250	171,000
St. Louis (S_3)	$0.85	700	225	825	133,875	490,875
		1,500			520,125	1,168,125
Atlanta (M_1)	$1.50	225	600	500	202,500	168,750
Boston (M_2)	$1.50	150	1,050	1,200	236,250	270,000
Jacksonville (M_3)	$2.25	250	800	300	450,000	168,750
Philadelphia (M_4)	$1.50	175	925	975	242,813	255,938
New York (M_5)	$1.50	300	1,000	1,080	450,000	486,000
	TOTALS	1,100			1,581,563	1,349,438

	Horizontal	Vertical
Numerator: $\Sigma(r * d * S)$ =	520,125	1,168,125
$+\Sigma(R * D * M)$ =	1,581,563	1,349,438
Sum	2,101,688	2,517,563
Denominator: $\Sigma(r * S)$ =	1,330	1,330
$+\Sigma(R * M)$ =	1,838	1,838
Sum	3,168	3,168
Grid Center	664	795

sourcing change

The second "what if" sensitivity analysis considers the elimination of a Buffalo supply source and increasing by 500 tons the amount the example company purchases from Memphis. Table 14–4 shows the effect of this sourcing change. With Memphis supplying all the material the company formerly purchased from Buffalo, the new least-cost location moves toward Memphis, or south and west of the original location. Similarly, a new market or a market experiencing a sales volume increase will draw the least-cost location.

conclusions

We can conclude from these sensitivity analyses that the rates, product volumes, and source/market locations do affect a plant's least-cost location. The least-cost location moves toward a market or source experiencing a rate or volume increase, and away from the market or source experiencing a decrease. Introducing a new market or source pulls the location toward the additional market or source.

warehouse in a city

Application to Warehouse Location in a City. A special case exists for applying the grid technique to the location of a warehouse in a city. The situation's uniqueness comes from the blanket rate structure, which applies the same rate from an origin to any point within the city or commercial zone. Thus, any location within a city's commercial zone incurs the same inbound transportation cost from a company's mix of suppliers used; that is, the cost of moving supplies to a warehouse within the same city does not affect the location decision.

TABLE 14–4 Impact of Supply Source Change on Least-Cost Location

Sources/Markets	Rate $/Ton-Mile (A)	Tons (B)	Grid Coordinates Hor.	Grid Coordinates Vert.	Calculations (A) ✱ (B) ✱ Hor.	Calculations (A) ✱ (B) ✱ Vert.
Buffalo (S_1)	$0.90	0	700	1,125	0	0
Memphis (S_2)	$0.95	800	250	600	190,000	456,000
St. Louis (S_3)	$0.85	700	225	825	133,875	490,875
		1,500			323,875	946,875
Atlanta (M_1)	$1.50	225	600	500	202,500	168,750
Boston (M_2)	$1.50	150	1,050	1,200	236,250	270,000
Jacksonville (M_3)	$2.25	250	800	300	450,000	168,750
Philadelphia (M_4)	$1.50	175	925	975	242,813	255,938
New York (M_5)	$1.50	300	1,000	1,080	450,000	486,000
	TOTALS	1,100			1,581,563	1,349,438

	Horizontal	Vertical
Numerator: $\Sigma (r * d * S)$ =	323,875	946,875
$+ \Sigma (R * D * M)$ =	1,581,563	1,349,438
Sum	1,905,438	2,296,313
Denominator: $\Sigma (r * S)$ =	1,355	1,355
$+ \Sigma (R * M)$ =	1,838	1,838
Sum	3,193	3,193
Grid Center	597	719

Since the supply volumes moving into the warehouse do not affect the location decision, the least-cost warehouse location within a city considers the cost of moving finished goods from the warehouse to the customers. We modify the grid technique equation as follows:

$$C = \frac{\sum_{1}^{n} R_i D_i M_i}{\sum_{1}^{n} R_i M_i}$$

If we assume that the cost of distributing (R) the commodity throughout the city is the same, R cancels out, reducing the equation to a ton-mile center as follows:

$$C = \frac{\sum_{1}^{n} D_i M_i}{\sum_{1}^{n} M_i}$$

As before, this modified grid technique enables the decision maker to eliminate certain areas of the city and to concentrate the analysis upon sites in the general vicinity of the least-cost location's grid coordinates. To determine a specific site for the warehouse, the decision maker must consider land and facility availability, expressway systems, and highway access in this general vicinity.

Transportation Pragmatics[14]

The previous discussion showed the importance of the transportation factor in the facility location decision. We simplified the rate structure focus on the transportation factor's locational pull. In this section, we examine how dropping these transportation simplifications affects facility location, directing attention specifically toward tapering rates, blanket rates, commercial zones, foreign trade zones, and in-transit privileges.

Tapering Rates. As we pointed out earlier, transportation rates increase with distance but not in direct proportion to distance. This *tapering-rate* principle results from the carrier's ability to spread certain fixed shipment costs, such as loading, billing, and handling, over a greater number of miles. As noted by Edgar M. Hoover, a tapering rate in a one-source, one-market situation pulls the location to either the source or the market but not to a point in between.

rates versus distance

To illustrate this effect, consider the data in Table 14–5 and Figure 14–7. In this example, we assume the rates to be constant (the same) for raw materials supplied at *S* and finished products sold at *M*. The rates in Table 14–5 increase with distance but not proportionally. For example, the shipping rate from *S* is $2.00 for 50 miles and $3.00 for 100 miles, a distance increase of 100 percent but a rate increase of only 50 percent.

Table 14–5 and Figure 14–7 indicate that a location at either *S* or *M* will result in a total rate of $3.70. At any other location the total rate is higher. Thus, the tapering rate pulls the location toward the source or the market.

Dropping rate constancy between raw materials and finished goods draws the location toward *M*, the market. In Table 14–6 and Figure 14–8, the rates for moving the finished product into the market are higher than those for moving raw materials. The location having the least total transportation cost is at *M*, where the total transportation rate is $3.70.

TABLE 14–5 Locational Effects of Tapering Rates with Constant Rate Assumption

Distance from *S* (miles)	Transport Rate from *S*	Distance to *M* (miles)	Transport Rate to *M*	Total Transport Rate
0	$0.00	200	$3.70	$3.70
50	2.00	150	3.50	5.50
100	3.00	100	3.00	6.00
150	3.50	50	2.00	5.50
200	3.70	0	0.00	3.70

FIGURE 14–7 Locational Effects of Tapering Rates with Constant Rate Assumption

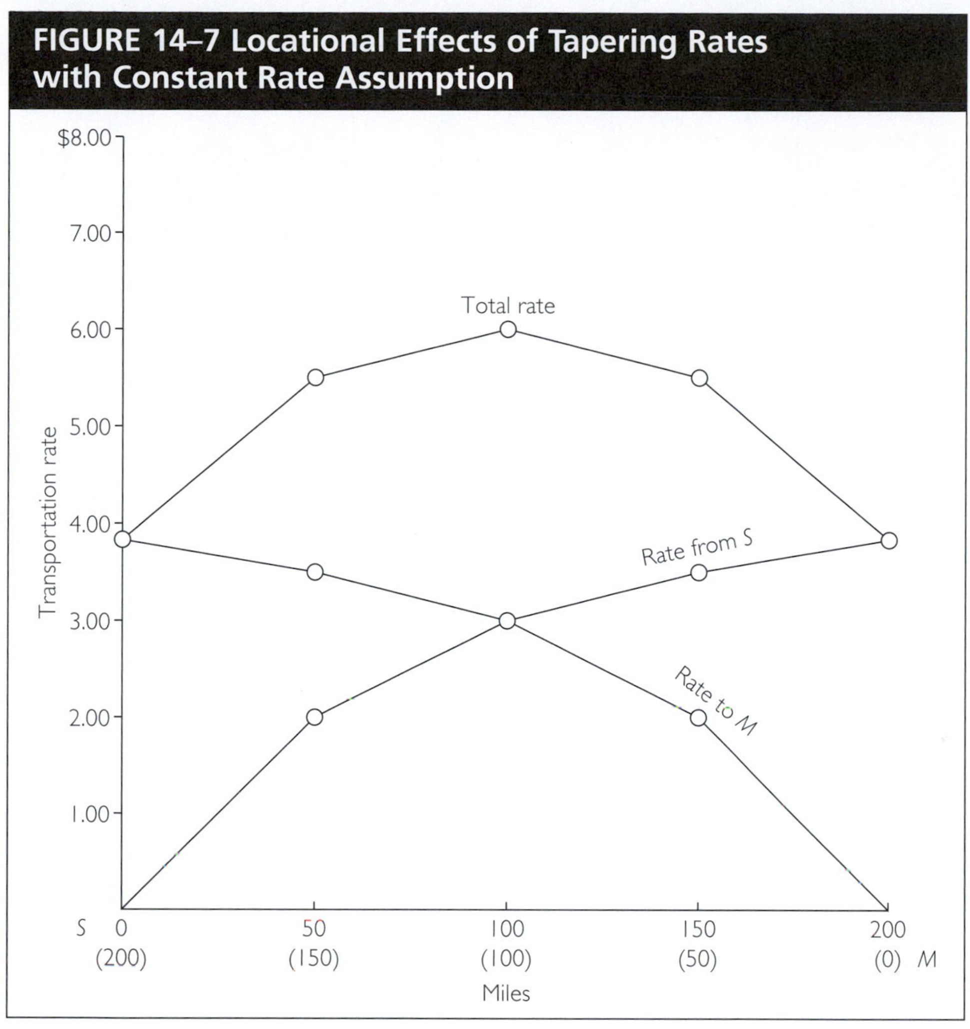

TABLE 14–6 Locational Effects of Tapering Rates without Constant Rate Assumption

Distance from *S* (Miles)	Transport Rate from *S*	Distance to *M* (Miles)	Transport Rate to *M*	Total Transport Rate
0	$0.00	200	$5.20	$5.20
50	2.00	150	5.00	7.00
100	3.00	100	4.50	7.50
150	3.50	50	3.50	7.00
200	3.70	0	0.00	3.70

FIGURE 14–8 Locational Effects of Tapering Rates without Constant Rate Assumption

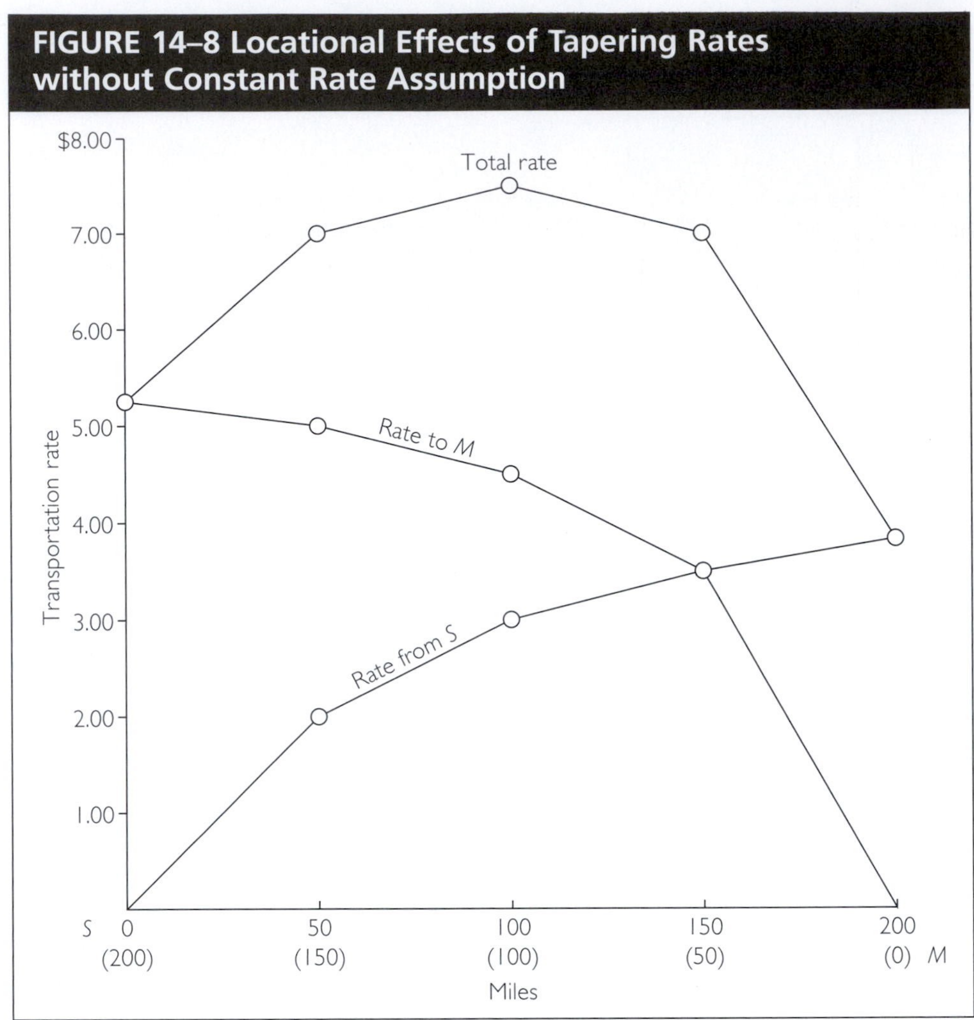

Blanket Rates. A noted exception to the preceding rate structure is the *blanket rate.* The blanket rate does not increase with distance; it remains the same from one origin to all points in the blanket area. The carriers establish such rates to ensure a competitive price for a product in a given area, thereby ensuring demand for the product and its transportation. An example of a blanket rate would be the same rate on wine traveling from the West Coast to all points east of the Rocky Mountains, enabling the West Coast wine to compete with imported wines entering the East Coast.

eliminate transportation factor

The blanket rate eliminates any transportation cost advantage or disadvantage that companies associate with a given location. In the case of the wine blanket rates, the West Coast wine producers can effectively compete in the East Coast market area with East Coast and foreign producers. The blanket rate, then, is a mutation of the basic rate-distance relationship that eliminates the transportation rate as a locational determinant; it is the exception rather than the rule in transportation rates.

Commercial Zones. A specific blanket area is the *commercial zone,* the transportation definition of a particular city or town. It includes the municipality itself plus various surrounding areas. The commercial zone rates that carriers quote to a particular town or city also apply to points in the surrounding area within the commercial zone.

transportation definition of a city

The commercial zone's locational impact appears near the end of the location decision process when a company selects a specific site. If the specific site is beyond the limits of a municipality's commercial zone, rates that apply to the city do not apply to the site. Also, a site outside the commercial zone reduces carrier availability, especially the availability of motor carriers that define their operating scopes in terms of point-to-point operations.

rates

carrier availability

Foreign Trade Zones.[15] As previously discussed, a *foreign trade zone* (FTZ) is a geographic area into which importers can enter a product and hold it without paying duties—and only paying duties or customs when is it shipped into U.S. customs territory. Specifically, the advantages of the FTZs include:

FTZs

- Deferred customs duties and federal excise taxes on imports
- No duties or quota payments on re-exported materials
- Choice of duty rates paid—based either on the rate for component parts or for the finished product
- Exemption from state and local inventory taxes or foreign and domestic goods that are to be exported

The availability of FTZ benefits can impact the design of a firm's logistics network. For example, Ryder Group operates a foreign-trade zone, Kelly USA, on the former Kelly Air Force Base in San Antonio, Texas. The Trade Processing Center operated by Ryder is a 40,000-square-foot facility with an on-site Mexican freight broker who serves as a liaison between Ryder's U.S. and Mexican operations. Also, the complex operates seven days a week with door-to-door services for over-the-road trucking, rail, air, and ocean transport of goods.

Transit Privileges. Basically, the *transit privilege* permits the shipper to stop a shipment in transit and to perform some function that physically changes the product's characteristic. The lower through rate from origin to final destination (the tapering-rate principle) applies, rather than the higher combination of rates from origin to transit point and from transit point to final destination.

stop shipment to perform processing

The transit privilege essentially makes intermediate locations, rather than just origins or destinations, optimum. The transit privilege eliminates any geographic disadvantage that companies associate with a producer's location. The intermediate point the carrier designates as a transit point enjoys the lower, long-distance through rate that applies at either the origin or the destination.

Like the blanket rate, the transit privilege is not available at all locations or for all commodities—only those sites and commodities the carrier specifies. If a commodity benefits from the availability of a transit privilege, the limited points specified by the carrier will be prime facility location alternatives.

Summary

- The logistics network design decision is of great strategic importance to logistics, the firm as a whole, and the supply chain.
- There are a number of factors that may suggest the need to redesign the logistics network.
- A formal, structured process for logistics network design is preferable; the potential impacts on cost and service justify a significant effort toward following a sound process.
- Numerous factors may affect the design of a logistics network and the location of specific facilities within the context of the network.
- Principal modeling approaches to gain insight into the topic of logistics network design include optimization, simulation, and heuristic models.
- The "grid" method represents a useful way to obtain a good, but not necessarily optimal, solution to a logistics facility location problem.
- The availability and cost of transportation affect the location decision in a number of significant and unique ways.

Study Questions

1. In what ways can the design of a firm's logistics network affect its ability to create value for customers through efficiency, effectiveness, and differentiation?
2. What are the steps in the process of logistics network design? Of these steps, which are most relevant to the task of selecting a specific site for a logistics facility?
3. Discuss the factors that cause a company to analyze the design of a logistics network or to reconsider the location of a particular facility.
4. Why are most location decisions analyzed by a team of managers instead of a single person? What types of teams are suggested as being helpful to the task of logistics network redesign?
5. What are the major locational determinants, and how does each affect the location decision?
6. Discuss the role of the logistics variable in the decision as to where to locate a plant or warehouse.
7. What are the principal types of modeling techniques that apply to the task of logistics network design and facility location? What are the strengths and limitations of each?
8. Describe the grid technique. What is its purpose, and how does it lead to the making of a decision? What are its strengths and limitations?

9. Using the grid technique, determine the least-cost location for the following problems:

(a)

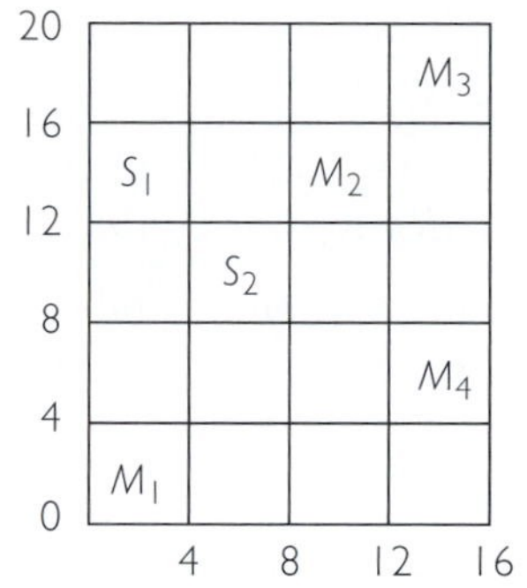

	Tons	Rate	Grid Coordinates (H, V)
S_1	200	0.50	2, 14
S_2	300	0.60	6, 10
M_1	100	1.00	2, 2
M_2	100	2.00	10, 14
M_3	100	1.00	14, 18
M_4	100	2.00	14, 6

(b)

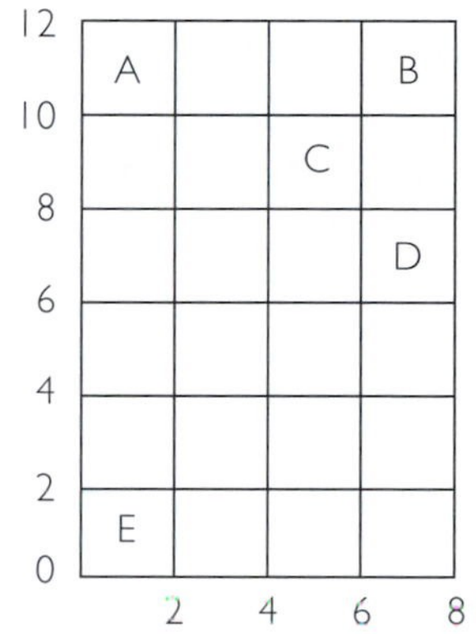

Customer	Tons	Grid Coordinates (H, V)
A	100	1, 11
B	300	7, 11
C	200	5, 9
D	500	7, 7
E	1,000	1, 1

10. Explain how tapering rates, blanket rates, commercial zones, foreign trade zones, and in-transit privileges affect the facility location decision.

NOTES

1. *Wall Street Journal* (6 April 1999): 1.

2. David Savageau, *Places Rated Almanac,* 6th ed. (Chicago, Ill.: Rand McNally, 1999).

3. E. S. Browning and Helene Cooper, "States' Bidding War over Mercedes Plant Made for Costly Chase," *Wall Street Journal* (24 November 1993): 1.

4. Ronald H. Ballou, *Business Logistics Management,* 3d ed. (Englewood Cliffs, N.J.: Prentice-Hall, 1992), 297.

5. Richard F. Powers, "Optimization Models for Logistics Decisions," *Journal of Business Logistics* 10, no. 1 (1989): 106.

6. SAILS™ (Strategic Analysis of Integrated Logistics Systems), (Manassas, Va.: Insight, Inc., 2001).

7. Robert E. Shannon, *Systems Simulation: The Art and Science* (Englewood Cliffs, N.J.: Prentice-Hall, 1975), 1.

8. Frederick S. Hillier and Gerald J. Lieberman, *Introduction to Operations Research,* 3d ed. (San Francisco, Calif.: Holden-Day, Inc., 1980), 643.

9. For an excellent overview of simulation modeling, see Donald J. Bowersox and David J. Closs, "Simulation in Logistics: A Review of Present Practice and a Look to the Future," *Journal of Business Logistics* 10, no. 1 (1989): 133–48.

10. Ronald H. Ballou, "Logistics Network Design: Modeling and Informational Considerations," *The International Journal of Logistics Management* 6, no. 2 (1995): 47.

11. For additional examples and a comprehensive perspective on heuristic modeling, see Ronald H. Ballou, "Heuristics: Rules of Thumb for Logistics Decision Making," *Journal of Business Logistics* 10, no. 1 (1989): 122–32.

12. Donald H. Ratliff and William G. Nulty, *Logistics Composite Modeling* (Atlanta, Ga.: Ratliff & Nulty, 1996), 38.

13. The content of this section has been adapted from Paul S. Bender, "How to Design an Optimum Supply Chain," *Supply Chain Management Review* (Spring 1997): 79–80.

14. Portions of this section are adapted from Edward J. Taaffe and Howard L. Gauthier Jr., *Geography of Transportation* (Englewood Cliffs, N.J.: Prentice-Hall, 1973), 41–43.

15. Margaret Gordetsky, "Ryder Puts Customers in the Foreign Trade Zone," *Transport Topics* (28 August 2000): 26.

CASE 14–1 ■ Fireside Tire Company

Fireside Tire Company, a manufacturer of radial tires for sport utility vehicles, sells its products in the automotive aftermarket and distributes them throughout the United States. Fireside has three tire production plants, located in Allentown, Pennsylvania; Toledo, Ohio; and Macomb, Illinois (see map). Normally, Fireside ships tires from its plants to distribution centers, but truckload-size purchases typically are transported directly from plants to customer locations. All shipments to a region move under truckload rates applying to a minimum weight of 40,000 pounds, or 400 cwt.

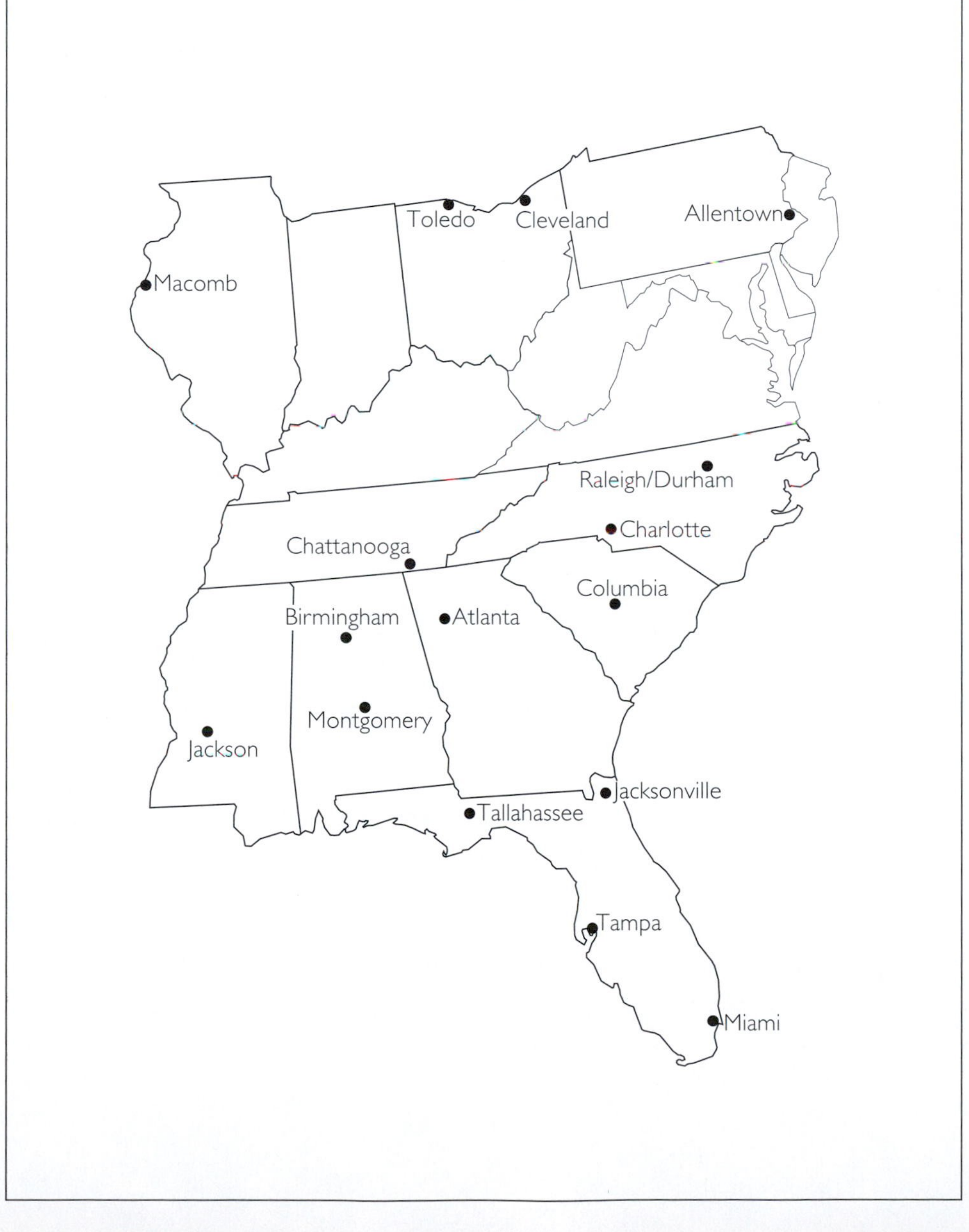

Fireside management is concerned about the most economical location for a distribution center to serve its southeastern region, consisting of North Carolina, South Carolina, Georgia, Florida, Mississippi, Alabama, and southeastern Tennessee. Although an Atlanta distribution center currently serves this region, Fireside management is concerned that the Atlanta location is not the most logistically sound alternative.

To help the logistics department conduct an analysis of this region's distribution center location using the grid method, Fireside's transportation department developed the following data:

2000 Shipments to Atlanta				**Grid Coordinates**	
From	**cwt**	**Rate/cwt**	**Mileage**	**Horizontal**	**Vertical**
Toledo	15,000	$2.20	640	1,360	1,160
Macomb	5,000	2.43	735	980	1,070
Allentown	11,000	2.52	780	1,840	1,150

2000 Shipments from Atlanta		**Grid Coordinates**	
To	**cwt**	**Horizontal**	**Vertical**
Chattanooga	2,700	1,350	650
Atlanta	3,500	1,400	600
Tampa	4,300	1,570	220
Birmingham	2,800	1,260	580
Miami	5,300	1,740	90
Jacksonville	5,100	1,600	450
Columbia	2,200	1,600	650
Charlotte	2,900	1,590	740
Raleigh/Durham	2,200	1,700	800

The transportation department also determined that total freight expenditures from the Atlanta distribution center during 2001 were $217,000 and that the average shipment distance was 330 miles.

Case Questions

1. Based on the available information, is Atlanta the best location for a distribution center to serve the southeastern region? If not, what would you recommend?
2. The Fireside transportation department projects a 25 percent rate increase in 2002 from all of its transportation providers. How will this affect the Atlanta location?
3. Marketing anticipates that the Raleigh/Durham market will grow by 3,000 cwt in 2003, and that Fireside will serve the growth from Allentown. How will this affect Atlanta as a location?

CHAPTER 15

SUPPLY CHAIN FINANCE

LEARNING OBJECTIVES

After reading this chapter you should be able to do the following:

- Convert cost savings into equivalent sales increase.
- Understand a company's income statement and balance sheet.
- Demonstrate the impact of supply chain strategies on the income statement, balance sheet, profitability, and return on assets.
- Understand and use the strategic profit model.
- Analyze the financial impact of supply chain service failures.
- Utilize the spreadsheet computer software program to analyze financial implications of supply chain decisions.

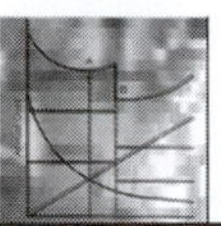

LOGISTICS PROFILE

CBL Book Distributors.com

CBL Book Distributors.com (CBL) is a new dot com company that began operation in 1995 for the sale and distribution of college textbooks and student supplies. During the first few years, CBL struggled with the normal technical glitches associated with an Internet-based company, but the concept of on-line purchasing of college textbooks proved immensely popular with college students. After obtaining information as to the textbook(s) required in a course, the students would go to their computers and place their orders, avoiding the dreaded long lines at the campus bookstore.

CBL's original mission was to be a low-price seller of college textbooks and instructional materials in the United States. The typical textbook price at CBL averaged 15 percent below that of the local bookstore, and supplies averaged 20 percent lower. When the cost of shipping was included, the landed cost of the textbook was about 10 percent lower and materials 15 percent lower than purchases at the local bookstore. This lower cost and the convenience of on-line purchasing resulted in double-digit sales increases every year.

Beginning in 1996, CBL made a profit and has done so every year since then. In 2001, CBL had sales of $150 million with a net income of $10.5 million. This net profit margin of 7 percent was above average for business-to-customer (B2C) Internet companies. However, net income as a percent of sales, or net profit margin, was lower than the previous years. In 1999, net profit margin was 10.3 percent and, in 2000, it was 9.1 percent. This profit margin trend was causing considerable concern with top management and CBL's stockholders.

Following release of the 2001 financial data, Markus Baseline, CEO, held a meeting with the executive committee consisting of the vice presidents of marketing, finance, information systems, and supply chain management. After reviewing the 2001 financial results and discussing the underlying causes for the lower net profit margin, each vice president was given the assignment of examining his/her respective area for process changes that would remove costs while maintaining the same level of service customers expected.

Particular attention was given to the supply chain function because supply chain cost increases exceeded those in other areas of the company. Mr. Baseline also pointed out that during the past year he had been receiving complaints from irate customers regarding late deliveries of orders and receipt of improperly filled orders (wrong items or not all items ordered). Lauren Fishbay, vice president of supply chain management, said she was aware of these problems and was working on solutions for order-fulfillment problems as well as the escalating shipping cost. She told the committee she would develop a strategic plan to address these issues and present it at the next monthly meeting.

Following the executive committee meeting, Ms. Fishbay gathered her operating managers to review the situation and explore alternatives. She asked Kate Southern, supply chain analyst, to prepare financial data emphasizing the supply chain process. Maggie Acture, warehouse manager, was asked to examine the nature and cause of the order-fulfillment problems and to suggest alternative solutions. Finally, Jon Moderne, transportation manager, was charged with examining the rising shipping costs and longer delivery times.

Prior to the supply chain operating managers' meeting, Lauren Fishbay received the following 2001 financial information from Kate Southern:

CBL Book Distributors.com Income Statement 2001

Sales		$150,000,000
Cost of goods sold		80,000,000
Gross margin		70,000,000
Transportation	6,000,000	
Warehousing	1,500,000	
Inventory carrying	3,000,000	
Other operating cost	30,000,000	
Total operating cost		40,500,000
Earnings before interest and taxes		29,500,000
Interest		12,000,000
Taxes		7,000,000
Net income		10,500,000

(continued on next page)

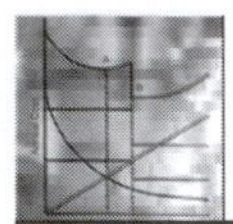

LOGISTICS PROFILE

CBL Book Distributors.com *continued*

CBL Book Distributors.com Balance Sheet
December 31, 2001

Assets	
Cash	$15,000,000
Accounts receivable	30,000,000
Inventory	10,000,000
Total current assets	55,000,000
Net fixed assets	90,000,000
Total assets	145,000,000
Liabilities	
Current liabilities	$65,000,000
Long-term debt	35,000,000
Total liabilities	100,000,000
Stockholders equity	45,000,000
Total liabilities & equity	145,000,000

Ms. Southern determined that the inventory carrying cost rate was 30 percent of the value of the average inventory held per year. The corporate tax rate was 40 percent. Total orders in 2001 amounted to 1.5 million ($150 million in sales at an average sale per order of $100). She estimated the lost sales rate to be 10 percent of the service failures caused by late transportation delivery and 20 percent of the service failures caused by improper order fulfillment. The cost of a lost sale per order is the gross profit per order, or $46.67 ($70 million gross margin divided by 1.5 million orders).

Maggie Acture concluded that the cost of a service failure, whether caused by order-fulfillment or delivery problems, resulted in an invoice reduction of $10 per order (to appease the customer) and a rehandling cost of $20 per order (to reship the order). Currently, CBL's order fill rate is 97 percent. The causes of the improper order fulfillment could be attributed to lack of warehouse personnel training. In the current economic environment, it is very difficult to obtain experienced warehouse workers, and many of the current warehouse employees do not have a high-school diploma. Other problems could be traced to a lack of discipline regarding order-picking procedures and the computer-generated pick slip. At least $100,000 was required annually for ongoing training.

Jon Moderne traced the escalating shipping costs to the 35 percent increase in residential delivery rates charged by CBL's ground delivery carrier for standard service (three to five days transit time). The residential delivery rates charged by other ground express carriers were comparable or higher. An alternative to reduce shipping costs was to switch to the U.S. Postal Service, but delivery times would increase. However, CBL's current on-time delivery performance is only 95 percent because of the longer order-processing times at the warehouse and longer transit times via the ground package carrier to residential delivery locations. By using the carrier's expedited ground service, CBL would improve service and on-time delivery to 96 percent and increase shipping cost by 10 percent.

Given this information, Lauren Fishbay was pondering what actions she should explore with the operating managers in preparation for the next executive committee meeting. She knew whatever course of action she proposed had to be financially sound and provide the greatest benefit to CBL's stockholders.

Introduction

Throughout the text, emphasis is given to cost and cost reduction. The systems approach emphasizes the need to examine the cost implications of a decision to all supply chain functional areas as well as other functional areas of the company. The implication of this focus on total cost is that lowering total costs will increase profitability.

significance

The importance of finance in the supply chain context is best shown by the significance current managers place on returning to school to study finance. In a recent survey, current logistics managers chose for a ninety-day course of study the following top four curriculum topics: information systems/technology (21 percent), E-commerce (16 percent), global business processes (15 percent), and financial applications (14 percent).[1]

In this chapter, our attention is directed toward the financial implications of various supply chain decisions. We examine the impact of cost reductions, inventory level changes, and other supply chain actions on profitability. A spreadsheet format for analyzing the financial implications of supply chain actions is introduced, along with the strategic profit model. To help with an understanding of financial terminology, Appendix 15A contains a glossary of common financial terms. First, the supply chain financial connection is examined.

The Supply Chain–Finance Connection

As noted in the Logistics Profile, CBL Book Distributors.com is focusing its attention on the supply chain process as a means to improving its financial performance. CBL recognizes the impact supply chain performance has on customer satisfaction and future sales. In addition, the effectiveness of the supply chain process impacts the cost of fulfilling customer orders and transporting these orders to the customer, both of which impact the overall landed cost of the product to the customer.

landed costs

More specifically, the supply chain process influences the flow of products from the vendor to the final point of consumption. The resources utilized to accomplish this flow process determine, in part, the cost of making the product available to the consumer at the consumer's location. This landed cost, then, impacts the buyer's decision to purchase a seller's product. For example, if supplier A's supply chain process is inefficient and A's landed cost is higher than its competitors, the buyer may buy from the lower-cost competitor, thereby reducing A's sales.

The cost of providing supply chain services not only affects the marketability of the product (via the landed cost, or price), but it also impacts profitability. For a given price, level of sales, and level of service, the higher the supply chain costs, the lower the company's profit. Conversely, the lower the supply chain costs, the higher the profits.

optimization

The decision to alter the supply chain process is essentially an optimization issue. Management must view the supply chain alternatives as to their ability to optimize the corporate goal of profit maximization. Some alternatives may minimize costs but reduce sales and, possibly, profits. Conversely, some alternatives may increase sales while increasing costs and reducing profits. By implementing supply chain alternatives that optimize profits, the decision maker is taking the systems approach and trading off sales and costs for optimum profits.

Supply chain management involves the control of raw material, in-process, and finished goods inventories. The financing implication of inventory management is the amount of capital required to fund the inventory. In most companies, capital is in short supply and capital needs to fund critical capital projects, such as new plants, plant modernization, and so on, are high. The higher the inventory level, the higher the capital devoted to inventory and the less capital available for other projects.

inventory minimization

The recent focus on inventory minimization is a direct response to the competing needs for capital and the difficulty some firms have in raising additional capital. Supply chain techniques such as just-in-time, efficient consumer response, and quick response are directed toward reducing a company's inventory level, thereby reducing capital invested in inventory and making more capital available to other projects. Many companies focus on reducing finished goods inventory because finished goods inventory has a higher value than raw material or in-process inventory and affords a greater potential for capital reduction per inventory unit reduction. For example, if the finished product has a value or $10.00 per unit and the raw material a value of $1.00/unit, the capital saving per unit is ten times greater for finished goods than raw materials.

cost of service

As indicated in previous chapters, the level of supply chain service provided has a direct bearing on customer satisfaction. The provision of consistent, low lead times builds strong customer satisfaction and loyalty. However, the cost of providing this service must also be examined in light of the overall profitability of providing a given level of service and the resulting sales. The supply chain manager must analyze the cost of providing improved supply chain service and the added profitability associated with the corresponding level of sales, the optimization issue referred to previously.

Finally, *efficiency* of the supply chain impacts the time required to process a customer's order. Order-processing time has a bearing on the total time elapsing between placement of the order and receipt of the customer's payment, the *order-to-cash cycle*. Typically, the invoice is sent to the customer after the order is processed and shipped. If the terms of sale are net thirty days, the seller will receive payment in thirty days plus the number of days required to process the order. The longer the order-processing time, the longer it takes to get the cash from the sale—the order-to-cash cycle. The longer the order-to-cash cycle, the higher the accounts receivable and the higher the capital investment in "sold" finished goods inventory, that is, capital is required to fund the accounts receivables (for "sold" finished goods inventory) while awaiting for the customers to pay for the items purchased.

The Sales–Cost Saving Connection

sales, cost, and profit

Throughout the text, attention is given to supply chain efficiency and cost reduction. While process efficiency and cost saving are worthy goals, top management generally refers to corporate improvements in terms of increases in sales and profit. This apparent conflict between the goals of top management and supply chain management can be readily resolved by converting cost savings into equivalent sales increases. To improve communication effectiveness with top management, it behooves the supply chain manager to relate efficiencies and cost savings in a language that top management uses, that is, sales and profits.

profit equation

It is often advantageous to transform cost savings into equivalent sales increases to connote to top management the effects of improved supply chain cost performance. To accomplish this we use the profit equation:

$$\text{Profit} = \text{Sales} - \text{Costs}$$

where

$$\text{Cost} = (X\%)(\text{Sales})$$

then

$$\text{Profit} = \text{Sales} - (X\%)(\text{Sales}) = \text{Sales}\ (1 - X\%)$$

where

$$(1 - X\%) = \text{Profit Margin}$$

$$\text{Sales} = \text{Profit} \div \text{Profit Margin}$$

sales equivalent

Assuming that everything else remains unchanged, a supply chain cost saving will directly increase profits by the amount of the cost saving. If a supply chain cost saving increases profit by the same amount, the sales equivalent of this cost saving is found by dividing the cost saving by the profit margin as shown in the preceding equations. For example, if cost is 90 percent of sales and the profit margin is 10 percent of sales, a \$100 cost saving is equivalent to sales of \$1,000:

$$\text{Sales} = \text{Cost Saving (Profit)} \div \text{Profit Margin}$$

$$\text{Sales} = \$100 \div 0.10$$

$$\text{Sales} = \$1{,}000$$

Table 15–1 provides examples of equivalent sales for different supply chain cost savings using the data found in the Logistics Profile for CBL. As shown in the table, CBL has a profit margin of 7 percent. Given this profit margin, a \$200,000 supply chain cost saving has the same effect as increasing sales by \$2,857,143, a 1.9 percent increase in sales. Likewise, \$.5 million and \$1 million supply chain cost savings have equivalent sales equal to \$7,142,857 (4.76 percent sales increase) and \$14,285,714 (9.52 percent sales increase), respectively.

profit margin

The lower the profit margin, the higher the sales equivalent for a given supply chain cost because it takes a greater sales volume to produce a given profit. Table 15–2 shows the equivalent sales of a given supply chain cost saving with varying profit margins. For a \$10,000 supply chain cost saving, the equivalent sales equals \$1 million for a company with a 1 percent profit margin but only \$50,000 for a company with a 20 percent profit margin. Supply chain cost savings have a much greater sales impact for companies with low profit margins.

In the following section, the financial implications of the supply chain strategies are discussed. Statements contained in the Logistics Profile for CBL Book Distributors.com are analyzed.

TABLE 15–1 Sales Equivalent of Supply Chain Cost Saving

	CBL 2001		Sales Equivalent for Cost Savings of		
	(000)	%	$200,000	$500,000	$1,000,000
Sales	$150,000	100.0%	$2,857,143*	$7,142,857†	$14,285,714‡
Total cost	139,500	93.0	2,657,143	6,642,857	13,285,714
Net profit	10,500	7.0	200,000	500,000	1,000,000

*$200,000 cost saving ÷ .07 profit margin

†$500,000 cost saving ÷ .07 profit margin

‡$1,000,000 cost saving ÷ .07 profit margin

TABLE 15–2 Equivalent Sales with Varying Profit Margins

	Profit Margins			
	20%	10%	5%	1%
Sales	$50,000	$100,000	$200,000	$1,000,000
Total cost	40,000	90,000	190,000	990,000
Cost saving/Profit	10,000	10,000	10,000	10,000

The Supply Chain Financial Impact

stockholder return

A major financial objective for a company is to produce a satisfactory return for the stockholders. This requires the generation of sufficient profit in relation to the size of the stockholders' investment to assure that the investors will maintain the investment in the company. If the return to the stockholder is too low, the stockholder will withdraw its investment from the company, lowering the stock value, and possibly setting the stage for financial disaster such as a takeover or bankruptcy.

net worth

The absolute size of the profit must be considered in relation to the stockholders' net investment, or net worth. For example, if Company A makes a profit of $1 million and Company B makes $100 million, it would appear that B is more profitable. But, if A has a net worth of $10 million and B $10 billion, the *return on net worth* for a stockholder is 10 percent ($1 million ÷ $10 million) and for B it is 1 percent ($100 million ÷ $10 billion).

return on assets

A company's financial performance is also judged by the profit it generates in relation to the assets utilized, or *return on assets.* A company's return on assets is a

FIGURE 15–1 Supply Chain Impact on Return on Assets

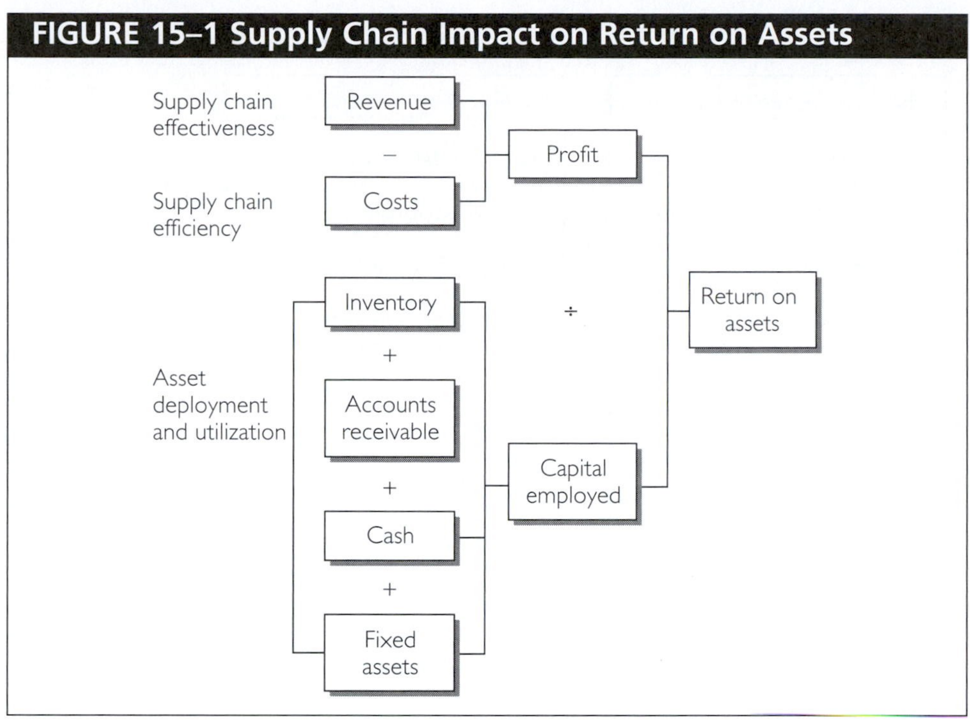

financial performance metric that is used as a benchmark to compare management and company performance to that of other companies in the same industry or similar industries. As with return on net worth, return on assets is dependent on the level of profitability of the company.

The supply chain process plays a critical role in determining the level of profitability in a company. The more efficient and productive the supply chain process is, the greater the profitability of the company. Conversely, the less efficient and less productive, the higher the supply chain costs and the lower the profitability. The decisions made by the supply chain manager directly impact the financial position of the company.

Figure 15–1 shows the financial relationship between supply chain management and return on assets (ROA). The effectiveness of supply chain service impacts the level of sales, and the efficiency affects the company's total cost. As we noted earlier, revenue minus cost equals profit, the first component in determining ROA.

The level of inventory held throughout the internal supply chain determines the assets devoted to inventory. The order-processing time, as well as the transit time, affects the time required to receive payment from a sale, thereby impacting the accounts receivable and cash assets. Finally, the supply chain decisions regarding the type and number of warehouses utilized impact fixed assets.

Lastly, Figure 15–1 shows that the calculation of ROA is the division of the profit realized by the capital (assets) employed (profit ÷ capital employed). As noted earlier, the higher the profits for a given level of assets (capital) utilized, the higher the ROA. Alternatively, the lower the capital employed for a given level of profit, the higher the ROA.

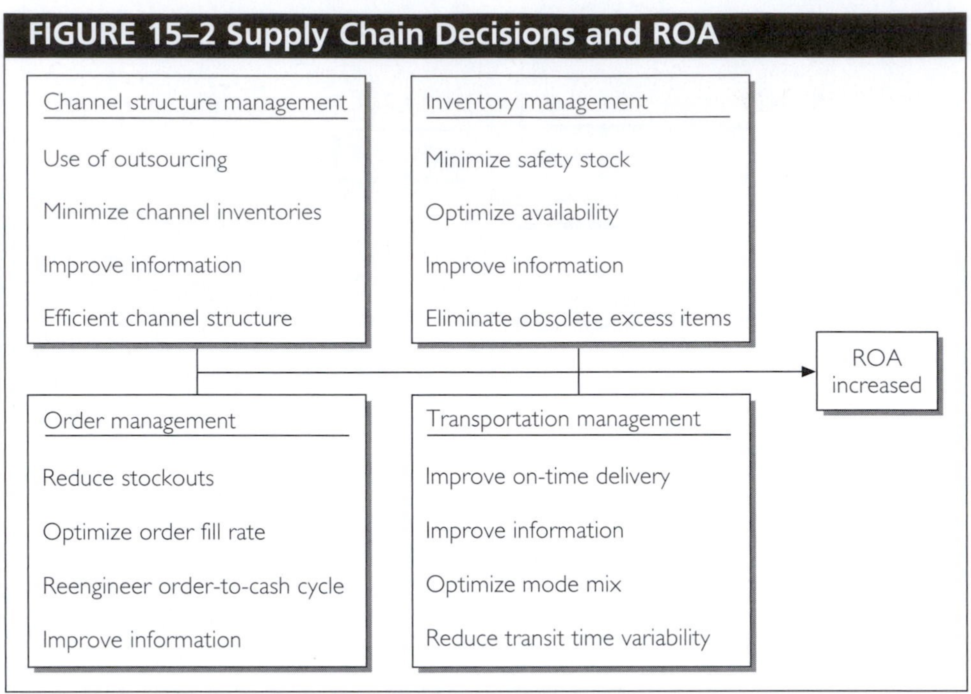

FIGURE 15–2 Supply Chain Decisions and ROA

The supply chain strategic areas affecting return on assets are summarized in Figure 15–2. The decisions the supply chain manager makes with regard to channel structure, inventory management, order management, and transportation management all have an effect on the level of assets employed or the level of profitability (sales incurred and supply chain cost incurred).

channel structure

Channel structure management includes the decisions regarding the use of outsourcing, channel inventories, information systems, and channel structure. Through outsourcing supply chain processes, the company may realize lower supply chain costs (outsourcing firm possesses greater supply chain expertise and efficiency), a reduction in assets (use of outsourcing firm's facilities and more efficient management of inventories), and increased sales (from improved and consistent supply chain service). Decisions that lower supply chain assets and/or improve sales through supply chain services improvements result in higher ROA.

channel inventories

Minimization of channel inventories results in a direct reduction in assets. The use of improved information systems enables the firm to monitor inventory levels, production schedules, and purchases to meet the current level of sales. Streamlining the channel structure through the elimination of unnecessary channel intermediaries—for example, dealing directly with the retailer and bypassing the wholesaler—may eliminate inventory from the channel, as well as reduce the channel cost of transportation and warehousing. The reduction in inventory results in a direct increase in ROA.

Inventory management decisions that reduce inventory (safety stock, obsolete, and/or excess items) and optimize inventory location (in relation to sales or use patterns) reduce the investment in the inventory asset. These decisions require analysis of sales data and inventory levels by location, which is readily available with current information systems.

ON THE LINE

HARD SELL

To professionals working in the field, the benefits of effective logistics management are abundantly evident and the potential bottom-line payback compelling. A short list might include reduced costs in such areas as inventory management, warehousing, and transportation; enhanced revenues through programs that assure higher product availability and more customized products; and significant improvements in corporate profitability. Yet these same managers still wrestle with the question of how to convince senior management that logistics is vital to a company's financial performance and therefore deserves continued investment.

To successfully communicate the value that logistics can bring to their organizations, managers must be able to show that logistics is vital to their companies' financial performance. James K. Wilson, president of Quantum International, a consulting firm based in Longmont, Colorado, uses the following example: "Let's say your company earns a dollar of profit for every $10 of sales. If logistics [efficiency] can save you a dollar without changing sales figures, then in effect you just went out and earned another $10 in sales," he says. "So an efficient logistics operation can deliver the value of another entire business division without ever making one additional sale. That's a message you need to communicate."

Dr. Stephen G. Timme, president of Atlanta-based FinListics Solutions, Inc., which develops seminars on finance and logistics, agrees. "By lowering costs and increasing asset utilization, the logistics manager frees up cash," he says. "This manager can go to his board of directors and say, 'If you want to expand your business, let me go get the money for you.' "

That approach commands attention in today's business environment, where senior management must improve earnings across an entire enterprise or supply chain in order to earn the kind of returns that keep shareholders happy. It also offers a solid incentive for companies to continue investing in their logistics organizations. "Over the last ten years, there has been increased pressure on companies to make a good return for their shareholders because the shareholders fund the company," Timme says. "They will let you reinvest profits in logistics only if they believe you will give them a good return."

Before logistics managers can sell value, of course, they must create it—and there are several ways to do this. Whirlpool Corp.'s logistics organization, for example, takes a three-pronged approach to contributing to the company's financial performance, says J. Paul Dittmann, vice president of global logistics. "We look at reducing operating costs. We also look at reducing working capital, which generally means lowering inventory. And we improve customer service through our ability to serve our dealer network and trading partners through such services as the 'perfect order,' " he explains.

Whirlpool defines the perfect order as one that is shipped complete, on time, and undamaged. It also must be invoiced correctly. "If we fall down in any one of these four areas, then we've disappointed our partners," says Dittmann. Senior management understands the importance of the perfect order because the financial implications of disappointing a trading partner include the reduction or loss of business.

Another way logistics managers can demonstrate logistics' impact on profits is to focus on asset utilization. "Most shareholders understand that if you reduce inventories, you reduce costs," says Timme. "But few understand that if you are more efficient with your assets, that affects how you price goods and the markets you go after."

He cites the example of Dell Computer. According to Timme, Dell utilizes its assets two to three times more efficiently than its competitors. "Therefore, Dell can price things slightly lower, advertise more, and remain more profitable than its competitors," he explains.

One of the biggest roadblocks to selling logistics value to upper management, says Dittmann, is the "business question of the next century: How do you create value in logistics—the ultimate, horizontal functions?" The answer, he says, is to hold everyone

(continued on next page)

ON THE LINE

HARD SELL *continued*

accountable for meeting common objectives and financial-performance measurements. Those measurements should apply throughout the supply chain, Dittmann believes. One challenge companies pursuing that strategy face is determining how to implement a measurement system that balances service- and cost-based objectives. "We don't want to drive performance in one area at the expense of another," Dittmann says.

Getting a broad-based overview of how logistics affects a company's overall financial performance can help resolve that dilemma. At Whirlpool, senior management gets that macro view by using EVA, or Economic Value Added, a trademarked financial-performance measurement developed by Stern Stewart & Co. of New York City. In simple terms, EVA represents the after-tax operating profit minus the cost of capital used to generate that profit. The cost of capital includes charges for both debt and equity. Under EVA, which basically measures how efficiently companies use capital to create wealth, shareholder value increases when an investment earns more than the cost of capital.

Another term for the same concept is "economic profit," which Timme defines as the net operating profit after taxes minus the capital charge. Economic profit increases through improvements to asset drivers—all of which can be influenced to some extent by logistics performance, Timme says.

"Whether it's called EVA or economic profit, more and more companies are using some type of return measure that ties together revenue, operating costs, and capital," says Timme. "If your company announces that it is going to be managed by economic profit, then you can do great things. Why not get up to speed on the concept so you can be in a position to tell your CFO how logistics can increase economic profit?" he suggests.

Ultimately, Timme concludes, the message logistics managers must convey to corporate leaders is this: "Logistics is not about cutting costs. It's a growth story."

Source: Adapted from Jim Thomas, "Hard Sell," *Logistics Management & Distribution Report* (February 1999). Copyright Cahners Business Information. Reprinted by permission.

order management Effective order management not only reduces supply chain costs but also supports improved sales, the combined effect being higher ROA. Reducing stockouts implies sufficient inventory available to meet demand and make the sale. Optimizing the order fill rate implies a reduction in order-processing time, which, as we discussed earlier, reduces the accounts receivable collection time. Reductions in the order-processing times, coupled with a reduction in the length of credit period extended to customers, reduce accounts payable and the cost of capital required to fund accounts payable. All of these reductions in time improve the ROA.

transit time Finally, reducing transportation transit time and the variability of transit time will have a positive impact on sales, as well as inventory levels. By providing low, consistent transit time, a seller can differentiate its product in the marketplace by lowering the buyer's inventory and stockout costs. This product differentiation should produce increased sales and a potential for increased profit. Modal optimization affords the opportunity to lower transportation cost by utilizing a lower-cost method of transportation that does not increase other costs above the transportation cost savings. Transportation management decisions, then, offer the opportunity to increase sales and lower inventories and costs, resulting in higher ROA.

FIGURE 15–3 CBL Distributors.com Income Statement: 2001

	Symbol	(000)	(000)
Sales	S		$150,000
Cost of goods sold	CGS		80,000
Gross margin	$GM = S - CGS$		70,000
Transportation	TC	$6,000	
Warehousing	WC	1,500	
Inventory carrying	$IC = IN * W$	3,000	
Other operating cost	OOC	30,000	
Total operating cost	$TOC = TC + WC + IC + OOC$		40,500
Earnings before interest and tax	$EBIT = GM - TOC$		29,500
Interest	INT		12,000
Taxes	$TX = (EBIT - INT)*.4$		7,000
Net income	NI		$10,500

FIGURE 15–4 CBL Distributors.com Balance Sheet: December 31, 2001

Assets	Symbol	(000)
Cash	CA	$15,000
Accounts receivable	AR	30,000
Inventory	IN	10,000
Total current assets	$TCA = CA + AR + IN$	55,000
Net fixed assets	FA	90,000
Total assets	$TA = FA + TCA$	$145,000
Liabilities		
Current liabilities	CL	$65,000
Long-term debt	LTD	35,000
Total debt	$TD = CL + LTD$	100,000
Stockholders equity	SE	45,000
Total liabilities and equity	$TLE = TD + SE$	$145,000

FINANCIAL STATEMENTS

It is now time to turn our attention to the income statement and balance sheet. We will use the data contained in the Logistics Profile for CBL Distributors.com. Figure 15–3 contains the CBL income statement, and Figure 15–4 shows the balance sheet for CBL. Both financial statements have been prepared using a spreadsheet software program, and the symbol column indicates the symbol and/or equation used for each of the entries.

sales, cost, and profit

CBL's *income statement* shows a net income (NI) of $10 million on sales (*S*) of $150 million, a profit margin of 7 percent. Gross margin (*GM*) is found by subtracting cost of goods sold (*CGS*) from sales (*S*). Earnings before interest and taxes (*EBIT*) are gross margin minus total operating costs (*TOC*). Net income (*NI*) is *EBIT* minus interest cost (*INT*) and taxes (*TX*). The supply chain costs include transportation (*TC*), warehousing (*WC*), and inventory carrying cost (*IC*). Inventory carrying cost is equal to average inventory (*IN*) times the inventory carrying cost rate (*W*).

assets and liabilities

The *balance sheet* in Figure 15–4 indicates CBL utilized total assets (*TA*) of $145 million to generate $150 million in sales. Total assets (*TA*) consist of $15 million of cash (*CA*), $30 million of accounts receivable (*AR*), $10 million of inventory (*IN*), and $90 million of net fixed assets (*FA*). These assets were financed by debt (liabilities) and stockholder equity; that is, the $100 million of total debt (*TD*), consisting of $65 million of current liabilities (*CL*) and $35 million of long-term debt, plus $45 million of stockholder equity (*SE*), paid for these assets.

FINANCIAL IMPACT OF SUPPLY CHAIN DECISIONS

largest financial impact

Based on the financial data given in Figure 15–3 and Figure 15–4, we can analyze the alternative supply chain actions available to Lauren Fishbay to improve CBL profitability. The basic supply chain alternatives are reductions in the areas of transportation, warehousing, and inventory costs. To determine the supply chain area that affords the largest financial impact and then the focus of our initial profit improvement efforts, we analyze the effect of a 10 percent reduction in transportation and warehousing costs and a 10 percent reduction in inventory.

Figure 15–5 shows the financial impact of a 10 percent reduction in transportation costs. First, for 2000, CBL had a net income of $10 million on sales of $150 million, or a profit margin of 7.0 percent. It utilized $145 million in assets to produce this profit, thereby generating a return on assets of 7.24 percent. The inventory turn rate for 2000 was 8.0, and transportation costs mounted to 4.0 percent of sales, warehousing costs 1.0 percent of sales, and inventory carrying costs 2.0 percent of sales.

functional cost reduction

If CBL can reduce transportation costs by 10 percent, net income will increase $360,000 to $10,860,000 and the profit margin will increase to 7.24 percent. ROA will increase from 7.24 percent to 7.49 percent. Transportation costs as a percentage of sales will decrease from 4.0 percent to 3.6 percent. Warehousing and inventory carrying costs as a percentage of sales will not change (assuming the transportation changes do not result in longer or undependable transit times that would cause inventory levels to increase).

Figure 15–6 and Figure 15–7 show the results of a similar analysis of a 10 percent reduction in warehousing cost and a 10 percent reduction in inventory. In each case, the comparison is made to the 2000 CBL performance; that is, transportation cost and inventory are computed at the 2000 level when the 10 percent warehouse cost reduction is analyzed. As would be expected, the reduction in warehousing cost and inventory results in increases in profit, profit margin, and ROA.

The analyses contained in Figure 15–5 to Figure 15–7 provide the input data necessary to answer the question regarding which of the basic supply chain alternatives will provide the greatest potential for increased profitability. Figure 15–8 contains a comparison of the financial results of the alternative supply chain strategies just examined.

FIGURE 15–5 Financial Impact of a 10 Percent Reduction in Transportation Cost

	Symbol	CBL, 2001 $(000)	Transportation Cost Reduced 10 Percent
Sales	*S*	$150,000	$150,000
Cost of goods sold	*CGS*	80,000	80,000
Gross margin	*GM = S – CGS*	70,000	70,000
Transportation	*TC*	6,000	5,400
Warehousing	*WC*	1,500	1,500
Inventory carrying	*IC = IN * W*	3,000	3,000
Other operating cost	*OOC*	30,000	30,000
Total operating cost	*TOC*	40,500	39,900
Earnings before interest and tax	*EBIT*	29,500	30,100
Interest	*INT*	12,000	12,000
Taxes	*TX*	7,000	7,240
Net income	*NI*	10,500	10,860
Asset deployment			
Inventory	*IN*	10,000	10,000
Accounts receivable	*AR*	30,000	30,000
Cash	*CA*	15,000	15,000
Fixed assets	*FA*	90,000	90,000
Total assets	*TA*	$145,000	$145,000
Ratio analysis			
Profit margin	*NI/S*	7.00%	7.24%
Return on assets	*NI/TA*	7.24%	7.49%
Inventory turns/year	*CGS/IN*	8.00	8.00
Transportation as percentage of sales	*TC/S*	4.00%	3.60%
Warehousing as percentage of sales	*WC/S*	1.00%	1.00%
Inventory carrying as percentage of sales	*IC/S*	2.00%	2.00%

profit margin

From Figure 15–8, it is evident that CBL profit margin will be increased the greatest amount by utilizing a supply chain alternative that reduces transportation costs. This is to be expected, because transportation cost is a larger percentage of sales than the other two supply chain functional areas, 4.09 percent of sales versus 1.0 percent and 2.0 percent for warehousing and inventory, respectively. If the cost to CBL to realize a 10 percent reduction in these functional areas is the same, it is prudent for Lauren Fishbay to dedicate her resources and efforts to realizing a reduction in transportation.

return on assets

The largest increase in ROA was generated by the transportation alternative. However, the inventory reduction alternative increased ROA by almost the same amount, 7.49 percent versus 7.42 percent. The financial benefit of an inventory reduction is twofold: (1) a reduction in the inventory carrying cost and (2) a reduction in assets. Annual inventory turns are increased with the inventory reduction strategy, requiring CBL to utilize less capital for inventory and making more capital available for other uses in the company. Thus, an inventory reduction strategy has a double effect on ROA by increasing profits and reducing assets deployed.

FIGURE 15–6 Financial Impact of a 10 Percent Reduction in Warehousing Costs

	Symbol	CBL 2001 $(000)	Warehousing Cost Reduced 10 Percent
Sales	*S*	$150,000	$150,000
Cost of goods sold	*CGS*	80,000	80,000
Gross margin	*GM = S – CGS*	70,000	70,000
Transportation	*TC*	6,000	6,000
Warehousing	*WC*	1,500	1,350
Inventory carrying	*IC = IN * W*	3,000	3,000
Other operating cost	*OOC*	30,000	30,000
Total operating cost	*TOC*	40,500	40,350
Earnings before interest and tax	*EBIT*	29,500	29,650
Interest	*INT*	12,000	12,000
Taxes	*TX*	7,000	7,060
Net income	*NI*	10,500	10,590
Asset deployment			
Inventory	*IN*	10,000	10,000
Account receivable	*AR*	30,000	30,000
Cash	*CA*	15,000	15,000
Fixed assets	*FA*	90,000	90,000
Total assets	*TA*	$145,000	$145,000
Ratio Analysis			
Profit margin	*NI/S*	7.00%	7.06%
Return on assets	*NI/TA*	7.24%	7.30%
Inventory turns/year	*CGS/IN*	8.00	8.00
Transportation as percentage of sales	*TC/S*	4.00%	4.00%
Warehousing as percentage of sales	*WC/S*	1.00%	0.90%
Inventory carrying as percentage of sales	*IC/S*	2.00%	2.00%

Another methodology available to perform the same financial analysis is the *strategic profit model.* The strategic profit model makes the same calculations that we made in the preceding spreadsheet analysis. Figure 15–9 contains the strategic profit model for CBL 2001 operations and the 10 percent transportation cost reduction.

asset turnover

return on equity

The strategic profit model shows the same results as those calculated in Figure 15–5. We added two ratios to the strategic profit model—asset turnover and return on equity. *Asset turnover* is the ratio of sales to total assets and indicates how the company is utilizing its assets in relation to sales. *Return on equity* indicates the return the stockholders are realizing on their equity in the company. Asset turnover was 103 percent for both scenarios, but return on equity increased from 23.33 percent ($10,500/$45,000) for the CBL 2000 scenario to 24.13 percent ($10,860/$45,000) with the reduced transportation cost scenarios.

risk

The preceding analysis and its conclusion examine only the returns from the alternative actions. We must also consider the risks associated with each. The conclusions we *cannot* make from the preceding analysis are those regarding the risks

FIGURE 15–7 Financial Impact of a 10 Percent Reduction in Inventory

	Symbol	CBL 2001 $(000)	Average Inventory Reduced 10 Percent
Sales	*S*	$150,000	$150,000
Cost of goods sold	*CGS*	80,000	80,000
Gross margin	*GM = S − CGS*	70,000	70,000
Transportation	*TC*	6,000	6,000
Warehousing	*WC*	1,500	1,500
Inventory carrying	*IC = IN * W*	3,000	2,700
Other operating cost	*OOC*	30,000	30,000
Total operating cost	*TOC*	40,500	40,200
Earnings before interest and tax	*EBIT*	29,500	29,800
Interest	*INT*	12,000	12,000
Taxes	*TX*	7,000	7,120
Net income	*NI*	10,500	10,680
Asset deployment			
Inventory	*IN*	10,000	9,000
Account receivable	*AR*	30,000	30,000
Cash	*CA*	15,000	15,000
Fixed assets	*FA*	90,000	90,000
Total assets	*TA*	$145,000	$144,000
Ratio Analysis			
Profit margin	*NI/S*	7.00%	7.12%
Return on assets	*NI/TA*	7.24%	7.42%
Inventory turns/year	*CGS/IN*	8.00	8.89
Transportation as percentage of sales	*TC/S*	4.00%	4.00%
Warehousing as percentage of sales	*WC/S*	1.00%	1.00%
Inventory carrying as percentage of sales	*IC/S*	2.00%	1.80%

FIGURE 15–8 Comparison of Supply Chain Alternatives

Ratio Analysis	CBL 2001 $(000)	Transportation Cost Reduced 10 Percent	Warehousing Cost Reduced 10 Percent	Inventory Reduced 10 Percent
Profit margin	7.00%	7.24%	7.06%	7.12%
Return on assets	7.24%	7.49%	7.30%	7.42%
Inventory turns/year	8.00	8.00	8.00	8.89
Transportation as percentage of sales	4.00%	3.60%	4.00%	4.00%
Warehousing as percentage of sales	1.00%	1.00%	0.90%	1.00%
Inventory carrying as percentage of sales	2.00%	2.00%	2.00%	1.80%

FIGURE 15–9 Strategic Profit Model for CBL 2001 and Reduced Transportation Costs

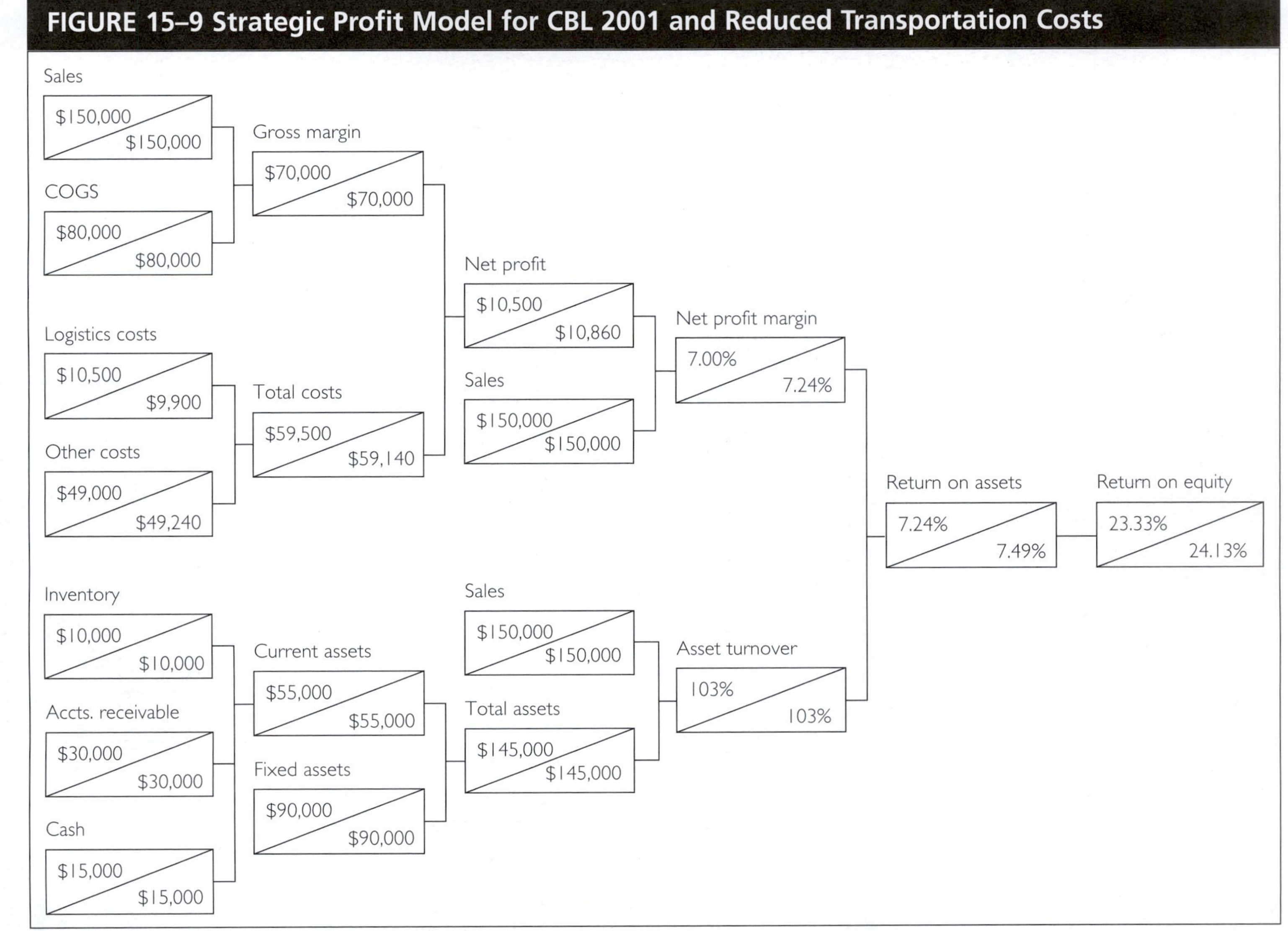

Note: Numbers above diagonal are CBL 2001, and below are reduced transportation costs.

SUPPLY CHAIN TECHNOLOGY

COSTING INFORMATION TECHNOLOGY

Before they would agree to spend $10,000 on a new dispatching and management system, the owners of B&D Transport in Springfield, Ohio, asked business manager Reggie Conley to do a cost-benefit analysis; but Conley ran into a Catch-22: Without more sophisticated software than he had, he lacked the tools to extract the kind of data he needed to justify a new system. "I couldn't come up with anything saying how much we were going to save. I knew we were going to save a lot of labor, but it was more of a feeling," he said.

Conley is not alone, and small family businesses like B&D are not the only ones that do not calculate precisely the expected return on investment before they buy information technology. While larger trucking firms are more likely to spend time and effort to understand the value of proposed IT investments, even some large firms implement new software simply because "they know they need something," said Mark Woodka, a senior vice president for business development at TMW Systems in Beachwood, Ohio.

Gut instinct can drive even fairly large purchases. J&J Machinery Transport in Charlotte, North Carolina, spent $120,000 on a new software and hardware package to manage its business without going through a formal analysis. The company's old computer system clearly was not providing the functions needed to analyze how well different portions of the business were performing, said Paul DePirro, controller at J&J. "We didn't necessarily run any numbers on how long it would take to pay for it; we just knew that we had to have it," he said.

Other trucking firms, however, bring a great deal of discipline to the justification process. Dallas & Mavis Specialized Carriers in Kenosha, Wisconsin, analyzed the potential savings before committing to a three-year lease of a $250,000 hardware and software package for document management. The company considered how long it was taking to get bills out and what it was spending on paper, photocopies, and postage, said Steve Salituro, director of finance.

It also included the benefits that would result when employees could spend more time making collection calls rather than digging paper out of the file cabinets. "It cut days out of our receivables and basically provided a cash flow improvement," he said. In addition, Dallas & Mavis predicted the imaging system would allow it to spend less on temporary employees or to expand its business without increasing staff, Salituro said.

A return-on-investment analysis convinced executives at Cornhusker Motor Line in Omaha, Nebraska, that with a new document-imaging system they could get bills out two days sooner, reducing interest costs. "That became a big number," said Jerry Beninato, Cornhusker's chief financial officer. The carrier also expected to cut a full-time position once the imaging system was in place. That prediction turned out to be half correct: Cornhusker was able to eliminate a half-time filing clerk. "But the efficiency we hoped for has definitely been there," Beninato said.

Source: Merrill Douglas, "Costing the Data System: Lacking Analysis, Tools, Some Go On Instinct," *iTech*, supplement to *Transport Topics* (July 2001): 29.

associated with the added cost necessary to realize the functional cost reductions, the additional capital required to achieve the reduction, and the service implications accompanying the changes. For example, to accomplish the transportation cost reduction, CBL may have to revert to a mode of transport that is slower. This could have a negative impact on customer satisfaction and result in lower sales. Or, the warehouse cost reduction may require the expenditure of $500,000 for automated materials-handling equipment that increases the assets deployed and reduces the ROA.

It should be noted that the preceding issues can be added to the financial analysis presented. For example, the added cost associated with reengineering the warehouse or any additional investment in fixed warehouse assets such as facilities or equipment can be added to the financial analysis along with the resulting warehouse cost savings.

Given our financial analysis and the preceding caveats, CBL has a better insight into the supply chain areas that will result in the greatest improvement in profitability and the accompanying risks (costs). In the next section, we address the financial implications of CBL's supply chain service failure issues.

Supply Chain Service Financial Implications

As noted in the Logistics Profile, CBL Book Distributors.com has experienced service failures in the service areas of *on-time deliveries* and *order fill rates.* The 95 percent on-time delivery rate means that only 95 percent of CBL orders are delivered when promised (on-time delivery). Also, only 97 percent of the orders are filled correctly. The alternative view of this service is that 5 percent of the orders are delivered after the promised delivery date and 3 percent of the orders are filled improperly.

service failure cost

The results of these supply chain service failures are added cost to correct the problem and lost sales. Figure 15–10 shows the methodology of determining the cost of service failures. When supply chain service failures occur, a portion of the customers experiencing the service failure will request that the orders be corrected and

FIGURE 15–10 Supply Chain Service Failure

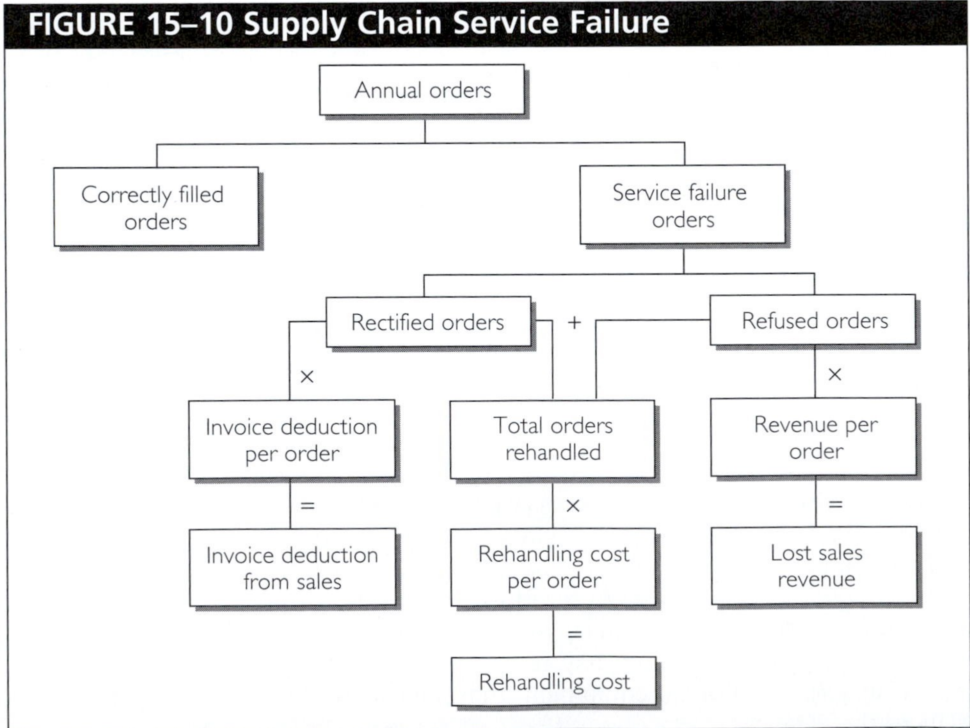

the others will refuse the orders. The refused orders represent lost sales revenue (refused orders times revenue per order) that must be deducted from total sales. For the rectified orders, the customers may request an invoice deduction to compensate them for any inconvenience or added costs. Finally, the seller incurs a rehandling cost associated with correcting the order such as reshipping the correct items and returning the incorrect and refused items (rectified orders plus refused orders times rehandling cost per order).

Referring to the data provided in the Logistics Profile for CBL on-time delivery and order fill rates, the financial impact of improving these two supply chain service metrics is given in Figure 15–11 and Figure 15–12. It is assumed that there are 1.5 million orders for the year, the revenue per order is $100, and the cost of goods per order is $53.33. Also, the lost sales rate for on-time delivery failures is 10 percent and, for order fill failures, 20 percent. The rehandling charge is $20 per rectified and refused order, and the invoice deduction is $10 per rectified order. The costs and assets are those provided in the Logistics Profile and used in the previous section. This pertinent information is contained within the boxed area of the spreadsheets in Figure 15–11 and Figure 15–12.

on-time delivery

Examining Figure 15–11, we note that the upper portion of the spreadsheet analysis determines the number of service failure orders, lost sales orders, rectified orders, and net orders sold. (The symbols provided in the second column are to assist the reader in creating the spreadsheet analysis.) At the 95 percent on-time delivery rate, 1,425,000 are delivered on time (.95 × 1,500,000 total orders) and 75,000 orders are delivered late (service failures). Of the 75,000 late orders, the customers will decline 7,500 (10 percent) and CBL will lose the sales on these orders, or $750,000 ($100 revenue/order × 7,500 lost orders). The rehandling cost is $1,500,000 ($20/order × 75,000 orders [rectified plus refused]), and invoice deduction is $675,000 ($10/order × 67,500 rectified orders).

In our example, the 1 percent improvement in on-time delivery (from 95 percent to 96 percent) results in net income falling by $56,997. The improved on-time delivery reduces invoice deductions by $235,000 and rehandling cost by $300,000, or a total cost saving of $535,000. However, to realize this cost saving of $535,000, transportation cost increases by 10 percent or $600,000. Since net income is reduced by $56,997 with the proposed strategy to switch to second-day ground delivery service, CBL will probably not consider this on-time delivery improvement option.

order fill rate

Examination of Figure 15–12 shows that the $100,000 cost to provide training to the warehouse personnel will improve the order fill rate from 97 percent to 98 percent and result in an increase in net income of $276,006. The combined savings of $420,000 (rehandling cost saving of $300,00 and invoice deductions saving of $120,000) are greater than the additional training cost of $100,000.

Given the two options—improve on-time delivery or order fill rate—CBL would be advised to implement the order fill improvement strategy.

strategic profit model

The strategic profit models of these two alternatives are given in Figure 15–13 and Figure 15–14. The profit margin, return on assets, and return on stockholder equity are greater with the order fill rate improvement strategy than with the on-time delivery strategy. For the order fill rate improvement from 97 percent to 98 percent, the ROE increases to 33.71 percent from 31.10 percent, the profit margin increases to 10.17 percent from 10.01 percent, and the return on assets increases to 10.46 percent from 10.27 percent.

FIGURE 15–11 Financial Impact of Improving On-Time Delivery

	Symbol	On-Time Rate 95%	On-Time Rate 96%
Annual orders	*AO*	1,500,000	1,500,000
Orders filled correctly	*OFC* = *AO* * %*CF*	1,425,000	1,440,000
Service failure orders	*SF* = *AO* – *OFC*	75,000	60,000
Lost sales orders	*LS* = *SF* * *LSR*	7,500	6,000
Rectified orders	*RO* = *SF* – *LS*	67,500	54,000
Net orders sold	*NOS* = *AO* – *LS*	1,492,500	1,494,000
Sales	*S* = *SP* * *AO*	$150,000,000	$150,000,000
Less: Invoice deduction	*ID* = *IDR* * *RO*	$675,000	$540,000
Lost sales revenue	*LSR* = *LS* * *SP*	$750,000	$600,000
Net sales	*NS* = *S* – *ID* – *LSR*	$148,575,000	$148,860,000
Cost of goods sold	*CGS* = *CG* * (*NOS*)	$79,595,025	$79,675,020
Gross margin (*GM*)	*GM* = *NS* – *CGS*	$68,979,975	$69,184,980
Rehandling cost	*RC* = *RCO* * *SF*	$1,500,000	$1,200,000
Transportation	*TC*	$6,000,000	$6,600,000
Warehousing	*WC*	$1,500,000	$1,500,000
Inventory carrying	*IC* = *IN* * *W*	$3,000,000	$3,000,000
Other operating cost	*OOC*	$30,000,000	$30,000,000
Total operating cost	*TOC*	$42,000,000	$42,300,000
Earnings before interest and tax	*EBIT* = *GM* – *TOC*	$26,979,975	$26,884,980
Interest	*INT*	$3,000,000	$3,000,000
Tax (40% * (*EBIT* – *INT*))	*TX*	$9,591,990	$9,553,992
Net income	*NI* = *EBIT* – *INT* – *TX*	$14,387,985	$14,330,988
Profit increase of 1% improvement			**($56,997)**

Input Data	95%	96%
%*CF*	95%	96%
Annual orders	1,500,000	1,500,000
SP = Revenue/order	$100	$100
CG = Cost of goods/order	$53.33	$53.33
Lost sales rate	10%	10%
RCO = Rehandling cost/order	$20	$20
IDR = Invoice deduction rate	$10	$10
Transportaiton cost	$6,000,000	$6,600,000
Warehousing cost	$1,500,000	$1,500,000
Interest cost	$3,000,000	$3,000,000
Other operating cost	$30,000,000	$30,000,000
Inventory	$10,000,000	$10,000,000
Cash	$15,000,000	$15,000,000
Acounts receivable	$30,000,000	$30,000,000
Fixed assets	$90,000,000	$90,000,000
W = Inventory carrying rate	30%	30%

FIGURE 15–12 Financial Impact of Improving Order Fill Rate

	Symbol	Order Fill Rate 97%	Order Fill Rate 98%
Annual orders	*AO*	1,500,000	1,500,000
Orders filled correctly	*OFC = AO * %CF*	1,455,000	1,470,000
Service failure orders	*SF = AO – OFC*	45,000	30,000
Lost sales orders	*LS = SF * LSR*	9,000	6,000
Rectified orders	*RO = SF – LS*	36,000	24,000
Net orders sold	*NOS = AO – LS*	1,491,000	1,494,000
Sales	*S = SP * AO*	$150,000,000	$150,000,000
Less: Invoice deduction	*ID = IDR * RO*	$360,000	$240,000
Lost sales revenue	*LSR = LS * SP*	$900,000	$600,000
Net sales	*NS = S – ID – LSR*	$148,740,000	$149,160,000
Cost of goods sold	*CGS = CG * (NOS)*	$79,515,030	$79,675,020
Gross margin (*GM*)	*GM = NS – CGS*	$69,224,970	$69,484,980
Rehandling cost	*RC = RCO * SF*	$900,000	$600,000
Transportation	*TC*	$6,000,000	$6,000,000
Warehousing	*WC*	$1,500,000	$1,600,000
Inventory carrying	*IC = IN * W*	$3,000,000	$3,000,000
Other operating cost	*OOC*	$30,000,000	$30,000,000
Total operating cost	*TOC*	$41,400,000	$41,200,000
Earnings before interest and tax	*EBIT = GM – TOC*	$27,824,970	$28,284,980
Interest	*INT*	$3,000,000	$3,000,000
Tax (40% * (*EBIT – INT*))	*TX*	$9,929,988	$10,113,992
Net income	*NI = EBIT – INT – TX*	$14,894,982	$15,170,988
Profit increase of 1% improvement			**$276,006**

Input Data	97%	98%
%*CF*	97%	98%
Annual orders	1,500,000	1,500,000
SP = Revenue/order	$100	$100
CG = Cost of goods/order	$53.33	$53.33
Lost sales rate	20%	20%
RCO = Rehandling cost/order	$20	$20
IDR = Invoice deduction rate	$10	$10
Transportaiton cost	$6,000,000	$6,000,000
Warehousing cost	$1,500,000	$1,600,000
Interest cost	$3,000,000	$3,000,000
Other operating cost	$30,000,000	$30,000,000
Inventory	$10,000,000	$10,000,000
Cash	$15,000,000	$15,000,000
Acounts receivable	$30,000,000	$30,000,000
Fixed assets	$90,000,000	$90,000,000
W = Inventory carrying rate	30%	30%

FIGURE 15–13 Strategic Profit Model for On-Time Delivery Improvement

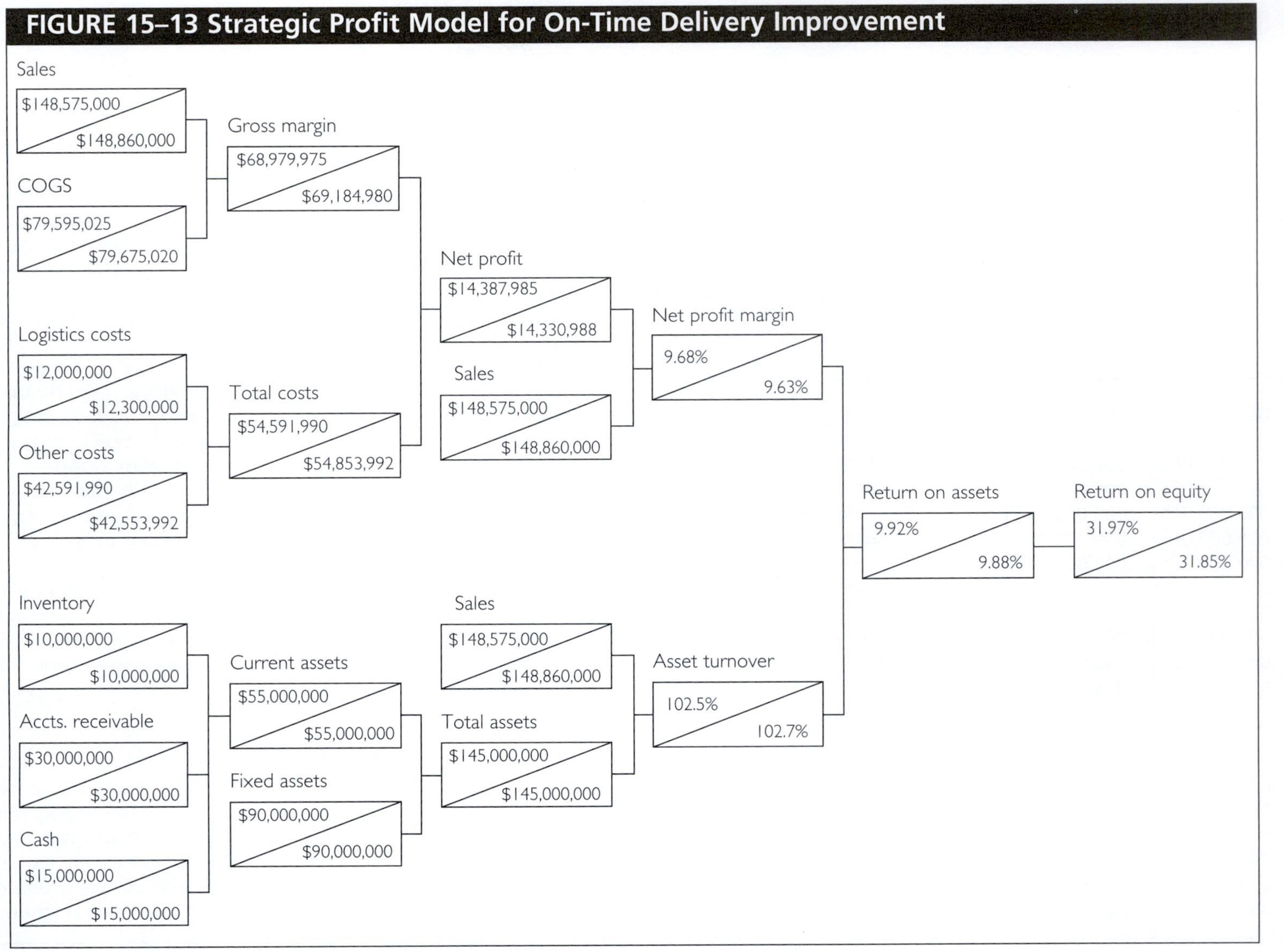

Note: Numbers above diagonal are for 95 percent on-time, and below are for 96 percent.

FIGURE 15–14 Strategic Profit Model for Order Fill Rate Improvement

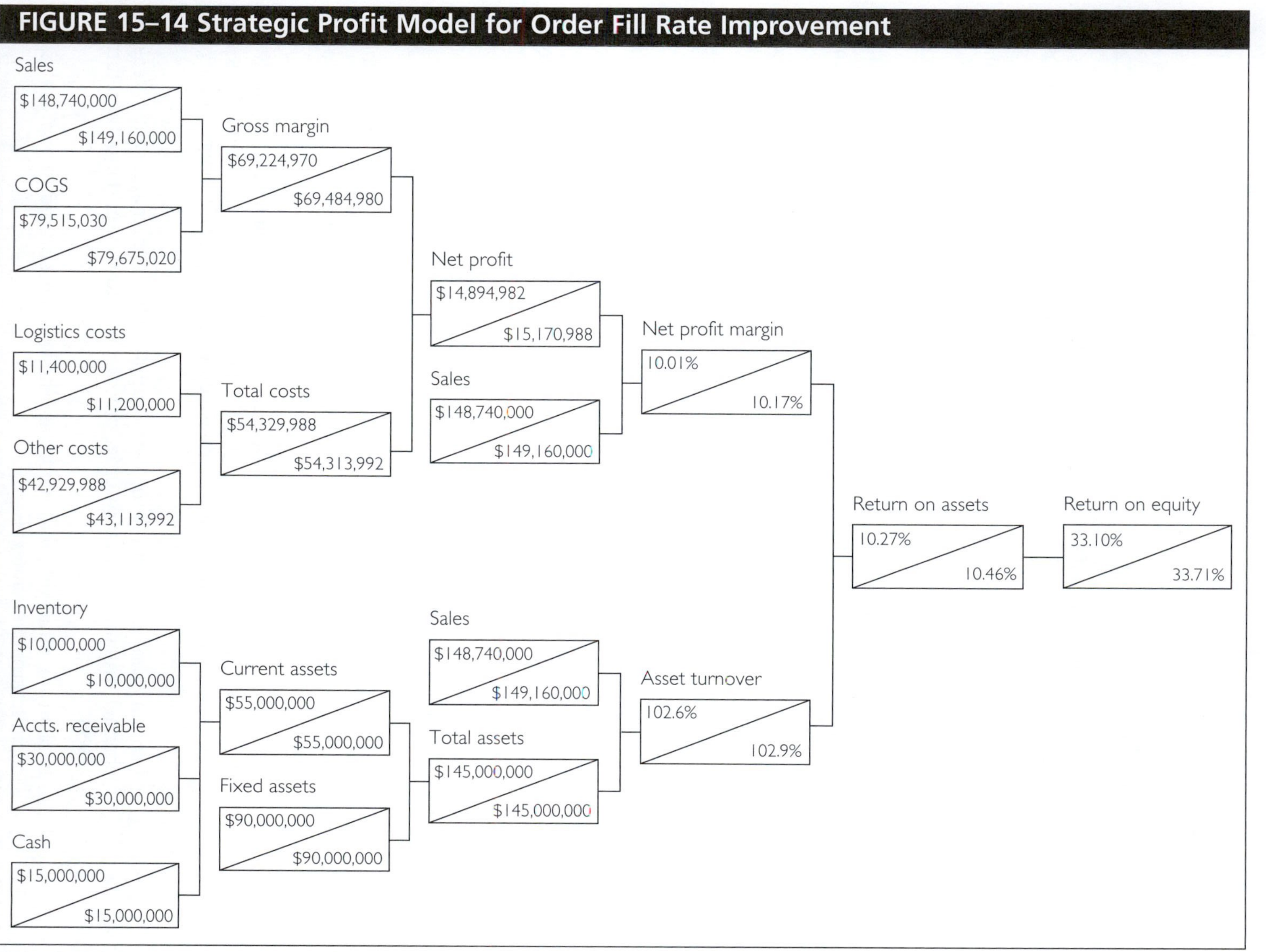

Note: Numbers above diagonal are for 95 percent on-time, and below are for 96 percent.

return to stockholders The financial goal for supply chain management is to increase return to stockholders. Examining alternative courses of action in light of the bottom-line impact (net income) and resultant return on equity accomplishes this goal.

Summary

- The supply chain influences the flow of products from vendor to final point of consumption, and the resources utilized in the process impact the cost of making the product available to the consumer.
- The equivalent sales increase for supply chain cost saving is found by dividing the cost saving by the company's profit margin.
- The lower the profit margin, the greater the sales equivalent of a given supply chain cost saving.
- Supply chain management impacts return on assets via decisions regarding channel structure management, inventory management, order management, and transportation management.
- The income statement shows the company sales, costs, taxes, and net income for a given time period.
- Alternative supply chain decisions should be made in light of the financial implications to net income, return on assets, and return on equity.
- The strategic profit model shows the relationship of sales, costs, assets, and equity; and it can trace the financial impact of a change in any one of these financial elements.
- Supply chain service failures result in lost sales and rehandling costs. The financial impact of modifications to supply chain service can be analyzed.

Study Questions

1. Discuss the impact supply chain management has on a company's profitability.
2. What is the relationship between supply chain management and a company's income statement and balance sheet?
3. Determine the sales equivalent of a $25,000 supply chain cost savings when the profit margin is (a) 20 percent, (b) 5 percent, and (c) 1 percent. What conclusions can be drawn between sales equivalent and profit margin for a given supply chain cost savings?
4. Explain the connection of the supply chain management areas of channel structure, inventory, order processing, and transportation to return on assets.
5. Explain the strategic profit model and how it can be used to analyze supply chain alternative strategies.
6. Using a spreadsheet computer software program, construct a supply chain finance model and calculate the profit margin; ROA; inventory turns; and trans-

portation, warehousing, and inventory costs as a percentage of revenue for the following:

Sales = \$200,000,000; Transportation cost = \$7,000,000;

Warehousing cost = \$1,600,000; Inventory carrying cost = 28 percent;

Cost of goods sold = \$70,000,000; Other operating costs = \$65,000,000;

Average inventory = \$10,000,000; Accounts receivable = \$30,000,000;

Cash = \$15,000,000; Net fixed assets = \$90,000,000;

Interest = \$10,000,000; Taxes = 40 percent of (EBIT – interest),

Current liabilities = \$65,000,000; Long-term liabilities = \$35,000,000; and

Stockholders equity = \$45,000,000.

7. Using the supply chain finance model developed for Problem 6, calculate the impact on profit margin; ROA; inventory turns; and transportation, warehousing, and inventory costs as a percentage of revenue for the following scenarios:
   a. Transportation costs increase 15 percent.
   b. Warehousing costs increase 15 percent.
   c. Average inventory increases 15 percent.
   d. Warehousing is outsourced with net fixed assets reduced 15 percent, inventory reduced 5 percent, warehousing cost = \$0, and outsourcing provider cost = \$1,200,000.
8. Develop a strategic model to depict the scenarios given in Problems 6 and 7.
9. Discuss the financial implications of supply chain service failures.
10. Construct a financial model to determine the redelivery/rehandling cost, lost sales, invoice deduction cost, and net income for the following: (a) On-time delivery increases from 98 percent to 99 percent with a 2 percent increase in transportation cost, and (b) Order fill rate decreases from 99 percent to 98 percent with operating cost remaining constant.

    Selling price/order = \$150/order; Gross profit/order = \$35/order; Lost sales rate: On-time delivery failure = 20 percent and Order fill failure = 25 percent;

    Annual orders = 200,000; Rehandling cost = \$100/order; Invoice deduction/service failure = \$75/order; Transportation cost = \$1,000,000; Average inventory = \$1,000,000;

    Interest cost = \$1,500,000; Inventory carrying cost rate = 25 percent/\$/Yr; Warehousing cost = \$750,000; Other operating cost = \$500,000; Cash = \$3,000,000; Accounts receivable = \$4,000,000; Fixed assets = \$30,000,000.

NOTE

1. Bernard J. Lalonde and Terrance J. Pohlen, "The Ohio State University 2000 Survey of Career Patterns in Logistics," *Council of Logistics Management Annual Conference Proceedings 2000*, 54.

CASE 15–1 ■ DVD4LESS.com

DVD4LESS.com is one of the many new firms that have a presence on the World Wide Web. It specializes in manufacturing and selling one type of high-end DVD player. By purchasing large volumes from a small number of suppliers, it receives a significant quantity discount. This reduced cost is passed on to its customers. DVD4LESS.com manages to sell its DVD player for $200 less than all its high-end competitors, thereby creating its competitive advantage.

DVD4LESS.com receives 112,000 orders for DVD players annually. Each DVD player sells for $500, of which $200 is retained as gross profit. Last year, it filled 97 percent of all orders correctly. Of the orders filled incorrectly, DVD4LESS.com estimates that 20 percent of the customers cancel the order and the remainder will accept a second shipment, which results in a rehandling cost of $20 per order. To maintain customer goodwill, the firm gives a $35 invoice reduction for *all* units rehandled.

DVD4LESS.com pays $1,950,000 annually for the transportation of its materials and delivery of its products. Its warehousing costs average $1,460,000 annually for the storage of its materials. DVD4LESS.com has $30 million of debt outstanding at an annual interest rate of 10 percent. The total cost for all selling and general administrative expenses (other operating costs) comes to $750,000, and $50,000 is held in cash at all times.

DVD4LESS.com has an average inventory of $5 million. This large inventory is partially attributed to its purchasing policy, and also to its inventory management system. The inventory carrying cost rate is estimated at 25 percent of the average inventory value per year. Its accounts receivable averages $250,000 throughout the year primarily due to sales to medium-sized retailers. DVD4LESS.com has a large fixed asset base. It is comprised of land, the manufacturing facility, machinery, and various administrative offices that are valued at $64 million.

DVD4LESS.com has explored a variety of options to improve its correct order fill rate. It is also interested in lowering its average inventory as a means to improve its overall profitability. After weeks of presentations and heated debates, the decision is made to outsource its warehousing operations and inventory management. Many third-party-logistics providers bid for the contract; in the end, it is awarded to Basileo Logistics for an annual cost of $500,000 (this is classified as other operating cost). By outsourcing, DVD4LESS.com manages to save $760,000 in warehousing expenses, reduces its average inventory by 30 percent, and now meets its 99 percent correct order fill rate. All other costs remain the same. The tax rate is 40 percent.

Case Questions

As the supply chain management analyst at DVD4LESS.com:

1. Calculate the net savings of the outsourcing of the warehousing and inventory management to Basileo Logistics.
2. Develop a strategic profit model of both the old system and the modified system reflecting the required adjustments. DVD4LESS.com's net worth is $30 million.

APPENDIX 15A

FINANCIAL TERMS

account receivable A current asset showing the amount of sales currently owed by customers.

balance sheet A snapshot of everything the company owes and owns at the end of the financial year in question.

cash cycle Time between payment of inventory and collection of cash from receivables.

cash-flow statement Shows cash receipts and payments from all company financial activities; earnings before interest, taxes, depreciation, and amortization (EBITDA).

cost of goods sold Total cost of the goods sold to customers during the period.

cost of lost sales The short-run forgone profit associated with a stockout.

current assets Cash and other assets that will be converted into cash during one operating cycle.

current liabilities An obligation that must be paid during the normal operating cycle, usually one year.

current ratio Current assets divided by current liabilities; measures company's ability to pay short-term debt with assets easily converted to cash.

debt-to-equity ratio Long-term debt divided by shareholder equity.

earnings before interest and taxes (EBIT) Sales minus cost of goods sold and operating costs.

earnings per share Net earnings divided by average number of shares outstanding.

gross margin Sales minus cost of goods sold.

income statement Summarizes revenues and expenses, reporting the net income or loss for a specific accounting period.

inventory carrying cost The annual cost of holding inventory; the value of the average inventory times the inventory carrying cost rate (W).

inventory carrying cost rate (W) The cost of holding one dollar of inventory for one year, usually expressed as a percentage and includes cost of capital, risk, item servicing, and storage space.

inventory turns Cost of goods sold divided by average inventory.

liquidity ratio Cash flow from operations divided by current liabilities. Measures short-term cash available to pay current liabilities.

net income (or loss) Final result of all revenue and expense items for a period; sales minus cost of goods sold, operating costs, interest, and taxes.

operating expense Every expense other than cost of goods sold, depreciation, interest, and income tax.

operating ratio Percentage of revenues used for operations; operating expenses divided by operating income.

order-to-cash cycle Time between receiving customer orders and collection of receivables.

profit margin Net income divided by sales.

return on assets Net income divided by total assets.

return on equity Net income divided by average stockholder's equity.

shareholder equity The difference between value of all things owned by the company and the value of all the things owed by the company; the investment made by the stockholders at the time the stock was originally issued plus all past earnings that have not been paid out in dividends. Sum total of shareholder's investment in a company, since it was formed, minus its liabilities.

working capital Current assets minus current liabilities. Working capital finances the business by converting goods and services to cash.

CHAPTER 16

LOGISTICS AND SUPPLY CHAIN CHALLENGES FOR THE FUTURE

LEARNING OBJECTIVES

After reading this chapter, you should be able to do the following:

- Understand what is meant by *strategy* and how it applies to logistics and supply chain management.
- Trace the stages in the evolution of strategic planning and its application to logistics and supply chain management.
- Have a working knowledge of how logistics and supply chain strategies have benefited individual business firms.
- Be able to explain the relevance and importance of several types of logistics and supply chain strategies.
- Identify and explain a number of macro trends that will impact the future of logistics and supply chain management.

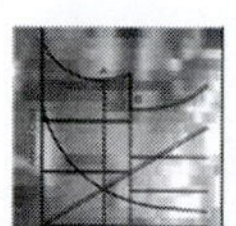

LOGISTICS PROFILE

Creating a State-of-the-Art VW Beetle Production Facility in Mexico

When Volkswagen AG decided to produce its new Beetle in Mexico, its goal was to transfer to that country the lean manufacturing techniques and supplier park concept employed at its SEAT subsidiary production facility in Martorell, Spain, one of the world's largest automotive production facilities in terms of daily output. The facility produces nearly 2,000 cars daily in seven different models with the support of its pre-assembly supplier park located 2.2 kilometers from the factory. The challenge faced by Volkswagen was how to export quickly and efficiently this extremely effective just-in-time (JIT) supplier park model to Puebla, Mexico.

That's when Volkswagen invited Exel, the global logistics and supply chain services provider that designed, engineered, and now operates the SEAT park, to work with them in Mexico. Exel had an established infrastructure in Mexico providing services to clients such as Procter & Gamble, which was expected to expedite the transfer process.

The SEAT Model

The SEAT Pre-Assembly Supplier Industrial Park in Spain was created near the factory to support its lean manufacturing strategy. Subassembly activities are carried out at the Park, guaranteeing JIT delivery and zero stocks at SEA assembly lines. Twenty-five suppliers are located there, providing parts or subassemblies. Exel is responsible for primary transport from the component suppliers' main plants to the Park, and also for warehousing, picking, subassembly and sequencing operations, and JIT deliveries to the SEAT assembly lines.

Replicating the Model in Mexico

In January, 1998, at Volkswagen's Mexican assembly plant in Puebla, Exel implemented the JIT sequencing operation, with limited modifications to the SEAT model. Currently, the Mexican plant produces more than 1,600 vehicles daily, including the Beetle and the Jetta. The operation provides parts and components to the assembly line with as little as one hour's notice. The Exel JIT sequencing operation is the cornerstone of a supplier industrial park that serves the Volkswagen assembly plant. Exel is responsible for the assembly, staging, and delivery of parts and components from more than a dozen suppliers in that industrial park to the assembly line. Parts delivery is scheduled to take place within 40 minutes of an order, with one car built every 40 minutes, 24 hours a day, 6 days per week. Parts are to be delivered directly to specific locations on the assembly line.

The end result is that Exel provides Volkswagen with expert logistics and supply chain management to support operations in a new, modular, JIT manufacturing environment. Actually, this represented the first Volkswagen Mexico manufacturing park logistics operation to be managed by a single supply chain specialist. Overall, the involvement of Exel in Volkswagen's Puebla, Mexico, operation demonstrates significant capability to transfer technology, human resources, and best practices on a global basis.

Source: Exel, 2000. Reprinted with permission.

Introduction

As should be evident from the content of the preceding fifteen chapters, the areas of logistics and supply chain management are changing quickly. Aside from many of the innovations and improvements that have occurred, there is evidence that firms are moving toward thinking of these areas as helping to create strategic, competitive advantage for firms and their customers. Thus, it can be said that these areas have become prime candidates for application of tried and proven approaches to strategic planning.

strategic issues

This chapter first provides an overview of strategic planning and provides a perspective on the principles of strategic planning as applied to logistics and supply chain management. Emphasis is on how competency in these areas can help to meet overall goals and objectives. Then, the focus is on strategy, specifically as it is related to four important areas: time-based, asset productivity, technology-based, and relationship-based. These represent four key areas in which firms are investing significant resources to help achieve competitive advantage through logistics and supply chain management. Last, a number of future directions are presented that will help you to look ahead and try to anticipate what tomorrow's logistics and supply chain challenges are likely to be. This is appropriate, since part of your responsibility will be to "step up" to these challenges and help your companies and your profession improve and move forward.

Overview of Strategic Planning for Logistics and Supply Chain Management

The terms *strategy, strategic, strategic management,* and *strategic advantage* have been used frequently throughout this text. The frequent use of these terms can be explained in part by the intensely competitive global environment that most firms are faced with today. Effective response to this changing environment requires a management focus that is future oriented and one that involves a continuing evaluation and analysis of the many underlying factors that drive the need for change.

Gaining some sort of strategic advantage over competitors is a key part of survival, and logistics has come to be recognized as having a role to play in helping to gain that competitive advantage. Understanding how we gain competitive advantage and how logistics can contribute is important. Initially, we examine the background and development of strategy. Then we discuss some generic or basic general strategies. Finally, we examine the types of logistics strategies that companies are utilizing to help their organizations gain competitive advantage.

It is no wonder that businesses talk strategy or reference strategic approaches. They must keep focused on a future course or direction and on positioning themselves to respond proactively. They must also achieve the necessary acumen to survive successfully, that is, to make a profit and have a sufficient return to add value for shareholders. Strategy is justifiably a part of our business lexicon.

Historical Perspective on Strategy

As has been indicated in previous chapters, strategy and strategic advantage have become a meaningful part of the company culture in most successful corporations that operate globally or that are affected by global competition. Economic survival is closely related to having a vision and understanding the effect that major drivers of change will have upon the mission of an organization. Logistics supply chains should play an important role in the strategic plans of companies.

economic imperative

It is important to note at the outset that good planning is not a new phenomenon in successful companies. Rather, there have been several phases of evolutionary development with respect to planning:

evolutionary development

- During the 1950s and 1960s, strategic planning typically meant investment planning. The prevailing doctrine was that diversity led to success and was a hedge against economic downturns. A broader array of products and/or services would, therefore, provide growth and stability.
- During the 1970s, strategic planning began to focus on internal growth opportunities, with an emphasis upon marketing research, product development, and brand management. Also, cost reduction strategies were developed for expanded national and international sales.
- During the 1980s, a combination of investment in other companies and internal growth opportunities were utilized. Strategic business units (SBUs) were developed; these were essentially components of the larger organization. The focus was upon predicting the impact of the forces of change and providing plans for the SBUs to become sources of growth in sales or sources of cash from profits to finance other SBUs that were moving up the growth curve.
- During the 1990s, the emphasis refocused somewhat to the development of plans for gaining strategic advantage in the marketplace and for defending against competitors seeking greater market share. Strategic planning became more team oriented and more comprehensive in terms of participation by company personnel. The planners were less likely to be a remote group that did not actively participate in decision making. It was a much more challenging era both because of the dynamics of the changes that were occurring and also because more individuals in the company were having an opportunity to provide input for changing existing practices and, perhaps, even to help change the direction of the organization.
- The early 2000s have seen strategic focus clearly move toward the development of effective, interfirm relationships that would help to create maximum value for the consumers or business buyers of products and services. In relation to this emphasis, corporate priorities clearly strive to improve business practices through synchronization, collaboration, and integration of activities and processes both within and among companies.

Before proceeding to discuss generic strategies, a discussion of the definition of strategy is appropriate.

Definitions

The term *strategy,* or *strategic,* is a derivative of the Greek word *strategos,* meaning "the art of the general," which is indicative of the word's military origins. In fact,

terminology

strategy and *tactics* are a part of both the military and the business lexicon, and an appropriate definition is provided of both terms:

- *Strategy* can be defined as a course of action, a scheme, or a principal idea through which an organization or individual hopes to accomplish a specific objective or goal. In other words, a strategy is designed to determine how someone is going to achieve something that has been identified as being important to future success.
- *Tactics*, on the other hand, refers to the operational aspects that are necessary to support strategy. Tactics are more likely to involve daily short-run operations that help achieve the strategy that has been identified or agreed upon in the organization. An example is useful to help clarify the essential differences between strategy and tactics.

cross-docking

Wal-Mart has been referred to on several occasions in previous chapters, and it provides a good example for this discussion of strategy. Wal-Mart's obvious goal as it was developing was to increase market share. The strategies that the company identified to accomplish this goal or objective were low prices to the consumer and high levels of customer service. Efficiency of logistics systems and effective functioning of the overall supply chain were critical to the realization of both strategies. Looking more closely at Wal-Mart's operations reveals that a tactic that has been deployed on a continuing basis is cross-docking at the numerous distribution centers in the overall logistics network. As indicated previously, *cross-docking* is a term that describes moving goods or freight through a distribution facility in twenty-four hours or less, that is, in and out in less than a day, if possible.

The tactic of cross-docking plays an important part in the strategies to have low prices and excellent customer service. Products move through the warehouse to the shelf for consumers to purchase in a timely fashion. This practice contributes to efficiency by helping to move product through facilities rapidly, thus increasing inventory turnover. That same speed of movement helps to achieve customer satisfaction by having stock available when and where the customer needs it.

internet capabilities

Best Buy is another well-known retailer of high-tech, consumer electronics and other products; it has effectively used its logistics and supply chain capabilities to improve customer service and market positioning. As indicated in Figure 16–1, Best Buy has successfully integrated its traditional store presence with its more recent, electronic capabilities using the Internet. Best Buy significantly coordinates and integrates its logistics strategies for these two complementary aspects of its business and even provides opportunities for its consumers to order products over the Internet and then pick them up at nearby stores.

inventory availability

Benetton is another well-known retailer that has used good logistics to achieve increased market share and higher levels of profit. Benetton's strategy was to develop a quick-response logistics system that would link manufacturing and the retail store, giving high levels of customer service by having the right stock available but with low in-store inventory. One of the tactics that the company uses is bar-coded cartons that can be moved swiftly through the warehouse to be transported, often by airfreight, to the retail location needing that inventory (SKU). Other tactics, including postponement, are also utilized to achieve efficiency and high levels of customer satisfaction.

Wal-Mart, Best Buy, and Benetton are good examples of companies that have increased market share through good logistics strategy or through strategies sup-

FIGURE 16–1 Best Buy: Integrating Retail and On-Line Sales

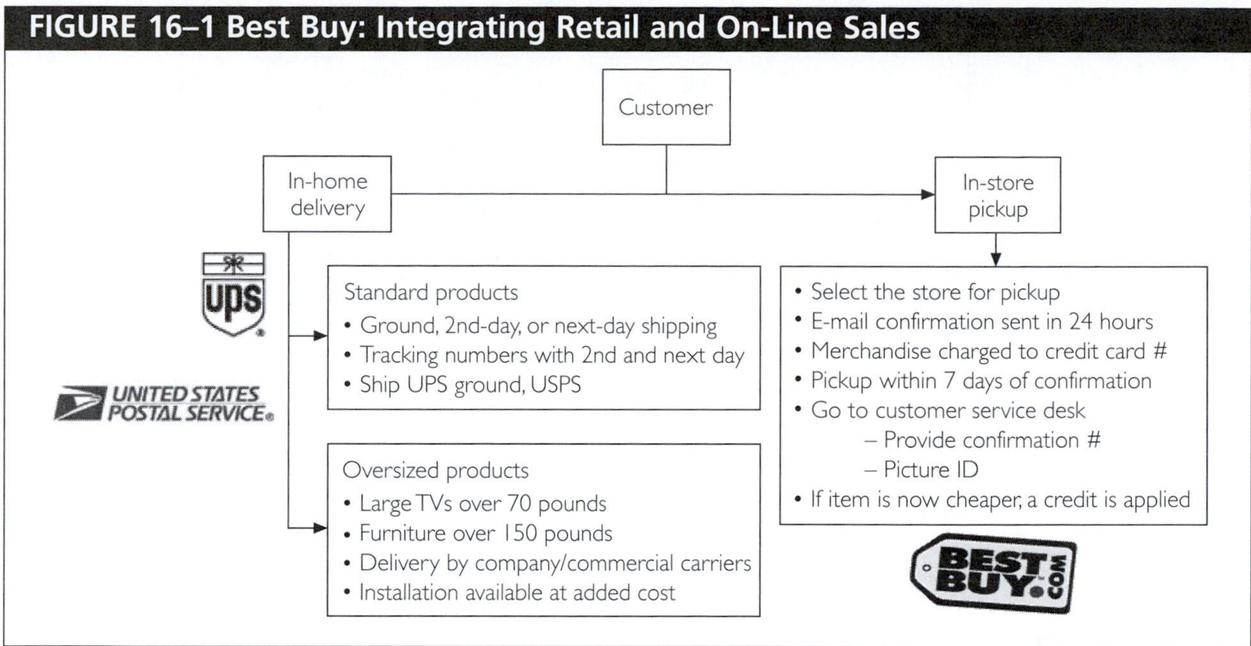

Source: Best Buy Co., Inc. Used with permission.

ported by good logistics tactics. Other examples that demonstrate the value of efficient and effective logistics strategies and tactics have been referred to in previous chapters, including Nabisco, Procter & Gamble, Becton Dickinson, Keebler, and so on. All of these organizations have logistics strategies and tactics to achieve corporate goals.

With strategy in mind, we turn to a review of basic or generic strategies that should shed some additional light on logistics strategy.

Strategy Classification

Porter's strategies

While there are several ways to classify strategy, one of the most popular is to use Porter's basic or generic strategies, namely, cost, differentiation, and focus (Figure 16–2). A strategy based upon *low cost* essentially stresses offering a product or service in the market at a price or cost lower than that of other competitors. This frequently used strategy was used by many Japanese producers when they entered the U.S. market. Products such as automobiles, televisions, computers, copiers, stereos, and so on were usually priced lower than those of their U.S. competitors. U.S. companies such as Wal-Mart and McDonald's have also used this strategy to gain higher market share. The increased market share means higher volumes of output, with economies of scale that reinforce the low cost/low price strategy; that is, firms continue to lower prices as costs are lowered through economies of scale.

low cost

In today's business environment, low price does not always translate to low quality, as even low-priced products or services require an acceptable level of quality. There have been certain instances of companies utilizing a strict, cost-based strategy; however, the product or service offering was so inferior that customers soon ceased purchasing the product. The foreign-produced Yugo automobile is a good example of such a situation. In fact, companies such as Toyota, Honda, Wal-Mart,

FIGURE 16–2 Strategies for Creating Value

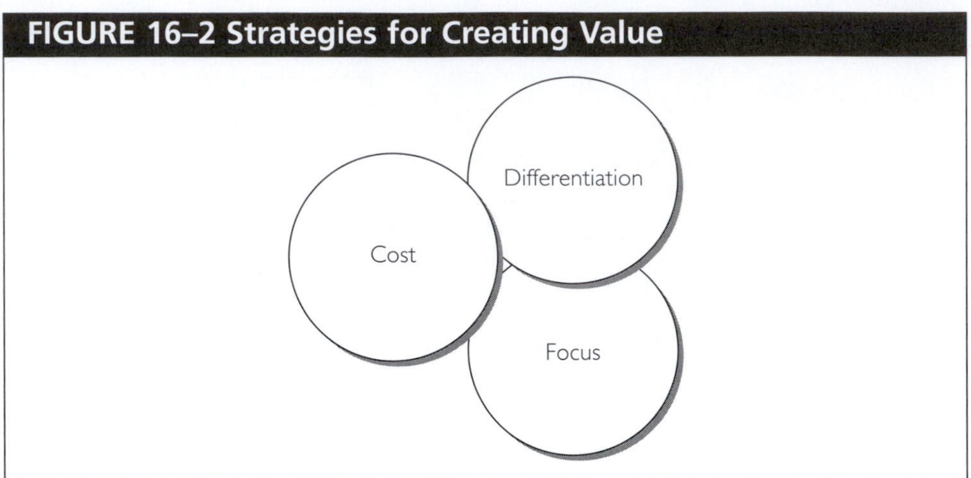

Source: Reprinted with the permission of The Free Press, a division of Simon & Schuster, Inc., from *Competitive Advantage: Creating and Sustaining Superior Performance* by Michael E. Porter. Copyright © 1985, 1998 Michael E. Porter.

and so on have continually stressed quality because it too can lead to lower costs, if implemented in an effective manner. Quality is considered consistent with their low-cost strategy. High quality and low cost are of great strategic value to companies such as these.

differentiation

The second type of basic strategy involves using *differentiation* to gain market share. The approach underlying differentiation is to make a product or service offering that is unique so that customers will be willing to pay a premium price. Typically, that involves providing a bundle of attributes with the offering that makes it more valuable to the customer than some other offering available at a lower price. When a customer buys a higher-priced article of clothing, automobile, or entertainment center, for example, she perceives that this higher price is worth it because of better fit, higher quality, longer product life, better service, or some other perceived value associated with the higher-priced item. This would be true, for example, of buyers of Lexus brand automobiles.

You can probably think of examples from personal experience in which you have paid for a higher-priced product because of its perceived extra value to you. From a strategic point of view, the differentiation approach requires good logistics to provide high-quality customer service. This may mean making deliveries on an appointment basis with a very tight window for delivery; being available twenty-four hours a day, seven days a week, to receive orders; or perhaps providing special pallet packs. Xerox Corporation, for example, in trying to compete against Canon, decided to differentiate its copiers by providing high levels of service for parts and repairs to minimize delay times when a machine needed repair. In some instances, that time frame for repair is two hours or less. The company did not feel that it could match Canon's prices. Therefore, differentiation through excellent customer service became its strategy.

focus

The third type of strategy is the *focus* strategy, which is based on identifying a smaller segment of the market or a market niche in which to utilize either the lower price or differentiation approach. Many small businesses are successful because they recognize the logic of this approach. It may be the local restaurant

FIGURE 16–3 The Generic Value Chain

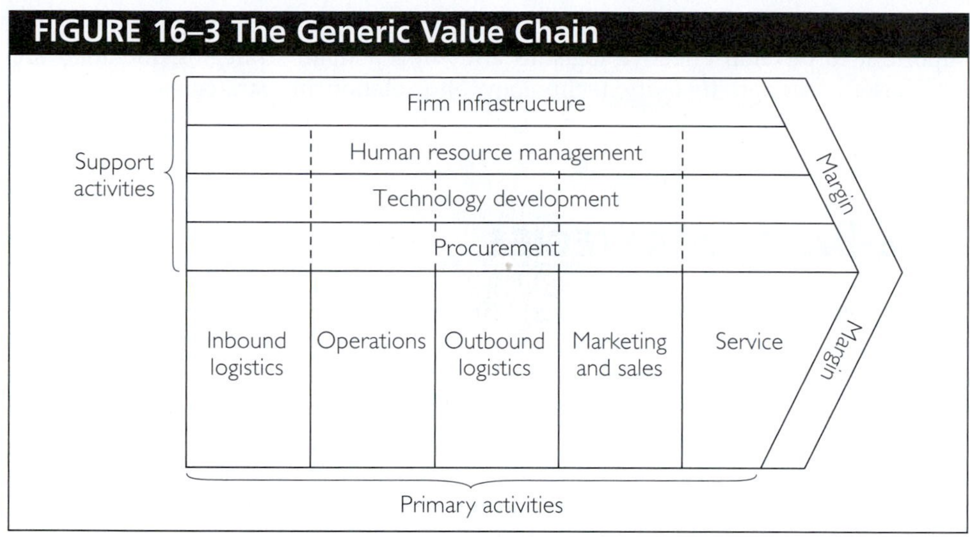

Source: Reprinted with the permission of The Free Press, a division of Simon & Schuster, Inc., from *Competitive Advantage: Creating and Sustaining Superior Performance* by Michael E. Porter. Copyright © 1985, 1998 Michael E. Porter.

that offers home delivery or the laundry that is open twenty-four hours a day. Even large businesses can capitalize on this approach by providing product or service offerings in different segments, with low cost in one or more market niches and differentiation in one or more others. Hotel chains are a good example of large companies using this approach. Marriott, for example, is among the medium-high price category of hotels, but it also has the Courtyard by Marriott hotels that offer lower prices to cost-conscious guests. In addition, Marriott Suites caters to a different group of customers, while Fairfield Inns, also owned by Marriott, offer low-end or budget-class rooms.

For companies that compete on price in some market segments and on differentiation or value in others, it is challenging to separately manage the systems needed to support these two contrasting market strategies. In the case of a company that is providing twenty-four-hour delivery in the high-price market as a customer service tactic to help differentiate a product, it would be a problem if that same level of service was provided in the low-price segment. Using our hotel example, if customers perceived that the Fairfield Inns were of the same quality as the Marriott, they would stay at the Fairfield Inn for a lower price. Therefore, it is important to effectively communicate to the marketplace the difference as to what is being provided or the distinction between the offerings will be blurred or lost.

value chain

In his discussion of these types of strategies, Porter presents the value chain (see Figure 16–3), which suggests that the corporation can be disaggregated into five primary activities and four support activities. The major point is that all of these activities have to be aligned effectively for the overall value chain to achieve the desired results. It is important to note in this context that logistics is prominently displayed as two of the five primary activities, namely, inbound and outbound logistics. The obvious conclusion is that logistics activities can play an important role in helping to develop and/or sustain competitive advantage. Also, inbound and outbound logistics need to be coordinated with the other primary activities and the support activities.

The next several sections provide details concerning four areas in which it is important to develop effective logistics and supply chain strategies. Included are time-based, asset productivity, technology, and relationship strategies.

Time-Based Strategies

Most people have heard the old adage "Time is money." The value of time can be measured in a number of different ways. For example, the earlier discussion of using the adapted EOQ model to make transportation modal choice decisions demonstrated that a choice of transportation with faster, more consistent transit times could help to reduce inventory and warehousing costs. Even though the faster mode of transportation may be more expensive, the net impact of savings in inventory and warehousing costs would be a reduction in total costs. This is an example of an effective strategy that is based on the trade-offs between transportation, inventory, and warehousing costs.

return on investment

When logistics improvements require a level of investment (e.g., facilities, technology, equipment, etc.), it is important not only that the net savings exist and be positive but also that they represent an acceptable return on use of the firm's investment resources. This means that company measures such as ROI, ROA, and economic profit should meet or exceed corporate standards and yardsticks to justify improving investment ideas.

cash-to-cash cycle

One aspect of time-based strategies that will receive additional attention in the future is the impact of logistics and supply chain improvements on cash flow. As transportation times continue to become shorter and more consistent, for example, there are significant savings in working capital that is tied up in inventories that are moving through the supply chain. Time-based improvements literally "free up" investment and the associated costs of carrying inventory throughout the supply chain. When viewing this from a total supply chain perspective, the objective has evolved to managing what is known as the "cash-to-cash cycle," defined as the time it takes to convert a dollar worth of raw materials into a dollar worth of sales in the marketplace. This metric is becoming one of the more sought after measures of overall supply chain performance. In addition to reduced investment in working capital, shorter, more consistent supply chain performance typically means that participating firms receive payments more quickly than otherwise. This, too, can be a major type of time-based benefit that may result.

Logistics-related strategies that shorten the length of the order and/or replenishment cycle have been the focus of much attention in recent years. Time-compression strategies have also received attention in the previous chapters in this text when inventory, transportation, warehousing, and so on were discussed. Before summarizing what has been stated in previous chapters, we examine some more general aspects of time reduction.

Reducing Cycle Time

Reductions in cycle time are based upon three factors: processes, information, and decision making. The previous discussion mentioned performing logistics-related processes faster and more consistently. If logistics is viewed as a series of *processes,* then those processes being performed faster will reduce cycle time, with the associated benefits already mentioned.

information technology

Another important source of reductions in cycle time has been provided by faster provision of *information.* The utilization of faster, more efficient forms of order transmission—EDI or the Internet, for example—can significantly reduce the time needed to complete the transaction. Also, the use of contemporary information technologies is becoming increasingly attractive as the costs of computer hardware and software, as well as overall connectivity, have been declining significantly. Timely, accurate information about sales, orders, inventory levels, transportation service, and so on leads to shorter cycle times and also reduces uncertainty about what is happening, which leads to lower inventory levels by reducing the need for safety stock. Thus, information has become a source of significant savings to many companies.

levels of approval

The final factor in reducing cycle time is *decision making.* In some organizations, this is the most important of the three factors. The critical issue is to empower individuals to make decisions relevant to their areas of expertise and responsibility. All too frequently, multiple levels of approval must be gone through before a decision can be made. One may refer to this as the *approval process* or, perhaps more realistically, as "*red tape.*" The important point is that preexisting levels of needed approval slow down the decision-making process, which can in turn lengthen the order cycle. The flat, lean organizations that are becoming more common in today's environment are frequently characterized by delegated decision making, which emphasizes decision making at the so-called "action" level, such as that of the customer service representative. While decision making at the lowest possible level in the company can lead to the making of some mistakes, the experience of companies like Procter & Gamble and others suggests that the risk is justified in terms of the time that is saved and the improvement that often takes place with respect to customer responsiveness.

The combination of improved (faster) logistics processes; faster and more accurate flow of information; and quicker, more responsive decision making can lead to dramatic reductions in lead time or cycle time. We turn now to a more specific discussion of logistics initiatives that have led to reductions in cycle time.

Time-Reduction Logistics Initiatives

Logistics professionals have used a number of important time-reduction initiatives. Among the more popular of these approaches is *cross-docking,* a concept that emphasizes flow of products through logistics facilities, rather than the use of storage. The relevance of cross-docking in today's logistics environment is clear; the concept typifies the types of initiatives that should be receiving attention today.

"push" to "pull"

In addition, other approaches such as *just in time* (JIT), *vendor-managed inventory* (VMI) and *continuous replenishment* (CRP) are all characteristic of contemporary approaches that help our logistics practices move from "push" to "pull." While these techniques are frequently discussed in the context of inventory strategies, they also have important implications for time reduction of the order cycle because they shorten the total time from vendor to delivery to customers.

Also, contemporary concern for visibility of product throughout the supply chain has renewed our emphasis on the utilization of information technologies for product tracking and tracing, optical scanning and bar coding, stock location, and so forth. In short, the imperative is for firms to develop the ability to know where all products may happen to be at any point in time. This information is needed not for its own sake but, more importantly, to know when shipments may be late, need expediting, and so forth Approaches like *efficient consumer response* (ECR), discussed earlier in the text, are also examples of effective time-reduction strategies or initiatives. The basic plan, as you will recall from earlier reading, is to reduce the length of time that grocery inventory spends in the pipeline, between the time it comes off the assembly line and when the final customer purchases the product. For a grocery chain, the average pipeline time was 104 days, and the goal was to reduce it to 61 days, which was quite an improvement. This initiative is obviously different from the others we have discussed in that it involves a whole group of companies that operate in the same supply chain. In today's business environment, groups of firms in various industries have formed their own, industry-specific organizations to accomplish a number of objectives such as these. Examples include Covisint (automotive), Transora (consumer packaged goods), and Converge (high tech).

anticipate customers' needs

Finally, there has been considerable recent interest in leveraging the power of effective demand planning and forecasting to more meaningfully move from "push" to "pull." Improved ability to diagnose and even anticipate customers' needs enables the logistics and supply chain processes to make a much more valuable contribution to the achievement of corporate goals and objectives. Recent interest in *collaborative planning, forecasting, and replenishment* (CPFR) also serves as an example of a highly useful, contemporary technology.

Increasingly, companies are changing from the traditional push approach to a pull approach, which is a demand-responsive system. The switch requires a major change in corporate culture that is frequently difficult to achieve. Not only does the change require a switch to a flexible, quick-change manufacturing environment, necessitating retraining of the manufacturing employees, it also requires that manufacturing operate at a less-than-optimal cost from time to time.

manufacturing impacts

In its purest form, the *pull approach* requires that products be manufactured only when an order is received. Obviously, this requires a fast manufacturing system. The ability to accomplish this feat essentially eliminates finished goods inventory, which can result in significant savings. Some very large companies are moving in this direction. Chrysler, for example, states that it can manufacture a car to order in fifteen days, which means that it fills a customer's order reasonably quickly. It is hoping to reduce that time to seven days within the near future. Chrysler's intent is to reduce dealer inventories. One of the Japanese auto manufacturers has a goal of being able to produce a car to order in three days. The achievement of these goals will significantly reduce the inventory of new cars.

responding to demand

Sears is moving to reduce the size of its retail furniture stores, which tend to be very large in terms of floor space. It will compensate by being able to produce furniture to order and deliver it within seven days after the order is received. Even some manufacturers of farm equipment, which is a seasonal product, are considering a change to a more demand-oriented manufacturing system. Pull systems are more challenging in such an environment because of the peak demand. These are just some of the many types of companies that have changed or are changing to a demand-responsive manufacturing and logistics system. Also note that a pull system is consistent with the time-compression strategies discussed previously.

An additional aspect of pull systems is that some companies use the concept of postponement to achieve a system that is close to a pure pull system. As was indicated, postponement involves not completely finishing products until an order is received. An example of this would be the food processor that adds labels to the "brights," or unlabeled canned goods, after the orders are received, enabling it to reduce inventory levels significantly. Even the auto industry is using a form of postponement by assembling basic component packages—for example, the wiring harnesses—in advance of orders and then assembling the auto to final specification. Considering the fast pace of technological change, the practice of postponement is essential to the success of the many businesses in the compute and high-tech businesses.

postponement

Overall, leading-edge companies have used a number of initiatives to improve their competitive position by reducing cycle time, producing significant benefits in terms of efficiency and effectiveness. Time-reduction strategies, because of the potential to reduce costs, improve cash flow, and enhance customer service, have been the focus of much attention and have enabled companies to gain a competitive advantage.

Asset Productivity Strategies

As indicated, companies are deeply concerned about making optimum use of logistics and supply chain resources. Thus, there has been a focusing of attention on return on assets (ROA) as one of the primary metrics that help to evaluate the success of logistics and supply chain capabilities. Companies can improve return on assets by increasing revenue earned or by earning the same level of revenue with a reduced investment in assets. Consequently, companies have been investigating approaches to improving asset productivity, or "doing more with less." Logistics is one of the important areas for improving asset productivity, and during the last ten to fifteen years many companies have been able to reduce logistics-related assets.

asset investment

Inventory Reduction

One of the first assets to receive attention has been inventory, and there is much evidence to indicate that companies have been successful in reducing inventory levels or investment. Some of the proven initiatives that focus on time reduction have the synergistic benefit of reducing investment in inventory. While JIT, QR, and ECR certainly would be among these, there are others that are also very valuable. One strategy that has been utilized in tandem with ECR is vendor-managed inventory (VMI); and the Procter & Gamble and Wal-Mart relationships provides a useful look at how this works. Essentially, P&G manages the level of inventory of its products in Wal-Mart's stores and monitors their movement through Wal-Mart's distribution cross-docking facilities. For each product stock-keeping unit (SKU), P&G decides when to ship and how much to ship to Wal-Mart. Other companies, such as Nabisco, have developed similar relations with some of their best customers. One of the major reasons for VMI is the reduction in inventory that both parties have been able to achieve.

inventory investment

Supply Chain Technology

The Need for Real-Time, Supply Chain Visibility

According to the U.S. Department of Commerce, the value of all business inventories in the U.S. totaled nearly 1.5 trillion dollars in 2000.* One primary driver for this obviously significant number is the fact that inventories are managed independently by individual managers in different enterprises across the continuum of any given supply chain. Inventory managers in each enterprise are focused on minimizing risk with a careful eye on costs. However, many times, the actual costs of the practices being used across the entire supply chain are not known. In addition, inventory quantities may be maintained at higher levels expressly to avoid any chance of a supply chain disruption— risk that could be managed with better inventory visibility. Manufacturers agree that huge gains to solving this problem will be realized with better visibility to all inventories in the supply chain, including access to an integrated view of product in facilities and in transit.† Although visibility software tools have made this type of information more accessible, technology alone will not solve the inventory management issues. Solutions that create the highest value also address the issues related to process and people.

An example of a visibility tool is BulkVision™ by Transentric. With this tool, manufacturers are able to obtain real-time visibility of both en-route and on-site inventory. With this level of visibility, the software is able to project when inventory levels will run out, thus allowing manufacturers to keep safety stocks to a minimum. A mineral company selected this tool in order to manage their customers' inventory. By using BulkVision, their customer service managers are able to continuously monitor the current and planned inventory consumption of each of their customers. Processes were set up so that, when BulkVision predicts that rail (their normal mode of transport) will not get required inventory to the customer in time, the mineral company can use other modes to meet the demand. With trained personnel and the appropriate processes in place, BulkVision allows this company to successfully manage its customer's inventory while increasing customer service levels and decreasing costs. This type of success has positioned Transentric to create additional technology tools (e.g., ItemVision™) that will provide companies with inventory visibility at the SKU level.

The preceding example provided a measurable benefit because the solution addressed the practical issues beyond the application of technology. To help companies accelerate value realization by taking a "whole solution" approach, Transentric has formed a unique alliance with Competitive Logistics (CL). CL is a full service supply chain solutions company that helps companies decrease logistics costs while delivering quality customer service and raising shareholder value. This partnership brings together two market leaders who are creating effective solutions for inventory management issues.

Companies are aggressively looking for solutions that offer both inventory visibility and the ability to take effective inventory management action. Enhanced by the possibility of collaboration, inventory visibility across the supply chain is becoming a reality. Once achieved, the benefits of improved supply chain performance will create sustained competitive advantage.

Source: Competitive Logistics, Inc., and Transentric, Inc.

*Robert V. Delaney and Rosalyn Wilson, *12th Annual State of Logistics Report©* (Washington, D.C.: Cass Information Systems, Inc. and ProLogis Trust, June 4, 2001).

†Research done by Urban Wallace & Associates, Inc. for Transentric indicate that of 100 manufacturing companies with sales between $100 million and $1 billion, greater than 80% cite that it is a priority of their company to improve the visibility of their inbound and outbound supply chain.

Facility Utilization

logistics facilities

There are a number of ways to describe logistics systems. For example, the logistics network can be viewed as being composed of a set of fixed facilities connected by links represented by transportation. The fixed facilities are supplier locations, plants, warehouses, distribution centers, and customer locations. Looking throughout the logistics network, it has become apparent that a high priority has been attached to the effective utilization of all of these types of facilities. Regardless of where a product may be in the logistics network, the objective is the same: "keep it moving." Only when product is at rest do the major kinds of waste and inefficiency begin to accrue. Along with this priority, all types of firms have subscribed to one way of characterizing the move to lean enterprises: "doing more with less." Many of the techniques and approaches we have been discussing do exactly that.

direct shipments

In addition, there have been other initiatives that have improved facility utilization or, more importantly, eliminated storage facilities altogether. One such initiative is the movement of shipments direct from manufacturers to retail stores, thus bypassing the traditional stop at or move through the distribution center. This strategy not only contributes to improved facility utilization but does so by reducing or eliminating the need for certain types of facilities. Many distribution centers, ones that previously were an important link between the manufacturers and retailers, are being bypassed in the interest of improving logistics and supply chain efficiency. When there no longer is a need for such facilities, it is said that "disintermediation" has occurred. While this is usually not good news for those involved in operating the distribution center, it does help to reduce cost and improve service to the customers, the combined effect being improved positioning in the marketplace for the manufacturer. The Amdahl Corporation is a good example of a company that has reduced the need for warehousing by direct plant shipments. Procter & Gamble is a good example of a large, Fortune 100 company that has achieved significant savings and asset productivity through direct shipments to retailers from manufacturer.

Equipment Utilization Strategies

improving utilization

Another area of asset investment for companies is logistics-related equipment such as materials-handling equipment used in warehouses and transportation equipment that is leased or owned by a company. Some reduction in the amount of this equipment has occurred because of the reduction in the number of distribution centers, discussed in the previous section. Companies have rationalized their facilities and improved their throughput, utilizing the initiatives discussed previously. In other words, as companies have reduced the number of warehouse facilities that they operate, there has been a natural reduction in the materials-handling equipment that is necessary. Also, the use of technology-based devices such as handheld computers, bar code scanning devices, and radio-frequency communications in logistics facilities has caused a general reduction in the need for additional assets to move and store product.

transportation improvements

In addition, transportation equipment is an important area in terms of asset investment. This has been another area of improvement for many companies. Since deregulation, many companies have reevaluated their position with respect to equipment ownership. Contract rates with railroads and motor carriers, more specialized service and equipment, lower rates, and so on have led companies to turn increasingly to the commercial sector for needed transportation services. As was explained earlier, transportation companies, particularly motor carriers, have become much more service oriented. Motor carriers frequently provide tailored service to large shippers in the current, highly competitive environment. With lower rates and better service, for-hire transportation service has become a much more attractive alternative for many shippers. These cost and/or service benefits, combined with a strategy to lower asset investment for increased productivity, can have a synergistic impact that can result in an increased reliance upon the for-hire carrier system to provide high-quality transportation service.

private fleet software

In addition to the improvements in productivity and efficiency made possible by the increased use of for-hire carriers, the companies that have continued to use private carriage in whole or in part to connect their nodes or fixed points have become more efficient in the utilization of their equipment. Many of them have duplicated the capabilities of commercial carriers, using software packages to schedule and dispatch their equipment more efficiently, installing direct communication links to drivers, consolidating shipments more effectively through load-planning software, and taking advantage of intermodal rail service for the line haul parts of their service needs. The net effect is similar to the observation that was made regarding warehouse facilities—companies have been able to do more with less. In summary, there has been significant improvement in asset productivity with respect to transportation equipment. The improvement has been made possible by increased reliance upon for-hire carriers and better utilization of companies' own equipment through the use of technology, computer software, and better management planning.

Third-Party/Contract Logistics Services

3PL services

Another key area of decision making that has had a dramatic impact on asset productivity is the use of third-party-logistics (3PL) services. This increasingly popular alternative has led many firms such as DuPont, Nabisco, Procter & Gamble, General Electric, General Motors, and others to use the services of capable 3PLs. The decision to utilize third-party or contract logistics companies has been fostered in part by the interest in reducing asset investment to improve asset productivity. An interesting aspect of 3PL use is that, while a customer may use a 3PL to help reduce commitment to its assets, the 3PL may focus its activity on "managing" the provision of logistics services and actually procure the "asset-based" services from selected contractors. While it is true that there must be some firms that actually provide the asset-based services, the response to this matter is more of a strategic and financial matter than one related to logistics operations.

The move to utilize a 3PL may be even broader than the reasoning discussed heretofore. Another rationale is the trend mentioned earlier of focusing upon core competencies as a strategy to operate more effectively and efficiently. Essentially, a company may feel that its expertise or core competency may, for example, be producing and marketing cookies and crackers. While it may be very capable of providing necessary inbound and outbound logistics services to support its products, the company may be even more effective if it focuses upon its two core competencies. While this rationale is commonly used to support the decision to use a 3PL, the move can be even more attractive if it can be demonstrated that, additionally, there will be cost savings and or improved asset productivity.

Frito-Lay

A good example of a large company that has used third-party logistics to its advantage is Frito-Lay, a subsidiary of Pepsico. Frito-Lay is a producer of snack foods, and it had traditionally relied upon its own fleet of trucks to ship products from its thirty-eight plants to its twenty-seven distribution centers. As the company expanded, the management decided that it was not economical to produce every product at every plant, and so the company started to specialize production at plants. However, it did not fully understand the impact of this new strategy upon the logistics system. Shipping distances grew increasingly longer from the specialized production facilities to the warehouses, and the company's private trucks usually had to return to their origin empty. Subsequently, Frito-Lay began to utilize an increasing number of common carriers to distribute its products to the distribution centers, but this did no go smoothly. Therefore, Frito-Lay decided to outsource the responsibility for managing its transportation operations to Menlo Logistics. Menlo has been able to reduce the carrier base by 50 percent and to negotiate discount rates with the remainder of the carriers on a national basis. The routing of trucks is handled by Menlo Logistics, which has a staff member on site at Frito-Lay's headquarters in Plano, Texas. Frito-Lay's transportation savings exceeded 10 percent the first year, which was significant in this highly competitive market arena.

4PL services

As a concluding comment regarding the use of 3PL providers, there is a current trend toward the involvement of 4PL providers, to help manage a number of 3PLs that may be involved with a company's operations. Aside from managing a number of 3PL operations, a 4PL is looked to for the provision of competencies relating to knowledge availability, information technology, and skills in forming and sustaining successful supply chain relationships. Figure 16–4 illustrates the approach that Accenture has taken with respect to the provision of 4PL services to its clients.

FIGURE 16–4 Fourth-Party™ Logistics

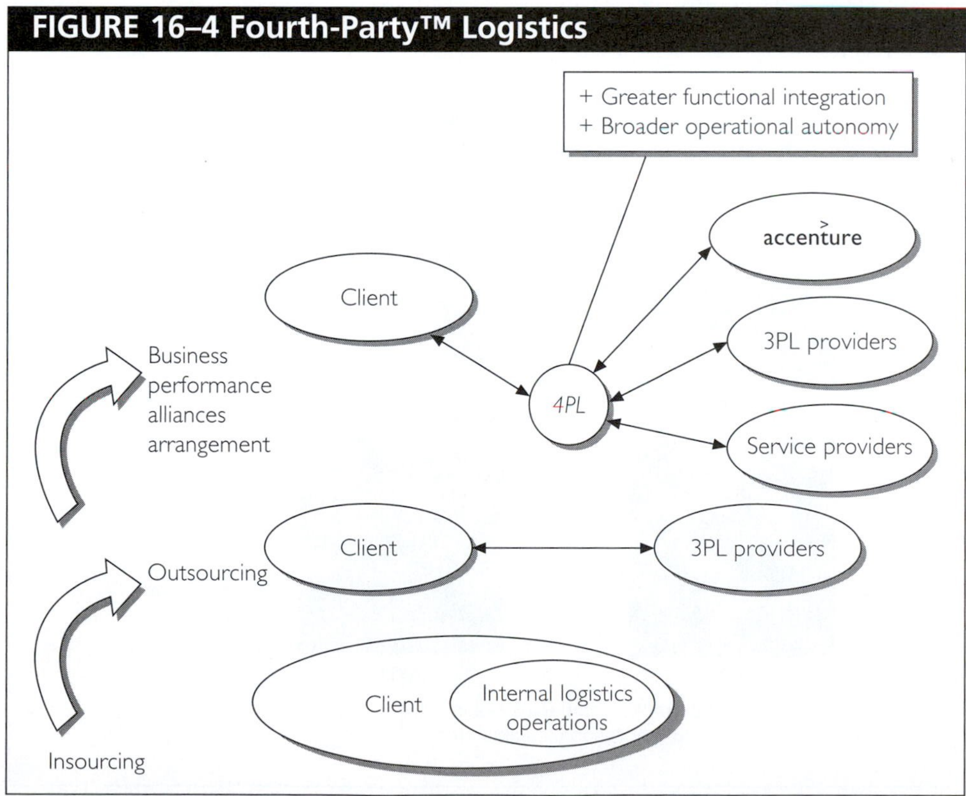

™ Registered trademark of Accenture.
Source: Accenture (used with permission).

Technology-Based Strategies

It has been evident for some time that the realization of future logistics and supply chain goals will depend significantly on the further development and utilization of information technologies. Whether it be in the form of hardware, software, or connectivity, these technologies will be the springboard for progress and innovation. Looking back at the content of this text, there are numerous areas in which evolving information technologies have been highlighted and discussed. Also, Chapter 12 was devoted fully to a treatment of contemporary information technologies that impact logistics and supply chain management.

"disruptive technologies"

Rather than try to repeat or summarize those key points, this section is directed toward some of the more significant future trends in technology and their likely impacts. As part of its annual survey of executives in the information technology area of a wide range of business firms, CSC Consulting tracks what it terms to be "disruptive technologies" in the IT area—those technologies that the respondents feel will not only help to make firms more competitive but that will change the very basis of competition. Table 16–1 identifies the trends as suggested in the year 2000 survey results, along with the types of implications for logistics and supply chain management. A look at these trends suggests that the logistics and supply chain areas of tomorrow will differ significantly from those in existence today.

e-commerce

Another notable trend in the technology area is the increased utilization of e-commerce and the further development and refinement of synergies between e-procurement and strategic sourcing. According to the information in Figure 16–5,

FIGURE 16–5 Shifts in Technology

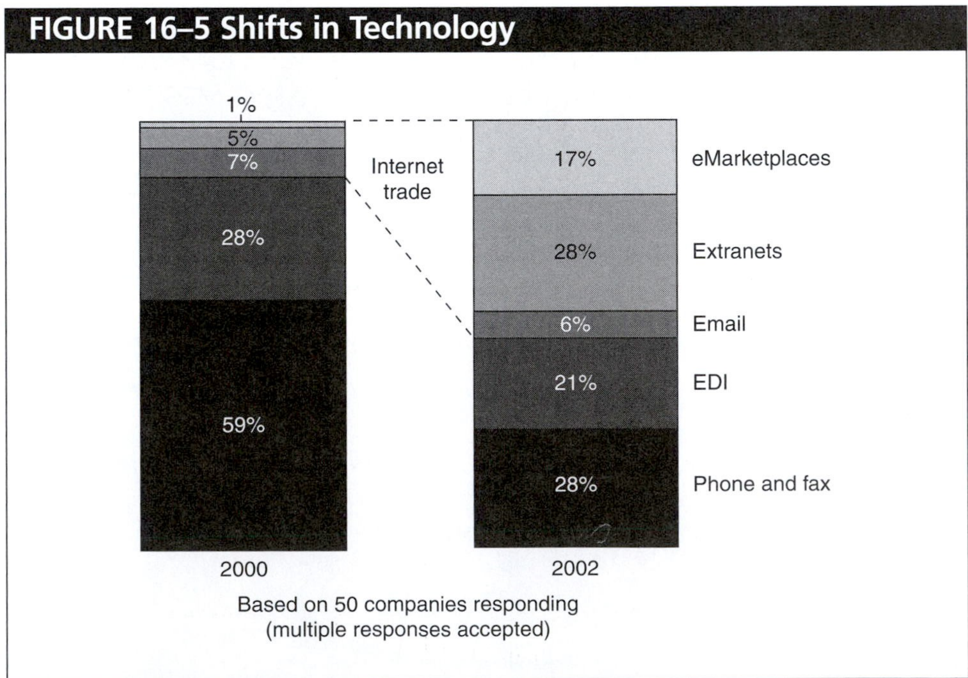

Note: Figure shows expected trends in direct materials purchasing from 2000 to 2002.
Source: On-Line Supply Chain Realities (Cambridge, Mass.: Forrester Research, Inc., 2000), 3.

TABLE 16–1 Disruptive Information Technologies

Disruptive Technologies	Description	Impacts on Logistics and Supply Chain
1. Ubiquitous bandwidth	Virtually unlimited network capacity	Facilitates "seamless" connectivity of people and processes throughout logistics and supply chain management
2. Smart environments	Computer technologies available in a wide range of applications	Assets will be "smart" assets (e.g., trucks will know when they need repair; buildings will personalize environments depending on which people are within; etc.)
3. Net-centric computing	Increasing connectivity as the Internet permeates systems and spawns new products, applications, and services	Availability of E-commerce–based markets for products and for logistics and supply chain services
4. Knowledge discovery and exploitation	Formalization of knowledge management programs	Enhanced efficiency of access to higher-quality knowledge pertaining to logistics and supply chain initiatives
5. High-performance computing	Significant enhancements to the power of computing to drive sophisticated collaborative environments	Facilitates use of comprehensive network design software and significantly increases the size and scope of problems that can be analyzed
6. Digital money and electronic micropayments	Use of digital capabilities to transfer cash on a wide scale	Significant reductions in length of cash-to-cash cycles
7. Privacy, security, and information survivability	Technological solutions that enhance security of information	Drives more meaningful collaboration and information sharing throughout the supply chain
8. Virtual spaces and simulation	Use of virtual reality to facilitate viewing and experiencing of various capabilities	Facilitates customer views of products to be purchased and visualizes logistics assets and efficiency of loading, usage, and so forth
9. Human-computer connection	Facilitating connectivity between people and technology	Interaction with computers by voice, rather than digitally or electronically
10. Miniaturization	Technologies that change the scale of products to very small versions of the original items	Manufacturers will become their own suppliers by replicating the materials they need

Source: "Emerging Trends and Disruptive Information Technologies," Computer Sciences Corporation, *The Era of Digital Disruptions: Exploring the Next Technology Wave* (Cambridge, Mass.: Computer Sciences Corporation, 2001). Available at http://www.csc.com

FIGURE 16–6 Strategic Sourcing and E-Procurement

• How Strategic Sourcing Aids E-Procurement	• How E-Procurement Aids Strategic Sourcing
– Reduces number and complexity of catalogs and maintenance cost – Focuses development work with preferred suppliers – Focuses catalog content and features on priorities – Prioritizes roll-out based on benefits – Develops "strategic" capabilities in personnel freed up by E-procurement – Addresses the necessary business process issues that can make E-procurement difficult to accomplish	– Encourages use of supplier agreements by eliminating "maverick" buying – Allows for increased volume estimates in negotiations by capturing more data on purchases – Frees up procurement resources to focus on strategic efforts – Takes advantage of potential cost incentives available from supplier for use of E-business – Aids in measuring performance

Source: "Integrating E-Procurement and Strategic Sourcing," *Supply Chain Management Review* (March/April 2000). Reprinted with permission of *Supply Chain Management Review,* a Cahners publication.

there are already significant shifts underway in terms of on-line capabilities to facilitate direct materials purchasing. For example, this diagram captures and quantifies the significant shifts from capabilities such as phone/fax and EDI to more contemporary technologies such as E-mail, Extranets, and E-marketplaces.

strategic sourcing

The ways in which strategic sourcing aids E-procurement, and vice versa, are indicated in Figure 16–6. Evident from this information is that strategic sourcing helps to simplify and streamline E-procurement activities. Alternatively, E-procurement assists strategic sourcing by fostering a more rational buying environment and by making more efficient and effective use of procurement-related resources.

electronic markets

Last, the movement toward electronic marketplaces will help to better distinguish between and enhance the capabilities of transactional versus collaborative capabilities. Among the activities included in the transactional category are: identifying new materials suppliers, finding and establishing prices for products and materials, and purchasing materials from suppliers. Examples of collaborative capabilities include: communicating delivery requests to suppliers, communicating production requirements to suppliers and optimizing production schedules, and managing and communicating engineering changes.

Relationship-Based Strategies

An area of significant strategic interest is that of relationships and relationship formation in the logistics and supply chain processes. Although the preceding chapters have provided a number of perspectives on this topic, experience to date suggests that major challenges lie ahead with respect to our ability to develop and sustain effective relationships. As indicated earlier, one of the major attributes of using the services of a 4PL is that this type of firm specializes in a number of areas,

FIGURE 16–7 Types of Collaboration

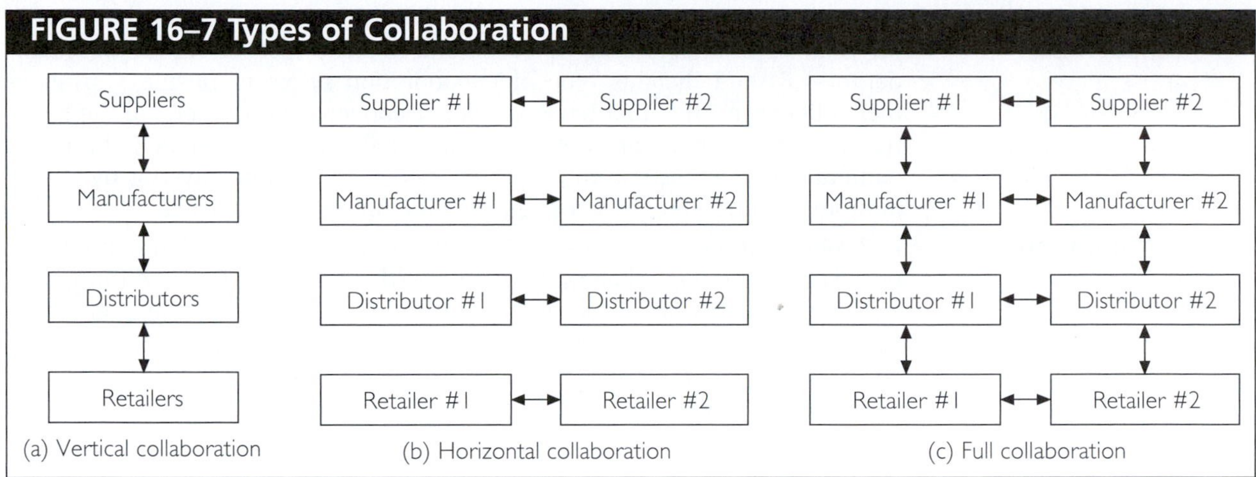

Source: C. John Langley Jr., Ph.D.

including relationship management. Thus, this area represents a critical challenge for future logistics and supply chain managers.

Collaboration

collaborative relationships

The contemporary topic of importance is "collaboration." Most simply, collaboration occurs when companies work together for mutual benefit. Since it is difficult to imagine very many logistics or supply chain improvements that involve only one firm, the need for effective relationships is obvious. Collaboration goes well beyond vague expressions of partnership and aligned interests. It means that companies leverage each other on an operational basis so that together they perform better than they did separately. It creates a synergistic business environment in which the sum of the parts is greater than the whole. It is a business practice that requires

- Parties involved to dynamically share and interchange information
- Benefits experience by parties to exceed individual benefits
- All parties to modify their business practices
- All parties to conduct business in a new and visibly different way
- All parties to provide a mechanism and process for collaboration to occur

Figure 16–7 provides illustrations of three important types of collaboration: vertical, horizontal, and full. Descriptions of these are included here:

vertical collaboration

- *Vertical collaboration* (see Figure 16–7a) refers to collaboration typically among buyers and sellers in the supply chain. This refers to the traditional linkages between firms in the supply chain such as retailers, distributors, manufacturers, and parts and materials suppliers. Transactions between buyers and sellers can be automated, and efficiencies can be significantly improved. Companies can share plans and provide mutual visibility that causes them to change behavior. A contemporary example of vertical collaboration is collaborative planning, forecasting, and replenishment (CPFR®), an approach that helps buyers and sellers to better align supply and demand by directly sharing critical information such as sales forecasts.

horizontal collaboration

- *Horizontal collaboration* (see Figure 16–7b) refers to a relationship that is buyer to buyer and/or seller to seller, and in some cases even between competitors. Essentially, this type of collaboration refers to business arrangements between firms that have *parallel* or cooperating positions in the logistics or supply chain process. Horizontal collaboration can help find and eliminate *hidden* costs in the supply chain that everyone pays for by allowing joint product design, sourcing, manufacturing, and logistics.

full collaboration

- *Full collaboration* (see Figure 16–7c) is the dynamic combination of both vertical and horizontal collaboration. Only with full collaboration do dramatic efficiency gains begin to occur. With full collaboration, it is intended that benefits accrue to all members of the collaboration. The development of agreed-upon methods for sharing gains and losses is essential to the success of the collaboration.

Value Nets[1]

Up until now, supply chains generally have been rigid and linear, manufacturing fixed product lines and pushing them slowly and sequentially through distribution channels in the hope that someone will buy them. Information, meanwhile, often moves erratically back up the chain. Time delays and multiple handoffs are common. As a result, supply and demand rarely match, resulting in lost sales and inventory buildups.

value net

Digital age supply chains, however, are leading to widespread changes in supply chains. In particular, the old supply chain is giving way to a new design that starts with the customer and is built around three powerful value propositions: high levels of customization, super service, and convenient solutions. This model is called a *value net* (Figure 16–8). The value net represents a way to move from a process step on the supply chain to a high-value relationship in a dynamic, interactive network focused on meeting end customers' needs.

FIGURE 16–8 Gateway's Value Net

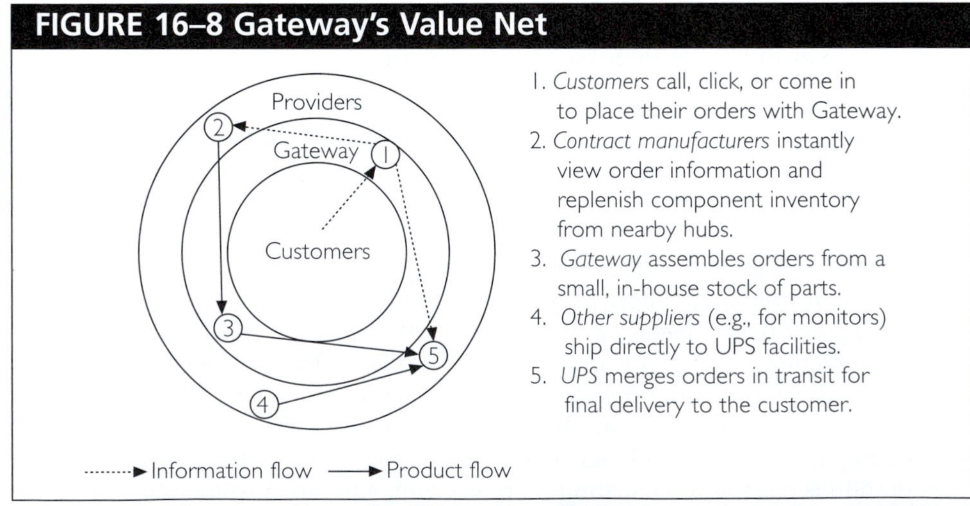

Source: David M. Bovet and Sridhar Thiagarajan, "Value Nets—The Potential for Transport Companies" (Lexington, Mass.: Mercer Management Consulting, 2000).

Value net design combines strategic thinking with the latest advances in digital supply chain management, forming itself first and foremost around the customer. Value nets view every customer as unique; rather than offering static products and average service, they allow customers themselves to choose the product/service attributes they value most, capturing real choices in real time and transmitting them digitally to other net participants. Pathways for information and materials flows are aligned with the service needs and priorities of distinct customer segments.

The company or business unit creating the value net is represented in Figure 16–8 by the inner ring around the customer: this unit controls customer touch points and manages the customer relationship. The outer ring represents a dynamic network of partner-providers that perform some or all of the activities required by the value net, such as sourcing, assembly, distribution, or delivery. For most traditional companies, developing a value net requires significant transformation. Besides information and organizational agility, a value net requires a high level of physical flexibility in order to deliver on the promise of greater customer choice, convenience/reliability, and speed. Such flexibility can be hard to achieve, and thus far only limited examples exist of completely integrated and successful value nets.

SYNTHESIS AND FUTURE DIRECTIONS

barriers to entry

As businesses move solidly into the 2000s, the areas of logistics and supply chain management clearly are receiving greater attention from senior corporate management. Also, while the evolution is far from complete, competency in these areas is viewed not only as a requirement of business but as a key to enhanced competitiveness and improved market positioning. Considering the improvements being made at selected companies today, there will be an increasing number of industries in which not having these competencies will become a barrier to entry.

In the interest of providing a concluding, high-level overview, this section considers several of the over-arching, macro trends that will continue to have significant impacts on logistics and supply chain management. Effective planning, operations, and control in the logistics and supply chain areas will be dependent on the extent to which individual companies have involvement with each of these.

Shift from Vertical to Virtual Integration

vertical versus virtual

One common thought is that the preferred business model for the years ahead will be that of virtual integration, in contrast to the more traditional vertical integration. The *virtual enterprise* can be thought of as "the selection, partnering, and integration of key intellectual capital across the enterprise or supply chain."[2] This model involves not necessarily outsourcing of logistics and supply chain capabilities, but simply making the right choices about which processes to retain in-house and which to outsource. It is also about partnering and aligning one's business with others that differentiate themselves by performance and continue to make capital asset investments in processes, technology, and intellectual capital.

ON THE LINE

MODUS MEDIA INTERNATIONAL

The experience of Modus Media International (MMI) highlights the benefits companies can realize by incorporating supply chain information systems that effectively address the knowledge gap. In 1997, MMI began transforming itself from a contract manufacturer to a supply chain management services company. When the transformation began, MMI was running its twenty-three operational "solution centers" on a collection of legacy and homegrown operating systems for finance, manufacturing, and distribution activities. The company wanted to create a world-class process and technology infrastructure to ensure that all of its operations ran on the same platform using the same global processes. In addition to allocating nearly 50 percent of its capital expenditures to build this globally consistent infrastructure, MMI established a worldwide process improvement team reporting directly to the newly created executive position of chief process and technology officer.

Key criteria set by MMI for the technology selection process included: only best-of-breed technology; off-the-shelf software; industry or de facto standard; externally supported, E-business enabled, and supportive of business modeling and scripting. Implementation priorities set by MMI began with first consolidating its existing logistics and finance systems to one globally consistent enterprise resource planning system, and second, adding new capabilities that would address the critical information gaps in sales, marketing, and content management. Other areas of emphasis included (1) development of a front-end call center and E-commerce services, (2) conversion of its legacy order-entry system to a true CRM (customer relationship management) system that is integrated with traditional back-end procurement, manufacturing, and distribution services, and (3) implementation of a supply chain information system that integrates the Internet into its information processes.

MMI has a prioritized, phased approach to transitioning its legacy-based systems to the single supply chain information system. The effort that began in 1997 was expected to end sometime in 2002. The results certainly will help to close the knowledge gap in its supply chain information systems.

Source: Adapted from Stephen M. Rutner, Brian J. Gibson, Kate L. Vitasek, and Craig M. Gustin, "Is Technology Filling the Information Gap?" *Supply Chain Management Review* (March/April 2001): 62. Reprinted with permission of *Supply Chain Management Review*, a Cahners publication.

According to Joan Magretta, reporting the content of an interview with Michael Dell of Dell Computers:

> Virtual integration harnesses the economic benefits of very different models. It offers the advantages of a tightly coordinated supply chain that has traditionally come through vertical coordination. At the same time, it benefits from the focus and specialization that drives virtual corporations. Virtual integration has the potential to achieve both coordination and focus. If it delivers on that promise, it may well become a new organizational model for the information age.[3]

Collaboration

Closely related to the topic of virtualization is that of collaboration. In the logistics and supply chain arenas of the future, the ability to develop effective collaborations will become a key to success. Particularly since many logistics and supply chain innovations are multiorganizational by definition, the knowledge and skill sets relating to the formation, sustainability, and evolution of collaborative relationships will be essential capabilities. The desired end result is a business environment in which overall results surpass what individual organizations could achieve by themselves.

collaborative logistics

Collaborative logistics provides complete visibility to the entire process flow, from beginning to end, to all participants. Members gain forward visibility throughout the supply chain, as well as the ability to create efficiencies as they establish and modify their relationships with their business partners. Although some organizations may find it challenging to meaningfully buy into the idea of collaborating with customers, suppliers, and even competitors, many are quickly adopting changes to accomplish this objective. Considering the imperative on creating value for the end-use customer or consumer, the need for collaborative relationships cannot be overstated.

Knowledge of Core Competencies

core competencies

Perhaps more than ever before, the ability of organizations and their people to have knowledge of "core competencies" and act accordingly is of utmost importance. In this context, we would say that an organization is core competent in a given area or process if each of the following three conditions are satisfied:

- *Expertise.* It just does not make any sense for an organization to claim core competency without the requisite knowledge and skill sets.
- *Strategic fit.* This assumes that the area of competency is one that is aligned appropriately with overall corporate strategy and unique areas of competitive advantage.
- *Ability to invest.* The firm must have the financial resources to invest in the area, and the financial results must be commensurate to what would be expected from any desirable investment of the firm's resources.

As organizations further develop the ability to diagnose and evaluate their own areas of core competency, they will be better equipped to determine opportunities in which outsourcing of logistics and supply chain resources may be a preferable strategy. All too often, firms have a narrow understanding of core competency, one that focuses only on the need for expertise rather than on the more complete picture. As a result, they tend to internalize activities and processes for which they should look for capable external providers and partners in the supply chain.

Technology and Connectivity

technology

The future of technology is yet to come. While this statement may sound a little strange, the important point is that we have just begun to conceptualize and experience the ultimate types of supply chain benefits and improvements that will result from our ability to leverage information technology. In a connected economy, where connectivity is a highly desired objective, technology becomes a strategic enabler. The ability of a company to select, implement, and utilize technology will be a key determinant of success or failure. The appropriate combination of information technologies, processes, and people is critical to generating a speed and continuity of innovation that is expected by the marketplace, as well as the growth, revenues, and profits that are demanded by the shareholders. Thus, technology must be viewed as an investment that is needed to satisfy the *information imperative* of the connected economy for velocity, visibility, rapid decisions, and operational flexibility.[4]

Managing-the-People Skills

managing people

Many successful companies have identified the effective management of their people as a key area of competency. Although the need for technology and interfirm relationships is obvious, none of the benefits will be experienced if the people and organizational issues are not properly addressed from the start. Good, multifunctional people, who understand the progressive environment of supply chain management, are at a premium.

The rise of the connected economy and the synchronization, collaboration, and integration that are becoming evident in supply chains are "blurring" traditional interfaces between organizations and people throughout the supply chain. In this type of business environment, people can become "free agents" whose knowledge is their most valuable asset. Just as it is important for organizations to know their core competencies, the same advice holds true for individual people. Thus, it will become increasingly important for people to manage their knowledge and skill sets and for organizations to recognize and strengthen relationships with their people.

Comprehensive Supply Chain Perspective

supply chain perspective

The overriding imperative is for firms to adopt a comprehensive supply chain perspective. Considering that most supply chains encompass multiple types of organizations and resources that must work together to create value for the end user or customer, the importance of a smoothly functioning supply chain is obvious. Also, and even though certain supply chain resources are significantly "upstream" from the end user or consumer, a far-reaching, comprehensive perspective on the overall supply chain will be essential. As organizations establish strategic priorities in the years ahead, the concern for supply chain imperatives will accelerate. Until we reach the point where all of the involved organizations and needed resources are working together as effectively as possible, the markets for the resulting products and services will remain unfulfilled.

SUMMARY

- Today's competitive global environment, with the rapid changes that it engenders, has necessitated that companies utilize strategic planning to survive.
- Strategic planning has gone through several stages of development. Today, the planning process taken by many companies focuses on a team-oriented approach to gain competitive advantage in the marketplace.
- Strategic planning also involves understanding the difference between strategy and tactics. Strategy focuses on how a given goal is going to be achieved

over the longer run, whereas tactics emphasize the short-run, operational aspects necessary to drive the strategy.

- There are three basic, generic strategies: cost, differentiation, and focus. Competency in logistics and supply chain management can help to achieve these objectives.
- One of the major strategies being implemented in today's environment is to reduce or compress order cycle time, which has the advantage of reducing inventory cost and improving customer service.
- There are numerous logistics-related initiatives that can help to improve cycle time, including cross-docking, just in time, vendor-managed inventory, continuous replenishment, efficient consumer response, and other technology-related time improvements.
- Another major focus of logistics-related strategies is the improvement of asset productivity. For logistics, the major focus has been on improving the utilization of inventory, facilities, and equipment. Third-party or contract logistics service companies have also become a factor in logistics strategy because of the opportunities to reduce cost, improve asset productivity, and improve customer service if used appropriately.
- The emergence of new and innovative technology-based strategies will result in dramatic changes to the ways we manage logistics and supply chain activities. Also, the move to strategic sourcing and the availability of E-procurement and electronic marketplace capabilities will have significant impacts.
- A final area of great strategic interest will be that of relationship-based strategies. Overall, the business environment will be characterized by a move to collaboration among business partners and more of a "network"-based approach to management of logistics and supply chain activities.
- Key characteristics of future change will include: a move from vertical to virtual integration, further development of collaborative capabilities, knowledge of core competencies, technology and connectivity, and a move to a comprehensive supply chain perspective.

STUDY QUESTIONS

1. What is meant by *strategy,* and how have business strategies evolved over the past fifty years?
2. How would you distinguish between *strategy* and *tactics?* Provide an example of each.
3. What are the three types of strategies? What would you think of a firm that did not evidence a commitment to any of these three types of strategies?
4. Explain the benefits of *time-based* logistics and supply chain strategies. What are some of the types of strategies that are included in this category?
5. What is the overall goal of *asset-based* strategies? In what ways does a move to third-party logistics facilitate or hinder accomplishment of this goal?
6. What are some of the more popular *technology-based* strategies?

7. Define *strategic sourcing* and *e-procurement*. In what ways do strategic sourcing and e-procurement reinforce the objectives of each other?
8. What is *collaboration*, and what are the differences between vertical, horizontal, and full collaboration?
9. Do you think that the concept of *value nets* refutes or reinforces the objectives of strategic sourcing? How?
10. What do you feel will be the strategic areas of greatest future interest to logistics and supply chain management?
11. How would you define *core competency*, and what do you feel are among the core competencies that firms should evidence in logistics and supply chain management?

NOTES

1. Much of the content of this section is taken from David M. Bovet and Sridhar Thiagarajan, "Value Nets—The Potential for Transport Companies," *Mercer on Transport & Travel* (Lexington, Mass.: Mercer Management Consulting, 2000); and from David M. Bovet and David G. Frentzel, "The Value Net: Connecting for Profitable Growth," *Supply Chain Management Review* (Fall 1999): 96–104.
2. Ernst & Young, *Proceedings of the Advantage '99 Executive Forum: Supply Chain Management in the Connected Economy* (Atlanta, Ga.: Ernst & Young, 1999), 11.
3. Joan Margretta, "The Power of Virtual Integration: An Interview with Dell Computer's Michael Dell," *Harvard Business Review* (March/April 1998).
4. Ernst & Young, op. cit., 53.

CASE 16–1 ■ Vector SCM

Vector SCM (supply chain management) is the lead logistics provider worldwide for vehicle manufacturer General Motors (GM). The company is a joint venture between GM and CNF, Inc., a $6 billion management company of global supply chain services. Founded in December 2000, Vector SCM draws from the supply chain expertise of all of CNF's operating companies: Con-Way Transportation, Emery Worldwide, and Menlo Logistics. Ultimately, the goal is for Vector SCM to provide GM with a seamless, integrated, end-to-end visibility of all material and vehicles moving within its worldwide supply chain through a common information technology system.

According to the group vice president, GM worldwide purchasing and production control and logistics, "Vector SCM will provide to GM solutions to the tremendous logistical challenges facing the automotive industry today. We have over 180 million pounds of material delivered to GM daily from 12,000 origins, and ship over eight million vehicles per year. Vector SCM will build the management tools to fulfill our requirements, accelerating the speed and reliability necessary to satisfy the changing demands of our customers."

GM is undergoing a company-wide effort known as *Order-to-Delivery.* The objective of this OTD objective is to provide accurate and reliable delivery of vehicles to customers and slash GM's order cycle time from its current level of more than sixty days to an average of fifteen to twenty. An intent of Vector SCM was to provide expensive supply chain engineering expertise along with advanced Web-based technologies to product end-to-end visibility of all materials and vehicles moving within GM's supply chain, while improving the overall logistics capability of GM and its affiliates.

As already mentioned, Vector SCM leverages the extensive supply chain engineering expertise of all of CNF's operating companies. The advanced, Web-based software technologies to be used by Vector SCM were developed by CNF. They include a supply chain visibility and compliance system called *Vector Vision* that will facilitate the management of all materials and finished vehicles in the GM pipeline, improving the reliability and flexibility of GM's production and distribution system.

At the time Vector SCM was formed, GM was using multiple third-party logistics providers, each with separate information technology systems that did not interface well. Once electronic data links are established from all of the service providers to the new Vector Vision system, Vector SCM will be able to optimize the materials network, increasing the speed at which materials move, and reducing costs.

The new company began its transition period in North America in early 2001. A goal was for Vector SCM to be expanded in varying degrees to other global regions as plans became more finalized. Ultimately, Vector SCM will function as GM's 4PL (fourth-party logistics) provider, managing all aspects of GM's supply chain including coordination among all 3PLs engaged by GM.

Case Questions

1. What was the underlying rationale for the formation of Vector SCM? What benefits does it create for General Motors Corporation and for CNF, Inc.?
2. According to Dr. Michael Porter, there are three basic types of strategy: low cost, differentiation, and focus. Looking at the Vector SCM from the perspective of GM, in what ways does it help to achieve each of these three types of strategy?
3. Consider the four primary areas in which it is important to develop logistics and supply chain strategies: time-based, asset productivity, information technology, and relationship-based. In what ways does Vector SCM involve aspects of each of these four areas?
4. Overall, what do you think is the most important motivation of General Motors to become involved in a joint venture as is suggested by Vector SCM? Would you expect to see more relationships such as this in the areas of logistics and supply chain management? Less? Why?

Source: Adapted from material in http://www.vectorscm.com and Ken Cottrill, "Sharing the Risks, Riches," *Traffic World* (December 18/25, 2001): 10–11.

Suggested Reading

Chapter 11 Logistics Relationships and Third-Party Logistics

Armstrong & Associates, Inc., *Armstrong's Guide to Third Party Logistics Services Providers*, 8th ed. (2000).

Bauknight, Dow, and Douglas J. Bade, "Fourth Party Logistics: Breakthrough Performance in Supply Chain Outsourcing," *Supply Chain Management Review* (Global Supplement, Winter 1999): 2–5.

Bowersox, Donald J., "The Strategic Benefits of Logistics Alliances," *Harvard Business Review* 90, no. 4 (July–August 1990): 36–45.

Ellram, Lisa M., "Life Cycle Patterns in Industrial Buyer-Seller Relationships," *International Journal of Physical Distribution and Logistics Management* 21, no. 9 (1991): 12–21.

Harps, Leslie Hansen, "Managing 3PL Relationships: Partnering for Performance," *Inbound Logistics* (July 1998): 26–40.

Lambert, Douglas M., Margaret A. Emmelhainz, and John T. Gardner, "Building Successful Logistics Partnerships," *Journal of Business Logistics* 20, no. 1 (1999): 165–182.

Langley, C. John Jr., "The Seven Immutable Laws of Collaborative Logistics," available at Nistevo.com.

Langley, C. John Jr., Brian F. Newton, and Gene R. Tyndall, "Has the Future of Third Party Logistics Already Arrived?" *Supply Chain Management Review* (Fall 1999): 85–95.

Langley, C. John Jr., and Brian J. Gibson, "Buyer Observations of the U.S. Third Party Logistics Market," *International Journal of Physical Distribution and Logistics Management* 26, no. 3 (1996): 38–46.

Lieb, Robert C., and Arnold Maltz, "What's the Future for Third Party Logistics?" *Supply Chain Management Review* (Spring 1998): 71–79.

Lynch, Clifford F., *Logistics Outsourcing: A Management Guide* (Oak Brook, Ill.: Council of Logistics Management, 2000).

Maltz, Arnold B., and Lisa M. Ellram, "Total Cost of Relationship: An Analytical Framework for the Logistics Outsourcing Decision," *Journal of Business Logistics* 18, no. 1 (1997): 45–66.

Rabinovich, Elliot, Robert Windle, Martin Dresner, and Thomas Corsi, "Outsourcing of Integrated Logistics Functions," *International Journal of Physical Distribution and Logistics Management* 29, no. 6 (1999): 353–373.

Sink, Harry L., and C. John Langley Jr., "A Managerial Framework for the Acquisition of Third Party Logistics Services," *Journal of Business Logistics* 18, no. 2 (1997): 163–190.

Skjoett-Larsen, Tage, "Third-Party Logistics—From an Interorganizational Point of View," *International Journal of Physical Distribution and Logistics Management* 30, no. 2 (2000): 112–127.

Stallkamp, Thomas T., "Chrysler's Leap of Faith: Redefining the Supplier Relationship," *Supply Chain Management Review* (Summer 1998): 16–23.

Chapter 12 Logistics and Supply Chain Information Systems

Bauknight, Dow N., "The Supply Chain's Future in the e-Economy . . . And Why Many May Never See It," *Supply Chain Management Review* (March/April 2000): 28–35.

Bundy, William, "Leveraging Technology for Speed and Reliability," *Supply Chain Management Review* (Spring 1999): 62–69.

Closs, David J., "Positioning Information in Logistics," Chapter 31 in *The Logistics Handbook* (New York: The Free Press, 1994): 699–713.

Computer Sciences Corporation, *13th Annual Critical Issues in Information Systems Management Survey* (Cambridge, Mass.: Computer Sciences Corporation, 2001). Available at www.csc.com.

Corini, John, "Integrating e-Procurement and Strategic Sourcing," *Supply Chain Management Review* (March/April 2000): 70–75.

Gustin, Craig M., Stephen M. Rutner, and Brian J. Gibson, "An Overview of Current Supply Chain Information Systems," presentation at *2000 Annual Conference of the Council of Logistics Management.*

Henriott, Lisa L., "Transforming Supply Chains into e-Chains," *Supply Chain Management Review* (Global Supplement, Spring 1999): 15–18.

Hickey, Kathleen, "The Way We Are: Logistics Technology Trends . . . Highlighted by Study," *Traffic World* (October 9, 2000): 39–41.

Kahl, Stephen J., "What's the Value of Supply Chain Software?" *Supply Chain Management Review* (Winter 1999): 59–67.

Krass, Louis John, "Building a Business Case for Supply Chain Technology," *Supply Chain Management Review* (Winter 1999): 18–27.

Langley, C. John Jr., "Information-Based Decision Making in Logistics Management," *International Journal of Physical Distribution and Materials Management* 15, no. 7 (1985): 41–42.

Rutner, Stephen M., Brian J. Gibson, Kate L.; Vitasek, and Craig M. Gustin, "Is Technology Filling the Information Gap?" *Supply Chain Management Review* (March/April 2001).

Stenger, Alan J., "Information Systems in Logistics Management: Past, Present, and Future," *Transportation Journal* 26, no. 1 (Fall 1986): 65–82.
Thompson, Richard H., and Karl B. Manrodt, *Logistics @ Internet Speed: The Impact of e-Commerce on Logistics* (Knoxville, Tenn.: Cap Gemini Ernst & Young and the University of Tennessee Press, 2000).

Chapter 13 Supply Chain Performance Measurement

Bowman, R. J., "From Cash to Cash: The Ultimate Supply Chain Measurement Tool," *Global Logistics and Supply Chain Strategies* (June 2001): 42–49.
Brower, Peter C., and Thomas W. Speh, "Using the Balanced Scorecard to Measure Supply Chain Performance," *Journal of Business Logistics* 21, no. 1 (2000): 75–94.
Digler, K. A., "Say Good-bye to the Weakest Link with Supply Chain Metrics," *Global Logistics and Supply Chain Strategies* (June 2001): 34–40.
Dreyer, D. E., "Performance Measurement: A Practitioners' Perspective," *Supply Chain Management Review* (September/October 2000): 62–69.
Kallio, J., T. Saarinen, M. Tinnila, and A. P. J. Vep-Säläinen, "Measuring Delivery Process Information," *International Journal of Logistics Management* 10, no. 2 (1999): 75–88.
Lapide, L., "What About Measuring Supply Chain Performance?" *Supply Chain Yearbook 2001:* 373–390.
Liberatore, M., and T. Miller, "A Framework for Integrating Activity Based Costing and the Balanced Scorecard," *Journal of Business Logistics* 19, no. 1 (1998): 131–154.
Lobse, M., and J. Ranch, "Linking CPFR to SCOR: Imation's Experience," *Supply Chain Management Review* (July/August 2001): 56–67.
Morell, J. A., "Metrics and Models for the Evaluation of Supply Chain Integration," *Supply Chain Yearbook 2001*: 408–426.

Chapter 14 Network Design and Facility Location

Arntzen, Bruce C., Daniel W. Mulgrew, and Garry L. Sjolander, "Redesigning 3M's Worldwide Product Supply Chains," *Supply Chain Management Review* (Winter 1998): 16–27.
Ballou, Ronald H., "Heuristics: Rules of Thumb for Logistics Decision Making," *Journal of Business Logistics* 10, no. 1 (1989): 122–132.
Ballou, Ronald H., "Logistics Network Design: Modeling and Informational Considerations," *International Journal of Logistics Management* 6, no. 2 (1995): 39–54.
Bender, Paul S., "How to Design an Optimum Worldwide Supply Chain," *Supply Chain Management Review* (Spring 1997): 70–81.
Bowersox, Donald J., and David J. Closs, "Simulation in Logistics: A Review of Present Practice and a Look to the Future," *Journal of Business Logistics* 10, no. 1 (1989): 133–148.
Geoffrion, Arthur M., and Richard F. Powers, "Twenty Years of Strategic Distribution System Design: An Evolutionary Perspective," *Interfaces* 25, no. 5 (September–October 1995): 105–127.
Mentzer, John T., "Approaches to Logistics Modeling," *Journal of Business Logistics* 10, no. 1 (1989): 104–105.
Powers, Richard F., "Optimization Models for Logistics Decisions," *Journal of Business Logistics* 10, no. 1 (1989): 106–121.
Ratliff, Donald H., and William G. Nulty, *Logistics Composite Modeling* (Atlanta, Ga.: Ratliff & Nulty, 1996), 38.
Savageau, David, *Places Rated Almanac,* 6th ed. (Chicago, Ill.: Rand McNally, 1999).
Schlegel, Gregory L., "Supply Chain Optimization: A Practitioner's Perspective," *Supply Chain Management Review* (Winter 1999): 50–57.

Chapter 15 Supply Chain Finance

Bowman, Robert J., "Does Wall Street Care about the Supply Chain?" *Global Logistics and Supply Chain Strategies* (April 2001).
Bowman, Robert J., "Finance and Logistics: Across the Great Divide," *Global Logistics and Supply Chain Strategies* (August 2000).
Buxton, Cindy, "The Financial-Logistics Connection: Supply Chain Financing," *Finlistics* (November 23, 1999).
Christopher, Martin, and Lynette Ryals, "Supply Chain Strategy: Its Impact on Shareholder Value," *International Journal of Logistics Management* 10, no. 1 (1999): 1–10.
Cockins, Gary M. "How Do You Measure Profits and Costs Across the Supply Chain?" *Council of Logistics Management Annual Conference Proceedings* (2000): 367–390.
Heskett, James L., W. Earl Sasser, Jr., and Leonard A. Schlesinger, *The Service Profit Chain* (New York: The Free Press, 1997).
Kaplan, Robert S., and Robin Cooper, *Cost & Effect: Using Integrated Cost Systems to Drive Profitability and Performance* (Cambridge, Mass.: Harvard Business School Press, 1997).
Keebler, James S., David A. Durtsche, Karl B. Manrodt, and D. Michael Ledyard, *Keeping Score: Measuring the Business Value of Logistics in the Supply Chain* (Council of Logistics Management, 1999).
Lambert, Douglas M., and Renan Burduroglu, "Measuring and Selling the Value of Logistics," *International Journal of Logistics Management* 11, no. 1 (2000): 1–17.
Ross, Stephen A., Randolph W. Westerfield, and Bradford D. Jordan, *Fundamentals of Corporate Finance,* 4th ed. (New York: Irwin McGraw-Hill, 1998).

Chapter 16 Logistics and Supply Chain Challenges for the Future

Anderson, David L., Frank F. Britt, and Donavon J. Favre, "The Seven Principles of Supply Chain Management," *Supply Chain Management Review* (Spring 1997): 31–43.

Bovet, David M., and Joseph A. Martha, "Lessons from the Innovators," *Supply Chain Management Review* (May/June 2000): 85–91.

Bowersox, Donald J., "Lessons Learned from the World Class Leaders," *Supply Chain Management Review* (Spring 1997): 61–69.

Cavinato, Joseph L., "A General Methodology for Determining a Fit Between Supply Chain Logistics and Five Stages of Strategic Management," *International Journal of Physical Distribution and Logistics Management* 29, no. 3 (1999): 162–180.

Delaney, Robert V., *12th Annual "State of Logistics Report"* (St. Louis, Mo.: Cass Information Systems, June 2001).

Fisher, Marshall L., "What Is the Right Supply Chain for Your Product?" *Harvard Business Review* (March–April 1997): 105–116.

Fuller, Joseph B., James O'Conor, and Richard Rawlinson, "Tailored Logistics: The Next Advantage," *Harvard Business Review* (May–June 1993): 87–98.

Langley, C. John Jr., "The Evolution of the Logistics Concept," *Journal of Business Logistics* 7, no. 2 (1986): 1–13.

Mentzer, John T., ed., *Supply Chain Management*, Chapter 1: "What Is Supply Chain Management (Thousand Oaks, Calif.: Sage Publications, 2001), 1–25.

Metz, Peter J., "Demystifying Supply Chain Management, *Supply Chain Management Review* (Winter 1998): 46–55.

Poirier, Charles C., "The Path to Supply Chain Leadership," *Supply Chain Management Review* 2, no. 3 (Fall 1998): 16–26.

Timme, Stephen G., and Christine Williams-Timme, "The Financial-SCM Connection," *Supply Chain Management Review* (May/June 2000): 32–43.

Selected Supply Chain Publications

Air Cargo World
(800) 717-0063
Web: http://www.aircargoworld.com

Air Force Journal of Logistics
(334) 416-4087

American Shipper
(800) 874-6422
Web: http://www.americanshipper.com

APICS—The Performance Advantage
(800) 392-7294
(770) 431-0867, ext. 212

Army Logistician
(804) 765-4761

Astralog
(404) 524-3555
Web: http://www.astl.org

Business Horizons
(203) 323-9606
Web: http://www.jaipress.com

Business Marketing
(312) 649-5417

Business Trucking
(888) 665-9887
Web: http://www.nptc.org

Business Week
(800) 635-1200
Web: http://www.businessweek.com

California Management Review
(510) 642-7159

Canadian Transportation/Logistics Magazine
(416) 442-2102

CFO
(617) 345-9700

Chain Store Age
(212) 756-5252

Chief Executive
(212) 687-8288

CIO
Web: http://www.cio.com

Council of Logistics Management Annual Conference Proceedings
(630) 574-0985
Web: http://www.clm1.org

Customer Service Newsletter
(212) 228-0246

Cycle Time Research
(901) 678-4973

Defense Transportation Journal
(703) 751-5011

Distribution
Merged with *Logistics Management and Distribution Report*
(800) 662-7776
Web: http://www.logisticsmgmt.com

Distribution Center Management
(212) 228-0246

The Economist
(202) 783-5753
Web: http://www.economist.com

EDI News
(301) 340-7788

EDI World
(954) 925-5900
Web: http://www.ecomworld.com

Export Today
(800) 824-9785

Exporter Magazine
(212) 587-1340
Web: http://www.exporter.com

Food Logistics Magazine
(212) 979-4825
Web: http://www.foodlogistics.com

Forbes
(800) 888-9896

Fortune
(800) 621-1771

Global Logistics & Supply Chain Strategies
(516) 829-9210
Web: http://www.Kellerpubs.com

Grocery Headquarters
(312) 654-2300

Harvard Business Review
(800) 274-3214

ID Systems
(603) 924-9631

Inbound Logistics
(212) 629-1560

Inc.
(617) 248-8000

Industrial Management
(800) 494-0460

Industry Week
(800) 326-4146
Web: http://www.industryweek.com

Intermodal Shipping
(770) 396-9676

International Business
(212) 683-2426

International Journal of Logistics Management
(904) 620-1050

International Journal of Physical Distribution and Logistics Management
(813) 974-6173

International Journal of Purchasing Materials Management
(800) 888-6276, ext. 401

Inventory Reduction Report/IOMA, Inc.
(212) 244-0360
Web: http://www.ioma.com

JOC Week
(800) 331-1341
Web: http://www.joc.com

Journal of Business Logistics
(630) 574-0985 (Council of Logistics Management)

Journal of Marketing
(312) 648-0536
Web: http://www.marketingpower.com

Journal of Supply Chain Management
(480) 752-6276
Web: http://www.napm.org

Logistica & Transporte
Fax 011-341-721-9021 (Spain)

Logistics and Transportation Review
1-888-4ES-INFO (437-4636)
E-mail: usinfo-f@elsevier.com

Logistics Management and Distribution Report
(formerly *Traffic Management;* merged with *Distribution* magazine)
(800) 662-7776
Web: http://www.logisticsmgmt.com

Logistics Technology News (newsletter)
(607) 770-4075
Web: http://www.ttpnews.com

Logistics World/IFS Publications
011-44-123485-3605 (United Kingdom)

Marketing Management
(312) 648-0536
Web: http://www.marketingpower.com

Material Handling Engineering
(216) 696-7000
Web: http://www.mhesource.com

Modern Bulk Transporter
(800) 441-0294

Modern Materials Handling
(800) 662-7776 or (303) 470-4000

Operations & Fulfillment
(203) 857-5656
Web: http://www.opsandfulfillment.com

Packaging Technology
PO Box 11570
Riverton, NJ 08076-1570

Parcel Shipping and Distribution
(608) 241-8777

Private Carrier
(703) 683-1300, ext. 204

Purchasing Magazine
(303) 470-4000

Purchasing Today
(480) 752-6276
Web: http://www.napm.org

Rail Industry Newsletter
(800) 331-1341

Refrigerated Transporter
(800) 441-0294
Web: http://www.refrigeratedtrans.com

Sloan Management Review
(800) 876-5764
Web: http://mitsloan.mit.edu/smr/index.html

Staging Area
(847) 934-5580

Supply Chain e-Business
(516) 829-9210
Web: http://www.kellerpubs.com

Supply Chain Management
(888) 622-0075
Web: http://www.mcb-usa.com

Supply Chain Strategy
(603) 891-9406
Web: http://www.pennwell.com

Traffic World
(800) 331-1341
Web: http://www.trafficworld.com

Transport Topics
(800) 517-7370
Web: http://www.ttnews.com

Transportation & Distribution
(216) 696-7000
Editor: Perry Trunick, (216) 931-9274

Transportation Journal
(717) 748-8515
Web: http://www.astl.org

Wall Street Journal
(800) 221-1940

Warehouse Management Technology
(607) 770-4075
Web: http://www.ttpnews.com

Warehousing Forum
(614) 488-3165

Warehousing Management
(800) 446-6551
Web: http://www.warehousemag.com

World Trade
(847) 291-5224
Web: http://www.worldtrademag.com

World Wide Shipping/WWS
(813) 920-4788

Directory of Trade and Professional Organizations in Logistics

Air Transport Association of America
1301 Pennsylvania Avenue, NW Suite 1100
Washington, DC 20004-1701
(202) 626-4000
Fax: (202) 626-4166
Web: http://www.air-transport.org

Airforwarders Association, Inc.
1200 18th Street, NW, Suite 901
Washington, DC 20036
(202) 466-1317
Fax: (202) 466-0226
Web: http://www.logcity.com/airfwdrasn

American Association of Port Authorities (AAPA)
1010 Duke Street
Alexandria, VA 22314-3589
(703) 684-5700
Fax: (703) 684-6321
Web: http://www.aapa-ports.org

American Marketing Association (AMA)
311 South Wacker Drive, Suite 5800
Chicago, IL 60606
(312) 542-9000
Fax: (312) 542-9001
Web: http://www.marketingpower.com

American Moving and Storage Association, Inc.
1611 Duke Street
Alexandria, VA 22314
(703) 683-7418
Fax: (703) 683-8208
Web: http://www.moving.org

American Productivity and Quality Center (APQC)
123 North Post Oak Lane
Houston, TX 77024
(713) 68 L-4020
Fax: (713) 681-8578
Web: http://www.apqc.org

American Society of Transportation and Logistics
229 Peachtree Street, Suite 401
Atlanta, GA 30303
(404) 524-3555
Fax: (404) 524-7776
Web: http://www.astl.org

American Trucking Associations, Inc.
2200 Mill Road
Alexandria, VA 22314
(703) 838-1866
Fax: (703) 684-5751
Web: http://www.trucking.org

APICS—The Educational Society for Resource Management.
5301 Shawnee Road
Alexandria, VA 22312
(703) 354-8851
Fax: (703) 354-8785
Web: http://www.apics.org

Argentina Logistics Management Association
Adolfo Asina 1170 P5 of 511
Buenos Aires, 1088
ARGENTINA
(541) 384-9096
Fax: (541) 384-9120

Asociacao Brasileira De Logistica (ASLOG)
Rua Gandavo 41
Sao Paulo 04023-000
BRAZIL
(55) 11-570-9060
Fax: (55) 11-573-1902

Asociacion de Ejecutivos de Logistica de Guatemala
Avenida del Ferrocarril 49-65
Zona 12
Guatemala City, GUA 01012
GUATEMALA
(502) 477-5511
Fax: (502) 479-4075

Asociacion De Logistica Empresarial (ALEM)
PO Box 172
Valencia 2001
VENEZUELA
(58)(41) 576 203
Fax: (58)(41) 575 748

Asociatia Romana De Logistica
Calea Grivitei, 393
Sector 1, Cod 78341
Bucuresti
ROMANIA
40 (1) 666-4531
Fax: 40 (1) 224-1370

Assn. Chilena Proveedores de Servicios Logisticos
Don Carlos Carlos 2986 of. 6
Las Condes
Santiago
CHILE
(562) 334-0827
Fax: (562) 231-1629

Associacao Portuguesa De Logistics (APLOG)
Praca Felix Correia No 2
Amadora 2720-228
PORTUGAL
(351) 21 499-0740
Fax: (351) 21 495-4404

Association for Transportation Law, Logistics and Policy (ATLLP)
19564 Club House Road
Gaithersburg, MD 20879
(301) 670-6733
Fax: (301) 670-6735
Web: http://www.transportlink.com/atllp

Association of American Railroads
50 F Street NW
Washington, DC 20001
(202) 639-2100
Fax: (202) 639-2286
Web: http://www.aar.org

Association of Management Consulting Firms (AMCF)
380 Lexington Avenue, 17th Floor
New York, NY 10168
(212) 551-7887
Fax: (212) 551-7934
Web: http://www.amcf.org

Associazione Italiana di Logistica (AILOG)
19-20124 Milano
ITALY
(392) 6671-0622
Fax: (392) 670-1483
Web: http://www.ailog.org

ATA Information Technology & Logistics Council
2200 Mill Road
Alexandria, VA 22314
(703) 838-1766
Fax: (703) 684-4328
Web: http://www.trucking.org

Bundesvereinigung Logistik e.v.
Joseph-von-Fraunhofer-Str 20
Dortmund 44227
GERMANY
(49) 231 9700 120
Fax: (49) 231 9700 464
Web: http://www.bvl.de

Canadian Association of Supply Chain & Logistics Management (CASCLM)
590 Alden Road, Suite 211
Markham, Ontario L3R 8N2
CANADA
(905) 513-7300
Fax: (905) 513-1248
Web: http://www.infochain.org

Canadian Wholesale Drug Association (CWDA)
5255 Yonge Street, Suite 505
Toronto, Ontario M2N 6P4
CANADA
(416) 222-3922
Fax: (416)222-8960
Web: http://www.cwda.com

Centro Español De Logistica (CEL)
Travessera de Gracia, 15, 1st, 1st
Barcelona 08021
SPAIN
34 (93) 201 0555
Fax: 34 (93) 208 0864
Web: http://www.cel-logistica.org

China National Association of Materials and Equipment
25 Yuetan North Street
Bejing 100384
CHINA
86 (10) 6839 2228
Fax: 86 (10) 6839 2433

Containerization and Intermodal Institute (CII)
195 Fairfield Ave, Suite 4D
West Caldwell, NJ 07006
(973) 226-0160
Fax: (973) 364-1212

Council of Logistics Management
2805 Butterfield Road, Suite 200
Oak Brook, IL 60523
(630) 574-0985
Fax: (630) 574-0537
Web: http://www.clm1.org

Delta Nu Alpha
530 Church Street, Suite 700
Nashville, TN 37219
(615) 251-0933
Fax: (615) 244-3170
Web: http://www.deltanualpha.org

Distribution Mgmt Association of the Philippines
PO Box 13254 Ortigas Center
Pasig City 1605
PHILIPPINES
63 (2) 671-8670
Fax: 63 (2)671-4793

Eno Transportation Foundation, Inc.
One Farragut Square S, Suite 500
Washington, DC 20006-4003
(202) 879-4700
Fax: (202) 879-4719
Web: http://www.enotrans.com

Express Carriers Association (ECA)
PO Box 4307
Bethlehem, PA 18018
(610) 740-5857
Fax: (610) 710-3174

Food Distributors International (IFDA)
201 Park Washington Court
Falls Church, VA 22046
(703) 532-9400
Fax: (703) 538-4673
Web: http://www.fdi.org

Food Marketing Institute (FMI)
655 15th St NW Suite 700
Washington, DC 20005
(202) 452-8444
Fax: (202) 429-8282
Web: http://www.fmi.org

German Society of Logistics
Joseph von Fraumhofer Str 20
Dortmund, 44227
GERMANY
49 (231) 9700-121
Fax: (231) 9700 464

Grocery Manufacturers of America, Inc.
1010 Wisconsin Avenue NW #900
Washington, DC 20007
(202) 337-9400
Fax: (202) 337-4508
Web: http://www.gmabrands.org

Health & Personal Care Distribution Conference, Inc.
1090 12 Street
Vero Beach, FL 32960
(561) 778-7782
Fax: (561) 778-4111
Web: http://www.hpcdc.org

Health Industry Distributors Association
66 Canal Center Plaza, Suite 520
Alexandria, VA 22314-1591
(703) 549-4432
Fax: (703) 549-6495
Web: http://www.ghv.com

Household Goods Forwarders Association of America
2320 Mill Road
Alexandria, VA 22314
(703) 684-3780
Fax: (703) 684-3784
Web: http://www.hhgfaa.org

Hungary Association of Logistics
Veres Palne u. 36
Budapest 1053
HUNGARY
(36) 1 317-2959
Fax: (1) 317-2959

Institute of Industrial Engineers (IIE)
25 Technology Park
Norcross, GA 30043
(770) 449-0461
Fax: (770) 263-8532
Web: http://www.iienet.org

Institute of Logistics and Transport
80 Portland Pl
London W1N 4DP
UNITED KINGDOM
44(0) 207 467-9400
Fax: 44 (0) 207 467-9440
Web: http://www.iolt.org.uk

Institute of Supply Management (ISM)
(formerly National Assn. of Purchasing Mgmt., Inc.)
PO Box 22160
Tempe, AZ 85285-2160
(480) 752-6276
Fax: (480) 752-7890
Web: http://www.ism.ws

Institut International De Mgmt Pour La Logistique
CH-1015 Lausanne
SWITZERLAND
41 (21) 693-2465
Fax: 41 (21) 693-5060
Web: http://imlwww.epfl.ch

Intermodal Association of North America (IANA)
7501 Greenway Center Drive #720
Greenbelt, MD 20770-6705
(301) 982-3400
Fax: (301) 982-4815
Web: http://www.intermodal.org

The International Air Cargo Association (TIACA)
3111 SW 27th Avenue
PO Box 330669, Coconut Grove
Miami, FL 33233-0669
(305) 443-9696
Fax: (305) 443-9698
Web: http://www.tiaca.org

International Customer Service Association (ICSA)
401 North Michigan Avenue
Chicago, IL 60611-4267
(312) 321-6800
Fax: (312) 245-1084
Web: http://www.icsa.com

International Safe Transit Association (ISTA)
1400 Abbott Road, Suite 310
East Lansing, MI 48823-1900
(517) 333-3437
Fax: (517) 333-3813
Web: http://www.ista.org

International Society for Inventory Research
Veres Paine u. 36
Budapest H-1053
HUNGARY
Phone and Fax: (36) 1 317-2959

International Society of Logistics
8100 Professional Place, Suite 211
Hyattsville, MD 20785
(301) 459-8446
Fax: (301) 459-1522

International Warehouse Logistics Association
1300 West Higgins Road, Suite 111
Park Ridge, IL 60068-5764
(847) 292-1891
Fax: (847) 292-1896
Web: http://www.iwla.com/home.asp

Intl. Association of Refrigerated Warehouses (IARW)
7315 Wisconsin Avenue, Suite 1200N
Bethesda, MD 20814
(301) 652-5674
Fax: (301) 652-7269
Web: http://www.iarw.org

Japan Institute of Logistics Systems (JILS)
Sumitomo Higashi-Shinbashi Bldg 3 Goukan
1-10-14 Hamamatsu-cho Minato-ku
Tokyo 105-0013
JAPAN
81 (3) 3432-3291
Fax: 81 (3) 3432-8681
Web: http://www.logistics.or.jp/jils/

Korea Logistics Society
154-10 Samsung-dong
Kangnam-gu
Seoul, 135-090
KOREA
(02) 3404-3007
Fax: (02) 3404-3039

Logistics Association of Australia-LAA
PO Box 249
Parramatta NSW 2124
AUSTRALIA
61 (2) 9635-3422
Fax: 61 (2) 9635-3466
Web: http://www.logassoc.asn.au

Logistics Institute of New Zealand
PO Box 75-345
Manurewa
NEW ZEALAND
64 (9) 267-1106
Fax: 64 (9) 267-9075

Logistiikka—Finnish Association of Logistics
Katajanokankatu 5 D 14
Fin-00160 Helsinki
FINLAND
(358) 179 567
Fax: (358) 177 675

Maria Association, Ltd.
Val Moscow 125047
RUSSIA
7 (095) 258-1237
Fax: 7 (095) 975-2027

Material Handling Equipment Distributors Assn.
201 US Highway 45
Vernon Hills, IL 60061-2398
(847) 680-3500
Fax: (847) 362-6989
Web: http://www.mheda.org

Material Handling Industry (MHI)
8720 Red Oak Boulevard, Suite 201
Charlotte, NC 28217-3992
(704) 676-1190
Fax: (704) 676-1199
Web: http://www.mhia.org

Materials Handling and Management Society
8720 Red Oak Boulevard, Suite 201
Charlotte, NC 28217-3992
(704) 676-1183
Fax: (704) 676-1199
Web: http://www.mhia.org/ps/ps_mhms_home.cfm

National Assn. of Purchasing Mgmt., Inc. (NAPM)
PO Box 22160
Tempe, AZ 85285-2160
(480) 752-6276
Fax: (480) 752-7890
Web: http://www.napm.org
(Note: NAPM changed its name to Institute for Supply Management on January 1, 2002.)

National Association of Wholesaler-Distributors (NAW)
1725 K Street NW
Washington, DC 20006
(202) 872-0885
Fax: (202) 785-0586
Web: http://www.naw.org

National Customs Brokers & Forwarders Assn. of America
1200 18th Street NW, Suite 901
Washington, DC 20009
(202) 466-0222
Fax: (202) 466-0226
Web: http://www.ncbfaa.org

National Defense Transportation Association (NDTA)
50 S. Pickett Street, Suite 220
Alexandria, VA 22304-7296
(703) 751-5011
Fax: (703) 823-8761
Web: http://www.ndtahq.com

National Industrial Transportation League (NITL)
1700 N. Moore Street, Suite 1900
Arlington, VA 22209-1904
(703) 524-5011
Fax: (703) 524-5017
Web: http://www.nitl.org

National Private Truck Council (NPTC)
66 Canal Center Plaza, Suite 600
Alexandria, VA 22314-1591
(703) 683-1300
Fax: (703) 683-1217
Web: http://www.nptc.org

National Society of Professional Engineers (NSPE)
1420 King Street
Alexandria, VA 22314
(703) 684-2856
Fax: (703) 519-3763
Web:http://www.nspe.org

National Tank Truck Carriers, Inc. (NTTC)
2200 Mill Road
Alexandria, VA 22314-4677
(703) 838-1960
Fax: (703) 684-5753
Web: http://www.tanktransport.com

National Wholesale Druggists' Association
PO Box 2219
Reston, VA 20190-0219
(703) 787-0000
Fax: (703) 787-6930
Web: http://www.HealthcareDistribution.org

Norwegian Association Purchasing & Logistics
PO Box 2602, St. Hanshaugen
0131 Oslo
NORWAY
(47) 222-01400
Fax: (47) 222-00650

Office Furniture Distribution Association, Inc. (OFDA)
PO Box 326
Petersham, MA 01366-0326
(978) 724-3267
Fax: (978) 724-3507

South African Institute of Materials Handling
PO Box 787549
Sandton, Gauteng 2146
SOUTH AFRICA
27 (11) 883-0339
Fax: 27 (11) 883 0716
Web: http://www.saimh.co.za

Supply Chain Council, Inc.
303 Freeport Road
Pittsburgh, PA 15215
(412) 781-4101
Fax: (412) 781-2871
Web: http://www.supply-chain.org

Swedish Materials Administration Forum (SMAF)
Box 608
Nacka S-13121
SWEDEN
(46) 8 718 1280
Fax: (46) 8 718 0025

Swedish National Association of Purchasing and Logistics
PO Box 1278
SE-164 29 Kista
SWEDEN
46 (8) 752-1690
Fax: 46 (8) 750-6410

Thai Logistics and Production Society (T-LAPS)
29/126 Ladprao 41 Road
Bangkok 10900
THAILAND
(662) 229 4255
Fax: (662) 541 8581

Tranportation Consumer Protection Council
120 Main Street
Huntington, NY 11743-6906
(516) 549-8984
Fax: (516) 549-8962

Transportation Intermediaries Association (TIA)
3601 Eisenhower Avenue, Suite 110
Alexandria, VA 22304
(703) 329-1894
Fax: (703) 329-1898
Web: http://www.southlandexpress.com

Transportation Research Board (TRB)
2101 Constitution Avenue NW
Washington, DC 20418
(202) 334-2936
Fax: (202) 334-2920
Web: http://www.nas.edu/trb

Transportation Research Forum
One Farragut Square South, Suite 500
Washington, DC 20006-4003
(202) 879-4701
Fax: (202) 879-4719

Truckload Carriers Association
2200 Mill Road
Alexandria, VA 22314
(703) 838-1950
Fax: (703) 836-6610
Web: http://www.truckload.org

Uruguayan Logistics Association (URULOG)
Av Rivera 2203/601
11600 Montevideo
URUGUAY
59 (82) 307-6873
Fax: 59 (82) 400-2100

VDI-FML
VDI-Gesellschaft Foerdertechnik
Materialfluss Logistik (VDI-FML)
Postfach 10 11 39
40002 Dusseldorf
GERMANY
49 (211) 6214-231
Fax: 49 (211) 6214-155

Vereniging Logistiek Management
PO Box 23207
3001 KE Rotterdam
NETHERLANDS
31 (10) 436-4155
Fax: 31 (10) 436-4625
Web: http://www.vlmnet.nl

Warehousing Education and Research Council (WERC)
1100 Jorie Boulevard, Suite 170
Oak Brook, IL 60523-2243
(630) 990-0001
Fax: (630) 990-0256
Web: http://www.werc.org

Case A1

Big Byte Computers, Inc.*

Jerry Cole, area manager at CBL Logistics, was escorting Jill Gallagher, a graduate student from a large local university, around the facility. CBL ran the outbound transportation activity inside of Big Byte Computers' (BBC) Jackson, Tennessee, plant. It was the usual one-hour tour where he got to show an outsider rows of warehouse space filled with pallets, a sorting and sequencing operation where various computer components were combined as per individual customer order, and outbound transportation staging.

Jerry always liked the idea of showing the facility, not only the physical goods portion but also the information technology aspect. CBL had been on-line with Big Byte Computers ever since they first started the relationship in the early 1990s. To no one's surprise, all of the terminals in the building were Big Byte products. Jill could not help but notice.

As the tour was coming to an end, Jerry turned to Jill and said, "That's about all there is to it. You could sum up this client relationship as one where they do what they do best, designing and making computers, and hire us to do what we do best, handle outbound transportation."

"But, I'm curious about one thing, Mr. Cole," asked Jill, "This looks like its a commodity business that you're in. Why doesn't Big Byte just put it out to bid and see if someone like a Menlo might be able to do it cheaper?"

"Big Byte is very aggressive in seeing that we continue to provide them with savings each year," explained Jerry. He then added, "That's probably one of the toughest aspects of this business. Not only do they put performance expectations on us that they could never have achieved themselves when this function was performed internally, but they constantly have the pressure on us to reduce costs each year."

"Your operation is impressive and you no doubt provide Big Byte with what they want," replied Jill, "But I just can't help but think there are other logistics activities that Big Byte would want you to do for them."

Jerry, perhaps just a little perplexed at how to respond to that issue, thought for a moment and finally turned to Jill and said, "We're doing about as much as I think we can do for them right now. CBL would need a whole range of other capabilities

*This case was prepared by William L. Grenoble, Robert A. Novack, and Richard R. Young, all of the Center for Supply Chain Research, The Pennsylvania State University. Reproduced with the permission of the Center for Supply Chain Research, The Pennsylvania State University.

in order to do more. Right now we operate with the customer's information systems, but that would likely have to change."

Then Jerry added, "Not only that, I don't think the distribution folks at Big Byte are willing to throw more in our direction. It seems to work as it is and I'm proud to say that I kind of like it just that way. We've got this thing here working like a well-oiled machine!"

"Not only that, but I really don't know what I'd do if they came and asked for more!" thought Jerry to himself as he walked Jill back to the front of the building.

COMPANY PROFILE

Big Byte Organization

Big Byte Computers (BBC) Inc., is a manufacturer/assembler of personal computer systems. Each system consists of a tower unit (central processor), monitor, keyboard, and printer. BBC has a reputation in the industry for high quality primarily because of several innovations it has made in its manufacturing processes. However, the products in a major segment of the industry have become commodity-like using all the same processors, keyboard, and monitors, thus forcing BBC to focus its attention on cost reduction and logistics service quality to differentiate its product line from that of its competitors. In recent months, BBC's main competitors have started offering home systems for less than $1,000, meaning that even more aggressive cost reductions are needed.

BBC has annual sales approaching $5 billion with overseas representing a mere 7 percent of the total. Domestically, BBC has three major customer groups: retail, distributor, and corporate accounts. Retail accounts for 45 percent of revenue; distributors, 40 percent, and corporate accounts, the remaining 15 percent. Although most of the systems that BBC offers are built to inventory, it does offer a limited number of options for custom-built systems for corporate accounts. An abbreviated set of financial statements can be found in Figure A1–1.

Logistics Organization

BBC recognized the importance of logistics and reorganized its transportation, warehousing, and inventory control activities into a logistics department. Purchasing still reports to manufacturing. The current organization consists of Mary Kissell, vice president of logistics; Herbert Conrad, director of transportation; Desmond Goh (Goh Tieng Beng), director of warehousing; and Scott Allen, director of production scheduling and inventory control.

Production reports to its own vice president, Ernesto Perez. Ryan Dunn, director of purchasing, reports directly to Perez. Although Allen has responsibility for both raw material and finished goods inventories with respect to inventory availability, Dunn retains control over raw material purchases. An organization table can be found in Figure A1–2.

Of BBC's annual transportation expenses of $75 million, the domestic outbound (finished goods to customers) is $65 million with the remaining $10 million for

FIGURE A1–1 Big Byte Computers, Inc., Selected Financial Data (in $ Millions, except Employees)

Income Statement	199Z	199Y	199X
Sales	4,997	3,801	3,271
Percent foreign sales	*8.1%*	*4.6%*	*4.3%*
Cost of goods	3,570	2,515	2,003
Gross profit	1,427	1,286	1,268
Selling, general & administrative	835	699	722
Research and development	207	201	197
Income tax provision	211	198	168
Net income	174	188	181
Balance Sheet	**199Z**	**199Y**	**199X**
Current Assets			
Cash and equivalents	465	371	298
Finished goods inventory	651	502	359
Parts & assembly inventory	434	308	211
Other current assets	1,551	1,137	914
Total current assets	3,101	2,318	1,782
Long-Term Assets			
Property, plant, & equipment	1,009	725	891
Other long-term assets	112	99	153
Total long-term assets	1,121	824	1,044
Total assets	4,222	3,142	2,826
Current liabilities	1,366	960	638
Long-term debt	153	70	73
Total liabilities	1,519	1,030	711
Stockholder equity	2,703	2,112	2,115
Employees	**199Z**	**199Y**	**199X**
	10,541	9,559	10,059

inbound (raw materials and components for manufacturing). Annual warehousing expenses are $25 million.

Logistics Network—Inbound

Despite its size, BBC has its only manufacturing/assembly facility in Jackson, Tennessee. As for product, BBC systems are relatively simple in their configuration,

FIGURE A1–2 Big Byte Computers, Inc., Corporate Logistics Group Organization Chart

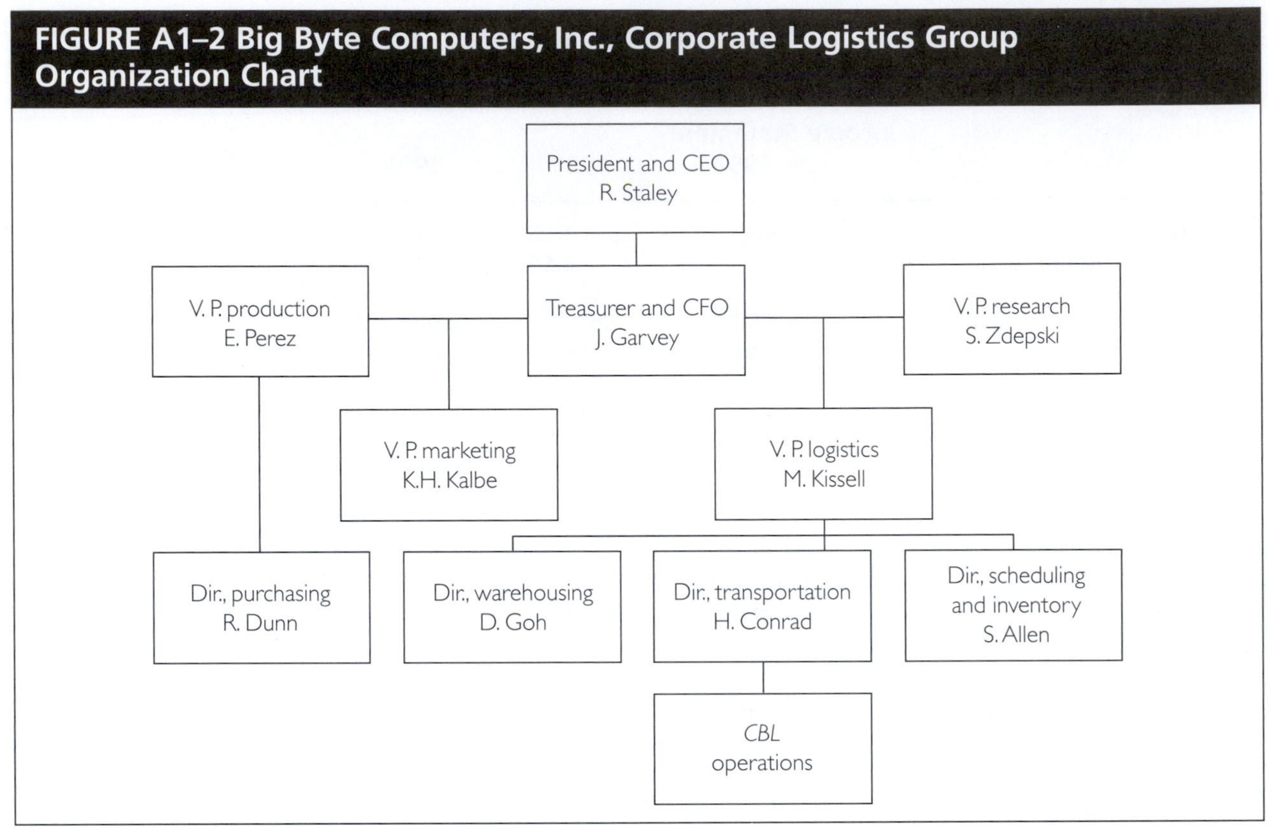

meaning that customers are offered only limited choices on items such as printers, keyboards, and monitors. The Jackson plant manufactures and installs the interior circuitry for the tower. All other components for the systems are sourced as follows:

Assembly Items	*Source Location*	*FOB Terms*
Case	Monterey, Mexico	Destination
CD/disk unit	Ft. Worth, Texas	Destination
Hard drive	St. Paul, Minnesota	Origin
Chips	Renton, Washington	Origin
Modem	Greensboro, North Carolina	Origin
Power supply	Dallas, Texas	Destination
Cable and wire	Nogales, Mexico	Destination
Peripheral Component	*Source Location*	*FOB Terms*
Keyboard/mouse	Columbus, Ohio	Origin
Printers	Torrance, California	Destination
Monitors	State College, Pennsylvania	Destination

BBC offers its customers configurations with two choices of monitors and three types of printers. Custom-built systems, however, offer configurations with special chips and hard drive capacities. Monitors, keyboards, and printers never enter the plant but are shipped directly from the supplier to BBC's distribution facility located next to the plant in Jackson. These are bundled with the completed tower

FIGURE A1–3 BBC Logistics Network

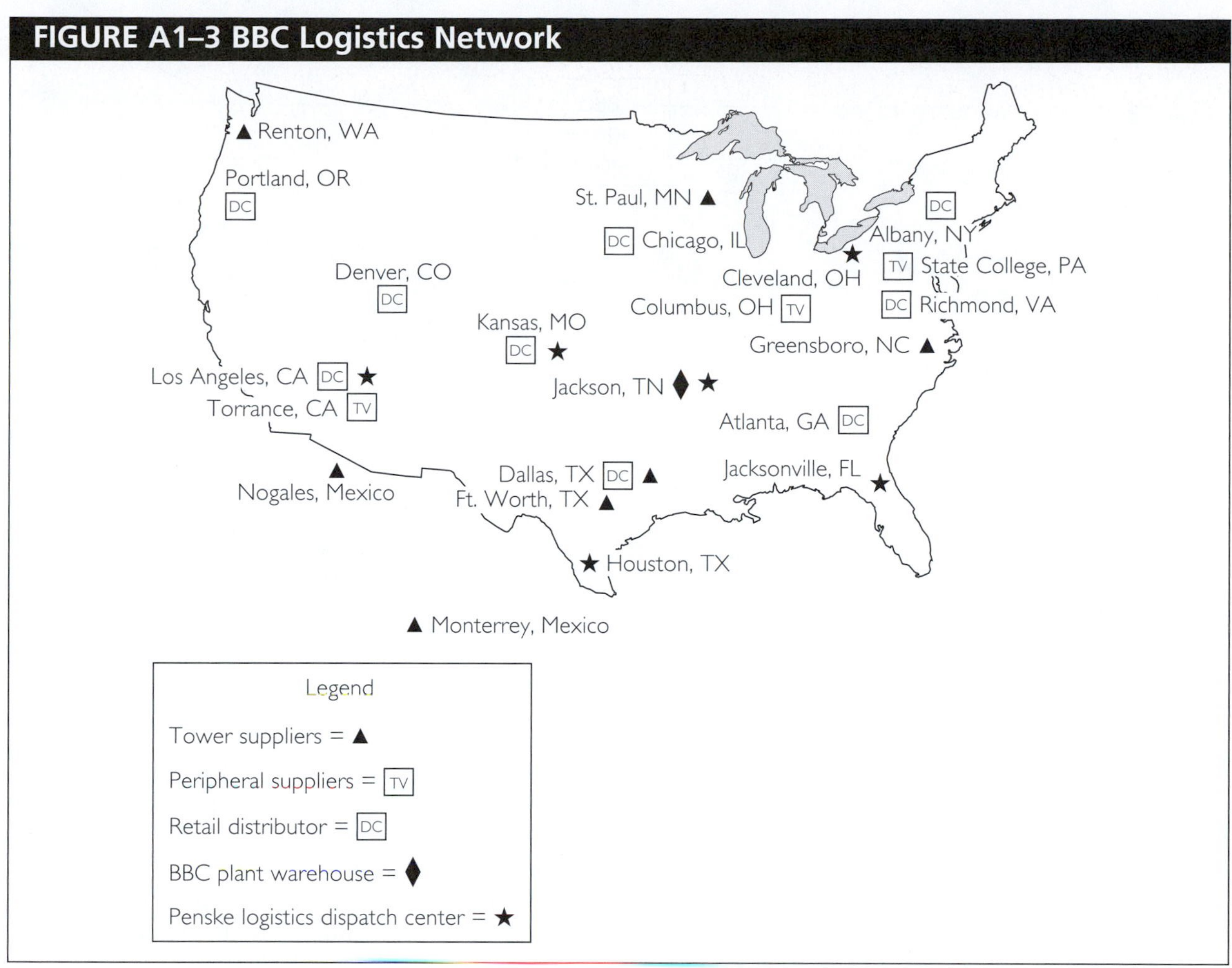

units from manufacturing to fill customer orders. Assembly items, however, are delivered to the plant from the supplier. Figure A1–3 and Figure A1–4 contain the BBC logistics network.

Current methods of transportation for inbound moves are as follows:

Peripheral Component	*Transportation Method*
Keyboard/mouse	LTL/truckload
Printer	Truckload
Monitors	Truckload

Assembly Item	*Transportation Method*
Case	Truckload
CD/disk drive	LTL
Hard drive	LTL
Chips	LTL and small package
Modem	LTL
Power supply	LTL
Cable and wire	LTL/truckload

FIGURE A1–4 BBC Supply Chain

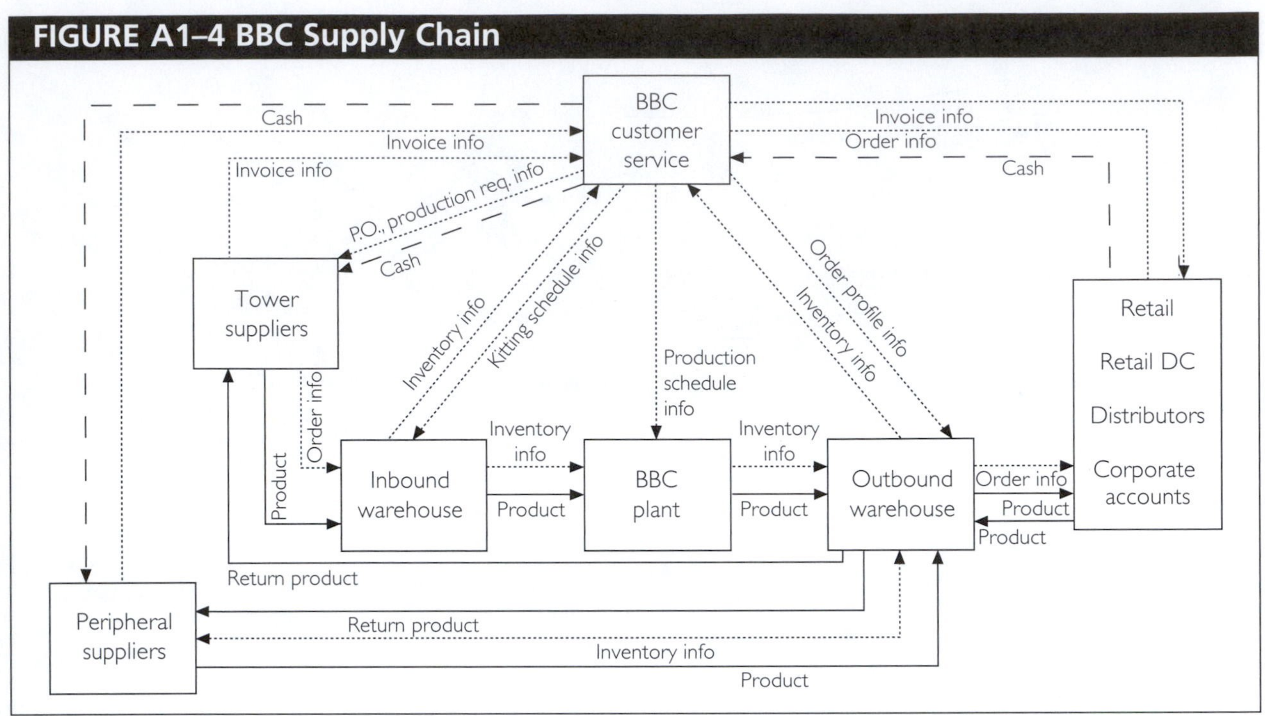

The tower unit is assembled on a line with materials and components controlled by an MRP system that releases an eighteen-day production forecast to suppliers with a guaranteed ten-day volume. While annual contracts specify volumes and delivery schedules for the tower components, BBC updates forecasts on rolling ninety and thirty-day basis. Individual releases against the contracts are currently placed manually by purchasing based on inventory records maintained by manufacturing.

The monitor, keyboard, and printer suppliers replenish the warehouse using a vendor-managed inventory (VMI) system. These items are bar coded by the supplier and scanned by BBC upon receipt and again in the warehouse when each is allocated to a particular customer. The second scanning removes the item from the record of available inventory, although not from the physical.

In manufacturing, warehouse personnel kit each tower assembly on the second shift while assembly component inventory is replenished on the first shift. Bar coding of tower components allows for a real-time inventory count for reordering purposes. Manufacturing carries in inventory approximately seven days of production materials.

Logistics Network—Outbound

All outbound shipments to customers are FOB destination from the warehouse in Jackson, Tennessee. BBC serves its markets through four distinct distribution channels:

Channel	*% Revenue*	*Transportation*
Direct to retail store	5%	LTL small package
Direct to retail DC	40%	Truckload
Wholesale distributor DC	40%	Truckload
Direct to corporate account	15%	LTL and small package

Major retail and distributor DCs are located in:

Richmond, Virginia	Atlanta, Georgia
Albany, New York	Chicago, Illinois
Kansas City, Missouri	Dallas, Texas
Denver, Colorado	Los Angeles, California
Portland, Oregon	

Distributors and retail DCs place orders with BBC customer service using EDI; retail store and corporate account customers by 800 voice and fax numbers. When a customer places an order, the order-management system will generate a projected delivery date. This date is based on inventory availability, production capacity availability, and lead times for component parts from suppliers and complete systems to the customers.

Daily orders are exploded and compared with a bill of materials file as well as the assembly components inventory file. When there will be insufficient quantities on hand, its interface with the purchasing system triggers purchase orders for component parts. The order system also interfaces with the available capacity file maintained by production planning in order to generate both daily and aggregate kitting schedules. All information systems currently in use at BBC are legacy systems that have either been internally developed or commercially available and substantially modified to accommodate BBC's requirements.

In addition to the outbound shipments of finished goods, the warehouse also currently handles customer returns for system component repairs and obsolete/damaged items for return to suppliers.

Current CBL Logistics Operations

CBL Logistics (CBL) has responsibility for outbound transportation. CBL operates a dispatch center located inside the Jackson warehouse. This center receives its daily order activity report through CBL's TMS (transportation management system). This system interfaces with the BBC order management system (OMS) and warehouse management system (WMS). The TMS consolidates shipments when appropriate, determines staging for LTL stop-offs, provides routing for CBL vehicles, generates transportation documentation, and routes shipments on contracted and common truckload and LTL carriers.

All contracts for outbound transportation are negotiated in conjunction with the BBC transportation department; all common carriers used are on a preferred carrier list supplied by BBC. The CBL dispatch center is kept current on the carrier routing schedule. The dispatch center is also responsible for sending ASNs to retail and distributor DCs.

In addition, the dispatch office is notified when a customer return must be picked up. If it cannot be picked up by a CBL driver making a return run, customers are allowed to make the return by either LTL or small parcel carrier as instructed on the return goods authorization (RA).

CBL equipment currently assigned to the BBC business consists of thirty-five tractors and fifty trailers. The trailers are clearly dedicated units and have been painted with the Big Byte logo; however, many of the tractors are rotated through the regional CBL fleet and are all in corporate yellow and carry no customer identification. Most of the dedicated routes handled are in the Southeast and Middle Atlantic states. These are all outbound only, as no purchased components are transported on backhauls.

The current contract between BBC and CBL is for a three-year period. Dashboard metrics for the CBL operation are as follows:

Metric	*8%*	*9% (Goal)*	*10% (Target)*
Deliver to promise	97%	98%	100%
Damage ($)	<5,000	<3,500	<2,000
Freight bill accuracy	92%	95%	98%
Cost reduction	2%	4%	6%
Customer complaints (due to transportation)	<10	<6	<2

Dashboard metrics are calculated at the end of each calendar quarter and are reviewed (1) internally by the BBC with the customers; (2) with CBL regional management, including Jerry Cole; and (3) with CBL headquarters in Reading. Performance is also shared with those carriers utilized for the quarter.

History of CBL Relationship

The current relationship between BBC and CBL goes back to mid-1992 when the then head of BBC distribution management, one of the predecessors of the present logistics activity, realized that BBC expertise could be better utilized in areas other than handling day-to-day transportation transactions. There were, in fact, several criteria that supported this position and had been earlier identified by a team of faculty members from a nearby university.

Decision to Outsource

BBC had been told that using its talent to perform various analyses could allow the company to better position itself by using logistics as a competitive weapon. Moreover, it would yield a better return than managing individual transactions for delivering BBC products to retailers, wholesalers, and direct customers. The obvious decision was to outsource the management of outbound transportation to an organization that had such an activity as one of its core competencies. The BBC distribution department would become the manager of a network, rather than the handler of the details.

Expectations for Outsourcing

Just before the holidays in late 1992, BBC having collected the data about its organization, customers and operations set out to identify who should be included on the list of firms who potentially could fill the role. Senior distribution management identified the following roles that such an outsource would need to fulfill:

- *Load planning.* Using BBC order processing systems, identify volumes of orders, applicable weights and cubes, and their destinations and promise dates. Where possible, consolidate into larger LTL or truckload shipments.

- *Carrier scheduling.* Arrange for carrier pickup schedules with an awareness for particular equipment needs. Modes included within the scope of the activity were truckload, less-than-truckload, small parcel delivery (e.g., UPS), a minimal amount of airfreight, and some small air express (FedEx). At the outset, international shipments, with the exception of trucks to Canada, were to be handled by a person in BBC's international group.
- *Dedicated fleet operations.* Where feasible, utilize a fleet of tractors and trailers dedicated to the outbound carriage of BBC products. Utilize this fleet where practical for transport of returned goods from retailer and wholesaler distribution centers.
- *Documentation.* Also using existing BBC systems, prepare bills of lading and distribute to the shipping dock areas at the Jackson DC.
- *Expediting, tracing, and tracking.* The successful outsource would take over these customer service liaison activities, much of which entailed obtaining proofs of delivery.
- *Loss and damage claims.* Receive notices of loss and damage from customers, investigate them, and file the necessary claim documents with carriers on a timely basis. BBC also built into this part of the specification the need to have the outsource collect loss and damage data and to regularly review it with the carriers involved.
- *Freight bill auditing and payment.* Receive carrier freight bills, pre-audit them for accurate rates, weights, origins and destinations, and discounts; and enter data into the freight bill payment system.
- *Performance reporting.* Over the years, BBC knew that it should be collecting more information about the performance of its various selected carriers, particularly on the loss and damage record; on-time performance for both pickup and delivery; the accuracy of their information, including billing as well as tracking and tracing; and their performance as seen by the customers. Whoever was to be selected would need to have the ability to promptly address all of these issues and relate them back to BBC for use in periodic carrier negotiations.

Selecting an Outsource

The growth of the third-party logistics business had grown significantly since its inception in the 1980s. Not that it was so much of an inception as it was a redefining what some firms felt their roles were vis-à-vis combining various elements of goods transportation and storage. It was specifically this element that made the selection process so difficult for BBC.

Once word was out that BBC was looking to develop a bidders list, all of the carriers who had at one time worked with BBC arranged for sales interviews. This was not just limited to the truckers, as 3PLs that had been formed by public warehouses, airlines, and household goods carriers also wanted consideration, as well as others who had never worked for BBC such as at least one railroad, a software company, and a pair of leasing companies. The list clearly had grown.

Internally, a team comprised of distribution, marketing, operations, and finance representatives was formed to spearhead the selection process. Each potential bidder had to meet some basic BBC criteria, including:

1. Be of a size to handle BBC's volume of business both now and in the future
2. Have sufficient knowledge of the transportation industry

3. Have the resources to add capabilities in the future
4. Be committed to continuous quality improvement
5. Have a culture that was consistent and would apparently mesh well with BBC's.

Using these criteria, the list shortened rapidly. By the time the request documents were to be distributed, there were only five firms in contention. Upon analysis of the quotations, a further round of interviewing, and the negotiation of some of the nebulous items in the specification, CBL emerged as the clear winner. A joint BBC-CBL implementation team commenced its work beginning in May 1993.

Implementation

Although simple in concept, the outsourcing proved to be difficult in its execution. Although the managers involved knew that they were not losing their jobs, indeed they were being redeployed into more interesting and challenging assignments; the period of transition contained some personal as well as operational challenges. This occurred in part because of the comfort level many found based in the routine of managing the transactions.

Implementation activities continued to move ahead. Shortly after the first of August, CBL people had moved into their new offices in the Jackson DC, systems had been reconfigured to allow CBL personnel terminal access, and a round of introductions had been made with those carriers whom BBC had in place at the time.

At this stage, however, it seemed almost impossible to disengage the BBC traffic personnel from their day-to-day transactional thinking. Finally, the one development that more or less saved the relationship occurred when Mary Kissell, by this point the new vice president of logistics at BBC, began handing out analytical projects with relatively short due dates for completion to various BBC members of the team.

Despite the start-up problems, everything seemed to work; in the words of Mary Kissell, "This whole arrangement is working better than when we were doing it! Sure there are problems, but we've all demonstrated a willingness to work though them." The success at this juncture was due to two factors: the due diligence done by BBC during the selection phase, and the commodity-like nature of the transportation functions that had been outsourced.

Added Responsibilities

In late 1994, after a little more than just a year's experience, it had become apparent that having CBL responsible for all outbound transportation made some sense. Not that it was that much of an issue because of its low volume, but the non-Canadian foreign shipments were also then included.

At the same time, BBC began giving CBL more responsibility for carrier selection and negotiation. Although they had been present in the BBC transportation contracting council since the beginning of the relationship, that presence had only been intended for them to be observers. Although the traffic department was to maintain its lead role, the CBL representatives were able to increasingly provide active input.

This move, too, was fraught with some political issues as some BBC people felt that they were foolishly surrendering some of their inherent prerogatives. After a while it was apparent that they were not giving up their responsibility, just some of their authority.

Contract Renewal

In late 1995, Jerry Cole—who had just been appointed as the head of the regional CBL activities that included not only BBC in Jackson but also several accounts in both Nashville and Memphis—was informed that BBC was planning to rebid the outbound transportation business that CBL had enjoyed since 1993. Jerry was clearly worded anytime anybody rebid anything but was particularly concerned about BBC for several reasons:

1. They were a high profile account, and it was beneficial for CBL to publicize them as such.
2. They were a somewhat new account, and CBL had spent a considerable amount in setting up and raising its performance to a level consistent with the customer's expectations.
3. They nicely complemented some of the other efforts that CBL was making in both the electronics industry and the Midwest, in general.

When the bid package was distributed, Jerry did learn that this time around there were only three bidders of which CBL was one. Without going through all of the detail on his response to this particular request, Jerry did win the bid for CBL and some time later learned that BBC really wanted to benchmark the services it was getting relative to the prices in the marketplace. By 1995, the market had shifted as many 3PLs reverted to their core businesses, leaving, at least for the most part, those who were pretty earnest about their roles.

Even between BBC and CBL, however, the business was shifting as the savings found as the "low-hanging fruit" had been pretty much plucked by this time; and Jerry was finding it all the more difficult to identify opportunities whereby CBL could continue to provide BBC with operational savings. So far, some of the things that had been implemented included:

1. Negotiating more realistic contracts with some of the carriers. This was possible because of the increased knowledge of the operation that CBL had as a result of collecting operating statistics and reporting performance measures to the carriers.
2. Finding ways to consolidate freight with other firms in the region, particularly with the distribution center replenishments.
3. Finding opportunities for carrier backhauls using other firms within the regions where the distribution centers were located.
4. Working with BBC and the carriers on packaging issues that served to reduce loss and damage while improving stowability factors in the trucks.

Now What?

Consequently, Jerry knew that the time was coming that he would need to be even more creative. Not only was BBC as aggressive as ever, but CBL Logistics was adamant about him growing the business within the region, increasing his penetration with existing customers, and improving in his profitability. Clearly, in his own words, Jerry summed it up as, "We're in a squeeze. The customer wants more for less money and Reading wants us to produce better returns on that. Something has to change!"

The Situation

A few days ago, the "next shoe" dropped. Jerry had been in the process of opening his morning mail and was quite surprised to find a request for proposal (RFP) from Big Byte. See Figure A1–5 for the details of the RFP.

"This is just great!" he said outloud and with more than just a bit of intended sarcasm. "And just when I thought things were going along on such a nice 'even keel,' too," he added.

Jerry's real thoughts were that Big Byte should have given him some advance warning that this was coming. That, of course, was not apparently the case.

The content of the RFP was surprising in itself. It was not typical of most RFPs, which usually put a piece of business up for grabs using a detailed specification of what was needed. Although the "carrot" of a major contract was held out, the specific request in this RFP was for prospective logistics service suppliers to study BBC's operations and to make recommendations on the different ways that support might be provided.

Moreover, it called for bidders to make presentations to BBC in two weeks. The three companies making the best presentations would be selected as finalists for "round two," which would be the development and implementation of the best ideas from all the presentations. The tone of the RFP was clear—BBC was looking for more than just outsourcing a commodity-like activity.

"This is really going to be a big deal!" came Jerry's thoughts. "Look who signed it," he added as his eyes dropped to the signature at the bottom of the last page.

It had been authored by Jack Garvey, BBC's chief financial officer. Moreover, it explicitly indicated that BBC was on a path to improve logistics capability and supply chain management through increased partnering with service providers. For CBL, this represented a double-edged sword: the opportunity for much more business was there, but the present business was also being placed at risk.

Later that morning, Jerry, clearly feeling the urgency that the RFP had sought to convey, called a meeting of his staff, not only to discuss how to respond but to consider what some of the implications would be for the CBL business in the region. In attendance were Joe Duff, manager of the logistics center handling the present BBC business; Cathy Porter, the regional financial analyst; and Ben Washington, the project manager who Jerry considered to be particularly adept at developing start-up initiatives for new business.

FIGURE A1–5 Big Byte Request for Proposal

BIG BYTE COMPUTERS, INC.
Large Capacity Systems Solutions for the Office and Home
Jackson, Tennessee

Request for Proposal

Improvements in Supply Chain Management

INTRODUCTION

Big Byte Computers (BBC) is a manufacturer of personal computer systems and peripherals. Annual revenues of the company approach $5 billion. The company is privately held, with corporate offices in Jackson, Tennessee.

Logistics and supply chain management play a key role in what is expected by customers of BBC and its products for two important reasons. First, the competitive nature of the PC business has put severe cost and profitability pressure on manufacturers. PCs have largely become a commodity, and all costs are important. Inbound and outbound supply chain costs are significant, and keeping them low allows improved competitiveness. Second, BBC's customers, many of which employ sophisticated, time-sensitive inventory and merchandising processes, are looking more and more to their suppliers to improve logistics service levels. In the computer industry, short product life cycles demand increased supply chain service performance and flexibility.

Recently, it has been decided to review the present state of supply chain management at BBC and to investigate what changes might be made to allow logistics activities and processes to provide more value for BBC and its customers. In particular, we are interested in expanding the role that third-party-logistics providers play.

An initial review has also raised several issues of concern to BBC management, and these issues, in turn, provide the focus for further study and action planning. The issues are as follows:

1. What is logistics and supply chain management for BBC? What supply chain activities (transportation, warehousing, inventory management, order management, etc.) are important to BBC in fulfilling its customer mission? What value do they add?
2. How do competitors and supply chain partners (suppliers and customers) organize for and manage logistics?
3. How efficiently and effectively is BBC performing in supply chain management? What are the proper metrics that should be in place to gauge performance? Are cost and service benchmarks available to point out areas of improvement?
4. Are there opportunities for logistics to add even more value to the products and services BBC markets? What are the important ways that logistics can make contributions in reducing cost and in improving product and service quality at BBC?

(continued on next page)

FIGURE A1–5 Big Byte Request for Proposal *(continued)*

5. How should supply chain management be organized at all levels—plant, operating division, and corporate? How can BBC's suppliers and customers be better integrated into logistics? How can third-party-logistics providers be better utilized?
6. What information systems are presently in place to support decision making for supply chain and integrated logistics management? What new systems or changes to present systems will be needed?
7. Once the opportunities for improvement have been identified, how best might they be implemented?

PURPOSE AND SCOPE

The purpose of this document is to invite several third-party-logistics organizations to propose a course of action to assist BBC in addressing the preceding issues. In seeking overall improvement, BBC envisions a multiple-step process. First, several third-party companies will be asked to make an initial presentation on what they believe are the right directions for BBC. After listening to the presentations, BBC will invite three of the companies to join BBC in pursuing further study and embarking on a plan for improvement. All three of these organizations will be compensated for their consulting input. A final "lead supply chain partner" will be selected from the three.

This improvement process has the following objectives:

- To gain a better understanding of current logistics processes through process analysis and mapping and to develop a plan for process improvement
- To make specific operational and procedural recommendations in regard to how logistics and supply chain management might be improved at BBC
- To develop recommendations for changing logistics organization in the company
- To identify changes to information systems that will facilitate performance improvement in logistics
- To develop a short-term, tactical plan (including target dollar savings) to implement suggested improvements

SUPPLIER SELECTION PROCESS

BBC has formed a team to guide the implementation of a plan for supply chain improvements. The sequential steps for the BBC team to select a supplier for the support described are as follows:

1. *Initial presentations.* Each interested supplier will make a broad presentation on possible improvements to the BBC supply chain.
2. *Supply chain study partner selections.* The initial presentations will be reviewed by team members, and three of the presenters will be selected to participate in a more comprehensive study of the BBC supply chain. The three organizations selected will be compensated for this effort.

FIGURE A1–5 Big Byte Request for Proposal *(continued)*

3. *Final improvement presentations.* The three suppliers will be asked to present their final recommendations to the BBC team. Each presentation period will be two hours in length. At least one hour should be allowed for questions from the team.
4. *Selection meeting.* The BBC team will meet to make a preliminary selection of a lead supply chain partner. Negotiations will then proceed with this supplier to finalize the arrangements and terms of the contract for the study.
5. *Notification.* All suppliers, whether they are selected or not, will be notified of the results of the selection.

Selection criteria have not been finalized by the team, but the successful supplier will display several, if not most, of the following attributes:

- Professionalism, trust, and credibility
- Supplier strategy
- Financial strength
- Process improvement capability
- Systems capability and long-term strategy
- Technical support
- Agility and flexibility
- Geographical coverage
- Creativity
- Implementation skills and success rate

INITIAL PRESENTATION REQUIREMENTS

It is requested that the initial presentations from suppliers contain the following elements:

1. A description of the current BBC supply chain and an overview of key supply chain processes
2. A list of recommendations for improving and reengineering the BBC supply chain
3. An estimate of the expected benefits of the recommendations
4. A list of the key barriers that might be expected in implementing the recommendations
5. For the three most important barriers, a list of initial action steps to overcome them

PRESENTATIONS

The initial presentations should not exceed fifteen minutes in length. Those selected as semi-finalists should be well prepared to field whatever questions may come from members of the selection team. Question-and-answer time is not included in the fifteen-minute limit.

The meeting lasted for the balance of the morning and finally broke up in early afternoon. Although there was much discussion, some of it impassioned, the salient parts of the dialogue went as follows:

Jerry: We have a lot to do get ready for our presentation to BBC. It appears that they are open to suggestions for third-party involvement across the entire spectrum of supply chain activities. This will probably be one of the most challenging projects that we, as a group, have ever worked on. Any suggestions as to where we should start?

Cathy: Well, I believe it's important that we don't think small on this one. Of course, it is clear that BBC isn't going to let us. I think we need to review the supply chain for BBC from suppliers to ultimate consumers and find the places where we as a third-party provider can add value.

Joe: A big advantage we have is our current relationship. We know BBC, their people, their suppliers, and their customers. We have a good reputation with them.

Jerry: Yes, but we have to be a little careful here. This RFP is not "Business as usual" with BBC. In fact, some of the things we might want to suggest doing may look like we're stepping on the toes of the people we work closely with. Nevertheless, I agree that we have to be very broad in our approach.

Ben: One of my concerns is that BBC's perception of us is that we may be too narrow. A lot of what we do for them and our other local customers is just transportation-based. We're great dedicated fleet operators and they know that. But, can we be seen as being able to offer capability in other aspects of supply chain management?

Cathy: Don't forget, though, that CBL in other areas is beginning to develop more comprehensive relationships with customers. Look at what we're doing with the General Motors "Lean Vision" account in Kansas City and with the Lucent Technologies business in Dallas. Within the company as a whole, we have a lot of good experience to draw on.

Ben: You're right. I visited Kansas City last month. It's impressive the way we're working with the GM plant on supplier relations, production planning, and inventory control, in addition to transportation for inbound parts. We have even been involved in quality rework.

Cathy: CBL also has other significant strengths in technology and our low cost of capital.

Joe: That last point is really a good one! I believe finding a way for a third party to both manage and own BBC's inbound and outbound inventory should be a key part of what we propose.

Cathy: I agree with the *managing* part, Joe, but the *owning* part is really scary. There will be a lot of risk. We will really, truly have to be fully integrated into BBC's supply chain processes. It may be feasible, though, if we can reduce inventories overall by shifting BBC from "make to stock" to "make to order." A few computer companies have started in that direction.

Joe: I believe our recommendations for improved supply chain technologies will have to be an important part of our plan. It will be hard to show improvement without making a lot of changes on the technology front.

Ben: One thing about the RFP that struck me is that developing the components for the initial presentation will be similar to using the improvement methods in our own quality program, such as DMAIC, BPMS, or PIP. Maybe we should enlist a "Master Black Belt" to join our team?

Jerry: Well, let me ask again: Where do we begin? Should we try to do some high-level diagrams of the BBC supply chain and some key processes like order management?

Ben: Probably as good a place as any to start. Somehow we need to develop a real clear picture of what BBC has right now.

CASE A2

KOBE AUTOMOBILE MANUFACTURING COMPANY INTEGRATED SUPPLY CHAIN*

For some time, Karl van Pelt, senior auditor for one of the world's largest public accounting firms, sensed a trend forming with the way his clients dealt with both suppliers and customers. Most troubling, however, was the lack of consistency in their business processes. "What's going on here?" he thought to himself. "In many respects, this goes against everything I have ever learned."

In fact, Karl had already spent countless hours with some of the firm's major clients attempting to explore this obvious shift further. During the past six months, he had visited Kobe Automotive at their headquarters in Japan as well as all of their major U.S. operations, both for finished vehicles (KAMCO) and parts distribution (KAPCO). As it turned out, Midwest Carbon Steel (MCS), another client, continued to grow in importance to Kobe.

Rereading the additional reports that both he and others had prepared for his client profiles, Karl realized that many questions remained unanswered. He jotted some ideas at the end of each, knowing that he would want to approach his colleagues about their thoughts.

The text of each of these reports with their various attachments follows.

---

*This case was prepared by William L. Grenoble, Robert A. Novack, Richard R. Young, and Joseph L. Cavinato, all of the Center for Supply Chain Research, The Pennsylvania State University. Reproduced with the permission of the Center for Supply Chain Research, The Pennsylvania State University.

CLIENT PROFILE

Client: Kobe Automobile Manufacturing Co.

Writer: K. van Pelt and R. A. Novack

Date: July 2, 1996

INTRODUCTION

Kobe Automobile Manufacturing Company (KAMCO) is a Japanese firm that exported its first automobile to the United States in 1972. These cars were the first true "economy" vehicles introduced to the American consumers. Because of their relatively low price and excellent fuel economy, these cars immediately took market share away from the Big Three automakers. United States government tariffs and taxes on imported automobiles eliminated the price advantage that KAMCO cars had in this country.

In 1981, KAMCO built its first U.S. manufacturing facility to once again become more price competitive with U.S. car manufacturers. Over the next few years, KAMCO automobiles developed a reputation for extremely high quality, far surpassing that of other domestic manufacturers. In fact, KAMCO's Starfire series became the #1 selling car in the United States in 1988, thus allowing KAMCO to be the market leader for quality and price in the United States. By 1995, KAMCO had produced and/or sold more than 5 million cars in the U.S., making it the fourth largest carmaker.

On a global scale, KAMCO has 73 production facilities in 40 countries that supply automobiles to over 150 national markets plus a supplier network based in 50 of these. This global supply chain complexity has posed a challenge to KAMCO in delivering not only cars to dealers but also parts to production facilities and dealers.

The parts business is separate, yet connected, to the manufacturing business. Two types of parts exist in the KAMCO global supply chain. First, original equipment manufacturer (OEM) parts are delivered from suppliers directly to manufacturing facilities to satisfy daily production needs. Second, spare parts flow from these same suppliers to Kobe Automobile Parts Company (KAPCO) in the North American market to be distributed to car dealers. Many of these parts (e.g., oil filters) are considered to be in the aftermarket and are subject to competition. Other parts (e.g., side view mirrors) are replacement parts and are specific to KAMCO automobiles. Selected financial and operating data are shown in Table A2–1.

KAPCO currently services a network of 1,300 dealers from 15 warehouses located in the United States. Spare parts are received from approximately 300 suppliers, most of whom are located in the United States. However, there are a small number of suppliers located in Canada, Mexico, and Japan. KAPCO's top fifty suppliers account for 90 percent of its dollar volume.

COMPETITIVE ISSUES

The nature of the global market, as well as their reputation for product quality, is causing several difficult competitive challenges to both KAMCO and KAPCO.

(continued on next page)

CLIENT PROFILE—KOBE *(continued)*

TABLE A2–1 Kobe Automobile Parts Company Selected Financial and Operating Data, 1995

1. Revenue	$15,000,000,000
2. Operating income	$405,000,000
3. Inventory	$7,500,000,000
4. Facilities (assets)	$165,000,000
5. Employees	
Salaried	400
Hourly	1,500
6. Inventory turns (system wide)	3
7. On-time delivery	90%
8. Order fill	94%
9. Freight expense	$80,000,000
10. Warehouse operating expense	$150,000,000

Labor

Japanese manufacturing facilities and distribution centers enjoy a union-free environment thus allowing more flexibility in job design, work assignments, and scheduling for changeovers. Lower wage rates and the higher productivity of this nonunion environment have allowed KAMCO and KAPCO to be very price competitive.

The U.S. automobile industry has had a long affiliation with the United Auto Workers (UAW) in its facilities. Although the relationship with U.S. manufacturers was well established, the UAW and the Japanese were not well acquainted. The Japanese quickly found that they faced higher wages and less flexibility with American workers. The UAW found the Japanese to be less willing to accept low productivity and rigid work rules. After several years of operation in the United States, both KAMCO and KAPCO have seemed to find an acceptable working relationship with the UAW, and vice versa. However, the union is still bargaining for changes.

Complexity

KAMCO and KAPCO have complex supply chains. KAPCO's, compounded by the dynamic nature of the demand for parts, has a three-echelon network. A national facility in Cincinnati holds all classifications of their 22,000 stock-keeping units (SKUs) and is used to replenish inventory at two regional distribution centers (DCs) located in Los Angeles and Atlanta, as well as at five district DCs in Hanover, Pennsylvania; Newark, New Jersey; Syracuse, New York; Portland, Maine; and Richmond, Virginia. The regional DC in Los Angeles supports inventory at the Portland, Oregon; Salt Lake City; and Phoenix district DCs. The Atlanta regional DC supports inventory at the Dallas; Chicago; Kansas City, Kansas; and Jacksonville, Florida, facilities.

This network receives parts from 300 suppliers and supports the needs of 1,300 dealers located throughout North America. DCs are connected by approximately fifty carriers, including rail, truckload (TL), less-than-truckload (LTL), and express carriers. Rail and TL are used for transfers between facilities. Express carriers, TL, and LTL provide inbound as well as outbound service to the dealers.

Cycle Time and Customer Service

OEM Darts availability is extremely important for manufacturing productivity. Most suppliers make daily deliveries to KAMCO's plant located in Urbana, Ohio. These deliveries are based on guaranteed production schedules supplied by KAMCO. Parts are combined with other components in a consolidation center located at the plant for timely delivery to the line. The plant holds only one-day raw material inventory.

KAPCO's cycle times differ from KAMCO's as their suppliers hold very little, if no, parts inventories. Supplier inventories are dedicated to OEM; hence, KAPCO orders are manufacturing orders (i.e., the supplier must manufacture to KAPCO's order). Since KAPCO places monthly orders, cycle times can be long and unpredictable despite the requirement that deliveries to dealers must be timely. The quality reputation of KAMCO automobiles requires the use of original KAMCO parts at the dealer level because these parts exceed the performance specifications of aftermarket competitors. Deliveries to dealers, therefore, are closely controlled as a missed delivery might result in a dealer or consumer buying a competitor's part at the local Walmart. The high level of dealer service results in 20 percent of all DC shipments to dealers by express carriers, although many dealers are on specific delivery schedules ("milk runs") to guarantee part availability. Some suppliers may bypass the network and deliver directly to dealers.

DCs are also required to inventory parts for discontinued models "for life." Although not held forever, the Kobe philosophy is to support its customers' needs for as long as their cars are running. KAPCO can offset holding some inventory by ordering small batches from suppliers, but much is held at DCs.

ISSUES

KAMCO and KAPCO managements have initiated the formation of several task forces to investigate the opportunities that exist in five different supply chain processes. The results from these task forces will help shape the strategic direction for the futures of both organizations.

Supplier Relationship Management

Relationships with all suppliers are initiated and maintained by KAMCO, although recently KAPCO representatives have been involved as well. The Japanese style of relationship management is used with all suppliers, that is, long-term mutually beneficial alliances as the norm. A single OEM supplier is selected to be the single source for a part or component for the life of the particular model. This OEM supplier will also support KAPCO's needs during the model life plus long after it being discontinued. Both KAMCO and KAPCO give all suppliers scorecards for identifying areas requiring improvement rather than failure.

Carriers and third-party suppliers are selected and managed by KAPCO for parts distribution operations. KAPCO maintains control over both inbound and outbound transportation and has adopted a "core carrier" concept in order to reduce the number of carriers used and to forge stronger alliances with them. Outbound shipments to dealers are made by dedicated contract carriage, while suppliers are given preferred carrier routing sheets for inbound to DCs. If a supplier fails to use the preferred carrier, it will be charged for any excess freight charges incurred.

(continued on next page)

CLIENT PROFILE—KOBE *(continued)*

Although the carrier base is not managed in the same Japanese tradition as the suppliers, KAPCO maintains close ties and demonstrates a high level of loyalty with its larger carriers. This appears to be changing toward a relationship for life because KAPCO has found that traditional contracts are not conducive to this type of relationship because most contract language punishes carrier failures but does not reward carrier success. Moreover, "backup" carriers are maintained to keep competitive pressures on the primary carriers. Typical carrier contracts last for three years, with one-year extensions. Carriers are currently selected based on on-time delivery, damage rates, price, and financial stability.

Outsourcing/Third Parties

Until three years ago, all of KAPCO's DCs were company owned and operated. The importance of control over order accuracy and cycle time drove this decision to invest in facilities and union labor. In 1993, KAPCO broke ground for a new DC with cross-docking potential that would be operated by a third-party-logistics organization. This new facility, located in Jacksonville, would provide an experiment for future outsourcing opportunities for KAPCO. Some executives feel, however, that warehousing is too risky to outsource because the third party might not provide the level of service interest that customers see as a priority.

Inasmuch as all of KAPCO's transportation needs are met by third-party providers, KAPCO does not own or operate any transportation vehicles. Dedicated milk runs, round-trip operations, and trailer spotting are some of the customized transportation operations provided. Transportation management has not been seen as an opportunity because selecting carriers and controlling delivery times are too critical to KAPCO's service mission. Ten people are employed in this function.

Carrier freight bills are sent to a third party for payment. Amounts charged are compared with negotiated rates. If the rates agree, a check is generated and sent to the carrier. If not, the bill is sent to KAPCO where it is made to reconcile with the carrier. Checks are generated on a transaction-by-transaction basis, that is, each separate freight bill will be paid by a separate check. KAPCO maintains a $100,000 minimum cash balance that is replenished weekly. This third party also generates several types of freight activity reports.

Price competition in the automobile and parts markets has forced KAMCO and KAPCO to search for cost-reduction alternatives. Two potential areas, especially for KAPCO, have been outsourcing of transportation management and warehousing. Management sees its core competency as quality parts, not logistics; hence, several third-party firms have been identified to potentially take over these functions. One specializes in buying and managing transportation. It has several other customers in the parts industry, and economy of scale is an advantage. The other firm focuses on managing warehousing assets. It both owns and leases warehousing space for its clients and offers both consolidation and transportation services. Logistics management at KAPCO sees these outsourcing efforts as a quick way to reduce both variable and fixed costs but that the efforts probably cannot match the service levels achieved with in-house staff.

Electronic Data Interchange (EDI)

Many industries have embraced electronic commerce to reduce errors and costs as well as to improve service across the total supply chain. KAMCO and KAPCO have only just begun to transmit and receive electronic messages with supply chain partners. Although customer invoicing and placing of some purchase orders with suppliers have provided a starting point, no EDI is currently being done with carriers as ordering and payment processes are still performed manually. Freight tracking uses carriers' systems and is passive rather than active. Advance ship notices (ASN) are not used with the carriers either inbound or outbound. Inbound on-time delivery rate is 60 percent.

Several suppliers and carriers have suggested electronic transmission of ASNs, bills of lading, freight bills, and payment remittance. KAPCO estimates that the investment in these EDI transmissions would approximate $500,000 plus annual operating costs of $100,000. Suppliers also cited statistics showing cost reductions from EDI. KAPCO remains skeptical of making this investment.

Evaluated Receipts Process

When a supplier sends a shipment to a KAPCO DC, an invoice is sent to KAPCO accounts payable. When the shipment is received, a receiving report is generated based on the bill of lading and an inspection of the actual shipment. The receiving report is sent to accounts payable (at the Cincinnati DC) to be matched with the invoice. If all documents match, a check is generated and either sent manually or electronically to the supplier. This process is also used to pay carriers. If documents do not agree, reconciliation is made with the supplier. Twenty-five people are employed in accounts payable.

An alternative is the evaluated receipts process and does not require suppliers to generate invoices. Rather, an agreement between supplier and receiver states the price and payment terms. When a supplier makes the shipment, an ASN is also issued to the receiving location that the receiver uses to generate a check to the supplier. Another method is to use the receiving report or packing list to initiate the payment process. Either could eliminate the need to reconcile documents manually with firms reporting 75 percent reductions in their accounts payable activities.

Several suppliers have requested that KAPCO begin use of the evaluated receipts process. KAMCO already utilizes this method with several large suppliers. Accounts payable fears that this process would reduce cash flow (by paying suppliers faster and possibly paying inaccurate bills), allow more mistakes in supplier billing by suppliers, and would not sufficiently reduce accounts payable costs.

Logistics Service Measurement

Logistics service measurement has not been consistent. While it controls both inbound and outbound transportation, it only passively monitors on-time deliveries. Table A2–2 summarizes those processes that are measured and those that are not. Many of the measurements are internal, for example, order fill and inventory turns. Only three measurements reach beyond KAPCO into the supply chain (customer satisfaction, customer retention, and supplier excellence). Although these measurements reveal much about logistics operations, they say little about the impact of logistics service on KAPCO or customer profits. Traditionally, the Japanese have regarded logistics as a "tax" on the business. This cost-focused view of logistics has forced KAPCO to continuously find ways to reduce logistics cost. Sometimes this can lead to sacrificing service. KAPCO's current on-time delivery rate to dealers is 90 percent,

(continued on next page)

TABLE A2–2 Kobe Automobile Parts Company Logistics Service Measurements

Internal Measures	Inbound	Outbound
1. On-time delivery	Yes	Yes
2. Invoice accuracy	No	No
3. Order cycle time	Yes	No
4. Order fill rate	Yes	Yes
5. Damage rates	Yes	Yes
6. Complaint resolution time	No	Yes
7. Inventory turns	Yes	Yes
8. Product returns	No	Yes
9. Transit time	No	No
10. Forecast accuracy	No	No
11. Back orders (%)	No	Yes
12. Tracking system accuracy	No	No
13. Product quality	Yes	No
External Measures	**Inbound**	**Outbound**
14. Customer satisfaction	—	Yes
15. Customer retention	—	Yes
16. Supplier excellence	Yes	—

although dealers will purchase parts in the aftermarket if a KAPCO part is not available. This reduces revenues as well as dealer satisfaction and consumer loyalty.

KAPCO's dealers have requested a 98 percent on-time delivery rate and a 99 percent order fill rate (the current rate is 94 percent). Achieving this will require an investment in information systems, facilities, and inventories. Logistics management has found it difficult to reconcile the marginal improvement in KAPCO and dealer profits from improved service requirements stemming from these investments.

OPTIONS

Management has given the directive to logistics to develop the ability to generate both income statements and balance sheets for its operations and investments. This was caused by the ability of the potential third-party firms to show KAPCO management the effects of outsourcing both the transportation management and warehousing activities on these financial statements.

Management has also begun serious consideration of forming KAPCO logistics as a separate profit center organization making them direct competitors to third-party organizations. KAPCO logistics now has the task of calculating its operations costs and the relationships of its service and costs to bottom-line results.

CLIENT PROFILE

Client: MCS Corporation

Writer: K. van Pelt and W. L. Grenoble

Date: July 18, 1996

INTRODUCTION

MCS Corporation (formerly Midwest Carbon Steel Company) is an integrated steel producer of flat-rolled carbon steel products. Its history dates back to 1927, when it was founded in Cleveland, Ohio. With $2.8 billion in sales in 1995, representing over 5 million tons of steel, it ranks in the top 10 of U.S. steelmakers. It is also one of the most profitable.

MCS operates two plants—its original plant in Cleveland and another facility in Gary, Indiana. The Cleveland Works facility, with production capacity of 3,500 tons, is located on a 3,100-acre site and employs 4,100 workers. The Gary Works has capacity of 1,800 tons, is on a 1,000-acre site, and employs 1,500 steelworkers. Both locations have coke ovens, blast furnaces, basic oxygen furnaces, continuous casters, and hot strip mills. Only Cleveland has a cold mill, at which final finishing for both locations is accomplished. The two operations are highly integrated. Scheduling is done jointly, and dedicated rail and truck transportation links the sites. A production process chart is shown in Figure A2–1.

MCS produces steel at the high end of the value spectrum—mostly coated and cold-rolled products. As such, it has tended to buffer itself from growing competition from minimills, which typically are involved in products more generic and commodity-like. More than 75 percent of its output in 1995 was aluminized, galvanized, zinc/zinc-iron coated, or terne coated.

In the late 1980s, MCS was disastrously unprofitable. Unfavorable business trends, competitive pressures, and weak management nearly bankrupted the firm. New management, put in place in 1991, has reversed fortunes. Major changes have been to increase focus on steelmaking, streamline operations, and to make strategic capital investments in the production process. Its turnaround was also aided by the production shift of foreign automakers, such as Toyota, BMW, Daimler-Benz, Honda, Nissan, and KAMCO to new U.S. facilities. The results have been to make MCS one of the most productive, efficient, and profitable steel producers. At $70/ton, its operating profit yield ranks second in the United States.

MCS's competitors include other integrated producers such as USX, Bethlehem, LTV, National, and Inland, as well as minimill operators such as Nucor (an integrated producer has coke ovens and blast furnaces to create iron from iron ore, while minimills produce steel from scrap only). Minimills have advantages in reduced capital requirements and nonunion labor but are often subject to fluctuations in commodity scrap prices.

The company's management believes its principal competitive advantages are the following:

- A focus on high value-adding products of excellent quality
- A strong base of productive employees and facilities
- A healthy balance sheet
- A vigorous commitment to customer service, which has fostered leading-edge integration with customers, and, in turn, high degrees of responsiveness and flexibility

(*continued on next page*)

Figure A2–1 MCS Corporation Steel Production Process

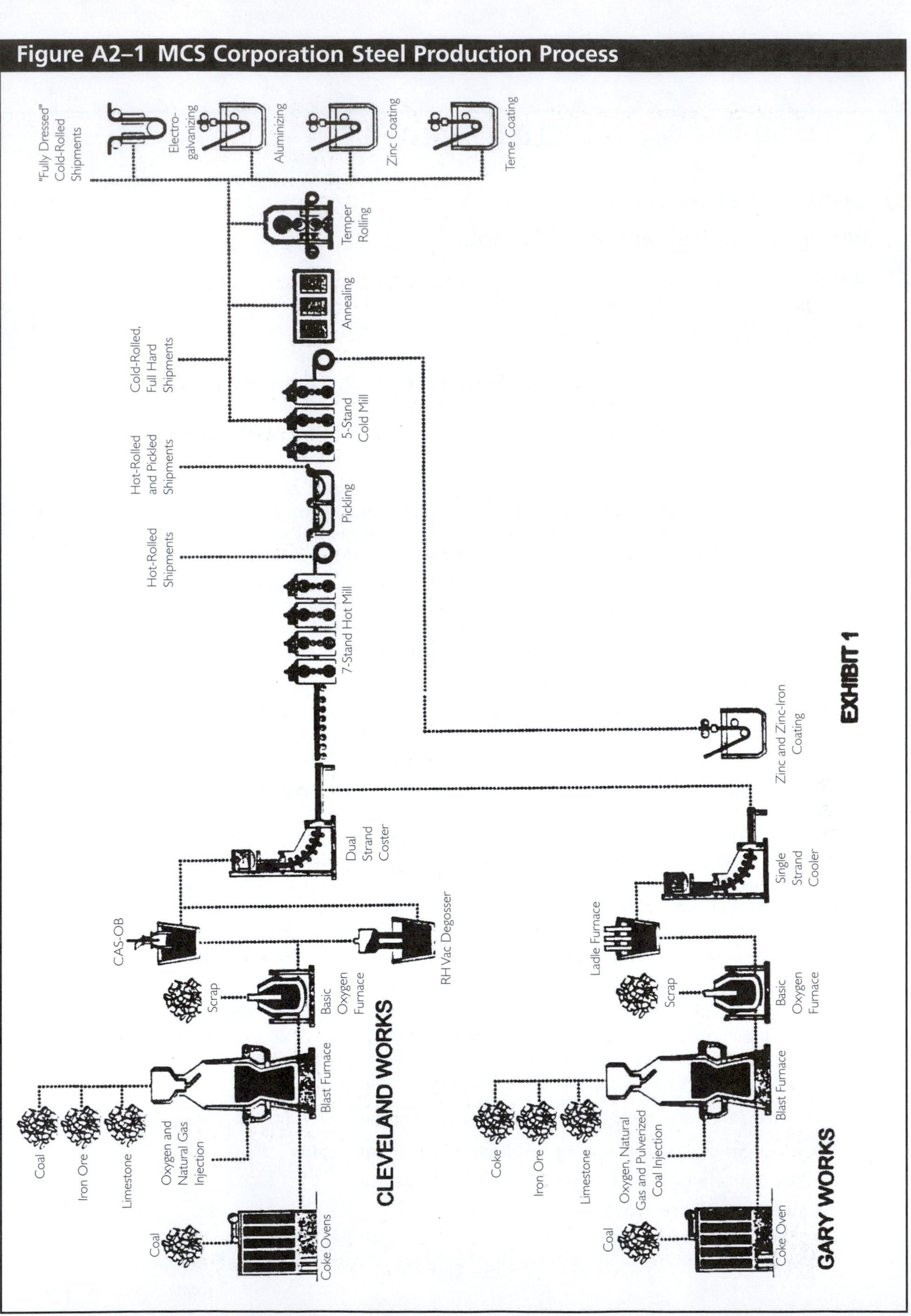

CLIENT PROFILE—MCS *(continued)*

Customers and Channels

The following is the mix of MCS's 1995 shipments to key market segments:

Segment	*$ Sales (M)*	*%*	*Tons*
Automotive	$1,178	42	1,960,000
Appliances	336	12	480,000
Construction	224	8	640,000
Distribution	1,066	38	2,095,000
Total	$2,804	100	5,175,000

In the automotive category, MCS sells to virtually all U.S.-located manufacturers. The "Big Three" represent 70 percent of automotive sales. General Motors is MCS's largest account. The distribution segment is made up of service centers and independent processors.

At $120 million, KAMCO is MCS's largest "implant" customer. This volume represents sales direct to KAMCO for U.S. production, as well as to parts manufacturers (such as Newtown, alias NAC) that sell to both KAMCO and KAPCO. KAMCO is able to leverage its own volume with that of its parts suppliers to purchase steel from MCS and other steelmakers at very competitive prices and terms. This arrangement is administered by KAMCO Trading Company and is known as the "KAMCO Steel System." KAMCO Trading buys the steel from MCS and resells it to its suppliers. MCS, though, has strong links to the parts producers and treats them as it would direct customers.

As depicted in Figure A2–2, the steel from MCS, which eventually ends up in KAMCO automobiles, can get there through several channels. First, it can be sold direct to KAMCO for OEM production. Second, it can be shipped to processors, who perform basic form changes such as slitting and blanking, and who, in turn, ship it to KAMCO or its suppliers. Third, shipments might be made to independent service centers that purchase, store, and convert it and then resell it to parts makers or OEM producers. Fourth, the steel might be shipped to any of the tiers of parts makers, who subsequently ship to a higher tier or to KAMCO or KAPCO.

MCS is extremely proud of the relationship it has developed with KAMCO. It was the first U.S. steel producer to be chosen as supplier to KAMCO. Learning the manufacturing methods and wisdom used by the automaker, as embodied in the "KAMCO way," has been important in MCS's success, even with other customers.

INDUSTRY ISSUES

Since the mid-1980s, when foreign steel producers deluged the U.S. market with high-quality, low-price product, U.S. steelmakers have been running hard and scared to get better. Many have failed, and many older, outmoded steel plants have been closed. On the other hand, though, many domestic producers, like MCS, have rallied and are reaching moderate degrees of success. The following is a short summary of key issues driving competitiveness and profitability.

(continued on next page)

Figure A2–2 Automotive Steel Supply Channels

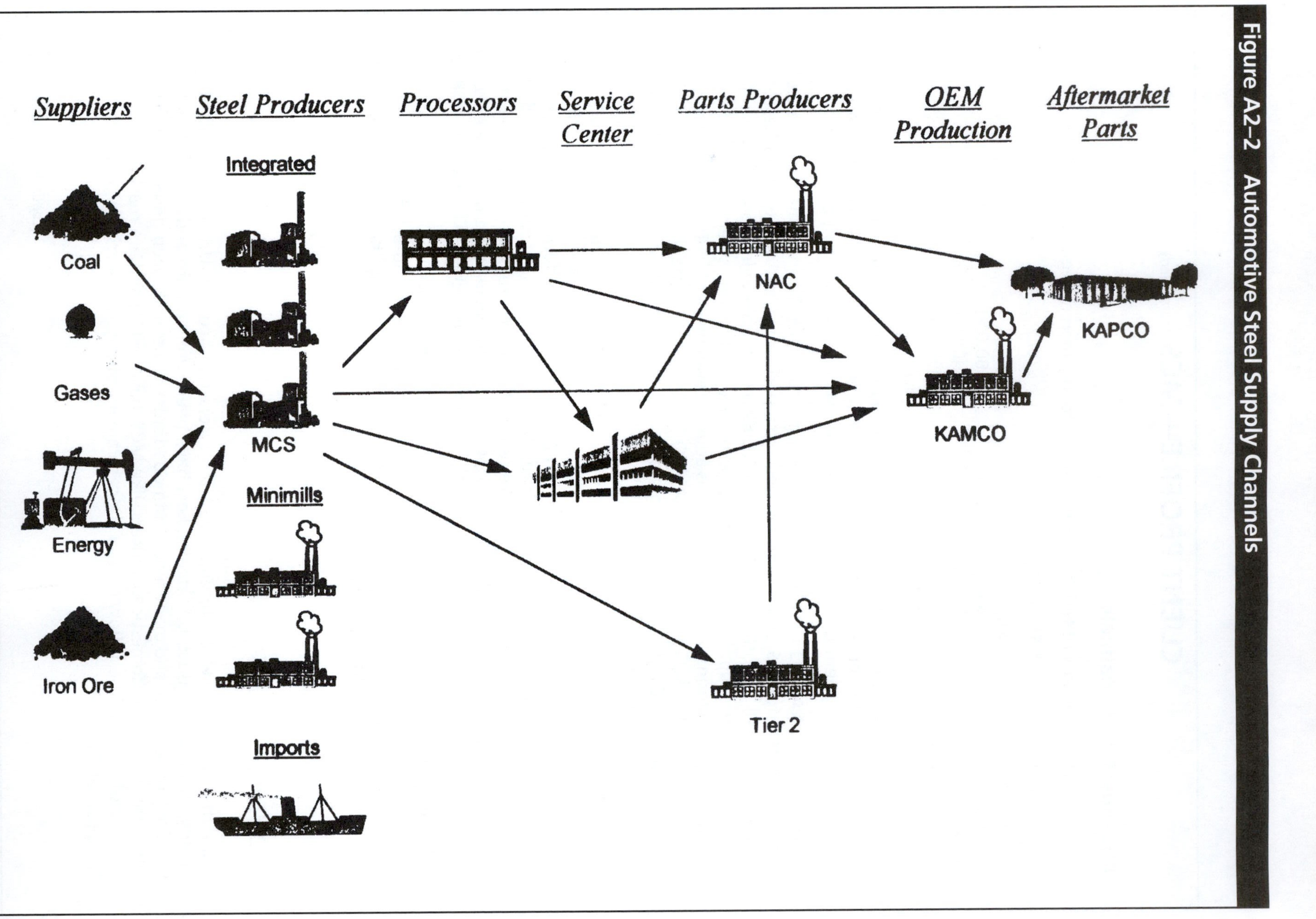

CLIENT PROFILE—MCS *(continued)*

Price Pressure

The Wall Street Journal recently noted, "Steel is a commodity. No matter how you roll it, cut it, or coat it, it is much the same, although variations in quality are important to some customers. To most, all that matters is price."[†] A major part of the problem is that the capital-intense structure and high fixed costs have driven producers to push out product, almost irrelevant of price or whether there is a waiting customer. The major producers are producing full bore but making little money.

Legacy Costs

The drastic trimming of facilities and workforces in the recent past has not been without ongoing cost effects. The shuttering and maintaining of old, environmentally contaminated plant sites are expensive. So is the burden of pension and insurance benefits for retirees and laid-off workers.

Environmental Compliance

The Clean Air Act of 1990 has also placed enormous strains on steel producers. The industry is now spending 15 percent of capital expenditures on environmental improvements. Strict standards for coke oven emissions, to be in place by 1998, have been particularly onerous.

Minimill Competition

As noted earlier, minimills have several advantages over integrated steel producers. They usually do not bear the legacy and environmental costs previously mentioned, and they usually operate with lower-priced labor. Their lower capital requirements also offer them more flexibility. They are growing rapidly and are causing industry supply to outstrip demand even more than usual.

Customer Requirements

Traditionally, makers of steel products, such as automakers and their suppliers, have looked to steelmakers only to deliver large steel coils to their manufacturing site on fairly comfortable schedules. Much steel production used to be on a "made-to-order" basis, rather than "made to inventory." Today, sophisticated manufacturers, perhaps exemplified by Japanese automakers such as KAMCO, are requiring their suppliers, and their suppliers' suppliers, to be as efficient and resourceful as they are—and to be integrated into their operations as if they were part of the same company. The philosophy and practice of "just in time" and "total quality management" have been driven down to all participants in the supply chain.

Steel customers are also asking producers to do more with the product. In some cases, slitting, blanking, and "cut-to-length" activities are being pushed back to steel producers. Many of these are activities the steelmakers recently "rationalized" out of their

[†]Earle Norton, "U.S. Steelmakers Run Mills Close to Capacity But Still Earn Little," *Wall Street Journal* (18 July 1996).

(continued on next page)

CLIENT PROFILE—MCS *(continued)*

operations, so they now are looking to third parties such as processors or service centers to perform them.

SUPPLY CHAIN ISSUES

Logistics and transportation play a key role in what is expected by customers of MCS and its products for two reasons. First, because of the low-value, high-density nature of most products, transportation expense is an important component of total product cost. Transportation expense in 1995 exceeded $450 million—over 15 percent of sales. Second, MCS's customers, many of which employ sophisticated, time-sensitive manufacturing processes, are looking more and more to their suppliers to improve logistics service levels.

Key supply chain activities at MCS include purchasing, inbound transportation, production scheduling, order management, inventory management, customer service, and outbound transportation. Organizationally, these activities reside in both the manufacturing and marketing departments.

Purchasing is responsible for the procurement of raw materials, energy, MRO (maintenance, repair and operating supplies), and capital expenditures. Principal raw materials and energy sources, which totaled $870 million in 1995, are iron ore, coke, limestone, scrap metal, natural gas, electricity, and industrial gases. Iron ore is sourced from Minnesota and South America. Two industrial gas producers have established operations contiguous to the MCS plants.

Inbound transportation of raw materials, which amounted to $260 million in 1995, is mainly by Great Lakes shipping and rail. A seasonal buildup of iron ore inventory is necessary to cover production needs during the winter months when shipping is not possible. Interplant transportation ($60 million) is mostly via rail, supplemented by a dedicated truck fleet. Outbound transportation is 70 percent truck, 25 percent rail, and 5 percent barge and was $130 million in 1995.

Raw materials are stored in yards and in transportation equipment at the plants. Warehousing of finished goods is accomplished both at the plants and at processors. Warehousing expense was $15 million in 1995. For key customers, such as those in the automotive industry, MCS maintains a 21- to 28-day supply of finished product. Average inventory levels for the year were as follows:

Raw materials	$205 million
MRO	50 million
Finished goods	178 million
Total	$433 million

A few important, current issues in front of logistics management at MCS follow.

Freight Bill Payment and Auditing

MCS is currently operating under a philosophy that requires management in all functional areas to consider outsourcing of all processes that are not considered "core competencies."

In this vein, the company recently outsourced the management of some fairly important activities, including information systems to EDS, the mail room and duplication activities to Kodak, MRO inventory management to Grainger, and traffic management for outbound truck deliveries to LogicCorp. Top management has a strong belief that the company needs to maintain a strong focus on steelmaking—and only steelmaking—and, indeed, this attitude has been a strong ingredient in MCS's recent success.

MCS has an internal department of six individuals who have the responsibility of matching bills of lading, proofs of delivery, and freight bills; verifying freight rates; authorizing payment; and handling carrier inquiries. The company pays nearly 200,000 freight bills per year. Accounts payable has begun to examine the feasibility of transferring the payment of freight bills to an outside specialist.

That investigation has yielded a few surprises. First, there are a number of well-respected companies that have been in the business of paying and auditing freight bills for a long time. A short list of major players includes Cass Logistics, Strategic Technologies, Barry & Lloyd, and TranZact. The industry developed because of the detail and complexity that is inherent in freight rates. Second, a few of the freight payment companies have evolved into being "third-party-logistics information resources." As a by-product of the bill payment process, they offer access to databases and detailed reports that are valuable in managing transportation. Transportation has been seeking this type of information capability. Third, a few of the freight payment companies have developed "paperless" arrangements, in which the carriers are paid immediately upon a notification that the delivery has been made, rather than generating and handling freight bills.

Several issues for MCS management to consider include:

- What factors should be taken into account in a study to examine whether MCS should outsource the payment of freight bills?
- Who should be involved with this decision?
- If outsourcing is decided upon as the logical step, how do we go about selecting a vendor?
- What will our internal and public auditors think about moving an important control activity to an outside resource? What will their concerns be?

Forecasting and Information Exchange

MCS recently empowered a small cross-functional team to examine and make improvement recommendations for the way MCS forecasts demand and plans production. The team includes Sally Wright, a sales rep; Dennis Poorman, an accountant; Kim Agnelli, from information systems; Pradeep Khan, marketing; and Eric Smoltz, production planning. A particular challenge to the team was to find a way to reduce the large inventories in place to support customers that operate on a JIT basis. Following is an internal MCS memorandum describing the discussion at the first meeting of the team.

MCS CORPORATION CLEVELAND, OHIO
Internal Memorandum

Date: 30 April 1996

To: Team members

From: Eric Smoltz

Subject: Demand forecasting and production planning team

In an attempt to capture the essence of the discussions from our first meeting, I am using a dialogue approach because it may best illustrate the relative functional stances that were represented. In the event that I have not properly captured your thoughts or positions, please contact me.

At our first meeting, we, members of the team, offered several different perspectives:

Sally: We really don't need to forecast demand. We are already getting lots of information from customers. Take, for example, NAC. They are a parts maker that is part of the KAMCO Steel System. NAC gets multiyear, annual, and monthly forecasts from KAMCO and then generates and sends a three-month forecast to KAMCO Trading, who then sends it on to me. We also get a weekly release from them on Fridays, which tells us what to ship for each day of the following week. Isn't this good enough?

Also, I'm not optimistic about being able to reduce inventory. There are huge penalties if we fail to deliver product on the days they specify. Our inventory is needed to make their JIT system work.

Kim: I'm a great believer in the premise that timely and accurate information can be used to replace assets such as inventory. There has to be a way that we can cut into all that product we are holding for customers such as NAC. Wouldn't getting forecasts and production schedules directly from KAMCO help?

Eric: That kind of information will help, but it might not be enough. We presently lock in our production schedule a month in advance. Also, part of the problem is the lack of visibility of inventory up through the supply chain. We have a good grasp of what we are holding here at the plant, but we don't always know what our processors are holding or how much a customer like NAC is holding. I have this belief that if we *did* know, if we were able to see it all, that we could at least cut out some of the duplication of safety stocks.

Pradeep: Isn't part of the challenge here *how* we get our information? If it were more systematized, couldn't we do more with it? Have we given enough thought to adding more capability with *electronic data interchange*—EDI?

Sally: That's a good thought. I believe that we are going to have to get more involved with EDI anyway. The "Big 3" recently put out an edict to their suppliers that says that the top-tier suppliers will have to implement EDI with *their* suppliers—and that's us.

CLIENT PROFILE—MCS *(continued)*

TABLE A2–3 MCS Corporation Selected Financial and Operating Data, 1995

1. Revenue	$ 2,804,000,000
2. Operating income	$ 362,000,000
3. Inventory	$ 433,000,000
4. Property, plant, equipment	$ 1,887,000,000
5. Employees	
Salaried	250
Hourly	5,900
6. Inventory turns	3.1
7. On-time delivery	(Not measured)
8. Order fill rate	98.5%
9. Freight expense	$ 450,000,000
10. Warehouse operating expense	$ 15,000,000

Dennis: EDI is awfully expensive to implement. There is hardware, software, and training. We are tight on resources. There will have to be more to justify it than just reduced inventories. Also, it's my understanding that EDI is just used to ship orders from one company to another. Is this what we need?

I wonder, too, what our outside auditors are going to think about EDI. Will they think that "going paperless" is a precursor to losing control and accountability?

Newtown Advance Components, Inc. (NAC)

Karl was also absorbed by the agenda he was preparing for his visit to one of Kobe's critical components suppliers. It was evident that this firm, Newtown Advanced Components, was key because it bridged steel, a basic process industry, and automobile assembly and parts distribution—a relationship that probably caused Newtown to endure a high level of complexity.

When he went to the client profile folder, he was disappointed to find only the sketchiest information—certainly nowhere near as complete as he found with KAMCO and MCS Corporation. So far, however, he was starting to see the intense interconnectivity between customers and suppliers.

"Sounds simple enough," thought Karl, "but then again not too different than the arrangement that GM has had with Saginaw, Rochester, or Delphi. The only difference is that Kobe doesn't own the whole enchilada. This visit should be interesting."

CLIENT PROFILE

Client: Newtown Advanced Components, Inc.

Writer: J. L. Cavinato and R. R. Young

Date: June 12, 1996

BACKGROUND

Founded in 1985, Newtown was capitalized by Kobe and Narita Advanced Components of Japan for the sole purpose of supplying complex components with each holding an initial 50 percent interest. Through his research, Karl knew that Narita was an important, long-term supplier of similar items to Kobe's Japanese operations. In Japan, their relationship goes back to 1949 when industrial activity was beginning to be rebuilt following the war.

Narita and Kobe have several similar ventures. The first was established in Australia during the mid-1980s and followed later with operations in Brazil and South Africa. A plant is currently under construction in the Ukraine, plus one is planned for the People's Republic of China.

Component manufacturers in general and NAC in particular produce automotive components that combine structural, electrical, and fluid-handling capabilities into a single unit in order to facilitate final vehicle assembly. Production requires expertise in multiple technologies such as metal stamping, welding, polymer injection molding, and assembly. The purchase of assembled components, such as electronics, is carried out where specific expertise or other scale economies must be achieved.

NAC sells to two Kobe units: KAMCO for OEM, and KAPCO for replacement parts furnished to authorized Kobe dealers. Exact replacement parts must be sourced from the producer of the OEM parts; however, the volume of the former far exceeds that of the latter. Production is always scheduled where parts orders are overruns of OEM. Distribution is simple as KAMCO has only two assembly plants and KAPCO fifteen regional warehouses.

Selected financial information and operating data can be found in Table A2–4.

The Visit

"Mr. van Pelt, we have been looking forward to your visit. My name is Masao Ishida. Please, my card." Karl accepted the card, presenting one of his own in return.

"Before discussing our agenda items, it might be helpful to take a plant tour. You can get a better idea of the product and the processes we employ to make it," said Ishida. Following his host onto the production floor, Karl immediately was struck by the amount of activity but also by the low levels of inventory, both raw materials as well as finished goods. The plant covered 300,000 square feet and contained modern equipment in a clean, well-maintained working environment. "Easy to do when you start from scratch," Karl said to himself.

TABLE A2–4 Newtown Advanced Components, Inc., Selected Financial and Operating Data for Calendar Year 1995

1. Revenue	$250,000,000
2. Operating income	$12,000,000
3. Inventory	$4,000,000
4. Initial capitalization	$50,000,000
5. Shareholders	
Narita Advanced Components	50%
Kobe Automotive (Japan) Ltd.	50%
6. Employees	
Salaried	65
Wageroll	500
7. Plants	
Number	1
Age	12 years
Square feet	300,000
8. Delivery performance (KAMCO only)	
Timeliness	100.0%
Quality	>99.9%

"How many different products do you make here?" Karl queried. "Fifteen major components for three different models, or forty-five in all. Since some individual items are used on more than one Kobe, there are not as many assembly items as you might think," came the reply.

They stood for a moment watching injection molded parts eject from a machine, the cavity close, and a new shot of resin get measured and injected. "There aren't that many molding machines here," said Karl. "How do you accommodate all of the various parts?"

Ishida answered, "It's really quite simple. We sourced special machines so that we could do changeovers in about twelve minutes. That's time from shutting down the machine, changing molds, restarting, and running acceptable parts. Our competitors take upwards of three hours." As Ishida was talking, Karl did notice that all of the machinery—stamping presses, molding presses, industrial robots and welders—had been sourced in Japan.

"What union represents the workers? I assume United Auto Workers," exclaimed Karl.

On the contrary, NAC is a nonunion operation. There are no job classifications here, and everyone earns the same hourly wage. NAC prides itself for being competitive in the area, and we are generous with benefits," came the reply, much to Karl's surprise. Ishida continued, "We have low turnover and a very steady level of staffing. Since our founding, we have never laid off any full-time associate because we use temporaries to accommodate the expansions and contractions of the market. We've had some minor union organizing efforts, but nothing of any consequence—what would it get anyone?"

(*continued on next page*)

CLIENT PROFILE—NEWTOWN *(continued)*

On the way back to the conference room, they passed a bulletin board full of process control charts; but it also contained three larger graphs that NAC was evidently pleased to display. Karl knew what statistical process control charts were but asked his host to explain the larger graphs.

"These are the basis for our profitability," said Ishida. "We need a safe working environment, so we measure reportable lost-time accidents. Below this target," he said pointing to a plot on the graph, "everyone gets a plant-wide bonus. We use the same technique on the other two charts in measuring deliveries and quality."

Karl stepped back to look more carefully at the whole chart. It was eight feet wide—clearly something that was intended for everyone to notice. In amazement, Karl said, "If I understand this correctly, you have only one month this year with any defects and no missed shipments."

Ishida smiled, "Quite correct. In March we shipped some mismarked product. It was only one pallet, but each part gets counted as a defect. Luckily we discovered it before the truck made its delivery and we were able to recover without Kobe being the one to discover the error."

"How did you recover? NAC clearly doesn't have any inventory. Besides, you needed to get the right components to Kobe," said Karl.

"In fact we do have some latitude. We normally will have one shift's requirement on hand here with Kobe keeping another half shift at their plant. Also, we keep two day's raw material inventory here and expect our suppliers to maintain a quantity equal to one shipment at their location," said Ishida with an apparent full command of the subject.

COMPETITIVE ISSUES

Upon returning to the conference room, Karl was keen to understand more about the role of NAC's suppliers. Sure, the production floor looked efficient enough, but he had seen enough just-in-time situations to know that all too frequently customers push inventories back up the supply chain onto their suppliers. Ultimately, it forced someone to become inefficient, or even worse, too expensive. Moreover, he had many misgivings about the close ties between Kobe and NAC.

"Thank you for the tour, Mr. Ishida. But, please tell me how much pressure does Kobe put on you to be competitive? It doesn't sound too serious when you're part of the family so-to-speak."

"On the contrary, Kobe is always pressing us for lower prices and quality improvements. They may not go out for competitive bids, but they expect that we will have a program of continuous improvement that will cut our costs and ultimately our prices. We practice price-based costing, not cost-based pricing. Kobe is extremely aggressive on this issue. Our relationship may be long and solid, but I must perform to their expectations, which are the same as those between Kobe-Japan and Narita," explained Ishida.

"Our two companies have very high levels of cooperation. For example, at Kobe's research and design center, it is common for us to have as many as twelve resident NAC engineers who work side-by-side with engineers from Kobe and their other major suppliers on the development of new models. These are called 'guest engineers' and are on our payroll. They guarantee that whatever Kobe designs we have the capability to supply, but also we have sufficient lead time to develop our own capability to do it well." Ishida elaborated, "This is not possible in your traditional three-bid purchasing system."

"OK, this sounds good so far. But what about your suppliers? How do you keep them honest? How do you know that your prices are competitive?" asked Karl.

"Perhaps the best thing to do is to call in our head of purchasing and you can ask him yourself," said Ishida.

A few minutes later, Karl was introduced to Hugh Koblenz. As purchasing manager, Hugh had spent time in the heavy truck segment of the industry and for a time worked in Europe.

Karl thought for a moment, formulating his question with some care. "I understand the relationship that NAC has with Kobe—it clearly goes back to Japan and has nearly a fifty-year track record. But what kind of relationships does NAC have domestically? All of the U.S. suppliers must operate on the traditional three-bid approach. How can this ever work?"

"Actually, Karl, it's quite easy," started Hugh. "Once suppliers get used to working with our methods, they rather like it. But, you're right—it is different, especially at first. Consider, for example, that we are presently looking to add a second customer. Before executing such a decision, we held many lengthy meetings with KAMCO management."

Karl nodded his head in agreement, and Hugh continued, "I know that you've been through the plant with Mr. Ishida so you understand what we make and how we make it. Our purchasing requirements are really rather limited—we need plastic resin, coils of steel, some small steel stampings, electronic assemblies, and paint for raw materials. Also, since most of our equipment is Japanese, we need to be aware of spare parts and tooling issues."

"OK," said Karl, "everyone's on board getting you competitive prices except the parts and tool suppliers—which leads me to ask why you sourced Japanese machinery in the first place. Obviously, both NAC and Kobe are Japanese firms and that's what they feel comfortable with, but was that such a good idea?"

"In fact, it was most logical," explained Ishida, "because Kobe started by satisfying the U.S. market with Japanese-built finished vehicles. The components supplied by NAC in Japan were made on the same equipment as you saw earlier; hence, when Kobe transitioned its manufacturing to the United States, they wanted the same quality no matter if a part was made here or there."

"I might add," said Hugh, "that this becomes even more important in the parts industry where one of ours might be used on a Japanese-built Kobe Starfire."

"All well and good, but doesn't the long supply line present problems for you, at least relative to what a domestic supplier could provide?" asked Karl. "Besides, I don't know if your argument holds water because the raw materials are sourced domestically!"

Hugh reached for a blank sheet of paper and said, "Let me show you the way we differentiate purchasing objectives. This is a simple way to explain our purchasing, and, while I first encountered it when a consultant visited with us when I worked for another firm in Germany, I have since seen it applied elsewhere, even in Japan." Hugh drew a simple two-by-two matrix on the paper and labeled one axis "risk"; the other, "value-added."

(*continued on next page*)

CLIENT PROFILE—NEWTOWN *(continued)*

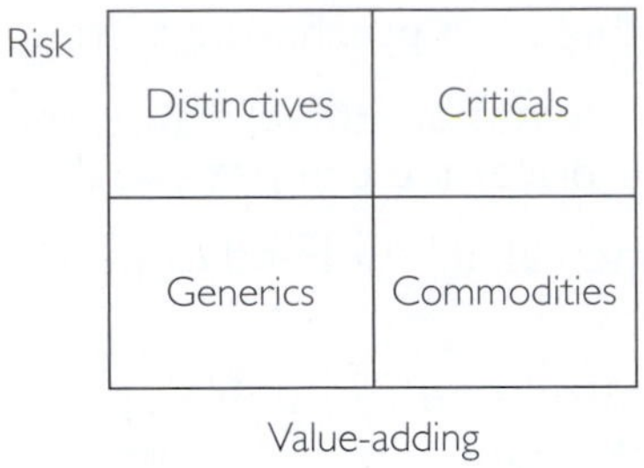

Risk		
	Distinctives	Criticals
	Generics	Commodities
	Value-adding	

Hugh then continued, "We can also call something that is value-adding an item that has higher profit potential, but what is important is the four combinations that this represents. For example, low risk and low value-adding potential should sound like something that we shouldn't spend a lot of effort on—many generic maintenance, repair, and operating (MRO) supplies fit this description. These are situations where the value of the goods is frequently less than the internal cost of processing a purchase order."

"OK," said Karl. "What about something that is low risk but high value-adding? How do you handle that?"

"In fact, there are some of those. For example, our paint is such a commodity because we can specify a solvent type and with computer color matching systems can achieve absolute interchangeability. Karl," said Hugh, "paint may be the only item I can buy on price and I use all of the suppliers on the market."

"Steel and plastic resins aren't in this category then?" asked Karl.

Hugh thought only a quick moment and said, "They approach it but really aren't. We've discovered that certain manufacturers's resins work better than others do in the molding presses. A savings on price doesn't do anything for us if it slows down the process and creates more scrap. As for steel, it's pretty much the same thing because we've learned that rolling oils, gauge tolerances, and specific heats from specific mills work better than others. If we bought on price, we'd probably hurt our own profitability. Quality, especially as performance, is important."

This was indeed a touchy subject because Ishida interjected, "These items are of such importance in terms of quality that KAMCO has taken the supplier relationships back in-house. They establish contracts, and we release from those."

"This is interesting stuff, but it sure complicates my life as an auditor. It means that each process is unique and every operation that I get to visit will require a different type of analysis. I'm not sure that I'm all that comfortable with what you just laid out before me!" complained Karl, but then he continued. "You were kind enough to explain this to me, but I think we have two more quadrants to discuss. Let's see. My guess is that the electronic assemblies are high risk and high value-adding. Performance in the customer's hands is important because failure could persuade the customer to buy a competitor's automobile next time around."

"Good call," said Hugh, "but, tell me, do I have any in the low-value, high-risk quadrant?"

"Probably not, although previously I would have thought that the spare parts for your Japanese equipment could have been such. I can sense that those do add value even though the risk may be higher than the domestic sources," said Karl.

"Another good observation," added Hugh, "but in fact we have no purchased items currently in that category. We once did, but it takes a constant effort to prevent that from occurring. Ishida explained to you about the guest engineers, and I can tell you that these guys are adamant that we don't paint ourselves into one of those corners."

"But what about services?" asked Karl. "I know that any organization, whether it is manufacturer or service provider, requires the use of outside services such as janitorial, equipment maintenance, and transportation. How do these fit into your matrix?"

"This indeed can be a difficult question. We've seen other organizations discuss this issue endlessly," interjected Ishida. "For example, we looked at plant housekeeping, you might call it janitorial service, and found that it represented a high level of risk when not present but also had the potential of adding great value. You saw that the plant is spotlessly clean and that all employees wear white uniforms. This is for a reason: neat premises tend to produce higher levels of quality. The color white is most revealing and is therefore the most demanding in terms of establishing discipline. As a consequence, we have no external janitorial service; each work area is responsible for its own."

"OK, so it's simple, but how do you exchange transactional information with Kobe and with suppliers?" asked Karl, again thinking of the EDI demands that many automakers had been placing on their suppliers.

"Well, we have two blanket orders—one each from KAMCO and KAPCO," explained Ishida. "Each provides a three-year forecast that is updated every three months. These are exploded by our bill of material and passed on to suppliers to allow them to make commitments to their suppliers and to allocate capacity. In the short term, Kobe provides us with weekly shipping schedules that we also pass on. With only one customer and just several suppliers, EDI does not make much sense for us. Constant contact does, and we view suppliers as our own external manufacturing capacity."

"But," interjected Karl, "you are still working on a transactional basis."

"Yes and no," came the reply. "We pay our suppliers on an order-for-order basis and match purchase orders, receipts, and invoices like everyone else. We also pay inbound carriers on that basis, but, having outsourced our distribution to a third party, we only pay them on a monthly invoice."

"So how do KAMCO and KAPCO pay NAC?" asked Karl. "Order-for-order or monthly invoice?"

"Monthly invoice," replied Hugh, noting that processing a great number of invoices does not add value even if it does improve cash flow—assuming, of course, that everyone pays according to the stated terms of sale. He added, "In Kobe's case, they use electronic funds transfer exactly on the invoice due date. With that kind of predictability, we know specifically what our cash flows will be."

(*continued on next page*)

CLIENT PROFILE—NEWTOWN *(continued)*

CLOSING

"Thank you for the tour and the candid conversation—although it may lead to more questions than you may have answers," said Karl.

"Please call us if there is anything else you want to know. We do not feel particularly unique in what we do," replied Ishida.

As Karl walked down the path to his car, he could not help thinking about the implications for public accounting in general and auditing in particular. As he drove back to his own office, he made several mental notes of what he now wanted to explore further, including:

1. How might physical flow time be a more relevant measurement than working capital?
2. How can benchmarking effectively trade off difficult issues such as the janitorial one where $14/hour workers were chosen over $6/hour cleaners?
3. How can OEM and aftermarket flow effectiveness be measured when these represent two distinct types of operation in a joint situation?
4. Can the quadrant approach to purchasing effectively be employed by auditors? If so, how? Or is it a model that is far too subjective in that it is at the mercy of the eye of the beholder?

IMPLICATIONS

Your task is to assist your colleague in formulating answers to these particular issues. Most importantly, what are the reasons for supply chain theory dramatically affecting the ways in which you look at manufacturing operations, both in these specific industries and in others?

Case A3

Lexington Supply Company*

Lexington

George Pappas, president and founder of Lexington Supply Company (LSC), was becoming increasingly concerned over the future direction of the business. "Somehow," he thought to himself, "I've got to learn more about how supply chain management is going to impact LSC. The discomforting fact is that such impact is probably going to arrive much sooner than either I or anybody else in this organization is willing to admit."

Company Background

Lexington Supply Company (commonly referred to as LSC) is a regional distributor of pipes, valves, and fittings located in Lexington, Kentucky. The owner and CEO of the company is George Pappas. George's father-in-law, Alex Gilardi, founded LSC in the mid-1950s; and George joined the company as its treasurer and CFO in 1968 after getting an MBA at Wharton. The business has grown significantly through the years and is now approaching $50 million in annual revenue. The company operates throughout the state of Kentucky, southwestern Ohio, and southern Indiana, but its core business is in the triangle formed by Lexington, Louisville, and Cincinnati. The main offices and warehouse are in Lexington, but there are branches in Louisville and Cincinnati.

LSC's main business is in the general market for maintenance, repair, and operating (MRO) supplies. Its principal customers are large factories or plants that purchase its principal product line (pipes, valves, and fittings—or PVF) mainly for facility and equipment upkeep.

The business originally focused on the Lexington market for smaller-diameter copper pipe (1″ to 3″ in diameter) used in residential and commercial plumbing applications. By 1960, revenues had grown to over $1 million.

---

*This case was prepared by William L. Grenoble, Robert A. Novack, and Richard R. Young, all of the Center for Supply Chain Research, The Pennsylvania State University. Reproduced with the permission of the Center for Supply Chain Research, The Pennsylvania State University.

In 1962, medium-diameter pipe (4″ to 10″) had been added to the product line and LSC decided to open a branch in Cincinnati to focus on the southern and central areas of Ohio. Both the Lexington and Cincinnati locations inventoried a full range of products, and there were little or no inventory transfers between sites.

By 1965, revenues approached $5 million. In this year, LSC added large-diameter pipe (greater than 10″), including ductile iron and stainless steel, to its product line. Some of these were kept in inventory, but many were special order from the manufacturers.

In 1970, revenues reached $8 million. This was also about the time when fittings (essentially elbows, flanges, nipples, tees, "Y" connectors, and end caps) and valves were added to the product line in response to customer requests. Since some customers had locations throughout Kentucky and Ohio, this product line expansion precipitated the decision to open their third branch, this one in Louisville.

As the complexity of the business increased, an inventory analysis was performed that resulted in several key decisions being made:

1. Only *A* and *B* inventory items for pipes and fittings were to be kept at Cincinnati and Louisville.
2. All pipe with diameters of 10″ or greater were held in Lexington.
3. Interbranch transfers were now required between Lexington and the other two sites.

Revenues hit $10 million by 1974 when LSC added large-diameter ball, gate, and butterfly valves to its product offering. Fast-moving valve products were located in all three locations, and the slow-moving (*C*) items were held only in Lexington. Expanding the product line, however, allowed many customers to consolidate orders, with the result being a dramatic revenue increase between 1974 and 1998.

Organization

As president, George Pappas has the following five key managers reporting directly to him (also see Figure A3–1). Each is based in Lexington; however, note that their subordinates may actually be located at one of the branches:

Jamie "J. G." Curtis, purchasing manager
Laura Ashton, chief financial officer (CFO)
Bob Packer, sales manager
Callie Pappas, operations manager
Sam Gilardi, inventory manager

Laura has responsibility for all billing, collections, and payment responsibilities for all three locations. These activities are centralized in Lexington and include four full-time and one part-time employee. For sales, LSC is divided into four sales territories, each having its own sales representative located in the field and its own customer service representative at Lexington. These eight individuals report to Bob Packer. Callie oversees three distribution center (DC) supervisors, one transportation supervisor, and three transportation clerks. The DC supervisors and the three transportation clerks are located at the field locations. Sam has three inventory clerks reporting to him from the field locations. J. G. has a centralized purchasing operation consisting of three buyers, one for each product line.

FIGURE A3–1 LSC Organization Chart

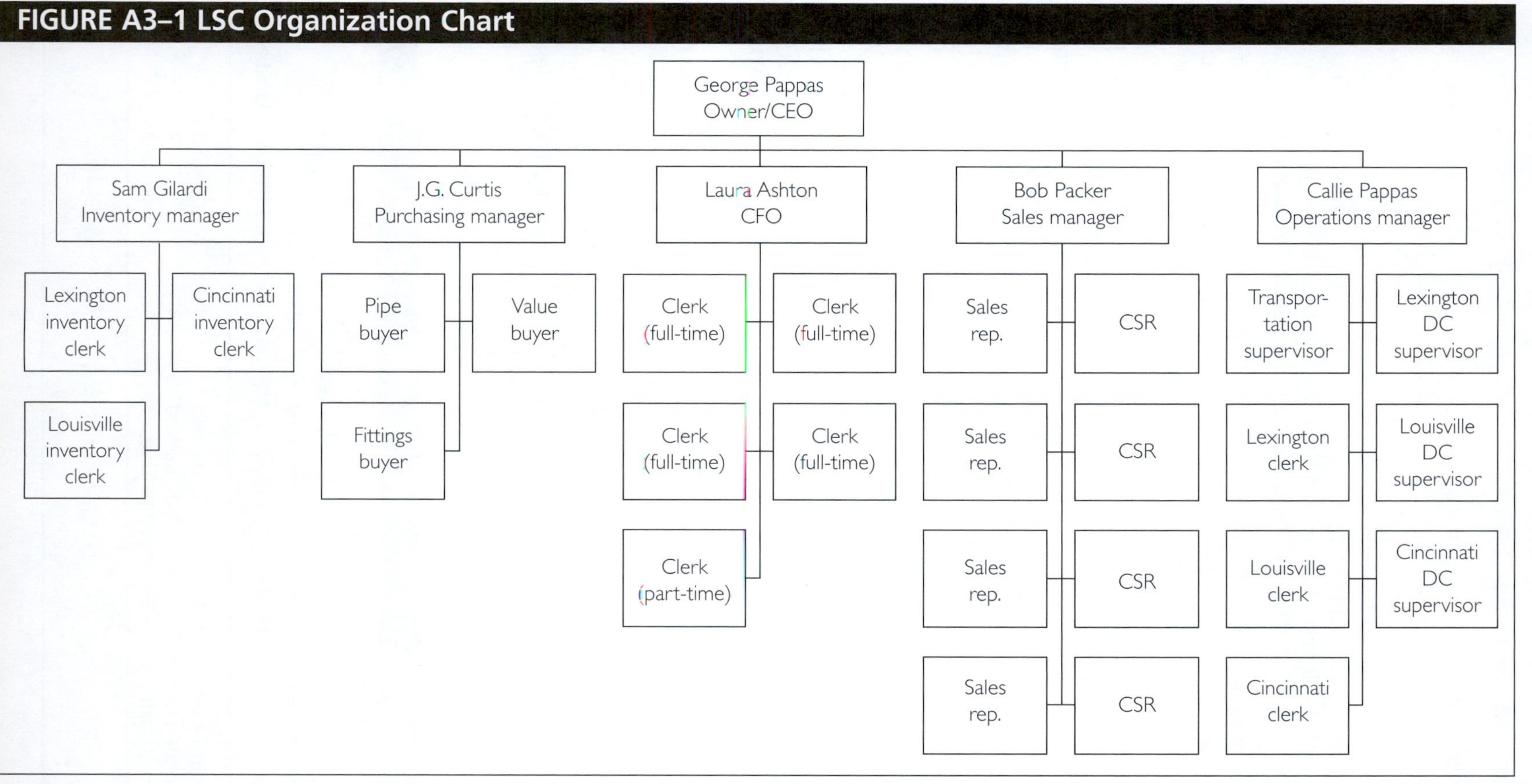

Supplier and Customer Bases

LSC suppliers are geographically dispersed across the United States. Suppliers for small- and medium-diameter pipe are located in Pittsburgh, Green Bay, and Minneapolis; large-diameter pipe suppliers in Flint, Michigan, and Huntsville, Alabama; and valve suppliers in Cleveland, Columbia, Georgia, Philadelphia, and Birmingham, Alabama. Each supplier carries a full range of sizes. Fittings suppliers are located in Toledo; Topeka, Kansas; and Houston. Like the valve suppliers, these suppliers also carry a full range of fittings, including different diameters and alloys.

Shipments of small and medium pipe are either less than truckload (LTL) or truckload (TL). Some of the TL moves are handled by 48′ or 53′ dry vans. Smaller-diameter pipe is loaded on returnable racks inside dry van trailers. LSC holds the racks until a full TL can be returned to the supplier. Because inclement weather has little effect on pipe, flatbed trailers carry TL medium- and large-diameter pipe orders. Flatbed trailers are difficult to obtain during certain times of the year because of demand swings in such industries as construction where the movement of structural steel and precast concrete can consume much of the available capacity. All regular orders for valves and fittings are shipped to LSC by LTL carriers. Special order valves for oversize pipe may be shipped either by TL or flatbed trailers. The shipment terms for inbound product are FOB origin.

LSC's customers are industrial plant sites ordering PVF suppliers for general maintenance, operations, and repair. LSC's service area is defined by Wheeling, West Virginia, and Roanoke, Virginia, on the east, Knoxville and Nashville on the south, St. Louis on the west, and Indianapolis and Columbus, Ohio, on the north. However, 70 percent of sales come from customers within a 135-mile radius of each LSC location. Driving this concentration is LSC's guarantee of next-day delivery within this area.

A private fleet of trucks is maintained for customer deliveries and interbranch transfers. Table A3–1 shows the kinds of vehicles, numbers of units, and base of operation. Tractor-trailer combinations each drive 50,000 miles per year at a unit cost of $1.45 resulting in $115,000 or $1,860,000 for the fleet when the cost of the additional five trailers is included. Seven straight trucks are also in the fleet for local deliveries of smaller orders. These are driven approximately 25,000 miles per year each at $0.85 per mile for a total cost of $297,000.

Table A3–1 Private Fleet Statistics

	Tractors		Trailers		
Location	Type	Units	Type	Units	Straights Units
Lexington, Kentucky	Tandem axle	3	48′ flatbed	4	3
Louisville, Kentucky	Tandem axle	2	48′ flatbed	3	2
Cincinnati, Ohio	Tandem axle	2	48′ flatbed	3	2
Total units		7		10	7

All routing and dispatching of LSC's fleet are done manually by the transportation clerks at the branches. A contract with a national LTL carrier is used for those customer shipments not made with the private fleet. Total cost per year of the contract is $150,000. The total combined inbound and outbound total annual transportation expenditures are $2,657,500, or about 5.3 percent of revenue.

Customer Interface

Customers place all orders by phone or fax through the customer service representatives (CSRs) in Lexington. There are currently no customers submitting orders by EDI.

Upon arrival of an order, the CSR checks inventory availability at the designated shipping branch. Each branch takes inventory at the end of the day and reports it to Lexington each evening. If the inventory is available to fill the order complete at the primary shipping branch, the inventory is allocated to that order. If only part of the inventory is available at the primary shipping branch, the CSR will look at inventory levels at other branches. In the case of *C* items, the CSR will always check availability at Lexington. If the *C* item is available in Lexington, it will be put on the next scheduled interbranch transfer. If the vehicle reaches the primary delivery branch in time to match up the *C* item with the rest of the order, the order will be shipped complete to the customer. If it is not on time, the primary branch will deliver it as a split shipment.

If LSC does not have the inventory at any location (e.g., a special order pipe), a purchase order is created and forwarded to the buyer assigned to that commodity and supplier for placement. All customer orders and transfer orders are faxed to the appropriate branch each night.

Once the customer order is confirmed, it is sent to billing so an invoice can be created and mailed to the customer. Customers traditionally begin the payment process when their purchase order is matched with the delivery receipt and the invoice. If this matching process is successful, the customer will generate a check and mail it to LSC. If it is not, the customer calls the CSR to rectify the discrepancy.

Supplier Interface

Inventory control at the branches uses a min/max system with ending inventories reported to Lexington nightly. Replenishment orders are generated by the branch inventory clerk but are typically placed by the appropriate buyer. LSC purchase orders are normally transmitted to the respective suppliers each morning by phone or fax. Special orders and emergency shipments are always telephoned. LSC has EDI capability for purchase orders but only uses this with its largest supplier, Ajax Valve. Normal replenishment orders have specified lead times from each supplier. If the promised lead time cannot be met, the supplier will notify LSC of the actual delivery date. On special order and emergency shipments, lead times are given to the buyer who subsequently informs the CSR and/or the delivering branch of the expected delivery date.

LSC uses a payment process that is very similar to the one used by its customers. Invoices are generated based on as-shipped dates and mailed to LSC for processing.

Ajax Valve, the current exception, has begun using EDI to send invoices to LSC and, while developing the capability, cannot yet receive funds this way (EFT). When the LSC branch receives the shipment, the delivery receipt is compared to the purchase order. If they match, these documents are sent to LSC Lexington to be matched with the invoice. If all documents match, a check is generated and mailed to the supplier.

Stevenson Carbon Corporation

"I'm not surprised at what you're telling me," said Joe Cioffi to the group of consultants seated around the table in the conference room. "I know we spend a lot of time on supplies purchases and we apparently don't get it right too often either. Maintenance at all of the plants has complained about purchasing for so many years that I started to believe that it was just cultural."

Joe looked through the hard copy of the presentation one more time, took a deep breath, and finally said, "OK, we know we have a problem. Supplies purchasing costs us too much, and the service is poor. So what can we do about it?"

Background

Stevenson Carbon was founded in 1910 by Duncan Stevenson, a Scottish immigrant who had earned a degree in chemistry at Edinburgh University. Believing that there was a better, more economical method to manufacture asphalt and related products, he established his first plant near Pittsburgh. The Stevenson Process, as it was called in the patent, took crude tar, a by-product of steelmaking, and fractionally distilled it into asphalt, refined pitch, and a lesser range of benzenoid chemicals.

As it turned out, Stevenson's timing could not have been better. The growing U.S. population required improved roofing materials for its expanding cities; and, not too many years later, large quantities of asphalt were needed to support road-building, which used a new material invented by a fellow Scot named MacAdam.

Although growth had pretty much leveled off by the 1990s, Stevenson was a profitable firm with sales approaching $620 million annually. In addition to Pittsburgh, the company had plants, generally found in close proximity to steel mills—namely, in Gary, Indiana; Paducah, Kentucky; Baltimore, Maryland; and Birmingham, Alabama. Crude tar was purchased from Bethlehem, USSteel, LTV, and AK.

The process was essentially a closed one, but, because of the heat employed as well as the very nature of the material, it demanded significant, continuous streams of supplies to keep in operation. A breakdown of the categorizes and their respective annual corporate expenditures can be found in Table A3–2.

Organization

Each plant had a purchasing agent; but, despite the name, each was only in charge of supplies as raw materials were negotiated at the corporate level and released as needed by the plant manager. Similarly, capital equipment was specified, sourced,

TABLE A3–2 Stevenson Carbon, Inc., Breakdown of MRO Expenditures

Pipe, valves and fittings	$5.2 million
Electrical supplies	1.2
Filters and strainers	1.2
Bearings	0.6
Welding & grinding supplies	0.4
Safety, health & environmental	0.2
Vehicle parts and tires	0.2
Misc. chemicals, cleaning, janitorial	0.1
Total	$9.1 million

and negotiated by the plant engineer; although, in this case, purchasing did issue the confirming purchase order.

Reporting directly to the plant manager, purchasing agents typically had four people working for them: usually a pair of purchasing clerks plus a pair of storeroom clerks, one of whom was considered lead clerk. This latter pair was responsible for receiving, put away, issues, maintaining inventory records, and occasionally delivering items to specific work sites.

Purchasing Process

Requisitions authorizing purchases arrive at purchasing from one of two sources: the storeroom or directly from the requisitioner. Direct requests are made when there is no known stock in the storeroom or when the requisitioners suspect that there are no stocks in the storeroom but may not have checked.

Established practice is for all items over $500 to be placed only after three quotations have been obtained. The purchasing agent or more likely one of the clerks will obtain quotes for items of much lesser value when they believe that greater savings potential exists. While price is an import driver of purchasing decisions, delivery will take precedence when supplies are urgently required. Although occasionally attempted, purchasing will not compromise on specified quality unless substantial savings may be available by doing so. Usually, such a decision becomes the basis for major political battles between purchasing and engineering—battles frequently needing resolution at the plant manager level.

Purchase order cycle time is an important consideration and, like many purchasing environments, most people "want it yesterday." The quoting process frequently slowed down cycle time as many times a supplier would need to make further inquiry and call the buyer back, or the buyer and seller would "play telephone tag"—all to the frustration of the maintenance technicians, but all to the detriment of purchasing's reputation.

But there was another source of irritation: maintenance felt that purchasing did not adequately understand the items they were being asked to buy; nor did they understand how those items were used within the plant. The problem—at least in the opinion held by the technicians—was that purchasing did not get out of its office to go learn these things. The purchasing agents more or less agreed with this view but claimed that they were too "snowed under" with work to be able to afford that particular luxury, however useful it might be.

Finally, there was the issue of supplier invoices. While Stevenson used a computerized general ledger system, accounts payable remained archaic with manual matches of purchase orders, receiving tickets, and supplier invoices being made at each plant. If all three exactly matched, an on-line voucher screen was prepared and transmitted to Pittsburgh where checks were printed and mailed. In those instances where exact matches were not achieved, purchasing was instructed to resolve the discrepancies, arrange for revised documentation, and return everything to accounting for vouchering. Current estimates reveal that in excess of 20 percent of the match attempts fail on first try.

Storeroom Process

All inventoried items are kept in locked storerooms. Whenever maintenance technicians require an item, they go to the storeroom, submit an approved requisition for the item in exchange for the its receipt, and return to their worksite, which in some situations may be close to a quarter-mile away. The requisition subsequently becomes the reordering authorization to replace in inventory the item that had been issued.

Frequently, however, the item may not be in stock, in which case the requisition is forwarded to purchasing where the item is sourced and an order placed. Other times, because of a pressing need, such as in the case of an emergency shutdown, the technician would request admission to the storeroom and attempt to "engineer on the fly" a solution to the problem from what appeared to be immediately available parts.

Some items in the storeroom are kept on the inventory system, but many have been in stock since before the system was implemented; hence, these records, some perhaps having been maintained on Kardex or others not at all, are unreliable at best. The result, of course, is that some items are found in two places in the storeroom: one where the system controls inventory; the other, where the old stores are kept. Either way, there appears to be much wasted effort in searching for items or for keeping unnecessarily large quantities on hand.

The Cost Meeting

"Look at this!" Geoff Staley, one of the staff consultants looking at MRO purchasing, exclaimed looking at the totals column on his computer spreadsheet. "It costs Stevenson over $251 per purchase order once we account for all the effort that goes into the total procurement cycle." (See Table A3–3.)

"There has to be something wrong with that," came Joe's reply in utter disbelief. "We ran a similar analysis about two years ago and felt that $68 was pretty close to 'right-on.'"

TABLE A3–3 Cost Elements of MRO Procurement Cycle

Defining the Purchase	$31
Defining the demand or need	
Prepare specification	
Qualification of suppliers	
Determining If Item in Stock	$57
Search inventory record	
Physically look in storeroom	
Ordering	$47
Solicit prices & determine availability	
Place orders & prepare documents	
Expedite orders	
Receive Orders	$26
Complete receiving ticket	
Contact requisitioner	
Put away in inventory	
Deliver/place item at jobsite	
Prepare Payment	$32
Receive invoices	
Match documents	
Input voucher data	
Print checks	
Mail checks	
Resolve mismatches	
Stores Inventory	$58
Inventory holding costs	
Putaway costs	
Retrieval costs	
Recordkeeping costs	
Total	$251

"But what did you include?" queried Bob. "Writing the requisition, submitting it to purchasing, placement of the order, receipt of the goods, and payment of the invoice?"

"That's exactly the way we measured it. Costs of operating the purchasing department and accounts payable plus some portion of time for completion of requisitions by the user, but that didn't amount to much," said Joe.

"But how much time does the technician take looking for the stuff he needs or calling various suppliers trying to find something that may work? You have to take a look at purchasing as a process that many people do small parts of. It's not just a department with a name on the door."

"That's true," replied Joe.

"Geoff also included inventory considerations. There's a lot of stuff in the storeroom that has been obsolete for years, and there's even more that you carry too much in inventory. All that eats into working capital but also puts a demand on storeroom space—space that the clerks claim they don't have."

"And don't forget the informal inventories," Geoff reminded the two others. "When maintenance guys strike out too often at the storeroom, they find ways to protect themselves such as building their own little cache of critical items. A friend of mine refers to these as the 'maintenance closets,' but they're really located all over the plant. It's like squirrels hiding nuts."

"OK, you've made your point," said Joe. "What else does your analysis show?"

"Well," began Geoff, "of the thousands of purchase orders we've looked at, the median had a face value of only $158. That means Stevenson is paying $251 to place an order for $158! Doesn't sound like a very good deal to me, especially when your internal customers are complaining about the service."

"I hear what you guys are saying, but what can we possibly do about it?"

"We've seen some interesting developments along this line. For one, some of the major oil companies such as Amoco have been implementing something called integrated supply. It takes purchasing out of the transaction loop by using some carefully selected suppliers who are connected to both you and to each other electronically. The idea is to simplify both the process and the supplier relationship to the point that they will maintain on-site inventories close to the point of use. The stocks are replenished on a pre-established schedule and summary billed to you monthly."

"You know, now that I think about it, there was an article in *Purchasing Magazine* about something like this being implemented at Bethlehem Steel," Joe thought outloud.

"That is one of the better-known ones," said Geoff. "But you already have a plant that's fooling with it but probably doesn't recognize it as such. Paducah has its pipe, valves, and fittings (PVF) wholesaler placing a locked trailer on the plant property. Each electrical foreman has a key and just takes what's needed. The supplier checks the usage and replenishes every Wednesday morning. Gus Schmidt (the Paducah chief engineer) seems to like it a lot."

"Let's see. What will it take to formally expand this into a formal program encompassing a full range of items and ultimately implementing at all of our plants?" affirmed Joe.

Lexington Meets with Stevenson

Bob Packer, sales manager for Lexington, in filling his role as the national accounts manager, called on Joe Cioffi at Stevenson's headquarters near Pittsburgh. The purpose of such a visit was (1) to maintain the long-standing relationship between the two firms, and (2) to gain a better insight for the potential demand that the Stevenson plants anticipated during the next calendar quarter or two.

"We're starting to rethink the process we use to purchase MRO," began Joe, catching Bob quite unaware. "We have too many suppliers, too many transactions, too many internal resources committed, and too few dollars expended. Something has got to give somewhere. We've already conducted some in-house seminars and developed a cross-functional team consisting of those individuals having a vested interest in the outcome, and held some exploratory meetings with some potentially interested suppliers"

"But we've been suppliers to Stevenson for years," responded Bob, admittedly a bit defensively. "Lexington has always given you competitive prices and superior service. I can even remember taking phone calls at home in the middle of the night to keep Paducah running."

"True enough, Bob, and we really appreciate that, but we've got to find a better way," continued Joe. "We've got some consultants working with a team down at the Paducah plant. They're looking to find ways where we can work smarter—you know, simplify the business-to-business processes and perhaps add some of the latest, and now much more affordable, information technologies. I think that they're going to be ready to issue a request for proposal in the not too distant future."

"Well, I can tell you, Joe. We have at least one supplier who seems to be thinking in that same direction. I'm sure we'll be in here again soon with some intriguing ideas."

"I don't want to sound threatening, Bob," began Joe, "but the market is changing. Those suppliers who can't come up with new relationships, new ways of doing business, or approaches that add value all the way through the supply chain are going to be the ones to fall by the wayside. We just can't afford to do business that way any more."

Bob, now furiously taking notes, was already formulating the wording for his call report. "It sure won't make George Pappas's day when he reads this one," he thought to himself.

Proposal for Supplier Collaboration

A few days ago, the principals of LSC had attended a major presentation from one of their leading suppliers, Ajax Valve Company, on the subject of "vendor-managed inventories." Sales of the Ajax line represent about 15 percent of LSC's overall sales. The presentation described a new to program to allow for better information sharing and collaboration between LCS and Ajax based on a new concept called *collaborative planning, forecasting, and replenishment,* or CPFR. Ajax's program was called FASTER, the acronym for *forecasting and scheduling technique for efficient replenishment.*

In addition to Ajax's presentation, George had also recently read about a CPFR program called HOPS, which Heineken USA had implemented with its distributors. He had been impressed that Heineken had taken the initiative to develop the supply chain capability on behalf of its distributors and that, apparently, it was producing benefits for all parties.

Key features of FASTER are as follows:

- Communications will be via the Internet and a Web browser. The main technology investment will be by Ajax, which will have to install a new server and collaboration software.
- The program will focus on the *A* items of Ajax that LSC carries. This would be approximately the top fifty SKUs that would represent 85 percent of sales.

- On a weekly basis, planners at Ajax and buyers at LSC would exchange sales, "on hands," and one-month and three-month forecasts for the items involved. Ajax would also forward the master production schedule for the following four weeks. Each would review the other's info for discrepancies.
- If there were discrepancies, the planner and buyer would exchange E-mail messages or phone calls to rectify.
- Based on the commonly agreed-to forecasts, Ajax would provide LSC with a weekly suggested replenishment order. LSC would review the order, add *B* and *C* items, and submit it.
- Order tracking would also be facilitated by the system.
- LSC sales info on *B* and *C* items would also be shared with Ajax. An expected future feature of the program would be for Ajax to take over warehousing and distribution of slow-movers.

Ajax's expectations were that FASTER would enable it and its distributors to reduce inventories, lower transaction costs, and cut lead times. A preliminary estimate of the cost to LSC to join FASTER was about $20,000 for hardware, software, and communications expenditures.

Planning for the Future

George Pappas called together his executive team to discuss the integrated supply and CPFR issues. He realized that LSC was at a critical juncture in its history. In the past "arm's-length transactions" were the rule in their relationships with both customers and suppliers. The world was changing now, and George felt pressure from both customers and suppliers to work more closely together toward common objectives. Assembled were Laura Ashton, Bob Packer, Callie Pappas, J. G. Curtis, and Sam Gilardi:

George: I appreciate your being able to join me on short notice. We are faced with making some key decisions, and everyone's input will be important. As you know, one of our largest accounts, Stevenson, has asked us to develop an integrated supply capability and one of our largest vendors, Ajax, is pushing us to participate in a new collaboration program. I don't believe these are isolated situations. I feel they might be trends that will shape the way we will operate with most of our customers and suppliers in the future.

Bob: I know that's true on the customer side. Many of our bigger customers are waking up to the opportunity to reduce their MRO purchasing costs through programs like integrated supply. We *do* have to do something now or it will soon be too late. You've seen my call report from Stevenson Carbon at Pittsburgh.

J. G.: The pressure is not as great from our suppliers, but it's there just the same. I believe Ajax is on the cutting edge with what they are proposing.

Callie: I have some concerns about the Ajax approach, but I, too, feel it's an opportunity we should look closely at.

George: What's bothering you?

Callie: Well, it's mostly technology adoption and partnering concerns. Are we really ready for this Internet stuff? Is the Internet ready? How will our roles change? Can we trust Ajax with the sensitive information we will be sending them? Do they really have our interests at heart, or is this just another program for a vendor to push inventory and cost back on us? How will we know if the program is working? Our measurement systems—forgive my language—really suck.

George: Callie, my first thoughts on these programs are that they are "must dos," which should be justifiable from a financial perspective. I think we can afford them. Or, put better, maybe we can't afford not to do them. What do you think?

J. G.: We need to give it serious consideration because I'm hearing these things elsewhere. I had a conversation with one of our stainless pipe suppliers who told me about a partnership that's forming near Cincinnati called RTSGroup, which means *real time supply.* As I understand it, it, too, uses an information technology solution to link noncompeting wholesalers together with a common business process. I think integrated supply is here right now!

George: Sounds like more evidence suggesting that maybe we need to look real hard about getting into this way of doing business.

Laura: George, you know it won't be easy. In particular, getting up and running with integrated supply will be expensive. My first thoughts, too, are that this will be a lot of effort and money for just one customer and one supplier. I think, also, that it would be prudent for us to do an informal cost-benefit analysis for both proposals. I think we have a good handle on what the costs are, but how about the benefits?

Sam: I realize that many of the benefits of integrated supply are soft, but I truly believe we will lose Stevenson and some other major accounts if we don't move forward. One of the "benefits" will definitely be avoiding lost customers and sales! Also, the window of opportunity with someone like this RTSGroup might close pretty quickly on us. They might select another PVF distributor for this area.

George: As you know, we have a board meeting next week, and I would like to discuss these issues with Alex and the outside board members. But, first, we need to do some more thinking. As a team, I'd like to propose we do the following for both of the projects:

1. Develop a list of the expected benefits.
2. Develop a list of what we feel will be the problems or "down sides."
3. Identify the key barriers that might be expected in implementing the programs.
4. For the three most important barriers, create a list of initial action steps to overcome them.

Careers in Logistics[1]

What Is the Role of Logistics in the Organization?

Logistics is critical to the success of every organization. Once considered an important, behind-the-scenes operational activity, logistics is now recognized as a strategic tool for creating customer value and loyalty. Companies like Wal-Mart, Coca Cola, and Nike attribute a great deal of their success to their global logistics systems. They realize that integrating activities within the organization and across the logistics pipeline, building strong relationships with product suppliers, and working with customer-focused logistics service providers are all critical to building a competitive advantage through logistics.

The scope of opportunities for logistics professionals is expanding. Logistics managers are involved in boundary and organization-spanning teams, strategic planning, alliance building, and a host of other activities that directly impact the success of their organizations worldwide. Because these roles are expanding, a career in logistics management can lead in many directions—including to the top of the company!

Who Works in Logistics Management?

The demand for logistics managers at all levels is excellent. *The Collegiate Employment Research Institute* reports that logistics is a field with more positions than graduates each year. *The Wall Street Journal* reports that senior logistics management talent is also in short supply. As logistics managers' roles and value have grown, the need for well-educated, talented professionals with a diverse array of skills has emerged.

The increasing importance of analytical, strategic, and technological activities also makes logistics an attractive career to more people. As a result, the number of minorities and women entering the field of logistics directly from high school, college, and from other fields is increasing rapidly. Another factor which contributes to the changing face of logistics is the value that organizations are placing

[1]The contents of this section are adapted from Brian Gibson, Marcia Gibson, and Stephen Rutner. *Careers in Logistics* (Oak Brook, Ill.: Council of Logistics Management, 2001). Used with permission.

on diversity today. Successful organizations realize that diversity gives them an edge in the highly competitive global marketplace. As a result they are recruiting a variety of people from all walks of life for their logistics management positions. This strategy is highlighted here by comments from two companies:

> It makes good business sense to have a workforce that reflects the marketplace at large. We recognize the value that a diverse management team brings to our company—the ability to reach out to the entire world.
>
> We recruit from a wide pool because we need all the skills that are out there. The bottom line is that our organization wants people with excellent skills, regardless of their ethnic background, gender, or age.

Clearly, logistics is a discipline worthy of attracting the best and the brightest people from all walks of life. Anyone with the education, skills, and drive to succeed can build a prosperous career in logistics management.

WHAT KINDS OF ORGANIZATIONS EMPLOY LOGISTICS MANAGERS?

Logistics involves so many critical business activities that nearly every Fortune 500 and Global 500 company can be considered a potential employer for logistics managers. The same can be said for smaller public and private companies around the world. From the largest automobile manufacturers to the smallest zipper producers, any company that purchases and/or sells products has a need for logistics professionals to manage the flow of product and information locally, nationally, and internationally. Service firms like hospitals and restaurant chains like McDonald's must also manage logistics activities.

Here is a sample of the types of businesses and organizations that you could work for as a logistics manager:

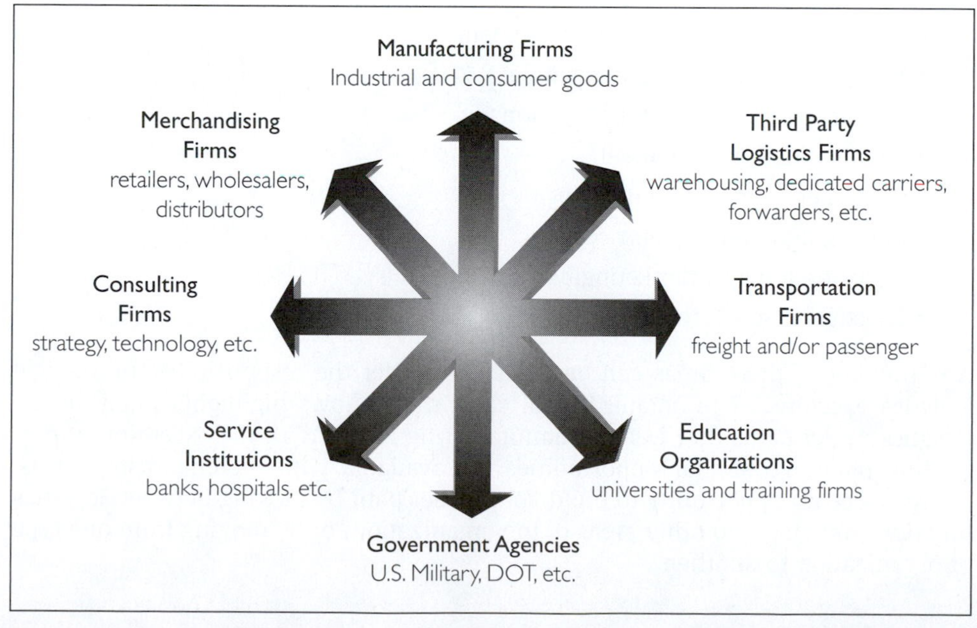

What Is the Most Common Career Path in Logistics?

No single career path dominates logistics management. In fact there are hundreds of potential career paths. Your career path will be largely influenced by your skills, interests, and personal decisions. It will also be impacted by the size, type, geographic scope, and organizational structure of the firm that you choose to work for.

A broad base of business skills, knowledge of the logistics process, and relevant internship/work experience will give you ample opportunity to begin your career with a manufacturer, retailer, carrier, third party logistics firm, or other organization. You will likely begin as a management trainee, analyst, or first line supervisor. As you demonstrate your managerial capabilities, you can progress to logistics positions of greater responsibility. You may also decide to gain experience in other parts of the organization.

One key to your success in this field is flexibility. You will work with people throughout your company—logistics, manufacturing, and marketing. Depending on the size of your company, your initial responsibilities may deal with one or more logistics functions. Some positions will require you to specialize in a specific area of logistics. There are numerous opportunities and career paths in this field—it is up to you to seek them out and develop the appropriate skills to be successful.

Your logistics career path can focus on a wide variety of functional areas. Some of these include:

- Logistics planning and analysis
- Transportation management
- Warehouse operations management
- Inventory planning and control
- Purchasing and materials management
- International logistics management
- Production planning and operations
- Supply chain management
- Customer service management
- Information systems and control
- Logistics services marketing and sales
- Logistics engineering

Any number of these areas can be combined under the responsibility of a single logistics executive. The organizational chart that follows highlights many of the logistics career paths that exist in manufacturing firms. With the exception of production planning, similar opportunities are available with merchandising firms. There is also an opportunity to build your career path by moving between logistics functions, moving into other areas of the organization, or by moving from one type of organization to another.

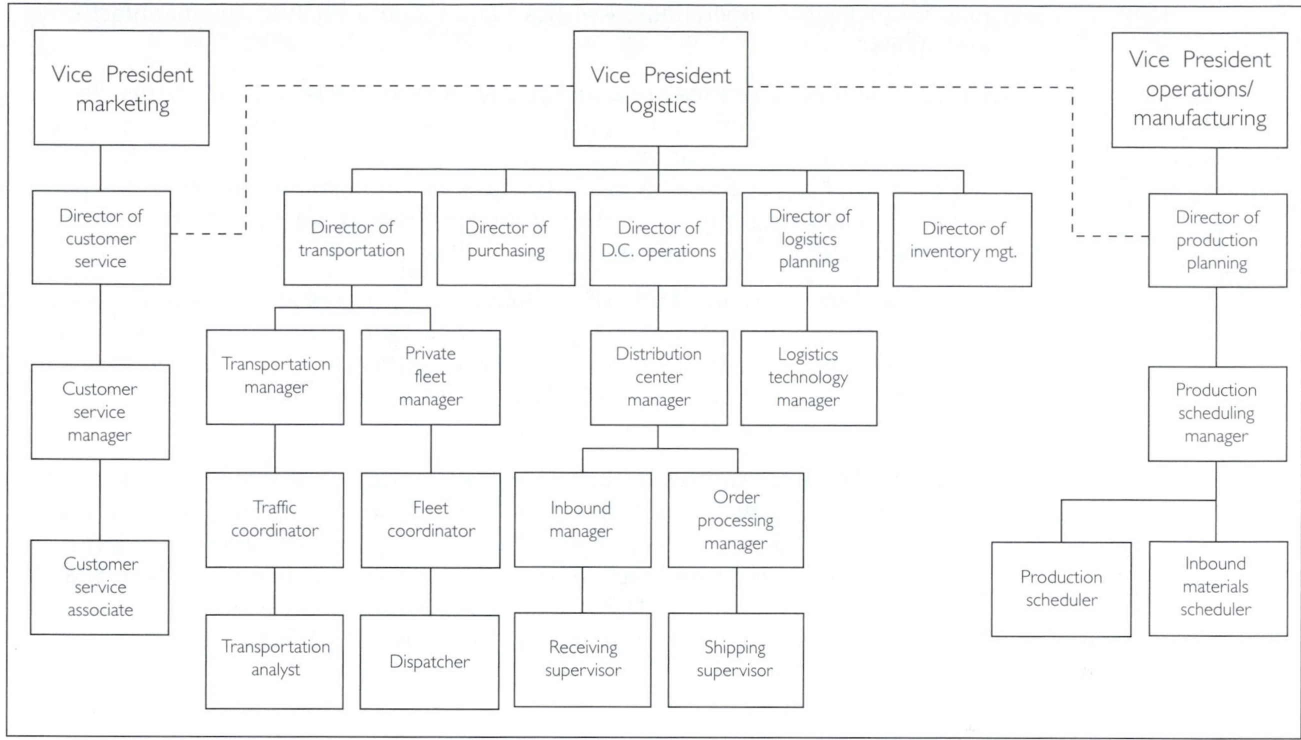

It is important to realize that not all organizations have a logistics department. Some organizations spread logistics functions across multiple departments. As a result, your career path may weave through marketing, manufacturing, operations, and/or specific product divisions. In these unique situations, you will still perform logistics functions and you may end up as the Vice President of Manufacturing or Marketing!

Where Do New Logistics Managers Get Started?

There are many potential starting points for a successful career in logistics. As discussed earlier, you can begin your career in many types of organizations, in numerous logistics activities, and virtually any location in the United States or the world depending on your skills and interests.

The career path profiles provided below are just a few examples of how new logistics professionals can get started. Remember that many other opportunities exist for you to embark upon a career in logistics.

Manufacturers and merchandisers offer excellent employment opportunities for new logistics managers. The opportunities, training and assignments are varied. Some manufacturers and merchandisers have formal training programs while others use on-the-job training to prepare new logistics managers. Initial assignments may be in logistics operations, logistics planning and analysis, or manufacturing operations.

Exceptional opportunities are emerging with third party logistics firms. Today, a growing number of manufacturing and merchandising firms are choosing to outsource their logistics activities. That's great news for the third party logistics firms but they need high-caliber, motivated people to manage the growth. Third party firms provide an excellent opportunity for you to start your career, take on new challenges, and advance your managerial skills.

Motor carriers, railroads, air carriers, and ocean carriers also offer a wide array of career options. Transportation represents the largest portion of logistics cost and has a great impact on the overall success of a logistical system. If the challenge of providing customers with cost effective quality service sounds interesting, then transportation management is for you.

Increasingly, opportunities in the fields of consulting and information technology have attracted individuals having skills and interest in logistics. Characteristically, firms in these fields are on the "leading-edge" of development in terms of creative ideas and improved technologies. These sectors are continually in search of new ideas and initiatives relating to logistics and supply chain management, and so they represent excellent career opportunities for those who are qualified and interested.

What Skills Do Logistics Managers Need?

As a logistics manager, you will work with people, processes, and information. Thus, you'll need a broad set of skills to build a successful career in logistics management.

Interviews with current logistics managers revealed that some of these skills and traits are universal while others are position-specific. You need to possess these universal skills to be successful in any logistics related position. They include:

- People skills
- Analytical skills
- Communication skills
- Computer skills
- Flexibility

Overall, the logistics profession offers a meaningful starting point for a career-minded individual. As more companies become aware of the strategic value of logistics, the attractiveness of this profession will continue to expand.

Glossary

ABC The classification of items in an inventory according to importance defined in terms of criteria such as sales volume and purchase volume.

ABC analysis The classification of items in an inventory according to importance defined in terms of criteria such as sales volume and purchase volume.

accessibility A carrier's ability to provide service between an origin and a destination.

accessorial charges A carrier's charge for accessorial services such as loading, unloading, pickup, and delivery.

action message An alert that an MRP or DRP system generates to inform the controller of a situation requiring his or her attention.

active stock Goods in active pick locations and ready for order filling.

activity-based costing (ABC) An accounting approach that provides businesses with better understanding of its costs, and therefore its profits. Capable ABC systems provide accurate cost information to the individual item level.

activity-based management (ABM) An extension of ABC costing that provides a comprehensive management framework and process to assure desired results.

advanced planning and optimization (APO) Software systems that aid businesses in effective decision making. These systems cover demand planning, supply planning, and manufacturing planning and scheduling in order to aid overall planning for the business.

advanced shipment notice (ASN) A list transmitted to a customer or consignor designating items shipped. May also include expected time of arrival.

agency tariff A rate bureau publication that contains rates for many carriers.

agglomeration A net advantage a company gains by sharing a common location with other companies.

aggregate tender rate A reduced rate offered to a shipper who tenders two or more class-related shipments at one time and one place.

air cargo Freight that is moved by air transportation.

air taxi An exempt for-hire air carrier that will fly anywhere on demand; air taxis are restricted to a maximum payload and passenger capacity per plane.

Airport and Airway Trust Fund A federal fund that collects passenger ticket taxes and disburses those funds for airport facilities.

all-cargo carrier An air carrier that transports cargo only.

American National Standards Institute (ANSI) Coordinates national electronic interchange of business transactions standards. ANSI itself does not develop standards. The Accredited Standards Committee (ASC) was chartered in order to develop uniform standards for electronic interchange of business transactions.

any-quantity (AQ) rate A rate that applies to any size shipment tendered to a carrier; no discount rate is available for large shipments.

Note: Some of the terms contained herein have been used with permission from Miles Group, Inc., a UPS Company.

artificial intelligence A field of research seeking to understand and computerize the human thought process.

auditing Determining the correct transportation charges due the carrier; auditing involves checking the freight bill for errors, correct rate, and weight.

automated guided vehicle system (AGVS) A computer-controlled materials handling system consisting of small vehicles (carts) that move along a guideway.

automated storage and retrieval system (ASRS) An automated, mechanized system for moving merchandise into storage locations and retrieving it when needed.

average cost Total cost, fixed plus variable, divided by total output.

average inventory The average inventory level over a period of time.

back order The process a company uses when a customer orders an item that is not in inventory; the company fills the order when the item becomes available.

backhaul A vehicle's return movement from original destination to original origin.

backup Making a duplicate copy of a computer file or a program on a disk or cassette so that the material will not be lost if the original is destroyed; a spare copy.

bar code A series of lines of various widths and spacings that can be scanned electronically to identify a carton or individual item.

bar code scanner A device to read bar codes and communicate data to computer systems.

barge The cargo-carrying vehicle that inland water carriers primarily use. Basic barges have open tops, but there are covered barges for both dry and liquid cargoes.

basing-point pricing A pricing system that includes a transportation cost from a particular city or town in a zone or region even though the shipment does not originate at the basing point.

batch picking The picking of items from storage for more than one order at a time.

benchmarking A management tool for comparing performance against an organization that is widely regarded as outstanding in one or more areas, in order to improve performance.

benefit-cost ratio An analytical tool used in public planning; a ratio of total measurable benefits divided by the initial capital cost.

best practice State-of-industry performance or application.

bill of lading A transportation document that is the contract of carriage between the shipper and carrier; it provides a receipt for the goods the shipper tenders to the carrier and, in some cases, shows certificate of title.

billing A carrier terminal activity that determines the proper rate and total charges for a shipment and issues a freight bill.

binder A strip of cardboard, thin wood, burlap, or similar material placed between layers of containers to hold a stack together.

blanket rate A rate that does not increase according to the distance a commodity is shipped.

bonded warehousing A type of warehousing in which companies place goods in storage without paying taxes or tariffs. The warehouse manager bonds himself or herself to the tax or tariff collecting agency to ensure payment of the taxes before the warehouse releases the goods.

boxcar An enclosed railcar, typically forty- to fifty-feet long, used for packaged freight and some bulk commodities.

bracing Supports used to secure a shipment inside a carrier's vehicle to prevent damage.

break-bulk The separation of a consolidated bulk load into smaller individual shipments for delivery to the ultimate consignee. The freight may be moved intact inside the trailer, or it may be interchanged and rehandled to connecting carriers.

broker An intermediary between the shipper and the carrier. The broker arranges transportation for shippers and secures loads for carriers.

buffer stock A quantity of goods or articles kept in storage to safeguard against unforeseen shortages and demands.

bulk area A storage area for large items which at a minimum are most efficiently handled by the palletload.

bundling An occurrence where two or more products are combined into one transaction for a single price.

business logistics The process of planning, implementing, and controlling the efficient, effective flow and storage of goods, services, and related information from the point of origin to the point of consumption for the purpose of conforming to customer requirements. Note that this definition includes inbound, outbound, internal, and external movements.

cabotage A federal law that requires coastal and intercoastal traffic to be carried in U.S.-built and -registered ships.

cage (1) A secure enclosed area for storing highly valuable items, (2) a pallet-sized platform with sides that can be secured to the tines of a forklift and in which a person may ride to inventory items stored well above the warehouse floor.

capital The resources, or money, available for investing in assets that produce output.

Carmack Amendment An Interstate Commerce Act amendment that delineates the liability of common carriers and the bill of lading provisions.

carousel A rotating system of layers of bins and/or drawers that can store many small items using relatively little floor space.

carrier A firm that transports goods or people.

carrier liability A common carrier is liable for all shipment loss, damage, and delay with the exception of that caused by act of God, act of a public enemy, act of a public authority, act of the shipper, and the goods' inherent nature.

carton flow rack A storage rack consisting of multiple lines of gravity flow conveyors.

cash against documents (CAD) A method of payment for goods of which documents transferring title are given to the buyer upon payment of cash to an intermediary acting for the seller.

category management Management of product categories as strategic business units. Examples in a food retailing operation, for example, might include: soft drinks; canned vegetables; fresh meats; health and beauty aids; etc.

center-of-gravity method Heuristic approach to facility location.

central processing unit (CPU) The physical part of the computer that does the actual computing.

centralized authority The restriction of authority to make decisions to few managers.

certificate of origin An international business document that certifies the shipment's country of origin.

certificate of public convenience and necessity The grant of operating authority that common carriers receive. A carrier must prove that a public need exists and that the carrier is fit, willing, and able to provide the needed service. The certificate may specify the commodities the carrier may haul, the area it may serve, and the routes it may use.

certificated carrier A for-hire air carrier that is subject to economic regulation and requires an operating certification to provide service.

channel of distribution A means by which a manufacturer distributes products from the plant to the ultimate user, including warehouses, brokers, wholesalers, retailers, etc.

charging area A warehouse area where a company maintains battery chargers and extra batteries to support a fleet of electrically powered materials handling equipment. The company must maintain this area in accordance with government safety regulations.

chock A wedge, usually made of hard rubber or steel, that is firmly placed under the wheel of a trailer, truck, or boxcar to stop it from rolling.

city driver A motor carrier driver who drives a local route as opposed to a long-distance, intercity route.

CL Carload rail service requiring shipper to meet minimum weight.

claim A charge made against a carrier for loss, damage, delay, or overcharge.

class rate A rate constructed from a classification and a uniform distance system. A class rate is available for any product between any two points.

classification An alphabetical listing of commodities, the class or rating into which the commodity is placed, and the minimum weight necessary for the rate discount; used in the class rate structure.

classification yard A railroad terminal area where railcars are grouped together to form train units.

coastal carriers Water carriers that provide service along coasts serving ports on the Atlantic or Pacific Oceans or on the Gulf of Mexico.

COFC Container on flat railroad car.

collaboration Multiple companies working together for mutual benefit.

collaborative logistics Logistics practice that encourages individual organizations to share information and resources for the benefit of all.

collaborative planning, forecasting and replenishment (CPFR) Seeks to enhance vendor managed inventory and continuous replenishment through a more proactive means of information sharing between supply chain partners. Supply chain partners collaborate on things like sales planning, promotions, forecasts, delivery means, and inventory levels throughout the supply chain to improve service and to drive revenue growth. Communication in CPFR encompasses the gamut from web-based systems to periodic face-to-face planning sessions.

commercial invoice A document created by the seller. It is an official document that is used to indicate, among other things, the name and address of the buyer and seller, the product(s) being shipped, and their value for customs, insurance and other purposes.

commercial zone The area surrounding a city or town to which rate carriers quote for the city or town also apply; the ICC defines the area.

commodities clause A clause that prohibits railroads from hauling commodities that they produced, mined, owned, or had an interest in.

commodity code A code describing a commodity or group of commodities pertaining to goods classification. This code can be a carrier tariff or regulating in nature.

commodity rate A rate for a specific commodity and its origin-destination.

common carrier A for-hire carrier that holds itself out to serve the general public at reasonable rates and without discrimination. To operate, the carrier must secure a certificate of public convenience and necessity.

common carriers duties Common carriers must serve, deliver, charge reasonable rates, and not discriminate.

common cost A cost that a company cannot directly assign to particular segments of the business; a cost that the company incurs for the business as a whole.

commuter An exempt for-hire air carrier that publishes a time schedule on specific routes; a special type of air taxi.

comparative advantage A principle based on the assumption that an area will specialize in producing goods for which it has the greatest advantage or the least comparative disadvantage.

consignee The receiver of a freight shipment, usually the buyer.

consignment Goods shipped to an agent/customer when an actual purchase has not transpired until the consignee agrees to release the consigned goods for production and payment.

consignor The sender of a freight shipment, usually the seller.

consolidation Collecting smaller shipments to form a larger quantity in order to realize lower transportation rates.

container A big box (ten- to forty-feet long) into which freight is loaded.

container freight station (CFS) Location designated by carriers for receipt of cargo to be packed in containers/equipment by the carrier. At destination, CFS is the location designated by the carrier for unpacking of cargo from equipment/containers.

contingency planning Preparing to deal with calamities (e.g., floods) and noncalamitous situations (e.g., strikes) before they occur.

continuous-flow, fixed-path equipment Materials handling devices that include conveyors and drag lines.

continuous replenishment (CR) System used to reduce customer inventories and improve service usually to large customers. The supplier receives point of sale information that gives data on current inventory and from this information the supplier prepares shipments to meet previously agreed upon inventory levels.

continuous replenishment planning (CRP) A program that triggers the manufacturing and movement of product through the supply chain when the identical product is purchased by an end user. A system used to reduce customer inventories.

contract carrier A for-hire carrier that does not serve the general public but serves shippers with whom the carrier has a continuing contract. The contract carrier must secure a permit to operate.

contract logistics Third party logistics relationship where a contract exists between provider of 3PL service and client.

conveyor A materials handling device that moves freight from one warehouse area to another. Roller conveyors utilize gravity, whereas belt conveyors use motors.

cooperative associations Groups of firms or individuals having common interests; agricultural cooperative associations may haul up to 25 percent of their total interstate nonfarm, nonmember goods tonnage in movements incidental and necessary to their primary business.

coordinated transportation Two or more carriers of different modes transporting a shipment.

core competency One of the company's primary functions that is considered essential to its success.

cost of capital The cost to borrow or invest capital.

cost of lost sales The forgone profit companies associate with a stockout.

cost trade-off The interrelationship among system variables in which a change in one variable affects other variables' costs. A cost reduction in one variable may increase costs for other variables, and vice versa.

courier service A fast, door-to-door service for high-valued goods and documents; firms usually limit service to shipments weighing fifty pounds or less.

crane A materials handling device that lifts heavy items. There are two types: bridge and stacker.

critical value analysis A modified ABC analysis in which a company assigns a subjective critical value to each item in an inventory.

cross-docking The movement of goods directly from receiving dock to shipping dock to eliminate storage expense.

currency adjustment factor (CAF) An added charge assessed by water carriers for currency value changes.

customer-centric value web model® Model of supply chain that represents how participants are related through information technologies.

customer order The seller's internal translation of their buyer's purchase order. The document contains much of the same information as the purchase order but may use different product IDs for some or all of the line items. It will also determine inventory availability.

customer service Activities between the buyer and seller that enhance or facilitate the sale or use of the seller's products or services.

customs The authorities designated to collect duties levied by a country on imports and exports.

customs broker A firm that represents importers/exporters in dealings with customs. Normally responsible for obtaining and submitting all documents for clearing merchandise through customs, arranging inland transport, and paying all charges related to these functions.

customs invoice A document that contains a declaration by the seller, the shipper, or the agent as to the value of the shipment.

cycle inventory An inventory system where counts are performed continuously, often eliminating the need for an annual overall inventory. It is usually set up so that A items are counted regularly (i.e, every month), B items are counted semi-regularly (every quarter or six months), and C items are counted perhaps only once a year.

cycle time The amount of time it takes to complete a business process.

decentralized authority A situation in which a company management gives decision-making authority to managers at many organizational levels.

decision support system (DSS) A set of computer-oriented tools designed to assist managers in making decisions.

deconsolidator An enterprise that provides services to un-group shipments, orders, goods, etc., to facilitate distribution.

dedicated contract carriage A third-party service that dictates equipment (vehicles) and drivers to a single customer for its exclusive use on a contractual basis.

defective goods inventory (DGI) Those items that have been returned, have been delivered damaged and have a freight claim outstanding, or have been damaged in some way during warehouse handling.

demand chain Another name for the supply chain, with emphasis on customer or end-user demand pulling materials and product through the chain.

demand management Focused efforts to estimate and manage customers' demand, with the intention of using this information to shape operating decisions.

demurrage The charge a railroad assesses for a shipper or receiver holding a car beyond the free time the railroad allows for loading (twenty-four hours) or unloading (forty-eight hours).

density A physical characteristic measuring a commodity's mass per unit volume or pounds per cubic foot; it is an important factor in ratemaking, since density affects the utilization of a carrier's vehicle.

density rate A rate based upon the density and shipment weight.

deregulation Revisions or complete elimination of economic regulations controlling transportation. The Motor Carrier Act of 1980 and the Staggers Act of 1980 revised the economic controls over motor carriers and railroads, and the Airline Deregulation Act of 1978 eliminated economic controls over air carriers.

derived demand The demand for a product's transportation is derived from the product's demand at some location.

detention The charge a motor carrier assesses when a shipper or receiver holds a truck or trailer beyond the free time the carrier allows for loading or unloading.

differential A discount offered by a carrier that faces a service time disadvantage over a route.

differentiation Ability to distinguish a capability from those of competing firms.

direct product profitability (DPP) Calculation of the net profit contribution attributable to a specific product or product line.

direct store delivery (DSD) A logistics strategy to improve services and lower warehouse inventories.

dispatching The carrier activities involved with controlling equipment; it involves arranging for fuel, drivers, crews, equipment, and terminal space.

distribution The physical path and legal title that goods and services take between production and consumption.

distribution center (DC) A post-production warehouse for finished goods held for distribution.

distribution channel The route by which a company distributes goods.

distribution channel management The organizational and pipeline strategy for getting products to customers. Direct channels involve company sales forces, facilities, and/or direct shipments to customers; indirect channels involve the use of wholesalers, distributors, and/or other parties to supply the products to customers. Many companies use both strategies, depending on markets and effectiveness.

distribution requirements planning (DRP) A system of determining demands for inventory at distribution centers and consolidating demand information in reverse as input to the production and materials systems. A computer system that uses MRP techniques to manage the entire distribution network and to link it with manufacturing planning and control.

distribution warehouse A finished goods warehouse from which a company assembles customer orders.

diversion A carrier service that permits a shipper to change the consignee and/or destination while the shipment is en route and to still pay the through rate from origin to final destination.

dock receipt A receipt that indicates a domestic carrier has delivered an export shipment to a steamship company.

domestic trunk line carrier A classification for air carriers that operate between major population centers. These carriers are now classified as major carriers.

double bottoms A motor carrier operation that involves one tractor pulling two trailers.

double-pallet jack A mechanized device for transporting two standard pallets simultaneously.

download To merge temporary files containing a day's or week's worth of information with the main data base in order to update it.

downsizing Reducing the size of a workforce, distribution network, etc., to achieve a broader set of objectives.

drayage A motor carrier that operates locally, providing pickup and delivery service.

drivers Compelling reasons to form a logistics relationship.

driving time regulations U.S. Department of Transportation rules that limit the maximum time a driver may drive in interstate commerce; the rules prescribe both daily and weekly maximums.

drop A situation in which an equipment operator deposits a trailer or boxcar at a facility at which it is to be loaded or unloaded.

dual operation A motor carrier that has both common and contract carrier operating authority.

dual rate system An international water carrier pricing system in which a shipper signing an exclusive use agreement with the conference pays a rate 10 to 15 percent lower than nonsigning shippers do for an identical shipment.

dumping This occurs when a product is sold below cost in a foreign market and/or when a product is sold at a lower price in the foreign market than in a domestic market, with the intention of driving out competition in the foreign market.

duties Taxes levied based on tariffs for imported goods.

duty drawback A refund of duty paid on imported merchandise when it is exported later, whether in the same or a different form.

economic order quantity (EOQ) An inventory model that determines how much to order by determining the amount that will minimize total ordering and holding costs.

economic value added (EVA) Popular financial performance measure that measures how effectively a firm is utilizing its assets. The greater the EVA measure, the more effective the firm is managing its assets. A measurement of shareholder value as a company's operating profits after tax, less an appropriate charge for the capital used in creating the profits.

economies of scale The reduction in long-run average cost as the company's size (scale) increases.

efficiency Extent to which processes and activities are productive in terms of resources consumed.

efficient consumer response (ECR) A customer-driven system where distributors and suppliers work together as business allies to maximize consumer satisfaction and minimize cost.

electronic data interchange (EDI) Computer-to-computer communication between two or more companies that such companies can use to generate bills of lading, purchase orders, and invoices. It also enables firms to access the information systems of suppliers, customers, and carriers and to determine the up-to-the-minute status of inventory, orders, and shipments.

end user The final buyer of the product who purchases the product for immediate use.

enterprise resource planning (ERP) A cross-functional/regional planning process supporting regional forecasting, distribution planning, operations center planning, and other planning activities. ERP provides the means to plan, analyze and monitor the flow of demand/supply alignment and to allocate critical resources to support the business plan.

event management Technology-based resource that enables firms to have visibility into their supply chains such that key "events" may be tracked, targeted, and measured continually. This provides opportunities to know when there is a real or potential problem with key or critical events.

ex works The price that the seller quotes applies only at the point of origin. The buyer takes possession of the shipment at the point of origin and bears all costs and risks associated with transporting the goods to the final destination.

exception-based management Focusing management attention on behaviors that are outside the expected norm, or "exceptions" to what was expected. This may be very effective when it helps to identify and diagnose problems at an early stage, and to seek corrective action.

exception rate A deviation from the class rate; changes (exceptions) made to the classification.

exchange Electronic marketplace that facilitates buying and selling of products and services.

exclusive patronage agreements A shipper agrees to use only a conference's member liner firms in return for a 10 to 15 percent rate reduction.

exclusive use Vehicles that a carrier assigns to a specific shipper for its exclusive use.

exempt carrier A for-hire carrier that is exempt from economic regulations.

expediting Determining where an in-transit shipment is and attempting to speed up its delivery.

expert system A computer program that mimics a human expert.

export declaration A document required by the Department of Commerce that provides information about an export activity's nature and value.

export sales contact The initial document in any international transaction; it details the specifics of the sales agreement between the buyer and seller.

exporter identification number (EIN#) A number required for the exporter on the Shipper's Export Declaration. A corporation may use their Federal Employer Identification Number as issued by the IRS; individuals can use their Social Security Number.

extensible markup language (XML) Standard language protocol which companies are beginning to use to share information across the web. It is anticipated that XML will eventually replace EDI.

facilitators Supportive corporate environmental factors that enhance partnership growth and development.

fair return A profit level that enables a carrier to realize a rate of return on investment or property value that the regulatory agencies deem acceptable for that level of risk.

fair value The value of the carrier's property; the calculation basis has included original cost minus depreciation, replacement cost, and market value.

FEU Forty-foot equivalent unit, a standard size intermodal container.

field warehouse A warehouse that stores goods on the goods' owner's property while the goods are under a bona fide public warehouse manager's custody. The owner uses the public warehouse receipts as collateral for a loan.

fill rate The percentage of order items that the picking operation actually found.

finance lease An equipment-leasing arrangement that provides the lessee with a means of financing for the leased equipment; a common method for leasing motor carrier trailers.

financial responsibility Motor carriers must have bodily injury and property damage (not cargo) insurance of not less than $500,000 per incident per vehicle; higher financial responsibility limits apply for motor carriers transporting oil or hazardous materials.

finished goods inventory (FGI) The products completely manufactured, packaged, stored, and ready for distribution.

firm planned order In a DRP or MRP system, a planned order whose status has been updated to a fixed order.

fixed costs Costs that do not fluctuate with the business volume in the short run.

fixed interval inventory model A setup wherein a company orders inventory at fixed or regular time intervals.

fixed quantity inventory model A setup wherein a company orders the same (fixed) quantity each time it places an order for an item.

flatbed A trailer without sides used for hauling machinery or other bulky items.

flatcar A railcar without sides, used for hauling machinery.

flexible-path equipment Materials handling devices that include hand trucks and forklifts.

F.O.B. A term of sale defining who is to incur transportation charges for the shipment, who is to control the shipment movement, or where title to the goods passes to the buyer; it originally meant "free on board ship."

focus Ability to identify a smaller segment of a market and to specialize resources and capabilities to meet the needs of this segment.

for-hire carrier A carrier that provides transportation service to the public on a fee basis.

forecasting Estimation of future phenomena, such as customer demand, transit times, seasonal usage of product, etc. Forecasts are used for long-term, mid-range, and short-term purposes.

foreign trade zone (FTZ) An area or zone set aside at or near a port or airport, under the control of the U.S. Customs Service, for the holding of goods duty-free pending customs clearance.

forklift truck A machine-powered device used to raise and lower freight and to move freight to different warehouse locations.

flow rack A storage method where product is presented to picking operations at one end of a rack and replenished from the opposite end.

form utility The value the production process creates in a good by changing the item's form.

fourth party logistics (4PL™) A firm that assembles and manages the resources, capabilities, and technology of its own organization with those of complementary service providers to deliver a comprehensive supply chain solution. (4PL™ is a registered trademark of Accenture, Inc.)

freight-all-kinds (FAK) An approach to rate making whereby the ante is based only upon the shipment weight and distance; widely used in TOFC service.

freight bill The carrier's invoice for a freight shipment's transportation charges.

freight forwarder A carrier that collects small shipments from shippers, consolidates the small shipments, and uses a basic mode to transport these consolidated shipments to a consignee destination.

Freight Forwarders Institute The freight forwarder industry association.

full-service leasing An equipment-leasing arrangement that includes a variety of services to support the leased equipment; a common method for leasing motor carrier tractors.

fully allocated cost The variable cost associated with a particular output unit plus a common cost allocation.

gainsharing Gainsharing is a system that includes (1) a financial measurement and feedback system to monitor company performance and distributed gains in the form of bonuses when appropriate, and (2) a focused involvement system to eliminate barriers to improved company performance. Gainsharing systems vary widely in terms of their design and the degree of which they are integrated into regular operating systems of the company.

gathering lines Oil pipelines that bring oil from the oil well to storage areas.

general-commodities carrier A common motor carrier that has operating authority to transport general commodities, or all commodities not listed as special commodities.

general-merchandise warehouse A warehouse used to store goods that are readily handled, are packaged, and do not require a controlled environment.

general order (GO) A customs term referring to a warehouse where merchandise not entered within five working days after the carrier's arrival is stored at the risk and expense of the importer.

globalization The process of making something worldwide in scope or application.

going-concern value The value that a firm has as an entity, as opposed to the sum of the values of each of its parts taken separately; particularly important in determining a reasonable railroad rate.

gondola A railcar with a flat platform and sides three to five feet high, used for top loading long, heavy items.

goods A term associated with more than one definition: (1) Common term indicating movable property, merchandise, or wares. (2) All materials used to satisfy demands. (3) Whole or part of the cargo received from the shipper, including any equipment supplied by the shipper.

grandfather clause A provision that enabled motor carriers engaged in lawful trucking operations before the passage of the Motor Carrier Act of 1935 to secure common carrier authority without proving public convenience and necessity; a similar provision exists for other modes.

granger laws State laws passed before 1870 in midwestern states to control rail transportation.

grid method Heuristic approach to facility location.

grid technique A quantitative technique to determine the least-cost center, given raw materials sources and markers, for locating a plant or warehouse.

Gross Domestic Product (GDP) A measure of a nation's output; the total value of all final goods and services a nation produces during a time period.

gross weight The total weight of the vehicle and the payload of freight or passengers.

guaranteed loans Railroad loans that the federal government cosigns and guarantees.

handling costs The cost involved in moving, transferring, preparing, and otherwise handling inventory.

hard copy Computer output printed on paper.

harmonized commodity description and coding system (Harmonized Code) An international classification system that assigns identification numbers to specific products. The coding system ensures that all parties in international trade use a consistent classification for the purposes of documentation, statistical control, and duty assessment.

hazardous materials Materials that the Department of Transportation has determined to be a risk to health, safety, and property; includes items such as explosives, flammable liquids, poisons, corrosive liquids, and radioactive material.

heuristic Modeling approach that may provide a "good" solution to a problem, but mathematically does not seek an optimum or best solution.

hi-low Usually refers to a forklift truck on which the operator must stand rather than sit.

Highway Trust Fund A fund into which highway users (carriers and automobile operators) pay; the fund pays for federal government's highway construction share.

highway use taxes Taxes that federal and state governments assess against highway users (the fuel tax is an example). The government uses the use tax money to pay for the construction, maintenance, and policing of highways.

hopper cars Railcars that permit top loading and bottom unloading of bulk commodities; some hopper cars have permanent tops with hatches to provide protection against the elements.

horizontal relationship Relationship that occurs between supply chain participants that have "parallel" or cooperating positions in the supply chain process. May be thought of as a service agreement between two or more independent logistics provider firms based on trust, cooperation, shared risk and investments, and following mutually agreeable goals.

household goods warehouse A warehouse that stores household goods.

hub A central location to which traffic from many cities is directed and from which traffic is fed to other areas.

hub airport An airport that serves as the focal point for the origin and termination of long-distance flights; flights from outlying areas meet connecting flights at the hub airport.

hundredweight (cwt) The pricing unit used in transportation; a hundredweight is equal to 100 pounds.

igloos Pallets and containers used in air transportation; the igloo shape fits the internal wall contours of a narrow-body airplane.

in-bond goods Goods held or transported in-bond under Customs control either until import duties or other charges are paid, or to avoid paying the duties or charges until a later date.

inbound logistics The movement of materials from suppliers or vendors into production processes or storage facilities.

incentive rate A rate that induces the shipper to ship heavier volumes per shipment.

INCOTERMS International terms of sale developed by the International Chamber of Commerce to define sellers' and buyers' responsibilities.

independent action A carrier that is a rate bureau member may publish a rate that differs from the rate the rate bureau publishes.

information system (I/S) Managing the flow of data in an organization in a systematic, structured way to assist in planning, implementing, and controlling.

inherent advantage The cost and service benefits of one mode compared with other modes.

integrated logistics A comprehensive, system-wide view of the entire supply chain as a single process, from raw materials supply through finished good distribution. All functions that make up the supply chain are managed as a single entity, rather than managing individual function separately.

intelligent marketplace Electronic resource that includes "smart" technologies that facilitate transactions between buyers and sellers of products and services.

interchange The transfer of cargo and equipment from one carrier to another in a joint freight move.

intercoastal carriers Water carriers that transport freight between East and West Coast ports, usually by way of the Panama Canal.

intercorporate hauling A private carrier hauling a subsidiary's goods and charging the subsidiary a fee; this is legal if the subsidiary is wholly owned or if the private carrier has common carrier authority.

interline Two or more motor carriers working together to haul a shipment to a destination. Carriers may interchange equipment but usually they rehandle the shipment without transferring the equipment.

intermittent-flow, fixed-path equipment Materials handling devices that include bridge cranes, monorails, and stacker cranes.

intermodal marketing company (IMC) An intermediary that sells intermodal services to shippers.

intermodal transportation The use of two or more transportation modes to transport freight; for example, rail to ship to truck.

internal water carriers Water carriers that operate over internal, navigable rivers such as the Mississippi, Ohio, and Missouri.

international import certificate A document required by the importing country indicating that the importing country recognizes that controlled shipment is entering their country. The importing country pledges to monitor the shipment and prevent its re-export, except in accordance with its own export control regulations.

interstate commerce The transportation of persons or property between states; in the course of the movement, the shipment crosses a state boundary.

Interstate System The National System of Interstate and Defense Highways, limited-access roads connecting major population centers.

intrastate commerce The transportation of persons or property between points within a state. A shipment between two points within a state may be interstate if the shipment had a prior or subsequent move outside of the state and the shipper intended an interstate shipment at the time of shipment.

inventory Raw materials, work in process, finished goods and supplies required for creation of a company's goods and services. The number of units and/or value of the stock of goods a company holds.

inventory carrying costs A financial measurement that calculates all of the costs associated with holding goods in storage, usually expressed as a percentage of the inventory value. It includes inventory-in-storage, warehousing, obsolescence, deterioration or spoilage, insurance, taxes, depreciation and handling costs.

inventory cost The cost of holding goods, usually expressed as a percentage of the inventory value; includes the cost of capital, warehousing, taxes, insurance, depreciation, and obsolescence.

inventory deployment A technique for strategically positioning inventory to meet customer service levels while minimizing inventory and storage levels. Excess inventory is replaced with information derived through monitoring supply, demand, and inventory at rest as well as in motion.

inventory in transit Inventory in a carrier's possession, being transported to the buyer.

inventory management Inventory administration through planning, stock positioning, monitoring product age, and ensuring product availability.

inventory turns The cost of goods sold divided by the average level of inventory on hand. The ratio measures how many times a company's inventory has been sold during a period of time. Operationally, inventory turns are measured as total throughput divided by average level of inventory for a given period.

inventory velocity The speed with which inventory moves through a defined cycle (i.e., from receiving to shipping).

irregular route carrier A motor carrier that may provide service utilizing any route.

ISO International Standards Organization.

joint cost A common cost in cases where a company produces products in fixed proportions and the cost the company incurs to produce one product entails producing another; the backhaul is an example.

joint rate A rate over a route that requires two or more carriers to transport the shipment.

just-in-time (JIT) inventory system An inventory control system that attempts to reduce inventory levels by coordinating demand and supply to the point where the desired item arrives just in time for use.

Kanban system A just-in-time inventory system used by Japanese manufacturers.

kitting The process by which individual items are grouped or packaged together to create a special single item.

knowledge management Capability to diagnose knowledge-based needs, and to provide resources to satisfy those needs.

lading The cargo carried in a transportation vehicle.

land bridge The movement of containers by ship-rail-ship on Japan-to-Europe moves; ships move containers to the U.S. Pacific Coast, rails move containers to an East Coast port, and ships deliver containers to Europe.

land grants Grants of land given to railroads to build tracks during their development stage.

landed cost The total cost of a product delivered at a given location; the production cost plus the transportation cost to the customer's location.

lash barges Covered barges that carriers load on board oceangoing ships for movement to foreign destinations.

LCL Less than carload rail service; less than container load.

lead time The total time that elapses between an order's placement and its receipt. It includes the time required for order transmittal, order processing, order preparation, and transit.

less-than-truckload carriers (LTL) Trucking companies that consolidate and transport smaller (less than truckload) shipments of freight by utilizing a network of terminals and relay points.

lessee A person or firm to whom a lessor grants a lease.

lessor A person or firm that grants a lease.

letter of credit An international business document that assures the seller that the bank issuing the letter of credit will make payment upon fulfillment of the sales agreement.

lighter A flat-bottomed boat designed for cross-harbor or inland waterway freight transfer.

line functions The decision-making areas companies associate with daily operations. Logistics line functions include traffic management, inventory control, order processing, warehousing, and packaging.

line-haul shipment A shipment that moves between cities and over distances more than 100 to 150 miles in length.

line item A specific and unique identifier assigned to a product by the responsible enterprise.

linear programming Popular, commonly-used modeling approach that seeks an optimum solution.

liner service International water carriers that ply fixed routes on published schedules.

link The transportation method a company uses to connect nodes (plants, warehouses) in a logistics system.

live A situation in which the equipment operator stays with the trailer or boxcar while it is being loaded or unloaded.

load factor A measure of operating efficiency used by air carriers to determine a plane's utilized capacity percentage or the number of passengers divided by the total number of seats.

loading allowance A reduced rate that carriers offer to shippers and/or consignees who load and/or unload LTL or AQ shipments.

local rate A rate published between two points served by one carrier.

local service carriers A classification of air carriers that operate between less-populated areas and major population centers. These carriers feed passengers into the major cities to connect with trunk (major) carriers. Local service carriers are now classified as national carriers.

localized raw material A raw material found only in certain locations.

locational determinant The factors that determine a facility's location. For industrial facilities, the determinants include logistics.

logbook A daily record of the hours an interstate driver spends driving, off duty, sleeping in the berth, or on duty but not driving.

logistics audit Examination of firm's logistics objectives, processes, activities, and results.

logistics channel The network of intermediaries engaged in transfer, storage, handling, and communications functions that contribute to the efficient flow of goods.

logistics (CLM 1999) Logistics is the process of planning, implementing, and controlling the efficient, effective flow and storage of goods, services, and related information from point or origin to point of consumption for the purpose of conforming to customer requirements. Activities include but are not limited to: warehousing, transportation, private fleet, inventory control, purchasing, production scheduling, customer service, and long range planning.

logistics data interchange (LDI) A computerized system that electronically transmits logistics information.

logistics information system An interacting structure of people, equipment, and procedures which together make relevant information available to the logistics manager for the purposes of planning, implementation and control.

long ton 2,240 pounds.

lot size The quantity of goods a company purchases or produces in anticipation of use or sale in the future.

LTL shipment A less-than-truckload shipment, one weighing less than the minimum weight a company needs to use the lower truckload rate.

lumping The act of assisting a motor carrier owner-operator in the loading and unloading of property; quite commonly used in the food industry.

mainframe An organization's central computer system.

maintenance, repair, operations (MRO) Materials sourced strictly to support maintenance, repairs, and daily operations (i.e., wrenches, lubricants, safety glasses, packaging, etc.).

major carrier A for-hire certificated air carrier that has annual operating revenues of $1 billion or more; the carrier usually operates between major population centers.

manifest A list of all cargoes that pertain to a specific shipment, grouping of shipments, or piece of equipment. Ocean carriers will prepare a manifest per container.

manufacturing resource planning (MRP II) The process of identifying, performing a needs analysis, and committing the resources needed to produce a product.

marginal cost The cost to produce one additional unit of output; the change in total variable cost resulting from a one-unit change in output.

marine insurance Insurance to protect against cargo loss and damage when shipping by water transportation.

market dominance The absence of effective competition for railroads from other carriers and modes for the traffic to which the rail rate applies. The Staggers Act stated that market dominance does not exist if the rate is below the revenue-to-variable-cost ratio of 160 percent in 1981 and 170 percent in 1983.

master production scheduling (MPS) Second input into the MRP. This shows how many end products will be produced within a designated period of time. The MPS breaks the aggregate-planning schedule into weekly production schedules for each particular part in the schedule.

material index The ratio of the sum of the localized raw material weights to the weight of the finished product.

materials handling Short-distance movement of goods within a storage area.

materials management The movements and storage functions associated with supplying goods to a firm.

materials planning The materials management function that attempts to coordinate materials supply with materials demand.

materials requirement planning (MRP) Predecessor to the new ERP systems. MRP was the first computerized information system developed specifically to aid in managing and scheduling materials to forecasted demand. It is a decision-making tool used to determine how much material to purchase and when to purchase it based on forecast. The MRP system allowed businesses to reduce inventory levels, use facilities more efficiently, and improve customer service.

matrix organization An organizational structure that emphasizes the horizontal flow of authority; the company treats logistics as a project, with the logistics manager overseeing logistics costs but traditional departments controlling operations.

measurement ton Forty cubic feet; used in water transportation ratemaking.

merger The combination of two or more carriers into one company that will own, manage, and operate the properties that previously operated separately.

micro-land bridge An intermodal movement in which the shipment is moved from a foreign country to the U.S. by water and then moved across the U.S. by railroad to an interior, nonport city, or vice versa for exports from a nonport city.

mileage allowance An allowance, based upon distance, that railroads give to shippers using private railcars.

mileage rate A rate based upon the number of miles the commodity is shipped.

mini-land bridge An intermodal movement in which the shipment is moved from a foreign country to the U.S. by water and then moved across the U.S. by railroad to a destination that is a port city, or vice versa for exports from a U.S. port city.

minimum weight The shipment weight the carrier's tariff specifies as the minimum weight required to use the TL or CL rate; the rate discount volume.

mixed loads The movement of both regulated and exempt commodities in the same vehicle at the same time.

modal split The relative use that companies make of transportation modes; the statistics include ton-miles, passenger-miles, and revenue.

MRO items Maintenance, repair, and operating items—office supplies, for example.

multinational company A company that both produces and markets products in different countries.

multiple-car rate A railroad rate that is lower for shipping more than one carload at a time.

national carrier A for-hire certificated air carrier that has annual operating revenues of $75 million to $1 billion; the carrier usually operates between major population centers and areas of lesser population.

National Motor Freight Classification (NMFC) A tariff that contains descriptions and classifications of commodities and rules for domestic movement by motor carriers in the United States.

nationalization Public ownership, financing, and operation of a business entity.

negotiations A set of discussions between two or more enterprises to determine the business relationship.

net weight The weight of the merchandise, unpacked, exclusive of any containers.

no location (No Loc) A received item for which the warehouse has no previously established storage slot.

node A fixed point in a firm's logistics system where goods come to rest; includes plants, warehouses, supply sources, and markets.

noncertificated carrier A for-hire air carrier that is exempt from economic regulation.

non-vessel-owning common carrier (NVOCC) A firm that consolidates and disperses international containers that originate at or are bound for inland ports.

on-line receiving A system in which computer terminals are available at each receiving bay and operators enter items into the system as they are unloaded.

operating ratio A measure of operating efficiency defined as operating expenses/operating revenues × 100.

optimization Modeling approach that seeks the "best" or optimum solution. The process of making something as good or as effective as possible with given resources and constraints.

order A type of request for goods or services.

order cycle The time spent and the activities performed from the time an order is received to the actual delivery of the order to a customer.

order cycle time The time that elapses from placement of order until receipt of order. This includes time for order transmittal, processing, preparation, and shipping.

order fill A measure of the number of orders processed without stockouts or the need to back order, expressed as a percentage of all orders processed in the distribution center or warehouse.

order fulfillment All steps included in the process that begins with receipt of a customer order, and ends with satisfaction of that customer through delivery of the order as specified. Process may be extended to include return product movement, or reverse logistics that may occur post-delivery.

order management system Principal means by which buyers and sellers communicate information relating to individual orders of product.

order picking Assembling a customer's order from items in storage.

order processing The activities associated with filling customer orders.

order processing system Component of order management system that deals most directly with the processing of individual orders.

ordering cost The cost of placing an inventory order with a supplier.

out-of-pocket cost The cost directly assignable to a particular unit of traffic and which a company would not have incurred if it had not performed the movement.

outbound consolidation (break-bulk) Consolidation of a number of small shipments for various customers into a larger load. Shipped to a location near the customers; then the small shipments are distributed to the customers.

outbound logistics The process related to the movement and storage of products from the end of the production line to the end user.

outsourcing Purchasing a logistics service from an outside firm, as opposed to performing it in-house.

over-the-road A motor carrier operation that reflects long-distance, intercity moves; the opposite of local operations.

overhead The general continuing costs of doing business. In logistics, refers mainly to fixed costs and fixed assets.

owner-operator A trucking operation in which the truck's owner is also the driver.

P & D Pickup and delivery.

packing list A document containing information about the location of each product ID in each package. It allows the recipient to quickly find the item he or she is looking for without a broad search of all packages. It also confirms the actual shipment of goods on a line item basis.

pallet A platform device (about four feet square) used for moving and storing goods. A forklift truck is used to lift and move the loaded pallet.

pallet wrapping machine A machine that wraps a pallet's contents in stretch-wrap to ensure safe shipment.

partnership Customized business relationship that produces results for all parties that are more acceptable than would be achieved individually.

passenger-mile A measure of output for passenger transportation that reflects the number of passengers transported and the distance traveled; a multiplication of passengers hauled and distance traveled.

peak demand The time period during which customers demand the greatest quantity.

pegging A technique in which a DRP system traces demand for a product by date, quantity, and warehouse location.

per diem A payment rate one railroad makes to use another's cars.

perfect order Refers to an order where all customer requirements are met upon delivery of the order (e.g., right time, right place, right quantity, right condition, and right documentation).

permit A grant of authority to operate as a contract carrier.

personal discrimination Charging different rates to shippers with similar transportation characteristics, or, charging similar rates to shippers with differing transportation characteristics.

physical distribution The movement and storage of finished goods from manufacturing plants to warehouses to customers; used synonymously with business logistics.

physical supply The movement and storage of raw materials from supply sources to the manufacturing facility.

pick/pack Picking and packing immediately into shipment containers.

pick-up order A document indicating the authority to pick up cargo or equipment from a specific location.

picking by aisle A method by which pickers pick all needed items in an aisle regardless of the items' ultimate destination; the items must be sorted later.

picking by source A method in which pickers successively pick all items going to a particular destination regardless of the aisle in which each item is located.

piggyback A rail-truck service. A shipper loads a highway trailer, and a carrier drives it to a rail terminal and loads it on a rail flatcar; the railroad moves the trailer-on-flatcar combination to the destination terminal, where the carrier offloads the trailer and delivers it to the consignee.

pin lock A hard piece of iron, formed to fit on a trailer's pin, that locks in place with a key to prevent an unauthorized person from moving the trailer.

place utility A value that logistics creates in a product by changing the product's location. Transportation creates place utility.

planned order In DRP and MRP systems, a future order the system plans in response to forecasted demand.

point of sale (POS) Technology that allows firms, in real time, to know what and where an item is being sold through scanning of individual barcodes when an item is purchased at the retail level. Using this information, businesses can improve product forecasting, make better purchase decisions, and reduce the chance that an item will be out of stock.

police powers The United States' constitutionally granted right for the states to establish regulations to protect their citizens' health and welfare; truck weight; speed, length, and height laws are examples.

pooling An agreement among carriers to share the freight to be hauled or to share profits. The Interstate Commerce Act outlawed pooling agreements, but the Civil Aeronautics Board has approved profit pooling agreements for air carriers during strikes.

port authority A state or local government that owns, operates, or otherwise provides wharf, dock, and other terminal investments at ports.

possession utility The value created by marketing's effort to increase the desire to possess a good or benefit from a service.

postponement The delay of final activities (i.e. assembly, production, packaging, etc.) until the latest possible time.

prepaid A freight term that indicates that charges are to be paid by the shipper.

present value Today's value of future cash flows, discounted at an appropriate rate.

primary-business test A test the ICC uses to determine if a trucking operation is bona fide private transportation; the private trucking operation must be incidental to and in the futherance of the firm's primary business.

private carrier A carrier that provides transportation service to the firm that owns or leases the vehicles and does not charge a fee. Private motor carriers may haul at a fee for wholly owned subsidiaries.

private warehousing The storage of goods in a warehouse owned by the company that has title to the goods.

process A series of actions, changes, or functions bringing about a result.

process improvement Designs or activities that improve quality or reduce costs, often through the elimination of waste or non-value-added tasks.

product Something that has been or is being produced.

product description The user's description of the product.

product ID A method of identifying a product without using a full description. These can be different for each document type and must, therefore, be captured and related to the document in which they were used. They must then be related to each other in context (also known as SKU, Item Code or Number, or other such name).

production planning The decision-making area that determines when and where and in what quantity a manufacturer is to produce goods.

productivity A measure of resource utilization efficiency defined as the sum of the outputs divided by the sum of the inputs.

profit ratio The percentage of profit to sales—that is, profit divided by sales.

proof of delivery (POD) Information supplied by the carrier containing the name of the person who signed for the shipment, the time and date of delivery, and other shipment delivery related information.

proportional rate A rate lower than the regular rate for shipments that have prior or subsequent moves; used to overcome combination rates' competitive disadvantages.

public warehouse receipt The basic document a public warehouse manager issues as a receipt for the goods a company gives to the warehouse manager. The receipt can be either negotiable or nonnegotiable.

public warehousing The storage of goods by a firm that offers storage service for a fee to the public.

pull ordering system A system in which each warehouse controls its own shipping requirements by placing individual orders for inventory with the central distribution center.

purchase order A document created by a buyer to officially request a product or service from a seller. It contains, among other things, the name and address of the buyer, the ship-to address, the quantity, product code (and expected price), requested ship or receipt date, sales and shipping terms, and other appropriate information.

purchase price discount A pricing structure in which the seller offers a lower price if the buyer purchases a larger quantity.

purchasing The functions associated with buying the goods and services the firm requires.

pure raw material A raw material that does not lose weight in processing.

push ordering system A situation in which a firm makes inventory deployment decisions at the central distribution center and ships to its individual warehouses accordingly.

quality control The management function that attempts to ensure that the goods or services that a firm manufactures or purchases meet the product or service specifications.

quick response A method of maximizing the efficiency of the supply chain by reducing inventory investment.

radio frequency (RF) technology Typically used in a warehouse or distribution center, RF technologies provide the communications capability between operating personnel (e.g., fork lift drivers, loading dock personnel, etc.) and centralized computer capabilities.

random access memory (RAM) Temporary memory on micro chips. Users can store data in RAM or take it out at high speeds. However, any information stored in RAM disappears when the computer is shut off.

rate basis number The distance between two rate basis points.

rate basis point The major shipping point in a local area; carriers consider all points in the local area to be the rate basis point.

rate bureau A carrier group that assembles to establish joint rates, to divide joint revenues and claim liabilities, and to publish tariffs. Rate bureaus have published single line rates, which were prohibited in 1984.

reasonable rate A rate that is high enough to cover the carrier's cost but not high enough to enable the carrier to realize monopolistic profits.

Recapture Clause A provision of the 1920 Transportation Act that provided for self-help financing for railroads. Railroads that earned more than the prescribed return contributed one-half of the excess to the fund from which the ICC made loans to less profitable railroads. The Recapture Clause was repealed in 1933.

reconsignment A carrier service that permits a shipper to change the destination and/or consignee after the shipment has reached its originally billed destination and to still pay the through rate from origin to final destination.

Reed-Bulwinkle Act Legislation that legalized common carrier joint ratemaking through rate bureaus; extended antitrust immunity to carriers participating in a rate bureau.

reefer A refrigerated vehicle.

reengineering A fundamental rethinking and radical design of business processes to achieve dramatic improvements in performance.

refrigerated warehouse A warehouse that is used to store perishable items requiring controlled temperatures.

regional carrier A for-hire air carrier, usually certificated, that has annual operating revenues of less than $75 million; the carrier usually operates within a particular region of the country.

regular-route carrier A motor carrier that is authorized to provide service over designated routes.

relay terminal A motor carrier terminal that facilitates the substitution of one driver for another who has driven the maximum hours permitted.

released-value rates Rates based upon the shipment's value. The maximum carrier liability for damage is less than the full value, and in return the carrier offers a lower rate.

reliability A carrier selection criterion that considers the carrier transit time variation; the consistency of the transit time the carrier provides.

reorder point A predetermined inventory level that triggers the need to place an order. This minimum level provides inventory to meet the demand a firm anticipates during the time it takes to receive the order.

reparation A situation in which the ICC requires a railroad to repay users the difference between the rate the railroad charges and the maximum rate the ICC permits when the ICC finds a rate to be unreasonable or too high.

replenishment The process of moving or resupplying inventory from a reserve storage location to a primary picking location, or to another mode of storage in which picking is performed.

replenishment cycle Similar to the order cycle, except it typically refers to inbound movements that may occur in the supply chain (e.g., inbound to manufacturing, distribution, or retail establishment).

reverse logistics The process of collecting, moving, and storing used, damaged, or outdated products and/or packaging from end users.

right of eminent domain A concept that, in a court of law, permits a carrier to purchase land it needs for transportation right-of-way; used by railroads and pipelines.

roll-on-roll-off (RO-RO) A type of ship designed to permit cargo to be driven on at origin and off at destination; used extensively for the movement of automobiles.

rule of eight Before the Motor Carrier Act of 1980, the ICC restricted contract carriers requesting authority to eight shippers under contract. The number of shippers has been deleted as a consideration for granting a contract carrier permit.

rule of ratemaking A regulatory provision directing the regulatory agencies to consider the earnings a carrier needs to provide adequate transportation.

safety stock The inventory a company holds beyond normal needs as a buffer against delays in receipt of orders or changes in customer buying patterns.

sales order See customer order.

salvage material Unused material that has a market value and can be sold.

schedule information Data concerning the service provided by an enterprise.

SCOR Developed by the Supply Chain Council as an attempt at standardizing processes for supply chain management and stands for Supply Chain Operations Reference Model. The idea behind SCOR was to provide a language that can describe, measure, and compare supply chain operations.

scrap material Unusable material that has no market value.

separable cost A cost that a company can directly assign to a particular segment of the business.

service The defined, regular pattern of calls made by a carrier in the pick up and discharge of cargo.

service contract A contract between a shipper and an ocean carrier or conference, in which the shipper makes a commitment to provide a minimum quantity of cargo over a fixed time period. The ocean carrier or conference also commits to a rate or rate schedule as well as a defined service level, such as space, transit item, port rotation, or other features.

service levels A set standard of operating procedures and outcomes as agreed upon by one or more enterprises involved in a transaction.

service provider An enterprise that offers and supplies goods or services.

service request A description of a specific service provided as an interface between layers (for example, transfer data).

service response A description of the response to a specific service request that reports the success or failure of the request.

setup costs The costs a manufacturer incurs in staging the production line to produce a different item.

ship agent A liner company or tramp ship operator representative who facilitates ship arrival, clearance, loading and unloading, and fee payment while at a specific port.

ship broker A firm that serves as a go-between for the tramp ship owner and the chartering consignor or consignee.

shipper The party that tenders goods for transportation.

shipper's agent A firm that primarily matches up small shipments, especially single-traffic piggyback loads, to permit shippers to use twin-trailer piggyback rates.

shippers association A nonprofit, cooperative consolidator and distributor of shipments that member firms own or ship; acts in much the same way as a for-profit freight forwarder.

shipping instructions A document detailing the cargo and the requirements of its physical movement.

short-haul discrimination Charging more for a shorter haul than for a longer haul over the same route, in the same direction, and for the same commodity.

short ton 2,000 pounds.

silo Departments and departmental functions operating autonomously.

simulation Modeling approach that involves designing a model of a real system and conducting experiments with this model for the purpose either of understanding the behavior of the system or of evaluating various strategies within the limits imposed by a criterion or set of criteria for the operation of the system.

sleeper team Two drivers who operate a truck equipped with a sleeper berth; while one driver sleeps in the berth to accumulate mandatory off-duty time, the other driver operates the vehicle.

slip seat operation A motor carrier relay terminal operation in which a carrier substitutes one driver for another who has accumulated the maximum driving time hours.

slip sheet Similar to a pallet, the slip sheet, which is made of cardboard or plastic, is used to facilitate movement of unitized loads.

slurry Dry commodities that are made into a liquid form by the addition of water or other fluids to permit movement by pipeline.

software A computer term that describes the system design and programming that the computer's effective use requires.

source A specific location or enterprise from where goods will be obtained.

special-commodities carrier A common carrier trucking company that has authority to haul a special commodity; the sixteen special commodities include household goods, petroleum products, and hazardous materials.

special commodity warehouses A warehouse that is used to store products requiring unique facilities, such as grain (elevator), liquid (tank), and tobacco (barn).

special customs invoice In addition to a commercial invoice, some countries require a special customs invoice designed to facilitate the clearance of goods and the assessment of customs duties in that country.

spot To move a trailer or boxcar into place for loading or unloading.

spur track A railroad track that connects a company's plant or warehouse with the railroad's track; the user bears the cost of the spur track and its maintenance.

staff functions The planning and analysis support activities a firm provides to assist line managers with daily operations. Logistics staff functions include location analysis, system design, cost analysis, and planning.

stage The act of locating goods at a specific location to prepare for movement.

statistical process control (SPC) A managerial control technique that examines a process's inherent variability.

status Information concerning the state or location of a defined item.

steamship conferences Collective ratemaking bodies for liner water carriers.

stock-keeping unit (SKU) A single unit that has been completely assembled. In a DRP system, an item is not considered complete until it is where it can satisfy customer demand.

stockless purchasing A practice whereby the buyer negotiates a purchase price for annual requirements of MRO items and the seller holds inventory until the buyer orders individual items.

stockout A situation in which the items a customer orders are currently unavailable.

stockout cost The opportunity cost that companies associate with not having supply sufficient to meet demand.

stores The function associated with storing and issuing frequently used items.

strategic alliance Relationship in which two or more business organizations cooperate and willingly modify their business objectives and practices to achieve long-term objectives.

strategic assessment Evaluation of overall supply chain with emphasis on strengths, weaknesses, opportunities, and strengths.

strategic planning Looking one to five years into the future and designing a logistical system (or systems) to meet the needs of the various businesses in which a company is involved.

strategic variables The variables that effect change in the environment and logistics strategy. The major strategic variables include the economy, population, energy, and government.

strategy A course of action, a scheme, or a principal idea through which an organization or individual hopes to accomplish a specific objective or goal. In other words, a strategy is designed to determine how someone is going to achieve something that has been identified as being important to future success.

stretch-wrap An elastic, thin plastic material that effectively adheres to itself, thereby containing product on a pallet when wrapped around the items.

sub-optimization Decisions or activities in a part made at the expense of the whole.

substitutability A buyer's ability to substitute different sellers' products.

supplemental carrier A for-hire air carrier having no time schedule or designated route; the carrier provides service under a charter or contract per plane per trip.

supply chain The physical, financial, and information networks that involve the movement of materials, funds, and related information through the full logistics process, from the acquisition of raw materials to delivery of finished products to the end user. The supply chain includes all vendors, service providers, customers, and intermediaries.

supply chain management (SCM) The integration of the supplier, distributor, and customer logistics requirements into one cohesive process to include demand planning, forecasting, materials requisition, order processing, inventory allocation, order fulfillment, transportation services, receiving, invoicing, and payment. Also, the management and control of all materials, funds, and related information in the logistics process from the acquisition of raw materials to the delivery of finished products to the end user.

supply-demand misalignment Occurs when supply and demand are not synchronized. May result in excess inventories or shortages of inventory.

supply warehouse A warehouse that stores raw materials; a company mixes goods from different suppliers at the warehouse and assembles plant orders.

surcharge An add-on charge to the applicable charges; motor carriers have a fuel surcharge, and railroads can apply a surcharge to any joint rate that does not yield 110 percent of variable cost.

switch engine A railroad engine that is used to move railcars short distances within a terminal and plant.

switching company A railroad that moves railcars short distances; switching companies connect two mainline railroads to facilitate through movement of shipments.

synchronization The state that is created when all supply chain processes and functions operate in coordination with each other.

system A set of interacting elements, variables, parts, or objects that are functionally related to each other and form a coherent group.

systems concept A decision-making strategy that emphasizes overall system efficiency rather than the efficiency of each part.

tactic Refers to an operational aspect that is necessary to support strategy. Tactics are more likely to involve daily short-run operations that help achieve the strategy that has been identified or agreed upon in the organization. An example may be useful to help clarify the essential differences between strategy and tactics.

tally sheet A printed form on which companies record, by making an appropriate mark, the number of items they receive or ship. In many operations, tally sheets become a part of the permanent inventory records.

tandem A truck that has two drive axles or a trailer that has two axles.

tank cars Railcars designed to haul bulk liquid or gas commodities.

tapering rate A rate that increases with distance but not in direct proportion to the distance the commodity is shipped.

tare weight The weight of the vehicle when it is empty.

tariff A publication that contains a carrier's rates, accessorial charges, and rules.

temporary authority Temporary operating authority as a common carrier granted by the ICC for up to 270 days.

terminal delivery allowance A reduced rate that a carrier offers in return for the shipper or consignee tendering or picking up the freight at the carrier's terminal.

terms of sale The details or conditions of a transaction including details of the payment method, timing, legal obligations, freight terms, required documentation, insurance, responsibilities of the buyer and the seller, and when the buyer assumes risk for the shipment.

terms of sale—Cost, Insurance, and Freight (CIF) The price quote the seller offers to transportation charges.

TEU Twenty-foot equivalent unit, a standard size intermodal container.

third party A firm that supplies logistics services to other companies.

third party logistics provider (3PL) An external supplier that performs all or part of a company's logistics functions.

three-layer framework A basic structure and operational activity of a company; the three layers include operational systems, control and administrative management, and master planning.

throughput A warehousing output measure that considers the volume (weight, number of units) of items stored during a given time period.

time-definite services Delivery is guaranteed on a specific day or at a certain time of day.

time/service rate A rail rate that is based upon transit time.

time utility A value created in a product by having the product available at the time desired. Transportation and warehousing create time utility.

timetables Time schedules of departures and arrivals by origin and destination; typically used for passenger transportation by air, bus, and rail.

TL (truckload) A shipment weighing the minimum weight or more. Carriers give a rate reduction for shipping a TL-size shipment.

TOFC (trailer-on-flatcar) Also known as piggyback.

ton-mile A freight transportation output measure that reflects the shipment's weight and the distance the carrier hauls it; a multiplication of tons hauled and distance traveled.

total average inventory Average normal use stock, plus average lead stock, plus safety stock.

total cost analysis A decision-making approach that considers total system cost minimization and recognizes the interrelationship among system variables such as transportation, warehousing, inventory, and customer service.

total quality management (TQM) A management approach in which managers constantly communicate with organizational stakeholders to emphasize the importance of continuous quality improvement.

tracing Determining a shipment's location during the course of a move.

tracking and tracing Monitoring and recording shipment movements from origin to destination.

trade lane The combination of the origin and destination points.

trading community Electronic resource that allows members of buying and selling communities to buy and sell their products and services in an interactive manner.

traffic management The buying and controlling of transportation services for a shipper or consignee, or both.

tramp An international water carrier that has no fixed route or published schedule; a shipper charters a tramp ship for a particular voyage or a given time period.

transit privilege A carrier service that permits the shipper to stop the shipment in transit to perform a function that changes the commodity's physical characteristics, but to still pay the through rate.

transit time The total time that elapses between a shipment's delivery and its pickup.

transportation management system (TMS) Logistics tool used to improve management of a firm's transportation processes both inbound and outbound. A TMS can help optimize the movements of freight into multiple facilities, assist in tracking the freight through the supply chain, and then manage the freight payment process to the user's carrier base.

transportation method A linear programming technique that determines the least-cost means of shipping goods from plants to warehouses or from warehouses to customers.

transportation requirements planning (TRP) Utilizing computer technology and information already available in MRP and DRP databases to plan transportation needs based on field demand.

transshipment problem A variation of the linear programming transportation method that considers consolidating shipments to one destination and reshipping from that destination.

travel agent A firm that provides passenger travel information; air, rail, and steamship ticketing; and hotel reservations. The carrier and hotel pay the travel agent a commission.

trunk lines Oil pipelines used for the long-distance movements of crude oil, refined oil, or other liquid products.

two-bin system An inventory ordering system in which the time to place an order for an item is indicated when the first bin is empty. The second bin contains supply sufficient to last until the company receives the order.

ubiquity A raw material that is found at all locations.

umbrella rate An ICC ratemaking practice that held rates to a particular level to protect another mode's traffic.

Uniform Communication Standard (UCS) Grocery industry standard transaction sets that allow computer-to-computer, paperless exchange of documents between supply chain partners.

Uniform Warehouse Receipts Act The act that sets forth the regulations governing public warehousing. The regulations define a warehouse manager's legal responsibility and define the types of receipts he or she issues.

unit cost The cost associated with a single unit of product. The total cost of producing a product or service divided by the total number of units.

unit train An entire, uninterrupted locomotive, car, and caboose movement between an origin and destination.

unitize To consolidate several packages into one unit; carriers strap, band, or otherwise attach the several packages together.

value added Increased or improved value, worth, functionality or usefulness.

value-added network (VAN) Clearing house for electronic transactions between trading partners.

value chain Sequence of activities that, when combined, define a business process. An example would be the sequence of activities from suppliers to manufacturers to retail stores that define the industry supply chain.

value net® New supply chain design that starts with the customer and is built around three powerful value propositions: high levels of customization; super service; and convenient solutions.

value-of-service pricing Pricing according to the value of the product the company is transporting; third-degree price discrimination; demand-oriented pricing; charging what the traffic will bear.

variability Uncertainty that may occur, for example, in the length of the order cycle.

variable cost A cost that fluctuates with the volume of business.

vendor A firm or individual that supplies goods or services; the seller.

vendor managed inventory (VMI) A customer service strategy used to manage the customer's inventory toward lower cost and improved service. VMI is used often between retailers and their suppliers and has been in use by some as early as 1985.

vertical integration Traditional ways that firms in the supply chain organizationally relate to one another.

vertical relationship Relationship that occurs between supply chain participants such as retailers, wholesalers, manufacturers, and suppliers, that have a "vertical" organizational relationship.

virtual integration The selection, partnering, and integration of key intellectual capital across the enterprise or supply chain. Offers the advantages of a tightly coordinated supply chain that traditionally has come through vertical coordination, and benefits from the focus and specialization that drives virtual organizations.

visibility The ability to access or view pertinent data or information as it relates to logistics and the supply chain.

warehouse management system (WMS) Helps to manage inventory of goods stored in a warehouse. The system can provide visibility of this inventory back to the manufacturing environment for replenishment (many times through a DRP system) and forward to order processing and management for allocation to a customer's order.

warehousing The storage (holding) of goods.

waterway use tax A per-gallon tax assessed barge carriers for waterway use.

weight break The shipment volume at which the LTL charges equal the TL charges at the minimum weight.

weight-losing raw material A raw material that loses weight in processing.

work in process (WIP) Parts and subassemblies in the process of becoming completed assembly components. These items, no longer part of the raw materials inventory and not yet part of the finished goods inventory, may constitute a large inventory by themselves and create extra expense for the firm.

zone price The constant price of a product at all geographic locations within a zone.

Name Index

Note: Italicized page numbers indicate illustrations or boxed text.

Subject Index

Note: Italicized page numbers indicate illustrations or boxed text.